DEC 0 4 2007

## DATE DUE

| March 3, 2011 | |
|---|---|
| | |
| | |
| | |
| | |
| | |
| | |
| | |
| | |
| | |
| | |
| | |
| | |
| | |
| | |
| | |
| | |

DEMCO, INC. 38-2931

ALSO BY ROBERT FISK

*The Point of No Return:*
*The Strike Which Broke the British in Ulster*

*In Time of War:*
*Ireland, Ulster and the Price of Neutrality, 1939–1945*

*Pity the Nation:*
*The Abduction of Lebanon*

# The
# GREAT WAR *for*
# CIVILISATION

# The
# GREAT WAR *for*
# CIVILISATION

## *The Conquest of the Middle East*

# ROBERT FISK

*Alfred A. Knopf   New York   2005*

THIS IS A BORZOI BOOK
PUBLISHED BY ALFRED A. KNOPF

www.aaknopf.com

All maps are drawn by Hardlines, except the Armenian Genocide, produced
by the Armenian National Institute (ANI), Washington, D.C. and the Nubarian
Library, Paris. © ANI, English Edition Copyright 1998.

Library of Congress Cataloging-in-Publication Data
Fisk, Robert.
The great war for civilisation : the conquest of the Middle East / Robert Fisk.
p.  cm.
Includes bibliographical references and index.
ISBN 1-4000-4151-1 (alk. paper)
1. Middle East—History, Military—20th century.   2. Middle East—History,
Military—21st century.   3. War and society—Middle East.   4. Middle
East—Colonization.   5. United States—Relations—Middle East.
6. Middle East—Relations—United States.   I. Title.
DS62.8.F53 2005
956.04—dc22          2005049813

Manufactured in the United States of America
Published November 15, 2005
Reprinted One Time
Third Printing, December 2005

*For Bill and Peggy,*
*who taught me to love books and history*

# Contents

*Acknowledgements* ix

*List of Maps* xiii

*Preface* xvii

1. "One of Our Brothers Had a Dream . . ." 3

2. "They Shoot Russians" 35

3. The Choirs of Kandahar 71

4. The Carpet-Weavers 92

5. The Path to War 139

6. "The Whirlwind War" 179

7. "War against War" and the Fast Train to Paradise 218

8. Drinking the Poisoned Chalice 259

9. "Sentenced to Suffer Death" 294

10. The First Holocaust 316

11. Fifty Thousand Miles from Palestine 356

12. The Last Colonial War 402

13. The Girl and the Child and Love 453

14. "Anything to Wipe Out a Devil . . ." 513

15. Planet Damnation 586

16. Betrayal 646

17. The Land of Graves 688

18. The Plague 716

19. Now Thrive the Armourers . . . 748

20. Even to Kings, He Comes . . . 789

21.  Why?                                                                    827

22.  The Die Is Cast                                                          888

23.  Atomic Dog, Annihilator, Arsonist, Anthrax, Anguish and Agamemnon  937

24.  Into the Wilderness                                                     999

     *Notes*                                                                1039

     *Select Bibliography*                                                  1061

     *Chronology*                                                           1069

     *Index*                                                                1073

# Acknowledgements

IN A BOOK OF THIS SIZE—which includes so many years of reporting—the decision over who should be thanked is almost impossible to take. I have decided, however, that acknowledgements should be given both to those who helped me in the direct knowledge that this book was being written over the past fifteen years—these are the vast majority of names listed here, including, for example, Yassir Arafat, Hizballah leader Hassan Nasrallah and Mikhail Kalashnikov, the inventor of the world's most popular automatic rifle—and a minority whose help in my past reporting shaped the text of this book before the final decision to write it.

I was also faced with the fact that those who did directly assist me in *The Great War for Civilisation* include the Good, the Bad and the Ugly. Can I place a suicide bomber's father alongside a Western humanitarian worker, or a heroic Iraqi who was tortured after resisting Saddam Hussein's nuclear ambitions in the same column as a man who handed his unsuspecting pregnant girlfriend a bomb to take onto an aircraft? Should the late Margaret Hassan, so cruelly murdered in Iraq, stand on the same page as Algeria's "exterminator" interior minister?

The most extreme example of this problem is Osama bin Laden. In my last two conversations with him, he knew I was writing this book and clearly spoke in that knowledge. So should a man held responsible for the greatest international crime against humanity in the Western world be dignified with an entry? Since his comments and thoughts were crucial to parts of the text, I place this on record. But he does not appear below. Others do.

So, in alphabetical order, here are those who must be thanked for their help, enthusiasm and disclosures over the past fifteen years and more. For guidance to the reader, some are listed by their titles or the specific nature of their assistance. Others will realise that this is my specific thanks personally to them. Joan Ablett of the Armenian Assembly of America; Reem Abul Abbas; Astrid Aghaganian, survivor of the 1915 Armenian genocide; Shojae Ahmmadavnde, Iranian soldier in 1984; Robert A. Algarotti, communications manager at Boeing Autonetics and Missile Systems Division; to Dr. Jawad al-Ali, children's doctor in Basra; Dorothy Anderson, for pointing out Lord Roberts's 1905 remarks on Afghanistan; Nimr Aoun, wounded survivor of the 1948 Palestinian dispossession; the late Yassir Arafat, chairman of the Palestinian Authority; Hanan Ashrawi of the Palestinian Authority; Tim Austin, former chief foreign sub-editor of *The Times;* the late Shapour Bakhtiar, the Shah of Iran's last prime minister; Peter Balakian of Colgate University; Siddiq Barmak, Afghan film-maker; Dr. Antony Barter for his father's letters on Iraq and the Armenians in the 1914–18 war; Zouaoui Benamadi of

*Algerie Actualite;* Zaka Berberian, Armenian Holocaust survivor; Shameem Bhatia; Mohamed Bouyali, brother of guerrilla leader Mustafa Bouyali; Lakhdar Brahimi; Ross Campbell for transcripts of *The Scotsman* reports on the end of the British Palestine Mandate; Pierre Caquet; Lieutenant "Sandy" Cavenagh, 3rd Battalion, the Parachute Regiment in 1956; Mustfa Cerić, the Imam of Bosnia; Ellen Sarkisian Chesnut for her memories of her Armenian father; Conor O'Clery of *The Irish Times;* Tony Clifton of *Newsweek;* Patrick Cockburn of *The Independent;* Warrant Officer Tim Corwin, Chinook pilot in Kurdistan in 1991; the late Fred Cuny, U.S. aid official; Jeannik Dami of the ICRC in Kuwait in 1991; Norman Davies for his analysis of Hitler's references to the Armenian Holocaust; Dr. John de Courcy Ireland for his memory of Armenian orphans; Dr. Nadim Dimeshkieh, former Lebanese diplomat; Leonard Doyle, foreign editor of *The Independent;* Eamon Dunphy of Irish radio; Iain R. Edgar of Durham University; Judge David A. O. Edward for his copy of the 1922 James Bryce lecture on the Great War and Armenia; Isabel Ellsen; Saeb Erekat of the Palestinian Authority; Jeanne Farchath; Bill and Peggy Fisk, my late parents; U.S. Major General Jay Garner, commander of U.S. forces in Kurdistan in 1991; Samir Ghattas, current Associated Press bureau chief in Beirut; Bassam and Saniya Ghossain, whose daughter was killed in the 1986 U.S. bombing of Iraq; Dr. Stephen Goldby for Foreign Office correspondence on UN sanctions; Terry Gordy of Boeing Defence and Space Group (Autonetics and Missile Systems Division); Ben Greenberger, Jewish settler on the West Bank; Dr. Selma Haddad, children's doctor in Baghdad; Dennis Halliday, head of the UN Oil-for-Food programme, 1997; Mullanah Sami el-Haq of the al-Haq madrassa in Pakistan; Amira Hass of *Ha'aretz;* the late Margaret Hassan of CARE in Iraq; Dr. Mercy Heatle; Philippe Heffinck of UNICEF, Baghdad in 1997; Mohamed Heikal, Egyptian journalist and author; Gavin Hewitt of the BBC; Sue Hickey, formerly of the Canadian Broadcasting Corporation (CBC), London; Nezar Hindawi, for his unconvincing attempt to explain why he gave his pregnant girlfriend a bomb to take on an El Al flight; Marjorie Housepian; Chafiq al-Hout and his wife, Bayan; Justin Huggler of *The Independent;* John Hurst, vice president of Lockheed Martin; the late King Hussein of Jordan; Alia al-Husseini, granddaughter of Haj al-Husseini, the former Grand Mufti of Jerusalem; Nadeen El Issa for his copy of the Paice and Martin Palestine Police report (also thanks to Peter Metcalfe); Abbas Jiha, who lost many of his family in the Israeli helicopter attack in Lebanon in 1996; Mikhail Kalashnikov, inventor of the Soviet AK-47 rifle; Mayreni Kaloustian, survivor of the 1915 Armenian massacres; the late Wassef Kamal, former assistant to Haj Amin in Nazi Germany; Al Kamhi, Lockheed's director of communications in 1997; Marwan Kanafini of the Palestinian Authority; Kevork Karaboyadjian, director of the Beirut Armenian Old People's Home; Viktoria Karakashian, survivor of the Armenian exodus from Alexandretta; Jamal Kashoggi, assistant to the Saudi ambassador in London; Haroutian Kebedjian, Armenian genocide survivor; Andrew Kevorkian for his unstinting help in tracing Armenian genocide information, and his late brother Aram for memories of his visit to his ancestral home in Turkey; Zainab Kazim for her letter on Shiism;

Sheikh Jouwad Mehdi al-Khalasi for his historical help on British rule in Iraq; Helen Kinsella, former foreign manager of *The Independent* for her indefatigable research; Zeina Khoury of the Associated Press; Josef Kleinman, Auschwitz survivor; Gerry Labelle of AP; the late professor Yeshayahu Leibowitz; George Lewinski, formerly of CBC, London; Mikael Lindval, former UNIFIL officer in southern Lebanon; Dr. David Loewenstein of the University of Wisconsin, Madison; Mrs Hilda Maddock for details of her father Private Charles Dickens in 1917; Dr. Grace Magnier of the Department of Hispanic Studies, Trinity College, Dublin, for her work on Andalusia; the late Ali Mahmoud, Bahrain bureau chief of the Associated Press; General Mansour, commander of Syrian military intelligence in Kimishli; Lara Marlowe of *The Irish Times;* Nabila Megalli, formerly of the Associated Press in Bahrain; Alf Mendes; Gerhard Mertins, German arms dealer; Peter Metcalfe; Abderahman Meziane-Cherif, former Algerian minister of interior; Tewfiq and Philippa Mishlawi of *Middle East Reporter* in Beirut; the late General (Ret'd.) Mohamed Abdul Moneim of *Al-Ahram;* Judy Morgan of CARE in Iraq, Harvey Morris of Reuters, *The Independent,* and now the *Financial Times;* Fathi Daoud Mouffak, Iraqi military cameraman in the Iran-Iraq War; Major Mustafa Murad of the Egyptian army in 1956; Anis Naccache for his memories of the Iranian Revolution and his wife, Battoul, for her translations of Iranian war poetry; Haj Mohamed Nasr, father of a Palestinian suicide bomber from Jenin; Sayed Hassan Nasrallah, chairman of the Lebanese Hizballah; Suheil Natour of the Democratic Front for the Liberation of Palestine; Guillaume Nichols for drawing my attention to Lloyd George's 1936 speech on Palestine; Nawaf Obaid whose Harvard thesis on the goals of Saudi Wahabists was so valuable; Mohmed Mahran Othman, blinded Egyptian guerrilla fighter in 1956; the late Srpouhi Papazian, Armenian genocide survivor; film-maker Nelofer Pazira; the late Dr. Abdul-Aziz Rantissi of Hamas; my colleague Phil Reeves of *The Independent* and now of National Public Radio; Rabbi Walter Rothschild for his encylopaedic knowledge of Lebanese railways; Martin Rubenstein, who drew my attention to a reference on the Armenian genocide in *The Road to En-Dor;* Mujtaba Safavi, former Iranian POW; Haidar al-Safi in Baghdad; the late and brilliant Palestinian scholar Edward Said, and his authoress sister Jean Makdissi for their help and suggestions over many years; Mohamed Salam, former Associated Press bureau chief in Baghdad; Dr. Kamal Salibi, formerly director of the Institute of Interfaith Studies in Amman; Mohamed Salman, former Syrian minister of information; Farouk al-Sharaa, Syrian foreign minister; Abdul-Hadi Sayah, the friend of Mustafa Bouyali; Martin Scannall for permission to quote from Kenneth Whitehead's *Iraq the Irremediable;* Clive Semple; Dr. Hussain Sharistani, Saddam Hussain's senior nuclear adviser; Don Sheridan; Private Andrew Shewmaker of the U.S. 24th Mechanized Infantry Division in the 1991 Gulf War; the Israeli historian Avi Shlaim; Amira el-Solh; Hans von Sponeck, Halliday's UN successor in the humanitarian office in Baghdad, 1999; Eva Stern of New York for her indefatigable search for the truth about the Sabra and Chatila massacre; Verjine Svazlian for her copy of Armenian Holocaust survivors' songs; Maitre Mohamed Tahri, Algerian human rights lawyer; Monsigneur Henri Teissier, Archbishop of Algiers; Alex Thomson of ITV; Dr. Hassan Tourabi in Khartoum; Derek Turnbull of Vickers; Karsten Tveit of Norwegian radio; Christopher J. Walker for his knowledge of all things Armenian; Jihad al-Wazzir; Garry Williamson of the Boeing Defence and Space Group; the late Christopher "Monty" Woodhouse, former SOE agent in Greece and British agent in Iran; and Dedi Zucker, Israeli Knesset MP.

My thanks must also go to Simon Kelner, the editor of *The Independent*, who encouraged me to write this book between assignments in Iraq and Lebanon and who turned an editor's blind eye towards my prolonged absences from the paper, and for allowing me to quote from my own dispatches to the paper over sixteen years; and to *The Times* of London for whom I worked as Middle East correspondent from 1976 until 1988; to *The Irish Times;* to the *London Review of Books* and to *The Nation* in New York for allowing me to quote from articles of mine which appeared in their pages; to the Canadian Broadcasting Corporation in Toronto for my recordings from the 1980 Soviet occupation of Afghanistan and from the Iran-Iraq War; to the Controller of Her Majesty's Stationary Office for British Government documents in the National Archives (Kew).

Especially, I must thank Louise Haines, my editor at Fourth Estate for her superhuman patience in nurturing this book for an astonishing sixteen years and Steve Cox, the most indefatigable copy-editor in the world. Lastly, my appreciation goes to Dr. Victoria Fontan, who wrote the chronology, formatted the bibliography and, with superhuman patience, archived 328,000 of my documents, notes and dispatches.

Inevitably, there are many to whom I owe my thanks but who cannot be named for their own security—subject to potential threat both from their enemies and from their own governments. They include members—serving and retired—of the armed forces of Egypt, France, Iran, Iraq (including the former second-in-command of the air force and two of his pilots), Israel, Jordan, Lebanon, "Palestine," Syria, Turkey, the United Kingdom and the United States.

And, of course, I add the usual author's caveat: none of the above is responsible for any errors or views expressed in *The Great War for Civilisation*.

# Maps

The Middle East        xiv–xv

Afghanistan        36

Iran        93

Iraq        140

The Sykes–Picot Agreement        143

The Iran–Iraq War        180

The Armenian Genocide        317

Israel/Palestine        357

Algeria        514

Saudi Arabia/Kuwait/Iraq        587

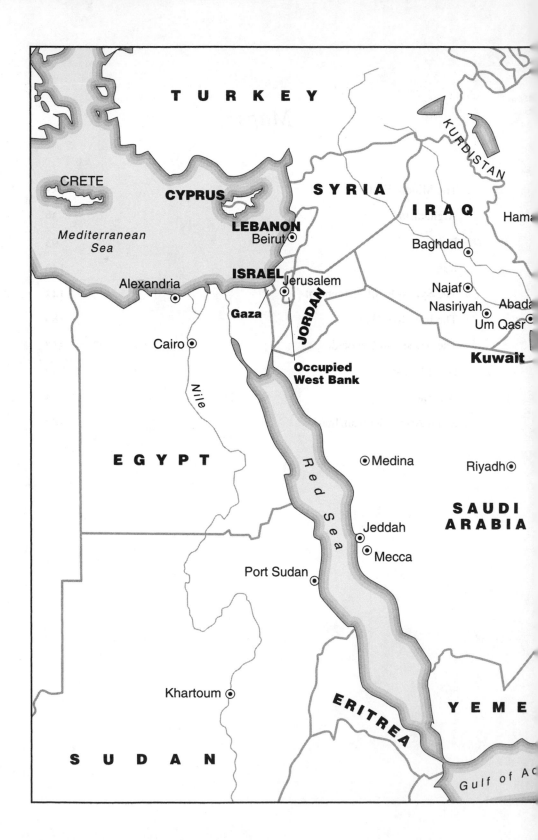

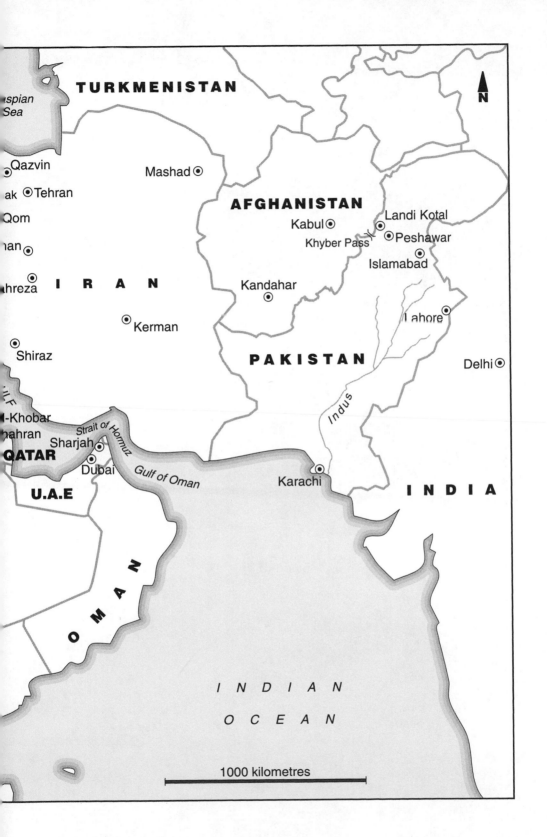

# *Preface*

WHEN I WAS A SMALL BOY, my father would take me each year around the battlefields of the First World War, the conflict that H. G. Wells called "the war to end all wars." We would set off each summer in our Austin of England and bump along the potholed roads of the Somme, Ypres and Verdun. By the time I was fourteen, I could recite the names of all the offensives: Bapaume, Hill 60, High Wood, Passchendaele . . . I had seen all the graveyards and I had walked through all the overgrown trenches and touched the rusted helmets of British soldiers and the corroded German mortars in decaying museums. My father was a soldier of the Great War, fighting in the trenches of France because of a shot fired in a city he'd never heard of called Sarajevo. And when he died thirteen years ago at the age of ninety-three, I inherited his campaign medals. One of them depicts a winged victory and on the obverse side are engraved the words: "The Great War for Civilisation."

To my father's deep concern and my mother's stoic acceptance, I have spent much of my life in wars. They, too, were fought "for civilisation." In Afghanistan, I watched the Russians fighting for their "international duty" in a conflict against "international terror"; their Afghan opponents, of course, were fighting against "communist aggression" and for Allah. I reported from the front lines as the Iranians struggled through what they called the "Imposed War" against Saddam Hussein—who dubbed his 1980 invasion of Iran the "Whirlwind War." I've seen the Israelis twice invading Lebanon and then reinvading the Palestinian West Bank in order, so they claimed, to "purge the land of terrorism." I was present as the Algerian military went to war with Islamists for the same ostensible reason, torturing and executing their prisoners with as much abandon as their enemies. Then in 1990 Saddam invaded Kuwait and the Americans sent their armies to the Gulf to liberate the emirate and impose a "New World Order." After the 1991 war, I always wrote down the words "new world order" in my notebook followed by a question mark. In Bosnia, I found Serbs fighting for what they called "Serb civilisation" while their Muslim enemies fought and died for a fading multicultural dream and to save their own lives.

On a mountaintop in Afghanistan, I sat opposite Osama bin Laden in his tent as he uttered his first direct threat against the United States, pausing as I scribbled his words into my notebook by paraffin lamp. "God" and "evil" were what he talked to me about. I was flying over the Atlantic on 11 September 2001—my plane turned round off Ireland following the attacks on the United States—and so less than three months later I was in Afghanistan, fleeing with the Taliban down a highway west of Kandahar as America bombed the ruins of a country already destroyed by war. I was in the United Nations General Assembly exactly a year after the attacks on America when George Bush talked about Saddam's non-existent weapons of mass destruction, and prepared to invade Iraq. The first missiles of that invasion swept over my head in Baghdad.

The direct physical results of all these conflicts will remain—and should remain—in my memory until I die. I don't need to read through my mountain of reporters' notebooks to remember the Iranian soldiers on the troop train north to Tehran, holding towels and coughing up Saddam's gas in gobs of blood and mucus as they read the Koran. I need none of my newspaper clippings to recall the father—after an American cluster-bomb attack on Iraq in 2003—who held out to me what looked like half a crushed loaf of bread but which turned out to be half a crushed baby. Or the mass grave outside Nasiriyah in which I came across the remains of a leg with a steel tube inside and a plastic medical disc still attached to a stump of bone; Saddam's murderers had taken their victim straight from the hospital where he had his hip replacement to his place of execution in the desert.

I don't have nightmares about these things. But I remember. The head blasted off the body of a Kosovo Albanian refugee in an American air raid four years earlier, bearded and upright in a bright green field as if a medieval axeman has just cut him down. The corpse of a Kosovo farmer murdered by Serbs, his grave opened by the UN so that he re-emerges from the darkness, bloating in front of us, his belt tightening viciously round his stomach, twice the size of a normal man. The Iraqi soldier at Fao during the Iran–Iraq War who lay curled up like a child in the gun-pit beside me, black with death, a single gold wedding ring glittering on the third finger of his left hand, bright with sunlight and love for a woman who did not know she was a widow. Soldier and civilian, they died in their tens of thousands because death had been concocted for them, morality hitched like a halter round the warhorse so that we could talk about "target-rich environments" and "collateral damage"—that most infantile of attempts to shake off the crime of killing—and report the victory parades, the tearing down of statues and the importance of peace.

Governments like it that way. They want their people to see war as a drama of opposites, good and evil, "them" and "us," victory or defeat. But war is primarily not about victory or defeat but about death and the infliction of death. It represents the total failure of the human spirit. I know an editor who has wearied of hearing me say this, but how many editors have first-hand experience of war?

Ironically, it was a movie that propelled me into journalism. I was twelve years old when I saw Alfred Hitchcock's *Foreign Correspondent*, a black and white 1940 creaky of patriotism and equally black humour in which Joel McCrea played an American reporter called John Jones—renamed Huntley Haverstock by his New York editor—who is sent in 1939 to cover the approaching war in Europe. He witnesses an assassination, chases Nazi spies in Holland, uncovers Germany's top agent in London, is shot down in an airliner by a German pocket battleship and survives to scoop the world. He also wins the most gorgeous woman in the movie, clearly an added bonus for such an exciting profession. The film ends in the London Blitz with a radio announcer introducing Haverstock on the air. "We have as a guest tonight one of the soldiers of the press," he says, ". . . one of the little army of historians who are writing history from beside the cannon's mouth . . ."

I never looked back. I read my father's conservative *Daily Telegraph* from cover to cover, always the foreign reports, lying on the floor beside the fire as my mother pleaded with me to drink my cocoa and go to bed. At school I studied *The Times* each afternoon. I ploughed through Khrushchev's entire speech denouncing Stalin's reign of terror. I won the school Current Affairs prize and never—ever—could anyone shake me from my determination to be a foreign correspondent. When my father suggested I should study law or medicine, I walked from the room. When he asked a family friend what I should do, the friend asked me to imagine I was in a courtroom. Would I want to be the lawyer or the reporter on the press bench, he asked me. I said I would be the reporter and he told my father: "Robert is going to be a journalist." I wanted to be one of the "soldiers of the press."

I joined the *Newcastle Evening Chronicle*, then the *Sunday Express* diary column, where I chased vicars who had run off with starlets. After three years, I begged *The Times* to hire me and they sent me to Northern Ireland to cover the vicious little conflict that had broken out in that legacy of British colonial rule. Five years later, I became one of those "soldiers" of journalism, a foreign correspondent. I was on a beach at Porto Covo in Portugal in April of 1976—on holiday from Lisbon where I was covering the aftermath of the Portuguese revolution—when the local postmistress shouted down the cliff that I had a letter to collect. It was from the paper's deputy editor, Louis Heren. "I have some good news for you," he wrote. "Paul Martin has requested to be moved from the Middle East. His wife has had more than enough, and I don't blame her. I am offering him the number two job in Paris, Richard Wigg Lisbon—and to you I offer the Middle East. Let me know if you want it . . . It would be a splendid opportunity for you, with good stories, lots of travel and sunshine . . ." In Hitchcock's thriller, Haverstock's editor calls him to his office before sending him to the European war and asks him: "How would you like to cover the biggest story in the world today?" Heren's letter was less dramatic but it meant the same thing.

I was twenty-nine and I was being offered the Middle East—I wondered how King Feisal felt when he was "offered" Iraq or how his brother Abdullah reacted to Winston Churchill's "offer" of Transjordan. Louis Heren was in the Churchillian mode himself, stubborn, eloquent, and an enjoyer of fine wines as well as himself a former Middle East correspondent. If the stories were "good" in journalistic terms, however, they would also prove to be horrific, the travel dizzying, the "sunshine" as cruel as a sword. And we journalists did not have the protection—or the claims to perfection—of kings. But now I could be one of "the little army of historians who are writing history from beside the cannon's mouth." How innocent, how naive I was. Yet innocence, if we can keep it, protects a journalist's integrity. You have to fight to believe in it.

Unlike my father, I went to war as a witness rather than a combatant, an ever more infuriated bystander to be true, but at least I was not one of the impassioned, angry, sometimes demented men who made war. I worshipped the older reporters who had covered the Second World War and its aftermath: Howard K. Smith, who fled Nazi Germany on the last train from Berlin before Hitler declared war on the United States in 1941; James Cameron, whose iconic 1946 report from the Bikini atom tests was perhaps the most literary and philosophical article ever published in a newspaper.

Being a Middle East correspondent is a slightly obscene profession to follow in such circumstances. If the soldiers I watched decided to leave the battlefield, they would—many of them—be shot for desertion, at least court-martialled. The civilians among whom I was to live and work were forced to stay on under bombardments, their families decimated by shellfire and air raids. As citizens of pariah countries, there would be no visas for them. But if I wanted to quit, if I grew sick of the horrors I saw, I could pack my bag and fly home business class, a glass of champagne in my hand, always supposing—unlike too many of my colleagues— that I hadn't been killed. Which is why I cringe each time someone wants to psycho-babble about the "trauma" of covering wars, the need to obtain "counselling" for us well-paid scribes that we may be able to "come to terms" with what we have seen. No counselling for the poor and huddled masses that were left to Iraq's gas, Iran's rockets, the cruelty of Serbia's militias, the brutal Israeli invasion of Lebanon in 1982, the computerised death suffered by Iraqis during America's 2003 invasion of their country.

I don't like the definition "war correspondent." It is history, not journalism, that has condemned the Middle East to war. I think "war correspondent" smells a bit, reeks of false romanticism; it has too much of the whiff of Victorian reporters who would view battles from hilltops in the company of ladies, immune to suffering, only occasionally glancing towards the distant pop-pop of cannon fire. Yet war is, paradoxically, a very powerful, unique experience for a journalist, an opportunity to indulge in the only vicarious excitement still free of charge. If you've seen the movies, why not experience the real thing? I fear that some of my colleagues have died this way, heading to war on the assumption that it's still Hollywood, that the heroes don't die, that you can't get killed like the others, that they'll all be Huntley Haverstocks with a scoop and the best girl. But you *can* get killed. In just one year in Bosnia, thirty of my colleagues died. There is a little Somme waiting for all innocent journalists.

When I first set out to write this book, I intended it to be a reporter's chronicle of the Middle East over almost three decades. That is how I wrote my previous book *Pity the Nation*, a first-person account of Lebanon's civil war and two Israeli invasions.* But as I prowled through the shelves of papers in my library, more than 350,000 documents and notebooks and files, some written under fire in my own

---

*\*Pity the Nation: Lebanon at War,* rev. ed. (1990; repr., Oxford: Oxford University Press, 2001), U.S. new edition entitled *Pity the Nation: The Abduction of Lebanon* (New York: Nation Books, 2002). Readers interested in the Lebanese civil war, the Israeli invasions of 1978 and 1982, the Qana massacre and other tragedies in Lebanon may turn to *Pity the Nation.* I have not attempted to rewrite the story of Lebanon here.

hand, some punched onto telegram paper by tired Arab telecommunications operators, many pounded out on the clacking telex machines we used before the Internet was invented, I realised that this was going to be more than a chronology of
eyewitness reports.

My father, the old soldier of 1918, read my account of the Lebanon war but
would not live to see this book. Yet he would always look into the past to understand the present. If only the world had not gone to war in 1914; if only we had not
been so selfish in concluding the peace. We victors promised independence to the
Arabs and support for a Jewish homeland in Palestine. Promises are meant to be
kept. And so those promises—the Jews naturally thought that their homeland
would be in all of Palestine—were betrayed, and the millions of Arabs and Jews of
the Middle East are now condemned to live with the results.

In the Middle East, it sometimes feels as if no event in history has a finite end,
a crossing point, a moment when we can say: "Stop—enough—this is where we
will break free." I think I understand that time-warp. My father was born in the
century before last. I was born in the first half of the last century. Here I am, I tell
myself in 1980, watching the Soviet army invade Afghanistan, in 1982 cowering
in the Iranian front line opposite Saddam's legions, in 2003 observing the first
American soldiers of the 3rd Infantry Division cross the great bridge over the
Tigris River. And yet the Battle of the Somme opened just thirty years before I was
born. Bill Fisk was in the trenches of France three years after the Armenian genocide but only twenty-eight years before my birth. I would be born within six years
of the Battle of Britain, just over a year after Hitler's suicide. I saw the planes
returning to Britain from Korea and remember my mother telling me in 1956 that I
was lucky, that had I been older I would have been a British conscript invading
Suez.

If I feel this personally, it is because I have witnessed events that, over the
years, can only be defined as an arrogance of power. The Iranians used to call the
United States the "centre of world arrogance," and I would laugh at this, but I have
begun to understand what it means. After the Allied victory of 1918, at the end of
my father's war, the victors divided up the lands of their former enemies. In the
space of just seventeen months, they created the borders of Northern Ireland,
Yugoslavia and most of the Middle East. And I have spent my entire career—in
Belfast and Sarajevo, in Beirut and Baghdad—watching the peoples within those
borders burn. America invaded Iraq not for Saddam Hussein's mythical "weapons
of mass destruction"—which had long ago been destroyed—but to change the map
of the Middle East, much as my father's generation had done more than eighty
years earlier. Even as it took place, Bill Fisk's war was helping to produce the century's first genocide—that of a million and a half Armenians—and laying the
foundations for a second, that of the Jews of Europe.

This book is also about torture and executions. Perhaps our work as journalists
does open the door of the occasional cell. Perhaps we do sometimes save a soul
from the hangman's noose. But over the years there has been a steadily growing
deluge of letters—both to myself and to the editor of *The Independent*—in which

readers, more thoughtful and more despairing than ever before, plead to know how they can make their voices heard when democratic governments seem no longer inclined to represent those who elected them. How, these readers ask, can they prevent a cruel world from poisoning the lives of their children? "How can I help them?" a British woman living in Germany wrote to me after *The Independent* published a long article of mine about the raped Muslim women of Gacko in Bosnia—women who had received no international medical aid, no psychological help, no kindness two years after their violation.

I suppose, in the end, we journalists try—or should try—to be the first impartial witnesses to history. If we have any reason for our existence, the least must be our ability to report history as it happens so that no one can say: "We didn't know—no one told us." Amira Hass, the brilliant Israeli journalist on *Ha'aretz* newspaper whose reports on the occupied Palestinian territories have outshone anything written by non-Israeli reporters, discussed this with me more than two years ago. I was insisting that we had a vocation to write the first pages of history but she interrupted me. "No, Robert, you're wrong," she said. "Our job is to monitor the centres of power." And I think, in the end, that is the best definition of journalism I have heard: to challenge authority—all authority—especially so when governments and politicians take us to war, when they have decided that they will kill and others will die.

But can we perform that task? This book will not provide an answer. My life as a journalist has been a great adventure. It still is. Yet looking through these pages after months of writing, I find they are filled with accounts of pain and injustice and horror, the sins of fathers visited upon their children. They are also about genocide. I used to argue, hopelessly I'm sure, that every reporter should carry a history book in his back pocket. In 1992, I was in Sarajevo and once, as Serb shells whiffled over my head, I stood upon the very paving stone upon which Gavrilo Princip stood as he fired the fatal shot that sent my father to the trenches of the First World War. And of course the shots were still being fired in Sarajevo in 1992. It was as if history were a gigantic echo chamber. That was the year in which my father died. This is therefore the story of his generation. And of mine.

Beirut, June 2005

# *The*
# GREAT WAR *for*
# CIVILISATION

# CHAPTER ONE

# "One of Our Brothers Had a Dream . . . "

They combine a mad love of country with an equally mad indifference to life, their own as well as others. They are cunning, unscrupulous, and inspired.

—"Stephen Fisher" in Alfred Hitchcock's
*Foreign Correspondent* (1940)

I KNEW IT WOULD BE LIKE THIS. On 19 March 1997, outside the Spinghar Hotel in Jalalabad with its manicured lawns and pink roses, an Afghan holding a Kalashnikov rifle invited me to travel in a car out of town. The highway to Kabul that evening was no longer a road but a mass of rocks and crevasses above the roaring waters of a great river. A vast mountain chain towered above us. The Afghan smiled at me occasionally but did not talk. I knew what his smile was supposed to say. Trust me. But I didn't. I smiled back the rictus of false friendship. Unless I saw a man I recognised—an Arab rather than an Afghan—I would watch this road for traps, checkpoints, gunmen who were there to no apparent purpose. Even inside the car, I could hear the river as it sloshed through gulleys and across wide shoals of grey stones and poured over the edge of cliffs. Trust Me steered the car carefully around the boulders and I admired the way his bare left foot eased the clutch of the vehicle up and down as a man might gently urge a horse to clamber over a rock.

A benevolent white dust covered the windscreen, and when the wipers cleared it the desolation took on a hard, unforgiving, dun-coloured uniformity. The track must have looked like this, I thought to myself, when Major-General William Elphinstone led his British army to disaster more than 150 years ago. The Afghans had annihilated one of the greatest armies of the British empire on this very stretch of road, and high above me were villages where old men still remembered the stories of great-grandfathers who had seen the English die in their thousands. The stones of Gandamak, they claim, were made black by the blood of the English dead. The year 1842 marked one of the greatest defeats of British arms. No wonder we preferred to forget the First Afghan War. But Afghans don't forget. *"Farangiano,"* the driver shouted and pointed down into the gorge and grinned at me. "Foreigners." *"Angrezi."* "English." *"Jang."* "War." Yes, I got the point. *"Irlanda,"* I replied in Arabic. *"Ana min Irlanda."* I am from Ireland. Even if he understood me, it was a lie. Educated in Ireland I was, but in my pocket was a small black British passport in which His Majesty's Principal Secretary of State for Foreign and Commonwealth Affairs required in the name of Her Majesty that I should be allowed "to pass freely without let or hindrance" on this perilous journey. A teenage Taliban had looked at my passport at Jalalabad airport two days earlier, a boy soldier of maybe fourteen who held the document upside down, stared at it and clucked his tongue and shook his head in disapproval.

It had grown dark and we were climbing, overtaking trucks and rows of camels, the beasts turning their heads towards our lights in the gloom. We careered past them and I could see the condensation of their breath floating over the road. Their huge feet were picking out the rocks with infinite care and their eyes, when they caught the light, looked like dolls' eyes. Two hours later, we stopped on a stony hillside and, after a few minutes, a pick-up truck came bouncing down the rough shale of the mountain.

An Arab in Afghan clothes came towards the car. I recognised him at once from our last meeting in a ruined village. "I am sorry, Mr. Robert, but I must give you the first search," he said, prowling through my camera bag and newspapers. And so we set off up the track that Osama bin Laden built during his jihad against the Russian army in the early 1980s, a terrifying, slithering, two-hour odyssey along fearful ravines in rain and sleet, the windscreen misting as we climbed the cold mountain. "When you believe in jihad, it is easy," he said, fighting with the steering wheel as stones scuttered from the tyres, tumbling down the precipice into the clouds below. From time to time, lights winked at us from far away in the darkness. "Our brothers are letting us know they see us," he said.

After an hour, two armed Arabs—one with his face covered in a kuffiah scarf, eyes peering at us through spectacles, holding an anti-tank rocket-launcher over his right shoulder—came screaming from behind two rocks. "Stop! Stop!" As the brakes were jammed on, I almost hit my head on the windscreen. "Sorry, sorry," the bespectacled man said, putting down his rocket-launcher. He pulled a metal detector from the pocket of his combat jacket, the red light flicking over my body in another search. The road grew worse as we continued, the jeep skidding backwards towards sheer cliffs, the headlights playing across the chasms on either side. "Toyota is good for jihad," my driver said. I could only agree, noting that this was one advertising logo the Toyota company would probably forgo.

There was moonlight now and I could see clouds both below us in the ravines and above us, curling round mountaintops, our headlights shining on frozen waterfalls and ice-covered pools. Osama bin Laden knew how to build his wartime roads; many an ammunition truck and tank had ground its way up here during the titanic struggle against the Russian army. Now the man who led those guerrillas— the first Arab fighter in the battle against Moscow—was back again in the mountains he knew. There were more Arab checkpoints, more shrieked orders to halt. One very tall man in combat uniform and wearing shades carefully patted my shoulders, body, legs and looked into my face. *Salaam aleikum*, I said. Peace be upon you. Every Arab I had ever met replied *Aleikum salaam* to this greeting. But not this one. There was something cold about this man. Osama bin Laden had invited me to meet him in Afghanistan, but this was a warrior without the minimum courtesy. He was a machine, checking out another machine.

IT HAD NOT ALWAYS BEEN THIS WAY. Indeed, the first time I met Osama bin Laden, the way could not have been easier. Back in December 1993, I had been covering an Islamic summit in the Sudanese capital of Khartoum when a Saudi journalist friend of mine, Jamal Kashoggi, walked up to me in the lobby of my hotel. Kashoggi, a tall, slightly portly man in a long white *dishdash* robe, led me by the shoulder outside the hotel. "There is someone I think you should meet," he said. Kashoggi is a sincere believer—woe betide anyone who regards his round spectacles and roguish sense of humour as a sign of spiritual laxity—and I guessed at once to whom he was referring. Kashoggi had visited bin Laden in Afghanistan during his war against the Russian army. "He has never met a Western reporter before," he announced. "This will be interesting." Kashoggi was indulging in a little applied psychology. He wanted to know how bin Laden would respond to an infidel. So did I.

Bin Laden's story was as instructive as it was epic. When the Soviet army invaded Afghanistan in 1979, the Saudi royal family—encouraged by the CIA—sought to provide the Afghans with an Arab legion, preferably led by a Saudi prince, who would lead a guerrilla force against the Russians. Not only would he disprove the popularly held and all too accurate belief that the Saudi leadership was effete and corrupt, he could re-establish the honourable tradition of the Gulf Arab warrior, heedless of his own life in defending the *umma*, the community of Islam. True to form, the Saudi princes declined this noble mission. Bin Laden, infuriated at both their cowardice and the humiliation of the Afghan Muslims at the hands of the Soviets, took their place and, with money and machinery from his own construction company, set off on his own personal jihad.

A billionaire businessman and himself a Saudi, albeit of humbler Yemeni descent, in the coming years he would be idolised by both Saudis and millions of other Arabs, the stuff of Arab schoolboy legend from the Gulf to the Mediterranean. Not since the British glorified Lawrence of Arabia had an adventurer been portrayed in so heroic, so influential a role. Egyptians, Saudis, Yemenis, Kuwaitis, Algerians, Syrians and Palestinians made their way to the Pakistani border city of Peshawar to fight alongside bin Laden. But when the Afghan mujahedin guerrillas and bin Laden's Arab legion had driven the Soviets from Afghanistan, the Afghans turned upon each other with wolflike and tribal venom. Sickened by this perversion of Islam—original dissension within the *umma* led to the division of Sunni and Shia Muslims—bin Laden returned to Saudi Arabia.

But his journey of spiritual bitterness was not over. When Saddam Hussein invaded Kuwait in 1990, bin Laden once more offered his services to the Saudi royal family. They did not need to invite the United States to protect the place of the two holiest shrines of Islam, he argued. Mecca and Medina, the cities in which the Prophet Mohamed received and recited God's message, should be defended only by Muslims. Bin Laden would lead his "Afghans," his Arab mujahedin, against the Iraqi army inside Kuwait and drive them from the emirate. King Fahd of Saudi Arabia preferred to put his trust in the Americans. So as the U.S. 82nd Airborne Division arrived in the north-eastern Saudi city of Dhahran and deployed in the desert roughly 500 miles from the city of Medina—the place of the Prophet's refuge and of the first Islamic society—bin Laden abandoned the corruption of the House of Saud to bestow his generosity on another "Islamic Republic": Sudan.

Our journey north from Khartoum lay though a landscape of white desert and ancient, unexplored pyramids, dark, squat Pharaonic tombs smaller than those of Cheops, Chephren and Mycerinus at Giza. Though it was December, a sharp, superheated breeze moved across the desert, and when Kashoggi tired of the air conditioning and opened his window, it snapped at his Arab headdress. "The people like bin Laden here," he said, in much the way that one might comment approvingly of a dinner host. "He's got his business here and his construction company and the government likes him. He helps the poor." I could understand all this. The Prophet Mohamed, orphaned at an early age, had been obsessed by the poor in seventh-century Arabia, and generosity to those who lived in poverty was one of the most attractive characteristics of Islam. Bin Laden's progress from "holy" warrior to public benefactor might allow him to walk in the Prophet's footsteps. He had just completed building a new road from the Khartoum–Port Sudan highway to the tiny desert village of Almatig in northern Sudan, using the same bulldozers he had employed to construct the guerrilla trails of Afghanistan; many of his labourers were the same fighters who had been his comrades in the battle against the Soviet Union. The U.S. State Department took a predictably less charitable view of bin Laden's beneficence. It accused Sudan of being a "sponsor of international terrorism" and bin Laden himself of operating "terrorist training camps" in the Sudanese desert.

But when Kashoggi and I arrived in Almatig, there was Osama bin Laden in his gold-fringed robe, sitting beneath the canopy of a tent before a crowd of admiring villagers and guarded by the loyal Arab mujahedin who fought alongside him in Afghanistan. Bearded, silent figures—unarmed, but never more than a few yards from the man who recruited them, trained them and then dispatched them to destroy the Soviet army—they watched unsmiling as the Sudanese villagers lined up to thank the Saudi businessman who was about to complete the road linking their slums to Khartoum for the first time in history.

My first impression was of a shy man. With his high cheekbones, narrow eyes and long brown robe, he would avert his eyes when the village leaders addressed him. He seemed ill-at-ease with gratitude, incapable of responding with a full smile when children in miniature chadors danced in front of him and preachers admired his wisdom. "We have been waiting for this road through all the revolutions in Sudan," a bearded sheikh announced. "We waited until we had given up on everybody—and then Osama bin Laden came along." I noticed how bin Laden, head still bowed, peered up at the old man, acknowledging his age but unhappy that he should be sitting at ease in front of him, a young man relaxing before his elders. He was even more unhappy at the sight of a Westerner standing a few feet away from him, and from time to time he would turn his head to look at me, not with malevolence but with grave suspicion.

Kashoggi put his arms around him. Bin Laden kissed him on both cheeks, one Muslim to another, both acknowledging the common danger they had endured together in Afghanistan. Jamal Kashoggi must have brought the foreigner for a reason. That is what bin Laden was thinking. For as Kashoggi spoke, bin Laden looked over his shoulder at me, occasionally nodding. "Robert, I want to introduce you to Sheikh Osama," Kashoggi half-shouted through children's songs. Bin Laden was a tall man and he realised that this was an advantage when he shook hands with the English reporter. *Salaam aleikum.* His hands were firm, not strong, but, yes, he looked like a mountain man. The eyes searched your face. He was lean and had long fingers and a smile which—while it could never be described as kind—did not suggest villainy. He said we might talk, at the back of the tent where we could avoid the shouting of the children.

Looking back now, knowing what we know, understanding the monstrous beast-figure he would become in the collective imagination of the world, I search for some clue, the tiniest piece of evidence, that this man could inspire an act that would change the world for ever—or, more to the point, allow an American president to persuade his people that the world was changed for ever. Certainly his formal denial of "terrorism" gave no hint. The Egyptian press was claiming that bin Laden had brought hundreds of his Arab fighters with him to Sudan, while the Western embassy circuit in Khartoum was suggesting that some of the Arab "Afghans" whom this Saudi entrepreneur had flown to Sudan were now busy training for further jihad wars in Algeria, Tunisia and Egypt. Bin Laden was well aware of this. "The rubbish of the media and embassies," he called it. "I am a construction engineer and an agriculturalist. If I had training camps here in Sudan, I couldn't possibly do this job."

The "job" was certainly ambitious: not just the Almatig connection but a brand-new highway stretching all the way from Khartoum to Port Sudan, a distance of 1,200 kilometres on the old road, now shortened to 800 kilometres by the new bin Laden route that would turn the distance from the capital into a mere day's journey. In a country that was despised by Saudi Arabia for its support of Saddam Hussein after his 1990 invasion of Kuwait almost as much as it was by the United States, bin Laden had turned the equipment of war to the construction of a pariah state. I did wonder why he could not have done the same to the blighted landscape of Afghanistan, but he refused at first to talk about his war, sitting at the back of the tent and cleaning his teeth with a piece of *mishwak* wood. But talk he eventually did about a war that he helped to win for the Afghans whom the Americans and the Saudis—and the Pakistanis—all supported against the Russians. He wanted to talk. He thought he was going to be interrogated about "terrorism" and realised that he was being asked about Afghanistan and—despite all the reserve and suspicion he felt towards a foreigner—that he wished to explain how his experience there had shaped his life.

"What I lived through in two years there," he said, "I could not have lived in a hundred years elsewhere. When the invasion of Afghanistan started, I was enraged and went there at once—I arrived within days, before the end of 1979, and I went on going back for nine years. I felt outraged that an injustice had been committed against the people of Afghanistan. It made me realise that people who take power in the world use their power under different names to subvert others and to force their opinions on them. Yes, I fought there, but my fellow Muslims did much more than I. Many of them died and I am still alive." The Russian invasion is often dated to January 1980, but the first Soviet special forces troops entered Kabul before Christmas of 1979 when they—or their Afghan satellites—killed the incumbent communist President Hafizullah Amin and established Babrak Karmal as their puppet in Kabul. Osama bin Laden had moved fast.

With his Iraqi engineer Mohamed Saad, who was now building the highway to Port Sudan, bin Laden blasted massive tunnels into the Zazai Mountains of Paktia Province for guerrilla hospitals and arms dumps, then cut a mujahedin dirt trail across Afghanistan to within 25 kilometres of Kabul, a remarkable feat of engineering that the Russians were never able to destroy. But what lessons had bin Laden drawn from the war against the Russians? He was wounded five times and 500 of his Arab fighters were killed in combat with the Soviets—their graves lie just inside the Afghan border at Torkham—and even bin Laden was not immortal, was he?

"I was never afraid of death," he replied. "As Muslims, we believe that when we die, we go to heaven." He was no longer irritating his teeth with the piece of *mishwak* wood but talking slowly and continuously, leaning forward, his elbows on his knees. "Before a battle, God sends us *seqina*—tranquillity. Once I was only thirty metres from the Russians and they were trying to capture me. I was under bombardment but I was so peaceful in my heart that I fell asleep. This experience of *seqina* has been written about in our earliest books. I saw a 120-millimetre mortar shell land in front of me, but it did not blow up. Four more bombs were dropped from a Russian plane on our headquarters but they did not explode. We beat the Soviet Union. The Russians fled . . . My time in Afghanistan was the most important experience of my life."

But what of the Arab mujahedin whom he took to Afghanistan—members of a guerrilla army who were also encouraged and armed by the United States to fight the Russians, and who were forgotten by their mentors when the war was over? Bin Laden seemed ready for the question. "Personally neither I nor my brothers saw evidence of American help," he said. "When my mujahedin were victorious and the Russians were driven out, differences started so I returned to road construction in Taif and Abha. I brought back the equipment I had used to build tunnels and roads for the mujahedin in Afghanistan. Yes, I helped some of my comrades come here after the war." How many? Osama bin Laden shook his head. "I don't want to say. But they are here with me now, they are working right here, building this road to Port Sudan."

A month earlier, I had been on assignment in the Bosnian war and I told bin

Laden that Bosnian Muslim fighters in the town of Travnik had mentioned his name to me. This awoke his interest. Each time I saw bin Laden, he was fascinated to hear not what his enemies thought of him but of what Muslim ulema and militants said of him. "I feel the same about Bosnia," he said. "But the situation there does not provide the same opportunities as Afghanistan. A small number of mujahedin have gone to fight in Bosnia-Hercegovina but the Croats won't allow the mujahedin in through Croatia as the Pakistanis did with Afghanistan." But wasn't it a bit of an anticlimax to be fighting for Islam and God in Afghanistan and end up road-building in Sudan? Bin Laden was now more studied in his use of words. "They like this work and so do I. This is a great project which we are achieving for the people here; it helps the Muslims and improves their lives."

This was the moment when I noticed that other men, Sudanese who were very definitely not among bin Laden's former comrades, had gathered to listen to our conversation. Bin Laden, of course, had been aware of their presence long before me. What did he think about the war in Algeria? I asked. But a man in a green suit calling himself Mohamed Moussa—he claimed to be Nigerian although he was a Sudanese government security agent—tapped me on the arm. "You have asked more than enough questions," he announced. So how about a picture? Bin Laden hesitated—something he rarely did—and I sensed that prudence was fighting with vanity. In the end, he stood on the new road in his gold-fringed robe and smiled wanly at my camera for two pictures, then raised his left hand like a president telling the press when their time was up. At which point Osama bin Laden went off to inspect his highway.

But what was the nature of the latest "Islamic Republic" to capture bin Laden's imagination? He maintained a home in Khartoum—he would keep a small apartment in the Saudi city of Jeddah until the Saudis themselves deprived him of his citizenship—and lived in Sudan with his four wives, one of them only a teenager. His bin Laden company—not to be confused with the larger construction business run by his cousins—was paid in Sudanese currency which was then used to purchase sesame, corn and sunflower seeds for export. Profits did not seem to be bin Laden's top priority. Was Sudan?

Certainly it boasted another potential Islamic "monster" for the West. Hassan Abdullah Turabi, the enemy of Western "tyranny," a "devil" according to the Egyptian newspapers, was supposedly the Ayatollah of Khartoum, the scholarly leader of the National Islamic Front which provided the nervous system for General Omar Bashir's military government. Indeed, Bashir's palace boasted the very staircase upon which General Charles Gordon had been cut down in 1885 by followers of Mohamed Ahmed ibn Abdullah, the Mahdi, who like bin Laden also demanded a return to Islamic "purity." But when I went to talk to Turabi in his old English office, he sat birdlike on a chair, perched partly on his left leg that was hooked beneath him, his white robe adorned with a tiny patterned scarf, hands fluttering in front of a black beard that was now flecked with white. He it was who had organised the "Popular Arab and Islamic Conference" which I had ostensibly arrived to cover, and within the vast conference centre in Khartoum I found gathered every shade of mutually hostile Islamist, Christian, nationalist and *inté-griste*, all bound by Turabi's plea of moderation. Shias, Sunnis, Arabs, non-Arabs, Yassir Arafat's Fatah movement and all of his Arab enemies—Hamas, Hizballah, the Democratic Front for the Liberation of Palestine, the Algerian Islamic Salvation Front, the FIS as they called themselves under their French acronym—the whole shebang, along with representatives of the Pakistan People's Party, the an-Nahda party of Tunisia, Afghans of all persuasions and an envoy from Mohamed Aideed of Somalia who was himself "too busy to come"—as a conference official discreetly put it—because he was being hunted by the American military in Mogadishu.

They represented every contradiction of the Arab world in a city whose British colonial architecture—of low-roofed arched villas amid bougainvillea, of tired, hot government offices and mouldering police stations—existed alongside equally dated revolutionary slogans. The waters of the Blue and White Niles joined here, the permanent way-station between the Arab world and tropical Africa, and Sudan's transition through thirteen years of nationalist rule—the *mahdiya*—sixty years of British-dominated government from Cairo and almost forty years of fractious independence gave the country a debilitated, exhausted, unresolved identity. Was it Islamic—after independence, the *umma* party was run by the son and grandsons of the Mahdi—or did the military regimes that took over after 1969 mean that Sudan was for ever socialist?

Turabi was trying to act as intermediary between Arafat, who had just signed the Oslo accord with Israel, and his antagonists in the Arab world—which meant just about everybody—and might have been making an unsubtle attempt to wipe Sudan off Washington's "state terrorism" list by persuading Hamas and Islamic Jihad to support Arafat. "I personally know Arafat very well," Turabi insisted. "He is a close friend of mine. He was an Islamist once, you know, and then slowly moved into the Arab 'club' . . . He spoke to me before he signed [the accord with Israel]. He came here to Sudan. And I am now putting his case to the others—not as something that is right, but as something of necessity. What could Arafat do? He ran out of money. His army stopped. There were the refugees, the ten thousand prisoners in Israeli jails. Even a municipality is better than nothing."

But if "Palestine" was to be a municipality, where did that leave the Arabs? In need, surely, of a leader who did not speak in this language of surrender; in need of a warrior leader, someone who had proved he could defeat a superpower. Was this not what the Mahdi had believed himself to be? Did the Mahdi not ask his fighters on the eve of their attack on Khartoum whether they would advance against General Gordon even if two-thirds of them should perish? But like almost every other Arab state, Sudan re-created itself in a looking glass for the benefit of its own leaders. Khartoum was the "capital city of virtues," or so the large street banners claimed it to be that December. Sometimes the word "virtues" was substituted with the word "values," which was not quite the same thing.

But then nothing in Sudan was what it seemed. The railhead, broiling in the midday heat, did not suggest an Islamic republic in the making. Nor did the squads of soldiers in jungle green drowsing in the shade of a broken station building while two big artillery pieces stood on a freight platform, waiting to be loaded onto a near-derelict train for the civil war in the south. Britain had long favoured the separate development of the Christian south of Sudan from which the Arabic language and Muslim religion were largely excluded—until independence, when London suddenly decided that Sudan's territorial integrity was more important than the separate development which they had so long encouraged. The minority in the south rebelled and their insurrection was now the central and defining feature of Sudanese life.

The authorities in Khartoum would one day have to explain a detailed list of civil war atrocities which had been handed to the United Nations in 1993 and which were to form the subject of a UN report the following year. Eyewitness testimonies spoke of rape, pillage and murder in the southern province of Bahr al-Ghazal as well as the continuing abduction of thousands of southern children on the capital's streets. According to the documents, the most recent atrocities occurred the previous July when the Sudanese army drove a railway train loaded with locally hired militiamen through territory held by the rebel Sudanese People's Liberation Army. Under the orders of an officer referred to in the papers as Captain Ginat—commander of the People's Defence Force camp in the town of Muglad in Southern Kordofan and a member of the Sudanese government council in the southern city of Wau—the militias were let loose on Dinka tribal villages along the length of the railway, destroying every village to a depth of ten miles on each side of the track, killing the men, raping the women and stealing thousands of head of cattle. Evidence taken from tribesmen who fled the village without their families included details of the slaughter of a Christian wedding party of 300 people near the Lol River. The documents the UN had obtained also alleged that government troops, along with loyal tribal militias, massacred large numbers of southern Dinkas in a displaced persons' camp at Meiran the previous February.

This was not, therefore, a country known for its justice or civil rights or liberty. True, delegates to the Islamic summit were encouraged to speak their minds. Mustafa Cerić, the imam of Bosnia whose people were enduring a genocide at the hands of their Serb neighbours, was eloquent in his condemnation of the UN's peacekeeping intervention in his country. I had met him in Sarajevo a year earlier when he had accused the West of imposing an arms embargo on Bosnian forces "solely because we are Muslims," and his cynicism retained all its integrity in Khartoum. "You sent your English troops and we thank you for that," he told me. "But now you will not give us arms to defend ourselves against the Chetniks [Serbs] because you say this will spread the war and endanger the soldiers you sent to help us." Cerić was a man who could make others feel the need for humility.

Thus even Sudan's summit had become a symbol of the humiliation of Muslims, of Arabs, of all the revolutionary Islamists and nationalists and generals who dominated the "modern" Middle East. The Hizballah delegates from Lebanon took me aside one night to reveal the fragility of the regime. "We were invited to dinner on a boat on the Nile with Turabi," one of them told me. "We cruised up and down the river for a while and I noticed the government guards on both banks watching us. Then suddenly there was a burst of gunfire from a wedding party. We could hear the music of the wedding. But Turabi was so frightened that he hurled himself from the table onto the floor and stayed there for several minutes. This is not a stable place." Nor was the façade of free speech going to lift the blanket of isolation which the United States and its allies had thrown over Sudan, or protect its more notorious guests.

Two months after I met bin Laden, gunmen burst into his Khartoum home and tried to assassinate him. The Sudanese government suspected the potential killers were paid by the CIA. Clearly, this was no place for a latterday Mahdi. Saudi Arabia stripped him of his citizenship later the same year. The Saudis and then the Americans demanded bin Laden's extradition. Sudan meekly handed its other well-known fugitive, Ilich Ramirez Sanchez—"Carlos the Jackal," who had seized eleven oil ministers at the OPEC conference in Vienna in 1975 and organised an assault on the French embassy in The Hague—to the French. But "Carlos" was a revolutionary gone to seed, a plump alcoholic now rotten enough to be betrayed. Bin Laden was in a different category. His followers were blamed for bomb explosions in Riyadh in November of 1995 and then at a U.S. barracks at al-Khobar the following year which in all killed twenty-four Americans and two Indians. In early 1996, he was permitted to leave for the country of his choice—and that was bound to be the one refuge in which he had discovered so much about his own faith.

AND SO IT WAS THAT ONE HOT EVENING in late June 1996, the telephone on my desk in Beirut rang with one of the more extraordinary messages I was to receive as a foreign correspondent. "Mr. Robert, a friend you met in Sudan wants to see you," said a voice in English but with an Arabic accent. I thought at first he meant Kashoggi, though I had first met Jamal in 1990, long before going to Khartoum. "No, no, Mr. Robert, I mean the man you interviewed. Do you understand?" Yes, I understood. And where could I meet this man? "The place where he is now," came the reply. I knew that bin Laden was rumoured to have returned to Afghanistan but there was no confirmation of this. So how do I reach him? I asked. "Go to Jalalabad—you will be contacted." I took the man's number. He was in London.

So was the only Afghan embassy that would give me a visa. I was not in a hurry. It seemed to me that if the bin Ladens of this world wished to be interviewed, *The Independent* should not allow itself to be summoned to their presence. It was a journalistic risk. There were a thousand reporters who wanted to interview Osama bin Laden. But I thought he would hold more respect for a journalist who did not rush cravenly to him within hours of his request. I also had a more pressing concern. Although the secret services of the Middle East and Pakistan had acted for the CIA in helping the Afghan mujahedin against the Russians, many of them were now at war with bin Laden's organisation, which they blamed for Islamist insurgencies in their own countries. Egypt, Algeria, Tunisia and Saudi Arabia all now suspected bin Laden's hand in their respective insurrections. What if the invitation was a trick, a set-up in which I would unwittingly lead the Egyptian police—or the infinitely corrupt Pakistani ISI, the ubiquitously named Inter-Services Intelligence organisation—to bin Laden? Even worse from my point of view, what if this was an attempt to lure a reporter who knew bin Laden to his death—and then blame the killing on Islamists? How many reporters would set off to interview bin Laden after that? So I called back the contact in London. Would he meet me at my hotel?

The receptionist at the Sheraton Belgravia called my room in the early evening. "There is a gentleman waiting for you in the lobby," he said. The Belgravia is the smallest Sheraton in the world, and if its prices don't match that diminutive title, its wood-panelled, marble-floored lobby was as usual that evening the preserve of elderly tea-sipping ladies, waistcoated businessmen with silver hair slightly over the collar and elegantly dressed young women in black stockings. But when I reached the lobby, I noticed a man standing by the door. He was trying to look insignificant but he wore a huge beard, a long white Arab robe and plastic sandals over naked feet. Could this, perhaps, be bin Laden's man?

He was. The man ran the London end of the "Advice and Reform Committee," a Saudi opposition group inspired by bin Laden which regularly issued long and tiresome tracts against the corruption of the Saudi royal family, and he dutifully sat down in the Belgravia lobby—to the astonishment of the elderly ladies—to explain the iniquitous behaviour of the House of Saud and the honourable nature of Osama bin Laden. I did not believe the man I was talking to was a violent personality. Indeed, within two years he would personally express to me his distress—and rupture—with bin Laden when the latter declared war on "Americans, 'Crusaders' and Jews." But in 1996, the Saudi hero of the Afghan war could do no wrong. "He is a sincere man, Mr. Robert. He wants to talk to you. There is nothing to fear." This was the line I wanted to hear; whether I believed it was another matter. I told the man I would check into the Spinghar Hotel in Jalalabad.

The most convenient flight into eastern Afghanistan was from India, but Ariana Afghan Airlines Flight FG315 from New Delhi to Jalalabad was not the kind that carries an in-flight magazine. The female passengers were shrouded in the all-enveloping burqa, the cabin crew were mostly bearded and the cardboard packet of litchee juice was stained with mud. The chief steward walked to my seat, crouched in the aisle beside me and—as if revealing a long-held military secret—whispered into my ear, "We will be flying at thirty-one thousand feet." If only we had. Approaching the old Soviet military airstrip at Jalalabad, the pilot made an almost 180-degree turn that sent the blood pumping into our feet, and touched down on the first inch of narrow tarmac—giving him just enough braking power to stop the jet a foot from the end of the runway. Given the rusting Soviet radar dishes and the wrecked, upended Antonov off the apron, I could understand why Jalalabad arrivals lacked the amenities of Heathrow or JFK.

When I trudged through the heat with my bags, I found that the bullet-scarred terminal building was empty. No immigration. No customs. Not a single man with a rubber stamp. Just six young and bearded Afghans, four of them holding rifles, who stared at me with a mixture of tiredness and suspicion. No amount of cheery *Salaam aleikums* would elicit more than a muttering in Pushtu from the six men. After all, what was this alien, hatless creature doing here in Afghanistan with his brand-new camera-bag and his canvas hold-all of shirts and newspaper clippings? "Taxi?" I asked them. And they looked away from me, back at the big blue-and-white aircraft which had jetted so dangerously into town as if it held the secret of my presence.

I hitched a ride with a French aid worker. They seemed to be everywhere. Jalalabad was a dusty brown city of mud-and-wood houses, unpaved earthen streets and ochre walls with the characteristic smell of charcoal and horse manure. There were donkeys and stallions and Indian-style "velo" rickshaws and Victorian bicycles and the occasional clapboard shop-front, Dodge City transferred to the subcontinent. Khartoum had nothing on this. Two of Engineer Gulbuddin Hekmatyar's local guerrilla commanders had turned up for their haircut at the same time the previous month and shot dead the barber and a couple of other men before deciding who was first in the queue. A third of all the children in Jalalabad hospitals were the victims of joy-shooting at weddings. It was a city ripe for Islamic discipline.

But it didn't put the agencies off. There was SAVE and the UN World Food Programme, UNDP, Médecins Sans Frontières, MADERA, the International Committee of the Red Cross, the OCHA Emergency Field Unit, the Sandy Gall clinic for orphaned children, the Swedish Committee for Afghans, the UNHCR and a German agronomist agency; and they were only the first few offices signposted off the highway to Kabul. Seven years after the last Soviet troops had left Afghanistan, four years after the communist government of President Mohamed Najibullah had been overthrown, the Afghan mujahedin victors of the war were slaughtering each other in Kabul. So what was the point? Were the agencies here to assuage our guilt at abandoning the Afghan people once they had served their purpose in driving the Russians from their land? The United Nations had a force of just two soldiers observing the chaos in Afghanistan—a Swede and an Irishman, both of whom stayed at the old Spinghar Hotel.

The Spinghar is a relic of the Afghanistan hippie trail, a high-ceilinged hotel of the 1950s with large rose gardens and tall palm trees which, even in winter, bask in the warmth of the winds coming up from the valley of the Indus. But in the torment of the summer heat of 1996—it is now mid-July—a roaring air conditioner plays Catch-22 with me: to cool my empty double room upstairs, I turn it on, but its tigerlike engine vibrates so loudly that sleep is impossible. So I switch it off. Yet when I turn to the only book beside my bed—*Plain Tales from the Raj*—the sweat runs down my arms and glues my fingers to the pages.

Then a rustle, a kind of faint, rasping sound, comes from the silent conditioner. I sit up and, five feet from my face, I see the dragon's head of a giant lizard looking at me from the cooled bars of the machine. When I raise my hand, the head disappears for a moment. Then it is back, a miniature armoured brontosaurus face that is followed now by a long, rubbery torso, grey-green in the dim afternoon sunlight, and big sucking feet that grip the plastic air-conditioning vents. Like an old silent film, it moves in jerks. One moment, I see its head. Then at shutter's speed, half its length of heavily-breathing rubberiness is out of the machine. A moment later, the whole half foot of creature is suspended on the curtain above my bed, swaying on the material, alien and disturbing, looking back at me over its fortresslike shoulder. What is it doing here? I ask myself. Then it scuttles out of sight into the drapery.

And of course, I switch on the air conditioner and swamp the room with a rush of ear-freezing cold air. And I curl up on the further bed and watch for movement at the top of the curtain rod. I am frightened of this thing and it is frightened of me. And only after half an hour do I realise that the bright screws on the curtain rail are its beady eyes. With rapt attention, we are watching each other. Are others watching me? I wake up next morning, exhausted, drenched in perspiration. The boy at the reception desk in a long shirt and a traditional *pakul* hat says that no one has called for me. Bin Laden has friends in Jalalabad, the tribal leaders know him, protect him, and even the man I met in London said that I should let "Engineer Mahmoud" know that I have arrived in Afghanistan to see "Sheikh Osama."

Engineer Mahmoud turns out to work for the city's Drug Control and Development Unit in a back street of Jalalabad. I might have expected the purist bin Laden to be involved with the eradication of drugs. In 1996, Afghanistan was the world's leading supplier of illicit opium, producing at least 2,200 metric tons of opium—about 80 per cent of western Europe's heroin. Afghans are not immune. You can see them in the Jalalabad bazaar, young men with withered black arms and sunken eyes, the addicts returned from the refugee camps of Pakistan, still-living witnesses to the corruption of heroin. "It's good for the Afghan people to see them," a Western aid official says coldly. "Now they can see the effect of all those poppy fields they grow—and if they are as Islamic as they claim they are, maybe they'll stop producing opium." He smiles grimly. "Or maybe not."

Probably not. The eastern Nangarhar province is now responsible for 80 per cent of the country's poppy cultivation—for 64 per cent of western Europe's heroin—and laboratories have now been transferred from Pakistan to a frontier strip inside Afghanistan, producing hundreds of kilos of heroin a day, fortified with anti-aircraft guns and armoured vehicles to withstand a military offensive. Local government officials in Jalalabad claim to have eradicated 30,000 hectares of opium and hashish fields over the past two years, but their efforts—brave enough given the firepower of the drug producers—seem as hopeless as the world's attempts to find a solution to drug abuse.

In Engineer Mahmoud's office, the problem is simple enough. A map on the wall depicts Nangarhar with a rash of red pimples along its eastern edge, a pox of opium fields and laboratories that are targets for Mahmoud's armed commandos. "We have been eradicating hashish fields, using our weapons to force the farmers to plough up the land," he proclaims. "We are taking our own bulldozers to plough up some of the poppy fields. We take our guns and rockets with us and the farmers can do nothing to stop our work. Now our *shura* [council] has called the ulema to lecture the people on the evils of drug production, quoting from the Koran to support their words. And for the first time, we have been able to destroy hashish fields without using force." Mahmoud and his ten-strong staff have been heartened by the United Nations' support for his project. On the open market in Jalalabad, the farmers were receiving a mere $140 for seven kilos of hashish, just over $250 for seven kilos of opium—around the same price they would have received for grain. So the UN provided wheat seeds for those farmers who transferred from drug production, on the grounds that they would make the same profits in the Jalalabad markets.

Only a few months earlier—and here is the strange geography that touched bin Laden's contacts—Engineer Mahmoud visited Washington. "The U.S. drugs prevention authorities took me to their new headquarters—you would not believe how big it is," he said. "It is half the size of Jalalabad city. And when I went inside, it is very luxurious and has many, many computers. They have all this money there—but none for us who are trying to stop the drug production." Engineer Mahmoud's senior staff received just under $50 a month and his senior assistant, Shamsul Hag, claimed that the drugs unit had to buy 4,000 kilos of maize seed to distribute to farmers the previous month. But the western NGOs in Jalalabad had little time for all this. "Haji Qadir, the governor of Jalalabad, went to the UN drugs people in Islamabad," one of them said, "and told him: 'Look, I have destroyed twenty thousand hectares of opium fields—now you must help me because the people are waiting for your help.' But it was more complicated than this. Farmers who had never grown poppies began to plant them so they could get free maize seed in return for destroying the fields they had just planted." Other aid workers suspected that the farmers were rotating their crops between wheat and drugs each season, the opium sold in return for increased payments, and for weapons that were recently transported in boxes through the Pakistan railway station of Landi Kotal on the Peshawar steam train to the Afghan border.

Poppy cultivation had become an agribusiness and the dealers for the Afghan drug barons now had technical advisers who were visiting Nangarhar to advise on the crop and the product, paying in advance, and so concerned about the health of their workers that they had given them face-masks to wear in the opium factories. Some said they even offered health insurance. This was capitalism on a ruthlessly illegal scale. And when I asked a European UN official how the world could compete with it, he drew in his breath. "Legalise drugs!" he roared. "Legalise the lot. It will be the end of the drug barons. They'll go broke and kill each other. But of course the world will never accept that. So we'll go on fighting a losing war."

Engineer Mahmoud would only shrug his shoulders when I repeated this to him. What could he do? I raised the subject of "Sheikh Osama" for the third time. The Sheikh wanted to see me, I repeated. I was not looking for him. I was in Jalalabad at the Sheikh's request. He was looking for me. "So why do you ask me to look for him?" Engineer Mahmoud asked with devastating logic. This was not a problem of language because Mahmoud spoke excellent English. It was a cocktail of comprehension mixed with several bottles of suspicion. Someone—I did not want to mention the man in London—had told me to contact Mahmoud, I said. Perhaps he could tell the Sheikh that I was at the Spinghar Hotel? Mahmoud looked at me pityingly. "What can I do?" he asked.

I sent a message through the Swedish UN soldier—he was the UN's sole radio operator as well as one of its only two soldiers in Afghanistan—and he connected me to the only person in the world I really trusted. There had been no contact, I said. Please call bin Laden's man in London. Next day a radio transmission message arrived, relaying the man's advice. "Tell Robert to make clear he is not there because of his own wish. He is only replying to the wish of our friend. He should make it clear to the Engineer that he is only accepting an invitation. The engineer can confirm this with our friend . . . Make it very clear he was invited and did not go on his own. This is the fastest thing. Otherwise he has to wait." Back I went to Engineer Mahmoud. He was in good form. In fact he thought it immensely funny, outrageously humorous, that I was waiting for the Sheikh. It was fantastic, laughable, bizarre. Many cups of tea were served. And each time a visitor arrived—a drugs control worker, an official of the local governor, a mendicant with a son in prison on drugs offences—he would be regaled with the story of the bareheaded Englishman who thought he had been invited to Jalalabad and was now waiting and waiting at the Spinghar Hotel.

I returned to the Spinghar in the heat of midday and sat by the lawn in front of the building. I had hidden in the same hotel sixteen years earlier, after Leonid Brezhnev had sent the Soviet army into Afghanistan, when I had smuggled myself down to Jalalabad and watched the Russian armoured columns grinding past the front gates. Their helicopters had thundered over the building, heavy with rockets, and the windows had rattled as they fired their missiles into the Tora Bora mountain range to the north. Now the butterflies played around the batteries of pink roses and the gardeners put down their forks and hoses and unspread their prayer rugs on the grass. It looked a bit like paradise. I drank tea on the lawn and watched the sun moving—rapidly, the movement clear to the naked eye—past the fronds of the palm trees above me. It was 5 July, one of the hottest days of the year. I went to my room and slept.

"Clack-clack-clack." It was as if someone was attacking my head with an ice-pick. "Clack-clack-clack-clack-clack." Ever since I was a child, I had hated these moments: the violent tugging of sheets, the insistent knock on the bedroom door, the screeching voice of the prefect telling me to get up. But this was different. "CLACK-CLACK-CLACK-CLACK-CLACK-CLACK-CLACK." I sat up. Someone was banging a set of car keys against my bedroom window. "Missssster Robert," a voice whispered urgently. "Misssster Robert." He hissed the word "Mister." Yes, yes, I'm here. "Please come downstairs, there is someone to see you." It registered only slowly that the man must have climbed the ancient fire escape to reach the window of my room. I dressed, grabbed a coat—I had a feeling we might travel in the night—and almost forgot my old Nikon. I walked as calmly as I could past the reception desk and out into the early afternoon heat.

The man wore a grubby, grey Afghan robe and a small round cotton hat but he was an Arab and he greeted me formally, holding my right hand in both of his. He smiled. He said his name was Mohamed, he was my guide. "To see the Sheikh?" I asked. He smiled but said nothing. I was still worried about a trap. The guide's name would be Mohamed, wouldn't it? He would suggest an evening walk. I could hear the later eyewitness evidence. Yes, sir, we saw the English journalist. We saw him meet someone outside the hotel. There was no struggle. He left freely, of his own accord. He walked out of the hotel gates.

I did, too, and followed Mohamed all the way through the dust of Jalalabad's main street until we arrived next to a group of gunmen in a pick-up truck in the ruins of an old Soviet army base, a place of broken armoured vehicles with a rusting red star on a shattered gateway. There were three men in Afghan hats in the back of the pick-up. One held a Kalashnikov, another clutched a grenade-launcher along with six rockets tied together with Scotch tape. The third nursed a machine gun on his lap, complete with tripod and a belt of ammunition. "Mr. Robert, these are our guards," the driver said quietly, as if it was the most normal thing in the world to set off across the wilds of Afghanistan's Nangarhar Province under a white-hot afternoon sun with three bearded guerrillas. A two-way radio hissed and crackled on the shoulder of the driver's companion as another truckload of Afghan gunmen drove up behind us.

We were about to set off when Mohamed climbed back down from the pick-up along with the driver, walked to a shaded patch of grass and began to pray. For five minutes, the two men lay half-prostrate, facing the distant Kabul Gorge and, beyond that, a far more distant Mecca. We drove off along a broken highway and then turned onto a dirt track by an irrigation canal, the guns in the back of the truck bouncing on the floor, the guards' eyes peering from behind their checkered scarves. We travelled like that for hours, past half-demolished mud villages and valleys and towering black rocks, a journey across the face of the moon.

Out of the grey heat, there loomed the ghosts of a terrible war, of communism's last imperial gasp; the overgrown revetments of Soviet army firebases, artillery positions, upended, dust-covered guns and the carcass of a burned-out tank in which no one could have survived. Amid the furnace of the late afternoon, there emerged a whole blitzed town of ancient castellated mud fortresses, their walls shot through with machine-gun bullets and shells. Wild naked children were playing in the ruins. Just the other side of the phantom town, Mohamed's driver took us off the track and began steering across shale and hard rock, the stones spitting beneath our wheels as we skirted kilometres of fields that were covered in yellow dust. "This is a gift from the Russians," Mohamed said. "You know why there are no people working this ground? Because the Russians sowed it with thousands of mines." And so we passed through the dead land.

Once, as the white sun was sliding into the mountains, we stopped for the gunmen on the back to pull watermelons from a field. They scampered back to the trucks and cut them up, the juice dripping through their fingers. By dusk, we had reached a series of cramped earthen villages, old men burning charcoal fires by the track, the shadow of women cowled in the Afghan burqa standing in the alleyways.

There were more guerrillas, all bearded, grinning at Mohamed and the driver. It was night before we stopped, in an orchard where wooden sofas had been covered in army blankets piled with belts and webbing and where armed men emerged out of the darkness, all in Afghan clothes and soft woollen flat hats, some holding rifles, others machine guns. They were the Arab mujahedin, the Arab "Afghans" denounced by the presidents and kings of half the Arab world and by the United States of America. Very soon, the world would know them as al-Qaeda.

They came from Egypt, Algeria, Saudi Arabia, Jordan, Syria, Kuwait. Two of them wore spectacles, one said he was a doctor. A few of them shook hands in a rather solemn way and greeted me in Arabic. I knew that these men would give their lives for bin Laden, that they thought themselves spiritually pure in a corrupt world, that they were inspired and influenced by dreams which they persuaded themselves came from heaven. Mohamed beckoned me to follow him and we skirted a small river and jumped across a stream until, in the insect-filled darkness ahead, we could see a sputtering paraffin lamp. Beside it sat a tall, bearded man in Saudi robes. Osama bin Laden stood up, his two teenage sons, Omar and Saad, beside him. "Welcome to Afghanistan," he said.

He was now forty but looked much older than at our last meeting in the Sudanese desert late in 1993. Walking towards me, he towered over his companions, tall, slim, with new wrinkles around those narrow eyes. Leaner, his beard longer but slightly flecked with grey, he had a black waistcoat over his white robe and a red-chequered kuffiah on his head, and he seemed tired. When he asked after my health, I told him I had come a long way for this meeting. "So have I," he muttered. There was also an isolation about him, a detachment I had not noticed before, as if he had been inspecting his anger, examining the nature of his resentment; when he smiled, his gaze would move towards his sixteen-year-old son Omar—round eyes with dark brows and his own kuffiah—and then off into the hot darkness where his armed men were patrolling the fields. Others were gathering to listen to our conversation. We sat down on a straw mat and a glass of tea was placed beside me.

Just ten days ago, a truck bomb had torn down part of the U.S. Air Force housing complex at al-Khobar in Dhahran, and we were speaking in the shadow of the deaths of the nineteen American soldiers killed there. U.S. secretary of state Warren Christopher had visited the ruins and predictably promised that America would not be swayed by violence, that the perpetrators would be hunted down. King Fahd of Saudi Arabia, who had since lapsed into a state of dementia, had foreseen the possibility of violence when American military forces arrived to "defend" his kingdom in 1990. It was for this very reason that he had, on 6 August that year, extracted a promise from then President George Bush that all U.S. troops would leave his country when the Iraqi threat ended. But the Americans had stayed, claiming that the continued existence of Saddam's regime—which Bush had chosen not to destroy—still constituted a danger to the Gulf.

Osama bin Laden knew what he wanted to say. "Not long ago, I gave advice to the Americans to withdraw their troops from Saudi Arabia. Now let us give some advice to the governments of Britain and France to take their troops out—because what happened in Riyadh and al-Khobar showed that the people who did this have a deep understanding in choosing their targets. They hit their main enemy, which is the Americans. They killed no secondary enemies, nor their brothers in the army or the police in Saudi Arabia . . . I give this advice to the government of Britain." The Americans must leave Saudi Arabia, must leave the Gulf. The "evils" of the Middle East arose from America's attempt to take over the region and from its support for Israel. Saudi Arabia had been turned into "an American colony."

Bin Laden was speaking slowly and with precision, an Egyptian taking notes in a large exercise book by the lamplight like a Middle Ages scribe. "This doesn't mean declaring war against the West and Western people—but against the American regime which is against every American." I interrupted bin Laden. Unlike Arab regimes, I said, the people of the United States elected their government. They would say that their government represents them. He disregarded my comment. I hope he did. For in the years to come, his war would embrace the deaths of thousands of American civilians. "The explosion in al-Khobar did not come as a direct reaction to the American occupation," he said, "but as a result of American behaviour against Muslims, its support of Jews in Palestine and of the massacres of Muslims in Palestine and Lebanon—of Sabra and Chatila and Qana—and of the Sharm el-Sheikh conference."

Bin Laden had thought this through. The massacre of up to 1,700 Palestinian refugees by Israel's Lebanese Phalangist militia allies in 1982 and the slaughter by Israeli artillerymen of 106 Lebanese civilians in a UN camp at Qana less than three months before this meeting with bin Laden were proof to millions of Westerners, let alone Arabs, of Israeli brutality. President Clinton's "anti-terrorism" conference at the Egyptian coastal town of Sharm el-Sheikh was regarded by Arabs as a humiliation. Clinton had condemned the "terrorism" of Hamas and the Lebanese Hizballah, but not the violence of Israel. So the bombers had struck in al-Khobar for the Palestinians of Sabra and Chatila, for Qana, for Clinton's hypocrisy; this was bin Laden's message. Not only were the Americans to be driven from the Gulf, there were historic wrongs to be avenged. His "advice" to the Americans was a fearful threat that would be fulfilled in the years to come.

But what bin Laden really wanted to talk about was Saudi Arabia. Since our last meeting in Sudan, he said, the situation in the kingdom had grown worse. The ulema, the religious leaders, had declared in the mosques that the presence of American troops was not acceptable and the government took action against these ulema "on the advice of the Americans." For bin Laden, the betrayal of the Saudi people began twenty-four years before his birth, when Abdul Aziz al-Saud proclaimed his kingdom in 1932. "The regime started under the flag of applying Islamic law and under this banner all the people of Saudi Arabia came to help the Saudi family take power. But Abdul Aziz did not apply Islamic law; the country was set up for his family. Then after the discovery of petroleum, the Saudi regime found another support—the money to make people rich and to give them the services and life they wanted and to make them satisfied."

Bin Laden was picking away at his teeth with that familiar twig of *mis-hwak* wood, but history—or his version of it—was the basis of almost all his remarks. The Saudi royal family had promised sharia laws while at the same time allowing the United States "to Westernise Saudi Arabia and drain the economy." He blamed the Saudi regime for spending $25 billion in support of Saddam Hussein in the Iran–Iraq War and a further $60 billion in support of the Western armies in the 1991 war against Iraq, "buying military equipment which is not needed or useful for the country, buying aircraft by credit" while at the same time creating unemployment, high taxes and a bankrupt economy. But for bin Laden, the pivotal date was 1990, the year Saddam Hussein invaded Kuwait. "When the American troops entered Saudi Arabia, the land of the two Holy places, there was a strong protest from the ulema and from students of sharia law all over the country against the interference of American troops. This big mistake by the Saudi regime of inviting the American troops revealed their deception. They were giving their support to nations which were fighting against Muslims. They helped the Yemeni communists against the southern Yemeni Muslims and are helping Arafat's regime fight Hamas. After it insulted and jailed the ulema eighteen months ago, the Saudi regime lost its legitimacy."

The night wind moved through the darkened trees, ruffling the robes of the Arab fighters around us. Bin Laden spread his right hand and used his fingers to list the "mistakes" of the Saudi monarchy. "At the same time, the financial crisis happened inside the kingdom and now all the people there suffer from this. Saudi merchants found their contracts were broken. The government owes them 340 billion Saudi rials, which is a very big amount; it represents 30 per cent of the national income inside the kingdom. Prices are going up and people have to pay more for electricity, water and fuel. Saudi farmers have not received money since 1992—and those who get grants now receive them on government loans from banks. Education is deteriorating and people have to take their children from government schools and put them in private education, which is very expensive."

Bin Laden paused to see if I had listened to his careful if frighteningly exclusive history lesson. "The Saudi people have remembered now what the ulema told them and they realise America is the main reason for their problems . . . the ordinary man knows that his country is the largest oil-producer in the world yet at the same time he is suffering from taxes and bad services. Now the people understand the speeches of the ulemas in the mosques—that our country has become an American colony. They act decisively with every action to kick the Americans out of Saudi Arabia. What happened in Riyadh and al-Khobar is clear evidence of the huge anger of Saudi people against America. The Saudis now know their real enemy is America." There was no doubting bin Laden's argument. The overthrow of the Saudi regime and the eviction of U.S. forces from the kingdom were one and the same for him. He was claiming that the real religious leadership of Saudi Arabia—among whom he clearly saw himself—was an inspiration to Saudis, that Saudis themselves would drive out the Americans, that Saudis—hitherto regarded as a rich and complacent people—might strike at the United States. Could this be true?

The air was clouding with insects. I was writing in my notebook with my right hand and swatting them away from my face and clothes with my left, big insects with wide wings and buglike creatures that would slap against my shirt and the pages of my notebook. I noticed that they were colliding with bin Laden's white robe, even his face, as if they had somehow been alerted by the anger emanating from this man. He sometimes stopped speaking for all of sixty seconds—he was the first Arab figure I noticed doing this—in order to reflect upon his words. Most Arabs, faced with a reporter's question, would say the first thing that came into their heads for fear that they would appear ignorant if they did not. Bin Laden was different. He was alarming because he was possessed of that quality which leads men to war: total self-conviction. In the years to come, I would see others manifest this dangerous characteristic—President George W. Bush and Tony Blair come to mind—but never the fatal self-resolve of Osama bin Laden.

There was a dark quality to his calculations. "If one kilogram of TNT exploded in a country in which nobody had heard an explosion in a hundred years," he said, "surely the exploding of twenty-five hundred kilos of TNT at al-Khobar is clear evidence of the scale of the people's anger against the Americans and of their ability to continue that resistance against the American occupation." Had I been a prophet, might I have thought more deeply about that fearful metaphor which bin Laden used, the one about the TNT? Was there not a country—a nation which knew no war within its borders for well over a hundred years—which could be struck with "evidence" of a people's anger, 2,500 times beyond anything it might imagine? But I was calculating more prosaic equations.

Bin Laden had asked me—a routine of every Palestinian under occupation—if Europeans did not resist occupation during the Second World War. I told him no Europeans would accept this argument over Saudi Arabia—because the Nazis killed millions of Europeans yet the Americans had never murdered a single Saudi. Such a parallel was historically and morally wrong. Bin Laden did not agree. "We as Muslims have a strong feeling that binds us together . . . We feel for our brothers in Palestine and Lebanon . . . When sixty Jews are killed inside Palestine"—he was talking about Palestinian suicide bombings in Israel—"all the world gathers within seven days to criticise this action, while the deaths of 600,000 Iraqi children did not receive the same reaction." It was bin Laden's first reference to Iraq and to the UN sanctions which were to result, according to UN officials themselves, in the death of more than half a million children. "Killing those Iraqi children is a crusade against Islam," bin Laden said. "We as Muslims do not like the Iraqi regime but we think that the Iraqi people and their children are our brothers and we care about their future." It was the first time I heard him use the word "crusade."

But it was neither the first—nor the last—time that bin Laden would distance himself from Saddam Hussein's dictatorship. Much good would it do him. Seven years later, the United States would launch an invasion of Iraq that would be partly justified by the regime's "support" of a man who so detested it. But these were not the only words which bin Laden uttered that night to which I should have paid greater attention. For at one point, he placed his right hand on his chest. "I believe that sooner or later the Americans will leave Saudi Arabia and that the war declared by America against the Saudi people means war against all Muslims everywhere," he said. "Resistance against America will spread in many, many places in Muslim countries. Our trusted leaders, the ulema, have given us a fatwa that we must drive out the Americans."

For some time, there had been a steadily growing thunderstorm to the east of bin Laden's camp and we could see the bright orange flash of lightning over the mountains on the Pakistan border. But bin Laden thought this might be artillery fire, the continuation of the inter-mujahedin battles that had damaged his spirit after the anti-Soviet war. He was growing uneasy. He broke off his conversation to pray. Then on the straw mat, several young and armed men served dinner—plates of yoghurt and cheese and Afghan nan bread and more tea. Bin Laden sat between his sons, silent, eyes on his food. Occasionally he would ask me questions. What would be the reaction of the British Labour Party to his demand that British troops must leave Saudi Arabia? Was the Labour opposition leader Tony Blair important? I cannot, alas, remember my reply. Bin Laden said that three of his wives would soon arrive in Afghanistan to join him. I could see the tents where they would be living if I wished, just outside Jalalabad, "humble tents" for his family. He told an Egyptian holding a rifle to take me to the encampment next day.

Then he pointed at me. "I am astonished at the British government," he said suddenly. "They sent a letter to me through their embassy in Khartoum before I left Sudan, saying I would not be welcome in the United Kingdom. But I did not ask to go to Britain. So why did they send me this letter? The letter said: 'If you come to Britain, you will not be admitted.' The letter gave the Saudi press the opportunity of claiming that I had asked for political asylum in Britain—which is not true." I believed bin Laden. Afghanistan was the only country left to him after his five-and-a-half-year exile in Sudan. He agreed. "The safest place in the world for me is Afghanistan." It was the only place, I repeated, in which he could campaign against the Saudi government. Bin Laden and several of his Arab fighters burst into laughter. "There are other places," he replied. Did he mean Tajikistan? I asked. Or Uzbekistan? Kazakhstan? "There are several places where we have friends and close brothers—we can find refuge and safety in them."

I told bin Laden he was already a hunted man. "Danger is a part of our life," he snapped back. "Do you realise that we spent ten years fighting against the Russians and the KGB? . . . When we were fighting the Russians here in Afghanistan, 10,000 Saudis came here to fight over a period of ten years. There were three flights every week from Jeddah to Islamabad and every flight was filled with Saudis coming to fight . . . " But, I suggested uncharitably, didn't the Americans support the mujahedin against the Soviets? Bin Laden responded at once. "We were never at any time friends of the Americans. We knew that the Americans support the Jews in Palestine and that they are our enemies. Most of the weapons that came to Afghanistan were paid for by the Saudis on the orders of the Americans since Turki al-Faisal [the head of Saudi external intelligence] and the CIA were working together."

Bin Laden was now alert, almost agitated. There was something he needed to say. "Let me tell you this. Last week, I received an envoy from the Saudi embassy in Islamabad. Yes, he came here to Afghanistan to see me. The government of Saudi Arabia, of course, they want to give the people here a different message, that I should be handed over. But in truth they wanted to speak directly to me. They wanted to ask me to go back to Saudi Arabia. I said I would speak to them only under one condition—that Sheikh Sulieman al-Owda, the ulema, is present. They have locked up Sheikh Sulieman for speaking out against the corrupt regime. Without his freedom, negotiation is not possible. I have had no reply from them till now."

Was it this revelation that made bin Laden nervous? He began talking to his men about *amniya*, security, and repeatedly looked towards those flashes in the sky. Now the thunder did sound like gunfire. I tried to ask one more question. What kind of Islamic state would bin Laden wish to see? Would thieves and murderers still have their hands or heads cut off in his Islamic sharia state, just as they do in Saudi Arabia today? There came an unsatisfactory reply. "Islam is a complete religion for every detail of life. If a man is a real Muslim and commits a crime, he can only be happy if he is justly punished. This is not cruelty. The origin of these punishments comes from God through the Prophet Mohamed, peace be upon him."

Dissident Osama bin Laden may be, but moderate never. I asked permission to take his photograph, and while he debated this with his companions I scribbled into my notebook the words I would use in the last paragraph of my report on our meeting: "Osama bin Laden believes he now represents the most formidable enemy of the Saudi regime and of the American presence in the Gulf. Both are probably right to regard him as such." I was underestimating the man.

Yes, he said, I could take his picture. I opened my camera and allowed his armed guards to watch me as I threaded a film into the spool. I told them I refused to use a flash because it flattened the image of a human face and asked them to bring the paraffin lamp closer. The Egyptian scribe held it a foot from bin Laden's face. I told him to bring it closer still, to within three inches, and I physically had to guide his arm until the light brightened and shadowed bin Laden's features. Then without warning, bin Laden moved his head back and the faintest smile moved over his face, along with that self-conviction and that ghost of vanity which I found so disturbing. He called his sons Omar and Saad and they sat beside him as I took more pictures and bin Laden turned into the proud father, the family man, the Arab at home.

Then his anxiety returned. The thunder was continuous now and it was mixed with the patter of rifle fire. I should go, he urged, and I realised that what he meant was that *he* must go, that it was time for him to return to the fastness of

Afghanistan. When we shook hands, he was already looking for the guards who would take him away. Mohamed and my driver and just two of the armed men who had brought me to these damp, insect-hungry fields turned up to drive me back to the Spinghar Hotel, a journey that proved to be full of menace. Driving across river bridges and road intersections, we were repeatedly stopped by armed men from the Afghan factions that were fighting for control of Kabul. One would crouch on the roadway in front of our vehicle, screaming at us, pointing his rifle at the windscreen, his companion sidling out of the darkness to check our driver's identity and wave us through. "Afghanistan very difficult place," Mohamed remarked.

It would be difficult for bin Laden's family, too. Next morning, the Egyptian turned up at the Spinghar Hotel to take me to the grass encampment in which the families of the returning Arab "Afghans" would live. It was vulnerable enough. Only a few strands of barbed wire separated it from the open countryside and the three tents for bin Laden's wives, pitched close to one another, were insufferably hot. Three latrines had been dug at the back, in one of which floated a dead frog. "They will be living here among us," the Egyptian said. "These are ladies who are used to living in comfort." But his fears centred on the apparent presence of three Egyptian security men who had been driving close to the camp in a green pick-up truck. "We know who they are and we have the number of their vehicle. A few days ago, they stopped beside my son and asked him: 'We know you are Abdullah and we know who your father is. Where is bin Laden?' Then they asked him why I was in Afghanistan."

Another of the Arab men in the camp disputed bin Laden's assertion that this was only one of several Muslim countries in which he could find refuge. "There is no other country left for Mr. bin Laden," he said politely. "When he was in Sudan, the Saudis wanted to capture him with the help of Yemenis. We know that the French government tried to persuade the Sudanese to hand him over to them because the Sudanese had given them the South American." (This was "Carlos the Jackal.") "The Americans were pressing the French to get hold of bin Laden in Sudan. An Arab group which was paid by the Saudis tried to kill him and they shot at him but bin Laden's guards fired back and two of the men were wounded. The same people also tried to murder Turabi." The Egyptian listened to this in silence. "Yes, the country is very dangerous," he said. "The Americans are trying to block the route to Afghanistan for the Arabs. I prefer the mountains. I feel safer there. This place is semi-Beirut."

Not for long. Within nine months, I would be back in a transformed, still more sinister Afghanistan, its people governed with a harsh and ignorant piety that even bin Laden could not have imagined. Again, there had come the telephone call to Beirut, the invitation to see "our friend," the delay—quite deliberate on my part— before setting off yet again for Jalalabad. This time, the journey was a combination of farce and incredulity. There were no more flights from Delhi so I flew first to the emirate of Dubai. "Fly to Jalalabad?" my Indian travel agent there asked me. "You have to contact 'Magic Carpet.' " He was right. "Magic Carpet Travel"—in a movie, the name would never have got past the screenplay writers*—was run by a Lebanese who told me to turn up at 8:30 the next morning at the heat-bleached old airport in the neighbouring and much poorer emirate of Sharjah, to which Ariana Afghan Airlines had now been sent in disgrace. Sharjah played host to a flock of pariah airlines that flew from the Gulf to Kazakhstan, the Ukraine, Tajikistan and a number of obscure Iranian cities. My plane to Jalalabad was the same old Boeing 727, but now in a state of much-reduced circumstances, cruelly converted into a freight carrier.

The crew were all Afghans—bushy-bearded to a man, since the Taliban had just taken over Afghanistan and ordered men to stop shaving—and did their best to make me comfortable in the lone and grubby passenger seat at the front. "Safety vest under seat," was written behind the lavatory. There was no vest. And the toilet was running with faeces, a fearful stench drifting over the cargo of ball-bearings and textiles behind me. On take-off, a narrow tide of vile-smelling liquid washed out of the lavatory and ran down the centre of the aircraft. "Don't worry, you're in safe hands," one of the crew insisted as we climbed through the turbulence, introducing me to a giant of a man with a black-and-white beard who kept grinding his teeth and wringing his hands on a damp cloth. "This," he said, "is our senior flight maintenance engineer." Over the Spinghar Mountains, the engineer at last sniffed the smell from the toilet, entered the tiny cubicle with a ratchet and attacked the plumbing. By the time we landed at the old airstrip at Jalalabad, I was ready to contemplate the overland journey home.

The immigration officer, a teenager with a Kalashnikov, was so illiterate that he drew a square and a circle in my upside-down passport because he couldn't write his own name. The airline crew offered me a lift on their bus into Jalalabad, the same dusty frontier town I remembered from the previous July but this time with half its population missing. There were no women. Just occasionally I would catch sight of them, cowled and burqa-ed in their shrouds, sometimes holding the hands of tiny children. The campus gates of Nangarhar University were chained shut, the pathways covered in grass, the dormitories dripping rain water. "The Taliban say they will reopen the university this week," the post office clerk told me. "But what's the point? All the teachers have left. The women can no longer be educated. It's back to Year Zero."

Not quite, of course. For the first time in years, there was no shooting in Jalalabad. The guns had been collected by the Taliban—only to go up in smoke a few days later in a devastating explosion that almost killed me—but there was a kind of law that had been imposed on this angry, tribal society. Humanitarian workers could travel around the town at night—which may be why some of them argued that they could "do business" with the Taliban and had no right to interfere in "traditional culture." Robberies were almost unknown. While prices were rising, at least there were now vegetables and meat in the market.

---

*The more dangerous the destination, the more fictional the name of the airline that flies there. The only direct flight from Beirut to the cauldron of occupied Iraq was run by another company called—yes, you guessed it—"Flying Carpet Airlines."

The Taliban had finally vanquished twelve of the fifteen venal Afghan mujahedin militias in all but the far north-eastern corner of the country and imposed
their own stark legitimacy on its people. It was a purist, Sunni Wahhabi faith
whose interpretation of sharia law recalled the most draconian of early Christian
prelates. Head-chopping, hand-chopping and a totally misogynist perspective
were easy to associate with the Taliban's hostility towards all forms of enjoyment.
The Spinghar Hotel used to boast an old American television set that had now been
hidden in a garden shed for fear of destruction. Television sets, like videotapes and
thieves, tended to end up hanging from trees. "What do you expect?" the gardener
asked me near the ruins of the old royal winter palace in Jalalabad. "The Taliban
came from the refugee camps. They are giving us only what they had." And it
dawned on me then that the new laws of Afghanistan—so anachronistic and brutal
to us, and to educated Afghans—were less an attempt at religious revival than a
continuation of life in the vast dirt camps in which so many millions of Afghans
had gathered on the borders of their country when the Soviets invaded sixteen
years before.

The Taliban gunmen had grown up as refugees in these diseased camps in Pakistan. Their first sixteen years of life were passed in blind poverty, deprived of all
education and entertainment, imposing their own deadly punishments, their mothers and sisters kept in subservience as the men decided how to fight their foreign
oppressors on the other side of the border, their only diversion a detailed and
obsessive reading of the Koran—the one and true path in a world in which no other
could be contemplated. The Taliban had arrived not to rebuild a country they did
not remember, but to rebuild their refugee camps on a larger scale. Hence there
was to be no education. No television. Women must stay at home, just as they
stayed in their tents in Peshawar. Thus it was to be at the airport when I eventually
left; another immigration officer now, perhaps only fifteen, was wearing make-up
on his face—he, like many Algerians who fought in Afghanistan, was convinced
the Prophet wore kohl around his eyes in Arabia in the sixth and seventh centuries
of the Christian era. He refused to stamp my passport because I had no exit visa—
even though exit visas did not exist in Jalalabad. But I had broken a greater rule. I
wasn't wearing a beard. The boy pointed at my chin and shook his head in admonition, a child-schoolmaster who knew wickedness when he saw it and directed me
towards the old plane on the runway with contempt.

On the lawn of the Spinghar Hotel, two children approached me, one a
fourteen-year-old with a pile of exercise books. In one of the books, in poor
English, was a hand-written grammar test. "Insert the correct [*sic*] voice," it
demanded: " 'He . . . going home.' Insert: 'had'/'was'/'will.' " I gently inserted
"was" and corrected "cerrect." Was this the new education of the Afghan poor?
But at least the boys were being taught a foreign language at their pitiful school.
The smaller child even had a Persian grammar which told—inevitably—of the life
of the Prophet Mohamed. But girl pupils there were none. One afternoon during
the same dreary days of waiting, when I was sitting on the porch drinking tea, a
woman in a pale blue burqa walked slowly up the driveway muttering to herself.
She turned left into the gardens but made a detour towards me. She was moaning,

her voice rising and falling like a seagull, weeping and sobbing. She obviously wanted the foreigner to hear this most sombre of protests. Then she entered the rose garden.

Did we care? At that very moment, officials of Unocal (the Union Oil Company of California) and its Central Asian Oil Pipeline Project were negotiating with the Taliban to secure rights for a pipeline to carry gas from Turkmenistan to Pakistan through Afghanistan; in September 1996, the U.S. State Department had announced that it would open diplomatic relations with the Taliban, only to retract the statement later. Among Unocal's employees were Zalmay Khalilzad—five years later, he would be appointed President George W. Bush's special envoy to "liberated" Afghanistan—and a Pushtun leader called Hamid Karzai. No wonder Afghans adopted an attitude of suspicion towards the United States. America's allies originally supported bin Laden against the Russians. Then the United States turned bin Laden into their Public Enemy Number One—a post that was admittedly difficult to retain in the Pentagon wheel of fortune, since new monsters were constantly being discovered by Washington, often in inverse proportion to its ability to capture the old ones. Now the Taliban were being courted. But for how long? Could bin Laden, an Arab whose political goals were infinitely more ambitious than the Taliban's, maintain the integrity of his exile alongside men who wished only to repress their own people? Would the Taliban protect bin Laden any more courageously than had the failed Islamic Republic of Sudan?

ON THE MOUNTAINSIDE, THE MACHINE continued his search of the machine. There was a cold moon now and, when the mist did not conceal its light, I could see the tall man's tight lips and the sunken hollows of his cheeks beneath his shades. On the frozen mountainside, he opened the school satchel that I always carry in rough countries and fingered through my passport, press cards, notebooks, the pile of old Lebanese and Gulf newspapers inside. He took my Nikon camera from its bag. He flicked open the back, checked the auto-drive and then knelt on the stones by my camera-bag and opened each plastic carton of film. Then he put them all neatly back into the bag, snapped the camera shut, switched off the auto-drive and handed me the bag. *Shukran*, I said. Again, no reply. He turned to the driver and nodded and we drove on up the ice track. We were now at 5,000 feet. More lights flashed until we turned a corner past a massive boulder and there before us in the moonlight lay a small valley. There were grass and trees and a stream of unfrozen water that curled through it and a clutch of tents under a cliff. Two men approached. There were more formal Arab greetings, my right hand in both of theirs. Trust us. That was always the intention of these greetings. An Algerian who spoke fluent French and an Egyptian, they invited me to tour this little valley.

We washed our hands in the stream and walked over the stiff grass towards a dark gash in the cliff face above us. As my eyes became accustomed to the light, I could make out a vast rectangle in the side of the mountain, a 6-metres-high air-raid shelter cut into the living rock by bin Laden's men during the Russian war. "It was for a hospital," the Egyptian said. "We brought our mujahedin wounded here and they were safe from any Russian plane. No one could bomb us. We were safe." I walked into this man-made cave, the Algerian holding a torch, until I could hear my own crunching footsteps echoing softly from the depths of the tunnel. When we emerged, the moon was almost dazzling, the valley bathed in its white light, another little paradise of trees and water and mountain peaks.

The tent I was taken to was military issue, a khaki tarpaulin roped to iron stakes, a flap as an entrance, a set of stained mattresses on the floor. There was tea in a large steel pot and I sat with the Egyptian and Algerian and with three other men who had entered the tent with Kalashnikovs. We waited for perhaps half an hour, the Algerian slowly acknowledging under my questioning that he was a member of the "Islamic resistance" to the Algerian military regime. I spoke of my own visits to Algeria, the ability of the Islamists to fight on in the mountains and the *bled*—the countryside—against the government troops, much as the Algerian FLN had done against the French army in the 1954–62 war of independence. The Algerian liked this comparison—I had intended that he should—and I made no mention of my suspicion that he belonged to the Islamic Armed Group, the GIA, which was blamed by the government for the massacres of throat-cutting and dismemberment that had stained the last four years of Algeria's history.

There was a sudden scratching of voices outside the tent, thin and urgent like the soundtrack of an old movie. Then the flap snapped up and bin Laden walked in, dressed in a turban and green robes. I stood up, half bent under the canvas, and we shook hands, both of us forced by the tarpaulin that touched our heads to greet each other like Ottoman pashas, bowed and looking up into the other's face. Again, he looked tired, and I had noticed a slight limp when he walked into the tent. His beard was greyer, his face thinner than I remembered it. Yet he was all smiles, almost jovial, placing the rifle which he had carried into the tent on the mattress to his left, insisting on more tea for his guest. For several seconds he looked at the ground. Then he looked at me with an even bigger smile, beneficent and, I thought at once, very disturbing.

"Mr. Robert," he began, and he looked around at the other men in combat jackets and soft brown hats who had crowded into the tent. "Mr. Robert, one of our brothers had a dream. He dreamed that you came to us one day on a horse, that you had a beard and that you were a spiritual person. You wore a robe like us. This means you are a true Muslim."

This was terrifying. It was one of the most fearful moments of my life. I understood bin Laden's meaning a split second each of his words. Dream. Horse. Beard. Spiritual. Robe. Muslim. The other men in the tent were all nodding and looking at me, some smiling, others silently staring at the Englishman who had appeared in the dream of the "brother." I was appalled. It was both a trap and an invitation, and the most dangerous moment to be among the most dangerous men in the world. I could not reject the "dream" lest I suggest bin Laden was lying. Yet I could not accept its meaning without myself lying, without suggesting that what was clearly intended of me—that I should accept this "dream" as a prophecy and a divine instruction—might be fulfilled. For this man—and these men—to trust me, a foreigner, to come to them without prejudice—for them to regard me as honest—that was one thing. But to imagine that I would join them in their struggle, that I would become one with them, was beyond any possibility. The coven was waiting for a reply.

Was I imagining this? Could this not be just an elaborate, rhetorical way of expressing traditional respect towards a visitor? Was this not merely the attempt of a Muslim—many Westerners in the Middle East have experienced this—to gain an adherent to the faith? Was bin Laden really trying—let us be frank—to recruit me? I feared he was. And I immediately understood what this might mean. A Westerner, a white man from England, a journalist on a respectable newspaper—not a British convert to Islam of Arab or Asian origin—would be a catch indeed. He would go unsuspected, he could become a government official, join an army, even—as I would contemplate just over four years later—learn to fly an airliner. I had to get out of this, quickly, and I was trying to find an intellectual escape tunnel, working so hard in digging it that my brain was on fire.

"Sheikh Osama," I began, even before I had decided on my next words. "Sheikh Osama, I am not a Muslim." There was silence in the tent. "I am a journalist." No one could dispute that. "And the job of a journalist is to tell the truth." No one would *want* to dispute that. "And that is what I intend to do in my life—to tell the truth." Bin Laden was watching me like a hawk. And he understood. I was declining the offer. In front of his men, it was now bin Laden's turn to withdraw, to cover his retreat gracefully. "If you tell the truth, that means you are a good Muslim," he said. The men in the tent in their combat jackets and beards all nodded at this sagacity. Bin Laden smiled. I was saved. As the old cliché goes, I "breathed again." No deal.

Perhaps it was out of the need to curtail this episode, to cover his embarrassment at this little failure, that bin Laden suddenly and melodramatically noticed the school satchel lying beside my camera and the Lebanese newspapers partially visible inside. He seized upon them. He must read them at once. And in front of us all, he clambered across the tent with the papers in his hand to where the paraffin lamp was hissing in the corner. And there, for half an hour, ignoring almost all of us, he read his way through the Arabic press, sometimes summoning the Egyptian to read an article, at others showing a paper to one of the other gunmen in the tent. Was this really, I began to wonder, the centre of "world terror"? Listening to the spokesman at the U.S. State Department, reading the editorials in *The New York Times* or *The Washington Post*, I might have been forgiven for believing that bin Laden ran his "terror network" from a state-of-the-art bunker of computers and digitalised battle plans, flicking a switch to instruct his followers to assault another Western target. But this man seemed divorced from the outside world. Did he not have a radio? A television? Why, he didn't even know—he told me so himself after reading the papers—that the foreign minister of Iran, Ali Akbar Velayati, had visited Saudi Arabia, his own country, for the first time in more than three years.

When he returned to his place in the corner of the tent, bin Laden was businesslike. He warned the Americans of a renewed onslaught against their forces in Saudi Arabia. "We are still at the beginning of military action against them," he said. "But we have removed the psychological obstacle against fighting the Americans . . . This is the first time in fourteen centuries that the two holy shrines are occupied by non-Islamic forces . . . " He insisted that the Americans were in the Gulf for oil and embarked on a modern history of the region to prove this.

"Brezhnev wanted to reach the Hormuz Strait across Afghanistan for this reason, but by the grace of Allah and the jihad he was not only defeated in Afghanistan but was finished here. We carried our weapons on our shoulders here for ten years, and we and the sons of the Islamic world are prepared to carry weapons for the rest of our lives. But despite this, oil is not the direct impetus for the Americans occupying the region—they obtained oil at attractive prices before their invasion. There are other reasons, primarily the American–Zionist alliance, which is filled with fear at the power of Islam and of the land of Mecca and Medina. It fears that an Islamic renaissance will drown Israel. We are convinced that we shall kill the Jews in Palestine. We are convinced that with Allah's help, we shall triumph against the American forces. It's only a matter of numbers and time. For them to claim that they are protecting Arabia from Iraq is untrue—the whole issue of Saddam is a trick."

There was something new getting loose here. Condemning Israel was standard fare for any Arab nationalist, let alone a man who believed he was participating in an Islamic jihad. But bin Laden was now combining America and Israel as a single country—"For us," he said later, "there is no difference between the American and Israeli governments or between the American and Israeli soldiers"—and was talking of Jews, rather than Israeli soldiers, as his targets. How soon before all Westerners, all those from "Crusader nations," were added to the list? He took no credit for the bombings in Riyadh and al-Khobar but praised the four men who had been accused of setting off the explosions, two of whom he admitted he had met. "I view those who did these bombings with great respect," he said. "I consider it a great act and a major honour in which I missed the opportunity of participating." But bin Laden was also anxious to show the support for his cause which he claimed was now growing in Pakistan. He produced newspaper clippings recording the sermons of Pakistani clerics who had condemned America's presence in Saudi Arabia and then thrust into my hands two large coloured photographs of graffiti spray-painted on walls in Karachi.

In red paint, one said: "American Forces, get out of the Gulf—The United Militant Ulemas." Another, painted in brown, announced that "America is the biggest enemy of the Muslim world." A large poster that bin Laden handed to me appeared to be from the same hand with similar anti-American sentiment uttered by *mawlawi*—religious scholars—in the Pakistani city of Lahore. As for the Taliban and their new, oppressive regime, bin Laden had little option but to be pragmatic. "All Islamic countries are my country," he said. "We believe that the Taliban are sincere in their attempts to enforce Islamic sharia law. We saw the situation before they came and afterwards and have noticed a great difference and an obvious improvement."

But when he returned to his most important struggle—against the United States—bin Laden seemed possessed. When he spoke of this, his followers in the tent hung upon his every word as if he was a messiah. He had, he said, sent faxes to King Fahd and all main departments of the Saudi government, informing them of his determination to pursue a holy struggle against the United States. He even claimed that some members of the Saudi royal family supported him, along with officers in the security services—a claim I later discovered to be true. But declaring war by fax was a new innovation and there was an eccentricity about bin Laden's perspective on American politics. At one point, he suggested in all seriousness that rising taxes in America would push many states to secede from the union, an idea that might appeal to some state governors even if it was hardly in the world of reality.

But this was a mere distraction from a far more serious threat. "We think that our struggle against America will be much simpler than that against the Soviet Union," bin Laden said. "I will tell you something for the first time. Some of our mujahedin who fought in Afghanistan participated in operations against the Americans in Somalia and they were surprised at the collapse in American military morale. We regard America as a paper tiger." This was a strategic error of some scale. The American retreat from its state-building mission in Somalia under President Clinton was not going to be repeated if a Republican president came to power, especially if the United States was under attack. True, over the years, the same loss of will might creep back into American military policy—Iraq would see to that—but Washington, whatever bin Laden might think, was going to be a far more serious adversary than Moscow. Yet he persisted. And I shall always remember Osama bin Laden's last words to me that night on the bare mountain: "Mr. Robert," he said, "from this mountain upon which you are sitting, we broke the Russian army and we destroyed the Soviet Union. And I pray to God that he will permit us to turn the United States into a shadow of itself."

I sat in silence, thinking about these words as bin Laden discussed my journey back to Jalalabad with his guards. He was concerned that the Taliban—despite their "sincerity"—might object to his dispatching a foreigner through their checkpoints after dark, and so I was invited to pass the night in bin Laden's mountain camp. I was permitted to take just three photographs of him, this time by the light of the Toyota which was driven to the tent with its headlights shining through the canvas to illuminate bin Laden's face. He sat in front of me, expressionless, a stone figure, and in the pictures I developed in Beirut three days later he was a purple-and-yellow ghost. He said goodbye without much ceremony, a brief handshake and a nod, and vanished from the tent, and I lay down on the mattress with my coat over me to keep warm. The men with their guns sitting around slept there too, while others armed with rifles and rocket-launchers patrolled the low ridges around the camp.

In the years to come, I would wonder who they were. Was the Egyptian

Mohamed Atta among those young men in the tent? Or Abdul Aziz Alomari? Or any other of the nineteen men whose names we would all come to know just over four years later? I cannot remember their faces now, cowled as they were, many of them, in their scarves.

Exhaustion and cold kept me awake. "A shadow of itself" was the expression that kept repeating itself to me. What did bin Laden and these dedicated, ruthless men have in store for us? I recall the next few hours like a freeze-frame film; waking so cold there was ice in my hair, slithering back down the mountain trail in the Toyota with one of the Algerian gunmen in the back telling me that if we were in Algeria he would cut my throat but that he was under bin Laden's orders to protect me and thus would give his life for me. The three men in the back and my driver stopped the jeep on the broken-up Kabul–Jalalabad highway to say their dawn *fajr* prayers. Beside the broad estuary of the Kabul River, they spread their mats and knelt as the sun rose over the mountains. Far to the north-east, I could see the heights of the Hindu Kush glimmering a pale white under an equally pale blue sky, touching the border of China that nuzzled into the wreckage of a land that was to endure yet more suffering in the coming years. Hills and rocks and water and ancient trees and old mountains, this was the world before the age of man.

And I remember driving back with bin Laden's men into Jalalabad past the barracks where the Taliban stored their captured arms and, just a few minutes later, hearing the entire store—of shells, anti-tank rockets, Stinger missiles, explosives and mines—exploding in an earthquake that shook the trees in the laneway outside the Spinghar Hotel and sprinkled us with tiny pieces of metal and torn pages from American manuals instructing "users" on how to aim missiles at aircraft. More than ninety civilians were ripped to bits by the accidental explosion—did a Taliban throw the butt of a cigarette, a lonely and unique item of enjoyment, into the ammunition?—and then the Algerian walked up to me in tears and told me that his best friend had just perished in the explosion. Bin Laden's men, I noted, can also cry.

But most of all I remember the first minutes after our departure from bin Laden's camp. It was still dark when I caught sight of a great light in the mountains to the north. For a while I thought it was the headlights of another vehicle, another security signal from the camp guards to our departing Toyota. But it hung there for many minutes and I began to realise that it was burning above the mountains and carried a faintly incandescent trail. The men in the vehicle were watching it too. "It is Halley's comet," one of them said. He was wrong. It was a newly discovered comet, noticed for the first time only two years earlier by Americans Alan Hale and Tom Bopp, but I could see how Hale–Bopp had become Halley to these Arab men in the mountains of Afghanistan. It was soaring above us now, trailing a golden tail, a sublime power moving at 70,000 kilometres an hour through the heavens.

So we stopped the Toyota and climbed out to watch the fireball as it blazed through the darkness above us, the al-Qaeda men and the Englishman, all filled with awe at this spectacular, wondrous apparition of cosmic energy, unseen for more than 4,000 years. "Mr. Robert, do you know what they say when a comet like this is seen?" It was the Algerian, standing next to me now, both of us craning our necks up towards the sky. "It means that there is going to be a great war." And so we watched the fire blaze through the pageant of stars and illuminate the firmament above us.

# CHAPTER TWO

# "They Shoot Russians"

*When you're wounded and left on Afghanistan's plains,*
*And the women come out to cut up what remains,*
*Jest roll to your rifle and blow out your brains*
*An' go to your Gawd like a soldier.*

—Rudyard Kipling,
"The Young British Soldier"

LESS THAN SIX MONTHS BEFORE THE OUTBREAK of the First World War, my grandmother, Margaret Fisk, gave my father William a 360-page book of imperial adventure, *Tom Graham, V.C., A Tale of the Afghan War.* "Presented to Willie By his Mother" is written in thick pencil inside the front cover. "Date Sat. 24th January 1914, for another." "Willie" would have been almost fifteen years old. Only after my father's death in 1992 did I inherit this book, with its handsome, engraved hardboard cover embossed with a British Victoria Cross—"For Valour," it says on the medal—and, on the spine, a soldier in red coat and peaked white tropical hat with a rifle in his hands. I never found out the meaning of the cryptic reference "for another." But years later, I read the book. An adventure by William Johnston and published in 1900 by Thomas Nelson and Sons, it tells the story of the son of a mine-owner who grows up in the northern English port of Seaton and, forced to leave school and become an apprentice clerk because of his father's sudden impoverishment, joins the British Army under-age. Tom Graham is posted to a British unit at Buttevant in County Cork in the south-west of Ireland—he even kisses the Blarney Stone, conferring upon himself the supposed powers of persuasive eloquence contained in that much blessed rock—and then travels to India and to the Second Afghan War, where he is gazetted a second lieutenant in a Highland regiment. As he stands at his late father's grave in the local churchyard before leaving for the army, Tom vows that he will lead "a pure, clean, and upright life."

The story is typical of my father's generation, a rip-roaring, racist story of British heroism and Muslim savagery. But reading it, I was struck by some remarkable parallels. My own father, Bill Fisk—the "Willie" of the dedication almost a century ago—was also taken from school in a northern English port because his father, Edward, was no longer able to support him. He too became an apprentice clerk, in Birkenhead. In the few notes he wrote before his death, Bill recalled that he had tried to join the British Army under-age; he travelled to Ful-

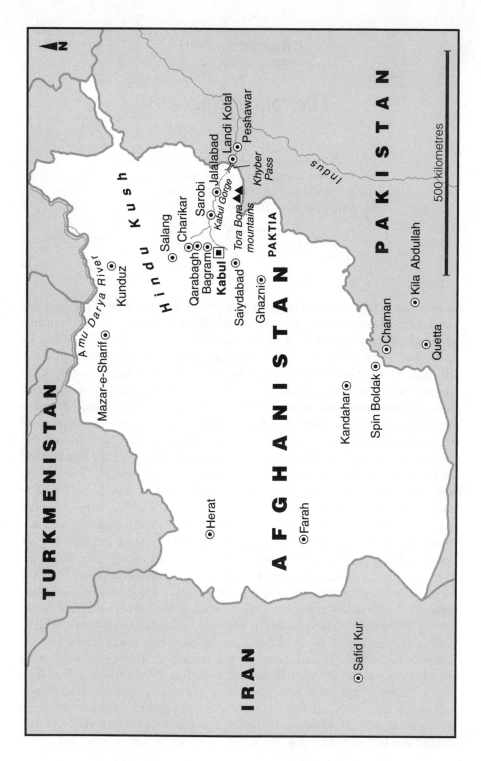

wood Barracks in Preston to join the Royal Field Artillery on 15 August 1914, eleven days after the start of Britain's involvement in the First World War. Successful in enlisting two years later, Bill Fisk, too, was sent to a battalion of the Cheshire Regiment in Cork in Ireland, not long after the 1916 Easter Rising. There is even a pale photograph of my father in my archives, kissing the Blarney Stone. Two years later, in France, my father was gazetted a second lieutenant in the King's Liverpool Regiment. Was he consciously following the life of the fictional Tom Graham?

The rest of the novel is a disturbing tale of colour prejudice, xenophobia and outright anti-Muslim hatred during the Second Afghan War. In the second half of the nineteenth century, Anglo-Russian rivalry and suspicion had naturally focused upon Afghanistan, whose unmarked frontiers had become the indistinct front lines between imperial Russia and the British Indian Raj. The principal victims of the "Great Game," as British diplomats injudiciously referred to the successive conflicts in Afghanistan—there was indeed something characteristically childish about the jealousy between Russia and Britain—were, of course, the Afghans. Their landlocked box of deserts and soaring mountains and dark green valleys had for centuries been both a cultural meeting point—between the Middle East, Central Asia and the Far East—and a battlefield.* A decision by the Afghan king Shir Ali Khan, the third son of Afghanistan's first king, Dost Mohamed, to receive a Russian mission in Kabul after his re-accession in 1868 led directly to what the British were to call the Second Afghan War. The First Afghan War had led to the annihilation of the British army in the Kabul Gorge in 1842, in the same dark crevasse through which I drove at night on my visit to Osama bin Laden in 1997. At the Treaty of Gandamak in 1879, Shir Ali's son Yaqub Khan agreed to allow a permanent British embassy to be established in Kabul, but within four months the British envoy and his staff were murdered in their diplomatic compound. The British Army was sent back to Afghanistan.

In Bill Fisk's novel, Tom Graham goes with them. In the bazaar in Peshawar—now in Pakistan, then in India—Graham encounters Pathan tribesmen, "a villainous lot . . . most of the fanatics wore the close-fitting skull-cap which gives such a

---

*Alexander the Great smashed through the Afghan tribes on his way to India and the land was subsequently ruled by the Kushans, the Persian Sassanians, the Hephthalites and then the Islamic armies whose initial conquests and occupation were fiercely resisted by the Hindu tribes. Genghis Khan invaded in 1219 and was so infuriated by the death of his grandson outside the besieged city of Bamiyan—where two giant 600-year-old Buddhas could clearly be seen, cut into the cliffs above the valley—that he ordered his Mongol army to execute every man, woman and child. Other empires were to extend their territory into what is now called Afghanistan. At the end of the fourteenth century, Timur-i-leng—"Timur, the club-footed," the Tamburlaine of Christopher Marlowe's blood-boltered play—conquered much of the land. The Timurids were succeeded by the Moguls of India and the Safavids of Persia. There were periodic rebellions by Afghan tribes, but the outlines of a country that could be identified as Afghanistan only emerged in 1747 when the leader of a minor Pushtun tribe, Ahmad Shah Durrani, formed a confederacy that subsequently invaded the north of India. Only under Dost Mohamed in the 1830s did Afghanistan take on the appearance of a single political nation.

diabolical aspect to its wearer." Within days, Graham is fighting the same tribesmen at Peiwar Kotal, driving his bayonet "up to the nozzle" into the chest of an
Afghan, a "swarthy giant, his eyes glaring with hate." In the Kurram Valley, Graham and his "chums"—a word my father used about his comrades in the First
World War—fight off "infuriated tribesmen, drunk with the lust of plunder." When
General Sir Frederick Roberts—later Lord Roberts of Kandahar—agrees to meet a
local tribal leader, the man arrives with "as wild a looking band of rascals as could
be imagined." The author notes that whenever British troops fell into Afghan
hands, "their bodies were dreadfully mutilated and dishonoured by these fiends in
human form." When the leader of the Afghans deemed responsible for the murder
of the British envoy is brought for execution, "a thrill of satisfaction" goes through
the ranks of Graham's comrades as the condemned man faces the gallows.

Afghans are thus a "villainous lot," "fanatics," "rascals," "fiends in human
form," meat for British bayonets—or "toasting forks" as the narrative cheerfully
calls them. It gets worse. A British artillery officer urges his men to fire at close-
packed Afghan tribesmen with the words "that will scatter the flies." The text
becomes not only racist but anti-Islamic. "Boy readers," the author pontificates,
"may not know that it was the sole object of every Afghan engaged in the war of
1878–80 to cut to pieces every heretic he could come across. The more pieces cut
out of the unfortunate Britisher the higher his summit of bliss in Paradise." After
Tom Graham is wounded in Kabul, the Afghans—in the words of his Irish-born
army doctor—have become "murtherin villains, the black niggers."

When the British suffer defeat at the battle of Maiwand, on a grey desert west
of Kandahar, an officer orders his men to "have your bayonets ready, and wait for
the niggers." There is no reference in the book to the young Afghan woman,
Malalai, who—seeing the Afghans briefly retreating—tore her veil from her head
and led a charge against her enemies, only to be cut down by British bullets. That,
of course, is part of Afghan—not British—history. When victory is finally claimed
by the British at Kandahar, Tom Graham wins his Victoria Cross.

From "villains" to "flies" and "niggers" in one hundred pages, it's not difficult
to see how easily my father's world of "pure, clean and upright" Britons bestialised its enemies. Though there are a few references to the "boldness" of Afghan
tribesmen—and just one to their "courage"—no attempt is made to explain their
actions. They are evil, hate-filled, anxious to prove their Muslim faith by "cutting
pieces out of the unfortunate Britisher." The notion that Afghans do not want foreigners invading and occupying their country simply does not exist in the story.

If official British accounts of Afghanistan were not so prejudiced, they nevertheless maintained the oversimplified and supremacist view of the Afghans that
Johnston used to such effect in his novel. An account of life in Kabul between
1836 and 1838 by Lt. Col. Sir Alexander Burnes of the East India Company—
published the year of the massacre of the British Army in 1842—gives a sensitive
portrayal of the generosity of tribal leaders and demonstrates a genuine interest in
Afghan customs and social life. But by the end of the century, the official *Imperial
Gazetteer of India* chooses to describe the animals of Afghanistan before it reports

on its people, who are "handsome and athletic . . . inured to bloodshed from child-hood . . . treacherous and passionate in revenge . . . ignorant of everything connected with their religion beyond its most elementary doctrines . . . "

Among the young Britons who accompanied the army to Kabul in 1879—a real Briton, this time—was a twenty-nine-year-old civil servant, Henry Mortimer Durand, who had been appointed political secretary to General Roberts. In horror, he read the general's proclamation to the people of Kabul, declaring the murder of the British mission diplomats "a treacherous and cowardly crime, which has brought indelible disgrace upon the Afghan people." The followers of Yaqub Khan, General Roberts declared, would not escape and their "punishment should be such as will be felt and remembered . . . all persons convicted of bearing a part in [the murders] will be dealt with according to their deserts." It was a Victorian version of the warning that an American president would give to the Afghans 122 years later.

Durand, a humane and intelligent man, confronted Roberts over his proclamation. "It seemed to me so utterly wrong in tone and in matter that I determined to do my utmost to overthrow it . . . the stilted language, and the absurd affectation of preaching historical morality to the Afghans, all our troubles with whom began by our own abominable injustice, made the paper to my mind most dangerous for the General's reputation." Roberts ameliorated the text, not entirely to Durand's satisfaction. He thought it merely "a little less objectionable."

Yet Durand sent a letter to his biographer's sister, Ella Sykes, which provided gruesome evidence that *Tom Graham* contained all too real descriptions of Afghan cruelty. "During the action in the Chardeh valley on the 12th of Dec.r 1879," he wrote almost sixteen years after the event, "two Squadrons of the 9th Lancers were ordered to charge a large force of Afghans in the hope of saving our guns. The charge failed, and some of our dead were afterwards found dreadfully mutilated by Afghan knives . . . I saw it all . . . " But Durand was well aware that the Afghans were not the "fiends in human form" of popular fiction. In 1893, he describes the Afghan army commander, Ghulam Hyder, as an inquisitive and generous man.

> Today we talked about the size of London, and how it was supplied with food . . . about religious prejudices, the hatred of Sunnis and Shias, the Reformation and the Inquisition, the Musselman [*sic*] and Christian stories of Christ's life and death, the Spanish Armada, Napoleon and his wars, about which Ghulam Hyder knew a good deal, the manners of the Somalis, tiger shooting . . .

Durand had been sent to negotiate with the Afghan king, Abdur Rahman—a nephew of Shir Ali—over the southern border of his country, to secure an agreed frontier between British India and Afghanistan. Durand's brother Edward had already helped to delineate the country's northern frontier with Russia—during which the Russians sent a force of Cossacks to attack Afghan troops on the Kushk

River—and Mortimer Durand found the king deeply unsympathetic to his northern neighbour. According to Durand's notes, Abdur Rahman announced that

> unless you drive me into enmity, I am your friend for my life. And why? The Russians want to attack India. You do not want to attack Russian Turkmenistan. Therefore the Russians want to come through my country and you do not. People say I would join with them to attack you. If I did and they won, would they leave my country? Never. I should be their slave and I *hate* them.

> Eighty-six years later, the Russians would find out what this meant.

I SAW THEM FIRST, those Russians, standing beside their T-72 tanks next to the runways at Kabul airport, fleece-lined jackets below white-pink faces with thick grey fur hats bearing the red star and the hammer and sickle of the Soviet Union. The condensation of their breath hung so thickly in the air in front of their mouths that I looked for cartoon quotations in the bubbles. On the trucks parked beside the highway into the city, they wore the steel helmets so familiar from every Second World War documentary, the green metal casks with ripples over the ears, rifles in gloved hands, narrowed eyes searching the Afghans unflinchingly. They drew heavily and quickly on cigarettes, a little grey smog over each checkpoint. So these were the descendants of the men of Stalingrad and Kursk, the heroes of Rostov and Leningrad and Berlin. On the tarmac of the airport, there were at least seventy of the older T-62s. The snow lay thickly over the tanks, icing sugar on cakes of iron, enough to break the teeth of any Afghan "terrorist."

The Soviets had invaded Afghanistan on Christmas Eve of 1979, but when I arrived two weeks later their armour was still barrelling down through the slush from the Amu Darya River, the Oxus of antiquity, which Edward Durand had agreed with the Russians should be the northern frontier of this frost-covered land. Save for a few isolated cities, the Soviet army appeared to have crushed all resistance. Along the highways south and east of Kabul, Russian military encampments protected by dozens of tanks and heavy artillery controlled the arteries between the rebellious provinces of south-eastern Afghanistan. An "intervention," Leonid Brezhnev had called his invasion, peace-loving assistance to the popular socialist government of the newly installed Afghan president Babrak Karmal.

"In all my life, I have never seen so many tanks," my old Swedish radio colleague from Cairo, Hans-Gunnar Erlandsson, said when we met. Hans-Gunnar was a serious Swede, a thatch of blond hair above piercing blue eyes and vast spectacles. "And never in my life do I ever want to see so many tanks again," he said. "It is beyond imagination." There were now five complete Soviet divisions in Afghanistan; the 105th Airborne Division based on Kabul, the 66th Motorised Rifle Brigade in Herat, the 357th Motorised Rifle Division in Kandahar, the 16th Motorised Rifle Division in the three northern provinces of Badakhshan, Takhar and Samangan and the 306th Motorised Division in Kabul with the Soviet para-troopers. There were already 60,000 Soviet troops in the country, vast numbers of them digging slit trenches beside the main roads. This was invasion on a massive scale, a superpower demonstration of military will, the sclerotic Brezhnev—Red Army political commissar on the Ukrainian front in 1943, he would die within three years—now flexing his impotent old frame for the last time.

But Russia's final imperial adventure had all the awesome fury of Britain's Afghan wars. In the previous week alone, Soviet Antonov-22 transport aircraft had made 4,000 separate flights into the capital. Every three minutes, squadrons of MiG-25s would race up from the frozen runways of Kabul airport and turn in the white sunshine towards the mountains to the east and there would follow, like dungeon doors slamming deep beneath our feet, a series of massive explosions far across the landscape. Soviet troops stood on the towering heights of the Kabul Gorge. I was Middle East correspondent of *The Times* of London, the paper whose nineteenth-century war correspondent William Howard Russell—a student of Trinity College, Dublin, as I was—won his spurs in the 1854–55 Anglo-Russian war in the Crimea. We were all Tom Grahams now.

I think that's how many of us felt that gleaming, iced winter. I was already exhausted. I lived in Beirut, where the Lebanese civil war had sucked in one Israeli army and would soon consume another. Only three weeks before, I had left post-revolutionary Iran, where America had just lost its very own "policeman of the Gulf," Shah Mohamed Pahlavi, in favour of that most powerful of Islamic leaders, Ayatollah Ruhollah Khomeini. Within nine months, I would be running for my life under shellfire with Saddam Hussein's Iraqi Army as it invaded the Islamic repub-lic. America had already "lost" Iran. Now it was in the process of "losing" Afghanistan—or at least watching that country's last pitiful claim to national inde-pendence melt into the Kremlin's embrace. Or so it looked to us at the time. The Russians wanted a warm-water port, just as General Roberts had feared in 1878. If they could reach the Gulf coast—Kandahar is 650 kilometres from the Gulf of Oman—then after a swift incursion through Iranian or Pakistani Baluchistan, Soviet forces would stand only 300 kilometres from the Arabian peninsula. That, at least, was the received wisdom, the fount of a thousand editorials. The Russians are coming. That the Soviet Union was dying, that the Soviet government was undertaking this extraordinary expedition through panic—through fear that the collapse of a communist ally in Afghanistan might set off a chain reaction among the Soviet Muslim republics—was not yet apparent, although within days I would see the very evidence that proved the Kremlin might be correct.

Indeed, many of the Soviet soldiers arriving in Afghanistan came from those very Muslim republics of Soviet Central Asia whose loyalties so concerned Brezh-nev. In Kabul, Soviet troops from the Turkoman region were conversing easily with local Afghan commanders. The high-cheekboned Asiatic features of some soldiers often suggested that their military units had been drawn from the Mongo-lian region. In Kabul and the villages immediately surrounding the city, no open hostility was shown towards the Soviet invaders in the daylight hours; so many

Russian units had been moved into the snow-covered countryside that Afghan troops had been withdrawn to protect the capital. But at night, the Soviets were pulled back towards Kabul and unconfirmed reports already spoke of ten Russian dead in two weeks, two of them beaten to death with clubs. In Jalalabad, 65 kilometres by road from the Pakistan border, thunderous night-time explosions bore witness to the continued struggle between Afghan tribesmen and Soviet troops.

For the next two months, we few journalists who managed to enter Afghanistan were witness to the start of a fearful tragedy, one that would last for more than a quarter of a century and would cost at least a million and a half innocent lives, a war that would eventually reach out and strike at the heart, not of Russia but of America. How could we have known? How could we have guessed that while an Islamic revolution had enveloped Iran, a far more powerful spiritual force was being nursed and suckled here amid the snows of early January 1980? Again, the evidence was there, for those of us who chose to seek it out, who realised that the narrative of history laid down by our masters—be they of the Moscow or the Washington persuasion—was essentially short-term, false and ultimately self-defeating. Perhaps we were too naive, too ill-prepared for events on such a scale. Who could grasp in so short a time the implications of this essentially imperial story, this latest adventure in the "Great Game"? We were young, most of us who managed to scramble into Afghanistan that January. I was thirty-five, most of my colleagues were younger, and journalism is not only an imprecise science but a fatiguing one whose practice involves almost as much bureaucracy as it does fact-gathering. I had spent Christmas in Ireland and returned to wartime Beirut on 3 January to prepare for my onward assignment to cover the continuing revolution in Iran. But no event could compare to the Soviet invasion of Afghanistan.

For a journalist, nothing can beat that moment when a great story beckons, when history really is being made and when a foreign editor tells you to go for it. I remember one hot day in Beirut when gunmen had hijacked a Lufthansa passenger jet to Dubai. I could get there in four hours, I told London. "Go. Go. Go," they messaged back. But this was drama on an infinitely greater scale, an epic if we could be there to report it. The Soviet army was pouring into Afghanistan, and from their homes and offices in London, New York, Delhi, Moscow, my colleagues were all trying to find a way there. Beirut was comparatively close but it was still more than three thousand kilometres west of Kabul. And it was a surreal experience to drive through West Beirut's civil war gunfire to the ticketing office of Middle East Airlines to seek the help of a Lebanese airline that now had only twelve elderly Boeing 707s and three jumbos to its name. Under the old travel rules, Afghanistan issued visas to all British citizens on arrival. But we had to work on the principle that with the country now a satellite of the Soviet Union, those regulations—a remnant of the days when Kabul happily lay astride the hashish tourist trail to India—would have been abandoned.

Richard Wigg, then our India correspondent, was in the Pakistani capital of Islamabad, Michael Binyon was in Moscow. The Lebanese airline had conceived of a plan to get me into Afghanistan, an ingenious plot that I sent through to London on the ancient telex machines in the Beirut Associated Press bureau, which regularly misspelled our copy. "Friends in ticketing section at MiddlehEast [*sic*] Airlines . . . have suggested we might try following: I buy single ticket to Kabul and travel in on Ariana [Afghan Airlines] flight that terminates in Kabul," I wrote. "This means that even if I get bounced, I will probably earn myself twelve hours or so in the city . . . because my flight will have terminated in Afghanistan and I can't be uput [*sic*] back on it . . . At the very worst, I would get bounced and could buy a ticket to Pakistan then head for Peshawar . . . Grateful reply soonest so I can get MEA ticket people to work early tomorrow (Fri) morning." London replied within the hour. "Please go ahead with single ticket Kabul plan," the foreign desk messaged. I was already back at the MEA office when *The Times* sent another note. "Binyon advises that Afghan embassies uround [*sic*] the world have been instructed to issue visus [*sic*] which might make things easier."

This was astonishing. The Russians *wanted* us there. Their "fraternal support" for the new Karmal government—and the supposedly hideous nature of his predecessor's regime—was to be publicised. The Russians were coming to *liberate* Afghanistan. This was obviously the story the Kremlin was concocting. For several years, I had—in addition to my employment by *The Times*—been reporting for the Canadian Broadcasting Corporation. I liked radio, I liked CBC's courage in letting their reporters speak their minds, in letting me go into battle with a tape recorder to "tell it like it is," to report the blood and stench of wars and my own disgust at human conflict. Sue Hickey came on the telex from CBC's London office. "Good luck keep ur eyes open in the back of ur head," she wrote. I promised her an Afghan silk scarf—bribery knows no bounds in radio journalism. "What is the Russian for 'Help I surrender where is the Brit Embassy?' " I asked. "The Russian for help is *'pomog,'* " Sue responded in her telex shorthand. "So there u shud not hv any trouble bi bi."

Ariana had a flight from Frankfurt to Kabul early on Sunday morning. Then it was cancelled. Then it was rescheduled and cancelled again. It would fly from Rome. It would fly from Geneva. No, it would fly from Istanbul. When I reached Turkey on MEA, the snow was piled round the Istanbul terminal and "Delayed" was posted beside the Kabul flight designator. There was no fuel for heating in Istanbul so I huddled in my coat on a broken plastic seat with all the books and clippings I had grabbed from my files in Beirut. My teeth were chattering and I wore my gloves as I turned the pages. We journalists do this far too much, boning up on history before the next plane leaves, cramming our heads with dates and presidents, one eye on the Third Afghan War, the other on the check-in desk. I pulled out my map of Afghanistan, green and yellow to the west where the deserts imprison Kandahar, brown in the centre as the mountains shoulder their way towards Kabul, a big purple-and-white bruise to the north-east where the Hindu Kush separates Pakistan, India, China and the Soviet Union.

The border between British India and Afghanistan was finally laid across the tribal lands in 1893, from the Khyber Pass, south-west to the desert town of Chaman (now in Pakistan), a dustbowl frontier post at the base of a great desert of sand and grey mountains a hundred kilometres from Kandahar. These "lines in the sand," of course, were set down by Sir Mortimer Durand and recognised by the great powers. For the people living on each side of the lines, who were typically given no say in the matter, the borders were meaningless. The Pathans in the southwest of Afghanistan found that the frontier cut right through their tribal and ethnic homeland. Of course they did; for the borders were supposed to protect Britain and Russia from each other, not to ease the life or identity of Afghan tribesmen who considered themselves neither Afghans nor Indians—nor, later, Pakistani—but Pushtun-speaking Pathans who believed they lived in a place called Pushtunistan, which lay on both sides of what would become known as the Durand Line.

The end of the First World War, during which Afghanistan remained neutral, left a declining British Raj to the south and an ambitious new Soviet communist nation to the north. Emir Amanullah began a small-scale insurrection against the British in 1919—henceforth to be known as the Third Afghan War—which the British won militarily but which the Afghans won politically. They would now control their own foreign affairs and have real independence from Britain. But this was no guarantee of stability.*

Reform and regression marked Afghanistan's subsequent history. My collection of newspaper cuttings included a 1978 report from *The Guardian*, which recalled how the Soviets had spent £350 million to build the Salang road tunnel through the mountains north of Kabul; it took ten years and cost £200 million a mile. "Why should they spend £350 million on a little-used roadway across the Hindu Kush?" the writer asked. "Surely not just for the lorry-loads of raisins that toil up the pass each day. The answer is no. The Salang Tunnel was built to enable Russian convoys . . . to cross from the cities and army bases of Uzbekhistan all the way over to the Khyber and to Pakistan . . . "

A nation of peasants relied upon tribal and religious tradition while only Marxists could provide political initiative. The violent overthrow of Mohamed Daoud in 1978 led to a series of ever harsher Marxist regimes led by Nur Mohamed Taraki and Hafizullah Amin, their opposing Parcham ("Banner") and Khalq ("People") parties cruelly executing their rivals. Rebellion broke out in rural areas of

---

*Influenced by the secular revolutions of Mustafa Kemal Atatürk in Turkey and Shah Reza in Persia, Amanullah instituted a series of worthy reforms—an elected assembly, a constitutional monarchy, secular education—which delighted the modern "West" but appalled the Islamic authorities who naturally saw in them the end of their feudal, indeed medieval, power. There was insurrection and Amanullah went into Italian exile. His kinsman Mohamed Nadir Khan did not make the same mistakes. He identified himself with the Muslim conservatives and created— a dangerous precedent, this, in a country of such disunity—a new and powerful army. He was assassinated in 1933, to be succeeded by his son Zahir. There followed a brief period of "democracy"—of free elections and a moderately free press—but in 1973 a coup brought Mohamed Daoud to power. Daoud turned to the Soviet Union for economic assistance, promulgated several liberal laws which found favour in the "West"—one encouraged the voluntary removal of the veil from women—but his virtual renunciation of the Durand Line led Pakistan, which had inherited the old frontier of the Raj, to close its border. Afghanistan was now ever more dependent on the Soviet Union.

Afghanistan and the army, increasingly mutinous despite its Soviet advisers, began to disintegrate. Taraki died of an "undisclosed illness"—almost certainly murdered by Amin's henchmen—and then, in December 1979, Amin in turn was shot dead. An entire Afghan army unit had already handed over its weapons to rebels in Wardak and there is some evidence that it was Amin himself who asked for Soviet military intervention to save his government. Soviet special forces were arriving at Afghan airbases on 17 December, five days after Brezhnev made his decision to invade, and it is possible that Amin was killed by mistake when his bodyguards first saw Soviet troops around his palace.

A quarter of a century later, in Moscow, I would meet a former Soviet military intelligence officer who arrived in Kabul with Russian forces before the official invasion. "Amin was shot and we tried to save him," he told me. "Our medical officers tried to save him. More than that I will not tell you." It is certainly true that the Soviet officer in charge of the coup, General Viktor Paputin, shortly afterwards committed suicide. On 27 December, however, it was announced that the increasingly repressive Amin had been "executed." Babrak Karmal, a socialist lawyer and a Parcham party man who had earlier taken refuge in Moscow, was now installed in Kabul by the Soviets. He had been a deputy prime minister—along with Amin—under Taraki; now he was the Trojan horse through whom the Soviets could protest that Afghanistan had been "freed" from Amin's tyranny.

It was below zero in Istanbul's Atatürk Airport. There was frost on the inside of the windows. I padded off to the empty check-in desk. There was a pamphlet lying there, a brochure from the Afghan Tourist Organisation. "Say 'Afghanistan' and you think of the friendliest country," it said on the back. "Say 'Ariana' and you've thought of the friendliest way of getting there." But the Afghan Tourist Organisation had not survived the purges. A thick black crayon had been drawn through the first page in a vain attempt to erase the name of "the Head of State of the Republic of Afghanistan Mr. Mohamed Daoud." The word "Democratic"—an essential adjective in the title of every undemocratic regime—had been penned in above the country's name and all references to the former royal family pasted over. Local tourist officials who had served Daoud and since disappeared suffered the same paper fate.

But the brand-new Ariana DC-10 arrived in Istanbul before dawn, its Afghan crew still flying with the American McDonnell Douglas technicians who had taught them to fly the aircraft. It was a bumpy, cold flight down to Tehran, the flight's last stop before Kabul. The Afghan crew ate their breakfast in first class before serving the passengers; the "friendliest way" of getting to Afghanistan. At Tehran's Mehrabad Airport, three Iranian Revolutionary Guards boarded and ordered two middle-aged men off the plane. They went, heads bowed, in fear. The Afghan crew would not reveal who they were. At dawn we took off for Kabul.

Afghanistan was cloaked in snow, its mountain ravines clotted white and black with rock. From 10,000 feet, I could see tiny Soviet helicopters turning the corners of the great gorges south of Kabul, fireflies dragging a brown trail in their wake. The airport was now a military base, the streets of the capital a parking lot for

Soviet armour; and these were not just Russian conscripts. The new ASU 85 infantry fighting vehicle belonged only to the Soviet Union's top divisions. Many of the soldiers held the newest version of the Kalashnikov rifle, the AKS 74. North of the city, the 105th Airborne Division had quite literally dug a maze of trenches—miles in length—across the plateau beneath the mountains. From a distance, they looked like soldiers standing along the front lines of the Western Front in those old sepia photographs which my father had taken sixty-two years earlier. Their commanders must have been hoping that this was the only obvious parallel between the two military campaigns.

When the Russians stopped my taxi, they stared at my passport, frowning. What was an Englishman doing in Kabul? At the Intercontinental Hotel, on a low hill above the city, there was no such puzzlement. The Afghan reception staff were all smiles, discreetly moving their eyes towards the plain-clothes Afghan cops lounging on the foyer sofas so that guests would know when to lower their voices. The intensity with which men from the Khad—the *Khedamat-e Etelaat-e Dawlati* or "State Information Services"—would watch us was fortunately only matched by their inability to speak much English. There was a snug little bar filled with bottles of Polish vodka and Czech beer and a large window against which the snow had sprawled thickly. The bedrooms were warm and the balconies a spy's delight; from mine, Room 127, I could look out across all of Kabul, at the ancient Bala Hissar fort—one of the fictional Tom Graham's last battles was fought there—and the airport. I could count the Soviet jets taking off into the afternoon sun and the explosions echoing down from the Hindu Kush and then the aircraft again as they glided back down to the runways.

In wars, I only travel with those I trust. Reporters who panic don't get second chances. Conor O'Clery of the *Irish Times* had talked his way up from the Khyber Pass through Jalalabad. He was already in the old telecommunications office down town, watching with an evil glint in his eye as the operator soldered the letter "w" back onto its iron stem inside the telex machine. Gavin Hewitt, a twenty-nine-year-old BBC television reporter, arrived with Steve Morris and Mike Viney, the smartest crew I've ever worked with, and a battered camera—these were the days of real film with its wonderful colour definition, now lost to the technology of videotape—and Geoff Hale. They were also the days of real crews when a soundman—in this case Morris—and a film editor, Hale, accompanied a reporter into the field. Hewitt had shrewdly found a beat-up old yellow Peugeot taxi, its front and back windows draped in plastic flowers and other artificial foliage behind which we thought we could hide when driving past Soviet or Afghan military checkpoints. For $100 a day, its driver, a certain Mr. Samadali, was ready to break all the rules and drive us out of Kabul.

So on the bright, white morning of 9 January 1980 we set out in our ramshackle Peugeot to watch the invasion of Afghanistan. We headed east towards the Kabul Gorge, deep into the crevasse at the foot of the Spinghar Mountains. The Soviet army was making its way down to Jalalabad and we threaded our way between their great T-72s and their armoured vehicles, each machine blasting hot, black smoke onto the snow from its exhausts. And beside the highway, the Afghan men watched, their faces tight against the cold, their eyes taking in every detail of every vehicle. They looked on without emotion as the wind tugged at their orange and green shawls and gowns. The snow spread across the road and drifted at their feet. It was two degrees below zero but they had come out to watch the Soviet army convoy hum past on the great road east to the Khyber Pass.

The Russian crews, their fur hats pulled down low over their foreheads, glanced down at the Afghans and smiled occasionally as their carriers splashed through the slush and ice on the mud-packed road. A kilometre further on, Soviet military police in canvas-topped jeeps waved them into a larger convoy in which more tanks and tracked armour on transporter lorries raced along the Jalalabad highway. They were in a hurry. The generals in Kabul wanted these men at the border with Pakistan—along the Durand Line—as fast as they could travel. Secure the country. Tell Moscow that the Soviet army was now in control. We drove alongside them for 16 kilometres, our car jammed between tanks and transporters and jeeps, the young Russian soldiers watching us from beneath their furs and steel helmets as the snow blew across us. Every kilometre, troops of the Afghan army stood on guard beside the dual carriageway and 8 kilometres out of Kabul the convoy passed through a Russian checkpoint, two Soviet soldiers standing to attention on each side of the road in long splayed coats of dark green.

The further we went, the safer we felt. We knew we were heading into danger; we were well aware that the Russians had already been attacked around Jalalabad. But once we had cleared the first suspicious police checkpoint in the suburbs of Kabul—we were, Hewitt fraudulently claimed with schoolboy innocence, merely touring the city—the next military post waved us nonchalantly through amid the convoys. If we had been allowed to leave Kabul, then we must have been given permission to be on this highway. That, at least, was what the Soviet and Afghan soldiers beside the road obviously thought. Who, after all, would countermand such permission? Thank God, we said, for police states. Our greatest concern was the speed we were forced to travel. The Russians moved fast, even their tank transporters overtaking each other at 80 kilometres per hour in the semi-blizzard, sometimes forcing civilian traffic to use the other carriageway, at one point almost crushing our diminutive taxi between a lorry and a tank.

All morning there had been rumours of a new battle at Jalalabad between the Russians and Afghan tribesmen. They were pushing armour out towards the city of Herat, close to the Iranian border, and back up towards Salang where a convoy had just been attacked. What the Soviets were representing as a move against "counter-revolutionary elements" in Afghanistan was clearly taking longer to complete than expected. The American contention that 85,000 Soviet troops had now entered the country from Tashkent and Moscow appeared to be correct. There could have been a hundred thousand.

Packed into Mr. Samadali's cramped Peugeot, we were recording history. Steve and Geoff sat in the back with Mike sandwiched between them, hugging the camera between his knees as Gavin and I watched the Soviet troops on their trucks. The moment we knew that no one was looking at us, I'd shout "Go!" and Gavin—he was, after all, the boss of our little operation—cried "Picture!" At this point, he and I would reach out and tear apart the curtain of plastic flowers and greenery, Mike would bring up the camera—the lens literally brushing the sides of our necks in the front—and start shooting through the windscreen. Every frame counted. This was the biggest Soviet military operation since the Second World War and Mike's film would not only be shown across the world but stored in the archives for ever. The grey snow, the green of the Soviet armour, the dark silhouettes of the Afghans lining the highway, these were the colours and images that would portray the start of this invasion. A glance from a Russian soldier, too long a stare from a military policeman, and Gavin and I would cry "Down!," Mike would bury his camera between his legs and we would let the artificial foliage flop back across the inside of the windscreen. "Don't let's be greedy," Gavin kept telling his crew. We all agreed. If we kept our cool, if we didn't become overconfident—if we were prepared to lose a beautiful shot in order to film again another day—then we'd get the story.

Above the little village of Sarobi, we stopped the car. Afghanistan's landscape is breathtaking in the most literal sense of the word. Up here, the sun had burned the snow off the astonishingly light green mountain grass and we could see for up to 50 kilometres east to the Khyber Pass, to the suburbs of Jalalabad, bathed in mists. For the descent to the Valley of the Indus was like walking from a snow-storm into a sauna. Hold your hand out of the window and you could actually feel the air grow warmer. Gavin was literally bouncing on his toes as he stood by the road, looking across the panorama of ridges and mountain chains. Far to the north we could even make out the purple-white snows on the top of the Pamirs. We were that close to China. And we felt, we young men, on the top of the world.

The tragedy of this epic had not yet gripped us. How could I have known that seventeen years later I would be standing on this very same stretch of road as Osama bin Laden's gunmen prayed beneath that fiery comet? How could I know, as I stood with Gavin on that hillside, that bin Laden himself, only twenty-two years old, was at that moment only a few miles from us, in the very same mountain chain, urging his young Arab fighters to join their Muslim brothers at war with the Russians?

We were halfway down the narrow, precipitous road through the Kabul Gorge when a car came towards us, flashing its headlights and skidding to a halt. The driver, unshaven and turbaned, knew only that there was "trouble" further on down the pass. He raised his hands in a gesture of ignorance and fear and then, having vouchsafed this vague intelligence, he drove off behind us at speed. In the mountains of Afghanistan, you do not take such warnings lightly. We all knew what happened to General Elphinstone's British army in this very gorge in 1842. So when we drove gingerly on down the road, we watched the rocks above us where the snowline ended and the crags gave cover for an ambush. We carried on like this for 15 kilometres without meeting another car until we reached Sarobi, where a group of decrepit old buses and a taxi stood parked beside a barber's shop. There was an

Afghan policeman standing in the road who referred in equally indistinct terms to an "ambush" ahead. The road had been blocked, he said. So beside the highway, with the mountains towering above us and the Kabul River carrying the melted snows in a thrashing torrent down the ravine below, we drank hot sweet tea until two Russian tanks came round the corner followed by two lorryloads of Afghan soldiers.

The tanks swept past to the south, their tracks cutting into the tarmac, the radio operators staring straight ahead. The soldiers, each holding a Kalashnikov rifle, gave two cheers as they passed through Sarobi but received no reply. We followed them further down the pass, out of the snowline and into the hot plains where the sub-zero temperatures and ice of the mountains were replaced by dust and orange groves beside the road. A lorryload of soldiers suddenly pulled across the highway and we heard gunfire up in the cliffs. We watched the soldiers scrambling up the rocks until we lost sight of them amid the boulders, figures from an old portrait of imperial hostilities in the Khyber. But we drove on behind the Russian tanks into the plain, and round a bend we came to a checkpoint and the site of the ambush.

For 400 metres, the trees that lined the road had been cut down. There were troops there now and two Russian armoured personnel carriers had already come up from Jalalabad and cleared most of the road. Tribesmen had fired out of the trees when the first civilian cars had stopped at the roadblock before dawn. They killed two people and wounded nine others, one in the back and chest. There was still a litter of glass across the highway but no one knew whether the tribesmen were bandits or whether they had mistaken the cars for Russian military vehicles in the dark. There was an old man by the road who thought he knew the answer. The men who carried out the ambush, he told us, were "mujahedin," "holy warriors." Gavin looked at me. We hadn't heard that word in Afghanistan before.

It was a reminder that the Soviet-backed authorities in Afghanistan could not even secure the main highway to Pakistan, although we noticed that the Afghan army was still allowed to play an important role in operations. The soldiers who checked our papers through the pass and manned the small concrete forts beside the gorge were all Afghans. Some of the tanks parked in the mountains outside Jalalabad were Afghan too, and only the Afghan army patrolled the city in daylight. Not a Russian was to be seen along the tree-lined, shady streets of this pretty town where horse-drawn carriages rattled with colonial grace over dirt roads, where shoeless peasant boys beat donkeys loaded with grain down to the little market. But the scene was deceptive and Jalalabad provided an important indicator to what was happening in other, remoter, towns in Afghanistan.

For despite the delightful serenity of the place, Pathan tribesmen in their thousands were shooting nightly at Afghan troops in the countryside outside Jalalabad. In the past six days, explosions had rumbled over the town at night and two large bombs had twice destroyed the electric grid and transformers carrying power into Jalalabad, whose population had had no electricity for five days. The curfew had been extended from 8 p.m. to 4 a.m. And during those hours of night, the Soviet army had been moving heavy armour through the town. There were now 1,400

Russian troops with T-54 tanks and tracked vehicles quartered in the old Afghan army barracks 5 kilometres east of Jalalabad on the road to Pakistan. If the Afghan army could not keep the peace, it seemed that the Russians were preparing to step in and pacify the countryside.

We drove back to Kabul before dusk and tried to visit the Russian-built military hospital. Through the iron fences, we could see soldiers with their arms in slings, walking with the aid of sticks or crutches. More ominously, a turboprop Aeroflot aircraft was parked at a remote corner of the Kabul airport and when we drove close to it, we could make out a Russian military ambulance next to a loading ramp at the front of the fuselage. In the years to come, the Russians would give a nickname to the aircraft that flew their dead home from Afghanistan: the "Black Tulip." Within eight years, the Russians would lose 14,263 combatants dead and missing, and bring home 49,985 wounded.

In the years to come, Gavin and I would remember our journeys out of Kabul in 1980 as a great adventure. We were a hunting party, off for an exciting day in the quest for images. We adopted the elderly Russian-built grain silo outside Kabul as a symbol of the Soviet Union's gift to the world—it represented, we thought, about a millionth of the Soviet Union's "gifts." "There was an innocence about our world," Gavin would recall more than twenty years later. "The grain silo was somehow typical. The more crumbling its presence, the more true our images were to their art form." Travelling with his crew, I became almost as possessive of their filmed report—as anxious to see them get a scoop a day for the BBC—as Gavin himself. For his part, Gavin wanted to ensure that I sent my reports for *The Times* safely out of Kabul each day. Our enthusiasm to help each other was not just journalistic camaraderie. Gavin was one of the only television reporters to reach Afghanistan and his dramatic film dispatches were shaping the world's perception of the Soviet invasion. William Rees-Mogg, the editor of *The Times*, and the deputy news editor, Ivan Barnes, watched all Gavin's reports, though they often took forty-eight hours to reach the screen. There were no satellite "feeds" in Kabul and we were forbidden to bring satellite dishes into the country. So Geoff Hale was hand-carrying cans of film out to London, commuting back and forth from Kabul every two days, a 13,500-kilometre round-trip at least three times a week. Gavin found that his own editors were reading my reports every day in *The Times* and eagerly waited for the pictures which they knew he would have—since Gavin had told them we travelled together. And his filmed reports were feeding my own editor's hunger for news from Afghanistan. We were two parasites, we used to claim, living off each other's work.

My own copy was reaching *The Times* in less expensive but almost equally exhausting form. The Intercontinental staff were instructed by the Afghan state security police not to allow journalists to send their reports over the hotel telex. I was thus reduced to sending messages to Ivan Barnes and to the deputy editor, Louis Heren, indicating how I planned to get my dispatch to London. Our New York and Washington bureaus were trying to call me by phone; so was Binyon in Moscow. But in all the weeks I spent in Kabul, I never received a single telephone call from anyone. Instead, I would wake up at four each morning and type up five copies of my story for *The Times*. I would give one copy to the Reuters news agency, which sent an Indian staffer to Delhi almost every day. I gave another copy to Reuters' Pakistani staffer who regularly flew to Peshawar and Islamabad. From there, they were asked to punch out my text and—since the paper subscribed to the news agency—send it to London. Another copy went to anyone travelling to the Soviet Union in the hope they would contact Binyon in Moscow. A fourth carbon went to Geoff for his regular flights to Britain.

The fifth was for a much more devious operation, one which—and still today I marvel that it worked—involved the Pakistani conductor of the daily old wooden bus that bumped down from Kabul to Jalalabad and on to Peshawar in Pakistan, where local hotel staff were standing ready to telex my pages to London. I set the scheme up on my third morning in Kabul. I had noticed the Peshawar bus on the highway south of the capital and learned that it left Kabul each morning at 6:30. I liked Ali, the conductor, an immensely cheerful Pathan with a green scarf and a round Afghan hat and a smile of massive pure white teeth who spoke enough English to understand both my humour and my cynicism. "Mr. Robert, if this hurts the Russians, I will carry your report to the very door of the Intercontinental Hotel in Peshawar. You give me money to pay their operators and when you leave Afghanistan, you will go to Peshawar with me and pay the telex bills. Trust me."

All my life in the Middle East, people have ordered me to trust them. And almost always I did and they were worthy of that trust. Ali received $50 a day, every day, to take my typed dispatch to Peshawar. The operators received $40 a day to telex it to London. Even in the worst blizzards down the Kabul Gorge, Ali's ancient bus made it through the snowdrifts and the Russian checkpoints. Sometimes I travelled with him as far as Jalalabad. The Afghan army had been told to stop journalists roaming the country in cars but they never thought to check the bus. So I would sit on the steps with Ali as we puttered and rocked down the Kabul Gorge, feeling the warmth of the countryside as we descended into the Indus Valley. I would stay at the Spinghar Hotel in Jalalabad, spend the morning driving into the rural villages in a motorised rickshaw—a cloth-covered cabin mounted on the back of a motorcycle—to investigate the results of the overnight fighting between the Russians and the mujahedin and then pick up Ali's return bus to Kabul in the afternoon. Ali never lost a single report. Only when I received a telegram from *The Times* did I realise how well he did his job. "MANY THANKS . . . FILES STOP TUESDAY'S LEAD PAPER<WEDNESDAYS CONVOYS FRONT PAGE STOP." When journalists have to smuggle their dispatches out of a country, they traditionally call the carrier a "pigeon." Ali was the best pigeon *The Times* ever had, his old bus its finest transport. And when one night, in the bar of the Kabul Intercontinental, a reporter from the *Daily Mail* admitted he had received a telegram from his editors in London with the angry demand "Does Fisk have cleft stick?" I added $100 to Ali's next payment.

Slowly, Gavin and I enlarged our area of operations. One hundred and fifty kilometres southwest of Kabul lay the more-than-one-thousand-year-old city of

Ghazni, clustering round the giant battlements of a Turkish fort destroyed by the British in the First Afghan War, a settlement on the road to Kandahar which was successively destroyed by Arab invaders in 869 and again by Genghis Khan in 1221. The Soviet army, we were told, had not yet reached Ghazni, so we took the highway south past the big Soviet guns that ringed Kabul and a European face beneath a Cossack-style hat waved us, unsmiling, through the last Russian check-point. Gavin and I were working our plastic foliage routine, pulling aside the ghastly purple-and-blue artificial flowers whenever a Soviet tank obligingly crossed our path so that Mike could run another two or three feet of film. At the tiny, windy village of Saydabad, 70 kilometres down the road, more Russian tanks were dug in beside the highway, their barrels pointing west, dwarfing the poor mud and wattle huts in which the villagers lived. There was a bridge guarded by four soldiers with bayonets fixed and then there was just an empty, unprotected road of ice and drifting snow that stretched down towards the provinces of Paktia and Ghazni.

The old city, when Gavin and his crew and I turned up in Mr. Samadali's Peugeot, looked like a scene from a medieval painting, walled ramparts set against the snow-smothered peaks of the Safid Kuh Mountains and pale blue skies that distorted all perspective. Indeed, there were no Russians, just a series of Afghan army lorries that trundled every half-hour or so down from the north to the Ghazni barracks, their red Afghan insignia a doubtful protection against attack by rebel tribesmen, their scruffily dressed drivers peering nervously from the cab. The Afghan army, notionally loyal to its new president and his Soviet allies, theoretically controlled the countryside, although it was clear the moment we entered Ghazni that some form of unofficial ceasefire existed between the local soldiers and the Pathan tribesmen. Afghan troops in sheepskin cloaks and vests—Ghazni is famous for the manufacture of such embroidered Pustin coats—were wandering the narrow, mud streets, looking for provisions beneath their turreted, crumbling barracks.

Almost a thousand years ago, Mahmud of Ghazni imposed his rule over most of Afghanistan, devastated north-west India and established an Islamic empire that consolidated Sunni Muslim power over thousands of square miles. Ghazni became one of the great cities of the Persian world whose 400 resident poets included the great Ferdowsi. But the city was now a mockery of its glorious past. Some of the battlements had long ago collapsed and ice had cracked the ancient walls in the sub-zero temperatures. Isolated from the outside world, its inhabitants were suspicious of strangers, a dangerous and understandable obsession that had reached a new intensity now that reports of the Soviet invasion had reached the city.

We had scarcely parked our car when a tall man with a long grey moustache approached us. "Are you Russian?" he asked, and a group of Pathans in blue and white headdress began to gather around the car. We told them we were English and for a minute or so there were a few friendly smiles. Gavin and I were to develop our own special smile for these people, a big, warm smile of delight to hide our dark concern. How good to see you. What a wonderful country. My God, how you must hate those Russians. All of us knew how quickly things could go wrong. It was only a few months since a group of Soviet civilian construction workers and their wives had decided to visit the blue-tiled Masjid Jami mosque in Herat—a place of worship since the time of Zoroaster—only to be seized by a crowd and knifed to death. Several of the Russians were skinned alive. Only the previous day, though I did not know it then, *The Times* had published a photograph of two blind-folded men in the hands of Afghan rebels. They were high-school teachers detained in the city of Farah, 300 kilometres west of Kandahar, and the man on the right of the picture had already been executed as a communist.

Mr. Samadali needed oil for his Peugeot, and from a cluttered, dirty, concrete-floored shop an old man produced a can of motor oil. Horses and carts and donkeys staggering under sacks of grain slithered through the slush and mud and then someone muttered "*Khar*" and the smiles all faded. *Khar* means "donkey" and though apparently humorous on first hearing, it is a term of disgust and hatred when used about foreigners. "They are calling you '*khar*,' " Mr. Samadali said desperately. "They cannot tell the difference between Englishmen and Russians. They do not want foreigners here. You must go." A larger group of Pathans had now arrived and stood in a line along a raised wooden pavement beside the street. There were no guns in their hands, although two had long knives in their belts. A middle-aged man came up to us. "Leave here now," he said urgently. "Don't stop for any-one. If you are stopped by people on the road, drive through them. You are foreigners and they will think you are Russians and kill you. They will find out who you are afterwards." We left Ghazni at speed. Were we really in danger? More than twenty-one years later, I would confront an almost identical group of angry Afghans and, almost at the cost of my life, I would discover just what it meant to incur their fury.

Frightening off strangers was one thing. Fighting a well-equipped modern army would be quite another. On the road north again, we noticed, high on the hill-sides and deep in the snow, a series of metal turrets with gun barrels poking from them. The Russians had already taken physical control of the highway even though they did not stand beside the road. Soviet tanks had been parachuted into the mountains north of Kabul and the artillery outside Ghazni had also been dropped from the air. Our plastic foliage twitched aside as we cleared the windscreen for Mike. We were becoming experts. Indeed, it was Gavin's contention that the Russians would inevitably learn about our stage-prop jungle and assume that all modern movies were produced like this, that a new generation of Soviet film-makers would insist on shooting all future productions through car windows stuffed with artificial purple flowers.

And there was plenty more to film in Afghanistan. Even before we arrived, the Karmal government had attempted to slink back into popular support by freeing Amin's political prisoners. But when the city prison in Kabul was opened, thousands of men and women arrived to greet their loved ones and began throwing stones at the young Soviet troopers around the walls. No one doubted that the previous regime was detested by the population; the newly installed Karmal officials lost no time in letting us know of their hatred. This, after all, was why we had been given visas to come to Afghanistan. In Peshawar, rebel groups had claimed that the Afghan army would fight the Russian invaders, but the 7th and 8th Afghan Divisions in Kabul, both of which were equipped with Soviet tanks, never fired a shot against Russian armour. Their Soviet advisers had seen to that.

On 11 January, however, the government's propaganda went disastrously wrong. Thousands of Afghans—relatives of inmates, many of them in long cloaks and turbans—gathered this time outside the Po-le-Charkhi prison, a grim fortress of high stone walls, barbed wire, jail blocks and torture cells, to witness the official release of 118 political prisoners. But enraged that so few had been freed, the crowd burst through an Afghan army cordon and broke open the iron gates. We ran into the prison with them, a Russian soldier next to me almost thrown off his feet. He stared, transfixed by the sight as men and women—the latter in the all-covering burqa—began shouting "*Allahu akbar*," "God is Great,"* through the outer compound and began to climb over the steel gates of the main prison blocks. Gavin and I looked at each other in wonderment. This was a religious as much as it was a political protest. On the roof of a barracks, a young Soviet officer with a Kalashnikov rifle began shouting in Russian that there were only eight people left inside the prison. Conor O'Clery of the *Irish Times* was in the yard in his big Russian greatcoat. He was based in Moscow and spoke good Russian and he turned to me with his usual irredeemable smirk. "That guy may claim there are only eight men left," he said. "I suspect we're going to find out he's lying."

For a moment, the crowd paused as the officer swung his rifle barrel in their direction, then heeded him no more and surged on through the second newly broken gate. Hopelessly outnumbered, the soldier lowered his weapon. Hundreds of other prisoners' relatives now smashed the windows of the cell blocks with rocks and used steel pipes to break in the doors of the first building. Three prisoners were suddenly led into the winter sunlight by their liberators, middle-aged men in rags, thin and frail and dazed and blinking at the snow and ice-covered walls. A young man came up to me in the prison as crowds began to break in the roof of a second concrete cell block. "We want Russians to go," he said in English. "We want independent Afghanistan, we want families released. My brother and father are here somewhere."

I squeezed into the cell block with the mob, and there were certainly more than the eight prisoners to which the Russian officer referred. Blankets had been laid on the stone floor by the inmates as their only protection against the extreme cold. There was a musty, stale smell in the tiny, airless cells. Across the compound, other prisoners waved through the bars of windows, screaming at the crowd to release them. One man in baggy peasant trousers bashed open a hatch in the metal

---

*Literally, "God is Greatest" or "God is the Greatest." Because in English the expression "is greatest" tends to be used about football teams rather than a divinity, I have used the less accurate but more traditional "God is Great" which more powerfully reflects the faith to Western ears.

roof of a cell and slid inside, shouting to his friends to follow him. I climbed through a window in the end of the same cell block and was confronted by at least twenty men, sitting on the floor amid chains and straw, eyes wide with horror and relief. One held out his hand to me. It was so thin I felt only his bones. His cheeks were sunken and blue, his teeth missing, his open chest covered in scars. And all this while, the Russian soldiers and the Afghan guards stood watching, unable to control the thousands of men and women, aware that any public bloodletting would cause irreparable damage to the Karmal regime. Some of the crowd abused the Russians, and one youth who said he was from Paktia Province screamed at me that "Russians are bombing and killing in south Afghanistan."

But the most notable phenomenon about this amazing prison break-in were the Islamic chants from the crowds. Several men shouted for an Islamic revolution, something the Russians had long feared in Afghanistan and in their own Muslim republics. Many of the youths looking for their relatives came from rural areas to the south of Kabul, where tribal rebellion had been growing for at least fourteen months. Altogether, the government had released more than 2,000 political prisoners in the previous two weeks—it was Babrak Karmal's first act as president—but the decision had the unintended effect of reminding the crowds of how many thousands of political prisoners were not being released, inmates who had long ago been executed under Amin.

Only in the early afternoon did Soviet soldiers form a line inside the main gate of Po-le-Charkhi with rifles lowered, apparently to prevent the hundreds of men and women from leaving. Conor pulled his greatcoat round him, hands in pockets, the very model of a modern KGB major-general, and walked straight up to the nearest officer in the line of troops. "*Dosvidanya*," he said in Russian. The officer and another soldier snapped smartly to attention and we walked out of the jail.*

That same day, Babrak Karmal held his first press conference, a dismal affair in which the new Soviet-installed president—the son of a high-ranking Pushtun army officer, a heavily built man with a prominent nose, high cheekbones and greying hair with the manners of a nightclub bouncer—denounced his socialist predecessor as a criminal and insisted that his country was no client kingdom of the Soviet Union. This was a little hard to take when the main door of the Chelsotoon Palace—in which this miserable performance was taking place—was guarded by a Soviet soldier with a red star on his hat, when a Russian tracked armoured vehicle stood in the grounds and when a Soviet anti-aircraft gun crew waited in the snow beside their weapons a hundred metres from the building. So when Babrak Karmal told us that "the only thing brighter than sunshine is the honest friendship of the Soviet Union," one could only regard it as a uniquely optimistic, if not Olympian, view of a world that Dr. Faustus would have recognised.

Even the Afghan officials clustered beside Karmal, however, must have wished

*True to the maxim that no prison ever loses its original purpose, Po-le-Charkhi was the scene of post-Taliban Afghanistan's first judicial execution in April 2004. The death sentence of the "bandit" was signed by the country's pro-American Pushtun president, Hamid Karzai.

for the presence of some subtle Mephistopheles to soften the rhetoric as the president's press conference descended into an angry and occasionally abusive shouting match. The questions that the Western journalists put to Karmal were often more interesting than his replies, but highlights of the affair had to include the following statements by Moscow's new man: that not one Soviet soldier had been killed or wounded since the Russian military "intervention" began; that the size of the "very limited Soviet contingent" sent to Afghanistan had been grossly exaggerated by the "imperialist Western press"; that the Soviet Union had supported the "brutal regime" of the late Hafizullah Amin because "the Soviet Union would never interfere in the internal affairs of any country"; and, finally, that Soviet troops would leave Afghanistan "at the moment that the aggressive policy of the United States—in compliance with the Beijing leadership and the provocation of the reactionary circles of Pakistan, Egypt and Saudi Arabia—is eliminated."

The full flavour of the press conference, however, could only be captured by quoting extracts. Martyn Lewis of ITN, for example, wanted to know about Karmal's election to the presidency after his predecessor had been overthrown in a coup.

LEWIS: "I wonder, could you tell us when and under what circumstances you were elected and—if that election was truly democratic—why is it that Russian troops had to help you to power?"
KARMAL: "Mr. Representative of British imperialism, the imperialism that three times blatantly invaded Afghanistan, you got a rightful and deserved answer from the people of Afghanistan."

This exchange was followed by a burst of clapping from Afghan officials and Soviet correspondents. Only after this excursion into three Afghan wars of the nineteenth and early twentieth centuries did Karmal reply to Lewis, telling him that during the Amin regime "an overwhelming majority of the principal members of the People's Democratic Party [PDP] of Afghanistan" had elected him president.* We had, of course, expected no less of Karmal, and his courageous—some might say foolhardy—assertion that "a true non-alignment for Afghanistan can be obtained with the material and moral help of the Soviet Union" accurately reflected Moscow's point of view.

The new man was once a bitter opponent within the PDP of Nur Mohamed Taraki, the assassinated president whose "martyrdom" Karmal now blamed on the CIA, and Gavin Hewitt experienced first-hand what it was like to be on the receiving end of the new dictator's anger. For when Gavin commented mildly that "there doesn't seem to be much support for you or the Russians in Afghanistan," Karmal drew in his breath and bellowed the first response that came into his head. "Mr.

---

*Lewis later went on to anchor ITN's evening news in London but also indulged himself by writing books about dogs and cats, a pastime that was probably more rewarding than reporting Karmal's press conferences.

Correspondent of the BBC—the most famous propaganda liar in the world!" he roared. That was all. The room collapsed in applause from the satraps around Karmal and uncontrollable laughter from journalists. "Well," I told Gavin, "old Babrak can't be that bad a guy—at least he got you down to a 'T.' " Gavin shot me a sidelong grin. "Just wait, Fiskers," he muttered. And he was right. Within hours, Karmal's absurd reply had gone round the world, proving that Moscow's new man in Kabul was just another factotum with a single message.

But it was a clear sign that our presence in Afghanistan would not be tolerated indefinitely. This was made clear to me some days later when three members of the Khad secret police turned up at the reception desk at the Intercontinental to see me. They all wore leather coats—*de rigueur* for plain-clothes cops in Soviet satellite countries—and they were not smiling. One of them, a small man with a thin moustache and a whining voice, held out a piece of paper. "We have come to see you about this," he snapped. I took the paper from him, a telegram bearing the stamp of the Afghan PTT office. And as I read the contents, I swallowed several times, the kind of guilty swallow that criminals make in movies when confronted with evidence of some awesome crime. "URGENT. BOB FISK GUEST INTERCONTINENTAL HOTEL KABUL," it said. "ANY POSSIBILITY OF GETTING TWO MINUTE UPDATE RE SOVIET MILITARY BUILDUP IN AFGHANISTAN FOR SUNDAY MORNING THIS WEEK? LOVE SUE HICKEY." I drew in my breath. "Jesus Christ!" I shouted. How could Sue have sent such a telegram? For days, I had been sending tapes to CBC, describing the atmosphere of fear and danger in Afghanistan, and here was Sue sending me an open telegram requesting details of Soviet military deployment in a state run by pro-Moscow communists. It was, I suspected, part of a very old problem. Somewhere between reporters and their offices in faraway London or New York there exists a wall of gentle disbelief, an absolute fascination with the reporter's dispatch from the war zone but an unconscious conviction that it is all part of some vast Hollywood production, that the tape or the film—though obviously not fraudulent—is really a massive theatrical production, that the Russian army was performing for us, the world's press, that the Khad—always referred to in news reports as the "dreaded" secret police—was somehow not that dreadful after all, indeed might be present in Afghanistan to give just a little more excitement to our stories.

I looked at the little man from Khad. He was looking at me with a kind of excitement in his face. He was one of the few who could speak passable English. And he had caught his man. The Western spy had been found with incontrovertible proof of his espionage activities, a request for military information about the Soviet army. "What does this mean?" the little man asked softly. Oh yes, indeed. What *did* this mean? I needed time to think. So I burst into laughter. I put my head back and positively gusted laughter around the lobby of the hotel until even the receptionists turned to find out the cause of the joke. And I noticed one of the cops grinning. He wanted in on the joke, too. I slowly let my laughter subside and shook my head wearily. "Look, this lady wants me to report for a radio show called *Sunday Morning* in Canada," I said. "There *is* no 'Soviet military buildup'—we all know that because President Karmal told us that only a 'very limited Soviet contingent' has come to Afghanistan. This lady obviously doesn't know that. I have to clear up this ridiculous situation and report the truth. I'm sorry you've been bothered with such a silly message—and I can certainly understand why you were worried about it." And I laughed again. Even the little cop smiled sheepishly. I offered him back the incriminating telegram. "No—you keep it," he snapped. And he wagged his finger in my face. "We know, you know," he said. I'm sorry, I asked, what did he know? But the lads from the Khad had turned their backs and walked away. Thank you, Sue. Weeks later, we dined out on the story—and she paid for the meal.

Yet it was all too easy to turn the Soviet occupation into a one-dimensional drama, of brutal Russian invaders and plucky Afghan guerrillas, a kind of flip-side version of the fictional Tom Graham's Second Afghan War. A succession of pro-Soviet dictators had ruled Afghanistan with cruelty, with socialist cant and pious economic plans, but also through tribal alliances. The Pathans and the Hazaras—who were Shia Muslims—and the Tajiks and the Ghilzais and the Durranis and the Uzbeks could be manipulated by the government in Kabul. It could bestow power on a leader prepared to control his town on behalf of the communist authorities but could withhold funds and support from anyone who did not. Prison, torture and execution were not the only way to ensure political compliance. But among the tribes, deep within the deserts and valleys of Afghanistan, the same communist governments had been trying to cajole and then force upon these rural societies a modern educational system in which girls as well as boys would go to school, at which young women did not have to wear the veil, in which science and literature would be taught alongside Islam. Twenty-one years later, an American president would ostentatiously claim that these were among his own objectives in Afghanistan.

And I remember one excursion out of Jalalabad in those early days of the Soviet invasion. I had heard that a schoolhouse had been burned down in a village 25 kilometres from the city and set off in an exhaust-fuming Russian-built taxi to find out if this was true. It was, but there was much worse. Beside the gutted school there hung from a tree a piece of blackened meat, twisting gently in the breeze. One of the villagers, urging my driver to take me from the village, told us that this was all that was left of the headmaster. They had also hanged and burned his schoolteacher wife. The couple's sin: to comply with government rules that girls and boys should be taught in the same classroom. And what about those Pakistanis and Egyptians and Saudis who were, according to Karmal, supporting the "terrorists"? Even in Jalalabad, I heard that Arabs had been seen in the countryside outside the city, although—typical of our innocence at that time—I regarded these stories as untrue. How could Egyptians and Saudis have found their way here? And why Saudis? But when I heard my colleagues—especially American journalists—referring to the resistance as "freedom fighters," I felt something going astray. Guerrillas, maybe. Even fighters. But "freedom" fighters? What kind of "freedom" were they planning to bestow upon Afghanistan?

Of their bravery, there was no doubt. And within three weeks of the Soviet invasion came the first signs of a unified Muslim political opposition to the Karmal government and its Russian supporters. The few diplomats left in Kabul called them "night letters." Crudely printed on cheap paper, the declarations and manifestos were thrown into embassy compounds and pushed between consular fences during the hours of curfew, their message usually surmounted by a drawing of the Koran. The most recent of them—and it was now mid-January of 1980— purported to come from the "United Muslim Warriors of Afghanistan" and bore the badge of the Islamic Afghan Front, one of four groups which had been fighting in the south of the country.

From the opened pages of the Koran, there sprouted three rifles. The letter denounced the regime for "inhuman crimes" and condemned Soviet troops in the country for "treating Afghans like slaves." Muslims, it said, "will not give up fighting or guerrilla attacks until our last breath . . . the proud and aggressive troops of the Russian power have no idea of the rights and human dignity of the people of Afghanistan." The letter predicted the death of Karmal and three of his cabinet ministers, referring to the president as "Khargal," a play on words in Persian which means "thief of work." The first man to be condemned was Asadullah Sarwari, a member of the Afghan praesidium who was Taraki's secret police chief, widely credited with ordering the torture of thousands of Taraki's opponents. Others on the death list included Shah Jan Mozdooryar, a former interior minister who was now Karmal's transport minister.

The "night letter" also included specific allegations that the Soviet army was "committing acts which are intolerable to our people," adding that Russian soldiers had kidnapped women and girls working in a bakery in the Darlaman suburb of Kabul and returned them next morning after keeping them for the night. A similar incident, the letter stated, had occurred in the suburb of Khair Khana, "an act of aggression against the dignity of Muslim families." When I investigated these claims, bakery workers in Darlaman told me that women workers who normally bake bread for Afghan soldiers had refused to work for Soviet troops and that the Russians had consequently taken the women from the bakery and forced them to bake bread elsewhere. But they were unclear about the treatment the women had received and were too frightened to say more. The authors of the letter said that Muslims would eventually overthrow Karmal and judiciously added that they would then refuse to honour any foreign contracts made with his government.* Then they added, hopelessly and perhaps a little pathetically, that their statements should be broadcast over the BBC at 8:45 p.m. "without censorship."

---

*Karmal was flown back to Moscow by the Russians in 1986 to be replaced by Mohamed Najibullah, the head of the Khad secret police. He was subsequently deposed by mujahedin factions and took shelter in the UN's Kabul offices in 1992, three years after the Soviet withdrawal. In 1996, the Taliban took Najibullah from his dubious protectors—"some men have come for you," one of the UN officials bleakly announced to Moscow's former servant—and, after emasculating the former secret serviceman, hanged him from a tree along with his brother, Afghan currency bills stuffed into his mouth and pockets. This was, no doubt, the fate that the "night letter"s' authors had hoped for Karmal—who was to die of cancer in 1996 in Moscow.

Still Gavin and I ventured out most days with Steve, Geoff, Mike and the faithful Mr. Samadali. We were halfway up the Salang Pass, 130 kilometres north of Kabul, on 12 January when our car skidded on the ice and a young Russian paratrooper from the 105th Airborne Division ran down the road, waving his automatic rifle at us and shouting in Russian. He had been wounded in the right hand and blood was seeping from the bullet-hole through his makeshift bandage and staining the sleeve of his battledress. He was only a teenager, with fair hair and blue eyes and a face that showed fear. He had clearly never before been under fire. Beside us, a Soviet army transport lorry, its rear section blown to pieces by a mine, lay upended in a ditch. There were two tracked armoured carriers just up the road and a Russian paratroop captain ran towards us to join his colleague.

"Who are you?" he asked in English. He was dark-haired and tired, dressed in a crumpled tunic, a hammer-and-sickle buckle on his belt. We told him we were correspondents but the younger soldier was too absorbed with the pain from his wound. He re-applied the safety catch on his rifle, then lifted up his hand for our inspection. He raised it with difficulty and pointed to a snow-covered mountain above us where a Russian military helicopter was slowly circling the peak. "They shoot Russians," he said. He was incredulous. No one knew how many Russians the guerrillas had shot, although a villager a mile further south insisted with undisguised relish that his compatriots had killed hundreds.

But the ambush had been carefully planned. The mine had exploded at the same time as a charge had blown up beneath a bridge on the main highway. So for almost twenty-four hours, half of a Russian convoy en route to Kabul from the Soviet frontier was marooned in the snow at an altitude of more than 7,000 feet. Russian engineers had made temporary repairs and we watched as the Soviet trucks made their way down from the mountains, slithering on the slush and packed ice: 156 tracked armoured vehicles, eight-wheel personnel carriers and 300 lorryloads of petrol, ammunition, food and tents. The drivers looked exhausted. The irony, of course, was that the Russians had built this paved highway through the 11,900-foot pass. That night, the U.S. State Department claimed that 1,200 Russian soldiers had been killed. It seemed an exaggeration. But the bloody-minded villager may have been right about the hundreds dead. A "very limited contingent," indeed.

Karmal's government held a "day of mourning" for those killed by "the butcher Amin." The British embassy even lowered its flag to half-mast. But only a few hundred people turned up at the yellow-painted Polekheshti Mosque to pray for their souls, and they were for the most part well-dressed PDP functionaries. Four young men who arrived at the mosque in northern Kabul and attempted to avoid the signing ceremony were reminded of their party duties by a soldier with a bayonet fixed to his rifle. They signed the book. The rest of Kabul maintained the uneasy tenor of its new life. The bazaars were open as usual and the street sellers with their sweetmeats and oils continued to trade beside the ice-covered Kabul River. In the old city, a Western television crew was stoned by a crowd after being mistaken for Russians.

Kabul had an almost bored air of normality that winter as it sat in its icy basin in the mountains, its wood smoke drifting up into the pale blue sky. The first thing all of us noticed in the sky was an army of kites—large box kites, triangular and rectangular kites and small paper affairs, painted in blues and reds and often illustrated with a large and friendly human eye. No one seemed to know why the Afghans were so obsessed with kites, although there was a poetic quality to the way in which the children—doll-like creatures with narrow Chinese features, swaddled in coats and embroidered capes—watched their kites hanging in the frozen air, those great paper eyes with their long eyelashes floating towards the mountains.

Gavin and I once asked Mr. Samadali to take us to the zoo. Inside the gate, a rusting sign marked "vultures" led to some of the nastiest birds on earth, skeletal rather than scrawny. Past the hog-pit, a trek through deep snow brought us to the polar bear cages. But the cage doors were open and the bears were missing. Even more disquieting was the silent group of turbaned men who followed us around the zebra park, apparently under the illusion we were Russians. It must have been the only zoo in the world where the visitors were potentially more dangerous than the animals. We even managed to find Afghanistan's only railway locomotive, a big early-twentieth-century steam engine bought by King Amanullah from a German manufacturer. It sat forlorn and rusting near a ruined palace, its pistons congealed together and guarded by policmen who snatched at our cameras when we tried to take a picture of this old loco—a doubly absurd event since there is not a single active railway line in all of Afghanistan.

Perhaps by way of compensation, the truck-drivers of Afghanistan had turned their lorries into masterpieces of Afghan pop art, every square inch of bodywork covered in paintings and multicoloured designs. Afghan lorry art possessed a history all its own, which took off when metal sheeting was added to the woodwork of long-distance trucks; the panels were turned into canvases by artists in Kabul and later Kandahar. Lorry-owners paid large sums to these painters—the more intricate the decoration, the more honoured the owner became—and the art was copied from Christmas cards, calendars, comics and mosques. Tarzan and the horse of Imam Ali could be seen side by side with parrots, mountains, helicopters and flowers. Three-panelled rail-boards on Bedford trucks provided perfect triptychs. A French author once asked a lorry-owner why he painted his coachwork and received the reply that "it is a garden, for the road is long."

Inevitably, Karmal tried to appease the mujahedin, seeking a ceasefire in rural areas through a series of secret meetings between government mediators and tribal leaders in Peshawar. A PDP statement announced that it would "begin friendly negotiations with . . . national democratic progressives and Islamic circles [*sic*] and organisations." This new approach, intriguing though doomed, was accompanied by a desperate effort on the part of the government to persuade itself that it was acquiring international legitimacy. Kabul newspapers carried the scarcely surprising news that favourable reactions to the new regime had come from Syria, Kampuchea and India as well as the Soviet Union and its east European satellites.

In a long letter to Ayatollah Khomeini, whose Islamic revolution in Iran the previous year had so frightened the Soviets, Karmal criticised the adverse Iranian response to his coup—it had been condemned by Iranian religious leaders—and sought to assure the Ayatollah that the murder of Muslim tribesmen in Afghanistan had been brought to an end with Amin's overthrow. "My Government will never allow anybody to use our soil as a base against the Islamic revolution in Iran and against the interest of the fraternal Iranian people," he wrote. "We expect our Iranian brothers to take an identical stance."

Iran, needless to say, was in no mood to comply. Within days of the Soviet invasion, the foreign ministry in Tehran had stated that "Afghanistan is a Muslim country and . . . the military intervention of the government of the Soviet Union in the neighbouring country of our co-religionists is considered a hostile measure . . . against all the Muslims of the world." Within months—and aware that the United States was sending aid to the guerrillas—Iran would be planning its own military assistance programme for the insurgents. By July, Sadeq Qotbzadeh, the Iranian foreign minister, was telling me that he hoped his country would give weapons to the rebels if the Soviet Union did not withdraw its army. "Some proposal [to this effect] has been given to the Revolutionary Council," he told me in Tehran. ". . . Just as we were against the American military intervention in Vietnam, we think exactly the same way about the Soviet intervention in Afghanistan . . . The Soviet Union claims that they have come to Afghanistan at the request of the Afghan government. The Americans were in Vietnam at the request of the Vietnamese government." But at this stage, Karmal had more pressing problems than Iran.

Desperate to maintain the loyalty of the Afghan army—we heard reports that only 60 per cent of the force was now following orders—Karmal even made an appeal to their patriotism, promising increased attention to their "material needs." These "heroic officers, patriotic cadets and valiant soldiers" were urged to "defend the freedom, honour and security of your people . . . with high hopes for a bright future." "Material needs" clearly meant back pay. The fact that such an appeal had to be made at all said much about the low morale of the Afghan army. No sooner had he tried to appease his soldiers than Karmal turned to the Islamists who had for so long opposed the communist regimes in Kabul. He announced that he would change the Afghan flag to reintroduce green, the colour of Islam so rashly deleted from the national banner by Taraki, to the fury of the clergy. At the same time—and Karmal had an almost unique ability to destroy each new political initiative with an unpopular counter-measure—he warned that his government would treat "terrorists, gangsters, murderers and highwaymen" with "revolutionary decisiveness."

For "terrorists," read "guerrillas" or—as President Ronald Reagan would call them in the years to come—"freedom fighters." Terrorists, terrorists, terrorists. In the Middle East, in the entire Muslim world, this word would become a plague, a meaningless punctuation mark in all our lives, a full stop erected to finish all discussion of injustice, constructed as a wall by Russians, Americans, Israelis,

British, Pakistanis, Saudis, Turks, to shut us up. Who would ever say a word in favour of terrorists? What cause could justify terror? So our enemies are always "terrorists." In the seventeenth century, governments used "heretic" in much the same way, to end all dialogue, to prescribe obedience. Karmal's policy was simple: you are either with us or against us. For decades, I have listened to this dangerous equation, uttered by capitalist and communist, presidents and prime ministers, generals and intelligence officers and, of course, newspaper editors.

In Afghanistan there were no such formulaic retreats. In my cosy room at the Intercontinental, each night I would spread out a map. What new journey could be made across this iced plateau before the Russians threw us out? With this in mind, I realised that the full extent of the Russian invasion might be gauged from the Soviet border. If I could reach Mazar-e-Sharif, far to the north on the Amu Darya River, I would be close to the frontier of the Soviet Union and could watch their great convoys entering the country. I packed a soft Afghan hat and a brown, green-fringed shawl I'd bought in the bazaar, along with enough dollars to pay for several nights in a Mazar hotel, and set off before dawn to the cold but already crowded bus station in central Kabul.

The Afghans waiting for the bus to Mazar were friendly enough. When I said I was English, there were smiles and several young men shook my hand. Others watched me with the same suspicion as the three Khad men at the Intercontinental. There were women in burqas who sat in silence in the back of the wooden vehicle. I pulled my Afghan hat low over my forehead and threw my shawl over my shoulder. Cowled in cigarette smoke from the passengers, I took a seat on the right-hand side of the bus because the soldiers on checkpoint duty always approached from the left. The bus growled up the highway towards Salang as the first sun shone bleakly over the snow plains. Gavin and I had now driven this road so many times that, despite its dangers, the highway was familiar, almost friendly. On the right was the big Soviet base north of Kabul airport. Here was the Afghan checkpoint outside Charikar. This was where the young Russian soldier had shown us the wound in his hand. Soldiers at the Afghan checkpoints were too cold to come aboard and look at the passengers. When Soviet soldiers made a cursory inspection, I curled up in my seat with my shawl round my face. Three hours later, the bus pulled over to the side of the highway just short of the Salang Tunnel. There were Russian armoured vehicles parked a few metres away and a clutch of soldiers with blue eyes and brown hair poking from beneath their fur hats. That's when things went wrong.

A Soviet officer approached the bus from the right-hand side and his eyes met mine. Then a man inside the bus—an Afghan with another thin moustache—pointed at me. He marched down the aisle, stood next to my seat and raised his finger, pointing it straight at my face. Betrayed. That was the word that went through my mind. I had watched this scene in a dozen movies. So, no doubt, had the informer. This man must have been working for the Afghan secret police, saw me climb aboard in Kabul and waited until we reached this heavily guarded checkpoint to give me away. Another young Afghan jumped from the bus, walked down the right side of the vehicle and then he too pointed at me through the window. Doubly betrayed. We were a hundred miles from Kabul. If I had cleared this last major *barrage*, I would have been through the tunnel and on to Mazar.

The Russian officer beckoned me to leave the bus. I noticed a badge of Lenin on his lapel. Lenin appeared to be glowering, eyes fixed on some distant Bolshevik dream that I would be forbidden to enter. "Passport," the soldier said indifferently. It was like the ghastly telegram Sue Hickey had sent me, further proof of my dastardly role in Afghanistan. In the 1980s, the covers of British passports were black, and the gold coat of arms of the United Kingdom positively gleamed back at the Russian. He studied it closely. I half expected him to ask me for the meaning of *"Dieu et mon droit"* or, worse still, *"Honi soit qui mal y pense."* He flicked it open, looked at the face of the bespectacled, tousled-haired Englishman on the third page and then at the word "occupation." The word "journalist" does not obtain many visas in the Middle East, and so the British Passport Office had been obliging enough to write "representative" in the space provided. The Russian, who could read about as much Latin script as I could Cyrillic, tapped his finger on the word and asked in painfully good English: "What do you 'represent'?" A newspaper, I owned up. "Ah, correspondent." And he gave me a big knowing smile. I was led to a small communications hut in the snow from which emerged a half-naked paratroop captain wearing shades. Captain Viktor from Tashkent showed no animosity when he was told I was a journalist, and his men gathered round me, anxious to talk in faltering but by no means poor English. There was a grunting from the engine of my bus and I saw it leaving the checkpoint for the tunnel without me, my betrayer staring at me hatefully from a rear window.

Private Tebin from the Estonian city of Tallinn—if he survived Afghanistan, I assume he is now a proud citizen of the European Union, happily flourishing his new passport at British immigration desks—repeatedly described how dangerous the mountains had become now that rebels were shooting daily at Soviet troops. Captain Viktor wanted to know why I had chosen to be a journalist. But what emerged most strongly was that all these soldiers were fascinated by pop music. Lieutenant Nikolai from Tashkent interrupted at one point to ask: "Is it true that Paul McCartney has been arrested in Tokyo?" And he put his extended hands together as if he had been handcuffed. Why had McCartney been arrested? he wanted to know. I asked him where he had heard the Beatles' music and two other men chorused at once: "On the Voice of America radio."

I was smiling now. Not because the Russians were friendly—each had studied my passport and all were now calling me "Robert" as if I was a comrade-in-arms rather than the citizen of an enemy power—but because these Soviet soldiers with their overt interest in Western music did not represent the iron warriors of Stalingrad. They seemed like any Western soldiers: naive, cheerful in front of strangers, trusting me because I was—and here in the Afghan snows, of course, the fact was accentuated—a fellow European. They seemed genuinely apologetic that they could not allow me to continue my journey but they stopped a bus travelling in the opposite direction. "To Kabul!" Captain Viktor announced. I refused. The people on that bus had seen me talking to the Russians. They would assume I was a Russian. No amount of assurances that I was British would satisfy them. I doubted if I would ever reach Kabul, at least not alive.

So Lieutenant Nikolai flagged down a passing Russian military truck at the back of a convoy and put me aboard. He held out his hand. "*Dosvidanya*," he said. "Goodbye—and give my love to Linda McCartney." And so I found myself travelling down the Hindu Kush on Soviet army convoy number 58 from Tashkent to Kabul. This was incredible. No Western journalist had been able to talk to the Soviet troops invading Afghanistan, let alone ride on their convoys, and here I was, sitting next to an armed Russian soldier as he drove his truckload of food and ammunition to Kabul, allowed to watch this vast military deployment from a Soviet army vehicle. This was better than Mazar.

As we began our descent of the gorge, the Russian driver beside me pulled his kitbag from behind his seat, opened the straps and offered me an orange. "Please, you look up," he said. "Look at the top of the hills." With near disbelief, I realised what was happening. While he was wrestling the wheel of his lorry on the ice, I was being asked to watch the mountain tops for gunmen. The orange was my pay for helping him out. Slowly, we began to fall behind the convoy. The soldier now hauled his rifle from the back of the cab and laid it between us on the seat. "Now you watch right of road," he said. "Tell if you see people." I did as I was told, as much for my safety as his. Our truck had a blue-painted interior with the word *Kama* engraved over the dashboard. It was one of the lorries built at the American-funded Kama River factory in the Soviet Union, and I wondered what President Carter would have thought if he knew the uses to which his country's technology was now being put. The driver had plastered his cab with Christmas cards.

At the bottom of the pass we found his convoy, and an officer—tall, with intelligent, unnaturally pale green eyes, khaki trousers tucked into heavy army boots—came to the door on my side of the truck. "You are English," he said with a smile. "I am Major Yuri. Come to the front with me." And so we trekked through the deep slush to the front of the column where a Soviet tank was trying to manoeuvre up the pass in the opposite direction. "It's a T-62," he said, pointing to the sleeve halfway down the tank's gun barrel. I thought it prudent not to tell him that I had already recognised the classification.

And I had to admit that Major Yuri seemed a professional soldier, clearly admired by his men—they were all told to shake my hand—and, in the crisis in which we would shortly find ourselves, behaved calmly and efficiently. With fractious Afghan soldiers, whom he seemed privately to distrust, he was unfailingly courteous. When five Afghan soldiers turned up beside the convoy to complain that Russian troops had been waving rifles in their direction, Major Yuri spoke to them as an equal, taking off his gloves and shaking each by the hand until they beamed with pleasure. But he was also a party man.

What, he asked, did I think of Mrs. Thatcher? I explained that people in Britain held different views about our prime minister—I wisely forbore to give my own—but that they were permitted to hold these views freely. I said that President Carter was not the bad man he was depicted as in the Moscow press. Major Yuri listened in silence. So what did he think about President Brezhnev? I was grinning now. I knew what he had to say. So did he. He shook his head with a smile. "I believe," he said slowly, "that Comrade Brezhnev is a very good man." Major Yuri was well-read. He knew his Tolstoy and admired the music of Shostakovich, especially his Leningrad Symphony. But when I asked if he had read Aleksander Solzhenitsyn, he shook his head and tapped his revolver holster. "This," he said, "is for Solzhenitsyn."

I squeezed into Major Yuri's truck, his driver and I on the outside seats, Yuri in the middle; and so we set off for Kabul. "England a good country?" he asked. "Better than Afghanistan?" No, Major Yuri did not want to be in Afghanistan, he admitted. He wanted to be at home in Kazakhstan with his wife and nine-year-old daughter and planned to take a return convoy back to them in three days' time. He had spent thirteen of his thirty years in the army, had not enough money to buy a car and could never travel abroad because he was an officer. It was his way of telling me that life in the Soviet Union was hard, that his life was not easy, that perhaps Comrade Brezhnev was not that good a man. Had not Brezhnev sent him here in the first place? When I asked questions he could not answer, he smiled in silent acknowledgement that he would have liked to be able to do so.

Amid a massive army, there is always a false sense of comfort. Even Major Yuri, his pale eyes constantly scanning the snowfields on each side of us, seemed to possess a dangerous self-confidence. True, the Afghans were attacking the Russians. But who could stop this leviathan, these armoured centipedes that were now creeping across the snows and mountains of Afghanistan? When we stopped at an Afghan checkpoint and the soldiers there could speak no Russian, Major Yuri called back for one of his Soviet Tajik officers to translate. As he did so, the major pointed at the Tajik and said, "Muslim." Yes, I understood. There were Muslims in the Soviet Union. In fact there were rather a lot of Muslims in the Soviet Union. And that, surely, was partly what this whole invasion was about.

The snow was blurring the windscreen of our truck, almost too fast for the wipers to clear it away, but through the side windows we could see the snowfields stretching away for miles. It was now mid-afternoon and we were grinding along at no more than 25 kilometres an hour, keeping the speed of the slowest truck, a long vulnerable snake of food, bedding, heavy ammunition, mixed in with tanks and carriers, 147 lorries in all, locked onto the main highway, a narrow vein of ice-cloaked tarmac that set every Soviet soldier up as a target for the "terrorists" of Afghanistan. Or so it seemed to the men on convoy 58. And to me.

Yet we were surprised when the first shots cracked out around us. We were just north of Charikar. And the rounds passed between our truck and the lorry in front, filling the air pockets behind them with little explosions, whizzing off into the frosted orchards to our left. "Out!" Major Yuri shouted. He wanted his soldiers defending themselves in the snow, not trapped in their cabs. I fell into the muck and slush beside the road. The Russians around me were throwing themselves from their trucks. There was more shooting and, far in front of us, in a fog of snow and sleet, there were screams. A curl of blue smoke rose into the air from our right. The bullets kept sweeping over us and one pinged into a driver's cab. All around me, the Soviet soldiers were lying in the drifts. Major Yuri shouted something at the men closest to him and there was a series of sharp reports as their Kalashnikovs kicked into their shoulders. Could they see what they were shooting at?

A silence fell over the landscape. Some figures moved, far away to our left, next to a dead tree. Yuri was staring at the orchard. "They are shooting from there," he said in English. He gave me a penetrating glance. This was no longer to be soldiers' small-talk. I listened to the crackle of the radios, the shouts of officers interrupting each other, the soldiers in the snow looking over their shoulders. Major Yuri had taken off his fur hat; his brown hair was receding and he looked older than his thirty years. "Watch this, Robert," he said, pulling from his battledress a long tube containing a flare. We stood together in the snow, the slush above our knees, as he tugged at a cord that hung beneath the tube. There was a small explosion, a powerful smell of cordite and a smoke trail that soared high up into the sky. It was watched by the dozen soldiers closest to us, each of whom knew that our lives might depend on that rocket.

The smoke trail had passed a thousand feet in height when it burst into a shower of stars and within fifty seconds a Soviet MiG swept over us at low level, dipping its wings. A minute later, a tracked personnel carrier bearing the number 368 came thrashing through the snow with two of its crew leaning from their hatches and slid to a halt beside Major Yuri's truck. The radio crackled and he listened in silence for a few moments, then held up four fingers towards me. "They have killed four Russians in the convoy ahead," he said.

We stood on the road, backed up behind the first convoy. One row of soldiers was ordered to move 200 metres further into the fields. Major Yuri told his men they could open their rations. The Tajik soldier who had translated for the major offered me food and I followed him to his lorry. It was decorated with Islamic pictures, quotations from the Koran, curiously interspersed with photographs of Bolshoi ballet dancers. I sat beside the truck with two soldiers next to me. We had dried biscuits and large hunks of raw pork; the only way I could eat the pork was to hold on to the fur and rip at the salted fat with my teeth. Each soldier was given three oranges, and sardines in a tin that contained about 10 per cent sardines and 90 per cent oil. Every few minutes, Major Yuri would pace the roadway and talk over the radio telephone, and when eventually we did move away with our armoured escorts scattered through the column, he seemed unsure of our exact location on the highway. Could he, he asked, borrow my map? And it was suddenly clear to me that this long convoy did not carry with it a single map of Afghanistan.

There was little evidence of the ambushed convoy in front save for the feet of a dead man being hurriedly pushed into a Soviet army van near Charikar and a great swath of crimson and pink slush that spread for several yards down one side of the road. The highway grew more icy at sundown, but we drove faster. As we journeyed on into the night, the headlights of our 147 trucks running like diamonds over the snow behind us, I was gently handed a Kalashnikov rifle with a full clip of ammunition. A soldier snapped off the safety catch and told me to watch through the window. I had no desire to hold this gun, even less to shoot at Afghan guerrillas, but if we were attacked again—if the Afghans had come right up to the truck as they had done many times on these convoys—they would assume I was a Russian. They would not ask all members of the National Union of Journalists to stand aside before gunning down the soldiers.

I have never since held a weapon in wartime and I hope I never shall again. I have always cursed the journalists who wear military costumes and don helmets and play soldiers with a gun at their hip, greying over the line between reporter and combatant, making our lives ever more dangerous as armies and militias come to regard us as an extension of their enemies, a potential combatant, a military target. But I had not volunteered to travel with the Soviet army. I was not—as that repulsive expression would have it in later wars—"embedded." I was as much their prisoner as their guest. As the weeks went by, Afghans learned to climb aboard the Soviet convoy lorries after dark and knife their occupants. I knew that my taking a rifle—even though I never used it—would produce a reaction from the great and the good in journalism, and it seemed better to admit the reality than to delete this from the narrative.* If I was riding shotgun for the Soviet army, then that was the truth of it.

Three times we passed through towns where villagers and peasants lined the roadside to watch us pass. And of course, it was an eerie, unprecedented experience to sit with a rifle on my lap in a Soviet military column next to armed and uniformed Russian troops and to watch those Afghans—most of them in turbans, long shawls and rubber shoes—staring at us with contempt and disgust. One man in a blue coat stood on the tailboard of an Afghan lorry and watched me with narrowed eyes. It was the nearest I had seen to a look of hatred. He shouted something that was lost in the roar of our convoy.

Major Yuri seemed unperturbed. As we drove through Qarabagh, I told him I didn't think the Afghans liked the Russians. It was beginning to snow heavily again. The major did not take his eyes from the road. "The Afghans are cunning people," he said without obvious malice, and then fell silent. We were still sliding along the road to Kabul when I turned to Major Yuri again. So why was the Soviet army in Afghanistan? I asked him. The major thought about this for about a minute

---

*From his executive office in London's Fleet Street—approximately 5,700 kilometres from Kabul—the managing director of Reuters, Gerald Long, dutifully fired off a letter to *The Times*, condemning me for holding the Kalashnikov. "Much though everyone will understand the natural instinct for self-preservation," he wrote, "he [Fisk] should have refused to carry the gun. If we are to claim protection for journalists reporting conflict, journalists must refuse to carry arms in any circumstances. Those who are responsible for the safety of journalists will instruct them to avoid avoidable risks. The risk to all journalists of any journalist carrying a gun is in my view greater than the doubtful protection a gun can give him." Despite the letter's odd syntax, I could not have agreed more. But how were we journalists supposed to "avoid avoidable risks" in Afghanistan? I had been trying to travel to Mazar on a bus, not to Kabul on a Soviet convoy.

and gave me a smile. "If you read *Pravda*," he said, "you will find that Comrade Leonid Brezhnev has answered this question." Major Yuri was a party man to the end.*

In Kabul, the doors were closing. All American journalists were expelled from the country. An Afghan politburo statement denounced British and other European reporters for "mudslinging." The secret police had paid Mr. Samadali a visit. Gavin was waiting for me, grim-faced, in the lobby. "They told him they'd take his children from him if he took us outside Kabul again," he said. We found Mr. Samadali in the hotel taxi line-up next day, smiling apologetically and almost in tears. My visa was about to expire but I had a plan. If I travelled in Ali's bus all the way to Peshawar in Pakistan, I might be able to turn round and drive back across the Afghan border on the Khyber Pass before the Kabul government stopped issuing visas to British journalists. There was more chance that officials at a land frontier post would let me back into Afghanistan than the policemen at the airport in Kabul.

So I took the bus back down the Kabul Gorge, this time staying aboard as we passed through Jalalabad. It was an odd feeling to cross the Durand Line and to find myself in a Pakistan that felt free, almost democratic, after the tension and dangers of Afghanistan. I admired the great plumes on the headdress of the soldiers of the Khyber Rifles on the Pakistani side of the border, the first symbol of the old British raj, a regiment formed 101 years before, still ensconced at Fort Shagai with old English silver and a visitor's book that went back to the viceroys.

But of course, it was an illusion. President General Mohamed Zia ul-Haq ran an increasingly Islamic dictatorship in which maiming and whipping had become official state punishments. He ruled by martial law and had hanged his only rival, the former president Zulfikar Ali Bhutto, less than a year earlier, in April 1979. And of course, he responded to the Soviet invasion of Afghanistan with publicly expressed fears that the Russian army planned to drive on into Pakistan. The United States immediately sent millions of dollars of weapons to the Pakistani dictator, who suddenly became a vital American "asset" in the war against communism.

But in Ali's wooden bus, it seemed like freedom. And as we descended the splendour of the Khyber Pass, there around me were the relics of the old British regiments who had fought on this ground for more than a century and a half, often against the Pathan *ghazi* fighters with their primitive jezail rifles. "A weird,

---

*All my dispatch lacked was a photograph for *The Times*. Major Yuri had taken pictures of me for his personal scrapbook—or for the KGB—but I had none of him. So when I trudged out through the packed snow to the gate of the Soviet army base back in Kabul and caught sight of a Russian hat, complete with red hammer and sickle badge and strap-up fur ear muffs, on a lorry driver's empty seat, I snatched it from the truck and stuffed it under my brown Afghan shawl. For years, I would proudly produce this memento of Soviet military power at dinners and parties in Beirut. But within ten years the Soviet Union had collapsed and tourists, alas, could buy thousands of identical military hats—along with those of Soviet generals and admirals and batteries of medals won in Afghanistan—in Moscow's Arbat Street for only a few rubles.

uncanny place . . . a deadly valley," a British writer called it in 1897, and there on the great rocks that slid past Ali's bus were the regimental crests of the 40th Foot, the Leicestershire Yeomanry, the Dorsetshires, the Cheshires—Bill Fisk's regiment before he was sent to France in 1918—and the 54th Sikhs Frontier Force, each with its motto and dates of service. The paint was flaking off the ornamental crest of the 2nd Battalion, the 10th Baluch Regiment, and the South Lancs and the Prince of Wales' Volunteers had long ago lost their colours. Pathan tribesmen, Muslims to a man of course, had smashed part of the insignia of a Hindi regiment whose crest included a proud peacock. Graffiti covered the plaque of the 17th Leicestershire Foot Regiment (1878–9). The only refurbished memorial belonged to Queen Victoria's Own Corps of Guides, a mainly Pathan unit whose eccentric commander insisted that they be clothed in khaki rather than scarlet and one of whose Indian members probably inspired Rudyard Kipling's "Gunga Din." The lettering had been newly painted, the stone washed clean of graffiti.

Peshawar was a great heaving city of smog, exhaust, flaming jacaranda trees, vast lawns and barracks. In the dingy Intercontinental there, I found a clutch of telex operators, all enriched by *The Times* and now further rewarded for their loyalty in sending my reports to London. This was not just generosity on my part; if I could re-enter Afghanistan, they would be my future lifeline to the paper. So would Ali. We sat on the lawn of the hotel, taking tea raj-style with a large china pot and a plate of scones and a fleet of huge birds that swooped from the trees to snatch at our cakes. "The Russians are not going to leave, Mr. Robert," Ali assured me. "I fear this war will last a long time. That is why the Arabs are here." Arabs? Again, I hear about Arabs. No, Ali didn't know where they were in Peshawar but an office had been opened in the city. General Zia had ordered Pakistan's embassies across the Muslim world to issue visas to anyone who wished to fight the Soviet army in Afghanistan.

A clutch of telexes was waiting for me at reception. *The Times* had safely received every paragraph I had written.* I bought the London papers and drank them down as greedily as any gin and tonic. The doorman wore a massive imperial scarlet cummerbund, and on the wall by the telex room I found Kipling's public school lament for his dead countrymen—from "Arithmetic on the Frontier"—framed by the Pakistani hotel manager:

> *A scrimmage in a Border Station—*
> *A canter down some dark defile—*
> *Two thousand pounds of education*
> *Drops to a ten-rupee jezail—*

---

*And printed all but one. Ivan Barnes had felt that a paragraph in a feature article in which I recorded how Gavin and I had come across a tribesman outside Jalalabad standing on a box and sodomising a camel was too much for *Times* readers.

# CHAPTER THREE

# The Choirs of Kandahar

No one spoke of hatred of the Russians. The feeling experienced . . .
from the youngest to the oldest, was stronger than hatred. It was not hatred,
for they did not regard dogs as human beings, but it was such repulsion,
disgust and perplexity at the senseless cruelty of these creatures . . .

—Leo Tolstoy, *Haaji Murat*

THE GHOSTS OF BRITISH RULE seemed to haunt Peshawar. In the bookshops, I found a hundred reprints of gazetteers and English memoirs. Sir Robert Warburton's *Eighteen Years in the Khyber* stood next to Woosnam Mills's yarns; "Noble Conduct of our Sepoys," "Immolation of Twenty-one Sikhs" and "The Ride of the Guides: How British Officers Die." Further volumes recalled the exploits of Sir Bindon Blood, one of whose young subalterns, Winston Churchill, was himself ambushed by Pathans in the Malakand hills to the north of Peshawar.* Not only ghosts frequented Peshawar. Unlike the Russian occupiers of Afghanistan, the British could not take their dead home; and on the edge of Peshawar, there still lay an old British cemetery whose elaborate tombstones of florid, overconfident prose told the story of empire.

Take Major Robert Roy Adams of Her Majesty's Indian Staff Corps, formerly deputy commissioner of the Punjab. He lay now beside the Khyber Road, a canyon of traffic and protesting donkeys whose din vibrated against the cemetery wall. According to the inscription on his grave, Major Adams was called to Peshawar "as an officer of rare capacity for a frontier. Wise, just and courageous, in all things faithful, he came only to die at his post, struck down by the hand of an assassin." He was killed on 22 January 1865, but there are no clues as to why he was murdered. Nor are there any explanations on the other gravestones. In 1897, for example, John Sperrin Ross met a similar fate, "assassinated by a fanatic in Peshawar City on Jubilee Day." A few feet from Ross's grave lay Bandsman Charles Leighton of the First Battalion, The Hampshire Regiment, "assassinated by a *Ghazi* at this station on Good Friday." Perhaps politics was left behind at death,

---

*As usual, Churchill saved his own thoughts for his last sentence: "One man was shot through the breast and pouring with blood; another lay on his back kicking and twisting. The British officer was spinning round just behind me, his face a mass of blood, his right eye cut out. Yes, it was certainly an adventure."

although it was impossible to avoid the similarity between these outraged headstones and the language of the Soviet government. The great-grandsons of the
Afghan tribesmen who killed the British were now condemned by the Kremlin as
"fanatics"—or terrorists—by Radio Moscow. One empire, it seemed, spoke much
like another.

To be fair, the British did place their dead in some historical context. Beneath a
squad of rosewood trees with their bazaar of tropical birds lay Privates Hayes,
Macleod, Savage and Dawes, who "died at Peshawar during the frontier disturbances 1897–98." Not far away was Lieutenant Bishop, "killed in action at
Shubkudder in an engagement with the hill tribes, 1863." He was aged twenty-two.
Lieutenant John Lindley Godley of the 24th Rifle Brigade, temporarily attached to
the 266th Machine Gun Company, met the same end at Kacha Garhi in 1919.

There were other graves, of course, innocent mounds with tiny headstones that
contained the inevitable victims of every empire's domesticity. "Beatrice Ann, one
year and 11 months, only child of Bandmaster and Mrs. A. Pilkington" lay in the
children's cemetery with "Barbara, two years, daughter of Staff Sergeant and Mrs.
P. Walker." She died three days before Christmas in 1928. Some of the children
died too young to have names. There were young men, too, who succumbed to the
heat and to disease. Private Tidey of the First Sussex died from "heatstroke" and
Private Williams of "enteric fever." E. A. Samuels of the Bengal Civil Service succumbed to "fever contracted in Afghanistan." Matron Mary Hall of Queen Alexander's Imperial Military Nursing Service—whose duties in Salonika and
Mesopotamia presumably included the Gallipoli campaign in Turkey as well as
the British invasion of Iraq in 1917—died "on active service."

There were a few unexpected tombs. The Very Rev. Courtney Peverley was
there, administrator apostolic of Kashmir and Kafiristan, who clearly worked hard
because beyond the British headstones were new places of interment for
Peshawar's still extant Christian community, paper crosses and pink flags draped
in tribal fashion beside the freshly dug graves. Many imperial graves exhibit a faith
that would be understood by any Muslim, the favourite from the Book of Revelation: "Blessed are the dead that die in the Lord." And there was a Gaelic cross on
top of the remains of Lieutenant Walter Irvine of the North West Frontier Police
"who lost his life in the Nagoman River when leading the Peshawar Vale Hunt of
which he was Master." No Soviet soldier would earn so romantic a memorial. On
the graves of the Russian soldiers now dying just north of this cemetery, it would
be coldly recorded only that they died performing their "international duty."

The local CIA agent already had a shrewd idea what this meant. He was a thin,
over-talkative man who held a nominal post in the U.S. consulate down the road
from the Peshawar Intercontinental and who hosted parties of immense tedium at
his villa. He had the habit of showing, over and over again, a comedy film about
the Vietnam War. Those were the days when I still talked to spooks, and when I
called by one evening, he was entertaining a group of around a dozen journalists
and showing each of them a Soviet identity card. "Nice-looking young guy," he
said of the pinched face of the man in the black-and-white photograph. "A pilot,

shot down, the mujahedin got his papers. What a way to go, a great tragedy that a young guy should die like that." I didn't think much of the CIA man's crocodile tears but I was impressed by the words "shot down." With what? Did the guerrillas have ground-to-air missiles? And if so, who supplied them—the Americans, the Saudis, the Pakistanis, or those mysterious Arabs? I had seen thousands of Russians but I had yet to see an armed guerrilla close up in Afghanistan. I wouldn't have to wait long.

Ali's bus returned to the border one warm afternoon and I walked back across the Durand Line to a small grubby booth on the Afghan side of the frontier. The border guard looked at my passport and thumbed through the pages. Then he stopped and scrutinised one of the document's used pages. As usual, I had written "representative" on my immigration card. But the thin man clucked his tongue. "Journalist," he said. "Go back to Pakistan." How did he know? There were visas to Arab countries in the passport which identified me as a journalist, but the Afghan official would not know Arabic, would have no idea that *sahafa* meant "journalist." A group of men shoved past me and I walked back to Ali. How did they know? Ali looked through my passport and found the page that gave me away. A visa to post-revolutionary Iran was marked with the word *khabanagor*—Persian for "journalist"—and Dari, one of the languages of Afghanistan, was a dialect of Persian. Damn.

I took a taxi back to Peshawar and sent a message to *The Times*: "Scuppered." But next day Ali was back at the hotel. "Mr. Robert, we try again." What's the point? I asked him. "We try," he said. "Trust me." I didn't understand, but I repacked my bags and boarded his friendly wooden bus and set off once more for the border. This was beginning to feel like a real-life version of *Carry On Up the Khyber*, but Ali was strangely confident I would be successful. I sat back in the afternoon sun as the bus moaned its way up the hairpin bends. There's an odd, unnerving sensation about trying to cross a border without the consent of the authorities. Gavin and I had experienced this at almost every checkpoint we came across in Afghanistan. Would they let us through or turn us round or arrest us? I suppose it was a throwback to all those war films set in German-occupied Europe in which resistance heroes and heroines had to talk their way past Nazi guards. The Afghan border police were not quite up to Wehrmacht standards—and we were no heroes—but it wasn't difficult to feel a mixture of excitement and dread when we arrived once more at the grotty little booth on the Afghan side of the frontier.

Yet before I had a chance to stand up, Ali was at my seat. "Give me your passport," he said. "And give me $50." He vanished with the money. And ten minutes later, he was back with a broad smile. "I will take you to Jalalabad," he said, handing me back my newly stamped passport. "Give me another $50 because I had to give your money away to a poor man." The Russians had invaded but they couldn't beat that most efficacious, that most corrupt of all institutions between the Mediterranean and the Bay of Bengal: The Bribe. I was so happy, I was laughing. I was singing to myself, all the way to Jalalabad. I'd even arranged with Ali that he would stop by at the Spinghar Hotel each morning to take my reports down to

Peshawar—and come back in the afternoon with any messages that *The Times* sent to me via Pakistan. I could meanwhile snuggle down in the Spinghar and stay out of sight of the authorities.

I need not have worried. Every night, the rebels drew closer to Jalalabad. Four days earlier they had blown up a bridge outside the town and that very first night, after dark, they opened fire on an Afghan patrol from the plantation behind the hotel. Hour after hour, I lay in bed, listening to machine guns pummelling away in the orange orchards, sending the tropical birds screaming into the night sky. But it was a Ruritanian affair because, just after the call for morning prayers, Jalalabad would wake up as if the battles had been fought in a dream and reassume its role as a dusty frontier town, its bazaar touting poor-quality Pakistan cloth and local veg-etables while the Afghan soldiers ostensibly guarding the market place nodded in fatigue over their ancient—and British—Lee Enfield rifles. I would take a rick-shaw out of town to look at a damaged tank or a burned-out government office, type up my report of the fighting for the paper, and at mid-morning Ali would arrive with the "down" bus—Peshawar being 4,700 feet lower than Kabul—to pick up my report.

The teashops, the *chaikhana* stalls on the main street, were filled with truck-drivers, many of them from Kandahar, and they all spoke of the increasing resis-tance across the country. South of Kandahar, one man told me, villagers had stopped some Russian construction engineers and killed them all with knives. I could believe it. For however brave the mujahedin might be—and their courage was without question—their savagery was a fact. I didn't need the fictional Tom Graham or Durand's account of the fate of the 9th Lancers to realise this. "We will take Jalalabad," a young man told me over tea one morning. "The Russians here are finished." A teenage student, holding his father's hunting falcon on his wrist— editors love these touches, but there it was, a real live bird of prey anchored to the boy's arm with a chain—boldly stated that "the mujahedin will take Jalalabad tonight or tomorrow." I admired his optimism but not his military analysis.

Yet their views were also to be found within the Afghan army. Lunching in a dirty restaurant near the post office, I found an off-duty soldier at the next table, eating a badly cooked chicken with an unfamiliar knife and fork. "We do not want to fight the mujahedin—why should we?" he asked. "The army used to have local soldiers here but they went over to the mujahedin and so the government drafted us in from Herat and from places in the north of Afghanistan. But we do not want to fight with these people. The mujahedin are Muslims and we do not shoot at them. If they attack some building, we shoot into the air." The young man complained bitterly that his commanding officer refused to give him leave to see his family in Herat, 750 kilometres away near the Iranian border, and in his anger the soldier threw the knife and fork onto the table and tore savagely at the chicken with his hands, the grease dribbling down his fingers. "Jalalabad is finished," he said.

Again, untrue. That very morning, the Afghan air force made a very noisy attempt to intimidate the population by flying four of the local airbase's ageing MiG-17s at low level over the city. They thundered just above the main boulevard, the palm trees vibrating with the sound of jet engines, and left in their wake a silence broken only by the curses of men trying to control bolting, terrified horses. The big Soviet Mi-25 helicopters were now taking off from Jalalabad's tiny airport each morning and racing over the town to machine-gun villages in the Tora Bora mountains. While I was shopping in the market they would fly only a few feet above the rooftops, and when I looked up I could see the pilot and the gunner and the rockets attached to pods beneath the machine, a big, bright red star on the hull, fringed with gold. Such naked displays of power were surely counterproductive. But it occurred to me that these tactics must be intended to deprive the guerrillas of sufficient time to use their ground-to-air missiles. American helicopter pilots were to adopt precisely the same tactics to avoid missiles in Iraq twenty-three years later.

If there was a military accommodation between the Afghan army and the mujahedin, however, the insurgents knew how to hurt the government. They had now burned down most of the schools in the surrounding villages on the grounds that they were centres of atheism and communism. They had murdered the school-teachers, and several villagers in Jalalabad told me that children were accidentally killed by the same bullets that ended the lives of their teachers. The mujahedin were thus not universally loved and their habit of ambushing civilian traffic on the road west—two weeks earlier they had murdered a West German lorry-driver—had not added much glory to their name. And the mujahedin lived in the villages—which is where the Russians attacked them. On 2 February, I watched as four helicopter gunships raced through the semi-darkness to attack the village of Kama and, seconds later, saw a series of bubbles of flame glowing in the darkness.

Each morning at eight o'clock, the tea-shop owners would tell the strange Englishman what had been destroyed in the overnight battles and I would set off in my rickshaw to the scene. Early one morning, I arrived at a bridge which had been mined during the night. It lay on the Kabul road and the crater had halted all Soviet troop movements between Jalalabad and the capital, much to the excitement of the crowd which had gathered to inspect the damage.

Then one of them walked up to me. "*Shuravi?*" he asked. I was appalled. *Shuravi* meant "Russian." If he thought I was Russian, I was a dead man. "*Inglistan, Inglistan,*" I bellowed at him with a big smile. The man nodded and went back to the crowd with this news. But after a minute, another man stepped up to me, speaking a little English. "From where are you—London?" he asked. I agreed, for I doubted if the people of Nangarhar would have much knowledge of East Farleigh on the banks of the Medway River in Kent. He returned to the crowd with this news. A few seconds later, he was back again. "They say," he told me, "that London is occupied by the *Shuravi.*" I didn't like this at all. If London was occupied by the Soviet army, then I could only be here with Russian permission—so I was a collaborator. "No, no," I positively shouted. "Inglistan is free, free, free. We would fight the Russians if they came." I hoped that the man's translation of this back into Pushtu would be more accurate than the crowd's knowledge of political geography. But after listening to this further item of news, they broke into smiles and positively cheered Britain's supposed heroism. "They thank you because your country is fighting the Russians," the man said.

It was only as the rickshaw bumped me back to Jalalabad that I understood what had happened. To these Afghan peasants, Kabul—only a hundred kilometres up the highway—was a faraway city which most of them had never visited. London was just another faraway city and it was therefore quite logical that they should suppose the *Shuravi* were also patrolling Trafalgar Square. I returned to Jalalabad exhausted and sat down on a lumpy sofa in a *chaikhana* close to the Spinghar Hotel. The cushions had been badly piled beneath a pale brown shawl and I was about to rearrange them when the tea-shop owner arrived with his head on one side and his hands clutched together. "Mister—please!" He looked at the sofa and then at me. "A family brought an old man to the town for a funeral but their cart broke down and they have gone to repair it and then they will return for the dead man." I stood up in remorse. He put his hand on my arm as if it was he who had been sitting on the dead. "I am so sorry," he said. The sorrow was mine, I insisted. Which is why, I suppose, he placed a chair next to the covered corpse and served me my morning cup of tea.

At night now, the local cops and party leaders were turning up at the Spinghar to sleep, arriving before the 8 p.m. curfew, anxious men in faded brown clothes and dark glasses who ascended to their first-floor lounge for tea before bed. They would be followed by younger men holding automatic rifles that would clink in an unsettling way against the banisters. The party men sometimes invited me to join their meals and, in good English, would ask me if I thought the Soviet army would obey President Carter's deadline for a military withdrawal. They were understandably obsessed with the deadly minutiae of party rivalry in Kabul and with the confession of a certain Lieutenant Mohamed Iqbal, who had admitted to participating in the murder of the "martyr" President Nur Mohamed Taraki. Iqbal said that he and two other members of the Afghan palace guard had been ordered to kill Taraki by the "butcher" Amin and had seized the unfortunate man, tied him up, laid him on a bed and then suffocated him by stuffing a pillow over his face. The three then dug the president's grave, covering it with metal sheets from a sign-writer's shop.

The party men were so friendly that they invited me to meet the governor of Jalalabad, a middle-aged man with a round face, closely cropped grey hair and an old-fashioned pair of heavily framed spectacles. Mohamed Ziarad, a former export manager at Afghanistan's national wool company, could scarcely cope with the morning visitors to his office. The chief of police was there with an account of the damage from the overnight fighting; the local Afghan army commander, snapping to attention in a tunic two sizes too small for him, presented an intimidatingly large pile of incident reports. A noisy crowd of farmers poured into the room with compensation claims. Every minute, the telephone rang with further reports of sabotage from the villages, although it was sometimes difficult for Mr. Ziarad to hear the callers because of the throb of helicopter gunships hovering over the trees beyond the bay window. It had been a bad night.

Not that the governor of Jalalabad let these things overwhelm him. "There is no reason to overdramatise these events," he said, as if the nightly gun battles had been a part of everyone's daily life for years. He sipped tea as he signed the reports, joking with an army lieutenant and ordering the removal of an old beggar who had forced his way into the room to shout for money. "All revolutions are the same," he said. "We defend the revolution, we talk, we fight, we speak against our enemies and our enemies try to start a counter-revolution and so we defend ourselves against them. But we will win."

If Mr. Ziarad seemed a trifle philosophical—almost whimsical, I thought—in his attitude towards Afghanistan's socialist revolution, it was as well to remember that he was no party man. Somehow, he had avoided membership of both the Parcham and the Khalq; his only concession to the revolution was an imposing but slightly bent silver scale model of a MiG jet fighter that perched precariously on one end of his desk. He admitted that the insurgents were causing problems. "We cannot stop them shooting in the country. We cannot stop them blowing up the electric cables and the gas and setting off bombs at night. It is true that they are trying to capture Jalalabad and they are getting closer to the city. But they cannot succeed."

Here Mr. Ziarad drew a diagram on a paper on his desk. It showed a small circle, representing Jalalabad, and a series of arrows pointing towards the circle which indicated the rebel attacks. Then he pencilled in a series of arrows which moved outwards from Jalalabad. "These," he said proudly, "are the counter-attacks which we are going to make. We have been through this kind of thing before and always we achieve the same result. When the enemy gets closer to the centre of Jalalabad, they are more closely bunched together and our forces can shoot them more easily and then we make counter-attacks and drive them off." What a strange phenomenon is the drug of hope. I was to hear this explanation from countless governors and soldiers across the Middle East over the coming quarter of a century—Westerners as well as Muslims—all insisting that things were getting worse because they were getting better, that the worse things were, the better they would become.

Mr. Ziarad claimed that only three Afghan soldiers had been killed in the past week's fighting around the city and—given the unspoken truce between the army and the mujahedin—the governor's statistics were probably correct. He did deny, however, that there were any Soviet troops in Jalalabad—only a handful of Russian agricultural advisers and teachers were here, he said—which did not take account of the thousand Soviet soldiers in the barracks east of the town. He was not concerned about the Russian presence in his country. "It is the bandit groups that are the problem and the dispossessed landlords who had their land taken from them by our Decree Number Six and they are assisted by students of imperialism. These people are trained in camps in Pakistan. They are taught by the imperialists to shoot and throw grenades and set off mines."

The governor still visited the nearest villages during daylight, in the company of three soldiers, to inspect the progress of land reform and Jalalabad's newly created irrigation scheme. But he understood why the reforms had created animosity. "We tried to make sure that all men and women had equal rights and the same education," he said. "But we have two societies in our country, one in the cities and one in the villages. The city people accept equal rights but the villages are more traditional. Sometimes we have moved too quickly. It takes time to arrive at the goals of our revolution."

Mr. Ziarad's last words, as we walked from his office, were drowned by the roar of four more Soviet helicopter gunships that raced across the bazaar, sending clouds of dust swirling into the air beside the single-storey mud-walled houses. He asked me if I would like to use his car to travel back to my hotel. In view of the angry faces of the Afghans watching the helicopters, I decided that the governor of Jalalabad had made the kind of offer it was safer to refuse. But the cops at the Spinghar were getting nosy, wanting to know how long I was staying in Jalalabad and why I didn't go to Kabul. It was time to let Jalalabad "cool down." As Gavin always said, don't get greedy.*

It was the Russians who were getting greedy. Hundreds of extra troops were now being flown into Kabul in a fleet of Antonov transport aircraft along with new amphibious BMB armoured vehicles. In some barracks, Russian and Afghan soldiers had been merged into new infantry units, presumably to stiffen Afghan army morale. New Afghan army trucks carried Afghan forces but Soviet drivers. There were more Karmal speeches, the latest of which attacked what he called "murderers, terrorists, bandits, subversive elements, robbers, traitors and hirelings." That he should, well over a month after the Soviet invasion, be appealing for "volunteer resistance groups" to guard roads, bridges and convoys—against the much more powerful and genuine "resistance," of course—demonstrated just how serious the problem of the insurgents had become and how large an area of Afghanistan they now effectively controlled.

The Russians could neither wipe out the guerrillas nor give hope to Afghan villagers that their presence would improve their lives. Large areas of Afghanistan were cut off from government-subsidised food and the Soviets were flying planeloads of grain—even tractors—into Kabul while one of their generals appeared at the Bagram airbase to claim that only "terrorist remnants" remained in the mountains. "Remnants"—*bakoyaye* in Dari—became the vogue word for the insurgents on Afghan radio. But to "reform" Afghanistan under these circumstances was impossible. The government was losing. It was only a matter of time. And the more the government said they were winning, the fewer people believed them. In the lobby of the Intercontinental, a Polish diplomat told me that he thought the Russians would need at least 200,000 troops to win their war.[†]

---

*Anxious to avoid incriminating Ali if he was forced to hand over my file on his journey to Peshawar, I sent a suitably oblique message about the policemen to *The Times*, telling them that I was having "Maigret problems"—a reference to Georges Simenon's famous French police inspector. But in time of war, journalists should never be too clever. Sure enough, someone on the foreign desk passed my message to CBC's London office who immediately sent back a telex sympathising over my "migraine" problems.

[†]At this time, many Afghans also believed that Polish, East German, Czech and other soldiers from the Soviet satellite states were arriving in their country to support Russian troops. These false rumours probably began when Russians were heard speaking German in the Kabul bazaar. But these were Soviet troops from the German-speaking area of the Volga.

Karmal's men had effectively closed down the capital's mosques as a centre of resistance. When I found the speaker of the Polekheshti Mosque in the centre of Kabul, a small man with a thin sallow face whose features betrayed his anxiety and who refused even to give his name, he declined to answer even the mildest questions about the welfare of his people. He arrived one minute before morning prayers, walking quickly across the ice-encrusted forecourt in his tightly wound silk turban and golden cap and leaving immediately after his devotions were completed. When I walked towards him, he immediately glanced over his right shoulder. And when I presented him with a list of questions in Pushtu—what was the role of Islam in Afghanistan since December, I asked him?—he waved the paper in the frozen air in a gesture of hopelessness.

"Your questions are all political," he yelped at me. "One of your questions is asking if the people are happy with the new regime of Babrak Karmal. I will answer no questions about him. I do not represent the people. I will answer only religious questions." It was predictable. As *khatib* of the Polekheshti, he had only to interpret the Koran, not to deliver sermons on the morality of his government. Since the *khatibs* had all been appointed by the revolutionary governments in the past two years, there was even less chance that he would unburden himself of any feelings about the Soviet Union's invasion. A few days after Taraki's coup in 1978, calls for a jihad were read out in Kabul's mosques. Any political independence among the Sunni Muslim clergy had been wiped out within days when police raided all the city's religious institutions and dispatched dissenting mullahs to the Po-le-Charkhi prison, whence they never emerged. But brutal repression did not alone account for the lack of any serious political leadership within the clergy.

A decapitated church can scarcely give political guidance to its flock, but the history of Islam in Afghanistan suggested that there would be no messianic religious leader to guide the people into war against their enemies. Shia Muslims, whose tradition of self-sacrifice and emphasis on martyrdom had done so much to destroy the Shah's regime, were a minority in Afghanistan. In the western city of Herat, posters of Khomeini and Ayatollah Kazem Shariatmadari could be found on the walls, but the Sunnis formed the majority community and there was a fundamental suspicion in Afghanistan of the kind of power exercised by the leading clergymen in Iran. Afghans would not pay national subservience to religious divines. Islam is a formalistic religion, and among Sunnis, the mosque prayer leaders had a bureaucratic function rather than a political vocation. The power of religious orthodoxy in Afghanistan was strong but not extreme, and the lack of any hierarchy among Sunnis prevented the mullahs from using their position to create political unity within the country. Besides, Islam was also a class-conscious religion in Kabul. The Polekheshti Mosque catered largely to the poor, while the military favoured the Blue Mosque and the remains of the country's middle-class elite attended funerals at the two-tiered Shah-Do-Shamshira Mosque.

The monarchy, so long as it existed, provided a mosaic of unity that held the country more or less together. And although the last king was ostentatiously toasted in the *chaikhana* now that more ominous potentates had appeared in

Kabul, the spendthrift rulers who once governed Afghanistan were never really popular. When the monarchy disappeared, the only common denominator was religion; it was identified with nationalism—as opposed to communism—which is why Karmal had reintroduced green into the colour of the national flag. All ministerial speeches, even by cabinet members known to be lifelong Marxists, now began with obsequious references to the Koran. The Afghan deputy prime minister had just visited Mazar to pray at the shrine of Hazarate Ali, the cousin and son-in-law of the Prophet Mohamed. But in Afghanistan—as in most rural countries—religion was regarded with deepest respect in the villages rather than in the towns and it was from the villages that the mujahedin came. Although it was a reactionary force—opposing the emancipation and equality of women and secular education—it focused the attention of the poor on the realities of politics in a way that had never happened before. It was not by chance that a joke made the rounds of Afghans in Kabul, that apart from the five traditional obligations of Islam, a sixth instruction must now be obeyed: every true Muslim should listen to the BBC. This would no longer be a joke, of course, if a new Islamic force emerged from within the resistance rather than the clergy.

So few journalists were now left in Afghanistan that no one paid much attention to the *Times* correspondent, who carried no cameras but still possessed a valid visa. In Kabul, I shopped for carpets in the bazaar among the off-duty Soviet soldiers who still felt safe walking along Chicken Street. The Russians bought souvenirs, beads and necklaces for wives and girlfriends, but the Tajik Soviet soldiers would go to the bookshops and buy copies of the Koran. I eventually purchased a 2-by-3-metre rug of crimson and gold that had been lying on the damp pavement. Mr. Samadali, who was still free to drive us within the Kabul city limits, cast his critical eye on my rug, announced that I had paid far too much for it—it is a function of all taxi-drivers in south-west Asia to depress their foreign clients by assuring them they have been ripped off—and tied it to the roof of his car.

From Kabul, I now once more took Ali's bus down to Jalalabad, planning to spend a night at the Spinghar before returning to Kabul. In the Jalalabad bazaar, I went searching for a satin bag in which to carry my massive carpet out of Afghanistan. After ensuring I knew the Pushtu for a satin bag—*atlasi kahzora*—I bought a large Hessian sack, along with a set of postcards of Jalalabad under the monarchy, a gentle, soporific town of Technicolor brilliance that was now lost for ever. I visited the Pakistani consulate in the town, whose staff—some of them at least—must already have been coordinating with the guerrillas. They spoke of Soviet fears that Jalalabad might partially fall to the rebels, that the highway to Kabul might be permanently cut. And the Pakistani diplomats did not seem at all unhappy at this prospect.

No sooner was I back at the Spinghar than the receptionist, in a state of considerable emotion, told me that the Russians were using helicopters to attack the village of Sorkh Rud, 20 kilometres to the west. I hired a rickshaw and within half an hour found myself in a township of dirt streets and mud-walled houses. I told the driver to wait on the main road and walked into the village. There was not a human to be seen, just the distant thump-thump sound of Soviet Mi-25 helicopters which I only occasionally saw as they flitted past the ends of the streets. A few dogs yelped near a stream of sewage. The sun was high and a blanket of heat moved on the breeze down the streets. So where was the attack that had so upset the hotel receptionist? I only just noticed the insect shape of a machine low in the white sky seconds before it fired. There was a sound like a hundred golf balls being hit by a club at the same time and bullets began to skitter up the walls of the houses, little puffs of brown clay jumping into the air as the rounds hit the buildings. One line of bullets came skipping down the street in my direction, and in panic I ran through an open door, across a large earthen courtyard and into the first house I could see.

I literally hurled myself through the entrance and landed on my side on an old carpet. Against the darkened wall opposite me sat an Afghan man with a greying beard and a clutch of children, open-mouthed with fear and, behind them, holding a black sheet over her head, a woman. I stared at them and tried to smile. They sat there in silence. I realised I had to assure them that I was not a Russian, that I was from Mrs. Thatcher's England, that I was a journalist. But would this family understand what England was? Or what a journalist was? I was out of breath, frightened, wondering how I came to be in such a dangerous place—so quickly, so thoughtlessly, so short a time after leaving the safety of the Spinghar Hotel.

I had enough wits to remember the Pushtu for journalist and to try to tell these poor people who I was. "*Za di inglisi atlasi kahzora yem!*" I triumphantly announced. But the family stared at me with even greater concern. The man held his children closer to him and his wife made a whimpering sound. I smiled. They did not. Fear crackled over the family. Only slowly did I realise that I had not told them I was a journalist. Perhaps it was the carpet upon which I had landed in their home. Certainly it must have been my visit to the bazaar a few hours earlier. But with increasing horror, I realised that the dishevelled correspondent who had burst in upon their sacred home had introduced himself in Pushtu not as a reporter but with the imperishable statement: "I am an English satin bag."

"Correspondent, journalist," I now repeated in English and Pushtu. But the damage had been done. Not only was this Englishman dangerous, alien, an infidel intruder into the sanctity of an Afghan home. He was also insane. Of this, I had no doubt myself. Whenever we journalists find ourselves in great danger, there is always a voice that asks "Why?" How on earth did we ever come to risk our life in this way? For the editor? For adventure? Or because we just didn't think, didn't calculate the risks, didn't bother to reflect that our whole life, our education, our family, our loves and happiness, were now forfeit to chance and a few paragraphs. Sorkh Rud was the "border station" into which Kipling's British soldier cantered, the street outside this house his "dark defile," the helicopter his enemy's jezail. The cliché tells us that life is cheap. Untrue. Death is cheap. It is easy and terrible and utterly unfair.

I sat on the carpet for perhaps ten minutes, smiling idiotically at the cold-faced family opposite me until a little girl in a pink dress walked unsteadily across the floor towards me and smiled. I smiled back. I pointed at myself and said "Robert."

She repeated my name. I pointed to her. What was her name? She didn't reply. Outside I heard a donkey clop past the gate and a man shouting. The sound of the helicopters had vanished. There was a wailing from far away, the sound of a woman in grief. I stood up and looked out of the door. Other people were walking down the street. It was like Jalalabad each daybreak, when the night of death turned magically into a day of toil and dust and blooming jacaranda trees. The war had washed over Sorkh Rud and now it had moved elsewhere. I turned to the family and thanked them for their unoffered protection. "*Shukria*," I said. Thank you. And very slowly the man with the beard bowed his head once and raised his right hand in farewell.

The rickshaw driver was waiting on the main road, fearful that I might have died, even more fearful, I thought, that I might not have survived to pay him. We puttered back to Jalalabad. That night the party leaders were back in the hotel with news that obviously disturbed them. The mujahedin had raided a student hostel of Jalalabad University, taken twenty girls from the building, and transported them to Tora Bora, where they were given money—1,000 afghanis, about $22—and a black veil and told to end their studies. The same day, a Russian technical engineer had been sent to the suburbs of Jalalabad to mend an electric cable that had been repeatedly sabotaged. When he was at the top of a pylon, someone had shot him dead and his body hung in the wires 10 metres above the ground for several hours while men and women arrived to gaze at his corpse.

I would leave next day on the first bus back to Kabul, a luxury bus that left at dawn, long before Ali's old vehicle ground into town. My visa had only another three days to run. The bus from Jalalabad was packed, not with the villagers and Pakistani businessmen who travelled on Ali's charabanc, but with Afghan government students, Parcham party apparatchiks travelling back to Kabul University after vacation. Even before we had left the suburbs of the city, they were ordering everyone to pull the curtains so that no one could be seen and they craned their necks at every bend in the road to squint through the cracks in case an ambush lay ahead. I didn't see how the curtains would help. A mystery bus would attract far more attention from the mujahedin than a vehicle with windows open and passengers asleep inside.

When we stopped 25 kilometres to the north to find the body of a dead man covered in a blanket being loaded onto a truck, the communist students gazed in silence and in horror. It was, according to a middle-aged Afghan on another bus, the corpse of a lorry-driver who had not stopped for the mujahedin. There were five buses bunched up together, all heading for Kabul, and they all stopped now at a *chaikhana* while their drivers debated whether to talk their way through the guerrilla roadblock up the road or turn back to Jalalabad. Two hours passed, the drivers unable to make up their minds, the young Afghan men ever more nervous. And with good reason. The mujahedin gave their prisoners only two options: they could join the resistance or face execution. Some of the Afghan boys were taking off their party badges. I could only feel sorry for them. Perhaps they joined Parcham for promotion at college or because their parents worked for the government. And for all the government's brutality and its reliance on foreign invaders, its functionaries had been trying to create a secular, equal society in the villages around Jalalabad. It was not the government that was burning the schools and killing the teachers.

Another hour drifted by, the heat rising, the students ever more depressed, the drivers basking in the sun. In wartime, in any great danger, indecision is a narcotic. Then labouring up the highway came Ali's wooden bus, the coat of arms of the North West Frontier Province proudly displayed on its flanks. "Why do you desert me?" Ali wanted to know. He pointed to his charabanc. "Mr. Robert, please come with us." So I took my usual seat on the right-hand side of his vehicle and the other buses moved out into the road like sheep behind us. "You are better with us, Mr. Robert," Ali said. "You should not be with them." I soon realised why.

Round a bend just 5 kilometres up the highway, in a narrow valley of rocks and small pines, six tall and sun-burned mujahedin stood astride the road. A seventh was perched on a rock, lazily waving his arm up and down to tell us to stop. We had been told that they were poorly armed, that they only dared appear at dusk, that they were frightened of government retaliation. But here were the mujahedin in the hot midday sun in their turbans and Afghan shawls, each holding a brand-new Kalashnikov, controlling the traffic on one of Afghanistan's most important highways. It was an audacious display of self-confidence and a fearful one for the students in the bus behind. There was no anxiety in Ali's bus and a Pakistani passenger—a cloth merchant from Peshawar—was so bored that he began a long and tiresome discussion about Pakistan's domestic politics.

Through the back window, however, I could see the students stepping off their bus onto the road. They stood there, heads lowered as if they were criminals, some trying to hide behind the others. Ali was chatting and joking with one of the guerrillas. The other drivers stood beside their buses expressionless. The gunmen were moving through the line of young Afghans. Some were ordered back on the bus. Others, white with fear, were told to form a line by the road. Three of them were tied up and blindfolded and taken, stumbling and falling, through the pine stands and towards the river that gurgled away to our right. We watched them until they and their captors had disappeared. The Pakistani cloth merchant clucked his tongue and shook his head. "Poor chaps," he said.

Ali climbed back aboard and announced that since this was a Pakistani bus, the mujahedin did not wish to trouble us. And as we drove away, a young guerrilla with a rose tied to his rifle waved vigorously at us through the window. At last I had seen them. Here were the "holy warriors" whom the CIA was now adopting, the "terrorists" and "bandits" and "counter-revolutionary subversive elements" as Karmal called them, the "remnants" as the Soviet general blandly dismissed them, Mr. Ziarad's "students of imperialism." But they didn't look like "remnants" to me. Their Kalashnikovs were the new AKS 74s that the Soviets had just brought into Afghanistan, and they were wearing new ammunition belts.

The Kabul Intercontinental was forlorn. Most Western journalists had been expelled or left. Gavin and his crew had gone. My visa would soon expire and there was no hope of acquiring another. In the hotel sales office, one of the female secretaries, Gina Nushin, pleaded with me to take her private mail out of the country. Nine months later, in Ireland, I would receive a cryptic note from her, thanking me for posting her letters; the stamp on the envelope depicted a smiling and avuncular President Taraki browsing through his morning papers. But a far more important letter had just reached Kabul, smuggled out of the Soviet Union by a Shia cleric who had been arrested after Taraki's 1978 revolution and who was believed to have been murdered by the Afghan secret police. The mullah, whose name was Waez and who had enlisted the help of a sympathetic Soviet worker and an Afghan student at Moscow University to take his letter by hand to Kabul, told his family that he and hundreds of other Afghans were being held prisoner in the Russian city of Tula, 200 kilometres south of Moscow. Waez was honoured among Sunnis as well as Shias for his opposition to communist rule.

Rumours that thousands of Afghans were being secretly held in the Soviet Union—in violation of international law—had been circulating for more than a year. Many of the families whom I watched as they angrily stormed the Po-le-Charkhi prison outside Kabul in January were looking for relatives who, it now appeared, might have been in Russia all along. According to the Waez letter, he and other Afghans jailed in Tula were referred to as "state prisoners," although all were seized in Afghanistan. In 1979 the U.S. ambassador to Kabul, Adolph Dubs, had been murdered by gunmen who, intriguingly, had initially demanded Waez's release in return for the diplomat's life. Were the Soviets unwilling to free Waez because this would reveal how many Afghans were held captive in Tula?

I knew that Afghanistan's government was forcing the last of us out of the country, but the door was still ajar and I thought there was a crack through which I might squeeze.* I made one last trip to Jalalabad with Ali, only to find my hotel the venue for a clandestine meeting between six senior Soviet officers and the Afghan interior minister, Saed Mohamed Gulabzoi, and his local officials, all anxious to prevent a full-scale siege of Jalalabad by the rebels. So dangerous was the highway that the Russians had to be flown down from Kabul by helicopter. I watched them arrive at the Spinghar, protected by security police in riot visors who erected belt-fed machine guns on tripods upon bar tables around the hotel's rose gardens. There were now 3,000 Soviet troops outside the town.

And the destruction of the villages around Jalalabad was now under way. Ali-singh and Alinghar outside Metarlam had been bombed by the Russians but a 40-kilometre journey into mujahedin-held territory in Laghman Province showed that every school and government office in the villages had been burned by the rebels. Several villagers said that up to fifty women and children had been killed in Soviet air raids in the previous three days. An old man with an unshaven face kept repeating the word "napalm," gesturing with his hands in a downwards, smothering motion. In one tiny village outside Metarlam, more than 200 men surrounded my taxi when they thought we were Russians.

---

*It was instructive to note that Soviet journalists had so much difficulty in conveying the reality of this early stage of the war that Moscow newspapers were reduced to printing extracts from Western dispatches, including my own.

The mujahedin were not without their humour. Two nights earlier, an Afghan truck-driver found a notice on the main road west. "In the name of God," it read, "this is for tanks." The driver journeyed on and promptly set off a landmine. An armed insurgent then turned up to demand that the lorry driver pay $350 for the explosives which he had just wasted. Far less amusing was a report from three independent sources in Jalalabad that a museum at Hadda containing a statue of Buddha—dating from at least the second century BC—had been destroyed, along with other priceless antiquities. What did this mean? And if the reports were true, what confidence could the world have that the giant 1,400-year-old Buddhas of Bamiyan might not one day be similarly destroyed? On my way back to Kabul, the guerrillas were back on the road, twenty of them this time, and there were no longer any roses attached to their rifles.

I WOULD, BRIEFLY, RETURN TO AFGHANISTAN in the summer of 1980, flying in to Kabul with a tennis racket and an unbelievable claim to be a tourist. The Khad attached a cop to me this time and I was taken under escort to the Intercontinental where I paid him off in return for a taxi ride around the capital. The dust hung in layers of heat over Kabul and the Soviet soldiers were now on the defensive, escorting civilian cars in long armoured convoys across the highways of Afghanistan, their airbase at Bagram now flying bombing sorties against the mujahedin every three minutes. Soviets now occupied senior "advisory" positions in all the Kabul ministries, their large black limousines gliding through the muggy streets of the city at midday, curtains pulled across the back windows and plain-clothes men peering from the front passenger seats. The occupants were not the large, bulky commissars of popular mythology but, for the most part, small, respectable men in glossy grey business suits, narrow, slightly unfashionable ties and hair thick with oil, family men from an autonomous republic with five-year plans to meet.

In the stifling summer, the Russian soldiers were wearing floppy, wide-brimmed sombreros and their trucks jammed the streets of Kabul. Their "limited intervention" had spawned a spring offensive—that tactic beloved of all generals confronted by an armed insurrection—which had now turned into a full-scale military campaign. Helicopter gunships stood in rows five deep at the Kabul airport. Four-engined Ilyushin transport aircraft en route to Tashkent turned all day over the city, trailing fuel exhaust as they banked sharply above the international airport to avoid ground-to-air missiles.

At the airport, the two faces of Afghanistan's revolution could be seen within 800 metres of each other. Above the main terminal building, the faded outline of January's triumphant greeting to Soviet troops could still be observed—"Welcome to the New Model Revolution"—although the 1.5-metre-high letters had long ago been taken down and the sun had bleached the red paint a drab pink. Just across the airfield, at the eastern end of the main runway, lay the other symbol of Afghanistan's revolutionary conflict: a Soviet SA-2 missile with a 130-kilogram warhead, a range of 50 kilometres and a maximum altitude of 50,000 feet; this was the same weapon used with devastating effect against U.S. B-52 bombers over Hanoi in the Vietnam War. And Vietnam was the word that more and more Afghans were using to describe their own conflict. President Carter and Mrs. Thatcher were urging the world to boycott the Olympics in Moscow.

Kabul's schoolchildren were refusing to attend classes since hundreds of them were taken ill; rebels, according to the government, had put sulphur in the schools' water supplies. A thousand children had been taken to the Aliabad Hospital in one week alone. At night, gun battles crackled around the city as gunmen attacked Russian patrols and rival Parcham and Khalq party members assaulted each other. A doctor who was a member of President Karmal's Parcham party was shot dead while visiting a patient at Bandeghazi—within the city limits—but the police could not discover whether he was killed by mujahedin or by Khalq agents. One of the cops assigned to me was a Khalq man who, in the privacy of the hotel elevator, suddenly burst out in anger: "It is bad here and I am sick. We want Soviet help— we need it. But if anyone stays longer than we want—anyone, and that includes the Soviet Union—we will shoot them."

On 14 June, Karmal ordered the execution of thirteen former Khalq functionaries for "hatching conspiracies against the state." Most were minor officials— Sidaq Alamyar, the ex-planning minister, for example, and Saeb Jan Sehrai, who was in charge of "border affairs"—while the deputy prime minister, Asadullah Sarwari, who was head of Taraki's secret service, remained untouched. His name was on the death list of the "night letter" pushed into diplomatic compounds four months earlier. I was lucky to have stolen forty-eight hours in Kabul, albeit under secret police surveillance. When I was taken back to the Kabul airport for my flight out, an Aeroflot jet was standing on the apron, its fuselage evidence for Mrs. Thatcher's profound cynicism towards the Soviets.

The aircraft bore Aeroflot's proud English-language slogan "Official Olympic Carrier" on both sides of its fuselage but from its doors it was disgorging Soviet combat troops, young men—some with blond hair—carrying their rifles in the hot sun as they walked down the steps to the tarmac. They looked happy enough—one raised his arms towards the sun and said something that made his comrades laugh—although their chances of returning home in similar mood had decreased in recent weeks. More than 600 seriously wounded Soviet servicemen had been admitted to the Kabul military hospital, another 400 to Soviet clinics near the bus station at Khair Khana; of these 1,000, 200 had died—and this figure only included those who died of wounds, not those who were killed in combat. The dead were loaded in square wooden coffins aboard Antonov-12 aircraft and no one knew what they contained until a young Soviet soldier was seen saluting one of the boxes. Even the Khad secret policeman who followed me so assiduously agreed that the Soviet army was experiencing "very big trouble."

BUT BACK IN THAT CHILL FEBRUARY of 1980, I still had two days of precious, lonely freedom before my visa expired and I was forced to leave Afghanistan. I decided this time to be greedy, to try once more a long-distance bus ride, this time to a city whose people, so we were told in Kabul, had rediscovered their collective faith in confronting the invaders of their country: Kandahar.

I took the bus before dawn, from the same station I had set out from on my vain trip to Mazar, wearing the same Afghan hat and hunched under the same brown shawl. Men and women sat together—they all appeared to be families—and the moment I announced my nationality, I was deluged with apples, cheese, oranges and the big, flat, sagging nan bread that Afghans use as an envelope to contain their food. When I gently expressed my concern that there might be "bad" people on the bus—the very word Khad usually had the effect of silencing any conversation for an hour—I was assured there were none. I would be safe. And so the passengers, with scarcely any English, gave me their silent protection on the fourteen-hour journey across the moonlike, frozen landscape to Kandahar.

It was an epic of a country at war. Our coach passed the wrecks of countless vehicles beside the road. Sixty-five kilometres west of Ghazni, the town from which Gavin and I and his crew had fled the previous month—it already felt another life ago—a convoy of civilian buses and trucks had just been ambushed. All of the vehicles were burning fiercely, sending columns of black smoke funnelling up from the snow-covered plains. Small, darkened mounds lay beside the buses, all that was left of some of their passengers. Soviet convoys passed us in the opposite direction, each vehicle carrying a Russian soldier standing in the back, pistol in hand. The Soviets were now too busy ensuring their own safety to worry about the civilians they had supposedly come to rescue from the "bandits."

In one village, three Afghan soldiers, including an officer, boarded our bus and tried to arrest a postman who had deserted from the army. There was a brutal fist-fight between soldiers and passengers until two uniformed conscripts who were smoking hashish in the back seats walked down the aisle and literally kicked the officer out of the vehicle. So much for the morale of Karmal's Afghan army. In another village, the passengers hissed at Soviet Tajik troops who were standing beside the barbed wire of a military depot. But the passenger behind tapped me urgently on the shoulder. "Look!" he gasped, and pointed to his forehead. I looked at his face and could not understand. "Look!" he said more urgently and placed his right hand flat on top of his head, as if it was a hat. Hat. Yes, there was something missing from the Soviet Tajik soldiers' grey fur hats. They had removed the red star from their hats. They stood looking at us, darker-skinned than their Russian comrades, bereft now of the communist brotherhood in which they had grown up.

I should have understood at once. If Soviet troops in Afghanistan—Muslim Soviet soldiers—would remove the very symbol of their country, the badge that their fathers had worn so proudly in the Great Patriotic War between 1941 and 1945, then already the cancer of Afghanistan must have eaten deep into their souls. They had been sent to war against their Muslim co-religionists and had decided that they would not fight them. No more telling portent of the imminent collapse of empire could have confronted me in Afghanistan. Yet my trek across the snow-lands was so vast, the dangers so great, my exhaustion so overwhelming that I merely jotted in my notebook the observation that the soldiers had "for some reason" removed their hat-badges.

A few miles further on, an Afghan soldier could be seen standing in the desert, firing into the dusk with a sub-machine gun at an enemy he could not possibly have seen. When our bus stopped at a *chaikhana* in the frozen semi-darkness, an old man from the burned convoy we had passed told us that of the 300 passengers taken from the buses, 50 were detained by more than 100 armed rebels, all of them told—quite openly—that they would "probably" be executed because they were party men. Each scene spoke for itself, a cameo of violence and government impotence that our frightened passengers clearly understood.

It was night when we entered Kandahar, the ancient capital of Afghanistan, our bus gliding past the shrine in which lay the cloak of the Prophet Mohamed, circling a set of nineteenth-century cannon that had belonged to General Roberts's army in the Second Afghan War. I was dirty and tired and checked into a seedy hotel in the old city, a place of cigarette smoke, sweat and overcooked meat. My bedroom was small, the sheets stained, the threadbare carpet smallpoxed with cigarette burns. But two big rust-encrusted doors led onto a tiny balcony from where I could see the moon and the stars which glistened across the winter sky.

I was lying on my bed when I first heard the sound. *Allahu akbar*. God is great. It was a thin, pitched wail. *Allahu akbar*. God is great. I looked at my watch. This was no fixed time for prayers. It was 9 o'clock. The curfew had just begun. *Allahu akbar*. Now the chant came from the next roof, scarcely 20 metres from my room, more a yodel than an appeal to the Almighty. I opened the door to the balcony. The cry was being carried on the air. A dozen, a hundred *Allahu akbar*s, uncoordinated, overlaying each other, building upon a foundation of identical words, high-pitched and tenor, treble and child-like, an army of voices shouting from the rooftops of Kandahar. They swelled in volume, a thousand now, ten thousand, a choir that filled the heavens, that floated beneath the white moon and the stars, the music of the spheres.

I saw a family, a husband and wife and a clutch of children, all chanting, but their voices were lost in the pulse of sound that now covered the city. This extraordinary phenomenon was no mere protest, a lament at the loss of freedom. When the Prophet entered Mecca in the year 630 of the Christian era, he walked to the great black stone, the Kaaba, touched it with his stick and shouted in a strong voice that supreme invocation of Islam. *Allahu akbar*. His ten thousand followers chorused those same words and they were taken up by members of the Prophet's own Quraishi tribe who had gathered on their roofs and balconies in Mecca. Now these same holy words were being chanted by another ten thousand voices, this time from the roofs and balconies of Kandahar. A Westerner—or a Russian—might interpret this as a semi-political demonstration, a symbolic event. But in reality, the choirs of Kandahar were an irresistible assertion of religious faith, the direct and deliberate repetition of one of the holiest moments of Islam. In the last year of his life, the Prophet had entered the newly purified shrine in Mecca and seven more times chanted *Allahu akbar*. In Kandahar, the voices were desperate but all-powerful, mesmeric, unending, deafening, an otherwise silent people recognising their unity in God. This was an unstoppable force, an assertion of religious identity that no Afghan satrap or Kremlin army could ultimately suppress.

Kandahar's earthly, political protests had little effect. Shopkeepers had closed down the bazaar for more than two weeks but a squad of Afghan soldiers forced its reopening by threatening to smash stores whose owners did not obey their orders. Afghan troops could be found chain-smoking in their trucks beside the Khalki-sherif Mosque. But the five rebel groups operating south of Kandahar had united and the otherwise obedient mullahs had told the city's Muslim population that they should be "aware of events"—an over-discreet but nonetheless unprecedented reference to the Soviet invasion.

And over the past few days, a series of poorly printed posters had made their appearance on the walls of the reopened bazaar. "The people are asleep," one of them admonished. "Why do you not wake up?" Another, addressed to Soviet troops, asked simply: "Sons of Lenin—what are you doing here?" Yet the poster addressed to the Russians was written in Pushtu—a language with which Soviet troops were unlikely to be familiar—and five days earlier the people of Kandahar had watched from those same balconies and rooftops as a column of tanks, tracked armoured vehicles and trucks drove through their city. The first tank was seen just after nine in the evening and the tail of the convoy only left Kandahar at four in the morning. Most of this Soviet convoy ended up along the road to Spin Boldak on the Pakistan border.

In Kandahar, food prices had doubled, inflation had cut into wages. Meat and rice prices in the city had risen by 80 per cent and eggs 100 per cent. A shopkeeper, an educated man in his fifties who combined a European sweater and jacket with traditional Afghan baggy trousers and turban, claimed that Karmal's government could not survive if it was unable to control food prices. "Every day the government says that food prices are coming down," he said. "Every day we are told things are getting better thanks to the cooperation of the Soviet Union. But it is not true." The man lapsed into obscenities. "Do you realise that the government cannot even control the roads? Fuck them. They only hold on to the cities."

This I already knew. And the journey back to Kabul, 450 kilometres across lagoons of snow and deserts held by marauding rebels, was evidence of the terrible future that Afghanistan would be forced to endure. From the windows of my bus I saw, 8 kilometres from the road, an entire village on fire, the flames golden against the mountain snows, while the highway was sometimes in the hands of gunmen—several, I noticed, were wearing Arab kuffiah scarves—or truckloads of cringing Afghan soldiers. The Russian troops were moving up the side roads now, spreading their army across the plains, driving imperiously into the smallest villages.

At one intersection, a Soviet patrol was parked, the soldiers in their BMB armoured vehicles watching us with routine disinterest, already counting their mission as something normal. This was now their land, their inheritance, dangerous, to be true, but a part of their life, a duty to be done. But their mission was as hopeless as it was illusory. "Even if they kill a million of us," an Afghan *bazaari* was to say to me later in Kabul, "there are a million more of us ready to die. We never allow people to stay in our country." Both statements were true.

Only days after I left Kabul, Afghan troops and security men brutally suppressed a mass demonstration against the Soviet invasion, shooting down hundreds of protesters, including women students, in the streets of the capital. Well over a million Afghans would be killed in the war against the Russians over the next nine years, at least 4 million would be wounded and 6 million driven out of the country as refugees—even before the Afghan war entered its further tragedy of civil conflict between the mujahedin, Taliban rule and subsequent American bombardment. What that suffering meant we would only discover later. The most efficient killers were the armies of landmines sown across the mountains and fields of Afghanistan by the Soviets. The war would cost the Russians, it has been estimated, around $35 billion—$2.5 billion worth of Russian aircraft were lost in one year alone—and the Americans claimed to have spent $10 billion on the conflict. Saudi Arabia, on its own admission in 1986, spent $525 million in just two years on Afghan opposition parties and their Arab supporters. Pakistani sources would later say that 3,000 to 4,000 Arab fighters were in action in Afghanistan at any one time throughout the war and that as many as 25,000 Arabs saw service in the fighting. Yet in the end, once the Russian bear had burned its paws and the Soviet Union was on its way to perdition, the Americans and their Arab and Pakistani suppliers abandoned Afghanistan to its fate and ignored the thousands of Arabs who had fought there. Nor did any Saudi prince risk his life for the Afghans, nor any Arab leader ever dare to go to war for his fellow Muslims there, nor did Yassir Arafat, who understood the meaning of dispossession, ever criticise the army of occupation that was to lay waste the Muslim lands between the Amu Darya and the Durand Line. Only Bin Laden and his men represented the Arabs.

I flew out of Kabul on a little Pakistani prop aircraft that bucked in the air pockets over the Hindu Kush and dropped me into the basking, bakery-hot airport at Peshawar from which Francis Gary Powers had set off twenty years earlier in his doomed U-2 intelligence plane over the Soviet Union. I was light-headed, overwhelmed to have watched history and survived, possessed of a schoolboy immaturity. Hitchcock's *Foreign Correspondent* had nothing on this.* At my hotel, a message from Ivan Barnes told me I had won an award for my reporting on the Iranian revolution. "Have a very big drink on me tonight . . . " he telexed. The editor announced a $1,000 bonus. A letter was to arrive with congratulations from my old soldier father. "Well done Fella," he wrote. I could not sleep.

Next morning, I indulged my innocence by riding the old British steam train

---

*But at least Hitchcock's "Huntley Haverstock" would go on seeing the war with his own eyes. Charles Douglas-Home would later express to me every editor's fear for a story uncovered. "Now that we have no regular coverage from Afghanistan," he wrote, "I would be grateful if you could make certain that we do not miss any opportunity for reporting on reliable accounts of what is going on in that country . . . We must not let events in Afghanistan vanish from the paper simply because we have no correspondent there."

back up the Khyber Pass, to take one last look at Afghanistan before I returned to Beirut. Engine-driver Mohamed Selim Khan, a brisk and moustachioed Pathan with a topi on his head and eighteen years' experience with Pakistan Railways under his arm, wiped his oil-cloth over the firebox of his sixty-year-old steam engine, knowingly tapped the lubricator—a Wakefield patent made in London EC4—and eased loco Number 2511 out of Peshawar's hot and smoky station. Every schoolboy would have loved SGS class no. 2511, and so did I. She had six driving wheels, a smokestack with a lid like a teapot, a rusting boiler under constant repair, a squadron of gaskets that leaked steam and a footplate that reeked of oil, smoke and freshly brewed tea. She made a noise like thunder and I clung like a child to the fittings of Mr. Khan's footplate.

The Ministry of Defence in Islamabad paid for the upkeep of the 60 kilometres of track—they might need it one day, to take their own army up to Landi Kotal if those Russian convoys spilled over the border—but its subsidy allowed us to hammer our way up the one-in-three gradient, the steepest in the world, black smoke boxing us into the more than thirty tunnels that line the route, a thin, shrieking whistle sending buffaloes, goats, sheep, children and old men off the track. At 3,000 feet, No. 2511 performed so sharp a turn above so sheer a ridge of boulders high above a spinning river that Mr. Khan and I grasped the iron doors of the cab to stop ourselves falling out. So we steamed into Landi Kotal from Jamrud Fort, our loco fuming in the sharp high-altitude breeze.

And when I jumped down from the footplate and crunched my way across the gravel of the permanent way, there were the pale blue mountains of Afghanistan shimmering to the north and west, sun-soaked and cold and angry and familiar and dangerous. I looked at them with attachment now, as one always does a dark land from which one has emerged alive. Up there, with Gavin and his crew, I had reached the top of the world. Never could I have imagined what we had given birth to in Afghanistan, nor what it held in store for that same world in twenty-one years' time. Nor the pain it was to hold for me.

# CHAPTER FOUR

# The Carpet-Weavers

> *. . . the Men who for their desperate ends*
> *Had plucked up mercy by the roots, were glad*
> *Of this new enemy. Tyrants, strong before*
> *In wicked pleas, were ten times now*
> *And thus beset with foes on every side,*
> *The goaded Land waxed mad; the crimes of few*
> *Spread into madness of the many, blasts*
> *From hell came sanctified like airs from heaven;*

—William Wordsworth,
*The Prelude,* 1805, Book Tenth

CHRISTOPHER MONTAGUE WOODHOUSE was asking himself if he had helped to create the Islamic revolution in Iran. He was an old man now, but you could see the energy that still gripped him, a tall, dignified, brave and ruthless seventy-nine-year-old. It was snowing that morning in Oxford in 1997, but he had come to the gate of his retirement home to greet me, his handshake a vise. He sat ramrod-straight in his library with the mind of a young man, answering my questions with the exactness of the Greek scholar he was, each sentence carefully crafted. He had been Britain's senior secret agent in "Operation Boot" in 1953, the overthrow of Iran's only democratic prime minister, Mohamed Mossadeq. It was "Monty" Woodhouse who helped to bring the Shah of Iran back from exile, along with his colleagues in the CIA, who set in motion a quarter-century in which the Shah of Shahs, "Light of the Aryans," would obediently rule Iran—repressively, savagely, corruptly and in imperious isolation—on our behalf. Woodhouse was a reminder that The Plot—the international conspiracy, *moamara* in Arabic—was not always the product of Middle East imagination. Woodhouse was in the last years of a life in which he had been a guerrilla fighter in Greece, a Tory MP and a much honoured Greek linguist and academic. Almost everyone who had destroyed Iranian democracy was now dead: CIA boss Allen Dulles, Robin Zaehner of the British Foreign Office, the two mysterious Rashidian brothers who organised the coup, Mossadeq himself and the last Shah of Iran. Except for Kermit Roosevelt, the senior CIA man in Tehran, "Monty" was the last survivor.

We had known each other for nine years, ever since *The Times* sent me to investigate the secret wartime history of former UN secretary-general and

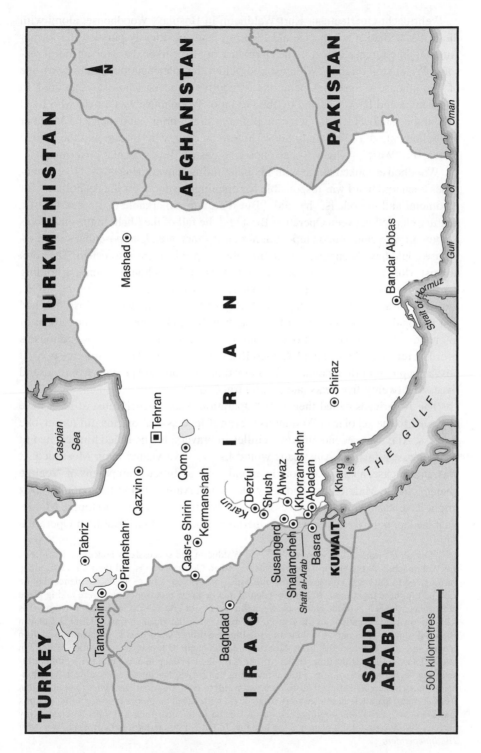

ex-Wehrmacht Oberleutnant Kurt Waldheim in Bosnia.* Woodhouse, along with
the brilliant British scholar Gerald Fleming, had relentlessly pursued the former
Austrian intelligence officer in the German army for personal as well as moral reasons; Waldheim's initial "W" appeared below the interrogation summary of one
of Woodhouse's Special Operations Executive officers who was captured in
Yugoslavia and later executed by the Gestapo. Woodhouse was a man who lived
first in the shadows—in the wartime Balkans and Tehran—and then as a Member
of Parliament, and I wanted to know, before he died, why Britain and the United
States, the "West"—why we—had chosen to destroy Iran's secular government.

Woodhouse looked at me with his penetrating, unwavering eyes. "I've sometimes been told that I was responsible for opening the doors for the Ayatollah—for
Khomeini and the others," he said. "But it's quite remarkable that a quarter of a
century elapsed between Operation Boot and the fall of the Shah. In the end it was
Khomeini who came out on top—but not until years later. I suppose that some better use could have been made of the time that elapsed." I was astonished. The coup
against Mossadeq, the return of the Shah, was, in Woodhouse's mind, a holding
operation, a postponement of history. There was also the little matter of the AIOC,
the Anglo-Iranian Oil Company—later British Petroleum—which Mossadeq had
just nationalised. You could tell from the way he spoke, the urgent movement of
his hands, that this had been one of the most exciting moments of Woodhouse's
life. The return of the young Mohamed Reza Shah Pahlavi was the ultimate goal. It
cost a couple of million pounds, a planeload of weapons and perhaps five thousand
lives. And twenty-five years later, it all turned to dust.

The Americans called their plot "Operation Ajax," which must at least have
appealed to the scholar in Woodhouse, even if its classical origins did not invoke
success; Ajax was second only to Achilles in bravery, but he killed himself in a fit
of madness, a fate the Americans would like to have visited upon Mossadeq. It
was, in any case, a long way from later and more ambitious campaigns of "regime
change" in the Middle East, and a few neo-conservatives in the Pentagon in 2003
might have dusted off the archives of the early Fifties to see how to topple Middle
East leaders before embarking on "Operation Iraqi Freedom." But then Operation

*During his time as UN secretary-general, Waldheim had successfully concealed his role in
the Wehrmacht's Army Group E in Yugoslavia, when German troops and their Croatian allies
participated in the mass killing of Serbs and Muslims. Although there was no evidence that he
took part in these massacres, Waldheim's denial that he knew that war crimes were taking place
in Bosnia at the height of the battles between the Nazis and Tito's Partisans in 1943 was at odds
with my own investigations in the region. When I visited the Bosnian town of Banja Luka in
1988, I discovered that one of Waldheim's intelligence offices stood next to a wartime execution
ground and only 35 kilometres from the extermination camp of Jasenovac—of which Waldheim
said he knew nothing at the time. In the Middle East, the UN's top man would later lecture political leaders on guerrilla warfare, without revealing that he was an expert in the subject. My abiding memory of leaving Bosnia that summer was a call to Ivan Barnes at *The Times* to tell him that
I saw so many parallels in modern-day Yugoslavia with Lebanon on the eve of conflict in 1975
that I believed a civil war would break out in Bosnia in the near future. Barnes laughed at my
naiveté. "We'll report it if it happens," he told me. In 1992, I was reporting the Bosnian war—for
*The Independent.*

Boot/Ajax—though it was undeniably about oil—was never intended to change the map of the Middle East, let alone bring "democracy" to Iran. "Democracy," in the shape of the popular and somewhat effete Mossadeq, was the one thing Washington and London were not interested in cultivating. This was to be regime change on the cheap.

The project had not attracted President Truman, but when Eisenhower arrived at the White House in 1953, America was already fearful that Mossadeq would hand his country over to the Soviets. The CIA end of the operation was run by the splendidly named Kermit Roosevelt—grandson of the buccaneering ex-president Theodore—and his victim was the very opposite of Saddam Hussein. "No nation goes anywhere under the shadow of dictatorship," Mossadeq once said—words that might have come from President George W. Bush's speechwriters half a century later. But one thing Mossadeq did have in common with the later dictator of Iraq; he was the victim of a long campaign of personal abuse by his international opponents. They talked about his "yellow" face, of how his nose was always running; the French writer Gérard de Villiers described Mossadeq as "a pint-sized trouble-maker" with the "agility of a goat." On his death, *The New York Times* would claim that he "held cabinet meetings while propped up in bed by three pillows and nourished by transfusions of American blood plasma." True, Mossadeq, an aristocrat with a European education, had a habit of dressing in pink pyjamas and of bursting into tears in parliament. But he appears to have been a genuine democrat—he had been a renowned diplomat and parliamentarian—whose condemnation of the Shah's tyranny and refusal to sanction further oil concessions gave his National Front coalition mass popular support. When Woodhouse arrived in Tehran—officially, he was the British embassy's "information officer"—Iran was already on the brink of catastrophe. Negotiations had broken down with the AIOC, whose officials, Woodhouse admitted, were "boring, pig-headed and tiresome." The British ambassador was, according to Woodhouse, "a dispirited bachelor dominated by his widowed sister" and his opposite number an American business tycoon who was being rewarded for his donations to the Democratic Party.*

"One of the first things I had to do was fly a planeload of guns into Iran," Woodhouse said. He travelled on the aircraft from the Iraqi airbase at Habbaniya—decades later, it would be one of Saddam Hussein's fighter-bomber stations, and later still a barracks for America's occupation army—and then bought millions of Iranian rials, handing them over at a secret location to the Rashidian brothers. They were to be the organisers of the mobs who would stage the coup. The guns would be theirs, too—unless the Soviet Union invaded Iran, in which case they were to be used to fight the Russians.

---

*Students of Saddam Hussein's later bestialisation should note that the U.S. ambassador's successor, Loy Henderson, wrote to the State Department of Mossadeq that "we are confronted by a desperate, a dangerous situation and a madman who would ally himself with the Russians." Replace the Russians with al-Qaeda and it could be President Bush or Prime Minister Blair in 2002.

"We landed in Tehran after losing our way over the Zagros Mountains. They were mostly rifles and Sten guns. We drove north in a truck, avoiding checkpoints by using by-roads. Getting stopped was the sort of thing one never thinks about. We buried the weapons—I think my underlings dug the holes. And for all I know those weapons are still hidden somewhere in northern Iran. It was all predicated on the assumption that war would break out with the Soviet Union. But let me clarify. When I was sent to Tehran, it was not for the purpose of political interference. In fact, political interference at the British embassy in Tehran was in the hands of a quite different personality, Robin Zaehner. He was very good company, very intelligent but very odd. His function was to get rid of Mossadeq. This only became my function when Zaehner despaired of it and left Tehran."

In fact, Zaehner, later to become professor of Eastern religions at Oxford, had been involved in Britain's disastrous attempt to raise a revolution in communist Albania, based in Malta, and later accused by American agents of betraying the operation—Woodhouse never believed this—and was now the principal liaison with the Shah. It was Zaehner who cultivated the Rashidian brothers, both of whom had worked against German influence in Iran during the Second World War. Iran was on the point of throwing the British embassy staff out of Tehran, so Woodhouse made contact with the CIA station chief in the city, Roger Goiran, "a really admirable colleague . . . he came from a French family, was bilingual, extremely intelligent and likeable and had a charming wife . . . an invaluable ally to me when Mossadeq was throwing us out." Once back in London, Woodhouse took his plans to the Americans in Washington: the Rashidians, along with an organisation of disenchanted army and police officers, parliamentary deputies, mullahs, editors and mobs from the bazaar, all funded by Woodhouse's money, would seize control of Tehran while tribal leaders would take over the big cities—with the weapons Woodhouse had buried.

Mossadeq rejected the last proposals for a settlement with the AIOC and threatened the Shah—who had already left Iran—and from that moment, his fate was obvious. Roosevelt travelled secretly to Tehran while Woodhouse met the Shah's sister Ashraf in Switzerland in an attempt to persuade her brother to stay on the throne. The Shah himself received a secret emissary bent on the same purpose, a certain General H. Norman Schwarzkopf—father of the Norman Schwarzkopf who would lead U.S. forces in the 1991 Gulf War against Iraq. The Shah went along with the wishes of his superpower allies. He issued a firman dismissing Mossadeq as prime minister, and two days after Mossadeq refused to obey and arrested Colonel Nimatullah Nassiri—who had brought the Shah's order—the mobs whom Roosevelt and Woodhouse had bought duly appeared on the streets of Tehran.

Woodhouse was always unrepentant. "It was all Mossadeq's fault. He was ordered by the Shah's firman to leave. He called out his own thugs and he caused all the bloodbath. Our lot didn't—they behaved according to plan. What if we'd done nothing? What would relations have been between Mossadeq and the mullahs? Things would only have got worse. There would have been no restoration of

AIOC. And the Shah would have been overthrown immediately, instead of twenty-five years later."*

In retirement, and still mourning his wife, Davina, who had died two years earlier, Woodhouse was now keeping his mind alert by translating into English a history of modern Greece by his old friend and fellow scholar, Panayotis Kanellopoulos.[†] It was easy to see him, a gentle old man who had just become the fifth Baron Terrington, as a romantic figure of history. Here, after all, was a man who knew Churchill and Eden and the top men in the CIA in Washington. But British agents who engineer coups can be remorseless, driven people. At one point in our conversation, Woodhouse talked about his own feelings. "I don't want to be boastful," he said. "But never—neither in Athens during the German occupation nor in Tehran during this operation—was I afraid. I was never afraid of parachuting, even in the wrong place. I ought to have been, I realise. And when I look back on it, a shudder comes over me. I was always fascinated by the danger and fascinated by the discoveries that come out of being in danger."

There was, I felt, a darker side to this resolve. In his autobiography, Woodhouse described how during his Second World War service in Greece, a gypsy was captured carrying an Italian pass and working for the Axis powers. With two Greek guerrilla leaders, Napoleon Zervas and Aris Veloukhiotis, Woodhouse formed a court martial. "The outcome was inevitable," he wrote. "We could not afford the manpower to guard a prisoner; we could not risk his escape. He was hanged in the village square."

Did Woodhouse still think about this youth? I put this question to him gently, at the end of our conversation as the gale outside hurled snow at the window of his library. There was a long silence and Woodhouse shook his head very slowly. "It was terrible—I felt terrible. I still bring the scene back to me from time to time. He was a wretched youth. He didn't say anything really—he was so shaken. He was a sort of halfwit. I was at the hanging. He was hanged from a tree. They simply pulled a chair from beneath his feet. I don't think it took long for him to die, I don't know exactly how long. We were only a hundred men or so—it was the early days of the occupation. If we had let him go, he would have told the Italians . . . He had been following us from village to village. After that, I told Zervas not to take any prisoners."

Woodhouse, I suspect, viewed the Iranian coup with the same coldness of heart. He certainly had as little time for Ayatollah Abul Qassim Kashani as he did for Mossadeq. Kashani was one of Khomeini's precursors, a divine—albeit of a slightly gentler kind—whose opposition to the British gave him nationalist cre-

---

*Unsurprisingly, the CIA announced in 1997 that almost all its documents on the Mossadeq coup had been destroyed in the early 1960s—"a terrible breach of faith with the American people," according to the former CIA director James Woolsey, who in 1993 had publicly promised that the Iran records would be made public. A CIA historian noted that there had been "a culture of destruction" at the agency in the early Sixties.

[†]When he died in 2001, it was Woodhouse's wartime career that was remembered. His obituary in *The Independent* (26 February 2001) made no mention of his Persian skulduggery.

dentials without making him an automatic ally of Mossadeq. Woodhouse was not impressed. Kashani, he said, was "a man no one really took seriously—he became a member of the Majlis [parliament], which was an odd thing for an ayatollah to do. He had no power base . . . Kashani was a loner. One didn't think of him in terms of any mass movement. He was a nuisance, a troublemaker." Others thought differently. Kashani, it has been said, spoke for the "democracy of Islam"; he was a man "completely fearless, unscrupulous, completely free from self-interest . . . With these qualities he combines humility and ready access, kindness and humour, wide learning and popular eloquence."* In November 1951, Kashani stated that "we don't want any outside government interfering in our internal affairs . . . The United States should cease following British policy otherwise it will gain nothing but hatred and the loss of prestige in the world in general and in Iran in particular." Much the same warning would be given to Britain in the Middle East fifty-two years later when Tony Blair's government followed American policy over Iraq.

Woodhouse was right in one way: after Mossadeq's overthrow and subsequent trial—he was given a three-year jail sentence and died under house arrest ten years later—Kashani moved into obscurity. Woodhouse would record how the Ayatollah later sent a telegram of congratulations to the Shah on his return to Iran. But Mossadeq's rule and the coup that ended Iran's independence in 1953 would provide a bitter lesson to the revolutionaries of 1979. If the Shah was ever to be dethroned, there could be no flirtation with constitutional rights, no half-measures, no counter-revolutionaries left to restore Western power in Iran. A future revolution would embrace more than five thousand dead; it must be final, absolute—and unforgiving. The spies, the ancien régime, would have to be liquidated at once.

There were also lessons for the Americans and British, and for the Shah, had they chosen to pay attention. The Shah would henceforth always be seen as a tool of the United States and Britain. The fall of Mossadeq, as James A. Bill has written, "began a new era of intervention and growing hostility to the United States among the awakened forces of Iranian nationalism." Woodhouse was to become deeply depressed by Khomeini's subsequent revolution. "I felt that the work we had done was wasted, that a sort of complacency had taken over once the Shah had been restored," he said. "Things were taken for granted too easily." After Mossadeq had been booted out, Allen Dulles praised Woodhouse for visiting Washington and persuading the Eisenhower administration to back the coup: "That was a nice little egg you laid when you were here last time!" he told the man from MI6.

But we don't go in for "little eggs" any more. More ambitious ideological projects, vast armies—and bigger egos—are involved in "regime change" today.

*Not that the future Ayatollah Khomeini at this stage was opposing the Shah. The American academic James A. Bill wrote of rumours that the future leader of Iran's Islamic revolution was one of those who urged the preeminent Shia cleric of the day, Ayatollah Sayed Mohamed Hussein Burujirdi, to support the Shah's political system. Iranian newspaper biographies of Khomeini in 1979 intriguingly left out any reference to his activities more than a quarter of a century earlier.

Maybe that's why they can fail so quickly and so bloodily. The coup against Mossadeq was the first such operation carried out by the Americans in the Cold War—and the last by the British. At least we never claimed Mossadeq had weapons of mass destruction. But the final word must go to the CIA's man, Kermit Roosevelt. "If we are ever going to try something like this again," he wrote with great prescience, "we must be absolutely sure that [the] people and army want what we want."

The "sort of complacency" which Woodhouse defined was based upon the security services which the Shah established after his return. Savak—*Sazman-i Etelaat va Amniyat-i Keshvar*, the "National Information and Security Organisation"—was to become the most notorious and the most murderous, its torture chambers among the Middle East's most terrible institutions. A permanent secret U.S. mission was attached to Savak headquarters. Methods of interrogation included—apart from the conventional electric wires attached to genitals, beating on the soles of the feet and nail extraction—rape and "cooking," the latter a self-explanatory form of suffering in which the victim was strapped to a bed of wire that was then electrified to become a red-hot toaster.* Mohamed Heikal, that greatest of Egyptian journalists, once editor of *Al-Ahram* and former confidant of Nasser, has described how Savak filmed the torture of a young Iranian woman, how she was stripped naked and how cigarettes were then used to burn her nipples. According to Heikal, the film was later distributed by the CIA to other intelligence agencies working for American-supported regimes around the world including Taiwan, Indonesia and the Philippines. Colonel Nimatullah Nassiri, the man who had served Mossadeq with the Shah's eviction order, controlled Savak for almost the last fifteen years of the monarch's reign and employed up to 60,000 agents. At one point, it was believed that a third of the male population of Iran were in some way involved in Savak, either directly or as occasional paid or blackmailed informants. They included diplomats, civil servants, mullahs, actors, writers, oil executives, workers, peasants, the poor and the unemployed, a whole society corrupted by power and fear.

For the West, the Shah became our policeman, the wise "autocrat"—never, of course, a dictator—who was a bastion against Soviet expansionism in south-west Asia, the guardian of our oil supplies, a would-be democrat—the "would" more relevant than the "be"—and a reformer dedicated to leading his people into a bright economic future. Over the next quarter-century, the international oil industry exported 24 billion barrels of oil out of Iran; and the "policeman of the Gulf"

---

*One of its victims was Massoud Ahmadzadeh, an engineer later executed by the regime. In 1972, Nuri Albala, a French lawyer, who attended his trial, described how Ahmadzadeh pulled up his pullover to show the marks of torture. "The whole of the middle of his chest and his stomach was a mass of twisted scars from very deep burns. They looked appalling . . . His back was even worse. There was a perfect oblong etched into it, formed by a continuous line of scar tissue. Inside the oblong, the skin was again covered in shiny scars from burning." Ashraf Dehqani, who escaped from prison after torture—she was an opposition militant—wrote of how she was raped by her Savak torturers and had snakes placed on her body.

was more important than ever now that the British were withdrawing from "east of Suez." But the Shah's rule was never as stable as his supporters would have the world believe. There was rioting against the regime throughout the 1960s and four hundred bombings between 1971 and 1975. In early 1963, Ayatollah Khomeini repeatedly condemned the Shah's rule. On 3 June, the day marking the martyrdom at Kerbala of Imam Hussein, the grandson of the Prophet, he publicly denounced the Shah's corruption and was promptly arrested and taken to Tehran. An outburst of popular anger confirmed Khomeini as a national opposition leader. Sixteen months later, on 4 November 1964, he delivered a speech in which he condemned a new law giving American forces immunity from prosecution for any crimes committed inside Iran. Henceforth, an American who murdered an Iranian could leave the country; an Iranian who murdered an Iranian could be hanged.* Next day, Khomeini was exiled to Turkey.

The Shah's "White Revolution" succeeded in alienating the middle classes by legislating for land reform and the clerics by increasing the secular nature of the regime, especially by giving electoral power to women. By 1977, less than two years before the Islamic revolution, the Shah was predicting that within ten years Iran would be as developed as western Europe, and shortly thereafter one of the five most powerful countries in the world. President Jimmy Carter's U.S. administration, burdened with a liberal desire to spread human rights across the globe but still anxious to maintain the Shah's power, continued the American policy of supporting the reforms that were causing so much unrest among Iranians. Israeli leaders paid frequent visits to Iran—David Ben Gurion, Moshe Dayan, Golda Meir, Abba Eban, Yitzhak Rabin and Yigal Allon all visited Tehran, often in secret. Iranian military officers travelled to Tel Aviv for talks with senior Israeli army officers. There were regular El Al flights between Tel Aviv and Tehran.

Like all absolute monarchs, the Shah constantly reinvented himself. In 1971, he invited world leaders to celebrate the thirtieth anniversary of his rule at a massive birthday bash in the ancient city of Persepolis, the capital of the Persian empire under Darius the First. The city would become "the centre of gravity of the world" and everyone and almost everything—from Imelda Marcos to U.S. Vice President Spiro Agnew, from King Hussein of Jordan to the fine wines and furnishings in the vast "big top" tent beside the ruins—was imported from abroad. The Shah was to be worshipped as spiritual heir to the empire of Cyrus the Great, whose rule included a landmass stretching to the Mediterranean, later extended to Egypt and east to the Indus River. Alexander the Great had conquered Persepolis in 330 BC and, so legend would have it, ordered its destruction at the request of a courtesan. For the Shah's "birthday," Iranian troops were dressed up as Medes and Persians, Safavids and Kajars and Parthians. All that was missing was any reference to the Prophet Mohamed and the Muslim invasions that brought Islam to Per-

---

*An almost identical law, passed by Paul Bremer, the U.S. proconsul in Baghdad after America's 2003 invasion of Iraq, brought widespread protests from Iraqis and helped mobilise popular opposition to the U.S. occupation.

sia. But that was the point. The Shah was presenting himself not as a Muslim but as the kingly inheritor of pre-Islamic Persia. Khomeini naturally condemned the whole binge as obscene.

This act of self-aggrandisement counted for nothing when the end came. Indeed, the very detritus of the banquet was effortlessly turned by the Ayatollah's regime into a symbol of emptiness. When the Shah, long exiled, was undergoing surgery in New York, I travelled down to Persepolis from Tehran and found his special tent, still standing beside the ruins of the city. I even lowered myself into his solid gold bath and turned on the solid gold taps. There was no water in them.

Nor did the Shah have Cyrus's blood in his veins. He had no such illustrious lineage—the Pahlavi dynasty was only founded in 1925—although there was a very firm blood tide that linked the various shahs of Iranian history. The Polish writer Ryszard Kapuściński has most eloquently conveyed the horrors of the eighteenth-century monarch Aga Mohamed Khan, who ordered the population of the city of Kerman to be murdered or blinded because they had sheltered the previous Shah. So the king's praetorian guard "line up the inhabitants, slice off the heads of the adults, gouge out the eyes of the children . . . Later, processions of blinded children leave the city . . . "

The Shah was finally persuaded by the Americans to allow the International Committee of the Red Cross into Iran's prisons in 1977; they were allowed to see more than 3,000 "security detainees"—political prisoners—in eighteen different jails. They recorded that the inmates had been beaten, burned with cigarettes and chemicals, tortured with electrodes, raped, sodomised with bottles and boiling eggs. Interrogators forced electric cables into the uterus of female prisoners. The Red Cross report named 124 prisoners who had died under torture. A year later, the Shah told the *Sunday Times* that on human rights "we have no lessons to learn from anybody."

When the Islamic revolution eventually came over Iran, we would often wonder at the Iranian capacity for both cruelty and sensitivity, for sudden anger and immense, long and exhausting intellectual application. In a country of violent history, its public squares were filled with statues of poets—Ferdowsi, Hafiz, Saadi—rather than conquerors, although the Shah and his father naturally occupied some substantial plinths. An Arab politician once compared Iranian persistence in adversity to the country's craft of carpet-weaving. "Imagine that one carpet, worked on by scores of people, takes about ten years to complete. A people who spend years in manufacturing just a single carpet will wait many more years to achieve victory in war. Do not take lightly the patience and perseverance of the Iranians . . . "

And so it was to be. Khomeini moved his exile from Turkey to the Shia holy city of Najaf in Saddam Hussein's Iraq, where he became outspoken in his support of the Palestinians. On clandestine tapes, his sermons were now circulated across Iran. Saddam Hussein had secured an agreement with the Shah that settled their mutual border along the centre of the Shatt al-Arab River on the Gulf and which also smothered the Kurdish insurrection in the north of Iraq, a betrayal at which both U.S. secretary of state Henry Kissinger and the Shah connived. When the Shah was unable to stanch the cassette sermons, Saddam was enjoined to deport Khomeini. This time he settled in Neauphle-le-Château outside Paris, where he was assured of the constant, almost fawning admiration of the international press, an institution for which he was later to show his contempt.

When the political earthquake eventually struck Iran, *The Times* was enduring a long industrial closure. It is the fate of journalists to be in the right place at the right time and, more frequently, in the wrong place at the wrong time. But to be in the right place without a newspaper to write for was journalistic hell. When I should have been reporting the martyrdom of tens of thousands of Iranians at the hands of the Shah's Javidan Guards—the "Immortals"—I was resigning from the National Union of Journalists who were, for all kinds of worthy socialist reasons, opposing the paper's philanthropic owner Lord Thomson in his dispute with his printers over new technology; the union ultimately trussed up *The Times* for sale to Rupert Murdoch. But the Canadian Broadcasting Corporation came to my rescue with a request for me to cover the Iranian revolution for a half-hour radio documentary. I packed the big tape recorder that CBC gave its reporters in those days—this was long before digitalisation—and a bag of cassettes and a notebook in case I could find a newspaper to print my reports.

The fall of the Shah was an epic. His downfall had about it something of a medieval morality play, even ancient tragedy. It might have qualified as Greek if the Shah had been a truly great man who fell from grace through a single flaw. But he was not a great man and his sins were many. Hubris was perhaps his greatest crime, although the Iranians saw things somewhat differently. Yet they sensed this mythic element in their revolution even before the King of Kings piloted his personal Boeing airliner out of Mehrabad Airport for the last time on 16 January 1979.

One of the most impressive of the revolutionary posters depicted the Shah in his full regalia, crown toppling from his balding head, hurtling towards the everlasting bonfire as the avenging Ayatollah swept above him on wings of gold. If ever a Middle Eastern potentate was so frequently portrayed as the Devil, surely never in Islamic art did a living human—Khomeini—so closely resemble the form of the Deity. Tramping through the snow-swamped streets of Tehran, I was stopped by a schoolboy outside the gates of Tehran University who wanted, for a few rials, to sell me a remarkable example of post-revolutionary graphic art. It was a cardboard face-mask of the Shah, his jowls slack and diseased, his crown kept in place only by two massive black horns. Push out the detachable cardboard eyes, place the mask over your own face and you could peer through the Devil's own image at the black chadors and serious-faced young men of central Tehran. The effect was curious; whenever a stroller purchased a mask—whenever I held it to my own face in the street—the young men would cry *Marg ba Shah*—"Death to the Shah"—with a special intensity. It was as if the cardboard actually assumed the substance of the man; the Devil made flesh.

Khomeini had already returned from Paris, and his Islamic revolution initially seduced the more liberal of our journalistic brethren. Edward Mortimer, an equally beached *Times* journalist—a leader-writer on the paper and a fellow of All Souls, he was also a close friend—caught this false romanticism in its most embarrassing form in an article in *The Spectator* in which he favourably compared the revolution to both the 1789 fall of the Bastille and the 1917 overthrow of the Tsar. To Mortimer, Charles Fox's welcome to the French revolution—"How much the greatest event it is that ever happened in the world! And how much the best!"—seemed "entirely apposite" in the Tehran household among whom he was listening to revolutionary songs broadcast from the newly captured headquarters of Iranian National Radio. The events in Iran, Mortimer wrote, "are a genuine popular revolution in the fullest sense of the word: the most genuine, probably, since 1917 anywhere in the world, perhaps *more* genuinely popular than the Bolshevik revolution was, and quite possibly . . . no less far-reaching in its implications for the rest of the world . . . Khomeini has himself defied religious conservatism, and is therefore most unlikely to want to impose it on the rest of society."

Now this was a journalism of awesome—one might even say suicidal—bravery. While I could not disagree with Edward's remarks on the far-reaching implications of the Iranian revolution, his trust in Khomeini's liberal intentions was born of faith rather than experience. Mossadeq's downfall had demonstrated that only a revolution founded upon the blood of its enemies—as well as the blood of its own martyrs—would survive in Iran. Savak had been blamed for the cinema fire in Abadan in August 1978 in which 419 Iranians were burned alive; the Shah, his enemies claimed, wanted Muslim revolutionaries to be accused of the massacre. Each period of mourning had been followed by ever-larger protest demonstrations and ever-greater slaughter. Street marches in Tehran were more than a million strong. Revolutionary literature still claims that the Shah's army killed 4,000 demonstrators in Jaleh Square in Tehran on 8 September. When Ayatollah Khomeini arrived back in Iran from Paris—the French, who had provided the wine for the Shah at Persepolis, provided Khomeini with the aircraft to fly him home—he was at once taken by helicopter to the cemetery of Behesht-i-Zahra. Four days later, on 5 February 1979, he announced a provisional government headed by Mehdi Bazargan. Iran might still become a democracy, but it would also be a necrocracy: government of, by and for the dead.

And once the martyrs of the revolution had been honoured, it was time for the Shah's men to pay the price. Each morning in Tehran I would wake to a newspaper front page of condemned men, of Savak interrogators slumping before firing squads or twisting from gallows. By 9 March, there had been forty death sentences handed down by revolutionary courts. None of his 60,000 agents could save Nimatollah Nassiri, the head of Savak; grey-haired, naked and diminutive, he lay on a mortuary stretcher, a hole through the right side of his chest. This was the same Nassiri who had brought the Shah's firman to Mossadeq to resign in 1953, the same Nassiri who had arranged the visits of Ben Gurion, Dayan and Rabin to Tehran. General Jaffar Qoli Sadri, Tehran's chief of police—once head of the notorious Komiteh prison—was executed, along with Colonel Nasser Ghavami, the head of the Tehran bazaar police station, and a man accused of being one of Savak's most savage torturers at Qasr prison, Captain Qassem Jahanpanar. All three had been sentenced in the evening and executed within twelve hours.

Many who faced the firing squad that March were found guilty of shooting at demonstrators during the great anti-Shah marches. On 11 March, Lieutenant Ahmed Bahadori was shot for killing protesters in Hamadan. In Abadan, four more ex-policemen were executed for killing a nineteen-year-old youth during demonstrations. On 13 March, revolutionary courts sent another thirteen men accused of being censors and secret police agents to the firing squad. Among them were Mahmoud Jaafarian, the Sorbonne-educated head of the Iranian National News Agency, and former television director Parviz Nikkhah. Before his death, fifty-six-year-old Jaafarian would say only that "I hope when I die my family and my countrymen will live in freedom." Nikkhah was believed to be the journalist who wrote the inflammatory article against Khomeini that provoked the first bloody religious riots in the holy city of Qom in 1978. One newspaper carried photographs of all eleven with their names written on cardboard around their necks. Jaafarian stares without hope at the camera. Nikkhah looks angrily to the right. The eyes of one ex-secret policeman are directed at the floor. In their minds, they must already be dead. *Kayhan* published two pictures of former Qom police officer Agha Hosseini. In one, he is tied to a ladder, his eyes covered in a white cloth, his mouth open and his teeth gritted as he prepares to receive the first bullets. In the other, his knees have buckled and he sags against the ladder.

Mehdi Bazargan appeared on television, condemning the kangaroo trials as a disgrace to "a wonderful revolution of religious and human values." Bazargan was angered in April when he heard that the Shah's former prime minister Amir Abbas Hoveyda had been taken from his prison—in which the Shah had confined him in a last attempt to curry favour with the revolution before fleeing the country himself—and charged with "corruption on earth" and "a battle against God." Only hours before Hoveyda was to go before a firing squad, Bazargan drove at speed to Qom to speak to Khomeini, who immediately set new rules for revolutionary courts. To no avail.

Hoveyda, an intellectual, urbane man whose interests included Bach, Oscar Wilde and James Bond and whose contempt for the corruption surrounding the Shah had earned him the trust of statesmen and diplomats—but not of ordinary Iranians—had been brought to the revolutionary court from his bed at Qasr prison just before midnight, bleary-eyed and pleading that "my doctor has given me a sedative and I can hardly talk, let alone defend myself properly." But he knew what was coming. "If your orders are for me to get condemned, then I have nothing more to say. The life of an individual is not worth much against the life of a whole nation." What does a "battle against God" mean? Hoveyda asked the court. If it meant that he was a member of the "system," then up to 700,000 people had worked in the Shah's civil service. "I had a share in this system—call it the regime of a battle against God if you so wish—and so did you and all the others," he told the court. He wanted time to gather evidence in his defence. "My hand is unstained both by blood and money," he pleaded. " . . . You have brought me here as prime minister while five prime ministers have left the country. Couldn't I also be walking on the Champs Elysées or in the streets of New York?" He had no control over Savak, he said. "In all Savak papers, if you find a single document showing that the prime minister had any role in the organisation, then I shall say no more in my defence." Hoveyda turned to the reporters in the audience. "What's the news?" he asked them. "I haven't seen any papers or heard the radio for some time."

Hoveyda was eventually sentenced to death as a "doer of mischief on earth." Immediately after the sentence, Ayatollah Sadeq Khalkhali, the "hanging judge" of the revolution, disconnected the telephones in the prison, locked the doors, and had Hoveyda dragged into the prison yard, tied to a stake and shot. "The first bullets hit him in the neck but did not kill him," William Shawcross wrote in his gripping account of the Shah's last days. "He was ordered by his executioner, a mullah, to hold up his head. The next bullet hit him in the head and he died." *Paris Match* was to carry a photograph of his corpse with a grinning gunman looking at it. Alongside, the magazine carried a picture of the exiled royal family swimming on Paradise Island. Put not your trust in Shahs.

In those early days of the revolution, Iran was in too much anarchy for the new authorities to control journalists. Revolutionary Guards on the roads would send foreign reporters back to Tehran, but they never thought to look for us on the trains. And with a student card—I was using my free time during the stoppage at *The Times* to take a Ph.D. in politics at Trinity College, Dublin—I bought an all-rail card that allowed me to travel across Iran by train. They were long revolutionary trains, the windows smashed, portraits of Khomeini and poster tulips—symbols of martyrdom—plastered over the rolling stock, their restaurant cars serving chicken, rice and tea for breakfast, lunch and dinner. Unable to write for my own newspaper, I sent a long letter to Ivan Barnes, the foreign news editor, to describe Iran's unfinished revolution. The Shah's acolytes, I told him, had usually been insufferably arrogant.

I found that this arrogance had disappeared with the revolution. I was treated with courtesy and kindness almost everywhere I went and found Iranians much more aware of the implications of world events than . . . the inhabitants of Arab countries. There was a straightforward quality about Iranians in the country as well as the towns that I couldn't help admiring. They were thirsting to talk about anything. The only trouble I had was on the train to Qum [*sic*] when a gang of Islamic Guards (green armbands and M-16 rifles) opened the compartment door and saw me recording a cassette with train sounds. I was immediately accused of being a CIA spy (what else?) but explained that I was a journalist working for Canadian radio. The interpreter, a leftist student who travelled with me everywhere . . . repeated the same thing and they relaxed a bit. I had been told in Tehran to always say *Deroot do Khomeini, marg ba Shah!* to anyone nasty ("Long live Khomeini, death to the Shah!"). I said my piece, at which the Khomeini guards all raised their right fists in the air and shouted their approval. Then they all shook hands with me with giant smiles and tramped off down the train to torment someone in another compartment.

From the desert to the north, Qom stands like an island of distant gold, the cupolas of its mosques and its plump, generous minarets an oasis of beauty at dawn. Like the spires of a medieval English university, its ancient centre appears to reach up to heaven. But my train pulled in after dark, the suburbs thick with exhaust and dust and vast crowds, dark-jacketed, bearded men and black-veiled women moving like a tide towards a grim red-brick building surrounded by big, muscular men with automatic rifles. My leftist student friend turned to me. "There is a trial," he shouted. "They are trying one of the Shah's men." I dumped my bag in a hotel crammed between shops opposite the Friday Mosque, pulled out my old clunker of a tape recorder and ran back to what was already called the "court."

Warrant Officer Rustomi of the Shah's Imperial Army sat on a metal-framed chair on the stage of the revolutionary court, his hands clasped in front of him and his gaze fixed on the wooden floor of the converted theatre where he was now on trial. He was a middle-aged man and wore an untidy grey-brown beard. He had long ago been stripped of his artillery regiment uniform, and he appeared in court in a creased green anorak and a pair of dirty jeans, a crumpled figure relieved only by the snappy pair of built-up French shoes on his feet. He looked for all the world like a bored defendant awaiting judgement for a minor traffic offence rather than a man who was waiting only for the legal niceties—if "legal" was the right word—of a death sentence. He was accused of killing anti-Shah demonstrators.

The Islamic court in Qom had dispatched its fifth victim to the firing squad only six hours earlier. He was a local policeman accused of killing demonstrators in the revolution, the man who had appeared on the newspaper front page, tied to the ladder, gritting his teeth in front of the firing squad. Someone had cruelly shown the newspaper to Rustomi; maybe it was the inevitability of his sentence that made him so calm, sitting up there on the platform above us. Every few minutes he would take a packet of American cigarettes out of his pocket, and a gunman with a rifle—yes, an American rifle—slung over his shoulder would step over to him obligingly with a match. Rustomi dragged heavily on the cigarettes and glanced occasionally over towards us with a kind of lifelessness in his eyes.

There were more than 600 men—no women—in the audience and most of them were talking of that morning's execution, although it was difficult to understand why the event should have occasioned any excitement. There had been no acquittals in the revolutionary courts and the only punishment handed out had been death. The crowd had come to watch the prisoner, to see if he cried or pleaded for life or walked defiantly to the firing squad, to watch the mighty fallen. George Bernard Shaw once claimed that if Christians were thrown to the lions in the Royal Albert Hall in London there would be a packed house each night. These excited men in the audience must have been wearing the same faces as the mobs that gathered before the guillotine during the French revolution.

You could see why death would be the only possible sentence as soon as Rustomi's trial started. An Islamic priest in long brown robes and a civilian lawyer appointed by the mosque walked onto the stage of the converted theatre and announced that they were to act as prosecuting counsel and judges. Rustomi did not even glance at them. They sat at two iron desks and behind them, fixed on to a starlike design of strip lights, was a crude oil painting of Ayatollah Khomeini. There was no doubt under whose authority this court was sitting.

The mullah made a brief address to the crowd, stating that the trial would be held according to the rules of the Koran, and that the prisoner should be allowed to reply to the charges against him. The mullah was a tall, distinguished man with a long white beard and a kind, honest face. The civilian lawyer looked angry and vindictive, and said something abusive to Rustomi before he sat down. The mullah waved a sheaf of papers in his hand; a series of written testaments by witnesses to anti-Shah demonstrations, each claiming that Rustomi had ordered his company of soldiers to fire at civilians.

One by one, the witnesses were called from the audience to give their evidence—a process occasionally interrupted by shouting at the back of the theatre where more men were pushing their way through the doors and fighting for places in the court. Rustomi pulled his chair up to the mullah's desk and listened. The first witness was a young man with his shoulder in plaster and the second witness limped onto the stage. They had seen Rustomi order his men to fire at the demonstrators, they claimed, and a third man ran onto the stage and yelled that Rustomi had broken through the door of a mosque and killed a boy hiding in the shrine. There was much discussion of dates and street names—there was, in fact, a genuine if chaotic attempt to define the events surrounding the shooting—before Rustomi stood up.

The crowd bayed at him and for several seconds the mullah did nothing. Rustomi looked down at us with an uncomprehending expression. He wanted to talk. Yes, he said, he had ordered his men to disperse the demonstrators, but he had told them to fire into the air. If anyone had been hit, it must have been a ricochet. There was a momentary silence in the court before another man, scarcely twenty years old, clambered onto the stage and pointed at Rustomi. "You're lying, you bastard," he screamed, before the judge ordered him off.

Rustomi fought his corner against obviously impossible odds. He had no defence counsel. He admitted that on another date, he had indeed fired his rifle into a crowd of people who were demanding the overthrow of the Shah. He had questioned the orders to open fire, he said, over his two-way radio, but his major had threatened him with a court martial if he did not obey. At this, an old man in the theatre leapt to his feet. "The Holy Koran does not allow any man to take that attitude," he shouted. "If a Muslim kills another Muslim in those circumstances he is not true to his religion." The old man went on and on, abusing Rustomi, and the mullah with the wise, kindly face nodded in an agreeable fashion and allowed the abuse to continue. Rustomi seemed on the verge of tears.

Then the civilian lawyer walked round and shouted "Liar!" in the prisoner's ear. For a dreadful moment I was reminded of those scratched archive films of the Nazi People's Court trying the plotters against Hitler's life in 1944 when Judge Roland Freisler swore at the defendants. At the end of the first day in Qom, the civilian lawyer walked over to me smiling. "It's a fair trial we're giving him," he said. "As you can see, we allow Rustomi to answer the charges." The court resumed next morning, and Rustomi watched unhappily as two members of his own riot squad condemned him as a murderer. Another soldier did bravely step forward to defend the prisoner, but he was ordered to shut up after being accused of muddling the date of the incident.

When the mullah called a break for lunch, a man of about thirty walked up to me outside the theatre. He was watched suspiciously by a group of Islamic Guards, gunmen wearing the distinctive green armband that showed they were appointed by the mosque. It turned out to be Rustomi's brother, and he was a frightened man. There was no way we could talk there on the pavement, so we walked down a street together, followed by the gunmen from the court. "Do you think this is a fair trial?" he asked. "My brother has no defence counsel. They told him to find one if he wants, but I have been to Tehran to the committee of lawyers, and I've spoken to twenty lawyers. Not one of them will take his case. This court has killed every prisoner it has tried." There was a sad pause while the man tried to stop himself from weeping. "My brother has a little boy. He has told the other children at his school that he will kill himself if the court killed his father." Then we said goodbye and Rustomi's brother walked off, the gunmen mincing after him. That same afternoon, I asked Ayatollah Kazem Shariatmadari, one of Khomeini's closest advisers, why Rustomi was allowed no defence counsel. The white-bearded Ayatollah sat cross-legged on rich ornamental carpets. "A prisoner at an Islamic court should be allowed a lawyer to defend him," he said. "I do not know what is going on at this trial at Qom—I do not know the circumstances of this trial. I do not know the answer to your question."

He was a gentle old man and a moderate among the divines in the city of Qom. But what did "moderate" mean any more? Shariatmadari simply had no idea what was going on in the courts, and I'm sure he preferred not to find out. I still have the tapes of the old man's excuses and—far more difficult to listen to—the recordings of the "trial," of the lawyer shrieking "Liar!" in Rustomi's ear, of the condemned man trying to explain his military rules, of his brother's tears outside the "court." They carry an authentic, painful reality, of injustice by the many against the few. Khomeini's ruling after Bazargan's frantic visit to Qom did not spare the prisoners brought into the converted theatre. Executions started again the morning after I left Qom, and although the identity of the victims was not at first made clear, one of them was a former soldier in the Shah's army. I knew his name.

There would be no counter-coups in this revolution, no "Operation Ajax," no CIA men operating from within the U.S. embassy to buy up the *bazaaris*. Indeed, very soon there would be no U.S. embassy. The demands for the return of the Shah were being made not for his restoration but in order to put him on trial. Only when the head of the snake had been cut off would the revolution feel safe. Just as the

Americans believed twenty-four years later that only the capture of Saddam Hussein would bring them tranquillity in Iraq, so Khomeini and his retinue were convinced that only the death of the Shah—preferably hanged as a criminal in Iran for "crimes against God"—would free Iran from its corrupt past.* In reality, the Shah was already dying from cancer. Many Iranians saw in his pathetic exile the true justice of God, his cancer the ultimate divine vengeance against one who had "sinned on earth." The Shah's gruesome odyssey through the hospitals of Central America, New York City and, eventually, Cairo gave grim satisfaction to the mullahs who had already ordered his assassination.

Not long after his departure, I had sat at the feet of Sadeq Khalkhali, the "hanging judge," as he listed those of the Shah's family who had been sentenced to death *in absentia*. Around him sat a score or so of Revolutionary Guards who had been maimed in the revolutionary war against the Kurds of north-western Iran, each of them clacking his newly fitted artificial metal fingers, hands and feet as the prelate outlined the fate that so surely awaited his aristocratic enemies. Khalkhali it was who had sentenced a fourteen-year-old boy to death, who had approved of the stoning to death of women in Kermanshah, who earlier, in a mental asylum, would strangle cats in his prison cell. Gorbeh, the "Cat," was what he was called. "The Shah will be strung up—he will be cut down and smashed," the Cat told me. "He is an instrument of Satan."

In fact, the Shah was a poor substitute for the Devil, scarcely even the equal of Faustus; for he sold himself for the promise of worldly military power and seemingly everlasting American support. The chorus of harpies that pursued the Shah halfway around the world were the bickering, greedy surgeons, doctors and nurses who bombarded the dying man with pills, blood platelets and false hope, agents of darkness who only too well represented the technology of the world to whom the Shah had long ago sold his soul. His erstwhile friends from that world—King Hussein of Jordan, King Khaled of Saudi Arabia, King Hassan of Morocco, the Swiss, the Austrians, President Carter and Margaret Thatcher—either terminated his residence, turned him away or broke their promise to accept him when they realised the political cost. It was sobering to reflect that his only true friend—the only potentate to honour his word to Carter when the Americans wanted the old man to leave New York—was President Sadat of Egypt. President Torrijos of Panama—who gave temporary refuge to the Shah and who wanted to seduce Queen Farah but was swiftly given the brush-off by the Shahbanou—produced the pithiest obituary of the "Light of the Aryans." "This is what happens to a man squeezed by the great nations," he said. "After all the juice is gone, they throw him away."

In the event, the Shah died in Cairo on 27 July 1980 and was lowered into a modest tomb in the al-Rifai mosque. Six years later, in the heat of summer, I went

---

*There were other odd parallels with America's later disaster in Iraq. The Shah, while still in power, always insisted that his enemies were "communists" and "fanatics." President Bush was always claiming that America's enemies were "Saddam remnants" and "foreign terrorists." Neither the Shah nor Bush could admit that they faced a popular domestic insurgency.

with an Iranian friend to look at his tomb. It was midday and there was only one guardian in the mosque, an old, silver-haired man who, for a pittance, promised to take us into the last resting place of the man who thought he was the spiritual descendant of Cyrus the Great. There was a single marble slab and, resting upon it, a handwritten poem declaring eternal faith in the Shah from a member of the Javidan Guards. A spray of withered roses lay on the tomb. The old guardian wandered up to us and muttered "*Baksheesh*." He settled for 50 piastres. In the end, it cost the equivalent of 40 cents to sit at the feet of the King of Kings.

The Islamic revolutionaries who now emerged behind Ayatollah Khomeini were oddly middle-class. Men like Sadeq Qotbzadeh, the head of the television service, later foreign minister—and later still, executed for allegedly plotting against the Ayatollah—were graduates of American universities. They spoke English with American accents, which meant that they could appear surprisingly at ease on the U.S. television networks. Many, like the new deputy prime minister Amir Abbas Entezam, flaunted their un-proletarian origins. "I am proud that this has been a middle-class revolution," Entezam announced to me one day. He leaned forward in his chair and tapped his chest. "I'm proud of that," he repeated. By ministerial standards, his was a modest office with only two desks, a sofa, a clutter of chairs and a telephone that purred unanswered in the corner. It would have been difficult to find anyone more middle-class than Entezam, with his American education and well-travelled career as an engineer. Yet in his way, he was telling the truth. For while the physical power behind the revolution lay in those colossal street demonstrations by the urban poor and the Islamic revivalists, it was the middle class from the bazaar, the tens of thousands of merchants from the Middle East's largest souk whom the Shah tried to tame with a system of guilds, that provided the economic backing for Khomeini's return. It was this merchant class and its alliance with the mullahs that emerged as the critical combination of secular and religious opposition.

That is why Iran's revolution had until now generally avoided the more traditional path of such events, the looting of the homes and property of the rich. That is why you could still take a taxi across Tehran and drive into the northern suburbs beneath the mountains to find that the luxury apartments and opulent town houses with their tree-shaded verandas and goldfish ponds had been left untouched. Accumulated wealth had not been appropriated by the state. By late March of 1979, however, this had begun to change. In the north of Iran, around the Caspian, factories were being taken over by workers—leftists had led the revolution east of Kurdistan and the mosque had never held sway there—and property was confiscated. The interim government appointed by Khomeini was receiving reports of further confiscations near Mashad and the pattern was beginning to spread to Tehran.

Just over a week earlier, Faribourz Attapour, one of the city's most prolific and outspoken journalists, was told that his father had been arrested. It turned out that Attapour Senior, who owned a small estate on the Caspian coast, had walked into his local Tehran bank to cash a cheque and had been detained by the cashier, who thought that if his customer looked rich then he must indeed be wealthy—and that if he was indeed wealthy, then he must also be corrupt. Old Mr. Attapour, who had been a soldier in the Imperial Army but retired from military service twenty-seven years earlier, was seventy years old and deeply in debt. Nonetheless, he was collected from the bank by a heavily armed revolutionary *komiteh* and freighted off to the Qasr prison. At least, that is where Faribourz Attapour thought his father was being held.

No official statement had been issued by the *komiteh* and even the government could not gain access to the jail. There were now an estimated 8,000 prisoners inside—there had been around 2,000 at the time of the Shah—and it took the Red Cross several weeks to gain admission. So it was not surprising that Attapour was angry. "This revolution has deteriorated into petty vengeance and tyranny," he said. "It can only be compared to the Jacobin Terror of the French revolution. The merchants in the bazaar have more money than my father but they do not care about his fate. Nor do the so-called religious leaders. I spoke on the telephone to the local ayatollah from our area of the Caspian and he said that my father must be corrupt because he was rich. He would not even let me answer his accusation on the telephone. He just hung up."

Attapour was daily expecting his own arrest, but three days after we spoke his journalistic voice was silenced when Tehran's two English-language newspapers announced that they were suspending publication. *The Tehran Journal*, for which Attapour wrote, gave economic reasons for its closure but for weeks revolutionary *komitehs* had been denouncing the paper as "anti-Islamic." Most of the staff had received anonymous phone calls threatening their lives. Attapour's parallel with the French revolution—so much at variance with Edward Mortimer's enthusiasm—was not lost on the most dogmatic of Iran's new regime. Dr. Salamatian, a political aide at the foreign ministry, found an agreeable comparison. There were fewer executions in Iran than in the French or Russian revolutions, he said. When I pointed out to him that there were no firing squads at all after the 1974 Portuguese revolution, he snapped back at me: "But in Portugal they were only getting rid of Caetano—we have been overthrowing more than two thousand years of monarchy." This was a curious response, since the idea that Persia had lived under a seamless monarchy for 2,300 years was a figment of the Shah's imagination, a myth propagated to justify his authoritarian rule.

That this rule *was* authoritarian was one of the few common denominators among those who supported the revolution, for the Left in Iran already realised that the clerics were installing themselves in power. "Why condemn us for hunting down the Shah's murderers?" Salamatian asked. "In the West, you kept the Nazi Rudolf Hess in prison in Germany. We regard the agents of Savak as Nazi-type criminals. You in the West put Nazis on trial. Why shouldn't we put our Nazis on trial?"

And how could one argue with this when reporters like Derek Ive of the Associated Press had managed, very briefly, to look inside a Savak agent's house just before the revolution was successful? He entered the building when a crowd stormed through the front door. "There was a fish-pond outside," he told me. "There were vases of flowers in the front hall. But downstairs there were cells. In each of them was a steel bed with straps and beneath it two domestic cookers. There were lowering devices on the bed frames so that the people strapped to them could be brought down onto the flames. In another cell, I found a machine with a contraption which held a human arm beneath a knife and next to it was a metal sheath into which a human hand could be fitted. At one end was a bacon slicer. They had been shaving off people's hands." Ive found a pile of human arms in a corner and in a further cell he discovered pieces of a corpse floating in several inches of what appeared to be acid. Just before the Shah's soldiers burst back into the rear of the building, he snatched some quick photographs of the torture apparatus.

After the revolution, we were able to meet some of the Shah's top Savak agents. Sitting in Evin prison in their open-neck shirts, winter cardigans and corduroys, drawing nervously on American cigarettes, the eighteen prisoners looked nothing like the popular image of secret policemen. From the moment they were brought into the room—a dingy, rectangular office that doubled on occasions as a revolutionary court—these middle-aged, over-friendly men either smiled or just stared at us as government officials described them as criminals.

But they had disturbing and sometimes frightening stories to tell. Hassan Sana, the economic and security adviser to the deputy head of Savak, talked of British intelligence cooperation with the Shah, a friendly liaison which, he claimed, prompted British agents to pass to their Iranian counterparts information about Iranian students in Britain. Sana, a chainsmoker with dark glasses and an apparent passion for brightly coloured shirts, said that British assistance enabled Savak to watch or arrest students on their return to Tehran from London.

He spoke, too, of how Savak agents were flown from New York by the CIA for lessons in interrogation techniques at a secret American military base, a mysterious journey that took four hours flying across the United States in an aircraft with darkened windows. We had earlier toured the Savak interrogation centre in central Tehran, where former inmates described how they had been tortured. A black-tiled room with a concrete floor was all that remained of the chamber—almost identical to the one Ive had discovered—where prisoners were roasted on beds over gas burners. In Evin, for one terrible moment, Mohamed Sadafi—a Savak agent who had been a weightlifter—was confronted by a man whose daughter died in Sadafi's personal custody.

"You killed my daughter," the man shouted. "She was burned all over her flesh until she was paralysed. She was roasted." Sadafi glanced briefly at the man. "Your daughter hanged herself after seven months in custody," he replied quietly. The father said there was not even a sheet in the prison from which an inmate could hang herself. Yes there was, Sadafi said. He had himself seen the laundry bills at Evin.

Upon such horror the Shah's regime was maintained, and upon such fearful scenes the revolution was fuelled. If there was a cause for surprise in Iran at this early stage of the new regime, it was not that the revolution had claimed so many victims among the Shah's retinue but that it had claimed so few. But the revolution was unfinished. It was not going to end at that friendly bourgeois stage at which the Portuguese grew tired, nor was there any common ground between the new Islamic Republic and the people's democracy that Iranian left-wing groups had been propagating. The Left was now more active—there were fire-fights in the streets every night—and the situation would only be exacerbated by Iran's constantly worsening social conditions. Even Khomeini described the country as "a slum."*

The security authorities of the new Islamic state remained convinced, however, that some in the new government regarded the United States as a potential partner rather than the "Great Satan" of the street demonstrations.

And they were right. After the U.S. embassy was seized in November 1979 by the "Muslim Students following the Line of the Imam," Iranian security men found tons of shredded U.S. diplomatic correspondence which they spent months reconstructing by laboriously pasting documents back together. The papers included an embarrassing quantity of material about Abbas Amir Entezam, the deputy prime minister, and his contacts with the U.S. government. At first this was on a formal basis—the American embassy remained open after the revolution and U.S. officials routinely met Iranian foreign ministry staff to arrange the repatriation of American military staff and civilians—and the embassy told Entezam in March 1979 that "the United States desires to normalize its relations with Iran at a steady pace." Entezam replied, according to the documents, that "his government also wanted a good relationship with the United States . . . the prime minister, Bazargan . . . had recently expressed this sentiment publicly."

Within a few days, however, Entezam was expressing his government's desire to "share intelligence information with USG [U.S. Government]." The Americans had, incredibly, already given Entezam a "paper on Afghanistan"—the Iranians were increasingly fearful that the Soviet Union might invade their eastern neighbour—but now Entezam explained that his government was more concerned about "internal security threats." According to the U.S. embassy report of a further meeting in May, Entezam said that "PGOI [Provisional Government of Iran] was concerned about possible meddling by Iraqis in Khuzestan province as well as activities of PLO and Libyans." Entezam said that "PGOI had information that George Habash [the leader of the Syrian-supported Popular Front for the Liberation of Palestine] had recently visited several Gulf countries . . . presumably with a view to causing trouble for Iran." The PLO's office in the southern Iranian city of Ahwaz was also causing concern but "shaking his head, he [Entezam] said his

---

*There were now 3.5 million people out of work—about 25 per cent of the workforce—and 50 per cent of the population lived in grossly overcrowded cities. The food shortages were not just caused by Khomeini's insistence that Muslims should in future refuse to eat frozen meat; they were brought about by Iran's proud refusal to import more foreign goods. Yet until the previous winter, the country had been relying on $2 billion of imported foodstuffs.

government could do nothing about it . . . because it was Khomeini's desire that it be opened."

This was incendiary material. Here was Entezam—who only a few weeks earlier was boasting to me about the "middle-class" nature of the revolution—discussing Iran's security fears with the CIA; not only revealing his own intelligence information but expressing his exasperation with the most revered Islamic figure in the country for endangering that security. In June, Entezam was asking for U.S. information on "Iraqi intentions towards Iran." By this time, there had been frequent artillery exchanges across the Iran–Iraq border, and the U.S. embassy chargé, "after remarking that he was not sure who cast the first stone . . . speculated on the possibility of the Iraqis attempting to create a 'prickly hedge' along Iraq's border with Iran *à la* one-time British policy on the Durand Line."

Bruce Laingen, the American chargé, held further meetings with Entezam and within weeks Entezam—known in the U.S. cable traffic by the rather unromantic code-name "SD/PLOD/1"—was receiving direct visits from senior CIA officials. When he became an Iranian ambassador based in Sweden, Entezam was given an intelligence briefing by CIA agent George Cave, who was later to be a leading figure in the 1985–86 Contra scandal. In Tehran there had been further meetings between the CIA and Bazargan, Entezam and Ibrahim Yazdi, the Iranian foreign minister. Cave himself later visited Tehran and agreed with Entezam that there should be briefings—again, I quote the reconstructed documents—"every three to six months, with spot information being passed if particularly important. Entezam asked if there could be a contact in Tehran to exchange information on a regular basis. (Note: Cave was introduced as senior briefing officer from intelligence community. Term CIA was never used.)"

When the American embassy in Tehran was invaded after the Shah had been admitted to the United States, the explosive nature of Entezam's CIA contacts was revealed in the shredded files that the young Iranian men and women were painstakingly pasting back together. Bazargan and Yazdi were discredited and Entezam arrested and put on trial for treason, barely escaping execution when he was given a life sentence in 1981. Entezam always maintained that he was a true revolutionary merely seeking to maintain relations with the Americans in the interests of Iran.

Massoumeh Ebtekar, among the principal "invaders" of the embassy, saw it quite differently. "The CIA apparently believed that it could manipulate any revolution or political establishment if it could successfully infiltrate its top ranks early on," she was to write. "In Iran, the agency was particularly intent on doing so. After all, it had plenty of past experience." According to Ebtekar, the "students of the Imam" also found counterfeit identity cards and passports for CIA agents in the embassy, including stamps and seals for airport entry and exit visas in Europe and Asia, as well as 1,000 false Ghanaian passports. Other documents dealt with pro-monarchists "who were involved in terror killings." But if another Operation Ajax was ever considered in Washington, it surely died in November 1979.

Our own life in those early weeks of the Islamic Republic was not without its humour. As long as Iran kept to the system of free visas operating under the Shah, we could enter and leave Iran as often as we wished—I even flew to Dublin for a weekend break, leaving Tehran on a Friday morning, returning by Monday night—and only slowly did the regime's new laws affect us. For months, at the Intercontinental Hotel in Tehran—later renamed Laleh, "Rose," after the symbol of revolution—we could still drink vodka with blinis. But the ban on alcohol was quickly imposed. I still possess a memorable note from the Tehran hotel management pushed under my door on 21 March 1979. "Due to the limited supply of alcoholic beverages in the country and the unexpected [*sic*] in the mark-ups in the price of these itesm [*sic*]," it said, "the management has no alternative but to a 20% increase. Thank you." Not long afterwards, a revolutionary *komiteh* invited journalists to watch the destruction of the remaining stocks of Satanic alcohol in the hotel's cellars. As film cameras whirred, gunmen hurled Pol Roger champagne bottles into the bottom of the empty swimming pool, along with the finest French wines and upended boxes of Gordon's gin. From the two-foot-deep field of glass at the bottom of the pool, the stench of alcohol permeated the hotel for days afterwards. A South Korean restaurant continued to elude the authorities, its staff burying cases of German beer in their garden. Clients had to wait for ten minutes until each beer can arrived at their table covered in earth.

And the middle classes so beloved of Entezam continued to entertain. One evening I was invited to dinner at a villa of marble stone floors and tasteless pseudo-baroque paintings in north Tehran where a young couple entertained several Iranian writers and myself with poetry-reading and a meal of pre-revolutionary abundance, along with obligatory glasses of home-made vodka. I was intrigued by the attractive hostess because she was rumoured to have been one of the Shah's last mistresses. Whenever the Shah wished to make love to a woman, it was said, she would be invited to a side door of his palace, would spend two hours with him in a discreet salon and—before leaving—would be presented with a Labrador puppy dog as a token of the King of Kings' affection. Given the grotesque reputation of the man, I often wondered why Tehran was not populated with hundreds of stray Labradors. I had dismissed all such thoughts when the dinner ended and I was saying goodbye to my hosts. It was at this moment that the kitchen door burst open and something vast and furry catapulted into me, to the consternation of the couple. I looked up to see the friendly face of a yellow Labrador, looking at me as if it had spent all evening waiting to make my acquaintance.

Just what life for the Shah was like emerged when the new information ministry, rejoicing in the name of the "Ministry of Islamic Guidance," asked us to take a look at the Niavaran Palace in north Tehran. If Richard the Third really did offer his kingdom for a horse, then the Shah of Iran paid for his freedom with a clutch of palaces, a heap of priceless Persian carpets, a Marc Chagall sketch, a 22-carat gold seventeenth-century model of a Chinese slave ship, a two-storey library, a set of pianos that would send a music college into ecstasy and two solid gold telephones.

Standing beneath the silver birches on the windy lawn of the Niavaran, an Iranian government official made one of the more historic sales of the century sound like nothing but a momentary hiccup in the progress of the revolution—which was what it would turn out to be. "We will put the contents up for auction," he announced. "Then the palaces will be turned into museums." So we were left to watch a turbaned mullah and two men armed with G3 automatic rifles as they pulled and tugged a 30-foot-square handwoven crimson-and-gold Isfahan rug across the inlaid wooden floor of the Shah's drawing room. Oriental princesses, plumed birds and exotic beasts of prey were tangled through the arabesque embroideries and each carpet was neatly tagged with an inventory number: proof that while the revolution might have its ups and downs, Iran's new rulers had a head for efficiency. In the previous few weeks, the Shah's carpets had reportedly raised $15 million.

One had to admit that the Shah had the most dreadful taste in furniture. French baroque chairs nestled against glass and steel tables while the most grotesque urns—mutated by some silversmith's black magic into ugly peahens—sat upon desks of delicately carved and mosaic-encrusted wood. Walls of cut glass with a powdering of dust upon them suggested a British cinema of the 1930s. This was how the Shah and his wife left their palace in January 1979 when they set off for a "holiday" and eternal exile.

Fate does not usually vouchsafe to ordinary folk the right to roam around a Shah's gilded palace, and strange things happen when mere mortals are let loose among such opulence. When the international press were invited into what Abolhassan Sadeq of the guidance ministry sarcastically called "the Shah's slum," there were scenes befitting the Ostrogoth descent on Rome. We tripped over piles of carpets and surged into the great library to discover what the Shah read in his spare time. There were leather-bound volumes of Voltaire, Verlaine, Flaubert, Plutarch, Shakespeare and Charles de Gaulle. The entire works of Winston Churchill rested against Coleridge's *Rime of the Ancient Mariner*—a work the Shah might have found suitable reading on his long journey of exile—and biographies of Mahatma Gandhi. *My People* by Abba Eban, the former Israeli foreign minister—in fact, his book was partly written by an editor of *Commentary* magazine—lay on a lowly shelf with the author's handwritten dedication to "His Imperial Majesty, the Shah of Shahs." On another rack were the Goebbels diaries.

In the Shah's personal office, the guards could scarce restrain us from dialling a line on the golden telephones. On a balcony above the living room, a youth with a rifle over his shoulder watched with an expression of perceptible concern while I played an execrable two-finger version of Bach's *Air on a G String* on a harpsichord presented to the Shah by King Baudouin and Queen Fabiola of the Belgians. Souvenir-hunters would be able to bid for the toys that once belonged to Princess Leila, the Shah's eight-year-old daughter. Miniature aircraft and toy bears lay near a cupboard not far from her four-poster bed. On a sideboard, there was a photograph of the American president's family with a handwritten greeting: "With best wishes, Rosalynn and Amy Carter." A blackboard carried Leila's first efforts at writing in chalk the European version of Arabic numerals. In the Shah's study, the desk calendar still registered 16 January, the day on which the monarch left his realm. In the golden ashtray I found five dusty cigarette ends, testimony to the last depressed hours of imperial rule.

We had been taken earlier to the slums of south Tehran in a heavy-handed though quite effective effort by the guidance ministry to point up the different lifestyles of the Shah and his people. Children played upon the earth floor of No. 94 Gord Najhin Place and women carried their washing over open drains. Tehran's slums were less poverty-encrusted than Cairo's tenements and the Shah's palace was modest by Saudi standards. But we got the point—even if the smell of sewage did mix oddly with the expensive perfumes of the ministry girls.

There was much that was odd about Tehran. The sheer normality of the great, dirty, traffic-clogged city was more astounding than the crisis in Iranian–American relations. For all the talk of fanatical mobs and economic chaos, I could still catch the Number 20 bus—a green-painted Leyland double-decker—into the centre of town, go shopping for French clothes in expensive stores or call in for a snack at the local Kentucky Fried Chicken. Iranians weaned on the American way of life could no longer buy Skippy peanut butter or Kraft cheese spread at the Forshagh Bozorg department store and, in keeping with Khomeini's views on the general appearance of women, French and American cosmetics had been banned. Tehran was not an attractive city by either Western or oriental standards. Its square blocks and the architectural poverty of the shop façades built in the 1960s gave the place a sterile, curiously eastern European air. Even Tehranis, however, were still having problems with their city's political geography, for nearly every main street in the capital had undergone an identity change in accordance with revolutionary instructions. Thus Pahlavi Street disappeared to become Dr. Hossein Fatimi Street, named after Mossadeq's foreign minister, who was executed two months after Operation Ajax.*

The Reuters news agency bureau in Tehran became a place of spiritual repair. When I first pushed open the door, I found its bureau chief, Harvey Morris, surrounded by clouds of thick cigarette smoke with an open bottle of Scotch on his desk and a look of pained surprise on his face. With his Mark Twain moustache and unruly hair, Harvey found the revolution as outrageous as it was brave, as farcical as it was cruel. He had to protect his staff from the *komitehs*, keep his Iranian freelancers out of prison and soft-soap the Ministry of Islamic Guidance. And it was the ministry that was causing him his latest crisis. "They've told me they want to know the history of the Reuters news agency," he announced with a frown. "So the great and the good at my London office have just sent me a tome about our esteemed founder, Paul Julius, Freiherr von Reuter, to give to the ministry. But it

---

*These changes were nothing to the problems afflicting the editors of the *Times Atlas* in London. On 13 December, I received a message from Barry Winkleman of Times Books asking for the new names of Pahlavidezh in Kurdistan, Reza Shah Pahlavi reservoir north of Dezful and Shahreza south of Isfahan. In Tehran, he wanted to know, "what was the old name of Taleghani Avenue?" Answer: Takht-e-Jamshid Street.

turns out that the good baron built half the bloody railways in this country and the Reuter Concession of 1872 granted British subjects a monopoly over the entire economic and financial resources of Iran. Christ! How can I tell the arseholes at the ministry that the founder of our news agency was worse than the fucking Shah?"

I saw his point. But Harvey was a smart guy, his laid-back, tired appearance a disguise behind which lay an able, humorous and sometimes a wicked mind. I would drop by to punch my copy on his wire machine each evening and tell him what I'd learned from my day's street reporting or my travels outside Tehran. He would tip me off on press conferences or scandals—like the one in which television head Qotbzadeh ordered his secretary to photocopy a bunch of official papers in which she had found a letter from his French mistress. The letter was duplicated a thousand times. My hotel phone would sometimes ring in the morning with a call from Harvey. "Fisky, you might just like to know that Khalkhali's lads have topped another bunch of folk for being 'corrupt on earth.' " Or, more frequently, he'd announce that there was "a demonstration outside the American embassy—better you than me!"

It is strange that the seizure of the U.S. embassy and its aftermath should have become so tedious an assignment for journalists. After all, it was to lead to an abortive U.S. military rescue mission and, ultimately, the destruction of Carter's presidency. It created a burning sense of humiliation within subsequent U.S. administrations that led America into a series of political and military disasters in the Middle East. Most of the U.S. diplomats and other American hostages remained captive for 444 days; they were only freed after the U.S. and Iranian governments agreed on a series of complex economic and banking arrangements, at which point the captives were taken to Mehrabad airport and escorted out of Iran by Algerian commandos.

Perhaps it was the impossible equation which the embassy occupation represented. The Americans were no more going to hand the Shah back to Iranian "justice" than the Iranians were going to release their captives until Washington had been sufficiently humbled. Removing the Shah from his New York hospital bed and dumping him in Panama was not going to satisfy the revolutionaries in Tehran. And so each day we would watch the tens of thousands of demonstrators, students, armed guards and members of Muslim organisations streaming past the embassy—now officially referred to as the "U.S. Nest of Spies"—hurling to heaven their demand for the Shah's immediate return and condemning President Jimmy Carter as a "warmonger." They became familiar to the point of monotony. Their cry of "Down with the Carter, Down with the Shah" would be taken up for six or seven minutes, interspersed with "Yankee go home." Hamburger stands, beetroot-juice sellers and postcard stalls cluttered the roadside.

The crowds were strategically placed to catch the television cameras, and journalists were allowed—indeed, encouraged—to approach the embassy and stare through the black wrought-iron gates. The hostages locked in the main embassy buildings—the men with their hands tied—could not be seen, although students had spray-painted slogans on the roof of the reception block. Just inside the fore-court, they now erected a painting 5 metres high, a symbolic work inspired by Joe Rosenthal's photograph of U.S. Marines raising the Stars and Stripes on Iwo Jima in 1945; in this case, however, Muslim revolutionaries had replaced the marines and they were struggling to raise a green Islamic flag, one end of which had mirac-ulously turned into a hand strangling the Stars and Stripes. The occupation had thus become theatre, complete with painted scenery. It was more than this. It was a carnival.

It was also a mistake to believe that this represented a falsehood. Individual Iranians expressed their contempt for the Shah all too eloquently—and all too often in American accents. "You wanna know why we want the damned Shah?" a student at Tehran Polytechnic University asked me. "Well, I tell you—it's 'cos that man stole fifty billion dollars from Iran." An Iranian air force private wandered up to join our conversation. "That bastard staged the biggest heist in history," he said. The airman's accent sounded like east side New York City, and it said more about Iran's relationship with America than any amount of political rhetoric. Never before, it seemed, had so many revolutionaries lived, worked or been educated in the country which they now held responsible for so much of their past suffering.*

During the Shah's rule, there were sometimes half a million Iranians in the United States. Many were at American universities or colleges; some were escap-ing from the Shah's regime. Many thousands were undergoing military training; one of the perks available to Iranian army officers was a regular free trip to New York on an Iranian air force jet. Dr. Ibrahim Yazdi, who had just resigned as for-eign minister, worked for seventeen years as a doctor in America, associating with Iranian students opposed to the Shah. Dr. Mustafa Chamran, who had been appointed assistant prime minister in July 1979 and was to die a "martyr" in the Iran–Iraq War, helped set up the Islamic Students Association in America in 1962, together with Yazdi and Sadeq Qotbzadeh, now the acting minister of "national guidance."

An Iranian girl who had studied journalism in New York—who had experi-enced, as she put it, the fruits of American democracy—demanded to know why Americans were prepared to support the Shah's regime when it had opposed indi-vidual freedom and dissent. "In the United States, we learned all about liberty and the freedom to say what we wanted to say. Yet America went on propping up the Shah and forcing him to squander Iran's wealth on arms. Why did it do that? Why was America a democracy at home and a dictator abroad?" There was, of course, a contradiction here. The fact that President Carter, whose campaign for human rights was well known in Iran, should have continued to honour America's politi-cal commitment to the Shah before the revolution—in however tentative a way—was regarded as hypocrisy. Yet the Carter administration was opposed to the anti-democratic nature of the Shah's regime and, within the limits of diplomacy, Carter had urged the Iranian monarch to liberalise his country.

---

*Ireland in 1920 also comes to mind.

Iranians argued that this was too ambiguous a position to respect, and it was difficult to read some of Carter's statements during the last months of the Shah's rule without sensing a certain naiveté in the American president. In November 1978, for example, Carter was describing the Shah as "a friend, a loyal ally"; he would say only that criticism of the Shah's police state was "sometimes perhaps justified," adding that he did not know the "details" of the criticism. Yet Iranian condemnation often seemed directed at the actions of previous American administrations: at the Eisenhower or Kennedy or Nixon governments. The students, when they shouted abuse about Carter, appeared to be voicing sentiments they once felt about the policies of Henry Kissinger, who had so powerful a role (as U.S. secretary of state) when they themselves worked and lived in the United States. Comparatively few had any experience of the Carter administration—except for the knowledge that Carter refused to deport the Shah to Iran. Few of the students outside the embassy gave much thought to the long-term outcome of the embassy occupation, to the possibility that it might result in the election of Ronald Reagan, who would take a much less tolerant interest in world affairs and now a much greater enthusiasm for Iran's external enemies.

Iranian reaction to the smaller "Satanic" powers was almost quixotic. At the British embassy, still daubed with paint from earlier demonstrations, a crowd arrived to express its satisfaction that Shapour Bakhtiar, the Shah's last prime minister, had not been given asylum in the United Kingdom. When the same demonstrators reached the French embassy—the country in which Bakhtiar had been given temporary residence—they expressed their appreciation at the sanctuary France had given Ayatollah Khomeini before the revolution.

But no political démarche could unscramble the U.S. embassy siege. The Europeans, the Papal Nuncio, Sean MacBride—a founder of Amnesty International—seventy-five ambassadors representing the entire diplomatic corps in Tehran: all found their appeals ignored. The ambassadors could not even visit Bruce Laingen, who was in the Iranian Foreign Ministry when the embassy was taken and remained there until his release in 1981. Ayatollah Khomeini sternly informed the Pope that "Jesus Christ would have punished the Shah." Iranian television broke into a showing of *The Third Man* to announce that Iran was halting its daily supply of 600,000 barrels of oil to the United States—a rather hurried response to the decision already taken by the Carter administration to suspend oil imports from Iran. On 14 November, Iran announced the withdrawal of $12 billion of government reserves from American banks and Carter promptly froze Iranian funds in the United States. Each new step reinforced the power of the theocracy governing Iran and reduced the influence of the leftists.

Half a million students gathered near Tehran University on 15 November in support of the Fedayeen, the left-wing guerrilla movement which was now illegal in Iran and which had not supported the embassy takeover. But inside the campus of Tehran University I found Mehdi Bazargan at Friday prayers, sitting in a grey sweater, cross-legged on the ground, and listening to Ayatollah Hussein Ali Montazeri, the head of the committee of experts who had just written the new Islamic constitution for Iran. He was telling his audience that "the will of the Iranian people was behind the occupation" of the embassy. Yazdi sat next to Bazargan, who had just resigned because the embassy siege had undermined his government. Article 5 of Montazeri's new constitution stated that a religious leader with majority support—"a just, pious, enlightened, courageous and sagacious person"—would become guardian of the nation. It was obvious that this arduous, not to say spiritually wearying role, would be given to none other than Ayatollah Khomeini.

In this new theocracy, there was going to be no place for the communist Tudeh party. After the overthrow of Mossadeq in 1953, the Shah had executed some of its leaders; others fled the country. Soon it would be the party's fate to be crushed all over again, this time by Khomeini. But in the winter of 1979, it was still officially supporting the Ayatollah—even if Nouredin Kianouri's office walls were the only ones in Tehran without a picture of the Imam. There was a copper-plate portrait of Lenin above the stairs and the secretary-general of Tudeh frowned when I asked him why the Ayatollah was not staring stiffly down upon his desk.

"The cult of personality does not exist here in Iran," I was told. "We are not like the English, who have a picture of the Queen hanging in every room." Kianouri laughed rather too much at this joke, aware that the parallel was somewhat inexact. He was a precise, faintly humorous man whose balding head, large eyes and bushy grey moustache made him look like a character from a great French novel, but the political language of this former professor—Tehran University and the East Berlin Academy of Architecture—had more in common with *Pravda* than with Zola. Tudeh was involved in "the radical struggle against imperialism" and "the struggle for the reorganisation of social life, especially for the oppressed strata of society." The party wanted a "popular democracy," not the bourgeois variety so popular in the West. And in so far as it was possible, Tudeh, Iran's oldest political party, wanted the same things as Ayatollah Khomeini. This was the theory and Kianouri held to it bravely. The truth was that Tudeh's views on the new Iran were almost exactly the same as those of the Soviet Union—which, for the moment, was in favour of the Ayatollah.

"We have criticised the establishment," Kianouri said. "We have made criticism over the position of liberty in the state and about the rights of women. We have criticised Islamic fanaticism—we are against the non-progressive ideas of those conservative elements. But for us, the positive side of Ayatollah Khomeini is so important that the so-called negative side means nothing. We think he is an obstacle to fanaticism: he is more progressive than other elements." I interrupted Kianouri. Three months ago, I said, Khomeini condemned Hafizullah Amin's Soviet-backed government in Afghanistan for struggling against Muslim rebels. Did this not represent a divergence of opinion? "That was three months ago," Kianouri replied. "But now the Ayatollah's outlook is different. He has new information on the situation there."

Was the Ayatollah therefore mistaken? "I did not use the word 'mistaken,' " Kianouri corrected me. "I said only that the outlook of the Ayatollah has changed and he now knows that the Muslim counter-revolutionary movement is a tool of

American CIA agents." Wasn't this a Soviet voice that was talking to me? Wasn't Tudeh, as its critics had claimed, just a mouthpiece for the Soviet Union? "This is not true. Cheap critics once accused Victor Hugo of being an English spy, and great figures have been called foreign agents because this is the form of insult used against the forces combating imperialism. Tudeh is not the official voice of the Soviet Union."

In my *Times* report of the interview, I suggested that the Ayatollah might soon accept less benignly the little criticisms of the Tudeh. All I got wrong was the time frame. It would be 1983, at the height of the Iran–Iraq War, before Khomeini turned his "progressive" attention to the party which wanted "popular democracy." When Vladimir Kuzichkin, a Soviet KGB major stationed in Tehran, defected to Britain in 1982, he handed over a list of Soviet agents operating in Iran—a list that was then shared with the authorities in Iran. More than a thousand Tudeh members were arrested, including Kianouri, who was quickly prevailed upon to admit that the party had been "guilty of treason and espionage for the Soviet Union." Kianouri appeared on Iranian television to say that he had maintained contact with Soviet agents since 1945 and that members of his party had been delivering top-secret military and political documents to the Soviet embassy in Tehran. Eighteen Soviet diplomats were expelled. Kianouri and his wife Mariam Firouz were sent to Evin prison for ten years; he died soon after his release. It was the end of the Left in Iran.

It was only in November of 1979 that I sat at last before Khomeini. Long ago, when Britain had an empire, the *Times* correspondent would have the ear of statesmen and warlords. Shahs and princes would demand to be interviewed. But a new empire now guaranteed that it was the American television anchormen, the boys from *The New York Times* and the journalists who played the role of mouthpiece for the State Department who got the interviews. The best I could do was to "piggyback," to team up with the men from the new *pax Americana* whom the Ayatollahs—who sniffed power as acutely as any politicians—wanted to talk to. So I travelled to Qom with two American television networks whose reporters —as opposed to their employers—I greatly admired, John Hart and Peter Jennings. It took courage for an American to report the Iranian revolution with compassion and fairness, and I had many times travelled with Hart in Tehran. "I think we can let young Bob come with us, don't you, Peter?" Hart noisily asked Jennings as I stood beside him. "I mean, he's not going to get in our way and it always feels good to help out the poor old Brits. Anyway, I'm sure young Bob will be grateful to America!" The sarcasm was forced, but he well understood my lowly status in the ranks of scribes.

It was a bright winter Sunday morning as we approached Qom, its blue-tiled domes and golden minarets twinkling in the light. I often thought that this was what our own European cities must have looked like in the Middle Ages, a sudden sprouting of spires and towers above a hill or along a valley. Before you reached the car repair shops and the lock-up garages and the acres of slums, Qom appeared mystical across the desert. We didn't need to call it a "holy" city in our reports; after the miles of grey, gritty dunes, it was a miracle of light and power. You could

understand how pilgrims, after days in the harshness of rock and gravel and powdered sand, would behold the cupolas and the reflected gold on the horizon and
renew their faith. *Allahu akbar*. From every loudspeaker in the city, floating down
upon every courtyard, came the same exhortation. Once, on a parched summer
midday, I had arrived in Qom to interview one of its clerics, and a Muslim
student—a Briton, by chance, who had converted to Islam—offered me chilled
water in a glittering bronze bowl. Outside the window, as I put my lips to the bowl,
a pink jacaranda tree swayed in the breeze. It was like pouring life into myself. No
wonder Khomeini had decided to return to Qom. This was the city from which he
had first assaulted the Shah. Here were born and here died the revolution's first
martyrs. They said he lived a humble life and they were right. I was shown
Khomeini's bedroom, a rough carpet on the floor, a mattress, a pillow, a glass for
his morning yoghurt.

It was an interesting phenomenon, this oriental desire to show the poverty of
their leaders. In Cairo, members of the underground Jemaa Islamiya would delight
in showing me the slums in which they spent their lives. Bin Laden had ordered his
men to show me the tents in which his wives would live. Now Khomeini's guards
were opening the door of the old man's bedroom. No palaces for the Imam;
because, as I quickly realised, he built his palaces of people. His faithful, the adoration on the faces of the dozens of men who pushed and shoved and squeezed and
kicked their way into the small audience room with its bare white walls, these were
the foundations and the walls of his spiritual mansion. They were his servants and
his loyal warriors, his protectors and his praetorian guards. God must protect our
Imam. And their devotion grew as Khomeini proclaimed that, no, he was *their* servant and, more to the point, he was the servant of God.

I didn't see him come into the room although there was a cry of near-hysteria
from the crowd as he entered. I glimpsed him for just a moment, advancing at the
speed of a cat, a small whirlwind of black robes, his black *sayed*'s turban moving
between the heads, and then he was sitting in front of me, cross-legged on a small
blue-and-white patterned carpet, unsmiling, grave, almost glowering, his eyes cast
down. I have always responded badly at such moments. When I first saw Yassir
Arafat—admittedly, he was no Khomeini—I was mesmerised by his eyes. What
big eyes you have, I wanted to say. When I first met Hafez el-Assad of Syria, I was
captivated by the absolute flatness of the back of his head, so straight I could have
set a ruler against it without a crack showing. I spent an evening at dinner with
King Hussein, perpetually astonished at how small he was, irritated that I couldn't
get him to stop playing with the box of cigarettes that lay on the table between us.
And now here was one of the titans of the twentieth century, whose name would be
in every history book for a thousand years, the scourge of America, the Savonarola
of Tehran, the "twelfth" Imam, an apostle of Islam. And I searched his face and
noted the two small spots on his cheek and the vast fluffy eyebrows, the bags under
his eyes, the neat white beard, his right hand lying on his knee, his left arm buried
in his robe.

But his eyes. I could not see his eyes. His head was bowed, as if he did not see us, as if he had not noticed the Westerners in front of him, even though we were the symbol—for the poor, sweating, shoving men in the room—of his international power and fame. We were the foreign consuls arriving at the oriental court, waiting to hear the word of the oracle. Qotbzadeh sat on Khomeini's right, gazing obsequiously at the man who would later condemn him to death, his head leaning towards the Ayatollah, anxious not to miss a single word. He, after all, would be the interpreter. So what of the embassy hostages? we wanted to know. Khomeini knew we would ask this. He understood the networks. His last, cynical remarks about newspapers in the final days of his life showed that he understood us journalists as well.

"They will be tried," he said. "They will be tried—and those found guilty of espionage will submit to the verdict of the court." Khomeini knew—and, more to the point, we knew—that since the revolution, everyone found guilty of spying had been sentenced to death. Then came what I always called the "slippery floor" technique, the sudden disavowal of what might otherwise appear to be a closed matter. "It would be appropriate to say," the Ayatollah continued, "that as long as they stay here, they are under the banner of Islam and cannot be harmed . . . but obviously as long as this matter continues, they will remain here—and until the Shah is returned to our country, they may be tried." The extradition of the Shah to Iran, Khomeini had decided, must dominate every aspect of the country's foreign policy. Of course, Hart and Jennings talked about international law, about the respect that should be paid to all embassies. The question was translated *sotto voce* by Qotbzadeh. Khomeini's reply was quiet but he had a harsh voice, like gravel on marble. It was President Carter who had broken international law by maintaining "spies" in Tehran. Diplomatic immunity did not extend to spies.

He thought for a long time before each reply—here, he had something in common with bin Laden, although the two men would have little reason to share more than their divided Islamic inheritance—and only when he used the word "espionage" did his voice lose its monotone and rise in anger. "Diplomats in any country are supposed to do diplomatic work. They are not supposed to commit crimes and carry out espionage . . . If they carry out espionage then they are no longer diplomats. Our people have taken a certain number of spies and according to our laws they should be tried and punished . . . Even if the Shah *is* returned, the release of the hostages will be a kind gesture on our part."

I still searched for the eyes. And at that moment, I realised he was staring at a point on the floor, at a single bright emanation, a ray of sunshine that was beaming through the high, dirty windows and was forming a circle of light on the carpet. His head was bent towards it as if the light itself held some inspiration. The left arm remained concealed in his gown. Was he watching this sun-point for some theological reason? Did it give focus to his mind? Or was he bored, tired of our Western questions, with selfish demands for information about a few dozen American lives when thousands of Iranians had been cut down in the revolution?

Yet he had clearly decided what to say to us long in advance of the interview. He would already have known that three of the Americans were to be released five hours later, two black members of the embassy's U.S. Marine guard contingent and a woman, Kathy Gross. But Khomeini simply came back, again and again, to the same argument. Rather like the U.S. television networks, he seemed to be obsessed by only one theme: retribution. He was not going to preach to us, to speak to us of God or history—or, indeed, his place in it. "Carter has done something against international law—someone has committed a crime and that criminal should be sent back to this country to be tried." His voice went on purging us. "As long as Carter does not respect international laws, these spies cannot be returned." Then he sprang up, a creature who had lost all interest in us, and the heap of men in the front rows collapsed over each other in the excitement of his departure. One of our drivers stepped forward—our own translator bent towards Khomeini and whispered that it would be the greatest moment in the driver's existence on earth if he could shake the Ayatollah's hand—and our driver held the Imam's right hand and kissed it and when he raised his head, tears streamed down his cheek. And Khomeini had gone.*

This was not just an anticlimax. This was bathos. When one of the freed U.S. Marines, Sergeant Ladell Maples, announced that night that the Iranian Revolution had been "a good thing," it was almost as interesting. And from that moment, I decided to read Khomeini, to read every speech he made—heavens above, the Islamic Guidance Ministry flooded us with his words—to see what had captured the hearts of so many millions of Iranians. And slowly, I understood. He talked in the language of ordinary people, without complexity, not in the language of religious exegesis, but as if he had been talking to the man sitting beside him. No, although he would not have known who Osama bin Laden was in 1979—the Saudi would not leave for Afghanistan for another month—Khomeini knew all too well of the dangers that the Saudi Wahhabi Sunni faith posed for the Shiite as well as the Western world. In his famous "Last Message" just before his death, when he had probably heard the name of bin Laden, Khomeini inveighed against "the anti-Koranic ideas propagating the baseless and superstitious cult of Wahhabism."

And he knew how to argue against those American conservatives who claimed—and still claim—that Islam is a religion of backwardness and isolation. "Sometimes with explicit but crude argument it is claimed that the laws of 1,400 years ago cannot efficiently administer the modern world," he wrote.

> At other times they contend that Islam is a reactionary religion that opposes any new ideas and manifestations of civilisation and that, at pres-

---

*Lessons in journalism. When I filed my report from Tehran that evening, I made a point of telling *The Times* that they must give due credit to the two American networks and should under no circumstances change the order in which I had placed our names in the dispatch, my own at the end. The foreign desk promised to ensure that this was done. Then, late at night, a sub-editor thought that *The Times* should have its own reporter in front of the U.S. networks and altered the order of names, giving the impression that the Americans had been "piggybacking" my own interview. I cursed the paper. Jennings cursed me. It was days before he forgave me for *The Times*'s unprofessional behaviour.

ent, no one can remain aloof to world civilisation . . . In fiendish yet foolish propaganda jargon, they claim the sanctity of Islam and maintain that divine religions have the nobler task of purging egos, of inviting people to ascetism, monkhood . . . This is nothing but an inane accusation . . . Science and industry are very much emphasised in the Koran and Islam . . . These ignorant individuals must realise that the Holy Koran and the traditions of the Prophet of Islam contain more lessons, decrees and commands on the rule of government and politics than they do on any other issue . . .

Harvey Morris was full of admiration for Khomeini when I arrived at his office to file my dispatch that night in November 1979. "You've got to hand it to the old boy," he said, drawing on another cigarette. "He knew how to handle you lot. Yes, our 'AK' knows exactly how to handle the kind of wankers we send down to interview him. Doesn't waste his time on serious theological stuff that we wouldn't understand; just goes straight to the point and gives us our bloody headlines." In his own cynical way, Harvey respected Khomeini. The Ayatollah knew how to talk to us and he knew how to talk to Iranians. And when they read out his "Last Message" after his death in 1989, Khomeini's words were humility itself. "I need your prayers and I beseech Almighty God's pardon and forgiveness for my inadequacies and my faults," he wrote. "I hope the nation, too, will forgive my shortcomings and failings . . . Know that the departure of one servant shall not leave a scratch on the steel shield that is the nation."

You could understand how Khomeini's followers were persuaded by his sanctity into an almost crude obeisance. I remember the way Qotbzadeh talked to me about him, his voice softening into an almost feminine purr as he tried to convince me that the Ayatollah's annoyance at the slow pace of the revolution did not imply any change of character. "The man is as holy as he was, as honest as he has ever been, as determined as he always was, and as pure as he has ever been." This was the man whose execution Khomeini would approve. What Qotbzadeh thought in front of the firing squad we shall never know.

"So, back to the 'den of iniquity,' eh, Bob?" Harvey had asked when I came panting into the Reuters office to file. The cigarette smoke was thicker than usual. There was another whisky bottle on the desk. "What's it like to be back in the 'centre of vice and Saturnalia'?" Harvey was right, of course. "Saturnalia" really was one of Khomeini's favourite expressions. And it was easy to mock the Iranian revolution, its eternal sermonising, the endless, unalterable integrity of its quarrel, its childlike self-confidence. Yet there was a perseverance about this revolution, an assiduousness that could be used to extraordinary effect once a target had been clearly identified. Nothing could have symbolised this dedication more than the reconstitution of the thousands of shredded U.S. diplomatic papers which the Iranians found when they sacked the American embassy.

A woman "follower of the Imam" was later to describe how an engineering student called Javad concluded that the shreds of each document must have fallen close together, and could thus be restored in their original form:

> He was a study in concentration: bearded, thin, nervous and intense. These qualities, combined with his strong command of English, his mathematical mind and his enthusiasm, made him a natural for the job . . . One afternoon he took a handful of shreds from the barrel, laid them on a sheet of white paper and began grouping them on the basis of their qualities . . . After five hours we had only been able to reconstruct 20–30 per cent of the two documents. The next day I visited the document centre with a group of sisters. "Come and see. With God's help, with faith and a bit of effort we can accomplish the impossible," he said, with a smile.

A team of twenty students was gathered to work on the papers. A flat board was fitted with elastic bands to hold the shreds in place. They could reconstruct five to ten documents a week. They were the carpet-weavers, carefully, almost lovingly re-threading their tapestry. Iranian carpets are filled with flowers and birds, the recreation of a garden in the desert; they are intended to give life amid sand and heat, to create eternal meadows amid a wasteland. The Iranians who worked for months on those shredded papers were creating their own unique carpet, one that exposed the past and was transformed into a living history book amid the arid propaganda of the revolution. High-school students and disabled war veterans were enlisted to work on this carpet of papers. It would take them six years to complete, 3,000 pages containing 2,300 documents, all eventually contained in 85 volumes.*

Night after night, as each edition was published, I pored over these remarkable documents, a living archive of secret contemporary history from 1972 to the chaos of post-revolutionary Iran by the nation that was now threatening military action against Iran. Here was Ambassador William Sullivan in September 1978, contemptuously referring to "the extremist coalition of fanatic Moslems led by Ayatollah Khomeini in Iraq (which has reportedly been penetrated and is assisted by a variety of terrorist, crypto-communist, and other far left elements) . . . " or listening to the Shah as he "persists in saying that he sees the Soviet hand in all the demonstrations and disturbances that have taken place." Some of the diplomatic analyses were just plain wrong. "Such figures as Ayatollahs Khomeini and Shariatmadari . . . have little chance of capitalizing on their wide following to win control of the government for themselves," one secret cable confides.

Other documents were deeply incriminating. Robert R. Bowie, deputy director

---

*It was typical of the bureaucracy of U.S. security that American journalists arriving back at JFK airport in New York from Tehran with the published volumes containing the embassy documents found the books seized by U.S. Customs on the grounds that they contained "restricted" government papers. What the people of Tehran could buy on the street for 15 rials a copy was forbidden to the people of America.

for national foreign assessment at the CIA, thanks Sullivan on 14 December 1978 for hosting a cocktail party that enabled him to meet the Shah and "to have some less formal conversations with several Iranian military and SAVAK people." A memorandum of the same date from the U.S. consulate in Isfahan records a conversation with Ibrahim Peshavar, the local director of Iranian television, in which Peshavar is asked "if it was true that his teams had covered demonstration [*sic*] toppling the Shah's statues, and had provided it to security forces for investigation. He said that it was covered, that NIRT [National Iranian Radio and Television] had decided not to run it on television, and that such films are routinely shared with 'other government agencies.' He . . . asked that I not spread the word."

Among the reconstituted files was a 47-page CIA booklet marked "Secret" and dated March 1979—written after the revolution but still, incredibly, kept in the embassy archives—on the internal structure of Israel's "Foreign Intelligence and Security Services." Israeli efforts to break the Arab "ring" encircling Israel, it said, had led to:

> a formal trilateral liaison called the Trident organisation . . . established by Mossad with Turkey's National Security Service (TNSS) and Iran's National Organisation for Intelligence and Security (Savak) . . . The Trident organisation involves continuing intelligence exchange plus semmi-annual [*sic*] meetings at the chief of staff level . . . The main purpose of the Israeli relationship with Iran was the development of a pro-Israel and anti-Arab policy on the part of Iranian officials. Mossad has engaged in joint operations with Savak over the years since the late 1950s. Mossad aided Savak activities and supported the Kurds in Iraq. The Israelis also regularly transmitted to the Iranians intelligence reports on Egypt's activities in the Arab countries, trends and developments in Iraq, and communist activities affecting Iran.

Some of the internal American memoranda showed a considerable grasp of political events and an understanding of Iran's culture—even if this wisdom was not acceptable back in Washington. George Lambrakis sent a memo to the State Department on 2 February 1979, pointing out that:

> Iranian govt spokesmen have for a long time peddled the charge that Khomeini's followers are for the most part crypto communists or leftists of Marxist stripe . . . to a considerable extent it is based on a fable that communists have been infiltrated as youths into the religious schools and now constitute the mullahs and other organizers of the religious movement . . .
>
> Westernization in Iran achieved a status and legitimacy under the two Pahlavi monarchs which has practically wiped out memories of the Islamic past for large numbers of people who went to school in the westernized Iranian school system and did their higher studies for the most part abroad . . . the Pahlavi Shahs have sought to brand the Islamic establish-

ment as an ignorant reactionary remnant of the past which is fast becoming obsolete. Steps were taken to render this a self-fulfilling prophecy. The govt has made efforts to cut off the mullahs from direct financial support by the people . . . Nevertheless it has become obvious that Islam is deeply embedded in the lives of the vast majority of the Iranian people. In its Shiite format it has over the years become strongly identified with Iranian nationalism . . . The Pahlavis attempted to supplant this ancient nationalism with a modern version based on a return to traditions, legends and glories of the pre-Islamic past . . .

An embassy assessment of Iranian society in 1978 reads like an account of Iraqi society before the fall of Saddam in 2003—would that the Americans had read it before their invasion of Iraq—and ends with conclusions that Khomeini could only agree with:

There is much in Iranian history to predispose both the ruler and the ruled to exercise and to expect authoritarian behaviour. There exists no tradition of the orderly transfer of authority, there has been no real experience with democratic forms . . . There is in Iran . . . an established tradition of a strong ruler at the head of an authoritarian government, and of general obeisance to any authority that manifests its will with force. The experience of the current Shah, for example, superficially suggests that political stability in Iran is best assured by authoritarian government, and that periods of the greatest political unrest arise when the ruler . . . shares authority, as during the Mossadeq crisis of 1951–53, or attempts to introduce additional freedoms, as with the liberalization programme of the mid-1970s . . . The inability of Iranian society to accommodate successfully to these social changes stems in large part from the long-standing and pervasive influence of religion and religious leaders . . . Shia Islam is not merely a religion; rather it is an all encompassing religious, economic, legal, social, and intellectual system that controls all aspects of life, and the sect's leaders, unlike their counterparts in Sunni Islam, are believed to be completing God's revelations on earth.

Although this essay reached profoundly inaccurate conclusions—"we do not foresee any likely circumstances in which a government controlled by religious leaders would come to power," its authors wrote—other contemporary documents could display remarkable shrewdness. John Washburn would write on 18 September 1978 that "the Shah's repression of religion in Iran has made Shiism's predominant groups dogmatic and conservative in the course of defending themselves, just as Roman Catholicism has become in Communist countries." As long ago as 1972, the then ambassador, Richard Helms, formerly head of the CIA, received a long "secret" memo on the Iranian "character" which suggested that Iran's repeated national humiliations had "engrained in the Iranian personality very marked negative characteristics" but "under foreign occupation (Arabs, Mongols, Turks) or manipulation (British, Russians), Iranians preserved their sense of nationhood through their culture . . . and their self-respect in cloistered and concealed private lives . . . The world outside was justifiably seen as hostile."

But it was the more prosaic efforts of U.S. diplomats that probably got closer to the truth. A note from U.S. consulates in Iran on 21 November 1978 reported public opinion outside Tehran. "Why, it is being asked, does Iran need F-14s when villagers less than five kilometres from Shiraz's Tadayon Air Force Base . . . still live without running water or electricity?"*

What none of the U.S. embassy archives predicted was the brutality of the Iranian revolution, the extraordinary cruelty that manifested itself among the so-called judges and jurists who were predisposed to torture and kill out of whim rather than reflection. At the end of the eight-year Iran–Iraq War, this would meet its apogee in the mass hangings of thousands of opposition prisoners. But its characteristics were clearly evident within days of the Shah's overthrow; and no one emphasised them more chillingly than Chief Justice Khalkhali, who had told me in December 1979 how he intended to "string up" the Shah. When he said that, and despite his ferocious reputation, I thought at first it was a joke, a cliché, an idle remark. Of course, it was nothing of the sort.

The Revolutionary Guards sitting around Khalkhali when I first visited the Hojatolislam had all been wounded while fighting Kurdish rebels in the north-west of Iran. It was hot in the little room in Qom and the bespectacled divine was wearing only pyjamas and a white apron. "You are from *The Times* of London?" he asked, glancing in my direction. "Well, look at these men." He paused and then began to giggle in a high-pitched voice. "The rebels did this. I will pull them out by the roots—I will kill all of them." In truth, Khalkhali did not look the part. He was a small man with a kindly smile—Islamic judges at that time all seemed to smile a lot—which he betrayed when making inappropriate jokes. Asked by a reporter two weeks earlier how he felt when the number of executions in Iran was decreasing, he replied with a chuckle: "I feel hungry." It would have been a serious mistake, however, to imagine that Iran's most feared judge—the "wrath of God" to his admirers—did not take his vocation seriously. "If an Islamic judge realises that someone is guilty of corruption on earth or of waging war against God," he said, "the judge will condemn the accused, even if he claims he is innocent. The most important thing in Islamic justice is the wisdom of the judge . . . Even if a man denies the charges against him, it means nothing if the judge decides otherwise."

---

*There seemed no end to these revelations. Among the last of the documents released by the government were secret papers inexplicably abandoned in the Iranian eastern desert on 24 April 1980, when the Americans aborted their attempt to rescue the embassy hostages, after a C-130 and a U.S. helicopter crashed into each other, killing eight U.S. servicemen. The documents, produced in book form by the Iranians—complete with fearful pictures of the fire-scorched bodies of some of the dead Americans—included dozens of high-altitude and satellite photographs of Tehran, emergency Iranian landing fields, maps, coordinates and codewords which the rescuers were to use in their transmissions to the U.S. aircraft carrier *Nimitz*.

Hojatolislam Khalkhali naturally had no time for reporters who asked why so many Iranians were executed after the revolution. "The people who were executed were the principal retainers of the previous hated regime. They had exploited this nation. They had been responsible for killings, tortures and unlawful imprisonment. I am surprised that you ask such questions." Khalkhali displayed equally little patience when asked if his much-publicised determination to engineer the assassination of the ex-Shah accorded with the principles of Islamic justice. "We know that America will not return the Shah," he said—with, it had to be admitted, a remarkable sense of realism—"so we have to kill him—there is no other choice. If it was possible to bring him here and try him, we would kill him afterwards. But since we cannot try him—and since we are sure that he should be executed—we will kill him anyway. No one tried Mussolini. And who tried the Frenchmen who were executed for collaborating with Hitler's soldiers in the Second World War?"

All the while he was talking, the Revolutionary Guards would massage their wounded limbs—or what was left of them—and exercise their artificial hands. The creaking and clacking of steel fingers punctuated the conversation as Khalkhali walked around the room, shoeless and sockless, or massaged his feet with his hands. How, I asked, did he personally feel when he sentenced a man to death? "I feel that I am doing my duty and what I am required to do by the Iranian people. That is why I have never been criticised by my people for these executions." But had he not refused to give Hoveyda or Nassiri, the ex-Savak boss, any right to appeal against his death sentence?

"They did appeal," he replied. "And they asked the Imam and the court to forgive them. Many people came to me and asked me to forgive these people. But I was responsible to the Iranian nation and to God. I could not forgive Hoveyda and Nassiri. They destroyed the lives of sixty thousand people." Khalkhali had, he claimed, ordered a commando squad to go to Panama where the Shah was now staying with his family in order to kill all of them. "I do not know if they have left Iran yet," he said, and then broke into that familiar chuckle as he ventured into Spanish. "They all have *pistolas*." Since the murder of the Shah's nephew in Paris almost two weeks earlier, Interpol—and Khalkhali's intended victims—were now paying a good deal of attention to the judge's threats. And Khalkhali obligingly listed the targets of his hit squads. "We are looking for Sharif-Emami [former prime minister], General Palizban, Hushang Ansari [former finance minister], Ardeshir Zahedi [former ambassador in Washington], Gholam Ali Oveissi [former martial law administrator], Gharabagi [former chief of staff in the Shah's army], Farah [the ex-empress], Hojabr Yazdani [a former banker], Valian [former minister of agriculture], Jamshid Amouzegar [former prime minister] and Shapour Bakhtiar [the Shah's last prime minister, now living in Paris]. We also want the Shah and his brother and Ashraf [the Shah's twin sister]. Wherever we can find these people, we will kill them."

Khalkhali was unashamed at publicly naming his own "hit list," and he was perfectly serious; more than a decade later, I would meet the head of the Iranian hit squad sent to Paris to murder Bakhtiar. So was Khalkhali really the "wrath of

God"? I asked. "I grew up in poverty and therefore I can understand poor people. I know all about the previous regime. I have read books about politics. The Imam ordered me to be the Islamic judge and I have done the job perfectly. That's why none of the Shah's agents in Iran has escaped my hands."*

It would be seven months before I saw Khalkhali again. His monstrous reputation had not been sullied by a temporary fall in the number of executions. By July 1980, his wrath was falling on new and more fruitful pastures. He stood now, this formidable judicial luminary, in the sunny courtyard of Qasr prison, brandishing a miniature pink plastic spoon, smacking his lips noisily and tucking into a large cardboard tub of vanilla ice-cream. For a man who had just ordered the first public execution in Tehran for fifteen years, he was in an excellent frame of mind.

Five days earlier, a gruesome new precedent had been set when four people—two of them middle-aged married women—were stoned to death in the southern Iranian city of Kerman. All had been condemned for sexual offences by one of Khalkhali's revolutionary courts, and within hours the condemned had been dressed in white cloth, buried up to their chests in the ground and bombarded with rocks as large as a man's fist. In a characteristic and typically unnecessary comment, the court later stated that all four had died of "brain damage." The women were condemned for being "involved in prostitution" and for "deceiving young girls." One of the men was convicted of homosexuality and adultery, and the other for allegedly raping a ten-year-old girl. Before execution, the four were ritually bathed and shrouded, a ceremonial white hood being placed over their heads. Local clergymen had visited the condemned and chosen the stones for the execution, varying in size between one and six inches in diameter. It took the two women and two men fifteen minutes to die.†

"I don't know if I approve of stoning," Sadeq Khalkhali said, flashing a grin at us journalists and at a group of startled diplomats who had also been invited to the Qasr prison. "But in the Koran, it is mentioned that those who commit adultery should be killed by stoning." The Hojatolislam dug his little spoon into the melting white ice-cream, oblivious to the bare-headed prisoners who trudged past behind him, heaving barrels loaded with cauldrons of vegetable soup. "We approve of anything the Koran says. What is the difference between killing people with stones and killing them with bullets? But throwing stones certainly teaches people a lesson." Khalkhali modestly disowned responsibility for the Kerman stonings—his bearded public relations man informed us that a man called Fahin Kermani had taken this weighty decision—but he agreed that he had ordered some fresh execu-

---

*By the time he died of heart disease and cancer in 2003, Khalkhali was thought to have sent at least 8,000 men and women to the gallows and the firing squad.

†This was believed to be the first time in living memory that Muslims had been stoned to death in the Middle East after a court hearing. Stoning was a common village punishment in Iran and other Islamic countries for hundreds of years, and in the nineteenth century, members of the minority Bahai sect were killed with stones in Shiraz and Tehran. But they died at the hands of mobs, not after a judicial trial. Prostitutes were stoned to death long before the time of the Prophet Mohamed and the Bible describes how Jesus Christ tried to stop the practice.

tions that morning. Seven men had been lined up at one end of Jamshid Street at five o'clock and shot down by a firing squad while a large crowd gawked from a distance. Many of those who died had been convicted of drug offences, and it was in his role as chief of the Iranian anti-narcotics squad that the Hojatolislam had welcomed us to Qasr prison to view his latest haul of contraband.

One could only be impressed. Khalkhali had piled it up in the prison mosque, a magnificent frescoed edifice with a cupola of red and blue tiles, now filled with tons of opium, kilogram sacks of heroin, large sticky slabs of hashish, stolen refrigerators, ornately carved backgammon boards, a 2½-metre wall of cigarettes—here I thought briefly of Harvey Morris in his Reuters "saturnalia"— thousands of bubble pipes, carpets, knives, automatic rifles and rows of champagne bottles (Krug 1972). The beautiful mosque literally reeked of hashish as Khalkhali made a triumphal tour of his loot, pushing his way past 20 tons of opium and at least 100 kilograms of heroin, each neatly packed into clean white sacks. It was inevitable that he would be asked whether the revolutionary courts were dealing enthusiastically enough with drug-dealers, and equally inevitable that the Hojatolislam would evince a broad smile—directed at the diplomats—before replying. "If we did what others wanted us to do, we would have to kill many people—which in my opinion is simply impossible," he said. "Things could end up in a crisis. If we were going to kill everyone who had five grams of heroin, we would have to kill five thousand people—and that would be difficult." In fairness, it should be added that the Ayatollah had made a fair start. In the past seven weeks, his courts had summarily dispatched 176 men and women to the firing squads for narcotics offences, many of them sentenced by Khalkhali himself in the innocuous tree-shaded concrete building 300 metres from the little mosque.

Khalkhali tried hard not to look like an ogre; he repeatedly denied that he was any such thing. His small, plump frame, grey beard and twinkling eyes give him a fatherly appearance, the kind of man who might have been more at home at the fireside in carpet slippers with the family cat purring beside him—just so long as the family cat survived. He joked frequently with us as he made his round of the mosque, good-naturedly poking his finger into the sacks of opium that lay beneath the main cupola. Every minute or so, a young man in a pale green shirt with a pistol tucked into his trousers would clamber onto a pile of heroin bags and scream "God is Great" at the top of his lungs, a refrain that would be taken up and echoed around the mosque.

"If you look at me, you don't see an inner struggle written all over my face," Khalkhali remarked as he emerged into the sunshine. "But I am actually a revolutionary person. I am chasing agents everywhere—in France, England and America. That is a fact. I am chasing them everywhere." He claimed a "200 per cent success" in stamping out drug-running in Iran and an 80 per cent victory in preventing international drug-trafficking—which was why the diplomats had been invited to the Qasr prison to listen to the judge. He claimed that an intercontinental mafia was operating a drug ring from Pakistan, Burma and Thailand, and described how a member of the ex-Shah's family allegedly used a private aircraft to fly drugs from Afghanistan to a small airfield outside Tehran. The captured opium, he said, might be used by the government for medical purposes. The hashish and heroin would be burned.

The Hojatolislam strode briskly from the courtyard towards a wire fence, but as he did so, something very strange happened. Dozens of black-veiled women— the wives and sisters of the very men whom the Ayatollah would soon be sentencing—ran across a lawn towards him, clutching babies and crying, "Hail to Khalkhali." The Hojatolislam affected not to notice them as the soldiers held them at bay, and he pushed his way through a gate in the fence. For a few moments, he talked of holding a formal press conference before entering his tiny courthouse. But then a policeman walked over to us and told us that the judge had become "angry." Sensing that a Hojatolislam's fury could embrace a journalist or two, we brought this most extraordinary public event to a hurried conclusion. We fled.*

For Westerners, Khalkhali represented a special danger. If the American hostages in the embassy were to be tried by an Islamic court, what if Khalkhali was let loose on them? All Khomeini's promises of protection could be reinterpreted now that the embassy documents were being slowly put back together to reveal that the Iranian claims of a "spy nest" in Tehran were not entirely without foundation. Thus when the Shah moved from the United States to Panama—a journey of which the Iranians were forewarned by three Western diplomats acting at Washington's request—the "Students of the Imam" put out a statement repeating the promise to "try" the Americans.† In the end, of course, there was no trial.

Inevitably, the Iranians lost their patience with the foreign journalists in Tehran. The day after the "trial" statement, Abolhassan Sadeq walked into the Iranian Ministry of Islamic Guidance with the troubled expression of a headmaster forced at last to deal with a persistently unruly class. Harvey Morris, shrouded in his usual smoke haze—mercifully for him, it was to be at least a decade before Iran would ban smoking in government buildings—knew what was coming. "Well, Fisky, we'll see who's going to get the order of the boot today," he murmured. The ministry contained an underground auditorium that looked uncomfortably like a school hall and there we waited to hear the worst. Sadeq, the school director, took his place at a desk on a small raised podium and stared down at us severely. We all knew that an expulsion or two was in the air.

---

*I was taping Khalkhali's prison tour for CBC radio, and on the cassette in my archives it is still possible to hear the Hojatolislam's lips smacking over his ice-cream as he discusses the finer points of stoning.

†The full flavour of the somewhat portentous statement released in English by the Pars News Agency on 16 December is best conveyed in the following extract: "In the name of God, the compassionate, the merciful and the Islamic nation of Iran—the Great Satan, the United States, this origin of corruption of West [sic], after being defeated by our great nation, is trying to give asylum to its corrupt servant, the runaway Shah, and to prevent justice being implemented . . . In order to free itself from its great political deadlock and befool its nation, the U.S. has embarked on a futile effort and has sent the criminal Mohamed Reza out of the U.S. and has delivered to its poppet [sic] Panama. We herebye [sic] announce that to reveal the treacherous plots by the criminal U.S. and to punish it, the spy hostages will be tried."

"Gentlemen," he began—Harvey always liked the "gentlemen" bit—"I want to share with you a bit of agony we are going through with regard to the foreign media. With great displeasure, we are expelling the entire *Time* magazine crew from Iran." It mattered little that the "entire" staff of *Time* in the country numbered just two. This was not how Sadeq saw things. There were over three hundred foreign journalists in Iran from more than thirty countries, he said, but *Time* had gone too far. He flourished a clutch of front covers from the offending organ, one of which carried an unflattering portrait of Khomeini.

"Since the problem of hostages came up," Sadeq said, waving the latest issue of *Time* in his hand, "this has done nothing but arouse the hatred of the American people. The front covers have been like a hammer on the brain. The magazine has created some very irrational reaction on behalf of the American people." *Time* was not the only news organisation to feel Iranian wrath. Eight days earlier, Alex Efthyvoulos, a correspondent for the Associated Press—a bearded part-Russian Cypriot who looked like Rasputin—had been expelled for allegedly distorting news of rioting in the Azerbaijani provincial capital of Tabriz. Even the British had fallen foul of Iranian anger. In early December, Enayat Ettehad of Iranian television had been watching BBC News in a London hotel and was angered by a report on the hostages in which Keith Graves described in unpleasant detail how their hands were bound with rope and how they were forbidden to speak to each other or receive news from the outside world. I wasn't surprised. Over the next two and a half decades, Graves would infuriate the Taliban, the Israeli army, the U.S. government, the IRA, the British army, NATO, the Egyptians, the PLO, the Hizballah, the Syrians, the Turks and even the Cypriots—the latter an astonishing achievement even for a man of Graves's abrasiveness—and survive them all. But the BBC was made to pay for it. Ettehad instructed Iranian television to refuse BBC crews any further use of satellite facilities. The BBC was forced to ship all their film unprocessed by air to London, where it usually arrived a day late. It was clear, however, that Ettehad was far more upset by the BBC's Persian-language radio service, and Sadeq brandished a sheaf of papers above his head—complaints, he said, about the Persian service from "all over Iran."

Sadeq was confident about his broadsides. He loudly referred to the fact that one of the two *Time* correspondents had once worked for the CIA. "Yet still I let him into Iran." He was referring to Bruce van Voorst, who worked as a CIA research officer in the late 1950s but who now said that he had severed all links with the agency—whose own activities in the country were now, thanks to the embassy documents, a national Iranian obsession. The American CBS network was in trouble for comparing the students in the embassy to the German Baader-Meinhof gang, the ABC network for a State Department analysis "that would make any Iranian look like an idiot." But there was a pettiness about the government's response to overseas coverage, a gut reaction that sprang from patriotic anger rather than forethought. Sadeq, who in argument was given to drawing unhappy parallels with events in American history, unconsciously revealed this when he reminded us that "in 1834, Colonel Travis defended the Alamo against the Mexican army and when he was told to surrender he replied with gunfire. He stood up for his principles. And that is what Iran is doing today." I heard Harvey Morris sigh. "Good God!" he exclaimed. "I thought Travis lost the battle of the bloody Alamo."

The revolution was a tempest and we were all trapped in its vortex. We interviewed Khomeini, we watched the epic demonstrations, we watched America writhing in impotence. U.S. warships entered the Gulf. Khomeini called for an army of tens of thousands of schoolboy volunteers to defend Iran. I travelled back from Iranian Kurdistan on a bus whose passengers spent an hour watching a weapons education programme on the coach's specially installed television: how to strip and reassemble an automatic rifle, how to pull a grenade pin, how to master the mechanism of a heavy machine gun. I swayed at the back of the fast-moving bus as the audience sat in silent attention. And today, I thought, we have naming of parts.

But I was seeking some other way of reporting Iran, away from the events which were so obstinately staged for our benefit, especially for American television reporters. I was in Harvey's office, staring at the stained map of Iran on his wall, when I had an idea. What if I closed my eyes and stuck a pin into the map and then travelled to the point I had marked and asked the people there about the revolution? "Close your eyes and I'll give you a pin," Harvey announced. "And I bet you stick it in bloody Afghanistan." He produced the pin, I closed my eyes, stabbed at the map and then opened my eyes again. The little sliver of silver had landed in the "h" of a village called Kahak, south-west of the city of Qazvin. I set off at dawn next morning.

Kahak was the sort of place no one ever goes to visit. It lay, a rectangle of mud and clay single-storey houses, at the end of a dirt road with only a gaggle of children and a dung-heap picked over by fat chickens to welcome a stranger. Through the dust and the heat haze to the north, the Alborz Mountains ran along the horizon, forming the lower lip of the Caspian Sea basin. Foreigners never saw Kahak, except perhaps the passengers on the night train to the Soviet frontier as it skirted the village orchards. Even then, it was doubtful if they would notice anything. Kahak was so small that its 950 inhabitants could not even support a mosque of their own.

A prematurely ageing man of sixty-four with a slick of perspiration running down his face from beneath his turban and a shirt front covered in dirt had to travel up from Qom to minister to the faithful. But he was a man capable of extraordinary energy as he walked nimbly around the heaps of manure and puddles of gilded, foetid water, talking about the village in a possessive, slightly rhetorical, almost sermonising way, his voice rising and falling in the cadences of a formal speech rather than a conversation. What had the revolution done for these people, I asked, and Sheikh Ibrahim Zaude pointed to the hard, unwatered land beyond the mud huts, a desert of grey, unyielding earth.

"The villagers own everything on both sides of the road," he said. "But they do not know how much land they have." The heat shimmered and danced on the dried-up irrigation ditches: there were no deeds of ownership, no papers and no legal covenants in Kahak now that the landlords had gone. Just when the landlords did depart was something that bothered Sheikh Zaude. "In the past regime," he explained, "there were two big landowners—Habib Sardai and Ibrahim Solehi. The villagers lived in very bad conditions. Some of them were so poor that they owed many debts but Sardai and Solehi came here and took their grain in payment. I remember seeing these villagers going to other villages to buy back their own grain at high prices. So the people had to borrow money for this and then pay interest on the loans." More than a dozen villagers gathered round us as Sheikh Zaude talked on. They were poor people, most of them Turkish in origin with high, shiny cheekbones. Their grey jackets were torn and their trousers frayed where the rubble and thorns in the fields had scratched them. They wore cheap plastic sandals. There was only one girl with them, a thirteen-year-old with dark hair who had wrapped herself shroud-like in a pink and grey chador.

"Then things improved for us," Sheikh Zaude said. "Sardai and Solehi left with the land reforms." There was no perceptible change in the mullah's face. He had been asked about that year's Islamic revolution but he was talking about the Shah's "White Revolution" seventeen years earlier when the monarch's reform laws ostensibly curtailed the power of the big landowners. Private holdings were redistributed and landowners could retain only one village. Poor farmers were thereby brought into the economy, although most labourers and farm workers remained untouched. Kahak, it was clear, did not entirely benefit from the Shah's "revolution." "There were good things for us in the reforms," Sheikh Zaude said. "The number of sheep owned by the villagers went up from two thousand to three thousand. But the village itself, instead of being owned by two men, was now run by the government agent, a man called Darude Gilani, a capitalist from Qazvin. He was a bad man and he collected rent by demanding half of the villagers' crops."

There was an old man with an unshaven chin and a cataract in his left eye who now walked to the front of the villagers. From his grubby yellow shirt and broken shoes, I could not have imagined that Aziz Mahmoudi was the village headman and the largest farmer. He looked at the mullah for a moment and said, very slowly: "Darude Gilani is in Qazvin prison now." Mahmoudi walked across the village square, followed by a small throng of schoolchildren. He pointed to a crumbling, fortified mud house with two storeys, a sign of opulence amid such hardship. "That is where Solehi used to live," he said, gesturing to the broken windows. "Now Gilani is gone too. He will not come back." There was no reason why Gilani would return, even if he was released from prison. For on the first day of the revolution the previous February, when the villagers saw the imperial army surrendering in Tehran on the screen of a small black-and-white television set, they walked down to the fields that Gilani still owned on each side of the railway line. There they planted their own barley as a symbol that the revolution had arrived in Kahak.

Above the blackboard in the village's tiny clay-walled schoolhouse was a poster of Ayatollah Khomeini. It depicted the Imam bending over the bars of a jail while behind him thousands of Iranian prisoners wait patiently for their freedom. One after another, the boys in the seventh-grade class stood up and recited their admiration for Khomeini. Jalol Mahmoudi was twelve but talked about corruption in the Shah's regime, Ali Mahmoudi, who at fourteen was head of class, launched into a long speech about the Imam's kindness to children. "I am very pleased with the Ayatollah because in the past regime I was not taught well—now there are three extra classes and we can stay at school longer." Master Ali might be expected to receive a firm clout round the back of the head from his colleagues for such schoolboy enthusiasm. But the other children remained silent until asked to speak. And I knew that if I had visited this same village in the aftermath of the 1953 coup against Mossadeq in which "Monty" Woodhouse had played so prominent a part, I would have heard the fathers of these same children talking about the corruption of Mossadeq and the Shah's kindness to children.

Karim Khalaj was a teacher in his late forties and he said little as we sat in the staff room. He poured cups of tea from a large silver urn and sweetened it by drinking the tea sip by sip and nibbling lumps of sugar at the same time. Outside, we walked across the dusty fields towards the railway line. He was briefly imprisoned in the Shah's time. He was fired from his job for complaining about a government teacher's bribery.

The wind was picking up and the trees in the orchard were moving. A far belt of smog moved down the horizon. Somewhere near Kahak, more than a quarter of a century earlier, "Monty" Woodhouse must have buried his guns. Did any of the villagers support the Shah? I asked Khalaj. "None," he said firmly. "At least I never knew any who did." Savak never came to the village. It was too small to capture anyone's attention. So whose picture hung above the blackboard in class seven before the Ayatollah returned to Iran? Mr. Khalaj shrugged. "They had to put a picture there. Of course, it was the Shah's."

# CHAPTER FIVE

# The Path to War

*Perfection, of a kind, was what he was after,*
*And the poetry he invented was easy to understand;*
*He knew human folly like the back of his hand,*
*And was greatly interested in armies and fleets;*
*When he laughed, respectable senators burst with laughter,*
*And when he cried the little children died in the streets.*

—W. H. Auden, "Epitaph on a Tyrant"

IN MARCH 1917, TWENTY-TWO-YEAR-OLD Private 11072 Charles Dickens of the Cheshire Regiment carefully peeled a poster off a wall in the newly captured city of Baghdad. It was a turning point in his life. He had survived the hopeless Gallipoli campaign, attacking the Ottoman empire only 250 kilometres from its capital of Constantinople. He had then marched the length of Mesopotamia, fighting the Turks yet again for possession of the ancient caliphate and enduring the "grim battle" for Baghdad. The British invasion army of 600,000 soldiers was led by Lieutenant General Sir Stanley Maude and the sheet of paper that caught Private Dickens's attention was Maude's official "Proclamation" to the people of Baghdad, printed in both English and Arabic.

That same 11 by 18 inch poster—now framed in black and gold—hangs on the wall a few feet from my desk as I write this chapter. Long ago, it was stained with damp—"foxed," as booksellers say—which may have been Dickens's perspiration in the long hot Iraqi summer of 1917. It has been folded many times, witness, as his daughter Hilda would recall eighty-six years later, "to having travelled in his knapsack for a length of time." She called it "his precious document" and I can see why. It is filled with noble aspirations and presentiments of future tragedy, of the false promises of the world's greatest empire, commitments and good intentions and words of honour that were to be repeated in the same city of Baghdad by the next great empire more than two decades after Dickens's death. They read now like a funeral dirge:

## PROCLAMATION

. . . Our military operations have as their object the defeat of the enemy and the driving of him from these territories. In order to complete this task I am charged with absolute and supreme control of all regions in which British

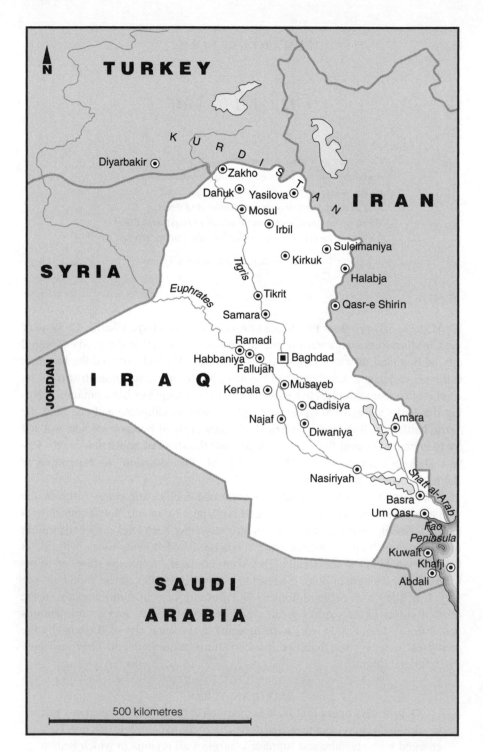

N

TURKEY

*K U R D I S T A N*

Diyarbakir ⊙

⊙ Zakho

Dahuk ⊙  ⊙ Yasilova

⊙ Mosul

IRAN

⊙ Irbil

SYRIA

⊙ Suleimaniya

⊙ Kirkuk

Halabja

*Tigris*

⊙ Qasr-e Shirin

*Euphrates*

⊙ Tikrit

Samara ⊙

Ramadi

⊙■ Baghdad

Habbaniya ⊙⊙
Fallujah

JORDAN

IRAQ

Kerbala ⊙  ⊙ Musayeb

⊙ Qadisiya

Najaf ⊙

Amara

⊙ Diwaniya

Nasiriyah ⊙

*Shatt al-Arab*

Basra ⊙
Um Qasr ⊙

*Fao
Peninsula*

Kuwait ⊙

Khafji ⊙

SAUDI

Abdali

ARABIA

500 kilometres

troops operate; but our armies do not come into your cities and lands as conquerors or enemies, but as liberators. Since the days of Hulagu\* your citizens have been subject to the tyranny of strangers . . . and your fathers and yourselves have groaned in bondage. Your sons have been carried off to wars not of your seeking, your wealth has been stripped from you by unjust men and squandered in different places. It is the wish not only of my King and his peoples, but it is also the wish of the great Nations with whom he is in alliance, that you should prosper even as in the past when your lands were fertile . . . But you, people of Baghdad . . . are not to understand that it is the wish of the British government to impose upon you alien institutions. It is the hope of the British Government that the aspirations of your philosophers and writers shall be realised once again, that the people of Baghdad shall flourish, and shall enjoy their wealth and substance under institutions which are in consonance with their sacred laws and with their racial ideals . . . It is the hope and desire of the British people . . . that the Arab race may rise once more to greatness and renown amongst the peoples of the Earth . . . Therefore I am commanded to invite you, through your Nobles and Elders and Representatives, to participate in the management of your civil affairs in collaboration with the Political Representative of Great Britain . . . so that you may unite with your kinsmen in the North, East, South and West, in realising the aspirations of your Race.

> (sd.) F. S. Maude, Lieutenant General,
> Commanding the British Forces in Iraq

Private Dickens spent the First World War fighting Muslims, first the Turks at Suvla Bay at Gallipoli and then the Turkish army—which included Arab soldiers—in Mesopotamia. My father, Bill, was originally in the Cheshire Regiment but was serving in Ireland the year Charles Dickens entered Baghdad, and would be sent to the Western Front in 1918. Dickens had a longer war. He "spoke, often & admirably," his daughter Hilda would recall, of one of his commanders, General Sir Charles Munro, who at fifty-five had fought in the last months of the Gallipoli campaign and then landed at Basra in southern Iraq at the start of the British invasion. But Munro's leadership did not save Dickens's married sister's nephew, Samuel Martin, who was killed by the Turks at Basra. Hilda remembers "my father told of how killing a Turk, he thought it was in revenge for the death of his 'nephew.' I don't know if they were in the same battalion, but they were a similar age, 22 years."†

The British had been proud of their initial occupation of Basra. More than

---

\*Grandson of Genghis Khan who destroyed Baghdad in 1258 as part of the Mongol campaign to subdue the Islamic world.

†For seventy years, Samuel Martin's gravestone stood in the British war cemetery in Basra with the following inscription: "In Memory of Private Samuel Martin 24384, 8th Bn., Cheshire Regiment who died on Sunday 9 April 1916. Private Martin, son of George and Sarah Martin, of the Beech Tree Inn, Barnton, Northwich, Cheshire." In the gales of shellfire that swept over Basra

eighty years later, a British Muslim whose family came from Pakistan sent me an amused letter along with a series of twelve very old postcards which were printed by *The Times of India* in Bombay on behalf of the Indian YMCA. One of them showed British artillery amid the Basra date palms, another a soldier in a pith helmet, turning towards the camera as his comrades tether horses behind him, others the crew of a British gunboat on the Shatt al-Arab River and the Turkish-held town of Kurna, a building shattered by British shellfire, shortly before its surrender. As long ago as 1914, a senior British official was told by "local [Arab] notables" that "we should be received in Baghdad with the same cordiality [as in southern Iraq] and that the Turkish troops would offer little if any opposition." But the British invasion of Iraq had originally failed. When Major-General Charles Townshend took 13,000 men up the banks of the Tigris towards Baghdad, he was surrounded and defeated by Turkish forces at Kut al-Amara. His surrender was the most comprehensive of military disasters and ended in a death march to Turkey for those British troops who had not been killed in battle. The graves of 500 of them in the Kut War Cemetery sank into sewage during the period of UN sanctions that followed Iraq's 1990 invasion of Kuwait when spare parts for pumps needed to keep sewage from the graves were not supplied to Iraq. Visiting the cemetery in 1998, my colleague at *The Independent*, Patrick Cockburn, found "tombstones . . . still just visible above the slimy green water. A broken cement cross sticks out of a reed bed . . . a quagmire in which thousands of little green frogs swarm like cockroaches as they feed on garbage." In all, Britain lost 40,000 men in the Mesopotamian campaign.

Baghdad looked much the same when Private Dickens arrived. Less than two years earlier, a visitor had described a city whose streets

> gaped emptily, the shops were mostly closed . . . In the Christian cemetery east of the high road leading to Persia coffins and half mouldering skeletons were floating. On account of the Cholera which was ravaging the town (three hundred people were dying of it every day) the Christian dead were now being buried on the new embankment of the high road, so that people walking and riding not only had to pass by but even to make their way among and over the graves . . . There was no longer any life in the town . . .

The British held out wildly optimistic hopes for a "new" Iraq that would be regenerated by Western enterprise, not unlike America's own pipedreams of 2003. "There is no doubt," *The Sphere* told its readers in 1915, "that with the aid of European science and energy it can again become the garden of Asia . . . and under British rule everything may be hoped."

The British occupation was dark with historical precedent. Iraqi troops who

---

during the 1980–88 war with Iran, the cemetery was destroyed and looted and many of the gravestones shattered beyond repair. When I visited the cemetery in the chaotic months that followed the Anglo-American invasion of 2003, I found wild dogs roaming the broken headstones and even the brass fittings of the central memorial stolen.

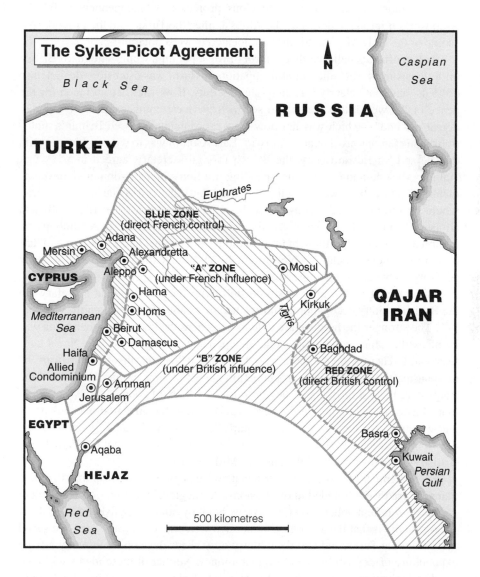

The Sykes-Picot Agreement

Caspian Sea

Black Sea

RUSSIA

TURKEY

Euphrates

BLUE ZONE
(direct French control)

Adana
Mersin
Alexandretta
Aleppo

CYPRUS

"A" ZONE
(under French influence)

Mosul

Mediterranean Sea

Hama
Homs
Beirut
Damascus

Kirkuk

Tigris

QAJAR IRAN

Haifa
Allied Condominium
Jerusalem
Amman

"B" ZONE
(under British influence)

Baghdad

RED ZONE
(direct British control)

EGYPT

Aqaba

HEJAZ

Basra
Kuwait

Persian Gulf

Red Sea

500 kilometres

had been serving with the Turkish army, but who "always entertained friendly ideas towards the English," found that in prison in India they were "insulted and humiliated in every way." These same prisoners wanted to know if the British would hand over Iraq to Sherif Hussein of the Hejaz—to whom the British had made fulsome and ultimately mendacious promises of "independence" for the Arab world if it fought alongside the Allies against the Turks—on the grounds that "some of the Holy Moslem Shrines are located in Mesopotamia."

British officials believed that control of Mesopotamia would safeguard British oil interests in Persia—the initial occupation of Basra was ostensibly designed to do that—and that "clearly it is our right and duty, if we sacrifice so much for the peace of the world, that we should see to it we have compensation, or we may defeat our end"—which was not how General Maude expressed Britain's ambitions in his famous proclamation in 1917. Earl Asquith was to write in his memoirs that he and Sir Edward Grey, the British foreign secretary, agreed in 1915 that "taking Mesopotamia . . . means spending millions in irrigation and development . . ." Once they were installed in Baghdad, the British decided that Iraq would be governed and reconstructed by a "Council," formed partly of British advisers "and partly of representative non-official members from among the inhabitants." Later, they thought they would like "a cabinet half of natives and half of British officials, behind which might be an administrative council, or some advisory body consisting entirely of prominent natives."

The traveller and scholar Gertrude Bell, who became "oriental secretary" to the British military occupation authority, had no doubts about Iraqi public opinion. ". . . The stronger the hold we are able to keep here the better the inhabitants will be pleased . . . they can't conceive an independent Arab government. Nor, I confess, can I. There is no one here who could run it." Again, this was far from the noble aspirations of Maude's proclamation eleven months earlier. Nor would the Iraqis have been surprised had they been told—which, of course, they were not— that Maude strongly opposed the very proclamation that appeared over his name and which was in fact written by Sir Mark Sykes, the very same Sykes who had drawn up the secret 1916 agreement with François Georges Picot for French and British control over much of the postwar Middle East.

By September of 1919, even journalists were beginning to grasp that Britain's plans for Iraq were founded upon illusions. "I imagine," the *Times* correspondent wrote on 23 September, "that the view held by many English people about Mesopotamia is that the local inhabitants will welcome us because we have saved them from the Turks, and that the country only needs developing to repay a large expenditure of English lives and English money. Neither of these ideals will bear much examination . . . from the political point of view we are asking the Arab to exchange his pride and independence for a little Western civilisation, the profits of which must be largely absorbed by the expenses of administration."

Within six months, Britain was fighting an insurrection in Iraq and David Lloyd George, the prime minister, was facing calls for a military withdrawal. "Is it not for the benefit of the people of that country that it should be governed so as to enable them to develop this land which has been withered and shrivelled up by oppression. What would happen if we withdrew?" Lloyd George would not abandon Iraq to "anarchy and confusion." By this stage, British officials in Baghdad were blaming the violence on "local political agitation, originated outside Iraq," suggesting that Syria might be involved. For Syria 1920, read America's claim that Syria was supporting the insurrection in 2004. Arnold Wilson, the senior British official in Iraq, took a predictable line. "We cannot maintain our position . . . by a policy of conciliation of extremists," he wrote. "Having set our hand to the task of regenerating Mesopotamia, we must be prepared to furnish men and money . . . We must be prepared . . . to go very slowly with constitutional and democratic institutions."

There was fighting in the Shiite town of Kufa and a British siege of Najaf after a British official was murdered. The authorities demanded "the unconditional surrender of the murderers and others concerned in the plot" and the leading Shiite divine, Sayed Khadum Yazdi, abstained from supporting the rebellion and shut himself up in his house. Eleven of the insurgents were executed. A local sheikh, Badr al-Rumaydh, became a British target. "Badr must be killed or captured, and a relentless pursuit of the man till this object is obtained should be carried out," a political officer wrote. The British now realised that they had made one major political mistake. They had alienated a major political group in Iraq: the ex-Turkish Iraqi officials and officers. The ranks of the disaffected swelled. Wilson put it all down not to nationalism but "anarchy plus fanaticism." All the precedents were there. For Kufa 1920, read Kufa 2004. For Najaf 1920, read Najaf 2004. For Yazdi in 1920, read Grand Ayatollah Ali al-Sistani in 2004. For Badr in 1920, read Muqtada al-Sadr in 2004. For "anarchy and fanaticism" in 1920, read "Saddam remnants" and al-Qaeda in 2004.

Another insurgency broke out in the area of Fallujah, where Sheikh Dhari killed an officer, Colonel Gerald Leachman, and cut rail traffic between Fallujah and Baghdad. The British advanced towards Fallujah and inflicted "heavy punishment" on the tribe. The location of this battle is today known as Khan Dhari; in 2003 it would be the scene of the first killing of an American occupation soldier by a roadside bomb. In desperation, the British needed "to complete the façade of the Arab government." And so, with Churchill's enthusiastic support, the British were to give the throne of Iraq to the Hashemite King Feisal, the son of Sherif Hussein, a consolation prize for the man whom the French had just thrown out of Damascus. Paris was having no kings in its own mandated territory of Syria. "How much longer," *The Times* asked on 7 August 1920, "are valuable lives to be sacrificed in the vain endeavour to impose upon the Arab population an elaborate and expensive administration which they never asked for and do not want?"

The British suffered 450 dead in the Iraqi insurgency and more than 1,500 wounded. In that same summer of 1920, T. E. Lawrence—Lawrence of Arabia—estimated that the British had killed "about ten thousand Arabs in this rising. We cannot hope to maintain such an average . . ."* Henceforth, the British

---

*Lawrence made no mention of his confident assertion to a cabinet committee two years earlier that "in Irak the Arabs expect the British to keep control."

government—deprived of reconstruction funds by an international recession and confronted by an increasingly unwilling soldiery, which had fought during the 1914–18 war and was waiting for demobilisation—would rely on air power to impose its wishes.

The Royal Air Force, again with Churchill's support, bombed rebellious villages and dissident tribesmen. So urgent was the government's need for modern bombers in the Middle East that, rather than freighting aircraft to the region by sea, it set up a ramshackle and highly dangerous transit system in which RAF crews flew their often un-airworthy bombers from Europe; at least eight pilots lost their lives in crashes and 30 per cent of the bombers were lost en route. In Iraq, Churchill urged the use of mustard gas, which had already been employed against Shia rebels in 1920. He wrote to Air Marshal Sir Hugh Trenchard, Chief of the Air Staff, that "you should certainly proceed with the experimental work on gas bombs, especially mustard gas, which would inflict punishment upon recalcitrant natives without inflicting grave injury upon them."

Squadron Leader Arthur Harris, later Marshal of the Royal Air Force and the man who perfected the firestorm destruction of Hamburg, Dresden and other great German cities in the Second World War, was employed to refine the bombing of Iraqi insurgents. The RAF found, he wrote much later, "that by burning down their reed-hutted villages, after we'd warned them to get out, we put them to the maximum amount of inconvenience, without physical hurt, and they soon stopped their raiding and looting . . ." This was what, in its emasculation of the English language, the Pentagon would now call "war lite." But the bombing was not as surgical as Harris's official biographer would suggest. In 1924, he had admitted that "they [the Arabs and Kurds] now know what real bombing means, in casualties and damage; they know that within forty-five minutes a full-sized village can be practically wiped out and a third of its inhabitants killed or injured."

Lawrence remarked in a 1920 letter to *The Observer* that "these risings take a regular course. There is a preliminary Arab success, then British reinforcements go out as a punitive force. They fight their way (our losses are slight, the Arab losses heavy) to their objective, which is meanwhile bombarded by artillery, aeroplanes, or gunboats." This same description entirely fits American military operations in Iraq in 2004, once the occupying powers and their puppet government lost control of most of Iraq. But Lawrence had, as a prominent member of the T. E. Lawrence Society put it, a maddening habit of being sardonic or even humorous about serious matters which was one of his less attractive traits. "It is odd that we do not use poison gas on these occasions," he wrote in the same letter. "Bombing the houses is a patchy way of getting the women and children, and our infantry always incur losses in shooting down the Arab men. By gas attacks the whole population of offending districts could be wiped out neatly . . ."

In a less unpleasant mood, however, Lawrence spoke with remarkable common sense about the Iraqi occupation. "The Arabs rebelled against the Turks during the war not because the Turk Government was notably bad," he wrote in a letter to *The Times* the same year, "but because they wanted independence. They did not risk their lives in battle to change masters, to become British subjects . . . but to win a show of their own. Whether they are fit for independence or not remains to be tried. Merit is no qualification for freedom."

Far more prescient was an article Lawrence published in the *Sunday Times* in August 1920 in words that might have been directed to British prime minister Tony Blair eighty-four years later:

> The people of England have been led in Mesopotamia into a trap from which it will be hard to escape with dignity and honour. They have been tricked into it by a steady withholding of information. The Baghdad communiqués are belated, insincere, incomplete. Things have been far worse than we have been told, our administration more bloody and inefficient than the public knows . . . We are today not far from a disaster.

Air Commodore Lionel Charlton was so appalled at the casualties inflicted on innocent villagers in Iraq that he resigned his post as Senior Air Staff Officer Iraq because he could no longer "maintain the policy of intimidation by bomb." He had visited an Iraqi hospital to find it full of wounded tribesmen, and after the RAF had bombed the Kurdish rebel city of Suleimaniya, Charlton "knew the crowded life of these settlements and pictured with horror the arrival of a bomb, without warning, in the midst of a market gathering or in the bazaar quarter. Men, women and children would suffer equally." It was to be a policy followed with enthusiasm by the United States generations later.

The same false promises of a welcoming populace were made to the British and Americans, the same grand rhetoric about a new and democratic Iraq, the same explosive rebellion among Iraqis—in the very same towns and cities—the identical "Council of Ministers" and the very same collapse of the occupation power, all followed historical precedent. Unable to crush the insurgency, the Americans turned to the use of promiscuous air assault, just as the British did before them: the destruction of homes in "dissident" villages, the bombing of mosques where weapons were allegedly concealed, the slaughter by air strike of "terrorists" near the Syrian border—who turned out to be members of a wedding party. Much the same policy of air bombing was adopted in the already abandoned democracy of post-2001 Afghanistan.

As for the British soldiers of the 1920s, we couldn't ship our corpses home in the heat of the Middle East eighty years ago. So we buried them in the North Gate Cemetery in Baghdad where they still lie to this day, most of them in their late teens and twenties, opposite the suicide-bombed Turkish embassy. Among them is the mausoleum of General Maude, who died in Baghdad within eight months of his victory because he chose to drink unboiled milk: a stone sarcophagus with the one word "MAUDE" carved on its lid. When I visited the cemetery to inspect it in the summer of 2004, the Iraqi guarding the graves warned me to spend no more than five minutes at the tomb lest I be kidnapped.

Feisal, third son of the Sherif Hussein of Mecca, was proclaimed constitutional monarch by a "Council of Ministers" in Baghdad on 11 July 1922 and a referendum gave him a laughably impossible 96 per cent of the vote, a statistic that would become wearingly familiar in the Arab world over the next eighty years. As a Sunni Muslim and a monarch from a Gulf tribe, he was neither an Iraqi nor a member of Iraq's Shia Muslim majority. It was our first betrayal of the Shias of Iraq. There would be two more within the next hundred years. Henceforth, Mesopotamia would be known as Iraq, but its creation brought neither peace nor happiness to its people. An Anglo-Iraqi treaty guaranteeing the special interests of Britain was signed in the face of nationalist opposition; in 1930, a second agreement provided for a twenty-five-year Anglo-Iraqi alliance with RAF bases at Shuaiba and Habbaniya. Iraqi nationalist anger was particularly stirred by Britain's continued support for a Jewish state in its other mandate of Palestine. Tribal revolts and a 1936 coup d'état created further instability and—after a further coup in 1941 brought the pro-German government of Rashid Ali al-Gaylani to power—Britain reinvaded Iraq all over again, fighting off Luftwaffe attacks launched from Vichy Syria and Lebanon—and occupying Basra and Baghdad.* British forces paused outside the capital to allow the regent, the Emir Abdullah, to be first to enter Baghdad, a delay that allowed partisans of Rashid Ali to murder at least 150 of the city's substantial Jewish community and burn and loot thousands of properties. Five of the coup leaders were hanged and many others imprisoned; one of the latter was Khairallah Tulfah, whose four-year-old nephew, Saddam Hussein, would always remember the anti-British nationalism of his uncle. The German plan for a second Arab revolt, this time pro-Axis and supported by the Grand Mufti of Jerusalem, Haj Amin al-Husseini—whose journey to Berlin will be told later in our story—came to nothing.

But Iraq remained an inherently weak state, young King Feisal the Second having no nationalist credentials—since he was anyway not an Iraqi—and since the government was still led by a group of former Arab Ottoman officials like Nuri es-Said, who contrived to be prime minister fourteen times before his most bloody demise. On 14 July 1958, Iraqi forces under Brigadier Abdul-Karim Qassim stormed the royal palace. Es-Said was shot down after trying to escape Baghdad dressed as a woman. Feisal, the regent and the rest of the royal family were surrounded by soldiers and machine-gunned to death after trying to flee the burning palace. Qassim's new military regime enraged the United States. Not only did Qassim take Iraq out of the anti-Soviet Baghdad pact but he threatened to invade Kuwait. He also failed to quell a mass Kurdish uprising in northern Iraq and was eventually brought down by another coup in February 1963, this one largely

---

*The Germans had no more success in Iraq than any other Western powers over the past century. They flew 24 Heinkels and Messerschmitts into Mosul but lost their top Luftwaffe liaison officer in a dogfight over Baghdad. Only when Iraqi resistance to British forces was collapsing did Hitler issue his Military Directive No. 30 on the Middle East. "The *Arab liberation movement* in the Middle East is our natural ally against England," it announced. "In this connection the rising in Iraq has special importance . . ."

organised by the Baath party—but with the active assistance of the CIA. Qassim was taken to the radio station in Baghdad and murdered. His bullet-riddled body was then shown on television, propped up on a chair as a soldier laughingly kicked its legs.

The Baath had been founded in Syria in 1941—inspired, ironically, by Britain's re-invasion of Iraq—as a secular, pan-Arab movement intended to lift the burden of guilt and humiliation which had lain across the Arab world for so many generations. During the centuries of Ottoman rule, Arabs had suffered famine and a steady loss of intellectual power. Education had declined over the years and many millions of Arabs never learned to read and write. *Baath* means "rebirth," and although its Syrian Christian founder, Michel Aflaq, was himself a graduate of the Sorbonne—and wore an outsize fez—it had a natural base among the poor, the villages and tribes and, of course, within the army. Saddam Hussein was an early adherent, and among the first Baathists to try to kill Qassim; his subsequent flight across Iraq, his own extraction of a bullet in his leg with a razor-blade, and his swim to freedom across the Tigris River—at almost exactly the same location where American Special Forces were to find him in 2003—was to become an official Saddam legend.

Despite splits within the Baath, Saddam Hussein emerged as vice-chairman of the party's Regional Command Council after a further coup in 1968. He would remain nominally the second most powerful man in Iraq until 16 July 1979, when President Ahmed Hassan al-Bakr, Saddam's cousin, retired. There followed the infamous dinner party at the presidential palace at which Saddam invited his own party cadres to denounce themselves. The execution of his Baathist colleagues began within days.

As Saddam had slowly been taking control of Iraq, the Kurdish insurrection began again in the north and President Sadat of Egypt, by his journey to Jerusalem in November 1977, took the most populous Arab country out of the Arab–Israeli conflict. The Camp David agreement made this final. So it was that Saddam would preside over what the Iraqis immediately called the "Confrontation Front Summit" in Baghdad. This involved turning the Iraqi capital—however briefly—into the centre of the Arab world, giving Saddam exposure on the eve of his takeover from President al-Bakr. A vast tent was erected behind the summit palace, five hundred journalists were flown into Iraq from around the world—all telephone calls made by them would be free as well as bugged—and housed in hotels many miles from Baghdad, trucked to a "press centre" where they would be forbidden any contact with delegates and watched by posses of young men wearing white socks. We knew they were policemen because each wore a sign on his lapel that said "Tourism."

The latter was supposed to occupy much of our time, and I have an imperishable memory of a long bus journey down to Kurna, just north of Basra, to view the Garden of Eden. Our bus eventually drew up next to a bridge where a foetid river flowed slowly between treeless banks of grey sand beneath a dun-coloured sky. One of the cops put his left hand on my arm and pointed with the other at this miserable scene, proudly uttering his only touristic announcement of the day: "And this, Mr. Robert, is the Garden of Eden."

Before the summit, a lot of Arab leaders were forced to pretend to be friends in the face of "the traitor Sadat." President Assad was persuaded to forget the brutal schism between his country's Baath party and that of al-Bakr and Saddam. The Syrians announced that Assad and al-Bakr would discuss "a common front against the mad Zionist attack against our region and the capitulationist, unilateral reconciliation of the Egyptian regime with Israel." Once in Baghdad, Assad, who had maintained an entire army division on his eastern border in case Iraq invaded—he already had 33,000 Syrian troops deployed in Lebanon—and al-Bakr talked in "an atmosphere of deep understanding," according to the Syrian government newspaper *Tishrin*. Unity in diversity. King Hussein of Jordan would have to travel to the city in which the Hashemite monarchy had been exterminated only twenty years earlier. Baath party officials were sent to the overgrown royal cemetery in Baghdad to scythe down the long grass around the graves of the Hashemites in case the king wanted to visit them. Even Abu Nidal, the head of the cruellest of Palestinian hit-squads, was packed off to Tikrit lest his presence in Baghdad offend the PLO leader, Yassir Arafat, from whom Abu Nidal had split in 1974.

And so they all gathered, old al-Bakr and the young Saddam and Arafat and Hussein and Crown Prince Fahd of Saudi Arabia. Reporters were banned from the conference chamber but photographers were allowed to view these men much in the way that visitors are permitted to see the embalmed body of Lenin. Masquerading as part of Michael Cole's BBC television crew, we walked into the chamber and shuffled along the rows of princes and presidents who sat in waxworks attitudes of concern and apprehension, past Arafat, who repeatedly and embarrassingly gave a thumbs-up to the cameras, past a frowning King Hussein and a glowering Saddam. I watched the future Iraqi leader carefully, and when his eyes briefly met mine I noted a kind of contempt in them, something supercilious. This was not, I thought, a man who had much faith in conferences.

And he was right. The Saudis made sure that they didn't anger the United States, and after three days of deliberation the Arab mountain gave forth a mouse. Egypt would be put under an economic boycott—just like Israel—and a committee would be dispatched to Cairo to try to persuade Sadat to renounce Camp David. To sweeten the deal, they were to offer him $7 billion annually for the next ten years to support Egypt's bankrupt economy. The unenviable task of leading this forlorn delegation to Cairo fell, rather sadly, to Selim el-Hoss, the prime minister of Lebanon whose own war-battered country was then more deeply divided than the Arab world itself. Sadat snubbed them all, refusing to meet the ministers. The money was a bribe, he accurately announced, and "all the millions in the world cannot buy the will of Egypt."

The nature of the Iraqi regime was no secret, nor was its ruthlessness. The British had already become involved in a trade dispute with the government in 1978 after Iraqi agents in London murdered Abdul Razzaq al-Nayef, a former Iraqi prime minister who had been condemned to death by the Baghdad authorities. A British businessman, a representative of Wimpey's, had been languishing for a month in Baghdad's central prison without any charges, and a British diplomat, Richard Drew, was dragged from his car in the city and beaten up, apparently by plain-clothes police.

But the search for "spies" within the body politic of Iraq had been established eleven years earlier, and to understand the self-hatred which this engendered in the regime—and Saddam's role in the purges—it is essential to go back to the record of its early days. After I first saw Saddam in Baghdad, I began to build up a file on him back home in Beirut. I went back to the Lebanese newspaper archives; Beirut was under nightly civil war bombardment but its journalists still maintained their files. And there, as so often happened in the grubby newspaper libraries of Lebanon, a chilling pattern began to emerge. At its congress in November 1968, the Baath party, according to the Baghdad newspaper *Al-Jumhouriya*, had made "the liquidation of spy networks" a national aspiration; and the following month, the newly installed Baath party discovered a "conspiracy" to overthrow its rule. It accused eighty-four people of being involved, including the former prime minister, Dr. Abdul Rahman al-Bazzaz, and his former defence minister, Major General Abdul Aziz Uquili. The charges of spying, a Lebanese newspaper reported at the time, "were levelled in the course of statements made in a special Baghdad radio and television programme by two of the accused, an ex-soldier from the southern port of Basra and a lawyer from Baghdad." The interview was personally conducted, according to the Beirut press, "by Saddam Tikriti, secretary general of the Iraqi leadership of the ruling Baath party." According to the same newspaper, "the interview was introduced by a recording of the part of the speech delivered by President al-Bakr in Baghdad on December 5th [1968] where he said 'there shall no longer be a place on Iraqi soil for spies.'"

The slaughter began within six weeks. At dawn on 27 January 1969, fourteen Iraqis, nine of them Jews, were publicly hanged after a three-man court had convicted them of spying for Israel. They claimed that Izra Naji Zilkha, a fifty-one-year-old Jewish merchant from Basra, was the leader of the "espionage ring." Even as the men were hanging in Liberation Square in Baghdad and in Basra, a new trial began in Baghdad involving thirty-five more Iraqis, thirteen of them Jews. Only hours before the January hangings, the Baath—of which the forty-year-old "Saddam Tikriti" was just now, according to the Lebanese press, "the real authority"—organised a demonstration at which thousands of Iraqis were marched to the square to watch the public executions and hear a government statement which announced that the party was "determined to fulfil its promise to the people for the elimination of spies." The *Baghdad Observer* later carried an interview with the revolutionary court president, Colonel Ali Hadi Witwet, who said that the court reached its verdicts regardless of the defendants' religion, adding that seven Jews had been acquitted. When the next batch of "spies" was executed on 20 February, all eight condemned men were Muslims. As usual, their conviction had been secret, although the night before their execution Baghdad radio broadcast what it claimed was a recording of the hearing. The condemned men had been accused of collecting information about Iraqi troop deployment. Their leader, Warrant Officer Najat Kazem Khourshid, was one of the eight, although his "trial" was not broadcast. Baghdad radio later told its listeners that "the Iraqi people expressed their condemnation of the spies."

By May 1969, the Baathist failure to suppress the Kurdish rebellion had led to the arrest of a hundred more Iraqis, including twenty-four who had served in the previous regime. One of these was the lord mayor of Baghdad, Midhat al-Haj Sirri, who was accused of leading a CIA intelligence network. Former ministers arrested included Ismail Khairallah, Fouad Rikabi, Rashid Musleh, Siddik Shansal and Shukri Saleh Zaki. The Baath leadership sought the "people's" opinion. Delegates to a meeting of farmers' trade unions roared their support when President al-Bakr declared that he was determined to "chop off the heads of the traitors." The lord mayor was duly brought to the Baghdad television studios to "confess" his role as a CIA agent while another defendant, Dr. Yussef al-Mimar—an ex-director general of the Ministry of Agrarian Reform—broke down and implicated former senior ministers in the defection of Mounir Rufa, an Iraqi air force pilot who had flown his MiG-21 fighter-bomber to Israel nearly three years earlier.

Al-Mimar also claimed that he was recruited into the CIA by an Iraqi businessman in Beirut in 1964, and ordered by a CIA front company masquerading as investment brokers first to open an investment business in Libya and then to secure an invitation to Baghdad for President Eisenhower's onetime secretary of the Treasury, Robert Anderson. How much of this "confession" bore any relation to the truth it is impossible to know. Four Iraqi civilians—Taleb Abdullah al-Saleh, Ali Abdullah al-Saleh, Abdul Jalil Mahawi and Abdul Razzak Dahab—had been hanged the previous month for spying for the CIA. On 15 May 1969, the Baathist regime hanged another ten men after one of them, Abdul Hadi Bachari, had appeared in a television "confession." They were accused of working for both Israel and the United States and included an army sergeant and an air force lieutenant.

In June, for the first time, a convicted "spy" told Iraqi television he had worked for British intelligence. Named as Zaki Abdul Wahab, a legal adviser to the Iraqi businessman in Beirut, he was accused in the Baghdad press of being "a British-American agent." By July, another eighty prominent Iraqis were on trial for espionage. They were merely the prelude to thousands of hangings, almost all for "subversion" and "spying." Eleven years later, when Saddam Hussein was confirmed in power, Iraqi hangmen were dispatching victims to the gallows at the rate of a hundred every six weeks. In 1980, Amnesty International reported the recent executions of 257 people.

In 1979 came Saddam's own arrest of five of the twenty-one members of his Revolutionary Command Council, accusing all of them of espionage for Syria, whose president had visited Baghdad only two months earlier for those talks of "deep understanding" with al-Bakr. The revolutionary court condemned the five men to death without appeal, and the very next morning, Saddam Hussein and several of his senior advisers went to the central prison and personally executed them. Saddam himself used his service revolver to blow out one of the victims' brains.

In the early days of the regime, the names of newly executed Iraqis would be read on state television every afternoon at 4 p.m. An old Iraqi friend of mine would recall for me in 2003 how her relatives were imprisoned and how, each afternoon, she would dose herself with morphine before sitting down in front of the television screen. "I don't know how I survived those broadcasts," she said. "The man who read the names had a thin face and sharp eyes and he read them out in a very harsh way. His name was Mohamed al-Sahhaf." This was the same Mohamed al-Sahhaf who, grey-haired and humorous, was minister of information during the 2003 American invasion of Iraq, the "Comical Ali" who provoked President George W. Bush to laugh at his claims that U.S. forces had not reached Baghdad when their tanks were crossing the Tigris River. From brutal apparatchik to friendly buffoon in just thirty years. He was later to record his memories for Al-Arabia satellite television—without recalling his days as spokesman for the hangman of Baghdad.

So what lay behind this ferocious passion for executions that Saddam manifested, this controlled cruelty that became part of the regime's existence?* I once asked this of Mohamed Heikal, as we sat on the lawn of his farm in the Nile Delta, wildly coloured birds cawing from the palm trees and a servant producing chilled beer in delicate mugs of blue glass.

"I will tell you a story, Robert," he began. Heikal's stories were always brilliant. With Heikal, you had to remain silent throughout. His recollections were a theatrical performance as well as a feat of memory, his hands raised before his face when he wished to express shock, eyebrows arching towards heaven, Havana cigar brandished towards me if he thought I was not paying sufficient attention; they were stories that usually had a sting in the tail.[†] Heikal knew Saddam Hussein—in fact, he knew almost every Arab leader and was probably treated with greater deference than most of them—but he had no illusions about the Baath party.

"On my first visit to Baghdad after the takeover of power, I met the minister of planning. He was a very nice, urbane, cultured man whom I immediately liked.

---

*Mesopotamia had been the seat of kindly rulers, but it is not difficult to find precedents for cruelty. During the African slave revolt in Iraq from 869 to 883, the Caliph Moutaded failed to persuade a slave leader called Mohamed "Chemilah" to denounce his comrades. "Even if you have my flesh roasted," Chemilah is said to have replied, "I will never reveal the name of the person in favour of whom I administered the oath and whom I recognise as an imam." The caliph said that he would administer the punishment Chemilah had just designated. The unfortunate man was said to have been "skewered on a long iron rod which penetrated him from his anus to his mouth; he was kept like this over a huge fire until he died, heaping invective and curses on the caliph, who attended his torture." Another version of his demise says that he was tied between three spears, placed over a fire and turned like a chicken "until his skin began to crackle." Then he was tied to a gallows in Baghdad.

[†]In *The Sphinx and the Commissar*, Heikal told of Nikita Khrushchev's reaction to his cigar-smoking. "Suddenly Khrushchev turned on me. 'Are you a capitalist?' he demanded. 'Why are you smoking a cigar?' 'Because I like cigars,' I said. But Khrushchev seized my cigar and crushed it out in the ashtray. I protested. 'A cigar is a capitalist object,' said Khrushchev . . . The

When I returned to Iraq some time later, I asked to see him again. But each time I asked a minister where he was, I would be sidestepped. 'You must ask the president this question when you meet him,' they would say. Every time I asked to see the minister of planning, it was the same reply. So when I came to see Saddam, I asked him if I could meet the minister of planning again. Saddam just looked at me. Why did I want to see him? he asked me. I said he seemed a very intelligent and decent man. Saddam looked at me very seriously and said: 'We scissored his neck!' I was taken aback. Why? I asked. What had he done wrong? Had Saddam any proof of wrongdoing? 'We don't need proof,' Saddam replied. 'This isn't a white revolution in Iraq. This is a red revolution. Suspicion is enough.' I was speechless. Oh yes, and Robert, that blue beer mug you are drinking from—it was given to me personally as a gift by Saddam Hussein. It is Iraqi glass." I put down the beer.

I am in Tehran now, in 1997, in a cheap hotel in the centre of the city and, later, at a cosy restaurant that serves jugs of cold drinking yoghurt, and sitting opposite me is Dr. Hussain Shahristani, holder of a doctorate in nuclear chemistry from the University of Toronto and formerly chief scientific adviser to Saddam's Iraqi Atomic Energy Organisation, a Shia Muslim married to a Canadian with three children. His story is so frightening, so eloquent, so moving and so terrible that it deserves to be told in full, in his own words, without a journalist's interruptions. The next pages therefore belong to Dr. Shahristani:

In 1979, there was a backlash by the regime in Iraq because of activists in the Shia community. By the summer, the regime had started large-scale executions and mass arrests. I voiced my concern about human rights at atomic energy meetings. I knew I was very crucial to their atomic energy programme—I thought that they would not arrest me for voicing my concern. I *wanted* Saddam to know what I said. I was wrong. A little earlier, the regime had arrested and executed one of my cousins, Ala Shahristani— he was on his honeymoon and had only been married for fourteen days. He was not associated with any party. He was arrested in the street and taken away and his wife and sister were brought to the torture chamber to see him. They had given him a hideous torture. They had filled him with gas through his rectum and then beaten him. They threatened his young wife in front of him and then they banged his head into the wall, so hard that the wall was shaking. Then they killed him.

By this time, Saddam was president and he came to see us and he told us that he was going to redirect us at the Atomic Energy Organisation, that we were going to work on what he called "strategic projects." Until July 1979, we had been involved on purely peaceful applications of atomic energy. I and my colleague, Dr. Ziad Jaafar, were Saddam's two advisers;

---

next time I interviewed Khrushchev, in 1958, I left my cigar outside. Khrushchev asked me where it was. 'I want to crush it again,' he said."

we were reputable, internationally trained scientists. We were also close friends. I discussed this with him. I said: "If Saddam wants military applications, no way am I going to continue with this organisation."

At that time, we didn't take it seriously because we knew Iraq had limitations. I assumed I would be just thrown out of the organisation. They came to the Atomic Energy Organisation when I was talking to the board of directors on December 4th 1979. They said: "Could we have a word with Dr. Hussain?" As I stepped outside, they put handcuffs on me, shoved me into a car and took me to the security headquarters in Baghdad. At security headquarters, they took me in to the director of security, Dr. Fadel Baraq, who was later executed by Saddam. He said that some people who had been arrested and brought to the headquarters had given my name. I denied any involvement in political parties, I said I was a practising Muslim but that I had never taken part in subversive activities.

Then they brought me to a man I knew, Jawad Zoubeidi, a building contractor. He had been so badly tortured, I hardly recognised him. Jawad said: "I know Dr. Hussain. He comes to the mosque and takes part in our religious activities." For them, "religious activities" meant anti-government activities. They said to me: "Better tell us all or you'll regret it." Then they took me to the torture chamber in the basement. They blindfolded me and pushed me down the stairs into the chamber. It was a big room. My hands were tied behind my back and I was pulled up into the air by my hands. After five minutes, the pain was so severe in the shoulders that it was unbearable. Then they gave me shocks on sensitive parts of my body. By the end of the beating you are naked. There were shocks on my genitals and other parts of my body.

After fifteen minutes they came to me and said: "Sign." I was in a very cold sweat. They know you'll faint. They brought me down and gave me a short rest. I fell asleep for a few minutes. But this went on day and night, day and night. It went on for twenty-two days and nights. Four of them did it, in shifts. Baraq, who had a Ph.D. in military psychology from Moscow, was standing there. At one point, he said: "Look, Dr. Hussain, I'll tell you what your problem is—you think you are smart enough and we are stupid. You may be smart in your own field but we know what we are doing. Just tell us what you know and get this over."

I knew Saddam. He knew me. But this could happen to me. I remember once, Saddam said to me: "You are a scientist. I am a politician. I will tell you what politics is about. I make a decision. I tell someone else the opposite. Then I do something which surprises even myself."

The torture techniques in Baghdad were routine and varied in severity. The electric shocks could be everywhere. But sometimes they would burn people on the genitals and go on burning until they were completely burned off. They did the same with toes. They sometimes beat people with iron on the stomach or the chest. But with me, they were very careful not to leave any sign on me. I saw one man and they had used an iron on his stomach. They used drills and made holes in bones, arms and legs. I saw an officer, Naqib Hamid, and they dissolved his feet in acid. There was another torture where they would put sulphuric acid in a tub. They would take a man and start by dissolving his hands. Once, the founder of the Dawa party,* Abdul Saheb Khail, was totally dissolved. Baraq said to me: "Have you heard about Khail—there is where we dissolved him."

In the final stages of torture, they have a table with an electrical saw. They can saw off a hand or a foot. The majority talk. The people who have refused to talk are exceptional. Adnan Salman, a head of the Dawa, refused to talk. He was brought in—I saw him—and by that time they had a lot of confessions by other men who had been tortured. Adnan Salman was a teacher. Adnan knew—he was prepared. He told them: "My name is Adnan Salman. I am in charge of the Dawa party and none of these people are responsible for our activities. These will be my last words to you. You will never extract a single word from me." They brought three doctors and told them that if Adnan died under torture they would be executed. He didn't utter a single word. Sometimes you would hear the doctors, so scared because they could not bring him back from unconsciousness. I was in another torture room and could hear everything. I was in Abu Ghraib prison when I heard Adnan had been executed. He had not died under torture.

One prisoner told me he was seventeen and was the youngest prisoner and so they made him sweep the corridors of the internal security head-quarters every morning at seven o'clock. He saw a peasant woman from the south with tattoos, he said, a woman from the marshes with a girl of ten and a boy of about six. She was carrying a baby in her arms. The prisoner told me that as he was sweeping, an officer came and told the woman: "Tell me where your husband is—very bad things can happen." She said: "Look, my husband takes great pride in the honour of his woman. If he knew I was here, he would have turned himself in." The officer took out his pistol and held the daughter up by the braids of her hair and put a bullet into her head. The woman didn't know what was happening. Then he put a bullet into the boy's head. The woman was going crazy. He took the youngest boy by the legs and smashed the baby's brain on a wall. You can imagine the woman. The officer told the young prisoner to bring the rubbish trolley and put the three children in it, on top of the garbage, and ordered the woman to sit on the bodies. He took the trolley out and left it. The officer had got into the habit of getting rid of people who were worthless.

I was taken to the revolutionary court. Muslim al-Jabouri was the judge and there were two generals on each side of him. They asked me my name and if I had anything to say. The charges were that I was a "Zionist stooge,"

*See pp. 162ff.

an "Israeli spy" and "working with the Americans" and "a collaborator with the Iranians." They realised I wasn't a member of the Dawa party. The court handed down a sentence they had decided before I was taken there—life imprisonment. My own defence lawyer called for my execution. He had only a written statement to make: "This person has closed the doors of mercy—give him the severest penalty." I said to the court: "This Iraqi state which you are governing, we established it with our blood. My father was sentenced by the British, as for me I am president of the Palestinian Association in Toronto. A person with this background cannot be an Israeli agent." The lawyer said: "So you are a Russian spy." I said: "I have a family tree—from the Prophet Mohamed's time, peace be upon him."

I was taken to Abu Ghraib prison and put in a small cell with forty people inside. By the time I left in May 1980, we were sixty people to a cell. I worked out that there were three death sentences for every prison sentence. So when a thousand people went to Abu Ghraib, that meant there were three thousand executions. That May, they took me to the Mukhabarat intelligence headquarters and now the torture was much worse. In the previous torture centre, they were allowed a 10 per cent death rate. Here they were allowed 100 per cent. The head was Barzan Tikriti, the head of Saddam's human rights delegation to Geneva. Dr. Ziad Jaafar was brought there because he told Saddam that the nuclear programme couldn't continue without me, without Dr. Shahristani. He said that Iraq needed Shahristani the chemist. Saddam took this as a threat. Jaafar was never shown to me. They tortured twenty people to death in front of him. So he agreed to return to work.

Then one day they came and shaved me and showered me, brought me new pyjamas, blindfolded me, put cologne on me, put me in a car and took me to a room in what looked like a palace. There was a bedroom, sitting room, videos, a television . . . Then one day Barzan Tikriti came with Abdul-Razak al-Hashimi—he was to be Iraqi ambassador to France during the Kuwaiti occupation in 1990. He was a Baathist, a very silly man with a Ph.D. in geology from the United States. He was the vice president of the Atomic Energy Organisation and he stood by the door like a guard. I just sat there, lying down, both my hands completely paralysed. A man arrived. He said: "You don't know me but we know you well. Saddam was extremely hurt when he heard you had been arrested—he was very angry with the intelligence people. He knows about your scientific achievements. He would like you to go back to your work at the Atomic Energy Organisation." I said: "I am too weak after what I have been through." He said: "We need an atomic bomb." Barzan Tikriti then said: "We need an atomic bomb because this will give us a long arm to reshape the map of the Middle East. We know you are the man to help us with this." I told him that all my research was published in papers, that I had done no research on military weapons. "I am the wrong person for the task you are looking for," I said.

He replied: "I know what you can do—and any person who is not willing to serve his country is not worthy to be alive."

I was sure I would be executed. I said: "I agree with you that it is a man's duty to serve his country but what you are asking me to do is not a service to my country." He replied: "Dr. Hussain, so long as we agree that a man must serve his country, the rest is detail. You should rest now because you are very tired." After this, I was kept in several palaces over a number of months. They brought my wife to see me, once at a palace that had been the home of Adnan Hamdan, a member of the Revolutionary Command Council who had been executed by Saddam. But they realised I wouldn't work for them and I was sent back to Abu Ghraib. I spent eight years there. I wasn't allowed books, newspapers, radio or any contact with any human being.

I knew I was doing the right thing. I never regretted the stand I took. I slept on the concrete floor of my cell, under an army blanket that was full of lice. There was a tap and a bucket for a toilet. I got one plate of food every day, usually stew without meat in it. I suffered from severe back pains from sleeping on the concrete. I made up mathematical puzzles and solved them. I thought about the people who had accepted the regime, who could have fought it when it was weak and did not. The more I thought about it, the more I was convinced I had done the right thing. I knew that my family would understand the reasons for it. I wished Bernice would take the kids and leave the country. That would have been much easier for me. She said that as long as I was alive, she would never leave the country.

Hussain Shahristani eventually escaped from Abu Ghraib during an American air raid in February 1990 after friends helped him disguise himself as an Iraqi intelligence officer, and he made his way via Suleimaniya to Iran. Bernice remembered a visit to her husband in prison when she could not recognise his face. "I could only recognise his clothes," she said. "But I knew it was him because I saw a tear running down his cheek."

Just two months after Dr. Shahristani's mind-numbing transfer from Abu Ghraib prison to the palace in 1980, Saddam decided to deny what he had already admitted to Shahristani the previous year: his plan to possess nuclear weapons. I watched this typical Saddam performance, staged on 21 July 1980, in front of hundreds of journalists—myself among them—in the hall of Iraq's highly undemocratic national assembly. Perhaps the chamber was just too big, because when he entered, the first impression was of a tiny man in an overlarge double-breasted jacket, a rather simple soul with a bright tie and a glossy jacket. He began not with the cheery wave adopted by so many Arab leaders but with a long, slightly stilted salute, like a private soldier desperately ill at ease among generals. But when Saddam spoke, the microphone—deliberately, no doubt—pitched his voice up into Big Brother volume, so that he boomed at us, his sarcasm and his anger coming across with venom rather than passion. You could imagine what it was like to be denounced before the Revolutionary Command Council.

With an autocrat's indignation that anyone should believe Iraq wanted to build an atom bomb—but with the suggestion that the Arabs were perfectly capable of doing so if they chose—he denied that his country was planning to produce nuclear weapons. He also condemned the Soviet invasion of Afghanistan and U.S. military involvement in the Gulf, sneered at the Syrian Baathist leadership, accused British businessmen of bribery and belittled accurate reports of Kurdish unrest in Iraq. "We have no programme concerning the manufacture of the atomic bomb," he said. "We have no such programme for the Israelis to thwart . . . we want to use atomic energy for peaceful purposes."

His argument was artful. "A few years ago, Zionists in Europe used to spread the news that the Arabs were backward people, that they did not understand technology and were in need of a protector. The Arabs, the Zionists said, could do nothing but ride camels, cry over the ruins of their houses and sleep in tents. Two years ago, the Zionists and their supporters came up with a declaration that Iraq was about to produce the atom bomb. But how could a people who only knew how to ride camels produce an atom bomb?" Iraq had signed the nuclear non-proliferation treaty, but no one asked if the Israelis were making atom bombs at their nuclear centre at Dimona in the Negev desert. "Arab nations are on the threshold of a new age and will succeed in using atomic energy. Millions of Arabs will be able to use this advanced technology." Saddam kept using the word "binary" over and over again, as if Iraq had just split the atom.

His statements were laced with references to the "Arab nation," and the ghost of Gamal Abdel Nasser—whose name he invoked on at least three occasions—was clearly intended to visit the proceedings. Regarding his own regime as an example of the purest pan-Arab philosophy, he clearly saw himself as the aspiring leader of the Arab world. But he could not resist, just briefly, hinting at the truth. "Whoever wants to be our enemy," he shouted at one point, "can expect us as an enemy to be totally different in the very near future." He had made his point: if the Arabs were able to use advanced nuclear technology in the near future and if Israel's enemy was going to be "totally different," this could only mean that he was planning to possess nuclear weapons. It was no secret that Iraq's Osirak reactor was expected to be commissioned in just five months' time.

Then came Iran. He believed, he said, in the right of the Iranian people to self-determination, but "Khomeini has become a murderer in his own country." At one point, Saddam began to speak of the 35,000 Iraqi Shiites of Iranian origin whom he had just expelled from Iraq—he did not mention the figure, nor the fact that many of them held Iraqi passports—and he suddenly ended in mid-sentence. "We have expelled a few people of Iranian origin or people who do not belong to Iraq," he began. "But now, if they want to come back . . ." And there he suddenly ended his remark. It was an oblique but ominous warning of the punishment Saddam intended to visit upon Iran's Islamic Revolution.

His press conference went on long into the night and into the early hours of the next morning. He spoke without notes and, although he would not regard the comparison as flattering, he often improvised his speech as he went along in much the same way that President Sadat of Egypt used to do. I noted in my report to *The Times* next day that "when the president smiled—which he did only rarely—he was greeted by bursts of applause from fellow ministers and Baath party officials." When several of us were close to Saddam after his speech, he offered his hand to us. In my notes, I recorded that it was "soft and damp."

Two years later, Richard Pim, who had been head of Winston Churchill's prime ministerial Map Room at Downing Street during the Second World War, used exactly the same words—"soft and damp"—when he described to me his experience of shaking hands in Moscow with Josef Stalin, upon whom Saddam consciously modelled himself. It was one of Stalin's biographers who noted in 2004 that in the 1970s Saddam had dutifully visited all of Stalin's fifteen scenic seaside villas on the Black Sea coast of Abkhazia, some of them Tsarist palaces; these were presumably the inspiration for the vast imperial—and largely useless— palaces which Saddam built for himself all over Iraq.*

For the West, however, Saddam was a new Shah in the making. That, I suspected, was what his press conference was all about. He would be a Shah for us and a Nasser for the Arabs. His personality cult was already being constructed. He was a new version of the Caliph Haroun al-Rashid, it was said in Baghdad—he would soon become a far more disturbing version of an ancient Arab warrior—and his face now appeared across the country, in Kurdish dress, in Arab kuffiah, in business suit, digging trenches in guerrilla uniform, revolver tucked Arafat-style into his trouser belt, on dinar banknotes. He was, a local poet grovellingly wrote, "the perfume of Iraq, its dates, its estuary of the two rivers, its coast and waters, its sword, its shield, the eagle whose grandeur dazzles the heavens. Since there was an Iraq, you were its awaited and promised one."

Saddam had already developed the habit of casually calling on Iraqis in their homes to ask if they were happy—they always were, of course—and my colleague Tony Clifton of *Newsweek* was himself a witness to this kind of Saddamite aberration. During an interview with the president, Clifton rashly asked if Saddam was never worried about being assassinated. "The interpreter went ashen-grey with fear and there was a long silence," Clifton was to recall. "I think Saddam knew some English and understood the question. Then the interpreter said something to him and Saddam roared with laughter and clapped me on the shoulder. He didn't stop laughing, but he said to me: 'Leave this room now! Go out onto the street! Go and ask anyone in Iraq: Do you love Saddam?' And he went on laughing. And all the people in the room burst out laughing. Of course, you couldn't really do that, could you? You couldn't go up to Iraqis and ask them that. They were going to tell you that they loved him."†

---

*Simon Sebag Montefiore found other parallels. Gori, Stalin's Georgian birthplace, was barely 800 kilometres north of Saddam's hometown of Tikrit. Both men were raised by strong, ambitious mothers, abused by their fathers; both were promoted by revered potentates whom they ultimately betrayed.

†Impossible though it was to assess Iraqi public opinion under Saddam, I could speak to old Iraqi friends in their homes. In a feature article filed to *The Times* on 30 July 1980, I noted that many Iraqis "admitted even in private that stability under President Hussain [*sic*] is preferable to the social chaos that might occur if the freedoms of liberal western thought were suddenly introduced." Twenty-four years later, their fears of anarchy proved all too real.

Saddam had inherited the same tribal and religious matrix as the British when they occupied Iraq in 1917. The largest community, the Shia, were largely excluded from power but constituted a permanent threat to the Sunni-dominated Baath party. Not only were their magnificent golden shrines at Najaf and Kerbala potent symbols of the great division in Islamic society, but they represented a far larger majority in Iran. Just so long as the Shah ruled Iraq's eastern neighbour, its religious power could be checked. But if the Shah was deposed, then the Baathists would be the first to understand the threat which the Shia of both countries represented.

Shiites have disputed the leadership of Islam since the eighth-century murder of Ali, son-in-law of the Prophet Mohamed, at Najaf and believe that Ali's descendants, the imams, are the lawful successors of Mohamed. Their fascination with martyrdom and death would, if made manifest in modern war, create a threat for any enemy. The Sunnis, adherents of the *sunnah* (practice) of Mohamed, became commercially powerful from their close association with the Mamelukes and the Ottoman Turks. In many ways, Sunni power came to be founded on Shia poverty; in Iraq, Saddam was going to make sure that this remained the case. This disparity, however, would always be exacerbated—as it was in the largely Sunni kingdom of Saudi Arabia—by an extraordinary geographic coincidence: almost all the oil of the Middle East lies beneath lands where Shia Muslims live. In southern Iraq, in the north-east of Saudi Arabia and, of course, in Iran, Shiites predominate among the population.

Saddam tolerated the Shah once he withdrew his support for the Kurdish insurgency in the north—the Kurds, like the Shia, were regularly betrayed by both the West and Iraq's neighbours—and agreed that the Iraqi–Iranian frontier should run down the centre of the Shatt al-Arab River. He had been prepared to allow Ayatollah Khomeini to remain in residence in Najaf where he had moved after his expulsion from Iran. The prelate was forbidden from undertaking any political activity, a prohibition that Khomeini predictably ignored. He gave his followers cassettes on which he expressed his revulsion for the Shah, his determination to lead an Islamic revolution and his support for the Palestinian cause. One of his closest supporters in Najaf was Hojatolislam Ali Akbar Mohtashemi—later to be the Iranian ambassador to Syria who sent Iranian Revolutionary Guards to Lebanon in 1982—who was imprisoned three times by the Iraqi authorities.* Khomeini's theological ambassador was Ayatollah Sayed Mohamed Bakr Sadr, one of the most influential and intellectual of the Shia clergy in Najaf, who had written a number of highly respected works on Islamic economy and education.

But Bakr Sadr also advocated an Islamic revolution in Iraq, relying—like Hussain Shahristani—on his own political importance to protect him from destruction.

---

*Mohtashemi was also imprisoned in Saudi Arabia and Kuwait, but told me years later that "none of this hindered or affected my beliefs or my determination and this made me even more resolute in my decision to fight and struggle against the United States of America, Israel and all the other proxy governments and states."

Once Khomeini was expelled by Saddam—to Turkey and ultimately to Paris—
Bakr Sadr was in mortal danger. With an Islamic revolution under way in Iran,
Saddam would have no qualms about silencing Khomeini's right-hand man in
Najaf, let alone his followers. They were to suffer first. Bakr Sadr, sick at his
home, was arrested and imprisoned in Baghdad—only to be released after widespread demonstrations against the regime in Najaf. The Baath then announced the
existence of the armed opposition Dawa party and pounced on Bakr Sadr's supporters. The Iranians were later to list the first martyrs of "the Islamic Revolution
of Iraq" as Hojatolislam Sheikh Aref Basari, Hojatolislam Sayed Azizeddin Ghapanchi, Hojatolislam Sayed Emaddedin Tabatabai Tabrizi, Professor Hussain
Jaloukhan and Professor Nouri Towmeh. The Baath decided to crush the influence
of the Shia theological schools in Najaf by introducing new laws forcing all teachers to join the party. Bakr Sadr then announced that the mere joining of the Baath
was "prohibited by Islamic laws." This determined his fate—although it was a fate
that Saddam was at first unwilling to reveal.

For months, reports of Bakr Sadr's execution circulated abroad—Amnesty
International recorded them—but there was no confirmation from the regime.
Only when I asked to visit Najaf in 1980 did a Baath party official tell the truth,
albeit in the usual ruthless Baathist manner. It was a blindingly hot day—23
July—when I arrived at the office of the portly Baathist governor of Najaf, Misban Khadi, a senior party member and personal confidant of Saddam. Just
before lunchtime on this lunchless Ramadan day, as the thermometer touched
130 degrees, the admission came. Had Ayatollah Bakr Sadr been executed? I
asked.

"I do not know an Ayatollah Bakr Sadr," Khadi said. "But I do know a
Mohamed Bakr Sadr. He was executed because he was a traitor and plotted against
Iraq and maintained relations with Khomeini. He was a member of the Dawa party.
He was a criminal and a spy and had a relationship with not just Khomeini but with
the CIA as well. The authorities gave his body back to his relatives—for burial in
Wadi Salam. The family have not been harmed. They are still in Najaf."

I remember how, as Khadi spoke, the air conditioner hissed on one side of the
room. He spoke softly and I leaned towards him to hear his words. This was
enough to send a tingle down the spine of any listener. Khomeini's lack of respect
for his former protectors now smouldered at the heart of the Baathist regime that
once did so much to help him. "Khomeini speaks about crowds of people flocking
to see Bakr-Sadr in his absence," Khadi said softly. "But in court that man admitted that he spied. He was hanged just over five months ago. But these are small
things to ask me about. We execute anybody who is a traitor in Iraq. Why do
reporters ask unimportant questions like this? Why don't you ask me about the
development projects in Najaf?"

This was a bleak, dismissive epitaph for the man who accompanied Khomeini
into fourteen years of exile. Wadi Salam—the Valley of Peace—is the cemetery
where so many millions of Shiites wish to be buried, within a few hundred metres
of the golden shrine of the Imam Ali. The family were permitted to give him a tra-

ditional Muslim funeral and he now lay in a narrow tomb amid the hundreds of thousands of tightly packed, hump-shaped graves whose swaddled occupants believe that their proximity to Ali's last resting place will secure the personal inter-cession of the long-dead holy warrior on the day of resurrection. But there was another grave beside that of Bakr Sadr, and it was a more junior Baath party offi-cial who took some delight in expanding the governor's brutal story.

"We hanged his sister, too," he said. "They were both dressed in white shrouds for their hanging. Bint Huda was hanged around the same time. I didn't see the actual hanging but I saw Bakr Sadr hanging outside the Abu Ghraib prison after-wards. They hanged him in public. He was in religious robes but with a white cloth over him and he was not wearing his turban. Later they took him down and put him in a wooden box and tied it to the roof of a car. Then he was taken back to Najaf. Why do you ask about him? He was a bad man."

The history of the Baath party in Iraq might be written in the blood of ulemas and their families and the demise of the Shia clergy was to become a fearful theme over the coming years. Already, Imam Moussa Sadr, the leader of the Shia com-munity in Lebanon and a relative of Bakr Sadr, had disappeared while on a visit to Libya in August of 1978. A tall, bearded man who was born in Qom and who looked younger than his fifty years, Moussa Sadr had been invited to Libya to observe the ninth anniversary celebrations of Colonel Ghadafi's revolution. All he would talk of in the Libyan capital of Tripoli, one Lebanese newspaper reported, was the situation in Iran. Had the Shah's Savak secret police seized Moussa Sadr? Had Ghadafi "disappeared" him for Saddam? He was supposed to have boarded Alitalia Flight 881 to Rome on 31 August, on his way back to Beirut. His baggage turned up on the carousel at Fiumicino Airport—but neither Moussa Sadr nor the Lebanese journalist travelling with him were on the plane. Many Shiites in Lebanon still believe that their imam will return. Others are today trying to bring criminal charges against Ghadafi. Moussa Sadr, who founded the Amal—Hope—movement in Lebanon, was never seen again.

In Najaf, the Shiites were cowed. No one openly mentioned Bakr Sadr's name in the ancient dusty city with its glorious mosque, built around the solid silver cas-ket of the Prophet's son-in-law. One stall-holder shrugged his shoulders at me with exaggerated ignorance when I mentioned Bakr Sadr. The banners in the streets of Najaf that boiling July all praised Saddam's generosity—each slogan had been personally devised by local shopkeepers, an Information Ministry functionary insisted—and in one road there hung a small red flag bearing the words: "May the regime of Khomeini, the liar and traitor, fall to pieces."

The elderly Grand Ayatollah Abulqassem al-Khoi, the rightful heir to the Shi-ite leadership in Najaf but a man who believed that the people should render unto God the things that are God's and unto Saddam the things that are recognisably Baathist, had lacked the necessary influence to smother the unrest—just as he would fail to control the mobs during the southern Iraqi uprising in 1991. There were to be no interviews with the old man. But the governor was quite prepared to take me to the house in which Khomeini had once lived. A single-storey terraced building with walls of flaking blue paint, it stood in a laneway suitably named Sharia al-Rasoul—the Street of the Prophet—in the southern suburbs of Najaf.

They tell you that the house has a varnished wooden front door and this is true; but the midday heat was so harsh that it sucked all colour from the landscape. The heat smothered us in the shade and ambushed us in fiery gusts from unsuspecting alleyways until all I could see was a monochrome of streets and shuttered houses, the fragile negative of a city dedicated to the linked identities of worship and death. Ayatollah Khomeini must have loved it here.

But the city was changing. The roads had been resurfaced, a construction project had erased one of Khomeini's old "safe" houses from the face of the earth, and Iraq's government was doing its best to ensure that the Shia now lacked nothing in this most holy of cities; new factories were being built to the north, more than a hundred new schools—complete with Baath party teachers—had been completed, together with a network of health centres, hotels and apartment blocks. The city's beaming governor drove me through the drained and sweltering streets in his white Mercedes, pointing his pudgy finger towards the bazaar.

"I know everyone here," Misban Khadi said. "I love these people and they always express their true feelings to me." Behind us, a trail of police escort cars purred through the heat. Khadi, though a Shiite, did not come from Najaf but from the eastern province of Diyala. He came to the Imam Ali mosque every day, he claimed, and gestured towards a banner erected over the mosaics of the shrine. It was from a recent speech by Saddam. "We are doubly happy at the presence here of our great father Ali," it said. "Because he is one of the Muslim leaders, because he is the son-in-law of the Prophet—and because he is an Arab."

Baathist officials made this point repeatedly. All the Iraqis of Iranian origin had already been expelled from Najaf—"if only you had telephoned me yesterday," Khadi said irritatingly, "I could have given you the figures"—and the message that Shia Islam is a product of the Arab rather than the Persian world constantly reiterated. Had not Saddam personally donated a set of gold-encrusted gates to the Najaf shrine, each costing no less than $100,000? The governor stalked into the bazaar across the road. Because it was Ramadan, the shutters were down, so hot they burned your skin if you touched them. But a perfume stall was still open and Khadi placed his mighty frame on a vulnerable bench while the talkative salesman poured his over-scented warm oils into glass vials.

"Ask him if he enjoys living in Najaf," the governor barked, but when I asked the salesman instead if he remembered Khomeini, his eyes flickered across the faces of the nearest officials. "We all remember Khomeini," he said carefully. "He was here for fourteen years. Every day, he went to pray at the mosque and all the people of Najaf crowded round him, thousands of them, to protect him—we thought the Shah would send his Savak police to kill him so we stood round Khomeini at the shrine." There was a moment's silence as the perfume seller's critical faculties—or lack of them—were assessed by his little audience.

"But here's a little boy who would like to tell you his view of Khomeini," said the governor, and an urchin in a grubby yellow *abaya* shrieked, "Khomeini is a traitor," with a vacant smile. All the officials acclaimed this statement as the true feelings of the people of Najaf. Khadi had never met Khomeini but confidently asserted that the imam had been a CIA agent, that even Grand Ayatollah Abolqassem al-Khoi of Najaf had sent a telegram to Qom, blaming Khomeini for killing the Muslim Kurds of northern Iran. Al-Khoi may have done that—his fellow teacher, Ayatollah Sahib al-Hakim, had been executed by the regime—but this did not spare his family. In 1994, just two years after al-Khoi's death, his courageous thirty-six-year-old son Taghi was killed when his car mysteriously crashed into an unlit articulated lorry on the highway outside Kerbala. He had been a constant critic of Saddam's persecution of the Shia and told friends in London the previous year that he was likely to die at Saddam's hands. At the demand of the authorities, his burial—and that of his six-year-old nephew who died with him—went without the usual rituals.

Four years later, Ayatollah Sheikh Murtada al-Burujirdi, one of Najaf's most prominent scholars and jurists, a student of the elder al-Khoi and another Iranian-born cleric, was assassinated as he walked home after evening prayers at the shrine of Ali. He had been beaten up the previous year and had escaped another murder attempt when a hand grenade was thrown at him. Al-Burujirdi had refused government demands that he no longer lead prayers at the shrine. Grand Ayatollah Ali al-Sistani, the principal *marja al-taqlid*—in literal Arabic, "source of emulation"—was still under house arrest and the Baathists were promoting the more pliable Sayed Mohamed Sadiq al-Sadr, cousin of the executed Sadiq. But Sadiq al-Sadr himself was assassinated by gunmen in Najaf nine months later after he had issued a fatwa calling on Shiites to attend their Friday prayers despite the government's objection to large crowds. Al-Khoi's son Youssef—Taghi's brother—blamed the Baathists, and rioting broke out in the Shia slums of Saddam City in Baghdad. But the history of Shia resistance did not end with the fall of Saddam. It was Sadiq al-Sadr's son Muqtada who would lead an insurrection against America's occupation of Iraq five years later, in 2004, bringing U.S. tanks onto the same Najaf streets through which Saddam's armour had once moved and provoking gun battles across Sadr City, the former Saddam City whose population had renamed it after the executed Bakr Sadr.

These were just the most prominent of the tens of thousands of Iraqis who would be murdered during Saddam's nearly twenty-four-year rule. Kurds and communists and Shia Muslims would feel the harshest of the regime's punishments. My Iraqi files from the late seventies and early eighties are filled with ill-printed circulars from the Patriotic Union of Kurdistan, from Iraqi trade unions and tiny opposition groups, naming thousands of executed men and women. As I thumb through them now, I come across the PUK's magazine *The Spark*, an issue dated October 1977, complaining that its partisans have been jointly surrounded by forces of Baathist Iraq and the Shah's Iran in the northern Iraqi village of Halabja, detailing the vast numbers of villages from which the Kurdish inhabitants had been deported, and the execution, assassination or torturing to death of 400

PUK members. Another PUK leaflet, dated 10 December 1977, reports the deportation of 300,000 Kurds to the south of Iraq. Yet another dreadful list, from a communist group, contains the names of 37 Iraqi workers executed or "disappeared" in 1982 and 1983. Omer Kadir, worker in the tobacco factory at Suleimaniya—"tortured to death"; Ali Hussein, oil worker from Kirkuk—"executed"; Majeed Sherhan, peasant from Hilla—"executed"; Saddam Muher, civil servant from Basra—"executed" . . . The dead include blacksmiths, builders, printers, post office workers, electricians and factory hands. No one was safe.

This permanent state of mass killing across Iraq was no secret in the 1970s and 1980s. Yet the West was either silent or half-hearted in its condemnation. Saddam's visit to France in 1975 and his public welcome by the then mayor of Paris, Jacques Chirac, who bestowed upon the Iraqi "my esteem, my consideration, and my affection," was merely the most flagrant example of our shameful relationship with the Iraqi regime. Within three years, agents at the Iraqi embassy in Paris would be fighting a gun battle with French police after their diplomats had been taken hostage by two Arab gunmen. A French police inspector was killed and another policeman wounded; the three Iraqi agents claimed diplomatic immunity and were allowed to fly to Baghdad on 2 August 1978, just two days after the killing. U.S. export credits and chemicals and helicopters, French jets and German gas and British military hardware poured into Iraq for fifteen years. Iraq was already using gas to kill thousands of Iranian soldiers when Donald Rumsfeld made his notorious 1983 visit to Baghdad to shake Saddam's hand and ask him for permission to reopen the U.S. embassy. The first—and last—time I called on the consulate there, not long after Rumsfeld's visit, one of its young CIA spooks brightly assured me that he wasn't worried about car bombs because "we have complete faith in Iraqi security."

Iraq's vast literacy, public health, construction and communications projects were held up as proof that the Baathist government was essentially benign, or at least worthy of some respect. Again, my files contain many Western press articles that concentrate almost exclusively on Iraq's social projects. In 1980, for example, a long report in the Middle East business magazine *8 Days*, written with surely unconscious irony, begins: "Iraqis who fail to attend reading classes can be fined or sent to prison where literary classes are also compulsory. Such measures may seem harsh, but as Iraq enters its second year of a government drive to eliminate illiteracy, its results have won United Nations acclaim."

In 1977, the now defunct Dublin *Sunday Press* ran an interview with former Irish minister for finance Charles Haughey in which the country's human rights abuses simply went unrecorded. It was not difficult to see why. "An enormous potential market for Irish produce," it began, "including lamb, beef, dairy products and construction industry requirements was open in Iraq . . . Charles Haughey told me on his return from a week-long visit to that country." Haughey and his wife Maureen, it transpired, had been "the guest of the 9-year-old socialist Iraqi government" so that he could inform himself "of the political and economic situation there and to help to promote better contact and better relations between Ireland and

Iraq at political level." Haughey, who had met "the Director General of the Ministry of Planning, Saddam Hussein," added that "the principal political aspect of modern Iraq is the total determination of its leaders to use the wealth derived from their oil resources for the benefit of their people . . ." The Baath party, the article helpfully informed its readers, "came to power in July 1968 without the shedding of one drop of blood."

The British understood the Iraqi regime all too well. In 1980, gunmen from the "Political Organisation of the Arab People in Arabistan"—the small south-western corner of Iran with a predominantly Arab population, which is called Khuzestan—had taken over the Iranian embassy in London; the siege ended when Special Air Service men entered the building, capturing one of the men but killing another four and executing a fifth in cold blood before fire consumed the building.* Less than three months later, however, on 19 July 1980, I was astonished to be telephoned at my Baghdad hotel and invited by the Iraqi authorities to attend a press conference held by the very same Arab group which had invaded the embassy. Nasser Ahmed Nasser, a thirty-one-year-old economics graduate from Tehran University, accused the British of "conspiring" with Iran against the country's Arabs and demanded the return to Iraq of the bodies of the five dead gunmen.

Nasser, a moustachioed man with dark glasses, a black shirt and carefully creased lounge trousers, spoke slowly and with obvious forethought when he outlined his group's reaction to the killings. "We will take our vengeance," he said, "because now our second enemy is England." He claimed that he had been sentenced to death *in absentia* in Iran. But his arrival for the conference in the heavily upholstered interior of the Iraqi Information Ministry made it clear that the Baghdad government fully supported his cause and must have been behind the seizure of the embassy in London. A senior official of the ministry acted as interpreter thoughout Nasser's resentful peroration against Britain and Iran.

The Arabs of Khuzestan had been seeking autonomy from Khomeini's regime, and many Arab insurgents in the province had been executed or imprisoned, Nasser said. It was to demand the release of the jailed men that the gunmen had attacked the embassy in London. Nasser agreed that there was a "link" between the insurgents and the Iraqi Baath party and we should have questioned him about this. "Iraq's Arab Socialist Baath Party's motto—one unified Arab nation—is a glorious motto and we are Arabs," he said. "We follow this motto." What did this mean? On reflection, we should have grasped its import: Saddam was preparing a little Sudetenland, another Danzig, a piece of Iran that he might justifiably wish to liberate in the near future.

But of course, we asked about the siege in London rather than the implications

---

*Days before the siege, I had visited the embassy to request a visa to Iran and was asked to leave my second passport at the mission. After the fire, I had to send a message to Ivan Barnes from Beirut to say that I "think we have to assume my second passport now smouldering with the charred corpses in the embassy." I decided I would use my first passport to acquire an Iranian visa from diplomats at Iran's embassy in Beirut "in the hope that they don't blow up too, making Fisky stateless" and—if no visa was forthcoming—that I would try to enter Iran without one.

of Iraq's support for the rebels. "When we went to the embassy in London, our aim was not to kill," Nasser said. "We were not terrorists. We selected the British government as our negotiator because Britain is a democratic country and we wanted to benefit from this democracy. The British knew—all the world knew—that we did not intend to kill anyone . . . But for six days, they did not answer our requests or publicise our demands. They cut off the telex and the telephone . . . They did not have to kill our youths—they could have taken them prisoner and put them on trial." Nasser blamed Sadeq Khalkhali, the Iranian judge, for the torture of Arabs in Khuzestan—"he employs torturers who break the legs and shoot the arms of prisoners before knifing them"—and claimed that Arabs in the province had first accepted the Iranian revolution because "it came in the name of Islam" but that they now wanted autonomy "just like the Kurds, Baluchis and Turks." When we asked how the Arabs in the Iranian embassy had brought their weapons into Britain, Nasser replied: "How did the Palestinians get guns into Munich? How do Irish revolutionaries bring guns to Britain? We are able to do the same." Again, no one thought to ask if the guns reached Britain in the Iraqi diplomatic bag. Nasser himself came from the Iranian port of Khorramshahr, for which he used the Arab name "al-Mohammorah." So was al-Mohammorah going to be Danzig?

Britain, however, made no protest to Iraq over the siege—or over the extraordinary press conference so obviously arranged by the Iraqi government in Baghdad. It was an eloquent silence. Of course, there were those who questioned Britain's cosy relationship with Iraq. There was an interesting exchange in the House of Lords in 1989—a year after the end of the Iran–Iraq War and shortly after the arrest in Baghdad of *Observer* journalist Farzad Bazoft and his friend, the British nurse Daphne Parish—when Lord Hylton asked how the British government "justify their action in guaranteeing new credits to Iraq of up to £250 million in view of that country's detention of British subjects without trial, refusal to release prisoners of war following the ceasefire with Iran and its internal human rights record." For the government, Lord Trefgarne replied that "the Iraqi Government are in no doubt of our concerns over the British detainee, Mrs. Parish, and over Iraq's human rights record . . . we are a major trading nation. I am afraid that we have to do business with a number of countries with whose policies we very often disagree . . . we do not sell arms to Iraq." Hylton's response—that "while I appreciate that this country is a trading nation . . . is not the price that we are paying too high?"—passed without further comment.

Bazoft, who was Iranian-born and held British identity papers but not citizenship, had visited the Iraqi town of Hilla in Parish's car in a hunt for evidence that Iraq was producing chemical weapons. He was arrested as he tried to leave Baghdad airport, accused of spying and put on trial for his life, along with Parish. A month later, Foreign Office minister William Waldegrave was noting privately of Iraq that "I doubt if there is any future market of such a scale anywhere where the UK is potentially so well placed if we play our diplomatic hand correctly, nor can I think of any major market where the importance of diplomacy is so great on our commercial position. We must not allow it to go to the French, Germans, Japanese,

Koreans, etcetera." He added that "a few more Bazofts or another bout of internal repression would make it more difficult." Waldegrave's words were written only months after Saddam's gassing of the Kurds of Halabja. Geoffrey Howe, the deputy prime minister, decided to relax controls on the sale of arms to Iraq—but kept it secret because "it would look very cynical if so soon after expressing outrage about the treatment of the Kurds, we adopt a more flexible approach to arms sales."

Bazoft was sentenced to death on 10 March 1990. *The Observer* attacked Saddam over the conviction—not, perhaps, a wise decision in the circumstances— and British foreign secretary Douglas Hurd offered to fly to Baghdad to meet the Iraqi president. Saddam, according to the Iraqi Foreign Ministry, "could not intervene while under political pressure." But by then, a grim routine had begun, one of which my own research back in Beirut had made me painfully aware. Back in 1968, convicted Iraqi "spies" would confess their guilt on television. Then they would be executed. In 1969, the lord mayor of Baghdad had confessed—on television—to "spying" and he had been executed. And Bazoft had appeared on television, and confessed to spying—only later did his friends discover that he had been tortured with electricity during interrogation. In February 1969, before the execution of eight "spies," Baghdad radio had announced that the Iraqi people "expressed their condemnation of the spies"—they were then put to death. In May 1969, the farmers' trade union delegates had applauded President al-Bakr's decision to "chop off" the heads of a CIA "spy ring." They were duly put to death. Now, on one of his interminable visits to Iraqi minority groups, Saddam asked in front of a large group of Kurds if they believed that the "British spy" should hang. Of course, they chorused that he should. It was the same old Baathist technique; get the people to make the decision—once they knew what it should be—and then obey the people's will.

On the morning of 15 March 1990, Robin Kealy, a British diplomat in Baghdad, was informed that Bazoft was to be executed that day. He arrived at the Abu Ghraib prison to find the young man still unaware of his fate, still planning a personal appeal for his life to Saddam. It was Kealy's mournful duty to tell Bazoft the truth. Kealy declined an invitation to be present at the hanging. Eight days later, four Heathrow luggage handlers heaved Bazoft's coffin off a regular Iraqi Airways flight to London. No Foreign Office representative, relative or friend attended at the airport. The coffin was taken to a cargo shed to await burial. His friend Daphne "Dee" Parish was given fifteen years. Bazoft's last words to Kealy were: "Tell Dee I'm sorry."

Throughout the early years of Saddam's rule, there were journalists who told the truth about his regime while governments—for financial, trade and economic reasons—preferred to remain largely silent. Yet those of us who opposed the Anglo-American invasion of Iraq in 2003 were quickly accused of being Saddam's "spokesmen" or, in my case, "supporting the maintenance of the Baathist regime"—this from, of all people, Richard Perle, one of the prime instigators of the whole disastrous war, whose friend Donald Rumsfeld was befriending Saddam

in 1983. Two years after Rumsfeld's initial approach to the Iraqi leader—followed
up within months by a meeting with Tariq Aziz—I was reporting on Saddam's
gang-rape and torture in Iraqi prisons. On 31 July 1985, Wahbi al-Qaraghuli, the
Iraqi ambassador in London, complained to William Rees-Mogg, the *Times* editor,
that:

> Robert Fisk's extremely one-sided article ignores the tremendous advances
> made by Iraq in the fields of social welfare, education, agricultural devel-
> opment, urban improvement and women's suffrage; and he claims, without
> presenting any evidence to support such an accusation, that "Saddam him-
> self imposes a truly terroristic regime on his own people." Especially out-
> rageous is the statement that: "Suspected critics of the regime have been
> imprisoned at Abu Ghoraib [*sic*] jail and forced to watch their wives being
> gang-raped by Saddam's security men. Some prisoners have had to witness
> their children being tortured in front of them." It is utterly reprehensible
> that some journalists are quite prepared, without any supporting corrobora-
> tion, to repeat wild, unfounded allegations about countries such as Iraq . . .

"Extremely one-sided," "without presenting any evidence," "outrageous,"
"utterly reprehensible," "wild, unfounded allegations": these were the very same
expressions used by the Americans and the British almost twenty years later about
reports by myself or my colleagues which catalogued the illegal invasion of Iraq
and its disastrous consequences. In February 1986, I was refused a visa to Baghdad on the grounds that "another visit by Mr. Fisk to Iraq would lend undue credibility to his reports." Indeed it would.*

So for all these years—until his invasion of Kuwait in 1990—we in the West
tolerated Saddam's cruelty, his oppression and torture, his war crimes and mass
murder. After all, we helped to create him. The CIA gave the locations of communist cadres to the first Baathist government, information that was used to arrest,
torture and execute hundreds of Iraqi men. And the closer Saddam came to war
with Iran, the greater his fear of his own Shia population, the more we helped him.
In the pageant of hate figures that Western governments and journalists have
helped to stage in the Middle East—peopled by Nasser, Ghadafi, Abu Nidal and, at
one point, Yassir Arafat—Ayatollah Khomeini was our bogeyman of the early
1980s, the troublesome priest who wanted to Islamicise the world, whose stated
intention was to spread his revolution. Saddam, far from being a dictator, thus
became—on the Associated Press news wires, for example—a "strongman." He
was our bastion—and the Arab world's bastion—against Islamic "extremism."

---

*My "utterly reprehensible" journalism at least had the merit of putting both sides' noses out
of joint. In the summer of 1980, Tony Alloway, the *Times* stringer in Tehran, told Ivan Barnes, the
foreign news editor, that he could not obtain accreditation for me in Tehran because Iranian officials "were extremely upset both by the arrival of Robert Fisk in Tehran without proper
visa . . . and by the copy he filed and vowed never to let him in again." The visa problem had been
caused by the burning of my second passport in Iran's own embassy in London.

Even after the Israelis bombed Iraq's Osirak nuclear reactor in 1981, our support for Saddam did not waver. Nor did we respond to Saddam's clear intention of driving his country to war with Iran. The signs of an impending conflict were everywhere. Even Shapour Bakhtiar, the Shah's last prime minister, was helping stoke opposition to Khomeini from Iraq, as I discovered when I visited him in his wealthy—but dangerous—Paris exile in August 1980.

It had been the bright idea of Charles Douglas-Home, the foreign editor of *The Times*, to chase the remains of the Shah's old regime. "I'm sure Bakhtiar's up to something," Charlie said over the phone. "Besides, he knows a lot—and his daughter is stunningly beautiful!" He was right on both counts, although Bakhtiar—so Francophile that he had joined the French army in the Second World War—looked more impressive in his photographs than he did in person. Newspaper pictures portrayed him as a robust man with full, expressive features, his eyes alight for the return of Iranian democracy. In reality, he was a small, thin man, his cheeks somewhat shrunken, his clothes slightly too large for him, a diminutive figure sitting on a huge sofa with seven heavily armed gendarmes outside to protect him.

Even in his Paris apartment, with the noise of the city's traffic murmuring away outside and the poplar trees swaying in the breeze beyond the sitting-room window, you could feel the presence of the Iranian assassination squads that Tehran had ordered to kill Bakhtiar. When they had called two weeks earlier under the command of a twenty-nine-year-old Lebanese Islamist called Anis Naccache, they left behind a dead woman neighbour, a murdered French policeman and a bullet-smashed door handle, a souvenir of bright, jagged steel that lay beside the little table next to Bakhtiar's feet.

This had not served to dampen Bakhtiar's publicly expressed hatred of Khomeini or his theocratic regime. He admitted to me, uneasily and only after an hour, that he had twice visited Iraq to talk to officials of the Baath party—an institution that could hardly be said to practise the kind of liberal democracy Bakhtiar was advocating—and had broadcast over the clandestine radio that the Iraqis operated on their frontier with Iran, beaming in propaganda against the regime. "Why shouldn't I go to Iraq?" he asked. "I have been in Britain twice, I have been to Switzerland and Belgium. So I can go to Iraq. I contacted people there. I was invited to deal with the authorities there. I have a common point with the Iraqi government. They, like other Muslim countries, are against Khomeini by a large majority. It is possible to work together. This radio that is on the border with Iran is broadcasting what the Iranian people like to listen to. It has broadcast my statements on cassette. That is the only possible way when a dictatorship is established somewhere."

Bakhtiar, like many Western statesmen, suffered from a Churchill complex, a desire to dress himself up in the shadow of history. "When Khomeini arrived in Iran, I said we had escaped from one dictatorship [the Shah's] but had entered an even more awful one. Nobody believed me. Now, they have plenty to complain about but they do not have the courage to say it. So why do people talk about a coup d'état? I know that I have people on my side in the army . . . I remember when I was a student in Paris, there was an English leader by the name of Winston Churchill who saw the dangers of dictatorship. Other people were very relaxed about it all and wanted to do deals with Hitler. But Churchill told them they were on the point of extinction. In the same way I knew that Mr. Khomeini could not do anything for Iran: he is a man who does not understand geography, history or the economy. He cannot be the leader of all those people in the twentieth century, because he is ignorant about the world."

The Shah had died in a Cairo hospital six days before my interview with Bakhtiar, although Bakhtiar seemed quite unmoved at his former king's departure. "The death of a person does not give me happiness. I am not the sort of man who dances in the streets because someone is dead and I am alive—I did not even do that when Hitler died. And God knows, I am an anti-fascist as you know yourself. The king was a sick man, a very sick man—and I think that even for him, death was a deliverance, morally and physically." What Bakhtiar wanted was a provisional government "which would go to Iran and which, under the 1906 constitution, would call for a constituent assembly, calmly and without emotion, and would study the different constitutions for Iran."

Bakhtiar was already painfully out of touch with Iran, unaware that Khomeini's revolution was irreversible, partly because it dealt so mercilessly with its enemies—who included Bakhtiar himself. Naccache and his Iranian hit squad had bungled the first attempt to kill him.* Just over eleven years later, on 8 August 1991, more killers arrived at Bakhtiar's home. This time they cut his head off. Accused of helping the murderers, an Iranian businessman told the Paris assize court that Bakhtiar "killed 5,000 people during his thirty-three days in power. Secondly, he was planning a coup d'état in Iran . . . thirdly, he collaborated with Saddam Hussein during the Iran–Iraq war . . ."[†]

---

*Many years later, Naccache would tell me that he and his gunmen—another Lebanese, two Iranians and a Palestinian—had "tried to attack Bakhtiar's apartment but we failed because the door was armoured. We just had little pistols. If you check the place, you don't know if it's armoured or not. There was a shootout with the French gendarmes who were guarding him. Two people were killed; I was wounded in the arm and thigh. No one saw this woman. The bullet went through her door and unfortunately hit the woman in the head. The shootout was with the policemen. When I was in hospital, the judge said there was a woman killed. I asked: What woman? I didn't understand. I said that's very bad. I felt very badly. We hadn't foreseen that at all. She was innocent but immediately I proposed, according to the principles of Islam, that funds should be paid to the victim's family in recompense, also to the family of the dead policeman." Naccache said that he led his men to kill Bakhtiar because "I felt there was a danger of a repeat of the coup against Mossadeq. That's why we decided to attack Bakhtiar. He was the head of a plot to do a coup d'état against the revolution and come back to Iran . . . I had no personal feelings against Bakhtiar. It was purely political. It was not an attempted assassination. A sentence of death passed by the Iranian revolutionary tribunal is carried out as an execution." According to Naccache, the proof of Bakhtiar's coup plot was furnished by an Iranian military officer who handed to the authorities the names of other officers involved with Bakhtiar; they were arrested and more than a hundred were executed.

†For years, the Iranian authorities openly accused Bakhtiar of planning a coup. A booklet published by the Ministry of Islamic Guidance in Tehran in 1981 stated that he had been "setting

Just as Saddam was planning the destruction of the Iranian revolution, so Khomeini was calling for the overthrow of Saddam and the Baath, or the "Aflaqis" as he quaintly called them after the name of the Syrian founder of the party. After learning of Bakr Sadr's execution and that of his sister, Khomeini openly called for Saddam's overthrow. "It would be strange," he wrote on 2 April 1980,

> if the Islamic nations, especially the noble nation of Iraq, the tribes of the Tigris and Euphrates, the brave students of the universities and other young people turned a blind eye to this great calamity inflicted upon Islam and the household of the Messenger of God, peace be upon him, and allowed the accursed Baath party to martyr their eminent personalities one after the other. It would be even more strange if the Iraqi army and other forces were tools in the hands of these criminals, assisting them in the eradication of Islam. I have no faith in the top-ranking officers of the Iraqi armed forces but I am not disappointed in the other officers, the non-commissioned officers or their soldiers. I expect them to either rise up bravely and overthrow this oppression as was the case in Iran or to flee the garrisons and barracks . . . I hope that God the Almighty will destroy the system of oppression of these criminals.

OPPRESSION LAY LIKE A BLANKET over the Middle East in 1980, in Iraq, in Iran, and in Afghanistan. And if the West was indifferent to the suffering of millions of Muslims, so, shamefully, were most of the Arab leaders. Arafat never dared to condemn the Soviet Union after its invasion of Afghanistan—Moscow was still the PLO's most important ally—and the kings and princes and presidents of the Arab world, who knew better than their Western counterparts what was happening in Iraq, were silent about Saddam's deportations and tortures and executions and genocidal killings. Most of them used variations of the same techniques on their own populations. In Syria, where the "German chair" torture was used to break the backs of opposition militants, the bloodbath of the Hama uprising lay less than two years away.*

In Iran, the authorities turned brutally against members of the Bahai faith whose 2 million members regard Moses, Buddha, Christ and Mohamed as "divine educators" and whose centre of worship—the tomb of a nineteenth-century Persian nobleman—lies outside Acre in present-day Israel. By 1983, Amnesty estimated that at least 170 Bahais had been executed for heresy among the 5,000 Iranians put to death since the revolution. Among them were ten young women, two of them teenagers, all hanged in Shiraz in June of 1983. At least two, Zarrin Muqimi and Shirin Dalvand, both in their twenties, were allowed to pray towards

---

the scene for his 1953 style return to Iran. By this time the American administration probably was thinking of an American Iran without the Shah . . ."

*See p. 814.

Acre before the hangmen tied their hands and led them to the gallows. All were accused of being "Zionist agents." Evin prison began to fill with women, some members of the Iraqi-supported Mujahedin-e-Khalq—People's Mujahedin of Iran—others merely arrested while watching political protests. They were ferociously beaten on the feet to make them confess to being counter-revolutionaries. On one night, 150 women were shot. At least 40 of them were told to prepare themselves for execution by firing squad by writing their names on their right hands and left legs with felt-tip markers; the guards wanted to identify them afterwards and this was often difficult when "finishing shots" to the head would make their faces unrecognisable. But Bahais were not the only victims.

Executions took place in all the major cities of Iran. In July 1980, for example, Iranian state radio reported fourteen executions in Shiraz, all carried out at eleven at night, including a retired major-general—for "making attacks on Muslims"—a former police officer, an army major charged with beating prisoners, an Iranian Jew sentenced for running a "centre of fornication" and seven others for alleged narcotics offences. One man, Habib Faili, was executed for "homosexual relations." Two days earlier, Mehdi Qaheri and Haider Ali Qayur were shot by firing squad for "homosexual offences" in Najafabad. Naturally, Sadeq Khalkhali presided over most of these "trials."

Amnesty recorded the evidence of a female student imprisoned in Evin between September 1981 and March 1982 who was held in a cell containing 120 women, ranging from schoolgirls to the very old. The woman described how:

> One night a young girl called Tahereh was brought straight from the courtroom to our cell. She had just been sentenced to death, and was confused and agitated. She didn't seem to know why she was there. She settled down to sleep next to me, but at intervals she woke up with a start, terrified, and grasped me, asking if it were true that she really would be executed. I put my arms around her and tried to comfort her, and reassure her that it wouldn't happen, but at about 4 a.m. they came for her and she was taken away to be executed. She was sixteen years old.

A frightening nine-page pamphlet issued by the Iranian Ministry of Islamic Guidance—but carrying neither the ministry's name nor that of its author—admitted that "some believe only murderers deserve capital punishment, but not those who are guilty of hundreds of other crimes . . . Weren't the wicked acts of those upon whom [the] death penalty was inflicted tantamount to the spread . . . of corruption . . . The people have indirectly seconded the act of the revolutionary courts, because they realise the courts have acted in compliance with their wishes." The same booklet claimed that trials of senior officials of the Shah's government had to be carried out swiftly lest "counter-revolutionary" elements tried to rescue them from prison.

Khomeini raged, against the leftists and communists who dared to oppose his theocracy, and the Great Satan America and its Iraqi ally. Why did people oppose the death penalty, he asked. ". . . the trial of several young men . . . and the execution of a number of those who had revolted against Islam and the Islamic Republic and were sentenced to death, make you cry for humanity!" The "colonial powers" had frightened Muslims with their "satanic might and advancement"—Khomeini's prescient expression for the "shock and awe" that U.S. defence secretary Donald Rumsfeld would call down on Iraq almost exactly twenty years later—and now communists were "ready to sacrifice [their] lives out of love of the party" while the people of Afghanistan were "perishing under the Soviet regime's cruelty."

Here Khomeini was on safe ground. From Afghan exile groups and humanitarian organisations there came a flood of evidence that Soviet troops were now carrying out atrocities in Afghanistan. Human Rights Watch was reporting by 1984 that it had become clear "that Soviet personnel have been taking an increasingly active role in the Afghan government's oppression of its citizens. Soviet officers are not just serving as 'advisors' to Afghan Khad agents who administer torture— routinely and savagely in detention centres and prisons; according to reports we received there are Soviets who participate directly in interrogation and torture." The same document provided appalling evidence of torture. A twenty-one-year-old accused of distributing "night letters" against the government was hung up by a belt until he almost strangled, beaten until his face was twice its normal size and had his hands crushed under a chair. ". . . mothers were forced to watch their infant babies being given electric shocks . . . Afghan men . . . were held in torture chambers where women were being sexually molested. A young woman who had been tortured in prison described how she and others had been forced to stand in water that had been treated in chemicals that made the skin come off their feet." After Afghans captured a Soviet army captain and three other soldiers in the town of Tashqurghan in April 1982, killed them, chopped up their bodies and threw them in a river, the brother of the officer took his unit—from the Soviet 122nd Brigade—to the town and slaughtered the entire population of around 2,000 people.

An exile publication of the Hezb Islami in Pakistan listed the murder in Afghanistan of twenty-six religious sheikhs, *mawlawi* and other leaders, often with their entire families, from Kabul, Kandahar, Herat, Konar and Ghazni. The Soviets always claimed their village raids were targeted at insurgents, "terrorists" or the "remnants" of the *dushman*—ironically, they would use the Afghan Persian word for "enemy"—but inevitably most of the victims would be civilians. It was a pattern to be repeated by U.S. forces in Iraq almost a quarter of a century later. Photographs in exile magazines showed the victims of Soviet napalm attacks, their faces burned off by chemicals. One Soviet officer who launched his career amid the Afghan atrocities was General Pavel Grachev, later to be Russian defence minister. He it was who would earn the sobriquet "the Butcher of Grozny," after forgetting the lessons of the Afghan war and the defeat of the Soviets by the mujahedin and Osama bin Laden's Arab fighters, by launching the Chechnya war on Boris Yeltsin's behalf and bragging that he could sort out the Chechens in a matter of days. Wiser counsels had warned that he would unleash a "holy war."

And now, across much of this landscape of horror in Muslim south-west Asia,

an epic of bloodletting was about to begin as an obsessive, xenophobic and dictatorial nationalist and secular Arab regime prepared to destroy the Muslim revolutionary forces that were bent on its destruction. As long ago as October 1979, the
documents found in the U.S. embassy in Tehran would reveal, the Iranian government feared that the Iraqis were being encouraged to foment further rebellion
among Iranian Kurds. Ibrahim Yazdi, the Iranian foreign minister, told American
diplomats that "adequate assurances had been given to Sadam Husayn [sic] with
regard to the Shia majority in Iraq" to calm his fears of Shia nationalism; but "if
Iraqi interference continued, Iran would have to consider agitating among the Iraqi
Shia community." By November, the Americans were reporting that the Iraqi
regime was convinced that Iran wished to pursue a claim to the Arab but largely
Shia island of Bahrain, which Saddam Hussein had thought he might negotiate
with Tehran after meeting Yazdi at a summit in Havana, but that the Iraqis now
believed real power lay in "the Iranian religious establishment which is hostile to
Iraq."

Just how militarily powerful the two regimes were in 1980 obsessed both sides
in the forthcoming struggle. Back in 1978, the Shah, boasting of his "very good
relations" with Saddam's Iraq, claimed that Iraq had "more planes and tanks than
Iran has," even though Iran had acquired 80 F-14 Tomcats from the United
States—to counter any strikes from the Soviet Union—which could counter MiG
high reconnaissance and fighter aircraft. All the Iranian F-14 pilots had been
trained in the United States. Before the Shah's fall, according to one of the documents discovered in the U.S. embassy in Tehran, America believed that:

> Iran's . . . military superiority over Iraq rests primarily on the strength of
> its Air Force, which has more high-performance aircraft, better pilot train-
> ing . . . and ordnance such as laser-guided bombs and TV-guided missiles
> that are unavailable to Iraq. The Iranian navy also is far superior to that of
> Iraq; it could easily close the Gulf to Iraqi shipping . . . The two states'
> ground forces are more nearly balanced, however, with each side possess-
> ing different advantages in terms of equipment and capable of incursions
> into the other's territory. The disposition of ground forces and the greater
> mobility of Iraqi forces could in fact give Baghdad a substantial numerical
> advantage along the border during the initial stages of an attack.

This was an all-too-accurate prediction of what was to happen in September
1980—and was presumably also known to Saddam Hussein and his generals in
Iraq. They would have been comforted to know that, according to the same assessment, Iran's reliance on U.S. equipment meant that "if U.S. support was withdrawn, the Iranian armed forces probably could not sustain full-scale hostilities for
longer than two weeks." But this was a woefully inaccurate forecast, which may
have led Saddam to take the bloodiest gamble of his career.

The revolution had certainly emasculated part of the Iranian army. Every general had been retired—more than 300 of the Shah's senior officers departed in

three weeks—and conscription had been lowered from two years to one. As they prepared for a possible American invasion during the hostage siege, the Iranians desperately tried to rebuild their army to a pre-revolution complement of 280,000 men. But pitched battles in Kurdistan meant that every Iranian army unit had been involved in combat by the autumn of 1980. The Revolutionary Guards, who would provide the theological military muscle in any defence of Iran, were—or so I wrote in a dispatch to *The Times* from Tehran on 26 November 1979—"zealous, overenthusiastic and inexperienced," while the army's firepower might have been considerably reduced. Its 1,600 tanks, including 800 British-made Chieftains and 600 American M-60s—all purchased by the Shah—sounded impressive, but the Chieftains, with their sophisticated firing mechanism, may have been down to half strength through lack of maintenance. The M-60s were easier to maintain. The new army was commanded by Major-General Hussain Shaker, who had been trained by the Americans at Fort Leavenworth.

The Islamic government in Tehran put more faith in its air force, mainly because air force cadets had played a leading role in fighting the Imperial Army during the revolution. In the days after the Shah's fall, the air force was the only arm of the services permitted to appear in uniform outside its bases. But the F-14s were in need of U.S. maintenance, and although pilots could still fly the older F-4 Phantom fighter-bombers, much of the U.S. and British radar system had broken down and the U.S. technicians who serviced it had long ago left Iran.*

For months in early 1980, there had been violent incidents along the Iran–Iraq border. Tony Alloway, our stringer in Tehran—increasingly isolated but still doggedly filing to us—was now reporting almost daily artillery duels between Iraqis and Iranians. In *The Times* on 10 April, he reported on tank as well as artillery fire across the border near Qasr-e Shirin. Sadeq Qotbzadeh, now the Iranian foreign minister, was quoted as saying that his government was "determined to overthrow the Iraqi Baathist Government headed by that United States agent Saddam Hussein." On 9 April alone, 9,700 Iraqis of Iranian origin were forced across the border into Iran with another 16,000 soon to be deported. Four hundred of the new arrivals were businessmen who complained that they had been falsely invited to the commerce ministry in Baghdad and there stripped of their possessions, loaded onto lorries and sent to the frontier.

In April, I got a taste of what was to come when pro-Iranian militiamen in Beirut fought street battles with pro-Iraqi gunmen. At the American University Hospital, I counted fifty-five dead, some of them civilians, as armed men, bloodstained bandages round their faces and arms, were brought to the hospital on trucks mounted with anti-aircraft guns. Clouds of smoke billowed up from the Bourj el-Barajneh Palestinian camp where six charred corpses were found inside an Iraqi Baath party office.

Often, the Iranians would complain that Iraqi aircraft had entered Iranian air-

---

*By 1987, the year before the Iran–Iraq War ended, the American government believed Iran had only five F-14s able to fly, along with just fifteen Phantoms.

space; in early July 1980, Iraqi jets passed above Kermanshah Province on two separate days, coming under fire from Iranian anti-aircraft guns. The pilots were presumably trying to locate Iran's ground-to-air defence positions. On 3 July *Kayhan* newspaper in Tehran was reporting that the Iraqi regime had set up a "mercenary army," led by an Iraqi officer, near Qasr-e Shirin. By August, regular artillery fire was directed across the border in both directions. Iranian claims that their villages were coming under constant attack were dismissed by Iraq as "falsehoods." The Iraqi Foreign Ministry, however, listed twenty shooting incidents—against Iraqi villages and ships in the Shatt al-Arab around Basra—between 18 and 22 September. Ever afterwards, Saddam Hussein would claim that the Iran–Iraq War began on 4 September, by which time Iraq had complained of artillery firing at its border posts and neighbouring oil refineries on ninety-eight occasions. Iraq denounced Iran for violating the Shah's 1975 agreement with Baghdad which set the two countries' common frontier along the Shatt al-Arab, declaring the treaty "null and void."

Although a major conflict seemed inevitable, the UN Security Council would not meet to discuss the hostilities until after the Iraqis invaded Iranian territory; Iraq had made strenuous efforts to prevent seven non-aligned members of the council from going to the UN chamber. Had Iran not been a pariah state after its seizure of the U.S. embassy, it could have obtained a favourable motion and vote. But in the end, UN Security Council Resolution 479 did not even call for a withdrawal of Iraqi forces from Iranian territory, but merely for a ceasefire—which would satisfy neither party. Iran was convinced that the whole world had now turned against its revolution and was supporting the act of aggression by Saddam.

Fathi Daoud Mouffak, a twenty-eight-year-old Iraqi military news cameraman, was to remember those days for the rest of his life. Almost a quarter of a century later, he was to recall for me in Baghdad how he set off one morning in September 1980 from the Iraqi Ministry of Defence towards a location near Qasr-e Shirin. "When we arrived we found our border checkpoints attacked and destroyed—and our Iraqi forces there were less than a brigade," he said. "We visited Qasr-e Shirin and Serbil Sahab. All our checkpoints there had been destroyed by artillery from the Iranians. We filmed this and we found many dead bodies, our martyrs, most of them border policemen. I had never seen so many dead before. Then we brought our films back to Baghdad." Across Iraq, Mouffak's newsreel was shown on national Iraqi television under the title "Pictures from the Battle." It provided a kind of psychological preparation for the Iraqi people, perhaps for Saddam himself. For on 22 September, on the first day of what the Iranians would call the "Imposed War," Saddam's legions with their thousands of tanks, armour and artillery swept across the frontier and into Iran on a 650-kilometre front.

## CHAPTER SIX

# "The Whirlwind War"

> GAS! GAS! *Quick, boys!—An ecstasy of fumbling,*
> *Fitting the clumsy helmets just in time;*
> *But someone still was yelling out and stumbling*
> *And flound'ring like a man in fire or lime . . .*
> *If you could hear, at every jolt, the blood*
> *Come gargling from the froth-corrupted lungs,*
> *Obscene as cancer, bitter as the cud*
> *Of vile, incurable sores on innocent tongues . . .*
>
> —Wilfred Owen, "Dulce et Decorum Est"

SADDAM HUSSEIN CALLED IT "The Whirlwind War." That's why the Iraqis wanted us there. They were victorious before they had won, they were celebrating before they had achieved success. Saad Bazzaz at the Iraqi embassy in London couldn't wait to issue my visa and, after flying from Beirut to London—Middle East journalism often involves vast round-trips of thousands of kilometres to facilitate a journey only a few hundred kilometres from the starting point—I was crammed into the visa office with Gavin Hewitt of the BBC and his crew and more radio and newspaper reporters than I have ever seen in a smoke-filled room before. We would fly to Kuwait. We would be taken from there across the Iraqi border to the war front at Basra. And so we were. In September 1980 we entered Basra at night in a fleet of Iraqi embassy cars from Kuwait City, the sky lit up by a thousand tracer shells. Jets moaned overhead and the lights had been turned off across the city, a blackout to protect all of us from the air raids.

"Out of the cars," the Iraqis shouted, and we leapt from their limousines, crouched on the pavements, hands holding microphones up into the hot darkness as the frail Basra villas, illuminated by the thin moonlight around us, vibrated to the sound of anti-aircraft artillery. The tracer streaked upwards in curtains, golden lines that disappeared into the smoke drifting over Basra. Sirens bawled like crazed geriatrics and behind the din we could hear the whisper of Iranian jets. A great fire burned out of control far to the east, beyond the unseen Shatt al-Arab River. Gavin, with whom I had shared most of my adventures in Afghanistan that very same year, was standing, hands on hips, in the roadway. "Jesus Christ!" he kept saying. "What a story!" And it was. Never again would an Arab army so welcome journalists to a battle front, give them so much freedom, encourage them to

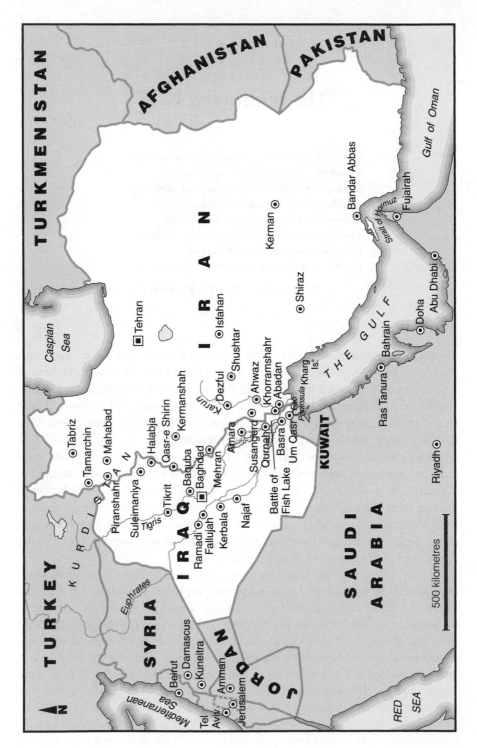

run and take cover and advance with their soldiers. In the steamy entrance of the Hamdan Hotel—the authorities had switched off power across Basra and the air conditioners were no longer working—the staff had turned on their battery-powered radios. There was a constant blowsy song, all trumpets and drums and men's shouting voices. *Al-harb al-khatifa, nachnu nurbah al-harb al-khatifa.* "The whirlwind war, the whirlwind war, we shall win the whirlwind war," they kept chanting.

We stood on the steps, watching the spray of pink and golden bullets ascending into the dark clouds that scudded across Basra. Somewhere to the east of the city, through the palm groves on the eastern banks of the Shatt al-Arab and all the way to the north, Saddam's army was moving eastwards through the night, into Iran, into the great deserts of Ahwaz, into the Kurdish mountains towards Mahabad. The Arab journalists who had accompanied us up from Basra were ecstatic. The Iraqis would win, the Iraqis would protect the Arab world from the threat of Iran's revolution. Saddam was a strong man, a great man, a good man. They were confident of his victory—even more confident, perhaps, than Saddam himself.

Yet the orders to give us journalists the freedom of the battlefield must have come from Saddam. We could take taxis without the usual "minders," all the way to the front if we wanted. The Ministry of Information would provide us with officials to escort us through road checkpoints if we wished. The Fao peninsula, that vulnerable spit of land south of Basra from which you can look eastwards across "the Shatt" at the palm-fringed shore of Iran? No problem. But when we reached Fao, it was under constant Iranian shellfire and the two deep-sea oil terminals 30 kilometres off the coast, Khor al-Amaya and Mina al-Bakr—the latter, one of the most modern in the world, had been opened only four years earlier—were already seriously damaged by Iranian ground-to-ground missiles. The Iraqis had not been able to silence the Iranian guns.

By 29 September 1980, exactly a week after the Iraqi invasion, Iranian shells were landing around Fao at the rate of one every twenty-five seconds and it was unsafe even to drive along the river promenade. The windows and doors of houses in the city rattled as each round exploded, hissing over the bazaar and crashing beyond the oil storage depots. In revenge, the Iraqis had attacked the huge oil terminal at Abadan, and for more than an hour I sat near the river, watching 200-metre gouts of fire shooting into the air over Abadan, a ripple of flame that moved with frightening speed along the bank of the river beneath a canopy of black smoke. An Iraqi official crouched next to me, pointing out the Iranian positions on the other shore. So much for the claims on Iraqi radio that its army had "surrounded" Abadan. In Basra, two Iranian Phantoms bombed a ship moored in the river, setting it on fire and splattering bullets along the waterfront walls, proof that the Iranian air force was still capable of daylight raids.

The Iraqis claimed to have shot down four Phantoms in five days, and the undamaged fuel tank of one aircraft—the American refuelling instructions still clearly readable on one canister in a local Baath party headquarters—was proof that their claim was at least partly true. The Iranians had damaged homes and schools in Fao—though their pilots could hardly be expected to distinguish between "military" and "civilian" targets during their high-speed low-level attacks.

Fao was almost deserted. I watched many of its inhabitants—part of the constant flow of millions of refugees which are part of Middle East history—driving north-west to Basra in a convoy of old wooden Chevrolet taxis, bedding piled on the roofs and chador-clad mothers and wives on the back seats, scarcely bothering to glance at the burning refineries of Abadan. They were Iraqi Shia Muslims and now they were under fire from their fellow Shias in Iran, another gift from Saddam.

Already I was beginning to realise that this war might not be so easy to win as the Iraqi authorities would have us believe. In Washington and London, the usual military "experts" and fossilised ex-generals were holding forth on the high quality of the Iraqi army, the shambles of post-revolutionary Iran, the extraordinary firepower of Iraq's largely Soviet equipped army. But on 30 September, eight days after their invasion, the Iraqis could only claim that they were 15 kilometres from Khorramshahr—the old Abbasid harbour which was Iran's largest port, and closer than "surrounded" Abadan.

I crossed the river from Basra, trailing behind convoys of military trucks carrying bridge-building equipment—the Iraqis had yet to cross the Iranian Karun River north of Khorramshahr—and headed into the blistering, white desert towards the Iranian border post at Shalamcheh. I overtook dozens of T-62 tanks and Russian-made armour and trucks piled with soldiers, all of whom obligingly gave us two-finger victory signs. The air thumped with the sound of heavy artillery, and on a little hill in the desert I came across the wrecked Iranian frontier station, stopped the car and gingerly walked inside. I was in Iran, occupied Iran. No problem with visas now, I thought. It's always an obscure thrill to enter a country with an invading army, knowing how furious all those pious little visa officers would be—those who kept me waiting for hours in boiling, tiny rooms, the perspiration crawling through my hair—if they could see me crossing their borders without their wretched, indecipherable stamps in my passport. Pictures of Ayatollah Khomeini had been ritually defaced on the walls of the Shalamcheh frontier station and a large pile of handwritten ledgers were strewn over the floor.

I have a fascination for the documents that blow through the ruins of war, the pages of letters home and the bureaucracy of armies and the now useless instructions on how to fire ground-to-air missiles that flutter across the desert and cover the floors of roofless factories. These books were written in Persian and recorded the names and car numbers of Iraqis and Iranians crossing the border at Shalamcheh. The last entry was on 21 September 1980, just a day before the Iraqi invasion. So although the Iraqis claimed that the war began on 4 September, they had allowed travellers—including their own citizens—to transit the border quite routinely until the very eve of their invasion.

An American camera-crew had pulled up outside the wreckage of the building and were dutifully filming the desecrated pictures of Khomeini, their reporter already practising his "stand-upper." "Iraq's army smashed its way across the Iranian frontier more than a week ago and now stands poised outside the strategic cities of Khorramshahr and Abadan . . ." Yes, cities were always "strategic"—at least, they always were on television—and armies must always "smash" through borders and stand "poised" outside cities. It was as if there was only one script for each event. Soon, no doubt, the Iraqis would be "fighting their way" towards Khorramshahr, or "poised" to enter Khorramshahr, or "claiming victory" over the Iranian defenders.

But who was I to talk? My CBC tape recorder hung over my shoulder and behind the border post stood a battery of Russian 155-mm guns, big beasts whose barrels pointed towards Khorramshahr and whose artillery captain walked up to us smiling and asked politely if we would like his guns to open fire. For a millisecond, for just that little fraction of temptation, I wanted to agree, to say yes, I would like them to fire, just the moment I had finished adjusting my microphone; and the captain was already turning to give the order to fire when a moral voice shouted at me—I had just imagined the tearing apart of an unknown body—and I ran after him and said, no, no, he should not fire, not for me, not under any circumstances.

But of course, I found a basin in the sand and sat down in it and leaned on the lip of the hole with my microphone on the edge and I waited as a desert gale blew over me and the sand caught in my hair and nose and ears and then, when the first artillery piece much later blasted a shell towards the Iranian lines, I switched on the recorder. I still have the cassette tape. The guns were dark against the sky as they bellowed away and I kept thinking of Wilfred Owen's description of the "long black arm . . . about to curse." And there were twenty, thirty long black arms in front of me, more still behind the curtains of sand. And there, I recorded, unwittingly, my own future loss of hearing, 25 per cent of the hearing in my left ear which I would never recover. That very moment is recorded on the cassette:

> We can see the gunnery officer just in front of us through this desert dust storm, feeding shells into the breeches of these big 155-mm Russian-made guns and preparing to cover their ears. The guns are so loud, they are leaving my ears singing afterwards—BANG—There's another one just gone off, a great tongue of fire about 20 feet—BANG—in front of it—BANG—They're going off all around me at the moment, an incredible sight, this heavy artillery firing right in the middle of a—BANG—there's another one, right in the middle of this dusty, windswept desert.

I can still hear that gun's distant echo in my ears as I write these words, a piercing tinnitus that can drive me crazy at night or when I'm tired or irritable or trying to listen to music or can't hear someone talking to me at dinner.

I turned on Iraqi radio. Further Iranian territory was about to "fall" and Iraqi generals were announcing a "last push" into Khorramshahr. Five days ago, the inhabitants of Basra were content to listen to news of the Iraqi advance on television, but now traders and shopkeepers in the city chose to supplement their knowledge by asking foreign journalists for information about the war. No one thought Iranian shells would still be falling on Iraqi soil this long after the invasion.

That evening, we were invited to tour Basra District Hospital, a bleak building of tiles and pale blue paint, a barrack-like edifice whose uniformity was relieved only by the neat flower-beds outside, the energetic doctors and, more recently, by the ubiquitous presence of Dr. Saadun Khalifa al-Tikriti, Iraq's deputy health minister. He was saluted and clapped on the back wherever he went, a short, friendly fellow with a mischievous smile and a large moustache. Everyone greeted Dr. al-Tikriti with exaggerated warmth, and when the minister made a joke, gales of laughter swept down the marble corridors. The Basra hospital had taken almost all the city's 500 wounded this past week but al-Tikriti had more than just his patients on his mind when he toured the wards. Foreign press correspondents were greeted with a short, sharp speech about the evils of civilian bombing, and the doctor stopped smiling and thumped his little fist on the table when he claimed that the Iranian air force deliberately killed Iraqi children.

He strode into a children's ward, a long, curtained room where tiny, awe-struck faces peered from beneath swaths of bandages while silent mothers stared with peasant intensity at the white-coated doctors. "Take, for example, this little girl," said the good doctor, pausing for a moment beside a child with beautiful round brown eyes and curled black hair. "She is only three years old and she has lost a leg." With these words, al-Tikriti seized the sheets and swept them from the child to reveal that indeed her left leg was nothing but a bandaged stump. The little girl frowned in embarrassment at her sudden nakedness but al-Tikriti had already moved on, preceded by a uniformed militiaman. In civilian life, the militiaman was a hospital dresser but his camouflage jacket and holstered pistol provided a strange contrast to the hospital as he clumped around the beds, especially when we reached the end of the second children's ward.

For there in a darkened corner lay a boy of five, swaddled in bandages, terribly burned by an Iranian incendiary bomb and clearly not far from death. There were plastic tubes in his nostrils and gauze around his chest and thighs, and his eyes were creased with pain and tears, the doors to a small private world of torment that we did not wish to imagine. The boy had turned his face towards his pillow, breathing heavily; so the militiaman moved forward, seized the little bandaged head and twisted it upwards for the inspection of the press. The child gasped with pain but when a journalist protested at this treatment, he was told that the militiaman was medically trained.

Dr. al-Tikriti then briskly ushered us to the next bed and the child was left to suffer in grace, having supposedly proved a measure of Iranian iniquity that he would certainly never comprehend. An air raid siren growled and there was, far away, a smattering of anti-aircraft fire. There were other wards, of Bangladeshi seamen caught by strafing Iranian jets, thin men who scrabbled with embarrassment for their sheets when Dr. al-Tikriti stripped the bedding from their naked bodies, a new generation of amputated, legless beggars for the streets of Dacca. There were oil workers caught in the cauldron of petroleum tank explosions, roasted faces staring at the ceiling, and for one terrible moment the doctors began to take off the bandage round a man's face. Al-Tikriti smiled brightly. "Some of these people speak English," he said, gesturing at the huddles on the beds. "Why not ask them what happened?"

No one took up the offer but Iraq's deputy health minister was already ushering his guests to the training hospital by the Shatt al-Arab, a six-storey block that looked more like a government ministry than a medical centre. Iranian cannon fire had punctured the fourth floor, wounding four patients, and the doctor claimed that this, too, was a deliberate attack, since the hospital had flown white flags with the red crescent on them. But the flags were only six foot square and the dark crescent painted upon the flat roof by the doctors merged with the colour of the concrete. Al-Tikriti pointed to the splashes of blood on the ceiling. "Arabs would never do this," he said. "They would never attack civilians." But as he was leaving the building, a battered, open-top truck drew up. There were two corpses in the back, half-covered by a dirty blanket, four bare brown feet poking from the bottom. The driver asked what he should do with the bodies but Dr. al-Tikriti saw no journalists nearby. "Take them round the back," he told the driver.

The first commandos of the Iraqi army broke through to the west bank of the Karun River on the Shatt al-Arab at 12:23 Iraq time on the afternoon of 2 October, four small figures running along the Khorramshahr quayside past lines of burned-out and derailed trucks, bowling hand grenades down the dockside. I was able to watch them through Iraqi army binoculars from just 400 metres away, peering above sandbags in a crumbling mud hut while an Iraqi sniper beside me blasted away at the Iranian lines on the other side of the Karun.

Pierre Bayle of Agence France-Presse was beside me, a tough, pragmatic man with a refusal to panic that must have come from his days as a French foreign legionnaire. "Not bad, not bad," he would mutter to me every time an Iraqi moved forward down the quayside. "These guys aren't bad." It was an extraordinary sight, an infantry attack that might have come from one of those romanticised oil paintings of the Crimean War, one soldier running after another through the docks, throwing themselves behind sandbags when rockets exploded round them and then hurling grenades at the last Iranian position on the riverbank. The Iranians fought back with machine guns and rockets. For over an hour, their bullets hissed and whizzed through the small island plantation on which we had taken refuge, smacking into the palm trees above us and clanging off the metal pontoon bridge that connected the island to the Iraqi mainland. Only hours earlier, the Iraqis had succeeded in crossing the Karun 4 kilometres upstream from the Shatt al-Arab, sending a tank section across the river and beginning—at last—the encirclement of the Iranians in Abadan. Iran's own radio admitted that "enemy troops" had "infiltrated" north of the city.

The Karun River runs into the Shatt al-Arab at a right angle and it was almost opposite this confluence—from the flat, plantation island of Um al-Rassas in the middle of the Shatt itself—that we finally watched the Iraqis take the riverfront. Behind them, Iraqi shells smashed into a group of abandoned Chieftain tanks, deserted by their Iranian crews when their retreat was cut off by the Karun. All morning and afternoon, the Iraqis fired shells into Abadan, an eerie, jet-like noise that howled right over our heads on the little island.

Shells travel too fast for the naked eye, but after some time I realised that their shadows moved over the river, flitting across the water and the little paddy-fields, then dropping towards Abadan where terrific explosions marked their point of impact. I could not take my eyes off this weird phenomenon. As the projectiles reached their maximum altitude before dropping back to earth, the little shadows—small, ominous points of darkness that lay upon the river—would hover near us, as if a miniature cloud had settled on the water. Then the shadow would grow smaller and begin to move with frightening velocity towards the far shore and be lost in the sunlight.

On the other bank of the river, one of these shells set a big ship ablaze; a sheet of flame over 100 metres in height ran along its deck from bow to stern. Its centre was a circle of white intensity, so bright that I could feel my face burning and my eyes hurting as I stared at it. At times, the din of Iraqi artillery fire and the explosion of Iranian shells around our little mud hut was so intense that the Iraqi troops crouched behind the windows and alleyways of the abandoned village on the island could not make themselves heard. An army captain—the small gold medallion on his battledress proof of his Baath party membership—was fearful that his riflemen might shoot into their own troops on the far side of the river, and repeatedly gave orders that they should turn their fire further downstream. One Iraqi sniper, a tall man with a broad chest, big, beefy arms and a scar on his left cheek, walked into our shabby mud hut holding a long Soviet Dragunov rifle with telescopic sights. He grinned at us like a schoolboy, scratched his face, placed his weapon at the broken window and fired off two rounds at the Iranians. Whenever a shell landed near us, the palm trees outside shook and pieces of mud fell from the ceiling.

At last, it seemed, the Iraqis might be marrying up reality with their propaganda. If they could take Khorramshahr and Abadan and so control both banks of the Shatt al-Arab, they would have placed their physical control over the entire waterway—one of the ostensible reasons for the war. There were reports that the Iraqis were now making headway towards Dezful, 80 kilometres inside Iran, as well as Ahwaz, although claims that they had already captured the Ahwaz radio station were hard to believe. They had originally captured it twelve days earlier, but journalists later watched it blown to pieces by Iranian shells. And there was no denying the ferocity of Iran's defence of Abadan. Even in Khorramshahr, they were still fighting, their snipers firing from the top of the quayside cranes.

The Iraqi soldiers in our hut had warned us of them as we were about to leave Um al-Rassas. Although they could not see us near the hut, the Iranians had a clear view over the top of the palm plantation once we arrived at the lonely iron bridge that linked the island to the western shore of the Shatt al-Arab. Pierre Bayle and I walked quickly between the trees, hearing the occasional snap of bullets but unworried until we reached the river's edge. There again, I could see the shadow of the shells moving mysteriously across the water. "Robert, we are going to have to run," Bayle said, but I disagreed. Perhaps it was the bright sunlight, the heavenly green of the palms that made me believe—or wish to believe—that no one would disturb our retreat across the bridge.

I was wrong, of course. As soon as we set off across the narrow iron bridge, the bullets started to crack around us, many of them so close that I could feel the air displacement of their trajectory. I saw a line of spray travelling across the river towards us—I was running now, but I still had the dangerous, childish ability to reflect that this was just how it looked in Hollywood films, the little puffs of water stitching their way at speed towards the bridge. And then they were pinging into the ironwork, spitting around us, ricochets and aimed shots. I actually saw a square of metal flattened by a round a few inches from my face. I ran faster but was gripped by a kind of stasis, a feeling—most perilous of all—that this cannot be happening and that if it is, then perhaps I should accept whatever harm is to come to me. Within seconds, Bayle was beside me, taking the cassette recorder from me, screaming "Run, run" in my left ear, physically pushing me from behind and then, when we neared the end of the bridge, grabbing me by the arm and jumping with me into the water of the Shatt al-Arab, the bullets still skitting around us. We waded the last metres to shore, scrambled up the bank and plunged into the palm grove as a cluster of mortar shells burst around the bridge, the shrapnel clanging off the iron.

Amid the trees, an Iraqi platoon was banging off mortars towards Khor-ramshahr. The sergeant beckoned to Pierre and myself, and there, amid his soldiers, we lay down exhausted in the dirt. One of his men brought us tea and I looked at Bayle and he just nodded at me. I thought at first that he was telling me how bad things had been, how closely we had escaped with our lives. Then I realised he was thinking what I was thinking: that Saddam had bitten off more than he could chew, that this might not be a whirlwind war at all but a long, gruelling war of aggression. When we returned to the Hamdan Hotel that afternoon, I typed up my story on the old telex machine, sent the tape laboriously through to London, went to my room and slept for fifteen hours. The smell of adventure was beginning to rub off.

So why did we go back for more? Why did I tell the *Times* foreign desk that although I was short of money, I would stay on in Basra? To be sure, I wanted to see a little bit more of this history I was so dangerously witnessing. If it was true that Saddam had grotesquely underestimated the effect of his aggression—and the Iranians were fighting back with great courage—then eventually the Iraqi army might heed Khomeini's appeal and revolt. This could mean the end of Saddam's regime or—the American and Arab nightmare—an Iranian occupation of Iraq and another Shiite Islamic republic.

But war is also a vicarious, painful, attractive, unique experience for a journalist. Somehow that narcotic has to be burned off. If it's not, the journalist may well die. We were young. I was fresh from the Soviet invasion of Afghanistan, already immersed in covering the Lebanese civil war and the effects of Israel's first 1978 invasion. I had covered the Iranian revolution, the very crucible of this Iraq–Iran conflict. This was my war. Or so I felt as we set off each morning for the Iraqi front lines. And thus it was one burning morning along the Shatt al-Arab, this time with Gavin and his crew, that I almost died again. Once more, I was carrying CBC's recording equipment and so—before writing these paragraphs—I have listened once more to that day's tape; and I can hear myself, heart thumping, when I first began to understand how frightening war is.

Most of the ships on the far side of the river were now on fire, a pageant of destruction that lent itself to every camera. But again, we had to approach the river through the Iraqi lines and the Iranians now had men tied by ropes to the cranes along the opposite riverbank who were holding rocket-propelled grenades as well as rifles. Here is the text of the audio-track that I was ad-libbing for CBC:

> FISK: We're walking through this deserted village now, there really doesn't seem to be anybody here, just a few Iraqi soldiers on rooftops and we can't see them. But there's a lot of small-arms fire very near. *Sound of gunfire, growing in intensity.* Yes, the car's just over there, Gavin.
> HEWITT: Down here.
> FISK: Yes, there they are. *Sound of shooting, much closer this time.* I'm beginning to wonder why I got into journalism. *My heartbeats are breaking up my commentary.* Going through the courtyard of what was obviously a school—there are school benches laid out here.
>
> *The sound of an incoming rocket-propelled grenade followed by a thunderous explosion that obliterates the commentary and breaks the audio control on the recorder.*
>
> FISK: Back over here, I think, round this way. *Dozens of shots and the sound of Gavin, the BBC crew and Fisk running for their lives, gasping for breath.* Just trying to get back to the car to get to safety. Ouch, that's too near. I think they can see us wandering around. Let's go! Let's go! There's . . .
> HEWITT (*to crew*): Yah, c'mon, c'mon, we're getting out of here. Can we go? Damn!

And then, listening to this tape, I hear us urging our Iraqi driver to leave, shouting at him to leave. "Go, just go!" one of us screams at him in fury and, once we are moving away, I talk into the microphone, giving a message to George Lewinski and Sue Hickey in the CBC office in London:

> George and Sue, I hope you've now listened to all that. Please, please, use as much as you can 'cos you can tell how dangerous it was. And please would you keep this cassette whatever happens—it's a memory I want to remember for the rest of my life, sitting in my Irish cottage. Whatever you do, don't throw it away!

The tape never made it. I gave it to our Iraqi taxi-driver in Basra to take across the border to send from Kuwait airport, but he was turned round at the frontier and arrived back four hours later outside our hotel, smiling ingratiatingly and holding my tape out of the driver's window like a dead fish. I later transmitted it down a crackling phone line. Heaven knows what the Canadians made of it—although I was later told that a truck-driver in Whitehorse, Yukon, pulled over to a phone booth, dialled CBC in Toronto and asked: "Was that for real?"

In one sense, it was. The recording was the actual sound of four comparatively young men risking their lives for . . . Nothing? I'm not sure that would be true. By putting our lives on the line, we did, I suspect, give an authenticity to our work that also gave us a credibility when we came to challenge what governments—or other journalists—claimed to be true. This experience had proved to me beyond all doubt that Iraq was not going to "win" this huge war. An Iranian artillery counter-attack was being sustained and, as I wrote that October—accurately but six years prematurely—"if this is carried to its logical conclusion, then it will not be Khorramshahr that is under shellfire from Iraqi guns but Basra that will be hit by shell-fire from the Iranians."

Across the Bailey bridge in Basra came now a steady stream of military ambulances. I ventured out to the border post at Shalamcheh again and there now were the Iraqi wounded, lying in the sand while an artillery battery beside them lobbed 155-mm shells across the border. An ambulance came bumping out of the desert and bounced to a halt in a sandy basin half surrounded by palm trees. They brought an infantryman out of it on a stretcher, pulled the blood-soaked bandages off his shoulder and laid him on a makeshift bed in the shade of the old police station. The man, shot by an Iranian sniper, was still in pain but he made no sound as three army medical orderlies fussed with drip-feed bags above him, the guns firing off a round every minute, a slamming explosion that shook the walls of the building and had the doctors wincing.

A second Iraqi casualty was brought out of the sands, a private from a tank crew who had been blasted from his vehicle, a severely shell-shocked soldier whose head lolled from side to side and whose knees buckled when his comrades carried him into the courtyard of the police station. The soldier with the shoulder wound moaned a little, and every time the big guns fired and the shells soared off towards Khorramshahr, the shell-shock victim rolled his eyes around, his arms flopping from side to side like a dummy with the stuffing knocked out of it.

The forward dressing station of the Iraqi army's southern front was a grim little place and the long smears of dried blood on the floor were witness to the sacrifice the Iraqi army was having to make for "The Whirlwind War." The senior medical orderly was quite matter-of-fact about it. "This is an old building and the Iranians have it on all their maps," he said. "They will fire at it and there will be more casualties." He gave me a mirthless grin. Three minutes later, the Iranian shells began coming in, sending the Iraqi gunners jumping into their pits.

The driver of an army jeep on the Khorramshahr–Shalamcheh highway—supposedly safe and long secure in Iraqi hands—was burned to death when Iranian shells rained down on his convoy. Not one major Iranian city had fallen to Baghdad and, with the exception of Qasr-e Shirin to the north, all that the Iraqis had so far captured was 3,000 square kilometres of brown, waterless desert, a shabby landscape of rock and sand from which the Iranians very sensibly withdrew to fight on from the hills.

When Gavin Hewitt and I asked to visit the military hospital in Basra, we were given permission within two minutes and nobody tried to prevent us talking to the wounded soldiers inside. All the casualties told the same stories, of surprise attacks by Iranian helicopter gunships—the Cobras sold to the Shah by the Americans—and Phantom jets suddenly swooping from the east. A badly burned tank crewman described how he heard the sound of jet engines only a second before a rocket hit his tank, covering a quarter of his body in blazing petrol. A private in the Iraqi army's transport command was blown from his jeep south of Ahwaz by a rocket fired from an Iranian helicopter; as he lay in the road, a Phantom appeared from the sun and bombed his colleagues who were staggering from the wrecked vehicle.

By 5 October, the Iraqis entered Khorramshahr at last, and we went with them. We found a burning, smashed city and just one old Arab Iranian—sole representative of the millions of Arabs of "Arabistan" whom Saddam was seeking to "save"—squatting on the stone floor of his mud home, a man with deep lines on his face and a white beard, brewing tea for an Iraqi soldier and ignoring the questions of strangers. He had been "liberated." This, after all, was the city where the representative of the Iranian embassy siege gunmen in London came from, the city he called al-Mohammorah. This was to be Saddam's Danzig, the desert beyond was his Sudetenland. The Iraqis were going to rescue the Arabs of Iran, but we could only walk down one main street of the city, a battered thoroughfare of broken telegraph poles and blackened, single-storey shops where tired Iraqi troops, their faces stained with mud, sat on doorsteps and talked under the cover of sheets of corrugated iron.

General Adnan Khairallah, the Iraqi defence minister and Saddam's first cousin, had offered a ceasefire to the Iranians—to show Iraq's "peaceful intentions" in front of the world rather than any Iraqi desire to withdraw from Iranian territory—but six and a half hours after the unilateral truce came into effect, the Iranians opened fire on occupied Khorramshahr. We had been sitting in the courtyard of a broken villa near the Karun River, listening to a Colonel Ramseh of the Iraqi army—his eyes bloodshot, head hanging with fatigue—as he claimed that his troops had taken control of the city and its harbour, when shells showered down onto the houses and orchards around us.

"Please go now because it is not safe," a brigadier pleaded as explosions began to crash around the bridge at the end of the street. An Iraqi commando was led through the gate, blood dribbling down his right cheek from a shrapnel wound. The Iraqi Special Forces soldiers—no longer laughing and making their familiar victory signs at journalists—sat round the edge of an empty fish pond and stared at us glumly. Iranian Revolutionary Guards were still holding out in the heavily damaged buildings on the western side of the Karun and they drove six Chieftain tanks past the central post office, firing shells at the nearest Iraqi command post until one of them was hit by a rocket. Running from the villa, I had just enough time to see an Iraqi tank, its barrel traversing wildly and its tracks thrashing through the rubbish along the street as it drove towards the centre of the city.

The Iraqis now had tanks positioned along the Khorramshahr waterfront. They must have entered the port very suddenly, for the docks were still strewn with empty goods wagons, half-empty crates and burning containers hanging from damaged cranes. From some of the containers, Iraqi soldiers were stealing the contents, making off with a bizarre combination of Suzuki motorcycles, footballs, Dutch cattle-feed and Chinese Ping-Pong bats.

The ships along the quayside had been under fire for days. The chief officer of the Yugoslav freighter *Krasica* leant over the after-deck of his bullet-flecked ship and grinned broadly. "Both sides shelled us all the time—for fifteen days," he shouted. "We sat down below, played cards and drank beer—what else could we do?" It must have been bad, because the man did not even look eastwards along the waterfront where smoke poured from a burning ship. The Italian freighter *Capriella* had had its bridge, funnel and superstructure gutted by fire. The crew of another Italian vessel had quenched the fires of a first bombardment but then fled to a Korean freighter whose crew refused to let them aboard; they were eventually given sanctuary on a Greek ship. The Chinese *Yung Chun* had rocket and bullet holes in its hull. Further east, there were larger vessels, all burning furiously.

None of these ships would ever sail again. They would remain, charred wrecks along the harbour-side, for eight more years. But in Basra, the ninety big freighters moored along the quays, their crews still aboard and keeping steam up for a quick escape if a real ceasefire took hold, would still be rotting away at the harbour almost a quarter of a century later. It was a mournful development for a port city founded by the Caliph Omar Ibn Khattab in 638, a harbour occupied by the British in 1914 and 1941 and 2003. British mercantile interests had been here since 1643, and behind the city's six stinking canals it was still possible to find the carved wooden façades and elaborate shutters of Ottoman houses. The Caliph Omar had decreed that no one should be permitted to cut down the city's date palms, although thousands of them now stood, decapitated or blackened by fire in plantations ribbed by streams into which nineteenth-century steamships had long ago been secreted, rotting museums of industrial technology which were no doubt launched with appropriate triumph when they went down the slipways of Birkenhead and Belfast two generations earlier. In what the Basra tourist office, in a moment of unfortunate enthusiasm, dubbed "the Venice of the East," it was still possible to come across the relics of empire. The Shatt al-Arab Hotel had been a staging post for the British Imperial Airways flying boats that would set down on the Shatt and deposit their passengers in a lounge still decorated with scale models of British-built ships.

Every day now, the Iraqis were learning that victory would not be theirs—not at least for weeks, maybe months, even years. The Iraqi army around Khorramshahr moved forward only 8 kilometres in ten days. In the city, an Iraqi army colonel in a paratrooper's red beret and carrying a swagger stick agreed with us that the Iranians were still fighting hard. Even as he spoke, a young soldier covered in blood was carried past us, the wounded man screaming that he was dying. "We thought the Iranians would not fight," another officer said to me that day. "But now I believe they will fight on, whatever happens."

Officially, no one would suggest such a thing. "You must come—you must come," a Ministry of Information minder shouted to us in the lobby of the Hamdan Hotel. "You must see the Iranian prisoners." It was to be the first display of prisoners by both sides in the war, a theatrical presentation that would eventually involve thousands of captured soldiers, a press "opportunity" which was a gross breach of the Geneva Convention. But we went along that bright October morning to see what the Iranians looked like. "Animals in a cell" was Gavin's apt comment.*

They were sitting in the far corner of a concrete-walled barrack hut, a dishevelled group of dark-haired young men, some in bandages and all in the drab, uncreased khaki uniform of the Iranian army. Unshaved, the seventeen men gaped at the television cameras as they sat on the bare mattresses that had been their beds for the past three days. "You are not permitted to talk to them," an Iraqi army major announced, and the Iranians looked again at the lenses and microphones that were thrust expectantly towards them. Asked by a journalist if any of the prisoners spoke English, a young bearded man below the latticed window said that he spoke German but the major shut him up. "They were taken prisoner at Ahwaz and Mohammorah," the major said. "What more do you want to know?"

But the prisoners talked with their hands and faces. About half had been injured, their heads and arms in bandages. A thin young man by the wall slyly made a victory sign with his fingers. Five prisoners had been told to hold copies of a Baghdad newspaper that pictured Saddam Hussein on the front page, but they had folded the paper in such a way that the portrait was no longer visible. The Iranian soldier who spoke German smiled and nodded at us as we were herded from the barracks hut. Then the Iraqi major announced that two prisoners would talk to us if we promised to take no pictures. Two sad, drawn young men, one with his chest bandaged in plaster, were eventually led into a messroom where a picture of Saddam, a Gainsborough reproduction and a bunch of pink plastic flowers vied for space along the wall.

The two soldiers were seated on steel chairs in the centre of the room while government officials and the major stood round them in order to "translate." The wounded prisoner clutched his hands nervously and began to shake. The major wagged his finger in front of the first soldier. "They are asking about your casualties," he said. The man shrugged and proclaimed his ignorance. "I am an Iranian soldier," he said quietly. Were the Iranian mullahs in charge of the Iranian army,

*We had to be careful with the freedom of reporting we were sometimes able to enjoy. Hewitt and his crew at one point hired a river boat to film on the Shatt al-Arab. Stopped by the Iraqi authorities, the boat's owner was taken away. "He will be punished," a remorseful Hewitt was told. He was advised that any protest on the boatman's behalf would only make this unknown "punishment" worse.

journalists asked, and the major translated this question as: "Aren't religious people influencing your officers?" It was true, the prisoner said sullenly. "The spirit of our soldiers is not what it used to be."

And what, the world's press wanted to know, did the two prisoners think of Ayatollah Khomeini? The major mistranslated the question thus: "Now that things have gone so badly for you, what do you think of Khomeini?" The first prisoner replied that "opinion" of the Ayatollah would not be the same after the war. But the wounded man glanced quickly at us and said that "if Ayatollah Khomeini brought on a war between two Muslim countries, this was wrong." The conditional clause in this reply was lost on the Iraqi major who then happily ordered the removal of the prisoners.

The Iraqi army, it seemed, would go to any lengths to display proof of victory and it spent a further hour showing off Iranian hardware captured in Khorramshahr. There was an American-made anti-tank launcher—made by the Hughes Aircraft Company and coded DAA-HOI-70-C-0525—a clutch of Soviet-made armoured vehicles and an American personnel carrier on which the Iraqis had spray-painted their own definitive and revealing slogan for the day. "Captured," it said, "from the racist Persian Asians." Captured armour was to become a wearying part of the now increasingly government-controlled coverage of the war.

They bussed us up to Amara, 160 kilometres north of Basra and only 50 kilometres from the Iranian border, to show us twenty Chieftain tanks seized on the central front around Ahwaz, a fraction of the 800 Chieftains that Britain had sold to the Shah. Some had been hit by shells or grenades but we clambered onto them. A partly damaged hulk was lying in a field with its hatch open, and in I climbed to sit in the driver's seat. A pouch on the wall to my left still contained the British Ministry of Defence tank manual—marked "Restricted" and coded WO 14557-1—although how the Iranian crews were supposed to translate the English was a mystery. I had sat there for a minute when it occurred to me that the crew probably did not survive their encounter with the Iraqis and I turned my head slowly to the gunner's seat to my right. And there, sure enough, lay the grisly remains of the poor young Iranian who had gone into battle a few days ago, a carbonised skeleton with the burned tatters of his uniform hanging to his bones like little black flags, the skull still bearing the faint remains of flesh.

But the Iraqis could not conceal their own losses. North of Basra I came across an orange-and-white taxi standing at a petrol station, the driver talking to the garage hand, not even bothering to glance at the long wooden box on top of his vehicle. Coffins in Iraq are usually carried on the roofs of cars, and all that was different in this case was that an Iraqi flag was wrapped around the box. A soldier was going home for burial.

According to the Baathist *Al-Thawra*, there had been only two Iraqi soldiers killed in the previous twenty-four hours, which meant that I had—quite by chance—come across 50 per cent of the previous day's fatalities. But there were four other taxis on the same road, all heading north with their gloomy cargoes, the red, white and black banner with its three stars flapping on the rooftop coffins. We did not use to see these cars in the early days of the war, nor the scores of military ambulances that now clogged the roads. On just one day in the first week of October alone, the army brought 480 bodies to the military hospital mortuary in Baghdad. If these corpses came from just the central sector of the battle front, then the daily toll of dead could be as high as 600 or 700. Even the Iraqi press was now extolling the glory that soldiers achieved when "sacrificing" themselves in battle, and Saddam Hussein, visiting wounded civilians in Kirkuk on 12 October, described their injuries as "medals of honour."

Iraqi television's lavish coverage of the conflict—the "Whirlwind War" theme music had now been dropped—was filled with tanks and guns and smashed Iranian aircraft, but there were no photographs of the dead of either side. When the station entertained its viewers with Gary Cooper in Hemingway's *For Whom the Bell Tolls*, the authorities clumsily excised a sequence showing the bodies of Spanish Republican troops lying on a road. Later the Iraqis would show Iranian corpses in large and savage detail.

Among the other British reporters in Basra was Jon Snow of ITN, whose courage and humour made him an excellent colleague in time of great danger but who could never in his life have imagined the drama into which he would be propelled in mid-October 1980. "Snowy," whose imitations of Prince Charles should have earned him a place in vaudeville,* was regularly reporting to camera from the bank of the Shatt al-Arab south of Basra. However, watching his dispatches in London was the owner of the Silverline shipping company, who had been desperately searching for six weeks for the location of his British-captained 22,000-ton soya bean oil carrier *Al-Tanin*.

And suddenly, there on the screen behind Snow's shoulder, he spotted his missing vessel, still afloat but obviously in the middle of a battle. The Foreign Office could do nothing to help, so the owner immediately asked Snow to be his official shipping agent in Basra and telexed his new appointment to him for the benefit of the Iraqi authorities. There were fifty-six souls aboard, nine of them British, and they had only one way of contacting the outside world; among the dozens of ships marooned in the city's harbour was a vessel captained by a Norwegian who was in daily contact with the *Al-Tanin* and who confirmed to Snow that the trapped captain and his crew were anxious to be rescued.

Snow decided to enlist the help of the Iraqi military and swim out to the ship at night to arrange the rescue of the crew. But neither the navy nor the Iraqi authorities in Basra could provide him with anything but a tourist map of the all-important waterway for which Saddam had partly gone to war. This, of course, was Snow's exclusive story—a "spectacular" if he brought it off, a human and political tragedy for the crew, Snow and ITN if it ended in disaster—but he told me privately of his difficulty in obtaining a map of the river. "Now listen, Fisky, old boy, if you can

---

*He claimed, accurately, that the Prince of Wales would pronounce "thousands and thousands of pounds" as "thicends and thicends of pines" and was able to perform variants of regal accents in situations of enormous peril.

find a decent map, I'll let you come along," he said. I immediately remembered my grandfather Edward, first mate on the *Cutty Sark*, and all that I had read about the merchant marine. Every ship's master, I knew, was required to carry detailed charts of the harbours and waterways he used. So I hunted down a profusely bearded Baltic sea-captain whose freighter lay alongside in Basra docks, and he agreed to lend me his old British Admiralty survey of the Shatt al-Arab. This magnificent document—a work of oceanographic art as much as technical competence—was duly photocopied and presented to the frogmen of the Iraqi navy.

All the elements of high adventure were in place: the *Al-Tanin*'s captain with the splendidly nautical name of Dyke, who thought up the rescue mission in the first place; Jack Simmons, the British consular official with a round face and small rimless spectacles who arrived unannounced in Basra but could get no help from the Iraqis. There was even a handsome major in the Iraqi navy, a grey-haired, quiet man who gallantly risked his life for the crew of the British ship. He never gave us his name, so Snow always referred to him warmly as "our Major." Then there was thirty-three-year-old Snow, his crew—cameraman Chris Squires and soundman Nigel Thompson—and Fisk, who would come to regard this as the last journalistic *Boy's Own Paper* story of his life. The rest of my reporting would be about tragedy.

The *Al-Tanin* had moored in the Shatt five weeks earlier to unload its cargo of cooking oil by lighter. But when the war began, it found itself—like all the other big ships in the river—trapped between two armies; machine-gun and rifle fire raked the waterway and on several days the crew watched low-level rockets skim the surface of the river around the *Al-Tanin*'s hull. Captain Dyke talked to Snow over the Norwegian captain's radio and suggested Snow should try a rescue attempt on 15 October. This would be "Operation Pear"; if it failed or was postponed, Snow could try again on 16 October when the rescue would become "Operation Apple." "Our Major," however, wanted to visit Dyke aboard the *Al-Tanin* to discuss the escape. Dyke agreed to what he called a "fibre ascent"—assuming any Iranian listeners to his conversation would not know this meant a rope—if they swam out to his ship.

At nine o'clock at night on 15 October, therefore, a strange band wound its way through the soggy, waterlogged plantation of an island on the Shatt al-Arab—not far from Um al-Rassas, from which Pierre Bayle and myself had made our own escape just a few days earlier. The major and two of his frogmen, Snow—in black wet suit with flippers in hand—Squires, Thompson and I. We must have made a remarkable spectacle, clopping along through the darkness of the tropical island to the stretch of river where we knew the *Al-Tanin* was at anchor, dragging with us a rubber boat for Snow's rescue attempt. In the darkness, we slipped off mud tracks into evil-smelling lagoons, slithered into long-forgotten dykes and lumbered over creaking, rotten bridges. Once, when we set the abandoned village dogs barking, Iranian snipers opened up on the plantation and for more than a minute we listened to the bullets whining around us at hip height as the Iranians tried to guess where the intruders were.

Even before we reached the riverbank, we could see the *Al-Tanin*, her super-structure fully lit up, her riding lights agleam, just as Captain Dyke had promised they would be. The ship's generators echoed through the hot palm forest and her bright orange funnel appeared surrealistically through the shadows of the tree trunks. Snow and the major were the first to see what was wrong. Dyke had told them to board his ship at 9:30 p.m. on the starboard side of the vessel, when the tide would have turned it towards the western, Iraqi bank of the river. He had illuminated the starboard hull for this reason. But it was the darkened port side of the *Al-Tanin* that faced us. Every Iranian could see the brightly-lit starboard of the ship right in front of the Iranian lines. Snow sat on the bank, squeezed into his flippers and stared at the ship. "Bugger!" he said. We all looked at Snow. He looked at the major. So did the frogmen. Snow would later come to regard the episode as "an act of unparalleled insanity." Squires, Thompson and I were all profoundly grateful we would not be part of this shooting match.

Then Snow slid into the muddy waters, the major and the two other naval frogmen beside him, clambering into their rubber boat, pushing and paddling it out into the river. So strong was the current—the tide was now at its height—that it took them twenty minutes to travel the 200 metres to the ship and at one point, staring at them through binoculars, I could see they were in danger of being taken right past the vessel and out into the open river. But they caught a ladder on the darkened port side and climbed aboard.

Snow first encountered members of the Filipino crew who appeared "terrified of the apparition" of the television reporter in black wet suit and flippers. But it was only when he met a surprised but otherwise exuberant Captain Dyke that Snow discovered he had not been expected for another three hours. Ships worked to GMT, not to local time, in their ports of call, and Iraqi time was three hours ahead of GMT. Had Snow and his Iraqi major turned up at half-past midnight according to Iraqi clocks—9:30 p.m. GMT—the illuminated starboard side of the ship would have faced Iraq.

Snow, the major and Dyke agreed that twenty-three of the ship's crew would head for the shoreline in a lifeboat at 3:30 a.m. and we watched Snow's rubber boat moving silently back across the river towards us. So we all sat through the long hours of darkness, watching the *Al-Tanin*'s riding lights reflecting on the fast-moving water as the big ship at last turned on the tide, and seeing—behind the vessel—the fires of Abadan. Distant guns bellowed in the night as the mosquitoes clustered round us for greedy company. At one point, Snow looked at me. "One does feel this tremendous sense of responsibility," he said. I was wondering how the Prince of Wales would pronounce that—the phrase was pure Prince Charles—when two red torch flashes sparkled from the ship's deck. "Operation Pear" had begun. Snow sent two lamp flashes back. A hydraulic winch—painfully loud over the river's silence—hummed away, followed by a harsh, metallic banging. The gate to the lifeboat had jammed. We could see the crew waiting on deck to disembark and we shared their feelings as the tell-tale hammer-blows echoed over the river towards the Iranians.

Then the lifeboat was down, its gunwales dipping towards us, carving ripples of water which the Iranians really should have seen. But when the boat thumped into the mud of our riverbank at 4 a.m., even the Iraqi frogmen lost their edge of fearful expectation as an English girl appeared on the slippery deck and asked: "Will someone help me ashore?" It was one of those quintessential moments so dear to Anglo-Saxons. The British were cheating danger again, landing on a tropical shore under a quarter moon with the possibility of a shell blowing them all to pieces and three young women to protect. And so delighted were we to see the little lifeboat that we tugged its crew onto the riverbank with enough noise to awaken every dozing Iranian on the other side. The Iraqi naval men grinned with happiness.

Thirteen crewmen had remained behind to guard their ship, and true to the traditions of what we thought then was a post-colonial world, only seven of the twenty-three crew who were rescued were actually British. The rest were a tough but cheerful group of Filipinos, small men with laughing eyes who hooted with joy when, with the British, we tugged them ashore and pushed them unceremoniously into an Iraqi army entrenchment behind us. Many of the Filipinos handed up to me their duty-free treasures, radios and television sets and—in one case—a washing machine which I dumped in the mud. They were hastily led off by Iraqi troops into the forest.

The first officer expressed his concern for those crewmen left aboard, the engineer announced that he would take a long holiday. Teresa Hancock, a crewman's bride from Stoke-on-Trent, had been honeymooning aboard and had celebrated her twenty-first birthday on the Shatt al-Arab three days earlier with a small party. But if ever there was a happy story, this was it. The Iraqi navy had acquitted itself with some glory—performing a genuinely humanitarian act with courage and professionalism—and "Snowy" got his scoop. Indeed, Snow announced that he would henceforth be known as *Al-Thalaj*—Arabic for "snow." As for "our Major," we went to thank him later and found him in his air-conditioned office, sipping yoghurt and grinning from ear to ear, knowing full well that he had—in the tradition of Sir Francis Drake—singed the Ayatollah's beard.

Snow packaged his film and gave it to me to take to Kuwait, where a private jet had been hired by America's NBC to take both their own and ITN's news film to Amman for satelliting to New York and London. As the Learjet soared into the air, the purser offered me smoked salmon sandwiches and a glass of champagne. From Amman I filed the story of the *Al-Tanin* to *The Times*. Then I sank into the deepest bed of the Intercontinental Hotel and woke to find a telex with a nudge-in-the-ribs question from the foreign desk in London: "Why *you* no swam shark-infested Shatt al-Arab river?"

But here the sweet stories must end. By the end of October, the Iraqis—realising that they were bogged down in the deserts of Iran with no more chance of a swift victory—were firing ground-to-ground missiles at Iranian cities. Early in the month, 180 civilians were killed in Dezful when the Iraqis fired a rocket into the marketplace. On 26 October, at least another hundred civilians were killed when the Iraqis fired seven Russian Frog-7 missiles at Dezful. The War of the Cities had begun, a calculated attempt to depopulate Iran's largest towns and cities through terror.

The outbreak of war in Iran had been greeted even by some of the theocratic regime's opponents with expressions of outrage and patriotism. Thousands of middle-class women donated millions of dollars' worth of their jewellery to Iran's "war chest." Captive in the Iranian foreign ministry, U.S. chargé d'affaires Bruce Laingen "knew something was happening when I heard a loudspeaker outside the foreign ministry playing American marching tunes—which the Iranians used on military occasions. I heard later that the Iraqis used them too. That night, there were anti-aircraft guns being used and the sky was full of tracer. They never seemed to hit anything. In fact, when we heard the air-raid sirens, we used to relax because we knew that the Iraqi planes had already been, bombed and flown away."

The Iranians, like Saddam, had to fight internal as well as external enemies during the war, knowing that groups like the Mujahedin-e-Khalq had the active support of the Iraqi regime. The strange death of the Iranian defence minister Mustafa Chamran on the battle front has never been fully explained. But there could be no doubt what happened when, just before 9 p.m. on 28 June 1981, a 60-pound bomb exploded at a meeting of the ruling Islamic Republican Party in Tehran, tearing apart seventy-one party leaders as they were listening to a speech by Ayatollah Mohamed Beheshti, chief justice of the supreme court, secretary of the Revolutionary Council, head of the IRP and a potential successor to Khomeini. When the bomb destroyed the iron beams of the building and 40-centimetre-thick columns were pulverised by the blast, the roof thundered down onto the victims. Among them were four cabinet ministers, six deputy ministers and twenty-seven members of the Iranian parliament, the Majlis.

Beheshti, who died with them, was an intriguing personality, his thin face, pointed grey beard and thick German accent—a remnant of his days as a resident Shiite priest in Germany—giving him the appearance of a clever eighteenth-century conspirator. When I met him in 1980, I noted that he employed "a unique mixture of intellectual authority and gentle wistfulness which makes him sound—and look—like a combination of Cardinal Richelieu and Sir Alec Guinness." He had for months been intriguing against President Bani-Sadr, although the date of the latter's formal removal gave Beheshti little time for satisfaction: he was murdered a week later.

He was a man with enemies, unmoved by Iran's growing plague of executions. "Don't you see," he explained to me with some irritation, "that there have been very few people sentenced to death because of their failures in the [Shah's] ministries. Those people who have been sentenced to death are in a different category—they are opium or heroin dealers." This was palpably untrue. Most of the executions were for political reasons. "When you study the history of revolutions," Beheshti said, "you will find that there are always problems. This is normal. When people here say they are unhappy, it is because they have not experienced a revolution before. There are problems—but they will be solved." Beheshti's loss was the most serious the revolution suffered—until the death of Khomeini in 1989—because he had designed the IRP along the lines of the Soviet Communist party, capable of binding various revolutionary movements under a single leader.

By coincidence, the bloodbath on 28 June cost the same number of lives—seventy-two—as were lost at the battle of Kerbala in 680 by Imam Hossein, his family and supporters, a fact that Khomeini was quick to point out. Saddam and America, he concluded, had struck again through the Mujahedin-e-Khalq. "Suppose you were an inveterate enemy to the martyred Beheshti," Khomeini asked sarcastically, ". . . what enmity did you bear against the more than seventy innocent people, many of whom were among the best servants of society and among the most adamant enemies of the enemies of the nation?" But on 5 August, Hassan Ayat, another influential Majlis deputy, was killed. On 30 August a second bomb killed President Mohamed Rajai, who had just replaced Bani-Sadr, and the new Iranian prime minister, Mohamed Javad Bahonar. The prosecutor general, Ayatollah Ali Quddusi, was murdered on 5 September and Khomeini's personal representative in Tabriz, Ayatollah Asadollah Madani, six days later.

The regime hit back with ferocious repression. Schoolchildren and students figured prominently among the sixty executions a day. One estimate—that 10,000 suspects were hanged or shot—would equal the number of Iranians killed in the first six months of the war with Iraq. Just as Saddam was trying to destroy the Dawa party as a militant extension of Shia Islam, so Khomeini was trying to eliminate the Mujahedin-e-Khalq as a branch of the Iraqi Baath. This duality of enemies would force both sides in the war to take ever more ruthless steps to annihilate their antagonists on the battlefield as well as in their prisons and torture chambers.

When I visited Tehran in the spring of 1982 to make my own investigations into these mass executions, survivors of Evin prison spoke to me of 8,000 hangings and shootings, of fourteen-year-old Revolutionary Guards brutalised by their participation in the killings. Among the 15,000 prisoners who were spared and were now being released—partly, it seemed, because of Amnesty International's repeated condemnation of Islamic "justice" in Iran—several vouchsafed accounts of quite appalling savagery. At one point after the Beheshti, Rajai and Bahonar murders, inmates were told to demonstrate their repentance by hanging their friends. There were three stages in this purgation: they could actually strangle their fellow prisoners, they could cut them down from the gibbet—or they could merely load their corpses into coffins. Prisoners thus emerged from Evin with souls purified but blood on their hands. Islamic socialism was almost wiped out; only a few leftists escaped death, capable of shooting at Iran's deputy foreign minister in April 1982. But the Mujahedin-e-Khalq was broken.

Saddam eventually claimed victory over Khorramshahr and the Iranians admitted they had "lost touch" with their forces still in the city. Henceforth the Iranians would call it Khuninshahr—the "City of Blood." The Iraqis never captured Abadan but Saddam invested tens of thousands of troops in Khorramshahr, and Iraq announced that it would become "another Stalingrad." This was an early version of the "mother of all battles" that Saddam always threatened but never fought. Fifteen months after the war began, the Iraqi army found that its supply lines were stretched too far and made a strategic decision to retreat, building a massive defensive line along its border with Iran and leaving behind it a carpet of destruction. Howeiza, with an Arabic-speaking population of 35,000, had been captured by the Iraqis on 28 September 1980, but when Iranian forces re-entered the empty town in May 1982 they found that it had been levelled; only two of its 1,900 buildings were still standing: a damaged mosque used as an observation post and a house that had been a command post. Even the trees had been uprooted. This is what the Israelis had done to the Syrian city of Kuneitra after the 1967 Middle East war. All of "Arabistan"—Khuzestan—whose liberation had been another of Saddam's war aims, was simply abandoned. The Iranians were winning. And Western journalists would now be welcomed in Iran as warmly as they once were in Iraq during the fictional "whirlwind war."

Dezful was the first major Iraqi defeat. In a blinding sandstorm, 120,000 Iranian troops, Revolutionary Guards and *Basiji* (mobilised) volunteers plunged through the desert towards the Iraqi lines in late March 1981, taking 15,000 Iraqi soldiers prisoner, capturing 300 tanks and armoured vehicles and recovering 4,000 square kilometres of Iranian territory. When I reached the scene of the Iranian victory, an almost total silence enveloped the battlefield. There were wild roses beside the roads south of Dezful and giant ants scuttled over the desert floor. Iranian artillerymen sat beneath their anti-aircraft gun canopies, glancing occasionally at the empty sky. The smashed tanks of the Iraqi army's 3rd Armoured Division, disembowelled by rocket fire, their armour peeled back as if by a can-opener, lay in the mid-afternoon heat, memorials already to what the dismissive Iranians insisted on calling "Operation Obvious Victory."

The silence of the desert indicated both the extent of Iran's success and the extraordinary fact that with scarcely a shot fired in return, the Iranian army had halted its advance along a geometrically straight line about 65 kilometres in length. It stretched from a ridge of hills north-west of Dezful to the swamps of Sendel, where Iraqi tanks and armoured carriers lay axle-deep in mud, driven there in frustration and fear by Saddam's retreating forces. The Iranians—at one point scarcely 5 kilometres from the Iraqi border—had effectively declared a halt to offensive action in the Dezful sector, forbidden to advance, on Khomeini's orders, across the international frontier.

Colonel Beyrouz Suliemanjar of the Iranian 21st Infantry Division was quite specific when he spoke to us, baton in hand, in his dark underground command post beneath a ridge of low hills. "According to the Imam's guidance," he stated with military confidence, "we are not allowed to cross the border." He patted a blue, straggling river on his polythene-covered map. "Our troops could cross this last river but our Imam will not let them. Our strategic aim is to push the enemy troops back to their territory. But we will not cross the frontier." Whenever the colonel spoke—with apparent modesty—about the surprise attack on 22 March, his junior officers along with a mullah, standing at the back of the dugout, chorused, "God is great—Down with America—Down with the Soviet Union." No military briefing could ever have been quite like this.

Khomeini had already promised that his armies would not invade neighbouring countries. Hojatolislam Ali Akbar Rafsanjani, the Majlis speaker, had given his word that Iran "harbours no territorial ambition against Iraq." All Iran wanted, according to Rafsanjani, was the satisfaction of four demands: the expulsion of Iraqi troops from all Iranian territory; "punishment of the aggressor"; compensation for war damage; and the return of war refugees to their homes. "Punishment of the aggressor," the Iranians made clear, meant the overthrow of Saddam Hussein—something that neither the Arabs nor the Americans would permit. That the Iranians sought an end for Saddam every bit as bloody as that dealt out to the 4,000 Iraqis estimated to have been killed at the battle of Dezful made this prospect even less likely.

The Iranians crammed John Kifner of *The New York Times* and myself into a Bell/Agusta helicopter gunship along with a bevy of mullahs—the pilots were trained in the United States, of course—and flew us across kilometre after kilometre of wreckage and corpses. A Cyclopean view of carnage, the whup-whup of the chopper blades, the sudden ground-hugging rush between hills and into wadis were so frightening that we placed superhuman faith in the pilot and thus became so confident that we almost enjoyed this flying madness. One pile of dead Iraqi soldiers had already been bulldozed into a mass grave—"Aggressor cemeteries," the signs said above these muddy crypts—but others still lay out in the sun in their hundreds. Many lay where they fell, in dried-up riverbeds, their decomposition clearly visible from our helicopter. Several times, the pilot hovered over a pile of corpses as the odour of their putrefaction wafted into the machine, overpowering and sickening, the mullahs screeching "God is Great" while Kifner and I held our breath. The dead were distended in the heat, bodies bloating through their shabby uniforms. We could see the Revolutionary Guards next to them, digging more mass graves for Saddam's soldiers.

When we landed behind what had been the Iraqi front line—they ran like ant-hills, catacombed with dugouts and ammunition boxes—there was almost no sign of incoming shellfire, none of the traditional "softening up" by heavy artillery that conventional armies employ. The Iraqi positions lay untouched, as if the occupants had been taken sleeping from their mattresses at night, leaving their trenches and revetments on display for the ghoulish visitors—us—who follow every war. The Iranians even invited us to enter the dugouts of their enemies. It was easy to see why. They were equipped with air conditioners, television sets, videos and cassette films and magazine photographs of young women. One officer maintained a fridge of beer, another had laid a Persian carpet on the concrete floor. This was Khomeini's "saturnalia" writ large. Saddam didn't want his soldiers to revolt—as Khomeini had now repeatedly urged them to—so he gave them every comfort. But how could such a pampered army fight when the Iranians stormed towards them in their tens of thousands?

The Iranians had learned that opposing massed Iraqi armour with poorly maintained Chieftain tanks was suicidal—the wreckage of dozens of Chieftains destroyed in the initial battles outside Dezful more than a year earlier still littered the desert. At Ein Khoosh, I padded round the broken Iraqi tanks for more than an hour. I noticed one whose severed turret had been blown clean off the base of the vehicle, landing with its gun barrel intact beside a small field. Around the turret and the decapitated tank stood a cluster of Iranian troops and peasants, all holding handkerchiefs over their mouths and noses.

The dead crew were unrecognisable, burnt paper creatures from another planet who still lay in their positions, the gunner's body crushed beneath the turret. A carpet of flies lay upon the scorched armour. An Iranian soldier looked to the sky and ran his hand briefly downwards over his short beard, a gesture of respect to God for the bloody victory that He had granted Iran over its enemies. But the tank itself had not been shelled to destruction—there was not a shell crater in the area, just a jagged hole in the armour near the turret plates. It had been destroyed by a hand-launched anti-tank rocket. In the desert, other Iraqi tanks had suffered an almost identical fate; they had "brewed up" on the battlefield after one point-blank round.

It was clear that the Iranians had used scarcely any heavy artillery or tanks in their six-day battle. They simply poured men into the Iraqi lines and caught their enemies off guard. The Iranians had been experimenting with human-wave attacks. The Iraqi front line had been overwhelmed by thousands of young men holding only rocket-propelled grenades and rifles. "The West fought two world wars and gave us their military manuals," an Iranian officer smugly remarked to me. "Now we are going to write tactical manuals for the West to read." We noticed the lack of Iranian corpses in the desert, but could not help seeing from our helicopter small tyre tracks across the sand. Could these be the motorcycles of the boy soldiers we had heard about, the fourteen-year-olds and their brothers who were encouraged to wear the sword of martyrdom around their necks as they drove through the Iraqi minefields to clear them for the infantry, dressed in heavy winter coats so that their shredded bodies would be held together for burial in their home villages? Kifner and I asked to see the youngest survivors of the battle, and the Iranians immediately understood what we wanted.

Under shellfire, they took us to a new Iranian front line of earthen revetments on the Dusallok Heights and we ran down these trenches like any soldiers of the 1914–18 war. The Iran–Iraq conflict was increasingly coming to resemble the great mire of death that entombed so many hundreds of thousands on the Somme and at Verdun. The dugout in which we sought shelter was small and a thick dust hung in the air. There were weapons on the mud and wooden-framed walls—a captured Iraqi machine gun and an automatic rifle—and a few steel helmets piled in a corner. The light from the sandbagged doorway forced its way into the little bunker, defining the features of the boys inside in two-dimensional perspective, an Orpen sketch of impending death at the front. There was no monstrous anger of the guns, only a dull, occasional vibration to indicate that the Iraqis had not abandoned all their artillery when they retreated from Dezful.

There, however, the parallels ended. For the youngest soldier—who welcomed us like an excited schoolboy at the entrance—was only fourteen, his voice unbroken by either fear or manhood. The oldest among them was twenty-one, an Islamic volunteer from Iran's "Reconstruction Crusade," who expounded the principles of martyrdom to us as the guns boomed distantly away. Martyrdom, I was made to understand, was a much-discussed subject in this dugout because it was much witnessed.

Yes, said the fourteen-year-old, two of his friends from Kerman had died in the battle for Dezful—one his own age and one only a year older. He had cried, he said, when the authorities delayed his journey to the battle front. Cried? I asked. A child cries because he cannot die yet? Were we now to have baby-wars, not wars which killed babies—we had specialised in them throughout the twentieth century—but wars in which babies, boys with unbroken voices, went out to kill? The fourteen-year-old's comments were incredible and genuine and terrifying at one and the same time, clearly unstaged, since we had only by chance chosen his dugout when we took cover from the shellfire outside.

There was no doubt which of these boy soldiers most clearly understood the ideology of martyrdom inside this claustrophobic bunker of sand and dirt. When I asked about the apparent willingness of Iranians to die in battle, the soldiers nodded towards a very young man, bearded and intense with a rifle in his hand, sitting cross-legged on a dirty rug by the entrance. In the West, he said, it was difficult—perhaps impossible—to understand Iran's apparent obsession with martyrdom. So did he *want* to die in this war?

The young man spoke loudly, with almost monotone passion, preaching rather than answering our question. Hassan Qasqari, soldier of the volunteer Reconstruction Crusade, was a man whose faith went beyond such questions. "It is impossible for you in the West to understand," he said. "Martyrdom brings us closer to God. We do not seek death—but we regard death as a journey from one form of life to another, and to be martyred while opposing God's enemies brings us closer to God. There are two phases to martyrdom: we approach God and we also remove the obstacles that exist between God and the people. Those who create obstacles for God in this world are the enemies of God."

There was no doubt that he identified the Iraqis with these theologically hostile forces. Indeed, as if on cue from God rather than the army of Saddam Hussein, there was a loud rumble of artillery and Qasqari raised his index finger towards heaven. We waited to hear where the shell would fall, fearing that direct hit that all soldiers prefer not to think about. There was a loud explosion beyond the trench, just beyond the bunker, the vibration shaking the dugout. Then there was silence. I could not imagine this speech in an Iraqi dugout. For that matter, I could not have heard it in any other army. Perhaps a British or American military padre might talk of religion with this imagination. And then I realised that these Iranian boy soldiers were all "padres"; they were all priests, all preachers, all believers, all—now I understood the phrase—"followers of the Imam." There was another pulsation of sound outside in the trench.

Qasqari seemed grateful for the shell-burst. "Our first duty," he proclaimed, "is to kill the enemy forces so that God's order will be everywhere. Becoming a martyr is not a passive thing. Hossein, the third Imam, killed as many of his enemies as possible before he was martyred—so we must try to remain alive." If we could not understand this, Qasqari explained, it was because the European Renaissance had done away with religion, no longer paying attention to morality or ethics, concentrating only upon materialism. There was no stanching this monologue, no opportunity to transfuse this belief with arguments about humanity or love. "Europe and the West have confined these issues to the cover of churches," Qasqari said. "Western people are like fish in the water; they can only understand their immediate surroundings. They don't care about spirituality."

He bade us goodbye with no ill will, offering Kifner and me oranges as we left his dugout for the dangerous, bright sand outside. How should we say goodbye to them? We looked into their eyes, the eyes of children who were, in their way, already dead. They had started on their jouney. The next shell landed a hundred metres behind us as we ran the length of the trench, a thunderous explosion of black and grey smoke that blew part of the roadway into the sky and frightened us, not so much for our peril but because it put martyrdom into a distinct and terrible perspective.

We returned to the jubilant city of Dezful just an hour before Saddam's revenge came screaming out of the sky, two massive blasts followed by towering columns of black smoke that spurted into the sky from one of the poorest residential areas of the city. It was the tenth ground-to-ground missile attack on Dezful since the start of the war, and by the time I reached the impact point the images were as appalling as they were banal. A baby cut in half, a woman's head in the rubble of her home, a series of arms and legs laid out beside each other next to a series of torsos in the hope that someone might be able to fit the correct limbs onto the right bodies. Hundreds of men dug through the crushed yellow bricks with their hands. Most Iranian homes in Dezful were built of these cheap, thin bricks, without concrete or structural support. They were made for destruction.

By early 1982, the Iranians were threatening to move across the border. Khomeini's promises of non-aggression—that Iran would not violate Iraqi national territory—had given way to a new pragmatism. If by entering Iraq the war could be ended, then Iranian troops would do what Iraq had done in September 1980 and cross the international frontier. Khomeini spoke repeatedly of the suffering of Iraqi Shiites, releasing their century-old political frustrations. Would he any longer be satisfied with just the head of Saddam? He would surely want an Iraqi regime that was loyal to him, a vassal state of Iran, or so the Arabs began to fear.

It was not hard to fathom what this might involve. The largest community in Lebanon—though not a majority—was Shia. Syria was effectively ruled by the Alawites, a Shia sect in all but name. If Iraq was to fall to its own majority Shiites, there could be a Shia state from the Mediterranean to the borders of Afghanistan, with both oil and the waters of the two great rivers of the Tigris and Euphrates. With both Iranian and Iraqi oil, Khomeini could undercut OPEC and control world prices, let alone dominate the waters of the Gulf and the Arab peninsula. That, at least, was the nightmare of the Arabs and the Americans, one that Saddam was happy to promote. Now he was portraying himself as the defender of the Arab lands, his war with Iran the new Qadisiya, the battle in AD 636 in which the Arab leader Saad bin Ali Waqqas vanquished the far larger Persian army of Rustum. In Baghdad's official discourse, the Iranians were now the "pagan Zoroastrians."

In Basra, the Iraqis had displayed their seventeen Iranian POWs to us. Now the Iranians took us to meet their Iraqi POWs—all 15,000 of them. At Parandak prisoner-of-war camp in northern Iran, they sat cross-legged on a windy parade ground in lines a quarter of a mile deep, many of them with well-trimmed beards, all of them wearing around their necks a coloured portrait of Ayatollah Khomeini. Their eyes moved in a way that only captivity can control, studying each other nervously and then staring at their prison guards, awed by the enormity of their surrender. When Iran's army chief of staff, grey-haired and bespectacled, told them of Iraq's iniquities, the Iraqis roared back: "Down with Saddam Hussein."

This was not brainwashing in the normally accepted use of the word. It was scarcely indoctrination. But there could be no doubt what the Iranians were trying to do at Parandak: to make Saddam's own soldiers more dangerous to his Baathist regime than the Iranian army that was fighting its way towards the Iraqi frontier. When Khomeini's name was mentioned, it echoed over the massive parade ground, repeated by thousands of Iraqi soldiers who then knelt in prayer and homage to the Islamic faith that overthrew the Shah.

True, there were some dissidents among the Iraqi troops, men who still retained their political as well as their Islamic identity. At the far back of one line of older prisoners—captives now for more than a year—an Iraqi soldier shouted "Saddam is a very good man," and a few of his comrades nodded in agreement. "The man did not say 'Saddam'—he was greeting you with the word 'Salaam,' " explained an Iranian official with the confidence of mendacity. Several hundred prisoners refused to pray. "They had probably not washed before prayers," said the same official. "They had not been purified."

From his residence in north Tehran, Khomeini had given specific instructions that Iraqi prisoners-of-war were to be well treated and given all the rights of captive soldiers. The POWs were visited by the International Red Cross, but they were also being lectured in Arabic each day by Iranian officers who explained to them that the United States, France, Britain and other Western nations had supported Saddam Hussein's 1980 attack on Iran. There were, naturally, no contradictions from their vast audience. When the Iraqi prisoners knelt to pray, they took Khomeini's portrait from around their necks, placed it upon the ground in front of them and rested their heads upon it. In the barracks, these men—including Iraqi paratroopers who arrived from the war front on the very day of our visit, still wearing their blue berets—were to be given weekly lessons by mullahs on the meaning of Islam. They were already receiving the daily Tehran newspaper *Kayhan*, specially printed in Arabic for their convenience.

When these prisoners eventually returned to Iraq, some of them, perhaps a goodly proportion, must have carried these lessons with them, an incubus for the overthrow of Saddam Hussein—or an inspiration to oppose any other army that dared to take control of their country in the years to come. We were not told how many of these young Iraqi soldiers were Shiites and what percentage were Sunni.

The Iranians would not permit us to speak to the prisoners, although they produced more than a hundred captives—or "guests" as they cloyingly called them—from Jordan, Lebanon, Tunisia, Nigeria and Somalia, who had been taken among the Iraqi prisoners. A bearded Lebanese librarian from Zahlé—a Christian town—claimed to have been forced to enlist while working in Baghdad. A Somali, Fawzi Hijazi, frightened but smiling, pleaded with me to tell his embassy of his presence. He had been a scholarship student at Baghdad University, he said, when he had been press-ganged into the Iraqi army. He had not been visited by the Red Cross. But at this point, an Iranian guard ordered him to stop speaking.

Now on our chaperoned visits to the Iranian front, we could see the country's newly established self-confidence made manifest. The Revolutionary Guard Corps had become the spine of Iran's military power, drawing on a huge pool of rural volunteers, the *Basiji*, the schoolboys and the elderly, the unemployed, even the sick. An official history of the Guard Corps was published in booklet form in Tehran during the war, claiming that it was "similar in many respects to the combatants of early Islam, in the days of the Holy Prophet . . . Among the important and prevalent common points of the two is . . . life according to an Islamic brotherhood; the story of the travellers and the followers. The travellers . . . migrated to the war fronts, and the followers . . . support their families in the cities during the war." An "important and popular activity" of the Guards, the pamphlet said, was "the military, political, and ideological training of the Baseej [*sic*], in which the limitless ocean of our people are organised."*

Both the "Guards" and the "travellers" were now in convoy towards the borders of Iraq, singing and chanting their desire to "liberate" the Iraqi Shia holy cities. One trail of trucks, jeeps and tanks 5 kilometres long, which I overtook near the Iranian city of Susangerd, was loaded down with thousands of *Basiji*, almost all of them waving black-and-green banners with "Najaf" and "Kufa" written across them. *Jang ba pirouzi*, they shouted at me when I took their pictures. "War until victory." Another convoy was led by a tank with a placard tied above its gun muzzle, announcing that it was the "Kerbala Caravan." These men, most of them, were going to their deaths in Iraq but they were doing so with an insouciance, a light-heartedness—a kind of brazen stubbornness—that was breathtaking.

I suppose the soldiers of the 1914 war had something of the same gaiety about them, the British who thought the war would be over by Christmas, the French who painted "Berlin" on the side of their troop trains, the Germans who painted "Paris" on theirs. In Frederic Manning's semi-autobiographical *Her Privates We*, a unit of British soldiers marching through a French village at night during the First World War awakes the inhabitants:

*An ominous sentence in the same document states that "one of the programmes [of the Guards], after the Baathist-imposed war, will be to disinfect Kurdistan of the hideous and mercenary elements of the U.S.-backed groups, such as the 'Democrat Party' (KDP), and in this way the Kurdistan region will become a totally Islamic area."

. . . doors suddenly opened and light fell through the doorways, and voices asked them where they were going.

"Somme! Somme!" they shouted, as though it were a challenge.

"Ah, no bon!" came the kindly, pitying voices in reply . . . And that was an enemy to them, that little touch of gentleness and kindliness; it struck them with a hand harsher than death's, and they sang louder, seeing only the white road before them . . .

No wonder that boy soldier on the Dusallok Heights had lectured me about spirituality and materialism. There comes a point, I suspect, in a soldier's life when the inevitability of death becomes more pressing than the possibility of life.

Now the Arab leaders who had expressed such confidence in Saddam were fearful that he might lose the war they had so cheerfully supported. King Hussein of Jordan arrived hurriedly in Baghdad for talks with Saddam, speaking boldly of standing "shoulder to shoulder" with the Iraqis but privately expressing his fears that their army would soon fall back even further, allowing the Iranians to enter Iraq. The Kuwaitis and Saudis bankrolled Saddam's new armoury. Egyptian-made heavy artillery shells were sent by air to Iraq from Cairo, overflying Saudi airspace.*

But the Arabs were not alone in their fears that Iraq might collapse. The United States had been furnishing Iraq with satellite imagery of the Iranian battle lines since the first days of the war, and a steady stream of unofficial U.S. "advisers" had been visiting Baghdad ever since. When Mohamed Salam, a Lebanese staff correspondent for the American Associated Press news agency in Beirut, was posted to Iraq in 1983, "Donald Rumsfeld was in Baghdad to meet Saddam and I was treated like a king, like all the people connected to the Americans. The Iraqis couldn't be more cooperative." At Muthanna, the old military airport in the centre of Baghdad, the Iraqis held an arms fair and "everyone was there, from the British to the South Koreans," he recalled. Around May 1985, a U.S. military delegation travelled to Baghdad with twelve ranking officers, according to Salam. "The embassy wouldn't talk about it. They stayed for three days and they came on a special Pan Am plane."

At the time, Salam—we had both covered the Lebanese civil war together—could not travel unaccompanied in Iraq, but he told me in Baghdad at the time how the Americans were concentrating on Iraq. "The U.S. is beginning to regard Iraq as its main card in the area . . . So far, Saddam has been successful in suppressing the communists, the Shiites and all the opposition. That suits the Americans quite well. King Hussein is useful in promoting Iraq to the West. But the U.S. would not want Iraq to be a post-war regional power. Nothing is clear at the embassy here. There's a USIS guy called Jim Bulloch, the deputy chief of mission is Ted Kattouf

*At first, according to *Al-Ahram*'s military affairs correspondent, the Iraqis sent European arms agents to Cairo to purchase the munitions "because they did not want us to know we were dealing with them. But when they asked for Soviet heavy artillery ammunition . . . we knew it was the Iraqis. We told the Iraqis that we Egyptians are a proud people, a dignified people, we must have *respect*. The Iraqis had to come to us in person and they did. They got the shells and they received our combat experience."

and Dean Strong is their military affairs man. But they're cut out of the loop of what the Pentagon is doing." Salam recalls now that he "saw satellite photos of the Iranian forces—I saw these pictures at the U.S. interests section in Baghdad in 1984."

Iraq's 15 million population was now facing Iran's 42 million, outnumbered on the battlefield itself almost five to one. Saddam's army could not fight against these odds in open battle—Dezful was proof of that—so a new and merciless logic was adopted in Baghdad. Iraqi troops would dig in along the front lines, embed their thousands of tanks in the earth and use them as mass artillery to wipe out the human-wave attacks. But in 1984, through the swamps of Howeiza and the rivers that run through the land of the Marsh Arabs, the Iranian Revolutionary Guards led an attack—along dykes and using power-boats—deep into Iraq. At one point—the Iraqis only admitted this eight months later but Salam was to see the evidence with his own eyes—the Iranians pushed armour across the main eastern Baghdad–Basra highway at Kurna. They had traversed the Tigris River and began destroying Iraqi tanks by firing at them from the highway bridges.

Baghdad's response was as successful as it was devastatingly cruel. Because he was one of the only journalists to witness the result, the account of what happened next belongs to Mohamed Salam:

There had been a major battle at Azair, Sada and Baida in the Howeiza marshes south of Amara—the Iraqi commander was Major General Hisham Sabah al-Fakhry. He got the Iranians into a pocket in the marshes then the Iraqis built a big dam to the east of them. It was still early '84. Al-Fakhry brought huge tanker trucks down and pumped fuel into the marshland and then fired incendiary shells into the water and started the biggest fire I've seen in my life. He burned and killed everything, the whole environment.

Then when the fire was out, he brought electrical generators and put huge cables into the marsh waters and electrified everything so that there was no source of life left in that place. When I was there, I needed to take a leak and walked over to an embankment and one of the soldiers said "Don't piss in the water" and pointed at the cables. He asked me: "Do you want to be a piss-martyr?"

Gutted bodies were floating everywhere, even women and children were among them—marsh people, people who knew what a toad was, people who'd lived among ducks and buffaloes and fished with spears, this civilisation was being wiped out. I saw about thirty women and children, all gutted open like fish, and many, many Iranians. The innocent had to die along with the living.

But petrol and electricity alone could not annihilate the invaders. In the battle of Qadisiya, Sardar and his fellow Arabs were astonished to see Rustum's army advancing towards them on massive animals they had never before seen, beasts six times the size of a horse with vast bones protruding from each side of their noses, their feet so great that they sank into the sand. Sardar told his archers to fire their arrows—and his soldiers to throw their spears—into the eyes of the elephants; to this day, the Iraqis believe that this was the key to their victory. So what was to be Saddam's weapon against the frightening hordes now moving into Iraq? What spear was poisoned enough for the "racist Persians"?

I AM ON AN IRANIAN military hospital train, trundling through the night-time desert north of Ahwaz, returning from another trip to the front, eating chicken and rice and drinking warm cola in the restaurant car. It is 1983. Rumsfeld is shaking hands with Saddam, asking to reopen the U.S. embassy. The train is slow, its un-oiled bogies shrieking on the curves, making heavy weather of the gradients, bumping over the unmaintained permanent way. Occasionally, a light moves slowly past the window, a distant village, no doubt with its own crop of martyrs. The man from the Ministry of Islamic Guidance is asleep, knowing that I cannot stray from a moving train.

But I cannot sleep and so I walk through the carriages. It is cold and the win-dows are shut against the night breeze off the desert but there is a strange, faint smell. At first I think it must be a deodorant, something to ameliorate the shitty stench of the blocked toilets at the end of each car. Then I pull open the connecting door of the next carriage and they are sitting in there by the dozen, the young soldiers and Revolutionary Guards of the Islamic Republic, coughing softly into tissues and gauze cloths. Some are in open carriages, others crammed into com-partments, all slowly dribbling blood and mucus from their mouths and noses. One young man—I thought he could be no more than eighteen—was holding the gauze against his face. It was already stained pink and yellow but in his left hand he was holding a Koran with a bright blue cover. From time to time, he laid the gauze on his knee and coughed and a new streak of red would run in a line from his nose and he would turn the page of the Koran with his right hand and put the cloth back to his face to sop up the new blood and then pick up the Koran to read again.

Carriage after carriage of them, they sit without talking, uncomplaining, accepting—so it seems—what has happened to them. Only after ten or fifteen min-utes do I realise that the smell that bothered me is not deodorant. It's a kind of sick perfume and the men are coughing it out of their lungs. I go to the windows of the carriages and start pulling them down, filling the corridors with the sharp night air. I don't want to breathe into my lungs what is coming out of theirs. I don't want to be gassed like them. I go on opening the windows but the soldiers don't look at me. They are enduring a private hell into which, thank God, I cannot be admitted.

IRAN'S OWN OFFICIAL HISTORY of the war says that Iraq first used chemical weapons against its combatants on 13 January 1981, killing seven Iranians. In 1982, the Iranians recorded eleven chemical attacks by Saddam's army, in 1983, thirty-one. Dr. Naser Jalali, a dermatologist and head of the dermatology ward at the Loqman al-Doleh Hospital in Tehran, examined a number of soldiers brought to the Iranian capital after a chemical weapons attack against Piranshahr and Tamarchin on 9 August 1983. "The injuries of those involved have been caused by exposure to toxic agents which have been released in the atmosphere in the forms of gas, liquid or powder," he said. ". . . the weapons of delivery had released a toxic chemical called 'Nitrogen mustard' or 'mustard gas.'" At around 9:30 in the evening of 22 October 1983, between Marivan and Sultan, an Iraqi artillery shell exploded on the Iranian lines, giving off a smell of kerosene. Next morning, eleven Iranians—soldiers, Revolutionary Guards and *Basiji*—were afflicted with nausea, vomiting, burning of the eyes, blurred vision, itching, suffocation and coughing. Taken to a medical centre, they were found to have blisters all over their skin. Between 21 and 28 October, three Kurdish villages sympathetic to Iran came under chemical attack; an Iranian medical report stated that "many villagers of this Kurdish district, including women and children, were severely injured." Between 28 December 1980 and 20 March 1984, the Iranian official history of the war lists sixty-three separate gas attacks by the Iraqis.

Yet the world did not react. Not since the gas attacks of the 1914–18 war had chemical weapons been used on such a scale, yet so great was the fear and loathing of Iran, so total the loyalty of the Arabs to Saddam Hussein, so absolute their support for him in preventing the spread of Khomeini's revolution, that they were silent. The first reports of Saddam's use of gas were never printed in the Arab press. In Europe and America, they were regarded as little more than Iranian propaganda, and America's response was minimal. Only in March 1984 did Washington condemn Iraq for using poison gas—but even that criticism was mild. It was 1985 before *The New York Times* reported that "United States intelligence analysts have concluded that Iraq used chemical weapons in repelling Iran's latest offensive." True to that paper's gutless style, even this report had to be attributed to those favourite sources of all American reporters—"Administration officials."

Preliminary evidence suggested that the Iraqis had been using bis-(2-chloroethyl) sulphide, a blistering agent that damages all human tissues. The *New York Times* report continued in the same cowardly fashion: "Iran flew purported [*sic*] victims of the attacks to Austria and West Germany, where some doctors were quoted as having said [*sic*] that the wounded showed signs of having been under attack by mustard gas . . ." The days before the *New York Times* report, U.S. secretary of state George Shultz had met the Iraqi foreign minister Tariq Aziz in Washington, but uttered no criticism of the chemical weapons attack. Despite the mass of evidence now available, my own paper, *The Times* of London, was still able to carry a photograph in March 1985 of an Iranian soldier in a London hospital covered in terrible skin blisters, with a caption saying only that he was suffering from "burns which Iran says [*sic*] were caused by chemical weapons."

Mohamed Salam was again one of the few correspondents to obtain first-hand, almost lethal evidence of this latest poison gas attack. Again, he should tell his own awesome story:

I was invited with Zoran Gramaciev of the Yugoslav Tanjug News Agency to go down to Basra where there had been a major offensive by the Iranians. The 3rd Army Corps under Major General Maher Abdul Rashed was faced by this huge attack, totally overwhelming, so the only way of handling it was by mass killing. Rashed had crushed the Iranian offensive. There had been no flooding, no fire, no electricity. Zoran and I wandered around the desert where all this had happened and we came across hundreds and hundreds of dead Iranians, literally thousands of them, all dead. They were still holding their rifles—just think, thousands of them dead in their trenches, all still holding their Kalashnikovs. They had their little sacks of food supplies still on their backs—all the Iranians carried these little sacks of food. There were no bullet holes, no wounds—they were just dead.

We started counting—we walked miles and miles in this fucking desert, just counting. We got to 700 and got muddled and had to start counting again. All the dead Iranians had blood on their mouths and beards, and their pants below the waist were all wet. They had all urinated in their pants. The Iraqis had used, for the first time, a combination of nerve gas and mustard gas. The nerve gas would paralyse their bodies so they would all piss in their pants and the mustard gas would drown them in their own lungs. That's why they spat blood.

We described all this in our reports, but we didn't know what it was. We asked the Iraqi soldiers. They had been eating—tomatoes and cucumbers—but when they weren't eating, they would wear gas masks. From that visit, I developed an infection in my sinus and went to see a friend of mine in Baghdad who was a doctor. He said: "This is what we call 'front line infection'—I would advise you to leave Iraq immediately." I went to see Eileen and Gerry [Eileen Powell and Gerry Labelle, a husband-and-wife AP team in Nicosia] and they put me into the Cyprus Clinic. They gave me antibiotic injections.

But what I saw was a killing machine. Zoran and I, in the end, we thought we had seen about 4,700 Iranian bodies. You know, the things that happened in that war, you would need centuries to write about it.

Every evening at 6 p.m., the Iraqis would broadcast their official war communiqué for the day. I remember word for word what it said in early 1985: *The waves of insects are attacking the eastern gates of the Arab Nation. But we have the pesticides to wipe them out.*

So where did the "pesticides" come from? Partly from Germany (of course). But on 25 May 1994 the Committee on Banking, Housing and Urban Affairs of the U.S. Senate produced a report, *United States Chemical and Biological Warfare-Related Dual-Use Exports to Iraq and their Possible Impact on the Health Consequences of the Gulf War*. The "Gulf War" referred to the 1991 war and liberation of Kuwait, but its investigations went all the way back to the Iran–Iraq War—which was itself originally called the "Gulf War" by the West until we participated in a Gulf war of our own and purloined the name. The committee's report informed the U.S. Congress about government-approved shipments of biological agents sent by American companies to Iraq since 1985. These included *Bacillus anthracis*— which produces anthrax; *Clostridium botulinum*; *Histoplasma capsulatum*; *Brucella melitensis*; *Clostridium perfringens* and *Escherichia coli* (*E. coli*). The same report stated that "the United States provided the Government of Iraq with 'dual use' licensed materials which assisted in the development of Iraqi chemical, biological, and missile-system programs, including . . . chemical warfare agent production facility plant and technical drawings (provided as pesticide production facility plans), chemical warhead filling equipment . . ."

In the summer of 1985, the Iraqi Information Ministry took Salam close to the Syrian border, where there was a quarry with the name Al-Qaem-ukashat. The government "minders" told Salam it produced fertilisers. "There was an American engineer there from Texas," he was to recall.

> I interviewed him and he said they were making fertilisers there. Actually, they were producing the mustard and nerve gas there. Many people in Iraq knew about this. There was a kind of artificial town next to it with a restaurant and chalets. The place was bombed by the Americans in the 1991 war. The regime people stayed there for a while immediately after the American invasion in 2003. But at the time they wanted us to write about this wonderful fertiliser plant. They laid on this big banquet with lots of wine and whiskey.

Hamid Kurdi Alipoor lies on his hospital bed in a semi-stupor, wheezing through cracked lips, his burned forehead artificially creased by his frown of pain. The nurse beside him—a girl in dark-framed spectacles wearing an equally black chador—pours water gently into his mouth from a plastic mug. The girl smiles at the young man as if she does not notice the dark skin hanging from his face or the livid pink burns around his throat. Something terrible has happened to him, but the Iranian doctors insist that I ask him to tell me his own story.

It is the same as that of many of the other 199 Iranian soldiers and Revolutionary Guards lying in torment in their beds in the Labbafinejad Medical Centre in Tehran. It is now February 1986. "I was in a shelter on the Iranian side of the Arvand [Shatt al-Arab] River," Alipoor says. "When the shell landed, I did not realise the Iraqis were firing gas. I could not see the chemical so I did not put my gas mask on. Then it was too late." He relaxes for a few moments, breathing heavily, the nurse holding out the cup to him again. How old is he? I ask. He looks at the girl when he replies. "Nineteen," he says.

Some of the other patients watch him from their beds, others are lying with their eyes congealed shut, a bowl of damp, pink swabs beside their pillows. They do not talk. All you can hear is the sound of harsh, laboured breathing. "The lungs are the real problem—we send them home when they improve and we can deal with the blood infections." Dr. Faizullah Yazdani, one of the senior medical staff at the hospital, is a small man with huge eyebrows who radiates cheerfulness among all the pain. "But they come back to us with lung problems. They cough a lot. And some have been attacked with nerve gas as well as mustard gas."

The Iranians very publicly flew some of their chemical warfare victims to London, Stockholm and Vienna for treatment, but Dr. Yazdani's wards are overflowing with patients. So far, only 7 of the 400 he has received have died. He still hopes to send 200 home, although many will never recover. According to the doctors, the Iraqis use mustard and tabun gas and nerve gas on the Iranians; they renewed their chemical attacks on a large scale on 13 February. When the victims are badly affected, they drown in their own saliva. Those who survive are brought choking to the long hospital trains, successors to the train of gas victims on which I travelled three years earlier. Now these trains are running from Ahwaz every twenty-four hours. "You cannot see the gas so it's often a terrible surprise," Dr. Yazdani says. "The soldier will smell rotten vegetables, then his eyes start to burn, he suffers headaches, he has difficulty seeing, then he starts crying, he coughs and wheezes."

The pain is physically in the ward as the doctor takes me round bed after bed of blistered young men, their strangely contorted bodies swathed in yellow bandages. The blisters sometimes cover their bodies. They are yellow and pink, horribly soft and sometimes as large as basketballs, often breeding new bubbles of fragile, wobbling skin on top of them. In bed sixteen, I come across a doctor who is also a patient, a thirty-four-year-old dermatologist from Tabriz called Hassan Sinafa who was working in a military hospital near the Shatt al-Arab on 13 January when a gas shell burst only 20 metres from him. I can tell he must have been wearing his gas mask at the time because it has left an area of unblemished skin tissue around his eyes and mouth, producing a cynical dark line around his forehead and cheeks. "There was nothing I could do," he says slowly, dosed in morphine. "I had my anti-gas clothes on but the shell was too close for them to protect me. I felt the burns and I knew what was happening."

He smiles. He had been brought safely to Tehran but it was two days before he gave the doctors permission to telephone his wife, at home in Tabriz with his twenty-month-old daughter. What did she say when she arrived at his hospital bed and saw him? I ask. "She has not come," he replies. "I told her not to—I don't want her or our baby seeing me like this."


THROUGHOUT ALL THESE YEARS, the Americans also continued to supply the Iraqis with battlefield intelligence so that they could prepare themselves for the mass Iranian attacks and defend themselves—as the U.S. government knew—with poison gas. More than sixty officers of the U.S. Defense Intelligence Agency were secretly providing members of the Iraqi general staff with detailed information on Iranian deployments, tactical planning and bomb-damage assessments. After the Iraqis retook the Fao peninsula from the Iranians in early 1988, Lieutenant Colonel Rick Francona, a U.S. defence intelligence officer, toured the battlefield with Iraqi officers and reported back to Washington that the Iraqis had used chemical weapons to secure their victory. The senior defence intelligence officer at the time, Colonel Walter Lang, later told *The New York Times* that "the use of gas on the battlefield by the Iraqis was not a matter of deep strategic concern."

The Iraqis had used gas to recapture Fao on 19 April 1988—to the virtual indifference of the world. Just a month earlier, on 17 and 18 March, during Operation *Anfal*—*anfal* means "booty"—the Iraqis had taken a terrible revenge on the Kurdish town of Halabja for allegedly collaborating with the Iranians during Iran's brief *Val Fajr 10* offensive in the area. For two days, Iraqi jets dropped gas, made from a hydrogen cyanide compound developed with the help of a German company, onto Halabja, killing more than 5,000 civilians. In Washington, the CIA—still supporting Saddam—sent out a deceitful briefing note to U.S. embassies in the Middle East, stating that the gas might have been dropped by the Iranians.

Humanitarian organisations would, much later, draw their own frightening conclusions from this lie. "By any measure, the American record on Halabja is shameful," Joost Hiltermann of Human Rights Watch was to say fifteen years afterwards. The U.S. State Department even "instructed its diplomats to say that Iran was partly to blame. The result of this stunning act of sophistry was that the international community failed to muster the will to condemn Iraq strongly for an act as heinous as the terrorist strike on the World Trade Center." In the United States, Halabja was mentioned in 188 news stories in 1988, but in only twenty in 1989. By 2000, Halabja featured in only ten news stories in the American media. But then it was reheated by the George W. Bush administration as part justification for its forthcoming invasion of Iraq. Halabja was remembered by journalists 145 times in February 2003 alone. In common with Tony Blair and many other Western leaders, Bush repeatedly emphasised that Saddam "is a person who has gassed his own people."

The possessive "his own" was important. It emphasised the heinous nature of the crime—the victims were not just his enemies but his fellow Iraqis, though that might not be the Kurds' point of view. But it also served to distance and to diminish Saddam's earlier identical but numerically far greater crimes against the Iranians, who had lost many more of their citizens to the very same gases used at Halabja. And since we, the West, were servicing Saddam at the time of these war crimes—and still were at the time of Halabja—the gassing of the Kurds had to be set aside as a unique example of his beastliness.

Nearly a decade after Halabja, the United States accused Iran of trying to acquire chemical weapons, and it was Ali Akbar Hashemi Rafsanjani, in charge of Iranian forces during a large part of the Iran–Iraq War, who—as outgoing president of Iran—formally denied the American claim. "We have had such a malicious experience of the use of chemical weapons by the Iraqis in the Imposed War that we would never wish to use or possess them," he said with unusual emotion in 1997. "At the time I was the sole commander of Iranian forces in the war. When we captured the Howeiza area, I witnessed such terrible scenes that I could never forget them. The people of Halabja cooperated with us after victory . . . Saddam had got away with using it on our people so he resorted to advanced chemical weapons which he then received from Germany and used these against those [Kurdish] people. These chemical substances were used and the people were harvested down on the ground. When you could smell this substance no one could survive. I saw terrible scenes there [in Halabja] and I hope this scene could never be repeated in any country."

I AM SITTING ON THE FLOOR of a tent in northern Iraq on 28 May 1991. Halabja was gassed three years ago. Around us, thousands of Kurdish refugees, victims of Saddam's latest ethnic cleansing—the repression that followed our instigation and then betrayal of the post-Kuwait Iraqi uprising—are languishing amid squalor and disease under U.S. military protection. The hillside is cold and streaks of snow still lie in the hollows around the tents, the air frozen, but thick with the thump of American Chinook helicopters transporting food and blankets to the refugee camp.

Zulaika Mustafa Ahmed is twenty-two and wears a white embroidered dress, a long skirt and a scarf over her dark hair. Her family are victims of the *Anfal* campaign during which perhaps 10,000 Kurds were murdered. Zulaika, married at the age of fourteen, was with her six children and her husband, Moussa Issa Haji, when the *Anfal* started and, like so many thousands of Kurds, they were obeying government instructions to report to their nearest town. "We were approaching Dahuk in our van when we were stopped by Iraqi soldiers," she says. "We were taken along with hundreds of other Kurds to Dahuk fort. They took us to the second floor where I saw Moussa being beaten with concrete blocks. I saw myself ten men who died after they were beaten with the blocks—I was standing only 6 metres away. Then they took them all away. I managed to speak to Moussa. I said to him: 'Don't be afraid, you are a man.' He answered: 'Please, you have to take care of my children. If they kill me, it doesn't matter.' What was I to say? They took him away and I have never seen him again. Sometimes I think I will never see my husband again—yes, sometimes I think this."

Zulaika returned to her village of Baharqa. "It was some days later. We were used to the aircraft. I had left the village early with three of my children—the other three were with their grandfather—to go to the fields but I saw the two aircraft come low over Baharqa and drop bombs. There was a lot of smoke and it drifted towards us on the wind. It covered the land. We were hiding ourselves behind a small hill but we saw it coming towards us. The smoke had a nice smell, like medicine. Then my smallest children, Sarbas and Salah, started to cry. They started having diarrhoea but it didn't stop. I couldn't help them so I took them to the hospital in Irbil. The doctors were afraid. They gave them injections and medicine but it was no use. Both of them started to go black, as black as asphalt, and they both died nine or ten days later. The older child, when he died, he was vomiting his lungs. I buried them in the village cemetery. A lot of children died there. Now, if I go back there, I would not be able to find them."

Zulaika says she will never marry again. How does she see her life, we ask. "I am living just to raise my children, that is all. In my dreams, I dream about my children who died. In one dream, I dream that my husband says to me: 'You didn't take care of the children as you promised. This is the reason why they died.'"

FOR SOME OF THE SOLDIERS in the Iraqi army—the perpetrators, not the victims—the memory of those chemical attacks will also remain with them for ever. It is now July 2004, almost a quarter of a century after the start of the Iran–Iraq war, sixteen years since the *Anfal* operation against the Kurds. Under the occupation of the Americans and its puppet government, Baghdad has become the most dangerous city on earth. Suicide bombings, executions, kidnappings are the heartbeats of the city. But I arrive at the little market garden behind Palestine Street to buy a fir tree for the balcony of my hotel room, something to keep me sane in the broiling heat of midsummer Iraq. The garden is a place of flowers and undergrowth and pot plants and it is ruled over by Jawad, a forty-four-year-old with a sharp scar on his forehead, but who knows he lives in *jenah*. *Jenah* means "heaven."

But Jawad, I quickly discover, has also lived in hell. When I ask about the scar, he tells me that a piece of Iranian shell cut into his head during a bombardment on the Penjwin mountain during the Iran–Iraq War. He was a radio operator and spent thirteen years in the Iraqi army. "I lost almost all my friends," he says, rubbing his hands together in a false gesture of dismissal. "What happened to us was quite terrible. And what happened to me. I can't remember the name of one of my dead friends—because the shell fragment in my head took my memory away."

Not all his memory, however. Jawad moves silently through the trees, only the trickle of water from a fountain and the back-cloth sound of Baghdad's traffic disturbing his journey. A white ficus tree, perhaps? Very good for withstanding the heat. A green ficus tree? The only fir trees for sale are so deeply rooted, they would take an hour to dig up. All his life, Jawad has worked in the market garden, along with his father. The heat accentuates the smells so that the smallest rose is perfumed, white flowers turning into blossom.

Yes, Jawad survived the entire Iran–Iraq War. He loathed Saddam, he says, yet he fought for him for eight terrible years. "I was at Ahwaz, I was at the Karun River, in the Shamiran Mountains, in the *Anfal* operation, at Penjwin. I was a conscript and then a reservist but I refused to become an officer in case I had to stay in the army longer." In my notebook, I put a line beside the word *Anfal*. Jawad had crossed the Iranian frontier in 1980. He had entered Khorramshahr and then, when Khorramshahr was surrounded, he had retreated out of the city at night.

"I first noticed the gas being used east of Amara. Our artillery were firing gas shells into the Iranians. I couldn't smell the gas but I soaked my scarf in water and held it to my nose. Because I was a radio operator, I had a lot of equipment round me that protected me from the gas. These were black days and we suffered a lot. After I was wounded, they insisted on sending me back to the front. I had a thirty-five per cent disability and still they sent me back to the war."

Jawad manoeuvres a dark green potted plant onto the path, waving his hands at the birds that spring from the undergrowth. If heaven really is a warm and comfortable garden, then Jawad lives in it. And the *Anfal* operation? I ask. Did he see the effects with his own eyes? Jawad raises his hands in an imploring, helpless way.

"We saw everything. Would you believe this, that when they started using the gas strange things happened? I saw the birds falling from the sky. I saw the little beans on the trees suddenly turning black. The leaves decayed in front of our eyes. I kept the towel round my face, just as I did near Amara."

And bodies?

"Yes, so many of them. All civilians. They lay around the villages and on the hillsides in clumps, as if streets of people had gathered at the same place to die. Some were scattered, but there were many women who held children in their arms and they all lay there dead. What could I do? I could say nothing. We soldiers were too frightened even to discuss it. We just saw so many dead. And we were silent."

CHAPTER SEVEN

# *"War against War"*
# *and the Fast Train to Paradise*

*What candles may be held to speed them all?*
*Not in the hands of boys, but in their eyes*
*Shall shine the holy glimmers of good-byes.*

—Wilfred Owen, "Anthem for Doomed Youth"


IN THE HUSH OF THE CURTAINED front room, the two former Iraqi pilots and the man who had been second-in-command of Saddam Hussein's air force sat in front of me in silence. The pilots spoke the heavily accented French they had learned while training on their Mirage fighter-bombers at Cherbourg. I had asked them about the USS *Stark*. But why now? they wanted to know. Why, sixteen years after an Iraqi Mirage had fired two missiles at the American guided-missile frigate in the Gulf—incinerating thirty-seven of its crew—did I want to know why they had almost sunk the ship? Why not discuss the growing anarchy in Baghdad under American occupation? That very morning in 2003, a car bomb had exploded outside the gates of the American headquarters at Saddam's former Republican palace.

All three men feared that I was a spy, that I was trying to identify the pilot who killed the young American seamen more than a decade and a half ago. Why else would I ask if he was still alive? I told them I would never betray any human being, that I was a journalist—not an intelligence officer—that I would no more hand them over to the Americans than I would hand Americans over to them. I knew that senior Iraqi air force personnel had all remained in contact with each other after the 2003 Anglo-American invasion, that they now constituted an air force without aircraft. But I also suspected, correctly, that many of these men were now involved in the anti-occupation insurgency. I tried to explain that this was the one Iraqi air force mission that changed the Middle East. Their colleague's actions on 17 May 1987 had—through one of those grotesque double standards which only Washington seemed able to produce—brought Iran to its knees.

The ex-general looked at me for almost another minute without speaking. Then he gave what was almost a mundane operational report. "I saw him take off from Shaiba," he said. "It was a routine flight over the Gulf to hunt for Iranian ships. There was a 'forbidden zone' from which we had excluded all ships and the *Stark* was in that zone. The pilot didn't know the Americans were there. He knew he had to destroy any shipping in the area—that's all. He saw a big ship on his radar screen and he fired his two missiles at it. He assumed it was Iranian. He never saw the actual target. We never make visual contact—that's how the system works. Then he turned to come home."

Seventy kilometres north-east of Qatar, the American Perry-class frigate's radar had picked up the Iraqi Mirage F-1 as it flew low and slowly down the coast of Saudi Arabia towards Bahrain. But Captain Glenn Brindel and his crew were used to Iraqi jets flying over them. Iraqi aircraft, he was to tell journalists later, were "deemed friendly." The green speck on the radar did not represent a threat. Because the *Stark* held a course almost directly towards the Iraqi Mirage, the frigate's superstructure blocked the anti-missile sensors and the Phalanx anti-missile battery which had the ability to pick up an incoming missile and fire automatically. But the system had anyway been switched to manual to avoid shooting down the wrong aircraft in the crowded Gulf. The captain would later claim that the detection systems were also malfunctioning. At 10:09 p.m., Brindel ordered a radio message to be sent to the pilot: "Unknown aircraft, this is U.S. navy warship on your 078 for twelve miles. Request you identify yourself." There was no reply. A minute later, the aircraft banked towards the north and rose to 5,000 feet. The crew in the *Stark*'s "combat information centre" failed to identify the two Exocet missiles with their 352-pound warheads which had detached themselves from the Mirage and were now racing towards them.

It was a lookout who first saw the rocket skimming the surface of the water towards the ship and telephoned Brindel. Two seconds later, the Exocet punched into the *Stark* at 600 mph and exploded in the forward crew's quarters, cremating several of the American seamen as they lay in their bunks. The second missile exploded thirty seconds later. More than a sixth of the frigate's crew were to die in less than a minute after the first Exocet spewed 120 pounds of burning solid missile fuel into crew sleeping quarters. The warhead failed to explode but smashed through seven bulkheads before coming to rest against the starboard hull plating. The second missile sent a fireball through the crew's quarters, its 3,500-degree burning fuel killing most of the thirty-seven victims, turning many of them to ash. The *Stark* filled with thick, toxic smoke, the temperature even in neighbouring compartments soaring to 1,500 degrees. Bunks, computers and bulkheads melted in the heat. One petty officer spent thirteen hours in a darkened magazine room spraying water on 36 missiles as a 2,000-degree fire raged only a bulkhead away. The ship burned for two days. Even after she was taken in tow, the fires kept reigniting.

Listing and flying the American flag at half-staff, the *Stark* was pulled towards Bahrain. Secretary of State Caspar Weinberger called the attack "indiscriminate." The Iraqi pilot, he said, "apparently didn't care enough to find out what ship he was shooting at." But there America's criticism of Iraq ended. Even before Saddam Hussein made his own unprecedented and contrite expression of remorse—and long before the U.S. Navy had begun its own three investigations into the attack—President Ronald Reagan decided to blame Iran. "We've never considered them hostile at all," he said of the Iraqis. "They've never been in any way hostile." The Gulf was an international waterway. "No country there has a right to try and close it off and take it for itself. And the villain in the piece is Iran. And so they're delighted with what has just happened."*

Listening to Reagan's words, one might have thought that Iran had started the war by invading Iraq in 1980, that Iran had been using chemical weapons against Iraq, that Iran had initiated the maritime exclusion zone in 1984 which started the tanker war in the Gulf—of which the *Stark* was indirectly a victim. Iraq was responsible for each of these acts, but Iraq was deemed "friendly." Only a few weeks before the near-sinking of the *Stark*, U.S. under-secretary Richard Murphy had himself visited Baghdad and praised Iraq's "bravery" in withstanding Iran, spraying its enemies with poison gas now a definition of Iraqi courage for Mr. Murphy. Reagan had rewarded the aggressor by accepting his excuses and referred to the nation that did not kill his countrymen as the "villain." It was an interesting precedent. When Iraq almost sank an American frigate, Iran was to blame. When al-Qaeda attacked the United States fourteen years later, Iraq was to blame.

All that was left was for Saddam himself to offer his condolences to the families of the dead Americans. They were not long in coming. "Rest assured that the grief which you feel as a result of the loss of your sons is our grief, too," the Iraqi leader wrote in a letter to the families of the dead, dated 22 May and printed on the stationery of Iraq's Washington embassy:

> On the occasion of the funeral ceremony of the victims lost in the grievous and unintentional incident that has happened to the American frigate *Stark*, I would like to express to you . . . my condolences and feelings of grief. All the Iraqis and I feel most profoundly the sorrow of moments such as these. Since we have ourselves lost a great many of our dear ones in the war which has been raging now for seven years, while the Iranian government still persists in . . . rejecting our appeals and those of the international community for the establishment of a just and lasting peace.

Even now, Saddam had to add his own propaganda line, although it neatly dovetailed with Reagan's own distorted view of the conflict. Iran's "rejection" of appeals from the "international community" alluded to Iran's refusal to accept UN Security Council ceasefire resolutions which failed to demand punishment for the "aggressor" nation. Pentagon spokesman Dan Howard also said Reagan's vilification of Iran was because of its refusal "to go to the bargaining table."† Shipping

---

*Far from gloating over the attack, the Iranian "war information headquarters" in Tehran called it a "serious and dangerous trap" laid by the Iraqis to draw Washington and Moscow into the war.

†In an emotional interview in which he kept breaking into tears—to the consternation of his press secretary, Anne O'Leary—U.S. ambassador to Bahrain Sam Zakhem insisted to me that "we never before had reason to feel the Iraqis would attack an American ship . . . our people feel it was a mistake. We paid very dearly for that mistake because the nature of the American people

officials in the Gulf always suspected that the Iraqis made their night-time attack on the *Stark* in the hope that the United States would believe an Iranian aircraft tried to destroy the frigate and would therefore retaliate against Tehran. In the event, they didn't need to waste their time with such conspiracy theories: America blamed Iran anyway. A few days later, Reagan called Iran "this barbarous country."

Saddam compared the American relatives of the *Stark* to the families of Iraqis killed during his aggression against Iran, thus turning the U.S. Navy personnel into the surrogate dead of his own atrocious war. Saddam's plaintive call for a "just and lasting peace" was almost Arafat-like in its banality. The final American abasement came when Washington dispatched a full-scale U.S. Navy inquiry team under Rear Admiral David Rodgers to Baghdad, where they were told they would not be permitted to question the Iraqi pilot who fired the two Exocet missiles; nor did the Iraqis agree with the Americans that the *Stark* was outside Iraq's self-imposed "exclusion zone" when it was hit. The Americans said the vessel was at least 10 nautical miles outside, Iraq claimed it was at least 20 nautical miles inside. Weinberger's call to produce the Iraqi pilot was ignored. Captain Brindel of the *Stark* was relieved of his command, his weapons officer was reprimanded and left the navy, and his executive officer disciplined for "dereliction of duty."

The Americans always assumed that the Iraqi pilot had been executed—hence Iraq's refusal to produce him—but the ex-deputy commander of the Iraqi air force insisted to me in Baghdad that this was untrue. "I saw him a few months ago," he said. "Like me, he's out of work. But he obeyed all our rules. We were fighting a cruel enemy. It was a mistake. We weren't going to get rid of one of our senior pilots for the Americans. The Americans were inside our 'forbidden zone.' We told them not to enter it again—and they obeyed."

A visit by a group of U.S. senators to the melted-down crew quarters on the *Stark* was sufficient to set them off in a spasm of rage at the one country that had nothing to do with the American deaths. Republican Senator John Warner, a former secretary of the U.S. Navy, described Iran as "a belligerent that knows no rules, no morals." Senator John Glenn was reduced to abusing Iran as "the sponsor of terrorism and the hijacker of airliners." Thus Saddam's attack on the *Stark* was now bringing him untold benefits. Americans were talking as if they were themselves contemplating military action against Iran.

Reagan pretended that the Americans were in the Gulf as peacemakers. "Were a hostile power ever to dominate this strategic region and its resources," he explained, "it would become a chokepoint for freedom—that of our allies and our own . . . That is why we maintain a naval presence there. Our aim is to prevent, not to provoke, wider conflict, to save the many lives that further conflict would cost us . . ." Most Americans knew, Reagan said, that "to retreat or withdraw would

---

is to give others the benefit of the doubt." If the Soviet Union wished to prove its own good intentions in the Gulf, Zakhem said, it could "stop the flow of arms of the eastern bloc nations to Iran . . . It's Iran which has refused to come to the negotiating table." So Iraq was "friendly"— and Iran had to be deprived of weapons to defend itself.

only repeat the improvident mistakes of the past and hand final victory to those who seek war, who make war." The Iranians, needless to say—the victims of Iraq's aggression—were those "who seek war, who make war," not "friendly" Iraq which had anyway been taken off the State Department's list of "international terrorist countries" in 1982, two years after its invasion of Iran and in the very year that Iran reported eleven Iraqi poison gas attacks against its forces. The truth was that the *Stark*—one of seven U.S. warships in the Gulf—was sailing under false pretences.

Iraq had placed its "exclusion zone" around Kharg Island in January 1984 because it was losing the land war it had initiated more than three years earlier; by attacking tankers lifting oil from Iran's Kharg Island terminal, Saddam hoped to strangle his antagonist economically. His aircraft henceforth fired at ships of any nationality that were moving to and from Iranian ports. Iran retaliated by targeting vessels trading with Iraq through the Arab Gulf states. Iraq's massive imports of arms for the war were transiting Saudi Arabia and Kuwait, whose funding of Iraq's war effort was close to $404 billion; any ship trading with either nation was now threatened with Iranian air attack. Between 18 April 1984 and 18 May 1987—the day after the *Stark* was hit—227 ships had been attacked in the Gulf, 137 of them by Iraq and 90 by Iran; several had been struck by missiles and repeatedly repaired, and of the 227 total, 153 were oil tankers. Between May 1981 and 18 May 1987, 211 merchant seamen, most of them foreigners, were killed on these ships, of which 98 were on oil tankers; it was a tiny figure compared with the hundreds of thousands of combatants in the land war, but it internationalised the conflict—as both Iraq and Iran probably hoped that it would.

American warships were now ostensibly keeping the sea lanes open for international shipping, to prevent the Gulf becoming, in Reagan's odd term, a "chokepoint." But U.S. vessels were not shielding Iranian tankers from Iraqi attack. Nor were they seeking to protect foreign oil tankers lifting Iranian oil for export at Kharg. America's mission in the Gulf was to protect only one side's ships—Iraq's—in the sea lanes. Already the Americans were proposing to escort Kuwaiti-flagged tankers in the Gulf, which did not carry Iranian cargo. They carried Iraqi oil for export. Iraq might not be able to gain any victories in its land war with Iran, but with American help, as the Iranians realised at once, it could win the sea war. Reagan claimed that the United States was fighting "war against war" in the Gulf. In fact, Washington was fighting a war against Iran.

Eleven days after the *Stark* was rocketed, the Iranians complained that a U.S. warship in the Gulf had "threatened" an Iran Air passenger jet flying from Shiraz to Doha, in Qatar, and ordered the pilot to alter course. My own investigation among Dubai air traffic controllers established that the American warning came from one of four naval vessels escorting a Kuwaiti-registered ship with a cargo of arms to Bahrain. "The incident provided just the sort of scenario for a . . . tragedy in the Gulf," I wrote in my dispatch to *The Times* that night. "Iran Air flies scheduled routes to both Doha, the capital of Qatar, and to the Gulf emirate of Dubai further east, regularly overflying the waters in which American . . . frigates patrol. Although the Iranians did not say so, the pilot probably flew unwittingly over a

U.S. naval unit which identified the plane as Iranian and ordered it to change course." The "tragedy" was to come exactly fourteen months later.

There were plenty of portents. Not long after the *Stark* was hit, I spent a day and a night on Gulf patrol with HMS *Broadsword*. Accompanying British ships through the Strait of Hormuz, Reagan's now famous chokepoint—the word "escort" was never used by the British—and discouraging the attentions of the Iranians might have seemed a simple matter in the dry memoranda that their naval lordships used at the defence ministry in London. But inside the glow-worm interior of the Type-22 class frigate, the radar monitors watched with feverish intensity for the transponder numbers of the civilian aircraft passing over *Broadsword*. "If you want to avoid burning up six sheikhs in their private jet, you've got to be bloody careful," one of them said.

At least the air conditioning was pumped into their little nest—for the computers, of course, not for them—but what afflicted most of the seamen in the Gulf was the heat. It burned the entire decks until they were, quite literally, too hot to walk on. British sailors stood on the edges of their shoes because of the scalding temperatures emerging from the steel. The depth-charge casings, the Bofors gun-aiming device, were too hot to touch. On the helicopter flight deck, the heat rose to 135 degrees, and only a thoughtless leading hand would have touched a spanner without putting his gloves on. It created a dull head, a desperate weariness, an awesome irritation with one's fellow humans on the foredeck.

Inside the ship—and their lordships would have appreciated the cleanliness of *Broadsword*'s galleys and mess decks and bunks and short, fearful advertisements warning of the dangers of AIDS in Mombasa port—the heat shuffled through the vessel faster than the seamen. The officer's mess was a cool 80 degrees. One glass of water and I was dripping. Open the first watertight door and I was ambushed by the heat, just as I was seven years earlier in the streets of Najaf. After the second door, I walked into a tropical smelter, the familiar grey monochrome sea sloshing below the deck. How can men work in this and remain rational? Or—more to the point—how could the Iraqis and Iranians fight in this sweltering air and remain sane?

"There's Sharjah airport," the radar officer said, and fixed the beam. "I'm listening to a plane landing now—commercial flight—but if I want to know about a specific plane, I ask for an IFF [identification, friend or foe?] and talk to Sharjah control." There were boards and charts and crayon marks on war-zone lines. The USS *Reid*—part of Reagan's Gulf flotilla—had just cut across the Iraqi "exclusion zone." So much for *Stark*'s insistence that it stayed outside. Two Soviet Natya-class minesweepers and a submarine depot ship were listed as outside the Hormuz Strait. Two British Hong Kong–registered ships were waiting for us on the return journey.

Night was no relief. At 4:15 a.m., *Broadsword* was in the Gulf of Oman, her engineers dragging a hawser from the support ship *Orangeleaf* riding alongside her, refuelling in the heat. The humidity cloaked us all. The deck was awash with condensation, the seamen's faces crawling with perspiration. The sweat crept through my hair and trickled down my back. Our shirts were dark with moisture. It came to all men, even to Russians. Off Fujairah, Moscow's contribution to the freedom of Gulf navigation—a depot ship and two minesweepers—nestled against each other on the warm tide, the Soviet sailors, glistening and half-naked on deck, waiting for the next inbound Kuwaiti tanker. Here was the principal reason why Reagan wanted to patrol the sea lanes, here was the real "hostile power" that he feared might "dominate" the Gulf. The two British freighters came alongside to be "accompanied" by *Broadsword*.

On the bridge, an Indian radio operator could be heard pleading over VHF with an Iranian patrol ship. "We are only carrying dates," he said. "Only dates." The Iranian was 30 kilometres away. An Iranian P-3 reconnaissance aircraft answered. "Be aware," boomed the tannoy throughout *Broadsword*, "that yesterday the Iraqis launched an Exocet attack on a Maltese tanker carrying oil from Iran. We can therefore expect the Iranians to retaliate . . ." A dog-day mist now swirled around the ship, leaving salt cakes across the flight deck. The two freighters were steaming beside us, an overheated version of every Second World War Atlantic convoy, because *Broadsword*, however unheroic in her humidity, was—like the American ships—a naval escort.

BACK IN 1984, WHEN IRAQ began this maritime conflict, the Gulf looked a lot simpler. The Arabs, protesting mightily at every attack by the Iranians and silent when the Iraqis struck at Iranian shipping, were almost as fearful of American involvement as they were of the Iranians. Saudi Arabia maintained a quiet relationship with Iran—just in case Iraq collapsed—while at the same time underwriting Saddam's war. Ostensibly, the Arabs remained neutral—"at war but skulking," as Churchill unfairly remarked about the Irish in the Second World War—and offered refuge to any ship's master who found himself under fire. Bahrain and Dubai would receive the crippled hulks of both sides' aggression, profiting from the millions of dollars in repairs that their shipyards would make in reconstituting the ships. By 1987, eighteen had been hit twice, six had been attacked three times and two—*Superior* and *Dena*—had the distinction of being rocketed and repaired four times in four years. As early as May 1984 there was a floating junkyard of mortally wounded vessels off Bahrain.

They called it the ships' graveyard and the term was cruelly appropriate. The great tankers that Iran and Iraq had destroyed were towed here in terminal condition, bleeding fuel oil into the warm, muddy brown waves in the very centre of the Gulf, a series of jagged holes in their scalded superstructure to show how they met their end. The Bahraini government even ran a patrol boat out to this maritime cemetery for journalists to understand what this war now represented. An Iranian Phantom hit the 29,000-ton *Chemical Venture* so accurately on 24 May that its missile plunged into the very centre of the bridge: there was a 12-metre sign there saying "No Smoking" in the middle of the superstructure; the rocket took out the letters "S" and "M." The tanker crews along the Gulf were growing restive over the dangers; by the end of May, up to twenty-five ships were riding at anchor off the Emirates alone, waiting for instructions from their owners, and you only had to take a look at the ruin of the *Al-Hoot* to understand why. The 117,000-ton supertanker was listing with a hole the size of a London bus along her waterline where an Iraqi missile had exploded three weeks earlier. The superstructure had been twisted back and outwards over the stern and the crew's quarters had simply melted down as if they were made of plastic rather than iron. The gash on the starboard side was so deep I could see daylight through it.

Just to the north lay the 178,000-ton *Safina al-Arab*, moving restlessly in the swell as a Swedish-registered tanker tried to take off the last of her crude oil. The stuff was everywhere, down the sides of the ship, across the water, turning even the foam on the waves dark. I could smell it from a mile away. The salvage crews—mostly Dutchmen—knew the risks but strolled the decks as if they were in harbour rather than sitting on bombs 115 kilometres out in the Gulf.

It was an isolated place.* On the map of the Middle East, the Gulf seemed just a crack in the landmass between the deserts of Arabia and southern Iran, but the seas could be rough and the horizon featureless save for the lonely and vulnerable tankers butting through the sirocco winds up to Ras Tanura and Kuwait. They had no convoys to sail in then, no protection from the air, and they crept in those days as close as they could to the southern shoreline. They passed us as we photographed the graveyard of their more unfortunate brethren, ill painted for the most part, plunging through the heat haze, targets of opportunity for either side in the upper reaches of the Gulf, depending on their masters and their ports of call.

The sea should have been polluted but it was alive with flying fish that landed on their tails, long yellow sea snakes that came up out of the green depths to look at us, and porpoises and even turtles. Big-beaked black cormorants effortlessly outflew our fast Bahraini patrol boat. The oil slicks came in thick, viscous patches and in long thin streaks that shredded their way up the pale blue water towards the wrecks. The only sign of President Reagan's concern in those days was the discreet grey majesty of the USS *Luce*, a Seventh Fleet missile cruiser that lay all day off the Mina Salman channel outside Bahrain harbour, a picket boat filled with armed sailors slowly circling it to ward off unconventional attackers—an idea before its time, since the USS *Cole* would not be struck by suicide bombers in Aden for more than another decade. Besides, the radio traffic from the *Luce*, clearly audible on our own ship-to-shore radio, seemed mostly bound up with the complexities of bringing new video films aboard for the crew. A few hours later, a smaller U.S. patrol craft moved into port and the *Luce* gently steamed off into the sweltering dusk, its in-house entertainment presumably updated.

But other American warships were—even then—playing the role of convoy

---

*Foreign correspondents on assignment add datelines to their names so that readers immediately know from where they are reporting. Sending dispatches from the oceans of the world is more problematical. I dutifully—and accurately—gave my dateline in the Gulf as "51 degrees 40 mins E, 26 degrees 40 mins N." The sub-editors of *The Times* changed this, with my permission, to "At Sea"—which pretty much summed up how most of us felt about the story.

escorts. This unofficial and unacknowledged protection was given no publicity in Washington, nor among the Arab states, coinciding with their own desire to keep the U.S. Navy over the horizon. Sometimes the escort was provided by the USS *John Rodgers*, a sleek, twin-funnelled missile cruiser that last defended American interests by bombarding the Chouf mountains of central Lebanon less than a year earlier. At other times, the USS *Boone*, a squat and rather cumbersome flat-topped missile carrier, came up by night from the Emirates and rested off Bahrain. Anyone who approached the warships by day—which we did, of course—would be confronted by a steel-helmeted U.S. sailor manning a fixed heavy machine gun.

U.S. Air Force cargo jets were already flying regularly into the airports of the Gulf states, carrying equipment so bulky that they were forced to deploy their giant C-48 droop-wing transports. These flights were being made to the countries that Reagan always called "our Arab friends," a definition that no longer included Lebanon—from which U.S. forces had been famously "redeployed to sea" three months earlier, following the bombing of the Beirut marine barracks and the killing of 241 U.S. servicemen—but which very definitely embraced the conservative oil states of the Gulf peninsula. If the Americans did become strategically involved—as they did three years later—then the Arab states would have to be portrayed, as I wrote in *The Times* in May 1984, "as the innocent party in the dispute: the Iranians, inevitably, will be the enemy." And so it came to pass. Was it not Iranian aircraft, the Iranian regime and ultimately Iranian ideology that threatened the security of the area? Again, we would be expected to forget that Iraq began the war and that Iraq was the first to order its air force to attack oil tankers in the Gulf.

In the autumn of 1980, when it seemed certain to them that Khomeini's regime would collapse in anarchy under the onslaught of the Iraqi army around Abadan, the Arab Gulf states—those very states which by 1984 were seeking UN censure of Iran for its air attacks on the shipping lanes—poured billions into Iraq's war funds. But now that Iran's Islamic revolution had proved more tenacious than they thought, the Arabs were stapling their hopes to a worthless peace mission to Tehran and Riyadh by Syria, the one Arab country which very shrewdly decided at the beginning of the war that its Baathist enemies in Baghdad—rather than Khomeini's mullahs—might prove to be the losers. The failure of the Arab Gulf states to draw the same conclusion had now led to a disjointed policy that was as impossible to follow as it would be to justify historically.

Sheikh Khalifa Sulman al-Khalifa, the Bahraini prime minister and brother of the emir, insisted to me in June of 1984 that Iraq did not start the war. "I believe that—Iraq likes to protect itself like any other nation . . ." he said. "Of course, a war starts with something. You never know how far it will go on either side. First there is fire and fire depends on wind and the direction in which the wind blows. Sometimes people get carried away—they think they are strong." This was the nearest he came to criticism of Saddam. Now Bahrain—like the rest of the Gulf Cooperation Council—was demanding a UN Security Council resolution that would condemn only Iran for air attacks in the Gulf. He was not in favour of U.S. intervention. "There are ways of helping us and one of them is to stop the supply of arms to the fighting parties from Europe and from the Far East countries." And this, it has to be remembered, came from the prime minister of a country that was enthusiastically bankrolling Saddam's aggression.

The Kuwaitis, who once denounced any foreign intervention on Gulf soil, had by November of 1983 reached the conclusion that the defence of the Strait of Hormuz was the responsibility of the countries that benefited from it—in other words, the West. Sheikh Ahmed al-Sabah, the foreign minister, was quoted in the Beirut newspaper *An-Nahar* as saying that the Gulf was an "international" region in which he could not object to foreign intervention. Then on 27 May 1984 Kuwait's ambassador to Washington was warning against American involvement because it might "prompt the Soviet Union to enter the area." This was a strange observation to come from the only wealthy Gulf state to permit a Soviet embassy in its capital and the one country which had hoped Soviet good will could be used on behalf of the Gulf states at the UN Security Council.

The Saudis, on the other hand, were still fearful of any American presence in the Gulf. U.S. bases on Gulf territory would run counter to the anti-Israeli crusade carried on by the sheikhdoms, while a prolonged American presence could quickly ignite the sort of fires that brought ruin upon the Americans and their client government in Lebanon. Reagan's strategic cooperation agreement with Israel had not been forgotten in the Gulf—and Israel had added fuel to the Gulf War by supplying arms to Saddam Hussein's Iranian enemy. This was long before Iran-Contra, when the Americans used Israel to channel weapons to Tehran.

The Soviets, after watching the destruction of the communist Tudeh party in Iran, were sending massive new tank shipments to Iraq. The Israelis had provided large quantities of small arms and ammunition to the Iranians. So had the Syrians. The French were still supplying Exocet missiles to the Iraqis while the North Koreans sold Soviet rifles to Iran. The Americans had been quietly re-establishing their relations with Baghdad—at this point, they were still increasing their "interests section" in the Belgian embassy in Baghdad—at the very moment when Saddam most needed the moral as well as the military support of a Western power. While George Bush was in Pakistan denouncing Iran's "oppressive regime," Saddam was reported to be hanging deserters by the roadside outside Baghdad.

On 29 May 1984 the first load of 400 Stinger anti-aircraft missiles and launchers arrived by air in Saudi Arabia from the United States. President Khamenei of Iran sarcastically warned Washington that Iran would "resist and fight" any U.S. forces sent to the battle zone. "If the Americans are prepared to sink in the depths of the Persian Gulf waters for nothing, then let them come with their faith, motivation and divine power," he said. As for the Gulf Arabs, he warned: "You will be neutral in the war only if you do not provide Saddam with any assistance. But a neighbour who wants to deliver a blow at us is more dangerous than a stranger, and we should face that danger." Well aware that the Arabs were still giving huge financial support to Iraq, the oil-tanker crews took Khamenei's threats seriously. Several vessels on the Kuwait run through the sea lanes north-west of Bahrain were now travelling by night for fear of Iranian air attack.

Covering this protracted war for a newspaper was an exhausting, often unre-warding business. The repetition of events, the Iraqi attacks on Kharg Island, the massing of hundreds of thousands of Iranian troops outside Basra, the constant appeals by both sides to the UN Security Council, the sinking of more oil tankers, had a numbing quality about it. Sometimes this titanic bloodbath was called the "forgotten war"—even though at times it approached the carnage of the 1914–18 disaster. I dislike parallels with the two greatest conflicts of the twentieth century. Can we really say, for example, that Saddam's decision to invade Iran in 1980 was a blunder on the scale of Hitler's Operation Barbarossa, the Nazi invasion of the Soviet Union in June 1941, which led to the deaths of 20 million Russians—when perhaps only a million Iranians died as a result of Saddam's aggression? Certainly, by the time it ended, the Iran–Iraq bloodletting had lasted as long as the Vietnam War. And Saddam's war was the longest conventional conflict of the last century, a struggle of such severity that the barrels of the Iranian army's guns had to be replaced twelve times before it ended in 1988.

My visits to the battle fronts, and to Tehran and Baghdad, seemed to have a "story-so-far" quality about them. Statistics lost their power to shock. In 1985 alone, Colonel Heikki Holma of the UN's inspection team in Iran estimated that 4,500 Iranians had been killed or wounded by chemical weapons. In two years, there had been at least sixty major chemical attacks by Iraq. The casualty figures were obviously on a Somme-like scale—again, I found myself unwillingly using the parallels of my father's war—but neither side would admit the extent of its own losses. By 1986 alone, a million had perished in the war, so it was said by the Western diplomats who rarely if ever visited the war front, 700,000 of them Ira-nian. The Iranians said that 500,000 Iraqis had been killed. There were—and here the figures could be partly confirmed by the International Red Cross—100,000 Iraqi POWs in Iran and around 50,000 Iranian POWs in Iraq. Both sides were together spending around $1.5 billion a month on the war.

In Iran, the conflict had changed the mood of the theologians trying to conduct the battle with Iraq. Only a year earlier, there were daily reports of torture and mass rape coming out of the grey-walled confines of Evin prison. But in April 1985, Hojatolislam Ali Ladjevardi, the Tehran prosecutor, was dismissed from his post together with many of his murderous henchmen; executions were now carried out almost exclusively on common criminals rather than enemies of the state. "The executions have been toned down," an Iranian businessman put it with mild sar-casm. "Now they only kill murderers and narcotics men. The worst they do to a girl who offends Islamic law is to cut her hair off." There was a growing acquies-cence—rather than acceptance—of the Khomeini regime that produced an irrita-ble freedom of speech; shopkeepers, businessmen, Iranian journalists, even conservative religious families could complain about the government without fear that they would be betrayed to the Revolutionary Guards.

It was part of an illusion. The Islamic Republic had not suddenly become democratic; it had cut so deeply into its political enemies that there was no focus of opposition left. In 1984 at least 661 executions were believed to have been carried out in Tehran, a further 237 up to Ladjevardi's dismissal. The figures were Amnesty International's, but the Iranians themselves admitted to 197 judicial killings between March 1984 and April 1985, claiming that they were all for drug offences. The introduction of a machine specially designed by Iranian engineers to amputate fingers was proudly announced by Tehran newspapers, proving that the revolution was as anxious as ever to exact punishment on those who contravened its laws.

Such public freedom of expression as still existed could be found in the Majlis, the institution that so many critics had once predicted would provide only a rubber-stamp parliament for Khomeini's decrees. There was a confrontation in parliament over a series of laws on land reform, trade and the budget. Conservative members led by Rafsanjani, the speaker, wanted to preserve the power of the clergy and the *bazaaris,* arguing for a liberal economy and no changes in land ownership. More radical members who claimed to follow "the line of the Imam" were demanding full government control of trade, land distribution and a number of social reforms that sounded like socialism. The result was government paralysis. Landowners refused to till their fields lest their property became profitable and was taken away by the state.

Khomeini had a final veto over all legislation, but his chief function now was to be a presence; he was the patriarch, produced for the relatives of martyrs or, more rarely, for foreign diplomats, a figure of solidity but no movement, of image rather than content, a mirror to past victory and what had gone before rather than to the future. His last meeting with diplomats was typical. More than sixty ambassadors, chargés and first secretaries were crammed into a minuscule room at the Ayatollah's residence and obliged to sit cross-legged on a slightly grubby carpet, a French embassy attaché suffering severe cramp as he perched on top of a Scandinavian chargé. In due course, Khomeini entered the room and delivered himself of a fifteen-minute speech in Farsi, without translation. "It didn't matter what he said," one of the ambassadors remarked acidly. "The old man sat there on a sheet on a raised dais and he was making only one point: that the Shah had received his guests in regal magnificence in his palace but that he, Khomeini, would receive us in humble circumstances."

But each night now, Khomeini was taken off to the bunkers beneath the Shah's old palace at Niavaran, the only air-raid shelter in all Tehran, to protect him from the war that was now his enduring legacy. As the Iraqi fighter-bombers soared unmolested over the capital, tens of thousands of his people would flee into the mountains by road. While Khomeini still demanded the overthrow of Saddam, his mullahs appeared on national television, begging the people of Isfahan, Shiraz, Ahwaz, Dezful and Tehran itself to contribute food and clothing for their soldiers at the front. Individual home towns were asked to resupply front-line units that came from their areas. In the marshes of southern Iraq, the Iranian *Basiji* clung on amid the hot mud and Iraqi counter-attacks.

The Iranians were now freighting their 600-kilo ground-to-ground missiles up to a new base at Sarbullzaharb in Kurdistan where North Korean engineers calibrated them for the flight to Baghdad. When they knew the rocket was approaching its target just over fifteen minutes later, the Iranians would announce the impending strike over national radio. For reporters, this could have a weird journalistic effect. "I'd be sitting in the bureau in Baghdad when Nabila Megalli would come through on my telex from Bahrain where she'd been listening to the radio," Samir Ghattas, Mohamed Salam's AP successor in Iraq, would recall. "She would say that the Iranians had just announced they'd fired a missile at Baghdad. I stayed on the telex line—we had no fax then—and the moment I heard the explosion in Baghdad, I'd write "Yes." The Iraqis would pull the plug five minutes later. It took twenty minutes for the rocket to travel from the border to Baghdad."

The Iraqi raids often provoked little more than a fantasy display of anti-aircraft fire from the guns around Tehran. The pilots could not identify any targets now that the Iranians had acquired new German SEL aircraft warning radar and switched off the electricity. On 2 June 1985, however, two bombs dropped by an Iraqi high-altitude Ilyushin-28 exploded on a large civilian housing complex in the Gisha suburb of the city, collapsing five entire blocks of apartments. From my hotel window—from where I had been watching the lights of the distant bomber— I saw two huge flashes of crimson light and heard a terrific roar, the detonation of the bombs becoming one with the sound of crashing buildings. Hitherto, the Iraqis had fired rockets onto Tehran, so this was a new precedent in the War of the Cities. At least 50 civilians were killed and another 150 wounded in the raid. When I arrived there, it was the usual story: the cheaply-made bricks of the walls had crumbled to dust and a four-storey building—home to sixteen families—had been blown to pieces by one of the bombs. A little girl in the block had been celebrating her birthday during the evening and many children were staying the night with her family when the bombs destroyed the girl's home. Angry Iranians gathered at the site next morning and the Revolutionary Guards were forced to fire into the air to clear the road.

In all of March and April of 1985, there were thirteen air raids on Tehran. Now there were thirteen a week, sometimes three a night. Only one Iraqi jet had been shot down—during a daylight raid in March—when an Iranian F-14 intercepted it over the capital. The Iraqi plane crashed into the mountains above Tehran, its pilot still aboard. Yet the Iranians could be forgiven for believing that the world was against them. In July, Iraq began to take delivery of forty-five twenty-seater Bell helicopters from the United States, all capable of carrying troops along the war front. The Reagan administration said, in all seriousness, that the sale of the Super Transports did not breach the U.S. arms embargo on the belligerents because "the helicopters are civilian" and because the American government would "monitor" their use. The sale had been negotiated over two years, during which the United States had been fully aware of Iraq's use of poison gas and its "cleansing" of the Kurds. I would later see eight of these same Bell helicopters near Amara—all in camouflage paint and standing on the tarmac at a military air base.

Yet still the martyrology of war could be used to send fresh blood to the front;

the child soldiers of Iran, it seemed, would be for ever dispatched to the trenches of Kerman and Ahwaz and Khorramshahr, each operation named *Val Fajr*—"Dawn"—which, for a Muslim, also represents the dawn prayer. We had *Val Fajr 1*, all the way up to *Val Fajr 8*. I would walk down to the Friday prayers at Tehran University during the war and I would often see these miniature soldiers—every bit as young and as carefree of life and death as those I had met in the trenches outside Dezful. The inscription on the red bands round the little boys' heads was quite uncompromising. "Yes, Khomeini, we are ready," it said. And the would-be martyrs, identically dressed in yellow jogging suits, banged their small fists against their chests with all the other worshippers, in time to the chants. This cerebral drumbeat—at least ten thousand hands clapping bodies every four seconds—pulsed out across the nation, as it did every Friday across the airwaves of Iranian radio and television. The audience was familiar, even if the faces changed from week to week: mullahs, wheelchair veterans of the war, the poor of south Tehran, the volunteer children and the Iraqi POWs, green-uniformed and trucked to the prayer ground to curse their own president.

Friday prayers in Tehran were a unique combination of religious emotion and foreign policy declaration, a kind of Billy Graham crusade and a weekly State of the Nation address rolled into one. A stranger—especially a Westerner—could be perplexed at what he saw, even disturbed. But he could not fail to be impressed. It was not the prayer-leader who acted as the centrepiece of this great theatre. Often this was Rafsanjani. He could discourse to his ten thousand audience on the origins of the revolution, superpower frustration in Lebanon and further Iranian military successes outside Basra. But this was almost a rambling affair. His hair curling from beneath his *amami* turban and his hand resting on an automatic rifle, Rafsanjani did not stir his audience to any heights of passion.

The congregation that June provided their own sense of unity, their voices rising and falling in cadence with a long chant in Farsi that attempted to integrate Islamic history with the struggle against Iraq, the little boys—some as young as ten—still banging their fists on their heads. Much Farsi verse rhymes and—by rhyming the English translation—these calls to war come across with an archaic, almost Victorian naiveté:

> *We are ready to give our lives, we are ready to go,*
> *And fight as at Kerbala against our foe.*
> *Imam Hossein said those around him were the best;*
> *Now you see with Khomeini we attest*
> *That Hossein and those around him are with us.*
> *In our way lies the honour of Islam*
> *As we follow the word of our Imam.*

There were some, the more youthful *Basiji*, who had already been chosen for martyrdom, thirteen- and fourteen-year-olds kitted out in tiny bright camouflage uniforms. They stood on each side of Rafsanjani's dais holding trays of toffees, each sweet wrapped in crimson cellophane. At a signal, they stepped among the rows of mullahs and war-wounded, the Revolutionary Guards in parka jackets and the elderly, unshaven, dark-suited men from south Tehran, and presented their trays of toffees. Each man carefully took a sweet without looking at the child in front of him, aware of the significance; for this was no interlude between prayers. It was a communion with doomed youth.

Then the boys walked soulfully back to their places on each side of the dais, hair cut short, large dark eyes occasionally turning shyly towards the mass of people. They were, the worshippers were told, aware of their mission. And they stood there, fidgeting sometimes, headbands slightly askew, but feet together at attention as any child might play at soldiers in his home. Rafsanjani made no reference to them. His message was more temporal and the formula was an old one, too familiar for words. Iraq was losing many men at the front. It was also losing much territory. To save the land, it had to lose more men. To save the men, it had to lose more land. So Iraq was losing the war. In just one week, Rafsanjani said, Iraq had lost six more brigades. The worshippers chanted their thanks to their army at the front.

Friday prayers were broadcast through loudspeakers along those very trench lines opposite Basra, piped through loudspeakers so that the Iranian soldiers could hear these ten thousand voices above the shellfire. They called for revenge against Iraq for its air raids on Iranian cities. Rafsanjani added a pragmatic note. "If you want to make yourselves useful," he told his nationwide audience, "you can dig air-raid shelters at home." The young boys stood listlessly on either side of him, perhaps aware that their homes were no longer their immediate concern.

Yet still Iraq hoovered up Iranian prisoners—by the thousand now, just as the Iranians had done before—and ostentatiously presented them to the world's press. Iraq opened a huge prison camp complex for its new POWs in the desert west of Baghdad, around the hot, largely Sunni cities of Fallujah and Ramadi, where there would be no Shia community to offer comfort and help should any of them escape. This was every man's Stalag, complete with a jolly commandant called Major Ali who wanted to introduce us to his model prisoners. The Iranian inmates crowded round us when we arrived, sixteen- and seventeen-year-olds, still in their drab, desert-yellow uniforms, happy prisoners according to the senior Iranian officer at Ramadi, Anish Tusi. How could they be otherwise? the camp's doctor asked. Why, look, they had schools, a library, a tuck shop, table tennis, basketball.

A portrait of Saddam Hussein smiled down benevolently upon them. "If you obey the camp rules, it will be better for you and for everybody else," a poster advised the prisoners in Farsi. "Obey the rules of the camp and the commander of the camp, and you will be treated as friends." Major Ali, smiling in the midday sun, gestured magnanimously towards the canteen. "Just see how well our prisoners eat," he said. We pushed inside a small hut where four Iranian *Basiji*—captured in the Howeiza marshes a year earlier—gently stirred two cauldrons of fish and roast chicken. "This camp is Ramadi Two," the jolly major said, "and all our camps at Ramadi are the same. The prisoners here are in such good conditions that they don't feel the need to escape."

A sharp eye detected an element of hyperbole. Ramadi One, for example, was surrounded by so much glistening barbed wire, 9 metres deep and 5 metres high, that there was scarcely room for the prisoners to lean out of their hut windows, let alone play basketball. Ramadi Three appeared to have none of those friendly tuck shops and prison libraries. Perhaps, too, the inmates of the other camps did not speak in quite such scathing tones of Ayatollah Khomeini. For the boy soldiers in Major Ali's Ramadi Two condemned Khomeini's regime with an enthusiasm that had the Baath party officials nodding sagely and the military police guards grinning with satisfaction.

Mohamed Ismaili, a twenty-year-old from Kerman, for example, admitted he had broadcast over Iraq's Farsi-language radio, telling his parents on the air that "this war is not a holy war." Ahmed Taki, who was only seventeen, was even more specific. A thin, shy youth with his head totally shaved, he was a *Basij* volunteer sent to the battle front a year ago. "I was in school when a mullah came to our class and told us we should fight in the battle against Iraq," he said. "I heard Khomeini say that all young people should go to the front. But now I know it is not a holy war." The stories were all similar, of schoolboys told that God would reward them if they died in battle, a spiritual inspiration that underwent a swift transition once they entered Ramadi Two.

For after uttering such statements, few of these Iranian prisoners could return home under the Khomeini regime, even if the war suddenly ended. Some of them admitted as much. The Iranians, of course, had persuaded hundreds of Iraqi POWs to speak with an identically heretical tongue about Saddam. Perhaps that is what both sides wanted: prisoners who could not go home.

Major Ali seemed unperturbed. "There are maybe sixty or seventy prisoners who still support Khomeini," he said. "That's not many—a very small percentage. Sometimes they mention him at their prayers—we never interfere with their religion." But the major did interfere with their news. The POWs could listen only to the Farsi service of Iraqi radio and television—hardly an unbiased source of information on the war—and the only outside information they were permitted to receive were the letters sent to them by their families through the International Red Cross. "Come and see the barracks," the major insisted. We walked into a hut containing a hundred teenagers, all in that same pallid, greyish-yellow uniform. They stood barefoot on the army blankets that doubled as their beds and the moment an Iraqi army photographer raised his camera, half of them bowed their heads. Their identity concealed, perhaps they could one day go home.

Each military setback for Iraq provided an excuse to break the rules of war once more. Faced with human-wave attacks, there was gas. Faced with further losses, there was a sea war to be commenced against unarmed merchantmen. A new and amoral precedent was set in early 1986—just after the Iranian capture of the Fao peninsula—when Iraq shot down an Iranian Fokker Friendship aircraft carrying forty-six civilians, including many members of the Majlis and the editor of the Iranian daily *Kayhan*, Sayad Hassan Shah-Cherghi.

The Iranians wanted to take journalists to Fao, but I for one refused to take the usual night-time C-130 Iranian military transport plane to the front. If the Iraqis were prepared to attack civilian aircraft, they would certainly shed no tears if they destroyed the international press as it travelled to witness Iraq's latest humiliation. So we took the train again, back down to Ahwaz and the war I had been covering for five and a half years.

Fao had a special meaning for me. It was at Fao that I first saw the Iran–Iraq War with my own eyes. It lay on a spit of land at the bottom of the Shatt al-Arab River, from which the Iraqi army had shelled Abadan. In those days, the Iraqis planned to take the eastern bank of the river and secure it for all time for Iraq. They had not only failed to capture the eastern bank; now they had lost part of the western bank—they had lost the port of Fao itself to the Iranians. The next target for the Iranians would be the great port of Basra with its Shia Muslim population and its straight roads north-west to the holy Shia cities of Kerbala and Najaf. I would be reporting if not from Basra itself, at least from the city in which I started off in this war.

I wasn't happy. There were frequent allusions in Tehran to "setbacks" in the Fao battle. Rafsanjani made a disturbing reference to Iran's need to hold on to Fao, while announcing that there were no plans to advance on Basra—which was odd because, if this was true, why bother to capture Fao in the first place? The Tehran newspapers described how the Iranian forces in Fao were "consolidating" their positions—always a sign that an army is in difficulties. Then when we arrived in Ahwaz and were taken to the nearest airbase for a helicopter ride to the front line, the two American-trained pilots packed the machine with journalists and mullahs—and then aborted the flight. There was too much wind on the river, one of them claimed. There was a bad weather forecast for the afternoon. A cleric arrived to order the men to fly. Gerry "G. G." Labelle of the Associated Press, with whom I had spent years in Beirut during the war, was sitting beside me on the floor of the chopper and we looked at each other with growing concern as the helicopter lifted off the apron, hovered 2 metres above the ground, turned to face due west— and then gently settled back onto the tarmac. Like so many journalists in time of war, we had been desperate to get to the front line—and even more desperate to find a reason to avoid going.*

Part of me—and part of Gerry—was of the "let's-get-it-over-with" persuasion. Hadn't I sped around the Dezful war front on an identical Bell helicopter scarcely a year before? Didn't John Kifner and I admit that we had enjoyed those heart-stopping, shirt-tearing, speed-gashing rides up the wadis and over those hundreds of burned-out tanks? Wasn't that what being a foreign correspondent in war was all about? Going into battle and getting the story and arriving home safe and sound and knowing you wouldn't have to go back next day? We climbed off the heli-

---

*James Cameron, one of my great journalistic heroes, describes precisely the same phenomenon in his brilliant account of the Korean War landing at Inchon in 1950. In the middle of the military landing craft heading for shore, he wrote, was "a wandering boat marked in great letters: 'PRESS,' full of agitated and contending correspondents, all of us trying to give an impression of determination to land in Wave One, while seeking desperately to contrive some reputable method of being found in Wave Fifty."

copter and I could see the relief on the pilots' faces. If they hadn't wanted to go, then there was something very, very wrong with this journey to Fao.

In the grotty hotel in Ahwaz that night, I didn't sleep. Mosquitoes came whining around my face and I ran out of bottled water, and the chicken I'd had for supper made me feel sick. "See you in the morning, Fisky," Labelle had said with a dark smile. Labelle was a New Yorker brought up in Arizona, a fast, tough agency man with a vocabulary of expletives for editorial fools, especially if they pestered him on the wire with childish queries about his reports. "How the fuck do I know if Saddam's fucking son is fighting in this fucking war when I'm on the Iranian front line getting shelled by the fucking Iraqis?" he was to ask me one day. "Sometimes I ask myself why I'm fucking working for this fucking news agency." But Labelle loved the AP and its deadlines and the way in which the wire bell would go ding-ding-ding-ding for a "bulletin" story. "I imagine you know, Fisky, that old AK has bitten the dust at last," he told me over the phone in 1989 when Ayatollah Khomeini died. "I guess that means no more war."

But on that hot and blasted morning in Ahwaz, after the mosquitoes and the sleepless night, I probably needed some of Labelle's saturating humour. As the ministry minders called us to return to the airbase, he gave me one of his mirthless Steve McQueen smiles. "Well, Fisky, I'm told it's a briefing at the usual bunker then a little mosey over the Shatt and a tourist visit to Fao. Lots of gunfire and corpses—should be right up your street." A few days earlier, a German correspondent had suffered a fatal heart attack during an Iraqi air raid on Fao. He and his colleagues had jumped for cover when the planes came in, but when they climbed back on to the truck on which they were travelling, the German had just stayed lying on the ground. The Iranians would later call him a "martyr" of the "Imposed War."

Labelle was right about the bunker. At the airbase, two Bell choppers with Iranian insignia on their fuselages were bouncing on the apron, their rotors snapping at the hot air, and into one of them we bundled, Labelle and I and maybe four other journalists and the usual crop of divines and, nose down, pitching in the wind, we swept over a date-palm plantation and flew, at high speed but only a few metres from the tree tops, towards that front line which all of us—save, I suppose, for our clerical brethren—had by now imagined as a triptych of hell. It was like a switchback, the way we cornered granaries and rose over broken electrical pylons and then fell into troughs of wind and sand and dust and turned like a buzzard over long military convoys that were moving down to the river. Labelle and I gazed down in a kind of wonderment. The sensation was so powerful, the act of flying in such circumstances such madness, that we were slipping into the same syndrome I had experienced at Dezful: To hell with the danger—just look at the war.

I saw the waters of the Shatt to our right—its paleness in the dawn light was breathtaking—and then, below us, coming up fast as if we were in a dive-bomber, a vast Iranian encampment of guns and mortars, earthworks and embrasures and tanks and armoured vehicles in the soggy desert, all swept by sand and smoke. The co-pilot, dressed in the beetle-like headset that the Americans supplied with their Bell helicopters, was scribbling something on a piece of paper as we made our final approach, the machine turning to settle next to a concrete bunker. The crewman was holding onto the machine with his right hand and scribbling with his left and I thought he must be writing an urgent message to the pilot until he turned to us and held up the paper with a grin. "We will kill Saddam," it said in English. Labelle and I looked at each other and Labelle put his mouth next to my ear. "Well, at least *he* knows what he fucking wants," he bellowed.

In the hot, noise-crushed air, I could see through the desert fog and rain that each dugout was decorated with a green banner bearing an Islamic exhortation. A middle-aged, slightly plump soldier ran to me smiling. "Death to England," he shouted and clasped my hand. "How are you? Do you want tea?" Ali Mazinan's bunker carried an instruction by the door, prohibiting the wearing of shoes. I walked in my socks across the woollen-blanketed floor as a 122-mm gun banged a shell casually towards Basra. A muezzin's voice called for prayer. It was like one of my taped CBC reports. "*Allah*-BANG-*akh*-BANG-*bar*," the voice sang amid the contentious gunfire. My map showed I was in what used to be a village called Nahr-e-Had.

Ali Mazinan clutched a wooden ruler in his right hand and pointed it lazily at the lower left-hand corner of a large laminated map, sealed to his dugout wall with minute pieces of Scotch tape. Mazinan wore a pair of thick spectacles with heavy black frames—they were at the time *de rigueur* for all self-respecting mullahs, Hizballah leaders, Revolutionary Guard officers and ministerial clerks—and was himself a Guard commander, one of the very men who captured Fao. "We won because we followed God's orders," he said. I would be meeting Mazinan again; he was to become a symbol to me of rash and dangerous journalistic missions.

How much land had he captured? we asked. Mazinan took a step towards the map, raised the ruler in his right hand again and slapped the palm of his left hand generously over the Fao peninsula. He didn't quite touch Kuwait but his index finger pointed towards Basra and his two middle fingers actually traversed the waterway, two fleshy pontoon bridges that spanned the Shatt above Abadan and gave the Iranians two quite mythical new bridgeheads into Iraqi territory. There was no talk of Iraqi counter-attacks. Instead, Mazinan's ruler flicked towards the map and traced the pale green strips that ran down each side of the riverbank. Both sides in the war produced dates, he said, and began a statistical analysis of their agricultural output. As he was speaking, the ministry men began to hand out dirty little plastic bags containing two tubes of liquid and an evil-looking syringe. "For nerve gas," one of them whispered in my ear, his finger poking the bottle with the green liquid. "For mustard gas," he said, indicating the bottle with the brown liquid. So here we were, kitted out with medical syringes for Saddam's poison gas before landing in Fao, listening to the local military commander as he briefed us on Iraq's 1979 date export production.

It is almost a relief to be told that we will now be taken to Fao. "Just think, Fisky," Labelle says wickedly. "In a short while, you'll have your dateline—'From

Robert Fisk, Iranian-occupied Fao.' " Outside beneath the high bright sun, the sand swirls around our faces, swamping our clothes and eagerly working its way down our collars. There is a clap of sound and the rush of another artillery shell whooshing off towards Basra. I climb into the helicopter as if in a dream. It has a maximum safety load of eight but there are nineteen of us aboard, most of them clamouring mullahs. When I must do something utterly insane, I have discovered, an unidentifiable part of my brain takes over. There are no decisions to be taken, no choices to be made. My brain is now operating independently of me. It instructs me to sit beside the open starboard door of the helicopter gunship and I notice Labelle squatting beside me, notebook in hand. Notebook? I ask myself in my dream. He's going to take notes on this suicide mission?

The growing rhythm of the rotor blades has a comforting effect, the gathering din slowly dampening the sound of the war. The crash of the artillery becomes a dull thump, the wind shears away from the blades, the first nudge off the ground and the sudden rise above the sand and it is the most normal thing in the world. We are immortal. Our helicopter moves round, faces east, then west then east again and then turns at 180 degrees to the ground, levels off and streaks between the artillery. And as we pass through the gun line—our door remains wide open because of the heat—there is a crack-crack-crack of sound and a long pink tulip of fire grows out of the gun muzzles, a barrage as beautiful as it is awesome. One of these big flowers moves inexorably past the starboard side of our chopper and for a moment I think I feel its heat. It hangs for a moment in the air, this magnificent blossom, until we overtake it and a line of palms curls beneath us and then the Shatt al-Arab, so close that the skids of the chopper are only a foot off the water.

I sit up and squint out of the pilot's window. I can see a smudge on the horizon, a black rime across the paleness of the river and a series of broken needles that stand out on the far shoreline. The water is travelling below us at more than a hundred miles an hour. We are the fastest water-skiers in the world, the rotors biting through the heat, sweeping across this great expanse of river; we are safe in our cocoon, angels who can never fall from heaven, who can only marvel and try to remember that we are only human. We fly through the smoke of two burning oil tanks and then Labelle bangs me on my foot with his fist and points to a mountain of mud and filth that the helicopter is now circling and onto which it gingerly, almost carelessly, sets down. "Go, go, go!" the pilot shouts and we jump out into the great wet mass of shell-churned liquid clay that tears off our shoes when we try to move and which sucks at our feet and prevents us even moving clear of the blades when the chopper whups back into the air and leaves us in a kind of noisy silence, Labelle and I trying to hold our trousers up, the mullahs' robes caked with muck and then, as the chopper turns fly-like in the sky, we feel the ground shaking.

It is vibrating as surely as if there is a minor earthquake, a steady movement of the soil beneath our feet. Smoke drifts across the mud and the shell-broken cranes of Fao port—the "needles" I had seen on the horizon—and the litter of burned-out Iraqi armour. Labelle and I struggle through the mire with the mullahs and an ascetic young man who turns out—of course—to be from the Ministry of Islamic

Guidance. We can hear the incoming shells now, a continuous rumble that makes no distinction between one explosion and the next, as if we have pitched up next to a roller-skating rink on which mad children roar endlessly over wooden boards. When we get to the quayside, littered with bits of mouldering bodies and hunks of crane and unexploded shells, Labelle comes staggering towards me, his feet caked in the glue-like mud. We are both exhausted, gasping for breath. "Well, Fisky," he wheezes grimly. "You've got your fucking dateline!" And he shoots me the Steve McQueen grin.

We walk a mile down the waterfront. There are burned oil storage tanks and captured artillery pieces; the earth and concrete are pulverised and there are Iraqi bodies lying in the muck. One soldier has lost his head, another his arms. Both were hit by grenades. Labelle and I find a basin of sand and cement near one of the cranes and shout to the man from the ministry. But as we walk to sit down in the dirt, I see another body in a gun-pit, a young man in the foetal position, curled up like a child, already blackening with death but with a wedding ring on his finger. I am mesmerised by the ring. On this hot, golden morning, it glitters and sparkles with freshness and life. He has black hair and is around twenty-five years old. Or should that be "was"? Do we stop the clock when death surprises us? Do we say, as Binyon wrote, that "they shall grow not old, as we that are left grow old"? Age may not weary them nor the years condemn, but their humanity is quickly taken from their remains by the swiftness of corruption and the jolly old sun. I look again at the ring. An arranged marriage or a love match? Where was he from, this soldier-corpse? A Sunni or a Shia or a Christian or a Kurd? And his wife. He could not be more than three days dead. Somewhere to the north of us, his wife is waking the children, making breakfast, glancing at her husband's photograph on the wall, unaware that she is already a widow and that her husband's wedding ring, so bright with love for her on this glorious morning, embraces a dead finger.

The man from the ministry is full of false confidence. No need to worry about air raids: the Iranian air force has put up fighter cover above Fao to protect the visiting foreign correspondents. Labelle and I look at each other. This is a whopper. No Iranian pilot is going to waste his time protecting the *khabanagoran*—the "journalists"—when his army is under such intense Iraqi fire to the north. A plane flies over at high altitude and the ministry man points up into the scalding heavens. "There you see, just like I said." Labelle and I know a MiG when we see one. It's Iraqi.

Coughing and bouncing on the muck, there then arrived a captured Iraqi army truck, into which we climbed. The second helicopter had brought another group of reporters from Nahr-e-Had who came slogging over the mud. It was tourism time. I could hardly recognise the Fao I'd driven through—in almost equal fear—five and a half years earlier. I could just remember the Iraqi army barracks that now had a banner floating over its entrance, reading "Islam means victory." The city was occupied by thousands of Revolutionary Guards. They waved at us, held up Korans and smiled and offered tea amid the ruins. The very name of Fao had acquired a kind of religious significance. "You will see there are no Iraqis left here," a young Pasdar officer told us, and he was as good as his word. The mud—"Somme-like mud" as I was to write melodramatically in my dispatch that night—consumed Fao, its roads, its gun emplacements, the base of its burning oil tanks, the dull grey and pale brown uniforms of the Iranian fighters, gradually absorbing the Iraqi bodies spread-eagled across the town. One Iraqi soldier had been cut neatly in half by a shell, the two parts of his body falling one on top of the other beside a tank. He, too, had a wedding ring. The Iraqi defences— 3-metre-high sandbag emplacements—stood along the northern end of Fao, their undamaged machine guns still fixed in their embrasures. Was it Iraqi indolence that allowed the Iranians to sweep through the city with so little opposition, even capturing an entire missile battery on the coast? Some of the mud-walled houses still stood, but much of the city had been destroyed. The Iranians displayed several Iraqi 155-mm guns which they were now using to shell the Basra road.

An elderly, grey-bearded man emerged from a ruined house on cue. *Jang ba piruzi,* he shrieked. War till victory, the same old chorus. The rain poured out of the low clouds above Fao, sleeking the old man's face. He wore a ragged red cloth round his forehead and waved a stick over his head. Members of Iran's "War Propaganda Department" had suddenly emerged from the bowels of a factory and turned to their foreign visitors in delight. "See—this is one of our volunteers. He wants to die for Islam in fighting Saddam." An old jeep pulled up alongside the man, a rusty loudspeaker on top. *Jang ba piruzi,* the machine crackled and the old man jumped up and down in the mud. Behind him, red flames rippled across the base of a burning oil storage depot where the Iraqis were shelling the Iranian lines.

Up the road there was now a curtain of fire and a wall of black smoke. From here came that drumbeat of sound, that seismic tremor which we had felt when we landed. The Iranians appeared to be nonchalant, almost childishly mischievous about their victory. On the back of our old Iraqi truck—we all noted the head-high bullet hole through the back of the driver's cab—an Iranian officer stood with a megaphone and pointed across the torrid Khor Abdullah strait towards the Kuwaiti island of Bubiyan. "Kuwait is on your left," he shouted. This was one of the reasons we had been brought to Fao. Here we were, inside Iraq with the Iranians, looking at the Arab country that was one of Iraq's two principal arms suppliers.

Bubiyan is 130 square kilometres of swamp and mud-banks, but a small Kuwaiti guard force was stationed there and the symbolism was obvious. "We hope Kuwait remains responsible during this conflict," the officer shouted again. Many of the newly dug Iranian gun-pits along the road to Um Qasr—a port still in Iraqi hands—had been newly equipped with artillery pointed directly across the narrow strait towards Kuwait. In the ghost town of Fao, the bodies would soon have to be buried if the wind and sand did not reach them first. On a vacant lot, there lay the wreckage of an Iraqi MiG, half buried in the liquid sand, its pilot's head poking from the smashed cockpit. A dead soldier was sitting next to the plane, as if preparing for our arrival.

We spent three hours waiting for our helicopter back to the east bank of the Shatt, Labelle and I sitting once more in our basin of sand with the dead soldier and his wedding ring a few metres away. We also discovered, as Labelle walked through the pieces of broken steel and body parts, puffing on his dozens of cigarettes—part of his charm was that he was a cigarette-smoking asthmatic—that there was a large unexploded bomb lying in the mud near us. "It has been defused," the ministry man lied. Labelle looked at it scornfully and lit another cigarette. "Fisky, it ain't going to explode," he muttered and began to laugh. Only one chopper came back for us. There was a shameful race through the mud by reporters and mullahs to find a place aboard and, as Labelle heaved me above the skids and behind the co-pilot, I saw some desperate soul's boot placed on the shoulder of a mullah, shoving at the scrabbling cleric until he fell backwards into the mud. Then we took off, back across the rippling waters of the Shatt, right over the army base at Nahr-e-Had and on to Ahwaz and the grotty hotel and the Ahwaz post office where there were no phone lines to London. So I called Tony Alloway in Tehran and dictated my report to him and he told me that *The Times* foreign desk had a message for me: the paper was full tonight—would my story hold till tomorrow?

The Iranians had occupied about 300 square kilometres of Iraqi territory south of Basra—their own claim of 800 square kilometres included territorial waters— and they would hold this land for almost two more years until Major-General Maher Abdul Rashed—whose 3rd Army Corps had gassed the Iranians in their thousands outside Basra in early 1985—battered his way back into the city in April 1988. But how did the Iranians capture Fao in the first place? They said it was a mystery known unto God, but years after the war I met the young Iranian war hero—a helicopter pilot—who had swum the Shatt al-Arab at night to reconnoitre the city when it was still under Iraqi control. He had devised an extraordinary plan: to place giant oil pipes beneath the river until they formed an underwater "bridge" upon which the Iranian trucks and fighters and artillery could cross with only their feet and the wheels of their vehicles under water. Thus the Iraqi defenders had seen, in the darkness, an Iranian ghost army walking and driving on the very surface of the water, crying "God is Great" as they stormed ashore. And how did Major-General Rashed retake Fao? "The Iraqis are strangely reluctant to explain how they staged last Sunday's attack," *The Observer*'s correspondent wrote on 24 April 1988. The Iraqis used their usual prosaic means; they drenched Fao in poison gas—as U.S. Lieutenant Rick Francona would note indifferently when he toured the battlefield with the Iraqis afterwards. The writer of the *Observer* report, who had been invited by the Iraqis to enter "liberated" Fao, was Farzad Bazoft. He had just two more years of his life to enjoy. Then Saddam hanged him.

Our train back to Tehran contained the usual carriages of suffering, half troop train, half hospital train, although mercifully without the victims of poison gas. The soldiers were all young—many were only fifteen or sixteen—and they sat in the second-class compartments, their hair shaved, eating folded squares of nan bread or sleeping on each other's shoulders, still in the faded yellow fatigues in which Iran's peasant soldiery were dressed. The wounded clumped on sticks down the swaying corridors, back and forth through the carriages, as if their exertion would relieve their pain.

One boy with cropped hair moved with an agonised face, grunting each time he put his weight on his crutches, staring accusingly at the compartments as if his comrades had personally brought about his ordeal. A youth in khaki trousers with an arm and hand wrapped in bandages sat disconsolately on a box by the carriage door, his back to the open window, hurling bottle caps over his shoulder into the desert north of Ahwaz, giggling to himself in a disturbing, fitful way.

It was a slow train that laboured for seventeen hours up from the Shatt al-Arab battle front, through the great mountains to the plains of Qom, a tired train carrying tired men home from a tired war. When darkness came, some of them left their crammed compartments and slept in the filthy corridors, so that I had to clamber over blankets and boots and backpacks and webbing to reach the broken buffet car with its chicken wings and tea and faded, blue-tinted photographs of the bearded man whom the soldiers had suffered for. They were kind, sad men, muttering "hallo" from their chipped Formica dinner tables and waiting for an acknowledgement before they smiled. "*Jang* good?" one asked pathetically in the corridor. Was war "good"? "Saddam finished," came another darkened voice. "Welcome to Iran."

A hundred kilometres north of Ahwaz, we had stopped at Shushtar, and on a windy platform Labelle and I fell into conversation with a civil engineer who tried to grasp the distance that separated him from his own countrymen. "I do not understand these people who say they want to die. I never knew people like this. These people say that if Khomeini wants them to die, they will die. What can you say to these people?"

The train pulled out of Shushtar late, its diesel engine roaring. And then, quite suddenly, our train climbed into a narrow valley and through the open window there were sheer-faced mountains with white peaks and ice glistening on the rock face, frozen rivers and stars. Just briefly, as we wound round a remote village, I saw a man and a woman standing on the roof of their home looking at us. His arm lay round her shoulders and she had no veil and her hair hung loosely over her shoulders. An ominous ridge—*Zard Kho*, a soldier said it was called, "Yellow Mountain"—towered over our train as it wormed its way through tunnels and along the river bends so tightly that you could see the locomotive's lamp far to the right as it illuminated the boulders and the dark torrents beneath. Here was a land for which these young men might be prepared to die. But for the man in the faded photograph in the buffet car? Yet the soldiers rarely looked out of the windows. A few read magazines, others smoked with their eyes closed, one read a tiny Koran, mouthing the words in silence.

There was an Ahwaz man on the train, a merchant going up to Tehran for a day, a round-faced, tubby figure who bemoaned his economic prospects but said that, yes, he was better off since the revolution because his family had become more religious. What did he think of the war? The man pondered this for a while, staring out at the moonlit waterfalls of the Bala Rud River, an innocent stream which—

like most of the soldiers on the train—would eventually make its way down to the mud of the Shatt al-Arab. "I think the Americans are behind it," he said from the gloom of the corridor. "The great powers want us to be weak but we will win the war." And the price? I asked him. The train heaved itself through a station with a white nameplate that announced a village called Tchamsangar. The man jerked his thumb over his shoulder to the compartments of slumbering young men. "They will pay the price," he said. Then he looked out at the stars and mountains and ice, and he added: "We will all pay the price. We can afford it."

Who would have believed that the United States would be flying anti-tank and anti-aircraft missiles to Iran? I should have done. Back in Lebanon, I had been trying, through the help of an Iranian intermediary, to secure the release of my colleague Terry Anderson, who had been held hostage by a satellite group of the Shia Muslim Hizballah movement for about a year. Anderson was the Associated Press bureau chief in Beirut and my best friend in the city; his apartment was in the same building as mine and we had travelled together on many hair-raising assignments.* The Iranians had started by demanding that I discover the whereabouts of three of their citizens taken hostage in Lebanon in 1982. But when I met with the Iranian intermediary at a Beirut restaurant in late May 1986, he bluntly told me that "his [Anderson's] people are in Tehran." I did not take this seriously. Only five years after the release of the U.S. embassy hostages in Tehran, no U.S. officials would travel to Iran.

I was wrong; doubly so. For quite by chance, I had stumbled onto the first evidence of the arms-for-hostages Iran–Contra scandal in September 1985 when— passing through Cyprus en route from Cairo to Beirut—an old friend who worked in air traffic control at Larnaca Airport tipped me off that a mysterious aircraft flying from Tabriz in northern Iran had been reported missing after it had passed over Turkey and suddenly turned south. My contact told me that Tel Aviv officials had personally telephoned the Cypriot air traffic controllers to confirm that the DC-8 cargo jet was safe on the ground at Ben Gurion airport after suffering "electrical failures."

Officially, however, the Israelis denied any knowledge of the aircraft—a sure sign that the plane was on a secret mission—and when the machine's purported American owners claimed in Miami that they had sold the aircraft the previous month to a Nigerian company, my interest only grew. The DC-8, bearing the U.S. registration number N421AJ, had identified itself to air traffic controllers as belonging to "International Airlines." The plane had originally filed a flight plan to Malaga in Spain, where a friendly airport official said that, although no DC-8 had been seen there, a Boeing 707—also claiming to belong to "International Airlines"—had touched down on 15 September from Tabriz and then taken off en route to another Iranian town which he said was called "Zal"—although no one was able to identify this location.

---

*Anderson would be held in Lebanon for almost seven years. He has recounted his ordeal in *Den of Lions* (Hodder, 1994). The author's account of Anderson's captivity can be found in *Pity the Nation*, pp. 584–627, 654–62.

Even when I first learned of these unorthodox flights, I should have been more suspicious. If Israel was sending or receiving freight aircraft to Iran, it was not exporting oranges or importing caviar. And as Israel's closest ally in the Middle East, Washington must have been involved. Had I connected this with the unexpected admission from my Iranian source that Anderson's "people" were in Tehran, I might have "broken" the Iran–Contra story. But it was a low-circulation magazine in Beirut, *Al-Shiraa*, which did that and the rest—to use the veteran cliché—is history. A naive group of White House officials inspired by the gullible but handsome Marine Lieutenant Colonel Oliver North—egged on by Israeli middlemen—persuaded President Reagan that American hostages in Beirut could be freed by Iran's surrogate allies in the Hizballah in return for a large supply of Hawk anti-aircraft missiles and TOW anti-tank weapons to Iran. Part payment for these arms—which breached Washington's arms embargo on Iran—would fund the right-wing Contra gunmen in Nicaragua whom Reagan and North so admired.

I had first heard North's name three months earlier when, travelling to Switzerland on an MEA flight out of Beirut, I found myself sitting next to Ahmed Chalabi, the senior financial adviser to Nabih Berri, the leader of the Shia Muslim Amal guerrilla movement in Beirut.* Berri had just managed to arrange the release of the passengers and crew of a TWA airliner that had been hijacked to Lebanon and Chalabi repeatedly told me that Berri was worth supporting because "the alternative is Hizballah and that is too awful to contemplate." We had only been in the air for twenty minutes when he said: "Robert, there's someone I'd like you to meet in Washington. His name's Oliver North." A sixth sense, partly induced by my distrust of Chalabi, led me to decline his invitation. But Chalabi must have talked of me to North who—under a scheduled mid-1986 meeting in his diary with Chuck Lewis, an AP staffer in Washington—wrote with his usual flair for inaccuracy "Robert Fiske." Some days later, Lewis called me in Beirut and asked if I would like to take a call from the colonel. I refused.

North's secret trip to Tehran with former U.S. national security adviser Robert McFarlane from 25 to 28 May 1986—a ridiculous but outrageously funny pastiche in which the Americans failed to realise they were participating in a hostage bazaar—did grave damage to the Reagan presidency and to America's relations with the Arab world. For a complete account of this folly, readers must turn to the Tower Commission report on the scandal; but for years afterwards, details of the clandestine weapons deals, in which "sterilised"—unmarked— Israeli aircraft flew missiles into Tabriz and Bandar Abbas airports, continued to emerge. Among the most revealing—because they demonstrate Iran's desperation at the very moment when they had just captured Fao—were extracts of conversations between Oliver North in Frankfurt and an unnamed Iranian government

---

*Chalabi would be convicted in Amman in 1992 for a $60 million banking fraud—which he denied after fleeing Jordan in the trunk of a friend's car—and eleven years later, the same Chalabi, now leader of the CIA-funded Iraqi National Congress, was the Pentagon's choice as the post-Saddam leader of Iraq. He was unceremoniously dropped after a public opinion poll suggested that only 2 per cent of Iraqis supported him. By 2005, however, he had become a deputy prime minister of "new" Iraq.

adviser in late February 1986. Tapes of these calls were made available to America's ABC television in October 1991, and appeared to have been recorded in Israel.

At one point, North appeals for the release of an American hostage in Beirut prior to any further delivery of weapons. Through an interpreter, the Iranian replies: "We must get the Hawk missiles. We must get intelligence reports of Iraqi troops strength. Iran is being destroyed. We need those missiles." At another point, North, trying to smother the reality of the guns-for-hostage arrangement, tells Iranian officials that "if your government can cause the humanitarian release of the Americans held in Beirut . . . ten hours immediately, ten hours immediately after they are released the airplane will land with the remaining Hawk missile parts."

The Americans received one hostage. The Iranians got millions of dollars' worth of missiles and, as Ali Akbar Rafsanjani revealed with smug delight in Tehran, a cake in the shape of a key—baked in Tel Aviv, though the Iranians didn't know this—a brace of Colt revolvers and a Bible signed by Reagan. I was in Tehran for this latest piece of grotesquerie. Rafsanjani had invited us to a press conference on 28 January 1987, where we found him staring at a pile of photocopied documents, each one bearing a small, passport-size photograph of Robert McFarlane. Rafsanjani ostentatiously ignored the dozens of journalists standing around him. He motioned to an aide who spoke fluent English and ordered him to approach an American reporter. He did, and moments later the correspondent, on cue, asked Rafsanjani what evidence he had that McFarlane entered Iran on an Irish passport.

Immediately, Rafsanjani seized the photocopies and brandished them over his head, handing them out like a rug merchant offering free samples. There on the right-hand side was McFarlane's mug-shot and the second page of what was clearly an Irish passport. "They forged them," Rafsanjani's secretary muttered as his master leaned back in his armchair and chuckled, the curl of brown hair beneath his mullah's turban giving him a sly, Bunteresque appearance. But one look at the photocopy convinced me this was no cheap forgery. I doubted very much if the CIA were capable of correctly spelling the colour of McFarlane's hazel eyes in the Irish language—cnodhonna—or even of spelling the Irish for Dublin correctly, Baile Atha Cliath, although the fabrication of McFarlane's fictional Irish name—"Sean Devlin"—lacked imagination. At least they'd made him a Catholic. Immediately after Rafsanjani's press conference had ended, I grabbed a taxi and raced with the photocopy to the Irish embassy, where the chargé, Noel Purcell-O'Byrne, sent it immediately to the Department for Foreign Affairs in Dublin. Far from being a forgery, McFarlane's passport had been one of several recently stolen from the Irish embassy in Athens.

As for the Bible, Rafsanjani positively beamed as he held it up to the multitude of journalists. The handwriting straggled across the page, the "g"s beginning with a flourish but the letters "o" and "p" curiously flattened, an elderly man's handiwork carefully copied from St. Paul's Epistle to the Galatians. "And the Scripture, foreseeing that God would justify the Gentiles by faith," it read, "preached the

gospel beforehand to Abraham, saying 'All the nations shall be blessed in you.' "
But there could be no doubting the signature: "Ronald Reagan, Oct. 3, 1986."

The Bible was sent long after the McFarlane mission. And only a month ago, Rafsanjani announced—he was talking about December 1986—a U.S. State Department official named Charles Dunbar had met Iranian arms dealers in Frankfurt in an attempt to open further discussions with the leadership in Tehran. Incredibly this was true, although Dunbar, who spoke Farsi, would later insist he had told an Iranian official in Frankfurt that arms could no longer be part of the relationship.

As for the Bible, said Rafsanjani, the volume was "being studied from an intelligence point of view," but "we had no ill-feeling when this Bible was sent to us because he [Reagan] is a Christian and he believes in this religion and because we as Muslims believe in Jesus and the Bible. For him, it was a common point between us. We believe that this quotation in the Bible is one that invites people of all religions to unity." The Iranians had refused to accept the gift of revolvers, Rafsanjani said. As for the cake, it had been eaten by airport guards.

But if McFarlane was Sean Devlin, there appeared to have been several Oliver Norths. There was Oliver North the Patriot, whom McFarlane would describe as "an imaginative, aggressive, committed young officer," Reagan's personally approved "hero." There was Oliver North the Man of God, the born-again Christian from the charismatic Episcopal Church of the Apostles who believed that the Lord had healed his wounds in Vietnam and who—in the words of one former associate at the National Security Council—"thought he was doing God's work at the NSC." There was Oliver North the Man of Action, able to work twenty-five hours in every twenty-four, dubbed "the Hammer" by Senator Dan Quayle's buddy Robert Owen, firing off memos from his state-of-the-art crisis centre in the White House.

And then there was Oliver North the thug, drafting directives that authorised CIA operatives "to 'neutralise' terrorists," supporting "pre-emptive strikes" against Arab states or leaders whom America thought responsible for such terrorism, supporting one gang of terrorists—the Contra "Freedom Fighters" of Nicaragua—with the proceeds of a deal that would favour another gang of terrorists, those holding American hostages in Beirut. The Oliver North that the Middle East got was the thug.*

Rafsanjani had only told Khomeini of the McFarlane–North visit after they had arrived in Tehran. Khomeini's designated successor, Ayatollah Hussein Ali Montazeri, was kept in total ignorance—which he seemed to resent more than the actual arms shipments. When the Majlis debated the scandal, Khomeini complained that their collective voice sounded "harsher than that of Israel." He wanted no Irangates in Tehran.

---

*The most comprehensive account of North's life and career, though it makes some naive errors about the Middle East and adopts a pro-Israeli view of the region, is Ben Bradlee Junior's *Guts and Glory: The Rise and Fall of Oliver North* (Grafton Books, London, 1988).

Covering the last years of the Iran–Iraq War, there were times when events moved so quickly that we could not grasp their meaning. And if we did, we took them at face value. However callously Saddam treated Iraqis, it was—because of the war—always possible to graft reasons of national security upon his cruelty. We knew, for example, that Saddam had completed a huge network of roads across 3,000 square kilometres of the Howeiza marshes and was cutting down all the reed bushes in the region—yet we assumed this was a security measure intended to protect Iraq from further Iranian attacks rather than a genocidal act against the Marsh Arabs themselves. Samir Ghattas succeeded in filing a report for the AP out of Baghdad—and there was no more repressive a capital for any journalist—in which he managed to hint to the world of the new campaign of genocide against the Kurds. His dispatch, on 5 October 1987, was carefully worded and partly attributed to Western diplomats—those anonymous spooks who use journalists as often as they are used by them—but anyone reading it knew that atrocities must be taking place. "Iraqi forces have destroyed hundreds of Kurdish villages in northern Iraq and resettled [sic] thousands of Kurds in a campaign against Iranian-backed guerrillas . . ." he reported.

Again, it was Saddam's struggle against Iran—the guerrillas were, of course, Kurdish—which was used to explain this war crime. Ghattas managed to finger Saddam's cousin, Ali Hassan al-Majid—"Chemical Ali" as he was to become known—as the man responsible, and quoted an unnamed ambassador as saying that as many as 3,000 villages might have been razed. He wrote of the dynamiting and bulldozing of villages and, mentioning Kurdish claims that the Iraqis were using poison gas, added that Iraqi television had itself shown a post-air-raid film of "bodies of civilians strewn on the ruined streets." Ghattas also noted that "most diplomats doubt there have been mass killings"—a serious piece of misreporting by Baghdad's diplomatic community.

In the Gulf, Saddam was now trying to end Iran's oil-exporting capacity. In August 1986 the Iraqi air force had devastated the Iranian oil-loading terminal at Sirri Island, destroying two supertankers, killing more than twenty seamen and forcing Iran to move its loading facilities to Larak Island in the choppy waters close to the Hormuz Strait. Almost at once, Iran's oil exports fell from 1.6 to 1.2 million barrels a day. Further Iraqi attacks on Kharg Island, less than a hundred miles from the front lines outside Basra, wreaked such damage that eleven of the fourteen loading berths had been abandoned. By November, the Iraqis were using their Mirage jets to bomb Larak, secretly refuelling in Saudi Arabia en route to and from their target. A series of new Iraqi raids on Iranian cities took the lives of 112 people, according to Iran, which responded with a Scud missile attack on Baghdad that killed 48 civilians, including 17 women and 13 children. Iraq blamed Iran for the hijacking of an Iraqi Airways flight from Baghdad to Amman on 25 December, which ended when the aircraft crashed into the desert in Saudi Arabia after grenades exploded in the passenger cabin. Of the 106 passengers and crew, only 44 survived. That same day, the Iranians staged a landing on Um al-Rassas, the Shatt al-Arab island from which Pierre Bayle and I had made such a close-run escape more than six years earlier.

A series of Iranian attacks on Kuwaiti-flagged ships prompted an offer of protection from the Soviet Union—which immediately provoked an almost identical proposal from President Reagan. Kuwait was now feeling the breath of war more closely. Iran's Silkworm missiles, fired from Fao, were soon to be landing on Kuwaiti territory. One night, I lay in my bed in the Kuwait Meridien hotel, unable to grasp why the windows and doors were perpetually rattling until I realised that the detonation of the Iranian guns outside Basra was blasting across the head waters of the Gulf and vibrating throughout Kuwait city. Almost daily, Kuwaitis would find the corpses of Iranians drifting in on the tide from Fao on the other side of the seaway.

As the Americans pushed in the United Nations for a worldwide arms embargo against Iran, Iranian government officials authorised a massive new weapons procurement programme. Hundreds of pages of documentation from the Iranian National Defence Industry Organisation (INDIO) shown to me by dealers in Germany and Austria listed urgent demands for thousands of TOW anti-tank missiles and air-to-air missiles for Iran's F-14 aircraft. The Iranians were offering $20 million for one order of 155-mm gun barrels, demanding more than 200,000 shells at $350 a shell.

King Hussein of Jordan, frightened that what he called "my nightmare"—the collapse of Iraq and an Iranian victory—might be close, hosted a secret meeting of Saddam Hussein and President Hafez el-Assad of Syria at a Jordanian airbase known only as "H4" in the hope that Assad might be persuaded to abandon his alliance with Iran. Nine hours of talks between the Iraqi and Syrian dictators, whose mutual loathing was obvious to the king, produced nothing more than an arrangement that their foreign ministers should meet, but such was the king's political stature that his failures always reflected well upon him. The worthiness of his endeavours always appeared more important than their results; was he not, after all, trying to bring about an end to the Gulf War by calling upon Arab leaders to unite?

Kuwait now accepted an offer by Reagan to re-flag its tankers with the Stars and Stripes. Washington decided to parade its new and provocative policy by escorting the huge 401,382-ton supertanker *Bridgeton* up the Gulf to Kuwait, a phenomenal story to cover, since television crews from all over the world were hiring helicopters in the United Arab Emirates to follow this mega-tanker to her destination. I flew into Dubai on 23 July 1987 on an MEA aircraft from Beirut and—true to form—the flight-deck crew invited me to sit in the cockpit. And from there, at 10,000 feet over the Gulf, I saw *Bridgeton*, putting half a knot onto her previously acknowledged top speed of 16½ knots while three diminutive American warships described 3-kilometre circles round her hulk. "Mother-hen surrounded by her chicks," I wrote scornfully in my notebook. The Americans closed to battle stations as they passed within range of Iran's Silkworm missiles and the island of Abu Moussa, where Revolutionary Guards maintained a base.

It was a fiasco. South-east of Kuwait and still 200 kilometres from its destination, the *Bridgeton* struck a mine on her port side and the U.S. naval escorts, anxious to avoid a similar fate to that of the *Stark* two months earlier, immediately slunk away in line behind the *Bridgeton*'s stern for protection. On board the escorting missile destroyer USS *Kidd*, the captain ordered armed seamen to the bow of his vessel to destroy any suspicious objects in the water by rifle-fire. Iranian fishing boats had been in the area before the *Bridgeton* was hit, but there was no way of identifying the mine. This permitted the Iranian prime minister, Mir-Hossein Moussavi, to praise the "invisible hands" which had proved the vulnerability of America's "military expedition." With her speed cut to a quarter and her port side number one compartment still taking water, the *Bridgeton* continued what was now a political rather than a commercial voyage towards Kuwait.

It transpired that the Americans had no minesweepers in the area, had not even bothered to look for mines in the 30-kilometre-wide channel where the tanker was struck, and now feared that their own warships were more vulnerable to mines than the vessels they were supposed to protect. Kuwaiti and American officials now sought to load the *Bridgeton* with crude oil, an overtly political act because, as one shipping agent asked contemptuously, "Who in their right mind would load his cargo onto a damaged ship?" The sorry tale of military unpreparedness was only made worse when Captain Yonkers, the U.S. naval officer in command of the three warships—the destroyer *Kidd* and two frigates—blandly admitted that he did not wish to sail back through the same sea lane because "one of the things I do not now have is the capability to defend my ships against mines." This statement was compounded by Rear Admiral Harold J. Bernsen, who told reporters accompanying the convoy that "it may sound incongruous, but the fact is [that] a large ship, a non-warship such as the *Bridgeton*, is far less vulnerable to a mine than a warship . . . if you've got a big tanker that is very difficult to hurt with a single mine, you get in behind it. That's the best defence and that's exactly what we did." Such statements provoked an obvious question: if the U.S. Navy could not protect itself without hiding behind a civilian vessel, how could it claim to be maintaining freedom of navigation in the Gulf?

For newspaper reporters, this was again a frustrating story. From the shore, it was impossible to see the tanker fleets or their escorts. Only by being in the air could we have any idea of the immensity of the conflict. The Iran–Iraq War now stretched from the mountains of Kurdistan on the Turkish border all the way down to the coastline of Arabia, the land that once belonged to the Sherif Hussein of Mecca whom Lawrence had persuaded to join the Allied cause in the First World War. The question was overwhelming: how could we write about this panorama of fire and destruction if we could not see it? The television networks with their million-dollar budgets flew their own planes. They needed pictures. We did not. But during the Lebanese civil war, which was now in its thirteenth year, I had befriended many of the American network producers and crews, often carrying their film to Damascus or Cyprus for satelliting to the United States. And the American NBC network now happily allowed me to fly in their helicopter out of Dubai—provided I acted as an extra "spotter" of ships in the heat-hazed sea lanes.

At least forty warships from the United States, France, the Soviet Union and Britain were now moving into station in the Gulf and the waters of the Gulf of

Oman outside Hormuz; America would have the largest fleet—twenty-four vessels, with 15,000 men aboard—including the battleship *Missouri*. The superlatives came with them; it was one of the biggest naval armadas since the Korean War and very definitely the largest U.S. fleet to assemble since Vietnam. They would all be guaranteeing the "freedom" of Gulf waters for "our Arab friends"—and thus, by extension, Iraq—but they would do nothing to protect Iran's shipping. It was scarcely surprising that the Iranians should announce their own "Operation Martyrdom" naval manoeuvres off the Iranian coast with the warning that "the Islamic Republic will not be responsible for possible incidents against foreign planes and warships passing through the region."

From my seat in NBC's chopper, I now had an aerial platform from which to observe the epic scale of the conflict. Off Dubai, we flew at almost mast height between a hundred tankers and gas carriers, moored across miles of sea, big creamy beasts, some of them, alongside dowdy freighters and rust-streaked tubs packed with cranes and haulage equipment. True, they were under orders to wait for a rise in the spot price of oil rather than to delay their voyages because of Iran's naval threats. But such was the blistering heat across the Gulf that we often blundered into warships in the haze without seeing them. "This is U.S. warship. Request you remain two nautical miles from U.S. warships. Over." The voice on the radio had a clipped, matter-of-fact East Coast accent but retained its unnecessary anonymity. "U.S. warship. Roger. Out."

When we saw them spread across 6 kilometres of gentle swell—three tankers in V-shaped formation, the four warships at equidistant points around them—they looked set for a naval regatta rather than a hazardous voyage up the Gulf. The foreign tankers lying across the ocean around them, some with steam up, others riding the tides for their masters' orders, were somehow familiar, faint echoes of those great convoys that set off through the Western Approaches forty-six years earlier. Three new American-registered ships—*Gas King*, *Sea Isle City* and *Ocean City*—were unremarkable symbols of Washington's political determination in the Gulf; ill-painted, a touch of rust on their hulls, the American flag not yet tied to their stern. The U.S. warships *Kidd*, *Fox* and *Valley Forge* lay line astern and abeam of them, a further American vessel standing picket. There was an element of theatre about it all, this neat little configuration of high-riding empty tankers and their grey escorts, lying in the hot sea, actors awaiting the curtain to rise upon their own farce or tragedy.

There was a small but sudden bright, golden light on the deck of the *Valley Forge* and an illumination rocket moved gracefully up over the sea then drifted untidily back towards the waves. "This is U.S. warship," the voice came back into our headsets, louder and more clipped. "You are inside two nautical miles. Request you clear. Over." Coming up at us from the *Valley Forge* now was a big anti-submarine helicopter, an SH 603 whose remarkable ascent was assisted by two oversize engines. It came alongside, its crew staring at us from behind their shades, a lone hand in the cavernous interior gesturing slowly in a direction away from the ships. Around nine in the morning, a sleeker warship with a long, flat funnel and Exocet missile launchers on her decks sailed slowly across the rear of the American convoy, a British frigate of the Armilla patrol, HMS *Active* keeping the sort of discreet distance from America's latest political gamble that British prime minister Margaret Thatcher would have approved of, at least one nautical mile from the nearest American ship.

Iran's anger was growing.* Its Revolutionary Guards began assaulting un-escorted merchant ships with rocket-propelled grenades, approaching them on power boats from small Iranian islands in the Gulf and then opening fire at close range. All this time, the margins of error grew wider. In mid-August, an American fighter aircraft over the Gulf fired two rockets at an Iranian "plane" that turned out to be nothing more threatening than a heat "band" in the atmosphere. Two weeks later, the Kuwaitis fired a ground-to-air missile at a low-flying cloud because humidity had transformed the vapour into the image of an approaching jet aircraft on their radar screens.

Crowds ransacked the Saudi embassy in Tehran but the "spontaneous" demonstration in protest at the Mecca deaths included some very professional locksmiths who stole $40,000 in cash from the embassy vault. In an effort to damage Iran's economy, the Saudis threatened oil price cuts, although this was a self-defeating weapon. Iraq, like Iran, relied upon its oil exports to help fund its war and, with scarcely any foreign currency reserves, Baghdad now owed $60 billion in foreign debts. Kuwait, one of Iraq's principal financial supporters, would see the $17 million in profits which it had obtained from its additional oil exports since the U.S. re-flagging of its tankers disappear overnight. The Arabs therefore remained as vulnerable financially as they often believed themselves to be militarily.

And now more mines were discovered in the Gulf. One exploded against the supertanker *Texaco Caribbean* off Fujairah in the Gulf of Oman, far outside the Arabian Gulf. The explosion ripped a hole in her number three tank large enough to drive through in a family car. There was more condemnation of Iran, but very little mention of the fact that the ship was carrying not Kuwaiti exports but Iranian crude oil from the offshore terminal at Larak. Like the Iraqi missile attack on the *Stark*—the assault that brought Washington to a frenzy of anger against Iran—now the Iranians were supposedly mining their own supertankers, again displaying that cold contempt for world peace of which they had always been accused. Sure enough, within two days, a British Foreign Office minister was talking of Tehran's "very irrational regime."

Two more mines were found by, of all people, an NBC crew. Steve O'Neil, fly-

---

*And not just because more Western nations were taking Iraq's side in the war. At least 317 Iranians had been killed during the annual *haj* at Mecca on 31 July 1987, shot down—so Iran claimed—by Saudi police. Initial reports suggested that the pilgrims were battered and crushed in a stampede through the narrow, oppressive streets near the great mosque as an Iranian political demonstration became fused with religious emotion and anger at the presence of black-uniformed Saudi security police. In 1986, the Saudis said they had discovered explosives in the bags of 113 male and female Iranian pilgrims, but they had received a promise from President Ali Khamenei that this would not be repeated in 1987.

ing low over the sea in our usual chopper, was looking through his view-finder when he glimpsed a large, spherical black shape disappearing past the helicopter's left skid. He was only a few metres from the water, flying at more than 150 kilometres an hour, but the object was too sinister—too familiar from a dozen war movies—to be anything other than a mine. A few hours later and in almost identical circumstances, a CBS crew found another mine, black-painted like the first but weighted down by a chain. Chinese military technicians working with the Iranians reported that Iran had built a factory near the port of Bandar Abbas to upgrade the old mines they were buying, mines that were originally manufactured—a short pause for imperial reflection here—in Tsarist Russia.

In April, the American warship USS *Samuel Bo Roberts* was almost sunk when it struck a mine while on Gulf patrol. On 21 September, Rear Admiral Bernsen, the same officer who had meekly agreed that his ships were better off using supertankers for their own protection, decided that sonar-equipped "Seabat" helicopters aboard the USS *Jarrett*—by historic chance, a sister ship of the *Stark*—should attack the Iranian naval vessel *Iran Ajr* after it was observed for thirty minutes laying mines in the Gulf 80 kilometres north-east of Bahrain Reporters later taken aboard the 180-foot Iranian vessel—an unromantic nine-year-old Japanese roll-on-roll-off landing craft—saw ten large black-painted mines bearing the serial number "Mo8" near the stern of the boat with a special slide attached to the deck so that the crew could launch them into the sea. Bullet holes riddled the deck, cabins and bridge structure, with trails of blood running along the galleyways. Three of the thirty-man Iranian crew were killed in the attack, two more were missing believed dead and another four wounded, two seriously. Rafsanjani said that the American claim of minelaying was "a lie," but it clearly was not, and the Iranians finally retracted their assertion that the *Iran Ajr* was an innocent cargo vessel. Saddam Hussein now had the satisfaction of knowing that the United States had aligned itself with Iraq as an anti-Iranian belligerent.

The United States followed up on its success against the Iranian minelayer just over three weeks later with a naval strike against two Iranian oil platforms 130 kilometres east of Qatar. Four U.S. guided missile destroyers firing 5-inch guns demolished the Rustum and Rakhsh platforms. Defence Secretary Caspar Weinberger called it a "measured response" to an Iranian missile attack on an American-flagged tanker the previous week. All that initially came from the Iranians was a distant Iranian voice pleading over a crackling radio for a naval ceasefire so that wounded men could be evacuated from one of the burning rigs. The two platforms had been used as military bases by Revolutionary Guards, the Americans claimed. Tehran warned, not very credibly, that the United States would receive a crushing response from Iran.

Because these military actions involved the Western powers, little attention was paid to the far more serious casualties still being inflicted in the land war, even when the victims were clearly civilians. On 12 October, for instance, an Iranian ground-to-ground missile allegedly aimed at the Iraqi defence ministry in Baghdad struck the Martyrs Place Primary School, 20 kilometres from the ministry, as children were gathering for morning class. The explosion killed 29 children and wounded 228 other civilians, a hundred of them critically. Iraq had just recommenced the use of chemical weapons against Iranian forces outside Basra, but this did not prevent the Iraqis capitalising on what they immediately condemned as an example of Iranian "bestiality."

BASRA HAD COME TO DEFINE this last and savage stage of the war. For the Iranians, it remained the gateway to southern Iraq, the very roads to the shrines of Kerbala and Najaf and Kufa beckoning to the Iranian soldiers and Pasdaran who were still boxed into the powdered ruins of Fao. Iraq was still able to maintain an army of 650,000 men spread through seven brigades from Suleimaniya down to the front line outside Fao. Presidential guards and special forces made up 30,000 of these troops and the "popular army" of conscripts and "volunteers" at least 400,000. An "Arab army" of 200,000, many of them Egyptians, constituted the rest of Iraq's strength. But by early 1987 the Iranians had massed a force of 600,000 just opposite Basra. It seemed inevitable that Field Marshal Saddam Hussein, President of Iraq, Prime Minister, Secretary General of the Regional Command of the Arab Baath Socialist Party, Chairman of the Revolutionary Command Council and friend of America, would have to make another of his famous retreats.

And when the Iranians did break through in January 1987 and made their dash for Basra, they wanted to show us. At night, we were taken up behind the Iranian lines, our bus crunching through wadis as the skyline was lit by artillery fire, hour after hour of grinding through the dark amid thousands of troops moving up to the line, the same old approaching fear of death and wounds settling over us. A few months earlier, a ministry minder had led a Reuters photographer into a minefield. Both were blown to pieces. The Iranians proclaimed the Reuters man a "martyr" and were only just prevented from sending his widow a glossy book of coloured photographs depicting other martyrs in various stages of dismemberment and putrefaction.

I spent the night on the sand floor of a deep, white-washed underground bunker. We were given juice and *dooq*—cold drinking yoghurt—and nan bread and cheese and tea, and I lay, as usual, sleepless beneath my blanket. Before six next morning, the Revolutionary Guards arrived to take us all to visit "the front" and I climbed wearily up the steep steps towards the sun and heat and the roar of gunfire and the heavy crumping sound of incoming shells. Dezful was Cinema-Scope. Fao was devastating. But this was an epic with a cast of thousands. Tanks and trucks and heavy guns were pouring westwards with hundreds of Iranian troops sitting on armour and lorries or marching alongside them. To my horror, I noticed that our escort would be none other than Ali Mazinan, the crazed and bespectacled Revolutionary Guards officer with an obsession about Iraqi date exports who had sent me off on the lunatic helicopter flight to Fao. He advanced towards me now with the warmest of smiles, embraced me in a grizzly-bear hug and kissed me on both cheeks. Never was Coleridge's "willing suspension of disbelief" more necessary to a correspondent. Poetic faith was about the best there was to cling on to in the next few hours.

The Fish Lake was a stretch of desert north of the Karun River but west of Shalamcheh—the border post where I had been partially deafened by the Iraqi gun batteries shelling Khorramshahr more than six years earlier—but now Shalamcheh was back in Iranian hands and its vast army was moving towards the Shatt al-Arab River and the city of Basra. Once more, I was in "Iranian-occupied Iraq," but in a desert that the Iraqis had flooded as they retreated. The Iranians were now advancing on a series of dykes above the waterlogged desert, under intense and constant shellfire from Iraqi artillery whose gunners quickly worked out their trajectories to hit the dykes.

The Iranians provided another army truck for the press, a Japanese open-top lorry with a pile of old steel helmets in one corner that we could wear when we reached the battlefield. Between earthworks and dugouts and lines of trenches we drove, the marching soldiery of the Islamic Republic walking beside us, grinning and making victory signs and holding up their rifles like conquering heroes. I suppose that's what they were, the victims at last overcoming their aggressors, the winners—or so they thought—after so many years of pain and loss. Over to my left, as we climbed onto a plateau of rock and sand, I suddenly saw the shining white warheads and fuselages of a battery of Hawk missiles, gifts from Oliver North, along with the spare parts which had now turned them into a new and formidable air defence for the victorious Iranian army.

And then we were on the causeway, a long, narrow, crumbling embankment of sand surrounded by lagoons of water filled with still-burning Iraqi tanks, overturned missile launchers, half-submerged Iraqi personnel carriers and dozens of bodies, some with only their feet protruding above the mire. Far more fearful, however, were the whine and crash of incoming shells as the Iraqis directed their artillery onto the dykes. I squeezed the old Russian helmet the Iranians had given me onto my head. In front of us, an Iranian truck burst into pink fire, its occupants hurling themselves—some with flames curling round their bodies—into the water. The convoy backed up and our lorry came to a halt. We would hear the splosh in the water beside us as the next shell hit the lagoon, sending a plume of water into the sky, cascading us with mud and wet sand.

Ian Black of *The Guardian*, one of the sanest reporters with whom one could go to war, was sitting opposite me on the truck, looking at me meaningfully through his big spectacles. "This," he said, "is *bloody* dangerous." I agreed. Around us, on little hillocks amid the great green-blue lakes of water, Iranian gunners fired off 155-mm shells towards Basra, shouting their excitement, throwing their arms around each other. The young Iranian boys did not even bother to keep their helmets on amid the shellfire. They lounged around the earthworks of the captured Iraqi front lines, smoking cigarettes, hanging out their washing, waving good-naturedly at us as the Iraqi artillery rounds hissed overhead. The explosions even made them laugh. Was it contempt for death or merely their reaction to our fear?

Another big splosh and Black and I hunched our shoulders, and sure enough there was an eruption of water and earth behind me and a downpour of muck and brackish liquid descended on us. The shells came five at a time, zipping over the breakwaters. On a similar trip a few hours earlier, the British correspondent of *U.S. News and World Report* had summed up his feelings under fire along the dykes with eloquent understatement. "I don't think," he said, "that I could take more than a day of this." The road surface was only a few feet above the water but the causeway seemed to stretch out to the crack of doom, a dwindling taper of sand that reached a horizon of fire and smoke. The strap of my helmet suddenly snapped and it slid off my head and bounced onto the floor of the truck. I picked it up and stuck it back on my head, holding it on with my left hand. But what was the point? If I was hit on the head, my fingers would be chopped off. Black was frowning. We were all concentrating. The idea of instant death was indeed a concentrating experience. And all the while, the army of boys and elderly volunteers and Revolutionary Guard commanders tramped past us in the sun as we ground slowly towards the battle front.

"War till victory," they kept screaming at us from the mud. Would I never hear the end of this? And when we had driven for perhaps 3 kilometres along those earthworks and reached and passed Shalamcheh, the ghastly Mazinan suddenly appeared beside our truck, pointing in a demented way towards the north-west. "Basra," he kept shouting. "BASRA! BASRA! BASRA!" Black and I peered through the smoke and flames and the waterspouts that were now rising eerily around us, volcanic eruptions that would carry the dark brown mud high into the sky, where it would hover for a second before collapsing on us. Black was looking at me again. A bit like *The Cruel Sea*, I said stupidly. "Much worse," he replied.

Mazinan was obsessed. "Come, come," he kept ordering us, and we crawled up to an embankment of mud that physically shook as the Iranians fired off their 155s from the waterlogged pits behind me. I peered over the lip and could see across an expanse of bright water the towers and factory buildings of Basra's suburban industrial complex, grey on the horizon, silhouetted for the gunners by the morning sun. A mob of boys stood around us, all laughing. "Why be afraid?" one asked. "Look, we are protected. Saddam will die."

A few hours earlier, Saddam Hussein had declared that the causeway here would be turned into a "furnace"—Black and I had a shrewd suspicion he meant what he said—in which the Iranians would perish. Yet this boy's protection consisted of just one red bandanna wound tightly round his head upon which was inscribed in yellow God's supposed invocation to destroy the Iraqi regime. "Good God," said God, I remembered God saying in John Squire's poem, "I've got my work cut out." Nor was the First World War a cliché here. With at least a million dead, the battle of Fish Lake was the Somme and Passchendaele rolled into one but with the sacrifice turned maniacally cheerful by Mazinan and his comrades. One small boy—perhaps thirteen or fourteen—was standing beside a dugout and looked at me and slowly took off his helmet and held a Koran against his heart and smiled. This was the "Kerbala 5" offensive. And this boy, I was sure, believed he would soon be worshipping at the shrine of Imam Hossein. It was, in its way, a sight both deeply impressive and immensely sad. These young men believed they were immortal in the sight of God. They were not fearless so much as heedless—it was this that made them so unique and yet so vulnerable. They had found the key, they had discovered the mechanism of immortality. We had not. So he was brave and laughing, while I was frightened. I didn't want to die.

The mudfields around us were littered with unexploded bombs, big, grey-finned sharklike beasts which had half-buried themselves in the soggy mass when the Iraqi air force vainly tried to halt "Kerbala 5." "We are winning," a white banner proclaimed above a smashed dugout whose walls were built with empty ammunition boxes and shell cases. Who could doubt it? The Iraqis had five defensive lines before Basra and the Iranians had overrun the first three. The Iraqi T-72s that had been captured by the Iranians were being dug back into their own revetments but with the barrels traversed, firing now towards Basra.

Mazinan claimed—truthfully—that the Revolutionary Guards had won this battle, that the regular Iranian army provided only logistics and fire support, that Iraq had lost 15,000 dead and 35,000 wounded, that 550 tanks had been destroyed and more than 1,000 armoured vehicles. But the Iranians, I unwisely protested, were still a long way from the centre of Basra. Mazinan's eyes widened behind his giant spectacles. "Come," he said. And I was propelled by this idiotic giant—who was in reality rather too rational when it came to religious war—towards another vast embankment of mud. We struggled towards the top of it. And down the other side. It was the third Iraqi line and we were now in front of it. Bullets buzzed around us. I remember thinking how much they sounded like wasps, high-speed wasps, and I could hear them "put-putting" into the mud behind me. Mazinan clutched my right arm and pointed towards the pillars of black smoke that hung like funeral curtains in front of us. "Do you see that building?" he asked. And through the darkness I could just make out the outline of a low, rectangular block. "That," Mazinan cried, "is the Basra Sheraton Hotel!"

The Iranians were using their artillery at three times the Iraqi rate of fire, the muzzle flashes streaking out across the water. Still the boys and the bearded old men lounged along the causeway, sometimes playing taped religious music from loudspeakers. Back on the truck, Black and I looked at each other. Brent Sadler and a crew from ITN had been taken to view a pile of Iraqi bodies in a swamp churned up by shells. "Very dangerous but I've got no option," Sadler told me with just a twinkle of death in his eye. "It's television—you know, we've got to have pictures." Sadler would survive, he always did. But Black wasn't so sure. Nor was I. "We would like to go now," I hollered at Mazinan. He raised his eyebrows. "Go," Black shouted at him. "We want to go, go, go." Mazinan looked at us both with something worse than contempt. "Why?" he roared. Because we are cowards. Go on, say it, Fisk. Because I am shaking with fear and want to survive and live and write my story and fly back to Tehran and go back to Beirut and invite a young woman to drink fine red wine on my balcony.

Mazinan nodded at the driver. Then he raised his right hand level with his face and closed and opened his fingers, the kind of wave one gives to a small child. Bye-bye, bye-bye, he said softly. He was mimicking the mother taking leave of her babies. And so our truck turned left off the dyke and chuntered down a long causeway towards the ruins of Khorramshahr.

In a factory warehouse, a thousand Iraqi prisoners were paraded before us, including Brigadier General Jamal al-Bayoudi of the Iraqi 506th Corps, who described how the Pasdaran and the *Basiji* clawed their way through swaths of barbed wire 60 metres deep to reach their third line of defence.* The Iraqis halfheartedly chanted curses against the very Iraqi leader for whom they had been fighting only a few days before. Several smiled at us when the guards were not looking. One of them muttered his name to me. "Please tell my family I am safe," he said softly. "Please tell them I did not die in the battle." A week later, I gave his name to the International Red Cross, who promised to relay his message to his parents.†

I returned from the battle of Fish Lake with a sense of despair. That small boy holding the Koran to his chest *believed*—believed in a way that few Westerners, and I include myself, could any longer understand. He knew, with the conviction of his own life, that heaven awaited him. He would go straight there—the fast train, direct, no limbo, no delays—if he was lucky enough to be killed by the Iraqis. I began to think that life was not the only thing that could die in Iran. For there was, in some indefinable way, a death process within the state itself. In a nation that looked backwards rather than forwards, in which women were to be dressed in perpetual mourning, in which death was an achievement, in which children could reach their most heroic attainment only in self-sacrifice, it was as if the country was neutering itself, moving into a black experience that found its spiritual parallel in the mass slaughter of Cambodia rather than on the ancient battlefield of Kerbala.

I would spend days, perhaps weeks, of my life visiting the cemeteries of Iran's war dead. Less than a year after the capture of Fao—the offensive that was supposed to lead Iran into Basra and then to Kerbala and Najaf—I was standing in the little cemetery of Imam Zadeh Ali Akbar on the cold slopes of the Alborz Mountains at Chasar, where they had been preparing for the next Iranian offensive. The

---

*A measure of the Iranian victory may be gained from the number of senior officers captured in the attack. Among them were Col. Yassir al-Soufi, commander of the 94th Infantry Brigade, Lt. Col. Mohamed Reza Jaffar Abbas of the 7th Corps' Rangers Special Forces, Staff Lt. Col. Walid Alwan Hamadi, second-in-command of the 95th Infantry Brigade, Lt. Col. Madjid al-Obeydi, second-in-command of the 20th Artillery regiment, Lt. Col. Selim Hammoud Arabi, commander of the 16th Artillery Regiment and Lt. Col. Jaber Hassan al-Amari, commander of the 3rd Infantry battalion, 19th Brigade. From their names, at least three of these officers were Shia Muslims.

†A captured pilot from the Iraqi 49th Air Force squadron at Nasiriyah, Abdul Ali Mohamed Fahd, said that Iran's air defences had improved significantly over the previous eleven months and forced Iraqi bombers to fly at much higher altitudes. His MiG-23 was apparently shot down by one of Oliver North's Hawk missiles. The same pilot also claimed that Soviet, French and Indian technicians were advising the Iraqi squadrons at Nasiriyah and that the Iraqis often used a Kuwaiti airbase to refuel during their bombing missions against Iranian oil tankers.

bulldozers had dug deep into the icy graveyard and there was now fresh ground—two football pitches in length—for the next crop of martyrs.

The thin, dark-faced cemetery keeper was quite blunt about it. "Every time there is a new Kerbala offensive, the martyrs arrive within days," he said. "We have three hundred already over there and twelve more last week. The graves of ordinary people we destroy after thirty years—there is nothing left—but our martyrs are different. They will lie here for a thousand years and more." His statistics told a far more apocalyptic story than might have appeared; for Chasar—distinguished only by an ancient, crumbling shrine—merely contained the war dead of one small suburb of north Tehran. Spread across the country, those 312 bodies become half a million, perhaps three-quarters of a million, perhaps far more. In the Behesht-i-Zahra cemetery outside the city, they lie in their tens of thousands.

They are nearly all young and they are honoured, publicly at least, with that mixture of grief and spiritual satisfaction so peculiar to Shia Islam. Take Ali Nasser Riarat. He was only twenty-one when he was killed at the battle of the Majnoon Marshes west of Howeiza in 1986; his photograph, pinned inside a glass-fronted steel box above his remains, shows him to have been a slim, good-looking youth with a brush moustache. His gravestone contains a message to his father, Yussef, and to his mother:

> Don't cry mother, because I am happy. I am not dead. I remember all that you have done for me. You gave me milk and you wanted me to sacrifice my life for religion. Dear father, don't cry and don't beat yourself because you will be proud when you realise I am a martyr . . .

Several other inscriptions express similar sentiments. Even the flowers laid on the grave of a young soldier called Zaman near the cemetery-keeper's hut carry such a declaration. "We congratulate you upon your martyrdom," it says, signed by "students and staff of the Tehran University of Science." Could there really be such joy amid the graves of Chasar? Those cruel steel boxes above the dead contain fresh flowers and plastic doves and real steel-tipped bullets, but the snapshots show the young men who die in every war, laughing in gardens, standing with parents outside front doors, perched on mountain tops, holding field binoculars. Lutyens would have understood the waste of twenty-five-year-old Sergeant Akbazadeh, who died in 1982 in Khorramshahr; of Mehdi Balouoch—a hand grenade carved on his gravestone—who was twenty-three when he was killed in Zakdan; of Mehrdrodi Nassiri, aged twenty-five, who was shot at Mehran in July of 1986. A twenty-four-year-old who died outside Basra a few days before—perhaps in the same battle of Fish Lake which I had witnessed—was pictured with his two little girls, one with her hair in a bow, curled up in his arms before he went to the front.

Was there no sense of waste? A man in his forties, bearded, unsmiling, shook his head. What of Owen's question about doomed youth? What passing-bells for these who die as cattle? "I only met one man who spoke like that," the Iranian said.

"He was an old man in hospital. He had his legs and one arm blown off by a bomb near Ahwaz. He had lost an eye. The bomb had killed his wife and children, his sisters and his brothers. He said he thought Saddam and Khomeini were both out for what they could get and did not care about their people. But he was the only man I ever heard who said those things."

Outside the chilly, intimate cemetery, there stood a shop selling books about martyrdom. Inside was a young Revolutionary Guard who had that day returned from the southern front. His name was Ali Khani. What did his parents feel when he was away? "I have three brothers as well as me at the front," he replied. "My mother and father know that if I am martyred, I will be still alive." But did his parents not wish him luck—not tell him to "take care" when he left for the war? "No," he said, a slight smile emerging at such Western sentiment. "They believe it is God's wish if I die." But would his parents not cry if he died? Ali Khani thought about this for a long time. "Yes, they would," he said at last. "And so did the Prophet Mohamed, peace be upon him, when his baby son Ibrahim died. But this is not a sign of weakness or lack of faith. It is a human thing."

# CHAPTER EIGHT

# Drinking the Poisoned Chalice

*. . . the sun shone*
*As it had to on the white legs disappearing into the green*
*Water; and the expensive delicate ship that must have seen*
*Something amazing, a boy falling out of the sky,*
*Had somewhere to get to and sailed calmly on.*

—W. H. Auden, "Musée des Beaux Arts"

IT IS A LONG WAY FROM WASHINGTON to the Mossan Food and Fruit Cold Store in Bandar Abbas. The Pentagon's clinical details of the last flight of Iran Air IR655 on 3 July 1988 cannot reflect the appalling human dimension of the charnel house in which I am standing, where three-year-old Leila Behbahani lies in her cheap, chipboard coffin. She was a very little girl and she still wears the small green dress and white pinafore in which she died three days ago when the United States Navy missile struck the Iranian Airbus over the Gulf, killing Leila and her 289 fellow passengers. She was pulled from the water only minutes after the explosion and she looks as if she has fallen asleep, her left wrist decorated with two bright gold bangles, her feet still in white socks and tiny black shoes. Her name is scrawled in crayon on the coffin lid that is propped up beside her. Her equally small brother—a dark-set, handsome boy with very short black hair—lies a few inches from her, cradled inside another plywood coffin.

Only the ice in their hair proves that they are awaiting burial. The central cold storage hall of the fruit depot is strewn with the same pale wooden coffins. "Yugoslav," it says on one. "Still unknown" on another. In a corner, a middle-aged man is peering at some corpses. He recognises three members of his own family— two he cannot find—and an Iranian in a pair of jeans trundles into the hall with three more coffins piled haphazardly on a trolley. There are fifty-eight intact corpses here, fringed by a row of human remains so terrible that they could only be described with accuracy in a doctor's report or a medical journal. Limbs, torsos, heads—eyes open—lie half-folded in blankets and plastic sheets. Iranian Pasdaran, normally the most voluble of revolutionaries, are reduced to silence. "Come, you are a lady," one says to a female reporter. "Come and see this woman who was killed." There is tampering in a coffin and a woman's face, pale with wet hair, emerges through the plastic sheets.

Yet if this might seem in Western eyes a gesture of bad taste, an intrusion into grief, there is no avoiding some terrible conclusions: that so many of the dead—sixty-six—were children, that some of the coffins are so very small, that one twenty-year-old girl lies in the same wooden box as her year-old baby. Fatima Faidazaida was found in the sea three hours after the Americans shot down the plane, still clutching her child to her breast; which is why the baby, Zoleila-Ashan, is beside her now. "That is why we put them in together," an Iranian official says quietly. "We found them together so they must stay together."

I come across another middle-aged man clutching a handkerchief to his face, walking unsteadily through the cold store, looking for his relatives. Several corpses he rejects; though terribly disfigured by the blast of the two American navy missiles that destroyed the aircraft, the bodies are clearly unknown to him. Only later does he discover his sister and brother-in-law beneath some plastic and kneel to touch their faces gently, weeping as he does so. Just a few hours ago, President Reagan has stated publicly that he has apologised enough for killing all these innocent people. His expressions of regret, he tells the world, are "sufficient."

It is extraordinary here in the boiling southern Iranian port of Bandar Abbas how the official explanations of condolence, sorrow and self-absolution in Washington seem both hollow and opportunistic. What in Washington is called a "tragedy"—as if some natural disaster overwhelmed these dead airline passengers around me—seems in Bandar Abbas to be an outrage. In the United States, it was possible for newspaper editors to suggest that the Airbus might have been on a suicide mission, that the pilot was deliberately trying to crash his passenger-packed airliner into the American frigate that shot it down. Even my own paper, *The Times*, has disgracefully made the same claim. But in Bandar Abbas, where the pilot's friends and colleagues have spoken openly to me without official prompting, these suggestions are offensive, obscene. An entire family of sixteen Iranians were on the Airbus, travelling to a wedding in Dubai, the children in their wedding clothes. They are still dressed in the same bright, joyful colours in the coffins in the cold store as Reagan sends a letter to Congress announcing that he now regards the matter of the Airbus destruction as "closed."

We walk in churchlike silence down the aisles of the dead, Westerners with no excuses, cameramen filming the dead in long-shot for audiences who will not be able to accept—to "cope"—with the reality of what the U.S. Navy has just done. Only those passengers obliging enough to have died without obvious wounds, or who were lucky enough to have been killed without their faces being disfigured by the explosion of the two Standard missiles fired at their plane by the USS *Vincennes*, would be honoured with photographs in Western newspapers. Our response was predictable: we didn't mean to do it; the destruction of the airliner was a mistake. But it was Iran's fault.

I can remember so well that phone call from *The Times*. I am holidaying in Ireland that bright warm summer Sunday, and I have spent the morning in Dublin, talking to John Grigg, the historian who will be writing volume VI of the history of *The Times* from 1966 to 1981, during which Rupert Murdoch took over the paper. Over coffee, I recall for Grigg my four years as a correspondent in Northern Ireland and—although it falls outside his volume—the infamous story of the "Hitler diaries." Murdoch had been bamboozled into serialising these totally fictitious papers—supposedly the Nazi Führer's ravings on Chamberlain, his mistress Eva Braun, *et al.*\*

"I'm sure you know what's happened," the duty desk editor says from London. "The editor wants to know how soon can you get to the Gulf." Every reporter hates that moment. What had "happened"? I hadn't listened to the news that morning. Sometimes it is possible to bluff this out, to reply vaguely and then hurriedly tune to the radio news to find out what I am supposed to know. This was not one of those occasions. "The Americans have shot down an Iranian passenger jet over the Gulf," came the voice over the phone. "The American ship was called *Vincennes* and it fired two heat-seeking missiles at the aircraft . . . They say it was a mistake." Well, they would, wouldn't they? I mean, the Americans could hardly claim that the airliner was packed with "terrorists." Or could they? Sure enough, the Pentagon was already suggesting that the pilot might have been trying to fly his plane into the American warship. The American ship's captain would travel to Bahrain to explain how he had fired at a civilian plane.

This was just the sort of "tragedy" I had predicted in my dispatch to *The Times* from the Gulf in May 1987, an American warship panicked into believing that a civil airliner was an attacking jet. What was it the *Broadsword*'s lieutenant commander had told me that sweltering night as his British radar operators were checking the transponder numbers over the Gulf? "If you want to avoid burning up six sheikhs in their private jet, you've got to be bloody careful." But this was not a private jet. This was a packed airliner which had been blasted out of the sky. I flew to Paris with Lara Marlowe, who would write a brilliant, scathing dispatch for the *International Herald Tribune* on the slaughter. Harvey Morris, now of *The Independent*, was at Roissy Charles de Gaulle airport, dragging on his usual cigarettes. "Now they've really copped it," he said, without explaining who "they" might be. The Iranians or the Americans? We would soon find out. We took the Emirates flight to Dubai—the nearest non-Iranian city to the scene of the mass aerial killing.

It was an eight-hour flight, hot and stuffy and crowded. In front of me sat a

---

\*The historian Hugh Trevor-Roper, Lord Dacre, had initially guaranteed their authenticity. I was passing by the foreign desk in London en route back to Beirut when the Reuters "bulletin" bell began to ping in the wire room and Ivan Barnes seized the copy. "Ah-ha!" he bellowed. "The diaries are forgeries!" The West German government, as it then was, stated that a forensic analysis confirmed the documents were postwar.

"Why don't you go and tell Charlie?" Ivan suggested. "I think Murdoch's with him at the moment." Barnes, who like me had always suspected the diaries were false, sat back with a wolfish smile on his face. "Let me know how they react," he said. I padded round to the editor's office and there was Charles Douglas-Home behind his desk and, on a sofa to his right, Rupert Murdoch. "Well?" Charlie asked. We had all been expecting a statement from the German government that morning. "They say they're forgeries, Charlie," I said, looking at the editor and pretending to ignore the owner of the newspaper. Charlie looked at his boss and so did I. "Well, there you go," Murdoch giggled after scarcely a moment of reflection. "Nothing ventured, nothing gained." That, I tell Grigg, also pretty much sums up American policy in the Middle East.

reporter for a London radio station, writing feverishly into his notebook. He was, he said, drafting his first report so that he could go on air the moment our flight landed next morning. And what, I couldn't help asking—since he had not even arrived in Dubai to make a single inquiry—would be the thrust of this dispatch? "The danger of the Iranians using suicide boats to take revenge on the Americans," he said. He readily admitted he was making this story up on the plane, but said he also planned to write a report suggesting that the Iranians would try to assassinate the captain of the *Vincennes*. When I asked if he shouldn't also be questioning American naval competency, he replied, "We might be challenged on that story." Already the machinery was turning. The Americans who had destroyed the passenger jet were the potential victims; the real victims—all of them dead—were the aggressors.

Iran Air flight IR655, piloted by Captain Mohsen Rezaian, had taken off from Bandar Abbas on a scheduled passenger flight to Dubai with 290 passengers. The Americans, as usual, got their version out first, although it would change many times over the coming days. We were told that the Iranian Airbus was not on a normal flight path, then that its pilot failed to respond to warnings from the Aegis-class cruiser USS *Vincennes*, then that the plane was diving towards the American warship and that its identification transponder was not working. Captain Will Rogers the Third, the captain of the *Vincennes*, believed—according to the Pentagon—that he was under attack by an Iranian F-14 Tomcat fighter aircraft. But the American story began to crumble when the Italian navy and another American warship, the frigate *Sides*, confirmed that the plane was climbing—not diving to attack—at the time of the missile strike.

So the story changed again. The Pentagon now said that the plane's transponder might not have been giving out correct signals. Later, this was subtly changed; the transponder was identifying the Airbus A300B2 as a military aircraft, because the Iranians had earlier changed the coding when they used the same plane to take troops to the war front—and had forgotten to revert to the civilian code afterwards. Why the Iranians would have used the Airbus to conceal their troop movements from the Iraqis but blown their own cover by obligingly giving the aircraft a military identification that would reveal its true purpose was never explained by the Pentagon. The all-important issue was to justify the frightfulness of what had happened, to talk of the "tragedy" of the passenger jet's destruction. Tragedies are forgivable. The advantage for the Americans was that the Iranian side of the story would never be fully told—because those most intimately involved were all dead.

In Dubai, I went straight to the British air traffic controllers who had so often helped me during the "tanker war." They had heard the radio traffic over the Gulf on that fatal Sunday morning—and their story was horrifying. For weeks, they told me, they had been appalled at the apparent lack of training and efficiency of U.S. naval personnel challenging civilian aircraft. The pilots of airliners on scheduled flights down the Gulf from Kuwait were being repeatedly and aggressively challenged by American warship crews who seemed not to know that they were cruising beneath established air lanes.

In one incident—well known to the controllers but kept secret from the press—a U.S. frigate had stationed itself off the Emirates coast and radio-challenged every civilian flight approaching Dubai International Airport. In desperation, the British duty controller at the airport called the U.S. embassy in Abu Dhabi and told American diplomats to instruct the ship to move away because it was "a danger to civil aviation." Civilian helicopter pilots off the coast had often complained that American warships challenged them on the wrong radio frequencies. The controllers in Dubai could hear some of the U.S. Navy's traffic. "Robert, the Americans knew at once that they'd hit a passenger airliner," one of them told me quietly. "There was another American warship close by—we have its coding as FFG-14. Its crew reported seeing people falling at great speed out of the sky."

I sat behind the Dubai control tower thinking about this. Yes, the passengers would all fall out of the sky like that, over a wide area, together, in clumps, in bits, from 10,000 feet it seemed. I could imagine the impact with the sea, the spouts of water, some of the passengers—no doubt—still fully conscious all the way down. Three days later, in the emergency Bandar Abbas mortuary, I would look at Fatima Faidazaida and realise with horror that she must have been alive as she fell from the heavens, clutching her baby as she tumbled and spilled out of the sky in the bright summer sun, her fellow passengers and chunks of the Airbus and burning fuel oil cascading around her. And she held on to her baby, knowing—could she have known?—that she must die.

From Dubai that Sunday night, I sent three reports to *The Times*, the longest dispatch a detailed account of the record of the U.S. Navy's constant misidentification of civil aircraft over the Gulf and the near-panic that the air-traffic controllers had heard over the airwaves from the American warships. The *Vincennes* had claimed it was under attack by Iranian Revolutionary Guards in motor boats at the time it destroyed the airliner. I knew that U.S. warships carried the timetables of civil airliners in their "combat information centres" (CICs). Had Captain Rogers and his crew not had time to look at their copy? Iran Air flight IR655 flew to Dubai every day from Bandar Abbas. Why should it become a target on 3 July?

Captain Rogers himself said that he would have to live for ever with the burden of his own conscience at what he had done. Four years later, he would publish his own account of the destruction of the Airbus.* This would include a vivid description of an attack on the *Vincennes* by Iranian motor boats, the first alert of an aircraft taking off from Bandar Abbas—a military as well as civil airport—and the information that the aircraft was issuing two transponder codes, one used by passenger aircraft, the other a military code "known to have been used by Iranian F-14 fighters." The plane was also being monitored by the frigate USS *Sides*, naval coding FFG-14—this was the ship whose crew, according to the Dubai traffic controllers, would see bodies falling out of the sky.

---

*Storm Center: The USS Vincennes and Iran Air Flight 655*, co-authored by Rogers and his wife, Sharon, and published by the Naval Institute Press at Annapolis, was later the subject of fierce debate among other U.S. naval officers, including the commander of the USS *Sides*.

Before the Airbus was 40 kilometres from his warship Rogers had sent a routinely worded warning—but addressed it to a fighter aircraft: "Iranian aircraft . . . fighter on course two-one-one, speed 360 knots, altitude 9,000 feet, this is USNWS [United States Navy warship] bearing two-zero-two from you, request you change course immediately to two-seven-zero, if you maintain current course you are standing into danger and subject to USN defensive measures . . ." Rogers says he asked for further identification of the aircraft when it was 25 kilometres from his vessel. At 9:54 and 22 seconds in the morning, he launched his two missiles. Twenty-one seconds later, they exploded against Rezaian's passenger jet, which vanished from the *Vincennes*'s radar screen. "The bridge reported seeing the flash of missile detonation through the haze," Rogers wrote. "There was a spontaneous cheer, a release of tension from the men." But crewmen on another U.S. warship would moments later see a large wing of a commercial airliner, with an engine pod still attached, crashing into the sea.

Later investigation would reveal that staff of the CIC on the *Sides* correctly identified the Airbus's commercial transponder code at virtually the same moment that Rogers fired. For Captain David Carlson, commanding the *Sides*, the destruction of the airliner "marked the horrifying climax to Captain Rogers' aggressiveness, first seen just four weeks earlier." On 2 June, two of Rogers's colleagues had been disturbed by the way he sailed the *Vincennes* too close to an Iranian frigate that was carrying out a lawful though unprecedented search of a bulk carrier for war materiel bound for Iraq. On the day the *Vincennes* shot down the Airbus, Rogers had launched a helicopter that flew within 2 to 3 miles of an Iranian small craft—the rules stated that the chopper had to be no closer than 4 miles—and reportedly came under fire. Rogers began shooting at some small Iranian military boats, an act that disturbed Captain David Carlson on the *Sides*. "Why do you want an Aegis cruiser out there shooting up boats?" he later asked in an interview with an ex-naval officer. "It wasn't a smart thing to do. He was storming off with no plan . . ." Rogers subsequently opened fire on Iranian boats inside their territorial waters. The *Vincennes* had already been nicknamed "Robocruiser" by the crew of the *Sides*.

When Carlson first heard Rogers announcing to higher headquarters his intention to shoot down the aircraft approaching his cruiser, he says he was thunderstruck. "I said to the folks around me, 'Why, what the hell is he doing?' I went through the drill again. F-14. He's climbing. By now this damn thing is at about 7,000 feet . . ." But Carlson thought that the *Vincennes* might have more information—and did not know that Rogers had been told, wrongly, that the aircraft was diving. Carlson regretted that he did not interrupt Rogers. When his own men realised the Airbus was commercial, "they were horrified." The official U.S. investigation report would later say that computer data and "reliable intelligence" agreed that Captain Rezaian's airliner "was on a normal commercial air traffic plan profile . . . on a continuous ascent in altitude from take-off at Bandar Abbas." *Newsweek* magazine would carry out its own investigation, branding the official report "a pastiche of omissions, half-truths and outright deceptions" and painting a dramatic picture of "an overeager captain, panicked crewmen and a cover-up . . ." In *Newsweek*'s report, books had been sliding off the shelves in the *Vincennes*'s information centre as it manoeuvred prior to the missile launching; little chance, then, that anyone had an opportunity to look up a scheduled airline timetable.

But in the immediate aftermath of the slaughter, the Americans stuck to the tale of total innocence. Vice President Bush appeared before the UN Security Council to say that the *Vincennes* had been rushing to the aid of a merchant ship under Iranian attack—which was totally untrue. British prime minister Margaret Thatcher described the destruction of the Iranian Airbus as "understandable." The Iranian consul in Dubai had a point when he asked me later whether Mrs. Thatcher would have considered it "understandable" if an Iranian warship had shot down a British Airways airliner over the Gulf and then claimed that it was an accident because its captain thought it was under attack by a U.S. jet. One key to the disaster lay in the American claims that a warning was sent to Captain Rezaian on both military and civilian wavelengths. Did Captain Rezaian hear these warnings? If not, why not?

The evidence of the aircraft's destruction was laid out for journalists on a parade ground at Iranian naval headquarters in Bandar Abbas. Pieces of engine cowling, wings and flaps had been scored and burned by metal fragments; a jagged hunk of wing flap had a 12-centimetre hole punched through its centre. A section of the passenger cabin wall 3 metres square had been perforated by metal shards. Several of the bodies I saw had scarlet and red burns on their flesh; these passengers must have been sitting in the centre of the aircraft, close to the two engines onto which the *Vincennes*'s heat-seeking missiles would have locked. Lying beside this wreckage was the nosecone of the Airbus, escape chutes, electrical circuitry and oxygen systems. The explosions had been catastrophic.

Three days after the Airbus was destroyed, I flew from Bandar Abbas to Dubai aboard the first Iran Air plane to resume operations on the route. It was, of course, flight IR655. I sat in the cockpit of the Boeing 707 alongside Captain Rezaian's former Airbus navigator. Captain Nasser, who had been flying with Rezaian until six weeks ago when he transferred to Boeings—an act that probably saved his life—had marked the point of Rezaian's destruction on his charts and insisted that his friend, on other flights over the Gulf with him, had always replied when he heard challenges from the U.S. Navy. "He was a sensible, very professional man," he said. "He would never make a mistake or play games with the Americans. What the Americans did was very crude—they must have panicked." Suggestions that Rezaian was on a suicide mission, Nasser added, were "disgusting." Rezaian had flown the Dubai route on at least twenty-five previous occasions and had been piloting Airbus aircraft for almost two and a half years. So what happened on that Sunday morning?

The answer was not difficult to discover. In our Boeing, Captain Asadapur, the pilot, had to communicate constantly with three traffic-control centres—Tehran, Bandar Abbas and Dubai—which he did in fluent English. While talking to them, he could neither send *nor receive* on the civilian 1215 radio band to which our

Boeing was tuned—the same wavelength on which the *Vincennes* said it tried to warn Captain Rezaian. Climbing from 12,000 to 14,000 feet—not descending in an "attack mode" as the Americans initially claimed—Rezaian would have been talking to Bandar Abbas when he was 50 kilometres out, when the first American missile blew off the port wing of his Airbus. Bandar Abbas ground control told me that Rezaian's last message was that he was "climbing to one-four-zero" (14,000 feet). If Rezaian could not hear the Americans on his civilian waveband, he was certainly not going to hear them on the military net, a challenge that was anyway intended for the non-existent F-14 which was supposed to be closing on the American cruiser.

Then there was the mystery of the transponder. On our Iranian flight, a green light glowed beside the co-pilot's left knee, showing that it was sending out our identification into the dark night above the Gulf. Any warship down there on the moonlit sea would know who we were. Asadapur repeatedly told Dubai control—for the benefit of all listeners—that we were flight IR655 "with forty-four souls on board." If the transponder was not working, the light would have been out. Asadapur said he would never take off without checking it. Hossein Pirouzi, the Bandar Abbas ground controller and airport manager on 3 July, told me he "assumed" Rezaian's transponder was working. Rezaian would scarcely have taken off without ensuring that it was glowing that comforting green light. Pirouzi, a middle-aged man with a smart brown moustache, wavy hair and a thorough training in air-traffic control from London's Heathrow Airport, said that he did not know a naval engagement was in progress at the time of Rezaian's take-off. But as we were later to discover, there was no battle as such taking place. "The Americans broadcast warnings every time they see a speeding boat—they go on 'red alert' when they see every plane," Pirouzi said. "The Americans have no right to be in the Gulf challenging our legitimate right to fly our air routes—so why should we reply to them?"

His comment was devastating. If Pirouzi's blithe assumption that the Americans would never fire at an Airbus was to be the basis of his air-traffic policy, how easy it was to understand why the U.S. naval crews, equally psyched up against the country which their president blamed for the Gulf War, should have panicked and fired at the first plane to approach their ship after they had engaged an Iranian patrol craft.

Was it panic, as *Newsweek* was to suggest four years later, that caused the officers of the *Vincennes* to misread the information on their own radar screens, to see an aircraft descending which was clearly ascending, panic and the oppressive heat that cloaks the bodies and energies of all naval crews in the Gulf? Besides, was not Iran the enemy? Was not Iran a "terrorist state"? Was it not, in Reagan's words, "a barbarous country"? Unknown to them, Captain Rezaian and his passengers over the Gulf were flying across a cultural and emotional chasm that separated America from Iran, a ravine so deep and so dangerous that its updraft blew an Iranian Airbus out of the sky.

Nothing could have illustrated this more painfully than the American response to the *Vincennes*'s killing of 290 innocent civilians. Citizens of Vincennes, Indiana, were raising money for a monument—not to the dead Iranians, but to the ship that destroyed their lives.\* When the ship returned to its home base of San Diego, it was given a hero's welcome. The men of the *Vincennes* were all awarded combat action ribbons. The air warfare coordinator, Commander Scott Lustig, won the navy's Commendation Medal for "heroic achievement," for the "ability to maintain his poise and confidence under fire" that enabled him to "quickly and concisely complete the firing procedure." Even *Newsweek* was constrained to describe this as "surreal." Rogers retired honourably in 1991. Less than a year after the destruction of the Airbus, the captain's wife, Sharon, was the target of a pipe-bomb which exploded beneath her Toyota van in San Diego. She was unharmed. Rogers was to write that the "centerpiece" of his book was formed by "the events of 3 July 1988 and 10 March 1989"—as if the bloodbath over the Gulf and the failed attempt on his wife's life were comparable, a suggestion contained on the book's cover, which described its contents as "a personal account of tragedy and terrorism."

In fairness, however, Rogers was to quote in full in his book a long and bitter handwritten letter which he received from Captain Rezaian's brother Hossein. "He was turned into the powder at the mid-air by your barrage missile attack and perished along with so many other innocent lives aboard, without the slightest sin or guilt whatsoever," Hossein Rezaian wrote.

> I was at the area of carnage the day after and unfortunately I saw the result of your barbarous crime and its magnitude. I used to be a Navy Commander myself and I had my college education in U.S. as my late brother did, but ever since the incredible downing I really felt ashamed of myself. I hated your Navy and ours. So that I even quit my job and I ruined my whole career . . . me and my family . . . could somehow bear the pain of tragedy if he [Mohsen] had died in an accident but this premeditated act is neither forgiveable nor forgettable . . . the U.S. government as the culprit in this horrendous incident, showed neither remorse nor compassion for the loss of innocent lives . . . Didn't we really deserve a small gesture of sympathy? Did you have to say a pack of lies and contradictory statements about the incident in a bid to justify the case? . . . or it was the result of panic and inexperience. I do appreciate your prompt response.

It was much to Rogers's credit that he gave this letter so much prominence in his book. "Despite the diatribe," he wrote, "the pain and grief pouring from this letter struck me hard. All of the sorrow and grief that had haunted me since July returned in force." He had wanted, Rogers said, to reply but a naval public rela-

---

\*The *Vincennes* was named after the south-western Indiana city whose French-built fort was captured by American forces under George Rogers Clark in 1779. The ill-fated *Stark* bore the name of General John Stark, who fought at Bunker Hill in 1775.

tions officer warned that return correspondence "could be used by the Iranian gov-
ernment as some sort of political lever." Again, the Iranians were the bad guys.
Hossein Rezaian's letter was handed over to the U.S. Naval Intelligence Service.
Who knows, maybe they read it.

There certainly wouldn't have been much to gain from reading my first report
on the massacre. When a newspaper had been so loyal to a reporter as *The Times*
had been to me over the past eighteen years—fighting off the British army in
Northern Ireland, the Israelis and Palestinians, the American authorities and the
Iranians and Iraqis whenever they complained about my reporting—there was a
natural inclination to feel great trust in my editors. If my reports were cut, this was
done for space reasons—I was usually given the chance to shorten my own
dispatches—or because a breaking news story elsewhere in the world was forcing
the paper's night editors to change the pages after the first edition. But cuts were
never made for political reasons.

Murdoch had already bought *The Times* when the Israelis invaded Lebanon in
1982, but I reported without any censorship on Israel's killing of up to 17,000
Lebanese and Palestinians—most of them civilians—and the subsequent butchery
of hundreds of Palestinian refugees by Israel's Christian allies. The Israeli
embassy had condemned my dispatches, as they did the reporting of any journalist
who dared to suggest that Israel's undisciplined army killed civilians as well as
soldiers. But under Charles Douglas-Home's editorship, no foreign correspondent
was going to have his work changed out of fear or bias or prejudice. His deputy,
Charles Wilson, was a tough ex-Royal Marine who could be a bully, but who did
not mince his words about Israel or any other country which tried to impugn the
integrity of the paper's journalists. "What a bunch of fascists," he roared when I
had proved to him that an Israeli statement condemning my work was riddled with
factual mistakes.

Israelis are not fascists, but it was good to have a deputy editor who was
unafraid of a reporter's antagonists. After Douglas-Home's death from cancer,
Wilson became editor. He remained a bully but could also be immensely kind. To
members of staff who suffered serious illness, he was a rock of strength and compassion. He wanted to be liked. He was immensely generous to me when, for personal reasons, I wanted to work for a year in Paris. But there was one afternoon in
Beirut when I had filed a long and detailed investigative report on torture at Israel's
Khiam prison in southern Lebanon. About an hour after I had sent my story, a foreign desk staffer came on the telex to ask if I could not add a paragraph to the
effect that allegations about torture of the kind I had described—beatings and electrical currents applied to the genitals—were typical of the propaganda put out by
Israel's enemies. I protested. I had United Nations evidence to support my investigation—all of which was subsequently confirmed in a compelling report by
Amnesty International. In the end, I inserted a paragraph which only strengthened
my dispatch: that while such allegations were often used against Israel, on this
occasion there was no doubt that they were true.

I had won this round, and thought no more about it. Then an article appeared on the centre page of *The Times*, which was usually reserved for comment or analysis. It purported to explain the difficulties of reporting the Middle East—the intimidation of journalists by "terrorists" being the salient argument—but then ended by remarking that anyone reporting from Beirut was "a bloodsucker." I was reporting from Beirut. I was based in Beirut as Middle East correspondent—for *The Times*, for goodness' sake. What did this mean? The foreign desk laughed it off. I did not. Was Wilson trying to "balance" my dispatches by allowing the enemies of honest reporting to abuse me in the paper? It seemed impossible. I don't believe in conspiracies. Besides, I knew Wilson often did not read the centre page of *The Times*.

But it was a much more serious matter on 4 July 1988, when I discovered that my lead report for *The Times*—which I had been asked to write for the front page—was not appearing in the next day's paper. All the investigative work on the panic and inefficiency of U.S. warship crews in the Gulf, all the evidence that U.S. personnel had been placing civilian airliners in peril for weeks—the long and detailed conversations with the Dubai air traffic controllers who had actually heard the radio traffic between U.S. naval officers as the *Vincennes* was shooting down the Airbus—had been for nothing. If there had been any doubts about my report, they should have been raised with me on the evening I filed. But there had been silence. Two other routine dispatches—on Iran's public reaction to the destruction of the plane and possible retaliation—were printed inside the paper.

Next morning, I spoke to Piers Ackerman on the foreign desk. He told me that my story had been dropped in the first edition for space reasons but that the later, reinserted and shortened version contained "the main points." When I asked if cuts had been made for political reasons, he said: "My God, if I thought things had reached that stage, I would resign." I told him that if it transpired that the cuts *were* political, *I* would resign. *The Times* took days to reach the Gulf and I would be away in Iran, so I had no chance to read the paper for several days. When at last I did see the later editions, every element of my story that reflected negatively on the Americans had been taken out.

Journalists should not be prima donnas. We have to fight to prove the worth of our work. Neither editors nor readers are there for the greater good of journalists. But something very unethical had taken place here: my report on the shooting down of the Iranian Airbus had been, in every sense of the word, tampered with, changed and censored. Its meaning had been distorted by omission. The Americans, in my truncated report, had been exonerated as surely as they had been excused by Mrs. Thatcher. This, I felt sure, was a result of Murdoch's ownership of *The Times*. I did not believe that he personally became involved in individual newspaper stories—though this would happen—but rather that his ownership spread a culture of obedience and compliance throughout the paper, a feeling that Murdoch's views—what Murdoch wanted—were "known."

I had been very struck by the fact that the foreign desk staffer who had been so keen to add the "propaganda" paragraph to my Khiam torture story was previously a very left-wing member of the National Union of Journalists—the very union which had done so much to undermine owner Lord Thomson's faith in *The Times* and to truss up the paper for Murdoch to buy. A socialist lion had now turned into a News Corp. mouse. I am neither a lion nor a mouse, but I can be a tough dog, and when I get a rope between my teeth I won't let go until I shake it and tug it something rotten to see what lies at the other end. That, after all, is what journalists are supposed to do. Further enquiries to the foreign desk of the paper elicited ignorance. Wilson's compliant foreign editor, George Brock, was unavailable to take my calls. Days had now passed since my original report was filed, the subs on that night were never on duty when I telephoned, Wilson had gone on holiday. But my concerns did not go away. It is one thing to have an article cut for space—or "trimmed" or "shaved" as the unpleasant foreign desk expression goes—but quite another to risk one's life for a paper, only to find that the courage necessary to report wars is not in evidence among those whose task it is to print those reports. And so in the Gulf that steamy summer, I lost faith in *The Times*.

I decided I would try to join a brash, intelligent, brave, dangerously underfunded but independent new newspaper called—well, of course—*The Independent*. It would be months before I persuaded Andreas Whittam Smith, the editor and part-owner, to take me aboard, or to "draw rations" as he was to put it, but within a year I would be reporting from the Middle East for a new editor, a new newspaper and new colleagues—although many of them would turn out to be fellow refugees from *The Times*.

Only after I had written to Wilson to tell him that I was resigning from *The Times*, however, did I learn that I had transferred my allegiance for the right reasons. Just after New Year of 1988, I received a call from one of the senior night editors on the paper. He wanted to talk to me about the *Vincennes* story:

At the Sunday 5 p.m. conference, I advised the editor that your story would make a "hamper" [a large box across eight columns at the top of the front page]. Wilson said he wanted to see the story. It was about the incompetence of the crew of the *Vincennes*. I read it and said to myself: this is the clearest story I've yet read about what really happened. Later I saw the editor on the back bench. Wilson said to me: "Is this the story you're talking about?" I said it was. He said: "There's nothing in it. There's not a fact in it. I wouldn't even run this gibberish." Wilson said it was bollocks, that it was "waffle." I remember saying to Charlie: "Are you sure? This is a terrific story." I was shocked. I've looked up my diary for the night of July 3rd. It says: "Shambles, chaos on Gulf story. Brock rewrites Fisk."

It didn't run in the first edition, but in the second edition the story ran but with all the references to American incompetence cut out. I looked it up on the screen. George [Brock] had edited the story. He had taken out all those references. At the top, he had written a note, saying that "under no circumstances will the cuts made in this story be re-inserted." I wanted to resign. I considered resigning over this. I didn't, and perhaps I should have done. I told Denis [Taylor] about this on the desk. He was disgusted. All the foreign desk knew about it. But none of them would do anything about it. They were frightened. Nobody told you about this. I thought: "Well, it might be better for the paper if Bob didn't know." I thought you might resign if you knew.

On the day I filed the first *Vincennes* story, I had spoken to Piers Ackerman, asking him to pass on to the leader writers my advice that—whatever our editorial response to the disaster—we should not go along with the line that Mohsen Rezaian had been a suicide pilot, which would, I said, be rubbish. Ackerman said he passed on the message. But our editorial subsequently said that the plane might have been controlled by a "suicide" pilot. This was totally untrue. And so was the thrust of my story, once it had appeared in bowdlerised form in the paper that same morning. Readers of *The Times* had been solemnly presented with a fraudulent version of the truth.

There are rarely consolation prizes for a journalist when a paper doesn't run the real story, but Vincent Browne, the hard-headed editor of the Dublin *Sunday Tribune*, an old friend and colleague from Northern Ireland, had none of Wilson's fears about events in the Gulf. He invited me to write the fruits of my investigations for his own paper. Half the next issue of the *Tribune*'s front page carried a photograph of an American Aegis-class cruiser firing a missile into the sky; superimposed on the picture was the headline "What Really Happened," with my full-page report inside. Which is how the people of County Mayo were allowed to read what subscribers to *The Times* of London could not.

It's easy for a journalist to become self-important about his work, to claim that he or she alone is the bearer of truth, that editors must stand aside so that the bright light of a reporter's genius may bathe the paper's readers. It's also tempting to allow one's own journalistic arguments to take precedence over the ghastly tragedies which we are supposed to be reporting. We have to have a sense of proportion, some perspective in our work. What am I doing—what is Fisk doing, I can hear a hostile reviewer of this book ask—writing about the violent death of 290 innocent human beings and then taking up five pages to explain his petty rows with *The Times*? The answer is simple. When we journalists fail to get across the reality of events to our readers, we have not only failed in our job; we have also become a party to the bloody events that we are supposed to be reporting. If we cannot tell the truth about the shooting down of a civilian airliner—because this will harm "our" side in a war or because it will cast one of our "hate" countries in the role of victim or because it might upset the owner of our newspaper—then we contribute to the very prejudices that provoke wars in the first place. If we cannot blow the whistle on a navy that shoots civilians out of the sky, then we make future killings of the same kind as "understandable" as Mrs. Thatcher found this one. Delete the Americans' panic and incompetence—all of which would be revealed in the months to come—and pretend an innocent pilot is a suicidal maniac, and it's only a matter of time before we blow another airliner out of the sky. Journalism can be lethal.

But I also ask myself if, standing in that charnel house in Bandar Abbas, I did not see the genesis of another mass killing, five months later, this time over the

Scottish town of Lockerbie. Within hours of the destruction of the Airbus on 3 July 1988, President Khamenei of Iran declared that Reagan and his administration were "criminals and murderers." Tehran radio announced: "We will not leave the crimes of America unpunished." And it continued: "We will resist the plots of the Great Satan and avenge the blood of our martyrs from criminal mercenaries." I didn't have much doubt what that would mean. Back in Beirut, I found no one who believed that the *Vincennes* had shot down the Iranian aircraft in error. I started to hear disjointed, disturbing remarks. Someone over dinner—a doctor who was a paragon of non-violence—speculated that a plane could be blown up by a bomb in the checked baggage of an aircraft. It was a few days before it dawned on me that if people were talking like this, then someone was trying to find out if it was possible.

The Iranians, after all, had a motive. The destruction of the Iranian passenger jet, whatever Washington's excuses, was a terrible deed. But would someone so wickedly plot revenge? I was in Paris when the BBC announced that a Pan Am jet had crashed over Lockerbie. This time it was 270 dead, including 11 on the ground. I didn't need to imagine the corpses—I had seen them in July—and not for a moment did I doubt the reason. There were the usual conspiracy theories: a cover-up CIA drug-busting scheme that had gone crazily wrong, messing with the evidence by American agents after the crash. And Iranian revenge for the Airbus killings.

In the United States, this was a favourite theory. The news shows repeated the video—taken by a U.S. Navy team—of the *Vincennes* firing its missiles on 3 July. Captain Rogers saw the film again, writing later that he "felt a knot in my stomach and wondered if it was ever going to stop." The parallel was relevant but had no moral equivalence. The annihilation of the Airbus had been a shameful mass killing but Lockerbie was murder. In Beirut, an old acquaintance with terrifying contacts in the hostage world calmly said to me: "It's [Ahmed] Jibril and the Iranians." Jibril was head of the Damascus-based "Popular Front for the Liberation of Palestine—General Command." Diplomatic correspondents in Washington and London—always the stalking horses for government accusations—began to finger the Iranians, the PFLP-GC, the Syrians. In Tehran, people would look at me with some intensity when I mentioned Lockerbie. They never claimed it. Yet they never expressed their horror. But of course, after the Airbus slaughter, that would have been asking a bit much.

In Beirut, the PFLP-GC became known, briefly, as "the Lockerbie boys." I didn't count much on that. But then, more than two years later, a strange thing happened. Jibril held a press conference in a Palestinian refugee camp in Beirut, initially to talk about the release by Libya of French and Belgian hostages seized from a boat in the Mediterranean. But that was not what was on his mind. "I'm not responsible for the Lockerbie bombing," he suddenly blurted out. "They are trying to get me with a kangaroo court." There was no court then. And no one had officially accused Jibril of Lockerbie. But scarcely nine months later, Saddam Hussein invaded Kuwait and the diplomatic correspondents no longer believed in the Syrian–PFLP-GC–Iranian connection. Now it was Libya that was behind Lockerbie. Iran was the enemy of the bestial Saddam, and Syria was sending its tanks to serve alongside the Western armies in the Gulf. Jibril's men faded from the screen. So did the only country with a conceivable motive: Iran.

In the aftermath of the shooting down of the Airbus, Ayatollah Hussein Ali Montazeri, who was intended to be Khomeini's successor, said that he was "sure that if the Imam orders, all the revolutionary forces and resistance cells, both inside and outside the country, will unleash their wrath on U.S. financial, political, economic and military interests." But the *Vincennes* attack finally convinced most of the Iranian leadership that the United States had joined the war on Iraq's side. The Americans had destroyed Iran's oil platforms, eliminated the Iranian navy and were now, it seemed, determined to use missiles against Iran's passenger planes, all of which had previously been targets for Saddam Hussein. Iran's economy was collapsing and, so Rafsanjani warned Khomeini, even the resupply of Iran's vast armies was impossible. There could be no more Iranian offensives against Iraq, Khomeini was told by the country's Revolutionary Guard Corps commander, Mohsen Rezai, until 1993. So to protect the Islamic revolution—to ensure its survival—Khomeini accepted UN Security Council resolution 598 and a ceasefire to take effect on 22 July 1988, "in the interests of security and on the basis of justice." For the old man, it was a personal as well as a military catastrophe. "Woe upon me that I am still alive," he concluded bleakly, "and have drunk the poisoned chalice of the resolution."

But worse was to come. Seven days after Khomeini's 18 July acceptance of the UN resolution, the Mujahedin-e-Khalq's "National Liberation Army" swept across the Iranian border in Iraqi-supplied tanks and armour to overthrow the Khomeini regime. It was the ultimate treachery and the Iranians fought back against their invaders—who were, of course, themselves Iranians—with fury; across Iran, the government's secret police began the wholesale liquidation of the Mujahedin's supporters. The Revolutionary Guards and the *Basiji*, many of whom felt betrayed by the ending of the war, turned upon the mujahedin, summarily hanging their captured militiamen in Bakhtaran, Kangavar and Islam Abad. Now thousands of mujahedin militants and their supporters in jails all over Iran—many of whom had long ago been tried and sentenced to many years of imprisonment— were to be re-tried and hanged.

"We ask the Leader to deal harshly with murderers and as soon as possible, rid the people of their presence," *Resalat* newspaper pleaded. Ayatollah Musavi Arde-bili, the head of the supreme court, gave a Freisler-like speech at Friday prayers in Tehran. The *monafeqin*—the "hypocrites"—he said, "don't know that people see them as less than animals. People are so angry with them; the judiciary is under extreme pressure of public opinion . . . people say they should all be executed . . . We will judge them ten at a time, twenty at a time, bring a file, take away a file: I regret that they say a fifth have been destroyed. I wish they all were destroyed . . ." "Hypocrites" was a word that embraced the idea of heresy or apostasy rather than mere double standards. To be one of the *monafeqin* was a capital offence.

Even before the war had ended, Iran's prison population was re-interrogated and divided into those who still recognised the resistance to the Islamic Republic and those who had repented—the *tavvab*—and between those who prayed and those who refused to pray. At some point, Khomeini ordered that political prisoners should be liquidated en masse. Although this order was kept secret, we know that Ayatollah Montazeri protested vehemently against the massacres, an act that ensured his dismissal as the future Imam. ". . . As to your order to execute the hypocrites in prison," Montazeri wrote in a private letter to Khomeini, "the nation is prepared to accept the execution if those arrested [are] in relation to recent events [i.e. the Iraqi-backed mujahedin invasion] . . . But the execution of those already in prison . . . would be interpreted as vindictiveness and revenge."

In some prisons, inmates were lined up on opposite sides of a corridor, one line to be returned to their cells after "repenting," the other taken straight to a mass gallows. On 30 July, Revolutionary Guards at Evin began their executions with mujahid women prisoners. The hangings went on for several days. Male communist prisoners were hanged at the mosque in Evin. "When [they] are taken to the Hosseinieh to be hanged," an ex-prisoner testified, "some [are] crying, some swearing and all shivering but hiding their shivering. Some smile hopelessly . . . a number of the guards vie with each other to do the hanging so as to score more piety. A few are upset by seeing so many corpses. Some prisoners fight and are savagely beaten. The execution is swift." The bodies of the hanging men were paraded in front of female prisoners to break their spirit. In Tehran alone, an Iran-based human rights group published the names of 1,345 victims of the "national disaster."

Exile magazines opposed to the regime would, years later, publish terrifying eyewitness accounts of the prison hangings. Up to 8,000 inmates may have been put to death in the summer of 1988, perhaps 10,000. Secret executions were followed by burials in secret graves. A former female prisoner was to recall how:

> One *tavvab* woman was taken from the block below us to witness the execution of her husband. She had seen the rope on her husband's neck and another woman who had her chador tied round her neck. She herself was due to be executed but had escaped that fate by being *tavvab* and surrendering . . . Afterwards she became psychologically unbalanced . . .

Another ex-prisoner wrote of a militant leftist prisoner called Fariba who was taken to a dungeon beneath Dastgerd prison to see her husband. This was Fariba's description:

> What I saw terrified me . . . There in front of me was Massoud, my husband, bent and sickly with eyes that flickered from deep black crypts. I screamed Massoud my darling, and leaped towards him. They held me back . . . A Pasdar warned: "Be silent! You can only look. You can only witness how accounts are settled here—or your place is next to him." . . . Massoud, hands tied behind his back, noose round his neck, standing on a stool, looked at me with his whole being. A tired look but full

of love, full of consciousness, trying to smile. In a weak and exhausted voice he said: "It was so good to see you Fariba!" . . . The voice of the interrogator rose from behind me . . . he said: "If you would be prepared to push the stool away and hang this apostate I will set you free this very second. I promise on my honour!" . . . I looked straight into the interrogator's eyes and screamed: "Do you have any honour? Fascist! Executioner!" . . . The Pasdars grabbed me. The interrogator pulled out his Colt and shot Massoud. Another Pasdar kicked the stool from under him. Between my distress and my unbelieving eyes Massoud was hanged . . .

There is overwhelming evidence from ex-prisoners that female prisoners who were virgins were raped by their interrogators before execution. Of 1,533 Iranian female prisoners who were hanged or shot in the two decades that followed the 1979 revolution and whose names have been catalogued by a German women's group—a fraction of the actual number of executed women—163 were twenty-one years old or under, 35 of them pregnant. The youngest was Nafiseh Ashraf Jahani, who was ten years old. Afsaneh Farabi was twelve, three girls were thirteen years old. Akram Islami was seventy. One woman, Aresteh Gholivand, was fifty-six when she was hanged and left six children behind her.

WHAT CAN ONE SAY TO THE FAMILIES of these thousands? We journalists have to take the regime seriously. We interview the ayatollahs and the hojatolislams and the more humble mullahs and we ask questions about human rights and we are lectured about the iniquities of the Shah and of our—Western—responsibility for his "Satanic" rule. Almost every Khomeini prison governor was imprisoned by the Shah. So, for that matter, were many of the mujahedin prisoners who were executed in 1988 and the years before. I am sitting in a north Tehran house and a widow is slowly turning the pages of a family photograph album. She points to a Kodak shot of a handsome young man in a brown shirt. "He was in the opposition and they arrested him. They killed him," she says simply. The young man in the picture seems to come alive as she speaks, leaning forward towards the camera, one arm draped round his sister's shoulder, the other in a gentle way around his mother. "His mother never got over it," the woman says. Her young daughter is watching in silence. She is perhaps five years old, a pert, cheerful little girl with fluffy brown hair and a pixie smile. "She wears a chador to school," her mother says. "Fereshteh, let's see what you look like when you go to school." Fereshteh runs into her bedroom and emerges in a kind of mourning, head to toe in black cloth, her hair invisible beneath the material. Then she becomes serious and walks slowly back to the bedroom to become a child again.

BUT NOT ONLY IN IRAN had the war masked a nation's internal killing machine. Amnesty was able to list the names of 116 people executed by Saddam's regime between 11 November and 31 December 1997, the youngest of them fourteen years old. In total during December 1997 and January 1998 at least 700 prisoners were executed in Abu Ghraib prison west of Baghdad, many of them bearing the marks of torture. The victims were from Baghdad, Suleimaniya and Baquba; most were under eighteen.

But for those millions who participated in the Iran–Iraq conflict—as for every soldier—the war never ended. After the 18 July 1988 ceasefire, Iran and Iraq would exchange 90,000 prisoners-of-war, but many other thousands would remain in captivity for almost another decade. Iran was still releasing POWs in 1997. At least 500 men, some of them held in prison camps for seventeen years, were freed by Iran in advance of the December 1997 Islamic summit conference in Tehran. But in 1999, Baghdad was still claiming that Iran held 20,000 of its soldiers, including 8,700 who it said were registered with the International Red Cross. Iran said that at least 5,000 of its own men were still POWs in Iraq.

When Khadum Fadel returned to Baghdad after sixteen years of incarceration, he could remember only sorrow and hunger and rheumatism in an Iranian camp surrounded by barbed wire and mines, often lying in chains. Many thousands of the Iraqi prisoners came home after ten years of near-starvation in Iranian camps, only to find that American-backed sanctions after the 1991 war in which they had played no part were now starving their families. A whole angry army of ex-prisoners—filled with hatred of Iran, of Saddam and of the United States— were now living in misery and impoverishment in Iraq. Amid the mud and sand, they and the millions of Iraqis who avoided both imprisonment and death had learned to live and to die. They learned to fight. Under the lethal imagination of their dictator, they held the line against Iran. They used their tanks as static gun platforms dug into the desert and they burned their enemies with gas or swamped them with tidal rivers or electrocuted them in the marshes. A whole generation of Iraqi lieutenants and captains came to regard war—rather than peace—as a natural element in their lives. If ever the day came when Saddam was gone, what would these lieutenants and captains and their comrades from the trenches do if they faced another great army? What would they be capable of achieving if they could use their own initiative, their own imagination, their own courage—if patriotism and nationalism and Islam rather than the iron hand of Baathism was to be their inspiration?

Of course, there were also the dead. More than three years before the war ended, Saddam began construction of a space-age monument to his greatest blunder. From the air it looked like a rocket platform. From the ground it had the appearance of a giant sea-shell, two acres of sloping, marble-topped concrete surmounted by an umbrella of cement. Visitors to Baghdad—and there were many tens of thousands of Iraqis who came here to try to mourn their lost relatives— climbed the lower lip of the structure, then descended into a fridge of air conditioning in a vault beneath the canopy. Here, said an inscription in gold Arabic letters, lay the unknown Iraqi warrior, the hero of the Arab nation, the martyr of the Second Qadisiya. Even five years after the end of the Iran–Iraq War, the memorial had still not been completed.

In 1993, I would visit the monument again to find an army of Iraqi stonemasons chipping into marble slabs, each slice—and there were thousands—containing the names of sixteen Iraqis who never returned from the titanic war. Private Ahmed Katem's name was neatly carved onto a slab, and alongside him Mohamed Jadi, Abdullah Ahmed and "combatant" Salah Younis. Saddam's martyrs were worthy, it seemed, of nothing but the highest honours; in Baghdad, they were building Saddam Hussein's "Vietnam wall." True, the marble was pale yellow rather than black. True, it was being constructed around the circular vault rather than below an ellipse near a presidential palace. True, the Iraqi "wall" was said to be Saddam's brainchild. But then again, America's dead in Vietnam numbered a mere 56,555; Saddam's between 1980 and 1988 might have reached a conservative half million.

At that time, Saddam's "martyrs' wall" remained an official secret in Iraq. No one had been told of its construction and the wall would be revealed only at its completion in 1995, when families would be able to grieve before the names of their loved ones. "It is forbidden for you to take photographs," a resolute young lady from the memorial's executive announced uncompromisingly when I requested a snapshot of the unfinished palisade of names. "We may give you no information. We cannot talk to you about this. We have no details, no figures. Nothing must be said until this is completed. This instruction comes from the highest authority." There was no doubt about who that might be. But could one not perhaps know just how many names would appear on the wall? The lady was adamant. "It is impossible to give any figure while so many of our soldiers remain prisoners of Iran, even five years after this war has ended."

Quite so. Nor were the dead of the Second Gulf War—of the battle between Iraq and the American-led armies in 1991—likely to be commemorated here. Nowhere in Baghdad were they officially remembered. For it was the eight-year Iran–Iraq War that had been enshrined in Baathist history as the most important, the most strategic, the most historic, the most glorious—more to the point, the most necessary—battle in Iraq's history. The more the Second Gulf War was questioned by Iraqis, the more the First Gulf War was off-limits to all criticism. Even the 1990 Iraqi draft constitution demanded that any future president must accept that the Iran–Iraq War "was the only way to guarantee the integrity of Iraq and the safety of its sacred places."

Thus might history be safely locked up. There were whole families, brothers, fathers and sons, listed together on the marble slabs of Saddam's martyrs' wall, the monstrous death toll broken up by carved quotations from the Koran, in their turn guaranteeing—as no constitution can—eternal paradise for those who were cut down by shells and bullets or who drowned in the mud at Howeiza and Fish Lake, Ahwaz, Khorramshahr, Qasr-e Shirin and Fao. In the defence of Fao, an Iraqi official blurted out to me in March 1993, Iraq lost 58,000 men.

Just one of the half million had been preserved—in chemicals that would supposedly prevent his decomposition for a hundred years—in a coffin suspended above the Unknown Soldier's Museum 5 kilometres away, draped in an Iraqi flag amid the tattered remains of his dead colleagues' battledress. Stained uniforms, ripped open by surgeons in their vain attempts to save Iraqi lives, were encased in glass, along with the long-dried bloody bandages of the deceased. "There are seventeen swords above us here—you see?" the young curator asked, pointing to the Arab swords suspended in black stone above the uniforms. "They represent the 17 July revolution and the stones represent the black hearts of our enemies." Plaques were displayed around the hall, donated by the military attachés of socialist Romania, East Germany, the Soviet Union, Somalia, nations which had since died as miserably as any soldiers commemorated here.

It was all so simple, like the exhibition that lay before the martyrs' wall. It portrayed in photographs the life—as attempted assassin, guerrilla fighter and leader—of one Saddam Hussein, from birth to Baathist throne. There was a picture of the mud hut in the Tikrit village of Ouja where he was born in 1937. There was the eight-year-old with a half frown who would one day lead the Arab Baath Socialist Party. A grainy photograph showed the young but creepily familiar features of a schoolboy Saddam, sitting on the step of a railway carriage. There were pictures of Abdul-Karim Qassim's bullet-riddled limousine after Saddam Hussein had tried to kill the dictator in Rashid Street. More snapshots showed Saddam with girl students in his Egyptian exile, standing aloof before the Pyramids. His wife Sajida smiles from a wedding photograph. Saddam beams into the camera while behind him the hammers and chisels are chipping away at their thousands of names. Rarely has a president been so closely associated with those he sent to their deaths. They are "Saddam's Qadisiya Martyrs." Note the possessive—his personal property. But the little exhibition trailed off rather unexpectedly. There were photographs of Baath party officials and of Saddam's homes—not of the interiors but of the outside walls, of steel-enforced gates and sentry boxes and perimeter fences. If power did not corrupt, it clearly loved high walls. The sunlight outside the great vault was blinding. Only after a few seconds did I notice, to the right, a massive courtyard filled with many more thousands of slabs, all awaiting the stonemasons' testimony of blood.

Throughout the war, however, a more serious though less ostentatious memorial stood west of Baghdad, in the dusty military town of Fallujah. Here, in a series of refrigerated sheds, the Iraqi army maintained one of the world's largest mortuaries, with space for 2,000 bodies at a time. It was to this dismal, hot little suburb that the families of Iraq's war dead came to identify their sons and husbands and fathers. But even here, the authorities sometimes could not cope with the bloodletting. After the slaughter in the Howeiza marshes in the spring of 1985, there were so many corpses to transport to Fallujah that the government confiscated the licences of every taxi-driver in Baghdad and ordered all of them to drive south to Basra to collect the body of a soldier. Only when the driver turned up at the refrigeration sheds with his cadaver was his licence restored. Even then, the dead were still lying across the mud flats in their thousands; relatives were taken to the front line to identify their next-of-kin as they lay on the battlefield. Some said 8,000 Iraqis died in the marshes that spring, others 14,000. Some said 47,000.

. . .

I ALWAYS GO BACK TO OLD WARS and talk to old soldiers. I go back to Northern Ireland, to Bosnia, to Serbia, to Algeria and southern Lebanon and Kuwait, to post-invasion Baghdad. I am trying, I suppose, to make sense of what I have witnessed, to place it in a context that did not exist for me when I was trying to stay alive, to talk to those with whom—however briefly—I shared these nightmares. I am looking, I think, for the kaleidoscope to stop turning, to see the loose flakes of memory reflected in some final, irremediable pattern. So that is what it was about! Sometimes, as I write this book, I hear the pieces of glass moving in the kaleido scope, like the sound of the hard drive in my laptop as I write, searching for applications and programmes, ticking towards a conclusion, a clear screen with an undisputed memory.

I can sit on my balcony above the sea in Beirut and remember with absolute clarity how the Iranians—when we didn't choose the train—would take us to their war in a Hercules C-130, blasting through the hot darkness to Ahwaz or Dezful, we journalists trapped in our bucket seats, sweating, notebooks and cameras on our laps, praying that the Iraqi air force didn't sniff the engine exhausts in the dank night. We'd fly into the desert air base, see the oil fires burning—Bosch-like in the purple dawn, thick and tasting of dark, uneatable, cancerous chocolate—and hear that heavy rumbling of the Somme-like guns, and fear for the next thirty-six hours: the night in the underground bunker with the dust rising from the floor, a day of driving through battle lines with the shells cracking over our heads, corpses stinking by the roadside, the young men with no helmets and Korans in their hands.

Seven years after the war ended, it was easier to go back to the battlefields. I just turned up one summer's morning in 1995 at Mehrabad Airport for Iran Air's flight IR417 to Ahwaz, ate hot rolls with marmalade on the Airbus—yes, another A300—as my guide from the Ministry of Islamic Guidance snored beside me and, an hour later, circled the butane gas flames above the refineries before picking up Gholamreza's Peugeot taxi to the deserts where we all lost years of our lives. The moment I pass the first sand revetments, the sun a white blister at seven in the morning, Gholamreza points into the grey immensity of dust and says: "Bang bang! *Jang.*"

*Jang*, of course, meant "war," and "bang," for all its clichéd, simplistic quality, is an accurate enough representation of the sound of the Iraqi field gun that destroyed so much of my hearing just across the desert to the west of here a decade and a half ago. As Gholamreza accelerates the Peugeot through the dawn, my tinnitus is ringing merrily away from that distant bombardment, as if those guns were still firing over these withered killing fields. To left and right of us, as the desert grows from grey to dun-coloured in the rising sun, the trenches and tank emplacements stretch away for scores of kilometres, some turned by farmers into windbreaks for corn, others untouched by a breeze in fifteen years, the track-marks of long-destroyed Iraqi and Iranian tanks still cut into the sand. Already it is 100 degrees in the shade; perspiration is slicking down my face. In the back of the car, the man from the Ministry of Islamic Guidance has fallen asleep.

Perhaps a million men died here and in the battle line that snaked over 900 kilometres to the north, to the snows of the Turkish border, almost twice the length of the 1914–18 Western Front and fought over for almost twice as long. A whole generation of Iranians and Iraqis walked up the line to death in villages that sound, to the survivors and to the families of the dead, as sombre as Ypres and Verdun and Hill 60, Vimy Ridge and Beaumont Hamel. The names of their calvaries are almost as familiar to me now: Kerman and Shalamcheh, Penjwin and Khorramshahr, Abadan and Fateh and Ahwaz and Fao and the battle of Fish Lake. The Iranians suffered most. I used to ask in my reports then, stunned by the resilience of the Iranian defenders, whether they had their Owens and Sassoons to write about war and the pity of war.

But—perhaps because the Iranians were so xenophobic, so alien in creed, so hostile to the West, even to us reporters who risked our lives to visit their trenches—we never really tried to understand their motivation, or the effect of this bloodbath upon their minds. Even today, we forget this. The Iranians do not. Did they, like so many soldiers in the First World War, return home broken in body and spirit, their faith abandoned in the blood-drenched desert? I asked a senior Revolutionary Guard Corps officer this question. What, I asked him over dinner in Tehran, was the worst moment of the war? "July eighteenth, 1988," he snapped back at me. "It was the day we accepted the UN resolution to end the war, when our Imam said he had to eat poison and accept a ceasefire. I was driving a two-and-a-half-ton truck to the front at Shalamcheh and I couldn't believe my ears when I heard the news on the radio. I drove off into the desert and switched off the engine and I lay down in the sand, on my back with the sun above me. And I asked God why I was here on this earth. This was the worst day of my life."

Gholamreza's car raced south, the temperature rising, past a massive stockade of decaying Iraqi armour and trucks, mile after mile of it, stretching to the horizon and beyond. An Iranian sentry stood guard at this enormous war park, a museum of Iraqi tanks and smashed vehicles that belittled anything we saw in the aftermath of Norman Schwarzkopf's puny offensive against the same army back in 1991. On the right, a great train of burnt, twisted carriages lay on its side next to the Ahwaz–Khorramshahr railway line. The Iraqis had crossed and recrossed this bit of Iran; the trenches and gun-pits streamed away from the road, thousands of them, each year of desert warfare grafted onto the next. With a telescope, you could see this webbed terrain from the moon. We crossed the brown waters of the Karun River; the last time I was here, there were corpses floating in its hot currents. It was 110 degrees; they fought in this heat, died in these ovenlike winds, rotted in less than three hours. No wonder they buried the Iraqis in mass graves and freighted home the Iranian dead in less than a day.

The poetry they wrote—for they did write war poems in their thousands, the peasant *Basiji* volunteers and the Pasdaran and the artists drafted to the front—was not like Owen's or Sassoon's. In the volumes of war verse in the Tehran bookshops, old soldiers thank God who has matched them with His hour. Rifling through the shops near Tehran University, I found the ghosts of Rupert Brooke and W. N. Hodgson in these fat volumes. Here, for example, is the Iranian poet Mohamed Reza Abdul-Malikian, writing his "Letter Home" from the Ahwaz–

Khorramshahr front, where twelve-year-olds led suicide attacks on the Iraqi wire:

> *Here on our front line,*
> *Our gift of sacrifice is strewn around,*
> *Their power greater than the Karun's waves.*
> *Right here, you can admire the children and old men*
> *Who crave to walk the minefields.*
> *It's here for all to see.*

There was something frightening in this: not just the terrifying image of child martyrdom, but what appeared—to my Western mind—to be a kind of stasis of maturity and development. True, Hodgson was writing like this in 1914:

> *Sons of mine, I hear you thrilling*
> *To the trumpet call of war . . .*
> *Steeled to suffer uncomplaining*
> *Loss and failure, pain and death.*

But by 1916, our war poets had comprehended the obscenity of war. Abdul-Malikian had written his lines after many more years of war. He hadn't lost his faith. Was this because he was fighting to defend his own country or because Islam does not permit doubt in a believer? Or was it because in Iran a poem is supposed to be something holy, words that are intended to be spiritual rather than provocative? We in the West wait to be moved by a poem—simple patriotism and faith were not enough for Sassoon or Robert Graves. Wouldn't they have said something more than Abdul-Malikian? After all, in the eight years that followed Saddam's invasion of 22 September 1980, the war had embraced both poison gas and missile attacks, the worst horror of the First World War and one of the most terrifying potential weapons of the Second.

When I first wrote in *The Independent* about the "stasis of maturity" in Abdul-Malikian's poem and the obscenity of war that pervaded the work of the later British war poets, I received a long and challenging letter from a British Muslim. If I wanted to comprehend the Iranian motivation and resilience, Zainab Kazim wrote, I must understand the meaning of the seventh-century battle of Kerbala:

> I doubt whether I would be inaccurate in saying that the Iranians—in general—were aware of and understood the horrors of war *before* they were involved in the Iran–Iraq bloodbath. I think that Shias, on the whole, know a great deal more about the reality of martyrdom than the average non-Shia. I remember trying to explain the tragedy of Kerbala to my British friends at school and being astonished by their reaction. After all, I had already visualised the images of baby Ali Asghar with an arrow in his neck, Abbas with his arms slashed off, Akbar with a spear through his

chest and Hussain picking up each body, weeping over it and carrying it back to the tents . . . I had imagined the ladies of Imam Hussain's family being led through the bazaars after their bereavements and speaking out against the rulers. I have grown up with this history and it was and is a part of me. Most Shias are well aware of the price one may have to pay for standing by one's principles . . .

Gholamreza's car was hissing on the melting tar of the desert road when the man from Islamic Guidance tapped me on the shoulder. "Look over to your right," he shouted. Gholamreza slowed the car, the blowtorch heat swarming through the open windows. There was a railway track beside the road, but beyond it was the detritus of an army in defeat: burned-out Iraqi tanks and armoured personnel carriers, barrels cracked open, machine guns rusting on tank turrets, Saddam's monsters still decomposing in the desert. We walked across the railway and past a quicksand—the man from Islamic Guidance walked into it, up to his knees—and found ourselves among the wreckage of a great battle. Many of these vehicles had been driven into the sand and bogged down by their terrified drivers, their steel tracks snapping on rocks and concrete emplacements, their interiors turned into cauldrons by rocket-propelled grenades.

I climbed onto a T-62 tank, eased open the turret and lowered myself inside. The gun's breech had been blown apart, the driver's seat melted. A million tiny flies moved around this scorched, claustrophobic gunner's compartment. Perched on top of the tank, I began taking photographs, but realised that I could find no colour through my camera lens. I put the camera down and still saw no colour. The sun, the sheer whiteness of the desert, had sucked colour out of my vision, turning Saddam's armour into a dull monochrome. The man from Islamic Guidance was talking, more to himself than to me, but in English so that I would understand. "Think that he came here, Saddam, to our land, think of his arrogance, to think he would get away with this . . . How can you not understand why we had to fight him?"

On the other side of the main road, I recognised the skeletal outline of a Russian-made truck and walked across to it. Only the front of the driver's cab remained, pin-pricked by a thousand shrapnel holes and rusted grey. Behind it, punched into the desert floor, was a massive crater littered with ammunition tins that had been torn apart by some long-ago explosion and, half buried in the sand, thousands of heavy machine-gun bullets, congealed and twisted into grotesque shapes—a direct hit on an ammunition lorry. On the lip of the crater was some flaky white powder, perhaps human bone. The man from Islamic Guidance was sitting on the sand nearby, exhausted.

We walked off into the desert. We found an Iranian helmet with a bullet hole through it, dozens of army boots, one of them torn off at the heel with something dark inside. There were shell holes filled with dirt, and barbed wire, and a line of dugouts behind a trench, the floors lined with the lids of wooden ammunition boxes, the sandbags burst open. Somewhere near here, the Iranian poet Ali Babchohi had written a strangely moving pocm about a dream in which an old man from Nachlestan—a date-growing region in the south of Iran—appeared before him in the desert:

> *Hey, look over there!*
> *I can see him with my own blind eyes.*
> *Do you see him?*
> *It's old Shir Mohamed from the coast at Nachlestan*
> *With the glint of the sun on his musket.*
> *. . . I saw him with my own blind eyes.*
> *And old Shir Mohamed said to me:*
> *"I came to plant my rifle*
> *Instead of wheat and barley*
> *Across my land of dates."*

A few days earlier, in Tehran, I had talked to university students about the war. They were attending a philosophy seminar, fourteen young men and three women. Half of the men had fought during the eight-year war, one of the women had been a military nurse. Ex-*Basiji* volunteers, soldiers and Revolutionary Guards, they had been trying to analyse an impenetrable essay by an American sociologist. Then they tried to explain what the war had meant to them and why I did not understand it.

Shojae Ahmmadvande was bearded and looked to be in his thirties, though he must have been younger; he was just eighteen when he was sent to the front at Mehran on the Iraqi border, 170 kilometres east of Baghdad, in 1984. He spoke slowly, choosing his words with infinite care. "My involvement in the war was a reflection of the nature of our Islamic revolution. It was based on a new interpretation of religion—getting involved in the war was a sacred duty. We were led by a prophet-like statesman so this is how we perceived the war. This was the reason for our overwhelming commitment. The war could not be separated from our religion. I saw many incidents that cannot be described. I ask myself: 'Was it real or not?' There were extraordinary scenes that touched me."

And here Ahmmadvande looked at the floor, speaking to the ground rather than to me.

There was one day at the beginning of our *"Val Fajr 5"* operation in 1984. We were in the Mehran area and I was sitting with several other soldiers on top of a small hill. There was a man sitting with us, about thirty or thirty-five years old. And suddenly we all noticed that his head had fallen forward, just a little. We didn't know what had happened. Then we saw blood running from his arm and then from his head. A bullet had hit him in the head. And at this moment, he turned slightly, knowing he was hit, and he put his hand in his pocket and took out a Koran and started looking at it, and the blood was all the while flowing down his arm. Three of us just stood there in amazement—we couldn't do anything—this man was almost gone, he was in the seconds before his death, and he had taken out his Koran and was looking at it. It was a scene I will never forget all my life, the power of his commitment.

There was a long silence, and then one of the women, at the end of the room, dressed in a black chador, spoke. "In general, we were very proud of what we did in the war. Our nation of Iran proved its sovereignty. We know how people have returned home after other big wars. I've read about it in Hemingway. But this did not happen in Iran during the war. You have to understand the importance of morality in our war—morality was better than food. You think the number of deaths and casualties are important—you work these statistics out on your computers—but my impression is that here people died regardless of the material worth of their lives. It was their Islamic faith that mattered."

Exactly how many men died in the war may never be known—the Iraqis have not given precise figures—but the man who was in charge of the Revolutionary Guards during the 1980–88 conflict insisted to me that the Iranians lost well under 500,000 men. Mohsen Rafiqdoost, who by 1995 was running a multi-million-dollar foundation for the war wounded and the families of dead soldiers, claimed to me that 220,000 Iranians were killed and 400,000 wounded. "We think the Iraqis lost five hundred thousand dead. We don't know how many of their men were wounded. In addition to our Iranian war dead, we lost seventy thousand dead in the Islamic revolution the year before the war began."

Even today, the figures must be constantly revised upwards. The bodies of at least 27,000 Iranian soldiers were found on the borders of Iraq after the end of the war in 1988. In July 1997—nine years after the ceasefire—Iran was holding mass funerals for another 2,000 soldiers whose remains had only recently been discovered near the frontier. Four hundred of them were given a state funeral in Tehran attended by President Mohamed Khatami, while the bodies of the other 1,600 were buried in ceremonies in twenty-two towns around the country. Many of the casualties died in the first months of the war when the Iraqi army entered Khorramshahr and attacked Abadan.

Among the soldiers trying to fight off the Iraqi invaders was Mujtaba Safavi. He told me his story as he sat in the back of a Tehran taxi, locked into one of the capital's fume-clogged, traffic-jammed streets.

I was captured about twenty miles outside Abadan. We were surrounded at night. We had no chance. They took us to a big prison camp in Iraq, in Tikrit, the home town of Saddam Hussein. Our first years there were very hard. They killed some of us, tortured others. It was a year before the Red Cross visited us, took our names and brought us books. The younger ones among us were stronger than the older ones. I think it was because the younger ones felt their life was still in front of them. But two of our men in the prison killed themselves; they couldn't stand it any more. You know, if you are a prisoner, you have got to be very, very strong. I learnt a lot about myself in the prison, about how strong I could be. When the Red Cross brought me letters from home, they were already a year old. I wrote letters back and my mother still has them, but I do not want to read them now. They will remind me of terrible days.

When I asked Mujtaba the date of his release, he said it was the year after the war ended, 1989. He had been in prison camps for ten years—longer than any British Second World War POWs. When we met in 1995, Iran still maintained that 15,000 of its soldiers were being held in Iraq, some of them fifteen years after their capture.

When Gholamreza reached Khorramshahr, he shook his head at the ruins still strewn across the city. Fought over for two years and bombarded by the Iraqis for another six years, its brick-built apartments and factories were turned to dust by repeated Iraqi counter-offensives. It was Iran's—not Iraq's—Stalingrad. In the centre of the city, by a waterway littered with overturned, burned-out cargo ships, next to a mosque whose blue tiles were still being repaired, was a small museum of photographs marking the thirteenth anniversary of the city's liberation. "The photographer who took these pictures was martyred later in the war," the guide said. His right hand gestured to a corpse on the floor.

The soldier's body was so graphically re-created in wax, the dark blood seeping through his back, his face buried in sand, his helmet covering most of his hair, that for a moment I believed the Iranians had preserved a real soldier's remains. Next to the sand pit with its "martyr" stood a large portrait of Ayatollah Khomeini beneath the legend: "Martyrdom Is the Highest Point in Human Life." The photographs were of splintered trees and smashed railway yards, of ruined mosques and pulverised homes and bodies in side streets.

Another poet who fought in the war caught the sense of fury when he wrote about Khorramshahr under Iraqi occupation. Parvis Habib Abadi used traditional Iranian symbols of love—the butterfly hovering round a candle—and the anger of Abu Zaher, loyal friend of the Prophet Mohamed, to illustrate his rage:

> *My friend, how lonely we are,*
> *Away from this city that was ours,*
> *The candle's guttered out, the butterfly consumed by fire*
> *Everywhere, in every alley, I see just ashes, rubble, blood,*
> *A head here, over there some long, blood-matted hair,*
> *No hands left to comb it with.*
> *So until the time that head is recomposed upon the corpse,*
> *I wear my clothes as a shroud, screaming like Abu Zaher*
> *To put fear in all my enemies.*

But one man who liberated Khorramshahr had not wanted to die. He sat with me in a restaurant in Abadan, munching on his fish and potatoes, his mouth open, making too much noise. "I was in the naval service of the army and we came in at the liberation. I didn't see many bodies. You know, most of the Iraqis surrendered, 20,000 of them—can you imagine it? All with their hands up, like this." And there in the restaurant, to the surprise of fellow diners, he stuck his hands on his head, palms down. "But we should have ended the war then, in 1982. Saddam had offered a ceasefire, the Saudis offered Iran $70 million to rebuild. If we'd have stopped then, Saddam would have been overthrown by his own people. But another group of people had the Imam's ear and Khomeini decided to continue the war until Saddam was destroyed, to fight for Najaf and Kerbala and capture Basra. It was a big mistake. I decided to keep clear of the war then and got a job in Tehran. It went on for another six years. And we didn't even win. We only got all our lost territory back when Saddam was facing you after his invasion of Kuwait."

This was a rare voice of dissent. During the war, I remember, the dead would talk to the living, a permanent rebuke to those who might find fault with the military conduct of the conflict. The Revolutionary Guards had a house magazine, *The Guardian of Islam*, which carried memorial tributes to their newly dead comrades under an unimpeachable text: "Count not as dead those killed in the cause of God—but alive and living with their Lord." Shortly before he fell on the Shatt al-Arab, Hossein Chair-Zarrin would write in ungrammatical Persian that "I am being dispatched for the first time to the front—I had heard about the attack so I wanted to take part in it . . ." But to his mother, he wrote as if already in the afterlife: "Dear Mother, your son has broken loose from the chains of [worldly] captivity, of slavery and self-betrayal . . . Yes, dear Mother, your child has become a captive of Islam and has reached obedience, devotion and sincerity—of course if God accepts."

I was to grow used to reading these testaments with their convictions and—for want of a better word—their self-righteousness. Abulhassan As-Haq was almost blithe in his will. "Martyrdom is not a rank that everyone deserves," he wrote just before his death. "I am writing this will even though I think the possibility of being martyred is remote—but anyway, there's no shame in a young man having that ambition. I'm not frightened of the day of resurrection . . . when the first drop of martyr's blood is spilt, all his sins are cleansed . . . Yes, my dear ones, death will eventually take us all—no one lives for ever in this world—so why give away this golden opportunity?"

Now Khorramshahr was being rebuilt. There were new schools, two new hospitals, new factories and apartment blocks under construction. But the port was still in ruins, its wrecked ships blocking the river. At the harbourside, I stood next to one hulk—the *Race Fisher*, registered in Barrow-in-Furness—taking photographs, until two cops in black shirts turned up. The man from Islamic Guidance sprang out of Gholamreza's taxi to rescue me. "They are suspicious of foreigners with cameras," he said meekly. "People were hurt very badly in this city."

I toured one of the new hospitals where a doctor told me that the war was a "necessary" event in his life, as in the lives of all who fought. "I was twenty-one at the time and had a friend, Hossein Sadaqat from Tabriz. He was an Azeri, a good friend, very loyal. And one day during an advance, he was hit in the head by something and his brains came out all over me. I was right beside him, you see. I didn't want to believe it. There were no last words, nothing. Then I got hit in the shoulder by a piece of eighty-millimeter mortar shell. I was half-conscious and felt nothing at first, the pain came later." He pulled up his shirt to show me the wound. All over Iran, men showed me wounds, in their arms, their necks, their legs. One man talked to me through a false jaw—the original had been shot off—while another coughed through his words. He had been gassed. But when I asked the doctor if it had been worth it—all the pain, suffering, sacrifice—his face lit up. "Of course. We were defending our earth and our Islamic heritage. And we were angry, angry at our enemy."

That was what the Dezful poet Ghaysar Amin Pour felt when his home city came under nightly air attack. Perhaps because of this anger, his poem seems closer to us than others, touched with spite, even cynicism:

> *I wanted to write a war poem*
> *But I knew it wasn't possible.*
> *I would have to put down my cold pen*
> *And use a sharper weapon.*
> *War poems should be written with the barrels of a gun,*
> *Words turned into bullets . . .*
> *Here it's always red alert,*
> *The siren never ends its moaning*
> *Over corpses that didn't finish their night's sleep,*
> *Where bat-like jets which hate the light*
> *Bomb the cracks in our blind blackout curtains . . .*
> *We can't even trust the stars in case they're spies,*
> *We wouldn't be surprised if the moon blows up . . .*

Sometimes, this sense of indignation becomes political. Here, for example, is what Yahya Fuzi—thirty-one years old now, twenty-four when he fought in the war—said at that same Tehran University philosophy seminar:

War taught us about why people in the West who say they believe in freedom and human rights were ready to relegate these ideas to the background during our war. This was a major lesson for us. When Saddam invaded us, you were pretty silent, you didn't shout like you did when Saddam invaded Kuwait ten years later. But you were full of talk about human rights when he went to Kuwait. The crimes of Saddam were much more publicised then.

Another student, bespectacled, interrupted:

In our revolution in 1979, anti-dictatorial slogans were our cries against the Shah. But the war with Iraq completed this process of nation-building. At the top of a hill under shellfire, we would have guys from Baluchistan and

Kurdistan and other provinces all together. We all had to defend the same hill. And we had a lot of immigrants because of the war, people from Khuzestan driven out of their homes by the Iraqis, who fled to Tehran and Tabriz. There was this interaction with the rest of the population, an ethnic infusion. In this war, we were isolated, abandoned by everyone else, so we came to the conclusion that it was good to be alone—and we learnt about our fellow citizens, we felt united for the first time.

The idea that the Iran–Iraq War was, in a sense, the completion of the Islamic revolution in Iran—at the least, an integral part of it—was widely felt. The middle classes, who tried their best to stay out of the war, cut themselves off from history. The sons of the rich, using their visas to Canada, the United States, Britain or France, saw no reason to participate in what they regarded as a war of madness. "I spent the war in Canada, watched it on television and was glad I wasn't there," a twenty-nine-year-old told me at a party in Tehran. I couldn't dispute his logic but I wondered whether it had not deprived the rich, the old guard Iranians who regretted the revolution, of their claim to Iran. They, too, were isolated by the war, because they refused to defend their country.

But it is the dead rather than the survivors who speak most eloquently. South of Tehran, at Behesht-i-Zahra, close to the tomb of the old man who sent them to die, lie tens of thousands of Iranians who returned in body bags from the war. Still they arrive there today, in plastic bags, a skull or two with a body tag, recovered from the battlefields as the Iranians go on digging for lost souls along the western front. New graves are still being dug for corpses yet to be found.

The tombs are not marked, like those of our world war dead, with simple, identical gravestones, but with slabs of inscribed marble, engraved pictures, photographs, flags, sometimes even snapshots taken by frightened comrades in the minutes after death, the shells still falling around them, pictures of bodies covered in blood. I had seen this before at Chasar in the mountains above Tehran. But this graveyard is on a galactic scale, the *Gone With the Wind* of cemeteries, Iran's city of the dead. There is even a fountain that squirts blood-red water into the sky, the polar opposite of Saddam's seashell and concrete monument in Baghdad, although both, in their way, possess the same dull, frightening sanctity.

So here lies Namatallah Hassani. "Born August 1st, 1960, martyred October 30th, 1983 at Penjwin, student of the Officer's College," it says on his grave. "You have to sacrifice yourself before love—that is to say, you must follow the Imam Hossein." A face printed on a cloth screen shows Hassani, young with a small goatee beard. And here lies Mohamed Nowruzbei, "Martyred 1986, place of martyrdom Shalamcheh," and Bassim Kerimi Koghani, "Born 1961, martyred April 22nd, 1986, place of martyrdom Fakeh."

Many of these young men wrote their last messages to their families just before they died, long rhetorical speeches that begin with flowery praise of Khomeini and then disintegrate into humanity when they finish with personal wishes to their family. "I hope that I have done my duty by sacrificing my blood in the name of Islam," wrote Mohamed Sarykhoni, born 1963, killed in action March 17th, 1984, at Piranshahr in Iranian Kurdistan. But then he goes on:

> Give my best wishes to my father and mother, my sisters, my brothers, my friends. I hope they have been satisfied with me. I ask God to protect, forgive and bless you. To my wife, I say: it's true that my life was very short and I couldn't do all that I intended to provide for you. But I hope this short time we were together will be a wonderful memory for you. Take care of my child because he is my memory—for you and for my family too.

They speak from among the dead, these men. Hassan Jahan Parto, who was twenty-one when he was killed at Maimak in 1983, writes to his parents: "I advise my generous father and my family not to cry if I am martyred—don't be sad because your sadness would disturb my soul." But they do cry, the families, praying over the graves each Friday afternoon, eating beside their dead sons and husbands and brothers.

Mustafa Azadi, a *Basij* volunteer, was fighting in the hot desert at Shalamcheh when he was given the news that his nephew Haj Ali Jasmani had been killed. He offers me dates at the graveside. "He was one of the first men to join the Revolutionary Guards, and he fought until his martyrdom. He was hit by a shell. I was in the battle front when I heard the news. We were close to each other but it wasn't possible for me to see his body. What do I think now? That all the martyrs have put a responsibility on our shoulders to defend our faith."

This sounds too anachronistic to us Westerners, too much like John McCrae's "In Flanders Fields," whose martyrs warn the living that "If ye break faith with us who die/We shall not sleep, though poppies grow/In Flanders fields." Today we have seen through this martyrocracy: dictatorship—as opposed to government—by the dead. We think now of waste rather than responsibility. Robert Parry, a British soldier of the Second World War who participated in "regime change" in Iraq and Persia—he was part of the occupation force in Baghdad and Basra after the overthrow of Rashid Ali in 1941—was to write to me in 2004 with his own observations about the "lie" that dead soldiers "gave their lives for their country":

> Some magnificent men did just that by volunteering for suicide missions. Others gave their lives to save comrades. But for the vast majority coming back alive was their sustaining hope. Death took them without asking whether or not they wished to *give*. I lost a cousin in the 1914–18 war. Little more than a boy, half-trained, he was marched up into the front line. Arrived there, and out of curiosity, he looked out over the parapet. A German sniper got him. No time, like Hamlet, to choose.
> To give or not to give. That is the question.

I had taken Mujtaba Safavi, the ex-POW, with me to Behesht-i-Zahra, and he translated for each mourner, slowly, sometimes very moved by their stories.

Bahrom Madani described his dead cousin Askar Tolertaleri, killed at Maout, as "fascinated by God." Mohamed Junissian saw his son Said just ten days before his death. "We were talking at home. And his mother asked him: 'Why are you going back to the front again?' My son said he had to defend his country. His mother said: 'But you can be more useful to us here.' He said it was good to be at home but that the enemy was in our land and we have to push them back. I agreed with him." An old man with a grey beard said he had lost his nineteen-year-old son Hormuz Alidadi in a minefield twelve years ago at Dashdaboz. "It was God's will," he said. "We thank God he fought for Islam and his country."

Mohamed Taliblou only got his son Majid's remains back in 1994, "a few bones" dug up in the mud at Penjwin. "I have no feelings. He went to defend Islam and his country. It was in 1985, and I heard he had been wounded. One of his friends who was with him at the front came to see me and said: 'I saw Majid fall down, but I didn't see if he died or not.' It was during a counter-attack by the Iraqis. He was killed by a single bullet."

Mohamed Reza Abdul-Malikian wrote of last goodbyes in a poem called "Answer":

> "Why are you fighting?" my son asked.
> And me with my rifle on my shoulder and my pack on my back,
> While I'm fastening the laces of my boots.
> And my mother, with water and mirror and Koran in her hand,
> Putting warmth in my soul.
> And again my boy asks: "Why are you fighting?"
> And I say with all my heart:
> "So that the enemy may never take your light away."

The war had been over seven years now. Iranian diplomats were visiting Baghdad. The sons of the revolution—those who came home from the war—didn't find a land fit for heroes; it was they who were now angrily denouncing corruption in President Khatami's new "civil-society" Iran. But they came back, it seemed, having found faith rather than lost it, after an ecstasy of martyrdom that must leave us—horrified at the slaughter of two world wars, fearful of even the fewest casualties when we at last intervened in Bosnia, fixated by our own losses in Iraq— aghast and shocked and repelled. We mourn lost youth and sacrifice, the destruction of young lives. The Iranians of the eight-year Gulf War claimed to love it, not only as a proof of faith but also as the completion of a revolution.

For Iraqi soldiers, the war remained a curse. Hussein Farouk, an Iraqi military policeman, remembers the ceasefire as the moment an officer told his men that if they wanted to take revenge for the death of loved ones, now was the time. "One of our soldiers went into an Iranian prison camp. He had a brother who was killed. He just chose one of the Iranians. Then he shot him. He was the only one who did this." Farouk recalled the day he was himself guarding a group of Iranian prisoners. "They were all standing together and one of them asked me for some water. Of course, I gave him water. But then he picked up some soil from the ground and mixed it with the water and swallowed it. I watched in amazement. Then after a little while, the Iranian walked away, right past the guards. I ran after him and asked him what he thought he was doing. The Iranian looked puzzled. 'What?' he asked. 'Can you still see me?' "

Fati Daoud Mouffak, the Iraqi cameraman who had filmed the first casualties on the border in 1980, found that his experiences grew more crippling as the war continued. "We would go to the headquarters on the central front and they would say 'battle in Fakr' and they'd tell us the direction and we would go to the front and find a hole in the sandbags and point our lens through it. I saw many martyrs of both sides—I considered that both Iraqis and Iranians were martyrs." Mouffak filmed Iraq's prisoners—"Some were very young, fourteen or fifteen, they had gone through the minefields on motorbikes and were captured"—and saw an act of heroism that briefly lifted his spirits: an Iraqi soldier running onto the battlefield under fire to rescue a wounded Iranian, lifting his enemy onto his shoulder and bringing him to safety in the Iraqi lines. But he was to see other, more terrible things.

Outside Basra, an Iraqi military intelligence officer was screaming at an Iranian prisoner, demanding to know when the next attack would start. "The Iranian wouldn't talk and so our officer said he'd cut off his ear if he didn't give the information he needed. We journalists tried to stop this but we were told that this was none of our business. The Iranian still remained silent. So the Iraqi intelligence man cut off his ear. Then all the other Iranian prisoners started to talk."

We were paid three dinars each day to be at the front—that was nine dollars then—and we would pay for our own food at a hotel behind the lines. We'd come back tired and start drinking gin and tonic and whisky. We had another cameraman with us, a friend of mine, Talal Fana. He was so worried that he never had breakfast; he just drank Iraqi *arak*—he wanted the power to die. He would get completely drunk—that was how he would go off to the front because he was sure he was going to die—but he survived. Many soldiers drank. At al-Mohammorah [Khorramshahr], one of our television cameramen Abdul Zahera was wounded in the hand and lost a finger. Abbas, another film crewman, was hit in the chest. In 1987, Abdul Zahera was killed filming on the front at Qaladis on a hill called Jebel Bulgha. Abbas was killed in Fao in 1988, in the last battle there.

At the battle of Shalamcheh, Mouffak was stranded between the Iraqi and Iranian front lines, trapped with Iraqi soldiers who would have to surrender, hiding in shell holes and protecting his drunken friend Talal. He was ordered to fly in a helicopter—on Saddam's personal orders—to film close-quarters battles between Iraqi and Iranian troops outside Basra, "so close that they were stabbing each other with bayonets and we could not see which was an Iraqi martyr and which was an Iranian martyr. Saddam had ordered me to take two rolls of Arriflex [film] and I

used two whole rolls and later Saddam rewarded me with $3,000 and a watch."
Attached to the 603rd Battalion of the Iraqi army in 1987, Mouffak found himself
climbing a mountain in Kurdistan to film the scene of an Iraqi victory. But, lost on
the mountain in the dark, he stumbled into a killing field. "There were so many
bodies, I couldn't tell whether they were Iraqis or Iranians."

In 1985, Mouffak was to lose his own brother.

Ahmed was twenty-nine and one of his comrades had a wife who was
expecting a child, so Ahmed volunteered to do his job for him while his
friend went to Baghdad to see his newborn. It was May 5th, 1985. My
brother escorted an ammunition convoy to the front and it was ambushed
and we never learned any more. I went to the front there and spoke to his
commanding officer, Lt. Col. Riad, and he said he did not know what happened. "I do not know his fate," he said to me. Perhaps there was an explosion. We got nothing. No papers. No confirmation. Nothing. I was in
Baghdad when the war ended in 1988. I heard shooting in the air. People
said that the war was over. I went to have a drink—whisky and beer. I
thought that people would be happy and we would survive. I thought of my
brother—we had a hope that he would return if he was a prisoner. We
waited for years and years but no one came. He was lost. There was no letter, nothing. He was married with two daughters and a boy and his family
still wait for him to come home. They are still waiting for news. Because
there was no body, because there were no details of his death, his name was
not even put on the war memorial.

Mouffak would survive to film Iraq's invasion of Kuwait and then, under sanctions and no longer able to buy his beloved Kodak film—he still believes that film
gives a definition that video will never provide—he was reduced to taping a documentary on reconstruction. Until, that is, he was reactivated as a news cameraman
to film the 2003 Anglo-American invasion of his country. Yet he remains, even
today, haunted by the brutality he witnessed, especially by two deeply painful
experiences during the war with Iran. In Suleimaniya in northern Iraq, Saddam's
army suffered a serious defeat on Maout mountain in 1987.

There were military police on the roads below the mountain and they had
express orders from Saddam: that anyone who was found retreating must
be executed. Unfortunately, they caught three soldiers and they were to be
shot. I didn't have to watch. But I was a witness. I couldn't film. They were
between twenty and twenty-six years old. All three said the same thing:
"Our brigades collapsed—we retreated with the commanders." They were
all crying. They wanted to live. They couldn't believe that they would be
executed. There were six or seven in the firing squad. Each of the men had
his hands tied behind his back. They just went on weeping, crying and sobbing. They were shot as they cried. Then the commander of the firing squad

went forward and shot each one of them in the forehead. We call this the "mercy bullet." I vomited.

Yes, the "mercy bullet," the *coup de grâce*. How easily the Iraqis learned from us. Outside Basra, another young soldier was accused of desertion and again Mouffak was a witness:

He was a very young man and the reporter from *Joumhuriya* newspaper tried to save him. He said to the commander: "This is an Iraqi citizen. He should not die." But the commander said: "This is none of your business—stay out of this." And so it was the young man's fate to be shot by a firing squad. No, he did not cry. He was blindfolded. But before he was executed, he said he was the father of four children. And he begged to live. "Who will look after my wife and my children?" he asked. "I am a Muslim. Please think of Allah—for Saddam, for God, please help me. I have children. I am not a conscript, I am a reservist. I did not run away from the battle—my battalion was destroyed." But the commander shot him personally—in the head and in the chest. Then he lit a cigarette. And the other soldiers of the Popular Army gathered round and clapped and shouted: "Long life to Saddam."

# CHAPTER NINE

# "Sentenced to Suffer Death"

*Et puis mon souvenir s'éteindrait comme meurt*
*Un obus éclatant sur le front de l'armée*
*Un bel obus semblable aux mimosas en fleur*

*And then my memory would fade*
*As a shell blooms, bursting over the front line,*
*Magnificent, like mimosa in blossom*

—Guillaume Apollinaire,
"Si je mourrais là-bas," written on
30 January 1915, Nîmes

WHEN I WAS A BOY, my father would take me on his knee and place one of my fingers on a very small dent in his forehead. Running from it was a thin, old scar. "That's where the Chink got me with the knife," he'd say. And there would follow an odd story about how Bill Fisk had to solve a problem with a Chinese man during the First World War and how after he was attacked he shot dead his assailant with a revolver. "My Dad shot a Chinese man," I used to tell my friends at school. I could never explain why.

My father had a strange relationship with the 1914–18 war. He rarely wanted to talk about his own brief participation in the conflict, but all his life he read every book on the subject. He read the poems of Wilfred Owen—who, like my father, lived in Birkenhead—and he studied every official history of the Western Front. I can still remember his gasps of horror as he was reading the first critical biography of Earl Haig and realised that a man he once regarded with veneration was a proven liar. In a nursing home where he was recovering from cancer in the mid-Eighties, I asked him to recall his own memories of the trenches. "All it was, fellah, was a great, terrible waste."

My father called me "fellah" from the first day he saw me in my cot. He had been reading P. C. Wren's saga of the French Foreign Legion, *Beau Geste*. When one of the heroes bravely suffers a wound in silence, his comrade calls him "stout fellah." Never realising that *fellah* was an Arabic word for peasant or farmer, Bill always addressed me as "fellah" or "the fellah"—which was irony enough, since I would be spending half my life in the Arab world. Indeed, I was in Beirut when Bill Fisk died in 1992 at the age of ninety-three, unafraid of death but an increasingly angry and bitter man. He had been faithful to my mother, Peggy—his second wife—and he never lied or cheated anyone. He paid his bills on time. For about thirty years, he was Borough Treasurer of Maidstone in Kent. Every Sunday morning, he would wait for my mother to accompany him to All Saints' Church, striding up and down the hallway singing the 23rd Psalm. "Though I walk through the valley of the shadow of death, I shall fear no evil." He was a patriot. In 1940, he unhesitatingly agreed to a request from MI6 to form a resistance cell in Kent when it seemed likely that German troops would invade south-eastern England. At school, I used to show off his plans—to the envy of every boy in my class—for blowing up Maidstone East railway bridge while a German troop train was passing. Had the Nazis arrived, of course, Bill Fisk would have been shot as a "terrorists." For years, Karsh of Ottawa's great photograph of Churchill speaking over the wartime BBC from Downing Street loomed over our sitting-room in Maidstone—until, after my father's death, Peggy mercifully replaced it with a gentle watercolour of the River Medway.

Unfortunately, there were two sides to Bill Fisk. While he was loyal to my mother, he was also a bully. He would check her weekly housekeeping expenses as she waited in fear at his side for a word of criticism. If I interrupted him, he would strike me hard on the head. And his patriotism could quickly turn racist. In later years, and to my increasing fury, he would call black people "niggers" and when I argued with him he would turn angrily upon me. "How dare you tell me what to say?" he'd shout, while Peggy stood wringing her hands in the doorway. "Nigger means black, doesn't it? Yes, I'm a racist, and proud of it. I am proud to be English."

My mother would try to soften his language and would sometimes end up crying. At the age of nine, I was sent away to boarding school. I hated it—its violence as well as its class distinctions—and pleaded with my father for weeks, for months, for years, to take me away. My mother appealed to him too. In vain. Boarding school would enable me to stand up for myself, he told me. I was to be a stout fellah. His pride when I passed exams was cancelled out by his ferocity when confronted by a son who would not obey him. My clothes, my ties, my shoes were all to be chosen by him. Years later, when I told him I was sick of hearing his racist abuse—he had taken to cursing the Irish—he threw a table knife at me. My mother once told me that Bill had punched a council official on the jaw when he thought the employee was making a pass at her. Only after Peggy's death did my aunt tell me that it was the Mayor of Maidstone whom father laid out.

I was usually an obedient child. My father was for me—as fathers are for all young children—a protector, as well as a potential tyrant. I liked him when he was self-effacing. I tried to soften his temper by calling him "King Billy," which somehow satirised his dominating personality. And when he called himself "King Billy"—acknowledging his flaws with self-deprecation—he became an ordinary human. He taught me to love books and history, and from an early age I learnt of Drake and Nelson, of Harold of England and of the Indian Mutiny. His choice of literature could range from *Collins's Children's History of England* to the awful

G. A. Henty. By the time I was sent to boarding school, I knew about the assassination of an archduke at Sarajevo that had started the First World War and I knew that the Versailles Treaty of 1919 brought an end to the First World War but failed to prevent a second. So it was that at the age of ten, the "fellah" was taken on his first foreign holiday—to France, and to those battlefields that still haunted my father's mind.

When my mother died in 1998, I discovered the little scrapbooks she had compiled of this 1956 holiday, a cheap album with a green fake leather cover in which she had stuck a series of small black-and-white snapshots: Bill and Robert standing by our car—an Austin of England, it was called, and I can imagine why my father chose it—outside Dover Marine station, waiting for the old British Railways boat, the *Shepperton Ferry*, to take us to Boulogne; Robert in his school pullover sitting beside Bill, the car boot open and a paraffin stove hissing beside us; Robert loco-spotting French steam trains; and Bill and Peggy together by the car, slightly out of focus, a picture that must have been taken by me.

But it was clear where my father's mind was. "Through Montreuil, Hesdin, St. Pol, Arras," Peggy wrote in the album as she mapped our journey, "to—Louvencourt." And beside the word "Louvencourt" was a photograph of a road, framed by tall trees, with on the far side a barn with a sagging roof. I knew what this was. My father spoke of it many times later; he had found the very house on the Somme in which he slept on 11 November 1918, the last day of the First World War. On our 1956 holiday, my father had been too shy to knock on the door. Another snapshot shows him standing before a memorial of 1914–18 to the French dead from Louvencourt. He is wearing the tie he always wore, at work and on holiday, for seventy-two years: the navy-blue and maroon tie of the King's Liverpool Regiment.

He was wearing that tie one night in our hotel in Beauvais, waiting for my mother to join him at the bar. I had been suffering from food poisoning and Peggy had stayed with me until my father suddenly opened my bedroom door and said to her: "I want to speak to you—now." I listened at the thin wall that partitioned my room from theirs. "How dare you leave me waiting like that? How dare you?" he kept asking her. Then I heard Peggy weeping. And my father said: "Well, we'll say no more about it." He used that same phrase many times to me in later years. Then he would refuse to talk to me for weeks afterwards as punishment for some real or imagined offence. He didn't talk to Peggy for several days after he was kept waiting at the hotel bar. In the holiday scrapbook, we are always smiling. There were other holidays and other snapshots later, always through the battlefields of what Bill called the Great War. We went to Ypres many times. And to Verdun. By then, my mother was taking early colour stock home movie film. And in those pictures, too, we were always smiling.

Although Bill was reluctant to speak of his war, I had several times pestered him to tell a few stories. He had, it turned out, been bitten by a rat in the trenches in 1918. For several nights he lay in a first aid station actually inside Amiens Cathedral, its roof blown off by German shellfire—he remembered looking up at the stars as medieval gargoyles stared back at him. He had once shown me a photograph he had taken of the Western Front, a tiny, inch-long picture of muck and dead trees. My father had—against every military rule—taken a camera to the war in 1918. It sounded quite unlike the Bill I knew, who was usually as subservient to authority as he was jealous of his power in his home. He didn't say much about the war in the trenches—he had only arrived in August 1918—but when, in 1976, I was leaving to cover the Lebanese civil war for *The Times*, Bill turned to me and said: "Remember, fellah, it's not the shells you have to worry about—it's the snipers you have to watch out for." Advice from the trenches of the First World War. And he was right.

Not long before he died, he told me of his first marriage—it had been a secret from me until I discovered in Maidstone cemetery one day, by chance, his first wife's grave. She had been a childhood sweetheart, but when he had married her she had not returned his love, not even on the first night of their marriage. Matilda Fisk died in 1944, during the Second World War, which is how Bill came in 1946 to marry Peggy. She was twenty-five. He was forty-six.

But there is another story he told me, an astonishing one, quite out of character. At the very end of the war in 1918, he said, he had been ordered to command a firing party to execute a soldier. He had refused. Then, with the war over, the army punished him by forcing him to help transport the corpses left lying on the front lines for burial in the great British cemeteries. All the time I knew him, Bill hated things that rotted. A dead bird, a dead dog in a road would make him turn away. My father's insubordination sounded unlike him. But I admired him enormously for it. Indeed, as the years went by, I came to the conclusion that my father's refusal to kill another man was the only thing he did in his life which I would also have done.

For my twenty-eighth birthday, he bought me William Moore's *The Thin Yellow Line*, one of the first histories of capital punishment on the Western Front. My mother told me that Bill had read the book from beginning to end in total silence. He had wanted me to read of the fate of the 314 men executed by the British in the Great War. It seemed to prey on his mind. Not long before he died, I asked him if he knew the identity of the doomed soldier he refused to shoot. He was an Australian, my father replied, who had got drunk and then murdered a French gendarme. Someone else had commanded the firing squad.

That was all. I once asked Peggy to talk to my father about the war, to interview him as if she were a journalist, to find out about this missing segment of his life. She promised that she would. Yet on his death in 1992, all I found were nine short pages of notes in his own handwriting—in pencil—about the history of his family. "Born 1899 at 'Stone House,' Leasowe, Wirral, Cheshire," it said. "Father, Master Mariner Born 1868. Mother, Market Gardner's [*sic*] daughter, born 1869. Earliest record [of the Fisks] Danish professor, came to England 1737. [I] attended Council School. Won Scholarship to High School. Father unable to support me there, so no alternative but to leave school and compete for work in Borough Treasurer's Department. Examination (25 entrants) for 6 shillings per week—was successful and commenced two weeks before my 14th birthday in 1913." So no wonder my schooling was so important to Bill. The notes failed to mention that his father Edward had once been first mate on the *Cutty Sark*, the great tea-clipper now permanently in a Greenwich dry dock. There was another short entry, recording that only after the First World War was over did Bill discover that his own grandfather—his father Edward's father—had also served in the same conflict, as a naval reservist at Zeebrugge in 1918, when the British blocked the Belgian harbour to prevent its use by German U-boats and destroyers.

It would be another six years before I learned more. For when my mother lay dying in the autumn of 1998, I found in the roof of her home in Maidstone a tin box of the kind that families sent to soldiers in the Great War with soap and shaving brushes. On the front, the words "Parfumery Chiyotsbaki" were stamped above a painting of a young, half-smiling woman with roses in her hair. Inside the box were dozens of photographs from the 1914–18 war. Some were postcard-sized pictures of Bill's long-dead army friends in the uniform of the King's Liverpool Regiment, all of them with the solemn faces of doomed youth. "Lads from Preston" it said on the back of a large card. Others had been taken by Bill with his illegal camera. One I had seen before—the picture of the shattered countryside of the Western Front. "North of Arras 1918," Bill had written on the back. Another showed a young officer on horseback with the words "Self on Whitesocks near Hazebruck" on the reverse side. There was a French money coupon and a photograph of fifty young soldiers with my father, hatless, lying sprawled at the front, hobnailed boots towards the camera. A dramatic snapshot showed the 4th Battalion of the King's Liverpool Regiment on parade in driving snow at Douai in northern France, bayonets fixed amid the blizzard, another—much faded and probably poorly developed—showed the Douai artillery school, a vast Napoleonic building confronting a parade ground filled with British troops and horses and gun carriages. "Major General Capper inspects 'B' Company," he had written on the back.

And there was a larger photograph of Bill Fisk, leaning against the windowsill of a house in Arras, dated August 1918. He was a tall, handsome man, a shock of dark hair, deep-set eyes, protruding nose, a faint smile on his face, right hand self-consciously pushed into his trouser pocket, the horse rampant insignia of the regiment on his lapel. He looked like the young Burt Lancaster. Aside from the handsome appearance, I had to admit he looked a little like me.

Another picture showed him in an open-top car with a man and a woman. And a snapshot showed him in the French countryside in civilian clothes but still in his Great War puttees, the cloth wraps that British troops wore around their legs to prevent trench water from pouring into their boots. Behind him, hanging on a branch, was a woman's hat. Had there been a wartime love affair? He never said and my mother never spoke anything of it. When Bill was in France, she was not even born. But on his death, I had found two tickets to the races at Longchamps in 1919. "Throw them away!" my mother had commanded me. She didn't like the thought that Bill had kept those tickets all those years.

The tin of photographs had been stored in a shoebox in the roof. But in my mother's desk downstairs I found pages of notes in her handwriting. It was the interview with my father she had promised to make at least a decade earlier. Bill had spoken more freely to her. He describes his excitement at being posted to France—an amazing reaction from a man whose friends from Liverpool had already died at Ypres—and the thrill of wearing his first officer's uniform. He received a grant of £50 and "scrounged" a Smith & Wesson revolver. "I thought I was a Field Marshal," he told my mother. He was sent to France in August of 1918. "When I first got to France there were thousands of Chinese there," he said. "They were brought there to repair the roads from shell holes, and they had been robbing a French provision train, and we were the next battalion . . . I was a junior subaltern at the time." Bill arrived at the Chinese encampment near Arras to find a group of huts surrounded by barbed wire.

When I got there they wouldn't let us in . . . but they would let me in [alone]. I said to this Chinese man who could speak English: "I've been sent to make inquiries about a French supply train [with] my platoon of 30 men." [He said] "You can come in, but not your men"—which I didn't think much of. I didn't like that "not your men" a little bit. But I went in and sat at a table and there were Chinks all round, and this fellow aimed a knife at my forehead between my eyes. I was trying to read something, leaning forward, when I felt this fellow opposite me moving . . . he would have got me in the back of the neck if I hadn't moved. Well, I shot him dead and made for the door, and ran like hell—they were streaming after me and the Sarge that was in charge of these 30 men opened fire—I don't know how many of the Chinks they killed. It's a good job they did.

Many of the incidents Bill related to Peggy were told in an off-hand manner. The rat had bitten him on the chest just outside Arras—one of thousands that swarmed around the lines. "Their teeth must have been poisonous because they were eating casualties and dead men [who] had . . . been laying out for a week or more in the sun . . . The hospital at Amiens was staffed by German prisoners and that was where a German prisoner that was looking after me . . . gave me a shell case and he had inscribed on it a drawing of the regimental battalion horse, [my] name and rank and I took it home." Then he added in reference to me that "the lad would have liked that, I'm sure he would." For years, the shell case sat on his mother's mantelpiece in Birkenhead but then disappeared long before I was born.

The armistice of November 1918 was only a ceasefire and tens of thousands of British troops stayed on in the filth of the front lines in case hostilities with the Germans resumed. At Dover and Folkestone, thousands of British troops refused to board the boats to France in 1919, but my father volunteered to serve an extra year. He told my mother of his long horse rides with his colonel through the broken cities of northern France as the victorious powers dismembered the old empires of Europe and the Middle East at Versailles. One of his horses was blind in one eye and rode in circles, dumping him in a French railway yard. He was sent to Cologne as part of the army of occupation, and to Le Havre to oversee the departure of the last British fighting troops from France.

But still there was so little on the war itself, the agony of the trenches in which I knew he had spent weeks. And nothing of the execution party he said he had refused to command. The last page of my mother's notes broke off in mid-sentence. Had Bill destroyed the rest? My family was now gone, and I had inherited few of my father's memories—save for those recollections to my mother and the cache of little snapshots. But there was one other way in which I could seek the missing months of my father's life. In January 1999, I walked into the British Public Record Office in the London suburb of Kew and asked for Bill's personal war service file—along with the war diaries of his two battalions—the 12th and 4th King's Liverpool Regiment.

I have to admit to a slight tingle in the back of my hands when the tiny reader's computer bleeped and I walked to the desk where a middle-aged civil servant handed me file no. WO374/24476. The cover read "2nd Lt. Wm Fisk." But almost at once, my hopes fell. Printed on the same cover were the words "weeded in 1936" and "weeded in 1955." A file that might have contained fifty or sixty pages was left with scarcely twenty. Bill's commission as an officer was intact, his civilian status listed as "assistant book-keeper." The War Office questionnaire even asked if Bill was "of pure European descent." "Yes," Bill had replied. I don't suppose he had much trouble with that one. Under "power of command," an officer had written: "V fair. He only needs experience." Bill's dates of posting to France, his transfer to his postwar battalion and his final embarkation by steamship from Boulogne back to Liverpool just before Christmas of 1919 were all there. But nothing more. What had been taken out of the files? Reference to a refusal to command an execution, perhaps? A small massacre of Chinese workers?

A separate PRO file on the Chinese showed there were 187,000 of them in France by 1918, paid by the War Department, many of them lured away from their homeland by false promises that they would not be in the firing line—a promise that was a lie. Documents in the files refer to them as "coolies," stating that they should be kept away from Europeans. At least ten were executed for murder, several of them not even given the dignity of a name—only a number—when they were shot at dawn by British troops. The war diary of one British regiment did make a single intriguing reference to Chinese involvement in the looting of "French provision trains."

Then my reader's computer bleeped again. The war diaries of the King's Liverpool Regiment had arrived from the archives. In the last months of the Great War, a massive German offensive that almost reached Paris was turned back by British, Canadian, French and newly arrived American troops. Bill's last battles were thus part of a great Allied counter-attack that would still be in progress when the conflict ended. Handwritten on flimsy paper that was crumbling at the edges, the battalion war diaries came in big cardboard boxes. Yet the pages of the 12th

Battalion's history from August 1918 seemed eerily familiar. It would be many hours before I realised why this was so.

There were brief, hurried reports in the war diaries of "hostile shelling" and "enemy gas shells causing four OR [other ranks] casualties." On 22 August there was a raid towards German trenches which ended in the capture of two German prisoners. "Most of the enemy's concrete emplacements were destroyed by our artillery fire." On 1 November the battalion was in billets at Rue St. Druon in Cambrai. I knew my father had been in Cambrai—he had told me it was burning when he entered it with a Canadian unit—but what caught my attention was the handwriting. It was identical to the handwriting on the back of the snapshots I had found in the loft of my mother's home. Even the little squiggles that Bill used to put under his capital "D's were there. I found them under the "D" of Douai.

Bill Fisk must have been the second lieutenant tasked to write up the battalion war diary each night; of course, he had been an "assistant book-keeper." Sometimes the entries were only a few words in length, a remark about the "inclement weather"—all his life, my father called rainy days "inclement," much to my amusement—but there were other, longer reports in the dry military language that Bill would have been taught to use. "Strong fighting patrols out by day and night," Bill was reporting in early October. ". . . Patrols active and touch constantly maintained with the enemy. During the morning of the 5th contact patrols moved N. and S. from newly gained positions . . . Hostile opposition entirely in the form of M.G. [machine gun] Fire; machine guns appeared to be very numerous." In the official diaries, Bill always referred to the Germans as "the enemy." All his life, he called them "the Bosche."

He had been billeted in Douai. Yes, I knew that. Because along with the tin of snapshots—which included a long-distance photograph of German prisoners being led away down a tree-lined road by Bill's comrades in the King's Liverpool Regiment—were hundreds of black-and-white postcards. Everywhere Bill was stationed, he bought these cheap photographs of the cities and towns and villages of northern France. Some showed the devastation caused by German shellfire. Most had been printed before the war—of medieval towns with tall church spires and cobbled streets and Flemish house façades, of delicate tramcars rattling past buildings with wooden verandas—and were even then, as Bill collected them, souvenirs of a France that no longer existed.

In his collection from Douai, there were twenty-four postcards, some of which Bill had obviously sent home to Edward and Margaret Fisk in Birkenhead, because he had written a line or two on the reverse side. On the back of a prewar photograph which showed a streetcar negotiating the Rue de Bellain—devastated in the recent fighting—he had written with irony: "Haven't seen any car here yet." A picture of the Place d'Armes—the clock tower of the town hall in the distance, a set of elegant nineteenth-century town houses to the right—carried Bill's caption: "The buildings to the right of the tower are ruined. Our mess is about 100 yards from the Tower (Hotel de Ville)." There was a picture of the medieval Porte d'Arras—"My billet is 50 yards from here—Will," he had written, adding a kiss for his mother Margaret. He had included a printed drawing of a huge couple in Middle Ages regalia which captured Douai's long and violent history.* Much easier for Bill to understand was a dramatic photograph—obviously published after the town's liberation by the British—showing German occupation troops in spiked helmets goose-stepping past their officers in the Place du Barlet. He sent it home to Birkenhead, writing angrily on the back: "The Bosche [*sic*] manner in entering a town."

Much more precise, however, was a beautifully framed photograph, taken through an archway, of a set of turreted brick buildings close to the town hall. On the pavement to the right of the postcard, Bill had marked a cross. "I have put a cross under our mess," he wrote on the back. "1606, Passage de l'Hotel de Ville." The street had obviously survived the First World War. I wondered if it had survived the Second. On one of our interminable pilgrimages around the battlefields, Bill had driven my mother Peggy and me through Douai—it must have been in the late 1950s—but I had no memory of visiting these houses. All I can recall is that a gendarme had whistled Bill to a halt when he drove his beloved Austin of England car the wrong way up a one-way street. Bill had even bought a tiny wooden model of a fat gendarme to celebrate the occasion when a pompous French policeman dared to criticise the driving of one of Douai's British liberators. The model stood for years on the windowsill of the sitting room in our Maidstone home.

Eighty-six years after Bill sent those postcards from Douai, I pushed them carefully into an envelope—"2nd Lt. William Fisk," I wrote on the cover—and set off once more for the French city that Bill had entered under German shellfire in 1918. I'm not sure what I hoped to find in Douai. A ghost of the town he entered, a few of the buildings still standing, perhaps, an old pavement upon which a soldier had trodden a generation before me, cobblestones that he had marked with a cross twenty-eight years before I was born. The TGV express from the Gare du Nord flashed through the rainswept countryside of northern France, water lashing the carriage windows, sliding into Douai in just over an hour. I had the vague idea that it might be possible to use Bill's pictures to discover the city, to graft his image of Douai—albeit badly damaged by the time he sent his postcards home—onto the present, to walk in Bill's footsteps. One of his postcards showed the city's railway station, a fine three-storey nineteenth-century construction in the Dutch style, the windows embroidered in dressed stone, with horses and carriages and an early motor vehicle in the forecourt. But the station into which my train glided was a box, a cheap block of late 1940s concrete whose ceiling was peeling away. On the back of the station picture in 1918, Bill had written something illegible: "This is . . . a little." The missing word looked like "humped." Perhaps he meant "bombed" or "damaged."

---

*"Monsieur Gayant, seigneur de Cantin, nommé Jehan Gelon, délivra au IXe siècle la Ville de Douai assiégée par les Northmans" (Gayant, Lord of Cantin, who was called Jehan Gelon, freed the City of Douai which was under siege by the Norsemen in the ninth century). Bill, who always carried a small French dictionary with him as a soldier, wrote sadly on the back of the card: "Don't know what this means."

I soon discovered why. "The British and Americans bombed the place to pieces in the Second World War," an old man in the station buffet told me. "The Germans destroyed Douai in 1914 and then in 1918 and then the Germans destroyed it again in 1940 and then the British and Americans bombed it in 1944. They wanted to stop the Germans using the railway to send reinforcements to Normandy after the landings." I stopped at a local bookshop. The sixtieth anniversary of D-Day—*Jour-J* in French—had provoked an army of new books on the German occupation, though strangely not a single volume about the city in the First World War. But a booklet on Douai's military history recorded how German troops had occupied the city on 31 August 1914—twenty-seven days after the outbreak of war, just over four months after Bill's fifteenth birthday—how they had been driven out and then returned on 2 October. As a railhead and a centre of the French coal-mining industry, Douai would become a strategic military objective. All Frenchmen between the ages of seventeen and fifty were ordered to leave and then, when resistance to the occupation began, the Germans took hostages. Twenty hostages, including seven women, were sent to Germany on 1 November 1916, another thirty-three—twelve of them women—to Germany and Lithuania in late December 1917. In all, 193 civilians died in German hands during the Great War.

The rain had lifted and I pulled Bill's postcards from the envelope. The bookshop was in the Rue St. Jacques and one of Bill's pictures showed the same street before the Great War. There was a tramline, a cart and more than thirty people—many of them women in long white aprons—standing on the pavement and in the street. In the postcard, the street bent to the left, just as it did in front of me. A three-storey building to the left of the street bore an extraordinary wooden balcony, a big carved trellis that hung over the tramline. And there it still was. The building was decayed, the windows dirty, but the balcony was still there. This was still, conceivably, Bill's Douai. I walked along the canal. Again, Bill's postcard of the same canal showed several Flemish-style buildings identical to those along the *quai* upon which I was walking. I turned left into a cobbled street, its low cottages clearly untouched for a century. Did Bill and his fellow soldiers march down this street in October 1918?

It began to rain again and the cobbles turned shiny. I buried the postcards back in their envelope. There are times when journalists want to be film directors, to re-create history from both archives and experience. I could see the King's Liverpool Regiment moving down this street in the rain, their helmets shiny, the smoke of shelled buildings rising behind the houses, the few civilians allowed to remain in the city by the Germans waving to the British soldiers who had freed them. Would Bill, innocent nineteen-year-old Bill, have waved back? Of course he would. He was a liberator, a hero. He must have felt that. It must have been good to be a British soldier in Douai in 1918.

Did he know its history? Did Bill realise that eight hundred years before he arrived in this city, its liege-lords had set off on the Crusades to the Middle East, to liberate Jerusalem? Surely he could never have known that a family of Crusaders of this city would eventually settle north of Jerusalem, in the country we now call

Lebanon, would intermarry with local Christians to form a Lebanese family which is today the "Douaihy" family? Why, just over a quarter of a century ago, I tried to question the leader of another Lebanese Crusader family, old Sulieman Franjieh— "Franj" comes from "French" and is the Arabic for "foreigner" or even "Westerner"—about his participation in the machine-gun massacre of members of the Douaihy family in the Lebanese town of Zghorta in 1957. They were shot down in a Lebanese church, but old Sulieman refused to discuss this with me. His militiamen fingered their Kalashnikov rifles when I pressed the subject, and so I never discovered what lay behind his cold, French Crusader savagery. In Lebanon, even when challenged by overwhelming Muslim power, the Christians have always fought each other.

And history's fingers never relax their grip, never leave us unmolested, can touch us even when we would never imagine their presence. Europe and the Middle East, the "West" and the Arab world, are so inextricably entangled that even in modern-day Douai, I can be confronted by my own journalistic story. For in a narrow lane-way opposite the canal, I stop a young man and ask him for directions to the city archives. He promises to help me, tells me we will go to his university to find the address, apologises for his lack of local knowledge because he is—at this point I suddenly recognised his accent as we spoke French—Lebanese. Raymond Haddad was a Lebanese Christian from the Beirut suburb of Ashrafieh, his father a police officer who spent weeks trying to arrange a civil war ceasefire between the Christian Phalangist militia and General Michel Aoun, the messianic Christian Maronite army commander who claimed in 1988 that he was the Lebanese prime minister. I had spent more than two years reporting this absurd, pointless, bloody inter-Christian conflict and here I was, more than 3,000 kilometres away, seeking help from a Lebanese Christian as I tried to walk in my father's footsteps through a far more terrible, more horrific war. Raymond Haddad listened to Bill's story— those who have experienced war show understanding of such historical research, if not always a lot of sympathy—and eventually took me to the Hôtel de Ville whose great clock tower dominated many of Bill's postcards.

A woman in the town hall immediately identified the street with the cross on the pavement that marked Bill's mess in 1918. The arch in the photograph had been destroyed by Allied bombing in 1944 but it was easy to find the buildings on the right of the picture. They were identical: the balconies, the mock-château steeples on the top, the curve in the pavement, the elaborate stone frames around the windows. Long ago, the authorities had plastered over some gashes in the stonework of the walls—the shrapnel marks of the 1944 bombing that destroyed the arch—but the street was otherwise untouched. I rang the doorbell of number 1606 in the passage. Bill had walked over this doorstep, I told myself. Not the middle-aged Bill I remembered as a child, not the angry old man who would intimidate my mother, but a young Bill who believed in life and happiness and patriotism and, maybe, in love.

I don't know what I expected to find. Did I think that 2nd Lieutenant Fisk would open the door to me, that a fifty-seven-year-old son would meet his nineteen-year-old father, still wearing the khaki uniform in which he had been photographed at Arras in August of 1918? The door opened—the same door which had led to Bill's mess—and a small, friendly Frenchman greeted me with suburban *politesse*, a lawyer, I imagined—I was right—who expressed appropriate but not over-enthusiastic interest in my story. Yes, this was clearly the same house in which Bill's mess had been located. M. Michel Leroy was an *avocat* and expressed himself with precision. His wrought-iron balcony, with its lower railing bulging towards the narrow street, was clearly the same as the one in Bill's postcard. But everything inside had changed. He had remodelled the rooms—which had themselves been internally reconstructed long after the First World War—when he had bought the house eight years ago. His parents now lived in the long, low room where Bill and his fellow junior officers had drunk their pints and smoked their pipes in their mess. M. Leroy looked at my bearded Lebanese friend—who had survived his own war—and then at me—who had survived Raymond's war and several others—and thanked me formally for my interest in his home.

But why should a citizen of Douai have shown any more sympathy towards me? In the Second World War, British and American air attacks had killed 342 civilians in the town on one night alone, 11 August 1944, and left many ancient buildings—including the school of artillery that Bill had photographed just over a quarter of a century earlier—in ruins. Some of the dead must have been liberated by Bill and his fellow soldiers in 1918, only to be killed by his countrymen twenty-six years later. Bill must have liberated some of the thirteen French Jews of Douai who were deported by the Nazis in 1942. Several of Douai's citizens were to die under Gestapo torture; the local resistance had been strongly supported by local miners, many of whom were communists.

So what was Bill's war worth? I asked myself as my TGV slid back towards Paris through the dripping countryside of the Somme. My train crossed the line of the old Western Front, from German-occupied France into British-held France. For four years, tens of thousands of men died to hold these trenches—mere faint waves in the fields today—and my carriage crossed them in just under ten seconds, a hecatomb gone by in a sixth of a minute. And as I sipped black coffee in first class, a tiny British military cemetery zipped past so quickly that I could not read "Their Names Liveth for Evermore" beneath the plain cement cross amid the graves.

My father had always told me that when he died, I would inherit his library, two walls of books in his Maidstone home to which he would constantly refer as the years condemned him. "I always have my books," he would say. He held all of Churchill's published work, including a two-volume biography of Marlborough which Churchill—through the intercession of a friend in the National Savings Movement—had signed for Bill. I still from time to time take this book from its shelf. "Winston S. Churchill" signed his name with a fountain pen that has slithered across the page with the same self-confidence as it did when its author wrote his reports of action on the Afghan border, when he initialled the decision to land at Gallipoli in 1915, when he wrote his encomium to the young pilots of the Battle of Britain in 1940. By the time of my father's death, my own library was much larger than Bill's—I never told him this, of course—but his vast horde of works on the 1914–18 war and its aftermath was irreplaceable. Some of them would be used as references for this book. The memoirs of Haig and Lloyd George and Allenby—who entered Jerusalem in 1917 only eight months after Maude marched into Baghdad—leaned against weekly picture magazines of the Great War and analyses of the redrawing of the postwar world's frontiers.

In all, it was to take my father's generation just twenty-three months to create these artificial borders and the equally artificial nations contained within them. The new state of Great Lebanon was torn from the body of Syria and inaugurated by General Henri Gouraud on 30 August 1920. The constitution of Yugoslavia, the so-called Kingdom of Serbs, Croats and Slovenes, was promulgated on 28 June 1921. And the Anglo-Irish Treaty that partitioned Ireland was signed less than six months later, on 6 December. The League of Nations approved Britain's Palestine Mandate—incorporating the terms of the Balfour agreement—on 22 July 1922, eleven months after King Feisal, the son of Sherif Hussein, was set up by the British as king of Iraq. And it is, as I often reflect, a grim fact of my own life that my career as a journalist—first in Ireland, then in the Middle East and the Balkans—has been entirely spent in reporting the burning of these frontiers, the collapse of the statelets that my father's war allowed us to create, and the killing of their peoples. It is still a quaint reflection on the spirit of that age that most of the redrawing of maps and setting up of nations was supposedly done on behalf of minorities, minorities who in almost every case but two—that of the Jews of Mandate Palestine and the Protestants of Northern Ireland—did not want their maps redrawn at all.

Croats and Serbs fell out at once. Fierce sectarian rioting broke out in Ireland while Irish nationalists embarked upon a brutal civil war among themselves. The French destroyed the Arab army of Syria, executed its defence minister and cruelly put down revolts across both Syria and Lebanon. Britain was faced by a nationalist insurrection in Iraq. And by the 1930s, the British in Palestine were fighting a revolt by Arabs incensed that their land was to be divided and given to Jews as a homeland. The promises of independence that T. E. Lawrence had made to the Arabs were of no worth. Lord Balfour's 1917 declaration on Palestine specifically stated that "His Majesty's government view with favour the establishment in Palestine of a national home for the Jewish people" with a throwaway addendum that "nothing shall be done which may prejudice the civil and religious rights of existing non-Jewish communities in Palestine." In reality, Balfour had no interest in consulting the Arabs of Palestine as to their future. Indeed, the same Lord Balfour took an almost equally complacent—though somewhat more open—attitude towards Northern Ireland. Balfour gave vital cabinet support to Belfast prime minister James Craig's proposal that, in view of the number of Catholics who might serve in the new Royal Ulster Constabulary, a paramilitary Protestant force should be formed from the old sectarian Ulster Volunteer Force. A sectarian Palestine and a sectarian Northern Ireland, a sectarian Lebanon—founded upon the power of a thin minority of Christian Maronites—and a Syria and an Iraq divided and ruled by sects and tribes, and a Yugoslavia based upon ethnic suspicion: these were among the gifts my father's war bestowed upon the world.

Even while the conflict was still entombing its generations, the empires—victors and losers-to-be—used their colonial subjects as cannon fodder. Alongside my father on the Somme fought the Indians. Alongside the French at Verdun fought the Algerians and the Moroccans. In the Ottoman armies fought the Syrians and Palestinians and the soon-to-be Lebanese. My Lebanese driver, Abed Moghrabi, would often recall how his father was taken from his marriage only hours after his wedding night to serve in Turkish uniform against Allenby in Palestine. The Somme, where my father spent the last months of the war, had already soaked up the blood of tens of thousands of Catholic Irishmen who had fought and been cut down in British uniforms while their brothers died under British gunfire—or before a British firing squad—in Dublin.* Padraig Pearse and James Connolly and John McBride—and, yes, Eamon de Valera—all indirectly helped to save Bill Fisk's life. In the aftermath of their Easter Rising of 1916, my father was sent to Ireland rather than to France, where he might well have died on the first days of the Somme. He was to fight Sinn Fein—the "Shinners"—rather than the "Bosche." At least for now.

A quarter of a century ago, I travelled with a young Irishwoman to the Belgian city of Ypres, where in stone upon the Menin Gate are inscribed the names of those 54,896 men who fought in the same British army uniform as my father—but whose bodies were never found. They were fighting, they believed, for little Belgium—little Catholic Belgium—which had been invaded by the German armies in 1914. Looking at all those names on the Gate, the young woman was moved by how many of them were Irish. "Why in God's name," she asked, "was a boy from the Station House, Tralee, dying here in the mud of Flanders?"

After a few minutes, an elderly man approached, holding a visitor's book. He asked if she would like to sign it. This was long before an economically powerful and self-confident Irish Republic would face up to the sacrifice its pre-independence soldiers made in British uniform. So my friend looked at the British army's insignia on the memorial book with considerable distaste. The Crown glimmered on the cover in the evening light. Belgian firemen—as they do every night—were about to play the Last Post within the gaunt interior of the Menin Gate. There was not much time to decide. But my friend could not forget the young man from Tralee. She was facing history, which was not as easy and com-

---

*The politics of partition necessitate some statistics here. The 36th (Ulster) Division were almost all Protestants from the nine northernmost counties of Ireland—six of them now constituting Northern Ireland—who would have had no sympathy with the 1916 Dublin Rising. Their appalling casualties of 32,186 killed, wounded and missing were inflicted on the Somme and at Ypres. The 10th and 16th Irish Divisions, most of whom were Irish Catholics—many born in Britain—fought in Gaza and Palestine as well as the Somme and Flanders. Together, they lost 37,761 killed, wounded and missing. In all, 35,000 Irishmen are estimated to have been killed in the 1914–18 war.

forting and comprehensible for her as it can be for those of us who always consider ourselves the winners of wars. In the end, she wrote in the book, in Irish, *do thiortha beaga*—"for little countries." How carefully she eased the dead Irish soldier's desire to help Little Belgium—one of my father's reasons for going to war—into the memory of a tragedy of another little country, how she was able to conflate Ireland into Flanders without losing the integrity of her own feelings.

I admired her for this. It is easy to sign up for war, to support "the boys," to editorialise the need to stand up to aggression, invasion, "terrorism," "evil"—and the First World War was replete with definitions of "evil"—but quite another thing to sign *off* on war, to shake free of history's grasp, of the dead hand which catches us by the arm and reminds us that there is work still to be done, anger to be used up, ferocity to be assuaged, ambitions to be fulfilled, frontiers to be redrawn, states to be created, peoples to be ruled—or destroyed. Thus the First World War and the Gallipoli landings, which helped to provoke Turkey's unparalleled genocide against the Armenian people—the first holocaust of the twentieth century—left those same Armenian people abandoned when peace was agreed at Versailles. It did the same to the people of Kurdistan. In Bill's Great War, we Europeans used chemical weapons for the first time, another development we would bequeath to the Middle East. And how easily do we forget that the West's first defeat by Islamic arms in the modern age came not at the hands of Arabs but of the Turks, at Gallipoli and at Kut al-Amara in Iraq.

The European superpowers were blind to so many of the realities that they were creating. One is reminded of Lloyd George's description of Lord Kitchener. "He was like one of those revolving lighthouses," he wrote, "which radiate momentary gleams of revealing light far out into the surrounding gloom and then suddenly relapse into complete darkness." For many Britons, the Great War is an addiction, a moment to reflect upon the passing of generations, of pointless sacrifice, the collapse of empire, the war our fathers—or our grandfathers—fought. In my case, it was the war of my father and my great-grandfather. But it was the results of Bill Fisk's war that sent me to Ireland and Yugoslavia and the Middle East. The victorious mapmakers were not all of one mind. The border of Northern Ireland was a sign of imperial decline, the frontiers of the Middle East a last attempt by Britain and France to hold imperial power. No, Bill could not be blamed for the lies and broken promises and venality of the men of Versailles. But it was his world that shaped mine, the empires of his day that created our catastrophe in the Middle East. His postcards were not the only inheritance passed on to me by my father.

So how much further could I go in my search for Bill's life amid those gas attacks and shelling and raids mentioned in the war diaries—across the very same no-man's-land that was portrayed so vividly in the tiny snapshot I had received from my father?

In his battalion war diaries, under the date 10–11 November 1918, my father had written the following: "At 07.30 11th instant message from XVII Corps received via Bde [Brigade] that Hostilities will cease at 11.0 today—line reached at that hour by Advanced troops to remain stationary." Then, later: "Billets in Louvencourt reached at 18.00 hours." My father had arrived at the barnlike cabin that was to be his home until the end of the following January. I turned again to the notes my mother had taken from him before he died. "There was a château [at Louvencourt]," he said. "And most of the officers were billeted in the château because the occupants had gone and the junior officers were put in these scruffy little farm houses. I found myself in a derelict cottage and to get into my room, I had to go through a room where an old 'biddy' was in bed. Every morning I had to go through her room . . . she was always sitting in bed smoking a pipe."

I discovered that Bill's memory could be defective. In the 4th Battalion records is the following: "DUISONS 11 June 1919. 2 companies quelled trouble at Chinese Compound Arras . . . 1 officer and platoon remained as guard." I suspect that this is the official, censored version of the shooting at the Chinese compound, that the "officer" is my father. Only the date is 1919, not 1918. Bill had got the year wrong.

But he had remembered Louvencourt with great vividness. And one freezing winter's day, the countryside etched by snow banks and the fields of white military cemeteries, I travelled the little road I had taken with my parents more than forty years earlier, back to Louvencourt on the Somme. I had my mother's snapshot from the family scrapbook with me, which showed the house where Bill was billeted. Again, I'm not sure what I expected to find there. Someone who remembered him? Unlikely. He had left Louvencourt sixty years earlier. Some clue as to how the young, free-spirited man in the 1918 photograph could have turned into the man I remember in old age, threatening to strike Peggy even when she began to suffer the first effects of Parkinson's disease, who had grieved her so much that she contentedly watched him go into a nursing home, never visited him there and refused to attend his funeral?

I found the house in Louvencourt, the roof still bent but the wall prettified with new windows and shutters. Unlike Bill in 1956, I knocked on the door. An old French lady answered. She was born in 1920—the same year as Peggy—and could not have known Bill. But she could just remember her very elderly grandmother—my father's "old biddy"—who lived in the house. There was an old, patterned tile floor in the living-room and it must have been there for a hundred years. Bill Fisk in his hobnailed boots and puttees would have walked through here. At the end of the cold street, past the church, I found the château, half in ruins behind a yellow and red brick wall, and I met the oldest man in the village—he had three front teeth left—who did remember the English soldiers here. Yes, the officers had lived in the château.* His home had been the infirmary for the battalion. He was six at the time. The English soldiers used to give him chocolates. Maybe, I thought, that's why he lost his teeth.

---

*After I first wrote about my father's billets in Louvencourt in *The Independent*, I received a letter from a reader who said she now owned the château. She was British and told me that many of the officers had carved their names on the table and walls in the basement. Bill's name, of course, was not among them.

I walked back up the road. Opposite the house where my father had spent those cold nights I found another very small British war cemetery. And two of the graves in it were those of men who were shot at dawn by firing squad. Private Harry Mac-Donald of the 12th West Yorks—the father of three children—was executed here for desertion on 4 November 1916. Rifleman F. M. Barratt of the 7th King's Royal Rifle Corps was shot for desertion on 10 July 1917. Their graves are scarcely 20 metres from the window of the room in which 2nd Lieutenant Bill Fisk lived. Did he know who they were? Had their graves, so near to him, spoken to his conscience when he was asked to command a firing party and kill an Australian soldier?

From Paris, I called up the Australian archivist in charge of war records in Canberra. No soldiers from Australian regiments were executed in the First World War, he said. The Australians, it seemed, didn't want Haig's men shooting their boys at dawn. But when the war ended, two Australians were under sentence of death, one for apparently killing a French civilian. The archivist doubted if this was the man Bill spoke of, but could not be sure. And—it would have pleased my father, I thought—the condemned man was spared. Alas, the truth was far more cruel.

Yet another *Independent* reader wrote to me, referring to the case of an Australian soldier, an artilleryman serving in the *British* army, who had indeed been sentenced to death for murder—for killing a British military policeman in Paris, not a French gendarme. His name was Frank Wills and his file was now open at the National Archives in London. Back I went to what was once called the Public Record Office, where the computer bleeper had been replaced by a screen; but when I read that file number WO71/682 was waiting for me, I knew that these papers would contain a part of Bill's life. If he did not read them, he must have been familiar with their contents. He must have known the story of Gunner Wills.

The story was simple enough, and the trial of No. 253617 Gunner Frank Wills of "X" Trench Mortar Battalion of 50 Division, Royal Field Artillery, was summed up in two typed pages. He had deserted from the British army on 28 November 1918—more than two weeks after the Armistice—and was captured in Paris on 12 March 1919. He and a colleague had been stopped in the Rue Faubourg du Temple in the 11th arrondissement by two British military policemen, Lance Corporals Webster and Coxon. It was the old familiar tale of every deserter. Papers, please. Wills told the British military policemen that his papers were at his hotel at 66 Rue de Malte. All four went to the Hôtel de la Poste so that Wills could retrieve his documents.

According to the prosecution:
the accused and L/Cpl Webster went upstairs. Shortly afterwards two shots were fired upstairs . . . the accused came down and ran out with a revolver in his hand, he was followed by L/Cpl Coxon and fired three shots at him. One of the shots wounded L/Cpl Coxon in the arm slightly. The accused made off . . . but was chased by gendarmes and civilians and arrested. The revolver was taken from him and found to contain five expended cartridges.

L/Cpl Webster was found at the top of the stairs, wounded in the chest, abdomen and finger; he was removed to hospital and died three days later . . .

The Australian soldier, the dead policeman, the involvement of French gendarmes, Paris. This must have been the same man whom Bill was ordered to execute. Gunner Wills had joined the Australian army in 1915 at the age of sixteen—he was Bill's age—and was sent to Egypt, to the Sinai desert and to the Dardanelles. Like Private Dickens, Gunner Wills took part in Churchill's doomed expedition to Gallipoli. He too fought the Ottoman Turks. But in 1916 he had been sent to hospital suffering from "Egyptian fever"—which left him with mental problems and lapses of memory. The prosecution at his court martial did not dispute this. Frank Wills was discharged from the Australian army in 1917, then travelled to England and—a grim reflection, this, on the desperation of the British army at this stage of the war—was allowed to enlist in the Royal Artillery in April 1918. He arrived in France before Bill Fisk. Unlike Bill, however, nineteen-year-old Frank Wills was already a veteran.

Wills, according to his own defence, had been drinking. "He came to Paris for a spree . . . Had no breakfast on 12th March, 1919 . . . He was not drunk, but getting on that way. Does not remember whether he fired at L/Cpl. Coxon or not. He knew the revolver was loaded, and had been loaded since November 1918." A sad, eight-page handwritten testimony signed with an almost decorative "F Wills" explained how the two British military policemen asked him if he was carrying a pass to be in Paris and how, when he arrived with them at his hotel,

I rushed up the stairs to my room. I found the door of the room locked. Within a few seconds I heard someone coming upstairs. I had my great coat over my arm at the time. In a pocket of the great coat I had a revolver with six rounds. The revolver was issued to me by my unit . . . I took the revolver out of my pocket in order to hide it under the carpet on the landing. I did not want to be arrested with a revolver in my possession as I had a large amount of money on me and I had been playing crown and anchor. I thought a more serious charge would be brought against me in consequence. Scarcely had I taken my revolver out of my pocket when someone came up the stairs . . . This person rushed at me and I then saw it was Cpl Webster. No conversation passed. Cpl Webster had me by the right wrist. I was frightened and excited and in wrenching my wrist the revolver went off twice. Cpl Webster then let go my wrist and gave me a blow on the head and knocked me down the stairs. I was stunned by the blow on the head . . . I found the revolver lying on the stairs in front of me. I picked up the revolver. I was under the impression that Cpl Webster was following me down the stairs. I was bewildered and greatly excited. When I reached the street I heard one shot go off as I reached the pavement. I do not remember what happened after that until I was arrested.

Wills's testimony was that of a very young and immature man. "When I left my unit," he wrote, "I had no intention of remaining away. I met some of my friends and they persuaded me to come away for a spree. I eventually got to Paris. I intended to go back to my unit after seeing Paris: there was very little work being done at the time and things were rather slow. I got mixed up with bad company and had been gambling and drinking heavily . . ." Wills was to repeat this admission of his drinking problems in his last testimony. He claimed he still suffered from memory lapses. He had no pass to be in Paris and had returned to his hotel room to get his belongings. The two shots had been fired because Corporal Webster had "wrenched" his wrist. After his arrest, he wrote, French police had driven him away in a taxi and only after one of the policemen had hit him with a bayonet had his memory returned. "I was not drunk but was getting on that way. The deficiency in memory is brought on by drink . . ." It was not difficult to picture the young man, drunk, desperate, slowly realising the terrible fate that might await him. And again, I wanted to see this place, if it still existed, the hotel, the stairs, the second floor where Wills had fatally wounded the British military policeman, the street where Wills was arrested by the gendarme.

I fly back to France yet again. The Rue de Malte remains, a narrow one-way street cut in two by a boulevard, still home to a clutch of small, cheap hotels. And incredibly, No. 66 is still a hotel, no longer the Hôtel de la Poste, now the Hôtel Hibiscus. What on earth can I find here? The receptionist is Algerian and I ask for a second-floor room, nearest the stairs, the room in which Wills stayed. The hotel has been many times modernised, its walls flock-papered; there is a television in the lobby that is tuned to a football match with a commentary in Arabic. But the staircase is original, along with its ornate banisters and big iron knuckles, the kind installed in so many French houses in the late nineteenth century.

I tell the Algerian why I have come here and he suddenly bombards me with questions. Why did Wills come to Paris? Why did he shoot the military police-man? His name is Safian and he tells me that for his university degree in Algiers he studied the effect on children of a massacre at a village called Bentalha. Bentalha. I know that name. I have been there. I have seen the blood of a baby splashed over a balcony in Bentalha, a baby whose throat had been slit by young men who killed hundreds of civilians in the village in 1997. The Algerian government blamed Islamists for the slaughter. But I had always suspected that the Algerian army was involved. I repeat this to Safian. "I have heard this," he replies. "There is much to clear up about this massacre. I had a friend, he said the military were there and they advanced and they stayed just short of where the massacre was taking place. They did nothing. Why? I cannot say too much. Remember, I am an Algerian." I remember. I remember the villagers who survived. They said the same thing to me, that the Algerian army refused to come to their rescue.

Like the sudden meeting with the young Lebanese man in Douai, the Mid-dle East reaches out again. The fear of an Algerian—of his country, of his government—is present in this cheap hotel lobby in Paris. The killing of a soldier here more than eighty years ago is a safer subject. I translate Wills's testimony for

Safian. He cannot understand why Wills shot Corporal Webster when he would have received a lesser charge for desertion. I climb the stairs twice. It only takes fifteen seconds to reach the second floor. When I run up the staircase, I reach it in five seconds—the length of time it must have taken Corporal Webster. Wills would have had no time to conceal his gun—if he intended to. The second floor is only 5 metres square. Here Frank Wills struggled with Webster and left him lying in his blood on the floor. I walk into Room 22, nearest the stairs, Wills's room, the last place he slept in freedom before his death. Here he kept his great coat and his service revolver. He had been drinking on the morning of 12 March 1919, probably in this room. Punch, cognac and "American grog," he had told the court. There had been an American soldier staying in the hotel who fled after the shooting. No one ever found out his identity. Was there an army mafia at work here? Who was running the gambling dens, providing the drinks? Who gave Wills the money he was found to be carrying—6,640 French francs in notes and ten gold Louis coins?

I sit on my bed in Wills's room and read again through his testimony, this young man whom my father was ordered to kill, his last words written to spare his life.

> I am 20 years of age. I joined the Australian Army in 1915 when I was 16 years of age. I went to Egypt and the Dardanelles. I have been in a considerable number of engagements there, & in France. I joined the British Army in April 1918 and came to France in June 1918. I was discharged from the Australian Army on account of fever which affected my head contracted in Egypt. I was persuaded to leave my unit by my friends and got into bad company. I began to drink and gamble heavily. I had no intention whatever of committing the offences for which I am now before the Court . . . I ask the Court to take into consideration my youth and to give me a chance of leading an upright and straightforward life in the future.

I could see how this must have affected Bill Fisk. Wills was not only the same age—he had been sent to France only two months before Bill arrived on the Somme. Wills had not deserted in time of war. But he had killed a British military policeman. I remember how Bill believed in the law, justice, courts, magistrates, policemen.

I walk out of the Paris hotel into the soft summer night. To the left is the street in which the two military policemen asked Wills and his colleague for their papers. A little further is the street called "Rue Albert" in the British documents—it is the Rue Albert Thomas—in which Wills was grabbed by the French gendarme and pushed into a taxi and—according to Wills—struck by a bayonet. By then, he had forfeited his life.

The Court Martial summary states that Wills was "sentenced to suffer death"; he was taken to the British base at Le Havre on the French coast on 24 May. Bill was based there in May 1919—he took two snapshots of the camp, one of them with a church-tower in the background—and was present when Wills arrived. In the British archives, I had turned to the final record of his execution with something approaching fear. Bill had spoken of his refusal to command the firing party. I believed him then. But the journalist in me, the dark archivist that dwells in the soul of every investigative reporter, needed to check. I think that Bill's son needed to know that his father did not kill Frank Wills, to be sure, to be absolutely certain that this one great act was real.

And there was the single scrap of paper recording Wills's death. Shot by firing squad. "Sentence carried out 0414 hours 27th May," it read. The signature of the officer commanding was not in my father's handwriting. The initials were "CRW." A note added that "the execution was carried out in a proper and humane manner. Death was instantaneous." Was it so? Is death really instantaneous? And what of Wills in those last minutes, in the seconds that ticked by between four o'clock and 4:14 a.m., how did a man of only twenty feel in those last moments, in the dark in northern France, perhaps with a breeze off the sea? Did Bill hear the shots that killed him? At least his conscience was clear.

Bill Fisk was born 106 years ago but still remains an enigma for me. Was the French woman with whom he picnicked a girl who might have made his life happy, who might have prevented him returning on the Boulogne boat to Liverpool eighty-six years ago, to his life of drudgery in the treasurer's office and his first, loveless marriage? Was she perhaps the real reason why he volunteered to stay on in France after the war?

The Great War destroyed the lives of the survivors as well as the dead. By chance, in the same Louvencourt cemetery close to Bill's old billet lies the grave of Roland Leighton, the young soldier whose grief-stricken fiancée, Vera Brittain, was to write *Testament of Youth*, that literary monument to human loss. Perhaps the war gave my father the opportunity to exercise his freedom in a way he never experienced again, an independence that society cruelly betrayed. His medals, when I inherited them, included a Defence medal for 1940, an MBE and an OBE for postwar National Savings work, and two medals from the Great War. On one of them are the dates 1914–1919, marking not the Armistice of November 1918, but the 1919 Versailles Treaty which formally ended the conflict and then spread its bloody effect across the Middle East. This is the medal that bears the legend "The Great War for Civilisation."

In Peggy's last hours in 1998, one of her nurses told me that squirrels had got into the loft of her home and destroyed some family photographs. I climbed into the roof to find that, although a few old pictures were missing, the tin box containing my father's Great War snapshots was safe. But as I turned to leave, I caught my head a tremendous blow on a roof-beam. Blood poured down my face and I remember thinking that it was Bill's fault. I remember cursing his name. I had scarcely cleaned the wound when, two hours later, my mother died. And in the weeks that followed, a strange thing happened; a scar and a small dent formed on my forehead—identical to the scar my father bore from the Chinese man's knife.

From the afterlife, Bill had tried to make amends. Amid the coldness I still feel towards him, I cannot bring myself to ignore the letter he left for me, to be read after his death. "My dear Fellah," he wrote:

I just want to say two things to you old boy. First—thank you for bringing such love, joy and pride to Mum and me. We are, indeed, most fortunate parents. Second—I know you will take the greatest possible care of Mum, who is the kindest and best woman in the world, as you know, and who has given me the happiest period of my life with her continuous and never failing love. With a father's affection—King Billy.

# CHAPTER TEN

# The First Holocaust

*Pile the bodies high at Austerlitz and Waterloo.*
*Shovel them under and let me work—*
*        I am the grass; I cover all.*

*And pile them high at Gettysburg*
*And pile them high at Ypres and Verdun.*
*Shovel them under and let me work.*
*Two years, ten years, and passengers ask the conductor:*
*        What place is this?*
*        Where are we now?*

*        I am the grass.*
*        Let me work.*

                    —Carl Sandburg, "Grass"

THE HILL OF MARGADA is steep and littered with volcanic stones, a place of piercing bright light and shadows high above the eastern Syrian desert. It is cold on the summit and the winter rains have cut fissures into the mud between the rocks, brown canyons of earth that creep down to the base of the hill. Far below, the waters of the Habur slink between grey, treeless banks, twisting through dark sand dunes, a river of black secrets. You do not need to know what happened at Margada to find something evil in this place. Like the forests of eastern Poland, the hill of Margada is a place of eradicated memory, although the local Syrian police constable, a man of bright cheeks and generous moustache, had heard that something terrible happened here long before he was born.

It was *The Independent*'s photographer, Isabel Ellsen, who found the dreadful evidence. Climbing down the crack cut into the hill by the rain, she brushed her hand against the brown earth and found herself looking at a skull, its cranium dark brown, its teeth still shiny. To its left a backbone protruded through the mud. When I scraped away the earth on the other side of the crevasse, an entire skeleton was revealed, and then another, and a third, so closely packed that the bones had become tangled among each other. Every few inches of mud would reveal a femur, a skull, a set of teeth, fibula and sockets, squeezed together, as tightly packed as they had been on the day they died in terror in 1915, roped together to drown in their thousands.

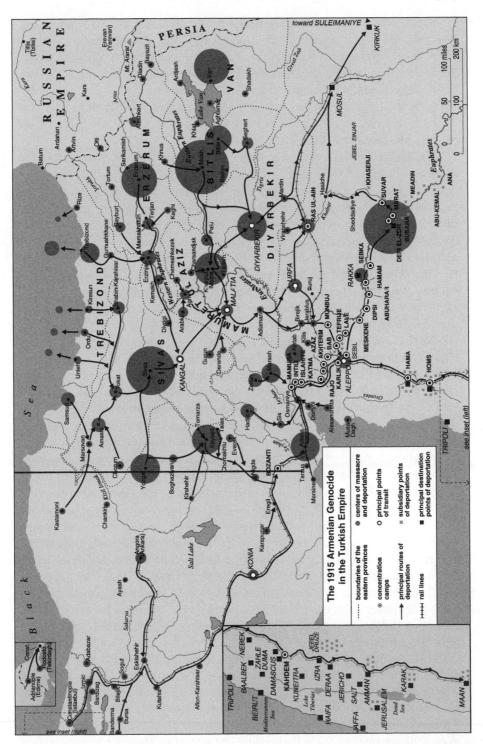

The 1915 Armenian Genocide
in the Turkish Empire

Exposed to the air, the bones became soft and claylike and flaked away in our hands, the last mortal remains of an entire race of people disappearing as swiftly as their Turkish oppressors would have wished us to forget them. As many as 50,000 Armenians were murdered in this little killing field, and it took a minute or two before Ellsen and I fully comprehended that we were standing in a mass grave. For Margada and the Syrian desert around it—like thousands of villages in what was Turkish Armenia—are the Auschwitz of the Armenian people, the place of the world's first, forgotten, Holocaust.

The parallel with Auschwitz is no idle one. Turkey's reign of terror against the Armenian people was an attempt to destroy the Armenian race. The Armenian death toll was almost a million and a half. While the Turks spoke publicly of the need to "resettle" their Armenian population—as the Germans were to speak later of the Jews of Europe—the true intentions of the Turkish government were quite specific. On 15 September 1915, for example—and a carbon of this document exists—the Turkish interior minister, Talaat Pasha, cabled an instruction to his prefect in Aleppo. "You have already been informed that the Government . . . has decided to destroy completely all the indicated persons living in Turkey . . . Their existence must be terminated, however tragic the measures taken may be, and no regard must be paid to either age or sex, or to any scruples of conscience."

Was this not exactly what Himmler told his SS murderers in 1941? Here on the hill of Margada, we were now standing among what was left of the "indicated persons." And Boghos Dakessian, who along with his five-year-old nephew Hagop had driven up to the Habur with us from the Syrian town of Deir es-Zour, knew all about those "tragic measures." "The Turks brought whole families up here to kill them. It went on for days. They would tie them together in lines, men, children, women, most of them starving and sick, many naked. Then they would push them off the hill into the river and shoot one of them. The dead body would then carry the others down and drown them. It was cheap that way. It cost only one bullet."

Dakessian knelt beside the small ravine and, with a car key, gently prised the earth from another skull. If this seems morbid, even obscene, it must be remembered that the Armenian people have lived with this for nine decades—and that the evidence of evil outweighs sensitivity. When he had scraped the earth from the eye sockets and the teeth, Dakessian handed the skull to little Hagop, who stood in the ditch, smiling, unaware of the meaning of death. "I have told him what happened here," Dakessian says. "He must learn to understand." Hagop was named after his great-grandfather—Boghos Dakessian's grandfather—who was himself a victim of the first Holocaust of the twentieth century, beheaded by a Turkish gendarme in the town of Marash in 1915.

In Beirut back in 1992, in the Armenian home for the blind—where the last survivors had lived with their memories through the agony of Lebanon's sixteen-year civil war, I would discover Zakar Berberian, in a room devoid of light, a single electric bar vainly struggling with the frosty interior. The eighty-nine-year-old Armenian cowered in an old coat, staring intently at his visitors with sightless eyes. Within ten years Zakar Berberian—like almost all those who gave me their testimony of genocide—was dead. But here is his story, just as he told it to me:

I was twelve years old in 1915 and lived in Balajik on the Euphrates. I had four brothers. My father was a barber. What I saw on the day the Turkish gendarmes came to our village I will never forget. I had not yet lost my eyesight. There was a market place in Balajik which had been burned down and there were stones and building bricks on the ground. I saw with my own eyes what happened. The men were ordered to leave the village—they were taken away and never seen again. The women and children were told to go to the old market. The soldiers came then and in front of the mothers, they picked up each child—maybe the child was six or seven or eight—and they threw them up in the air and let them drop on the old stones. If they survived, the Turkish soldiers picked them up again by their feet and beat their brains out on the stones. They did all this, you see? In front of their mothers. I have never heard such screaming . . . From our barber's shop, I saw all these scenes. The Turkish soldiers were in uniform and they had the gendarmerie of the government with them. Of course, the mothers could do nothing when their children were killed like this. They just shouted and cried. One of the children was in our school. They found his school book in his pocket which showed he had the highest marks in class. They beat his brains out. The Turks tied one of my friends by his feet to the tail of a horse and dragged him out of the village until he died.

There was a Turkish officer who used to come to our shop. He sheltered my brother who had deserted from the army but he said we must all flee, so we left Balajik for the town of Asma. We survived then because my father changed his religion. He agreed to become a Muslim. But both my father and my mother got sick. I think it was cholera. They died and I was also sick and like a dead person. The deportations went on and I should have died but a Turk gave me food to survive.

Berberian was eventually taken to a children's orphanage.

They gave me a bath but the water was dirty. There had been children in the same bath who had glaucoma. So I bathed in the water and I too went blind. I have seen nothing since. I have waited ever since for my sight to be given back to me. But I know why I went blind. It was not the bath. It was because my father changed his religion. God took his revenge on me because we forsook him.

Perhaps it was because of his age that Berberian betrayed no emotion in his voice. He would never see again. His eyes were missing, a pale green skin covering what should have been his pupils.

So terrible was the year 1915 in the Armenian lands of Turkey and in the deserts of northern Syria and so cruel were the Turkish authorities of the time that it is necessary to remember that Muslims sometimes risked their lives for the doomed Armenian Christians. In almost every interview I conducted with the elderly, blind Armenians who survived their people's genocide, there were stories of individual Turks who, driven by religion or common humanity, disobeyed the quasi-fascist laws of the Young Turk rulers in Constantinople and sheltered Armenians in their homes, treating Armenian Christian orphans as members of their own Muslim families. The Turkish governor of Deir es-Zour, Ali Suad Bey, was so kind to the Armenian refugees—he set up orphanages for the children—that he was recalled to Constantinople and replaced by Zeki Bey, who turned the town into a concentration camp.

The story of the Armenian genocide is one of almost unrelieved horror at the hands of Turkish soldiers and policemen who enthusiastically carried out their government's orders to exterminate a race of Christian people in the Middle East. In 1915, Ottoman Turkey was at war with the Allies and claimed that its Armenian population—already subjected to persecution in the 1894–96 massacres—was supporting Turkey's Christian enemies. At least 200,000 Armenians from Russian Armenia were indeed fighting in the Tsarist army. In Beirut, Levon Isahakian—blind but alert at an incredible 105 years old—still bore the scar of a German cavalry sabre on his head, received when he was a Tsarist infantryman in Poland in 1915. In the chaos of the Bolshevik revolution two years later, he made his way home; he trudged across Russia on foot to Nagorno-Karabakh, sought refuge in Iran, was imprisoned by the British in Baghdad and finally walked all the way to Aleppo, where he found the starving remnants of his own Armenian people. He had been spared. But thousands of Armenians had also been serving in the Ottoman forces; they would not be so lucky. The Turks alleged that Armenians had given assistance to Allied naval fleets in the Mediterranean, although no proof of this was ever produced.

The reality was that a Young Turk movement—officially the "Committee of Union and Progress"—had effectively taken control of the corrupt Ottoman empire from Sultan Abdul Hamid. Originally a liberal party to which many Armenians gave their support, it acquired a nationalistic, racist, pan-Turkic creed which espoused a Turkish-speaking Muslim nation stretching from Ankara to Baku—a dream that was briefly achieved in 1918 but which is today physically prevented only by the existence of the post-Soviet Armenian republic. The Christian Armenians of Asia Minor, a mixture of Persian, Roman and Byzantine blood, swiftly became disillusioned with the new rulers of the Turkish empire.*

Encouraged by their victory over the Allies at the Dardanelles, the Turks fell upon the Armenians with the same fury as the Nazis were to turn upon the Jews of Europe two decades later. Aware of his own disastrous role in the Allied campaign against Turkey, Winston Churchill was to write in *The Aftermath*—a volume almost as forgotten today as the Armenians themselves—that "it may well be that the British attack on the Gallipoli Peninsula stimulated the merciless fury of the

---

*The Armenians, descended from ancient Urartu, became the first Christian nation when their king Drtad converted from paganism in AD 301, and had to defend their faith against the Persians, who were Zoroastrian before becoming Muslim, and then the Arabs. The Turks arrived from central Asia in the eleventh century. Armenia and Greece were both Christian nations within the Ottoman empire.

Turkish government." Certainly, the Turkish victory at the Dardanelles over the British and Australian armies—Private Charles Dickens, who peeled Maude's proclamation from the wall in Baghdad, was there, and so was Frank Wills, the man my father refused to execute in 1919—gave a new and ruthless self-confidence to the Turkish regime. It chose 24 April 1915—for ever afterwards commemorated as the day of Armenian genocide—to arrest and murder all the leading Armenian intellectuals of Constantinople. They followed this pogrom with the wholesale and systematic destruction of the Armenian race in Turkey.

Armenian soldiers in the Ottoman army had already been disbanded and converted into labour battalions by the spring of 1915. In the Armenian home for the blind in Beirut, ninety-one-year-old Nevart Srourian held out a photograph of her father, a magnificent, handsome man in a Turkish army uniform. Nevart was almost deaf when I met her in 1992. "My father was a wonderful man, very intelligent," she shouted at me in a high-pitched voice. "When the Turks came for our family in 1915, he put his old uniform back on and my mother sewed on badges to pretend he had high rank. He wore the four medals he had won as a soldier. Dressed like this, he took us all to the railway station at Konya and put us on a train and we were saved. But he stayed behind. The Turks discovered what he had done. They executed him."

In every town and village, all Armenian men were led away by the police, executed by firing squad and thrown into mass graves or rivers. Mayreni Kaloustian was eighty-eight when I met her, a frail creature with her head tied in a cloth, who physically shook as she told her story in the Beirut blind home, an account of such pathos that one of the young Armenian nursing staff broke down in tears as she listened to it.

I come from Mush. When the snow melted each year, we planted rye. My father, Manouk Tarouian, and my brother worked in the fields. Then the Turkish soldiers came. It was 1915. They put all the men from the village, about a thousand, in a stable and next morning they took them from Mush—all my male relatives, my cousins and brothers. My father was among them. The Turks said: "The government needs you." They took them like cattle. We don't know where they took them. We saw them go. Everybody was in a kind of shock. My mother Khatoun found out what happened. There was a place near Mush where three rivers come together and pass under one bridge. It is a huge place of water and sand. My mother went there in the morning and saw hundreds of our men lined up on the bridge, face to face. Then the soldiers shot at them from both sides. She said the Armenians "fell on top of each other like straw." The Turks took the clothes and valuables off the bodies and then they took the bodies by the hands and feet and threw them into the water. All day they lined up the men from Mush like this and it went on until nightfall. When my mother returned to us, she said: "We should return to the river and throw ourselves in."

What Mayreni was describing was no isolated war crime. It was a routine. At the Kemakh Gorge, Kurds and troops of the Turkish 86th Cavalry Brigade butchered more than 20,000 women and children. At Bitlis, the Turks drowned more than 900 women in the Tigris River. So great was the slaughter near the town of Erzinjan that the thousands of corpses in the Euphrates formed a barrage that forced the river to change course for a hundred metres.

The American ambassador to Constantinople, Henry Morgenthau, himself a Jew, described what happened next in a telegram to the U.S. State Department:

> Reports from widely scattered districts indicate systematic attempt to uproot peaceful Armenian populations and through arbitrary arrests, terrible tortures, wholesale expulsions and deportations from one end of the Empire to the other accompanied by frequent instances of rape, pillage, and murder, turning into massacre, to bring destruction and destitution on them. These measures are not in response to popular or fanatical demand but are purely arbitrary and directed from Constantinople in the name of military necessity, often in districts where no military operations are likely to take place.

Mayreni Kaloustian, along with her mother Khatoun, her sisters Megad, Dilabar, Heriko and Arzoun and her two youngest brothers Drjivan and Feryad, set off on the death march from Mush the day after the men were murdered at the river.

> First we travelled in carts hauled by bulls. Then we had to walk for so many weeks. There were thousands of us. We begged food and water. It was hot. We walked from the spring and we did not stop until St. Jacob's Day, in December. I was only twelve and one day I lost my mother. I did not see her again. We went to Sivas. Then the Russians came, the army of the Tsar, and they reached Mush and blew up the bridge where my father was killed. We tried to go back to Mush but the Russians were defeated. Then my brothers and sisters and I all caught cholera. They died except for Arzoun and myself. I lost her, too. I was taken to an orphanage. You can never know what our life was like. The Turks let the bandits do what they wanted. The Kurds were allowed to kidnap the beautiful girls. I remember they took them away on horses, slung over the saddles. They took children. The Turks made us pay for water.

It is now largely forgotten that the Turks encouraged one of their Muslim ethnic groups to join them in this slaughter. Thus tens of thousands of Armenians were massacred—amid scenes of rape and mass pillage—by the Kurds, the very people upon whom Saddam Hussein would attempt genocide just over sixty years later. On the banks of the Habur River not far from Margada, Armenian women were sold to Kurds and Arab Muslims. Survivors related that the men paid 20 piastres for virgins but only 5 piastres for children or women who had already been raped. The older women, many of them carrying babies, were driven into the river to drown.

In 1992, 160 kilometres south of Margada, in a hamlet of clay huts 30 kilometres from the Iraqi frontier—so close that in 1991 the Syrian villagers could watch Saddam's Scud missiles trailing fire as they were launched into the night skies above their homes—I found old Serpouhi Papazian, survivor of the Armenian genocide, widow of an Arab Muslim who rescued her at Deir es-Zour. A stick-like woman of enormous energy, with bright eyes and no teeth, she thought she was a hundred years old—she was in fact ninety-two—but there could be no doubting her story.

I come from Takirda, twelve hours by horse from Istanbul. I was fifteen at the time. The Turks drove us from our home and all my family were put on a filthy ship that brought us from Konya to the coast and then we went to Aleppo—my mother Renouhi and my father Tatios, my aunt Azzaz and my sisters Hartoui and Yeva. They beat us and starved us. At Aleppo, my mother and Auntie Azzaz died of sickness. They made us walk all the way to Deir es-Zour in the summer heat. We were kept in a camp there by the Turks. Every day, the Turks came and took thousands of Armenians from there to the north. My father heard terrible stories of families being murdered together so he tattooed our initials in the Armenian alphabet on our wrists so that we could find each other later.

Tattooed identities. The grim parallels with another genocide did not occur to old Serpouhi Papazian. She was rescued by an Arab boy and, like so many of the Armenian women who sought refuge with non-Turkish Muslims, she converted to Islam. Only later did she hear what happened to the rest of her family.

The Turks sent them all north into the desert. They tied them together with many other people. My father and my sisters were tied together, Yeva and Hartoui by their wrists. Then they took them to a hill at a place called Margada where there were many bodies. They threw them into the mud of the river and shot one of them—I don't know which—and so they all drowned there together.

Ten years after the Armenian Holocaust, Serpouhi returned to the hill at Margada to try to find the remains of her father and sisters. "All I found in 1925 were heaps of bones and skulls," she said. "They had been eaten by wild animals and dogs. I don't even know why you bother to come here with your notebook and take down what I say." And Boghos Dakessian, in a bleak moment among the place of skulls on Margada hill, said much the same thing. One of the skulls he was holding collapsed into dust in his hands. "Don't say 'pity them,' " he told us. "It is over for them. It is finished." Serpouhi remembered the river running beside the hill—but Isabel Ellsen and I had at first found no trace of bones along the banks of the Habur

River. It was only when we climbed the hill above the main road to Deir es-Zour—almost 2 kilometres from the water—to survey the landscape, that we made out, faintly below us, the banks of a long-dried-up river. The Habur had changed its course over the previous seventy-five years and had moved more than a kilometre eastward. That is when Isobel found the skulls. We were standing on the hill where Yeva and Hartoui were murdered with their father. And it occurred to me that, just as the Euphrates had changed course after its waters became clogged with bodies, so here too the Habur's waters might have become choked with human remains and moved to the east. Somewhere in the soft clay of Margada, the bodies of Yeva and Hartoui lie to this day.

But the Armenian killing fields are spread wide over the Syrian desert. Eighty kilometres to the north, east of the village of Shedadi, lies another little Auschwitz, a cave into which Turkish troops drove thousands of Armenian men during the deportations. Boghos Dakessian and I found it quite easily in the middle of what is now a Syrian oilfield. Part of the cave has long since collapsed, but it was still possible to crawl into the mouth of the rock and worm our way with the aid of a cigarette lighter into its ominous interior. It stretched for over a kilometre underground. "They killed about five thousand of our people here," Dakessian said with a statistician's annoyance at such imprecision. "They stuffed them in the cave and then started a bonfire here at the mouth and filled the cave with smoke. They were asphyxiated. They all coughed till they died."

It took several seconds before the historical meaning of all this became apparent. Up here, in the cold, dry desert, the Turks turned this crack in the earth's crust into the twentieth century's first gas chamber. The principles of technological genocide began here in the Syrian desert, at the tiny mouth of this innocent cave, in a natural chamber in the rock.

There are other parallels. Enver Pasha, the Turkish war minister,* told Morgenthau that the Armenians were being sent to "new quarters," just as the Nazis later claimed that the Jews of Europe were being sent east for "resettlement." Armenian churches were burned like the synagogues of Nazi Europe. The Armenians died on what the Turks called "caravans" or "convoys," just as the Jews of Europe were sent on "transports" to the death camps. In southern Turkey, the Turks did sometimes use railway cattle wagons to herd Armenian men to their mass graves. The Kurds played the same role of executioners for the Turks that Lithuanians and Ukrainians and Croatians would later assume for the Nazis. The Turks even formed a "Special Organisation"—Teshkilat-i Makhsusiye—to carry out exterminations, an Ottoman predecessor to Hitler's Einsatzgruppen, the German "Special Action Groups."

Armenian scholars have compiled a map of their people's persecution every bit as detailed as the maps of Europe that show the railway routes to Auschwitz-

---

*When Enver held the city of Edirne during the calamitous Balkan wars, thousands of babies were named after the future mass murderer; Enver Hoxha, the mad dictator of Albania, was one, Anwar Sadat, the sane dictator of Egypt, another.

Birkenau, Treblinka, Dachau and the other Nazi camps. The Armenians in Sivas were driven to Malatya, from Malatya to Aleppo; or from Mush to Diyarbekir to Ras al-Ain or—via Mardin—to Mosul and Kirkuk. It is a flow chart of suffering, some of the "convoys" of humiliation and grief driven 150 kilometres south from Marash to Aleppo, then another 300 kilometres east to Deir es-Zour and then north—back in the direction of Turkey for another 150 kilometres up the Habur River and past the hill of Margada. Armenians were deported from the Black Sea coast and from European Turkey to the Syrian desert, some of them moved all the way south to Palestine.

What was at once apparent about this ethnic atrocity was not just its scale—perhaps two hundred thousand Armenians had been slaughtered two decades earlier—but the systematic nature of the Holocaust. A policy of race murder had been devised in wartime by senior statesmen who controlled, as one historian phrased it, the "machinery of violence, both formal and informal." Like the Jews of Europe, many Armenians were highly educated; they were lawyers, civil servants, businessmen, journalists. Unlike the Jewish Holocaust, however, the world knew of the Turkish genocide almost as soon as it began. Viscount James Bryce and the young Arnold Toynbee were commissioned to prepare a report for the British government in 1915, and their work, *The Treatment of Armenians in the Ottoman Empire 1915–1916*—700 pages of eyewitness accounts of the massacres—was to become not only a formative history of the slaughter but the first serious attempt to deal with crimes against humanity. Much of the testimony came from American missionaries in Turkey—the "non-governmental organisations" of the era—and from Italian, Danish, Swedish, Greek, U.S. and German diplomats and records.*

U.S. diplomats were among the first to record the Armenian Holocaust—and among the bravest eyewitnesses—and their accounts in State Department archives remain among the most unimpeachable testimonies of the Armenians' fate. Leslie Davis, the thirty-eight-year-old former lawyer who was American consul in Harput, has left us a terrifying account of his own horseback journeys through the dead lands of Armenia. Around Lake Goeljuk and in the space of just twenty-four hours, he saw "the remains of not less than ten thousand Armenians." He found corpses piled on rocks at the foot of cliffs, corpses in the water and in the sand, corpses filling up huge ravines; "nearly all the women lay flat on their backs and showed signs of barbarous mutilation by bayonets of the gendarmes . . ." On one of his excursions, Davis came across a dying Armenian woman. When she was

---

*The powerful Anglo-Armenian Association lobby group had been founded by Lord Bryce in 1890 and maintained constant pressure on the British government to ensure equal rights for Armenians within the Ottoman empire. A special supplement to the *Anglo-Armenian Gazette* of April 1895, in the possession of the author, contains a harrowing account of the massacre of Armenians at Sasun, a tub-thumping message of support from Lord Gladstone—"mere words, coming from the Turk, are not worth the breath spent in uttering them"—and a demand for a European-officered gendarmerie to protect "Armenian Christians." Their religion, rather than their minority status in the empire, was clearly the spur to British sentiment.

offered bread, she "cried out that she wanted to die." An Armenian college teacher called Donabed Lulejian who was rescued by Davis passed through a village littered with the bodies of men, women and children, and wrote an essay of pain and dignity—a "benediction," in the words of the Armenian historian Peter Balakian:

> At least a handful of earth for these slain bodies, for these whitened bones! A handful of earth, at least, for these unclaimed dead . . .
> We dislike to fancy the bodies of our dear ones worm-ridden; their eyes, their lovely eyes, filled with worms; their cheeks, their kiss-deserving cheeks, mildewed; their pomegranate-like lips food for reptiles.
> But here they are in the mountains, unburied and forlorn, attacked by worms and scorpions, the eyes bare, the faces horrible amid a loathsome stench, like the odour of the slaughter-house . . .
> There are women with breasts uncovered and limbs bare. A handful of earth to shield their honour! . . . Give, God, the handful of earth requested of Thee.

Germans, too, bore witness to the massacres because officers of the Kaiser's army had been seconded to Turkey to help reorganise the Ottoman military. Armin Wegner, a German nurse and a second lieutenant in the retinue of Field Marshal von der Goltz, disobeyed orders by taking hundreds of photographs of Armenian victims in the camps at Ras al-Ain, Rakka, Aleppo and Deir es-Zour. Today these fearful pictures of the dead and dying comprise the core of witness images. The Germans were also involved in building Turkey's railway system and saw with their own eyes the first use of cattle trucks for human deportation, men packed ninety to a wagon—the same average the Germans achieved in their transports to the Nazi death camps—on the Anatolian and Baghdad railways. Franz Gunther, a Deutsche Bank representative in Constantinople—the bank was financing the Turkish railway projects—sent a photograph of a deportation train to one of his directors as an example of the Ottoman government's "bestial cruelty."

Across the world—and especially in the United States—newspapers gave immense prominence to the genocide. From the start, *The New York Times* distinguished itself with near daily coverage of the slaughter, rape, dispossession and extermination of the Armenians. Its first reports appeared in the paper in November 1914. "Erzerum fanatics slay Christians," ran a headline on 29 November. Ambassador Morgenthau's representations to the Turkish government were published on 28 April 1915, under the words "Appeal to Turkey to stop massacres." By 4 October, *The New York Times* was headlining "Tell of Horrors done in Armenia" above a long dispatch containing details of atrocities, of torture, deportations and child-killing. On 7 October the paper's headline ran "800,000 Armenians counted destroyed . . . 10,000 drowned at once." Morgenthau's memoranda and Bryce's speeches to the House of Lords were given huge coverage. *The Nation* carried a series of powerful editorials, calling upon Berlin—the United States still being a neutral in the war—to stop the killings by its Turkish ally. Narratives of the mass murders were still being published in *The New York Times* in June 1919, almost eight months after the war ended; "Armenian girls tell of massacres," read the paper's headline on 1 June. Even in the Canadian city of Halifax, the local paper carried almost weekly reports on the genocide. A volume containing dispatches on the destruction of the Armenians which appeared in the *Halifax Herald* runs to 352 pages.

Rarely have ethnic cleansing and genocidal killings been given publicity on this scale. British diplomats across the Middle East were themselves receiving first-hand accounts of the massacres. In the former Ottoman city of Basra, Gertrude Bell, who would later be Britain's "Oriental Secretary" in Baghdad, was filing an intelligence report on the outrages received from a captured Turkish soldier.

> The battalion left Aleppo on 3 February and reached Ras al-Ain in twelve hours . . . some 12,000 Armenians were concentrated under the guardianship of some hundreds of Kurds . . . These Kurds were called gendarmes, but in reality mere butchers; bands of them were publicly ordered to take parties of Armenians, of both sexes, to various destinations, but had secret instructions to destroy the males, children and old women . . . One of these gendarmes confessed to killing 100 Armenian men himself . . . the empty desert cisterns and caves were also filled with corpses . . . The Turkish officers of the battalion were horrified by the sights they saw, and the regimental chaplain (a Muslim divine) on coming across a number of bodies prayed that the divine punishment of these crimes should be averted from Muslims, and by way of expiation, himself worked at digging three graves . . . No man can ever think of a woman's body except as a matter of horror, instead of attraction, after Ras al-Ain.

Even after the United States entered the war, its diplomats continued to compile reports on the atrocities. J. B. Jackson, formerly the American consul in Aleppo, wrote in July 1915 of a group of more than 1,000 women and children from Harput who were handed over to Kurds:

> who rode among them, selecting the best-looking women, girls and children . . . Before carrying off those finally selected and subdued, they stripped most of the remaining women of their clothes, thereby forcing them to continue the rest of their journey in a nude condition. I was told by eyewitnesses to this outrage that over 300 women arrived at Ras al-Ain . . . entirely naked, their hair flowing in the air like wild beasts, and after traveling six days afoot in the burning sun . . . some of them personally came to the Consulate (in Aleppo) and exhibited their bodies to me, burned to the color of a green olive, the skin peeling off in great blotches, and many of them carrying gashes on the head and wounds on the body . . .

The Armenian Holocaust was recorded, too, in countless private letters and diaries—some of them still unpublished—written by Europeans who found themselves in Ottoman northern Syria and southern Turkey. Here, for example, is an extract from a long account written by Cyril Barter, a British businessman who was sent out of Iraq to Aleppo under Turkish guard in 1915:

> I may tell you that two days south of Deir [es-Zour] we met the first fringe of Armenian refugees, and for the next three months I was seeing them continually. To attempt to describe their plight would be impossible. In a few words, there were no men of between sixteen and sixty among them, they had all been massacred on leaving their homes, and these, the remainder, old men, women and children were dying like flies from starvation and disease, having been on the road from their villages to this, the bare desert, with no means of subsistence, for anything from three to six months . . . It was a nightmare to me for a long time afterwards.

Barter would later submit a report to the Bryce Commission—which originally printed it anonymously—in which he recorded how carts would be taken through Aleppo for newly dead Armenians, the bodies "thrown into them as one would throw a sack of coal." Barter, too, would be a witness to the railway deportations, describing how Turks would drive Armenians from their places of refuge and "hustle them down to the railway station, pack them into the trucks like cattle and forward them to Damascus and different towns in the Hidjaz."

A British prisoner of war in Turkey, Lieutenant E. H. Jones, was to recall the fate of the Armenians of Yozgat, where he himself was held in a POW camp. "The butchery had taken place in a valley some dozen miles outside the town," he wrote. "Amongst our sentries were men who had slain men, women, and children till their arms were too tired to strike. They boasted of it amongst themselves. And yet, in many ways, they were pleasant enough fellows." As late as 1923, an Irish school-boy, John de Courcy Ireland, the future nautical writer and historian, would visit Castel Gandolfo outside Rome, where he would see Armenian refugee children, "dark, fascinating to look at but very quiet in spite of the disorder in which they swarmed."

As the survivors of the Armenian Holocaust have died, so their children have taken up their story. A number of Armenians not only escaped death in the 1915 deportations but were confronted by a second massacre in the Greek-held Turkish city of Smyrna—now Izmir—in 1922. "My father, Sarkis, not only survived the Syrian desert but barely made it out of Smyrna alive," his daughter Ellen Sarkisian Chesnut wrote to me.

> . . . he and two friends came to Smyrna just when Attaturk [sic] and his men had taken it over. Arrested and taken to an abandoned railway yard with several hundred Greeks and Armenians, they were subjected to rounds and rounds of machine gun fire. He survived the onslaught because he fainted. Later he was not so lucky when with fixed bayonets the Turkish soldiers repeatedly stabbed the dead and dying. Wounded badly on his forehead and leg, he nevertheless got up and made for the quay.

Ahead of him he saw two young girls trembling with fright and dazed by what they had seen. He could not leave them there. He grabbed ahold of their hands and the three of them ran for their lives. What they saw on the quay would stay with my father for the rest of his days. Tens of thousands of people crammed together in terror, with the flames of the dying city drawing ever closer. And yet . . . there was no help forthcoming from the British, French and American warships. But, in the distance, my dad saw that another ship was taking people on board. The three of them would have to jump into the water and swim for it. They did and were rescued by Italian sailors.

The first writer to call the Armenian genocide a holocaust was Winston Churchill, including in a list of Turkish wartime atrocities the "massacring [of] uncounted thousands of helpless Armenians, men, women and children together, whole districts blotted out in one administrative holocaust . . . beyond human redress." For Churchill:

the clearance of the race from Asia Minor was about as complete as such an act could be . . . There is no reasonable doubt that this crime was planned and executed for political reasons. The opportunity presented itself for clearing Turkish soil of a Christian race opposed to all Turkish ambitions, cherishing national ambitions that could be satisfied only at the expense of Turkey, and planted geographically between Turkish and Caucasian Moslems.

Acknowledging that British and American interest in the "infamous" massacre of the Armenians "was lighted by the lamps of religion, philanthropy and politics," Churchill said that the atrocities "stirred the ire of simple and chivalrous men and women spread widely about the English-speaking world."

But there were other, less chivalrous men whose interest in the Armenian Holocaust—gleaned at first hand—would prove to be a useful experience in a new and brutal Europe. Franz von Papen, for example, was chief of staff of the Fourth Turkish Army during the 1914–18 war and served as Hitler's vice chancellor in 1933. During the Second World War, he was the Third Reich's ambassador to Turkey. Another German who knew the intimate details of the Armenian genocide was Lieutenant General Hans von Seeckt, who was chief of the Ottoman General Staff in 1917. He laid the groundwork for the Wehrmacht in the 1920s and was honoured by Hitler with a state funeral on his death in 1936. Much more sinister was the identity of a young German called Rudolf Hoess, who joined the German forces in Turkey as a teenager. In 1940 he was appointed commandant of Auschwitz, and he became deputy inspector of all Nazi concentration camps at SS headquarters in 1944.

In a work of remarkable scholarship, the Armenian historian Vahakn Dadrian identified Max Erwin von Scheubner-Richter as one of the most effective Nazi mentors. Scheubner-Richter was German vice-consul in Erzerum and witnessed

Turkish massacres of Armenians in Bitlis province, writing a long report on the killings for the German chancellor. In all, he submitted to Berlin fifteen reports on the deportations and mass killings, stating in his last message that with the exception of a few hundred thousand survivors, the Armenians of Turkey had been exterminated (*ausgerottet*). He described the methods by which the Turks concealed their plans for the genocide, the techniques used to entrap Armenians, the use of criminal gangs, and even made a reference to the Armenians as "these 'Jews of the Orient' who are wily businessmen." Scheubner-Richter met Hitler only five years later and would become one of his closest advisers, running a series of racist editorials in a Munich newspaper which called for a "ruthless and relentless" campaign against Jews so that Germany should be "cleansed." When Hitler staged his attempted coup against the Bavarian government, Scheubner-Richter linked arms with Hitler as they marched through the streets and was shot in the heart and killed instantly by a police bullet.

We do not know how much Hitler learned of the Armenian Holocaust from his friend, but he was certainly aware of its details, referring to the genocide first in 1924 when he said that Armenians were the victims of cowardice. Then in August 1939 he asked his rhetorical and infamous question of his generals—in relation to Poles—"Who, after all, is today speaking of the destruction of the Armenians?" There have been repeated attempts—especially by Turkey—to pretend that Hitler never made such a remark but Dadrian has found five separate versions of the question, four of them identical; two were filed in German High Command archives. Furthermore, German historians have discovered that Hitler made an almost identical comment in a 1931 interview with a German newspaper editor, saying that "everywhere people are awaiting a new world order. We intend to introduce a great resettlement policy . . . remember the extermination of the Armenians." And there came another fateful reference to the century's first genocide when Hitler was demanding that the Jews of Hungary be deported; he ended a tirade to Admiral Horthy, the Hungarian regent, in 1943 with a remark about "the downfall of a people who were once so proud—the Persians, who now lead a pitiful existence as Armenians."

Historical research into the identity of Germans who witnessed the destruction of the Armenians and their later role in Hitler's war is continuing. Some Armenian slave labourers—male and female—spent their last months working to complete a section of the German-run Baghdad railway and were briefly protected by their German supervisors. But other German nationals watched the Armenians die— and did nothing.* What was so chilling about Hitler's question to his generals, however, was not just his comparison—the whole world knew the details of the Turkish destruction of its Armenian population—but his equally important knowledge that the perpetrators of these war crimes were rewarded with impunity.

---

*At a conference in Beirut in 2001, Professor Wolfgang Wippermann of the Free University of Berlin introduced evidence that many German officers witnessed the Armenian massacres without intervening or helping the victims.

In the immediate aftermath of the First World War, Turkish courts martial were held to punish those responsible and Turkish parliamentarians confessed to crimes against humanity. A Turkish military tribunal, unprecedented in Ottoman history, produced government records that were used as evidence at the trial. One exchange over the telegraph had a Nazi ring to it. An official says of the Armenians: "They were dispatched to their ultimate destination." A second voice asks: "Meaning what?" And the reply comes back: "Meaning massacred. Killed." Three minor officials were hanged. The triumvirate itself—Jemal, Enver and Talaat— was sentenced to death in absentia.

But the Turkish courts lacked the political will to continue, and the Western allies, who had boldly promised a trial of the major Turkish war criminals—the Armenian mass killings were described as "crimes against humanity" in an Allied warning to the Ottoman government in May 1915—lacked the interest to compel them to do so. Indeed, what was to come—the systematic attempt, which continues to this day, to deny that the mass killings were ever perpetrated—is almost as frightening as the powerlessness of the Allies who should have prosecuted those who devised the Armenian genocide. Talaat Pasha, the former interior minister, was assassinated in Berlin by an Armenian whose family had died in the genocide. Soghomon Tehlirian's trial and subsequent acquittal in 1921 meant that details of the Armenian Holocaust were widely known to the German public. Franz Werfel, the German-Jewish novelist, wrote a prophetic warning of the next Holocaust in his account of Armenian resistance to the Turkish killers, *The Forty Days of Musa Dagh*. He lectured across Germany in 1933, only to be denounced by the Nazi newspaper *Das Schwarze Korps* as a propagandist of "alleged Turkish horrors perpetrated against the Armenians." The same paper—and here was another disturbing link between the Armenian Holocaust and the Jewish Holocaust still to come—condemned "America's Armenian Jews for promoting in the U.S.A. the sale of Werfel's book."

Already, the century's first genocide was being "disappeared." Winston Churchill continued to emphasise its reality. In 1933, the same year that Werfel toured Germany, Churchill wrote that

> the Armenian people emerged from the Great War scattered, extirpated in many districts, and reduced through massacre, losses of war and enforced deportations adopted as an easy system of killing . . . the Armenians and their tribulations were well known throughout England and the United States . . . Their persecutors and tyrants had been laid low by war or revolution. The greatest nations in the hour of their victory were their friends, and would see them righted.

But the Armenians would be betrayed. The archives tell a bitter story of weakness and impotence and false promises. Here, for example, is Clause 1d of the Treaty of Sèvres between the Allied and Ottoman governments of 10 August 1920:

Turkey recognised Armenia as an independent state, and consented to accept President [Woodrow] Wilson's arbitration with regard to the boundary between the two states.

And here is Article 64 of the same treaty:

> If within one year . . . the Kurdish peoples shall address themselves to the Council of the League of Nations in such a manner as to show the majority of the population of these areas desires independence from Turkey, and if the Council . . . recommends that it should be granted to them, Turkey hereby agrees to execute such a recommendation and to renounce all rights and title over these areas.

Wilson's Fourteen Points were the United States' first attempt at a "new world order" and included honourable demands. Point Five insisted upon:

> a free, open-minded and absolutely impartial adjustment of all colonial claims . . . the interests of the populations concerned must have equal weight with the equitable claims of the government whose title is to be determined.

And Point Twelve clearly referred to the Armenians and the Kurds:

> The Turkish portions of the present Ottoman Empire should be assured a secure sovereignty, but the other nationalities which are now under Turkish rule should be assured an undoubted security of life and an absolutely unmolested opportunity of autonomous development . . .

Wilson did subsequently award the Armenian republic large areas of modern-day Turkey—including the provinces of Erzerum and Van—but the Turks and the Bolsheviks together destroyed it before the end of December 1920. Unlike a later president, however, Wilson was in no position to send a "desert storm" and drive out these armies and prevent yet another massacre of Armenians. The Kurds, who had been among the cruellest perpetrators of the Armenian genocide, were equally doomed. Enthusiasm for a British-protected Kurdish state that would act as a buffer between Turkey, Iran and Iraq was extinguished when Britain decided to win over Arab opinion in Iraq by including Kurdish areas in the state and when it became obvious that the emerging Soviet Union might benefit from the creation of a puppet Kurdish state.

American isolationism meant that the Armenians were to be abandoned. The Turks attacked a French army in Cilicia, drove them out of Marash and massacred another fifty thousand Armenians who believed they were living under French protection. A further massacre occurred in Yerevan. Of the Treaty of Lausanne, which registered the final peace between Turkey and the Great Powers, Churchill was to write: "history will search in vain for the word 'Armenia.'"

Yet it is important to remember that the one country which—in the immediate aftermath of my father's war—chose a truly democratic alternative to the Middle East was the United States of America. I am not just referring to the Fourteen Points, in themselves a powerful argument for democratic development. In a speech to Congress, Wilson stated that "people and provinces are not to be bartered about from sovereignty to sovereignty as if they were mere chattels and pawns in a game." U.S. diplomats and missionaries spread across the old Ottoman empire argued eloquently that the Arabs of the empire should be set up—without Turkey—as one "modern Arab nation," as they called it, to develop and progress in the world. Another powerful argument came from the King-Crane commission, set up under Wilson, which sailed to the Middle East to actually ask the peoples of the region what they wanted.

It was not Wilson's fault that illness and an increasingly isolationist American public caused a withdrawal from world affairs by the United States. In retrospect, however, that withdrawal—at a time when America was non-partisan in the Middle East—was one of the great tragedies of our time. We Europeans took over the area. And we failed. When the United States re-entered the region a quarter of a century later, it did so for oil and, shortly thereafter, as an almost unquestioning supporter and funder of Israel.

Lord Bryce, whose report on the Armenian genocide had done so much to enlighten public opinion, lamented in a lecture tour of the United States in 1922 that Allied failure to enforce the disarmament of the Turkish army had led the Turks to recover "their old arrogance." And in a most enigmatic phrase, he suggested there was more than war-weariness behind the Allied refusal to provide restitution to the Armenians. "Why the Turkish Government, which had in 1915 massacred a million of its Christian subjects . . . why after these crimes that Government should have been treated by the Allies with such extraordinary lenity— these are mysteries the explanation whereof is probably known to some of you as it is to me," he said. "But the secret is one which, as Herodotus says of some of those tales which he heard from the priests in Egypt, is too sacred for me to mention." The Armenians, Bryce said, had suffered more than any other peoples in the 1914–18 war and had been "most cruelly abandoned."

What was the secret of which Bryce claimed privileged knowledge? Was this a mere rhetorical flourish to explain the Allies' postwar irresolution? Or did he think that Britain and France wanted Turkey as an ally in the face of the newly created Bolshevik state that might soon threaten the oilfields of the Middle East? In Transcaucasia, British troops initially opposed the Bolsheviks—"smelling the oil of Baku," as one observer of the time put it—and for a short time preserved the independence of Georgia, Azerbaijan and a truncated Armenian state. But when Britain withdrew its troops in 1920, the three nations fell to the Soviet Union. In Turkestan, where we were interested in preventing Germany from gaining access to cotton supplies, British forces actually fought the Russians with the assistance of Enver Pasha's Turkish supporters, an odd exchange of alliances, since Tsarist Russia had been an ally of Britain until the 1917 Revolution.

In just one corner of their former Turkish homeland, the Armenians clung on;

in the province of Alexandretta and the now broken fortress of Musa Dagh, 20 kilometres west of Antioch, whose people had withstood the siege about which Werfel wrote his novel. Alexandretta fell under French colonial rule in the far north of Syria and so, in 1918, many thousands of Armenians returned to their gutted homes. But to understand this largely forgotten betrayal, the reader must travel to Aanjar, a small town of sorrow that blushes roses around its homes. From the roadside, smothering the front doors, all the way up Father Ashod Karakashian's garden, there is a stream of pink and crimson to mock the suffering of the Armenians who built this town on the malarial marshes of eastern Lebanon in 1939. They are proud people, holders now of Lebanese passports, but holders, too, of one of the darkest secrets of the Armenian past: for they were "cleansed" from their homeland twice in a century, first in 1915, then in 1939. If they blame the Turks for both evictions, they blame the French as well. And Hitler. Mostly they blame the French.

Father Karakashian's sister Viktoria was just ten in 1939, but she remembers her family's second disaster, a miniature genocide compared to the one in 1915, but nonetheless terrible. "The French army escorted us all the way," she said. "But we were dying. My brother Varoujan was only a year or two old, but I saw him die in my mother's lap in the truck. Like many of us, he had malaria. The French didn't seem to know what to do with us. They took us first for forty days to Abassid in Syria. Then they put us on ships for seven days. We landed at Tripoli [in northern Lebanon] and the French put us on a cattle train to Rayak. From Rayak, they brought us to Aanjar and here we remained."

Like most of the Armenians of Aanjar, Father Karakashian and his sister were born in Musa Dagh, the Armenian fortress town which is now in south-eastern Turkey and which held out for forty days against overwhelming odds during the genocide. Rescued by French and British warships, the Armenians of Musa Dagh were cared for in Egypt, then sent back to their home town with the French army after the 1914–18 war. And there they lived, in part of the French Mandate of Syria, until 1939, when the French government—in a desperate attempt to persuade Turkey to join the Allies against Hitler—"gave" Musa Dagh and the large city of Alexandretta back to the Turks.

The Karakashian children were born after the 1915 Holocaust, but many of their neighbours have no parents or grandparents. Even when they arrived in Aanjar—which was then in the French Mandate of "Greater Lebanon"—they continued to suffer. "There were plagues of mosquitoes and this place was a wilderness," Father Karakashian says. "The French gave each man twenty-five Lebanese pounds to break the rocks and build homes for themselves. But many people caught malaria and died." In the first two years of their ordeal—in 1940, when most of Europe was at war—the Armenians of Aanjar lost a thousand men and women to malaria. Their crumbling gravestones still lie to the north of the town.

The walls of Saint Paul's church in Aanjar are covered with photographs of the Armenian tragedy. One—taken in 1915—shows the survivors of the Musa Dagh siege climbing desperately onto the deck of an Allied warship. Another shows

French officers welcoming Armenian dignitaries back to Alexandretta, along with several men of the French army's "Armenian Brigade." In the 1930s, they built a memorial to the siege—it has since been destroyed by the Turks—and when they were forced to leave yet again before the Second World War, the Armenians took their dead, Serb-style, with them. The corpses of eighteen of the "martyrs" of the 1915 battle—whose bodies had been left untouched by the Turks until the French came with the Armenians in 1918—were stuffed on to trucks in 1939 together with the refugees, and brought to Aanjar along with the living. They rest now in a marble sarcophagus next to Saint Paul's church. "In eternal memory," it says in Armenian on the marble.

But memory has been softened for the people of Aanjar. "In the first ten years after leaving Alexandretta, the people—there were six thousand deportees who came here—wanted to go back," Father Karakashian said. "Then after the Second World War, a lot of our people emigrated to South America. Now we don't want to return. But I went back last year for a holiday. Yes, there is a tiny Armenian community left in our former bit of Turkey around Musa Dagh, thirty families, and they've just renovated the Armenian church. The Turks there are polite to us. I think they know what happened and they respect us because they know they are on our land."

The shame of France's surrender of the *sanjak* (provincial district) of Alexandretta—including Musa Dagh—is one of the largely untold stories of the Second World War. Fearing that Turkey would join the German Axis as it had in the 1914–18 war, France agreed to a referendum in Alexandretta so that the Armenian and Turkish inhabitants could choose their nationality. The Turks trucked tens of thousands of people into the *sanjak* for the referendum, and naturally the "people" voted to be part of Turkey. "The French government made the decision to give the place to Turkey and of course the Armenians realised they couldn't live there any more and requested from the French government that they be taken away and given new homes," the priest says. "They wanted to be rid of the Turks. So they left. The French made an agreement in their own interests. I blame the French." So the *sanjak* of Alexandretta became the Turkish province of Hatay, and the city of Alexandretta became Iskenderun. And the final irony was that Turkey did join the Allied side against Hitler—but only in the last days of the European conflict, when Hitler was about to commit suicide in his Berlin bunker and the Reich was in ashes. The sacrifice of Alexandretta was for nothing.

Nor have its ghosts departed. In 1998, the Turkish prime minister Mesut Yılmaz launched a warning against the Syrians who were assisting the communist Kurdistan Workers Party (PKK) guerrillas operating across the border. He chose a ceremony to mark the French handover of Alexandretta to announce that "those who have their eyes fixed on Turkish territory are suffering from blindness—not even a square centimetre of this country will be taken from it." Yet Alexandretta had been Armenian. So much for the Treaty of Sèvres.

The world is full of bigger and smaller genocides, some of which we know of from massive testimony and others to which we have blinded ourselves as surely as the Armenian refugee children lost their sight in the vile baths of the refugee homes to which they were taken in 1916. Mark Levene has written extensively about one of the lesser-known genocides—hands up, readers of this book, if you already know of it—when in 1933 the army of the nascent Iraqi state launched an exterminatory attack on members of the Assyrian community. Near the city of Dahuk, the soldiers massacred the entire population of a village called Summayl. The few surviving women were later gang-raped, and Kurds, who formed the predominant ethnic group in the region, joined in the mass killings—in some cases, no doubt, the very same Kurds who had looted and slaughtered the Armenians just across the Turkish border eighteen years earlier. This all happened in British-run Iraq and the local administrative inspector, a Colonel R. S. Stafford, reported to London that Iraqi officers had decided upon the killings with a view to the Assyrians being "as far as possible . . . exterminated." These Assyrians had been driven from Turkey after genocidal attacks on their villages, had sought sanctuary in Persia, and were then taken by the British to live near Mosul in what would be the new Iraqi state.

Levene has traced this pattern of confrontation with the Iraqi state all the way from 1933 to the Assyrian killings in Saddam's Anfal campaign of 1988. But even after the initial massacres, the British stifled an inquiry at the League of Nations by suggesting that it could lead to the collapse of King Feisal's regime, and promptly offered their bombs to the new Iraqi air force for their anti-Assyrian campaign—*after* the initial killings. The British also warned that a public inquiry might incite "an outbreak of xenophobia directed at foreigners"—something they only succeeded in doing seventy years later.

Any discussion of genocide in *The Independent* shows just how much it dominates the public mind. After writing about the Armenian Holocaust, the chairman of the Latvian National Council in Britain wrote to remind me that up to 11 million people died in the "terror famine" in the Ukraine between 1930 and 1933. "There will be no Holocaust Day for them," he said. What of the deaths of millions of Muslims expelled from the Balkans and Russia in the nineteenth century, "part of Europe's own forgotten past," as a historian has put it? Readers urge me to examine King Leopold II's Congo Holocaust, in which millions died—beaten or from physical exhaustion, famine or disease—in effective slave labour camps in the last century. And how are we to deal with those Spaniards who claim, with good reason, that Franco's annihilation of 30,000 political and military opponents—still buried in 600 mass graves across Spain—was a form of genocide?

When the historian Norman Davis wrote to me in 1998 to remind me that Hitler's question about the Armenians—"Who, after all, is today speaking of the destruction of the Armenians?"—was asked in relation to the Poles and first recorded by the Berlin bureau chief of the Associated Press, Louis Lochner, in August 1939, Davis concluded that "one is tempted to add—'and who, after all, speaks today of the annihilation of Poles?'" But sure enough, there was a book written anonymously just after the Second World War with a preface by, of all people, T. S. Eliot, which records the suffering of the millions of Poles deported to death and starvation by the Soviet army which had entered Poland shortly after the 1939 German invasion. And there is one passage in this book which always moves me, in which a Polish mother hopes that the deportation train will leave in the night:

> for the track went round a low hill just beside the homestead, and she hoped that the children need not see it and feel all their sorrow freshly burst out again. Unfortunately, the train left during the day. As the homestead came in sight, they saw neighbours and other members of the family standing on the hill and the parish priest with a crucifix in his hand . . . As the chimneys, the orchard, and the trees came clearly into sight, Tomus cried out in a terrible voice, "Mammy, Mammy, our orchard, our Pond, our . . . cow grazing! Mammy why do we have to go away?

That departure, the innocence of Tomus, his affection for the family cow, the growing awareness of the mother that the deportation train will pass their home, and that child's question echoes those of millions of other voices that would be heard on these same railway tracks as Hitler's Holocaust of the Jews gathered momentum in the months and years to come, just as they carried back to the Armenian Holocaust twenty-four years earlier. It was a Polish-born Jew, Raphael Lemkin, who in 1944 coined the word "genocide" for the Armenians, an act which helped to put in place the legal and moral basis for a culture of human rights.

So with all the evidence, the eyewitness accounts, the diplomatic reports, the telegrams, the bones and skulls of a million and a half people, could such a genocide be denied? Could such an act of mass wickedness as the Armenian genocide be covered up? Or could it, as Hitler suggested, be forgotten? Could the world's first Holocaust—a painful irony this—be half-acknowledged but downgraded in the list of human bestiality as the dreadful twentieth century produced further acts of mass barbarity and presaged the ferocity of the twenty-first?

Alas, all this has come to pass. When I first wrote about the Armenian massacres in 1993, the Turks denounced my article—as they have countless books and investigations before and since—as a lie. Turkish readers wrote to my editor to demand my dismissal from *The Independent*. If Armenian citizens were killed, they wrote—and I noted the "if" bit—this was a result of the anarchy that existed in Ottoman Turkey in the First World War, civil chaos in which countless Turks had died and in which Armenian paramilitaries had deliberately taken the side of Tsarist Russia. The evidence of European commissions into the massacres, the eyewitness accounts of Western journalists of the later slaughter of Armenians at Smyrna—the present-day holiday resort of Izmir, where countless British sunbathers today have no idea of the bloodbath that took place on and around their beaches—the denunciations of Morgenthau and Churchill, were all dismissed as propaganda.

Güler Köknar, head of the Assembly of Turkish American Associations, wrote to my editor, Simon Kelner, to claim that Armenians "had defected *en masse* to fight for the enemy, served as Fifth Columnists, and commenced a civil war against Ottoman Muslims." Ms. Suna Çakır wrote to tell me that claims of an Armenian genocide were "purely fabricated . . . a mere figment of the imagination." Aygen Tat of Washington, D.C., emailed my paper to say that an article I wrote about the Armenian genocide was "a fraud." The Hitler quotation was "fabricated" and "there never was an Armenian Holocaust or Genocide but there was a Turkish massacre by Armenians and their Czarist Russian masters." Tat's final line was to ask "why blame Turkey and the Turks for events that occurred in 1915?" Ibrahim Tansel said interestingly that the "so called Armenian genocide was partially response [sic] of villagers. In fact to avoid more bloodshed Armenians were moved from Anatolia to Lebanon." This flood of mail was performing something very disturbing: it was turning the perpetrators of the Armenian genocide into the victims and the victims into murderers and liars.

Each new letter—and some were clearly organised on a "round robin" basis—would add to the store of denial. S. Zorba of Rochester, New York, referred to "100-year-old unfortunate victims of the unfortunate event," which he later identified as "the alleged genocide." Other emails denounced me as "wicked" and one, after condemning my "ignorance" and "arrogance," finished with a very revealing line. "May be there was a genocide but it is not your duty to judge. It is up to historians to find out the reality." This was to become a weary refrain, repeated—incredibly—even by Israeli politicians, of whom more later.

But these remarks should not be seen in isolation. They were supported by Turkish diplomats. Korkmaz Haktanır, the Turkish ambassador to London, complained in a letter to *The Independent* that "many members of my family and their community suffered and died at the hands of Armenian terrorists." He enclosed two photographs of the bodies of horribly mutilated women, killed by Armenians—according to his captions—in the villages of Subatan and Merseni Dere in 1915. Fisk had shown, he asserted, "an eagerness to reopen old wounds"—which at least provided an admission that there were wounds inflicted in the first place.

Haktanir's opposite number in Israel, Barlas Özener, made an even more extraordinary démarche—in view of the country in which he was serving—in a letter to the *Jerusalem Post Magazine* in which he accused the author of an article on Armenia's "Genocide Denied" of an attempt to rewrite history. "The myth of 'Armenian Holocaust' was created immediately after World War I with the hope that the Armenians could be rewarded for their 'sufferings' with a piece of disintegrating Ottoman state," he wrote. What survivors of the Jewish Holocaust were supposed to make of this piece of "denialism" was beyond comprehension. The journalist, Marilyn Henry, had, according to Özener, "used her pen" to target "the new Knesset and the new Israeli government and Turkish–Israeli relations."

But Turkish diplomats need have no fear of Israel's opprobrium. When a Holocaust conference was to be held in Tel Aviv in 1982, the Turkish government objected to the inclusion of material on the Armenian slaughter. Again incredibly, Auschwitz survivor Elie Wiesel withdrew from the conference after the Israeli foreign ministry said that it might damage Israeli–Turkish relations. The conference went ahead—with lectures on the Armenian genocide—after Shimon Peres vainly asked Israel's most prominent expert in genocide, Israel Charny, not to include the Armenian massacres.

Peres was to go much further—and deep into the moral quagmire of Holocaust denial—in a statement he made prior to an official visit to Ankara as Israeli foreign minister in April 2001. In an interview with the Anatolia News Agency, Peres said that "we reject attempts to create a similarity between the Holocaust and the Armenian allegations. Nothing similar to the Holocaust occurred. It is a tragedy what the Armenians went through but not a genocide." If a position should be taken about these "allegations," Peres said, "it should be done with great care not to distort the historical realities." These astonishing comments by Peres—which flew in the face of all the facts that he must himself have been aware of, all the witness testimony, all the direct German links between the 1915 genocide and the Jewish extermination—received a powerful response from Charny, who is an Israeli academic of absolute integrity.

"It seems to me . . ." Charny wrote in a personal letter to Peres, "that you have gone beyond a moral boundary that no Jew should allow himself to trespass . . . it may be that in your broad perspective of the needs of the State of Israel it is your obligation to circumvent and desist from bringing up the subject with Turkey, but as a Jew and an Israeli I am ashamed of the extent to which you have now entered into the range of actual *denial of the Armenian Genocide*, comparable to the denials of the Holocaust." Charny reminded Peres that at a conference on the Jewish Holocaust in Philadelphia in 2000, a large number of researchers, including Israeli historians, signed a public declaration that the Armenian genocide was factual, and that a 1997 meeting of the Association of Genocide Scholars voted a resolution that the Armenians suffered "full-scale genocide." Nor did Charny flinch in his fine two-volume *Encyclopedia of Genocide*, which includes forty-five pages of factual testimony and contemporary diplomatic and journalistic accounts of the Armenian slaughter, especially from *The New York Times*, and—unusually—large quotations from original Turkish sources. One of them, the distinguished Turkish historian Ahmed Refik, who served in the intelligence service of the Ottoman general staff, stated categorically that "the aim of *Ittihad* [the Turkish leadership of the Committee of Union and Progress] was to destroy the Armenians."

Charny rightly pointed out that Peres's denial was founded upon his wish to advance Israeli–Turkish relations—relations that Turkey itself endangered when it interfered with Charny's 1982 genocide conference in Tel Aviv. According to Elie Wiesel, he was told "by an Israeli official . . . that the Turks had let it be known there would be serious difficulties if Armenians took part in the conference."

So for the Armenians, is there to be no justice, no acknowledgement of the terrible crime committed against them, no restitution, no return of property, no apology? Just a million and a half skeletons whose very existence the Turks still try to deny? Is Turkey so fearful, so frightened of its own past that it cannot do what Germany has done for the Jews—purged itself with remorse, admission, acknowledgement, reparations, good will? As Jonathan Eric Lewis of the Remarque

Institute at New York University has asked, "how can the destruction of a huge portion of the Ottoman Empire's merchant class be anything other than a central issue in Turkey's modern history? The lands, homes, and property of the Armenians are now in the hands of those who have benefited from past crimes. The fear of having to pay reparations is but one of the many reasons why the Turkish government refuses to acknowledge the genocide."

Yet still the denials continue. When Pope John Paul II dared to refer to "the Armenian genocide, which was the prelude of future horrors," the Turkish newspaper *Milliyet* libelled him on its front page with the headline: "The Pope has been struck with senile dementia." Dr. Salâhi Sonyel, claiming—falsely—that Hitler's question about the Armenians is a forgery, tried to disconnect it from the Nazi genocide by pointing out correctly that the German Führer was talking about the Poles, not the Jews. It sounds a strong line—until you remember that one-third of all Poles in 1939 were Jewish, the very section of the population Hitler intended to exterminate. This is the same Sonyel who entitled one of his essays: "How Armenian Propaganda against the Ottoman Caliphate swayed the gullible Christian World." The *real* difference between the Armenian Holocaust and the Jewish Holocaust, of course, is that Germany has admitted its responsibility while successive Turkish governments have chosen to deny the Armenian genocide.

In the United States, Turkey's powerful lobby groups attack any journalist or academic who suggests that the Armenian genocide is fact. For Turkey—no longer the "sick man" of Europe—is courted by the same Western powers that so angrily condemned its cruelty in the last century. It is a valued member of the NATO alliance—our ally in bombing Serbia in 1999—the closest regional ally of Israel and a major buyer of U.S. and French weaponry. Just as we remained silent at the start of the persecution of the Kurds, so we now prefer to ignore the twentieth century's first Holocaust.

This scandalous denial now even infects journalists. When the Pope visited Armenia in September 2001, the Associated Press felt constrained to tell its subscribers that "Turkey firmly denies Armenian charges that Ottoman Turk armies were involved in a genocide, a word that came into general use only after World War II." Quite apart from that wonderful word "firmly"—if the Turks are "firm" about it, you see, maybe they are right!—the word "charges" is a disgraceful pieces of journalism, and the reference to Lemkin's definition (which was made *during*, not after, the Second World War) fails to acknowledge that he was referring to the Armenians. The BBC, covering the same papal visit, also showed contemptible standards when it told listeners that "more than a million Armenians were killed as the Ottoman empire broke up." Note how the Armenians were killed rather than massacred and how this mysteriously took place during the breakup of the Ottoman empire—which is in any case factually incorrect, since the empire briefly continued after the First World War.

Most outrageous of all, however, has been *The New York Times*, which so bravely recorded the truth—and scooped the world—with its coverage of the Armenian genocide in 1915. Its bravery has now turned to cowardice. Here, for example, is a key paragraph from a 25 March 1998 *New York Times* report, by Stephen Kinzer, on the 70,000 Armenians who survive in present-day Turkey:

> Relations between Turks and Armenians were good during much of the Ottoman period, but they were deeply scarred by massacres of Armenians that pro-Ottoman forces in eastern Anatolia carried out in the spring of 1915. Details of what happened then are still hotly debated, but it is clear that vast numbers of Armenians were killed or left to die during forced marches in a burst of what is now called "ethnic cleansing."

Now I have a serious problem with this paragraph. First of all, the figure of a million and a half Armenians—or even a million Armenians—the all-important statistic that puts the Armenians in the genocide bracket, indeed marks them as victims of the first holocaust of the last century, has totally disappeared. We are left with what Kinzer calls "vast numbers" of killed which, I suppose, keeps *The New York Times* out of harm's way with the Turks. Then genocide is reduced to "ethnic cleansing," a phrase familiar from the Serb wars against the Muslims of Bosnia and the Albanians of Kosovo, but on an infinitely less terrible scale than the massacres of 1915. And note how this was a "burst" of "ethnic cleansing," a sudden, spontaneous act rather than a premeditated mass killing. Note, too, the reference to "pro-Ottoman forces" rather than the dangerous but real "Turkish forces," or even "Turkish Ottoman forces," that he should have been writing about. Then we are told that the issue is "hotly debated." How very "fair" of *The New York Times* to remind us that a campaign exists to deny the truth of this genocide without actually saying so, a lie every bit as evil as that most wicked claim that the Jewish Holocaust never happened. Another of Kinzer's articles was headlined: "Armenia Never Forgets—Maybe It Should."

I have my suspicions about all this. I think *The New York Times'* reporter produced this nonsense so as to avoid offending the present Turkish government. He didn't want his feature to be called "controversial." He didn't want to stir things up. So he softened the truth—and the Turks must have been delighted. Now let's supply a simple test. Let us turn to that later and numerically more terrible Holocaust of the Jews of Europe. Would Kinzer have written in the same way about that mass slaughter? Would he have told us that German–Jewish relations were merely "deeply scarred" by the Nazi slaughter? Would he have suggested—even for a moment—that the details are "hotly debated"? Would he have compared the massacre of the Jews to the Bosnian war? No, he would not have dared to do so. He should not have dared to do so. So why was he prepared to cast doubt on the Armenian genocide?

Kinzer was back to his old denial tricks in an article in *The New York Times* on 24 April 2002, about the proposed Armenian Genocide Museum in Washington:

> Washington already has one major institution, the United States Holocaust Museum, that documents an effort to destroy an entire people. The story it

presents is beyond dispute. But the events of 1915 are still a matter of intense debate.

Here we go again. The Jewish Holocaust is "undeniable," which is true. But its undeniability is used here to denigrate the truth of the Armenian Holocaust which, by inference, is not "beyond dispute" and is the subject of "intense debate." The "hotness" of the debate and its "intensity" again give force in both of Kinzer's articles to the idea that the Turkish denial may be true. The same slippage reappeared in *The New York Times* on 8 June 2003, when a famous photograph of Armenian men being led by Turkish gendarmes from an anonymous town in 1915 carried the caption "Armenians were marched to prison by Turkish soldiers in 1915." Scarcely any Armenians were marched off to prison. They were marched off—prior to the deportation, rape and massacre of their womenfolk and children—to be massacred. The town in the picture is Harput—the photograph was taken by a German businessman—and the men of Harput, some of whom are in this remarkable picture, were almost all massacred. But *The New York Times* sends these doomed men peacefully off to "prison."

Nor is *The New York Times* alone in its gutlessness. On 20 November 2000, *The Wall Street Journal Europe*, perhaps Israel's greatest friend in the U.S. press—though there are many other close contenders—went in for a little Holocaust denial of its own. While acknowledging the "historical fact that during World War I an estimated 600,000 Armenians, possibly more, lost their lives, many in forced deportations to Syria and Palestine orchestrated by Ottoman armies," it goes on to say—and readers should not smile at the familiarity of this wretched language—that "whether the majority of these deaths were the result of a deliberate policy of extermination or of other factors is a matter of contentious scholarly debate." Here is the same old vicious undercutting of truth. The Armenians "lost their lives"—as soldiers do, though rarely have journalists referred to massacre victims in quite so bland a phrase—in deportations "orchestrated" by "Ottoman armies." Once more, the word "Turkish" has been deleted. "Orchestrated" is a get-out phrase to avoid "perpetrated," which would, of course, mean that we were talking about genocide. And then at the end, we have our old friend the "debate." The truth of the Armenian genocide is "hotly" debated. Then it is subject to "intense" debate. And now this debate is "contentious" and "scholarly."

And I think I know the identity of the "scholar" whom the *Journal* had in mind: Heath Lowry, Atatürk Professor of Ottoman and Modern Turkish Studies at Princeton University, who has written several tracts—published in Turkey—attempting to discredit the Armenian genocide. Peter Balakian and the historian Robert Jay Lifton have done an excellent job of investigating Lowry's work. Lowry went to Turkey with a Ph.D. in Ottoman Studies, worked at a research institute in Istanbul and lectured at Bosphorus University, returning to America in 1986 to become director of the Institute for Turkish Studies in Washington, D.C. The American institute was set up by the Turkish government; from here Lowry wrote op-eds and essays denying the 1915 genocide, and lobbied Congress to defeat Armenian genocide commemorative resolutions.

What was astonishing, however, was that when the Turkish ambassador to Washington, Nüzhet Kandemır, wrote to Robert Jay Lifton to complain about references to the Armenian genocide in his new book *The Nazi Doctors*, the diplomat accidentally enclosed with it a letter from Lowry to the embassy which was an original draft of the ambassador's letter to Lifton himself; Lowry, in other words, was telling the Turkish ambassador how to object to the genocide references in Lifton's book, adding for good measure that he had "repeatedly stressed both in writing and verbally to Ankara" his concerns about the historians whose scholarship had been used by Lifton; they included the indefatigable Vahakn Dadrian. What was Lowry doing, advising the Turkish government how to deny the Armenian Holocaust?

There are other chairs of Turkish studies at Harvard, Georgetown, Indiana, Portland State and Chicago. To qualify, the holders must have performed research work in archives in Turkey (often closed to historians critical of that country) and have "friendly relations with the Turkish academic community"—something they are not going to have if they address the substance of the Armenian genocide. The University of California at Los Angeles had the courage to turn down a chair. All holders, of course, believe that "historians" must primarily decide the truth, an expression that precludes evidence from the dwindling survivors of the massacres. All this prompted 150 Holocaust scholars and historians to call upon Turkey to end its campaign of denial; they included Lifton, Israel Charny, Yehuda Bauer, Howard Zinn and Deborah Lipstadt. They failed. It was Elie Wiesel who first said that denial of genocide was a "double killing." First the victims are slaughtered—and then their deaths are turned into a non-event, an "un-fact." The dead die twice. The survivors suffer and are then told they did not suffer, that they are lying.

And big guns are brought into action—almost literally—to ensure that this remains the case. When the U.S. House of Representatives proposed an Armenian Genocide Resolution in 2000, asking President Clinton in his annual Armenian commemoration address to refer to the killings as genocide—it had the votes to pass—Turkey warned Washington that it would close its airbases to American aircraft flying over the Iraqi "no-fly" zones. The Turkish defence minister, Sabahattin Çakmakoğlu, said that Turkey was prepared to cancel arms contracts with the United States. The Israeli foreign ministry took Turkey's side and President Bill Clinton shamefully gave in and asked that the bill be killed in the Senate. It was.

All across the United States, this same pressure operates. In 1997, for example, the Ellis Island Museum removed photographs and graphic eyewitness texts of the Armenian genocide from an exhibition. It had done the same thing in 1991. In 2001, the Turkish consul-general in San Francisco objected to the use of a former First World War memorial cross as an Armenian memorial to the genocide. When I investigated this complaint in San Francisco, it turned out that a so-called "Center for Scholars in Historical Accuracy; Stanford Chapter"—which, it turned out, had nothing to do with Stanford University—had claimed in an advertisement in the *San Francisco Chronicle* that such a memorial would become "a political advertisement to preach their [Armenian] version of history which is roundly disputed among objective scholars and historians." Turks even circulated flyers to the local

Chinese American Democratic Club—in Chinese—warning it that the memorial could lead to "an historical dispute that happened in the past." So now the "debate" had become a "dispute," but I knew who those "objective scholars" must be.

Holocaust denial is alive and well in the United States—Armenian Holocaust denial, that is. The historian Bernard Lewis, who is a strong supporter of Israel and a favourite of President George W. Bush, no longer accepts that genocide was perpetrated against the Armenians and his views in the United States go largely unchallenged. In France, however, where genocide denial is an offence, there was an outcry from Armenians; Lewis was convicted by the High Court in Paris of committing "an error" (*une faute*) because he said that the word "genocide" was "only the Armenian version of this story." But when in 2000 the French Senate proposed to acknowledge the Armenian genocide of 1915, the French foreign ministry secretary-general responded with a statement that might have come from the Turkish embassy. Loïc Hennekinne said this was not the work of parliament and that history "should be interpreted by the historians." It all sounded horribly familiar, but the Senate did pass their vote in November and the French National Assembly formally recognised the Armenian genocide two months later.

Then the sky fell. In revenge, the Turkish government cancelled a $200 million spy satellite deal with the French company Alcatel and threw the arms company Giat out of a $7 billion tank contract. The newspaper *Türkiye* supported the proposal of forty-two Islamist deputies in the Turkish parliament to vote to recognise "the genocide of Algerians by the French"—a real *touché*, this, for a country that has been almost as reticent about its cruelty in the 1954–62 Algerian war as it has about its Second World War Vichy past—and reminded readers of the first wholesale massacres of Muslim Algerians around Kerrata in 1945.

President Jacques Chirac was always frightened of the Armenian mass killings. At a 1999 press conference in Beirut—where tens of thousands of Armenian descendants of the first Holocaust live—he refused to discuss the proposed assembly resolution on the genocide. "I do not comment on a matter of domestic politics when I'm abroad," he said. Would that, I asked myself as I listened to this dishonourable reply, have been Chirac's response to a condemnation of the Jewish Holocaust? In 2000, the best Chirac could do was to declare that he understood the "concerns" of Armenians.* Turkey's application to join the European Union opened the question again. In the assembly on 14 October 2004, François Bayrou asked why the European Commission had made so much of the criminalisation of adultery in the new Turkish penal code—it was subsequently withdrawn—but ignored article 305, passed by the Turkish parliament, which states that prosecution for "anti-national plots" included, according to the Turkish commission of justice, "asking for the recognition of the Armenian genocide."

---

*Strangely enough, the French national airline Air France had no qualms about discussing the Armenian bloodbath. In 1999, its own onboard airline magazine ran an article about a photographic exhibition of the mass killings, referring to "the genocide, still denied by the Turks today." Yet Air France continued to be allowed to fly unhindered to Turkey.

But for sheer political cowardice, it would be hard to beat the performance of British prime minister Tony Blair—he who was so eager to go to war with Serbia and Iraq to end human rights abuses—when he proclaimed in 2000 that there would be an annual Holocaust Memorial Day in Britain. It would be, he said, a day to remember the Nazi genocide against the Jews. He made not a single reference—not a single pathetic remark—about the murder of one and a half million Armenians in 1915. Was it not a British government that published the Bryce report? Armenian leaders immediately protested against this grotesque omission and demanded the inclusion of their own Holocaust. The British government's response was as weasel-worded as it was shaming.

Neil Frater of the Home Office's "Race Equality Unit"—the very name speaks volumes about the politically correct orientation of Blair's administration—said that the atrocities were "an appalling tragedy" and that the government extended its "sympathies" to the descendants of the victims. His "unit" had asked the "Holocaust Memorial Day Steering Group" to consider the matter but "after full and careful consideration" had decided not to change their plans for the Day. The steering group, Frater said, wanted "to avoid the risk of the message becoming too diluted if we try to include too much history." The purpose of Holocaust Day, he preached, was to "ensure a better understanding of the issues [of genocide] and promote a democratic and tolerant society that respects and celebrates diversity and is free of the influence of prejudice and racism."

So now, it seemed, mere mention of the Armenian genocide might "dilute" the "message" of Holocaust Day! All this had come about because of a "consultation exercise" in Whitehall. How typical it was of the Blair government to hold a "consultation exercise" to decide which ethnic group would have the privilege of having its suffering commemorated and which would be ruthlessly excised from the history books. At no point, of course, did the deadly word "Turkey" appear in Frater's correspondence. But he wrote another letter of astonishing insensitivity to Armen Lucas, a prominent Armenian businessman in France, repeating the same mantra of sympathy for the Armenians but adding that the British government had considered requests to examine other atrocities, including "the Crusades, slavery, colonialism, the victims of Stalin and the Boer War." The Armenian genocide was now lumped in by the government with Pope Urban II's eleventh-century war against the Muslims of the Middle East. The principal of the Armenian Evangelical College in Beirut, deploring Frater's committee decision, argued powerfully that "any serious commemoration must include the aetiology of genocide, particularly those of the twentieth century, especially if the oblivion of one encouraged the next one."

The BBC were asked to produce the official Holocaust Day commemoration, but when Lucas raised the omission of the Armenians with Daniel Brittain-Catlin, the BBC producer in charge, Brittain-Catlin admitted that the Home Office had "retained overall editorial control." There then followed a breathtaking example of political arrogance. "Our historical frame of reference," Brittain-Catlin announced, "does not include the period of 1915–20, and in terms of the event it was never in our brief to survey all 20th century atrocities." However, he added, an outside broadcast on BBC2 "is likely to include reference to, however briefly, the Armenian genocide." Note how the letter avoids the real issue. Lucas was not asking whether the BBC's "historical frame of reference"—whatever that is supposed to be—included the Armenian genocide, but why it did not do so. If it was never in the BBC's "brief" to survey all twentieth-century atrocities, the question is why not—and why not the Armenians? In the end, they were to be consigned—all those hundreds of thousands of slaughtered men, raped women and murdered children—to a reference, "however brief." Brittain-Catlin did at least call the massacre of the Armenians a "genocide," although I suspect this was a bureaucratic slip. But it would be hard to devise a more patronising letter to a man whose people were so cruelly persecuted.

All this obfuscation was based on a cynical premise by the Blair government, namely that it could get away with genocide denial to maintain good relations with Turkey. The message was very clear in 1999 when the British government stated, in a House of Lords reply, that "in the absence of unequivocal evidence to show that the Ottoman administration took a specific decision to eliminate the Armenians under their control at the time, British governments have not recognised the events of 1915 and 1916 as 'genocide.' " Now if this statement is true—if there is no "unequivocal evidence" of genocide in 1915—then the government must believe that the Bryce report; Churchill; Lloyd George; the American diplomats posted across the Ottoman empire at the time of the massacres; Armin Wegner, the photographer of the Armenian Holocaust; and the scholar Israel Charny—not to mention the actual survivors and the 150 professors who signed a declaration that the 1915 slaughter was genocide—are or were all frauds. This is clearly not true. Baroness Ramsay of Cartvale, who delivered this meretricious statement for the British government, claimed that few other governments "attributed the name 'genocide' to these tragic events. In our opinion that is rightly so because we do not believe it is the business of governments today to review events of over 80 years ago with a view to pronouncing on them . . . And who would benefit from taking such a position?"

Certainly not Tony Blair. But another part of the statement is even more disturbing—and indicative of the Blair government's immoral attitude towards history—when it suggests that Armenia and Turkey should "resolve between themselves the issues which divide them . . . we could not play the role of supportive friend to both countries were we to take an essentially political position on an issue so sensitive for both." So acknowledging or denying genocide is a "political" issue. The mass killings are now the "events." And governments cannot review events of "over 80 years ago" and take a position on them. What this means is that if in the year 2025 a new and right-wing Germany—from which heaven preserve us—were to deny the Jewish Holocaust, the British government might stand back and say that it could not take a position on "events" that happened eighty years earlier, that the Jewish community would have to "resolve" this matter with the Germans. That is the logic of claiming that the powerful Turkish successor to the Ottoman genociders must resolve this "sensitive" matter with the descendants of the Armenian victims.

The British were now also following Israel's practice of dissociating the Armenian Holocaust from the Jewish Holocaust, creating a uniqueness about the Jewish experience of persecution which no other ethnic group was to be permitted to share. Israel's ambassador to the Armenian state crassly said the same thing in 2002.\* So, two years later, did the British ambassador to Armenia.

But it is easy to be self-righteous. When Blair refused to acknowledge the Armenian genocide, I wrote a series of angry articles in *The Independent*, saying that Holocaust Day was to be an Armenian-free, Jewish-only affair. Yes, the word took a capital "H" when it applied to Jews. I have always agreed with this. Mass ethnic slaughter on such a scale—Hitler's murder of 6 million Jews—deserves a capital "H." But I also believe that the genocide of other races—of any race— merits a capital "H." So that's how I wrote it in a long centre-page article in my paper. Chatting to an Armenian acquaintance, I mentioned that I had done this. It would be the "Armenian Holocaust" in my report. Little could I have imagined how quickly the dead would rise from their graves to be counted. For when my article appeared in *The Independent*—a paper which has never failed to dig into the human wickedness visited upon every race and creed—my references to the Jew- ish Holocaust remained with a capital "H." But the Armenian Holocaust had been downgraded to a lower-case "h." "Tell me, Robert," my Armenian friend asked me in suppressed fury, "how do we Armenians qualify for a capital 'H'? Didn't the Turks kill enough of us? Or is it because we're not Jewish?"[†]

*The Independent* is the most outspoken paper in Britain in its demand that Turkey admit the truth about the Armenian killings. When the Turkish embassy officially complained in August 2000 that an exhibition at the Imperial War

---

\*Rivka Cohen, the Israeli ambassador in Yerevan, said on 5 March 2002 that while the Armenian genocide was "a tragedy," the (Jewish) Holocaust "was a unique phenomenon, since it had always been planned and aimed to destroy the whole nation." Understandably, the Armenian government in Yerevan issued a diplomatic note of protest.

[†]There are no conspiracies on *The Independent*'s copydesk; just a tough, no-nonsense rule that our articles follow a grammatical "house" style and conform to what is called "normal usage." And the Jewish Holocaust, through "normal usage," takes a capital "H." Other holo- causts don't. No one is quite sure why—the same practice is followed in newspapers and books all over the world, although it was the centre of a row in the United States, where Harvard turned down a professorial "Chair of Holocaust and Cognate Studies" because academics rightly objected to the genocide of other peoples—including the Armenians—being heaped in a bin called "cognate." But none of this answered the questions of my Armenian friend. To have told him his people didn't qualify for a capital "H" would have been as shameful as it would have been insulting.

"Common usage" is a bane to all of us journalists, but it is not sacred. It doesn't have to stand still. My father, I told my editor, had fought in what he called the "Great War"—but common usage had to be amended after 1945, to the "First World War." What's in a name? I asked in my paper. What's in a capital letter? How many other skulls lie in the sands of northern Syria? Did the Turks not kill enough Armenians? From that day, *The Independent* printed Holocaust with a capital "H" for both Jewish and Armenian genocides.

Museum in London should make textual changes to references about the Armenian killings—"a messy and painful affair" was the most Turkish diplomat Mehmet Akat could bring himself to say of the genocide—an *Independent* editorial said that "it almost beggars belief." Imagine, the paper said, "the German government declaring that, although a number of Jews died in the Second World War, it was because of poor health and as a result of the fighting."

But even the Imperial War Museum could bow to Turkey. When it staged another exhibition, *Crimes Against Humanity*, just over a year later—the very expression first used in 1915 about the Armenians—it included an entire panel in the Armenian section containing Turkey's denial that the mass murders ever took place. "What is shocking," one of our readers commented after visiting a museum dedicated to Muslims murdered by Armenians at the Turkish town of Yeşilyayla, "is that the very language of how we respond to the Jewish Holocaust has been appropriated and applied not to the murdered Armenians but to the Turks themselves." Turkey had already tried to undermine the authenticity of the photographic evidence of the genocide, demanding that the Hulton Getty picture library withdraw three famous pictures of the Armenian dead—including an iconic portrait by the brave German Armin Wegner of an Armenian girl and two smaller children lying dead amid garbage in 1915—on the grounds that there was no genocide. Hulton withdrew the pictures for three days but the agency's general manager, Mathew Butson, dismissed the Turkish objections. "I think that because of their application to join the EU, the Turks want to 'clean' their history," he said. "But this isn't the way to do it!"

Back in the United States, Armenians demanded compensation from U.S. companies with whom their families—murdered in 1915—had insured their lives. If it took Jewish Holocaust survivors forty years to gain recompense from such companies, it took the Armenian Holocaust survivors and descendants eighty-five years. New York Life Insurance agreed to settle a class-action suit for $20 million, but even then its chairman, Sy Sternberg—who said that a third of the claims were settled after the murders—used the neutral language favoured by Turkey. Prompt payment had been made on claims, he said, "when it became clear that many of our Armenian policyholders perished in the tragic events of 1915." Perished? Tragic events? Several companies in the United States initially declined to pay out because "no one came forward" to make claims. Andrew Kevorkian, one of the most outspoken British Armenians on 1915, asked: "What did they expect? That the Turks would write a little note—'To Whom It May Concern'—stating the date of the murder each time they killed these men and women?"

When the Armenian community in the United States asked George W. Bush for his policy on their genocide if he were elected president, he stated on 19 February 2000 that "the Armenians were subjected to a genocidal campaign . . . an awful crime in a century of bloody crimes against humanity. If elected President, I would ensure that our nation properly recognizes the tragic suffering of the Armenian people." Once he became president, however, Bush lost his courage, failed to honour his promise to the Armenian community and resorted to the usual weasel-words. Addressing Armenians on 24 April 2001, the eighty-sixth anniversary of the start of the slaughter, Bush no longer used the word "genocide." Instead, it became "one of the great tragedies of history"; he talked only about "infamous killings" and "the tragedy that scarred the history of the Armenian people" and their "bitter fate" at "the end of the Ottoman Empire."

On the same day a year later, Bush called the genocide "an appalling tragedy," talked about "horrific killings" but referred only to "this horrendous loss of life." Again, "genocide" had disappeared and there was even a mystifying remark about "the wounds that remain painful for people in Armenia, in Turkey, and around the globe." In April 2003 it was "a horrible tragedy" and "a great calamity" but one which—for some reason best known to Bush—reflected "a deep sorrow that continues to haunt them and their neighbours, the Turkish people." This was preposterous. The Turkish government was denying the genocide—not feeling sorry about it. In the words of the Armenian National Committee of America, Bush, despite his calls for "moral clarity" in international affairs, had "allowed pressure by a foreign government to reduce the President of the United States to using evasive and euphemistic terminology to avoid properly identifying the Armenian genocide . . ."

This, it should be remembered, was the same president who thought he was fighting a "war against terror," who claimed he was fighting "evil" but who, when confronted with inescapable evidence of both terror and evil on a scale outreaching anything perpetrated against Americans, got cold feet and ran away from the truth. Indeed, there are times when the very existence of the Armenian genocide—for so many nations around the world—seems to have become far more dangerous than the weapons of mass destruction Bush and Blair lied about in Iraq. In this parallel but more realistic universe, it is the Turks who are telling Bush and Blair: You are either with us or against us. And both men have lined up alongside the Turks to deny history.

So now let me shine some sad, wintry sunlight over the West's miserable, cowardly and dangerous response to the twentieth century's first Holocaust. The genocide of 1915 was "forcefully remembered" at Westminster Abbey in 1996 when Sir Michael Mayne, the Dean Emeritus of Westminster, commissioned an Irish artist to carve a stone to lie outside the west doors. "REMEMBER," the inscription reads, "all innocent victims of oppression, violence and war." Round the edge is written: "Is it nothing to you, all you that pass by?" Queen Elizabeth unveiled the stone in the presence of men and women who had suffered in Auschwitz, Rwanda, Bosnia, Siberia, Soweto and Armenia. Among them was eighty-nine-year-old Yervant Shekerdemian, who as a boy experienced the Armenian massacres and lost most of his family in the genocide.

And after the months of mean refusal to acknowledge the truth of history, an outpouring of public anger eventually forced the Blair government, at the very last moment, to give way and allow more than twenty Armenians to attend the first Holocaust Memorial Day in 2001. Shekerdemian and another genocide survivor, Anig Bodossian, were belatedly invited. The Armenian Bishop in Britain was given a place of honour with other senior clergy, including the Chief Rabbi, and was among those who lit a candle before Blair and other politicians.

Not long afterwards, on Turkish television, an extraordinary event took place. A Turkish writer and historian, Taner Akçam, lectured his people on the facts—the reality—of the 1915 Armenian genocide. In front of a nationwide audience, he advised penitence. "If you can't bring yourself to describe it as genocide, call it a massacre if you want," he said. "But it was a crime against humanity . . . Ask forgiveness from the Armenian people and . . . make a commitment that in Turkey, political dissent and disagreement should no longer be treated as an offence."

These were difficult, treacherous things for a Turkish audience to hear. So Akçam was interrupted during the bitter six-hour television debate on 3 February 2001. "How dare you let this man speak? Shut him up!" came an imperious voice over a phone link-up. It was Semra Özal, widow of former Turkish president Turgut Özal. But Dr. Akçam did not give up. "Unless we distance ourselves from the perpetrators of this crime, which *was* a genocide, we will never be able to relieve ourselves of this terrible burden," he said. He used the Turkish for genocide—*soykırım*—throughout the programme. "The constant refrain of 'We are not guilty,' and the parallel blaming of the Armenians, the victims, very much hurts the cause of Turkey," he said. Akçam even quoted Mustafa Kemal Atatürk, the founder of the Turkish state, who on 23 April 1920 denounced the "Armenian massacres" as "a shameful act."

Hikmet Çiçek, the editor of *Aydınlık*, immediately denounced Akçam as a "traitor," but other journalists were more courageous. Columnist Ertuğrul Özkök of *Milliyet* had written the same day that the perpetrators of the Armenian genocide were "our Pol Pots, Berias and Stalins and the sooner we call their crimes to account . . . the better our chances of redeeming ourselves from this scourge of being accused of genocide."

Almost exactly three years after Akçam's television "debate," more than 500 Turkish intellectuals—university teachers, authors, writers and human rights officials—protested at a new school history curriculum which ordered teachers to denounce to their children "the unfounded allegations" of the Armenians. Nor was this the first time that Turkish intellectuals had confronted their government. Three Turks were prosecuted in Istanbul in March 1994 for translating into Turkish and publishing 15,000 copies of a French book on the Armenian genocide. The book had been banned in January of that year by the Istanbul State Security Court No. 3, and they had been accused of inciting "belligerency, racial and territorial segregation and undermining the territorial integrity of Turkey." An Armenian Rights Group campaigned for the three Turks.

During the Jewish Holocaust, the Jews of Europe found their "righteous gentiles," the non-Jewish men and women living under Nazi occupation who risked their lives to save those of Jews. And the ghosts of another group of saviours pass through the pages of the massive Bryce report on the Armenian Holocaust. Two American witnesses record how orders arrived for Tahsin Bey, the governor of Erzurum, in 1915, instructing him "that all Armenians should be killed. Tahsin refused to carry this out and, indeed, all through the time he was reluctant to mal-treat the Armenians, but was overruled by *force majeure*."*

Armenians themselves are taught at school of the brave governor of Aleppo, Jelal Pasha, who said he was a governor, not an executioner—who said "it is the natural right of a human being to live." He saved thousands of lives. But it is the small man—the good Turk—who occasionally shines out of the Bryce report. On the deportation to Ras al-Ain, Maritza Kedjedjian was the witness to the rape of young women by Kurds. "When they were going to carry off another girl," she wrote later, "I asked Euomer Çavuş, a Mardin man, to help us." *Çavuş* means he was a Turkish army sergeant. Maritza goes on:

> He stopped them at once and did not let them take [the girl] away . . . The Kurds from the surrounding villages attacked us that night. Euomer, who was in charge of us, immediately went up to the heights and harangued them in Kurdish, telling them not to attack us. We were hungry and thirsty and had no water to drink. Euomer took some of our [drinking] vessels and brought us water from a long way off . . . The wife of my brother-in-law . . . had a baby born that night. The next morning we started again. Sergeant Euomer left some women with her and kept an eye on her from a distance. Then he put the mother and the new-born child on a beast, and brought her to us in safety.

Could there be a more moving story from the bloody fields of the Armenian Holocaust? And so I return to my original question. Should not the Armenians commemorate all those brave Turks who acted out of compassion and refused to obey orders? Though these Turks were painfully few in number, Armenians would be acknowledging their humanity. And how would the Turks react? By refusing to honour these courageous fellow Turks? Or by remembering their courage and thus—by the same token—accepting the fact of the Armenian genocide? Taner Akçam deserves such a gesture. So does Sergeant Euomer.

SO DO THE ARMENIANS. In 2002, Aram Kevorkian sent me an account of his visit to Chunkoush, the Armenian town in Turkey where his father Karnig was born. He found the rubble of the Armenian homes of ninety years ago, and the still standing wreckage of two Armenian churches. And he went to the ravine where his people had been murdered in April 1915. "There the Armenians had been forced to undress, their hands had been tied, and their throats slit or their heads shattered with axes, and their bodies thrown into the pits." Kevorkian stood and read from Yeats's poem of hope, "Lapis Lazuli":

---

*Elsewhere, it should be noted, Tahsin Bey does not appear in so favourable a light; but wasn't Oskar Schindler a member of the Nazi party?

*On their own feet they came, or on shipboard,*
*Camel-back, horse-back, ass-back, mule-back,*
*Old civilisations put to the sword.*
*Then they and their wisdom went to rack:*
*No handiwork of Callimachus,*
*Who handled marble as if it were bronze,*
*Made draperies that seemed to rise*
*When sea-wind swept the corner, stands;*
*His long lamp-chimney shaped like the stem*
*Of a slender palm, stood but a day;*
*All things fall and are built again . . .*

It is 1992, and I am at Margara on the border of Turkey and Armenia—the real Armenian state, free at last of its dark Soviet cloak—and I look at the snow-peak of Mount Ararat beyond the Turkish border; for Ararat, the national symbol of Armenia, is inside Turkey, a place to be looked at and wondered at from afar. I stand in the garden of Levon Karapegian, and above his tomato bushes and potato beds, his cucumbers and sick-looking cherry trees, I see a Turkish flag drooping in the midday heat on top of a wooden guard post. "Sometimes I see the Turkish soldiers standing over there by the little tree on the other side of the fence," Karapegian says. What Armenian, I ask myself, wants to live within 6 metres of the nation whose Ottoman rulers annihilated his people?

There are not many villagers left; today they are outnumbered by the storks that nest on the disused factory crane, on the telegraph poles, on the roof of the crumbling public library, on top of the marble podium commemorating those Armenians who fell in the 1941–45 "Great Patriotic War" against Hitler. Karapegian is a teacher of Armenian history at the local secondary school, educating the great-grandchildren of those who survived the genocide and fled—in most cases from villages scarcely 25 kilometres away on the other side of the Turkish border—between 1915 and 1918.

As I sit with Levon Karapegian and his family at a table in their garden, eating plates of cherries, a cuckoo calls from beyond the trees, from Turkey, from what the family call western Armenia. And his wife points to a line of poplars behind the Turkish guard post. "That was our family home," she says. "I remember my father putting me on his shoulders when I was small and telling me how my grandfather planted all those trees."

Five years later and 3,500 kilometres away, the sea mist curling over the Sussex dunes on a damp English evening, Astrid Aghajanian is pouring tea for me from a big, heavy pot. She is one of the last survivors. Eighty-two years ago, the Turks shot her grandfather, grandmother and uncle.

What was left of the family all walked and walked. At a village one night, my father who had been deported with us came to see us. He told my mother that he thought he was being allowed to say goodbye, that he would be shot with the other men. I remember my mother told me that my father's last words were: "The only way to remember me is to look after Astrid." We never saw him again. It was a long march and the Turks and Kurds came to carry off girls for rape. My mother would run from one end of the column to the other each time she saw them attacking us. My other grandmother died along the way. So did my newly-born brother Vartkes. We had to leave him by the roadside. One day, the Turks said they wanted to collect all the young children and look after them. Some women, who couldn't feed their children, let them go. Then my mother saw them piling the children on top of each other and setting them on fire. My mother pushed me under another pile of corpses. She buried herself with me under those bodies. Even today I cannot stand to be in darkness or to be on my own. My mother saved me from the fire. She used to tell me afterwards that when she heard the screams of the children and saw the flames, it was as if their souls were going up to heaven.

Astrid Aghajanian's mother eventually carried her to a Bedouin camp and, after reaching Aleppo—with the help of a Turkish officer—she remarried and moved to the newly mandated territory of Palestine. In Jerusalem young Astrid was to meet her future husband Gaspar, whose family had lived in Palestine for generations. But her Armenian agony had not ended. They were forced to flee the 1948 Arab–Israeli war and took refuge in Jordan—where Gaspar Aghajanian secured British citizenship—and then moved to Cyprus. But when the Turks invaded the island in 1974, after the Greek coup d'état, the couple were dispossessed once again. Astrid was now a refugee from the Turks twice in the same century. The Turkish army moved into what had been their family home. Could history torture anyone more than this?

It could. The Aghajanians received money for their lost home, but when Gaspar demanded compensation for the couple's possessions—Persian carpets, furniture, an ancient coin collection, photographs of massacred relatives from 1915, a piano and a large library of valuable books all stolen by the Turks—he received a letter from the British Foreign Office stating that "the Turkish Cypriot authorities . . . enacted 'legislation' to exclude claims made by those persons who were deemed to have Greek or Greek Cypriot connections. They have now extended this exclusion to cover claims by persons deemed to be of Armenian descent."

The couple were never Greek Cypriots and never asked for Greek Cypriot passports. "We were full British citizens," Gaspar Aghajanian says. "But we were refused compensation on grounds of our ethnic background." When he heard that Margaret Thatcher, the British prime minister, was to visit Turkey in 1990 for ceremonies marking the 1915 Gallipoli battle—another full-circle of the catastrophe—Astrid's husband wrote to his MP to complain, adding that his wife was a survivor of the Armenian genocide. Back came a letter from Foreign Office minister Francis Maude, saying—and here the reader of this book may be permitted to scream—that while the government "regard the loss of so many lives as a tragedy . . . we have long considered that it would not be right to raise with, or attribute to, the present Turkish government acts which took place 75 years ago during the time of the Ottoman empire . . ."

Catch-22 is a cliché compared to this. In order to maintain relations with Turkey, the British government no longer acknowledges that the Armenian genocide happened. But it cannot obtain compensation for the Aghajanians because the Turks refuse to compensate British citizens of Armenian descent—because of the 1915 Armenian genocide. To this day, the couple have received nothing for their possessions.

If there was any international kindness to be bestowed upon the Aghajanians, however, it came in 2003 when a young Turkish woman, a student from Chicago, asked to see them. The girl, whose identity it is still better to protect, had moved from Turkey to the United States and found herself living among Armenians and insisted on hearing the story of their genocide. She began academic work to discover what happened in 1915. One afternoon she came to the little bungalow in Shoreham in southern England and expressed her sorrow to Astrid, and her remorse for what her Turkish people had done. She gently produced a tape recorder. And so Astrid Aghajanian's memories—of her father's last goodbye, of the death of her baby brother and of the burning children whose souls went up to heaven—are now safeguarded by a young Turkish woman.*

In Beirut, the Armenian home for the blind—now for all elderly Armenians— is warmer now than it was during the last days of the civil war. There are new doors and central heating, although all the Holocaust survivors I met there in 1994 are dead. There are only two new patients who are survivors. There will be no more. One is an old lady who can only remember the songs her mother taught her of the horrors of the march and the deportation. She squeals them out in Turkish because she never learned Armenian, so that the staff have to find a nurse who speaks the Turkish language to translate. I know these songs. They have been meticulously collected by an Armenian academic:

> *Bunches and bunches of roses are coming,*
> *Death is hard to bear for me,*
> *Wake up, sultan, tyrant sultan!*
> *The whole world is weeping blood!*

Down the corridor, a very old man is lying on a bed. He is Haroutioun Kebedjian. He is holding in his left hand a Bible in Braille and his right hand is fingering the embossed paper letters. He greets me with a smile, sightlessly. It is now the year 2000 and he is ninety-three years old, so he was eight when he survived the Armenian Holocaust. His memory is as clear as his emotions:

---

*She later wrote to the Aghajanians. "I will do my best to continue working on the recognition of the genocide," she said in her letter, "and make a difference, even a small one."

We lived in Dortyol. My father was called Sarkis and my mother was Mariam. There were ten children including me and my brothers and sisters. The Turks collected all the people with their donkeys and horses. We were to go to Aleppo and Ras el-Ain. But they started killing us on the way. The Turks forced us to the Habur River and by the time we got there, there was only my mother and my sister and me left. They told the women and the men to take off all their clothes. My sister was eighteen and a man on a horse came and grabbed her and put her on his horse. He did this in front of us. It happened in front of my eyes. I was not blind then. And they started to beat my mother. As she begged them not to take my sister, the Turks beat her to death. I have always remembered that as she died, she screamed my name: "Haroutioun! Haroutioun!" Later an Arab Bedouin took me to his house and I stayed there for three years. The war was over and then people came saying they were looking for Armenian orphans. I said I was Armenian, so they took me to Aleppo. There I caught a virus that affected my eyes. I was suddenly blind and I was only eleven years old. Until I was twenty-three, I was filled with rage because the Turks took my sister and beat my mother in front of my eyes until she died. But when I was twenty-three, I felt this was not the right way to be a man, so I began to pray to God so He would see me. I was making peace with myself. Now I am ready to meet my God. I am at peace. Last year when the big earthquake happened in Turkey, it killed so many Turks. And I prayed to God for those Turks— I prayed for those poor Turkish people.

# CHAPTER ELEVEN

# Fifty Thousand Miles from Palestine

> *And be these juggling fiends no more believ'd,*
> *That palter with us in a double sense;*
> *That keep the word of promise to our ear,*
> *And break it to our hope.*

—Shakespeare, *Macbeth*, V, viii, 23–26

IN A CORNER OF THE PALESTINIAN "Martyrs' Cemetery" in west Beirut, surrounded by the graves of Palestinian guerrillas and Syrian soldiers who fell victim to Israel's 1982 invasion of Lebanon, there stands a raised tomb, surrounded by a cheap concrete wall. A bunch of withered flowers lies on the marble slab, which has been chipped by shrapnel and partly damaged at its base, as if someone has tried to break into the vault. But the Arabic script on the lid is still legible:

> The tomb of . . . Grand Mufti Al Haj Mohamed Amin al-Husseini,
> leader of the Palestinian Arab Higher Committee,
> President of the Supreme Muslim Council.
> Born Jerusalem 1897. Died Beirut 4th July 1974.

Photographs in that summer's memorial issue of *Palestine*, the quarterly political magazine Haj Amin founded more than a decade earlier, show mourners at the graveside, less than a year before the start of the Lebanese civil war. Chafiq al-Hout, the Palestine Liberation Organisation's ambassador to Beirut, and a clutch of former Lebanese prime ministers can be seen standing by Hassan Khaled, the Lebanese Grand Mufti; and just to their left, the figure of Yassir Arafat, sunglasses covering his eyes, the familiar kuffiah atop his younger but still unmistakable face, a handkerchief pressed to his mouth.

Archive pictures in the same issue show the Grand Mufti—the supreme religious officer and the most important elected Muslim leader in Palestine—sitting proudly among Palestinian fighters during the 1936 Arab revolt against British rule in Palestine and, dressed in a gold-fringed robe, alongside the Palestinian delegate to the League of Nations in Geneva. A tall man with broad, serious eyes and a carefully trimmed beard, he exudes, even in old photographs, something of the charisma of which his supporters still speak. Those who knew him talk of his unusual, bright blue eyes.

**Occupied Territory**

- - - - West Bank
- Palestian area
- Palestian main city
- ○ Israeli settlement

N

Netanya

Jenin

Tulkarm

Tubas

Nablus

Qalqilya

Salfit

Tel Aviv

**WEST BANK**

Jericho

Ramallah

Jerusalem

**ISRAEL**

Bethlehem

Hebron

Dead Sea

16 kilometres

But there are other archive photographs that *Palestine* did not choose to print, pictures far more troubling than those of the last farewell to a man described at his funeral as "Sheikh of the rebels, Imam of the Palestinians." These snapshots show Haj Amin sitting in a high-backed armchair, dressed in turban and black robes, listening attentively to a short-haired man with a brush moustache who is dressed in a military jacket, a man who is gesticulating with his left hand. A German eagle holding a swastika is stitched on Adolf Hitler's left sleeve. The place is Berlin, the date 28 November 1941. There are other pictures of the time: of Haj Amin at Nazi rallies in Berlin, Haj Amin greeted by Heinrich Himmler, Haj Amin, right hand raised in the Nazi salute, inspecting newly recruited Bosnian Muslims who had joined the Wehrmacht.

Perhaps it is not surprising that more than thirty years after his death, the very name of Haj Amin al-Husseini, Grand Mufti of Jerusalem, can still ignite both passion and hatred among Palestinians and Israelis. Recall the dedication with which he pursued the cause of Arab Palestine, his refusal to compromise when the British mandate government demanded the partition of his homeland, and Israelis will ask you why you do not condemn Haj Amin as a Nazi war criminal—which is how they portray him today in the Holocaust memorial at Yad Vashem, west of Jerusalem. Examine the motives for his flirtation with Hitler, question what Palestinians sometimes refer to uncomfortably as Haj Amin's "German period," and Palestinians will ask you why you wish to support the campaign of "Zionist" calumny against the old man's memory. Merely to discuss his life is to be caught up in the Arab–Israeli propaganda war. To make an impartial assessment of the man's career—or, for that matter, an unbiased history of the Arab–Israeli dispute—is like trying to ride two bicycles at the same time. "My advice to you is to write about Haj Amin when you retire," one of his former associates warned me when I asked him for his memories of the Grand Mufti. "It could be dangerous for you to produce such a biography."

Certainly, the name of Haj Amin rarely appeared in Yassir Arafat's speeches in the last quarter of the twentieth century, and not only because of Haj Amin's cooperation with the Nazis. Relaxing in a Beirut garden in July 1994, the Palestinian scholar Edward Said suggested to me another reason for this reticence. "I was sitting with Arafat in 1985 when he placed his hand on my knee, gripping it very tight. And Arafat said: 'Edward, if there's one thing I don't want to be, it's to be like Haj Amin. He was always right, and he got nothing and died in exile.' " But in 1990, Arafat was to follow a curiously similar destiny. Just as Haj Amin travelled to Baghdad and then to Berlin—believing that Hitler could guarantee Palestine's independence from British rule and Jewish immigration—so the PLO leader travelled to Baghdad to embrace Saddam Hussein after Iraq's invasion of Kuwait, convinced by Saddam's promise to "liberate" the land he called Palestine. Little wonder, perhaps, that Haj Amin's ghost sent a chill through the old retainers of the PLO. In 1948, the Grand Mufti of Jerusalem even set up a short-lived Palestine government in what was left of his country—like Arafat's rump administration, it met in the seedy confines of a Gaza hotel.

The facts of Haj Amin's life are well documented. Born in Jerusalem in the closing years of the Ottoman empire to a family that traced its ancestry back to the Prophet, he was educated at Islamic schools and at Al-Azhar University in Cairo before serving, briefly, as an officer in the Turkish army during the First World War, the war in which the British made their two conflicting promises. To the Arabs, they promised independence in return for an Arab alliance against the Turks. To the Jews, Lord Balfour declared Britain's support for a Jewish national home in predominantly Arab Palestine. From these betrayals, Haj Amin emerged an Arab nationalist and an uncompromising opponent of Jewish immigration into Palestine.

Blamed for inciting violence against both the Jews and British in 1920, Haj Amin fled to Transjordan and then to Damascus, where he was feted as a national hero. Ironically, it was the British—impressed by his family's status and his nationalist standing among Arab Palestinians—who engineered his election to the post of Grand Mufti. Haj Amin swiftly internationalised the Palestine question among Muslim nations and secured election to the newly created Supreme Muslim Council, which controlled Muslim endowments, courts and religious institutions. He was, needless to say, only one among many Arabs who would be raised to advantage by the Western powers—then bestialised when he no longer followed their policies.

Like King Hussein of Jordan in 1992, Haj Amin embarked on a project to restore the Dome of the Rock and Al-Aqsa mosques in Jerusalem, an undertaking that earned him enormous popularity in the largely rural areas of Palestine. "His major sources of power were the imams of the mosques and the villagers," Chafiq al-Hout remembered. "The Arabs in the municipalities were for the English. To us laymen, the heads of the municipalities were traitors because they were against Haj Amin." In August 1928, speeches by Haj Amin and other Muslim leaders to Arab villagers incited rioting in which sixty Jews were murdered in Hebron.

Among Haj Amin's Arab opponents was Raghib al-Nashashibi, the mayor of Jerusalem, one of many Palestinians who would find themselves unable to accept a man who would never—ever—compromise. In 1930, the British seemed prepared to restrict Jewish immigration and land purchase in Palestine. But when Haj Amin insisted that an Arab "national government" be created as well, the British lost interest. When the British arrested the leading Palestinian nationalists during the 1936–39 Arab revolt, Haj Amin fled secretly to Lebanon. Just before the outbreak of the Second World War, the British, amenable again to the Arab cause, called an Arab round-table conference to discuss Palestine. Haj Amin—who was prohibited from attending the talks by the British—insisted that Britain "stop trying to build a Jewish national home and give independence to Palestine." The conference failed. A subsequent British White Paper agreed to abandon Balfour's promise to the Jews and offered a state with an Arab majority within ten years. Haj Amin again turned down what Malcolm MacDonald, the British colonial secretary, called a "golden opportunity." Later, Arafat would be accused of almost identical intransigence when he did not obey Israeli or American wishes.

Fearful of arrest in French-Mandate Lebanon, Haj Amin fled again, this time to Iraq, where he was received as a Palestinian hero and swiftly broke his promise to the prime minister, Nuri es-Said, not to meddle in domestic politics. Believing that a British victory would doom Palestine, he supported the pro-Axis Rashid Ali al-Gaylani as es-Said's successor and wrote Hitler a long and angry letter, outlining the plight of Arab Palestinians in the face of what he called "world Jewry, this dangerous enemy whose secret weapons—finance, corruption and intrigue—were aligned with British daggers" and finishing with wishes for Hitler's "shining victory and prosperity for the great German people . . ."

Nadim Dimeshkieh, later Lebanon's ambassador to the United Nations, was a teacher in Baghdad at the time and frequently visited Haj Amin. "I suppose it was a great mistake to involve himself in Iraqi politics," Dimeshkieh would recall more than half a century later. "The people he involved himself with were wild and irresponsible. But where was he to turn? To America? To Britain? He was hoping that Iraq would support Germany and that this would put the Arabs in a better negotiating position over Palestine when the war ended in Hitler's favour. Haj Amin would keep on saying to us: 'Well, let's hope Germany doesn't lose the war.'"

When Britain invaded Iraq in 1941,* Haj Amin tried to organise a brigade of Palestinians living in Baghdad to fight alongside the Iraqis; elements of this organisation went to Abu Ghraib to confront the invading force, only to find that the Iraqis had already collapsed. So Haj Amin fled once more, to Iran, where he requested asylum in Afghanistan. But he rejected Kabul's permission to cross the frontier and took the ultimate, politically fatal step of escaping across Turkey to Axis Europe. It was then that Haj Amin became, in Palestinian eyes, a hostage to history, a man forced by patriotism to turn to the only ally available to him. For survivors of the Jewish Holocaust—and for Jews around the world—his act was unforgivable.

By the mid-1990s, the only survivor of the hothouse world of Arab wartime Berlin society still alive was eighty-seven-year-old Wassef Kamal, who had been a supporter of Haj Amin in Baghdad and had made his own way to Nazi Germany via Vichy Syria, Turkey and Bulgaria in 1941. "Most of the Palestinians and Arabs in Germany gathered round Haj Amin and Rashid al-Gaylani, who had also reached Berlin," he recalled for me in 1994:

> Most of them preferred the Grand Mufti. I became one of his senior assistants in Berlin and we decided to create an organisation, the "Society of Arab Students in Germany." Haj Amin was considered almost a head of state by the Italian and German governments. There was an agreement— that the Axis governments would give temporary loans to Haj Amin and Rashid [al-Gaylani]—to be repaid by the newly formed Arab states after an Axis victory. The two men were given salaries. I was treated like a refugee, but we received four times the rations given to German citizens and were

*See Chapter Five.

treated very nicely. But all the efforts of Haj Amin and Rashid to convince Hitler and Mussolini to make a treaty with Arab leaders guaranteeing a future independent Arab state and the destruction of the Zionist "national home," failed. All they would say on German radio was: "We are with the Arab people and for their independence." But they *never* agreed to a formal treaty.

When Haj Amin finally met Hitler in November 1941, the Grand Mufti obtained a verbal agreement from the Führer that "when we [Germany] have arrived at the southern Caucasus, then the time of the liberation of the Arabs will have arrived—and you can rely on my word." Disregarding the fact that Hitler's "word" was often a lie, Haj Amin recorded how Hitler insisted that the Jewish "problem" would be solved "step by step" and that he, Haj Amin, would be "leader of the Arabs." But Hitler refused publicly to recognise the claim to independence of the Arab states, partly because Mussolini was in no mood to lose his colony of Libya.

Wassef Kamal was to recall:

There was no agreement reached so we concluded we were more or less forced to work for the Axis. When Rommel began winning battles in Libya and was about to enter Egypt, the Germans came to us and believed the Axis would be victorious in the Middle East. Hitler and Mussolini approached Haj Amin and Rashid, saying: "Our armies will soon enter Egypt and also Iraq via the Caucasus. Rashid, you will go with our armies from Russia, Haj Amin, you will go with the Italian army via Egypt to Palestine." Haj Amin called us together. He said: "Prepare yourselves, get military uniforms and be ready to enter Egypt with me." But I said to him: "Your eminence, in the past Sherif Hussein [leader of the 1916 Arab Revolt against the Turks] had a treaty with the British—and, in spite of this treaty, the British betrayed us with the secret [Sykes–Picot] agreement with France. And now," I said, "we have not even a *treaty* with these people. How can we go when we have nothing in our hands? I will not go. I will not be a party to this." Three or four others agreed with me. But Haj Amin began to prepare himself—to go through Libya to Egypt. But slowly, slowly, the Axis lost.

Haj Amin now enthusiastically went to work for the Nazi propaganda machine. Arabs would later experience great difficulty and embarrassment in explaining these actions. In his biography of Haj Amin, Taysir Jbara devotes only four pages to his collaboration with the Nazis under the anaemic title "The Mufti in Europe," arguing that Haj Amin had as much right to collaborate to save his Palestinian homeland from the British and Jewish immigrants as the Zionists had to collaborate with Germany to save Jewish lives. Israelis have sometimes exaggerated his collaboration in order to portray him as a war criminal. And it can be argued that a man may make a pact with the Devil. Two of Haj Amin's former comrades repeated to me that tired—and irritating—Arabic proverb that "The enemy of my enemy is my friend." Churchill readily allied himself to one of the most murderous dictators of the twentieth century, Josef Stalin, transforming the monster into "Uncle Joe" until the defeat of Germany. The Lebanese Phalange militia, founded in 1936 after its leader had been inspired by the "discipline" of Nazi Germany, acted as Israel's militia allies in 1982. Anwar Sadat worked as a spy for Rommel yet he became, in later years, the darling of the West—though not of Egypt—for making peace with Israel. And it is true that the principal aim of Haj Amin was to gain the independence of Palestine after a German victory and, in the meantime, to prevent Jews from going to Palestine.

But amid the evil of the Holocaust, Haj Amin's moral position seems untenable. There is, too, in the archives of the wartime BBC Monitoring Service, a series of transcripts from Nazi radio stations that cast a dark shadow over any moral precepts Haj Amin might have claimed. Here he is, for example, addressing a Balfour Day rally at the Luftwaffe hall in Berlin on 2 November 1943: "The Germans know how to get rid of the Jews . . . They have definitely solved the Jewish problem." And on Berlin radio on 1 March 1944: "Arabs, rise as one man and fight for your sacred rights. Kill the Jews wherever you find them. This pleases God, history and religion." On 21 January that year, Haj Amin had visited Ante Pavelic's ferocious Fascist state of Croatia—which included present-day Bosnia— where he addressed Muslim recruits to the SS with these words, so sharply in contrast with sentiments expressed in his postwar memoirs: "There are also considerable similarities between Islamic principles and National Socialism, namely, in the affirmation of struggle and fellowship . . . in the idea of order."

He even played a role in fomenting hatred between Bosnian Muslims and the largely Serb-led partisan force fighting the Germans in Yugoslavia, an anger that burst forth again in the atrocities of 1992. On 26 May 1944, the BBC Monitoring Service recorded Haj Amin describing Tito as "a friend of the Jews and a foe of the Prophet." In 1943 he received from Heinrich Himmler, the architect of the Holocaust, a telegram recalling for him that "the National Socialist Party had inscribed on its flag 'the extermination of world Jewry.' Our party sympathises with the fight of the Arabs, especially the Arabs of Palestine, against the foreign Jew." Radio Berlin later reported that Haj Amin had "arrived in Frankfurt for the purpose of visiting the Research Institute on the Jewish problem."

Did Haj Amin know about the Jewish Holocaust? According to his most meticulous biographer, Zvi Elpeleg—a former Israeli military governor of Gaza who is respected as a historian even by Haj Amin's surviving family—"his frequent, close contacts with leaders of the Nazi regime cannot have left Haj Amin with any doubt as to the fate which awaited the Jews whose emigration was prevented by his efforts." In July 1943, when the extermination camps were already in operation in Poland, Haj Amin was complaining to Joachim von Ribbentrop, the German foreign minister, about Jewish emigration from Europe to Palestine in the following words: "If there are reasons which make their removal necessary, it would be essential and infinitely preferable to send them to other countries where they would find themselves under active control as, for example, Poland . . ." Before his death, Haj Amin was to write that "the Germans settled their accounts with the Jews well before my arrival in Germany," a statement that is factually and historically untrue.

Wassef Kamal would insist that Haj Amin did not encourage the annihilation of the Jews. "He was of course involved in stopping the emigration of Jews to Palestine but he had nothing to do with the extermination policy. When I was in Berlin with him, I saw many Jews. The only sign of foreigners there was that Russians would have an *Ost* band on their clothes and the Star of David was worn by the Jews. They used to move about. I think it was a secret then, what was happening . . ." Three months before he died, Haj Amin met Abu Iyad, one of Arafat's lieutenants, in Beirut. Of their conversation, Abu Iyad was to write:

> Haj Amin believed that the Axis powers would win the war and would then grant independence to Palestine . . . I pointed out to him that such illusions were based on a rather naive calculation, since Hitler had graded the Arabs 14th after the Jews in his hierarchy of races. Had Germany won, the regime which it would have imposed on the Palestinian Arabs would have been far more cruel than that which they had known during the time of British rule.

Alia al-Husseini, Haj Amin's granddaughter, recalled for me how her grandfather, in his last years, spoke of Hitler's true aims. "He said that after the Jews, the Germans would destroy the Arabs—he knew this. But what could he do? You must understand that Haj Amin lived at a time when everyone was against him." Rifaat el-Nimr, one of the founders of the PLO and subsequently a prominent Beirut banker, vainly tried to enlist the support of Haj Amin for the young PLO after the 1967 Arab–Israeli war. "I don't think it was a mistake he had relations with Herr Hitler," he said. "In 1916, the British lied to the Arabs about independence. In 1917, we had the Balfour declaration. Would the British or Americans have given Haj Amin anything if he had *not* gone to Herr Hitler?" But el-Nimr admitted that Haj Amin "hated the Jews" because "they stole his homeland."

As the Allies closed in upon Germany, Wassef Kamal and Haj Amin found themselves commuting between the ever more dangerous city of Berlin and the resorts of northern Italy that remained under Axis control. Kamal remembered one afternoon, standing on the lawn of the hotel with Haj Amin, looking far up into the heavens and watching "thousands and thousands" of American and British bombers heading for Germany. Haj Amin returned to Berlin, travelled down to Obersalzburg and then decided to seek asylum in neutral Switzerland. The Swiss turned him back and so the Grand Mufti of Jerusalem surrendered to the French. He was briefly imprisoned in Paris before being, with French complicity and American ignorance, smuggled to Cairo under a false name on an American military aircraft.

For eight dramatic days in 1948, Haj Amin helped to create a Palestine government in Gaza before the final collapse of the Arab armies and the annexation of the West Bank by Jordan. This was Israel's "War of Independence" and Palestine's *nakhba*—the "catastrophe" in which around three-quarters of a million Arab Palestinians were driven from their homes or fled into a refugee exile from which they would never return. "Haj Amin should have accepted the UN partition plan," his former admirer Habib abu Fadel would say. "So many nations went along with it and the Russians were among the first. He did not think about the future." Haj Amin's political life had been in vain. He courted and then disliked Colonel Nasser—whose troops now occupied Gaza—and he later hated and then courted King Hussein of Jordan, whose army occupied the West Bank. Returning in 1959 to Lebanon for his final exile, Haj Amin moved into a mountain villa, dispensing wisdom and memories to the Palestinians who came to see him, refusing to join any political movements lest he be dwarfed by them.

Chafiq al-Hout, who wanted the Grand Mufti's power to be enhanced among the Palestinian refugees of Lebanon, asked if he could advise the old man, but was rebuffed when he visited the villa at Mansourieh in the early Fifties and was later beaten up by Haj Amin's thugs in Beirut. "He was like all those tamed Ottoman subjects," he recalls. "He spoke slowly, in whispers, listening, aware of himself twenty-four hours a day. He was like a man on the stage. He could not be interrupted. There were no jokes . . ." His granddaughter Alia remembers him as a family man, scolding her parents when they tried to stop her laughing with friends during the Grand Mufti's afternoon siestas. "He used to say our laughter was music," she says.

Haj Amin spent his last years listening to the music of the Egyptian singer Um al-Khaltum and to the Arabic service of the BBC. Forgiving the past, al-Hout invited him as guest of honour to his wedding—to a young woman, Bayan, whose father was one of Haj Amin's early comrades and who would write her Ph.D. thesis on the Grand Mufti. Haj Amin's journey to Nazi Germany, Bayan al-Hout says, was "a very stupid act—he could have found someone else to take care of negotiations with Hitler. He used to believe that he was responsible for all Muslims in the world; he used to feel an Islamic responsibility. In Bosnia, they looked upon him as a great leader . . ."

Within two years of his death in 1974, the Christian Phalangist militia stormed into his empty villa, stealing his files and diaries—there is a rumour in Beirut that the Israelis possess them now—while fifteen Christian refugee families moved into the wrecked house. They were still there when I visited the house twenty years later, repairing cars in an underground garage beneath what was Haj Amin's study. He was more kindly treated by the latest of his biographers, Elpeleg, who wrote not just of his "enormous failures" but also his "impressive achievements for the Palestinian national movement."

When he died of a heart attack, the Israelis refused Haj Amin's request to be buried in Jerusalem and it was left to al-Hout to arrange his funeral in Beirut. "To my surprise, I found that the new Palestinian leadership in the PLO did not regard this as a great event. I thought there should be some continuity in our history, that we should 'close a chapter,' so to say. I told Arafat he should attend." At the funeral, al-Hout praised Haj Amin as a "religious fighter." Al-Hout remembers the speech. "We used then to look upon his grave as that of a martyr. But then the Lebanese war came and we had so many hundreds of martyrs' graves that we forgot about his."

Not everyone did. Although the al-Husseini family tried to maintain the tomb, the Lebanese Shiite Amal militia—at war in 1985 with their PLO enemies in the Beirut camps—believed that Palestinian weapons had been hidden in Haj Amin's grave. So they chiselled open the marble lid and looked inside. There were no guns; just the Grand Mufti of Jerusalem in a decaying white shroud.

The Arab–Jewish struggle, from the conflicting British promises of Bill Fisk's 1914–18 war—of independence for the Arab states, and of support for a Jewish national home in Palestine—to the establishment of the state of Israel on Palestinian land following the Jewish Holocaust and the Second World War, is an epic tragedy whose effects have spread around the world and continue to poison the lives not only of the participants but of our entire Western political and military policies towards the Middle East and the Muslim lands. The narrative of events— both through Arab and Israeli eyes and through the often biased reporting and commentaries of journalists and historians since 1948—now forms libraries of information and disinformation through which the reader may wander with incredulity and exhaustion. As long ago as 1938, when the British still governed Palestine under a League of Nations mandate, the eminent historian George Antonius was warning of the dangers of too much reliance on the vast body of literature already in existence, and his words are no less relevant today:

> ... it has to be used with care, partly because of the high percentage of open or veiled propaganda, and partly because the remoteness of the indispensable Arabic sources has militated against real fairness, even in the works of neutral and fair-minded historians. A similar equality vitiates the stream of day-to-day information. Zionist propaganda is active, highly organised and widespread; the world Press, at any rate in the democracies of the West, is largely amenable to it; it commands many of the available channels for the dissemination of news, and more particularly those of the English-speaking world. Arab propaganda is, in comparison, primitive and infinitely less successful: the Arabs have little of the skill, polyglottic ubiquity or financial resources which make Jewish propaganda so effective. The result is, that for a score of years or so, the world has been looking at Palestine mainly through Zionist spectacles and has unconsciously acquired the habit of reasoning on Zionist premises.

Most of the last thirty years of my life have been spent cataloguing events that relate directly or indirectly to the battle for Palestine, to the unresolved injustices that have afflicted both Arabs and Jews since the 1920s and earlier. British support for an independent Arab nation was expressed when Britain needed Arab forces to fight the Turks. The Balfour declaration giving support for a Jewish national home was made when Britain needed Jewish support—both politically and scientifically—during the First World War. Lloyd George, who was British prime minister in 1917, would often fantasise upon the biblical drama being played out in Palestine, saying that he wanted Jerusalem for Christmas in 1917—he got it, courtesy of General Allenby—and referring in his memoirs to "the capture by British troops of the most famous city in the world which had for centuries baffled the efforts of Christendom to regain possession of its sacred shrines." That Lloyd George should have reflected upon Allenby's campaign as a successor to the Crusades—"regaining possession" of Jerusalem from Muslims—was a theme that would run throughout the twentieth century in the West's dealings with the Middle East; it would find its natural echo in George W. Bush's talk of a "crusade" in the immediate aftermath of the international crimes against humanity of 11 September 2001.

In those memoirs, Lloyd George makes scarcely any reference to the Balfour declaration—and then only to suggest that it was a gesture made to reward the prominent Zionist Chaim Weizmann for his scientific work on acetone, a chemical essential in the making of cordite, and therefore to the British war effort. Weizmann's name, Lloyd George would enthuse, "will rank with that of Nehemiah in the fascinating and inspiring story of the children of Israel." Nehemiah was responsible for the fifth-century BC rebuilding and restoration of Jerusalem, a task he accomplished after his release from captivity by the Persian king Artaxerxes. But at almost the same time Lloyd George was writing this panegyric—in 1936— he was speaking far more frankly about the Balfour Declaration in the House of Commons during a debate on the Arab revolt:

It was at one of the darkest periods of the war that Mr. Balfour first prepared his Declaration. At that time the French Army had mutinied; the Italian army was on the eve of collapse; America had hardly started preparing in earnest. There was nothing left but Britain confronting the most powerful military combination that the world had ever seen. It was important for us to seek every legitimate help that we could get. The Government came to the conclusion, from information received from every part of the world, that it was very vital that we should have the sympathies of the Jewish community . . . We certainly had no prejudices against the Arabs because at that moment we had hundreds of thousands of troops fighting for Arab emancipation from the Turk. Under these conditions and with the advice they received, the Government decided that it was desirable for us to secure the sympathy and cooperation of that most remarkable community, the Jews, throughout the world. They were helpful to us in America to a very large extent; and they were helpful even in Russia at that moment because Russia was just about to walk out and leave us alone. Under those conditions we proposed this to our Allies. France, Italy, and the United States accepted it . . . The Jews, with all the influence that they possessed, responded nobly to the appeal that was made.

The French army's mutiny and potential collapse on the Italian front, it seems, had more to do with promises for a Jewish "national home" than did Nehemiah. But now the Arabs "were demanding practically that there should be no more Jewish immigration," Lloyd George complained to the Commons. "We could not accept that without dishonouring our obligations. It was not as if the Arabs were in a position to say that Jewish immigration is driving them, the ancient inhabitants, out . . ." But Lloyd George grasped, if with too little gravity, where the problem lay:

> The obligations of the Mandate were specific and definite. They were that we were to encourage the establishment of a National home for the Jews in Palestine without detriment to any of the rights of the Arab population. That was a dual undertaking and we must see that both parts of the Mandate are enforced.

But both parts of the British Palestine Mandate could not be enforced, and Nazi Germany's persecution of its Jews in 1936, which Lloyd George specifically mentioned, would turn into the Holocaust that would ensure the existence of an Israeli state in Palestine—whatever "the rights of the Arab population." By 1938, George Antonius was saying quite clearly that "the establishment of a Jewish state in Palestine, or of a national home based on territorial sovereignty, cannot be accomplished without forcibly displacing the Arabs . . ." Antonius wanted an independent Arab state "in which as many Jews as the country can hold without prejudice to its political and economic freedom would live in peace, security and dignity, and enjoy full rights of citizenship." Fearing "an unpredictable holocaust of Arab, Jewish and British lives," help for the Jews of Europe, he said, must be sought elsewhere than in Palestine:

> The treatment meted out to Jews in Germany and other European countries is a disgrace to its authors and to modern civilisation; but posterity will not exonerate any country that fails to bear its proper share of the sacrifices needed to alleviate Jewish suffering and distress. To place the brunt of the burden upon Arab Palestine is a miserable evasion of the duty that lies upon the whole of the civilised world. It is also morally outrageous. No code of morals can justify the persecution of one people in an attempt to relieve the persecution of another. The cure for the eviction of Jews from Germany is not to be sought in the eviction of the Arabs from their homeland; and the relief of Jewish distress may not be accomplished at the cost of inflicting a corresponding distress upon an innocent and peaceful population.

It is astonishing that such remarks—so prescient in view of the Palestinian disaster a decade later—could have been written in 1938. Yet there were others who foresaw future disaster in equally bleak terms. Only a year earlier, but reflecting upon the future, Winston Churchill had written of the impossibility of a partitioned Palestine and had written—far more prophetically—of how:

> the wealthy, crowded, progressive Jewish State lies in the plains, and on the sea coasts [of Palestine]. Around it, in the hills and the uplands, stretching far and wide into the illimitable deserts, the warlike Arabs of Syria, of Transjordania, of Arabia, backed by the armed forces of Iraq, offer the ceaseless menace of war . . . To maintain itself, the Jewish State must be armed to the teeth, and must bring in every able-bodied man to strengthen its army. But how long would this process be allowed to continue by the great Arab populations in Iraq and Palestine? Can it be expected that the Arabs would stand by impassively and watch the building up with Jewish world capital and resources of a Jewish army equipped with the most deadly weapons of war, until it was strong enough not to be afraid of them? And if ever the Jewish army reached that point, who can be sure that, cramped within their narrow limits, they would not plunge out into the new undeveloped lands that lie around them?

If Palestine should be partitioned, Churchill concluded, "I find it difficult . . . to resist the conclusion that the . . . [partition] scheme would lead inevitably to the complete evacuation of Palestine by Great Britain." And so, as they say, it came to pass.

John Bagot Glubb, commanding the Arab Legion from 1939, would comment movingly that "the Jewish tragedy owed its origin to the Christian nations of Europe and America. At last the conscience of Christendom was awake. The age-long Jewish tragedy must cease. But when it came to the payment of compensation in expiation of their past shortcomings, the Christian nations of Europe and America decided that the bill should be paid by a Muslim nation in Asia."

Antonius would have had the world settle Jewish refugees in countries other than Palestine—we know that the British considered Uganda—while we also know that prewar Zionist committees were contemplating the "transfer"—ethnic cleansing—of Palestine's Arabs to, among other locations, the Djezaira area of Syria, the very deserts around Deir es-Zour and Aleppo in which the Armenian deportees "had ended their miserable existences" twenty years earlier. It was in this atmosphere of suspicion, paranoia and immense suffering that the Arabs and Jews watched the Second World War overwhelm Europe, the former fearful that Britain would eventually sanction an Israeli state on their lands, the latter observing the annihilation of their race in Europe while the British sought to block even those few Jewish refugee ships that made a run for the Promised Land. This was the world in which Haj Amin, the Grand Mufti, set off to Germany and urged Hitler to end Jewish emigration to Palestine. But at what cost?

HERE THE MORAL COMPASS begins to spin at ever-increasing speed. Why did the Palestinians have to bear the fate of Britain's First World War promise to a people whose ancestors lived on their land two thousand years before? Why did this new flood of Muslim refugees have to pay this price, then—like the Armenians—be told that they were the aggressors, and those who dispossessed them the victims? For in the decades to come, the Palestinians would be the "terrorists" and those who took their lands would be the innocent, the representatives of a Phoenix nation rising from the ashes of Auschwitz. In the eyes of the world—especially in 1948, in a world grown weary of war and familiar with the millions of refugees who had washed across Europe—what was the lot of 750,000 Palestinian refugees when measured against the murder of 6 million Jews?

It is April 2002, a bright spring morning in west Jerusalem, and I am in the small, neat apartment where Josef Kleinman and his wife, Haya, live in what might seem—if we did not know its historical significance—to be just another tree-stroked suburb. Kleinman is excited, an instantly generous man who, asked to tell about the blackest days of his life, leaps from his chair like a tiger. "I will show you my museum," he says, and scampers into a back room.

He returns with a faded old khaki knapsack. "This is the shirt the Americans gave me after I was freed from Landsberg on April twenty-seventh, 1945." It is a crumpled, cheap chequered shirt whose label is now illegible. Then he takes out a smock of blue-and-white stripes and a hat with the same stripes running from front to back. "This is my uniform as a prisoner of Dachau," he says. Familiar from every 1945 newsreel, from *Schindler's List* and from a hundred other Holocaust movies, it is a shock to touch—to hold—this symbol of a people's destruction. Josef Kleinman watches me as I hold the smock. He understands the shock. I am thinking: this was in Dachau. This was produced by the Nazis. This is part of the real, dysentery-soaked, cyanide-gassed history of extermination, every bit as much a witness to inhumanity as those Armenian bones that Isabel Ellsen and I had keyed out of the Syrian mud ten years ago. In the newsreels, the concentration-camp smocks are black and white, but the actual mass murder of the Jews of Europe was performed in colour. Blue and white. The same colours as the Israeli flag. On the front of the smock is the number 114986.

Down in the entrance to Kleinman's block of flats, there are flyers reminding tenants of the forthcoming Holocaust Day. Givat Shaul is a friendly, bright neighbourhood of retired couples, small shops, flats, trees and some elegant old houses of yellow stone. Some of the latter are in a state of dilapidation, a few are homes. But one or two bear the scars of bullets fired long ago, on 9 April 1948, when another people faced their own catastrophe. For Givat Shaul used to be Deir Yassin. And here it was, fifty-four years ago, that up to 130 Palestinians were massacred by two Jewish militias, the Irgun Zvai Leumi and the Stern Gang, as the Jews of Palestine fought for the independence of a state called Israel. The slaughter so terrified tens of thousands of Palestinian Arabs that they fled their homes en masse—just a few of the 750,000—to create the refugee population whose vale of sorrow lies at the heart of the Israeli–Palestinian war.

Back in 1948, around the old houses that still exist close to the Kleinmans' home, Palestinian women were torn to pieces by grenades thrown by Jewish fighters. Two truckloads of Arab prisoners were taken from the village and paraded through the streets of Jerusalem. Later, many of them would be taken back to Deir Yassin and executed. Their mass grave is believed to lie beneath a fuel-storage depot that now stands at one end of the Jerusalem suburb. So a visit to the Kleinman home raises an unusual moral question. Can one listen to his personal testimony of the greatest crime in modern history and then ask about the slaughter that cut down the Palestinians at this very spot, when the eviction of the Arabs of Palestine, terrible though it was, comes nowhere near, statistically or morally, the murder of 6 million Jews? Does Josef Kleinman even know that this year, by another of those awful ironies of history, Holocaust Day and Deir Yassin Day fall on the same date?

Josef Kleinman is no ordinary Jewish Holocaust survivor. He was the youngest survivor of Auschwitz and he testified at the trial of Adolf Eichmann, head of the special "Jewish Section" of the SS, who ran the Nazi programme to murder the Jews of Europe. Josef Kleinman even saw Dr. Josef Mengele, the "Angel of Death," who chose children, women, the old and the sick for the gas chambers. At the age of just fourteen, he watched one day as Mengele arrived on a bicycle and ordered a boy to hammer a plank of wood to a post. Here is part of Kleinman's testimony at the Eichmann trial:

> We weren't told what was to happen. We knew. The boys who couldn't pass under the plank would be spared. Those boys whose heads did not reach the plank would be sent to the gas chambers. We all tried to stretch ourselves upwards, to make ourselves taller. But I gave up. I saw that taller boys than me failed to touch the plank with their heads. My brother asked me: "Do you want to live? Yes? Then do something." My head began to work. I saw some stones. I put them in my shoes, and this made me taller. But I couldn't stand at attention on the stones. They were killing me.

Josef Kleinman's brother, Shlomo, tore his hat in half and Josef stuffed part of it into his shoes. He was still too short. But he managed to infiltrate the group who had passed the test. The remainder of the boys—a thousand in all—were gassed. Mengele, Josef Kleinman remembers, chose Jewish holidays for the mass killing of Jewish children. Kleinman's parents, Meir and Rachel, and his sister had been sent directly to the gas chambers when they arrived at Auschwitz from the Carpathian mountains, in what is now the Ukraine. He survived, along with his brother—who today, a carpenter like Josef, lives a few hundred metres away in the same suburb of Givat Shaul/Deir Yassin. Josef Kleinman also survived Dachau and the gruelling labour of building a massive bunker for Hitler's secret factory, constructed for the production of Germany's new Messerschmitt Me 262 jet fighter aircraft.

After his liberation by the Americans, Kleinman made his way to Italy and then to a small boat that put him aboard a ship for Palestine, carrying illegal Jewish immigrants who were to try to enter the territory of the dying British Mandate. He could carry only a few possessions. He chose to put his Dachau uniform in his bag—he would not forget what had happened to him. Turned back by the British, he spent six months in the Famagusta camp on Cyprus, eventually ending up in an immigrants' camp at Atlit in Palestine. He arrived in Jerusalem on 15 March 1947, and was there when Israel's war of independence broke out. He fought in that war—but not at Deir Yassin. I mention the name, almost in passing. But both Josef Kleinman and Haya nod at once.

"There are things which have been written that were wrong about Deir Yassin," he said. "I was in Jerusalem and I saw the two truckloads of prisoners that came from here. Some reports say Arabs were killed, others that they were not. Not all the people were killed. There is much propaganda. I do not know. The Arabs killed their Jewish prisoners. There didn't have to be much fighting for the Arabs to leave."

But when he saw those Arabs leaving, did they not, for Josef Kleinman, provide any kind of parallel—however faint, given the numerically far greater and infinitely bloodier disaster that overtook the Jews—of his own life? He thinks about this for a while. He did not see many Arab refugees, he said. It was his wife, Haya, who replied. "I think that after what happened to him—which was so dreadful—that everything else in the world seemed less important. You have to understand that Josef lives in that time, in the time of the Shoah. Of the twenty-nine thousand Jews brought to Dachau from other camps, most of them from Auschwitz, fifteen thousand died."

But is it just about the enormity of one crime and its statistical comparison to the exodus of Palestinians in 1948? A group of Jews, Muslims and Christians have long been campaigning for Deir Yassin to be remembered—even now, at the height of the latest Palestine war. As one of the organisers put it, "Many Jews may not want to look at this, fearing that the magnitude of their tragedy may be diminished. For Palestinians there is always the fear that, as often before, the Holocaust may be used to justify their own suffering." The Kleinmans do not know of this commemoration—nor of the organisation's plans for a memorial to the Palestinian dead not far from their home in the suburb of Givat Shaul. Josef Kleinman won't talk about the bloodbath in Israel and Palestine that continues while we are talking. But he admits he's "on the right" in politics and voted for Ariel Sharon at the last Israeli election. "Is there any other man?" he asks.

Yet Josef Kleinman's memory of Deir Yassin is imperfect. Red Cross records and the dispatches of foreign correspondents of the time make it quite clear that the villagers of Deir Yassin were murdered and that some of the women were disembowelled. All over that part of Mandate Palestine which was to become Israel, there were little massacres—sometimes initiated by the Arabs, more frequently by Jewish fighters who were transmogrifying into the Israeli army as the war progressed—and just one small and tragic story gives an idea of what happened during the dispossession of Palestinians.

It is the year 2000 and I am in a rain-soaked village in southern Lebanon, a place of poverty and broken roads called Shabriqa. And eighty-five-year-old Nimr Aoun rolls up his trouser leg to show the twisted ligament and muscle where an

Israeli bullet tore into him fifty-two years earlier. Aoun's story is a tale of two betrayals, because he was a victim not only of the Israelis but of the two Mandate powers—Britain and France—who were supposed, in the aftermath of the First World War, to protect him. He comes from a village called Salha—now 2 kilometres inside Israel on the other side of the Lebanese frontier—and was the only survivor of an Israeli massacre of the male villagers.

The story of Salha and six other villages—En-Naame, Ez-Zouk, Tarchiha, El-Khalsa, El-Kitiyeh and Lakhas—goes back to 1923, when the British ruled Palestine and the French ruled the newly formed state of Lebanon. The two imperial powers were doing a little frontier-changing for their own ends and Paris decided to cede to London a few square miles of Lebanon—the British Mandate of Palestine was moved slightly north to take in the seven villages. A grubby deal lay behind this transaction. Old records in Beirut show that the land was handed over in exchange for a contract granted to a French company to drain marshland in the region for commercial use. At the time, it was called—I preferred not to tell old Nimr Aoun this—"the Good Neighbourhood" agreement. And it doomed every villager.

Nimr Aoun was no longer a Lebanese under the French Mandate. He was now a Palestinian under the British Mandate—although neither the Aoun family nor any of the other villagers were consulted about the matter. Anyway, Aoun remembers the British fondly. He was a farmer who married a girl of thirteen, and had nine children, living amid the cornfields of Salha. But his voice rises in pitch when he comes to 1948, the British departure and the arrival of the Jewish army outside the village. "They showered us with leaflets saying that, if we surrendered, we would be spared," he says. "The women and children had already fled. So we believed the leaflets and surrendered. But the Israelis had lied. They cursed us and made seventy of us stand together."

What happens next is confirmed in Israeli archives. The historian Benny Morris writes that in an Israeli attack called "Operation Hiram," after "light resistance" by Arabs near Salha, ninety-four of the villagers were blown up in a house on 30 October 1948. Nimr Aoun has a different version of events, but one given veracity by his scars:

> When we were all standing together, they opened fire on us. There were thirteen tanks all round the area. We had no chance. What helped me was that after I was shot in the leg, I fell under piles of bodies. They were on top of me and most of the bullets were hitting my friends. I was bleeding so much, I felt nothing. When night came, I pulled my way out and crawled past one of the tanks and then through long grass until I found a donkey.

Nimr Aoun heaved himself onto the animal's back and rode painfully north to the Lebanese village of Maroun, where he was given medical treatment. A government official prevented doctors from amputating his leg, which is why Nimr Aoun can still hobble around his home at Shabriqa, 40 kilometres from the site of the once-Lebanese village of Salha in which only a long low building survives today. Most of the land is now covered by Israeli apple orchards.

Until 1998, Nimr Aoun and the other few survivors from the "seven villages" of 1948 were treated as Palestinians with Palestinian documents. Then the Lebanese government—not immune to the political advantages of such an act— awarded them all Lebanese citizenship. Aoun produced for me his new Lebanese identity card, the image of a cedar tree close to his passport picture. He started life as a citizen of the Ottoman empire, became a Lebanese under the French, turned into a Palestinian under the British, became a Palestinian refugee from Israel and, at the very end of his life, was Lebanese once more.

My files on the last years of the British Mandate are packed with letters from British army veterans, interviews with former Jewish and Arab fighters, along with hundreds of contemporary newspaper clippings. It is a story of anarchy and pain and—to use Israel's current use of the word—"terrorist" attacks and bombings, most of them by the Jewish Haganah and Irgun and Stern gangs. A British Colonial Office pamphlet of 1946 reads like an account of the first year's Iraqi uprising against American occupation in 2003: attacks on road and rail bridges, the kidnapping of British officers and clandestine radio stations broadcasting propaganda for the insurgents. "The action of blowing up the bridges expressed the high morale and courage of the Jewish fighters who carried out the attack," the document reports Kol Israel as broadcasting on 18 June 1946.

Undisciplined British army raids—against Arabs as well as Jews—provoked ruthless revenge operations. The bombing of British headquarters at the King David Hotel in Jerusalem by the Irgun on 22 July 1946, killing ninety-one British, Jewish and Arab civil servants, was only the most infamous of the assaults carried out against the occupying power. British soldiers opened fire on civilians in the streets of Tel Aviv and when—after the British went ahead with the hanging of three Jewish Irgun fighters—the Irgun hanged two British army hostages, there were anti-Semitic attacks across Britain. Intelligence Corps Sergeants Mervyn Paice and Clifford Martin spent days hidden underground by their captors in the city of Netanya while the Irgun repeatedly threatened their execution. Paice's father wrote a pleading letter to the Irgun leader Menachem Begin—later, the prime minister of Israel who would order the brutal Israeli invasion of Lebanon in 1982—just as the relatives of Western hostages would appeal to Iraqi kidnappers in 2003 and 2004. I possess a photocopy of a statement from the "Court of the Irgun Zvai Leumi in Palestine" which was found pinned to the chests of the two men after they had been murdered. It says that the "court" found Paice and Martin guilty of "(a) illegal entry into our homeland. (b) Belonging to a British Terrorist Criminal Organisation known as the British Military Occupation Forces . . . the judgement was carried out on 30th July 1947. The hanging of the two spies . . . is an *ordinary legal action* of a court of the Underground which has sentenced and will sentence the criminals who belong to the criminal Nazi-British Army of Occupation."

Attached to this document is a British Palestine Police report on the finding of the bodies of the two sergeants in a eucalyptus grove:

They were hanging from two eucalyptus trees about five yards apart. Their faces were heavily bandaged so it was impossible to distinguish their features . . . Their bodies were a dull black colour and blood had run down their chests which made it appear at first that they had been shot . . . the press were allowed to take photographs of the spectacle. When this had been done, it was decided to cut down the bodies. The RE [Royal Engineers] captain and CSM [colour sergeant major] lopped the branches off the tree which held the right hand body, and started to cut the hang rope with a saw . . . As the body fell to the ground, there was a large explosion . . . The two trees had been completely blown up and their [sic] were large craters where the roots had been. One body was found horribly mangled about twenty yards away . . . The other body had disintegrated, and small pieces were picked up as much as 200 yards away.

The Irgun published tracts in poor English, urging British soldiers that if they wished to stay in Palestine, the best way to do so would be to "risk your life every day so that the [British] Government may have ten more years to make up its mind to claar [sic] out of Palestine." The British broke many of the rules of war. A British member of the Palestine Police was to describe how, when British soldiers travelled on the railway line from Lydda, "we usually had a gangers' trolley preceding us with several prisoners on board—for them to enjoy the explosion of mines laid along the line."

There is a fierce irony in all this. Israel came into being after a classic anti-colonial guerrilla war against an occupation army; yet within fifty years, Israel's own army—now itself the occupation force—would be fighting an equally classic anti-colonial guerrilla war in the West Bank and Gaza. The connection, however, often seems lost on the Israeli government. On 6 November 1944, Jewish gunmen assassinated Lord Moyne, the British minister-resident in Cairo, a former colonial secretary and close friend of Churchill. Moyne, who had favoured partition in Palestine, had upset Palestinian Jews because in 1942 he had urged the Turks to turn back the *Struma*, a ship carrying Jewish refugees from the Holocaust;* he had also made a number of racist remarks about Jews, although few could argue with his observation that "the Arabs, who have lived and buried their dead for fifty generations in Palestine, will not willingly surrender their land and self-government to the Jews."

Moyne's murder prompted Churchill to reflect that "if our dreams for Zionism should be dissolved in the smoke of the revolvers of assassins and if our efforts for its future should provoke a new wave of banditry worthy of the Nazi Germans, many persons like myself will have to reconsider the position that we have maintained so firmly for such a long time." Yet in 1975 the two murderers, Eliyahu Hakim and Eliyahu Bet Zuri, were given a state funeral in Israel with a public

---

*Shortly after it was refused passage through the Bosporus, the ship exploded and 767 of its passengers were drowned.

lying-in-state attended by the prime minister and a military funeral attended by the deputy prime minister and two chief rabbis. Moyne's son was to ask former Haganah officer David Hacohen: "Why then did your people murder my father? . . . In the end Palestine was partitioned and you are now consolidating your state on the basis of that partition, yet none of you has been assassinated for accepting this solution."

This question—of honouring one's own murderers while condemning the other side's killers as "terrorists"—is one that lies at the core of so many modern conflicts, yet one that both the Israelis and the Palestinians have failed to understand. Equally, the 1948 war threw up extraordinary portents of other, later, Middle East wars—of events that we regard as causes of present danger but which have clearly been a feature of conflict in the region for longer than we like to imagine.

In 1997, a Palestinian humanitarian group in Scotland decided to mark the fiftieth anniversary of the UN Partition resolution, the end of the British Mandate, the Israeli war of independence and the Palestinian *nakhba* by publishing a day-by-day account of events in Palestine throughout 1948, largely drawn from the pages of the *Scotsman*—a project that sometimes yielded devastating results. Here, for example, is a dispatch "from a Special Correspondent recently returned from the Middle East," which appeared in the paper on 13 September 1948:

A new danger to law and order is emerging in the Middle East. It comes from a loosely formed association of Arab terrorist gangs of hot-headed xenophobic young men who have sworn to rid their countries of all Westerners and of course particularly of British and Americans. Open threats have already been made to Europeans living in Damascus, Baghdad and Cairo—oil men mostly—that if they continue to have business relations with the Jews they will be killed . . . The backbone of this new terrorist organisation is provided by young Palestinian Arabs. They have seen their country overrun . . . and have lost everything they possessed—homes, property, money, jobs; they have nothing further to lose. They feel they have been let down by the British and the Americans, by the United Nations, and also, to some extent, by the other Arab countries. They now realise there is a grave danger that the present situation in Palestine, with the Jews in total possession of the best part of the country, will be generally recognised and legalised . . .

Another disturbing light into the future was cast in an article by Patrick O'Donovan which had appeared in *The Scotsman* on 14 July 1948:

The war [of independence] began as a simple war of survival—or so it seemed to the Jews. There was a set of figures that every little sunburnt child knew by heart—"700,000 Jews against 30 million Arabs plus the support of Britain." It seemed a victory every time a Jewish settlement survived an attack . . . but the Arabs proved less effective. And the Jewish consent to the continuation of the truce was flouted. (It makes no difference that the consent was certainly given in the knowledge that the Arabs would first refuse.) The Jews have been freed from any obligation to hold their hand. If Count Bernadotte's* efforts fail, then the Jews will wage a war which frankly will aim at acquiring a maximum of Arab land, much of which will be retained because it will be empty of Arabs and occupied by Jews . . . In Haifa . . . they have opened a ghetto for the Arabs. Four of the meaner streets have been wired off and, just like the Jews in Medieval Cracow, Christian and Muslim Arabs must sleep and live here under guard. Business men can apply for passes if they wish to emerge during the day . . . it would be hard to visualise a more subdued and frightened population than the Arabs left in Israel . . .

Although the extent of Palestinian dispossession often appears to be a newly discovered fact of Middle East history—at least until "new historians" like Benny Morris researched Israeli government archives of the time—the British press reported the *nakhba* in graphic detail. On 25 October, for instance, *The Times* reported from Beersheba that:

The Arab villages are deserted, their miserable houses have been looted, and many are burnt. The inhabitants, estimated to be about 20,000—a number which has been swollen considerably by refugees from the north—have fled, and no one knows, or apparently cares, where they have gone. It is obvious that most have fled in panic, leaving behind their cloaks, sheepskins, and blankets so necessary if they are to survive the cold nights of the Hebron hills . . . in Beersheba itself, once a thriving centre for camel trading, a few inhabitants remain, and at present members of the Israeli Army are systematically looting those houses which survived the bombing. It is perhaps an ancient and tacitly accepted rule of war that troops should make themselves comfortable at the expense of the vanquished, but it is difficult to excuse the behaviour of some, who ridicule Islamic devotions in a desecrated mosque . . . holy books have been torn and strewn upon the floor . . . Such a scene is disappointing to those who had gratefully observed the care taken by the Israeli Army to guarantee the sanctity of Christian holy places elsewhere, and by those correspondents who today visited the Imperial war cemetery just outside the town. In spite of the difficulties under which they worked, the Arab caretakers to the last obviously attended the graves of the British and Australian soldiers who died here in 1917, and English flowers are still blooming in desert sands.

---

*Count Folke Bernadotte, the UN mediator, had engineered several truces. On 17 September 1948, he was assassinated in Jerusalem by the Stern Gang, who regarded the Swede as a British agent. One of the three men who sanctioned the murder was Yitzhak Shamir, another future Israeli prime minister.

Desecration and murder were not tools of one side in this war. When the Israelis captured East Jerusalem in 1967, they discovered that Jordanian troops had used Jewish gravestones for lavatory floors. Ambushes and killings cut down many Jewish civilians, although Israel's advance into the Arab villages of Galilee was accompanied, as contemporary research in Israel has proved, by massacres and—sometimes—the rape of young Arab women. But if Israeli historians have proved the truth of this, Arab historians have remained largely silent about their own side's iniquities in this and other wars.

In my book on the Lebanon war, I have written at great length about the Palestinian dispossession of 1948, the subsequent history of those Palestinian homes that were vacated by their fearful inhabitants and the fate of the 750,000 Palestinian refugees and their millions of descendants today, many of whom rot in the squalor of camps in Lebanon, Syria, Jordan and in the occupied West Bank and Syria.* Following their travail, the task of reporting their hopeless political leadership, their victimisation—most cruelly demonstrated when they were turned into the aggressors by an all-powerful Israel and, later, an even more hegemonic United States—and their pathetic, brave and often callous attempts to seek the world's sympathy has been one of the more depressing experiences in journalism. The more we wrote about the Palestinian dispossession, the less effect it seemed to have and the more we were abused as journalists.

The 1956 Suez war, the 1967 Six Day War—and Nasser's blind folly in taking on the might of the Israeli army—the 1973 Middle East conflict and the 1982 invasion of Lebanon all further crushed the Palestinians, indirectly and, usually, directly. In 1967 the West Bank and Gaza fell under Israeli occupation, so that Israel at last had the entire former British Mandate of Palestine under its control, the "Palestine" in which Balfour had promised support for a "national home" for the Jews—and Balfour, let us remember, made no mention of how much of Palestine an Israeli state could have. The Arab "friends" of Palestine turned out to be as woeful in their military as they were in their political ambitions. Fighting with numerically overwhelming odds on their side, the Arab armies were repeatedly mauled by the superior firepower, ruthless tactics and morale of the Israelis, an advantage reinforced by every Israeli's understanding that he or she could never afford to lose a single war. The Egyptian army's initial success in 1973—Arabs could not at first believe the newsreel film of captured Israeli soldiers on the Bar Lev line—was later lost to Egyptian military indecision. Only the Lebanese Hizballah, with its Iranian and Syrian support, proved that Israel could be beaten. Israel's military retreat out of its occupation zone in Lebanon in 2000 and the dismantlement of its torture prison at Khiam remains one of the most significant military events in the Arab–Israeli war—although the Israelis, being the losers, have never chosen to regard it as such and the Americans, as their friends, refused to learn its lessons.

---

*\*Pity the Nation: Lebanon at War* (Oxford University Press, 2001)—in the United States, *Pity the Nation: The Abduction of Lebanon* (New York: Nation Books, 2002), especially pp. 12–47, 161–400.

For throughout these long years, there was one outstanding, virtually unchanging phenomenon which ensured that the Middle East balance of power remained unchanged: America's unwavering, largely uncritical, often involuntary support for Israel. Israel's "security"—or supposed lack thereof—became the yardstick for all negotiations, all military threats and all wars. The injustice done to the Palestinians, the dispossession, the massacres, not only the loss of that part of Palestine which became Israel—and is internationally recognised as such—but also the occupation of the remainder of the Mandate territory and the bloody suppression of any and all manifestation of Palestinian resistance: all this had to take second place to Israel's security and the civilised values and democracy for which Israel was widely promoted. Her army, which often behaved with cruelty and undiscipline, was to be regarded as an exemplar of "purity of arms" and those of us who witnessed Israel's killing of civilians were to be abused as liars, anti-Semites or friends of "terrorism."

Report the wanton use of violence by Palestinians—aircraft hijackings, attacks on illegal Jewish settlements and then, inevitably, suicide bombings on the innocent, the executioner with explosives strapped to his or her body—and that was "terror" pure and simple, dangerously present but comfortably isolated from reason, cause or history. As long as they were accused of crimes that had been committed because they hated Israel or hated Jews or were brought up as anti-Semites (despite being Semites themselves), or paid to carry out "terror," or because they hated "democracy" or represented "evil"—most of these explanations would later be adopted by the Americans about their Arab enemies—then Palestinians were outside the boundaries of reason. They couldn't be talked to, could not be negotiated with. You cannot "negotiate with terrorists."

"Terrorism" is a word that has become a plague on our vocabulary, the excuse and reason and moral permit for state-sponsored violence—*our* violence—which is now used on the innocent of the Middle East ever more outrageously and promiscuously. Terrorism, terrorism, terrorism. It has become a full stop, a punctuation mark, a phrase, a speech, a sermon, the be-all and end-all of everything that we must hate in order to ignore injustice and occupation and murder on a mass scale. Terror, terror, terror, terror. It is a sonata, a symphony, an orchestra tuned to every television and radio station and news agency report, the soap-opera of the Devil, served up on prime-time or distilled in wearyingly dull and mendacious form by the right-wing "commentators" of the American east coast or the *Jerusalem Post* or the intellectuals of Europe. Strike against Terror. Victory over Terror. War on Terror. Everlasting War on Terror. Rarely in history have soldiers and journalists and presidents and kings aligned themselves in such thoughtless, unquestioning ranks. In August 1914, the soldiers thought they would be home by Christmas. Today, we are fighting for ever. The war is eternal. The enemy is eternal, his face changing on our screens. Once he lived in Cairo and sported a moustache and nationalised the Suez Canal. Then he lived in Tripoli and wore a ridiculous military uniform and helped the IRA and bombed American bars in Berlin. Then he wore a Muslim imam's gown and ate yoghurt in Tehran and planned Islamic revolution. Then he wore a white gown and lived in a cave in

Afghanistan and then he wore another silly moustache and resided in a series of palaces around Baghdad. Terror, terror, terror. Finally, he wore a kuffiah headdress and outdated Soviet-style military fatigues, his name was Yassir Arafat, and he was the master of world terror and then a super-statesman and then, again, a master of terror, linked by his Israeli enemies to the terror-*Meister* of them all, the one who lived in the Afghan cave.

Here, personified, was everything loyal and everything miserable about the Palestinian dream. I have a tape recording of Arafat, sitting with me on a cold, dark mountainside outside the northern Lebanese port of Tripoli in 1983, where the old man—he was always called the old man, long before he was elderly—was under siege by the Syrian army, another of the Arab "brothers" who wanted to lead the Palestinian cause and ended up fighting Palestinians rather than Israelis. Even worse, the Syrians had suborned some of "their" Palestinians to join them in the siege. Just a year before, Arafat and his PLO had withstood an eighty-eight-day siege in the Lebanese capital of Beirut by the Israeli army, led by Defence Minister Ariel Sharon. Now Arafat's fortunes have crumbled again. The tape hisses and occasionally, far away, shells thump into a hillside. I play it again, listening to the wind cracking past the microphone:

ARAFAT: I will not be away from my freedom fighters while they are facing death and dangers from death . . . It is my duty to be beside my freedom fighters and my officers and my soldiers.

FISK: A year ago, you and I talked in west Beirut. Here we are on a windy hilltop outside Tripoli, fifty miles further away from the border of Israel, or the border of Palestine, and people within Fatah are rebelling.

ARAFAT: You see, I give you another proof that we are a nut that is not easy to be cracked. I hope that you still remember what Sharon had mentioned in the beginning of his invasion. He was dreaming that within three or five days he would liquidate or smash the PLO, our people, our freedom fighters—and here we are. The siege of Beirut, the battles of the south of Lebanon, this miracle, eighty-eight days, the longest Arab–Israeli war—and after that we have this war of attrition against the Israeli army, not only the Palestinians—definitely—we and our allies—our allies, the Lebanese—are participating in this war of attrition and we are proud—I am proud—that I have this brave alliance.

FISK: Fifty miles further from Palestine!

ARAFAT: What is the difference to be fifty miles or to be fifty thousand miles? One metre outside the border of Palestine, I am far away.

FISK: But I think it was Mr. Sartawi* who once said that if you keep having

---

*Isaam Sartawi, a PLO official and heart surgeon who successfully urged Arafat to negotiate with moderate Israelis, had been murdered in Portugal in April of 1983—just under two months before my conversation with Arafat—by gunmen paid by Abu Nidal's "Fatah Revolutionary Council." The claim of responsibility was made in that "beating heart of Arabism" which was even now besieging Arafat: Syria.

victories like last year's victory in Beirut, you'll hold your next year's
meeting of the Palestine National Council in Fiji . . .
ARAFAT: Please! Please! Don't give me this example! He is one of our
brave martyrs, a brave martyr. But he was nervous [*sic*], he was not giving
exact expression . . .

Arafat was a dreamer, which was a popular characteristic for Palestinians who
had only dreams to give them hope. If compromise was required of him, he could
talk to Israelis, even hint at acceptance of the partition of Palestine. "I will accept
even one square inch of my land," he would say; geographic proportion was not his
strong point. But if one of the PLO's more outlandish satellites embarrassed the
Palestinians—and the world—by murdering an innocent, Arafat would step in to
prevent further tragedy, thus acquiring prestige from the crimes of his own organisation. Nowhere was this better illustrated than in the 1985 voyage of the *Achille
Lauro*, an Italian cruise liner from which four teenage members of the "Palestine
Liberation Front," a PLO splinter outfit run by Mohamed Zeidan (Abul Abbas),
intended to storm ashore at Haifa when the vessel called at the Israeli port, seize
Israeli hostages and demand the release of Palestinian prisoners in Israeli jails.

Discovered by crew members before reaching Israel, the gunmen took over the
ship, holding its 476 passengers and 80 crew at their mercy and then coldly murdering a sixty-nine-year-old crippled Jewish pensioner, Leon Klinghoffer, whose
body was unceremoniously tipped over the side—still in his wheelchair—off the
Syrian coast. Unaware of the murder, Arafat flew to Cairo to assume his usual pose
of humanitarian leader. He ordered the hijackers to bring the *Achille Lauro* to
Egypt and the first newspaper reports from Port Said—including my own for the
London *Times*—spoke of how Arafat had played "a major part in bringing about a
peaceful conclusion to a crisis which had involved the United States, Syria and
Egypt." By the time the ship, lit up like a Christmas tree under the half-moon,
steamed pompously into the Suez Canal before dawn, we all knew what had
happened.

Nicholas Veliotes, the American ambassador in Cairo, was emotionally talking
to his diplomats about "those sons of bitches" who had murdered Klinghoffer as
dawn revealed the big ship following a tiny pilot boat to take station off the colonial
stucco offices of the Suez Canal Authority. When other foreign ambassadors
emerged from the vessel after visiting their nationals among the passengers, the
full story was revealed. "This American man was on the deck," the Austrian ambassador, Franz Bogan, told us. "I don't know why he was there. He was in a wheelchair. It was night. The captain told me that when he heard the shots, he leaned over
the side of the bridge and saw one of the terrorists with blood on his clothes."

Then the sun rose across the canal and revealed a dark slick of what appeared
to be paint down the side of the superstructure just below "A" deck: it was Leon
Klinghoffer's blood, sprayed across the side of the ship as the murdered old man
was pushed overboard. Egypt put the hijackers, along with Abul Abbas, aboard an
Egyptair Boeing and flew them out of a military base near Cairo en route to Tunis,

where the PLO maintained its headquarters. But the Americans in turn hijacked the plane—"air piracy," President Mubarak of Egypt angrily called what turned out to be another of Colonel Oliver North's doomed adventures—and forced it to land at a NATO airfield in Italy. Here armed Italian troops at gunpoint prevented U.S. forces seizing the Palestinians; Abul Abbas was passed on to Yugoslavia. His later story was as intriguing as it was deadly. Ritually forgiven by the Israelis, he was allowed into Gaza after the 1993 Oslo agreement as a mini-statesman to vote in Palestinian elections but—ten years later—was living in Baghdad, where he was seized by U.S. troops who claimed, of course, that they had arrested "a major terrorist leader." Months later, the Americans would admit, without any apology, that he had "died of natural causes" in their custody in Iraq.

Less than three years after the *Achille Lauro* fiasco, Yassir Arafat was turning up in Strasbourg to address socialist members of the European parliament. The local daily paper was asking—like the pro-Israeli demonstrators outside—when Arafat intended to "give up terrorism"—as if "terrorism" was a health complaint, like alcoholism. What was significant, however, was that within twenty-four hours the same paper was talking about Arafat's "triumph." Instead of being pilloried on his first visit to Strasbourg, the PLO leader was lionised. He had called for peace with Israel. He had conveyed Israel's Jews greetings on the occasion of the Jewish new year—and he had done this not in Arabic but in Hebrew. He wanted a state in the West Bank and Gaza—this, remember, was September 1988, and he thought that being a friendly "ex-terrorist" would help his cause.

I cornered Arafat later—his eyes would always follow me like a wolf when I prowled up to ask a question—and when I asked him if any Palestinian refugee would be allowed to live in a West Bank state, any one of the 5 million Palestinians whose families originally came from that part of Palestine that is now Israel, he was not amused. Every Palestinian could have a passport, he told me lamely. Yes, but could they live in a new Palestinian state? "At least they can be buried there," Arafat replied. It was an unfortunate answer, as his aides immediately realised. Sitting to his left, they immediately interrupted the PLO leader—but Arafat repeated his earlier, unwise reply: "At least Palestinians can be buried in Palestine."

But could any Palestinian go and live in Palestine? I repeated again. Palestinians were interested, surely, in living in Palestine, not in dying there. What use was the land to them if they could only touch it when it became their grave? I tried a fourth time. Could the Palestinian diaspora go and live in Arafat's West Bank state? There was muttered conversation with his aides. "Definite," he boomed out. "It is his [*sic*] right." Which was both the correct reply and the wrong reply. Correct because it *should* be the right of any Palestinian to live in his or her country. Wrong because Arafat would never permit the millions of the Palestinian diaspora to enter the West Bank. The population of "Palestine" would then outnumber Israel—and this the Israelis would never allow. Nor, therefore, could Arafat. By December 1988, he was accepting the partition of Palestine. This was not how he presented his case to the United Nations special session in Geneva. To this august body—and especially to the Americans—he was accepting the existence of the state of Israel. But in his speech to the UN and at his press conference afterwards, he effectively renounced any idea of returning to the borders of Mandate Palestine. The land that now belonged to Israel would remain Israel's, despite the three-quarters of a million Palestinians who had fled their homes there.

Then came Arafat's classic and characteristic error: his support of Saddam Hussein after the 1990 Iraqi invasion of Kuwait. It was a decision taken in a moment of emotion rather than reason. Saddam, the hero of the Iran–Iraq War, he who had held the line against the Persian horde, he who was not afraid to fire his missiles at Israel: was this not a worthy partner in the cause of Palestinian state-hood? Arab historians may one day question whether their leaders should use emotion less and reason rather more when deciding the fate of their people. West-ern leaders have veered wildly between the two, coldly advancing their imperial designs on the collapse of the Ottoman empire, cruelly calculating when they planned to invade Suez, pragmatic when they decided to liberate Kuwait, trapped by politics and guilt in their support for Israel, insanely emotional when they invaded Iraq. Arafat was emotional. He represented a people who had been dispos-sessed and occupied for more than four decades yet who were still portrayed in America—and in the media in general—as dangerous, mindless "terrorists," a "threat" to the nation which had taken their homes and property and, since 1967, had occupied every square metre of their land.

But his greatest error, his support for Saddam, was to give him his greatest and hollowest victory. Financially cut off by the wealthiest Gulf Arab states—especially Kuwait itself—and derided by the world, Arafat shared the fate of King Hussein of Jordan: he was now weak enough to be accepted as a "peace partner" by Israel. The Palestinians were not at first allowed to represent themselves. President George Bush Senior's Middle East "peace" was to permit the Palestinians to attend the Madrid Middle East conference only as part of a Jordanian delegation, a delega-tion moreover in which Arafat was very definitely not invited to participate. But in October 1991, the Arabs and the Israelis—the latter, under Prime Minister Yitzhak Shamir, with considerable reluctance—did gather in the Spanish capital under the auspices of Bush's "new world order." Not that anyone wanted to wield the cane.

It was George Bush Senior's right hand, slicing downwards in that familiar, supposedly decisive gesture of resolution, which defined a critical moment in the narrative of Middle East "peace." "Let *them* sort it out," he pleaded, ". . . we're not here to impose a settlement." Less than twenty-four hours before he was to enter the eighteenth-century folly of the Palacio Real for the opening of the conference, here was the American president breezily handing responsibility for the future to the peoples who inhabit what in Bush-speak was now repeatedly called "that trou-bled corner of the world."

Those who wished to revisit history, of course, remembered another palace and another peace conference in which victors had shared out the spoils of the con-quered. The Palacio Real in Madrid was not Versailles, but there were some dis-tinct parallels. Mikhail Gorbachev was there, the "loser" in the Cold War, a smiling, compliant figure, agreeing demurely with all of the American president's remarks. It was the future of Gorbachev's former Arab allies that would be under discussion in this Bourbon mansion.

No one could dispute the difference in scale. More than 10,000 delegates attended the Paris peace conference of 1919. Armenia, the most bloody of victims, had forty independent delegations. King Feisal even supported the Zionist cause—and the Zionists wanted a nation that stretched deep into what is now southern Lebanon. In Madrid more than seventy years later, the delegates were fewer, the public larger. Six thousand journalists and television crew members arrived in Madrid, most of whom would not see Messrs. Bush, Gorbachev and the Middle East luminaries in the flesh. They would sit instead in a hen-coop auditorium and watch the peacemakers on giant television screens, the bleak equivalent of William Orpen's final portrait of Lloyd George and Clemenceau in the Versailles Hall of Mirrors.

At least the nations of the Middle East were represented in Madrid. From Paris, Feisal had been taken on a tour of the 1914–18 war battlefields and then briskly betrayed by the British and French. The Zionists had to wait twenty-nine years for the Balfour Declaration to be honoured. But Woodrow Wilson—while in Paris—had stuck to his Fourteen Points. American diplomats in Madrid, however, noted George Bush's refusal to comment on UN Security Council Resolutions 242 and 338, which called for Israeli withdrawal from occupied Arab land and which, for the Arabs, were the touchstone of any peace treaty. He would not talk of "land for peace," nor would the obedient Mikhail Gorbachev. The man who in 1990–91 sent half a million soldiers to enforce a UN Security Council Resolution—which called for another Middle East army, Iraq's, to withdraw from another occupied Arab land, that of Kuwait—felt able to dismiss the darkness of history. "It's not my intention to go back to years of differences," was what Bush said.* For the Americans, the present was the future; for the Arabs and Israelis, the present was also the past. It was they rather than the Americans who recalled that Jews and Muslims once lived together in peace in Spain. The Palacio Real was built on the site of a castle that the Arabs constructed to protect Toledo.

At least the delegations in Madrid all agreed about God. President Bush had

---

*UN Security Council Resolution 242 of 22 November 1967, which emphasised "the inadmissibility of the acquisition of territory by war," demanded "the withdrawal of Israeli armed forces from territories occupied in the recent conflict," the "termination of all claims or states of belligerency and respect for the acknowledgement of the sovereignty, territorial integrity and political independence of every State in the area and their right to live in peace within secure and recognized boundaries." The latter implied an Arab recognition of Israel's right to exist. Israel, with its continuing colonisation of the West Bank and Gaza, repeatedly pointed out that the UN's demand for withdrawal employed the word "territories" without the definite article—and thus meant that Israel did not have to withdraw from *all* the territories it had occupied in 1967. It is inconceivable that the framers of 242 intended that Israel should pick and choose which bit of occupied land they would leave and which they would keep. Israel's claim that it was permitted to keep Arab territory because the 1967 conflict had been an act of aggression by the Arabs and that the territories had been occupied during a defensive war was undermined by the UN resolution's emphasis on "the inadmissibility of the acquisition of territory by war." Israelis and Arabs continue to nit-pick over the semantics of this short and perfectly succinct resolution.

publicly sought His assistance at the start of the conference. Prime Minister Shamir of Israel credited Judaism with the belief in one God. Foreign Minister Abu Jaber of Jordan reminded the conference that God had "created mankind as tribes so that they may know each other." Haidar Abdul Shafi of Palestine invoked God the most merciful, the most compassionate. "May God guide our steps and inspire us," prayed Foreign Minister Farez Bouiez of Lebanon. God was about the only personality who received a clean bill of health at the start of the Madrid peace conference.

The English language, in which most of the conference delegates chose to speak, did not. If clichés could produce peace, the last shots would already have been fired in the Middle East. The pursuit of peace was "relentless" (Shamir), the "shackles of hatred" had to disappear (Abu Jaber), there was "light at the end of the tunnel" (Abdul Shafi), a "new dawn" (Syrian foreign minister Farouk al-Sharaa) that would emerge from "a long night of darkness" (Abu Jaber again). The quotations were almost a relief: the Koran and Albert Einstein, the Prophet Isaiah and Yassir Arafat, Mark Twain, the Jewish philosopher Yehuda Halevy and the Palestinian poet Mahmoud Darwish were all recited with approval by the appropriate delegates. The creator of Huckleberry Finn was enlisted by Shamir to prove that Palestine was a wilderness before Israel's existence, Darwish's poetry to explain why a Palestinian homeland could no longer be represented by a refugee's suitcase. Noble ideals were brandished like knives: "human rights," "freedom," "justice," "peace," "reconciliation," "the integrity of nations," "international legitimacy."

At times, it seemed as if degrees of suffering rather than legitimacy were supposed to deliver peace. Shamir recalled the expulsion of the Jews (but not the Muslims) from Spain, and the Jewish Holocaust. The Arabs acknowledged the sins of Nazi Germany but asked why they should pay the price for them. The Palestinian exodus of 1948 and 1967 and the grief of occupation obsessed Abdul Shafi. Lebanon's sixteen years of civil war and two Israeli invasions were recalled by Bouiez. There was, too, a kind of equilibrium of omission. Shamir wanted to know why the Arabs had ignored UN Resolution 181 which provided for a state called Israel.* Abu Jaber demanded Israel's adherence to Resolution 242. But beneath the substratum of rhetoric, another imbalance appeared. The Arabs wanted their land back and then they wanted peace with Israel. The Israelis wanted peace but wanted to keep some of the Arab land. Talk of territory would be "the quickest way to an impasse," said Shamir. But when Abdul Shafi referred to Israel's "dream of expansion," the fingers of Shamir's left hand drummed on the table.

The 1st of November 1991 became Madrid's day of rage. The mullahs in Tehran, who that very week had organised their own "day of rage" against the

---

*It was typical of the mood of anger in Madrid that no one pointed out that UN Resolution 181 of 1947, while it called for the partition of Palestine—which the Arabs rejected—laid down borders that Israel ignored once it had expanded its territory after the 1948 war.

Middle East talks in Madrid, must have loved it. Saddam Hussein may have been tempted to uncork a magnum. For inside the banqueting hall of the Palacio Real, the last day of the first session of the peace conference was little more than a disgrace. Had I not been there, I would never have understood the nature of the venom that the Arabs and Israelis displayed towards each other. It was not so much the mutual accusations of "terrorism" that created so shameful a spectacle. It was not the extraordinary decision of the Israeli prime minister to stomp out after making the first speech because, he claimed, he wanted to return to Israel by the Sabbath. Nor was it even the Syrian foreign minister's decision to brandish an old British Mandate poster of a young Jewish "terrorist" called Yitzhak Shamir. It was because the Israelis and Arabs used the peace conference to talk about war.

Shamir accused the Syrians of hijacking aircraft, murdering civilians and subjecting their Jewish community to a life of "perpetual terror." The Palestinians, he said, had a leader "who collaborated with the Nazis for the extermination of the Jews during the Holocaust"—even Haj Amin al-Husseini, it seemed, had a place at the Madrid conference table—while Farouk al-Sharaa accused Shamir of lying and Israel of hijacking and shooting down civilian airliners. Then up came the old poster of "terrorist" Shamir. "He is 32 years old," al-Sharaa quoted from the British wanted poster. "He is 1.65 metres tall . . ." Arabs and Israelis alike sat transfixed, perspiration condensing on their faces under the television lamps. There was something mesmeric about this fixation with the Middle East's murderous history. "1.65 metres," one kept thinking. So Shamir was over five feet tall when he was thirty-two years old. Not 1.64 metres, mind you. Al-Sharaa wanted to be precise.

U.S. secretary of state James Baker suggested they were merely posturing for the cameras. They were not. Watching the faces at the T-shaped table—sullen, watchful, suspicious, occasionally images of suppressed fury—it was clear that they really hated each other. Had automatic weapons been available to the delegates, there might have been a rush for the doors. Around the walls of the banqueting hall, arrogant busts of the great Caesars stared down with marble implacability at this lamentable failure of spirit. Shamir had already left, of course. A Jew is allowed to break the Sabbath if human life is at stake but he had chosen to depart the conference—negotiations that might save countless lives—without listening to the other delegates. However sincere his reasons, it was as if Shamir had excused himself for a dentist's appointment. "Friday is a holy day for us," Abdul Shafi reminded the Israeli with dignity. "But we chose to stay in this conference today rather than go to our religious rites."

Syria's criticism of Israel, Shamir had said earlier, "stretches incredulity to infinite proportions." How dare al-Sharaa condemn Israel's human rights record when Syria was "one of the most oppressive regimes in the world"? "Lies," responded al-Sharaa. Israel's accusations were "a total forgery." The Israelis had murdered the first UN negotiator to arrive in the region, he said. Maybe all of us journalists, I began to wonder, will in future have to arrive at peace conferences with a "fact kit." Yes, it will inform us, the Jews of Syria were not all free to leave the country—and were treated badly under previous regimes—but they are free to practise their religion today. Yes, the Israelis did shoot down a Libyan civilian air-liner after it strayed into Israeli airspace. Yes, the Israelis forced a civilian airliner carrying Syrian government officials to land at Tel Aviv. Yes, Syria has an atro-cious human rights record. Yes, Shamir and his colleages in the Jewish Stern and Irgun gangs murdered civilians. Yes, a Jewish hit squad murdered Count Folke Bernadotte in 1948. Yes, Haj Amin al-Husseini encouraged Hitler and Himmler to prevent Jewish emigration to Palestine and thus probably helped to doom thou-sands of European Jews.

But this was supposed to be a peace conference, a place of compromise, not a murder trial. Abdul Shafi emerged with credit, still pleading for an end to Jewish settlements, accepting Israel's need for security, insisting that "it is the solution that brings about peace, not the other way round." Egyptian foreign minister Amr Moussa besought delegates to avoid "passionate speeches" and condemned Shamir's "wild dreams of expansion." Yet it was a sorry enough affair, and the response to it was deeply inadequate.

Officially, the Madrid peace conference was meeting under the auspices of the United States, the Soviet Union—hence Gorbachev's presence—and the United Nations. But in the auditorium beside the palace, there was no doubt who was run-ning the show. The Americans had a bank of offices manned by hundreds of State Department officials. The United Nations had two offices, a bunch of bureaucrats and a fax machine. The Russians had one office, three officials and no fax machine. Shamir would later admit that his sole intention at Madrid was to prevar-icate. Real work—real proposals for peace—was put together by the Arabs in the luxury hotels to which they had been appointed around Madrid.

Syria, for example, had drawn up an eleven-point plan for the Middle East which demanded a comprehensive and total Israeli withdrawal from all occupied Arab lands but which also accepted a demilitarised zone on both sides of the Israeli–Syrian frontier and the continued existence of an unspecified number of Jewish settlers under Arab sovereignty in a "liberated" Palestinian West Bank. In other words, Syria, which lost the Golan Heights in 1967 and was always por-trayed as the most intransigent of the Arab "confrontation" states, was even at this early stage prepared to contemplate the maintenance of some Jewish settlements on Arab land. The plan, which represented Syria's maximum demands, followed a confidential letter of assurance to President Hafez Assad from Secretary of State Baker in which, according to the Syrians, the United States refused to accept the Israeli annexation of Golan, its annexation of East Jerusalem or the legality of Israeli settlements on the West Bank.

The Syrian proposals, which tolerated no deviation from UN Security Council resolutions 242, 338 and 425,* were drawn up after Baker had visited Damascus to

---

*Resolution 338 of 1973 was essentially a reiteration of 242. Resolution 425 called for an Israeli withdrawal from southern Lebanon. Israel retreated from its occupation zone in Lebanon in 2000, twenty-two years after 425 had been voted by the Security Council.

talk to Assad. The Syrian president told Baker that UN resolutions were not "up for discussion" but had to be implemented in full, adding that "if you had let Iraq discuss the implementation of UN resolutions, the Iraqi army would still be occupying Kuwait." Assad's all-or-nothing approach to Israeli withdrawal was also influenced by America's separate "letter of assurance" to the Lebanese government which, again according to the Syrians, might allow Israel to stage its withdrawal from Lebanon, claim it had given "land for peace," and then refuse to give up Golan, the West Bank and Gaza. If any UN resolutions were dropped, Assad told his delegation, he would regard Madrid as "null and void."

While not suggesting that all Jewish settlements could stay on the West Bank, Syria was prepared to contemplate Jewish residents in the territory who could have free passage to and from Israel but who would not be permitted to fly the Israeli flag over their settlements and who would have to accept Arab sovereignty. "If the Israelis refuse to accept this," al-Sharaa said to me privately, "then we could demand Arab flags and sovereignty over Israeli Arab villages inside Israel." But the Syrians could also be uncompromising. They would not accept what the Americans called "confidence-building measures"—the presence of military observers, an end to propaganda campaigns—before the start of Israeli withdrawal from occupied Arab land. There would be no end to the Arab economic boycott of Israel and no agreements on water resources until the Israelis had undertaken "a comprehensive withdrawal from occupied territories."

In their private discussions with the Americans, the Syrians had also insisted that they would negotiate on the Palestinian question as well as on Golan in order to prevent the Israelis exploiting what Damascus feared was the weakest Arab team at the conference, the joint Jordanian–Palestinian delegation. The Palestinian right to "self-determination"—the all-important phrase that implied future statehood—must be "in association" with Jordan rather than "within Jordan." The Syrians said a private letter from Baker to Assad also refused to recognise the Israeli expansion of Jerusalem's administrative area. All Jewish settlements built around East Jerusalem since 1967—which the Israelis now claimed were part of the city (and thus part of Israel)—would be regarded as part of the West Bank, where the United States regards settlements as illegal. East Jerusalem itself must revert to Arab sovereignty but the Syrians would be willing to study "administrative procedures" which would allow all religions—including, of course, Israeli Jews—access to the Holy City. Syria believed that 60 per cent of Israel's water resources came from the West Bank, Golan and southern Lebanon—which is why Assad wanted the Israelis to negotiate with the Arabs as equal partners in talks only after a military settlement—when Israel would no longer be able to make unacceptable demands.

Behind the Palestinians on the joint Jordanian–Palestinian delegation, of course, Arafat's leadership was not hard to discern. Though banned from Madrid—indeed, the Israelis would hunt for any evidence that the "terrorist" PLO was influencing the likes of Abdul Shafi or that most urbane of academics, Hanan Ashrawi—Arafat had met Assad prior to the talks and given his promise that UN resolutions must be rigidly adhered to, an obligation he would betray within two years. A Palestinian official quoted Assad as telling Arafat that "we will barricade ourselves behind international legitimacy because our demands are consistent with international legitimacy."

President Bush's electoral defeat in 1992 sapped the Middle East talks of their momentum. If they were one of the few foreign policy achievements of the Bush administration, President-elect Clinton's initial remarks were hardly encouraging. The only promise he made at his first press conference was an almost offhand comment that he would "keep the Middle East peace process on track" and do "whatever I can to make sure there is no break in continuity." The phrase "peace process" was already a cliché, and in the years to come, peace—like a creaking railway carriage constantly derailed on a branch line—was always being put back "on track." These were slim pickings for the Israelis, Palestinians, Jordanians, Syrians and Lebanese now wasting hours in their Washington hotel suites. By the second week of November 1992, their meetings at the State Department had been dominated by a farcical episode at the multilateral talks in Ottawa when the Israelis agreed to resume negotiations only when they were told that one of the Palestinian delegates—to whose presence they objected because he had been a PLO member—was eligible to participate because his membership of the Palestine National Council had "lapsed."

In Washington, I found the chief Syrian delegate, Mouaffaq Alaf, depressed that Clinton seemed to have no grasp of the issues involved in the talks—even if the new president was going to sidestep his pre-election promise to move the U.S. embassy in Tel Aviv to Jerusalem. "At least the Bush administration was involved in this for four years and the peace process was linked to the personal efforts of Mr. Bush and Mr. Baker," Alaf moaned. "But . . . any president, even if he comes with preconceived ideas not based on fair or balanced information, will very soon come to know more about the facts of the situation in the light of *American* interests."

Arab delegates now feared more than ever that the amount of time it was taking to reach any agreement would prove increasingly damaging at home. In private, the Palestinians admitted that opposition to their participation in the talks was growing daily more violent in the West Bank and Gaza. The Syrians were deeply concerned at the effect on Syrian Muslim fundamentalist sentiment of any apparent failure at the talks. The detail in which they were now negotiating was excruciating. It took the Palestinian delegate Saeb Erekat, for example, months to persuade the Israeli delegation to stop calling the occupied West Bank by the biblical title of "Judaea and Samaria"—names that annulled the word "Palestine" from the Israeli narrative—and this was only achieved when Danny Rothschild, an Israeli delegate, leaned towards Erekat across a State Department table and said he would call them "territories" if the Palestinians would stop calling them "occupied." Another compromise was reached: the Palestinians would refer to "Palestinian Occupied Territories" only by their acronym, "POT."

That it took a whole year of negotiations merely to reach this level of verbal horse-trading was an unhappy commentary on the talks. The Palestinians wanted to talk about land; the Israelis wanted to talk about "devolved functions." The Palestinians wanted to talk about "transition autonomy"; the Israelis wanted to talk about "interim autonomy." The Palestinians wanted to talk about a country called Palestine; the Israelis would not hear of it. Jerusalem remained an unmentionable subject during these "interim talks," open for negotiation only in the final stages of the negotiations.

The problem for the Palestinians was that the Israelis wanted to talk about "double territoriality" and overlapping jurisdictions. The Israelis would not have Jewish settlers ruled by Arabs in an autonomous "Palestine." Nor would they accept the separation of East Jerusalem from Israel. Even though by 1992 Israeli taxi-drivers would no longer cross the city at night, Jerusalem had to remain the "permanent and unified capital of Israel." The Israelis had come forward with "Arab zones," "security zones," "settler zones," and an area where both Palestinians and Israelis were supposed to "cooperate" together. An Israeli spokeswoman in Washington said that her government realised that Arab-owned land existed in these areas and was willing to recognise this ownership, provided it was backed up by land and property deeds. But she said that most of the land was "disputed." "Whose law is supposed to prevail in it? Israeli law? Jordanian law from before the 1967 war? British Mandate law? Ottoman law?"

The Palestinians would not accept this. An infuriated Erekat, still waiting for talks to restart in Washington, could scarcely control his anger when I called on him. "We are willing to give security guarantees. But it was the Israelis who created this problem in the first place. It was the Israelis who created the settlements. It was they who set up what they call 'security zones' on our land. Since 1967, only the Israelis have access to deeds and laws on West Bank land. Why should we have to accept all this overlapping of functions? We should be given more rather than less power. Then we will have the authority to rule our people and give the security guarantees that the Israelis say they need."

Inevitably, the Palestinian delegates in Washington were playing the role of a conquered people, unable to make substantive concessions—since their land was occupied—but asked to match the concessions of their occupiers by reducing their own demands for autonomy. "When I go into that room at the State Department and see Rothschild, the man they call the 'coordinator of the territories,'" one of the Palestinian officials said, "I feel as if I am sitting down with my own jailer." And the Israeli response? "We are not on trial at these talks," one of their delegates told me angrily. "This is not a trial where we discuss who did what to whom. *History* created this problem."

The Arabs, I wrote in a dispatch from Washington in November 1992, were fearful that Israel would reduce their strength by cutting a deal with individual Arab states, just as it did with Egypt in 1979. "Hence Syria is worried that Jordan will make a separate agreement with Israel and Arafat has said he fears Syria may do the same . . . Already Jordan has drafted an agenda for final peace negotiations with Israel, agreeing to the two countries' mutual security . . . and to settle the conflict over two slivers of Jordanian territory . . ."

Within months, it would be revealed that "cutting a deal" was exactly what Israel was doing—but with the Palestinians rather than the Syrians and Jordanians. The Palestinian delegates to the Washington talks were taken aback to discover that Arafat had behind their backs opened his own secret channels to the Israelis and was even now negotiating for a separate but fatally similar peace plan. All that the Arabs had achieved—or worked to achieve in Washington—disappeared overnight. But the problems that had confronted them, the details that bedevilled them in all those long months since that gloomy conference in Madrid, would now turn up in the fatally flawed Oslo agreement of 1993. Arafat and his ill-trained officials—with not one lawyer among them—would now attempt to overcome arguments framed by Israel's best-educated and shrewdest negotiators, lured on by the chimera of a Palestinian state and a capital in Jerusalem that they would never—ever—be given.

It wasn't difficult to see why both the Israelis and Arafat saw common cause in a secret deal. Israel's occupation was growing ever more brutal and the increasing strength of the religious Palestinian militias, especially Hamas, was frightening both the Israelis and the Palestinian leadership. For years, the Israelis had encouraged Hamas in its building of mosques and social services as a rival to the "terrorist" PLO and the leadership of the exiled "super-terrorist" Arafat. Just as America helped to create Osama bin Laden and Saddam Hussein, so Israel nurtured Hamas and its leadership of imams and self-righteous fighters who now demanded Palestine—all of Palestine—for the Palestinians. In the end, what saved Arafat from obscurity was the power of these Islamic rivals among the Palestinians, and the degree to which they were bleeding Israel in the occupied territories. Without the opposition of Hamas and Islamic Jihad, the Israelis would have had no desire to withdraw. Without their existence—without those uncompromising pan-Islamic demands that far outstripped Arafat's aspirations—the Israelis would have had little interest in recognising the PLO or giving back a speck of Palestine to Arafat.

GAZA. 20 APRIL 1993. The Israelis will not let the ambulances through. The United Nations have been turned away. As the smoke rises from the Tofah suburbs of Gaza City, the Israelis have even told the fire brigade to go away. We could hear the explosions all day, punctuated by rifle fire and the throb of a helicopter gunship that circled the slums. The Israelis are busy losing their war in Gaza. Of course, it did not feel like that to the Palestinians. For Abdul-Rahman al-Shebaki, groaning in front of the X-ray machine at the Al-Ahli hospital with a fragment of Israeli high-velocity bullet lodged three inches from his heart, the Israelis were doing what they wanted in Tofah. "I walked into the street during the curfew—I was very close to the soldiers—and I'd thought they'd let me go home," al-Shebaki told me as Dr. Salah Saf applied a wad of bandages to the area below his heart.

The nurses produced a series of X-ray photographs that showed an ominous white smudge perforating al-Shebaki's diaphragm, an image held up to the light before his angry, muttering family and friends. The twenty-one-year-old Palestinian had seen the Israeli soldier who shot him clean through the chest. Even before al-Shebaki had been brought out of Tofah, the fury of the Palestinians had been palpable. "Why are you here?" a bearded Palestinian asked me as I cowered in a pharmacy, trying to avoid arrest by the Israeli major who had already brandished a "closed military area" prohibition document in my face and ordered me out of Salahedin Street. "We need help," the Palestinian shouted. "You've just come here to watch us dance." We had already watched the first prisoners taken out of Tofah, heads bowed in the back of an Israeli jeep.

The Israelis would not say why they were raiding Tofah, but no one in Gaza City doubted they were searching for the Palestinian gunmen who had knifed and axed to death Ilan Feinberg two days earlier as he sat in the offices of the European Cooperation for Development agency. The "Popular Front for the Liberation Front" 's so-called Red Eagles—how often we have to use "so-called" in the Middle East's self-generating wars—had claimed responsibility for murdering the Israeli lawyer, quite possibly with the intention of provoking the Israelis into just the kind of military operation that would further embitter thousands of Palestinians. If so, they were successful.

What did all this achieve? I asked the Israeli major just that question as we stood in Salahedin Street, Palestinian urchins preparing to set light to the first tyres of the day scarcely a hundred yards away. Wasn't Gaza simply a hopeless case, I asked, a war that was already lost to Israel? "What do you suggest we do?" the officer asked wearily. "What *can* we do?" Well, how about leaving Gaza? "It's a political question," he replied. And he was right. For no matter how many slums were blown up in revenge for Feinberg's murder, no matter how many Palestinians were arrested, no matter how many ambulances were made to wait outside the curfewed "military areas," the Israelis had lost the war in Gaza. The walls were heavy with the graffiti of hatred, claims of "collaborator" executions, threats of fire and blood from Hamas and the PLO's Fatah guerrillas. The moment the Israelis left a street, it reverted to Palestinian control.

Next day, we found out what had really happened in Salahedin Street, what that major wanted to conceal from us. The Israelis had found an armed Hamas gunman in Tofah, a man called Zakaria Sharbaji, who belonged to the Hamas "Qassem Brigade," and they had killed him with a light anti-armour weapon. Palestinians had made off with his head and the Israelis had kept his body—which, of course, created problems for Sharbaji's widow and parents in the Jabaliya refugee camp. His blood still lay across the smashed breeze-block hut in which he was killed along with some remarkably undamaged pages from a Koran which— so his sympathisers unconvincingly claimed—had fallen from his pocket at the moment of death. "They picked up the bones from his head and the brains and took them away," a visitor to the newly established shrine remarked. "But the Israelis had already taken the corpse."

No one denied that the thirty-year-old "martyr"—his baby was only six months old—was a member of Hamas. For three months, so they said in Tofah, he

had been on the run from the Israelis, hiding in Jabaliya and then in Tofah. Which
was why, with their usual penchant for a little collective justice, the Israelis cleared
the surrounding streets and blew up no fewer than seventeen Palestinian houses—
homes to perhaps 200 people—within the space of just twelve hours. Those were
the explosions I had heard from Salahedin Street. The rubble of Sharbaji's last hiding place was therefore the scene of much shrieking and rage from almost a thousand Palestinians who gathered to view the wreckage of broken walls and roofs,
fire-scorched furniture, shredded mattresses and clothes, smashed fridges, washing machines and television sets which the Israelis left behind them. Where, one
wondered, did punishment end and vandalism begin?

It was not a matter that Sharbaji's parents were likely to debate. Unable to
retrieve either part of their son's body, they nonetheless chose to mourn his death
at their home in Jabaliya camp, a step to which the Israelis had their own unique
response. Jabaliya, they decided, was under curfew. Jabaliya would become—and
the phrase had long been part of the lexicon of Gaza—a "closed military area."

This expression should be studied with great care. For in Gaza, a "curfew"
existed—or was brought into being—whenever an Israeli officer produced a piece
of paper and scribbled a name, date and hour onto it. It happened to me when we
tried to visit Sharbaji's parents. An Israeli border police patrol stopped my car with
that imperishable command: "No pictures." Where, I asked, was the law that prevented us taking photographs in Gaza? Quick as a flash, out came a printed sheet
from the pocket of the green-uniformed policeman, an Israeli Arab in dark glasses
who swiftly filled in the words "Jabaliya," "April 21st," and "0600 hours" beneath
the title "Closed Military Area." Would we like to take a picture of him signing the
piece of paper? Of course we would. Kafka had nothing on this.

This whole charade had little effect on the streets of Gaza City. No sooner were
stones thrown at the Israelis from behind the smoke of burning tyres than the first
wounded were carried, yelping with pain, into the Al-Ahli hospital. One man
arrived with a plastic-coated bullet buried deep in his thigh, another with blood
streaming from a bullet wound in his ankle. The doctors routinely administered
local anaesthetics, probed the wounds of the victims and brought out the bullets
one by one, clinking them neatly onto a metal tray in the operating theatre.

Before dark that night, uniformed and hooded men—two of them carrying
axes—appeared at the corpseless funeral rights for Zakaria Sharbaji in a wasteland
of sand in the very centre of Gaza City. They took me to a shabby street where a
cheap concrete breeze-block was lying in a square foot of newly smoothed sand
below the wall of a tenement. "Here we buried our martyr's brain," a bearded
Hamas official confided with solemnity, then pointed to a tree. "Over there we
buried some pieces of his jaw." There was a pause. "Would you like us to dig them
up to show you?"

For three days, the shooting continued in Gaza City, the Palestinian victims—
armed men, stone-throwers, kids, passers-by—gunned down as if gun battles were
rainstorms, something from which you could shelter indoors if you wished, something that was no longer dreadful or unreal or even un-normal. In the chaos and

hysteria of the Shifa hospital, it was impossible to ask the doctors, overwhelmed in bloodstained gowns amid the din of screams and shouting, for the identities of each victim. By the hour of curfew on 24 April, 27 Palestinians with gunshot wounds had been brought to the hospital, another 13 to Rafa hospital and another 25 to the Al-Ahli clinic, a total of 65 wounded by the Israelis in scarcely three hours. Trails of blood ran across the entrance to the Shifa hospital. Most of the wounded had still been demonstrating against the destruction of the homes in the Tofah district.

When I arrived at the hospital shortly after 6 p.m., distraught relatives were already shouting and weeping at the entrance. Young men and a small boy lay on the beds, blood covering their legs or chests, while another man, his clothes cut open, his chest streaked with blood, lay gasping on a table. His chin showed the mark of a bullet hole. On a screen above his bed, a green track described a wild stock exchange index. Life up, life down, life functions impaired. "The bullet entered his brain—he is critically ill," a nurse shouted as doctors thrust a tube down the man's throat and pushed a drip-feed needle into his arm. They were pushing their fingers into his mouth, trying to stop the man swallowing his own tongue. But he died in front of us, his eyes tight shut, his head lolling to the right, the doctors stunned by their failure to keep the man alive. The heartbeat on the screen now registered a thin green line. Within less than a minute, male relatives—all bearded and shouting religious chants—swept his shrouded body into the back seat of an old white Peugeot car. A crowd at the front of the hospital watched the car race away and chorused: "Kill the Jews." This was the "Palestine" that Arafat was now supposed to inherit.

THE OSLO AGREEMENT, hatched in secret, heavy with unguaranteed dreams, holding out false promises of statehood and Jerusalem and an end to Israeli occupation and Jewish settlement building, was greeted by the world's statesmen—and by most of the world's journalists—as something close to the Second Coming. The "handshake on the White House lawn" between Yitzhak Rabin and Yassir Arafat on 13 September 1993 became a kind of ideology. Critical faculties had no place here. Enough of blood and tears. The wolf also shall dwell with the lamb—just who was the wolf and who the lamb was not vouchsafed to us—and they shall beat their swords into ploughshares. No one noticed that of the three men on the White House lawn, it was President Bill Clinton who quoted the Koran. No one, for that matter, asked how a bunch of Norwegian politicians—some of whom had little practical experience of the Middle East—could have helped to produce this supposed miracle. "Peace," briefly, could sell as many newspapers as war. And any of us who dared to suggest that Oslo was a tragedy for the Palestinians—and, in the end, for the Israelis—was accused of being anti-peace or "pro-terrorist."

Under an "interim status" agreement, Arafat and his PLO cronies could create a "Palestinian Authority" in Gaza and Jericho and then, subject to a long and intricate timetable of withdrawal by the Israeli army, in the other major cities of the

West Bank. But only a "permanent status" agreement five years later would resolve the future of Jerusalem, Jewish settlements and the "right of return" of at least 3 million—perhaps 5 million—Palestinian refugees. In other words, the statehood which Arafat believed—and which the world was led to believe—was inevitable had to be taken on trust. The Israelis and Palestinians had to marry before proving their faithfulness, and had to accept the word of a father-in-law—Bill Clinton, who as an American president would inevitably be the protector of Israel's interests—that the marriage would work.

Before that handshake, Arafat had visited President Mubarak of Egypt and I travelled to Alexandria to look at the old man of the mountain, the PLO chairman who had once talked of being fifty thousand miles from Palestine but who now believed he was "going home." Standing beside Mubarak in Alexandria, he looked a truly pathetic figure. His once-plump torso had shrivelled to near-starvation proportions while the ubiquitous, angry scowl of pride with which he used to address his audiences had been replaced by a constant, almost simpering smile. "The fingers of Egypt are on many pages of this plan," he said of the proposal that would give him and his discredited PLO two little Palestines amid Israeli occupation. The word "fingers" made the plan sound like a crime—which many Palestinians suspected it was, although their voices were rarely broadcast in America or Europe—but Arafat was oblivious to this. He was trying to be nice to Mubarak. In fact, he was trying to be nice to everyone. He was now to accept, formally and on paper, the partition of Palestine which he had always refused and to shake hands, as Middle East journalist David Hirst so pointedly wrote, "with the prime minister of the Jewish state which he had once made it his sacred mission to remove from the face of the earth."

A decade before, in Lebanon, Arafat and I had discussed a partitioned Palestine. "We will be united and we will have our state," he said, although he would not admit then that he would relinquish 78 per cent of Mandate Palestine to the Israelis. I reminded him that Michael Collins, who fought so bloodily for Irish independence from Britain, was forced to accept only twenty-six of the thirty-two counties of Ireland and to abide by an oath of allegiance to his former colonial master. Did he know, I asked, that the Irishmen who fought for independence broke apart because of that agreement? "I will settle on any corner of my land," Arafat repeated, but then asked what happened to Collins. I told him that he was cut down by the very same Irishmen with whom he had fought the British. Collins was an infinitely more honest man than Arafat, but the Palestinian leader listened in silence. And a coldness came over his face when I described how the British army, preparing to leave Dublin, supplied the field guns for Collins's men to destroy their former comrades. What, I asked Arafat, if he ended up with the Americans or Israelis supplying him with the guns to destroy those of his colleagues who rejected a settlement? "Never!" Arafat cried. "Never!"

His predicament seemed unending—although quite unappreciated by Arafat himself. Perhaps it was his vanity that had led him into this trap. Or his advancing years. At sixty-four, Arafat and the middle-aged men who surrounded him—overweight, grey-haired cronies who had grown fat in Beirut—were reaching a point where they might never see Palestine, let alone rule it, where the mythology they had grafted onto their lives might never be made real, where the story of their fight for survival and recognition might not be completed. All their lives in exile, they had waited for the triumphal end of their epic story, the entry into "liberated" Jerusalem, the final CinemaScope dream come true.

Or could I be wrong? With a few exceptions—and Edward Said was the most courageous—the "experts" and the Middle East "analysts" and the old reporters who had spent decades covering these squalid Arab–Israeli wars were convinced that the geopolitics of the Middle East had changed for ever. Charles Richards, *The Independent*'s own Middle East editor, became angry when questioned about his own absolute, unquestioning faith in the Oslo agreement. "Things have changed, Robert," he said irritably down the phone to me as I set off from Egypt to the Israeli-occupied West Bank in September 1993 to find out if this was really true. I landed at Ben Gurion airport, drove to Jerusalem and set off next morning down the long road from Jericho through Hebron to Israel's south-eastern border, the closest a Palestinian could get to the Gaza Strip.

And I found they were already building the Arafat trail. The Palestinian construction worker on the sweltering slope beneath the town of Ubeidiya was less charitable as he sat in the shade of his truck on the dust-covered track. "This road is the graveyard of the Palestinian people," Imad Eid said. "Just look at the road—look where it is and you will understand why I say this." A corroded black kettle hissed away malevolently on a gas burner beside him.

"They'll let Arafat travel this road down from Jericho to Gaza and that way he won't be able to pass through Jerusalem," Eid said, his finger tracing the switchback trail of dust through the rocks of the wadi below. "This is what the Israelis want." The five men sitting beside him nodded in agreement. All were Palestinians, helping to build the road that would exclude them as well as Arafat from the city he still thought would one day be his capital.

The road looks as ugly as its apparent purpose. It careens sharply through rocks outside Abu Dis, tips down into a sun-baked valley and traverses a frothing sewer on a concrete bridge. Eid and his colleagues were widening the trail, preparing a new metalled road after two decades of frost have crumbled its surface. The Israelis had told them it must be repaired in time for the winter rains so that the Palestinians of Ramallah, Nablus or Jenin in the north of the West Bank might travel to Hebron in the southern half of the Israeli-occupied territories without passing through Jerusalem, turning their current temporary exclusion from the holy city—initiated after the start of the first Palestinian intifada uprising—into permanent exile.

What could be presented as a humanitarian gesture—how cruel it would be to prevent the Palestinians of the north from visiting the Palestinians of the south just because Jerusalem was temporarily closed to them by the Israelis—was thus also a devastating political act. Once Imad Eid and his workers had finished pouring tarmacadam onto the track, the people of the West Bank could not possibly demand transit rights through Jerusalem; a perfectly good alternative road would be available to them.

How easily the traps were laid. A three-hour drive from Jericho to Hebron, less than 50 kilometres apart, on this road showed just how treacherous Arafat might find his political "corridor." The first 10 kilometres of my journey were through a Jewish "Palestine," a wadi that started from Jericho's Aqabat Jaber refugee camp, past underground Israeli military emplacements and the desolate Byzantine cistern at Manzil Jibr and finished by the Jewish settlement at Wadi Qilt. They were extending the housing project there when I arrived, smoothing out the lawns of Wadi Qilt's Israeli "tourist village" where the on-site manager, a military veteran of the Lebanon war who had tried to destroy Arafat in Beirut eleven years earlier, predicted nothing but civil war between the Arabs of Palestine.

The highway from Wadi Qilt to Jerusalem was a canyon of Jewish settlements, row upon row of European-style houses—part of the great concrete "ring" around East Jerusalem—which have changed the contours of the Arab land that Arafat still claimed to remember. But he was not going to reach Jerusalem. Instead, there was that snaking, hot little road to Ubeidiya and to the villages further south where a different Palestinian Arab voice was represented on the walls. "No to the conspiracy to sell Palestine," was plastered over the side of a grocery store. "Whoever gives up Jerusalem will not represent our people" and—a more sinister announcement beside a cemetery—"Those who give our rights to the Jews will not be spared." But on the heights before you reach the ancient home of another local leader who feared betrayal—King Herod's palace is now no more than a pile of stones—the Palestinian leader would be granted just one very distant view of Jerusalem, 8 kilometres away, the Dome of the Rock and the Ottoman walls just visible through a crack in the hills, close enough to taunt him with its presence, far enough away to ensure despair. "There is no solution without Jerusalem," old Aida Jadour remarked with near-contempt as he sat in the square of Si'ir village, just out of sight of the third-holiest city of Islam. "If Arafat comes through here . . . we will not welcome him. We cannot accept that our children should die in the intifada for nothing more than Jericho and Gaza."

No one on the road south spoke in favour of Arafat's acceptance of an "interim" solution. At Harsina Jewish settlement outside Hebron—where new caravan homes arrived two months earlier, as Arafat was being persuaded to make his accord with Israel—an Israeli military convoy moved into the city, headlights blazing in the sun, soldiers sitting on the trucks with their rifles pointing at the Arab shops. On a pavement beside a group of Israeli border guards—green berets askew, shouting at anyone who tried to break yet another curfew—sat six Palestinian men, all informers according to the knowledgeable youth who directed me to them, all yellow-eyed and staring, one of them drooling.

"Cocaine," one of them giggled. It probably was; informers were said to be "hooked" on drugs by their Israeli intelligence controllers, although the Israelis routinely denied this. Yet even these sad creatures condemned Arafat out of hand: "treachery," one of them muttered. He had spent fourteen years in Israeli prisons before reluctantly signing up with Shin Bet. Difficult though it might be, I couldn't help feeling sorry for Yassir Arafat that hot afternoon on the West Bank. The most optimistic remark of the day came from a Palestinian who would identify himself only as Bassam. "If you are a small collaborator, the Israelis will help you in a little way," he said. "But if you are a big collaborator like Arafat, they may let you visit Jerusalem."

It was to prove much, much worse than this—and Arafat never would be allowed to visit Jerusalem—but the world's euphoria knew no bounds. I wrote an article based on my journey from Jericho to Hebron which ran in *The Independent* under the headline: "Arafat's road to Gaza is 'graveyard of the Palestinians.' " Yet next day, in my room at the King David Hotel in Jerusalem, I received a call from Harvey Morris—the same Harvey Morris who had been the garrulous Reuters bureau chief in Tehran fourteen years earlier and who was now my foreign news editor. "Fisky, you have been setting the cat among the proverbial pigeons," he said. "The great and the good here are wondering if you've got it right." I could imagine the nonsense that Charles Richards had been churning out about the inevitability of peace. "Not him, me old mate," Harvey replied. "I think it's our esteemed editor who's asking if you're not up to speed." I told Harvey that if Andreas Whittam Smith—who always loyally printed my reports despite the verbal missiles hurled against him—believed that, he should call me himself. He did, a few minutes later. "I don't doubt you're accurately reporting the pessimism being expressed, Robert," he said. "But is that the whole picture? My Jewish friends say this is wonderful news and that there will be peace with the Palestinians." I forbore to ask Whittam Smith what his Muslim friends were telling him.

But inside the Beit Agron—Temple of Truth to the Jerusalem press corps—the Israelis kept their files on Yassir Arafat. Assiduously collected from the Arabic press in the days when he was supposedly the personification of Arab evil—the days when Menachem Begin regarded him as "Hitler in his lair"—there were pages and pages of Arafat's rhetoric, promises and demands and threats. Here were all those weary, hopeless proclamations that we listened to over the years as the PLO chairman, sweating and shouting and sometimes weeping with emotion, addressed his Fatah guerrillas and the destitute of the Palestinian camps. "The land of Palestine is the homeland of the Palestinians, and the homeland of the Arab nation from the Ocean to the Gulf," he had announced in 1989. ". . . the PLO offers not the peace of the weak, but the peace of Saladin." Not any more. "The Palestinian uprising will in no way end until the attainment of the legitimate rights of the Palestinian people, including the right to return." Not any more. "There will be no peace other than through . . . the right to return, self-determination, and establishment of a Palestinian state with its capital at Jerusalem." Not any more.

Arafat liked to use children as props. One cloyingly hot night in Lebanon, in an olive grove high above one of his battlefields, he met a group of journalists to talk about the PLO's future. What, we asked politely, did the future hold? And Arafat seized a twelve-year-old in a tiny guerrilla uniform, pressed his lips for several seconds to the boy's cheek and said: "This is our future." Even his colleagues were embarrassed. There was nothing improper about Arafat's gesture. It was the empti-ness of it, the lack of intellect, the inappropriateness of response that troubled them. If this was how Yassir Arafat chose to talk about the future of his nation, they must have asked themselves, how would he react when he really had to nego-tiate Palestinian statehood?

Now we know. Like his celibate "marriage to the revolution"—which in 1991 turned into an unhappy marriage to a twenty-eight-year-old Palestinian Christian less than half his age—Arafat's promises were reveries, statements of happy intent for the good of his people, the most recent of which had been ground down in Nor-wegian drawing rooms to give him Jericho and the slums of Gaza. How could he dream dreams now? At the height of the Israeli siege of Beirut in 1982, a swelter-ing moment of crisis in the PLO's existence when the Israelis beat down on the encircled city with Sarajevo-like brutality, a visitor presented Arafat with a coloured jigsaw puzzle of Jerusalem to while away the hours in his bunker. The PLO chairman saw the television cameras and held up the lid of the jigsaw in front of him. "Ah yes, of course," he said. "This is my city. This is my home. This is where I was born."

More dreams. Arafat was not born in Jerusalem, not even—as some of his comrades claimed—in the Khan Younis refugee camp in Gaza, but in Cairo in 1929, the fifth of seven children of a Palestinian merchant called Abdul Raouf al-Qudwa al-Husseini who was killed fighting the Israelis twenty years later. Before his father's death, former friends say, Arafat spent hours each day studying the Koran. He was to be briefly inspired by the Egyptian Muslim Brotherhood while studying engineering at Cairo University; but he combined nationalism with reli-gion when he decided—with a vanity that would become familiar—to change his name. He abandoned his original first name, Rahman, and chose "Yassir" after an Arab killed by British Mandate troops in Palestine. "Arafat" is the name of the sacred mountain outside Islam's holiest city of Mecca.

Thus did he reinvent his name, just as he was to reinvent Palestine for the mil-lions of refugees who looked to him for hope. In the end, Arafat came to realise that something was better than nothing. Early in 1993, he took a call from Alija Izetbegovic, the Bosnian Muslim president, asking for Arafat's advice on the now-aborted Vance–Owen peace plan. "Are they offering you any land?" Arafat asked down the phone. Told by Izetbegovic that they were, but that it was too little, Arafat replied: "Take it! Take it! Accept!" Izetbegovic did not. Arafat saw the ter-rible results.

In his theatrically arranged kuffiah headdress,* his khaki uniform and his silly pistol, Arafat was now a strangely dated figure, a revolutionary from the past who would soon have to put aside childish things. Even the word "revolutionary" sounded odd. Arafat's revolution was now over. For the half-million Palestinian refugees in Lebanon who could now never return to their 1948 homes in what is

---

*Arafat always carefully arranged his kuffiah in the shape of Mandate Palestine, the "Negev desert" of this cloth map always concealing his right ear.

now Israel—for the final settlement of Oslo was scarcely going to allow them to "return" to Haifa and Netanya and Galilee—it was a betrayal. "I could accept him," an Israeli soldier told me as he was helping to impose another curfew on Hebron in early September of 1993. "Compared to the others, he wasn't that bad a terrorist." What an obituary on the revolutionary life of Yassir Arafat.

Revolutionaries are supposed to be intellectuals. Robespierre, Lenin, Marx, Trotsky, Atatürk, Nasser, Castro, Guevara: they wrote books or talked grand philosophy amid their struggles. Not so Arafat. He could rarely be seen reading books, let alone writing them. What he had, however, was single-mindedness. There was a certain self-dedication in this—and a lot of arrogance—but it was a great strength. From start to finish, it was Palestine, Palestine, Palestine. For the Palestinian poor, his uniform and headdress—fancy dress to Westerners and Israelis—were necessary, part of the binding of the spirits amid exile. But those spirits were now to be abandoned.

I was in Egypt when first word of the Oslo agreement leaked out, and I called Mohamed Heikal. Arafat, I suggested, was like a man with a mortgage trying to sell his house back to the bank. "You're wrong," Heikal admonished me. "Arafat has already sold the house—twice over!" And from the very start—from those speeches on the White House lawn on 13 September—it was possible to see how Oslo would unravel. Israeli prime minister Rabin spoke movingly of his new "peace partners." "Let me say to you, the Palestinians, we are destined to live together on the same soil on the same land," he said. Arafat's speech was more specific, as if he knew what would lead "this historic hope" to catastrophe. "Enforcing the agreement and moving toward the final settlement, after two years, to implement all aspects of UN Resolutions 242 and 338 in all their aspects, and resolve all the issues of Jerusalem, the settlements, the refugees and the boundaries will be a Palestinian and an Israeli responsibility," he said.

"All aspects"? And then, a repetition, "in all aspects"? Jerusalem? Settlements? Refugees? He was asking the Israelis for gifts but offering no more than "peace" in return. He called it "the peace of the brave"—Arafat picked up the phrase from Clinton—and probably did not at first realise that this was an echo of General Charles de Gaulle's "peace of the brave," the final agreement that gave Algeria its independence. The parallel was more painful than Arafat—or the Israelis—understood.

In Beirut, Chafiq al-Hout, the PLO's ambassador to Lebanon who organised Haj Amin al-Husseini's funeral back in 1974, received a phone call from Arafat. "He has changed the charter of the PLO, he has given up the right of return of about three million Palestinian refugees and it was all done in secret," he cried to me in despair. "It is not my PLO which now exists. Arafat telephoned me and called me 'brother,' but I cannot go on. I told him there had been no Palestine National Council meeting to discuss this. I said we did not know the details of this agreement. UN General Assembly Resolution 194 of 1948 said that the Palestinians could return to homes in what is now Israel. Now Arafat has given it all up. I have resigned. I am no longer an ambassador."

· · ·

WHEN SHAKR YASIN lays the front-door key on the table of his Lebanese refugee slum hut, it glows a dull gold, the handle worn smooth, the bit glimmering in the light—as it must have done when he and his family fled their home in Palestine in 1948. From a black tin tube, Yasin, who was only five when he was made a refugee, pulls out a thick, torn wad of British Mandate deeds—British royal coat of arms at the top—to the Yasin family property, a house in the village of Ezzib, 10 kilometres from Acre, and a clutch of citrus groves. "I kept these because I believed I would one day go home," he says. "But now I know the truth. Arafat has not included the 1948 refugees in his peace plan with Israel."

Nineteen forty-eight. The date is sprinkled through every conversation in the huge, crammed, boiling, angry camp at Ein el-Helweh in Sidon, through every complaint and every formal speech. Almost all Lebanon's Palestinians are refugees—or the children or grandchildren of refugees—of the Arab exodus that followed the original partition of Palestine. Some 65,000 of them live in the squalor of Ein el-Helweh. "The television and the papers say this is a wonderful peace but they never mention us," Mohamed Khodr mutters as he limps along the alleyways that pass for roads in Ein el-Helweh. "Our leaders are liars. They told us we would go home. But the peace agreement will only cover some of the Palestinians who became refugees in the 1967 war. What are we supposed to do?" Khodr was an eight-year-old when he travelled out of Palestine and into Lebanon on the same dilapidated truck as the Yasin family, just four days before the declaration of the state of Israel.

Another 1.5 million of the 1948 refugees were scattered now across camps in Jordan and Syria, a further million in Gaza and the West Bank, some of whom will find themselves in Arafat's little statelets. But they will not be going "home." An estimated 3 million Palestinians—approximately half the entire Palestinian population—will not enjoy the "right of return" because their homes were in what is now Israel. In Ein el-Helweh, however, the towns and cities from which the refugees fled, frozen in time, each slum quarter named after the lost towns. Refugees from Acre live in a group of streets called "Acre," those from Haifa in "Haifa," those from Hittin in "Hittin." Yasin lives in "Acre" because this was the nearest town to Ezzib. For twenty-seven years, he was a guerrilla in Arafat's Fatah army, crossing the Israeli border at night in 1969, surviving the Israeli invasions of 1978 and 1982, even the camps war of 1985 and 1986, certain of Arafat's promise of a return to "Palestine."

"There was never a day we didn't hope and live in hope," he says. "One of my brothers was killed in 1981, by a shell fired at Sidon by Israel's militia allies. We suffered so much, we couldn't afford to lose hope. My father believed in God and his country. He wouldn't let himself believe he wasn't going home. Yes, we are for peace. We want peace. But it must be a decent peace and not this agreement which is unfair to us. I came from Ezzib, my father was from there, my grandfather and great-grandfather are buried there. We must all go back to our villages."

It is hopeless, of course. Hopeless to explain that Israel would never allow 3 million Palestinians across its frontiers, hopeless to remind 1948 Palestinians that 400 of their villages were destroyed by the Israelis in the two years that followed their exodus, that in most cases their "home" no longer exists. Yasin knows this as a fact but does not comprehend it. His mother, Mariam, remembers the day she, Tewfiq and their fifteen children fled, and the clothes and lentils and oil she left behind in the house—because she thought she would be able to return in a week, a month at the outside.

"It was a village house, whitewashed with a big brown front door and wooden stairs," she remembers. "It was pretty with the lemon trees round it. But a friend of ours managed to go back briefly some years ago and found that all our homes had been destroyed, even ours. The only building left is an old stone house that was at one end of the village. The Israelis have turned it into a hotel."

Yasin picks up his key and turns it in his hand, clutching the bit in his fingers as if he is opening a door. "For twenty days now, since we first heard about all this, we've been living on our nerves, us Palestinians here," he says. "Still I don't know my fate. I hope that in the agreement—somewhere—Abu Amar [Arafat] says there is going to be something for those of 'forty-eight, that we can go back to our homeland." Yasin weighs the family key in his hand—a key to a house that no longer exists—as if it might provide an answer. "I am the keeper of this key, this treasure, for over forty-five years. I have safeguarded this metal cylinder containing all these papers and deeds so that one day we could find a solution to our problem . . . I wouldn't have carried these things for so long—looked after them under shells—if there was no hope . . ."

# CHAPTER TWELVE

# *The Last Colonial War*

*And the Lord spake unto Moses in the plains of Moab by
Jordan, near Jericho, saying,
Speak unto the children of Israel, and say unto them, When ye
are passed over Jordan into the land of Canaan;
Then ye shall drive out all the inhabitants of the land from
before you, and destroy all their pictures, and destroy all their
molten images, and quite pluck down all their high places:
And ye shall dispossess the inhabitants of the land, and dwell
therein: for I have given you the land to possess it . . .
But if ye will not drive out the inhabitants of the land from
before you; then it shall come to pass, that those which ye let
remain of them shall be pricks in your eyes, and thorns in your
sides, and shall vex you in the land wherein ye dwell.*

—The Bible, Numbers 33:50–53, 55

BEN GREENBERGER DOESN'T TRUST the Arabs. He doesn't trust the Americans.
He doesn't trust a lot of Israeli politicians either. Only God unites the Jewish people with their land. God, I have to say, occupies a lot of space in my Middle East
notebooks. It is spring 1992. The Oslo agreement is just eighteen months away.
Judaea and Samaria are safe—for the moment.

The land in Greenberger's case happens to be Arab—it lies just inside the
occupied West Bank—but the deputy mayor of the Jewish settlement of Ma'ale
Adumim, the largest in the West Bank, doesn't accept this at all. His face betrays
not a scintilla of doubt about the propriety of building new Jewish homes on the
hills of rock and poppies that stretch out towards the Mount of Olives. His manner
conveys more than conviction. The Arabs would claim it was fanaticism, although
they would be wrong. Righteousness is the word that comes to mind.

"Of course it's our land," he says in his New Jersey accent, pale blue eyes
studying my face. How dare I question this assumption? "If Tel Aviv is Jewish then
Hebron is more Jewish. It's unfortunate that other people live there. But we'll all
have to learn to live with that." It is the Arabs who refuse to compromise, whose
leaders are demanding the return of Arab land—"Jewish land," Greenberger
insists—as the first stage in the liquidation of Israel. "I don't trust them. By all
means, let the Palestinian Arabs have "autonomy," let them govern their own lives,

but that does not mean a state. This should all be Israeli. We should have annexed this place in 1967. If we had done so, we would not have these problems with the Arabs now."

Listening to Greenberger, a forty-two-year-old lecturer in law at the Hebrew University, one keeps asking: Are you sure? And: Are you quite certain? But of course, he is absolutely, irrevocably, morally certain of everything he says. "Every Jewish child who studied his history and Bible recognises this as being the only place which the Jewish people can claim as their home. If Israel today was within its 1967 borders and if Israel was looking with prying eyes towards Hebron, I agree there would be no excuse to start a war for it. But a war was forced on us in 1967. We won and now I find myself in land which I consider mine. So why should I leave?"

There is nothing odd about such views. If Ma'ale Adumim is still expanding— its 16,000-strong Jewish population will grow by 25 per cent in the next year with two-room homes at $90,000 apiece—the settlement of Efrat on the Hebron road, with 3,500 inhabitants, is set to expand almost twice that fast in an area of almost daily confrontation between Arab and Jew. And Bob Lang, native of Manuet, New York, graduate of the University of Wisconsin and resident of Efrat, makes Greenberger sound like a moderate.

"If there is a Jewish people, Judaea and Samaria are their home," he says. "To tell a Jew he cannot live in Hebron is to deny the existence of the Jewish people and the history of the Jewish people. Ninety per cent of the places mentioned in the Bible are in Judaea and Samaria. So if anything, Judaea and Samaria should form the state of Israel, rather than the coastal strip which is where the Philistines came from—from which we get the name 'Palestine.' " Lang talks with the fierce energy and speed of a true believer, his language at once passionate and biblical. "The land is mine. I feel it in my bones. It's mine. My grandfather thought he had a home in Germany. He fought for Germany in the First World War but then he fled after Hitler's Kristallnacht when the synagogues were burned. But here is our land, whether our homes are here or not. It is Jewish land and I feel the history in my bones. I need no other guidebook here but the Bible. When the bulldozers are working to make new homes, they always hit ancient sites—and always those ancient sites are Jewish."

Of course, there is a problem. More than 1.7 million Arabs also live in the West Bank and Gaza Strip, which were never part of modern Israel—and their first intifada rebellion owed more to the presence of 115,000 Jewish settlers than to any other phenomenon. Not one state recognises Israel's right to continue holding the occupied territories a quarter of a century after their capture; and although Israel has not annexed them, it has allowed Greenberger and his fellow settlers at Ma'ale Adumim to buy their homes on forty-nine-year leases. Is it any surprise that President George Bush—and we are talking about Bush Senior here, of course—has conditioned U.S. loan guarantees to Israel on a freezing of settlements?

Greenberger and Lang want an end to this shilly-shallying. Forgo U.S. government aid. Ignore Israeli as well as Arab calls for land for peace. Nothing less than outright Israeli sovereignty over the land—annexation—will do. "No wonder we have these problems," Lang says. "The status quo today is no good. As long as the Arabs living here think they will one day have a Palestinian state, they have no reason to come to terms with us. So Israel should stop the military occupation and annex it all outright and tell the Arabs: 'Your nationalist rights on this side of the River Jordan are finished.' The Arabs will accept this when they realise we are serious. After the 1948 war, Arabs in Galilee lived under police control until 1956 when they came to the conclusion that Israel was here to stay. They decided that the only way forward could be by becoming citizens—which they did in 1957."

If there appears to be an element of generosity buried deep in this ferocious solution, you only have to listen to Greenberger's version of this scenario to understand its true meaning. "When Arabs in Israel were granted citizenship after 1948," he says, "it was an evolving process. With a firm hand, that process can be repeated in Judaea and Samaria. If we persevere—once everyone realises there is no turning back—we'll end this problem." But what if the Arabs don't realise this? And what is this "firm hand" of which Greenberger speaks? "Every country has a police force," he replies ominously. "If there were problems, we'd deal with them."

It is something of a relief to find Israelis eloquent and brave enough to challenge this colonial mentality, although Dedi Zucker, a liberal member of the Knesset and leader of the Civil Rights Movement, is very much in a minority; he is the sort of man—broad-minded, bespectacled, academic in appearance—whom visitors to Israel seek out to hear what they want to hear. This is *our* Israel, we say to ourselves when we meet folk like Zucker. This is the Middle Eastern democracy we want to believe in, the one that represents our Western values, the one whose army really *does* abide by a doctrine of "purity of arms," that really doesn't support this loathsome colonial project of building houses for Jews on Palestinian Arab Muslim land. But Zucker has few illusions about the desire of Israeli governments to continue building colonies in the occupied territories, and no doubt at all about what the colonists represent.

"They are a new type of Israeli," he says. "They have about them the element of victim—of people who think of themselves as victims—despite the fact that these 'victims' have potential nuclear weapons. There is an element of the Israeli macho. And another origin is that of reviving the old archetype of the Israeli pioneer who goes to new lands and tries to conquer them by blood, by education, by bringing children to them. This fits some of the American ethos of going West surrounded by wild enemies . . . In a very narrow way, you can see a settler who lives—and whose kids live—in daily danger. But this narrow perspective does not recognise the fact that the settlers were injected there by the state as fingers of occupation. The fourth element is religious fundamentalism. We are talking about a 'clan' whose orientation is the holy books—they are isolated from modernism, in arrogant opposition to Western philosophies and Western achievements." For Zucker, there is no alternative but re-partition, with two countries achieving part of their nationalist ambitions. "Settlers," he says sternly, "will have to decide between their Zionism—their ambition to live in the Jewish state—and their desire to live in a place that is religiously important. Most would prefer to live among Israelis."

Rare indeed are the Israelis who regard the colonists as a threat to the existence of Israel, although Yeshayahu Leibowitz has been warning since Israel's 1967 victory that permanent occupation of the West Bank would contaminate his country. The ninety-year-old former editor of the *Encyclopaedia Hebraica* was once head of the Department of Biological Chemistry and Professor of Neurophysiology at Hebrew University. He is a guest professor in the philosophy department, a role he carries into the logic with which he argues in his small library in East Jerusalem.

"We must start with fundamentals—beyond theory, beyond ideology, even beyond faith," he says. "In relation to this country we call *Eretz Israel* and they call 'Palestine,' two peoples are in existence, each of them deeply conscious in their mind—and feeling in their bones—that this country is *their* country. And history cannot be amended or corrected. From this terrible situation, there is one of only two possible results and there is no third." Professor Leibowitz, stooped in his chair, his *kippa* almost falling off his bald head, pauses for a long time at this point. He has no political influence, but it is not hard to see the moral authority which has made him so influential among young left-wing Israelis.

"One of these two peoples conquers and occupies the other country and deprives the other people of the right of national independence. The Arabs tried to do this in 1948 and they lost. But since 1967, we have done this—and this situation has brought about all the contemporary horrors. The domination of the state of Israel over another people can be maintained only by violence. The only alternative is partition. Both parties will have to renounce a claim to the entire country. Partition is technically very difficult, but psychologically it's even more difficult— because both peoples have a very deep consciousness that this country is their country. But it is an absolute necessity if we are to avoid a catastrophe."

Leibowitz does not claim partition should be carried out along the original borders the United Nations laid down for Israel. Nor does he forget that Jordan annexed the West Bank after the 1948 war, that the Arabs did not allow "Palestine"—as a state originally envisaged by the UN—to exist.

"But I state unequivocally that we are responsible for the terrible situation we have today, just as the Arabs were responsible for the war of 1948 when we had the whole world behind Israel. And if there is no partition, if—*if*—the existing situation continues, two consequences are unavoidable: internally, the state of Israel will become a full-fledged fascist state with concentration camps not only for the Arabs but even for Jews like me. And externally, we will have a war to the finish against the Arabs, with the sympathy of the entire world on the Arab side. This catastrophe can be averted only by partition. It will be psychologically very difficult to renounce our claim to Jerusalem as the sovereign capital of Israel. For if partition is realised, then Jerusalem will have to be partitioned too."

It is not difficult to see why the Jewish colonists—even, perhaps, most Israelis—dismiss the old professor who fled Germany for British Mandate Palestine in the early years of the Third Reich, before the worst Nazi persecution of the

Jews. Greenberger calls Leibowitz a "media freak." Leibowitz sees Greenberger and his fellow colonists as the greatest danger to the state. The two men present opposing versions of reality, a reality that one is trying to create and the other is desperate to avoid. But one has God and logic on his side. The other has God and a bulldozer.

OSAMA HAMID set off to blow himself to pieces just after saying his prayers at the Bilal mosque. All his friends claimed that he was an unlikely car bomber, but Hamdi Hamid was not surprised when he was told of his son's death. "He talked a lot about martyrdom, about dying in battle against the Israelis," the old man said as he sat by the wall of the mosque where he had last seen his son. "He told me that if he became a martyr in this cause, he would attain a higher place in paradise." Hamid had prepared himself for death three months to the day after Arafat's handshake on the White House lawn.

Every few seconds, a weeping relative or friend would interrupt Hamdi Hamid's remarks to embrace the father of the second Palestinian "martyr" in forty-eight hours. Just a day earlier, Anwar Aziz had driven a bomb-laden ambulance into a jeepload of Israeli troops in the Gaza Strip, wounding three of them; for six hours after the explosion, his blackened and shrivelled corpse lay on the roadside while his friends recalled his preparation for death—a ritual washing and praying at his local mosque—and their much-trumpeted pride in his departure.

For the Israelis, it had been a frightening week: the suicide bomber—the fearful, unstoppable instrument of mass destruction which had helped to drive Israel's occupation army back to the south of Lebanon a decade earlier—had come of age in Gaza. Another two would-be suicide bombers were captured during the week and their explosives defused. Israeli prime minister Yitzhak Rabin understood what this meant. "Since Hamas became strong a year or more ago, we have witnessed suicide attacks for the first time," he told a Knesset meeting in Jerusalem on 13 December 1993. "Palestinians, until Hamas, did not do it—just as the Lebanese did not do it before Hizballah."

He did not, of course, remind his audience that it was Israel that originally encouraged the creation of Hamas as an opponent of the PLO. Nor could he have known that, only hours after his prescient warning, Osama Hamid, a twenty-five-year-old pharmacist at Gaza's Islamic University, would have shaken hands with his unsuspecting father at the Bilal mosque and set off—his bomb in the trunk of his car and a Kalashnikov rifle on the passenger seat—on the second suicide mission of the week.

The brothers and cousins who were comforting his father afterwards—a group of hard young men in black leather jackets—all spoke of his growing interest in religion. Walid Hamid tried to describe his dead cousin in one of those barren sketches that always emerge after a suicide bombing. "He read the Koran all the time and he gave speeches in the mosque about the need to die in the war against Israel. He never smiled. He played table-tennis from time to time, but that was all.

The Israelis kept arresting him. He spent four years in jail as a Hamas member and he was always being beaten." On the walls of the Bilal mosque, the family had pasted a series of coloured snapshots of Osama Hamid. They showed a bespectacled, bearded young man posing melodramatically on one knee with a Kalashnikov in his hand and a Koranic inscription behind his head. But the Hamas posters announcing the death of their latest "martyr"—the seventh Palestinian suicide bomber to have attacked the Israelis—did not hint at the failure of his mission.

For, far from killing his enemies, Osama Hamid headed down a road in the Sejaya area of Gaza in the hope of ramming his car into an army truck—only to find himself being chased by an Israeli border patrol which noticed that he was driving a stolen car. Instead of stopping, Hamid tried to shoot his way out but was killed instantly by two Israeli bullets.

"Osama was against the Arafat peace," his father remarked as the muezzin wailed prayers across the fly-blown streets around the funeral tent. "He said it would never be implemented but he had talked of dying for the liberation of Palestine weeks before that. The last time I saw him, he asked me if there was anything I and his mother wanted. He didn't spend the night at home. And next day I heard what he did." The man paused, aware that his son was—in Israeli eyes—a "terrorist." "I am proud of him," Hamid Hamdi said.

But why do such young men set off so easily for their deaths? On the day of Osama Hamid's funeral, I found five Palestinian men in the Shifa hospital, covered in blood from stomach and leg wounds. The Israelis shot them but provided no explanation. Half an hour later, on the road out of Gaza, I was stopped by soldiers who were screaming at a group of youths. Beside the soldiers was the corpse of a Palestinian. "The Israelis tried to arrest him," one of the young men told me. "The Palestinian pulled out an axe and attacked them. The Israelis shot him dead." The Israeli army later confirmed that they had killed eighteen-year-old Ashraf Khalil when he attacked a soldier with a hatchet.

The "Arafat peace" was what it was now called; Osama Hamid believed that Oslo would never be implemented, and he was right. The very first signs were made manifest in Cairo on 12 December 1993, when Arafat agreed to hold a joint press conference with Rabin at which—so he thought—the first Israeli withdrawals would be announced. But the moment I saw Arafat, I guessed what had happened. All the old fire had been knocked out of him. Usually, Arafat loved the television lights—he was, after all, now "President of Palestine"—but he stared unblinking, almost frightened, at the battery of cameras. For once he had nothing to tell us, not even a scrap of cheer to brighten the eve of what he had repeatedly called a "sacred day." He could announce no Israeli withdrawal from occupied territories, no agreements on the release of Palestinian prisoners, on road passages for Jewish settlers in the West Bank and Gaza or on the size of the Palestinian "autonomous zone" of Jericho. The word "Jerusalem" did not pass his lips. Asked if there would be negative repercussions in the occupied territories because of the failure of the PLO and the Israelis to meet the withdrawal deadline, Arafat gloomily replied: "I hope not."

We knew something had gone wrong in the talks between Arafat and Rabin the moment the Israeli prime minister walked into the room, equally grave-faced, flanked by unsmiling negotiators. The words came out in Rabin's familiar drawl but without the vigour he showed those three short months ago at the White House. He talked of "difficulties" over security, over those settlers' passages, over the "frontiers" to be drawn between Palestinian "autonomous zones" and Israeli-occupied areas.

Of course, he told us it would make no difference. A delay of ten days before further talks would help to clarify the issues. "I don't see any reason why, if we reach agreement in ten days from now . . . there will be any difficulty in achieving, in the time frame of the negotiations, the implementation of 'Gaza–Jericho first.'" In other words, the first Israeli withdrawal could still be completed by April 1994. Arafat was left talking about "some points of diversity" and "some differences." Having failed to demand international guarantees for the Oslo accord, he had pleaded with the Norwegians to put pressure on the Israelis to start their withdrawal on 12 December. He had pleaded with Clinton's secretary of state, Warren Christopher, to urge Israel to make at least a token withdrawal on his "sacred day." And with growing concern, the PLO learned that U.S. diplomats in the Middle East—always a reliable weather vane when plans start to go awry—were beginning, even now, to distance themselves from the agreement that the world was encouraged to applaud as the potential end of a hundred years of conflict. There were, the diplomats suggested, "holes" in the Articles of Agreement signed on 13 September 1993. The accord, U.S. embassies were telling American correspondents, should be seen as a "step" on the road to peace, rather than an end in itself.

None of this prevented "our" experts—all those who believed that Israel and the United States would sustain the peace—from maintaining their flawed analysis that the Israelis would carry the day for peace. *The Independent*'s Middle East editor, Charles Richards, managed to tell readers on 14 December that "the historic breakthrough is irreversible . . . Mr. Rabin has made up his mind. He carries the country with him. And it is Israel as usual that is calling the shots, not the Palestinians." The Israeli delay, however, was to become a feature of the coming years and would contribute substantially towards the collapse of the Oslo agreement. Indeed, within twenty-four hours of that depressing press conference, Rabin would say that "it would be a mistake to think that an agreement would be signed within the next ten days."

Back in Hebron, I found Hamas men talking of renewing the intifada, of their "triumph" in understanding the nature of Arafat's "surrender." Newly painted graffiti on the walls beside Hebron University threatened the settler who killed a Palestinian civilian in November. "The Islamic Movement of Hamas will kill the man who killed Talal Bakri," warned a slogan in black paint. "Our guns are speaking and we will strike down the seller of our country." The "seller," of course, was Arafat. Ibrahim, collecting a plastic bag of flat Arab loaves from the bakery on the main street of Hebron—most Palestinians preferred not to divulge their family names—declared himself a Hamas supporter. "We thank Rabin for refusing to help Arafat," he said. "And you see that now the Israeli army wants to talk not to the PLO but to us."

And remarkably, Ibrahim was correct. For the Israeli army itself—again, to the detriment of Arafat—admitted opening a "dialogue" with Hamas in which Hamas officials met with Brigadier General Doron Almog, the Israeli commander of the Gaza Strip. General Almog talked of how Hamas preferred "the continuation of the Israeli occupation over Arafat's control under autonomy." Yet even Hamas was mystified as to why the Israelis would do so much to undermine the PLO leader. The truth, of course, was that within the Israeli army there were those who were dedicated to destroying the Oslo agreement—just as there were Israelis murderous enough to kill their own prime minister in 1995 to extinguish all hope of agreement with the Palestinians.

Arafat had meanwhile to explain his secret escapades to his fellow Arabs. Yet again, I travelled to Cairo for this embarrassing performance, a one-man stand by Arafat at the 100th session of the powerless Arab League. "Antics" was the word used by one Levantine delegate—readers may guess which nation he belonged to—and Arafat did indeed appear before his fellow Arabs in the manner of a schoolboy who had much to explain. Why, they wanted to know, did he negotiate behind their backs after claiming that all Arabs should negotiate with Israel together? What about the "comprehensive" peace which all Arab leaders—including Arafat himself—had demanded?

He carefully placed a pair of spectacles on his face and read from an equally carefully prepared script. Arabs, he said, must "confront" the "New World Order" lest they be excluded. Palestine would always remain part of the Arab nation. "Though we bear the pain and words of our nation and its aspirations towards the future, we are standing at the threshold of a new stage of our history," Arafat lectured. Yes, there would be an independent Palestinian state with Jerusalem as its capital. There would be debates in the Palestine National Council. But after all, it was long ago that the PLO had decided "to set up a state on any part of liberated Palestine."

And then came the blow. "After twenty-two months, no progress was being made on the Palestinian and Israeli talks [in Washington] while the Israeli oppression on our occupied Palestinian people was growing worse." He had undertaken secret talks "to break the deadlock, to bridge the gap in the dead end" of the Washington peace talks. So that was it. The Arabs were supposed to feel grateful to Arafat who had single-handedly saved the entire "peace process" by starting his own secret negotiations with Israel. At the other end of the room, Farouk al-Sharaa, the Syrian foreign minister—President Assad's grey-suited policeman at the back of the hall—sat smoking Silk Cut cigarettes, his aides taking notes. Here was a school report that would make very interesting reading, one that the headmaster, back in Damascus, would find most unsatisfactory. But there was no end to the Arafat admissions.

"In order to confront the Israeli intransigence," he told us all, "we had to retreat away from the terms of reference of the negotiating process." The Palestinians were "on the verge of a new era." An Arafat history lesson reminded us of the first Zionist Congress in Switzerland in 1897, but at last the world acknowledged that the people of Palestine "have lived on this land since the beginning of time." No, the whole solution was not to be had just yet. "The phased process is regaining a dear part of our Palestine, in Jericho and Gaza, and the establishment of Palestinian self-government . . . What is most important is not the text or the start of Israeli withdrawal but that the executive Palestinian Authority will cover all the occupied territories." Only through this solution—Arafat's deal—could a "comprehensive" peace come about. Arafat made no mention of Palestinian critics, of armed Islamic opposition. Of those millions of Palestinians left out of his agreement with Israel, Arafat said: "I will tell you later what will happen to those 1948 refugees." He never did.

When he went to make his excuses to Assad in Damascus, the Syrian leader took his place on Arafat's right and sat in silence while the PLO chairman explained his secret agreement with Israel. Then Assad told Arafat, slowly and in a low, harsh voice: "You are sitting on the chair that Sadat sat on when he came to see me before his peace treaty with Israel—and look what happened to him." Sadat's murder in 1979—by one of his own soldiers—had lain over every Arab leader since. In 1982, the Lebanese president-elect, Bashir Gemayel, had expressed his desire for peace with Israel—and died within weeks in a bomb explosion during a Phalangist party meeting in Beirut. Abdul Khalim Khaddam, the Syrian vice president, would later privately describe the Oslo agreement as "the worst document the Arabs have signed since the 1948 partition of Palestine."

From the start, we did not appreciate how stubbornly Oslo was opposed by right-wing Israelis as well as by Islamist—I suppose we might also call them right-wing—Palestinians. The degree of Arafat's betrayal somehow obscured the extent of Rabin's treachery in the eyes of the Israeli colonists in Gaza and the West Bank. So when Baruch Goldstein, an Israeli army reserve officer in uniform, decided to massacre Palestinian worshippers in the mosque at Abraham's tomb in Hebron on 25 February 1994, we—journalists, Americans, Europeans, Israelis—did not know how to react. The "terrorists" were supposed to be Arabs. But Goldstein was an educated man, an American-born doctor—for heaven's sake—who must have known that his mission was suicidal. The survivors of the slaughter literally beat and strangled and tore him to death.

First reports spoke of more than fifty Palestinians dead in Hebron—the figure was accurate. After Goldstein had cut down more than two dozen Palestinians and wounded up to 170 others in the blood-spattered mosque, Israeli troops shot and killed at least another twenty-five enraged Palestinians outside who pelted them with stones and tried to break through the military cordon that was supposed to protect the sacred area—though it had failed to protect the worshippers. But within thirty-six hours, the Associated Press altered the statistics. Goldstein himself had killed only twenty-nine Palestinians—and this then became the "total" figure for the bloodbath. The other twenty-five dead became a "cut-out," another story, the aftermath of the killings rather than part of the total death toll.

The identity of the Israeli suicide killer underwent an even more mysterious transformation. "Just imagine if this crime had been committed by a Palestinian in a synagogue," Arafat's newly resigned ambassador in Beirut, Chafiq al-Hout, said to me. "Imagine this: almost fifty Israelis slaughtered by a lone Palestinian gunman. What would have been the world's reaction this morning? Answer me! What would have been the world's reaction?" It was a difficult question. For a start, the world would have called the gunman a "terrorist." Any group with which he was associated would have been dubbed a "terrorist group." Any country harbouring such a "terrorist group" would have been threatened with immediate sanctions. And the American president would no doubt have condemned the deed, quite rightly, as a "wicked crime."

But that, of course, was not the case. Goldstein was an Israeli. He was an Israeli reserve soldier. He was a Jewish settler. And only two Western news reports called him a "terrorist." Goldstein was associated with the right-wing Jewish Kach movement. But the Kach was legal in Israel. It had offices in New York. And President Bill Clinton—following the policy of previous U.S. administrations when an Israeli, rather than a Palestinian, was to blame for a massacre—described the slaughter at the Tomb of the Patriarch as "a gross act of murder," which it clearly was, but also a "terrible tragedy." It was the same old weasel phrase. The victims were not victims of terrorism but of tragedy, of some natural disaster, a tidal wave, perhaps, or an earthquake.

Down the road from al-Hout's home in Beirut, around the Palestinian refugee camp at Mar Elias, black flags snapped from lamp-posts, telephone wires and walls. "You damned people helped the Zionists," a woman screamed at me. "We don't count for you. We are animals." In the cramped offices of the "Democratic Front for the Liberation of Palestine," Suheil Natour's voice growled in fury. "I wonder why the West was prepared to act to protect the Bosnians when sixty-eight of them were killed in the Sarajevo market," he said. "And then I wonder why, when almost the same number of Palestinians are killed in and around a mosque, you people do nothing to protect us. The Palestinians are so weak that the Israelis repeat their crimes against us."

It should be said that the Arab states, so loud in their condemnation of the Hebron massacre, had little moral authority to point the finger of guilt. Egypt could denounce the murders, but its police force was systematically torturing hundreds of Muslim prisoners in Cairo and Assiout. Jordan could condemn the bloodshed while forgetting the slaughter of infinitely more Palestinians by the Jordanian army in 1970. Syria could denounce Israel while ignoring the thousands exterminated by Syrian special forces in Hama in 1982. Israelis, too, had a list of atrocities to hold against the Palestinians: a bomb that killed 12 Israelis in a Jerusalem market in 1968; a Palestinian-inspired shooting at Tel Aviv airport that killed 25 people, including several Israelis, in 1972; the deaths of 11 members of Israel's Olympic team at Munich the same year; the killing of 16 civilians at Kiryat Shmona in 1974; the killing of 21 children at Maalot in 1974. It is a sign of just how dangerously the whole "peace process" folly would collapse that these figures would seem mild by comparison with what was to come.

But the special fury of Arabs in 1994—of ordinary Arabs, not their unelected leaders—was directed at the double standards of the West. Why were we so surprised at the murders in Hebron? I was repeatedly asked. Had we forgotten the 1982 Sabra and Chatila massacre by Israel's Phalangist allies which left up to 1,700 Palestinians dead? Had we forgotten how, every time a Palestinian murdered an Israeli, he was a "terrorist," but every time an Israeli murdered a Palestinian he was a "deranged Jewish settler," an "American immigrant," or from a group of "underground Jewish fighters," but never, with two exceptions, a terrorist?

Trawling through my archives in the aftermath of the Hebron massacre was therefore a very unsettling experience. On 9 April 1948, the Irgun gunmen—"terrorists" by any measure—who committed the Deir Yassin massacre were described by the Associated Press as "radical underground Jewish fighters." In October 1956, forty-three Palestinian civilians in the Israeli town of Kafr Kashem were massacred by Israeli troops for innocently breaking a curfew. Then there was the Sabra and Chatila bloodletting. Curiously, the latter does not appear in the Associated Press list of major "attacks between Israelis and Palestinians" since 1948. Yet Israel's own Kahan commission of inquiry, which held Sharon "personally responsible" for the killings, noted that over a period of thirty-six hours, Israeli soldiers around the camps witnessed some of the killings by Lebanese Phalangists—and did nothing. On 20 May 1990 an Israeli soldier lined up a group of Palestinian labourers at Rishon Lezion and murdered seven of them with a submachine gun. This slaughter was fully covered by the international press, of course, although the word "terrorist" was not used. The soldier, it was explained, was "deranged." Five months later, Israeli police opened fire on Palestinians in Jerusalem, killing nineteen men. As U.S. secretary of state, it was James Baker's lot to comment on this massacre. But he did not call it a "massacre." He spoke of it as a "tragedy," the same word Clinton was to use after the Hebron outrage.

This list of horror is not comprehensive, but a pattern emerges from it. When Palestinians massacre Israelis, we regard them as evil men. When Israelis slaughter Palestinians, America and other Western nations find it expedient to regard these crimes as tragedies, misunderstandings, or the work of individual madmen. Palestinians—in the generic, all-embracing sense of the word—are held to account for these terrible deeds. Israel is not. Thus, over the years, a strange confusion has emerged in the Western response to Israeli misdeeds, a reaction that is ultimately as damaging to Israel as it is to the West itself. When Israeli soldiers or settlers murder Palestinians, they are semantically distanced from their country.

Baruch Goldstein held the rank of major in the Israeli army reserve. But in news reports of the time, his identity underwent a now familiar transmogrification. No longer referred to as an Israeli soldier, even though he was wearing his army uniform and carrying his military-issue rifle when he set out to kill, he was now called "an American Jewish immigrant." In the space of just twelve hours, the United States had been gently touched by the man's guilt; and by the same process, his Israeli identity had begun to fade. Yet when Israel as a state was clearly involved in the taking of innocent Arab life—in the massive air raids on Beirut in 1982, for example, in which the Israeli air force was, in early June of that year, killing more than 200 civilians a day—moral guilt was also avoided. These were not "terrorist" actions; they were military operations against "terrorist targets."

The same skewed semantics were applied to the July 1993 Israeli bombardment of southern Lebanon. In revenge for the killing of nine Israeli soldiers inside its occupation zone in Lebanon, Israel attacked the villages of southern Lebanon, killing more than 100 men, women and children—almost double the number of innocents killed by Goldstein—and putting 300,000 refugees on the road to Beirut. As one of the few reporters in Lebanon at the time, I watched women and children shrieking with pain in the hospital wards, their bodies tormented with burns from Israeli phosphorus shells. This "operation" cost, according to the Israeli finance minister, $33 million, a bill that Washington helped to underwrite. And President Clinton's reaction? He blamed the Hizballah—which killed the nine Israeli soldiers—for all the deaths, then called on "all sides" to exercise "restraint."

Amid this obfuscation, a new rationale had been laid out in the Middle East, one which—on a far greater geopolitical as well as geographical scale—continues to this day. It goes like this: America is running a "peace process." Anyone supporting it is a friend. That includes Israel and, for the time being—unless he had to metamorphose back into being a "super-terrorist"—it included Arafat as well. It also included Egypt and Jordan and Saudi Arabia. But any Arab who believed that the Arafat–Rabin agreement was flawed—or who believes today that Washington's monumentally ambitious and hopeless plans for Iraq and the entire Middle East are based upon lies or deceit—anyone who opposed this policy, objected to it, disagreed with it—however nonviolently—or said anything that might damage it, was treated as an enemy. Or, more specifically, in the words of the U.S. press, an "enemy of peace."

Thus, by extension, anyone opposing America's policy in the region—which also means anyone opposing Israel—is an enemy of peace. The all-embracing phrase leads to grotesque distortion. When those Palestinian protesters demonstrated against the Israeli dynamiting and rocketing of seventeen houses in the Tofah district of Gaza in 1993, CNN showed a tape of one of the young men stoning Israeli troops. But CNN's commentary described the young man as "protesting at the peace process." If he was fighting Israelis, he must have been an "enemy of peace." Even if that had been his cause of complaint, it was clearly regarded as illegitimate.* Yet it was the PLO–Israeli Oslo agreement that—in many Palestinian eyes—permitted Israel to keep both troops and settlements in the West Bank and Gaza Strip. It was Arafat, for tens of thousands of his detractors, who "legitimised" the Jewish settlements, from which came the killer who massacred the

---

*When I questioned CNN's Jerusalem bureau chief about this meretricious commentary, he replied that the film was "generic." I grasped at once what this meant. The film was "generic" because the violence was "generic," because Palestinians were a "generically" violent people. They protested, threw stones, objected to "peace" and were therefore, I suppose, anti-Israeli, anti-American, anti-peace and, of course, "pro-terrorist."

Palestinians of Hebron. Because American newspapers and television networks also did not want to be regarded as "enemies of peace," many in the West still did not realise just how disastrously Arafat's "peace" accord with Israel was disintegrating, nor why Israel was being directly blamed by Palestinians for the Hebron massacre. The Israeli government denied any involvement in the slaughter. But that did not mean that Israel was not *responsible* for the slaughter. For it was Israel's policy of colonisation, Israel's arming of the colonisers, and the subsequent Palestinian resistance to that occupation, which led directly to the killings in Hebron. If the murderer's act was an "individual" one, it was also inevitable. In any environment where opponents of Israel are dehumanised into "terrorists," where Israeli criminals are treated on a different moral plane from Palestinian criminals, such crimes will be committed. Goldstein saw Arabs as "terrorists"— the same corrosive word that had led the Israelis into their Lebanon adventure in 1982 and which persuaded the Americans to embark upon their folly in Iraq twenty-one years later—and walked into the Hebron mosque to exorcise the demons that we had all helped to create for him.

Arafat, too, had his demons. And when the old conjuror turned up, late as usual, in Gaza, he had another illusion to foist upon us. His face was the same as it was in Beirut twelve years earlier, when he claimed victory over the victorious Israelis and inspected his troops on the quayside before fleeing Lebanon. He looked older, the cheekbones more pronounced, but the eyes were the same as he pushed his way through the frenzied crowd, halfway between ecstasy and fear. Only minutes before, a young gunman had shrieked through a police Tannoy that Arafat would lead them to Jerusalem, and many of the Palestinians seemed to believe it.

The illusions thickened. Arafat had come, he told us in that packed, sweating square in Gaza two hours later, "to build a homeland, a nation of freedom, equality and democracy." Who could deny these Palestinians their dreams after the terrible years of occupation? Yet who could deny the familiar scenes on the road, from the Egyptian border-crossing point at Rafah: the screaming gunmen, the armed youths joy-firing from the car windows, the horse bolting in panic outside Khan Younis, its cart crashing into the olive tree by the roadside? Lebanon came to mind.

Even before Yassir Arafat staged his homecoming before the world's television cameras, there were Palestinian *mukhabarat* security men on the roads, pistols in their belts, overweight and suspicious, the very same apparatchiks—as they happily reminded me at one checkpoint—that once ruled the streets of Beirut. There could be advantages in this. Journalists were urged to watch every second of Arafat's triumphal arrival in "Palestine"; but, in faithful imitation of their oppressors, Palestinian officials would only allow journalists with Israeli credentials—or papers issued by the "Palestinian Authority" in Gaza—to reach the border at Rafah. My Beirut press card—issued by the Lebanese government—was of no use. *The Independent's* brilliant young correspondent in Jerusalem, Sarah Helm, had all the right documents. "Don't worry, Robert," she told me and a colleague as we stood in the muck at the roadside, forbidden to proceed to the Egyptian frontier.

"When I get to Rafah, I'll find an official, come back and rescue you." She did not.* But a tall, lean Palestinian with a Kalashnikov rifle came to our rescue. "Mr. Robert? Is this Mr. Robert from Beirut?" he asked. "You don't remember me? You gave me tea outside your home during the Beirut siege." And I had the vaguest of memories of an exhausted, frightened young gunman with his arm in bandages sinking onto the porch of my home in 1982 and begging for water. Now it was my turn to do the begging. "Of course, you will come to Rafah with us," he said. The gunman and his colleagues from Beirut were now all soldiers; another conjuring trick, like the parade at Rafah of smartly dressed men from the Palestinian navy—their drill immaculate, their dressing impeccable—who did not have a fishing boat to their name. But we had arrived just in time to witness this splinter of history.

And there was Arafat, a Hitler to the Israeli settlers down the road in Gush Qatif who had been so slow to recognise his transformation from "terrorist" to "statesman." He might have driven over the border in his usual fatigues and kuffiah, but Arafat quickly realised that the reception awaiting him—of esteemed and elderly village dignitaries sitting in the heat—was not worthy of his time. He swept past them in a mob of security men, greeting only the widow of his old comrade Abu Jihad—assassinated by the very nation whose troops were now watching him from the roadside.

"Never," said one of those Israeli soldiers to me—a veteran of the Lebanon war, wearing the purple beret of the Givati Brigade—"did I ever imagine in all my life that I would have to help protect Yassir Arafat." Across that same road, I found Captain Abu Shamra, a Palestinian Lebanon veteran with the black beret of the Palestine Liberation Army on his head, who insisted that in Beirut he never, ever doubted that he would "return to Palestine." The old conjuror had confounded the Israeli, but not the Palestinian.

It had taken him nearly all of ten months since he first shook hands with Rabin to negotiate his entry into "Palestine." But it was easy to be churlish that hot morning of 2 July 1994. Standing with his head through the sunroof of his car as it raced towards Gaza, Palestinian women and children waving to him from the palm groves, Yassir Arafat was seen by his bodyguards to be crying uncontrollably. As his voice echoed later round the hot concrete façades of Gaza City, we heard him address himself to his enemies among both the Israelis and the Palestinian Hamas movement. For the Israelis, he announced that illusive "peace of the brave." For Hamas, he praised the courage of their imprisoned leader, Sheikh Ahmed Yassin. He saluted the "steadfastness" of the Palestinians in the refugee camps of Lebanon, Syria and Jordan without mentioning that his peace agreement doomed them to remain for ever in their misery. Then he told the crowds they would "all pray together in Jerusalem."

Had Arafat not seen the Israeli soldiers along his route into Gaza City, dug in

---

*A Palestinian driver subsequently arrived back in our dust bowl with a handwritten note from Sarah, the kind of message one doesn't want to receive from colleagues. It read: "It seems you cannot come further so I will stay here. Almost no journalists are here. Sorry guys. Have fun. Love S."

behind their earth revetments in combat jackets, belt-fed machine guns pointing at the highway? Had he not noticed the forest of Israeli flags—before any Palestinian flags—as he entered his homeland? Did he not see the notice announcing that entry to the Palestinian "autonomous" area was "by co-ordination with the Israel Defence Force"?

His rule crept slowly across Gaza City. First came the commercial eulogies, the cloying praise of the new Palestinian president in advertisements printed on the front and back pages of the morning papers, eulogies from mayors and restaurant owners and construction company managers who, no doubt, hoped to earn a few contracts from the Palestinian "authority." "Congratulations to our brother and leader Yassir Arafat and all his brothers on their return to our precious Palestine," the Raghab Mutaja Company of citrus exporters and motor importers of Gaza announced. "We thank you for starting to build a Palestinian state with its capital in Jerusalem."

Down at the Palestine Hotel, Arafat was holding court with his servants, the Fatah leaders who ran the resistance battle against Israeli occupation—and whose absolute loyalty he must have in the coming years. He met the Jerusalem consuls of Britain, France and Germany—whose countries' financial assistance he needed almost as much as he did the support of his gunmen. Escorted by dozens of armed men, he drove through the refugee camp of Jabaliya—where the first intifada against Israeli rule began—and addressed thousands of refugees in a decrepit schoolhouse. "With our soul, with our blood, we sacrifice ourselves for you," came the tired response. No, Arafat roared back, in future they must shout that they sacrifice themselves "for Palestine." Aware at last of the deep and widespread dissatisfaction with the Oslo peace accords, he now spoke more ruefully about them. "The agreement we have made is not to our taste," he said as an Israeli helicopter flew over the schoolhouse. "But it's the best we've got at a time when the Arab predicament could not be worse." All the while, Arafat's men covered the crowd with their Kalashnikovs.

"Arafat's men" soon became a common expression in Gaza. Some of them were Gazans, but many were Palestinians who played no part in the resistance, who rotted away in Baghdad or Cairo or grew old fighting in Lebanon's internecine wars. They had arrived here now to rule Gaza with many of the characteristics of their countries of exile. The Palestinian soldiers and policemen who came from Egypt adopted that special mixture of Ottoman bureaucracy and British colonial arrogance that rubbed off on the Egyptians a hundred years ago. The Palestinians who spent too much time in Baghdad shouted and gave orders. "They want to use the stick," as one Gazan put it. Those who lived in Lebanon were more acquiescent, prepared to turn a blind eye to transgressions or even take a bribe or two.

In Omar Mukhtar Street, they were sitting outside the police station manning a set of ancient typewriters, trying to organise a new car registration scheme. Palestinians were handing over Israeli military papers in return for a document headed "Palestine Authority." But the symbols of statehood do not give a nation reality.

Anyone walking through the streets of Shati or Jabaliya camps in Gaza quickly realised that most of Arafat's new Gaza subjects—perhaps 90 per cent of them—did not come from Gaza at all.

They were refugees—or the children of refugees—from that part of southern Palestine that is now southern Israel, having lived for almost half a century amid the rubbish pits and squalor of Gaza waiting for Arafat to honour his promise of sending them home to Ashkelon or Beersheba. Just as the Galilee Palestinians had washed up in the camps of Lebanon, Syria and Jordan, so the Palestinians from the south had ended up in the wasteland of Gaza, over which—unlike the other locations to the north—Arafat would now have to rule. But they, too, had now to face the reality that they would not be able to go "home," indeed that they must live on in Gaza with two-thirds of the original Israeli occupation force who were still guarding Jewish settlements here and patrolling the borders of the nation that those newspaper advertisements lauded so fulsomely.

In Shati camp, the day after Arafat's arrival in Gaza, I found Ibrahim, a taxi-driver from the town of Ramleh which is now in Israel, standing at the door of his slum home, waiting to catch sight of Arafat. "Ten years ago, I drove my mother to Ramleh and she found her home and I knocked on the front door," he said. "There was a Jewish family inside. The Israeli man asked us to come in and said 'Welcome to our home.' And my mother—and it was her home, remember, that she was driven out of—broke down in tears. The Israelis were kind to us and understood that this had been our family's property. My mother died a year later. No, I know I'll never get our home back. Anyway it has been destroyed now for a new estate. Maybe I'll get compensation. And maybe also some statement from the Israelis that they took our homes away in 1948."

Elsewhere in Shati, men from Beersheba, Jaffa and Lod said that yes, they really did believe they would one day return to these towns—now in Israel—"with God's help." That, of course, is not what the Israelis had in mind for them. The Israelis wanted to see an orderly, well-policed "autonomous area" on their doorstep—and had chosen Yassir Arafat for the job. A few hours later, I was trekking through the sand dunes back to my run-down hotel when two plain-clothes men in a green saloon car stopped me in Shati. The PLO's security men were suspicious, abrupt. "What are you doing here? Where are you from? Give me your papers!" they demanded. Arafat's "Palestine," I reflected, might, after all, turn out to be just another typical Arab state.

To his economic advisers, Arafat had promised Palestinian postage stamps in three weeks, passports in three months. "There will be no problems with the Israelis about this," one of those advisers commented wistfully to me as he strode the sand-encrusted lawn of my hotel. "The protesters don't matter. The Israelis are now what we call the 'enemy-friends.' " It was an exclusive point of view. In Gaza, PLO officials now talked about the "good Jews" with whom they could negotiate, the honest Israelis they could trust. But the moment I drove out of Gaza, en route across Israel and the West Bank to Arafat's other borough of Jericho, all the old double standards reasserted themselves. At the Erez crossing between Gaza and

Israel, two elderly Palestinian women were forced to sit on the pavement in the sun while their papers were checked, hands upraised and begging an Israeli officer to allow them to pass. An Israeli border policeman forced a Palestinian with out-of-date papers to stand beside his car while he screamed abuse at him.

That morning's *Jerusalem Post* maintained the same double standards. The front page announced the wounding of an Israeli Jew by Arab "terrorists" while the back page carried a smaller article reporting that "Jewish extremists" might have been responsible for the murder of a Palestinian Arab. My Israeli Arab taxi-driver watched fearfully as a squad of bearded Israelis in yarmulkas erected a huge banner across the Ashkelon–Tel Aviv highway intersection calling for Arafat's assassination. Yet within four days of his appearance in Gaza, Arafat was performing the same trick all over again, this time in Jericho.

It was such stuff as dreams are made on—Yassir Arafat arriving by air in the West Bank escorted by an Israeli helicopter gunship; Yassir Arafat, microphone in his right hand like a crooner, pleading to be heard as his supporters stormed the platform in "free Jericho"; Yassir Arafat promising an "industrial revolution" in the oldest city in the world; Yassir Arafat solemnly swearing in a "government" whose "Minister of Jewish Affairs"—himself a Jew—was the only cabinet member not to recognise the state of Israel. Was there anything left to surprise us, now that the old man had arrived in his ramshackle capital? His features had become so familiar that only now, on the last day of his first return to "Palestine," did we notice that his pepper-and-salt beard now matched the black-and-white kuffiah on his head. His habit of raising his eyebrows to compensate for his small eyes gave him the appearance of a surprised walrus, a characteristic caught with uncanny and cruel accuracy by the amateur wall artists of Jericho.

His rasping voice, which grew ever harsher as he sought to shout down the crowds until he lost it altogether, and the constantly moving, whiskery features somehow made him appear both passionate and at the same time outrageous. "Listen to me! Listen to me," he screamed. "I have returned to Palestine . . . Don't touch those people"—this to the Palestinian police who were manhandling the crowds. "Stay calm . . . just hear me, listen to me like Dr. Saeb told you to . . . listen to me . . . in 1948, the Israelis said they had found a land without people and that they were a people without land . . . listen to me . . . now we remind them that nobody can erase the Palestinian people . . . I want to tell you we are devoted to a just peace, committed to it . . . I want to know who is preventing people from coming here to Jericho today . . . unity, unity, unity . . . we shall pray in Jerusalem— till we pray in Jerusalem, till we pray in Jerusalem."

It was painful to transcribe his speech—and to hear that failing voice, his ideas and phrases crashing into each other—as a lone, massive woman pushed her way through the armed security men and shrieked her desire to embrace "the President of Palestine." Arafat stood stunned but suddenly relented and the lady was hauled to the dais. She hurled herself at Arafat who recoiled in horror and then, with a frozen smile, put his arms around her.

He had spotted the real problem when he demanded to know who "prevented"

Palestinians from coming to Jericho. For after the crowds had broken through the security fences and trampled through the journalists and photographers, it was evident—and it must have been even more so to Arafat as he stood above us—that the field behind was empty. Not half, perhaps not a quarter of the people of Jericho had bothered to turn out to see him. There were rumours that the Israeli army had turned back busloads of West Bankers—an Israeli soldier on the nearest checkpoint admitted he had stopped them but then said the opposite; settlers certainly stoned cars on the Jerusalem–Jericho road. But a million Palestinians lived in the West Bank. There were no curfews to keep them at home. Those who gathered to greet Arafat were fewer than the Lebanese who gathered to bid him farewell from Beirut after the 1982 siege.

Most Palestinians had already gathered the purpose of Arafat's return. The Hebron massacre had been followed by a bloody bus bombing in the Israeli town of Afula—a "terrorist" attack, CNN was quick to tell us—and the Palestinian leader was clearly required to put an end to "terror." As the months and years went by, this became the agenda tabled by Israel and the Americans—and the usual, compliant journalists—and the question itself became a cliché: can Arafat control his own people? That Arafat was supposed to *represent* his people, rather than control them, was a point never made by journalists or Western politicians. Nor did anyone ask whether Sharon could "control" his own increasingly shambolic army as it gunned down Palestinian child stone-throwers ever more frequently with live bullets.

The "Palestinian Authority" was at times prepared to do the same. By November 1994, Arafat was participating in a form of parallel theatre. While his own policemen were shooting down Palestinians during violent protests by Hamas and Islamic Jihad in Gaza, the Israelis were shooting down Palestinians in both Gaza and the West Bank. Within days, Arafat was reduced to the claim made by all Middle East despots when they are attacked by their own people: his opponents, he said, were participating in "a foreign plot." It was an essential part of the Arafat story—anything to avoid the reality that those Palestinians who hated Arafat's rule were home-grown and objected not so much to the notion of peace but to what they saw as the grotesque injustice of the "Declaration of Principles" that Arafat had been so quick to sign a year before. "Foreigners" are always a card in the hand of those who will not confront the identity of their opponents; the Americans were to use just such a lame excuse when they faced an all-out Iraqi insurgency in 2003 and 2004 and 2005. The beauty of the trap into which Arafat had driven with such messianic confidence must already have been clear to him. If he refused to confront the Islamic movements opposed to Oslo, this would prove that he could not be trusted with more territory—as he was entitled to receive under the Oslo agreement. On the other hand, if he fought the Islamists into a civil war, the ensuing chaos would provide proof that Arafat presided over anarchy—which was also good reason why he should be given no more territory. And the longer the Palestinians waited for Israeli withdrawals, the weaker Arafat became.

In the years to come—as the conflict between Israelis and Palestinians degen-

erated into Palestinian suicide bombings, Israeli air attacks, extrajudicial executions, house destruction and further massive Israeli land expropriation—the Palestinians would be blamed by both Israel and the Americans for their failure to
"control" violence and to accept a deal that would have given the Palestinians a
mere 64 per cent of the 22 per cent of Mandate Palestine that was left to negotiate
over. So before we embark on this shameful story of tragedy and loss, it is vital to
establish that Israel reneged on every major accord and understanding that was
signed in the coming years.

UNDER THE OSLO AGREEMENT, the occupied West Bank would be divided into
three zones. Zone A would come under exclusive Palestinian control, Zone B
under Israeli military occupation in participation with the Palestinian Authority,
and Zone C under total Israeli occupation. In the West Bank, Zone A comprised
only 1.1 per cent of the land, whereas in Gaza—overpopulated, rebellious, insur-
rectionary—almost all the territory was to come under Arafat's control. He, after
all, was to be the policeman of Gaza. Zone C in the West Bank comprised 60 per
cent of the land, which allowed Israel to continue the rapid expansion of settlements for Jews and Jews only on Arab land. Arafat, as Edward Said was the first to
point out, had already conceded Jerusalem; he had already agreed that it would be
discussed only during "final status" talks. It thus fell outside the "zoning" system,
remaining entirely in Israeli hands.

The truth was that Oslo—far from holding out the possibility of statehood for
the Palestinians—allowed Israel to renegotiate UN Security Council Resolution
242. Whereas 242 demanded the withdrawal of Israeli forces from territory captured during the 1967 war, Oslo permitted the Israelis to decide from which bits of
the remaining 22 per cent of "Palestine" they would withdraw. The "zoning" system represented this new Israeli reality. The Israelis had the maps—Oslo, incredibly, was negotiated without proper maps on the Palestinian side—and the Israelis
decided which zones would be "given" to the Palestinians at once and which
would be haggled over later.

Indeed, a detailed investigation in 2000 of Israeli withdrawals under the Articles of Agreement would prove that not a single one of these accords had been
honoured by the Israelis since the 1991 Madrid conference.* In the meantime, the

---

*The Oslo II (Taba) agreement, concluded by Rabin in September 1995—two months before
he was assassinated—promised three Israeli withdrawals: from Zones A, B and C. These were to
be completed by October 1997. Final status agreements covering Jerusalem, refugees, water and
settlements were to have been completed by October 1999, by which time the occupation was
supposed to have ended. In January 1997, however, a handful of Jewish settlers were granted 20
per cent of Hebron, despite Israel's obligation under Oslo to leave all West Bank towns. By October 1998, a year late, Israel had not carried out the Taba accords. Israeli prime minister Benjamin
Netanyahu negotiated a new agreement at Wye River, dividing the second redeployment
promised at Taba into two phases—but he only honoured the first of them. Netanyahu had
promised to reduce the percentage of West Bank land under exclusively Israeli occupation from

number of settlers illegally living on Palestinian land had risen in the seven years since Oslo from 80,000 to 150,000—even though the Israelis, as well as the Palestinians, were forbidden to take "unilateral steps" under the terms of the agreement. The Palestinians saw this, not without reason, as proof of bad faith. Little wonder that by 1999, Edward Said, who had for many years shown both compassion and understanding for Arafat's brave role as the sole representative of a forgotten and dispossessed people, felt able to describe the Palestinian leader not only as "a tragic figure" but as "the Pétain of the Palestinians."

From Beirut, I would journey every few months via Cyprus or Jordan to Arafat's little fiefdoms in Israel—still in a formal and sometimes actual state of war with Israel, there were no direct flights from Lebanon—and each trip would reveal two parallel but totally contradictory narratives: the awesome optimism of the United States and Western correspondents that Israeli–Palestinian peace was a certainty (albeit that the "peace process" was always being put "back on track") and the steady deterioration of all hope among Palestinians that they would ever achieve statehood, let alone a capital in East Jerusalem. A trip to Gaza on 8 August 1995 was pure Alice through the Looking Glass.

"By the blood of our martyrs, take your cars from the race-track," a man in a white shirt screamed. "Take away your cars or we will burn them. Abu Amar is coming." In the old days, Palestinians were asked to perform stirring deeds for the blood of their martyrs. But the dead of the Palestinian revolution had never hitherto been summoned to sort out a parking problem. It was Arafat's sixty-sixth birthday and they had laid on a party for him at the beach racetrack, complete with a flurry of Arab steeds ridden by members of the "Palestinian Society of Equitation" of which President Arafat of Palestine also happened to be the honorary secretary. And when he came, preceded by blue police cars and jeeploads of gunmen and soldiers and security men, it had to be said that the chairman looked his age. He was tired, very tired, his eyes puffy from lack of sleep—angry meetings of the Palestinian Authority now dragged on till dawn—and his old generals and colonels in their faded uniforms with their eagles and crossed swords on equally faded epaulettes looked like men of the past, smoking too much, for ever fingering their moustaches. About the only fit creatures at the party were the horses that pranced past the Palestinian leader as he sat down on a blue-and-pink armchair beneath an awning and stared out across the Mediterranean. He did, it's true, try to look happy.

He embraced children, kissing a girl four times on the cheek, a little boy in a military uniform five times on the cheek and once on the hand. He had already opened the new children's park named after his eleven-day-old daughter Zahwa—

---

72 per cent to 59 per cent, transferring 41 per cent of the West Bank to Zones A and B. But at Sharm el-Sheikh in 1999, Israeli prime minister Ehud Barak reneged on the agreement Netanyahu had made at Wye River, fragmenting Netanyahu's two phases into three, the first of which would transfer 7 per cent from Zone C to Zone B. All implementation of the agreements stopped there.

"The Amusement Park of Palestine's Zahwa," it was cloyingly called—and a children's zoo with a mangy lion for the entertainment of Palestinian youth. And when the Palestinian boy scouts trooped past him, Arafat was on his feet saluting them. He saluted the girl guides, too, saluted the Palestinian Kung Fu society, all dressed out in black overalls and white headbands, saluted a child acrobat. And when a rider persuaded his mount to kneel before the president of Palestine, Arafat leapt to his feet and saluted the horse.

He laughed and grinned his way through a musical performance of *dabkeh* dancers and actors who rhetorically discussed the difficulties of the "peace process." "We have Gaza and Jericho because of your presence," they chorused confidently. "Jerusalem will come back to us with Abu Amar's efforts," they went on, less confidently. "Do we want to sell this land?" one actor asked. And his colleague replied: "I will not forget Jerusalem or Haifa or Bisan." And the crowd roared because half of Jerusalem and all of Haifa and Bisan are in present-day Israel, not in Gaza or the West Bank. And at the end, before the races began, the actors embraced, old friends who disagreed about the peace but would never fight each other. Arafat clapped and laughed. Ah yes, if only it was that easy, if only there was no need for the Palestinian midnight security courts and the twenty-five-year prison sentences and the after-dark arrests that were now part of life in Gaza for those who disagreed with Arafat. Then the president of Palestine opened the races while his men handed out baskets of sweet wafers to the hundreds of sheikhs and family leaders who sat beneath the awning. The people ate, the horses raced. Yes, the old man gave his people bread and circuses to mark his birthday.

For Arafat was running a little dictatorship down in Gaza, with the total approval of Israel and the United States. Under the pretext of stamping out "terrorism" on Israel's behalf, he now had more than ten competing Palestinian intelligence services under his command, a grand total exceeded only by Arab leaders in Baghdad and Damascus. New press laws effectively muzzled Palestinian journalists, many of whom were "invited" to security headquarters in Gaza City for after-dark meetings with plainclothes intelligence officers who now liaised with the Israeli security services.

Ostensibly aimed at Hamas and Islamic Jihad, both of whom had carried out suicide bombings against the Israelis, the carapace of new "security" measures being lowered over every aspect of Gaza life meant that Arafat was turning into just another Arab despot. The secret midnight courts were sentencing alleged Hamas members to up to twenty-five years in prison while at least three Palestinians died in custody. In April 1995 a newly-released prisoner was shot dead by Arafat's police in what many Palestinians regarded as an extrajudicial execution; he was said to have seventy bullets in his body.

Around Arafat there were now constructed "Military Security," "Political Security," "National Security" and "Preventive Security" units, along with a Palestinian intelligence service and a praetorian guard of three more paramilitary organisations: Amn al-Riyassi (presidential security), Harass al-Riyassi (presidential guard) and Force 17, the special security unit that had charge of Arafat's personal protection. In time-honoured Arafat fashion, the heads of these different outfits were encouraged to suspect and hate each other. Colonel Mohamed el-Musri, a former officer in the Popular Front for the Liberation of Palestine, for example, would collaborate only with his nominal boss, General Youssef Nasser, the head of the Palestinian police force. "Preventive Security" was run by Colonel Mohamed Dahlan, an officer who had developed close relations with the Israeli intelligence services even though his men were largely composed of "Fatah Hawks"—who played a leading role in the first armed uprising against Israeli occupation—and former long-term prisoners of the Israelis. All heads of security were summoned each night to hear Arafat discourse upon their duties and the dangers to his statelets, a meeting which they now called "The Lecture."

Far from condemning the ever-increasing signs of despotism on the other side of their border, the Israelis lavished only praise on Arafat's new security measures. U.S. State Department spokesmen, while making routine reference to their "concern" for human rights, welcomed and congratulated Arafat on the vitality of his secret midnight courts—a fact bitterly condemned by Amnesty International. Equally secret meetings of Arafat's inner cabinet, which led to mass arrests of political opponents, were ignored by the U.S. administration.

That Arafat's cabinet did meet in secret was revealed only when the Palestinian leader signed a series of harsh new measures against the press on 25 June 1995. Of the fifty Articles, the thirty-seventh stated that it was "strictly prohibited" for journalists to publish "the minutes of the secret sessions of the Palestinian National Council and the Council of Ministers of the Palestine National Authority." To comprehend these new press laws, it was necessary to visit Marwan Kanafani, special adviser to the president—the president of Palestine, of course—who happened to be the brother of the militant (and murdered) poet Ghassan Kanafani.

"We closed *Al-Watan* because of the report about the president," he announced to me. "The editor was arrested for something else—he is under arrest, yes. He is being questioned. We have also closed *Al-Istiqlal*. They have been involved in disinformation." And Kanafani glanced at his computer screen as if it contained the very law under which Imad al-Falouji, editor of the Hamas newspaper, was taken from his home the previous Saturday morning by plainclothes PLO security men. Al-Falouji's sin, it seems, was to have carried a small news item on his paper's back page which claimed to quote a report from *The Independent* that Yassir Arafat had sold to a French company the right to use the name of his newly-born daughter Zahwa on its products. In fact, my paper had carried no such report, but its provenance was of no interest to the PLO.

"Hamas only printed this article to hurt the credibility of President Arafat," Kanafani said with contempt. "Nobody believes it. President Arafat is a very generous man—he'd never do such a stupid thing. This has only been done to discredit the president. Yes, I talked with the president about it. His response was more in sorrow than in anger. I hope the suspension will be temporary. I hope the writers of that paper understand that this kind of 'news' has got nothing to do with what is called 'the people's right to know.' Why, I know of three news agencies which refused to carry the story." Writers on magazines like this were hurting the basis of the development and freedom of the press.

"We don't have any taboos here," he said. "Yes, these State Security courts, do you know whom they embarrass most, who complains most? The Palestinians. And me. I don't like them. Yes, they have passed a lot of sentences, some of them harsh. Yes, there are rules that the public are not allowed to attend. But these are just the regulations that go with these courts. And under current conditions here, we may have certain rules that may not be democratic. But didn't Britain have special courts when it was at war? We're almost in a state of war against those who don't want us to implement peace here. It's a very critical situation. When 1.2 million Palestinians are punished for what one or two [militants] have done, then we are in a state that calls for extraordinary measures. We are trying to punish justly those who are jeopardising the security, property, lives and human rights of the Palestinian people."

This was quite a speech. And this, I kept telling myself, was Arafat's special adviser. But more was to follow:

The Declaration of Principles signed in Washington was based on three words: land for peace. We will do anything humanly possible to satisfy Israel's security needs. But they must do everything humanly possible to satisfy our need for land. President Arafat knew when he signed this agreement that there were big holes in it. And the Israelis got praise for making peace. Rabin shared the Nobel prize with President Arafat. But now when we come down to the nitty-gritty, the Israelis want both peace and land. And if they want to keep their soldiers in the West Bank to protect settlements and keep most of our land under different pretexts, then we're not going to have peace. Yassir Arafat took a lot of chances for this. He took personally all the decisions that were necessary, yes, including arrests and unpopular decisions, as well as raising the hopes of our people . . . He did this because he believes in peace. Heads of state don't take these chances but leaders do—and he is a leader. He wants it to work but he is exhausted. He is worried. He is not satisfied that the peace process is moving.

Which is clearly what al-Falouji also thought. So I paid a call on General Youssef Nasser, commander of the Palestinian police, hero of Golan, PLO fighter in Lebanon, refugee from 1948 Palestine. And when I walk through General Nasser's door—its Israeli security lock snapping open at the touch of a card—there is the great bespectacled man, all smiles, overweight but smartly uniformed, a big clammy hand extended in welcome. He is an optimist. "How do you think we're doing in the Palestinian Authority?" he asks. So I mention the endless delays in implementation of the Palestinian agreements with Israel, the continued presence of Israeli troops in Gaza, the suicide bombs, the deaths in custody, Amnesty International . . .

"All peace treaties are imposed by a leverage of power and so is this one," the general replies. "But look, after 1917, the 'world order' of the period gave the Jews a homeland and divided us. In 1948, another 'world order' created the state of Israel and nullified the Palestinians from both the geographic and demographic map. But now we have managed to re-locate ourselves on the international map and re-establish our identity as Palestinians . . . The Palestinian entity is now international, created under the same resolutions that created Israel."

But this is not true, I tell the general. Israel was internationally recognised by the United Nations; no UN resolutions safeguard the PLO's agreement with Israel. "OK," General Nasser replies. "OK—but no one can shoulder the responsibility of destroying the peace process. The Jewish settlers have two options: to evacuate [Palestinian territory] or to become Palestinian citizens. Israel can't have both the peace and the land . . . Things are not easy, it's true. But there is an existing reality—a fact: three million Palestinians are on the ground in the West Bank and in Gaza. Israel has two choices: independence for the Palestinians or a complete merger with the Palestinians—but they can't keep on with their imperialistic policy . . ."

This was wilful self-delusion, a characteristic normally reserved for Israelis. Israel was backed by the world's only surviving superpower. No Israeli settler would elect to become a Palestinian and very few settlers would leave the West Bank. The responsibility of "destroying the peace process" would be easy to shift onto Israel's antagonists, the Palestinians—as indeed it would be in the years to come—the moment Israel decided that the next suicide bombing was one too many.

"Arafat is finding out what it's like to be Israel's man," one of his detractors told me in the cool of one August evening in Gaza that summer of 1995. "The Israelis know that he is a dictator and that the more internal power he has, the more he will do their bidding. So they approve of all this. They don't want a real democracy because Arafat might lose elections—and a new leader might not obey their wishes. Now they are even turning Arafat against Assad of Syria by persuading the PLO to claim part of the Golan Heights as Palestinian . . . And all the while Jewish settlements continue to be built . . ."

I have sought in vain to discover the origin of our journalistic use of the word "settlements." By its nature, the expression is almost comforting. It has a permanence about it, a notion of legality. Every human wants to "settle," to have a home. The far more disturbing—and far more accurate—word for Israel's land-grabbing in the West Bank and Gaza since 1967 is colonising. Settlers are colonists. Almost all the Israelis in the West Bank are living on someone else's land. They may say that God gave them the land, but those Palestinians who legally owned that land—who had property deeds to prove it, since the British Mandate, since the Ottoman empire—are not allowed to appeal to God. Successive Israeli governments have supported this theft of property, and by 2003, 400,000 Israeli Jews were living in the occupied territories in explicit violation of Article 49 of the Geneva Convention—which states that "the Occupying Power shall not deport or transfer parts of its own civilian population into the territory it occupies."

In all the long, fruitless negotiations with the Palestinians, the Israelis would always maintain that the return of any territory was "giving" land for peace—as if the occupied territories were legally Israeli property of which it could dispose if it was generously minded. So it is important to recall that the policy of implanting Jewish colonists on occupied Arab land since 1967 has been consistently and enthusiastically supported by successive Israeli governments.

As long ago as 1978, the U.S. administration under President Carter was condemning the growth of Jewish settlements in the West Bank and Gaza, asking why 9,000 Israelis were now living in the occupied territories in thirteen "unofficial" colonies when the Israeli prime minister, Menachem Begin, supposedly wanted to make peace with President Sadat of Egypt. Already, thirty-nine settlements had been built since the 1967 war. In November 1978 the Jewish Agency drew up a plan—and here I will quote from *The Guardian*'s highly biased report of the time—for "housing 16,000 Israeli families in 84 new *villages* on the West Bank of the Jordan, and a further 11,000 families in existing *outposts*" (my italics). The project would cost $1.5 billion and would be completed within five years—the deadline set for what was intended to be the end of a "transitional period" of Palestinian self-rule. Readers must here understand that the language and hopes of "peace" in the Middle East are a debased coinage. This "transitional period" had nothing to do with the later Oslo agreement but applied to the Begin–Sadat Camp David summit of 1977 which ultimately provided no "self-autonomy" for the Palestinians.

In May 1979, President Carter was appealing for Israeli "restraint" in expanding settlements because they were "inconsistent with international law and an obstacle to peace." But, he said—and here was a refrain that would be used by successive U.S. administrations as successive Israeli governments ignored them— "there is a limit to what we can do to impose our will on a sovereign nation." In December of the same year, there was a muted protest by Palestinians against an Israeli government decision to move a settlement onto Arab land near Nablus. In his coverage of the demonstration—the Arabs spread prayer rugs over a neighbouring road because the local Israeli military governor forbade the protest to be held in a mosque—*The Times* of London correspondent in Tel Aviv referred to the West Bank only by its Jewish name of "Samaria."

There was, in fact, an oddly subdued quality to the reporting of these successive land thefts by Israel. On 14 March 1980, for example, Christopher Walker of *The Times* was writing that "friction between Israel and Egypt over Jewish settlements in the occupied territories has been increased by the Israeli decision to seize 1,000 acres of land in east Jerusalem to build a new Jewish suburb. Two thirds of the land is owned by Arabs." That this was a scandal, rather than a cause of mere "friction," over a "suburb," scarcely came across. When in the same year Israel passed a "Basic Law" declaring Jerusalem its capital, the UN Security Council passed Resolution 476, stating that Israeli actions to change the status of Jerusalem "constitute a flagrant violation of the Fourth Geneva Convention." It had no effect. In March of that same year, the last Arab family living in the old Jewish quarter of Jerusalem—Ayub Hamis Toutungi's house overlooked both the Wailing Wall and the Al-Aqsa mosque—was forced to accept compensation for his property and leave. "I am a Jerusalemite," Toutungi protested in Hebrew. "I want to remain here. When a Jew loves Jerusalem, it is considered a spiritual value. An Arab who loves Jerusalem is suspected of supporting the PLO." The Israeli writer Amos Elon protested at this "violence." To no avail.

When the world was unimpressed by the "Basic Law" which upheld Israel's claim to Jerusalem as its capital, the Israeli authorities proceeded to seize land— 1,000 acres for a $600,000 settlement (or "suburb" as *The Times* called it again)— in March 1989. By now, 60,000 Jews lived in "Arab" East Jerusalem, more than 50 per cent of the area's 100,000 Arab population. In the following year, Israeli prime minister Yitzhak Rabin said he would hold onto occupied Arab land for the new wave of Soviet Jewish immigrants arriving in Israel, explaining that "past leaders of our movement left us a clear message to keep the land of Israel from the [Mediterranean] sea to the River Jordan for the generations to come . . ."

The moment the Oslo accord was revealed, the Israeli Likud party foresaw the end of Jewish colonies on Palestinian land. Benjamin Netanyahu claimed that "these Israeli islands, isolated in a PLO sea, will not last long." He need not have worried. On 27 September 1994—when 140 Jewish colonies already existed in the West Bank but when the Oslo agreement was only a year old—Israeli prime minister Rabin approved the construction of an extra 1,000 apartments at the settlement of Alfei Menache close to Jerusalem. By 1996, 86.5 per cent of East Jerusalem had been removed from Palestinian residents' control and use; 34 per cent of East Jerusalem land was expropriated for the building of Jewish colonies. The Jerusalem municipality announced plans to build another 70,000 new housing units over the next ten years. Then came the opening of the "archaeological tunnel" from the Wailing Wall—attended by Irving Moskowitz, a Florida multi-millionaire who owns hospitals and a bingo parlour in California—which ran beneath Muslim East Jerusalem; violent protests against the opening of the tunnel, which was paid for by the Israeli Ministry of Religious Affairs, left 43 Palestinians and 11 Israeli soldiers dead.

In February 1997, Israel approved the construction of a massive new Jewish colony at Jebel Abu Ghoneim, with 3,546 houses and a population of 25,000 Israelis in just the first stage of the project. The hill upon which the settlement was subsequently built is outside East Jerusalem—which Palestinians had once hoped would be their capital. Palestinian protests were ignored and the United States vetoed a UN Security Council resolution calling on Israel to abandon construction. In the same month, the Israeli Housing Ministry announced the sale of land for 5,000 new Jewish homes inside existing colonies in the West Bank and Gaza Strip. Benjamin Netanyahu's claim that the Jebel Abu Ghoneim colony—its identity changed to Har Homa in Hebrew—would be matched by the construction of 3,015 houses for Palestinians was denounced as "disinformation" by human rights groups. They pointed out that 18,000 permits for Palestinian homes had been promised in 1980—yet not a single one had been honoured seventeen years later.

Nor was this huge illegal colonial expansion—which continued throughout the Oslo "peace process"—without active encouragement from within the United States. On 18 April 1997, *The New York Times* carried a full-page advertisement signed by ten Christian "spiritual leaders"—including Pat Robertson and Jerry Falwell—all supporting "the continued sovereignty of the State of Israel over the holy city of Jerusalem . . . we believe that Jerusalem or any portion of it shall not be negotiable in any peace process. Jerusalem must remain undivided as the eternal capital of the Jewish people." This "spiritual" message claimed that Israel had "demonstrated sensitivity to the concerns and needs of all Jerusalem's residents, including the Palestinians' and that Israel's right to Jerusalem as a sovereign capital came by "divine mandate."*

Under Netanyahu, the Israeli authorities seemed almost anxious to enrage their Palestinian opposite numbers and to further undermine Arafat. When in 1997 the UN proposed a new resolution urging member states to "actively discourage" settlement-building on Arab land, Netanyahu's spokesman, the piano-playing David Bar Ilan, described the proposal as "shameful" and "morally bankrupt" because it ignored world dangers while condemning what he mischievously called "the building of apartments for young couples." U.S. secretary of state Madeleine Albright was positively mouselike when in September 1997 she urged Israel to "refrain from unilateral acts, including what Palestinians perceive as the provocative expansion of settlements." Such words were clearly understood. If the continued building of Jewish colonies on stolen Arab land during the Oslo "peace process" was merely "what Palestinians perceive" to be provocative, then what on earth did the United States perceive them to be?

If they weren't building homes for Israelis on Palestinian land, the Israelis were busy demolishing Palestinian houses. Between the signing of the Oslo accord in 1993 and March 1998, 629 Palestinian homes were destroyed by Israeli bulldozers, 535 in the West Bank and 94 in Jerusalem, more than a third under an Israeli Labour government and the rest under Likud. Another 1,800 demolition orders were waiting to be carried out. Palestinian outrage at this wholesale attempt to force them out of Jerusalem—in many cases because Israel would not issue building permits for Arabs living there—was merely exacerbated by the April 1999 decision of an Israeli ministerial committee to recommend building an additional 116,000 houses for colonists over the next twenty years.

The Labour government of Ehud Barak—billed as the most liberal and pro-Palestinian Israeli administration since Rabin's—colonised the West Bank ten times as fast as Netanyahu's Likud government. Just a day after "final status" negotiations opened between Israelis and Palestinians in September 1999, Barak—visiting the now vast colony of Ma'ale Adumim—announced that "we

---

*Readers who wanted to test this particular mandate were referred to Genesis 12:17, Leviticus 26:44–45, Deuteronomy 7:7–8, Samuel 7:12–16, I Kings 15:4, Psalms 89:34–37 and 105:8–11. "The battle for Jerusalem has begun," the ad said, "and it is time for believers in Christ to support our Jewish brethren . . ."

will not remove a settlement which has 25,000 people and which . . . all the Israeli governments helped to develop . . . Every house built here, every tree, is part of Israel for ever, that's clear." By November 2000, the Israeli pressure group Peace Now discovered that the Barak administration was planning to spend another $210 million on colonies the following year.

The final, damning statistics were inescapable. Between 1967 and 1982, a mere 21,000 colonists had moved into the West Bank and Gaza. In 1990, the total was 76,000. By 2000, seven years after the Oslo accord, it stood at 383,000, including those settlers in annexed East Jerusalem.* On 17 May 2001, René Kosimik, the head of the International Red Cross delegation to Israel and the Palestinian territories, felt it necessary to remind the world that under the Geneva Convention, "the installation of the population of the occupying power into the occupied territories is considered as an illegal move and qualified as a 'grave breach' . . . The policy of settlement as such in humanitarian law is a war crime." Yet still, even as Arafat was dying in 2004 and when Israel's "security" wall was stealing its way across yet more Arab land, the occupation and dispossession of Palestinians continued.

More than any other event, this huge colonial expansion proved to Palestinians that Oslo was a sham, a lie, a trick to entangle Arafat and the PLO into the abandonment of all that they had sought and struggled for over a quarter of a century, a method of creating false hope in order to emasculate the aspiration of statehood. For the settlers, of course, Oslo was a threat to that very same government-backed colonial project of which they were a part. When Israeli prime minister Yitzhak Rabin pressed on with the "peace process" after successive suicide bombings by Palestinians, he became, for the colonists, part of the same "terror" that Arafat and the PLO represented. On 24 July 1995, for example, a suicide bomber killed seven Israelis on a Tel Aviv bus; on 22 August a woman suicide bomber blew herself up at the rear of a Jerusalem bus, blasting herself and four other passengers to pieces. The day after the second bloodbath, Rabin said this would not deter him from "fighting extreme Islamic terrorism and continuing the negotiations" with the Palestinians. Just two months later, Rabin was denounced as a traitor at a Jerusalem rally at which Benjamin Netanyahu was the principal speaker. Leaflets distributed at the rally showed Rabin dressed as a Nazi officer. A video of the gathering showed a woman stabbing a picture of Rabin with a knife.

A definitive biography of Rabin has still to be written. The Israeli historian Avi

*Israeli leaders were not the only ones to try to avoid confronting this physically obvious blockade on the road to peace. In 2000, John Hume, Northern Ireland's only statesman, advised Palestinians and Israelis that "your challenge is not one of geographical turf, but rather the construction of agreed institutions . . ." The Irish version of the "peace process," however, does not travel well. A "turf" war—two groups of people arguing over the same piece of real estate—was precisely what this Middle East conflict *was* about. The nearest Irish approximation to the Israeli–Arab struggle would be an attempt to mediate an end to violence after the seventeenth-century dispossession of the Catholics. Urging the Protestant landlords and the mass of impoverished Irish Catholics to construct "agreed institutions" would not have commended itself to either side.

Shlaim has shrewdly noted that he "inflicted more punishment and pain on the Palestinians than any other Israeli leader." As chief of staff in 1967, Rabin captured the West Bank. For the next twenty-five years, he tried to hold onto the occupied territories by brute force, which "earned him his reputation inside Israel as a responsible and reliable politician." Under his premiership, Israeli soldiers were allowed to break the bones of Palestinian protesters, a practice that continued until an Israeli cameraman inconsiderately filmed Israeli soldiers snapping the legs of a Palestinian prisoner. That Rabin continued colonising, even after Oslo, suggests that he wanted to give Arafat the honour of ruling those areas of the West Bank and Gaza that the Israelis did not need for security or for further settlement—a totally different interpretation than Arafat's. But on 4 November 1995, after telling a Tel Aviv rally that "the path of peace is preferable to the path of war," Rabin was assassinated by a twenty-five-year-old Israeli religious student called Yigal Amir who was an admirer of Baruch Goldstein, the Hebron mosque murderer. At his trial, Amir said that once he was aware that something represented a religious commandment, "there is no moral problem. If I was conquering the land now, I would have to kill babies and children, as it is written in [the Book of] Joshua." Change the religion, and this could have been the voice of a Palestinian suicide bomber.

The parallels were facile, of course. As I was checking out of the King David Hotel in Jerusalem early one morning, the chief cashier, an Orthodox Jew with an impressively long beard who always wished me safety on my return to Beirut—the Lebanese capital was for him a "terror centre"—asked whether he reminded me of anyone I knew. "Don't I look a bit like some of the Hizballah?" he asked with a broad smile. And I had to admit that, yes, he did look a bit like some of the Shia Muslim militants of Lebanon. Beards have something to do with orthodoxy, with fundamentalism in the most literal sense of the word, just as the "covering" of women—Orthodox Jewish women, Muslim women, Christian nuns—seemed to be a feature of the three Middle East religions. What is it, I used to ask myself, about hair, the growing of hair, the concealment of hair, male hair as a symbol of manhood, female hair as a devilish trap for men, the length of beards or the shape of beards? Why did Christ, in all those Bible pictures, always have a beard? Why did every Shiite imam in Iran sport a growth around the chin, white and fluffy or stubbly or tangled, an undergrowth of hair every bit as complex as the moral exegesis or treatise on Islamic jurisprudence which had earned him his place in the clerical hierarchy? Was a beard meant to symbolise wisdom or commitment or manhood, or was it supposed to earn respect?

When Yitzhak Rabin illegally deported almost 400 Palestinian Hamas and Islamic Jihad supporters to Lebanon in 1992, he created an Islamic university on the slopes of Mount Hermon. Refused permission by the Lebanese government to travel north into the rest of the country, the Palestinians—many of them university teachers, engineers, clerics—were marooned in the summer heat and winter snows in a mountain wasteland called Marj al-Zahour, the "Field of Flowers," and here they discussed modern Islam and philosophy and learned their Korans by rote and kept the fast of Ramadan beside a narrow, broken road down which, almost nine hundred years earlier, Saladin was said to have ridden on his way to Jerusalem. Abdul-Aziz Rantissi of Hamas would hold court here, and so would Sheikh Bassam Jarrar and some of the future leadership of Hamas and Islamic Jihad. Jarrar would ask me what good could come of a secret "peace" deal that dishonoured those who had died in the first (1987–1993) Palestinian intifada struggle. The deportees would beg for newspapers but as the months passed, the Hizballah and other sympathetic Lebanese Muslim groups furnished them with generators and television sets and books. There was even a university tent "library," as well as a tent mosque and a tent infirmary. An entire male Islamic society grew up beside the great cartwheel cornucopia rocks of Marj al-Zahour.

"I will miss this beauty," one of them said to me before he was allowed to return to "Palestine"—and to an Israeli prison—in 1994. "The rocks here will have some special place in our minds in the future." They gave me family phone numbers in Ramallah and Hebron and Jenin and asked me to call on them when next I visited "Palestine." So many had negotiated with Israeli officials that one even gave me Shimon Peres's home telephone number.

And so, one cold December day in 1995, I walked up the drive to Hebron University and found Sheikh Jarrar, one of the "graduates" of the Field of Flowers. He was thinner, no longer dressed in the *abaya* that protected him from the snows sweeping across Lebanon, but in a new leather jacket, his beard neatly trimmed as he sat in the students' union office. There were other Hamas supporters from Marj al-Zahour around him, greyer than I remembered them but still listening to their teacher with the same rapt attention they gave him during history lessons in the big tent at the freezing University of Marj al-Zahour. "It changed us all," he said. "Marj al-Zahour had an effect on all of us. It has made me more relaxed because I realise the world noticed our plight and made me realise there were still values."

He paused a lot during our meeting in the crowded students' office, aware perhaps that all those bearded faces would be looking for inconsistencies as well as wisdom in their history teacher. Here, after all, was a Westerner who had known Sheikh Bassam Jarrar in exile, a reporter from a decidedly different culture who might know things they did not know about how those 400 Palestinians behaved in their exile two years before. "Because the world proved to be less of a jungle than we thought, a lot of us have doubts about evaluating our experience in southern Lebanon," Jarrar continued. "Our political speech was modified. In Marj al-Zahour, I had to talk to people from different cultures. We had to find a language that was convincing to others, not just to ourselves. That's why we developed a certain language."

And the PLO–Israeli agreement that the exiles had so scornfully dismissed back in the snows of their mountain encampment? "Any solution is connected to the concept of justice," Jarrar replied. "If there are mistakes in the plan, it won't last long. There is a possibility that there will be peace, but there will also be a lot of violence. Everybody believes that this is a superpower solution that is not based on justice . . . Israel will not deal with us with justice." All the young men around the room nodded obediently when Jarrar returned to a familiar theme: the massive, all-embracing power of Washington, whose interference in international affairs was dictated solely by the interests of the United States—in Bosnia as well as in the Middle East. "Bosnia is in the heart of Europe, it's a special case. The solution they have reached is to keep the Muslims under supervision and to prevent third parties like the Islamists from gaining any power. But Palestine is in the heart of the Islamic world and here the Americans are looking after their interests in the Middle East—oil and Israel."

I pushed Sheikh Jarrar back to the subject of Jerusalem, of which he had spoken so many times at Marj al-Zahour. "Arafat maybe will be able to take control of some areas annexed to Jerusalem. The West Bank will be split into cantons by the Israelis who have built all these bypass roads for the settlers which divide up our land. Some of the settlers will leave but others will stay, especially in settlements in the Jordan valley, in the north-west, and in all those areas where the settlements are already virtual cities." He was half-right. Arafat would be offered some meagre suburbs of Jerusalem. No settlers would leave—indeed, they would increase in number—but the settler roads would divide up the Palestinian land and ensure that no Palestinian state could come into being.

Out in the hallway, hundreds of students clustered round the noticeboards of the militant Palestinian groups. To the Islamist board were pinned dozens of snapshots of Hamas and Islamic Jihad "martyrs," holding pistols and automatic rifles and heavy machine guns. "That's Bassam Imasalni," another Marj al-Zahour veteran said, pointing to the portrait of a slightly bearded man with dark, serious eyes. "He was trapped in his home by the Israelis but came out fighting with his rifle— he only died because there were too many of them."

Was it self-deception or self-delusion that allowed us to believe that a just "peace" was still on offer? I look back over my own reports from the Middle East in the second half of the Nineties with a mixture of tiredness and horror. "The marriage is over," I wrote in June 1996. "The show has long drawn to a close. The divorce was made final the moment Bibi Netanyahu became prime minister. The solemn and official agreements signed by the PLO and Israel turn out to be of no interest to the new Israeli government: the Israeli withdrawal from Hebron has not been honoured. Final status talks which were supposed to decide the future of Jerusalem and the Jewish settlements still expanding across the occupied Palestinian West Bank have become an irrelevancy."

And then, in December 1996, I find myself writing that "an explosion is coming in the Middle East, a detonation that may well change the region for ever. We in the west have largely chosen not to heed the signs of impending calamity, preferring instead to pretend that the long-dead and deeply flawed 'peace process' still has life in its decaying body . . . but the Arab world is bracing itself for the shock wave of terrible events." What on earth, I ask myself today, did I think that explosion would be? I must have imagined that the "explosion" would detonate in the Middle East, inside Israel or Palestine. But I have a tape of an interview with a CBC anchorman in Toronto in November 1998 in which again I talk of "an explosion to come."

Torture and death in custody, arbitrary arrest and detention without trial, executions and unfair trials by both Israelis and Palestinians: five years after the Oslo agreement, could there have been a more wretched indictment of the "peace" than the report that Amnesty International published? So rapidly were human rights being sacrificed in the hopeless search for "security" between Israel and the PLO that the November 1998 report was too late to record the latest atrocities: two Palestinians shot by a PLO firing squad for murder and the apparent beating to death by Yassir Arafat's henchmen of Hussein Ghali, who called at a Gaza police station to make a complaint. Amnesty's own words were more eloquent than any reporter's notes:

> . . . killings of Palestinians by Israeli security services or settlers have led to suicide bombings and the deaths of Israeli civilians. These have led to waves of arbitrary arrests, incommunicado detention, torture and unfair trials. The Palestinian population have been the main victims of such violations . . . the Occupied Territories have become a land of barriers, mostly erected by Israeli security services, between town and town and village and village.

Methods of torture used by the Israelis included *shabeh* (sleep deprivation while shackled in painful positions and hooding), *gambaz* (forced to squat for more than two hours), *tiltul* (violent shaking that had already killed a Palestinian prisoner)* and *khazana* (imprisonment in a cupboard). Other methods included beatings, pressure on the genitals and exposure to heat and cold. "There is general acceptance by the international community," Amnesty said, "that Israel has legalised the use of torture." Torture by Yassir Arafat's authority included beatings, suspension from the wrists, burning with electricity or cigarettes, along with tortures learned from the Israelis, especially *Shabeh*. Twenty Palestinians had died in Palestinian Authority custody since the Oslo agreement, most of them during or after torture. Among those routinely tortured were "security detainees," suspected collaborators and those Palestinians who had sold land to Jews.

Amnesty was especially concerned about extrajudicial killings. They included the murder of Hani Abed, a Hamas member suspected of murdering two Israeli soldiers, who was killed in a Gaza car bomb; Fatih Shikaki, the Islamic Jihad leader shot dead in Malta, and Yahya Ayash, a Hamas bomb-maker killed by a booby-trapped mobile telephone. His death, during a self-proclaimed Hamas ceasefire, provoked another round of suicide bombings. Among the many inno-

---

*A Scottish pathologist confirmed in 1995 that a Palestinian who died in Israeli custody, Abed Samed Hreizat from Hebron, suffered fatal brain injuries when his head was forcefully jerked during "shaking" by Israeli Shin Bet agents on 22 April that year. In an Israeli special commission report on interrogation, retired justice Moshe Landau sanctioned the use of "moderate physical pressure" against Palestinians. In 1997, Palestinian military intelligence turned up at Nablus hospital with a detainee called Youssef Baba, who had been burned on the arm and thighs with the electric element used to boil water. His wounds had become gangrenous; he was later returned to prison, where he died on 31 January.

cents killed by the Israelis was eight-year-old Ali Jawarish. The organisation quoted Joel Greenberg of *The New York Times*, who later told the Israeli human rights group B'Tselem that he saw Israeli troops fire at the boy during a demonstration.

> I saw one of the soldiers kneeling and aiming his gun at the children . . . In my opinion it was a rubber [coated] bullet . . . but I am not certain . . . When the soldiers retreated I noticed a boy aged about nine or ten lying motionless on the ground . . . I saw . . . a wound on the right side of the forehead and a lot of blood flowing. Later the doctors at Muqassed Hospital and at Beit Jala told me that the child's brain had spilled out.

There was now a weird symbiosis about this bloody conflict. The greater the violence in Israel–Palestine, the darker the political future, the more optimistic the West would become about the "peace process" which was once more, of course, to be put "back on track." This was, I suppose, an unconscious dress rehearsal for the Anglo-American invasion of Iraq in 2003. As the results of that illegal military operation became steadily more disastrous, so the Americans and the British would repeat their absolute confidence that the invasion was worthwhile, the aftermath predictable and the final result a mixture of "freedom" and "democracy." So, too, "Palestine" and Israel in 1998.

In May of that year, I travelled to London to watch the continued myth-making of Middle East peace played out around Downing Street. A police helicopter purred lazily over us when Benjamin Netanyahu came out of Number 10 to tell us how grateful he was to Tony Blair. The chopper drifted back in the English spring sunshine when Yassir Arafat in turn emerged from Downing Street to thank Blair for his commitment to the "peace process." How they loved Tony. How they hated each other. And all the while, behind us, loomed the fateful building in which Lord Balfour had composed Britain's 1917 declaration of support for a Jewish national home in Palestine.

Bibi, immaculate as ever in dark suit and thick white hair, told us there could be progress if both sides showed "flexibility." Israel, he claimed, "had already gone the extra mile." The Palestinians took the view that Netanyahu's extra mile was the distance that Israel's latest Jewish colony had extended into occupied Arab land. Arafat—ashen-faced, lower lip quivering, his kuffiah for once untidy— warned only that "Netanyahu must take the responsibility of . . . the chaos that might take place in the region if the result of these talks is not positive."

A mile away, through the empty London bank holiday streets, the Israeli prime minister talked to U.S. secretary of state Madeleine Albright in the sumptuous suites of the Grosvenor Park Hotel. The foyer, with its fake log fire and oil painting of ice skaters, looked ominously like the smoking room of the *Titanic*; and within minutes, there was Israel's spokesman, David Bar Ilan, with his ice-cold public school accent, strolling through the lobby to tell journalists—in response to Arafat's statement—that "if the formula is 'land-for-terrorism,' we can't go on with this." It was the language of children that both sides spoke, the language of threat and false compromise. How Netanyahu and Arafat loved peace, strove for peace. But they could not even bring themselves to talk to each other. Arafat was so weakened that all he could do, pathetically, was accept Washington's demand for a further 13.1 per cent Israeli withdrawal from the West Bank, in itself a grotesque diminution of what the Oslo accords demanded. In Grosvenor House, Madeleine Albright—the supposedly tough-talking secretary of state who used all the anger of a sheep to persuade the Israelis to try to stop building settlements on occupied Arab land and adhere to the Oslo timetable—tried to persuade Netanyahu to cede more than 9 per cent of Palestinian land to Arafat in the next handover of territory. In vain.

So much for the Palestinian state. But outside Number 10, the networks were telling their viewers—in the words of the man from the BBC—that Netanyahu had "little room for compromise" because of his divided cabinet. There was no hint in his broadcast that Israel was not abiding by the terms of the signed Oslo agreement. Bar Ilan spelled out the situation all too well. Israel wanted more security from Arafat and demanded that he reduce the number of his Palestinian policemen. Better security, fewer policemen. Who dreamed up these crazy formulas?

There was a moment that captured the hopelessness of the Middle East "peace process." On a sofa just outside the coffee salon of the Churchill Hotel in London on the second day of the talks, I came upon a familiar figure slumped on the sofa. There was no obvious security, no policemen, just the tall, dark-haired State Department spokesman and the woman sitting white-faced with exhaustion in the corner of the settee. Madeleine Albright looked on the point of collapse. Only hours before, she had telephoned Arafat to plead her excuses. She could not come to see him as agreed, she said. She was simply too tired to drive over to Claridge's for their meeting. Arafat burst into laughter when the call was over. Never mind that his own state of health—shocking to behold when only a few feet from him, his right hand clutching his shaking left hand, his lower lip moving helplessly when he wasn't speaking—was far worse than Mrs. Albright's. But when it came to Netanyahu a few hours later, Albright was off in her limousine to meet the Israeli prime minister at his own hotel.

What came over most strongly—even more shocking than the state of Arafat's health—was Albright's fear of Netanyahu, indeed perhaps of Israel. Arafat and the PLO had already accepted America's conditions for the 11 May 1998 invitation to meet President Clinton in Washington. Netanyahu had not responded. He was flying back to Israel to "consult" his cabinet. But when Albright talked to us all later—hesitant and sometimes confusing or forgetting questions—she was all praise for the Israeli leader who was forging ahead with Jewish settlements on the land Arafat wanted as part of his Palestinian state. Netanyahu was "encouraging." He had produced "new ideas." He was enthusiastic. He was "helpful." She was very grateful to Netanyahu. "It is obviously up to Israel to decide what its security demands are"—goodbye, then, to those Palestinian policemen. But when we asked

Albright what all those "new ideas" were, we were informed that "more details do not help us to move forward."

This was meaningless. Yet still she talked of "progress"—I counted the word at least eighteen times in just a few minutes. And so did Tony Blair in his own appearance before the press. Here was another of those verbal punctuation marks, its increasing frequency making its use ever more suspect. Arafat said he had "heard" from Albright that there had been "progress." It was when I asked him if he did not now regret signing the Oslo accords that the old man's eyes suddenly widened and his voice took on its old strength. "The peace agreement I signed was the peace of the brave," he replied. "I signed with my partner Yitzhak Rabin, who paid for his life with this peace. It is our firm duty that we continue with the just endeavour we signed with Mr. Rabin and Peres." There was no mention of Netanyahu. And in what Netanyahu and Albright said, there was no mention of the "peace of the brave"; with inappropriate flippancy, Albright remarked of America's peace-making efforts that "it's up to the parties [to decide] as to whether we are serving the vegetables well." Perhaps that would be written on Oslo's tombstone.

At an autumn 1998 private dinner party in the White House with junior members of the Jordanian royal family, President Clinton unburdened himself of a few thoughts on Benjamin Netanyahu. There were fewer than a dozen guests and he was talking to men and women who would sympathise with his remarks. "I am the most pro-Israeli president since Truman," he announced to his guests. "But the problem with Bibi is that he cannot recognise the humanity of the Palestinians." Stripped of its false humility—Clinton was surely *more* pro-Israeli than Truman—the president had put his finger on Netanyahu's most damaging flaw: his failure to regard the Palestinians as fellow humans, his conviction that they are no more than a subject people. This characteristic comes across equally clearly in his book *A Place Among the Nations*, which might have been written by a colonial governor. Clinton got it right. He understood the psychological defect that lay at the heart not just of Netanyahu's policies but of the whole Netanyahu government.

Yet within just a few days, he was presiding over yet another "peace" accord—at Wye—which effectively placed the Palestinians in the role of supplicants. The main section in the Wye agreement was not about withdrawals but about "security"—and this was liberally laced with references to "terrorists," "terrorist cells" and "terrorist organisations," involving, of course, only Palestinian violence. There was not a single reference to killers who had come from the Jewish settler community.

Arafat's torture was exquisite. Each new accord with Israel involved a subtle rewriting of previous agreements. Madrid—with all its safeguards for the Palestinians—turned into Oslo—no safeguards at all, and a system of Israeli withdrawal that was so constructed that deadlines no longer had to be met. This turned into the 1997 Hebron agreement—which allowed Jewish colonists to stay in the town and made an Israeli withdrawal contingent upon an end to anti-Israeli violence. In 1998 the Wye agreement even dropped the "land for peace" logo. It was now billed as the "Land for Security" agreement, "peace" being at least temporarily unobtainable. Peace means respect, mutual trust, cooperation. Security means no violence—but it also means prison, hatred and, as we already knew, torture. In return, the Palestinians could have 40 per cent of their territory under their control—as opposed to the 90 per cent they expected under Oslo. And the CIA, that most trustworthy and moral of institutions, would be in the West Bank to ensure that Arafat arrested the usual suspects.

The Palestinian Authority had not prevented Hamas from attacking Israelis—any more than Israel could prevent it from doing so before Oslo—but now, miraculously, they would succeed with the help of the CIA. Palestinians holding illegal weapons would be disarmed. The thousands of Jewish settlers on Palestinian land who had weapons—and who condemned even the watered-down version of Wye as "treachery"—would not be disarmed. Israelis should have been able to live without fear. So should Palestinians. But security comes from peace, not the other way round. And 3 per cent of the Palestinian land from which Israel would now withdraw was to become—perhaps the most farcical of Oslo's many manifestations—a "nature reserve" upon which Palestinians could not build homes. One wondered what kind of wild animals were supposed to roam inside this protected area. And what kind of wild animals would now roam outside its walls.

No word in Wye, then, of the Jewish "terror organisations," no hope of controlling settler groups that would attack Palestinians in the future. In July 2001, for example, one such group—a "terror" group by Israel's own definition, although the international press called them "guerrillas" or "vigilantes"—fired dozens of bullets into a car carrying eight Palestinians home from a pre-wedding party in the small town of Idna on the West Bank. Mohamed Salameh Tmaizeh and his relative Mohamed Hilmi Tmaizeh died on the spot. Five others were wounded. The third fatality was Diya Tmaizeh, a baby just three months old. This is not an excuse for Palestinian violence or "terror"—a Palestinian sniper also killed a Jewish baby at a settlement in Hebron—but there was a vital difference. Palestinians were to be disarmed. Jewish colonists were not.

How did the United States allow this to happen? Ignorance, weakness in the face of Israel's powerful American lobby groups, intellectual idleness when confronted by issues of massive complexity: all these may provide a clue. But it was a general irresponsibility that pervaded U.S. policy. Clinton wanted to be the author of a "peace" that he stubbornly refused to guarantee. We heard the old refrain from Clinton, that while Washington could "bring the parties together," it was for "the parties themselves" to take the "hard decisions." Thus Israel, infinitely the more powerful of the two parties—Palestinian tanks, after all, were not occupying Tel Aviv—could act as it wished within or outside the framework of the Oslo accord. Off the record, we would be told—like the Jordanian dinner guests at the White House—of Clinton's exasperation with Netanyahu.* Publicly, he would be silent.

---

*Not least when Netanyahu threw in the release from an American prison of the Israeli spy Jonathan Pollard—who had been sending Pentagon secrets to Israel—as part of his demands for success at Wye. Pollard, a Jewish American working as a U.S. intelligence analyst, had been sentenced to life in March 1987. In 1995, Ehud Barak even made him an Israeli citizen. Clinton, after cringingly saying that he would "seriously review" Pollard's case, at least managed to refuse Netanyahu's demand.

Yet when Palestinian violence was inflicted on Israelis, Clinton was in lionlike mode, calling the killers "yesterday's men" in Amman, and at Wye lecturing the world on the "hate" that would undoubtedly greet the latest success for "peace."

Sloppy use of language was also one of the most dangerous aspects of successive American "peace" accords. Clinton was good on cliché and rhetoric but—ironically, in view of his pedantry in responding to the grand jury about his relationship with Monica Lewinsky—lazy when it came to points of detail. Despite all the handshakes and platitudes at Wye, for example, both Palestinians and Israelis went home with diametrically opposite ideas of what had been achieved. Netanyahu was able to assure Jewish colonists that there would be no Palestinian state, while Arafat's men could persuade their few remaining supporters that another Israeli withdrawal would be another step towards statehood. No sooner had Netanyahu returned to Israel than his foreign minister, Ariel Sharon, urged settlers to "seize every hilltop they can" in the West Bank.

In a real battle of wits between equal partners, Arafat might have made a few Netanyahu-like conditions: no continuation of the "peace process" unless Israel renounced its exclusive claim to Jerusalem as a capital—which precluded "final status" talks; no more Jewish settlements on occupied Arab land; no more negotiations until Netanyahu ended Jewish settler attacks on Palestinians. But Arafat could not do that—and Washington would not talk to him if he did. So the Wye talks probably ended any Palestinian hope for a just peace. Israel would be allowed to go on building more Jewish settlements on occupied land, confiscating Palestinian identity papers, demolishing Palestinian homes. And Arafat—for perhaps 14 per cent of the 22 per cent of mandate "Palestine" that was left—had promised to protect the Israelis who were building the settlements, confiscating the identity papers and demolishing the homes.

All the while, U.S. "peace envoys" continued to visit Netanyahu and Arafat as part of America's "impartial" stewardship of the Middle East "peace." Every Palestinian knew that the four principal members of this team were Jewish. There was no public discussion in the Western press of the ethnic makeup of the American team. Nor, in principle, should there have been. American foreign service officers or appointees—like any other citizens of a democracy—should hold their posts regardless of their ethnic or racial origins. But Dennis Ross, the lead negotiator, was a former and prominent staff member of the most powerful Israeli lobby group, the American Israel Public Affairs Committee (AIPAC). This was rarely mentioned in the American press, but was surely a matter of vital importance. If the chief negotiator had been the ex-staffer member of an Arab lobby group, Israel would have made its views known at once. And if all four main negotiators had been Muslims, be sure that this would be a matter of legitimate discussion in the world's press. In the Israeli press, however, the membership of the American team *was* a matter of comment. When the Ross delegation came to Jerusalem, the Israeli newspaper *Maariv* called it "the mission of four Jews" and talked about the Israeli connections of the men. Israeli journalists noted that one of them had a son undergoing military training in Israel. It was the Israeli writer and activist Meron Benvenisti who highlighted this in *Ha'aretz*. The ethnic origin of U.S. diplomats sent to the Middle East to promote peace, he wrote,

> may be irrelevant, but it is hard to ignore the fact that manipulation of the peace process was entrusted by the U.S. in the first place to American Jews, and that at least one member of the State Department team was selected for the task because he represented the view of the American Jewish establishment. The tremendous influence of the Jewish establishment on the Clinton administration found its clearest manifestation in redefining the "occupied territories" as "territories in dispute." The Palestinians are understandably angry. But lest they be accused of anti-Semitism, they cannot, God forbid, talk about Clinton's "Jewish connection" . . .

Nor did we as journalists dare to raise this issue. To do so would have brought the inevitable charges of anti-Semitism, racism, bias. It was quite acceptable for Israel's supporters to raise issues of family or national origin if others criticised its actions. When, for example, the UN Secretary General, Boutros Boutros-Ghali, instructed his military adviser, Dutch Major General Franklin van Kappen, to conduct an investigation into the Israeli massacre of 106 Lebanese refugees at the UN base at Qana in southern Lebanon in 1996, a pro-Israeli newspaper condemned the decision on the grounds that van Kappen came from a country which had surrendered its Jews to the Nazis in the Second World War. Yet when a former AIPAC staff member was appointed America's top peace negotiator, no questions were asked. Thank God, I often remark, for Israeli journalism.

Every few months in the Middle East, the Chamberlain bell is rung. "Peace in our time," it tolls. And anxious not to be blamed for its failure, the Arabs and Israelis leap to express their support. The moment Ehud Barak was elected Labour prime minister of Israel in 1999, the satellite television boys and girls—along with the ever-supine BBC World Service—were putting the "peace process" back "on track" once more, even though Barak had made it clear that Jerusalem must remain the united capital of Israel, that major Jewish settlements would stay and that no Palestinian refugees from 1948 could expect to return to their original Arab villages.

Barak wanted talks with the Syrians, and the same old negotiating routine was quickly re-established. The Syrians still wanted the return of all of Golan. But why wouldn't the Syrians accept just a bit of Golan? Or Golan with the settlements? Or part of Golan plus an unknown number of Israeli troops to maintain early warning stations? The world was reminded that Syria had "threatened" Israel from Golan before the 1967 war.* But Assad called Barak an honest and "strong" man, for he,

---

*This "threat" was thrown into doubt when an Israeli reporter, Rami Tal, revealed to the newspaper *Yediot Ahronoth* in 1997 that Moshe Dayan, the defence minister who conquered Golan in 1967, had told him in a series of interviews before his death that many of the Israeli–Syrian firefights were deliberately provoked by Israel, and that the kibbutz residents who pressed the government to take Golan did so less for security than for the farmland.

too, did not want to be blamed for any new failures. When Clinton travelled to meet Assad when Labour was previously in power in Israel, Syria had been portrayed as the nation that rejected peace, "the spanner in the works," in the words of CNN's reporter. In truth, nothing had changed. Israel wanted diplomatic relations and economic links with Damascus before any discussion of how much of Golan might be returned to Syria. Having watched Arafat writhing with this equation— only to find that having recognised Israel and compromised the very idea of statehood, Israel would decide Palestine's future—Assad was not enamoured of the idea that this was, in Clinton's own words, a "golden opportunity" to make peace. It was a familiar scenario. Accept Israel's version of peace and Syria could be overwhelmed by conditions she could not meet. Refuse, and Syria would be blamed for opposing peace and become an enemy of peace and—ergo—an enemy of the United States.

The pumpkin of the Oslo agreement could never be turned into the golden carriage of peace, but it took the collapse of the Arafat–Barak talks at Camp David in 2000 to prove this true. Even then, Clinton was reduced to claiming that the Oslo negotiations were "based" on UN Security Council Resolutions 242 and 338— which was not what Oslo said at all—and even Arafat must have realised that the end had come when Madeleine Albright made her preposterous offer of "a sense of sovereignty" over Muslim religious sites in Jerusalem. Only the silly villages that Arafat might have controlled outside his would-be capital would have "virtually full sovereignty," according to the Americans. There then followed the wilfully misleading leaks to the effect that Arafat had turned down 95 per cent of "Palestine"—in reality around 64 per cent of the 22 per cent of "Palestine" that was left. Barak would not give up Jerusalem or abandon the settlements. Arafat would not make the "concession" of ceding Israeli control over all of Jerusalem. So the sons of Abraham acknowledged what so many Israelis and Palestinians knew all along: that Oslo didn't work. Clinton predictably saw fit to praise the stronger of the two parties; he spoke of Barak's "courage" and "vision," but merely of Arafat's commitment. So much for America's role as "honest broker" of the Middle East peace. Offered virtual sovereignty to secure virtual peace, the Palestinian leadership—corrupt and effete and undemocratic—preferred failure to humiliation.

Arafat thus returned to a hero's welcome in Gaza. For once, the old man had not offered another capitulation. He had stood up to the United States. And Israel. He was a "Saladin." "Saladin of the century," no less. It was all sorry stuff. This Saladin was not going to gallop into Jerusalem. Instead, the city was to be the scene of repeated carnage as Jew and Arab Muslim attacked each other in the coming months. In September 2000, Ariel Sharon marched to the Muslim holy places—above the site of the Jewish Temple Mount—accompanied by about a thousand Israeli policemen. Within twenty-four hours, Israeli snipers opened fire with rifles on Palestinian protesters battling with police in the grounds of the seventh-century Dome of the Rock. At least four were killed and the head of the Israeli police, Yehuda Wilk, later confirmed that snipers had fired into the crowd when Palestinians "were felt to be endangering the lives of officers." Sixty-six Palestinians were wounded, most of them by rubber-coated steel bullets. The killings came almost exactly ten years after armed Israeli police killed 19 Palestinian demonstrators and wounded another 140 in an incident at exactly the same spot, a slaughter that almost lost the United States its Arab support in the prelude to the 1991 Gulf War.

Sharon showed no remorse. "The state of Israel," he told CNN, "cannot afford that an Israeli citizen will not be able to visit part of his country, not to speak for the holiest for the Jewish people all around the world." He did not, however, explain why he should have chosen this moment—immediately after the collapse of the "peace process"—to undertake such a provocative act. Stone-throwing and shooting spread to the West Bank. Near Qalqiliya, a Palestinian policeman shot dead an Israeli soldier and wounded another—they were apparently part of a joint Israeli–Palestinian patrol originally set up under the terms of the Oslo agreement. "Everything was pre-planned," Sharon would claim five weeks later. "They took advantage of my visit to the Temple Mount. This was not the first time I've been there . . ."

JUST OUTSIDE JERUSALEM, a Jewish settler from Efrat was screaming abuse at a group of Israeli soldiers. His car had been stoned by Palestinian children on a nearby hill. He demanded military intervention at once. "Are you one of the journalists that lies like CNN?" he rounded on me. "You people should write that a rock is like unto a lethal weapon. It's the same as a bullet. Someone who throws a rock at a bus is trying to murder fifty people." It was an instructive little outburst, for it turned the children on the hill behind Beit Jalla into mass murderers, gunmen without guns, worthy of the biblical fury so beautifully captured in that phrase "like unto a lethal weapon." It was obviously not only Palestinians who believed in "days of rage." The anger was just as palpable among Israelis this October of 2000, even if the sense of proportion—or lack of it—was profoundly disturbing. Again and again, in Israel, the bestialisation—and fear—of Palestinians betrayed a total inability to grasp reality: you might think that Israel was under Palestinian occupation, that Israelis were being shot down in their dozens by Palestinian "security forces," that Palestinian tanks and helicopters were blasting away at Israeli towns, that Yassir Arafat had taken time out from diplomacy, something that Barak had publicly declared his intention to do.

What was going on now in the occupied territories was a form of low-intensity warfare which was, week by week, creeping into an armed conflict between two peoples. The Palestinians now believed they had nothing to lose by fighting the Israelis. Trapped in their autonomous villages, a whole society under town arrest, they no longer had anything to gain by their silence or their acquiescence. A young Palestinian woman who worked for one of Arafat's security outfits explained it with candour. "Arafat has to go on fighting—he mustn't give in now. The intifada will force the Israelis to understand that Oslo is dead and that only a total withdrawal from the West Bank and Gaza and East Jerusalem will bring peace." When I pointed out to her that Arafat was not doing the "fighting"—that it was the Palestinians and their various satellite organisations that opposed Oslo that were providing "Palestine" with its dead—she changed her argument. "We must make sure that the people and the Palestinian Authority are together and united," she said, "when the real fighting starts."

"Real" fighting? What did that mean? Ten years ago, Ariel Sharon—then the outcast ex-defence minister shamed by Sabra and Chatila—said that Israeli tanks might one day have to shell Nablus or Ramallah. How we roared with laughter then. Yet now, a decade later, with Sharon on the verge of returning to the Israeli cabinet, those tanks were indeed shelling Palestinian towns. Tanks fired into Ramallah. Helicopter gunships rocketed Palestinian towns so frequently that their attacks no longer made headlines. And in those towns and in the foetid streets of Gaza, I found not a soul who wanted the new intifada to end. Nor did I find a Palestinian family that did not watch the Lebanese Hizballah's Manar television station, satellited from Beirut, beaming into the occupied territories a constant message: in Lebanon, Israel was driven from occupied land because its people fought for liberation; they believed in God; they were not afraid to die. And now Lebanon is free. Why not the West Bank and Gaza and Jerusalem?

This was a powerful but dangerous lesson to send to the Palestinians. For Gaza is not southern Lebanon, and Ramallah and Beit Jalla are not Tyre and Sidon. Jerusalem is not Beirut. But Oslo had proved so great a betrayal for the Palestinians, their trust so perverted by Israel's continued settlement building and land confiscation and its refusal to allow the Palestinians a capital in part of Jerusalem, that politics was no longer a viable instrument of progress. Faithfully continuing the bankrupt policy of beating the Arabs into submission—the policy that destroyed Israel in Lebanon—the Israelis responded to stones with bullets, to bullets with missiles. But in their hovels, the Palestinians of Gaza could absorb this punishment. They knew that if the Israelis wanted to invade Palestinian land, all of it—an idea floated by the less balanced Jewish settlers but later to be adopted by Sharon himself—then they would have perpetual war.

Nor was there much doubt that the terrible threats of Islamic Jihad to resume their war of suicide bombs were real. Nabil Arair might have failed to kill any Israelis with a bicycle bomb in Gaza but there were many others ready to take his place. Jerusalem's buses were already travelling three-quarters empty. The suicide bombers had struck—even before setting off their bombs. Hamas now ruled Gaza. Needless to say, Israel's once close relations with Hamas were no longer mentioned in news reports from Jerusalem.

So—and here I use the rubric of the Israelis, faithfully parroted by CNN and the BBC—did Arafat "control his own people"? The question was pointless, for the Palestinians now controlled Arafat. Their despair mirrored his own conviction that Oslo was dead; their fury at the Israeli killing of so many Palestinians paralleled Arafat's anger at both the Americans and Israelis. Their political explosion occurred—it was a fact—and Arafat could only acknowledge it by repeating the foundation of those talks so long ago in Madrid: that the only just peace lies in the direct and total implementation of UN Security Council Resolution 242. He said as much at the end of October 2000. Responding to Barak's call for a "political separation" between Palestinians and Israelis, Arafat said that he was "for a political separation that is based on the 1967 borders and international resolutions . . . and will lead to the setting up of a Palestinian state."

And how did Israelis respond to the Palestinians one month into the new intifada? "Palestinians are racist," said a letter-writer to the *Jerusalem Post*, a paper that ran a feature article on child victims with the memorable headline: "Child Sacrifice Is Palestinian Paganism." Yes, Palestinians are pagans, racists, child-sacrificers, "terrorists," animals, "serpents"—this from Barak in September 2000. But—a tragedy for both Palestinians and Israelis—they were likely to fight on, even if their Israeli antagonists were armed by the Americans.

For the Palestinians, this fact was no political point-scoring. Just after dark on 27 October 2000, at least two missiles smashed into the corner of the Ksiyeh family home in Beit Jalla, the first blasting a cavity in the wall, the second flying right through the hole and punching through the corridor floor before exploding in a neighbour's kitchen. An Israeli helicopter gunship fired both missiles and the evidence was there for all to see. One of the missiles was a Hellfire manufactured by Lockheed Martin. The second was a more modern projectile, carrying the U.S. designation number 93835C4286 and manufactured in June 1988. It wasn't hard, looking at the metal computer strips with their tell-tale factory markings, to see why the people of Beit Jalla didn't weep over the seventeen American sailors of the USS *Cole*, attacked by al-Qaeda suicide bombers in Aden just over two weeks earlier.

Yet the villagers here—60 per cent of them Christian—were not vengeful people; and the Palestinian gunmen firing across the valley at the Jewish settlement of Gilo were not from Beit Jalla. The Palestinian hamlet with its fine dressed-stone Orthodox churches, frescoes of St. George and the Dragon and massive, thick-furred street cats was not exactly a battlefield, but it now stood on a West Bank front line, regularly punished by Israel for the bullets that smacked through the windows of the Jewish settlers across the wadi. A week earlier, gunmen—almost certainly a Tanzim militia unit—fired first at the Israelis. In return a Merkava tank—I could see it sleeping under a blue tarpaulin on the opposite hillside—put three shells into one of Beit Jalla's narrow streets. One blasted into Margot Zidan's garage, destroying her brand-new VW Golf and crushing the ancient stone gateway above. War and the hand of God exclude insurance payments. Another shell blew a hole in the second floor of Jamil Mislet's home down the road.

The Plot—the essential ingredient in any Middle East folly—now engulfed this tourist-pretty village. The local Palestinian version went like this: true, some Tanzim men fired rifles from between the houses, but Israel also sent Palestinian collaborators with guns into the village to fire at the settlement and thus provide the Israelis with an excuse to deploy four Merkava tanks on the other hill. The Israeli version of the Plot was even more ingenious: the Palestinian Authority deliberately provoked Israeli gunfire onto Christian homes in the hope of bringing the Vatican onto the Palestinian side in the new intifada.

The truth seemed more prosaic. The settlement of Gilo, on the heights above Beit Jalla—*Gilo* is the Hebrew version of *Jalla*—is in sight of Jerusalem; and by targeting its houses, the Palestinians were sending a message to the Israeli government: settlements are part of the new war, even colonies which are part of "Jewish" Jerusalem. However, the Christian and Muslim villagers also claimed that the most recent attack—the double missile strike on the Ksiyeh family home—was unprovoked, that there had been no shooting from the town before the assault. Which is why they were taking no chances. Three workmen were building a parapet of concrete blocks around the local telephone switching box at one end of Beit Jalla. Pasted to a telegraph pole next to it was a photograph of thirteen-year-old schoolboy Mrayad Jawaresh, who had died a week earlier while returning home from school to the neighbouring refugee camp. He smiled out of the picture in his school tie, another child "martyr"—killed by gunfire, provenance unknown—to support the Palestinian cause.

Margot Zidan's daughter Ghadir made a clucking sound with her tongue as she looked at the portrait. "You people protect the Israelis and blame us for this," she said. "You say we are responsible for killing our own children. But this is not true. We are one people here. There is no difference between Christian and Muslim." And the latter was most certainly true. Walking from house to house in Beit Jalla, Christian families took me to Muslim homes, Muslim children to the houses of Christian friends—without prior arrangement or introduction. But did the villagers support the Palestinians who fired into Gilo? They would shrug when I asked this question. "These men have silly little guns and they fire from between our homes," one said. "What can we do? But how can we stop the Israelis? They know it's not us that's shooting at them."

Routine. That is what insurrection is about. A routine of violence that continues until it is suddenly and irreversibly detonated to a new and more bloody routine. Ramallah was the scene of what journalists liked to call "clashes." A "clash," you see, is an act in which Palestinians can die without anyone being held responsible—as in "Three Palestinians were killed in clashes yesterday." Perhaps they were killed by their own people—or expired due to over-exertion during protests. When Israelis were killed, the culprits were usually identified as Palestinians. Not so when the victims were themselves Palestinians. So I drove across to Ramallah to watch a "clash" day.

Clash. How amorphous, dull, indifferent, how very politely neutral the word sounds. But Israelis and Palestinians use it when they speak in English. And the "clash point" was an equally neutral stretch of roadway below the City Inn Hotel, its bedrooms now occupied by Israeli soldiers with sniper rifles. Across the muddy construction site to the north is an unfinished apartment block in which Palestinians also occupy bedrooms, with their own rifles. And up the road, towards the setting afternoon sun, is the day's "clash."

It is called Ayosha junction and it is also the place—if you are a Muslim and if you are religious and if you believe in "martyrdom"—where a live round may just send your soul to paradise. For the Israeli soldiers fire so many rubber-coated steel bullets—as well as live rounds—that they have a fairground's chance of hitting someone holding a stone. As for the bullets shot across the valley at the Palestinian gunmen, they appear to have little effect. The casualties are usually the stone-throwers.

It has a choreography all its own. A few burning tyres in the morning to enrage the Israeli soldiers in their clapped-out jeeps. Then two or three or four funerals for the previous day's Palestinian stone-throwers—capital punishment now being an unquestioned, routine penalty for chucking stones at Israelis—and then another "clash" at Ayosha junction. The tyres were already burning when they freighted Hossam Salem to the cemetery near his home, a cortège of black-dressed women, serious, bespectacled men and cars in which a convoy of trucks had become entangled. There was the old wooden coffin and a squad of men shouting *Allahu akbar*, then a bright orange lorry bearing the words "Bambini Fruit Juice," then a group of women carrying green flags which announced that there was no God but God and Mohamed was his Prophet. And, of course, everyone was remembering the unmarried twenty-four-year-old who worked in his father's grocery store and who—at Ayosha junction, of course—received a bullet full in the face scarcely eighteen hours before.

"He was religious, he had a big beard when he died and he was with Hamas," a family friend told me. "He was a supporter of Hamas for a long time, then he became more 'active' three months ago. All his family are with Hamas. When the Jerusalem intifada began three weeks ago, his brothers all said he would be a martyr. He also said he would be a martyr. Yesterday, he just said goodbye to his mother and went to Ayosha where there was a clash." Active? Did Hossam Salem carry a gun? No one knew. But he was throwing stones and his grisly post-death portrait—a massive coloured photograph taken in the morgue—showed that the front of Hossam Salem's face, much covered with a fluffy beard, had been powerfully stove in below the nose. Did he go to paradise? I asked a middle-aged man with a grey moustache and thin-framed spectacles. "If you are a real believer, then you go to paradise. I believe he went there, *inshallah*."

The mourners drifted away from the little mosque where a group of nineteenth-century buildings of pale grey stone spoke of an earlier, gentle, Ottoman Ramallah. And within an hour, more candidates arrived to take Hossam Salem's place at the "clash point." There were at least four hundred young men throwing and catapulting stones down the road—forget the cliché about "rock-throwing," these were garden-size stones, about five inches wide—and the Israeli soldiers were hiding behind their armoured jeeps and firing tear gas back at the Palestinians in a slow, almost lazy way.

One of the Israelis sat in the back of his jeep 3 metres from me, pulling on a cold can of Pepsi-Cola. Then he heaved himself from the vehicle, fixed a grenade to his rifle and fired it into the air above the jeep. It soared like a constellation, plummeting 400 metres down in a trail of white smoke to burst amid the crowd.

Then his colleague, with an equally casual effort, used the door of the jeep to aim his rifle and fired off a rubber-coated steel bullet that bounced and skipped down the road. The Israelis were on the edge of Oslo's Area A (total Palestinian occupation) and the Palestinians were in Area C (Israeli control) of the West Bank and the truly ridiculous theatre played out here showed just how insane the Oslo agreement had been. If the Israelis left, the Palestinians would stop throwing stones. If the Palestinians left, the Israelis would drive away. But each side was here because the other side was here—and because Area A and Area C had to be defended.

Every few seconds, the cartridge case of a rubber-coated bullet would ping at my feet. Then a Molotov cocktail would blaze harmlessly in a rusting telegraph pole, and a rain of stones would patter on the road. At mid-afternoon, an ambulance drove at speed into the centre of the highway to retrieve a stone-thrower who had been hit. And so it went on, more "clashes" for Clinton to bewail before the microphones in Washington. And I was struck, listening to his words on my radio in Ramallah, by the sheer vacuity—the absolute other-planet irrelevance—of what Clinton said. He wanted the young people of one side to re-establish contact with the young people of the other—as if these "clashes" were taking place in a vacuum, despite the wishes of thousands of young Palestinians and Israelis. The problem was that the soldier drinking Pepsi-Cola and the soldier firing the tear gas and the young man with the Molotov cocktail and Hossam Salem *are* the young people. Salem didn't want to join Clinton's merry reunion of youth. He wanted to go to paradise. And the Israelis were quite prepared to send him there. So, I wrote, let's keep calling them "clashes," child's play, just a little routine violence from which we can all withdraw and jump aboard the Oslo train once it's been put back on its little toy track. Or from which you can speed your way—if you believe in it—straight to heaven.

In every village, a tragedy. I drive into Yabad in the West Bank. Who's ever heard of Yabad? I can't even find it on a map, a forgotten hamlet south-east of Jenin. But the story is easy to write. They grew up together, they attended the same school together, they slept in the same room together, they became partners in the same village restaurant together. And on 29 October 2000, they were shot dead together by the Israelis and next day, in the small graveyard on the windy hilltop above Yabad, Bilal and Hilal Salah were buried together.

The brothers were hit, according to their family, by 50-calibre bullets as they shouted abuse at an Israeli army unit on the road below their village. "Bilal's brains spilled out of his head onto the ground just here," his eldest brother, Zuheir, said on the embankment of rubbish-strewn earth above a Jewish settlers' road. "We took Bilal to the hospital and it was only then that we realised Hilal was missing. When we got back, we found him lying just ten metres away. He had also been hit in the head. They had died together." Zuheir insisted that the brothers—Bilal was twenty-one, Hilal two years younger—were doing no more than shouting at the Israeli soldiers on the road beneath them, although one villager said that stones had been thrown at the Israelis by some of the seventeen youths on the embankment. Stone-throwing, as every Palestinian knows, is a capital offence. Hunks of concrete had been laid around the blood-stained earth where the brothers died.

It was the intifada in microcosm, a lunatic mixture of exaggerated Israeli fear and hopeless sorrow. On the road below, Israeli soldiers—perhaps the killers of Bilal and Hilal Salah—had warned me against visiting the village. "I wouldn't go there," their officer said bleakly. "There's a funeral." But the funeral was long over, and all I found was a circle of middle-aged men weeping in a room full of framed Korans and red plastic flowers, and the brothers' mother, Sada, sitting on the floor and crying beneath a cheap pink blanket. The two youths were Yabad's first "martyrs." "The soldiers guard five Jewish settlements near here and we are exposed to gunfire every day and fifty-calibre bullets are not normal ammunition," Zuheir Salah said. "Those bullets go right through cinder-blocks and we had to close the school in case bullets came inside." The family story was as mundane as it was ultimately tragic. Bilal and Hilal Salah had four brothers and five sisters; Zuheir, like their dead father, was a labourer. Only two days before their deaths, they had put up the nameplate on their café, the "Flowered Traffic Circle Restaurant." The family had already printed up a set of postcard portraits of the dead brothers, their heads surrounded by handwritten Koranic inscriptions and the insignia of Arafat's Palestinian Authority.

Down on that fatal road, the villagers lit tyres in protest at the killings, but by late afternoon the black smoke had drifted off over the stone fields, leaving coils of rusting wire on the burned tarmac. All around Yabad were the same pathetic signs of opposition to Israel's continued occupation. High up on the hills around the village, the red roofs of Jewish settlements glowed in the afternoon sun, their army-escorted convoys throbbing along the settlers' roads. Did their inhabitants know that, just across from them, Bilal and Hilal Salah were being lowered into their graves?

Israelis are more introspective about their history than Palestinians; they find it easier to be self-critical, but then that is one of the luxuries of being the winner, the occupier, the master. Halfway to Jerusalem, as our minibus began to climb the hill from the plains east of Tel Aviv, Simon began telling me about his Israeli war service. At seventy-three, his army life was over, but he'd fought in 1967 and 1973 and ended up in Beirut in 1982, landing on the beaches north of Sidon. Mercifully, there was no talk of "terrorists," only of peace, and when his wife asked why the Palestinians should not have Arab East Jerusalem as the capital of their new state—and this, remember, just four weeks after the death of the Oslo agreement— I wondered if there wasn't an undiscovered Israel.

The bus was negotiating the sharp curves around Harel and we could see the remains of the 1948 Jewish convoy by the highway, left as a memorial to the struggle of the Jews to keep open the road to Jerusalem more than half a century ago. That was when Simon's wife announced that everything had gone wrong in 1967. "We got used to the land we had taken then, to being in occupation. That made the Lebanon invasion easier, to be an occupier. We shouldn't have occupied someone else's land." Then she suddenly asked me about Mohamed al-Dura, the twelve-year-old shot dead by Israeli soldiers on 30 September as he cowered in his father's arms in Gaza. "What was he doing at the time?" she asked sharply. "Why was he on the street?" In fact, he had accompanied his father to buy a car—because the father had to walk to the Gaza border at two each morning for permission to work in Israel—and had been returning home when they were trapped by gunfire.* But I understood the implication of these questions at once: if Mohamed al-Dura did not have good reason to be on the streets of Gaza at the time—if he had been participating in a demonstration—then maybe the little boy had got what he deserved, another child sacrifice born of "Palestinian paganism."

This disconnection from reality comes in many forms. After I landed at Ben Gurion Airport in late October 2000, the young female Israeli immigration officer cheerfully asked me to remember that Israel was "a small country threatened by people from outside who want to take it." I suggested that the Palestinians had been living in "Palestine"—or modern-day Israel—for generations, that they were not "outside" (save those who had been expelled from their lands by Israel) and that UN Security Council Resolution 242 might, in the end, bring real peace. "What is 242?" she wanted to know.

How strange that 242—whose three figures alone are shorthand for any Palestinian who wants to refer to the UN resolution demanding an Israeli withdrawal from occupied lands—would mean nothing to a young, educated Israeli immigration officer. Oslo, of course, had a meaning for her, the very word used with such contempt by the Palestinians of the occupied territories. Deir Yassin would not. The same disconnection creeps into the Israeli and Western press.

Israelis are invariably "murdered" or "lynched" by Palestinians—often a perfectly accurate description, especially of the two Israeli reservists butchered in a Ramallah police station and then hurled from a window—but Palestinians were inevitably killed in those "clashes" with which I was so familiar. Reuters dutifully followed this skewed narrative. On 30 October 2000, its report on killings by Israeli troops in the occupied territories referred to Palestinians wounded in "stone-throwing clashes" and "killed in earlier clashes," adding that the "clashes" began on 28 September, that "the clashes have halted peace talks" and that Israeli Arabs have complained about "the killing of their brethren in clashes." But when on the same day an Israeli security guard was shot dead, his killer was accurately described by Reuters as a "suspected Palestinian gunman." On the same day, the Associated Press reported "Palestinian shooting attacks on Jewish settlements" but spoke of a Palestinian who was, of course, merely shot in "clashes."

---

*The video and photographs of the twelve-year-old falling lifeless into his father's arms became one of the iconic images of the second intifada, and the Israelis quickly erased all trace of the killing by demolishing the wall behind which they had taken cover. An Israeli military investigation then attempted to prove that Palestinians had been responsible for their deaths—and successfully persuaded America's CBS channel to air their bogus "findings" on its *60 Minutes* programme. "One gets the impression," Israeli Knesset member Ophir Pines-Paz bravely pointed out, "that instead of genuinely confronting this incident, the IDF [Israel Defence Force] has chosen to stage a fictitious re-enactment and cover up the incident by means of an enquiry with foregone conclusions and the sole purpose of which is to clear the IDF of responsibility for al-Dura's death." Western reporters who investigated the killings concluded that Israelis had shot both the son and the father, who survived, although the Israeli soldiers responsible may not have been able to see them behind the wall.

This double standard of Israeli and foreign reporting would find its way into the most unexpected of places. Staying at the King David Hotel in Jewish West Jerusalem, I found myself watching the hotel's home-video history on the television in my room. So what did the video tell about the destruction of the British military headquarters in this very same hotel by Menachem Begin's bombers, an act which—if committed by Palestinians—would be described by Israelis as an act of bestial terrorism? Well, the video proudly boasted that the King David was "the only hotel in the world that was bombed by a future prime minister" and referred to the perpetrators—whose victims included at least 41 Arabs, 28 British and 17 Jews—as "activists" who were dedicated to their cause.

Ariel Sharon is condemned as a "hawk" in the Israeli press, a "right-winger," a man who has wilfully sacrificed the lives of Israeli soldiers in war—but not, in Israeli newspapers, as the man chiefly responsible for the Sabra and Chatila massacre. This inversion of moral horror reminded me of the Serbs who loathed Slobodan Milošević for Serbia's economic collapse and the loss of Kosovo—but not for his ethnic cleansing of half a million Kosovo Albanians—and of Israel's ethnic cleansing of three-quarters of a million Palestinians in 1948, most of whom ended up in the muck of Gaza.

Every day now, we reporters would go to watch these fierce battles between stone-throwers and Israeli soldiers—"clashes," of course—and the Israeli tear-gas grenades were falling like Chinese fireworks one day near the Karni crossroads when my mobile phone rang. There had been a bomb in Jerusalem. One of the Palestinian policemen watching the stone-throwers was listening to my call. "How many dead?" he asked. Two, I said. The man looked disappointed. "Is that all?" he asked. There wasn't much compassion in Gaza for the enemy who used to be Yassir Arafat's "partner in peace."

Gaza is so physically tiny that it has to be a place of contrasts. At midday, I am sitting amid long grass, amid lemon and fig trees, bushes of pomegranates and gardenia, listening to one of Arafat's most trusted lieutenants telling me of George Tenet's threats. Indeed, the head of the CIA—so frequent a visitor to Gaza—seemed strangely present, because my host knows the CIA boys well. Then, a couple of hours later, I am back at Karni and I am watching an Israeli soldier run from the border fence and squat in the muddy dunes to take aim at a boy holding a slingshot. There is a high-pitched crack, the thwack of a bullet hitting something and the youth is on the ground, two men running towards him with a stretcher. The rifle cracks again and, just once, I hear the bullet literally whizz through the air to my right. Yes, Arafat's man had told me in his orchard, the CIA knew that the Israelis were deliberately trying to kill stone-throwers. "We have shown them the statistics and taken them to watch these unequal battles," he said. "Personally, they agree with us that the Israelis are shooting at the upper part of the body. But the CIA obey their American political masters."

From the orchard, with its fruit flies and sparrows, to the mud of Karni was possibly 1,500 metres. And it was interesting how the threats and anger of Camp David fitted in so naturally with the blood and tyre-shrieking ambulance down the road. Arafat's officer did not restrain his words. The story had come to him from Arafat himself, at the very end of the Camp David talks which had brought us all—within weeks—to the catastrophe that now embraced "Palestine." And, some would say, Israel as well:

> Tenet had gone to Arafat with a warning: "We can make new borders, we can make peoples, we can make new regimes." This is what Tenet told Arafat at Camp David. And when Arafat would not make the capitulation that Clinton and Barak wanted, Tenet threatened Arafat. Tenet said: "So you will go back to the Middle East alone." He meant that Arafat would not have the support of the CIA. And Arafat replied: "If this is the case, you are most welcome to come to my funeral—but I won't accept your offers."

Round us, the flies and birds moved through the hot trees. Arafat's grey-haired factotum chewed his way through a mandarin, the juice dribbling down his chin, occasionally taking calls on his mobile phone as his two sons picked olives off a tree behind us. "You have to understand that . . . the worst is yet to come," he said. "We may have a few days of less trouble. But that is all. We know how to start things and we don't know where it will end. But we believe that if it lasts longer, the results will be better. Nobody knows how the mechanism of war develops." He felt more comfortable with the "sacred" right of return of refugees—perhaps a symbolic 100,000 in ten years, he suggested—and with the influence of his boss. "At the start, we advised the Israelis that they had no partners for peace except Arafat. Yes, he controls Palestine. But if Barak controls the Israeli army, why doesn't he control the Jewish settlers who are on the loose with guns?" I mentioned Oslo. "It died with Rabin," he replied.

At Karni, Arafat's officer had ordered restraint. A flock of police captains swept their arms in front of the crowd of youths halfway down the road. "Go back up there," they shouted. There was a momentary movement in the crowd; then the policemen were ignored. About 400 youths stood on the narrow road and advanced together in a mass, shoulder to shoulder, almost falling off the edge of the track, offering the Israelis a target they could not miss, seeking that very "martyrdom" that the Israelis—and most of us—could not understand. It was an extraordinary scene. A group had unified without a word of command for a commonly understood goal. They wanted to be targets. The Israelis obliged. A cluster of teargas canisters failed to shift the crowd; a single live round fired into the pack of people did the trick. There were shouts and a stretcher bobbing through the screaming youths and an ambulance driving through the dust for the Shifa hospital.

Yet behind us, at the top of the road, a man was selling orange ices and bread filled with thyme for the tired stone-throwers and black-uniformed policemen. The television crews were standing there in their spaceman blue flak jackets and helmets, along with ambulance crews and truck-drivers and families from the concrete hovels across the highway. Anyone can turn up in Gaza to watch tragedy and farce. This is Shakespeare, Scott Fitzgerald and pantomime rolled into one, revenge and vaudeville. No wonder, I think as I drive back to Jerusalem, that Palestinian poetry is so bitter. "All I possess in the presence of death/Is pride and fury," wrote Mahmoud Darwish.

No one understands this better than Hanan Ashrawi. She bursts into her Ramallah home with an energy born of total exhaustion, jet-lagged, angry, scornful of Israel and Western journalists in about equal measure, complaining of toothache, wolfing through chicken, potatoes and hot peppers, her white cat Labneh watching aloofly from the carpet. The future will be difficult. "It's not just 'the dark night of the soul' when you have the resurgence of hostilities and a loss of faith in the 'peace process,' " she says. Oslo is dead. That is what she means. Only UN resolutions are left.

Palestine's most famous woman—with the exception of Yassir Arafat, Palestine's most famous citizen—has just returned from lecturing American universities on the catastrophe now befalling her people, trying to persuade the Gore and Bush foreign policy teams in this American election month to comprehend the realities of the Middle East, condemning the powerful American press for its biased reporting of the new Israeli–Palestinian conflict. A member of the original 1991 Madrid Palestinian team, Ashrawi's job as an English literature don allows her to speak with unique eloquence and contempt. Outside, a November gale buffets her villa, the wind moving the trees in the small back garden.

When I ask if it's all over for Oslo, she nods. When I ask if the UN's Security Council Resolution 242 is now the only possible peace, she nods twice more, between gulps of tabouleh and rice. When I ask if that means the closing down of all Jewish settlements on occupied Arab land and the return of East Jerusalem, her voice sharpens. "All the settlements will have to go—the moment you accept otherwise, you have legitimised the acquisition of territory by force. The basis of Oslo was 242 . . . but Oslo violated that. It reinterpreted 242. The Israelis never respected any of the Oslo withdrawal timetable. What is happening now is a result of Oslo. We've been saying this would happen, we've been warning this would happen, that there would be an implosion or explosion. And now we're proven right, it's too late and there's a tragic loss of life."

To listen now to Hanan Ashrawi—a voice of moderation and humanity—is to experience the historical shock of what has happened in the Middle East these past six weeks. "The Palestinian people feel victimised by this 'peace process,' " she says angrily. "The 'process' is reinvented all the time to suit Israel. And America thinks all the time that as long as there is a 'process,' God is in his heaven. Now the Americans are indulging in crisis management and individual legacies—the people involved in Washington have come to the end of their careers."*

*Less than two weeks later, Ashrawi will write an open letter to President Bill Clinton. "It has been our experience, Mr. President, that most American public officials, once out of office, begin to suffer pangs of conscience and inexplicable urges to express contrition in the form of public confessions pertaining to the injustice suffered by the Palestinian people. With an honest desire to spare you the fate of other high officials who develop after-the-fact immaculate hindsight and a drive for justice, I would like to point out that there is still world enough and time to speak out—better yet, to *act* now." Ashrawi knew Clinton would not do so. What she could not have known was that, when he did "speak out" once he was no longer president, he would blame the Palestinians.

It's also clear that Ashrawi would like the careers of several reporters to come to an end. "When I visited *The Washington Post*, I asked them what had happened to the idea of journalistic integrity. There's now a total disjunction between the pictures of what is happening—the Palestinian casualties—and the language; this is the product of America's processed language and the Israeli spin machine." Ashrawi leans back on the sofa in exhaustion. "Now we are all being fed well-worn phrases: 'peace process,' 'back on track,' 'ceasefire,' 'time out,' 'put an end to violence,' 'Arafat to restrain/control his people,' 'do we have the right peace partner?' This is a racist way of looking at the Palestinians and it obscures the fact that we've suffered an Israeli occupation all along. When newspapers ask if Palestinians deliberately sacrifice their children, it's an incredibly racist thing to do. They are dehumanising the Palestinians. The press and the Israelis have rid us of the most elemental human feelings in a very cynical, racist discourse that blames the victims. Of course we love our children. Even animals care about their children."

The phone rings—it's like a clock chime in the Ashrawi home in Ramallah, the chirruping of the mobile, the repeated, tiring explanation of why Oslo does not work—and only after a minute of silence can she continue. "I always said Oslo could lead to a disaster or a state. It's not an agreement, remember. It says specifically that it is a 'declaration of principles.' The danger was always that the 'peace of the brave' could turn into the 'peace of the grave.' " The new intifada will continue—"in different shapes, different forms"—Ashrawi says. "We are not fond of mass suicide, but we want the right to resist occupation and injustice. Then the moment we say 'resist,' the Israelis pull out the word 'terrorist'—so a child with a stone becomes the 'legitimate' target for Israeli sniper fire and a high-velocity bullet."

On the floor, Labneh is purring. The food is gone. Ashrawi has almost fallen asleep. The television news announces two more Palestinians killed by Israeli bullets. In the first month of the new intifada, a hundred Palestinians, including twenty-seven children, were killed by Israeli soldiers and border police. But the most alarming statistic is the contrast between the losses of the two sides. By 2002, 1,450 Palestinians will have been killed in the al-Aqsa intifada. Israel will have lost 525 lives, just over a third of the Palestinian death toll. And the Palestinians are the aggressors.

# CHAPTER THIRTEEN

# The Girl and the Child and Love

*Blood and destruction shall be so in use,*
*And dreadful objects so familiar,*
*That mothers shall but smile when they behold*
*Their infants quarter'd with the hands of war,*
*All pity chok'd with custom of fell deeds.*

—Shakespeare, *Julius Caesar*, III, i, 265–72

WHENEVER AMIRA HASS TRIES to explain her vocation as an Israeli journalist—as a journalist of any nationality—she recalls a seminal moment in her mother's life. Hannah Hass was being marched from a cattle train to the concentration camp of Bergen-Belsen on a summer's day in 1944. "She and the other women had been ten days in the train from Yugoslavia. They were sick and some were dying by the road. Then my mother saw these German women looking at the prisoners, just looking. This image became very formative in my upbringing, this despicable 'looking from the side.' It's as if I was there and saw it myself." Amira Hass stares at me through wire-framed glasses as she speaks, to see if I have understood the Jewish Holocaust in her life.

In her evocative book *Drinking the Sea at Gaza*, Hass eloquently explains why she, an Israeli journalist, went to live in Yassir Arafat's garbage-strewn statelet. "In the end," she wrote:

> my desire to live in Gaza stemmed neither from adventurism nor from insanity, but from that dread of being a bystander, from my need to understand, down to the last detail, a world that is—to the best of my political and historical comprehension—a profoundly Israeli creation. To me, Gaza embodies the entire saga of the Israeli–Palestinian conflict; it represents the central contradiction of the state of Israel—democracy for some, dispossession for others; it is our exposed nerve.

It is the summer of 2001. Amira Hass is sitting on the windowsill of my colleague Phil Reeves's home in Jerusalem and behind her the burnished dome of the Al-Aqsa mosque glitters in the sunlight. Yet she lives not in Jerusalem but in Ramallah—with the Palestinians whom many of her people regard as "terrorists," listening to the Palestinian curses heaped upon "the Jews" for their confiscations and dispossessions and murder squads and settlements—which makes her among the bravest of reporters. Her daily column in *Ha'aretz* blazes with indignation at the way her own country, Israel, is mistreating and killing the Palestinians. Only when I meet her, however, do I realise the intensity—the passion—of her work. "There is a misconception that journalists can be objective," she tells me, the same sharp glance to ensure my comprehension. "Palestinians tell me I'm objective. I think this is important because I'm an Israeli. But being fair and being objective are not the same thing. What journalism is really about—it's to monitor power and the centres of power."

If only, I kept thinking, the American journalists who report in so craven a fashion from the Middle East—so fearful of Israeli criticism that they turn Israeli murder into "targeted attacks" and illegal settlements into "Jewish neighborhoods"—could listen to Amira Hass. She writes each day an essay about despair, a chronological narrative that she does not abandon when talking about her own life. She begins at the beginning, her mother a Sarajevo Jew who joined Tito's partisans, who was forced to surrender to the Nazis when they threatened to kill every woman in the Montenegrin town of Cetinje, her father Avraham spending four years in the Transnistria ghetto in the Ukraine, escaping a plague of typhus that killed up to 50 per cent of the Jews, only to lose his toes to frostbite.

"When he came to Israel as a communist activist after the war, he was involved in lots of strikes and demonstrations. In the early Fifties, the Israeli police arrested him and he was brought before a judge who demanded to know why he'd refused to give his fingerprints. My father put his feet without toes on the desk of His Honour the Judge and said: 'I have already given my fingerprints.' " Avraham, Amira Hass says, combined a strong Jewish and secular identity; he was a socialist but never a Zionist.

The story of Hannah and Avraham is essential to an understanding of Amira. They fought for their right to be equal in the Jewish diaspora and had wanted to stay in the lands of Europe which had turned into mass graves. "Many of these people returned to their countries after the war—and the inhabitants there accepted the ordeal of the Jews far too easily. My mother went back to Belgrade as part of [Milovan] Djilas's [communist] group. It was a new regime in Yugoslavia. But when she went to register as a citizen of Belgrade, the woman clerk said: 'But you emigrated.' You see, the Germans had deported her and they always officially recorded that their deportees had 'emigrated.' The clerk took the Germans at their word." It was a common experience. Amid total destruction—in which entire families had been extinguished by the Nazis—the vacuum created by the Jewish Holocaust was too much to bear.

"My parents came here to Israel naively. They were offered a house in Jerusalem. But they refused it. They said: 'We cannot take the house of other refugees.' They meant Palestinians. So you see, it's not such a big deal that I live among Palestinians." Hass became a journalist by default. She had survived on odd jobs—she once worked as a cleaner—and travelled to Holland. "I sensed there the absence of Jewish existence. And this told me many things, especially about my attitude to Israel, how not to be a Zionist. This is my place, Israel, the language, the people, the culture, the colours . . . "

Hass dropped out of the Hebrew University where she was researching the history of Nazism and the attitude of the European left to the Jewish Holocaust. "I was stuck. The first intifada broke out and I didn't want to sit in academia while all this was happening. I used *wasta*—you know that Arabic word?—to get a copyediting job on the *Ha'aretz* newsdesk in '89." *Wasta* means "pull" or "influence." *Ha'aretz* is a liberal, free-thinking paper, the nearest Israel has to *The Independent*. When the Romanian revolution broke out, Hass pleaded to be sent to cover the story—she had many contacts from a visit to Bucharest in 1977—and much to her surprise, *Ha'aretz* agreed, even though she'd only been three months with the paper.

"When I'd gone to Romania before, I felt I had this philosophical responsibility to taste life under this socialist regime. It was a thousand times worse than I imagined. There was this terrible pressure—life under Israeli occupation is not as bad as life under Ceausescu's Romania. It was unbelievable suffocation. So I covered the revolution for two weeks and then went back to the paper. *Ha'aretz* didn't know if I could write—I knew I could. But I also knew never to look for what all the other journalists are looking for."

In 1990, with her parents' support, she joined a group called "Workers' Hotline," which assisted Palestinians who were cheated by their Israeli employers. "During the Gulf War, I reached Gaza under curfew—I'd gone to give Palestinians their cheques from Israeli employers. That's when my romance with Gaza started. No Israeli journalist knew or covered Gaza. My editor was very sympathetic. When in 1993 the 'peace process' broke out"—Hass requests the inverted commas round the phrase—"*Ha'aretz* suggested I cover Gaza. One of the editors said: 'We don't want you to live in Gaza.' And I knew at once that I wanted to live there."

From the start, Hass recalls, there was "something very warm about the Palestinian attitude—there was a lot of humour and self-humour in these harsh conditions." When I suggest that this might be something she had recognised in Jews, Hass immediately agrees. "Of course. I'm an east European Jew and the life of the *shtetl* is inbuilt in me. And I guess I found in Gaza a *shtetl*. I remember finding refugees from Jabaliya camp, sitting on a beach, looking at the waves. I asked them what they were doing. And one said he was 'waiting to be forty years old'— so he'd be old enough to get a permit to work in Israel. This was a very Jewish joke."

But Hass found no humour in the Israeli policy of "closure," of besieging Palestinian towns and throttling their economy and people. "I spotted as early as 1991 that the policy of 'closure' was a very clever step by the Israeli occupation system, a kind of pre-emptive strike. The way it debilitates any kind of Palestinian action and reaction is amazing. 'Closure' was also a goal: a demographic separation which means that Jews have the right to move about the space of mandatory Palestine. The 'closure' policy brought this to a real perfection."

Hass found herself fascinated with the difference between Palestinian image and reality. "Their towns were being portrayed in the Israeli press as a 'nest of hornets.' But I really wanted to taste what it means to live under occupation—what it is like to live under curfew, to live in fear of a soldier. I wanted to know what it was like to be an Israeli under Israeli occupation." She has used that word "taste" again, just as she did about Romania under dictatorship. She says she was still thinking about her mother's trip to Belsen. "It was this idea of not intervening, not changing anything. And luckily, this combined in me with journalism." Hass is possessed of the idea that change can only come through social movements and their interaction with the press—an odd notion that seems a little illogical.

But there is nothing vague about her vocation. "Israel is obviously the centre of power which dictates Palestinian life. As an Israeli, my task as a journalist is to monitor power. I'm called 'a correspondent on Palestinian affairs' but it's more true to say that I'm an expert in Israeli occupation." Israeli reaction, she says, is very violent towards her. "I get messages saying I must have been a *kapo* [a Jewish death-camp overseer for the Nazis] in my first incarnation. Then I'll get an email saying: 'Bravo, you have written a great article—Heil Hitler!' Someone told me they hoped I had breast cancer. 'Until we expel all Palestinians, there will be no peace,' some of them say. I can't reply to them—there are thousands of these messages."

But many Israelis tell Amira Hass to keep writing. "People misled themselves into believing that Oslo was a peace process—so they became very angry with the Palestinians. Part of their anger is directed at me. Israelis do not go to the occupied territories. They do not see with their own eyes. They don't see a Palestinian village with a settler on its land and a village that has no water and needs government permission even to plant a tree, let alone build a new school. People don't understand how the dispersal of Jewish settlements dictates Israeli control over Palestinian territory."

As her mother lay dying in the spring of 2001, Amira Hass was fearful that she would be trapped by the Israeli siege of Ramallah—where she still lives—and spent hours commuting the few miles to Jerusalem to be with her. Now she is alone. The woman who taught her to despise those who were "looking from the side" died just two months before we met. Yet for journalists who try to tell the truth about the world's last colonial war, Hass remains an inspiration. She lectures in America, turns up on countless radio talk shows and interviews, her inexhaustible reporting ever more astute and passionate. How typical that it should be a Jewish woman who writes more eloquently than any other reporter about the Palestinians. How admirable that it should be a Jewish woman, an older but equally committed New York Jew, who can fight for justice for the Lebanese civilians whose lives were destroyed in Israel's "Grapes of Wrath" bombardment of southern Lebanon in 1996, whose own research work into the Qana massacre should be far superior to anything written by an Arab author.

When Eva Stern's grandfather Aaron Hersh climbed off the transport at Auschwitz extermination camp in 1944, along with her mother Hannah and two aunts from their ultra-orthodox Jewish family, he was still holding his prayer shawl. "A Polish prisoner warned him he'd die if he didn't hand it over, but he refused," Eva Stern says. "Then a German officer ordered my grandfather to give the shawl to him while he was waiting in line for selection for the gas chambers. He again refused. So he shot my grandfather in the head. That's how he died."

In the warmth of a Manhattan hotel lobby, Stern speaks quickly, in an almost subdued voice, recalling the terrible story which her mother told her of the family's journey from Czechoslovakia to Auschwitz. "She was only seventeen and tried to save one of her sister's children by holding it in her arms. But another prisoner snatched it away and gave it back to her sister—because they would all die if Mengele saw both women with a child. So her sister and her children were all selected to die. And my mother lived. At least seventy members of her family were murdered. She was taken to Ravensbruck concentration camp and was eventually liberated by the Red Army. The incident with the child had the greatest impact on her. I can honestly say that my mother hasn't slept for fifty years." But it is the death of her grandfather Aaron Hersh—a Talmudic scholar by the age of twenty who was shot after refusing to surrender his *tallit*—that has marked Eva Stern's life.

With anger painfully suppressed, she opens a thick file on the seat beside her. Entitled *Israel's Operation "Grapes of Wrath" and the Qana Massacre*, it is her own work, a compilation of news reports and photographs of Israel's 1996 bombardment in which more than 170 civilians were killed, 106 of them at Qana, 55 of them children. Stern flicks her finger in fury at one of the pictures; it shows Israeli soldiers standing in front of their battle tanks on the Lebanese border. The caption reads: "Israeli soldiers briefly halt their shelling to commemorate Holocaust Day." And Stern looks at me so that I can see the extent of her fury.

"What would my grandfather say of this?" she asks. "What were those Israelis *thinking* as they were putting on their prayer shawls? Were they praying: 'Father who art in heaven, help me to kill as many *Arabushim* as possible'? Do they now have a right to kill without any guilt?" *Arabushim*—a racist term for Arabs in the Hebrew language—was later used in an Israeli newspaper interview by one of the artillerymen who fired into the UN base at Qana. Stern has included an English translation of the interview from *Kol Ha'ir* in her file, a set of documents that she has sent to the UN, to the Lebanese delegation to the UN, and to the most prominent American journalists in New York. She hoped to persuade the latter to mark the first anniversary of the Qana massacre. Her sense of outrage is as brave as it is lonely; although many American Jews are troubled by the behaviour of Israel's right-wing government and the bloody adventures in which Israel has been involved in Lebanon and in "Palestine," most do not take kindly to Stern's concern for the truth to be told. But she is unremitting:

> My feelings started slowly. I always had a problem with unquestioned obedience to authority—that's why I always got into trouble in class. And when I thought about the atrocities committed by the Israelis, I felt that as an American taxpayer and an American Jew, I had an obligation to speak out. If ordinary Germans living under total oppression can be held respon-

sible for the crimes committed by the Nazis—because they did not speak out—how much more responsible are we who live in a country where we have the freedom to speak out? If ordinary Germans were guilty for not speaking out, then surely we are also guilty in remaining silent about Qana. Because we don't live in fear of death squads. What I am doing is not courageous—it is the decent thing to do. If enough decent Germans had spoken out at the time, perhaps the Holocaust would not have happened. I'm not saying that the level of atrocities committed by the Israelis is on the same scale or in any way comparable to those of the Nazis. Of course not. But I know that I have paid as a taxpayer for the shells that rained down on Qana. And therefore if I'm silent, I'm no better than those Germans. Israel claims to be the representative of the Jewish people. It's important for people to know that they clearly do not speak for world Jewry. They clearly do not speak for me. So I have a duty to speak out.

A secretary in a Manhattan corporate law firm—she was educated in an ultra-orthodox Brooklyn girls' school—Eva Stern was encouraged in her campaign by Noam Chomsky, that most irascible and brilliant of America's philosophers and linguists, and by the work of former Warsaw Ghetto survivor Israel Shahak, whose history of Israel she quotes by heart. "He wrote that 'any support of human rights in general by a Jew which does not include the support of human rights of non-Jews whose rights are being violated by the "Jewish state" is as deceitful as the support of human rights by a Stalinist.' That really influenced me."

Stern's father, Chaim, was a Hungarian Jew who also survived the concentration camps. "My mother was his cousin and he married her in 1949. I was born seven years later. My parents are still alive and know my feelings about Israeli atrocities. They are sort of ambivalent about it. They believe I'm right in condemning it. But because of what they went through, they believe all the world is anti-Semitic. So when there's a terrorist attack against the Israelis, they are unable to see it in the context of the Arab–Israeli dispute. I strongly condemn any terrorist attack. But my parents see it in terms of 'the Arabs are anti-Semitic and that's why there's a terrorist attack.' I refuse to condemn my parents for these feelings. They see all Germans, for example, as Nazis—because in their experience, they only met Nazis. And for most Palestinians, the only Jews they know of are the oppressors. The Palestinians in the refugee camps . . . probably never met a decent, moral Jew."

But Eva Stern's attempt to persuade American journalists to mark the anniversary of the Qana slaughter met with little more than indifference. Not a single major mainstream American newspaper carried a paragraph—not even a brief news report—on the UN-attended ceremony held in Lebanon to mark the first anniversary of the bloodbath. Unlike Eva Stern, American journalists remained silent. So did her bosses. The house magazine of her Manhattan corporate law firm encourages employees to write about their interests and out-of-hours work. Stern wrote a passionate account of her inquiries into Qana—and into the 1982 massacre

of Palestinians at Sabra and Chatila. An official of the firm later declined to publish her article—on the grounds that it was "sensitive" and "might be misunder-
stood."

Not long after I met Eva Stern, a letter arrived in my mail in Beirut from Nezar
Hindawi. Remember the name? Hindawi was the Palestinian who on 17 April
1986 gave his unsuspecting and pregnant Irish girlfriend Anne-Marie Murphy a
bomb to take on board an El Al jet at London Heathrow Airport. The 1.5 kilograms
of Semtex would have destroyed the aircraft, killing all on board, including the
young chambermaid who fondly believed that Hindawi would be arriving in Israel
a few days later to marry her. After seeking the protection of Syrian security men
in London, he decided to give himself up. At the Old Bailey six months later,
he was given forty-five years in prison, the longest sentence in British criminal
history.

Which is why his letter to me carried the address of Her Majesty's Prison
Whitemoor in Cambridgeshire. It was polite but carried a persistent message: if
IRA killers imprisoned for "political" crimes could be freed, then he—Nezar
Hindawi—should also be released. In his poor English, he wrote: "My case is a
political as you know, no one will go to blow up an aircraft for personal matter. I
do believe that if it was not an Israeli aircraft and not in UK I would not have that
sentenced which it is the longest in UK's recent history." The first problem for me
in Hindawi's letter was not political. Many IRA men—and Protestant paramilitary
killers—in Northern Ireland discovered, after years in prison, a profound sense of
unease and contrition for the terrible deeds they committed. Even old Gusty
Spence, the first of "Loyalism"'s sinister murderers, came out of Long Kesh a
born-again Christian. Yet not a hint of remorse did I find in Hindawi's letter to me,
not a single tiny clue that he might feel sorry for what he had tried to do. The
clause "no one will go to blow up an aircraft for personal matter" was chilling, I
was to write in *The Independent*, his "categorisation of evil" quite clear. It would
be unforgivable for him to blow up a plane for "personal" reasons—if, I suppose,
he hated the passengers—but not, it appears, for political reasons if the passengers,
even his pregnant girlfriend Anne-Marie Murphy, were of no personal interest.

Referring to his own case as "history," Hindawi continued:

> The PLO and Israel made a peace deal with Jordan. Even the relation
> between Syria and UK is in its best in all aspects . . . look what happened
> after the peace deal in N. Ireland, the British Government transferred all
> IRA prisoners to N. Ireland and lots of them been released . . . I wrote to
> the Prime Minister Tony Blair, Jack Straw, Robben [*sic*] Cook, Ken Living-
> stone MP, Tony Benn MP, D. Skinner MP and others asking them to release
> me . . . I have not reply yet.

Nor was I surprised. For an Irish peace which a majority of people in both
Britain and Ireland support, the old Thatcherite policy of criminalising all villains
was abandoned. There were child-killers, wife-murderers, mafia murderers and hit

men—who must stay in prison—and "political" killers, "political" murderers and "political" hit men who were now going home. Like it or not, that's how most wars end. There's a kind of crossing-off of sin. The men we have dubbed "terrorists"— Jomo Kenyatta, Menachem Begin, Archbishop Makarios, Gerry Adams and, yes, Yassir Arafat—have an odd habit of turning up for talks at Downing Street and tea with Queen Elizabeth, or chats in the White House.

But where does that leave prisoners from other wars? In theory, the PLO–Israeli peace could have had some effect on Hindawi. But the peace was now dead and Hindawi wrote—though somewhat obliquely—that he thought he was working for the Syrians.* I didn't respond directly to him. But I wrote an article about his letter in which I said I wanted "to know a bit more about the real Nezar Hindawi"—and how a man—whomever he thought he was working for—could hand a bomb to the young girl who loved him, the woman who carried his child, knowing that it represented their doom and that of all those with her. I sent Hindawi a copy of the article. More than three months later, I received another letter from him. It was both angry and agitated, written from the depths of historical indignation. Although crippled by his English, Hindawi made a metaphorical attempt to reconstruct the betrayals of the Middle East—in which he flagellated himself as the instrument of "terrorism," inviting Britain and France to take up their mandates and create the state of Israel:

I thought it may be good for you to know "a bit more about the real Nezar Hindawi" . . . it seems to me that you have not found that "bit" . . . I am Nezar Hindawi who invited the EMPERORS of England and France to Arabia—Middle East—to slice the CAKE and to teach the Arab how to play Cricket. But the most important point for the invitation was to found or to fill "a Land without a people for a people without a Land." So, the Emperor of England brought from Europ "a people without a land for a Land without a people" as I request. For that "people" I gave them that slice of the cake and they named it "Israel." Free of charge. But the cricket game [is] still on. It is so long. It need time to end. The referee went away

---

*He certainly took refuge at the London home of Syrian security men. Hindawi signed a statement for police, saying he had been given the bag containing the bomb by an officer working for General Mohamed el-Khouly, the head of Syrian air force intelligence. In court, Hindawi retracted this statement, claiming he had been forced to sign it unread and believed he was part of a conspiracy by Israeli agents to damage Syria. He was convicted and Britain broke off relations with Damascus. Israel condemned "Syria's central role in terrorism," though I do remember a strange incident a few days later when I met the outgoing British ambassador to Syria in the VIP lounge at Damascus airport. There was some evidence, he said, that the Israelis "knew the bomb was being brought to Heathrow." He would say no more. Had the Israelis learned of the bomb by tapping Syrian embassy phones? Had they been tipped off by British security? Had they encouraged the Syrians to involve themselves in a bomb plot? No Israeli government would bomb its own aircraft. But if they knew about it in advance, the Israelis could, once the bomb arrived at Heathrow, arrest Anne-Marie Murphy and end up "proving" that Syria was a "centre of international terror."

for good. Do you think he may come to stop the game? That game, I am the founder of it. I am Nezar Hindawi, the founder of and the head of the HAGANAH, IRGUN, STERN GANG the terrorist organisations and by my direct orders, unleashed a campaign of terror and violence that deliberately targeted only civilians . . . I ordered the blowing up of the King David Hotel in Jerusalem which resulted in the death of about 90 British. I . . . ordered the invasion of Lebanon and West Beirut and did the Massacres at Sabra and Chatila Camps . . . Some more information for you, Dear Mr. Robert Fisk about Nezar Hindawi and his evil works, I am Nezar Hindawi responsible for killing, tortures and the disappearance of more than 4,000 people in Chile, NOT General Augusto Pinochet. I am the responsible of keeping the sanctions on Iraq . . . Now you may undestand Nezar Hindawi and his evil works.

My use of the word "evil"—before its meaning had been contaminated by George W. Bush—had riled Hindawi. But there was no doubting the meaning of his letter. Little criminals like Hindawi were locked up for forty-five years. Big criminals—Menachem Begin, Pinochet, Britain and France in their long colonial histories—get away with murder. There was a section of his handwritten letter in which he praised "Greater Syria," the Ottoman province which included Jordan, Palestine and present-day Syria—*Asham—Biladu Asham*—which existed in the "days before I send the invitation to the Emperors of England and France . . . "
He wrote that he was proud of his "love" for Syria.

I [was] just born in Part of Syria which [is] called Jordan. But does Jordan make a state? Is it really a state? It is part of Syria and one time it must return to its Mother, to its heart, to Syria, that is [a] tru [*sic*] fact and you may see it in your time . . . I have a great bright history I am so proud of it. I do not want to write about personal things, this belongs to me only, also this is why I do not want to reply to what you wrote about the girl and the child and love . . . I regard these things as something personal, once the time will allow me to say about this things [*sic*], make sure you will be one of whom will I tell them . . .

Hindawi ended by expressing his "love" for President Hafez el-Assad of Syria.
There is much more I would like to know about this case, not least why Hindawi's defence lawyer, Gilbert Gray QC, argued at his 1986 trial that "another nation may take retribution" if Hindawi was convicted—a remark which Sir William Mars-Jones, who sentenced the accused to forty-five years, said "should never have been made." Was this "nation" supposed to be Syria? A psychologist might also have much to say about Hindawi's refusal to discuss "the girl and the child and love" because that, surely, is what this whole drama revolves around. Hindawi will confront the political tragedy of the Middle East—and the hypocrisy of a world that will sentence lesser would-be murderers to forty-five years but

allow those held responsible for mass murder to go free—but not the immediate and all too relevant issue of his own moral conscience. Yes, I am waiting for Hindawi to tell me about "the girl and the child and love." And so, too, is Anne-Marie Murphy who, eighteen years after Hindawi tried to smuggle her and her unborn child onto the El Al flight at Heathrow with a bomb, gave her first newspaper interview to complain that Hindawi had been granted legal aid to demand a parole board review of his sentence:

> That man is pure unadulterated evil. You are talking about someone who has never shown a flicker of remorse or once said "sorry" . . . What about the human rights of all the people on that plane he was trying to murder? He held me in his arms and kissed me on both cheeks. The next time I saw him, he said we would be getting married. With that he smiled and stood there waving goodbye . . . He carried this bag all the way to the airport and then give [sic] it to me as I was about to go through. He left me at Terminal One because he said his flight was going from Terminal Three. I remember going past the sniffer dogs and two security check points before a guard asked me to step aside for a moment. Then when they opened the bag and looked inside my whole world fell apart.

If I was to enter Hindawi's mind—I am not sure I want to, and I await more letters from Whitemoor prison on this matter—would I not find the same logic as that employed by Yigal Amir, Rabin's killer, who could quote the Book of Joshua to justify how "if I was conquering the land, I would have to kill babies and children"? Is this not the same rationality—or lack of it—that allows a Palestinian suicide bomber to see his or her victims before the switch is pressed and the explosives detonated? The suicide bomber eliminates their own life but has the fearful privilege of looking at the future dead, the soldiers or—let us speak frankly—the Israeli children in the pizzeria or the girls on the bus who are about to be eliminated from the world. The Israelis and the White House tried to diminish the self-destructive element of suicide bombers by fatuously calling them "homicide bombers," which is ridiculous; all bombers, suicidal or otherwise, are homicidal. The difference is that the suicide bomber not only takes their own life—and thus becomes a "martyr" for Palestinian groups—but is an executioner. They see those about to die. They hold in their hands, however briefly, the life and death of innocents. Whether they press the button is their choice. Hindawi, of course, was not planning to press any buttons. Anne-Marie Murphy was going to be the button. And history—if we are to believe his letters to me—was the detonator.

I AM STANDING IN THE DUST and rubble of Khan Younis Palestinian refugee camp at the beginning of that year of 2001. April 15, it says in my notebook, along with the words: "In any other place, it would be a scandal, an outrage." If Palestinians had wilfully destroyed the homes of 200 Israelis, I wrote in my report to *The*

*Independent* that night, there would be talk of barbarism, of "terrorism," grave warnings to Arafat from the new American president, George W. Bush, to "curb violence." But it was the Israelis who destroyed the homes of at least 200 Palestinians in Gaza on that Easter Sunday morning of 2001, bulldozing their furniture, clothes, cookers, carpets and mattresses into the powdered concrete of their hovels until one end of Khan Younis looked as though it had been hit by an earthquake. So of course it was not "terrorism." It was "security."

The old sat like statues amid the rubbish tip that the Israelis had made of their houses. Many of them, like seventy-five-year-old Ahmed Hassan Abu Radwan, had been driven from their homes in Palestine—in his case from Beersheba—in 1948; now they were dispossessed by the same people for the second time in fifty-three years, this time courtesy of Ariel Sharon. Maybe it is impossible to shame history. What happened in Khan Younis—however the Israelis dress up their vandalism with talk of "security"—was a disgrace. This was house destruction—no, let us call it "home destruction"—on a hitherto unprecedented scale as a battery of bulldozers was sent to pulverise this part of Khan Younis above the sea from where—according to the Israeli army—shots had been directed at their occupying soldiers. As the machines careered up the road from the coast just after midnight, thousands of Palestinians ran screaming from their huts and concrete shelters.

Many of them fled to the nearest mosque, where they seized the loudspeakers and appealed to their neighbours "to take arms and resist." To the apparent surprise of the Israeli army, that is just what their neighbours did. As Palestinian rifles were turned on the bulldozers, at least two Israeli tanks raced up the same road and began firing shells into the nearest apartment blocks. An Apache helicopter gunship appeared out of the darkness, launching missiles into the same buildings. And as old Ahmed Hassan Abu Radwan and his family remember all too clearly, a crane suddenly moved out of the darkness, a platoon of Israeli soldiers in the bucket from where—once the crane's chain had hauled the container to its highest point—the troops opened fire.

The gun battle lasted for four hours and left two Palestinians dead and thirty wounded, twelve of them critically, among them a Reuters camera crew who were filming it when a shell exploded against the wall behind which they were standing. Ariel Sharon, the biggest bulldozer of them all, had taught the Palestinians another lesson. But picking one's way through the muck and dust of thirty-five houses, it didn't take long to realise that the lesson they had grasped was not quite the one Israel had intended. Mariam Abu Radwan, a cousin of old Ahmed, put it eloquently: "We have no life any more. This is the destruction of our life. Let them shoot us—please let them shoot us—and we can die here. And let the Israelis die too. No one is looking after us—no Arab countries, no foreign countries either."

One of the dead was Riad Elias, a Palestinian security forces officer—who was presumably fighting the Israelis when he died—but the second, Hani Rizk, was identified to me as a cleaner at the local Naser Hospital, the same hospital to which his body was taken before his funeral that Sunday afternoon. Ibrahim Amer, a thirty-five-year-old agricultural worker who says he was hit in the back and side by machine-gun bullets from the helicopter as he ran—he now lay in blood-soaked pain in one of the hospital's beds—saw Rizk running in the street "when a spray of bullets from the helicopter ricocheted against a wall and hit him—he had at least twelve bullets in his body." Had Palestinians been shooting at the Israelis from these houses? Ask anyone amid the rubble and they would invariably say that they "never saw anyone"; which is not quite the same as saying that no one ever fired from here. But this was more than disproportionate; the Israeli operation was a deliberate attack on civilians.

Ahmed Hassan Abu Radwan, like many of his cousins, was a Bedouin farmer when the Israelis advanced towards his Beersheba home in 1948 where he lived with his father Hassan, his mother Shema and his four brothers. Since then he has lived in poverty in Khan Younis and was sleeping in his seven-room complex of hovel-huts with his wife Fatma and their twenty-three children and grandchildren when he heard the Israeli bulldozers. "What has happened to me now was what happened to me fifty years ago," he said. "I feel a kind of madness. Peace now? I don't think so. The Jews gave us many words but they don't keep their word."

As usual, shots were fired into the air at the two funerals that Sunday afternoon. Just three hours earlier, Wail Hawatir, a Palestinian military doctor, was buried, victim of the previous night's helicopter attack on what the Israelis called a "Palestinian naval base"—the Palestinians, of course, have no navy and no ships—so the day began and ended in familiar Gaza fashion: with funerals. Needless to say, Mr. Bush was silent.

As both he and Clinton were silent while Israel perfected its system of executions against Palestinians deemed worthy of death for their role in Hamas or Islamic Jihad or any other organisation which opposed Israeli occupation of the West Bank or Gaza. There was nothing new in this campaign of extrajudicial executions. When the Israelis came for Arafat's lieutenant, Abu Jihad—Khaled al-Wazzir—in Tunis in 1988, they employed up to 4,000 men for the assassination. There was an AWACS plane over Tunis, two warships in the Mediterranean, a Boeing 707 refuelling aircraft, forty men to go ashore and surround the home of Arafat's PLO deputy commander, and four men and an officer to murder their victim.

Abu Jihad's son Jihad al-Wazzir, now living through the second intifada inside Gaza, recalled for me in detail how his father was executed. "First they killed the bodyguard who was asleep in the car outside—then they killed the gardener and the second bodyguard. My dad was writing in his office and went into the hall with a pistol. He got off one shot before he was hit. My mother remembers how each of the four men would step forward and empty an entire clip of bullets from an automatic weapon into my dad—like it was a kind of ritual. Then an officer in a black mask stepped forward and shot him in the head, just to make sure."

Now Israel's murder squads come cheaper: a computer chip that activates a bomb in a mobile telephone, a family collaborator, a splash of infrared on the roof of a car to alert an Israeli Apache pilot to fire a Hellfire missile into the Palestinian's vehicle. It's long-range assassination. It is an internationally illegal war in which the Palestinians have themselves been guilty in the past. Back in the 1970s, Israeli and PLO agents murdered each other in Europe in a policy of retaliation and counter-retaliation that enraged European security forces. In Beirut, two of the Israelis involved in murdering Palestinian leaders were called Ehud Barak and Amnon Shahak. Shahak would later become Israeli military commander in Lebanon in 1982. It was Barak who, as prime minister, relaunched Israel's murder squads.

Hamas and Islamic Jihad have their own murderers; their suicide bombs slaughter civilians as well as soldiers, hitherto unknown victims rather than individual Israeli intelligence officers. But Israel's killers take innocent lives too. A helicopter attack on a Palestinian militant in 2001 tore two middle-aged Palestinian women to pieces; the Israelis did not apologise. The nephew of a man murdered by the Israelis in Nablus later admitted to the Palestinian Authority that he had given his uncle's location to the Israelis. "They said they were only going to arrest him," he told his interrogators. "Then they killed him." When Ariel Sharon ordered the killing of a Hamas official in Gaza, an Israeli jet flattened an apartment block, killing seventeen civilians, including nine children. Sharon regarded the attack as a victory against "terror."

Al-Wazzir, now an economic analyst in Gaza, believed that people who did not believe themselves to be targets were now finding themselves under attack. "There's a network of Israeli army and air force intelligence and Mossad and Shin Bet that works together, feeding each other information. They can cross the lines between Area C and Area B in the occupied territories. Usually they carry out operations when IDF [Israeli Defense Forces] morale is low. When they killed my father, the IDF was in very low spirits because of the first intifada. So they go for a 'spectacular' to show what great 'warriors' they are. Now the IDF morale is low again because of the second intifada . . . "

Palestinian security officers in Gaza were intrigued by the logic behind the Israeli killings. "Our guys meet their guys and we know their officers and operatives," one of the Palestinian officials tells me. "I tell you this frankly—they are as corrupt and indisciplined as we are. And as ruthless. After they targeted Mohamed Dahlan's convoy when he was coming back from security talks, Dahlan talked to Foreign Minister Peres. 'Look what you guys are doing to us,' Dahlan told Peres. 'Don't you realise it was me who took Sharon's son to meet Arafat?' " Al-Wazzir understands some of the death-squad logic. "It has some effect because we are a paternalistic society. We believe in the idea of a father figure. But when they assassinated my dad, the intifada didn't stop. It was affected, but all the political objectives failed. Rather than demoralising the Palestinians, it fuelled the intifada. They say there's now a hundred Palestinians on the murder list. No, I don't think the Palestinians will adopt the same type of killings against Israeli intelligence. An army is an institution, a system; murdering an officer just results in him being replaced . . . " The murder of political or military opponents was a practice the Israelis honed in Lebanon where Lebanese guerrilla leaders were regularly blown up by hidden bombs or shot in the back by Shin Bet execution squads, often—as in the case of an Amal leader in the village of Bidias—after interrogation. And all in the name of "security."*

I RETURN TO THE AYOSHA JUNCTION and the "clashes." Stones bang onto the roofs of the Israeli jeeps, skitter over the road, ping off the metal poles of long-collapsed advertisement hoardings. I watch a young soldier open the door of his jeep every minute or so, take careful aim with his rifle, fire, and retreat back inside. He does this for half an hour, then looks back at me. "Where are you from?" he asks. We might have been in a bar, on a beach, coming across each other in some-

---

*There is a rich seam of information on Israel's policy of assassinating its opponents inside Israel, the West Bank and Gaza. As long ago as 1984, two of four Palestinian bus hijackers were bludgeoned to death by Shin Bet operatives after they had been interrogated, an admission made only when press photographers produced pictures of the two men being led, very much alive, from the bus. The then Israeli defence minister Yitzhak Shamir described the killings as "a mishap." In 1991, Palestinian lawyers and human rights groups began the re-examination of dozens of cases of Palestinian men shot dead during the first intifada after Israeli television revealed the existence of Israeli army hit squads. In early 1992, Israeli witnesses testified that they had seen Israeli soldiers in civilian clothes opening fire on masked Palestinians who were spray-painting graffiti on a wall in Dura near Hebron.

Amnesty International's 21 February 2001 report on *Israel and the Occupied Territories: State Assassinations and Other Unlawful Killings* is a carefully researched account of Israel's extrajudicial murders which includes the death of forty-nine-year-old Dr. Thabet Thabet, a former Fatah activist who was later named as a PLO representative to the 1991 Madrid peace talks and who developed many friendships with members of the Israeli peace movement. Thabet, a Tulkarem dentist, was shot dead in his car by Israeli troops on 31 December 2000. The Israelis later claimed he was a commander of a Tanzim cell who "instructed people where to carry out attacks," a highly unconvincing explanation for the murder of a Palestinian who had attended the funeral of an Israeli soldier, the son of an Israeli peace campaigner he had befriended. The killing of Hamas and Islamic Jihad leaders then became routine, helped by a ruling from one of Israel's chief rabbis. "Jewish religious law," Rabbi Israel Meir Lau claimed on 27 July 2001, "gives its . . . full support to the policy of active killings which the government and security forces maintains today in order to prevent terrorists from planning and carrying out attacks in Israel." On the same day, the spiritual leader of the Ultra-Orthodox Shas party, Rabbi Ovadia Yossef, announced in a sermon broadcast over Israeli army radio that Arabs were reproducing like insects and should go to hell. "In the old city of Jerusalem, they're swarming like ants," he said. "They should go to hell—and the Messiah will speed them on their way."

The Israeli human rights group B'Tselem condemned the "immoral and illegal practice" of killing wanted Palestinians in the occupied territories. In 1993, the U.S.-based Human Rights Watch calculated that 120 Palestinians had been killed by covert Israeli units since December 1987. When a Mossad hit squad tried to murder Khaled Mashaal, a Hamas official, in Jordan in 1997—Israelis criticised the attack not because it was illegal but because it had failed—even President Mubarak of Egypt felt constrained to call the tactics "immoral." Israel had already been shocked by earlier revelations that its security men had murdered dozens of Egyptian soldiers in the 1967 Middle East war. Their mass grave had been discovered in Sinai; Rabin called the war crime an "aberration."

Death always involved double standards. In 1998, for example, Israel's social security system said it could not compensate the family of a Palestinian killed by a Jewish gunman because under Israeli law an Arab murdered by a Jewish "terrorist" is not considered a victim of terrorism while a Jew killed by an Arab is.

one's office. England. The twenty-one-year-old grins. "I'm from Queens, New York, and now I'm at Ayosha junction, Ramallah—quite a journey! This is more fun than Queens." Fun? Do I hear him right? Fun? "Well, at least here you don't get shot while waiting at the traffic lights." He grins. "My name's Ilan."

The stones keep thundering off the metal roofs of the jeeps. Gas grenades soar through the hot sky towards youths hiding behind the skeleton of a bus, using slingshots—I can see them clearly through the smoke—to give their stones velocity. The Israeli firing—rubber-coated bullets for the most part—makes my ears sing, tinnitus from Iraqi guns mixed with Israeli rifles, louder than any shooting in the Hollywood movies from which Ilan seems to have taken his script. I am taken aback by the line about the traffic lights. Surely there's more chance of getting killed at the lights in the West Bank than in New York.

"Israel is a great place," Ilan says. But this is not Israel. And it occurs to me, watching these young men in their grimy olive-green fatigues, that their ritual had been practised. Two soldiers twist gas grenades onto their colleagues' rifles. A soldier points out a running youth to a colleague who fires a round in his direction. An ambulance moves towards the youth, lying now on the road. And one of the soldiers claps another on the back. Major Shai arrives in another jeep to watch this miserable spectacle, a thirty-four-year-old accountant from Tel Aviv whose Ray-Banned driver is an insurance agent when he isn't watching stone-throwers in Ramallah. In the back of the jeep, cradling his rifle on his knees, sits a twenty-one-year-old business management student of Moroccan origin, happily arguing politics with Shai, more interested in marrying his girlfriend in six months' time than in the outcome of today's theatre at Ayosha. The arguments are familiar. Shai shakes his head—he actually calls the confrontation "a ritual"—but thinks the Israeli army "couldn't give way." Give way? But this isn't Israel. I venture a heretical thought, that in ten years Israel will be back behind its 1967 frontiers—I don't believe it now—and, amazingly, Shai agrees. The student in the jeep does not. "If we pull out of here, we show we're weak. Then the Arabs will want all of Israel and they'll be trying to get Haifa and Tel Aviv."

It's the same weary argument I used to hear from Israeli soldiers in Lebanon. If we stay, we're strong. If we leave, we're weak. The Arabs only understand strength. At one point, Shai nods towards the stone-throwers and says: "They are animals." Why? I ask. "You saw what they did to our two soldiers in Ramallah police station." Yes, every Israeli has that image engraved in his mind. Not the destroyed children, not Mohamed el-Dura collapsing dead under a hail of Israeli bullets, but the savage murder of the two Israeli reservists. Photographs of their grotesquely mutilated faces are widely available on the Internet. Many soldiers have seen them. "You media are partly responsible for the image we have," Shai says. "You make this place out to be a war zone with nothing but stones and shooting." But it was Sharon, I say, who did that. It was Sharon who kept telling the world that Israel was "under siege," that Israel was being assaulted by "international terror."

Shai takes a call on his mobile from his family. "They're on the beach," he says. "And that's where we should be." And it dawned on me that these soldiers had an alternative in life. Shai could be on the beach. The soldier in the back could be with his girlfriend. But the Palestinians on the other side of the firing line couldn't go anywhere. They were locked in, trapped, under real siege. The degradation of life has been an incremental process, just as the war has moved incrementally from pain to bloodbath.

Wasn't this just what happened in the 1954–62 Algerian war? It began as a nuisance—trees cut down to block roads, railways sabotaged, Algerian crowds hurling stones at French troops—and ended in a welter of bombs and village massacres. There was plenty of torture, too, personally conducted by senior French officers. And plenty of drumhead executions of Algerians by Algerians. So, too, the Palestinian intifada descends into anarchy. From stone-throwing to suicide bombing, from snipers to bomber pilots. Palestinians are daily tortured by Israeli officers in the Russian compound in Jerusalem. Palestinians are regularly—and publicly—shot for collaboration.

In late July 2000, the Israelis fire a missile into the office of a Hamas official in Nablus. The rocket, American-made, of course, killed two small Palestinian children. A hundred thousand mourners call for retaliation. An Israeli bus-driver called Menashe Nuriel, en route from Jerusalem to Kiryat Shmona, stops to pick up a seventeen-year-old Palestinian. He thinks the man looks suspicious, notices wires coming from a bag in his hand and wrestles him off the bus while forty-six passengers look on in astonishment. The bag contains three 81-mm mortar shells and explosives that would have killed every passenger on the bus. "If it doesn't happen today, it will happen tomorrow," the Israeli policeman outside the Damascus gate tells me. But if Palestinian retaliation is such a certainty, I ask the man, why kill the Hamas official in Nablus? He shrugs. "It is a war and we know what war is. You don't need to worry. This is safer than London." But it's not.

Jerusalem is a city of illusions. Here Ariel Sharon promises his people "security" and brings them war. On the main road to Ma'ale Adumim, inside Israel's illegal "municipal boundaries," Israelis drive at over 100 mph. In the Old City, Israeli troops and Palestinian civilians curse each other before the few astonished Christian tourists. Loving Jesus doesn't help to make sense of the Arab–Israeli conflict. Gideon Samet got it right in *Ha'aretz*. "Jerusalem looks like a Bosnia about to be born. Main thoroughfares inside the Green Line . . . have become mortally perilous . . . The capital's suburbs are exposed as Ramat Rachel was during the war of independence . . . " Samet is pushing it a bit. Life is more dangerous for Palestinians than for Israelis. Terrorism, terrorism, terrorism. "I suggest that we repeat to ourselves every day and throughout the day," Sharon tells us, "that there will be no negotiations with the Palestinians until there is a total cessation of terrorism, violence and incitement."

But this does not mean, of course, that Israel's death squads have to stop murdering with their usual impunity or that Israeli settlers must stop shooting Palestinian civilians. Only that Palestinian suicide bombers must stop killing innocent Israelis. A Palestinian lawyer waves a copy of *The Wall Street Journal* in front of my face. "Your newspapers lay the groundwork of our suffering," he shouts at me. I want to disown all possible connection with the paper of Manhattan's ultra-right but its editorial fills me with dismay. It praises Sharon's "subtlety" because "suddenly, enemy terrorists" are "being brought down en route to their mischief . . . this is war waged in twilight . . . subtle, but not less deadly." Enemy? Brought down? No reference in *The Wall Street Journal* to the two children "brought down" in the attack on the Hamas office.

First come the changes in air pressure, then the drumroll of tank fire. I look out of the window, across the Kidron Valley to the Dome of the Rock shimmering in floodlights above the old city. It is long past dark but the Israeli–Palestinian war has now become a familiar sound in Jerusalem as the tanks fire on Beit Jalla. Only hours earlier, the Israelis had tried to murder Marwan Dirya, a member of Force 17 in Ramallah. They fired two ground-to-ground missiles at his car in a bougainvillea-smothered street, missed with the first shot—giving Dirya just enough time to hurl himself from the vehicle—and hitting the car with the second. Dirya was immediately called a "leading terrorist" by the Israelis. Had the Dirya murder attempt prompted the resumption of Palestinian attacks from Beit Jalla? And if so, what was the Israeli helicopter attack on a Palestinian police station in the Gaza town of Rafah meant to be?

No sooner have I arrived to look at the cinders of Dirya's car in Ramallah—the Israelis had a clear shot from a big military encampment and an illegal settlement on a neighbouring hilltop—than a Palestinian struck back. A member of Hamas? Islamic Jihad? A young man driving a black car speeds past one of Tel Aviv's main army bases and sprays with bullets a group of soldiers who are leaving for lunch. He, like the Israelis, is trying to murder his enemies. He wounds ten men before an Israeli shoots the gunman in the head and he crashes into a lamp-post. The first shooting assassination attempt by Palestinians inside Israel in twelve months is another lightning new statistic to add to the war.

A day later, I am driving at speed north up the Tel Aviv highway, the fastest way to reach Tulkarem if I don't want to get snarled up in the Israeli checkpoints outside Ramallah. "If you turn right, walk three hundred metres, then turn left," the Israeli soldier tells me on the border of the West Bank, "you'll find the son-of-a-bitch at the checkpoint." But the son-of-a-bitch isn't there. The Palestinian policeman at the Tulkarem junction didn't want to die in any more "mistaken" Israeli ambushes, and the road is just a sultry, midday pageant of tyres, stones, empty Israeli cartridges and rotting sandbags. A torn Palestinian flag hangs over the empty checkpoint. But not far beyond lies anger as hot as the sun. It is 6 August 2001. They are preparing to bury Amr Hassan Khudeiri and they are looking for the man who betrayed him.

Amr Khudeiri was the young Hamas "activist"—for which read "guerrilla"/ "terrorist"/"extremist"/"militant" or whatever—who was burned alive when an Israeli pilot in an American-made Apache maintained Israel's policy of state murder by firing three American-made missiles into Khudeiri's car. The manufacturer of the missile was not in doubt. But was it Khudeiri's car? The Fatah security man standing outside the row of Ottoman-built shops is more interested in the car than the missile.

"There was nothing left of him—atomised, burned alive," he says. "He was just ashes. But we have the information that there was some kind of strange paint on the roof of the car." He says this with his eyebrows raised, as if it was a question rather than a small but critical piece of intelligence. I ask about the missile. The Fatah guy opens his car door, takes something from the back seat and hands me a hunk of iron—perhaps six inches long—with two metal tubes attached to it and a code number which reads: 18876-13411923-14064. I have seen this shaped missile engine part and numeral configuration in Lebanon. Always it belongs to Lockheed missiles fired from Apaches. So Lockheed had a role in Khudeiri's death, although that doesn't interest the Fatah man.

"Khudeiri wasn't driving his own car," he says. "He had borrowed it. And the owner took the car to Israel last week. He is missing now. We are trying to find him.* The helicopter came over the bridge outside the town and fired the three missiles. We think there was some infrared paint on the roof." The message is easy: Fatah thinks Khudeiri was betrayed by a collaborator, probably the owner of the car, who had allowed the Israelis to splash some infrared on the roof to guide the missile. "Or maybe there was a 'bleeper' of some kind, a computer code."

This same afternoon, the Israeli police announce that they have arrested a Palestinian who was preparing to be a suicide bomber in Tel Aviv. Al! he needed were the explosives that were supposed to have been brought by Amr Hassan Khudeiri. Or so they say. Israeli "security" stories often turn out to be economical with the truth. But in Tulkarem, there are quite a few truths lying about. The first is that there was more than one body. The corpse I see taken from the smaller mosque bound in a Palestinian flag, a cloth round its head, revealing only a mouth and a moustache, turns out to be not Khudeiri but Mohamed Meziad, a twenty-year-old

---

*Preferring to avoid the deeply flawed trials which had condemned nine alleged collaborators to death, Arafat's intelligence operatives were now murdering Palestinians suspected of spying for Israel, killing at least twenty men between December 2000 and August 2001. Palestinian police no longer investigated the killings of men believed to have worked for the Israeli intelligence services and who in some cases helped Israel to murder Palestinian militants. Bassam Abu Sharif, one of Arafat's special advisers, admitted to me that "these people who were shot, they were killed by intelligence, under orders, because of very certain information and recorded confessions. All these people were shot by Palestinian intelligence in areas not under our security control. All were shot in Area B or Area C where they were protected by Israeli security." Kassem Khleef, found dead at a checkpoint near al-Ram on 12 November 2000, had been accused of providing Shin Bet with the movements of Hussein Abayat, assassinated three days earlier. Adnan Fathi Sultan was shot in the neck and chest by armed men who dragged him from his Bethlehem home on 17 December 2000 because they believed he had colluded with the Israelis to murder Yousef Abu Sway five days earlier. On 30 July 2001, sixty-eight-year-old Jamal Eid Shahin—the oldest victim so far—received a call at his house in Beit Sahour from men wearing Palestinian police uniforms; they asked him to follow them into the street. There they shot him eleven times and reportedly assaulted his corpse with a hammer. By the summer of 2001, a total of eighteen Palestinians had died in Palestinian prisons since 1993, often under torture by interrogators trained by the CIA.

Fatah man shot dead by the Israelis—but totally unreported—just twenty-four hours ago. I watch the mouth and the moustache bobbing off between the crowds to the second mosque where Khudeiri's somewhat humbler remains are also awaiting burial. When four Hamas members—cloaked head to foot in green gowns with eye-slits and "martyrdom" swords strapped to their backs—walk from the mosque with a wooden stretcher, the green shroud upon it seems to protect very little of substance.

Sitting on the pavement is a middle-aged man, shaking and perspiring. "He saw what happened to his friend yesterday—he saw him turning into ashes," his cousin tells me. It's the usual funeral. There are 10,000 mourners, a loudspeaker screaming *Allahu akbar*, and ferocious bursts of automatic gunfire from young men, often shooting rifles and pistols at the same time. They make their way through the delicate, decaying houses of Tulkarem, past the market whose vendors and donkeys are squeezed between trayloads of plums, lettuce, cauliflowers, onions, tomatoes, potatoes, pears, apples and watermelons. Life amid death.

There is more shooting at the graveside where Khudeiri's father, Mansour, a dignified figure with short grey hair who is a senior teacher at Tulkarem College, embraces hundreds of mourners. So does his equally unsmiling but unweeping son, Amr's brother, a green ribbon draped round his neck as he puts his arms across the shoulders of old men, teenagers and gunmen. The body is lowered into the grave and Abbas Zeyid, the local Hamas leader, makes a short but very revealing speech. "Our dear son and brother Amr loved his parents," he says. "Just five minutes before he left home for the last time, Amr said to them: 'My dear mother and father, if I die, you must not cry for me.' " The thousands round the grave lift their eyes at this and murmur *Allahu akbar* again. Prescience? Or was Amr Khudeiri on a mission from which he did not expect to return, a mission he undertook—fatally—in someone else's car?

The crack of the explosion comes as a shock from over a kilometre away. I am eating in a bar in West Jerusalem and I turn to the Israeli waitress and say the two words "suicide bomber" and she nods and her right hand moves involuntarily to her mouth. I give her more shekels than the meal can be worth and set off running up Jaffa Street, towards a great dirty smudge of brown and grey smoke that is streaming upwards. I get there just as police and soldiers pour out of jeeps and cars. Outside the Sbarro restaurant, there lies a plump lady with her brains bursting through her head. A child—perhaps three, perhaps five—is so mutilated that its eyes have been blasted out of its face. It is the atrocity every Israeli has been waiting for. A Palestinian suicide bomber, a crowded, air-conditioned pizzeria just before two on an ovenlike West Jerusalem afternoon. There is blood and glass all over the street, on the stretchers of the Magen David ambulances, on the faces of those who have survived. I count two dead until I see another woman with a table leg sticking out of her stomach. Three dead. Then five. Jens Palme, a German *Stern* magazine photographer, counts ten corpses in two minutes. Yehuda, a Jewish holidaymaker from Barcelona—first-name anonymity is one of the few things Israelis and Arabs wish to share here—saw "a soldier flying through the air, right up in the air, disintegrating" and "body parts flying around in the smoke." Many of the corpses are very small. More than half the dead are Israeli children. "Unforgivable" is the word that comes to mind. What did the child with no eyes do to the Palestinians?

My mobile starts to ring. Mobiles are ringing all over the street, on the belts of the cops and soldiers, in the hands of crying shop assistants, on the pavements, on the still intact corpses, harsh shrilling tones and merry jingles and mockeries of Beethoven. Radio Belfast is talking to me. Belfast? I ask myself amid this butchery. Belfast. One bomb alley calling another bomb alley. A girl with an Ulster accent tells me that Islamic Jihad have claimed the bombing. There is a fire engine crunching through the glass and I'm too overwhelmed to take in the irony that someone in Northern Ireland is telling me who blew up the café next to me in Jerusalem. Islamic Jihad made a phone call to the Agence France-Presse in Amman. I talk into the phone, the sound of alarm bells and shouting forcing me to raise my voice in the live interview as I recount what I've seen and I notice some of the Israelis beside the road listening to me with growing anger.

The corner of Jaffa Street and King George's Street is not the place to argue the causes of this horror. A reminder of the two Palestinian children who died in the helicopter missile attack in Nablus—one aged two, the other five—or of the dozens of Palestinian child stone-throwers shot dead by Israeli troops, or of the youngest victim of this war, a Palestinian baby murdered by Jewish settlers—would be setting fire to anger. For the Israeli crowd now gathered outside the boutiques and shoe shops of Jaffa Street, this is further—perhaps final—evidence that the "terrorist" Arafat wants them all dead, burned alive, liquidated.

High above us, two tiny white Israeli helicopters chunter through the hot air and a group of whey-faced youths are pushed into a police van. Arrested? Or was it for the Arabs' own protection? On Jaffa Street, I can hear the authentic voice of Jewish West Jerusalem, enraged, shocked, explicit. "I saw a two-year-old on the floor, in bits," a young man shouts. Alexander, he says his name is, a Jewish estate agent who spends half the year in Antwerp. "This was a little baby. What did he know of life? He knew nothing. He was in pieces. It was unbelievable." A number of Orthodox Jews gather round Alexander, black hats, white shirts, ringlets, nodding their heads vigorously. "When one or two Palestinians die, you press people say it's the end of the world. But the Palestinians terrorise our whole country. If we are going to have a war, so—we have a war. What more do the Palestinians want? When we offer them a finger, they want the whole hand. We offered them ninety-eight per cent of their land." I note the word "their." It's not 98 per cent. But why not 100 per cent? At this moment, it's an obscene thought.

David, a Jerusalem businessman, talks about "barbarism" and plays the role of catalyst to a crowd of furious shopkeepers crushed around him. "If Arafat can't control his people, then we have to go in there and take the place and sterilise it . . . The party's over and maybe they'll have to be put back under occupation. We're refighting the war of 'forty-seven. The Arabs think they have limited liability. But if they lose, they go crying to the world for help." I don't want to think what "sterilise" means. Up the street, the police ribbons are fluttering in the warm breeze like cordons round a fairground, the sun splashing over a million shards of glass, cops in flak jackets looking for the ultimate point of fear of all ordnance officers: the second bomb. But suicide bombers carry only one charge, round their waist. By now, the Palestinian Authority reacts and its inevitably incompetent—and incomprehensible—spokesmen are trying to remind the world of Palestine's casualties, of a "warmonger" [sic] called Sharon "who wanted only war, not peace." They are saying this at the wrong time, in the wrong place.

Then comes the day of lamentation. Even before the fourteen funerals begin, Israelis know the dead as if they are their own families—as, in a sense, they are. Long before five members of the Schijveschuurdr family are buried at the Givat Shaul cemetery outside Jerusalem—the same Givat Shaul that is, or was, Deir Yassin—Israelis have all seen the snapshot in the morning papers, a photograph of a bar mitzvah ceremony with two small girls in white and a middle-aged man wearing spectacles. Their father, Mordechai, and mother, Tzirli, both came from families of Holocaust survivors, families who had lived through the Nazi horrors only for a son and daughter to be torn apart by a Palestinian suicide bomber in West Jerusalem.

Outside the Sbarro pizzeria, Israelis light hundreds of candles. There is much talk of revenge—as there is at the funerals—and a growing anger that Sharon's overnight seizure of Palestinian offices in Jerusalem and the bombing of the Ramallah police headquarters falls far short of the retaliation Israelis expect. Fuelling this bitterness are reports on Israeli television of Palestinians celebrating the massacre on the streets of Ramallah. The reports are all true. Among the hovels of the Ein el-Helweh refugee camp in Lebanon, Palestinians even dance the traditional *dabkeh* in their satisfaction at the killings.

The Schijveschuurdrs' badly wounded ten-year-old daughter Leah attends the burials of five members of her family. Determined to see them lowered into their grave, she arrives on a stretcher, staring at the bright midday sky, a nurse monitoring her intravenous drip, more than two thousand Israelis standing around her. Mordechai and Tzirli and their children, two-year-old Chemda, Avraham, who was four, and Raya, fourteen, were all killed by the nail-studded bomb. Leah's surviving sister Hamda was also badly hurt in the explosion. The dead also included Judith Shoshana Greenbaum from New York, who was four months pregnant, ten-year-old Yocheved Shoshan, eight-year-old Tamara Shimshawily, and her mother, Lily. The oldest victim was Freida Mendelson, who was sixty-two.

When in the early hours of that morning the Israeli army had stormed into the Jerusalem Palestinian offices at Orient House and raised the Israeli flag on the roof of the venerable old mansion with its tracery windows and pitched roof, they did more than occupy the very symbol of the original "peace process," the building from which the Palestinians set out for the 1991 Madrid peace conference. Inside the Israelis found filing cabinets of documents and maps, the very archives of the "final status" negotiations that were supposed to bring eternal peace to the Middle East. Thus did a dream die when the soldiers broke through the front door.

Faced with the real threat of the suicide bomber, Sharon's men then squandered the world's sympathy by claiming that Orient House—with its elderly, pontificating officials, its "peace process" archives and its constant trail of foreign diplomatic visitors—was, in the words of Dore Gold, the Israeli government's official spokesman, "a virtual hub and nerve centre of terrorists." Even Gold's revealing insertion of the word "virtual" did not fool Israelis who asked—not unreasonably—why, if Orient House was such a "terror centre," it had not been raided, trashed, closed down, occupied or destroyed years ago. "We can hunt down their terrorists in the back streets of Ramallah, but we didn't know until now that 'terrorist HQ' was just a stone's throw from *shabbak* [Israeli secret service] offices," an Israeli journalist remarked sarcastically to me. "What are we supposed to believe next?" The headquarters of Shin Bet in the Russian compound in Jerusalem stands about a thousand metres from Orient House. If Gold was to be believed—and he was not—Israel's cops, who have stood outside the building for eight years, must have been breathtakingly inefficient to have allowed all those "terrorists" to pop in and out of their "nerve centre" for almost a decade.

The usual sense of disproportion set in. Two Palestinians killed by Israeli soldiers in Gaza on the day after the Sbarro bombing were buried amid scenes of grief and anger. Most Israelis were unaware of their deaths. Yet while many Western newspapers were urging the Sharon government on to bloody revenge, it was an Israeli journalist who provided the most generous and thoughtful response to the massacre of Israelis. Gideon Levy asked in *Ha'aretz*:

> What should the residents of the village of Aanin feel about the killing of Mustafa Yassin, a village resident, right in front of his wife and infant daughter? And what should the family of Majad Jalad, a five-year-old boy who is hovering between life and death, think after soldiers shot him in the stomach? . . . And what about the tens of thousands of Palestinians whose lives have become hell because of the closure and the siege? What feelings are being implanted in them and what buds of calamity will they produce?

Levy wrote that it was "time to tell the truth: the victims of this *intifada* are victims of the settlement enterprise . . . "

How many more Palestinian suicide bombers were waiting to die? After Sbarro—and the earlier annihilation of twenty-one young Israelis at a Tel Aviv nightclub—every Israeli was asking this question. On 12 August 2001, Mohamed Nasr climbed from a taxi and walked towards the terrasse bar of the Wall Street Café at Kiryat Motzkin north of Haifa and blew himself up, wounding twenty Israeli teenagers. Aharon Roseman, the café owner, said he saw Nasr walking towards the palm-tree-lined terrasse. "He approached a waitress, pulled up his shirt to reveal the explosives attached to his belt and asked the woman: 'Do you know what this is?' She screamed one word—'Terrorist!' I grabbed a chair and threw it at him and ran behind a wall—that's what saved me." In the exaggerated but frightening language of Islamic Jihad, Sheikh Abdullah Shami, one of its officials, stated that Nasr had been "able to penetrate into the heart of Zionism with all its security measures—we will continue our fight, our struggle, our operations, until we reach our goal of complete freedom."

The implications are awesome. Not only did Nasr kill himself just after Arafat had ostentatiously arrested four "activists"; Nasr's father, Mahmoud, revealed at his West Bank home of Qabatya that his son had been working for Arafat's own security services until just six weeks ago. Qabatya. I spend almost a quarter of an hour trying to find the village on a map—so many little dirt towns are now marked red on my "bomber's map"—and eventually discover the name close to Jenin. The sun burns the road to Qabatya; three youths and a mangy dog watch me suspiciously when I park on the corner of a rubbish-clothed hill. "The house of the martyr?" one of the boys asks before I have said a word. And his hand points to a single-storey hut with bare concrete walls.

I've sat in these rooms before, the broken fathers always trying to show pride in the death of the young men whose portraits stare down from the glossy posters on the wall, but who set off to kill the innocent, the relatives anxious to add their twopence of praise. "Chivalrous" is the word they keep using about Mohamed Nasr. When I ask his father what he believes his son was thinking as he walked towards the Wall Street Café and touched the detonator on his waist, he just raises his arms in a helpless way. "I don't know," he replies. They all say that. The family agrees that the saddest thing about his death was the time of his birth. "He was the first boy to be born after seven girls," his cousin Siham says. "Think of it. Seven girls and then Mohamed arrived and now he has gone."

Old Haj Mahmoud Nasr sits cross-legged on the floor wearing a white headdress, elbows resting on a patterned cushion. He acknowledges his son was a ninth-grade drop-out; he was kind, he says, he kept some sheep but had no money to marry. "All I knew was that he was active in the first intifada." But Mohamed Nasr's life and death contain a lesson for both Palestinians and Israelis. A thin, long-faced youth with a short beard, he was born into occupation and despair, shot through the thigh when he was fifteen after throwing stones at Israeli soldiers in 1988. Qabatya is a rocky village, its old stone houses as hard as its people. When the men there found a collaborator among them, they burned his house and hanged him from an electricity pole. Nasr drifted into a job with the Palestinian Authority—with Moussa Arafat's military intelligence services—as a prison guard, watching over Islamic Jihad and Hamas men whom Moussa's cousin Yassir Arafat had locked up in Jenin on Israel's orders.

One of them was Iyad Hardan, an intelligent, tough Jihad member whom Israel's death squads wanted to kill. He was studying at an open university and would regularly be freed from jail to attend classes. On 5 July he went to make a call from a pay phone in Jenin. The moment he lifted the receiver, it blew his head off. It was a turning point in Mohamed Nasr's life. He liked the prisoners he guarded. "He had come to admire Hardan," another cousin—also Mohamed—recalls. "He was sad for days afterwards. He was angry like everyone else. I remember him saying that 'We are from God and we go back to God.' Then he started talking to us about how he wanted to be a martyr." Other members of the family remember darker words. "Damn those who are behind this," Mohamed Nasr said. A few days later, in mid-July, he threw in his job, complaining that he hadn't been paid for a month. It must have been then that he first took up with Islamic Jihad. He was, as they say, "chosen," prepared for the "martyrdom" he claimed to seek, told how to strap explosives round his waist. His family insist they had no idea of this. That, too, is what they all say.

Perhaps it is the truth, although Jenin's school for suiciders seems to have been a sloppy affair, its Islamic Jihad cells containing at least one mole. A collaborator had prepared Hardan's murder and at least one of the men Islamic Jihad sent to die had already changed his mind and given himself up to the Israelis. Not Mohamed Nasr. "On the Sunday morning, he didn't have breakfast but he attended noon prayers," Siham says. "He took a bath, changed his clothes and said to his father: 'Do you want anything from me?' Then he asked to see his nephew, little Islam."

Islam is only four months old. Was Mohamed Nasr seeking some love of life in the child, having already abandoned his own? "He liked children." It is Siham talking again. "He liked playing with them. He took coffee but didn't shave that day. He was wearing a beige shirt, white trousers and black boots. He didn't say where he was going. Yes, he had a mobile phone. He took it with him."

Not long after three that afternoon, Nasr picked up a taxi near Haifa. The Israelis had already set up roadblocks in the city—another collaborator appears to have warned them that a suicider was on his way—but they never found Nasr. The driver was to recall later how Nasr had been uncertain of his destination. "Three times, he made calls on his mobile and said 'I can't find the place,' " the taximan said afterwards.

When he was asked about the taxi fare, Nasr said he didn't care how much it cost. Which made the driver even more suspicious as he dropped him off close to the Wall Street Café. Was he reflecting in those last seconds that the Israelis he was trying to kill might have included children, perhaps as young as four-month-old Islam? Did he question the morality of trying to erase the lives of innocents? That his twenty-eight years on earth were about to end? His cousin Mohamed has pondered this question. "There would have been no thought about himself," he says. "He would think of many things except himself—he couldn't think about himself because he wanted to die. Any person who has accepted this form of sacrifice doesn't think about himself."

The Israelis took their revenge by raiding Jenin two days later and destroying its police station, unaware—or failing to comprehend—that it was their own murder of Hardan that sent Mohamed Nasr on his frightening mission. The killing of Hardan—intended to strike fear into Islamic Jihad—had the opposite effect. It turned Mohamed Nasr into a suicide bomber.

I once asked the head of the Lebanese Hizballah movement if he could explain to me how the mind of a suicide bomber works. It was his first Western television interview. Sayed Hassan Nasrallah was dressed in his black turban and robes. He had formerly been the Hizballah's military commander in southern Lebanon

and from his legions had emerged the first Arab suicide bombers who would
after more than a decade and a half—sap the morale of Israel's retreating army of
occupation. Explain to me as a Westerner, I asked him, how a man can immolate
himself.

> There are qualities which our fighters have. He who drives his truck into
> the enemy's military base to blow himself up and to become a martyr, he
> drives in with a hopeful heart, smiling and happy because he knows he is
> going to another place. Death, according to our belief, is not oblivion. It is
> not the end. It is the beginning of a true life.
>
> The best metaphor for a Westerner to try to understand this truth is to
> think of a person being in a sauna bath for a long time. He is very thirsty
> and tired and hot and he is suffering from the effects of the high tempera-
> ture. Then he is told that if he opens the door, he can go into a quiet, com-
> fortable room, drink a nice cocktail and hear classical music. Then he will
> open the door and go through without hesitation, knowing that what he
> leaves behind is not a high price to pay, and what awaits him is of much
> greater value. I cannot think of another example to explain this idea to a
> Westerner.

Nasrallah enjoyed metaphors, similes, like the Hizballah's "martyr" posters
which so often show the dead in paradise, surrounded by rivers and tulips and
weeping willows. Is that where the suicide bombers really believe they are going?
To the rivers and the honey and the trees and—yes, of course—the virgins? Or the
quiet, comfortable room with a cocktail and classical music?

The idea that sacrifice is a noble ideal—and let us, for a moment, put aside the
iniquity of murdering children in a Jerusalem pizzeria—is common to Western as
well as Eastern society. Our First World War calvaries in France are covered with
commemorations to men—Bill Fisk's dead comrades—who supposedly "laid
down their lives" or "gave their lives" for their country—even though most died in
appalling agony, praying only that they would live. When, years after our conversation, Nasrallah's own son was killed in a suicidal assault on an Israeli army position in southern Lebanon, the Hizballah leader insisted that he receive not
condolences but congratulations. Nasrallah appeared on Lebanese television,
laughing and smiling, beaming with delight as he spoke to well-wishers on the
phone. His son's young fiancée also expressed her pride in her dead husband-to-
be. But she did not smile.

If the idea of self-sacrifice is thus explicable, it is clearly not a natural phenomenon. In a normal society, in a community whose people feel they are treated
equally and with justice, we regard suicide as a tragic aberration, a death produced—in the coroner's eloquent lexicon—when "the balance of the mind is disturbed." But what happens when the balance of a whole society's mind has been
disturbed? Walking with a friend through the wreckage of the Sabra and Chatila
refugee camp in Beirut in the year 2000, I could only wonder at the stability of the

survivors who still lived there amid the concrete huts and the football-sized rats. They have been homeless, many of them, since their original dispossession fifty-two years ago. If I lived there, I tell my friend, I would commit suicide. And that is the point.

When a society is dispossessed, when the injustices thrust upon it appear insoluble, when the "enemy" is all-powerful, when one's own people are bestialised as insects, cockroaches, "two-legged beasts," then the mind moves beyond reason. It becomes fascinated in two senses: with the idea of an afterlife and with the possibility that this belief will somehow provide a weapon of more than nuclear potential. When the United States was turning Beirut into a NATO base in 1983, and using its firepower against Muslim guerrillas in the mountains to the east, Iranian Revolutionary Guards in Baalbek were promising that God would rid Lebanon of the American presence. I wrote at the time—not entirely with my tongue in my cheek—that this was likely to be a titanic battle: U.S. technology versus God. Who would win? Then on 23 October 1983 a lone suicide bomber drove a truckload of explosives into the U.S. Marine compound at Beirut airport and killed 241 American servicemen in six seconds. This, I am sure, was the suicide bomber to whom Nasrallah was referring, the one who drives into the military base "smiling and happy." I later interviewed one of the few surviving American marines to have seen the bomber. "All I can remember," he told me, "was that the guy was smiling."

I spent months studying the suiciders of Lebanon. They were mostly single men, occasionally women, often the victims of Israeli torture or the relatives of family members who had been killed in battle with Israel. They might receive their orders while at prayer in the *masjid* or mosque in their south Lebanese villages. The imam would be told to use a certain phrase in his sermon—a reference to roses or gardens or water or a kind of tree. The cleric would not understand the purpose of these words, but in his congregation a young man would know that his day of "martyrdom" had arrived.

In Gaza, even before the Oslo agreement, I discovered an almost identical pattern. As in Lebanon, the would-be "martyr" would spend his last night reading the Koran. He would never say a formal goodbye to his parents. But he would embrace his mother and father and tell them not to cry if he were one day to die. Then he would set off to collect his explosives. Just as Mohamed Nasr had done in Qabatya.*

Yet there is a terrible difference with the suicide bombers of Palestine. However terrifying, the Japanese kamikaze—"divine wind"—pilots of the Second World War attacked battleships and aircraft carriers, not hospitals. The Lebanese largely followed this priority: they usually went for military targets. I was puzzled

*Amira Hass, the *Ha'aretz* correspondent, told me that although she had visited the houses of suicide bombers in Gaza, she did not, during the first year of the second intifada, choose to do so because "as an Israeli, I can't be objective." She only rarely went to the homes of "martyrs." "I made one story about a child—I really wanted to show how he was killed, that he was not a danger to the soldier who killed him. The family was not happy with an Israeli journalist."

why the Lebanese should have been queuing to watch *Pearl Harbor* when it opened in Beirut in July 2001—until I saw the young men studying the cinema stills of equally young Japanese pilots tying their "martyrdom" bandanas around their foreheads. In similar fashion, often with headbands containing a Koranic quotation, the Hizballah targeted the Israeli army and its militia allies. They blew up entire barracks and killed soldiers by the score. The Palestinians learned from all this. But more and more, their suicide bombers—including the women bombers who emerged in more recent years—have targeted Israeli civilians. A battleship or an Israeli tank is one thing; a three-year-old waiting for his young mother to cut his pizza for him quite another.*

Amnesty International devoted a whole report to the targeting of civilians by Palestinian suicide bombers. Between September 2000 and July 2002, at least 350 civilians, most of them Israeli, had been killed in over 128 attacks by Palestinian armed groups or individuals. "Civilians should never be the focus of attacks, not in the name of security and not in the name of liberty," Amnesty said. "We call on the leadership of all Palestinian armed groups to cease attacking civilians, immediately and unconditionally." The oldest victim of a suicide attack, according to Amnesty, was Chanagh Rogan, killed in a Passover bombing at a Netanya hotel on 27 March 2002. She was ninety years old.[†]

I called a Palestinian friend in Ramallah to ask about this, to ask how young Palestinians could rejoice in the streets at the pizzeria massacre. She expressed her abhorrence at what happened—she was genuine in this—but tried to explain that Palestinians had suffered so many civilian casualties since the first intifada began that they found joy in any suffering inflicted on their enemy. There was a feeling, she said, that "they should suffer too"; which, of course—and the principle applies, though not the historical parallel—is exactly how Air Chief Marshal Sir Arthur Harris's area bombing of German civilians was explained in Britain. They should suffer too. And save for a few souls like the bishop of Chichester, blitzed Britons supported Harris all the way. But I go back to my own reaction when I

---

*The most shameful explanation of Palestinian suicide bombing was concocted by Tom Friedman, an old friend but an increasingly messianic columnist for *The New York Times*. Palestinians, he wrote, had not chosen suicide bombing out of "desperation" but because "all they can agree on as a community is what they want to destroy." They had lost sight of the sacredness of human life, he claimed, because they were blinded by "narcissistic rage." He advised the Palestinians to adopt "nonviolent resistance, à la Gandhi." But peaceful protests by Palestinians have always been ignored or suppressed. When Palestinians and other Arab nations took their case against Ariel Sharon's land-grabbing wall to the International Court at The Hague in 2004—surely a "Gandhi-an" technique of seeking justice—Israel simply refused to heed the court's ruling. Friedman made no comment on this.

†Recording these details, a Quaker magazine, reporting the work of an international Quaker working party on the Israeli–"Palestine" conflict, notes that "we have been disturbed to find that within Israel the option of 'transfer'—that is, the ethnic cleansing of large numbers of Palestinians from the occupied territories, or even of Palestinian citizens from inside Israel itself—is now discussed openly by politicians, intellectuals, religious leaders and many other segments of society . . . we condemn this idea and any other proposal that fails to respect the equal worth of all of God's children."

reached the blitzed Sbarro pizza house. Unforgivable. I ask again: What did that eyeless, dead Israeli child ever do to the Palestinians? Could not the Palestinian bomber, in his last moments on earth, recognise this child as his daughter, his baby sister, his youngest cousin? Alas, no. He was too far down the road to his own death, too buried in his own people's tragedy. His was not an act of "mindless terror," the words Israeli spokesmen use as they try to deceive both the world and their own people. He was the logical product of a people who have been crushed, dispossessed, cheated, tortured and killed in terrible numbers. The pressure cooker of the West Bank was his sauna. And he passed through the door.*

If only—how often we use that phrase about the Middle East—if only the United States administration had seriously addressed the Arab–Israeli dispute in 2001, instead of wasting its energies in the creation of another war in the region, how much might have been gained, how much suffering alleviated, how much the pain of future history might have been spared us. In February 2001, Palestinians and Israelis were fighting a civil war. And what did the United States do? It bombed Iraq. What did the new secretary of state Colin Powell do? He arrived in the Middle East not to confront the furnace of the war in Israel and "Palestine," but to "re-energise" sanctions against Iraq and reforge the anti-Iraqi Arab coalition that ceased to exist more than a decade before. There's a story—probably apocryphal—that as the Red Army stormed into Berlin in 1945, German civil servants were still trying to calculate the Third Reich's paperclip ration for 1946. Powell was now the paperclip man.

Already he had sent instructions to U.S. embassies in the region that they were no longer to refer to the occupied Palestinian territories as "occupied." They were henceforth to be referred to as "disputed." And immediately the American media—and quite a number of British newspapers—fell into line. I recall a phone interview with the BBC World Service in early 2001—they had called me on my mobile while I was sitting in a traffic jam in East Beirut—in which I was "twinned" with an Israeli government spokesman in Jerusalem. And the moment I referred to the "Israeli-occupied territories," an Israeli voice boomed back: "But Mr. Fisk, the territories are *not* occupied by Israel!" I waited for a second. Aha, I countered, so you mean that the soldiers who stopped me on the road between Ramallah and Jenin last week were Swiss! Or were they Burmese? But this was no laughing matter. An occupied territory might generate violent resistance which could demand

---

*If Hizballah helped to construct that gateway, then the Palestinians surely passed it on to the Iraqi insurgents of 2003 and 2004. Suicide bombers were to appear daily on the streets of the major cities of Iraq, a country which had hitherto had no record of self-annihilation in its various insurgencies against foreign rule. In Iraq, too, civilian lives lost their sanctity for both sides. If the bombers or their controllers felt any compassion for the hundreds of innocent men and women torn apart by their attacks on American and British convoys, police stations, barracks, hotels and occupation headquarters, they never expressed any sorrow. The Sunni resistance, in the words of one of its progenitors, was not "overly worried" about civilian casualties because the insurgents were prepared to "pay any price" to destroy the occupation. But revolutions in guerrilla warfare, however brutal, do not cross frontiers unless the people who wish to adopt them have a cause.

international legitimacy. But violence used over a "dispute"—a real estate problem, something that might be settled in the courts—was obviously illegitimate, criminal, mindless; indeed, it could be portrayed as the product of that well-worn libel, "mindless violence." Powell—and the Israelis, of course—wanted to delegitimise the intifada.

All of this, however, obscured a momentous change within Arab society: the one great transition I have witnessed in almost thirty years reporting the Middle East. When I first visited the West Bank scarcely nine years after the 1967 war, there was in the occupied territories an Israeli-controlled Palestinian police militia, an army of collaborators—they even wore black berets—who "controlled" a supine and humiliated Palestinian people. North of the Israeli border, a Lebanese population lived in fear of Israeli military invasion. Israeli troops had only to cross the frontier to send a quarter of a million Lebanese civilians fleeing in panic to Beirut. To the east, millions of Iraqis lived in grovelling obedience to the Baath party.

Today, the Arabs are no longer afraid. The regimes are as timid as ever, loyal and supposedly "moderate" allies obeying Washington's orders, taking their massive subventions from the United States, holding their preposterous elections, shaking in fear lest their people at last decide that "regime change"—from within their societies, not the Western version imposed by invasion—is overdue. It is the Arabs as a people—brutalised and crushed for decades by corrupt dictators—who are no longer running away. The Lebanese in Beirut, under siege by Israel, learned to refuse to obey the invader's orders. The Hizballah proved that the mighty Israeli army could be humbled. The two Palestinian intifadas showed that Israel could no longer impose its will on an occupied land without paying a terrible price. The Iraqis first rose up against Saddam and then, after the Anglo-American invasion, against the occupation armies. No longer did the Arabs run away. The old Sharon policy into which the American neo-conservatives so fatally bought before the 2003 invasion of Iraq—of beating the Arabs till they come to heel or until they "behave" or until an Arab leader can be found "to control his own people"—is now as bankrupt as the Arab regimes that continue to work for the world's only superpower.

This is not to recommend the social and military "people's" revolutions which have occurred in the Middle East. But in Lebanon, "Palestine" and Iraq, the suicide bomber has become the symbol of this new fearlessness. Once an occupied people have lost their fear of death, the occupier is doomed. Once a man or woman stops being afraid, he or she cannot be made to fear again. Fear is not a product that can be re-injected into a population through re-invasion or harsher treatment or air attacks or walls or torture.

As the wreckage of the Oslo agreement rusted away, the once viable alternatives were also being slowly dismissed. For years, critics of the Oslo agreement pointed to the vital, undeniable UN Security Council Resolution 242. But now even this alternative is losing its appeal. More and more among Palestinians I hear the words that so frighten Israelis: that they must have "all" of Palestine, not just the lands taken by Israel in 1967. In Gaza in the autumn of 2000, I actually encountered this transition in progress. A Palestinian computer trainee began by telling me that UN Resolution 242 was the only path to real compromise and peace. But by the end of his increasingly bitter peroration, he began talking about Haifa and Acre and Ashkelon, cities which are in Israel, not in the nation of "Palestine" that Arafat was prepared to accept.

And all the while, reading back through my own reports as I write this book, I come across frightening little portents. "Do the Americans realise the catastrophe that is about to overwhelm the region?" I find myself asking in a feature filed to *The Independent* on 25 February 2001. "Have they any idea of the elemental forces that may be unleashed in the coming months?" Again, I ask myself why I wrote these words. Less than six and a half months before those elemental forces did explode, what did I expect? And I remember that friend of mine in Ramallah, the one who tried to explain the Palestinian reaction to suicide bombers by saying that Palestinians felt that their enemies "should suffer too."

And so, as I pull my files from the shelves, my notebooks from Beirut and Israel and "Palestine," I hear the clock ticking towards 11 September 2001, the calendar spitting out the dates. I have a hard copy of a long report filed from Jerusalem on 28 August 2001. There are just two weeks left to go.


THERE ISN'T A SCRAP OF INAS Abu Zeid left. She was only seven and the "martyrs" posters already going up around Khan Younis show her to have been a delicate-featured girl. But there isn't a trace of her amid the fragments of corrugated iron and plastic, nor in the soft brown Gaza sand. Inas had been atomised, turned to dust in a millisecond. "I will show you where the missile came from," a boy tells me, pointing far across the sand to where a few miserable concrete huts, with rag windows and flapping, sand-caked washing, stand near the horizon. "The Israelis fired from behind those houses. It was a tank."

Was it so? I say this to myself, not as a question but as another of those remarks you find yourself making in Gaza. Lie? Truth? They matter when a war has grown so brutal, so cruel as this. Inas's father, Sulieman, died with her. So did his six-year-old son, also named Sulieman. I don't think I've come across a war in which children are killed so quickly. If it's not an Israeli baby in a Palestinian sniper's crosshairs, it's two pesky Palestinian kids stupid enough to stand outside a Hamas office when the Israelis have chosen to blow the place away, or schoolkids who decide to take an early afternoon pizza, or Inas and Sulieman junior who got in the way or—if Hamas was lying and the Israelis are telling the truth—were turned to wet dust by their father's bomb.

The Palestinian Authority has made a clean sweep of the Abu Zeids' backyard. If he was making a bomb, it has disappeared, like Inas. I poke around amid the desert trash. How could an Israeli missile fly over the other huts, turn the corner outside the Abu Zeids' backyard, pass over the yard walls and then dip below the plastic roof to blast the family apart? But who would make a bomb with his two tiny children standing next to him? Or maybe there was a bomb hidden at the back of the yard and Inas or Sulieman Junior touched it.

A crowd has gathered around us, unsmiling, suspicious. It's not so easy now to investigate these deaths. "I'm Norwegian but Palestinians have started to look at me in the street and talk about me as if I'm an American," a smiling aid worker says to me. "They blame the Americans for what the Israelis do. And now they blame the Europeans because we do nothing to help them." Which is exactly what happened in Lebanon. The Norwegian lady is right. I was watched as I walked through the street in Gaza City, scrutinised by youths in Rafah. At Kalandia—just outside Jerusalem, on the road to Ramallah—a Palestinian boy of perhaps twelve looks at my car's Israeli registration plates, picks up an iron bar and smashes it as hard as he can onto the back mudguard. Two men in a truck—we are all waiting at one of Israel's humiliating checkpoints—jeer at me.

Everywhere, you notice the signs of collapse, of incipient anarchy. The Gaza wall murals used to depict Yassir Arafat's beaming, ugly mug and pictures of the Al-Aqsa mosque. Now they are filled with exploding buses and dead children and Israeli soldiers on their backs with blood squirting from their heads. "They don't even talk about Arafat any more," a Palestinian café owner says to me as three horse-drawn water carts clop lazily past us. "There's only one joke going the rounds about him. Arafat is at Camp David and the Israelis are demanding that he 'ends the violence.' And Arafat replies: 'I can't end the violence until I can stop my lips from trembling.' " Arafat's growing senility is a source of deepening concern. Not far from Hebron, I meet a prominent Palestinian figure, important enough to require anonymity, who shakes his head in despair. "What can Arafat do now? His marriage is in bits—he's only seen his wife for three minutes in the past ten months. His child needs a father and he's not there. And he's allowing the whole place to tribalise and disintegrate. There is complete disintegration here."

It's true. On the road south of Nablus, a yellow Palestinian taxi is hit by a stone—apparently thrown by an Israeli driver in an oncoming car, or that's what the Israeli cops thought—and careers off the road. Its driver, Kemal Mosalem, is killed outright. But when his body arrives at the Rafidiyeh hospital, his family believe he has been killed by a rival Palestinian clan led by Ali Frej. The Frej family then ambush the grieving Mosalems with Kalashnikov rifles. Among the four Palestinian dead is Ali Frej and a Fatah official who had been part of Jibril Rajoub's local "preventive security" unit. Six others are wounded. These are Arafat's people. They are killing each other. And Arafat remains silent.

Yet here's the thing. Ariel Sharon keeps saying that Arafat is a murderer, a super-terrorist, the leader of "international terror," linked to Osama bin Laden, a man who gives orders for the murder of kids in pizza parlours. And the Israeli public are buying this, their journalists front-paging it, their people repeating it, over and over. Talking to Israelis—in taxis, on aeroplanes, in cafés—I keep hearing the same stuff. Terror, murder, filth. Like a cassette. Where have I heard this before?

In Gaza, I cannot fail to remember Beirut in 1982. Gaza now is a miniature Beirut. Under Israeli siege, struck by F-16s and tank fire and gunboats, starved and often powerless—there are now six-hour electricity cuts every day in Gaza—it's as if Arafat and Sharon are replaying their bloody days in Lebanon. Sharon used to call Arafat a mass murderer back then. It's important not to become obsessed during wars. But Sharon's words were like an old, miserable film I had seen before. Every morning in Jerusalem, I pick up the *Jerusalem Post*. And there on the front page, as usual, will be another Sharon diatribe. PLO murderers. Palestinian Authority terror. Murderous terrorists.

Each day I travel to the scene of new Israeli incursions. The Israelis bomb Palestinian police stations, Palestinian security annexes, Palestinian police checkpoints. Why the police? I drive round the Gaza Strip with an old friend from the Beirut war, a European aid worker who still bears the webbed scar of a Lebanese bullet in his arm and stomach—the round punctured his spleen and liver. "Now if you look to your right, Bob, there's the police station that the Israelis bombed two weeks ago," he says. There's a mass of burned-out rooms and a crumpled office. "And just round the corner here is the police post the Israelis hit last week." More trashed buildings. "And down that road you can just see the Palestinian offices that were hit in July." After the early raids, the Palestinians would do a quick rebuilding and repainting job. Now they no longer bother. But how can Arafat "arrest the murderers" if the Israelis are going to destroy all his police stations?

There was a story told to me by one of the men investigating Sharon's responsibility for the Sabra and Chatila massacre, and the story is that the then Israeli defence minister, before he sent his Phalangist allies into the camps, announced that it was Palestinian "terrorists" who had murdered their newly assassinated leader, president-elect Bashir Gemayel. Sharon was to say later that he never dreamed the Phalange would massacre the Palestinians. But how could he say that if he claimed earlier that the Palestinians killed the leader of the Phalange? In reality, no Palestinians were involved in Gemayel's death. It might seem odd in this new war to be dwelling about that earlier atrocity. I am fascinated by the language. Murderers, terrorists. That's what Sharon said then, and it's what he says now. Did he really make that statement in 1982? I begin to work the phone from Jerusalem, calling up Associated Press bureaus that might still have their files from nineteen years ago. He would have made that speech—if indeed he used those words—some time on 15 September 1982.

One Sunday afternoon, my phone rings in Jerusalem. It's from an Israeli I met in Jaffa Street after the Sbarro bombing. An American Jewish woman had been screaming abuse at me—foreign journalists are being insulted by both sides with ever more violent language—and this man suddenly intervenes to protect me. He's smiling and cheerful and we exchange phone numbers. Now on the phone, he says he's taking the El Al night flight to New York with his wife. Would I like to drop by for tea?

He turns out to have a luxurious apartment next to the King David Hotel and I notice, when I read his name on the outside security buzzer, that he's a rabbi. He's angry because a neighbour has just let down a friend's car tyres in the underground parking lot and he's saying how he felt like smashing the windows of the neighbour's car. His wife, bringing me tea and feeding me cookies, says that her husband—again, he should remain anonymous—gets angry very quickly. There's a kind of gentleness about them both—how easy it is to spot couples who are still in love—that is appealing. But when the rabbi starts to talk about the Palestinians, his voice begins to echo through the apartment. He says several times that Sharon is a good friend of his, a fine man, who's been to visit him in his New York office.

What we should do is go into those vermin pits and take out the terrorists and murderers. Vermin pits, yes I said vermin, animals. I tell you what we should do. If one stone is lobbed from a refugee camp, we should bring the bulldozers and tear down the first twenty houses close to the road. If there's another stone, another twenty ones. They'd soon learn not to throw stones. Look, I tell you this. Stones are lethal. If you throw a stone at me, I'll shoot you. I have the right to shoot you.

Now the rabbi is a generous man. He's been in Israel to donate a vastly important and, I have no doubt, vastly expensive medical centre to the country. He is well-read. And I liked the fact that—unlike too many Israelis and Palestinians who put on a "we-only-want-peace" routine to hide more savage thoughts—he at least spoke his mind. But this is getting out of hand. Why should I throw a stone at the rabbi? He shouts again. "If you throw a stone at me, I will shoot you." But if you throw a stone at me, I say, I won't shoot you. Because I have the right not to shoot you. He frowns. "Then I'd say you're out of your mind."

I am driving home when it suddenly hits me. The Old and New Testaments have just collided. The rabbi's dad taught him about an eye for an eye—or twenty homes for a stone—whereas Bill Fisk taught me about turning the other cheek. Judaism is bumping against Christianity. So is it any surprise that Judaism and Islam are crashing into each other? For despite all the talk of Christians and Jews being "people of the Book," Muslims are beginning to express ever harsher views of Jews. The sickening Hamas references to Jews as "the sons of pigs and monkeys" are echoed by Israelis who talk of Palestinians as cockroaches or "vermin," who tell you—as the rabbi told me—that Islam is a warrior religion, a religion that does not value human life. And I recall several times a Jewish settler who told me back in 1993—in Gaza, just before the Oslo accords were signed—that "we do not recognise their Koran as a valid document."

I walk out of *The Independent*'s office and home in the Jerusalem suburb of Abu Tor to find my car surrounded by glass. Now it's my turn to get angry. The driver's window has been smashed, the radio torn out. It is plastered with "TV" stickers—in the hope that Palestinian gunmen and Israeli soldiers will not open fire. Abu Tor is mostly Arab, although *The Independent*'s house is right on the old green line, Arabs to the right of the front door, mostly Jews to the left. I drive down to the Hertz agency, sitting on piles of glass. The girl tells me that to avail myself of Hertz's insurance, I have to report the robbery to the police. She tells me to go to the Russian Compound.

Now I know about the Russian Compound from Amnesty's reports. This is where most of the Israeli torture goes on, the infamous "shaking" of suspected Palestinian "terrorists." It should be an interesting trip. The moment I park my car, a loudspeaker shrieks at me in Hebrew. A cop tells me that for security reasons I have to park round the corner. No trouble with that. I watch two big police vans with sealed windows pass through the security barrier. I park and return to the door. "Where was your car robbed?" I am asked. Just outside the office, in Abu Tor, I reply. The policewoman shrugs. "Well, what do you expect?" she asks. I understand what she means. Arabs rob, don't they, they steal car radios as well as blow up pizzerias? I wait for an hour. There is no cop to make out a report, although there are more than 200 policemen surrounding Orient House, a few hundred metres across the city.

There's a daily demonstration just down the road from Orient House. The television cameras are there but this doesn't stop the border police turning on several Palestinian youths. They are beaten in front of the cameras, groined and punched and headlocked by six cops. One is laid in a van where he is held down so that another policeman can stamp on his testicles. A young Israeli security man can't take his eyes off this vile scene. He is bending down low—right in front of me—to see where the other cop's boot is landing between the youth's thighs. How can they do this in front of the cameras? I keep asking myself. And then the dark thought occurs to me: that the Israeli police want the cameras to film this, they want the Palestinians to see what happens to them when they oppose Israel, when they demonstrate, when they object—as one boy does—by holding up a paper Palestinian flag.

I think it's the psychological shock of violence that always hits first, the sudden realisation that human beings intend to hurt each other. It afflicts everyone in this conflict. I have been attending the funeral of a Hamas man in Tulkarem and am returning to my taxi which is parked on the Israeli side of the line. On the map of the West Bank and Gaza—a broken window of settler roads and frontiers—Tulkarem is in Palestinian-controlled Area A and my taxi is in Israeli-controlled Area C. When I'd gone from C to A in the morning, the road was a litter of rubbish and stones. But when I return, there is a battle in progress, kids throwing stones at Israeli positions, burning tyres, rubber-coated steel bullets thwacking back through the trees.

I am tired and hungry and impatient to return to Jerusalem. So I grab the boys beside the burning tyres and tell them I am a journalist, that I have to cross back through the line. I find two more sinister figures lurking in a wrecked bus shelter. I tell them the same. Then I walk between the burning tyres towards the unseen Israelis, slowly, almost a dawdle. Then a stone lands at my feet. Just a very small stone but it lands with a nasty little crack. Then when I turn round, another hisses past my face. One of the Palestinian boys begins to shriek with laughter. Stones. I have never thought of them as enemies before. In a few months' time, they will hit me, many of them, and almost kill me. But that will be later, after the calendar clicks round to the date that is waiting for us all and that I can only vaguely ascertain now as an "explosion."

I keep walking slowly and realise that I will have physically to dodge each well-aimed stone calmly, as if it is perfectly normal for the *Independent* correspondent to be stoned by Palestinians on a hot summer's afternoon. The road runs parallel with Area A now, and a teenager with a slingshot comes crashing through the trees—I can hear the whirr of the rope. The stone comes towards me so fast I can't duck in time but it misses me by about a foot and smashes into the iron wall of an Israeli factory. The crash makes me look round. I am in the middle of an abandoned garden shop, surrounded by pots and cement eagles and deers and giant pots. One of the eagles has lost its head. Three more stones, maybe eight inches long. I realise what has happened. The Palestinians know I am a foreign journalist—I have shown them my Lebanese press card. But the moment I cross the line, I have become an Israeli. The moment they can no longer distinguish my face, they no longer care. I am an Israeli because I am on the Israeli side of the line. And I wonder what my friend the rabbi would have done.

Back in Jerusalem, I work the phone again, trying to track down that elusive quotation. If you call people animals, terrorists, vermin, can you be surprised when they behave so violently? Is it any wonder that Arafat is himself tribalising the rubbish dumps he still controls, playing the Musris and Nabulsis of Nablus off against each other, backing the Shakars of Nablus and the Shawars of Gaza, placating Hamas and Islamic Jihad by saying nothing?

On the way to Jenin, I and a colleague from the *Daily Telegraph* are stopped by Israeli border guards. On the sweaty road, we call the Israeli army press office for permission to pass. There's a small Jewish settlement up the hill, all red roofs and luscious foliage. It's strange how naturally we treat these little land-thefts now. The border guards are bored. One of them switches on the jeep's loudspeaker and hooks the mike to his mobile phone and begins playing the music "hold" button. Three lines of the 1812 Overture, three lines of Beethoven's Fifth, three lines of Handel's Water Music, all squawking out at high decibels, distorted and high-pitched, spilling its high-tech destruction of the world's greatest composers over the sweltering road with its lizards and bushes and garbage.

It's a relief to find sanity. On a flight into Tel Aviv, I find myself sitting next to an Israeli paratroop officer. I give him my own assessment—an intifada that will go on until 2004. He says it will last well into 2006. "And in the end, we'll be back on the 'sixty-seven border and give them East Jerusalem as their capital." And then he adds: "But given the way we're treating them, I'd be surprised if they'd settle for that." I ask a Palestinian in Rafah what he thinks. "2005, 2006, what difference does it make? But I tell you one thing. After this intifada is over, there will be a revolt against Arafat. How did he ever allow this to happen? How did he ever think he could win?" There will be no revolt, of course. Sharon will trap Arafat in Ramallah. And Arafat will die.

I am driving again through Gaza. Beside the road, a group of middle-aged men are sitting under a green awning; some have their heads in their hands, others are just looking at the sand. They are mourning Mohamed Abu Arrar, shot in the head by an Israeli soldier while throwing stones. He was thirteen. Every wall has become a mosaic of posters, dead youths, dead old men, dead children, dead women, dead suicide bombers; usually they have a coloured photograph of the Al-Aqsa mosque behind their heads, a building most of them will never have seen.

Just outside Khan Younis, the Israelis have bulldozed acres of citrus groves and houses—for "security" reasons of course, since there is a Jewish colony in the background—and left yet another bit of "Palestine" looking like the moon. "Well, they say it's for 'security,' " a European official tells me. "But I have a question. There were three houses standing over there, one of them was finished and lived in, the other two were still just walls and roofs. The Israelis said they could be used for ambushes. So a bulldozer comes and totally demolishes the completed home and then only destroys the staircases of the two unfinished homes. Now, how can that be for 'security'?"

Down at Rafah, the truly surreal. A man in his forties steps out of a tent right on the border—the Egyptian flag behind him almost touching the Israeli flag—and asks me if I would like to see the ruins of his toy shop. And there it is, right beside the tent, a tumble of concrete blocks, model telephones, lampshades, clocks, toy helicopters and one large outsize till. "The Israelis destroyed it in May and I stayed until the very last moment, running into that alleyway when the tanks arrived," he says. Mohamed al-Shaer, it turns out, is a Palestinian with an Egyptian passport. "I've got one house over there behind the palm tree"—here he points across the frontier wall—"and I'm here to guard this property." He's allowed to pass back and forth like other dual-citizenship Rafah residents because of a 1906 agreement between the Ottoman empire and Britain which he proceeds to explain in complex and unending detail. Behind him, children are flying kites—and each time a kite floats over the frontier wire, an Israeli soldier fires a shot. It cracks across the muck and sand and the children shout with pleasure. "Cra-crack," it goes again. "They always shoot at the kites or the kids," Mohamed al-Shaer says. He learned his English as a computer programmer in Cairo and explains fluently that the real reason he stays is that he has a relative whom he distrusts, that the relative lives on the Palestinian side of Rafah and might re-register the land on which the shop was built as his own if Mohamed returned to Egypt.

Every night, Palestinians shoot from these streets at the Israelis—which is why the Israelis destroyed Mohamed al-Shaer's shop. "These were the bullet holes from last night," he says, showing me three fist-size cavities in the wall of the nearest building. "I could hear the bullets going over my tent." I wonder how I can write the picture caption to the photograph I've taken of al-Shaer: "A Palestinian at war with his relative, sitting in a tent next to a demolished toy-shop, watches the Israelis shooting at kites."

I call up Eva Stern in New York. Her talent for going through archives convinces me she can find out what Sharon said before the Sabra and Chatila massacre. I give her the date that is going through my head: 15 September 1982. She comes back on the line the same night. "Turn your fax on," Eva says. "You're going to want to read this." The paper starts to crinkle out of the machine. An AP report of 15 September 1982. "Defence Minister Ariel Sharon, in a statement,

tied the killing [of the Phalangist leader Gemayel] to the PLO, saying 'it symbolises the terrorist murderousness of the PLO terrorist organisations and their
supporters.' "

Then, a few hours later, Sharon sent the Phalange gunmen into the Palestinian
camps. Reading that fax again and again, I feel a chill coming over me. There are
Israelis today with as much rage towards the Palestinians as the Phalange nineteen
years ago. And these are the same words I am hearing today, from the same man,
about the same people.

BUT WHO ARE THOSE PEOPLE? In the taboo-ridden world of Western journalism,
every effort continues to be made not only to dehumanise them but to de-culture
them, de-nation them, to dis-identify them. A long article by David Margolick in
*Vanity Fair* explains Israel's policy of "targeted killing"—the murder of Palestinians chosen by the Israelis as "security" threats—although Margolick never mentions the word "murder." Some of Israel's "targeted killing" operations, he says,
are "dazzling." Yet nowhere in the article is it explained where the Palestinians
come from, why they are occupied—or why Jewish colonies are being built on
their land. In the *Mail on Sunday*, Stewart Steven writes that "there is no language
known as Palestinian. There is no distinct Palestinian culture. There is no specific
Palestinian dress. Palestinians are indistinguishable from other Arabs." Jerusalem,
he adds, "was never visited by Mohamed." Palestinians speak Arabic but with a
distinctive Palestinian accent. There *is* a Palestinian culture of poetry and prose
and—among women—of national dress. Physically, many Palestinians are recog-
nisable by their height, the darkness of their skin—if they come from the south—
and their facial features. It could equally be said that there is no language known as
American, that American culture is of English origin, that there is no specific
American dress, that Americans are indistinguishable from other Westerners. Legend, not the Koran, has it that Mohamed visited Jerusalem. Perhaps he did not. But
Christians do not deny the holy nature of the Vatican or Canterbury Cathedral just
because Christ never visited Italy or England.

Far more disturbing and vicious paradigms of this contempt for Palestinians
regularly appear in Western newspapers. In the *Irish Times*, for example, Mark
Steyn felt able to describe the eminently decent Hanan Ashrawi as one of a number of "bespoke terror apologists." A visit to the West Bank in 2003, Steyn wrote,
"creeped me out." It was "a wholly diseased environment," a "culture that glorifies
depravity," which led the author to conclude that "nothing good grows in toxic
soil."

Once the identity of Palestinians has been removed, once their lands are subject to "dispute" rather than "occupation," once Arafat allowed the Americans and
Israelis to relegate Jerusalem, settlements and the "right of return" to "final status"
negotiations—and thus not to be mentioned in the meantime, for to do so would
"threaten" peace—the mere hint of Palestinian resistance can be defined as "terrorism." Inside this society there is a sickness—"disease," "depravity," "toxic

soil." Buried in Palestinian hearts—in secret—must remain their sense of unresolved anger, frustration and resentment at a multitude of injustices.*

Within hours of the 11 September 2001 attacks on the United States, Ariel Sharon turned Israel into America's ally in the "war on terror," immediately realigning Yassir Arafat as the Palestinian version of bin Laden and the Palestinian suicide bombers as blood brothers of the nineteen Arabs—none of them Palestinian—who hijacked the four American airliners. In the new and vengeful spirit that President Bush encouraged among Americans, Israel's supporters in the United States now felt free to promote punishments for Israel's opponents that came close to the advocacy of war crimes. Nathan Lewin, a prominent Washington attorney and Jewish communal leader—and an often-mentioned candidate for a federal judgeship—called for the execution of family members of suicide bombers. "If executing some suicide bombers' families saves the lives of even an equal number of potential civilian victims, the exchange is, I believe, ethically permissible," he wrote in the journal *Sh'ma*.

One could only wonder how Lewin's plan could be put into practice. Would the suicide bomber's wife—or husband—be put to death first? Or the first-born? Or the youngest son? Or perhaps granny would be hauled from her armchair and done away with while the rest of the family looked on. Lewin's argument, predictably, rested on scripture. "The biblical injunction to destroy the ancient tribe of Amalek served as a precedent in Judaism for taking measures that were 'ordinarily unacceptable' in the face of a mortal threat." Alan Dershowitz, the Harvard Law School professor who favoured the limited use of torture to extract information, said that Lewin's proposal was a legitimate if flawed attempt to strike a balance between preventing "terrorism" and preserving democracy. Other American Jewish leaders forcefully condemned Lewin's opinion as reprehensible and pointed out that scholars had ruled that the lessons of Amalek could not be applied to contemporary events lest the arguments "go all the way and suggest that the Palestinian nation as a whole has earned the fate of Amalek."

Not that the Palestinians themselves were averse to death sentences for their own people, albeit that the targets were Israel's collaborators. On 9 August 2000, for instance, it took just twenty minutes for Judge Fathi Abu Srur to decide that Munzer Hafnawi should be executed. At 10 o'clock he sat in his plastic chair, hands clasped between his knees, his gaze moving steadily over the seething crowd in the Nablus Palestinian courtroom, his solemn brown eyes avoiding the mother of the young Palestinian whose murder by the Israelis he had allegedly arranged. His lawyer, Samir Abu Audi—appointed by the Palestinian Authority— sat meekly below the bench, head bowed, in silence. By 10:20, Judge Abu Srur had ordered the execution of the accused and Hafnawi was crouching like an animal at the feet of his prison guards.

*In Korea, a country with its own vault of sadness and betrayal, this feeling is translated as *han*. A writer on Korea has concluded that "it is likely the misfortune of all small countries to experience injustice at the hands of larger, more powerful neighbours. The Irish cultivate their version of *han* towards the English; Polish *han* is directed at the Russian and German neighbours that have long wrestled for control of the land that lay between them."

This wasn't rough justice. It wasn't even tragic farce. It was a drumhead court which allowed the public to scream and wolf-whistle at the grey-bearded, forty-three-year-old defendant the moment the judge announced that, according to Jordanian Criminal Article 111 of 1960—a nice judicial Hashemite touch, this—his sentence was "to execute the criminal." As the guards dragged Hafnawi towards the court door, several men leaned over the barrier to beat their fists on his head. "Your excellency the President," the crowd bayed—the president being Arafat— "execute the spy at once!" No one in the Nablus court was likely to forget the smiles on the faces of the men when "death by bullets" was demanded by the prosecution, and the hoots of derision towards the doglike, humiliated creature in the open-neck white shirt and beige trousers who clung to the legs of his jailers.

The evidence, on the face of it, seemed damning. Hafnawi, the court was told, had graduated through the Popular Front for the Liberation of Palestine, through Fatah and then into Hamas solely to betray his comrades to Israeli killers. He had admitted in a signed confession that he had worked for the Israelis since 1979, but it was the murder of twenty-five-year-old Hamas member Mahmoud Madani on 19 February 2000 that did for him. Hafnawi owned a clothing store and employed Madani, who had been shot dead on his way to Hafnawi's shop from the mosque; the judge referred to an eleven-page "confession"—one could imagine the immutable fairness with which this was obtained—and to Hafnawi's acknowledgement that the Israelis had asked him to collect information on Madani; Hafnawi had told interrogators that he "didn't know the Israelis were going to execute Madani."

The defendant began to perspire. Beads of sweat began to appear around the corners of his eyes. Then a stream of perspiration ran from behind his ears and poured down his neck. Two policemen linked their arms with his. He was a dead man. Without the help of the defendant, the judge solemnly announced, Madani could not have been murdered by the Israelis. "It is illogical to say he was not responsible because he was not at the scene of the crime," the judge told the angry crowd of spectators and Madani's mother. "He played a major role in committing the crime because of his links with the Israelis . . . " There were eyewitness statements and security force evidence—Hafnawi had ordered his wife to delete the called numbers on his mobile phone when the police came for him a few hours after the killing—and this was the third and final sitting of the court.

As the moment of sentencing approached, the crowd were like stones. "This defendant, who was a citizen of the homeland but whose loyalty was not to the homeland, sold himself—his eyes and ears—to the usurpers of his homeland." Judge Abu Srur paused in these words. "What sort of man is he? Didn't he think about his roots?" There was no decorum about it. No "silence in court" when the judge and his two colleagues—one an army colonel, the other a captain—left the room. In the bright midday sun outside, Madani's mother, Nihad, told me she was "very happy" at the sentence, but wanted it carried out at once. "My son was a hero," she said. "He arranged two acts of martyrdom in Tel Aviv and he was planning another six attacks. He was a captain in the Hamas Ezzedine Brigade. I bless God. My heart is at ease now." A neighbour interrupted to abuse the convicted murderer. "Let him die slowly," he cursed. Mrs. Madani turned upon him. "I prefer to kill him myself," she said. Hafnawi and Madani, it transpired, had been imprisoned together by the Israelis. Stool-pigeon. Collaborator. Traitor. Hafnawi's family, as they say, was not in court. But these legal theatres would not last. It was the Palestinian mob who would ultimately decide on "justice," once the last shreds of the Oslo agreement had been blown away.

Hebron, four months later. I drive there on a settlers' road—Israeli registration plates, of course—then clamber over an abandoned Israeli checkpoint and just walk after all the other Palestinian men, women and children who are moving like a tide into the city. The first body is hanging upside down, one grey left foot tied to the electricity pylon with wire, his right leg hanging at an obscene angle, his head lolling below what remains of a black shirt. This was Moussa Arjoub of Doura village. The second body is infinitely more terrible, a butcher's carcass, again hanging by a left leg, but this time his almost naked torso riven with stab marks into which Palestinian boys of ten or twelve, whooping with glee, are stubbing cigarettes. This was Zuheir al-Mukhtaseb. His head is almost severed from his remains, moving slightly in the wind, bearded, face distorted with terror.

He reminds me of those fearsome portraits of Saint Sebastian, all arrows and open wounds. But Zuheir al-Mukhtaseb is reviled, not honoured, screaming children and middle-aged Palestinian men roaring with delight when stones thump off the collaborator's bloody corpse. "This is a lesson to all here." I turn around to find a portly man with a big brown beard, gesturing towards another revolting bag of flesh behind me. "This was Mohamed Debebsi. This is a lesson for the people. Everyone should see this." As I watch, a group of youths with grinning faces hurls the corpse into a rubbish truck.

What do you do when a people go mad with joy at such savagery? At first, I cannot write the description of what I see into my reporter's notebook and instead draw sketches to remind me of what I am seeing. *Allahu akbar,* roars that awful crowd. There are girls on rooftops, young men in suits and ties staring at the corpses from only 3 metres away, boys throwing stones to finish the decapitation of Zuheir al-Mukhtaseb. And the street where this—let us call it by its name and say, this pornography—is taking place? Sharia *Salam.* The Street of Peace.

The three men had been imprisoned in the local jail—sentenced so long ago that many of the crowd could not remember the date—for collaborating with Israel's occupation forces. Did they guess their fate, a few hours earlier, when they heard an Israeli Apache helicopter firing its four missiles, the power of the explosions audible in their Palestinian Authority prison a few hundred metres away?

The Israelis had sent a helicopter death squad to eliminate Marwan Zalum, one of the heads of the Al-Aqsa Brigades in Hebron, the four missiles—another gift from Lockheed Martin of Florida, according to the bits I found—turning his Mitsubishi car into a fireball. Zalum, who was forty-three and married, with a little girl called Saja, died at once—to a chorus of delight from the Israeli army. He was, they said, "the equivalent of an entire armed militia"—a ridiculous exaggeration—and they referred to suicide bombings arranged by his men and the "hundreds of shooting attacks," including the deaths of Shalhevat Pas, a Jewish infant murdered by a Palestinian sniper in March 2001, and of an Israeli civilian—a settler—killed three months later. Three times, the Israeli army's death squad admission talked of "Jewish communities" when it meant Jewish settlements on Arab land. And true to the morality of such statements, it failed to mention that Samir abu-Rajab, a friend of Zalum, was also killed with him by Israel's American-made missiles.

No matter. By 9:30, the Al-Aqsa Brigades and probably Hamas and no doubt a vast rabble of Palestinian corner-boys decided to revenge themselves by slaughtering Israel's three Palestinian collaborators who sat, helpless, in the local jail. A civil engineer watching the crowds told me that they were dragged to the scene of the car explosion, beaten insensible by the mob and then shot by gunmen.

So the people of the Hebron suburb of Ein Sara arrived to celebrate this revolting scene. A few touched the corpses, others stood by the roadside to throw stones. It was a meat shop, the kids climbing the electricity pylons to pose beside this butcher's work for friends with camcorders. And how they cheered when the refuse truck moved through the crowds in front of a German-donated fire engine. After Debebsi's bloody remains were flung into the back, the lorry moved to the pylon where Mukhtaseb was hanging. His head almost parted from his body as it was thrown into the grey-painted vehicle to another cry of satisfaction from the crowd.

So the citizens of the nascent Palestinian nation behaved in anger and fury and terrible pleasure at their revenge on Israel for the killing of Zalum and abu-Rajab. And on the way back to Jerusalem, of course, one could well imagine the reaction of the inhabitants of those illegal Jewish settlements of Efrat and Neve Daniel and Gush Etzion with their neat red roofs and water sprinklers. Savagery, barbarism, beasts acting like beasts. And one knew what the Palestinians thought. Those three men worked for Israel, for the country which has occupied their land for thirty-five years. "They probably did it for money," a Palestinian driver mumbled at me. All three collaborators were married men. It was said in Hebron that they would be refused a Muslim grave. And one wondered how brutalised the Palestinians must become before they inherit a state.

But what state was there to inherit? On 29 March 2002, the Israelis launched an attack on the West Bank which, for the press, they called "Operation Defensive Shield."* Two days earlier, a Hamas suicide bomber had walked into a hotel in the Israeli coastal town of Netanya and blown up a roomful of people celebrating the Jewish Passover, killing twenty-eight civilians, most of them elderly, some of them survivors of the Jewish Holocaust. It was the worst mass killing of its kind of Israeli civilians since the start of the intifada. In all, between 1 March and 1 April 2002, forty Israeli civilians were slaughtered. So the stated purpose of this Israeli

---

*Like the American and British armies, the Israelis often announce a "media" title for their operations which bears no relation to the actual military codename. Thus Israel's 1982 invasion of Lebanon was officially called "Operation Peace for Galilee"—a propaganda legend that gullible journalists happily disseminated—while its real codename was "Operation Snowball." Unlike "peace," snowballs increase in size and power as they roll downhill.

assault, according to the Israeli army, was to eradicate the infrastructure of "terrorism." Inevitably, their first strike was against Arafat himself, marooned in his old British fortress in the centre of Ramallah. Unable to bamboozle my way through the Israeli roadblocks on the highway from Jerusalem, I drove up to the illegal Israeli colony of Psagot, from where I had an Israeli-eye view of this new battle to destroy the Palestinian Authority. It was the looking-glass again. March the thirty-first, 2002, and here I was, amid a heavily armed settlement crammed with troops—friendly, offering to share their food with me—looking down on the start of "Palestine" 's latest tragedy. Grey smoke rose in a curtain over Arafat's headquarters, drifting high above two minarets and then smudging the skyline south of Ramallah.

"I guess he's blown himself up," an Israeli paratrooper said with contempt. "That guy is finished." We stood on the edge of the settlement—just 400 metres from the first houses of the newly reoccupied Palestinian city—surrounded by Merkava tanks, Magah armoured vehicles and jeeps and trucks and hundreds of reservists tugging blankets and mattresses and guns from the backs of lorries. "It's only just beginning, you know that?" the paratrooper asked. "They are idiots down there. They should know their terrorism is over. We're never going back to the '67 borders. Anyway, they want Tel Aviv." A clap of sound punched our ears, a shell exploding on the other side of the hill upon which Ramallah lies. I wandered closer to the city, through a garden of daffodils and dark purple flowers, to where an Israeli boy soldier was standing.

"I want to go home," he said blankly. I said that twenty seemed to be too young to be a soldier. "That's what my mother says." He was eating matzo bread with salami, staring at the empty streets of Ramallah. "They've locked themselves in their homes," he said. "Do you blame them?" I didn't. But it was a strange morning, sitting with the Israeli soldiers above Ramallah, a bit like those awful viewing platforms that generals would arrange for their guests in the Napoleonic wars, where food and wine might be served while they watched the progress of the battle. There was even a settler couple, cheerfully serving hot food and coffee to the reservists. The woman held out a bowl of vegetables and cheese for me. "My daughter's at Cambridge University," she said gaily. "She's studying the history of the Crusades." A bloody business, I remarked, and her companion happily agreed. Religious wars are like that. That's when I saw the four Palestinians.

Just below us, next to the garden with the daffodils and the purple flowers, three of them were kneeling on the grass in front of a group of Israeli officers. All were blindfolded, their hands tied behind them with plastic and steel handcuffs, one of them with his jacket pulled down over his back so that he could not even move his shoulders. The Israelis were talking to them quietly, one of them on one knee as if before an altar rather than a prisoner. Then I saw the fourth man, middle-aged, trussed up like a chicken, stretched across the grass with his blindfolded face lying amid a bunch of flowers. The paratrooper shrugged. "They all say they've done nothing, that they're innocent, that we just came into their homes and took them without reason. Well, that's what they say."

I mentioned the prisoners to the two friendly settlers. They nodded, as if it was quite normal to discover four men bound and blindfolded in the garden. When I asked the twenty-year-old about them, he shrugged like the paratrooper. "They're not my prisoners," he said, and I thought of Amira Hass and her contempt for those whom she saw "looking from the side." I walked round the corner of the building to the lawn upon which the Palestinians were being questioned. Another prisoner was repeatedly bowing his head before a door and his shoulders moved as if he was weeping.

None of it worried the soldiers. In their own unique "war on terror," these prisoners were "terrorists." Another soldier eating a plate of greens said that he thought "all the people down there" were "terrorists." Terrorists, terrorists, terrorists. In front of us a Merkava passed, roaring down the hill below in a fog of blue smoke, its barrel gently dipping up and down above its hull. More troops arrived in more trucks, assault rifles in their hands. Radio shacks were being erected, armoured vehicles positioned above Ramallah. On the road back to Jerusalem, I pass a rusting old bus opposite Ma'ale Adumim, its windows covered in wire. Hands were gripping the wire and behind them, twenty or thirty faces could be seen through the mesh. The Palestinian prisoners were silent, looking out of the windows at the massive Jewish colony, watching me, dark faces in shadow, guarded by a jeepload of Israeli troops.

A few minutes later, I stop to buy bread and chocolate at a Palestinian grocery store in East Jerusalem. The shoppers—men for the most part, with just two veiled women—are standing below the store's television set, plastic bags of food hanging from their hands. Israeli television does not flinch from telling the truth about its casualties. "The toll so far appears to be fourteen dead," the commentator announces. The Palestinians of Jerusalem understand Hebrew. A camera aboard a helicopter is scanning the roof of a Haifa restaurant, peeled back like a sardine can by a Hamas suicide bomber's explosives. A boy shakes his head but an elderly man turns on him. "No," he says, pointing at the screen. "That's the way to do it."

And I think of the girl in Cambridge who is studying the Crusades, and what a bloody business we agreed it was. And how religious wars tend to be the bloodiest of all.

Whenever the Israeli army wants to stop us seeing what they're up to, out comes that most preposterous exercise in military law-on-the-hoof: the "Closed Military Area." As in Lebanon in 1982, as in Gaza in 1993, as in all Israel's campaigns of occupation—so in 2002; and, as usual, the best reaction was to go and look at what the Israelis didn't want us to see. In Ramallah, I could see why they didn't want reporters around. A slog down a gravel-covered hillside not far from an Israeli checkpoint, a clamber over rocks and mud and a hitched ride to the Palestinian refugee camp of al-Amari on the edge of Ramallah told a story of terrified civilians and roaring tanks and kids throwing stones at Israeli jeeps, just as they did before Oslo and all the other false hopes that the Americans and Israelis and Arafat brought to the region.

It was a grey, cold, wet day for Sharon's war on terror, and it was a doctor who gave me a lift in his ambulance to the centre of Ramallah, driving slowly down side roads, skidding to a halt when we caught sight of a tank barrel poking from behind apartment blocks, for ever looking upwards at the wasplike Apaches that flew in pairs over the city. The centre was a canyon of fast-moving tanks, armoured personnel carriers with their hatches down and wild shooting from both Israelis and Palestinians. While the bullets crackled across the streets, the Israeli army drove its APCs and Merkavas—and a few old British Centurions, unless my eyes deceived me—around the roads at such high speed that they could scarcely have seen a "terrorist" if he'd waved at them from the steps of the local supermarket. Oslo had come to this.

Whenever they saw a Westerner, a journalist or a "peace activist"—the latter distinguished by lots of earrings, Palestinian scarves and in one case a nose-ring—the Palestinians of Ramallah would creep from their front doors and wave to us and offer us coffee. A child ran across a field, chasing a horse, and an old man drove a mule up a side road with a broad smile. And I realised then, I think, that it was these ordinary people—the families and the old man and the child with the horse—who were the real resistance to the Israelis, those who refuse to be intimidated from their very ordinary lives rather than the poseurs of Fatah and the Al-Aqsa Brigades.

There came from the Palestinians a litany of evidence of vandalisation and theft by Israeli soldiers. "Baseless incitement whipped up by the Palestinian Authority," went the Israeli reply, but it was almost all true. Israeli soldiers had defecated over office floors, destroyed thousands of dollars' worth of fax and photocopying machines in Palestinian ministries and schools and—far more seriously—stolen tens of thousands of dollars' worth of jewellery and cash from private Palestinian homes. Ramallah is a middle-class town; and, unfortunately for the Israeli army, many of the Palestinian families whose money was taken also held American citizenship. For reporting this looting by an army that is supposed to believe in "purity of arms," I was attacked as a "liar" and "anti-Semitic" by Israel's so-called friends. Yet within days, the Israeli army itself would admit that "there were indeed wide-scale, ugly phenomena of vandalism . . . the extent of the looting was much greater than could have been expected . . . " In Ramallah, this included the "systematic destruction" of computers. Israeli journalists published similar reports—without enduring racist abuse.

In the coming few days, Israeli forces would pour into Tulkarem, Nablus and other cities.* But it was in Jenin that the Israelis met their fiercest resistance and committed what can only be described as individual war crimes. Again, they forbade all journalists to enter Jenin as they smashed their way into the ancient souk

---

*Amnesty International's statistics showed that between 27 February and June 2002, which included two major Israeli offensives and the reoccupation of the West Bank, nearly 500 Palestinians were killed, many during armed confrontations, although 16 per cent of the victims—more than 70—were children. From the first Israeli incursions in March until June 2002, more than 250 Israelis were killed, including 164 civilians of whom 32 were children. More than 8,000 Palestinians detained during this period, according to Amnesty, were "routinely subjected to ill-treatment" and 3,000 Palestinian homes were demolished.

and the refugee camp that forms part of the city centre. Palestinian gunmen fought back tenaciously. There was no doubt that Jenin was a centre of suicide bombers—I had several times interviewed their families in the area—and there is equally no doubt that the Israelis met formidable resistance.* By 9 April, the Israelis had lost twenty-three soldiers in the fighting. And it was they who first gave the impression that there had been a massacre of civilians inside the city.

The IDF's official spokesman, Brigadier General Ron Kitrey, said early in the battle that there were "apparently hundreds" of dead. Israeli "military sources"—the anonymous screen behind which Israeli colonels briefed military correspondents of the Israeli press—said there was a plan to move bodies out of the camp and bury them in a "special cemetery." Refrigerated trucks were taken to Jenin. When two Palestinian rights groups appealed to the Israeli High Court to prevent the removal of the bodies because they would be interred in a mass grave in the Jordan Valley which would dishonour the dead, the court issued an interim order supporting the plaintiffs. All this time, journalists were kept out of Jenin, along with humanitarian workers and the International Red Cross.† At a press conference, an Israeli brigade chief of staff, Major Rafi Lederman, stated that—contrary to newspaper reports—the Israeli armed forces did not fire missiles from American-made Cobra helicopters. This was totally untrue. The ruins of Jenin, when journalists did eventually enter, were littered with parts of air-to-ground missiles—made in the United States, of course—and Western defence attachés who visited the scene said that the Israelis were not telling the truth about the Cobras. Then, as our Jerusalem correspondent Phil Reeves wrote, "the Palestinian leadership . . . instantly, and without proof, declared that a massacre had occurred in Jenin in which as many as 500 died. Palestinian human rights groups made matters worse by churning out wild, and clearly untrue stories."

This then became the all-important theme of Israel's response to the killings in Jenin. "There was no massacre," Benjamin Netanyahu shouted at a pro-Israeli rally in Trafalgar Square. And since then, the story of Israel's massive, brutal incursion into Jenin has focused not upon what actually did happen in that terrible episode of Palestinian and Israeli history but upon the supposed "lie" of the massacre. It was the "lie," not the facts, that became the story. The journalists had "lied." I had "lied"—during a lecture series across the United States in the late spring of 2002, I was repeatedly accused of lying about the "massacre" in Jenin—even though I was in Los Angeles at the time, had not witnessed the killings and had never used the word "massacre." There were enough real massacres attributable to Israel without inventing any more.

---

*Though not so formidable that the old Palestinian guerrilla hands who had endured the six weeks' siege of Beirut in 1982 showed any admiration for them. "Why didn't they *fight*?" one of them asked me in Lebanon a month later.

†The Israelis said the Red Cross were allowed to enter but that they chose not to do so. The Red Cross said this was untrue. The Israelis then claimed they had a video of Red Cross officials declining the Israeli offer. But when we demanded to see this video, the Israeli authorities failed to produce it. Few journalists believed that it existed.

But my *Independent* colleagues, Justin Huggler and Reeves, carried out their own meticulous investigation of the Jenin killings. They did not describe them as a massacre but they concluded that nearly half of the fifty identified Palestinian dead were civilians, including women, children and the elderly. Individual atrocities occurred, *The Independent* concluded, atrocities that Israel was trying to hide "by launching a massive propaganda drive":

. . . Hani Rumeleh, a 19-year-old civilian, had been shot as he tried to look out of his front door. Fadwa Jamma, a nurse staying with her sister in a house nearby, heard Hani's screaming and went to help. Her sister, Rufaida Damaj, who also ran to help, was wounded but survived. From her bed in Jenin hospital, she told us what happened.

"We were woken at 3:30 in the morning by a big explosion," she said. "I heard that one guy was wounded outside our house. So my sister and I went to do our duty and to help the guy and give him first aid. There were some guys from the resistance outside and we had to ask them before we moved anywhere . . . Before I had finished talking to the guys the Israelis started shooting. I got a bullet in my leg and fell down and broke my knee. My sister tried to come and help me. I told her, 'I'm wounded.' She said, 'I'm wounded too.' She had been shot in the side of her abdomen. Then they shot her again in the heart . . . she made a terrible sound and tried to breathe three times."

Ms Jamma was wearing a white nurse's uniform clearly marked with a red crescent, the emblem of Palestinian medical workers, when the soldiers shot her. Ms Damaj said the soldiers could clearly see the women because they were standing under a bright light, and could hear their cries for help because they were "very near." As Ms Damaj shouted to the Palestinian fighters to get help, the Israeli soldiers fired again: a second bullet went up through her leg into her chest . . .

Jamal Feyed died after being buried alive in the rubble. His uncle, Saeb Feyed, told us that 37-year-old Jamal was mentally and physically disabled, and could not walk . . . When Mr. Feyed saw an Israeli bulldozer approaching the house where his nephew was, he ran to warn the driver. But the bulldozer ploughed into the wall of the house, which collapsed on Jamal . . .

In a deserted road by the periphery of the refugee camp, we found the flattened remains of a wheelchair. It had been utterly crushed, ironed flat as if in a cartoon. In the middle of the debris lay a broken white flag. Durar Hassan told us how his friend, Kemal Zughayer, was shot dead as he tried to wheel himself up the road. The Israeli tanks must have driven over the body, because when Mr. Hassan found it, one leg and both arms were missing, and the face, he said, had been ripped in two.

Mr. Zughayer, who was 58, had been shot and wounded in the first *intifada*. He could not walk, and had no work. Mr. Hassan showed us the pitiful single room where his friend lived, the only furnishing a filthy mattress on the floor . . . Mr. Hassan did his washing; it was he who put the white flag on Mr. Zughayer's wheelchair.

"After 4 pm I pushed him up the street as usual," said Mr. Hassan. "Then I heard the tanks coming, there were four or five. I heard shooting, and I thought they were just firing warning shots to tell him to move out of the middle of the road." It was not until next morning that Mr. Hassan went to check what had happened. He found the flattened wheelchair in the road, and Mr. Zughayer's mangled body some distance away, in the grass.

So when does a bloodbath become an atrocity? When does an atrocity become a massacre? How big does a massacre have to be before it qualifies as a genocide? How many dead before a genocide becomes a holocaust? Old questions become new questions at each killing field. The Israeli journalist Arie Caspi wrote a scathing article in late April which caught the hypocritical response to the Jenin killings with painful accuracy:

Okay, so there wasn't a massacre. Israel only shot some children, brought a house crashing down on an old man, rained cement blocks on an invalid who couldn't get out in time, used locals as a human shield against bombs, and prevented aid from getting to the sick and wounded. That's really not a massacre, and there's really no need for a commission of enquiry . . . whether run by ourselves or sent by the *goyim*.

The insanity gripping Israel seems to have moved beyond our morals . . . many Israelis believe that as long as we do not practice systematic mass murder, our place in heaven is secure. Every time some Palestinian or Scandinavian fool yells "Holocaust!," we respond in an angry huff: This is a holocaust? So a few people were killed, 200, 300, some very young, some very old. Does anyone see gas chambers or crematoria?

These are not idle questions. Nor cynical. Not long after Sharon's failed attempt to stop the suicide bombers of Hamas and Islamic Jihad, on 27 April 2002, Palestinian gunmen broke into an illegal Jewish settlement built on Arab land at Adora on the Palestinian West Bank. Five-year-old Danielle Shefi was shot in her bedroom along with her mother and two brothers. Danielle was killed, her mother survived. Up the road, Katya Greenberg and her husband, Vladimir, were sprayed with bullets as they lay in bed. In the little girl's bedroom, there were smears of blood and three bullet holes just above Danielle's bed. Her mother had been shot as she ran to protect her daughter. In all, four Israelis—including two armed settlers who fought back—were dead, and eight wounded.

One would have to have a heart of stone not to be moved by the terrible fate of Danielle Shefi. She was only five. But if at least two dozen Palestinians dead in Jenin was not a massacre, how should we describe the four Israelis dead at the Adora settlement? Well, the official Israeli army spokesman, Major Avner Foxman, said of the Adora killings: "For me, now I know what is a massacre. This is a massacre." The Canadian *National Post* referred to the Palestinian assault as being "barbarous," a word it never used about the killing of Palestinian civilians. I don't like the mathematics here. Four dead Israelis, including two armed settlers, is a massacre. I'll accept this. But twenty-four Palestinian civilians killed, including a nurse and a paraplegic, is not a massacre. (I am obviously leaving aside the thirty or so armed Palestinians who were also killed in Jenin.) What does this mean? What does it tell us about journalism, about my profession? Does the definition of a bloodbath now depend on the religion or the race of the civilian dead to be qualified as a massacre? No, I didn't call the Jenin killings a massacre. But I should have done.

Yet our responsibility does not end there. How many of our circumlocutions open the way to these attacks? How many journalists encouraged the Israelis—by their reporting or by their wilfully given, foolish advice—to undertake these brutal assaults on the Palestinians? On 31 March 2002—just three days before the assault on Jenin—Tom Friedman wrote in *The New York Times* that "Israel needs to deliver a military blow that clearly shows terror will not pay." Well, thanks, Tom, I said to myself when I read this piece of lethal journalism a few days later. The Israelis certainly followed Friedman's advice.

When Sharon began his operation "Defensive Shield," the UN Security Council, with the active participation and support of the United States, demanded an immediate end to Israel's reoccupation of the West Bank. President George W. Bush insisted that Sharon should follow the advice of "Israel's American friends" and—for Tony Blair was with Bush at the time—"Israel's British friends," and withdraw. "When I say withdraw, I mean it," Bush snapped three days later. But he meant nothing of the kind. Instead, he sent Secretary of State Colin Powell off on an "urgent" mission of peace, a journey to Israel and the West Bank that would take an incredible eight days—just enough time, Bush presumably thought, to allow his "friend" Sharon to finish his latest bloody adventure in the West Bank. Supposedly unaware that Israel's chief of staff, Shoal Mofaz, had told Sharon that he needed at least eight weeks to "finish the job" of crushing the Palestinians, Powell wandered off around the Mediterranean, dawdling in Morocco, Spain, Egypt and Jordan before finally fetching up in Israel. If Washington fire-fighters took that long to reach a blaze, the American capital would long ago have turned to ashes. But of course, the purpose of Powell's idleness was to allow enough time for Jenin to be turned to ashes. Mission, I suppose, accomplished.

Once he had at last arrived in Jerusalem, the first thing Powell should have done was to demand a visit to Jenin. But instead, after joshing with Sharon, he played games, demanding that Arafat condemn the latest suicide bombing in Jerusalem in which six Israelis had been killed and sixty-five wounded, while failing to utter more than a word of "concern" about Jenin. Was Powell frightened of the Israelis? Did he really have to debase himself in this way? For this looked like the end-game in the Arab–Israeli dispute, the very final proof that the United States was no longer worthy of being a Middle East peacemaker. But no, that would come in 2004, when Bush would effectively destroy UN Security Council Resolution 242.

It seemed there were no barriers that could not be broken. If this was a war on terror, I wrote in my paper that awful spring, then Jesus wasn't born in Bethlehem. When a group of Palestinian fighters barricaded themselves in the Church of the Nativity, the Israelis laid siege to them and Bethlehem turned into a battlefield. The first to die was an eighty-year-old Palestinian man, whose body never made it to the morgue. Then a woman and her son were critically wounded by Israeli gunfire. A cloud of black smoke swirled up in the tempest winds from the other side of Manger Square, a burning Israeli armoured vehicle, although—running for our lives as bullets crackled around us—we had no time to look at it. Harvey Morris—reincarnated now, not as my foreign news editor but as the *Financial Times* correspondent, expletives mercifully undeleted—was with me as we pounded through the rain that guttered in waves across the Israeli tanks that were grinding between Ottoman stone houses, smashing into cars and tearing down shop hoardings.

A "Closed Military Area" had been declared once more by the Israelis. Jesus, we assumed, must have had to deal with a Roman version of closed military areas—but he had God on his side. The people of Bethlehem had no one. They waited for some statement from the Pope, from the Vatican, from the European Union. And what they got was an armoured invasion. "They've sent the whole fucking army," Harvey remarked with commendable exaggeration. All morning, we watched the Merkavas and APCs stealing their way through the ancient streets, searching for the "savages" of "terror" whom Sharon had just told the world about. We sat in the home of a Palestinian Christian woman, Norma Hazboun, watching her television upon which we could see "Palestine" collapsing around us. Palestinian intelligence offices had been attacked in Ramallah. Shells started falling on Deheishi camp. We knew that already—Deheishi was so close that the windows vibrated. Sharon was on the screen, offering to let the Europeans fly Arafat out of Ramallah, provided he never returned to the land he called "Palestine." Offer refused.

More shooting now from outside our window. A tank came down the road, its barrel clipping the green awning of a shop and then swaying upwards to point directly at our window. We decamped to the stairwell. Had they seen us watching them? We stood on the cold, damp stairs then peeked around our window. Two Israeli soldiers were running past the house as another tank shuddered up the street, absorbing a little car into its tracks and coughing it out in bits at the back of its armour. We knew all about these tanks, their maximum speed, the voice of their massive engines, their rate of fire. We respected them and hated them in equal measure. We had spent almost an hour walking the back streets to avoid the "Closed Military Area," dirty, dank, black streets with angry tanks in the neighbouring highways. One raced across an intersection while we stood, in blue-and-black flak jackets marked with "TV" in huge taped letters, arms spread out like ducks to show we carried no weapons.

We sat snug now by Norma Hazboun's gas fire, trapped in the home of the professor of social sciences at Bethlehem University. The newsreader stumbled on his words. Iran and Iraq might stop oil exports to force the Americans to demand an Israeli withdrawal from the West Bank. Harvey and I coughed in simultaneous contempt; Iran and Iraq would do no such thing. Arafat's Ramallah headquarters was on fire. An Israeli soldier was dead in an APC on the other side of Manger Square, hit by a rocket. That was presumably the burning vehicle we'd seen an hour ago. Colin Powell said that the Americans would still recognise Arafat as Palestinian leader, even if he was in Europe. Harvey burst forth again: "But if he's in Europe, he won't be the fucking Palestinian leader, will he?"

Outside the house, beside a cluster of lemon trees, two Israeli armoured carriers pulled up, their crews desperately trying to pump fuel through a hose from one vehicle to the other before Palestinian snipers picked them off. The bullets snapped around them within seconds and the two frightened soldiers threw themselves off the roofs to the shelter of a shop. Then my mobile rang. An English voice, a lady from Wateringbury in Kent—Peggy and Bill had lived in the next village above East Farleigh, one stop down the Paddock Wood–Maidstone West railway line—but Liz Yates was not in Kent. She was in the Aida refugee camp with nine other Westerners, trying to help the 4,000 Palestinian refugees there by asking their consulates to pressure the Israelis into withdrawing. Some hope. In the end, the consulates had to rescue the Westerners.

At least a hundred Palestinian civilians were now seeking sanctuary with the twenty gunmen in the Church of the Nativity.* I took another call, this time from Sami Abda. On Tuesday, he told me, Israeli soldiers had come to his house in the centre of Bethlehem and—though warned by a neighbour that his home was filled with women and children—the Israelis claimed that "terrorists" were in the building and opened fire on the Abda household. Sami Abda was crying as he spoke to me and these are his exact words:

> They fired eighteen bullets through our front door. They hit my mother Sumaya and my brother Yacoub. My mother was sixty-four, my brother was thirty-seven. They both fell to the floor. I called everyone I could to take them to the hospital. But there was no one to help us. They were dying. When an ambulance came, an Israeli officer refused permission for it to enter our street. So for thirty hours we have lived with their bodies. We put the children into the bathroom so they could not see the corpses. Help us, please.

That insistent question—What is sacred?—could be asked by anyone in the Holy Land that spring of 2002. And by anyone who read the *Jerusalem Post*: it printed a whole page of tiny photographs of the dozens of Israeli civilians torn to

---

*The Bethlehem siege provided another "first" when BBC Television World News, unable to cover the fighting round the church with its own cameras, repeatedly used Israeli army video footage—without announcing its provenance.

bits by Palestinian suicide bombers in just one month. One teenage Israeli girl was the same age as the Palestinian girl who destroyed her life. It was a page of horror and misery. Yes, the Palestinians' suicide campaign was immoral, unforgivable— the word that came to me outside the Jerusalem pizzeria—insupportable. One day, the Arabs—never ones to look too closely in the mirror when it comes to their own crimes—will have to acknowledge the sheer cruelty of their tactics. But since the Israelis never attempted to confront the immorality of shooting to death child stone-throwers or the evil of their reckless death squads who went around murdering Palestinians on their wanted list—along with the usual bunch of women and kids who get in the way—is this any wonder?

And so I am back in Gaza, sitting in another of those mourning tents, this time for two fourteen-year-old schoolboys and their fifteen-year-old friend, Internet surfers in the local cyber café, one of them idling his hours away drawing children's cartoons, all of them football enthusiasts. Hours after they had been shot dead by the Israeli army near the Jewish colony of Netzarim, their fathers received back the three young bodies. All had been shot. And all, they said, had been driven over by an armoured vehicle which—in Ismail Abu-Nadi's case—had cut his corpse in half.

Knife-wielding suicide bombers approaching the Jewish settlement, according to the Israeli army and—of course—*The New York Times*. But even Hamas, creator of the unscrupulous campaign of suicide bombing, admits that the three schoolchildren—all ninth-graders in the Salahedin School in Gaza City—had naively planned to attack the settlement of their own accord and with, at most, knives. It urged preachers and schoolteachers to tell children that they should never embark on such wild schemes again.

And when the three fathers talked to me, they told a story of waste and tragedy and childhood anger at Israel's bloody invasion of the Jenin refugee camp. "I spent all last night asking myself why my son did this," Mohamed Abu-Nadi told me as we sat among the mourners outside his middle-class home. "Did Ismail need money? No. Did he fail at school? No. He was first in his class. Were there problems with his family or friends? No. I asked myself the same question over and over. Why? Can you tell me?"

A painful question to be asked by a distraught father. Did Ismail want to die? His father said this would have been impossible until "three or four months ago." That was when the schoolboy, born in Abu Dhabi and a fluent English-speaker, began to ask his father why the Palestinians were given no outside help in their struggle for a state. "He asked me: 'Why is it that only the Palestinians cannot have a state? Why doesn't America help? Why don't the other Arab states help?' " Bassem Zaqout, the father of fifteen-year-old Yussef—none of the fathers had met, though their sons all attended the same school—also thought the Jenin bloodshed influenced his son. "He used to draw pictures and cartoons and wrote Arabic calligraphy. I never thought this could happen. But we watched all the news programmes about Israel's reoccupation—Palestinian television, Al-Jazeera from Qatar, CNN—and maybe he saw something . . . When I came back from evening prayers on Tuesday, he had left the house. I had no idea why. Now I think the boys were walking towards the Jewish settlement with some kind of idea of attacking the Israelis there. But he never touched a weapon. When we got his body back yesterday, it was in a terrible state. Dogs had been at it in the night and his face was unrecognisable because it had been crushed by a heavy vehicle driving over it."

Adel Hamdona's fourteen-year-old son Anwar was returned to him in the same condition. The father's description was cold, emotionless. "He didn't have a face. His legs had been severed. He had been driven over several times and had been pretty well disembowelled." Anwar's body, too, had been gnawed by dogs. "He was just a boy, a child. I am a teacher at his school. At five in the evening, he told his mother he was going to an internet café to surf the net. When he hadn't come home by nine, I felt something was wrong. Then we heard shooting from Netzarim . . . "

And there's a clue as to why Adel Hamdona felt that "something was wrong." For Anwar had begun talking to his family about "martyrdom." "The events here had an effect on the boy. He was always talking about the suicide operations, about martyrs and the concept of martyrdom. He used to want to become a martyr. I had a suspicion that a few years later, when he grew up, he might do this—but not now." Ismail Abu-Nadi, it turns out, left what appears to be a goodbye note to his parents. "One of his friends brought me a paper he had written," his father acknowledged. "On the paper, Ismail had said: 'My father, my mother, please try to pray to God and to ask for me to succeed to enter Netzarim and to kill the Israeli soldiers and to drive them from our land.' I could not believe this. At his age, any other boy—and I've been to England, the United States, India, Pakistan—yes, any other boy just wants to be educated, to be happy. To earn money, to be at peace. But our children here cannot find peace."

As for the condition of the bodies, none of the fathers wanted to speculate on the reasons. Would the Israelis deliberately mutilate them? It seems unlikely. Or did they, after shooting the three schoolboys, avoid the risk that one might still be alive—and with a bomb waiting to go off—by driving over their remains? And when their bodies were crushed, were they all dead? Ismail Abu-Nadi's father drew a simple message—meaningless to Tom Friedman, I guess—about their deaths: "If there is no future, there is no hope. So what do you expect a boy to do?"

But even Abdul-Aziz Rantissi, the Hamas leader in Gaza, was anxious to dissociate his movement from the boys' death, although his words were not without a disturbing message of their own. "I think the crimes of the Israelis pushed the boys to pursue acts of revenge without awareness. They were so young in age, they did not realise they could not do anything at the settlement . . . I've made a call to preachers in the mosques and to teachers to explain to the children that their role in all this has not yet come . . . "

Rantissi keeps touching his beard. I used to talk to him in the Field of Flowers in southern Lebanon but now he is on the run from Israel's killer squads, constantly interrupted by the phone as he sits in a Gaza office, his young bodyguard, Kalashnikov nursed upside down on his knee, handing him a big military two-way radio receiver. I think—but I do not say so—that this is to protect the Hamas leader. Mobile phones are traceable to within a few feet. Israel's death squads are masters of analogue and digital technology. Am I watching for an Apache helicopter? Do Israel's victims ever see the missiles streaking towards them?

Not that Rantissi has any illusions. "It's something to be expected so far as we are concerned. But the one thing I can say is something that can only be understood by someone who holds the Islamic faith the way I do. We believe that our lifetime is always predicted and that our death has already been determined by God, and this cannot change. There are many different reasons that could lead to the end of a person's life—a car accident, cancer, a heart attack—so I'm not saying I'm making a choice to shorten my life. But the preferred way of ending my life would be martyrdom." Rantissi would get his wish.

My eyes glance again towards the window. Of his fifty-five years, Rantissi has spent twenty-six in prison or in exile on the Lebanese mountainside. In those days, he was still trying to learn how to run Hamas. Now he talks coolly—coldly, frighteningly—about suicide bombers and death. Hamas has its own death squads. They kill soldiers, but women and children too, and the old and the sick. "Up till now, in these two intifadas, the Israelis have killed more than two thousand Palestinians. Following the killings in Nablus and Jenin, the number of children killed has passed the three hundred and fifty mark. This proves that the Israeli side is intentionally committing massacres against civilians." I have been down this path before. Every time you ask a Hamas leader to confront the wickedness of suicide-bombing civilians, you are taken down the statistics trail. What about the kids in the pizza parlour, the old folk at the Passover dinner?

"We are fighting people who violated our land," he replies, very quickly. "They are all soldiers or reserve soldiers. It was reserve soldiers in Jenin who killed civilians—these are people who in ordinary life are Israeli doctors and lawyers. They were civilians just hours before they went into Jenin. But of course, our fighters have orders not to kill civilians, especially the children."

Orders to avoid killing children? Or is this just a numbers game? The military phone pips again and Rantissi talks for several minutes. Is he in touch with Hamas leaders in the West Bank? He smiles bleakly. "There is some communication on a political level with leaders in the West Bank, yes. But they are wanted men and besieged and underground." This, I note in the margin of my notebook, is the first time Hamas has acknowledged the effects of the Israeli reoccupation. "You take Hassan Youssef, a political leader in Ramallah—he is calling me for information about what is going on. But ultimately Sharon will not be able to put an end to resistance. When the Israelis deported four hundred and sixty of us in 1993 and arrested another fifteen hundred Hamas members the same day, they said they had 'put an end' to resistance and to Hamas. After that, Yahyia Ayash"—the Hamas bomb-maker later assassinated by the Israelis—"escalated the resistance."

Marj al-Zahour, the Field of Flowers, the University of Islam, seems a long way away. Rantissi disagrees. "It was a stage that changed the Palestinian struggle.

It changed the history of Hamas for ever. Before that, it was a local movement. After our exile on the hillsides of Lebanon, it became an international organisation known all over the world. We received the benefits of Israel's mistakes." Rantissi speaks with considerable self-confidence. And there is no doubt who his chief enemy is. "Sharon wanted to rip up the Oslo papers. He is exercising his power over the Palestinian people—destroying or wilfully killing them—in order to compel them to leave. He wants to break our will so that we will accept his humiliating conditions. He also wants to create a conflict between the Palestinian Authority and the people." And Gaza? Rantissi laughs. "I want to remind you of something Rabin once said—that he longs to wake up one day to find Gaza swallowed up by the sea."

It is strange how often Arafat's opponents speak of Rabin—with whom Arafat thought he had signed the "peace of the brave"—and Arafat's nemesis Sharon in the same sentence. Rabin was commander of the Israeli units that captured Lod (Lydda) and Ramleh in July 1948 and who gave the order for the expulsion of up to 60,000 Palestinian Arabs, most of them women and children, an unknown number of whom died during their flight. Rabin's published memoirs were to recall the Israeli conquest of Lod:

> We walked outside. Ben Gurion [the Israeli prime minister, appointed two months earlier] accompanying us. [Haganah commander Yigal] Allon repeated his question "What is to be done with the population?" B.G. waved his hand in a gesture which said "Drive them out!"
>
> Allon and I held a consultation. I agreed that it was essential to drive the inhabitants out. We took them on foot towards the Bet Horon road, assuming that the [Arab] Legion would be obliged to look after them, thereby shouldering logistic difficulties which would burden its fighting capacity, making things easier for us ... The population of Lod did not leave willingly. There was no way of avoiding the use of force and warning shots in order to make the inhabitants march the 10 to 15 miles to the point where they met up with the Legion.

Certainly Rantissi assessed Sharon's contempt for Oslo correctly, though he might have looked more closely at Sharon's record. Ever since he was elected in 2001, Sharon's supporters in the West have tried to turn him into a pragmatist, another de Gaulle; the same theme was replayed when he suggested in 2004 that Israel should abandon the Jewish settlements in Gaza, a step which his own spokesman revealingly admitted would put any plans for a Palestinian state into "formaldehyde." In truth, Sharon is more like the French putschist generals in Algeria. They, too, used torture and massacred their Arab opponents. His career spells anything but peace. Sharon voted against the peace treaty with Egypt in 1979. He voted against a withdrawal from southern Lebanon in 1985. He opposed Israel's participating in the Madrid peace conference in 1991. He opposed the Knesset plenum vote on the Oslo agreement in 1993. He abstained on a vote for peace with Jordan in 1994. He voted against the Hebron agreement in 1997. He condemned the manner of Israel's retreat from Lebanon in 2000. By 2002 alone, Sharon had built thirty-four new Jewish colonies on Palestinian land.

Sharon's involvement in the 1982 Sabra and Chatila massacres continues to fester around the man who, according to Israel's 1993 Kahan commission report, bore "personal responsibility" for the Phalangist slaughter. So fearful were the Israeli authorities that their leaders would be charged with war crimes that they drew up a list of countries where they might have to stand trial—and which they should henceforth avoid—now that European nations were expanding their laws to include foreign nationals who had committed crimes abroad. Belgian judges were already considering a complaint by survivors of Sabra and Chatila—one of them a female rape victim—while a campaign had been mounted abroad against other Israeli figures associated with the atrocities. Eva Stern was one of those who tried to prevent Brigadier General Amos Yaron being appointed Israeli defence attaché in Washington because he had allowed the Lebanese Phalange militia to enter the camps on 16 September 1982, and knew—according to the Kahan commission report—that women and children were being murdered. He only ended the killings two days later. Canada declined to accept Yaron as defence attaché. Stern, who compiled a legal file on Yaron, later vainly campaigned with human rights groups to annul his appointment—by Prime Minister Ehud Barak—as director general of the Israeli defence ministry.* The Belgian government changed their law—and dropped potential charges against Sharon—after a visit to Brussels by U.S. defence secretary Donald Rumsfeld, the man who famously referred on 6 August 2002 to Israelis' control over "the so-called occupied area which was the result of a war, which they won." Rumsfeld had threatened that NATO headquarters might be withdrawn from Belgian soil if the Belgians didn't drop the charges against Sharon.

Yet all the while, we were supposed to believe that it was the corrupt, Parkinson's-haunted Yassir Arafat who was to blame for the new war. He was chastised by George Bush while the Palestinian people continued to be bestialised by the Israeli leadership. Rafael Eytan, the former Israeli chief of staff, had referred to Palestinians as "cockroaches in a glass jar." Menachem Begin called them "two-legged beasts." The Shas party leader who suggested that God should send the Palestinian "ants" to hell, also called them "serpents." In August 2000, Barak called them crocodiles. Israeli chief of staff Moshe Yalon described the Palestinians as a "cancerous manifestation" and equated the military action in the occupied territories with "chemotherapy." In March 2001, the Israeli tourism minister, Rehavem Zeevi, called Arafat a "scorpion." Sharon repeatedly called Arafat a "murderer" and compared him to bin Laden. He contributed to the image of Palestinian inhumanity in an interview in 1995, when he stated that Fatah sometimes punished Palestinians by "chopping off limbs of seven–eight

---

*Again, to no avail. In January 2003, Yaron was in Washington, presenting Israel's defence "needs" to justify a request for $4 billion in "special defence aid."

year old children in front of their parents as a form of punishment." However brutal Fatah may be, there is no record of any such atrocity being committed by them. But if enough people can be persuaded to believe this nonsense, then the use of Israeli death squads against such Palestinians becomes natural rather than illegal.*

Largely forgotten amid Sharon's hatred for "terrorism" was his outspoken criticism of NATO's war against Serbia in 1999, when he was Israeli foreign minister. Eleven years earlier he had sympathised with the political objective of Slobodan Milošević: to prevent the establishment of an Albanian state in Kosovo. This, he said, would lead to "Greater Albania" and provide a haven for—readers must here hold their breath—"Islamic terror." In a Belgrade newspaper interview, Sharon said that "we stand together with you against the Islamic terror." Once NATO's bombing of Serbia was under way, however, Sharon's real reason for supporting the Serbs became apparent. "It's wrong for Israel to provide legitimacy to this forceful sort of intervention which the NATO countries are deploying . . . in an attempt to impose a solution on regional disputes," he said. "The moment Israel expresses support for the sort of model of action we're seeing in Kosovo, it's likely to be the next victim. Imagine that one day Arabs in Galilee demand that the region in which they live be recognised as an autonomous area, connected to the Palestinian Authority . . . " NATO's bombing, Sharon said, was "brutal interventionism." The Israeli journalist Uri Avnery, who seized on this extraordinary piece of duplicity, said that "Islamic terror" in Kosovo could only exist in "Sharon's racist imagination." Avnery was far bolder in translating what lay behind Sharon's antipathy towards NATO action than Sharon himself. "If the Americans and the Europeans interfere today in the matter of Kosovo, what is to prevent them from doing the same tomorrow in the matter of Palestine? Sharon has made it crystal-clear to the world that there is a similarity and perhaps even identity between Milosevic's attitude towards Kosovo and the attitude of Netanyahu and Sharon towards the Palestinians." Besides, for a man whose own "brutal interventionism" in Lebanon in 1982 led to a Middle East blood-

---

*And woe betide the diplomat or journalist who points this out. In 2001, the Simon Wiesenthal Centre in Paris accused the Swedish president of the European Union of "encouraging anti-Jewish violence." For her to condemn Israel for "eliminating terrorists," the centre wrote in a letter to the Swedish prime minister, "recalls the Allied argument during the Second World War, according to which bombing the railways leading to Auschwitz would encourage anti-Semitism among the Germans." Sweden was making "a unilateral attack against the state of the survivors of the Holocaust." And the Swedish EU president's crime? She had dared to say that "the practice of eliminations constitutes an obstacle to peace and could provoke new violence." She had not even called the Israeli murder units "death squads." The Swedes did not apologise. But nor did they correct the misuse of historical facts. The principal Allied excuses for not bombing the Auschwitz and Birkenau camps included "technical difficulties," the belief that the task should fall to the Soviet air force, and the contention that all means should be directed to the overthrow of Nazi Germany—which would be "the positive solution to this problem." The latter reasons—inadequate and shameful in the light of history though they are—would not, of course, have made the Wiesenthal Centre's note to Stockholm as unpleasant as it was clearly intended to be.

bath of unprecedented proportions, Sharon's remarks were, to say the least, hypocritical.*

As Sharon sent an armoured column to reinvade Nablus, still ignoring Bush's demand to withdraw his troops from the West Bank, Colin Powell turned on Arafat, warning him that it was his "last chance" to show his leadership. There was no mention of the illegal Jewish settlements. There was to be no "last chance" threat for Sharon. The Americans even allowed him to refuse a UN fact-finding team in the occupied territories. Sharon was meeting with President George W. Bush in Washington when a suicide bomber killed at least fifteen Israeli civilians in a Tel Aviv nightclub; he broke off his visit and returned at once to Israel. Prominent American Jewish leaders, including Elie Wiesel and Alan Dershowitz, immediately called upon the White House not to put pressure on Sharon to join new Middle East peace talks. "This is a tough time," Wiesel announced. "This is not a time to pressure Israel. Any prime minister would do what Sharon is doing. He is doing his best. They should trust him." Wiesel need hardly have worried. Only a month earlier, the Americans rolled out their first S-70A-55 troop-carrying Black Hawk helicopter to be sold to the Israelis. Israel had purchased twenty-four of the new machines, costing $211 million—most of which would be paid for by the United States—even though it had twenty-four earlier-model Black Hawks. The logbook of the first of the new helicopters was ceremonially handed over to the director general of the Israeli defence ministry, the notorious Amos Yaron, by none other than Alexander Haig—the man who gave Begin the green light to invade Lebanon in 1982.

Perhaps the only man who now had the time to work out the logic of this appalling conflict was the Palestinian leader sitting now in his surrounded, broken, ill-lit and unhealthy office block in Ramallah. The one characteristic Arafat shared with Sharon—apart from old age and decrepitude—was his refusal to plan ahead. What he said, what he did, what he proposed, was decided only at the moment he was forced to act. This was partly his old guerrilla training, a characteristic shared by Saddam. If you don't know what you are going to do

---

*Variations on the Sharon theme were to emerge in the Israeli press. Although Israel furnished humanitarian aid to Kosovo Albanians—an act which Sharon said he supported—the fear that NATO's campaign could be transposed to the Middle East persisted. ". . . there is something to the question raised by Foreign Minister Ariel Sharon about a future Israeli response to the possibility that Arabs in the Galilee will demand their own separatist framework," Dan Margalit wrote. " . . . One can assume that Israel would never behave like the Serbs and engage in massacres while forcibly evicting the population across the border. But what exactly is the level of evil that allows NATO to attack a sovereign state that is protecting its sovereignty?" As a journalist in Serbia at the time, I asked the same question about Serbia's "sovereignty," not least because NATO inserted a mischievous clause in its prewar peace proposals to Milošević that would force him to accept NATO troops across all of Serbia. But Margalit's description of Serbia's massacres "while forcibly evicting the population" was a word-perfect description of Israel's own behaviour in 1948. There was also a Kinzer-like diminution of history in Margalit's throwaway remark that "the massacres of Albanians undertaken by Slobodan Milosevic" were "somewhat reminiscent of the Turkish massacres of Armenians . . . terrible crimes but not a Holocaust."

tomorrow, you can be sure that your enemies don't know either. Sharon took the same view.

As they took over the offices of the Palestinian Authority, the Israeli army looted its equipment and archives. *Ha'aretz* reported that soldiers were "fighting for the spoils" of their West Bank operations after seizing dozens of British-made Land Rovers; the vehicles were passed on to the Israeli army's logistics division on orders from the chief of staff, Shoal Mofaz. It was unclear whether the vehicles were paid for with EU money. The Israelis also got their hands on thousands of documents which showed just how far Arafat had lost control of the guerrilla organisations flourishing amid the Palestinians on the West Bank. But the Israelis then went public with translations and accounts of their contents which were deliberately misleading and, in one case, untrue. Journalists dutifully reprinted the Israeli version of the archives—that they showed Arafat's hand in "terror" and his use of EU money to fund "terrorism"—but when *The Independent* undertook a thorough translation of the papers, it became clear that the Israelis had presented a fraudulent account of their contents.* Next day, however, Sharon ostentatiously presented the "Arafat terror file" to Bush in front of the cameras at the White House—and was gratefully thanked for this "evidence" by the American president.

Amid what the Palestinian writer Jean Makdisi has accurately called "terrorology"—Edward Said's sister was referring to the "twisted version of Middle East reality" that right-wing academics like Stanley Kurtz wished to impose on U.S. universities—it was no surprise to learn that an Israeli officer had been advising his men, prior to the reoccupation of the West Bank, to study the military tactics adopted by the Nazis in the Second World War. According to the Israeli newspaper *Maariv*, the officer said that "if our job is to seize a densely packed refugee camp or take over the Nablus casbah, and if this job is given to an [Israeli] officer to carry out without casualties on both sides, he must before all else analyse and bring together the lessons of past battles, even—shocking though this might appear—to analyse how the German army operated in the Warsaw ghetto."

What on earth did this mean? Did this account for the numbers marked by Israelis on the hands and foreheads of Palestinian prisoners in early March 2002? Did it mean that an Israeli soldier was now to regard the Palestinians as subhumans—which is exactly how the Nazis regarded the trapped and desperate Jews of the Warsaw ghetto in 1943? Did the Americans have any thoughts about all this? Who were the forces of "terror" in Warsaw sixty-two years ago? The Jews fighting for their lives, or Brigadeführer Jürgen Stroop's SS troops?

In all, the Israeli human rights group B'Tselem estimated that between 1987

---

*In a Palestinian document detailing the case of Mahmoud Freih, a seventeen-year-old who set a bomb for an Israeli tank in Gaza, the Israeli "translation" stated that he had been protected by the Palestinian Authority. In fact, the original Arabic document stated clearly that the Palestinian Authority had prevented the bombing of the tank by cutting the wire to the detonator before finally inducing Freih to join Arafat's men.

and May 2003, a total of 3,650 Palestinians and 1,142 Israelis were killed, an over-all death toll of 4,792. But statistics alone cannot do justice to the suffering of children. By 1993, 232 Palestinian children, aged sixteen and under, had been killed by Israeli soldiers during the first intifada. However, in just twelve months ending on 30 September 2002, at least 250 Palestinian children and 72 Israeli children had been killed. In one of its most shocking reports on the Israeli–Palestinian war, Amnesty International condemned both sides for their "utter disregard" for the lives of children. The solemn list that Amnesty amassed showed just how ingrained child-killing had become. There was Sami Jazzar, shot in the head by an Israeli soldier on the eve of his twelfth birthday in Gaza, eleven-year-old Khalil Mughrabi, killed by an Israeli sniper in Gaza—one of his friends survived after being shot in the testicles by a high-velocity round—and there was ten-year-old Riham al-Ward, killed in her Jenin schoolyard by an Israeli tank shell. Then there were Raaya and Hemda—fourteen and two years old—killed with their parents by the Palestinian suicide bomber who attacked the Sbarro pizzeria in Jerusalem, Shalhevet Pas—she was just ten months old—shot by a Palestinian sniper in Hebron, and Avia Malka, killed by Palestinians who shot and threw grenades at cars in Netanya. She was nine months old.

The most terrible incident—praised by Sharon at the time as a "great success"—was the attack by Israel on Salah Shehada, a Hamas leader, which slaughtered nine children along with eight adults. Their names gave a frightful reality to this child carnage: eighteen-month-old Ayman Matar, three-year-old Mohamed Matar, five-year-old Diana Matar, four-year-old Sobhi Hweiti, six-year-old Mohamed Hweiti, ten-year-old Ala Matar, fifteen-year-old Iman Shehada, seventeen-year-old Maryam Matar. And Dina Matar. She was two months old. An Israeli air force pilot dropped a one-ton bomb on their homes from an American-made F-16 aircraft on 22 July 2002.*

What war did Sharon think he was fighting? And what was he fighting for? Throughout the latest bloodletting, the one distinctive feature of the conflict—the illegal and continuing colonisation of occupied Arab land—was yet again a taboo subject, to be ignored, or mentioned in passing only when Jewish settlers were killed. That this was the world's last colonial conflict, in which the colonisers were supported by the United States, was undiscussable, a prohibited subject, something quite outside the brutality between Palestinians and Israelis which was, so we had to remember, now part of America's "war on terror." This is what Sharon had dishonestly claimed since 11 September 2001. The truth, however, became clear in a revealing interview Sharon gave to a French magazine in December of

---

*Reality did not always win over propaganda. Amnesty's 2002 report said that despite repeated claims to the contrary, "no judicial investigation is known to have been carried out into any of the killings of children by members of the Israeli Defence Force in the occupied territories, even in cases where Israeli government officials have stated publicly that investigations would be carried out." Yet just over two years later, Michael Williams, an editor of *The Independent on Sunday*, felt able to "applaud the rigour with which it [Israel] applies the rule of law to the actions of its military . . ."

that year, in which he recalled a telephone conversation with Jacques Chirac. Sharon said he told the French president that:

> I was at that time reading a terrible book about the Algerian war. It's a book whose title reads in Hebrew: *The Savage War of Peace*. I know that President Chirac fought as an officer during this conflict and that he had himself been decorated for his courage. So, in a very friendly way, I told him: "Mr. President, you have to understand us, here, it's as if we are in Algeria. We have no place to go. And besides, we have no intention of leaving."

# CHAPTER FOURTEEN

# *"Anything to Wipe Out a Devil . . . "*

This thief who slinks along walls in the night to go home, he's the one. This father who warns his children not to talk about the wicked job he does, he's the one.

This evil citizen who hangs about in courtrooms, waiting for judgement, he's the one. This individual caught in a neighbourhood raid, whom a rifle butt pushes to the back of the truck, he's the one. He's the one who goes out of his house in the morning unsure whether he'll make it to the office. And he's the one who leaves work in the evening, uncertain he'll arrive home.

. . . This man who makes a wish not to die with his throat cut, he's the one. This body on which they sew back a severed head, he's the one. He's the one whose hands know no other skill, only his meagre writing . . .

He is all of these, and a journalist only.

—Saïd Mekbel, "The Rusty Nail," *Le Matin,* 1994

ROGER TARTOUCHE GRINS at visitors from beneath his steel French army helmet, head turned slightly to the left, his battledress buttoned up to the neck. "Died for France, December 4th, 1960," it says above his grave. The photograph printed onto the marble headstone shows such a confident young man, aware at the moment of his death, no doubt, that in just five days Charles de Gaulle would arrive in Algiers to assure the future of *Algérie française.* "Me today, you tomorrow" is inscribed over the iron gates of the old French cemetery at St. Eugène. Algerians outside the graveyard wall would do well to visit this monument to pride and tragedy. So might other Arabs—and the Jews of Israel.

They are all here, the Spahis and Zouaves, the forgotten cavalry of *la grande armée*, the schoolteachers and engineers who believed Algeria was for ever French, professors and civil servants along with their matronly wives from Metz, Lille and Rouen, their portraits—in some they smile, in others they think of mortality—pathetic in the most literal sense of the word; dead rulers in their Sunday best. Still untouched by vandals who might soon have good cause to desecrate his eternal resting place, Colonel d'État-Major Alexandre Edouard Constant Fourchauld (born Orléans, 19 August 1817) lies beneath a heavy marble stone commemorating his subjugation of the Muslims who dared to oppose French rule. His bronze bust depicts a frightening, high-cheekboned man with a bushy moustache,

514

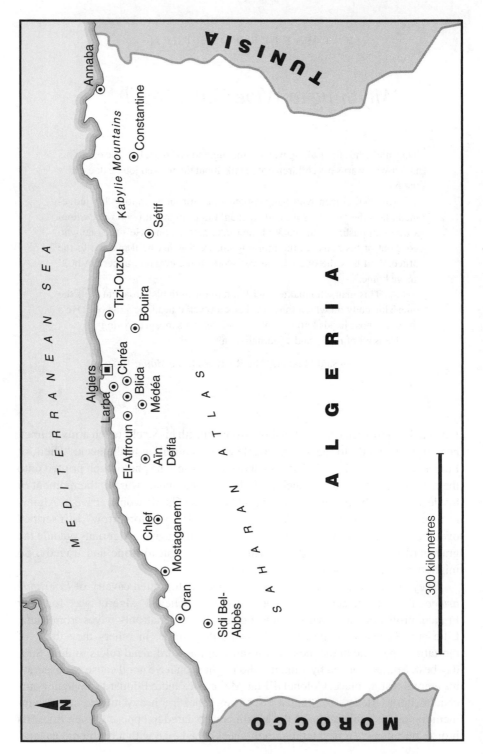

a military képi pushed rakishly to the side of his head, his campaigns listed beneath: "Grand Kabyle 1854, Djudjura 1857, Marocco 1859, Alma Palestro 1871, El Amra 1876 . . . " Hero of Sevastopol and the Franco-Prussian War, he died in his country, France, in a city called Algiers.

From this same city, Fourchauld's fellow countrymen went to die on other French soil. René and Edgar Guidicelli were both cut down on the Western Front, René while charging German trenches on the Marne on 25 September 1915, Edgar by shellfire on the same battlefield almost exactly three years later. Both men stare shyly from their photographs, both in dress uniform, "for ever remembered by their mother and father." The French embassy pays for a *gardien* at St. Eugène, just as it does for the neighbouring non-Christian cemetery, for the graves not of Muslims but of thousands of French citizens of the Jewish faith who also believed that Algeria belonged to France, their memorials—in Hebrew as well as French—still undamaged and protected in this Arab, Muslim, capital.

How many catastrophes lie in this little plot of land? William Lévy "died for France, June 16th, 1940, at Arpajon (Seine-et-Oise) at the age of 30," presumably facing Hitler's last assault on the wreckage of the French army. He has humorous eyes in his photograph, the confident expression of a man who thought he would live into old age. A tiny synagogue "dedicated by the Israelite community of Algiers to their children who died on the field of honour" contains dozens of photographs of desperately young men in French uniform, most of them killed before they knew how disgracefully their country would treat their fellow Jews.

Down a narrow path, history comes closer to the visitor. "Here lies Jules Roger Lévy, victim of terrorism, June 3rd, 1957, aged 34" . . . "here lies Albert Sarfati, victim of terrorism, February 20th, 1962, at the age of 42 . . . " Most poignant of all, "here lies Josette Smaja, aged 24, near her fiancé Paul Perez, knifed to death [*assassiné par arme blanche*], June 9th, 1957." Citizens of *la France d'Outre-Mer*, they counted themselves among the *pieds noirs*.* It is a cold, blustery January in 1992. Their graves are a terrible warning for the Algeria whose authorities and army officers are as adamant now in opposing an Islamic republic as were the French in opposing a liberated Algeria.

The gaunt nineteenth-century Eglise de Notre Dame de la Mer stands on a hill above the cemeteries, its bronze statue of Christ—*Christus Resurgens*—torn down and smashed before Christmas 1991. On the mosaic above the altar is written a revealing, quasi-colonial prayer. "Our Lady of Africa, pray for us and the Muslims." A French priest from Montpellier ministers to the three hundred or so ancient Catholic *pieds noirs* who never left. At the tiny chapel of Ste. Thérèse in

*Theories abound on the origin of the term *pied noir*. In his history of the Algerian war of independence, Alistair Horne says the expression may have come from the black polished shoes worn by the French military, or from the metropolitan French idea that the African sun burned the feet of the *colons* black. More recently, an Algerian told me that the name was given to poor Spanish immigrants who lived in a quarter of the Moroccan capital of Rabat but who allegedly never washed their feet. When French citizens moved into the same area, they inherited the name and then brought it with them to Algeria.

the Bab el-Oued district of Algiers, fifteen of them gather each Saturday, receiving communion, assuring each other that they will never leave.

A woman of sixty-nine from Saumur—"because I live here, you must not know my name"—accepts history with fatalism. She is small, with a round face and fluffy, curly white hair. "De Gaulle was not a bad man," she says. "He first of all said he 'understood' us and I think he meant that Algeria would stay French. But when he toured the area and saw the situation with his own eyes, he realised France could not stay here. He did not betray us. He just changed his mind. My husband and I stayed because it was our home. He died three years after independence but Algiers was still my home, its harbour and sea and hills which I love. My daughter Josette married an Algerian and converted to Islam. Now she has a Muslim name, Zaiya. Yes, I am happy in my old age. I have many friends, even in the Islamic Salvation Front I have friends." She smiles warmly, without the anxiety or fear which I now catch on Algerian faces. Then she says, very gently: "To each person, their destiny." This is a woman who is living on the cusp of a fearful tragedy. An orgy of throat-cutting and terror, a civil war that will cull 150,000 lives, is waiting for her and every foreigner in Algeria and then every journalist, every government official, every Islamist, every policeman, every shopkeeper, every husband, wife and child.

The lady from Saumur lived through the last years of France's colonial dream-turned-nightmare, though the dream lasted well over a hundred years. It lives on, even now, in the antiquarian bookshops of Paris. Here you can buy postcards of nineteenth-century Algeria in which French bungalows nestle behind beech trees on streets filled with French girls in long dresses and young Frenchmen in straw hats. A coloured card shows an *épicerie* in the town of Souk-Ahras where French citizens stroll in the rue Victor Hugo. There are dull and overbearing French churches in tiny towns and square stone fountains and pretty French trains gliding into ornate French railway stations. In many of the cards, the little French towns of Algeria appear empty, their chapels and *mairies* and offices part of a stage-set in which the actors have yet to appear. When Algerians are in the photograph, they usually stand or sit to the side of the camera lens, long-bearded or wearing head-scarves, a romantic part of the scenery, like the palm trees and the usually distant mosques. A magnificent photograph taken in Oran in 1910 shows more than a hundred French men, women and children sitting and standing on the terrasse of the "Grand Café Continental"; only one figure—apparently a tea-boy on the far left of the picture—might be Algerian. In that year, Algeria's population included 400,000 French, 200,000 other foreigners (most of them Spanish, Maltese and Italians) and 4,500,000 Algerian Muslims. On each postcard, there is a five-centime French stamp bearing the image of Marianne, that governessy old mother of the French nation.

In Paris today, you can buy a glossy monthly magazine produced for the *pieds noirs* and their families—originally founded with the support of the putschist French general Edmond Jouhaud and that eloquent proponent of *Algérie française*, Jacques Soustelle—whose pages are filled with photographs of the neat, orderly cities the French built across the tenth-largest country in the world which they believed to be part of France. The magazine is dedicated to the *"pieds noirs* of yesterday and today" and to "the Harkis and their friends."* Flicking through page after melancholy page, it is not difficult to grasp the schizophrenic nature of French Algeria. In Sidi Bel Abbès, for example, the quarters of the city included Alexandre Dumas, Bonnier, Les Trembles, Deligny and Boulet—but also Oued Imbert, Oued Sefioun, Tessalah and Sidi Yacoub. In Biskra, a vast statue of Monseigneur Charles Lavigerie stood in the city centre in honour of the bishop of Algiers who tried to evangelise Algeria and founded the order of the *Pères Blancs.* For although France's invasion of Algeria in 1830 was intended to distract attention from the domestic problems of the Bourbons and avenge a slight to the French consul—the reigning Dey of Algiers struck him in the face with a fly-whisk and called him "a wicked, faithless, idol-worshipping rascal"—it quickly became a Christian crusade.

The *pieds noirs* would later come to believe that their mission in Algeria was to "civilise" an otherwise barbarous land, hence the constant emphasis on administration, justice, education and modern technology. But contemporary evidence and the literature published in the early years of the French conquest tell a different story. For when the Comte de Bourmont, the lieutenant general commanding the French expeditionary force to Algeria, arrived off the North African coast with forty-two destroyers, frigates and corvettes and sixty other vessels in May 1830, he issued a proclamation of almost wearying familiarity:

> Soldiers, civilised nations of both [new and old] worlds are watching you; their thoughts are with you; the cause of France is the cause of humanity; show that you are worthy of this noble mission. Let no excess tarnish the banner of your exploits; merciless in combat, you must be compassionate and magnanimous after victory; this is in your interest as much as it is your duty. So long oppressed by a rapacious and brutal soldiery, the Arab will see you as liberators; he will beg to be our ally . . .

Eighty-seven years before General Maude's proclamation to the people of Baghdad, insisting that the British army had invaded Iraq as liberators rather than conquerors, and 173 years before President George W. Bush and Prime Minister Tony Blair invaded the same country with the same excuses—and the firm belief that they would be welcomed by the local Arab population—the French poured ashore in the gentle, sheltered bay of Sidi Fredj with identical illusions to commence the long and sombre history of colonial Algeria. The French army would spend the next fifty years suppressing an insurgency; fifteen of them would be spent fighting the brilliant, tough young Algerian resistance leader Abdelkader.

---

*The Harkis were the loyal Algerian auxiliaries of the French army who were to be betrayed by their masters in 1962—left behind to be butchered by their fellow countrymen or dumped in misery in the south of France.

Both sides committed atrocities and even French society was shocked to learn that its troops had asphyxiated 500 Algerian men, women and children by lighting a fire at the mouth of the cave in which they had taken refuge—a horrible prelude to the same fate which was visited by the Turks upon thousands of Armenians during the 1915 genocide. Between 1831 and 1839, the French lost 1,412 soldiers in battle in Algeria; a nightmare portrait of the land came from a French diplomat in 1841:

> The country is without commerce; the circulation of the caravans is suspended . . . the plough is forsaking the fields . . . the Arabs, bent on deeds of blood and decapitation, approach even the gates of Algiers.

Was it through self-delusion or false optimism that Léon Galibert, writing a history of Algeria only three years later, could describe with admiration the missionary works of the French Catholic Church—"because they strongly emphasise the consolidation of our authority in Algeria"—and its desire to conquer Islam:

> On December 24th 1832, one of the most beautiful mosques of Algiers, situated in Divan Street, was consecrated to the Catholic faith. Religious services began with the heavenly solemnity of a midnight mass . . . Here a new era starts for the Church of Africa. Not only have the ceremonial pomp and magnificence of the Catholic church made the natives realise that their conqueror believes in God and has a religion; the church's growing benevolent activities, from which they benefit, has made them understand that this religion is eminently merciful and the friend of man . . . Cardinal Pacca, in his journal dedicated to the Catholic world, makes a point of giving due praise to the efforts that France has made to spread Christianity throughout its possessions. "I saw on the coasts of Africa . . . the spirited French nation restoring the banner of the crucifix, reinstating the altars, converting infidel mosques in temples consecrated to the Almighty, and building new churches. Moreover, I saw on the coasts of Africa a holy priest followed by zealous followers, not only being welcomed by acclamations and shouts of glory on the part of the Catholics, but also respected and venerated by the infidels, Arabs and Bedouins . . . In Constantine, where we can already find 5,000 Catholics . . . a beautiful mosque was transformed into a Church, and renamed Our Lady of Sorrows . . . thanks to the French intervention, Christianity is reconquering in this part of Africa the power that it had acquired in the early age of the Church."

The Church regarded this proselytism as a re-establishment of Christianity in a country where St. Vincent de Paul's Catholic mission had first been established in 1646. Less Christian sentiments, however, applied to the territory which the French intended to settle. Typical was Saïd Bugeaud's statement before the National Assembly in 1840: "Wherever there is fresh water and fertile land, there one must locate the *colons*, without concerning oneself to whom these lands belong." France's own progress as a democracy shaped and reshaped its policies in Algeria, its imperial status constantly challenged by its own liberalism. If Algerians did not have a vote in the parliament of the mother country, however, they were expected to bear an equal sacrifice in the face of France's enemies; it was not only the *pieds noirs* who went to fight and die on the Western Front in the First World War. In the vast war cemeteries of northern France, Algerian tombstones bearing the half-moon of Islam can be found in their thousands, usually separated from the French dead but within the same cemetery enclosure. Their fate provoked widespread unrest in Algeria, although this went largely unreported at the time. Indeed, one has to search through French monographs of the postwar period to find any serious examination of this insurgency. "Despite the [1914] victory of the Marne, worries and prejudices magnified into terrible stories of the battle of Charleroi," one author wrote on the centenary of the French invasion of Algeria in 1830.

> In particular, it was said that we had sacrificed our Muslim troops; that we did not have any more soldiers in Algeria; that our capacity for troop reinforcements had vanished and that the conscripts would be sent under fire as soon as they were drafted. Incidents of resistance mushroomed in three areas, and at the beginning of October, in the mixed *commune* of Mascara, there occurred the rebellion of the Beni Chougrane [tribe] which occurred some days after demonstrations by the people of Sidi Daho . . . emphasising the region's hostility to recruitment.

Algerians, it seemed, were worthy of dying for France, but not of participating in its democracy, a view expressed without much subtlety by one of France's most experienced governor generals in 1926:

> There's no doubt that to give everyone the right to vote—for which few actually care—would not in itself resolve the native problem. It's perfectly commendable for those who are already 20th-century men to claim this right, but we have to be aware that the rest, who choose to maintain respectable traditions, barely achieve the level of maturity [*réalisent à peine*] of the 13th century . . .

Cruelty and oppression marked the last years of French rule. Around the walls of the "Museum of the Martyrs" in Algiers today, beneath the massive concrete wings of the memorial to well over a million Algerians killed in the 1954–62 war of independence against the French, the visitor can see all he wants of this terrible struggle. The museum curator plays Beethoven's Pastoral Symphony and Brahms's Violin Concerto in C over the audio system as if it is necessary to soften the evidence of barbarity. There are French military documents demanding the arrest of guerrilla leaders. There are shackles, whips and guns. Forty-three-year-old posters, printed in secret by the National Liberation Front—the FLN—

inform the resistance movement that it is "the beacon of African socialism." There are monochrome photographs of Algerian "martyrs" and tortured men, their faces shattered or running with blood at the hands of General Jacques Massu's 10th Parachute Division. And there is a showcase filled with the paraphernalia of the French military police, of bullets and cartridges and a small metal object in the shape of a pineapple, labelled: "U.S. Mark 2 Defensive Fragmentation Grenade."

Most historians agree that the massacre at Sétif in 1945—when European settlers and French gendarmerie and troops slaughtered around 6,000 Muslims in revenge for the Muslim murder of 103 Europeans—helped to provoke the original struggle for independence. They also agree that France's subsequent attempts to introduce reforms came too late; not least because "democratic" elections were so flagrantly rigged by the French authorities that Muslims could never achieve equality with French Algerians. Once the FLN declared war in 1954, "moderate" Muslim Algerians were silenced by their nationalist opponents, including a largely forgotten Islamic independence movement, the "Association of Ulemas," which saw the struggle as religious rather than political. The first FLN attacks were puny. A French gendarme would be murdered in the outback, the *bled*—from *balad*, the Arabic for a village—or in the mountains of Kabylie. The FLN began a campaign of cutting down telegraph poles and setting off small bombs in post, airline and government offices. As the war intensified, up to 500,000 French troops were fighting in the cities and mountains, especially in Lakhdaria, east of Algiers, using air strikes and employing helicopters to hunt down guerrilla bands. Sometimes the guerrillas were successful—the wreckage of a French helicopter shot down in the *bled* is today on display in the "Museum of the Martyrs."

Some Algerians claim that in fact a million and a half Algerians may have been killed in the eight-year war that ended in 1962, albeit that 500,000 of these may have been slaughtered by their own comrades in internecine fighting. The conflict was one of betrayal of Muslim Algerians by each other, of French Algerians by their own government, specifically—in the minds of so many *pieds noirs*—by de Gaulle. The guerrillas murdered, raped and mutilated captured French soldiers and civilians. The French army murdered prisoners and massacred the population of entire villages. They, too, raped.

The war of independence became the foundation of modern Algerian politics, a source of violent reference for both its supposedly socialist and corrupt *pouvoir* and those opposed to the government. The war was dirty but could always be called upon as a purifying factor in Algerian life. The revolutionary government of Algiers commissioned Gillo Pontecorvo to make a film of the initial 1954–57 uprising and *The Battle of Algiers* remains one of the classic movies of guerrilla struggle and sacrifice. There is a dramatic moment when Colonel Mathieu, a thin disguise for the real-life General Massu, leads the captured FLN leader Larbi Ben M'Hidi into a press conference at which a journalist questions the morality of hiding bombs in women's shopping baskets. "Don't you think it is a bit cowardly to use women's baskets and handbags to carry explosive devices that kill so many innocent people?" the reporter asks. Ben M'Hidi replies: "And doesn't it seem to you even more cowardly to drop napalm bombs on defenceless villages, so that there are a thousand times more innocent victims . . . Give us your bombers, and you can have our baskets." Mathieu is publicly unrepentant at using torture during interrogation. "Should we remain in Algeria?" he asks. "If you answer yes, then you must accept all the necessary consequences." The film contains many lessons for the American and British occupiers of Iraq; nor was it surprising when in early 2004 the Pentagon organised a screening for military and civilian experts in Washington who were invited by a flier that read: "How to win a battle against terrorism and lose the war of ideas."

If the war was a constantly revived theme for Algerians, however, it was for almost three decades wiped from the French collective memory. For years, *The Battle of Algiers* was banned in France, and when it was eventually shown, cinemas were fire-bombed. It took thirty years before a French film director interviewed the forgotten conscripts of the conflict in which 27,000 French soldiers died. Bertrand Tavernier's *La Guerre sans nom* showed the veterans breaking down in tears as they expressed their sorrow at killing Algerians. In the same year, 1992, the Musée d'Histoire Contemporaine held its first exhibition on the war and published a 320-page guide that did not attempt to hide the war's brutality. In 2000, President Jacques Chirac rejected calls for a formal apology for the use of torture by French soldiers during the war. When long-retired General Paul Aussaresses, who was coordinator of French intelligence in Algiers in 1957, published his memoirs in 2001 and boasted of the Algerians he had personally executed, Amnesty International demanded an investigation by the French government. Aussaresses claimed that François Mitterrand, who was Socialist minister of the interior at the time, was fully aware of the tortures and executions being carried out by French forces in Algeria. But the contemporary Algerian government maintained what an Algerian journalist called "a cowardly silence" over Aussaresses's revelations, not least because its own security services had long practised the same tortures on their own people which Aussaresses and his henchmen had visited upon Algerians. Even in Paris, Algerians died by the hundreds when they protested in October 1961 against a night curfew imposed on them by the police. French cops ferociously assaulted the demonstrators and as many as 300 may have been murdered, their corpses washed up next day in the Seine. To this day, the authorities have not opened all their archives on this massacre, even though the prefect of police responsible for the repression was Maurice Papon, who was convicted in April 1998 for crimes against humanity during the German occupation.

Just as the original French claim to have invaded Algeria to "liberate" its people has a painfully contemporary ring, so too do the appeals for support advanced by the French government to the U.S. administration during the Algerian war of independence. France, the Americans were told, was fighting to defend the West against jihad, against "Middle Eastern Islamic fanaticism." This, the French claimed, was a clash of civilisations. They were wrong, of course—

the French were fighting a nationalist insurgency in Algeria, just as the Americans found themselves fighting a national insurgency in Iraq—but the Islamic content of the 1954–62 independence struggle has long been ignored, not least by the Algerian government that found itself fighting an Islamist enemy in the 1990s.

MOHAMED BOUYALI HELD OUT to me the snapshot of his dead brother. "It was taken when Mustafa was already on the run. The government never got a picture of him wearing his beard. This is a historic photograph." Algeria was already collapsing into a terrifying new war as we spoke in July 1992, a conflict so fearful that the picture he handed me was never given back to him. When I returned to Algeria, Mohamed Bouyali's home was in an area controlled by the Groupe Islamique Armé (GIA—Islamic Armed Group) and even my Algerian driver refused to visit the house. So Mustafa Bouyali's snapshot lies on my desk as I write these words. It is a grainy but powerful print, because he has a big face and a thick beard and his eyes are boring hard and suspiciously into the camera, the eyes of a wanted man. In 1992, his brother and I were sitting in his high, bright airy home in the Algerian village of Ashour from which Mustafa Bouyali had fled just over ten years earlier, never to return.

The picture is slightly out of focus, the paper on which it is printed creased and grubby. It must have been shown many times to trusted family friends, the image of an honoured "martyr" since that rain-drenched night of 3 January 1987 when the Algerian army ambushed Bouyali on the Larba road and a soldier shot him in the head. It is a poor snapshot, unframed, though it would be difficult to overestimate the effect this man has had on Algeria's modern history.

His story has rarely been told in the West, let alone publicly discussed in Algeria. Yet he was the man who provided the inspiration for the armed groups that would assault Algeria's government in the 1990s. He was the catalyst behind the Islamic guerrilla movement that was then assassinating police officers across Algeria, 120 in the previous six months alone. Here in the village of Ashour, in the breezy house with its hot, synthetic velvet sofa and vinyl-covered table and peach trees outside the back door, was the missing historical link between Algeria's savage war of independence and the increasingly merciless civil war of the 1990s, a reference point for Algeria's betrayal and the continuity of its tragedy. Because Bouyali was both a loyal guerrilla fighter for the FLN against France and an Islamic guerrilla fighter against the FLN government that replaced French rule, his activities call into question the meaning of Algerian history. How could a man imprisoned by the French, a *maquisard* in the FLN's National Liberation Army, have chosen to lead another, Islamic maquis against his former comrades?

Mustafa Bouyali was born in Ashour on 27 January 1940, and joined the FLN at the age of sixteen, collecting funds for the nationalist guerrilla movement in his own village, part of the 6th zone of the FLN's Wilaya 4 district. In 1958 he was arrested by the French police at the little house in Ashour and imprisoned for two years. On his release, the French tried to force him into their army, but after three months he escaped from their barracks at Blida and was appointed an FLN officer in Algiers. His old wartime comrade Abdul-Hadi Sayah, who was arrested by the French at the same time, remembers Bouyali, even then, as an "Islamic militant." According to Sayah, Bouyali found within the FLN "a way to make jihad against the French—he held this Islamic view even when he was in the FLN."

His brother Mohamed agrees, although when he produces another, older photograph of his brother it shows Bouyali in FLN guerrilla uniform, dressed in a camouflage tunic, a poncho hat and army boots, posing melodramatically as if about to attack an enemy, holding an old breech-loading rifle in front of him. The picture has been painted in the manner of the time, the uniform a bright green, the sky a clear blue, the face an unhealthy yellow. The glass on the picture is cracked. There were other equally unknown FLN sympathisers at this time. One of them, who conspired to blow up a French government building, was called Abassi Madani. He spent most of the war in prison.

There was no doubting the bitterness that the war engendered. To their horror, the French discovered that hundreds of their own "loyal" Muslim troops were defecting to the FLN side, taking their weapons with them. French prisoners of the FLN were found with their eyes gouged out and their severed genitals stuffed in their mouths. The French responded with mass arrest operations, interning thousands of Algerian men in desert camps without trial. Death sentences were imposed on captured guerrillas; the condemned were usually guillotined, unless it became politically expedient to impose lighter sentences. After de Gaulle returned to office from his exile in Colombey-les-Deux-Eglises, he arrived in Algeria to give apparent support to the *pieds noirs*—*Je vous ai compris*, he told them—and then proceeded to negotiate with the FLN and to turn against the French army which had helped to bring him back to power. In 1960, de Gaulle negotiated, in person, with three leaders from the FLN's Wilaya 4 district—Bouyali's sector— and most of the subsequent assassination attempts against de Gaulle, a total of twenty-four in three years, were made by Frenchmen, some from within the security forces.

The historical similarities are uncanny, for all but one of these incidents were repeated in some form in Algeria in the first seven months of 1990. Over and over, the Algerian government followed the tragic path of the old French administrations. Nor was this by chance. The French, after all, had taught the Algerians that elections could be rigged. The French historian Annie Rey-Goldzeiguer has described how "we really contaminated the Algerians. We taught them that they could play with democracy, cheat democracy . . . We were first-rate professors of anti-democracy." And while the Algerian authorities played the role of their former French governors, the Islamist opponents of the Algerian regime mimicked, over and over again, the activities of the old FLN.

Algerians were cheated of the fruits of independence by their wartime leaders. In the last months before liberation, the maquis of the "interior"—the men who had to fight the most ruthless French paratroop units—objected to the way in which the "exterior" leadership in Tunis and then in Tripoli—men like Ahmed

Ben Bella and Houari Boumedienne—tried to impose policy upon the future Algerian state. The quixotic three-year post-independence rule of Ben Bella angered Bouyali, now an FLN functionary who worked in the national Algerian electronics company SONALEC. "Mustafa's first dispute was over the 'exterior' men's right to decide Algeria's future," Mohamed Bouyali said. "It was his first disagreement with the system. He didn't want to obey the Tripoli 'charter'—he wanted a congress of the FLN *inside* Algeria." At the end of 1963, he took up with the maquis again, along with the Front des Forces Socialistes, the FFS, with Hocine Aït Ahmed, Mohand Oul-Hadj and Krim Belkacem; but after six months of fighting, Ben Bella promised them there would be a fair representation inside the government, of both "interior" and "exterior" men. By 1992, Hocine Aït Ahmed was leader of the FFS. Oul-Hadj, a Kabyle veteran, avoided the fate of his colleague Belkacem, who was later strangled in a Frankfurt hotel, apparently on Boumedienne's orders.

Bouyali returned to civilian life, holding an FLN political post in the Algiers Casbah—until Boumedienne's coup d'état against Ben Bella in 1965. According to his wartime friend and colleague Sayah, Bouyali refused to send the ritual telegram of congratulations to Boumedienne's new "revolutionary council." "He said he refused to support a coup d'état. But the FLN supported the coup. I agreed with my friend Mustafa Bouyali. We both thought that the Algerian revolution was over. We thought the Algerian people had suffered enough. It was time for everyone in Algeria to be consulted about their future. We wanted democracy."

Sayah recalls how Bouyali and other old FLN comrades who objected to Boumedienne's dictatorship met secretly in private homes—sometimes in Sayah's own bungalow on the outskirts of Algiers—to discuss a future Algeria and the possibility of an Islamic state. Sayah, who was recovering from pleurisy when I met him and spoke in short, breathless sentences, was still emotional about that time. "You must see that what's happening now in Algeria is the direct result of the opposition that Bouyali started in 1965. Our opposition wanted to work for a future, a democratic future, without bloodshed. Islam was a fundamental part of our belief—even when we fought the French. In our case, our nationalist feelings were not as strong as our Islamic feelings. The French came [in 1830] and destroyed our mosques and prevented us from speaking our language freely, the language of the Koran. Now again, under Boumedienne, we had no freedom. Our meetings were religious, yes. Our conversations in secret always started with readings from the Koran and we said *Allahu akbar* as we did when we went into battle during the war with the French. The Islamic trend was very strong in us . . . We purposely didn't give our movement a name because Boumedienne's military security apparatus was very strong and it would have been easier for them to arrest us if they could identify us all in one way."

Sheikh Mahfouz Nahnah, who in 1992 led the Hamas party (no relation to its Palestinian namesake), Sheikh Ahmed Sahnoun, the last survivor of the old "Association of Ulemas" who was now the imam of the Cité de la Concorde mosque outside Algiers, and two religious figures who were to die under house arrest—Abdul

Latif Soltani and Sheikh Mousbah—were Bouyali's associates in these secret meetings, although they soon gave their movement a name, the "Group of Values" (*al-kiam*). The Algerian government banned the movement when it publicly opposed Nasser's execution of the Islamic theologian Saïd Qotb in Egypt—a condemnation which embarrassed Boumedienne's regime.

According to Mohamed Bouyali, his brother also began lecturing to Muslims in his local mosque in Ashour, assisted by a more senior figure, Abdul-Hadi Doudi, who was in 1992 the imam of the Marseille mosque. "Mustafa talked about Islam as a system of government—so this meant he talked about politics. His speeches were about political education in Islam. He denounced corruption and even used to cite the names of corrupt people in the regime . . . The whole village would be closed on Fridays because so many people came to hear Mustafa and Abdul-Hadi."

In December 1978, Boumedienne died, to be succeeded by Chadli Bendjedid, whose rule was equally dictatorial and more openly corrupt than his predecessor's. The police began to keep watch on Bouyali. "Government men turned up at the mosque and started taking down car registration numbers, to intimidate the people who were listening to Mustafa," Mohamed Bouyali says. "They filmed the crowd. They repeatedly asked Mustafa to go to the police station for interrogation. They did this every day—until 3 October 1981. When he went in to work that day, plain-clothes policemen tried to kidnap him, and his fellow workers rescued him. Mustafa fled to his grandfather's house. He was sure the police wanted to abduct him and that he would 'disappear.' "

Friends later acted as intermediaries to arrange a meeting between the police and Bouyali. He was told that the incident had been a "mistake." According to his brother, the head of the Algerian national security police warned Mustafa Bouyali that he was "getting involved in politics." "Mustafa replied: 'But for me, the whole of life is politics. When you breathe, when you eat—that's politics.' " In February 1982, according to the Bouyali family, Mustafa's file was transferred from the security police to Algerian military intelligence, an ominous sign. On 28 April, he escaped over the wall of his home in Ashour while armed plain-clothes men waited at his front gate to arrest him as he left to lead dawn prayers at the mosque.

"Now he was really on the run and he started making contacts for military action," Mohamed Bouyali recalls. "He spoke to most of the scholars—to Sheikh Nahnah, Ali Belhaj, Sheikh Ahmed Sahnoun, Abassi Madani. He said that he would take up military action, that they should speak in the mosques. He found his old maquis friends in the mountains, hundreds of them, and formed armed groups. Mustafa contacted the youth of Bab el-Oued and started making bombs." Nahnah played no military role and Sahnoun was elderly, but Belhaj and Madani were to become leaders of the Front Islamique du Salut (FIS—Islamic Salvation Front).

In late 1982, Bouyali shot and wounded a police officer at a road checkpoint, and the government struck against all his supporters; 47 were arrested between mid-December and early January 1983, another 103 by May. In the years to come, he would stage robberies to raise funds. His group attacked the police academy for weapons. Sayah, who sorrowfully left Bouyali when his friend turned to armed insurrection, claims that the police had much earlier taken their revenge on Bouyali by shooting dead one of his brothers in front of the man's children—and that it was this that drove Bouyali to abandon dialogue in favour of war. "He took to the mountains . . . in the Mitidja, in Medea, in Lakhdaria, across the country, even to Sétif. There were pitched battles, a real war."

It was a secret war that the world never heard of. There were more government ambushes. One of Bouyali's principal lieutenants, Abdelkader Chebouti, was captured and condemned to death—but he was reprieved by Chadli Bendjedid and returned to fight with Bouyali's maquis after his leader's demise. Dozens of Bouyali's comrades were fighting an "Islamic war" against the Soviet army in Afghanistan, where they came to admire Abdullah Azzam, an Islamic Palestinian guerrilla leader who was assassinated by a car bomb in 1989. Another of their heroes in Afghanistan was an Egyptian fighter named Shawki el-Islambouli, the brother of the man who assassinated President Sadat of Egypt in October 1981.

When Bouyali was finally run to ground, the Algerian newspapers recorded only the death of a "terrorist." "His driver gave him away," Mohamed Bouyali says. "Mustafa was travelling in the mountains near Larba, late at night in a rain storm. His driver had been arrested and then released some days before—usually Mustafa stayed away from people who had been detained in case they had been turned against him. The driver had been tortured. They were going down this road when Mustafa noticed the driver switching his lights onto high beam and down again and his friends heard him shout: 'Traitor!' At that moment, bullets were fired from both sides of the road and Mustafa was killed along with five of his men." According to Sayah, Mustafa Bouyali's last earthly act was to execute his driver by shooting him in the head, seconds before he himself was hit in the forehead by a bullet.

But Bouyali's posthumous legacy was far more violent. When Chadli Bendjedid's troops killed up to 500 demonstrators who were demanding democracy in Algiers in 1988, the event helped to give birth to the FIS, among whose leadership were Madani and Belhaj, Bouyali's old associates. The event was, in its way, as cataclysmic as that long-ago massacre at Sétif. President Bendjedid found himself facing pressure for reform, not unlike the French authorities before the independence war. When the military cancelled the second round of national elections in 1992—after a first round which showed that the FIS would win—this suppression of democracy was every bit as cynical as the French rigging of their own elections in Algeria. Bendjedid was fired by the generals. The FIS was banned and a guerrilla war of growing intensity began.

These "new" *maquisards* of 1992 were initially men who had fought with Bouyali in the mountains, and they used the same methods as the old FLN against the French. They cut down telephone and electricity poles and planted bombs in post, airline and government offices. They assassinated policemen. The government responded—as the French had done in the face of the FLN—by calling their enemies "terrorists." Thousands of Algerian troops, including paratroopers—

many of them trained by their old colonial masters in France—began hunting down Bouyali's old comrades and young disciples in Lakhdaria, Djemila, Sidi Bel-Abbès and Jijel, just as the French Régiment de Chasseurs Parachutistes hunted the FLN in these same locations more than three decades earlier. During these operations, which received virtually no publicity in or outside Algeria, dozens of soldiers defected to the Islamic "resistance" along with their rifles, just as the French Tirailleurs Algériens once crossed to the FLN.

Thus had the betrayal of the revolution against France led to a historical repetition. As the FLN's dictators corrupted their country, so their original victory came to be seen as a betrayal, their francophone, Western (if originally Soviet-style) clique a poor copy of the old French colonial regime. Their French culture—what Algerians refer to as "the damned inheritance"—suggested that nothing had changed. Algeria's unemployed young grew tired of the false promises of the independence war, sick of hearing about the revolution, weary of remembering dead heroes who brought them only destitution and homelessness. By 1992, more than 75 per cent of the Algerian population had been born after the independence war. Was it therefore any surprise that among the first targets of the Islamists were the ageing survivors of that war? Every day in the Algerian press there were death notices for the old mujahedin of 1954–62, *anciens combattants* who had been found with their throats slit in the towns and villages in which, for more than thirty years, they had been honoured as old soldiers. The fury of the young was even vented on their graves; to their shock, the Algerian government found the tombs of FLN "martyrs" torn open, their bones—smashed by French bullets three decades earlier—now broken to pieces with stones by Algerians who were supposed to honour their memories.

It was not surprising that future Algerian governments were forced to acknowledge the extent of the threat that now faced them. When the Algerian prime minister Mokdad Sifi asked me in 1995 if I knew who Bouyali was, it was a kind of watershed, an understanding of Bouyali's historical role, of the connections that bound him to the past as well as the present. The 1954–62 conflict was a civil war as well as an independence war against the French; afterwards, Algeria was locked into a steel corset by years of postwar dictatorship, just as Tito locked Yugoslavia into his iron embrace after the Second World War. When the iron rusts, history picks up where it left off. Hence both the Algerian government and its armed opponents looked backwards rather than forwards. The authorities made Boumedienne-like promises of future prosperity, democracy and popular support. The Islamists assaulted culture and the arts and talked of a caliphate. Even Hassan Turabi, the Sudanese prelate who, so the Algerian government claimed, had most seriously influenced the Islamists, admitted to me in 1992 that he could not understand the Muslim leadership in Algeria. "They will not talk about the future," he lamented. "I spoke to Abbas Madani before the elections . . . And I asked him: 'What's your programme like? What are you going to do after the elections? Have you started a dialogue with the French? . . .' And he just said: 'No, no, we just want to win the elections.' "

Within months of the latest insurgency, the Algerian government, in effect run by a coterie of privileged and immensely powerful army officers, cast around the Middle East for inspiration in their struggle against "fundamentalist terrorism." They produced books and pamphlets on the roots of Islamic revivalism in an effort to persuade diplomats and foreign journalists that the roots of Algeria's "terrorism" lay in the Egyptian Muslim Brotherhood, in Pakistan, in Saudi Arabia. In 1995, the interior minister even claimed that the Lebanese Hizballah, the Iranians and the Palestinian Hamas movement had made contact with the Algerian GIA at a meeting in Tripoli in northern Lebanon. The story was the fantasy of a French novelist—who alleged "Syrian intelligence" as his source—which had been recycled in a *New York Times* story out of Paris. The Algerians searched everywhere—anywhere—for some way of proving that the Algerian insurgency was not Algerian. Like the Americans in Iraq ten years later, their enemies had to be foreigners, aliens, dark figures who had crossed the frontiers to fight the forces of democracy.

Both sides had complementary illusions. Many Frenchmen had thought they were fighting communism in Algeria when they were in fact fighting nationalism—or Islam, if Bouyali's comrades and the French propagandists of the time are to be believed. The Islamic "resistance" now believed the independence war had been partly a religious jihad which—given the weight of documentary evidence to the contrary—it clearly was not for most of the participants. Bouyali's former supporters—those who left him when he went into the mountains—still believe that if only successive Algerian governments had talked to their opponents rather than imprisoned them, the crisis could have been resolved. Instead, those who chose to fight with weapons turned the memory of Mustafa Bouyali into an inspiration for further struggle. His brother Mohamed has one other photograph of him. It is a coloured snapshot of Bouyali in his last months, sitting cross-legged on the floor of a mountain cave, reading a Koran that lies open in front of him—with a French sub-machine gun propped against the wall on his right. And of course, today I remember another armed Islamist who sits on the floor of a cave and reads a Koran with a gun beside him.

Did Bouyali doom his people to re-enact the dreadful war that ended in 1962? In July 1992, Bouyali's old comrade Abdelkader Chebouti was captured again, along with another former Bouyali supporter, Mansouri Meliani, after a gun battle in Ashour. They were caught only a few hundred metres from Bouyali's unmarked grave.

"Democracy"—which in the Algerian context must always, like "Palestine," be used in quotation marks—came to an end on 12 January 1992, when the government effectively introduced martial law and stripped the FIS of its democratic election victory by cancelling the second round of the poll due to be held four days later. I had arrived in Algiers with a visa to cover the election that was no longer going to take place. Thus having been encouraged to witness Algeria's "experiment in democracy," I checked into the old French Hôtel Saint Georges, once Second World War headquarters to General Dwight D. Eisenhower—now the Hôtel el-Djezair—only to find Chadli Bendjedid announcing his resignation on the old and flickering television set in the hotel bar. Government "minders" who had been groomed to extol to us the wonders of Algerian "democracy" had suddenly to be reprogrammed to explain how "democracy" could only be protected by suspending "democracy." This was hard work. To destroy a Vietnamese village in order to save it was one thing. To destroy democracy in order to save it, quite another.

The army had pushed Chadli Bendjedid from the presidency and a five-man "Council of State"—including Algeria's most powerful general, Khaled Nezzar—soon announced it would run the country. Although it appeared to have no constitutional legality, this "Council" needed a symbolic figure to sit on its throne; in desperation, the authorities called in a hero of the past, a man of destiny who would return from exile to lead Algeria in its hour of need. Just as de Gaulle had returned from Colombey-les-Deux-Eglises, so Mohamed Boudiaf, veteran of the 1954–62 war and one of the founders of the FLN, must come back to Algeria. He told his people he understood their needs, just as de Gaulle said he understood the French Algerians. There would be no Islamic republic in Algeria.

Algeria's Islamist leaders—stunned to find the army in control of the country they thought they were about to rule—warned that they would not tolerate any attempt to cancel the second round of elections. But a quiet coup d'état had left the generals rather than the politicans in charge of the army, and paramilitary police checkpoints had now been set up on all main roads into the capital. Troops and armoured personnel carriers were positioned around government buildings—the prime minister's office, the foreign ministry, the post office, the treasury and radio station—and Algerian commandos with fixed bayonets patrolled the southern streets of the capital. The acting leader of the FIS, Sheikh Abdelkader Hachani, denounced the country's new rulers as thieves who had "stolen the liberty of the Algerian people." The army, he said, "must side with the people." Even Sheikh Nahnah, whose moderate plumage ensured his freedom from arrest, felt it necessary to say that "the greatest violence is done when a state attacks its own people." The new regime, he said, was a "dictocracy."

I took one of Algiers' yellow-painted taxis downtown that first morning of "dictocracy," to a shabby ground-floor room in rue Larbi Ben M'Hidi where an exhibition every bit as distressing as the "Museum of the Martyrs" was showing to a packed house. Here Beethoven and Brahms were replaced by a grotesquely amplified voice reciting verses from the Koran. Yet this display of much more recent history provided by the FIS contained some grim parallels with the other museum on the hill. Here again were the broken faces of dead and beaten men—in colour this time—yet they were not the victims of the 1954–62 war against the French but the dozens of Algerians who were shot down in the streets of Algiers by Algerian troops in the 1988 riots. There was even a showcase—ironically of the same size and layout as the case in the "Museum of Martyrs"—containing bullets and cartridges fired by the Algerian army. One of the cartridges was clearly marked: "Federal Laboratories Inc. Saltsburg, Pennsylvania 15681 U.S.A."

It was not the Western provenance of these weapons that was important—

though the anti-Western resentment within the FIS had been growing daily—but the pattern of repression which they represented. It was as if French colonial rule bequeathed not freedom but military force to the Algerians. Under the FLN's post-independence dictatorship, the Algerian security services practised many of the same tortures as their French predecessors—"electricity with oriental refine-ments," as one victim put it to me—and the French had themselves learned how to make men and women talk in the dungeons of the Gestapo during the Second World War. It was a genealogy of horror, one that would be expanded if Algeria were to be faced with an Islamist uprising.

FIS supporters could explain their anger very simply. They had been encour-aged to participate in these elections. The West had repeatedly said that power should come through the ballot box rather than through revolution—Islamist or otherwise—and the FIS had dutifully played the democratic card. The FIS abided by the rules—and made the mistake of winning the election. This was not what the *pouvoir*, or its Western supporters, intended. France was happy to avoid the night-mare of an Islamic "catastrophe" on the southern shore of the Mediterranean. The Americans did not want another Islamic revolution along the lines of Iran. So much for democracy.

Of course, it was not that simple. The FIS sought power without responsibility. Their repeated demands for an Islamic republic alienated the 26 million other Algerians whom they would have to represent once they achieved power. And their assumption of "rightness"—their unquestionable faith in their own Islamic path with all its social sharia laws—could be breathtaking. So could their grasp of his-tory. "All our martyrs against the French died for Islam," a young FIS acolyte told me outside the Bab el-Oued mosque. "The independence war was an Islamic struggle." This was the Bouyali doctrine.

In reality, the body politic of Algeria was not threatened in the way that Chadli Bendjedid's pitiful television appearance suggested. The Algerian constitution was so cleverly devised that even if the FIS had dominated parliament, it would not have been able to take over the government. For it was the president who chose ministers—and ministers who drew up the political programme. If that programme was twice rejected by parliament, there had to be new general elections. In other words, the government itself—for which, read the army—would continue to con-trol Algeria. Once again, however, the authorities did not want to talk to the oppo-sition. They did not want a democracy unless they could be the winners. They wanted to lock their opponents up. And within three days of the declaration of martial law, the FIS announced that fifty-three of its members—including three who gained seats in the first round of elections—had been arrested by the army.

Hachani shrewdly adopted the role of a constitutionalist, suggesting that all 231 deputies—including 188 FIS members—elected in the December first round should form a "parallel" parliament. "A political process has to be resumed," he said, although Hachani's words were diminished by the appearance at his press conference of Amar Bramia, the coach to Algeria's national athletic team, who gave an unpleasant account of his arrest and ill-treatment at the hands of the army on 13 January. He said he had been taken to the Ministry of Defence in Algiers because he had been identified at a FIS rally, and had been forced to remove his trousers before being severely beaten. "They threatened to rape my wife if I told anyone what happened," he said. "I am . . . telling this to the press so that the Algerian people should know what sort of people are in power."

But what sort of people supported the FIS? From outside, the apartment blocks of Bab el-Oued are pigeon lofts, tiny rectangular windows stuffed with drying bed-clothes and tired mattresses, the flats eight storeys high, thirty abreast, the exterior walls streaked with grime, more than three and a half thousand souls sleeping ten to a room. Walk the gaunt, grey corridors, deafening with the shriek of children, and you can see bunks, floor to ceiling, in each room as if the inhabitants live in a barracks. Which, in a sense, they do. Modern police stations have been erected on the roads above Bab el-Oued, the security forces a permanent army of occupation. No wonder the people there never regarded the Popular Democratic Republic of Algeria as either popular or democratic. The acronym "FIS," that cold, wet January of 1992, was on every wall.

"Why are you foreigners so surprised we voted for the FIS?" The thirty-nine-year-old shopkeeper, unshaven, in an old grey sweater and worn shoes—anonymous in these days of ghostly martial law—pointed eastwards in the direction of Algiers airport, where Mohamed Boudiaf, the grand old man of the independence war, was about to land after twenty-eight years of exile in Morocco. "If I was at the airport and had a gun, I'd shoot Boudiaf. How dare they impose this old man on us after our election victory? What has he got to do with us? I had never heard of him until they said he would be the new leader of Algeria." Nor could the shopkeeper be expected to know of Boudiaf. He was only nine years old when the French left Algeria and freed Boudiaf from prison. With 70 per cent of Algeria's 26 million people under the age of thirty-five—44 per cent were under fourteen—only a quarter could remember the guerrilla war with France.

But Algeria's "conversion" to Islam was ambiguous. The Algerian flag bears the half-moon of Islam. The first words of the Koran are printed above Article One of the Algerian constitution. Article Two declares that "Islam is the state religion." But the theological renaissance that millions of Algerians experienced over the previous decade bore no resemblance to the ruling FLN's formal adherence to the faith. FIS members recalled that they began to follow Islam in earnest around ten years earlier—in 1982, when Bouyali went on the run and started his guerrilla campaign, when a new group of young preachers appeared in the Algiers mosques, men who refused to maintain political discretion in the face of the government's economic mismanagement. In retrospect, the collapse of oil prices and the further impoverishment of Algeria's youth guaranteed the rise of fundamentalism—though the FIS rejected the word "fundamentalism" as a Western invention.

Akli, for example, worshipped at the Kabul mosque in Belcourt—the attendance of ex-guerrillas who fought the Soviets in Afghanistan gave the building its name—and remembered when his religion began to dominate his life. "The discussion of Islam started around the end of the Seventies, in cafés, in the streets—yes, even in bars. It filled a void in Algerian society. Our people were growing poorer. I had always thought of an Islamic republic as a dream, but for me it became a reality. The West tells us that the problems of the Third World are economic, but I came to realise through Islam that this is untrue, that in fact it is the people who must change."

Akli is a biologist, and a fascination with science characterised much of the FIS's thinking. Educated FIS supporters almost invariably turned out to be skilled engineers or communications technicians. Without exception, every bookshop in Algiers now displayed a special section on Islamic literature. Alongside each section were shelves of scientific works. All twenty-two of the FIS's candidates in the December parliamentary elections were graduates, fifteen of them scientists. In an Algerian Islamic republic, the government was more likely to be led by technocrats than by mullahs. Party supporters claimed that Islam and science were not only compatible but complementary, that both involved absolute truth and understanding.

Science could also be used to mislead. In July 1991 the FIS smuggled a laser device into Algeria in the diplomatic bag of an Arab embassy and at a night-time open-air rally at Bab el-Oued wrote the word *Allah* on the clouds above the city. Many of those present claimed they had witnessed a miracle. But the FIS was no party of ignorance. Another Bab el-Oued man—unemployed and again anonymous, since he rightly expected a civil war and mass arrests—could not suppress his rage at the attempts by ex-presidents Boumedienne and Bendjedid to repress the depth of religious feeling. "They thought they could keep our allegiance by building mosques—dozens of mosques all over Algeria, even Islamic universities in Algiers and Oran," he said. "Bendjedid's wife started appearing in photographs wearing the *hidjab* covering before she disappeared from public view. But you don't love Islam by building mosques. We have to practise our religion in our lives. We were inspired when a preacher, a militant preacher, came forward and abandoned discretion in the Eighties. His name was Mustafa Bouyali. He was shot by the police."

Bouyali. This was long before I had met Bouyali's family or researched his life. It was one of the first times I had heard his name. The FIS denied a military role, although already there were reports that several armed cells existed like satellites around the movement. One such group was said to be made up of "Kabulis," who had fought in Afghanistan. Another was believed to be called the Al-Quds (Jerusalem) Brigade. But the FIS would not speak of this.

"Don't provoke anyone, stay calm. There must be no violence." There were perhaps 30,000 Muslim worshippers in the narrow, broken streets around the breeze-block Sunna mosque, and they obeyed the instruction so literally that they scarcely spoke to each other when they completed their Friday prayers. Sheikh Abdelkader Hachani told his congregation—thousands of them kneeling on prayer mats on the very roads and pavements of Bab el-Oued—that at least 500 young men had already been arrested by the police and army. The riot police along the seafront, visors up, night-sticks in their hands, had been picking them out for four hours already.

I saw one of them, a youth of maybe fifteen, unshaven, shouting in protest as he was dragged by the collar across the highway outside the headquarters of the security police, his expression both pleading and angry. A paramilitary cop pushed him into a mini-bus already filled with young bearded men. It looked as if the police were trying to provoke the massive crowd. But for Hachani to have abandoned his address would have conceded victory to Mohamed Boudiaf. Although still in Morocco, he had been installed as head of Algeria's "Council of State," declaring that he would not allow anyone "to use Islam to take over the country." In the event, Hachani—his voice blasting from dozens of loudspeakers through the cramped streets—repeated his contention that Boudiaf was an unconstitutional leader, claiming that the spokeswoman of the U.S. State Department had given her approval to the new Algerian regime.

It must have been the first time in history that the name of Margaret Tutweiler had echoed forth from an Algerian mosque. George Bush's post–Gulf War "New World Order" had devised Boudiaf's coup d'état in order to prevent the creation of an Islamic republic, Hachani insisted. The multitude, cross-legged on their crimson and blue mats, listened in absolute silence, with such rapt attention that between Hachani's words it was possible to hear the chanting of other prayers from other mosques floating over the city. Watching those thousands of faces with their intense eyes, and the tears—real tears—that literally dripped from their faces as they prayed, one could only ask if old Boudiaf could stand up to this total, frightening, sense of purpose.

"Algeria is threatened," Boudiaf had told his countrymen a few hours earlier. "I will do everything I can to resolve the problems of Algeria's youth . . . Islam in this country belongs to everyone, not just to a few . . . I pray God he will unite us to bring us out of this crisis." But at the Sunna mosque, Hachani's audience were muttering equally fervent prayers. "Islam will conquer," one of the FIS supporters whispered as he surveyed the riot police at the bottom of the street. "Boudiaf and these government people will die—and they will go to hell." It was not said as a turn of phrase but with determination, as if he could actually ensure the destination of those he wished to doom.

Not all those in the streets of Bab el-Oued were FIS supporters. On some of the wrought-iron balconies were young women without scarves, long hair over their shoulders, a hint of jewellery showing on their wrists. They were courageous women, refusing to accept what so many of the men in their streets would no doubt demand of them in an Islamic republic. They were ignored by the thousands of FIS men who chose not to look up at the balconies; nor, when they left, did the worshippers even deign to glance at the soldiers in helmets, riot shields in front of them, who stood beside the iron dragon's-teeth checkpoints. Bab el-Oued had been cordoned off by Boudiaf's troops and policemen. "Besieged Bab el-Oued," Hachani called it, although it did seem as if it was Boudiaf's absent authority that might be under siege.

Algiers. *Alger la Blanche*. If its white walls were now stained with damp, it exerted an unusual magnetism over all who arrived in the city. It was like a place you knew from a previous life, whose hilly streets and shuttered villas and trees— even the smell of fish at *la pêcherie* at the end of the old French naval pier—had been waiting all along for your visit. "Sire, there is a war with Algiers," the French minister for war wrote to his emperor on 14 October 1827, after the fly-whisk assault on France's consul. "How can it end in a manner that is useful and glorious for France?" Algiers was always a city to be captured rather than loved by those who did not possess her. After Ben Bella's victorious guerrilla army took control in 1962, they attacked the heart of this soft Mediterranean city by erecting brown concrete monuments to socialism amid the Haussmanlike boulevards of the old town, vast offices that mocked the *petit Paris* which the French had cultivated for 132 years.

Wandering around Algiers reminded me of that first visit to France with Bill and Peggy in 1956. The still-proud nineteenth-century streets, the bumpy roads, the dented cars, the faulty plumbing and stinking drains, the railway stations with their cut stone walls and steeply sloping roofs, even the cheap, unpainted railway carriages with their corrugated silver steel sides, were a mirror image of French provincial cities in the late 1950s, embellished only by the shoddy postwar housing of the Fourth Republic. It was almost as if time stopped when Algeria's million *pieds noirs* went flocking aboard the hastily commandeered transatlantic liners that took them "home" to metropolitan France three decades before. At the Saint George Hotel, the waiter would arrive each morning with a classic French breakfast; orange juice, croissants and a silver pot of coffee. Yet the juice came not from the country's orchards but from a tin of Italian substitute, the croissants tasted like cardboard, the coffee had no taste at all.

Perhaps that is what happens when the culture of one country becomes fossilised into the fabric of a city it no longer owns. The bookshops still sold the works of Zola, Gide and Camus, himself a *pied noir*, whose masterpiece *L'Etranger* is set in Algeria. Some of the finest Algerian authors still wrote in French; typically, one of the country's most admired writers, Rachid Mimouni, had written his most recent novel, *Une peine à vivre*, in self-imposed exile in France. It was about dictatorship, the love of power and the power of love.

Drop by Le Restaurant Béarnais in rue Burdeau and you would find the customers discussing their horror of theocracy and their fears for their broken-backed democracy in Parisian French. The menu is in French not Arabic, the *plat du jour* is *steak au poivre*, the favourite wine a fine Algerian claret whose name, *Cuvée du Président*, had taken on new meaning since Bendjedid's resignation. Journalists from *Algérie Actualité*, one of the country's seventy-three new newspapers—all printed on a government press and thus easy to close down—are crowded round a corner table, smoking and sipping beer. They regard the threat of the FIS with the fascination of intellectuals. One of the ironies of the FIS is that the party itself uses the acronym for its own name in French, the Front Islamique du Salut.

"There is one thing you must understand about the FIS," the paper's editor,

Zouaoui Benamadi, says. "Only Islamic movements are capable of breaking the government systems that exist in the Arab world. But who are these people? What are these strange clothes they wear? They have beards and wear white caps and shortened trousers to show their allegiance to the FIS. But we have beautiful national clothes in Algeria. We have the burnous, a big woollen robe. Where does it come from, this curious dress of theirs?" Benamadi, a small, brown-haired man with large glasses—clean-shaven, in a sports jacket and tie, he looks like a French socialist—returns to his editorial office in a nineteenth-century apartment building a hundred metres from the restaurant. Its high ceilings, glossy yellow paint and broken mosaic floor exude a kind of poor elegance. A sub-editor brings in the printer's proof of the next day's editorial and Benamadi examines it with a priest's concentration. "From one day to the next, rural Algeria—the Anti-Berber Algeria—is supposed to become Afghan," he has written. " . . . to change our clothes, to change our eating habits, to change our customs, including the very way we bury our dead . . . the result: the desertion en masse of the middle classes, of our vitality, of those who do greatest service to our national life."

I visit the Kouba mosque at Friday prayers and find the answers to some of Benamadi's questions. True, the FIS is against alcohol, against singing at weddings, against mourners eating special meals on the first, seventh and fortieth days after death, against spoken prayers at funerals. True, the FIS has developed a "uniform" of beards and shortened trousers. The latter are supposed to symbolise a good Muslim's desire to wash before prayers without allowing water to touch the bottom of his clothes. But among the worshippers' heads as they rise and fall to their prayers are hundreds of Afghan hats, the rolled cloth head covering of the mujahedin guerrillas. For the Afghan connection—noticed but not sufficiently recognised by other Algerians—is vital to an understanding of the Islamists.

Pick up a taxi in Bab el-Oued and its significance becomes clear. The driver and his friend both have beards. Their impromptu conversation tells the story. "We wanted to go to Afghanistan to fight," the driver says. "They are mostly Sunni not Shia Muslims there. They fight communism. More important, they want an Islamic republic. The Hezb Islami is very good. We want to fight for them. Many hundreds of our friends went to Afghanistan to fight. Now our government tries to stop them. Two Algerians and three Palestinians returning to Algiers from Afghanistan were arrested at the airport when they got here. It is easy to go to Afghanistan. We go over to that building for visas." We are on the avenue Souidani Boudjema, passing an ill-painted office with an unpolished brass plaque which says: "Embassy of Pakistan."

Gulbuddin Hekmatyar, the leader of the Hezb Islami, has complained about the Algerian government's sudden lack of enthusiasm for his movement, but the real danger of the FIS's war in Afghanistan is not religious. It is in learning about the potential Islamic republic. Much more seriously, its young men are learning how to fight. In Afghanistan, they are taught how to use Kalashnikovs, mortars, even tanks—they can learn to drive T-55s and T-62s, exactly the same kind of tanks that the Algerian army uses.

"Fascists," the old FLN man cries. A gentle, kindly man, he has no doubt about the necessity of depriving the FIS of its hard-earned, genuinely democratic victory in the first round of elections. We are sitting at a dinner table, talking to men who have no moral qualms about switching off the engine of democracy in the interests of public order. We sip red wine, they have orange juice. The food—Algerian soup, *langoustine*, *ossobuco*—is served by liveried waiters. Our hosts speak impeccable French, their words uttered more slowly as they become more angry. "You people want to talk about democracy," the old FLN man says—he was a student at the start of the war of independence—"but this is not a philosophy lesson for us. If the FIS came to power, there would be a civil war in Algeria. There would be terrible bloodshed. We are having to deal with a real problem. How wonderful it would be, you might think, to have an Islamic republic in Algeria. How democratic of you! But we cannot allow a civil war to take place. We have a responsibility to our country, to our people."

His younger companion runs through the equations of this morality. Out of 26 million Algerians, the FIS gained only 3.2 million votes in December 1991. One million voting cards were spoiled, another million failed to reach the electorate. In the 1990 municipal elections, the FIS gained 4.3 million votes. Could we not therefore see how their support was declining? Out of 13 million eligible voters, the FIS's December victory represented only 23 per cent of the population. How could they have been permitted to win a second round of elections? "These people really want an Islamic republic and our people will not accept this. The FIS will be dictators. They use the system of the Nazis."

It was a supreme and terrible irony that in the rest of the Arab world, the situation is reversed. In Egypt, in Jordan, in Syria, it is the liberal, democratic elite who bemoan the lack of democracy in their countries, and the vast toiling mass of Muslims who suffer its consequences in silence. In Algeria in 1992, it was a popular Islamic movement that demanded democracy while the middle-class intelligentsia produced convoluted reasons for its postponement. The tragedy was that Boudiaf might have been right. The FIS had shown no urge to tolerate the millions of Algerians who did not want an Islamic republic, for the Francophile, middle-class Algerians, many of whom could not even speak Arabic fluently, for the liberated female population of the cities, for the Muslim Berber community—25 per cent of the population—who speak Tamazirte and who are not Arabs.

On 23 January, Algeria's Channel Three pop radio gave a fair reflection of the government's policy. The first item on its hourly news broadcast was the prime minister's international appeal for $8 billion in loans to ease the country's 20 per cent unemployment and supplement food supplies. Then, almost as an afterthought, came a brief report on the arrest of Abdelkader Hachani. The government's plan was obvious: encourage the people with talk of good economic times to come and treat the suppression of the FIS as of secondary importance, an unhappy but necessary result of the party's foolishness in winning 188 of the seats in the first election. Hachani had anyway been detained on the orders of General Khaled Nezzar, the defence minister, for calling upon the Algerian army to rebel against the government.

Hachani had done just that. Two days before his arrest, I had been given a copy of his cyclostyled appeal, addressed to the "Popular National Army" and signed in Hachani's own handwriting. For good measure, police and troops moved into the offices of the daily *Al-Khabar*, which had printed the desertion appeal, and arrested the journalists working on the newspaper. Hachani himself was stopped by plain-clothes police while driving in his own car in the Belcourt district of Algiers and taken off to Blida prison to join Abassi Madani and Ali Belhaj, the two principal leaders of the FIS. At the very same hour, the prime minister, Sid-Ahmed Ghozali, announced that no speeches "of a political nature" would in future be allowed in the country's mosques and that no demonstrations would be permitted in the vicinity of mosques. As usual, there were historical precedents behind the latest arrests. In 1930, the French dissolved Algeria's first twentieth-century independence group—the "North African Star"—whose leader, Messali Hadj, called himself an "Islamo-nationalist" and ran a newspaper called *El-Umma* which celebrated "the revival of Islam." Hadj was imprisoned for trying to reconstitute a dissolved association and later condemned to a year in a French prison for "provoking soldiers to disobey orders with the intention of creating anarchy."

Algerian government spokesmen talked each day about *calme et sérénité*. In the streets, the shopkeepers talked about the "explosion" to come. We all felt it, the absolute certainty that you couldn't obstruct democracy without creating violence. On 20 January a brigadier in the Algerian gendarmerie was shot dead. Forty-three-year-old Amari Aïssa was married with four children. Crowds of youths had thrown stones at military checkpoints outside Algiers and soldiers had to fire warning shots in the air to disperse them. "Anyone can kill a policeman," an official commented offhandedly when I asked for some indication of the government's concern. "People kill policemen from New York to Nepal. It is a criminal act and will anyway reflect badly on the FIS. Every time a policeman is killed, his village turns out for the funeral and the people turn against the FIS." Only a criminal matter. Nothing that couldn't happen in the United States. But no one suspends elections in America. And Brigadier Aïssa wasn't murdered by the mafia. Within three weeks, seven days of rioting between police and FIS supporters—in which at least 50 people were believed to have been killed and 200 wounded—prompted Boudiaf's military-controlled "Council" to proclaim a state of emergency. In the slums of Algiers there were clandestine calls for a "holy war" against Boudiaf's authorities. Almost the entire FIS leadership was already under arrest, the party's head office in Algiers had been closed down and sixty imams had been detained.

The meltdown comes faster than we expected. The Casbah, Algiers, 15 February 1992. Somewhere amid Bouznad Hadi's scorched home—around the charred bedclothes, the burned electrical wiring, the blackened stone staircase—lies the Truth. The veiled Algerian women crying in the tight alleyways outside the house are sure they knew what that is. So is Bouznad Hadi's cousin, holding a generator lamp in his right hand as he tells how four of the innocent inhabitants were incinerated by Algerian army rocket fire. So is the Algerian government, which states that its soldiers only attacked the house because shots had been fired at them from the building. You can witness the same scenes in Belfast or in the West Bank. But in the Algiers Casbah, its implications are far more serious. For the difference between truths here symbolises the gulf between the people and a government fearful of civil war. Are the people going to believe that Bouznad Hadi and his friends were "martyrs" or "terrorists"?

The fruit merchant's home lies in the very heart of the Casbah, where winding stone steps meander between wooden and mud-baked walls, where even narrower alleyways lead to old domed houses so buried in layers of habitation that they are almost underground. No one disputes that five men were in the house in the early hours of the previous day. Nor does anyone dispute that Algerian army paratroopers—neighbours saw their red berets in the semi-darkness—surrounded Bouznad Hadi's tiny dwelling some time between 2 and 3 a.m.

This, however, is where truth becomes a little slippery. The government says the soldiers came under fire from the building; but the doorway is too low to be seen from the nearest pathway and there are no windows facing the only alleyway down which the soldiers could have been walking. There is a hole above the door, apparently caused by a rocket-propelled grenade, and the authorities are content to let it be known that five militants of the FIS were killed inside.

Claw your way in darkness up the stone stairs of the interior and, in a room containing several charred beds, you will find Bouznad Hadi's cousin. No names are forthcoming, least of all for the bearded, thoughtful young man who will arrive during the morning. "They were all innocent," says the cousin. "There had been no shooting. The men were asleep. My cousin had only married recently—his wife is four months pregnant. When we found the dead, they were unrecognisable. They had been totally burned." There is a French woman radio reporter on the landing, thrusting her microphone into the cousin's face. "Are you telling the truth?" she snaps. I'm not sure he is, but this is no way to treat a man who has just lost his relative; this is not the time to practise the art of tough investigative journalist, here in this house of the dead.

But no one can explain why the pregnant wife and other female relatives were not in the house at the time. Another man arrives, a brother-in-law of Hadi. "The authorities could have taken them alive," he says. "The house was surrounded. But the soldiers burst in, they shot dead a man in the corridor and then fired a grenade into this room. Two of the dead men were lying on the ground. They had been wounded earlier."

Wounded earlier? Could these two men have been among the attackers who murdered six policemen in the Casbah a week ago, at least one of whom was wounded when he made his escape? "Definitely not!" the brother-in-law says at once. "They were shot during street demonstrations." But the soldiers obviously knew the wounded men were there. They had been betrayed; even the brother-in-law admitted ruefully that "someone told the soldiers the wounded men were here." Then the bearded man arrives. "It was revenge by the army," he says in a soft, dangerous voice. "When they came into the house, one of the soldiers shouted: 'We will do to you what you did to us at Guemmar.' " Guemmar is the border post where Muslim gunmen shot dead as many as fifteen Algerian soldiers in 1991. For the bearded man, standing in the semi-darkness, muttering "revenge" again and again, the matter is clear cut. "Of course they could have taken them alive. But they wanted to kill them all, including the wounded. We can't take wounded men with beards to hospital because they are then arrested and tortured. So they were sheltering here."

Outside in the alleyways, more women have gathered, weeping quietly, joined by dozens of watchful young men. History shoulders its way gently towards us, as it always seems to in Algeria. One of the men asks if we know the significance of the house only 300 metres up the same claustrophobic street, another "martyrs" house. It was in this other building that FLN guerrillas—including the fugitive Ali La Pointe, the "hero" of Pontecorvo's *The Battle of Algiers*—and some of their children preferred to be blown to pieces by French paratroopers rather than surrender. Early on the morning of 14 February 1992, "Paras" of a different nationality returned to the Casbah, and another legend was born.

No one ever discovered how many angels could dance on the end of a pin. But an even more pressing theological question weighed heavily upon FIS supporters the day Boudiaf came home: how long does it take to shave off a man's beard? Down at Ali's coiffeur on the end of Rahmouni al-Tayeb Street, they could hack off an Islamic beard in about five minutes. But as the seventy-five-year-old proprietor tells us, FIS men sometimes talk a lot during their necessary shave. This can prolong the process by ten minutes but will still cost only 15 Algerian dinars, a mere 60 U.S. cents, and is well worth the price to avoid summary arrest and imprisonment. Which was why, in the streets of Algiers, only brave men and fools now sported the long, pointed Muslim beards which were, until a week earlier, the symbol of the FIS. The tonsorial change therefore had grave political—even military—implications for the Algerian government. By shaving off their beards, the Islamists had gone underground.

The proof lay all over Ali's floor, a mass of thick brown and black hair, a carpet of human fur, which he swiftly dispatched into the garbage with a stout industrial broom. Ali was too frightened to give his family name but far too proud to resist advertising his craft as he squatted on his doorstep where two sleek grey cats were purring in the sunshine. Never before had his profession played so prominent a role in Algerian politics. "Shaving a beard is like flying an aircraft," he said. "Or . . . "—and here there was a combination of cynicism as well as mischief in his smile—"it is like writing an article. The skill is in your hands. I get around five beards a day to shave although I couldn't open last Friday because of the shooting. But most of these people shave off their beards at home." Wisely so. For the Algerian intelligence services, however, the disappearance of the beard created another problem; in order to mingle in the streets, many of their agents had adorned their own cautious faces with a full growth of poorly groomed hair. Less than a week earlier, one such bearded security operative, dressed in a long *khamis* shirt, was known to have seized an imam near the Bab el-Oued mosque. In the local police station, the agent dutifully shaved off the right half of the imam's beard, adding—according to the preacher—"We will get all of you in the end." An ambitious undertaking now that the barbers of Algiers had made their extra profits.

The people of Algiers were asked to give a tumultuous welcome to the returning prodigal. But when Mohamed Boudiaf, tall, frail, his features thin and elderly, arrived at the airport that bears the name of his late and hated rival, Houari Boumedienne, only a few taxi-drivers, porters, journalists and FLN functionaries were there to greet him. The only sign of enthusiasm came from three groups of Berbers in traditional brown robes who stood near the arrivals lounge and thumped away joylessly on high-pitched drums under the eyes of secret policemen. Boudiaf was driven through empty streets to the office of the vacated presidency where, with his hand on the Koran, he accepted the unconstitutional office of leader of the "Council of State." He promised to continue what he called "the democratic process" without explaining how he could do this when the democratic process—like the president and parliament—no longer existed.

For the press to be let loose on a seventy-two-year-old pensioner who was until a month ago the owner of a Moroccan brick factory should have been a trial for a man who was supposed to lead Algeria to its salvation. But for all of two hours, Mohamed Boudiaf proved to be a hard, almost aquiline man, soaking up the camera flashes like sunlight, reproving journalists who dared to talk of "repression," appealing to Western nations to help Algeria in its hour of need. He condemned his predecessors in government. He demanded obedience to the law. He admitted the incarceration of at least 6,000 young Algerians in desert prison camps—another copy-cat act of imprisonment from French colonial days—and claimed that "respect for democracy must not lead to the destruction of democracy."*

In just four days, another fifty Muslim demonstrators were killed by police in Algerian cities. Abdelkader Moghni, the most important of the FIS candidates to be elected in December and the one man who might have been able to renegotiate its position within the political establishment—even talk to the government—was imprisoned. But Boudiaf did not want to talk to the FIS. There was a growing suspicion in Algeria that the "Council of State" would prefer to provoke the FIS into

*No language protects politicians from flights of fancy about democracy and Islam. I leave it to readers to spot the non sequiturs in the following extracts from Boudiaf's Algiers press conference on 16 February 1992—which he gave in Arabic and French—as well as his self-delusionary optimism and incomprehension of what drove so many Algerians to support the FIS. "The halting of the electoral process was made necessary in order to safeguard democracy," he said. "The electoral process was stopped because it had come to represent a danger to Algeria. But the state of emergency had nothing to do with any restriction of fundamental freedoms . . . The situation is improving day by day. Algeria has become fed up with Fridays of terror and doubt . . . In Islam, tolerance, understanding and modesty can go together with democracy. A 'closed' Islam, which harks back to thirteen or fourteen centuries ago, cannot work with democracy. In Iran, is there or is there not democracy? I leave it to you to decide . . . people are not being hanged here. If we had followed the election principle, we would have had hanging in Algeria . . . Islam should not accept extremism. Mosques should be a place of preaching, of rest and moderation. Religion has its place, but democracy is a march towards a modern society which includes political pluralism."

armed insurrection—and thus "prove" that the party was never interested in con-stitutional politics, that the annulment of the January elections prevented a coup d'état by the Islamists rather than by the army. Certainly, more *groupuscules* of armed men began to emerge. An organisation naming itself "Faithful to the Promise" called for a jihad, claiming that this was a continuation à la Bouyali of the independence war. Boudiaf concentrated his anger on two targets: the FIS, and the corruption which had driven so many Algerians to despair of the democracy they had been promised. The first of his targets would despise him. The second would kill him.

And the moment Boudiaf died, on 29 June 1992, we all got it wrong. I was in Moscow, sitting in a hotel room that overlooked the Kremlin wall after returning from the Nagorno-Karabakh war on the edge of Armenia, when the phone rang and Harvey Morris, still my foreign news editor, came on the line from London. "They've topped Boudiaf," he said with his usual sensitivity. "Looks like your Islamic mates have done 'im in." And I believed him. In fact, we all thought, when we heard that three bullets had cut Boudiaf down while he addressed a public meeting in the eastern Algerian city of Annaba, that the FIS—or some armed group sympathetic to the movement—had carried out the death threat uttered by so many Islamists. At least one organisation, Islamic Jihad, had promised that an "all-out war" against the Algerian government would start on 30 June. They had promised to kill "a thousand" policemen and soldiers but—so I portentously announced in *The Independent*—"they struck a day early and decapitated instead the entire structure of government authority which had been created to destroy them."

I didn't have any doubts about who "they" were, didn't ask myself why we had never heard before from an Algerian Islamic Jihad, even though its name had been used by other groups in Lebanon and the occupied Palestinian West Bank and Gaza. I couldn't go back through my Algerian reporting notebooks—because they were in Beirut and I was in Moscow—in which I might have traced some antago-nism towards Boudiaf, not just from the FIS but from wealthy members of the *pouvoir*, even among the military, who feared his anti-corruption campaign. Only when I returned to Algiers two weeks later did I discover that there was grow-ing evidence that the old president might not, after all, have been killed by Islam-ists. In the weeks before his death, Boudiaf made powerful secular enemies inside Algeria—at least one of them reportedly linked to ex-President Chadli Bendjedid—and even Boudiaf's widow now said that she did not believe that the FIS committed the crime. Less than three weeks after the murder, the interior min-ister, General Larbi Belkheir—who with General Nezzar had formed the most powerful duo in Boudiaf's "Council"—was sacked by the new prime minister, Belaïd Abdesselam, for a "lapse" in security. Some lapse.

Boudiaf was killed by one of his own bodyguards, Second Lieutenant Lem-barek Boumarafi. State television cameras were taping the president's address at the moment of his death and Belkheir announced that Boumarafi had acted alone. He had fired two bullets into Boudiaf's head and a third into his back. What was not known at the time was that the president's anti-corruption campaign had already netted a retired Algerian army major-general and a prominent business-man and associate of Chadli Bendjedid in the southern city of Tamanrasset. And only days before Boudiaf was assassinated, a senior officer responsible for one of the investigations was himself mysteriously murdered. There were also rumours that Boudiaf—following the precedent set by de Gaulle of negotiating with the FLN—was trying to open a private dialogue with moderate FIS officials.

A quiet visit to an acquaintance in Algerian state television proved that some of the videotape of Boudiaf's killing had been suppressed by the authorities. Eye-witnesses in Annaba claimed that four separate television cameras taped the scene at the moment of the assassination. The footage shown around the world, in which Boudiaf could be seen uttering his last words and then lying dead on the ground with blood on his chest, was censored. My source was explicit:

> The cameras filmed the actual moment of the killing and they censored the scene when the bullets hit Boudiaf. The tape showed his brain exploding when the bullets hit him in the head—you cannot show something so terri-ble on television. There is another tape which shows the arrest of Boumarafi. In this, Boumarafi says on camera: "I killed Boudiaf, knowing of his heroic past and that he was a good man. But he didn't do enough against the mafia. And he opposed the choice of the people. I belong to no political party but I belong to the Islamic movement." Boumarafi was so self-confident, so sure of himself—he spoke so well and was so charis-matic—that the authorities feared he would become a hero if the tape was shown on television.

If this account was correct, then Boudiaf's murder might indeed have involved Islamists. But the events surrounding Boumarafi's arrest were extremely puz-zling—especially if the authorities really believed him to be a fundamentalist mur-derer. One account said that he had been able to escape from the Annaba conference hall but later surrendered peacefully to the police. Curiously, the army—which tried the leaders of the FIS in a well-publicised military court hear-ing in Blida two weeks later—refused to take responsibility for Boumarafi, claim-ing instead that he must be tried by a civilian court. Boumarafi was now incarcerated in the civilian prison at Annaba—by chance, the home town of Chadli Bendjedid—while local journalists were able to find out little about his life. He was twenty-six and, so it was rumoured, used to be a bodyguard for President Bendjedid. He was trained for his job in the presidential security unit by Italian Carabinieri.

It was Boudiaf's actions in the months before his assassination, however, that showed he was not afraid of being unpopular. Perhaps to the surprise of the old FLN and army hands who originally supported him, Boudiaf had in May ordered the arrest of retired Major-General Mustafa Beloucif, who was charged before a military tribunal at Blida with misuse of state funds. Boudiaf also ordered the arrest of a prominent businessman on corruption charges; the man was allegedly involved in the illegal sale of subsidised food and smuggling. One of the officers dispatched to conduct this investigation was a lieutenant in the security forces; only days before Boudiaf's murder, he was assassinated in an Algiers street.

Already one Algerian newspaper columnist had dubbed Boudiaf's assassination "Algeria-gate" and hinted that details of his death might be covered up like the murders of FLN dissidents Mohamed Kider, shot in a Madrid street in 1967, and Krim Belkacem, the 1970 Frankfurt strangulation victim. In the daily *El Watan*, Laïd Zaghlani recalled that details of the death of Algerian foreign minister Mohamed Benyahyia—shot down along with his delegation over the Iran–Iraq frontier in 1982 during an attempt to end the war—were kept secret "to protect the nation's supreme interests." More likely, this was done to protect Saddam Hussein—but that is another story.

It was now popular in Algeria to attribute Boudiaf's assassination to the "mafia," an opaque term used to indicate the social and political class that enriched itself at the expense of the country during Chadli Bendjedid's twelve-year rule. Former prime minister Abdel-Hamid Brahimi's claim that bribes of $26 billion— the equivalent of Algeria's foreign debt—were paid to government officials over a decade had entered popular folklore. Boudiaf's supporters even claimed that there was an alliance between the "mafia" and the Islamist movements. The one thing they wanted, however, they most certainly would not get.

"We demand to know the whole truth about the assassination of our martyr Mohamed Boudiaf—raise your hands with me and say you want the truth." The words drifted over the pile of brown clay and dying wreaths under which lay the last, bullet-cracked remains of the assassinated president. And Boudiaf's *anciens combattants* comrades—the gunmen and bombers and couriers who more than thirty years earlier had freed their land from Massu's paras—raised their right hands by the grave and said, firmly and loudly: "I do."

Age confers dignity and gentleness upon the most ruthless of men and women. White-haired, head bowed in homage to his dead leader, Omar Boudaoud looked like just another old soldier, the kind of stooped figure you might see by an English war memorial any Remembrance Sunday. Yet Boudaoud was the man who led the FLN inside France, who organised the blowing up of fuel dumps, the derailment of a train at Cagnes-sur-Mer, the killing of four gendarmes in Lyon, the attempted assassination of Algerian governor-general Jacques Soustelle. Can men with so bloody an inheritance expect the truth? There was Abu Bakr Belkaïd, for example, freedom fighter, fellow inmate with Boudiaf at Fresnes prison in 1956, mourning the lost opportunities of Algeria. "Things are more serious now," he said. "President Boudiaf was clean—he had been in exile, far from the establishment, before he became our leader. He came here to modernise our country, to give us a clear path. Yes, I hope we will know the truth about his martyrdom. But will we? Do we know who killed Kennedy? Do we?"

Madame Boudiaf was there; she who said that she did not think "for a single moment" that the FIS had murdered her husband. Cloaked in green and white, face hidden behind sunglasses, she stood before the pile of earth, then embraced Belkaïd and sobbed in his arms, ignoring the marble catafalque next to her husband's grave. "Houari Boumedienne, 1932–1978," it said. Boudiaf had turned down Boumedienne's offer to be president after the 1962 liberation because he did not want to be a figurehead; he opposed Boumedienne from his Moroccan exile. There were other, identical, catafalques in the same row as Boudiaf's grave, each containing an honoured warrior, their names inscribed on each without comment or verbal homage; you needed memory and a history book to understand their meaning. There was Larbi Ben M'Hidi (murdered by French paratroopers in March 1957). There was Ferhat Abbas (exiled by his own FLN). There was Abane Ramdane (brutally murdered—probably strangled—in 1957 by his FLN colleagues near Tangiers). There was Belkacem, the Frankfurt murder victim, and Aït Hamouda Amirouche and Sid el-Hawass (FLN leaders of Wilaya 4—Bouyali's sector—both killed by the French in 1959). With so many bullet-smashed bones and broken necks inside these graves, could anyone expect to learn the truth about the cemetery's newest "martyr"?

Such was the demand for truth, light and discovery in the humid graveyard of El-Alia. No one pointed the finger, of course. No one blamed Islamists or the "mafia" or the old FLN. Behind the gravestones stood a bunch of soldiers, a few blue-uniformed policemen and a scattering of unshaven young men in jeans holding sub-machine guns, ammunition clips in their trouser belts. For security, of course. Just like the bodyguards who protected Mohamed Boudiaf in Annaba, one of whom shot him in the head and back.

Boudiaf's death was the moment when Algeria's war turned savage. The BBC, when it wished to air atrocity film, would give due warning to viewers of what it called "a nervous disposition." Readers are thus duly given the same warning before they wade through the following blood-drenched pages of this book. For within two years, a largely unreported tragedy was unfolding across Algeria, its nature—an insurrection by Muslim militants denied an election victory—well known, but its dimensions growing daily more fearful with bloodletting on a scale unknown since independence from France. By 1994, up to 4,000 violent deaths had been officially recorded and large areas of Algeria were falling each night under the control of an increasingly cohesive military organisation, the "Armed Islamic Movement." If the previous two years were a playback of Algeria's "savage war of peace" with France, the bloodbath now unleashed held terrible precedents for the Anglo-American occupation of Iraq a decade later.

The families of security forces personnel—and in some cases the officers themselves—were now forced to retreat each night into government compounds for their own protection. Despite full-scale battles with the Islamists, the Algerian army and paramilitary police were unable to protect the growing number of victims cut down so brutally. The word "cut" was all too accurate. Many of those assassinated by "Islamists" were dispatched with knives, left on garbage tips or roadsides with their heads almost severed from their bodies. Professors and journalists, soldiers and Muslim militants, policemen and local government officials were slaughtered daily. The notebooks of my frightening visits to Algeria were now filling up with details of these gruesome, wanton killings. On 27 January 1994, a twenty-four-year-old unemployed man in the village of Kasr el-Boukhari was totally decapitated and his head left on the steps of a disused cinema. "An example," his murderers said in a fly-sheet pasted on village walls, "to all those who violate the morality of Islam." On the eve of a "national conference" of political parties—the FIS, needless to say, was excluded—a policeman was stabbed to death in front of a group of children in Annaba. On the night the conference ended, Islamists assassinated seven civilians in Djidjel province, one of them Dr. Ferhat Chibout, a professor of history, who was shot down in front of his parents, his wife and two children.

As usual, the outside world cared more about foreign than domestic victims of the war, a fact shrewdly grasped by the killers. Their promise to "execute" all citizens of "Crusader states" culminated in early January 1994 in the murder of the twenty-sixth Westerner in Algeria, a female French consular official whose death led at once to the suspension of all visas to France. Monique Afri's murder was followed by the killing of Raymond Louzoum, a sixty-two-year-old Tunisian-born Jew who had been living in Algiers for thirty years. An optician who had married a Muslim woman and was seeking Algerian citizenship, he played French officers in a series of films about the independence war. Two bullets were fired into Louzoum's head in Didouche Mourad Street in the very centre of Algiers city.

Not that the Muslim insurrection had a monopoly on killing. It was in late 1993 that an Algerian human rights group first claimed that the government was using death squads in its struggle with the Islamists. A French intelligence intercept of an Algerian police assault on a Muslim stronghold provided clear evidence of an officer ordering his men to take no prisoners. In December 1993, "Islamists"—and at this point, we should perhaps start putting quotation marks around that word—killed twelve army recruits in their camp near Sidi Bel-Abbès. In early January 1994, a soldier was stopped at a routine police checkpoint outside Algiers. He showed his army pass—and immediately had his throat cut. The checkpoint was false; the "policemen" were gunmen in police uniform. Or were they? These *faux barrages* were becoming ever more frequent and creeping closer to the capital each week. It soon became all too obvious to the few journalists still travelling to Algiers that in many cases the killers were real policemen—working for the government by day and the insurrection by night.

Already the army was using tanks and helicopters against "Islamist" units in the mountains of Lakhdaria. It had little choice, because the insurgents were now moving across Algeria in company strength. When a dozen Croat guest workers had their throats cut in December 1993, they had no chance of escape; their executioners were among fifty armed men who stormed their accommodation shacks outside Oran. At times, Algeria's cities were close to mass panic. Bread queues in Algiers were outnumbered only by the thousands of Algerians desperate to leave their country who stood outside the French embassy day and night until Monique Afri's murder closed down the visa section. Nor did the authorities allow Algerians to forget what civil war would mean. Every day, state television repeated news film of the post-Soviet slaughter in Kabul, MiG jet fighters bombing the Afghan capital, corpses of women and children lying in the streets. If you do not remain united behind your government, the unspoken message went, then this will be Algiers and Oran and Constantine and all the other cities of Algeria. But how far could the authorities go in frightening a people into supporting a government?

Within a year, the government was sending a delegation of high-ranking Algerian army intelligence officers on a tour of Arab capitals, notably Cairo and Damascus, in the hope of learning how to combat "Islamist" guerrilla armies. In Egypt—where real Islamists had killed President Sadat—they learned how Egypt's paramilitary police stormed the hideouts of armed insurgents in the sugar-cane fields around Assiout and Beni Suef before interrogating the survivors under torture or hanging them after sentences in military courts. In Damascus, they learned first-hand of how Syrian special forces with artillery and tanks killed thousands of Muslims in the rebellious city of Hama in 1982, pulverising its ancient streets and mosques. At the end of December 1994, the Algerian army staged an identical assault on the Muslim stronghold around Aïn Defla—about the same size as Hama—with artillery and tanks, and slaughtered up to 3,000 alleged GIA men. Again, there were no prisoners.

It would be intriguing to know how many times these Middle Eastern conflicts have been used as school classes for other, later military campaigns. During the 1954–62 Algerian war the French gave the Israeli government unprecedented access to their war against the FLN. Yitzhak Rabin, who was then Israeli army chief of staff, Uzi Narkiss, the Israeli military attaché in Paris, and Chaim Herzog, who was then director of Israeli military intelligence, were taken to visit a naval commando unit based in southern France, the French commando training centre in Corsica, and to Algeria itself where, according to Herzog, "we watched the bitter struggle against the FLN." Forty years later, the Pentagon sent a delegation to Israel to study Israeli army tactics during the Palestinian intifada, so they could adopt these lessons in their own battle with Iraqi insurgents—which they did with predictably disastrous results. In some derivative and unconscious way, the Americans in Iraq may thus have been copying—at second hand—France's equally deplorable tactics in the Algerian war of independence.

"The Plot," so deeply buried in the psyche of all Algerians and all Arabs—and indeed, in the U.S. administration of George W. Bush since 2001—now took on a disturbing shape. The GIA convinced themselves that French military aid and political encouragement for the regime—most notably from the intrigue-loving and authoritarian French interior minister, Charles Pasqua—constituted a declaration of war against Algerian Muslims by the old "Crusader" states of Europe. The Algerian government persuaded themselves that the United States was now supporting the GIA. Why else, they asked, would Washington allow a spokesman for the FIS, Anwar Haddam, to run an office in Washington? Why else would the Americans urge "dialogue" with the Islamists, something they would never do with Israel's Muslim enemies? Washington obviously wanted to create "moderate" Islamic regimes in North Africa—rather than democracies which they would not be able to control. Or so read "The Plot."

In Algeria itself, fear was becoming a disease. "I went to a relative's funeral in Oran in December—he died a natural death—but in the funeral a sheikh mentioned an Algerian woman who had just been murdered along with her Belgian husband." There was silence at the dinner table; this was not a moment to rattle our knives and forks over the hot spicy peppers and tomatoes. "The sheikh didn't talk about the murdered Belgian—he ignored him. But of the woman, he said: 'If she hadn't married a foreigner, this wouldn't have happened.' "

He paused for the horror of the statement to sink in. "How can we reason with people like this? How can we let people like this sheikh come to power? A lot of our problem here was our education system. The FLN taught children that history began in 1962, after the war of independence. They were not taught about Abdelkader, our warrior who fought the French. But the people rejected the FLN and their version of history. So the only thing that was true to them was the Koran—which gave the fundamentalist leaders increased power. They were like the sheikh in the Oran mosque; they could take any sentence from the Koran and light bonfires with it."

The bonfires are everywhere. I do not tell our host that I have seen a postmortem photograph of the Belgian man and his murdered wife. The Algerian government has issued a vile dossier of decapitated corpses, colour snapshot after colour snapshot of slit throats and bullet-punctured corpses from Algeria's mortuaries. The grey-haired woman lies on a mortuary floor, a bullet hole on the right of her mouth, eyes partially opened, right breast exposed above a white shroud. Her husband, in only his underpants, has bullet holes in his chest, shoulder and face. His eyes are staring at the camera as they must have stared at the killers when they came to the family home at Bouira on 29 December 1993. Opposite them lies a young Frenchman, murdered at Bir Khadem on 23 March 1994, his short black hair still neatly parted, looking downwards at the two bullet holes in his chest. Is that, I ask myself, what he did at the moment of death? Did he feel the metal streaking into his chest and glance downwards in surprise to see what had smashed his heart?

Turn the pages and it gets worse. The Croat guest workers overwhelmed outside Oran had their throats cut. They are not neat little slits in the neck, an invisible razor blade that might have rendered death swift and merciful. Their throats have been hacked open, sawed through, the blood pouring over their chests. One of them, a young man, is grimacing in pain, his suffering written across his dead face, his lips pursed as he tries to cope with the pain. Whoever carved their way into his throat went on slicing away until they reached the top of his backbone. You can see the white of the bone at the back of his neck.

Other bodies are a butcher's shop of blood and flesh, their faces hacked off, their arms stripped of flesh. In some cases, only the severed heads appear in the photographs. The left eye of Djillali Nouri, murdered on 28 August 1994 in Aïn Defla, is open wide, looking at the blanket upon which his head is resting, in horror, as he must have gazed upon the assassin's knife. And after a while, this pornography of cruelty becomes banal. The head of Ahmed Haddad, murdered on 13 May 1994, is lying on a tiled shelf, blood dripping from the base of the skull, a human hand steadying the head with two fingers lest it roll off onto the floor. Halima Menad was a young woman, killed at Aïn Defla on 23 July 1994, her long dark hair and half-open eyes still containing a ghost of beauty, her ringlets bathed in the gore of her cut-open neck. Yamina Benamara, another young woman decapitated near Oran on 11 April 1994, was left lying on the floor of her home in her nightclothes. Her body lies on a cheap, orange and blue carpet, partially covered with a cushion. Her head, part of her neck still adhering to her chin, lies on another carpet, eyes closed. Other photographs record the burning of factories, the wreckage of schools, buses, trucks.

Everyone joins the porno market of death. In Middlesex, a FIS front organisation publishes its own grisly photos, a heavily bearded "Islamist" riddled with holes; "victim of torture," it says in the caption, "whose body and neck were drilled with a sharp instrument. He sacrificed his life and everything dear to him." The man's eyes are open in a quite natural way, looking straight into the camera as if anxious to explain just how terrible his suffering must have been. There are carbonised corpses, a girl in her twenties bathed in blood, a bald man with a bullet hole in his cranium. Instead of wrecked factories, this booklet contains coloured photographs of the desert prison camps in which thousands of young Algerians are incarcerated, photographs of Algerian cops interrogating young men in the streets of Algiers. The government's handbook of decapitation claims that 15,000 men and women have been murdered; most of them had their heads chopped off. The FIS pamphlet says that "since the Junta's coup d'état, 60,000 Muslims have been killed." Above the photograph of a young man lying in a halo of blood, it says: "As for those who are slain in God's cause, never will he let their deeds go to waste . . . Holy Koran, 47, verse 4."

It will be ten years before I see this kind of butchery again. For every one of these photographs could have been taken in the mortuaries of Iraq in and after 2003. So could the snapshots of burned trucks and destroyed factories.

And of course, before I start to ask just who carried out these crimes against humanity—for they cannot all be the work of the GIA or renegade FIS members— I ask myself a more prosaic, more obvious, more terrible question. What kind of man—for the killers are all men—could hold young Nabila Rezki, with her short frizzy hair and tip-tilted nose and lovely face, to the floor of her home in Aïn Defla on 23 July 1994, and carve open her neck as if she were a sheep or a chicken? What about the cries of horror, the shrieks of pain, the desperate, hopeless appeals for mercy that must have been uttered before the knife sank in? What about "the girl and the child and love"?

And after a few minutes, it dawns on me that the attention I pay to this horror, the detail I find in the photographs, makes me complicit in these crimes. I remember how the Iranian Revolutionary Guards would hand round photographs of the dead Airbus passengers in the refrigerated Bandar Abbas warehouse in 1988, studying the minutiae of suffering, the ant-tracks of blood on the bodies, the eyes still looking sightlessly from the faces. Again, they remind me of medieval paintings, of Hieronymus Bosch's skewered corpses, of Goya's raped and eviscerated victims of French cruelty, of praying, arrow-pierced saints. Once, in a Kosovo field, I found an Albanian man's head lying in the grass, lopped off by an American air force bomb dropped on his refugee convoy, staring up at the sky; and I thought to myself, very coldly, that this must have been a common sight in Tudor England or anywhere in fifteenth-century Europe. Later, I met the young woman who had found the head and who had placed it on the grass because she thought that it would give the dead man more dignity if the face of his severed head was able to look at the sky.

We travel to Algeria now in fear, we few journalists. Lara Marlowe of *Time* magazine and I work out a routine. If we visit a shop, we must stay only four minutes to buy our fruit or teabags or books. Five minutes would give someone enough time to bring the killers. We hide our faces in newspapers when we are trapped in downtown traffic. We walk between the car and the front door of a family home with manic, Monty Python speed, the journalists of silly walks, characters in an old silent movie, our terror forcing us to move with high-speed normality. Ring the doorbell, watch the street in a casual, breathless way, curse the occupants for not answering the moment we ring. At dinner, we look at our watches. Curfew is at 11:30. The minute hand that creeps past eleven makes our smiles stiffen, our desire to flee all the greater. Cops want to escort us through the cities, policemen who sometimes wear hoods. "For your protection," they say. Yes, but who wants to be seen travelling with a policeman wearing a balaclava, a *cagoule*, to be identified with the men who are arresting the young of Algiers and who are—the proof starts to mount in ever more horrifying evidence—tortured, quite often to death?

We travel to Blida, to the old French town in what we will soon call "the triangle of death." Yes, we love these racy names. Ten years later, in Iraq, we would start talking about "the Sunni triangle"—which wasn't all Sunni and wasn't a triangle at all—and then, inevitably, we would create in our pages an Iraqi "triangle of death." The Blida version took only half an hour to reach. On 30 January 1994, the policemen there wore hoods and carried automatic rifles. The walls were spray-painted "FIS." And the body of Sheikh Mohamed Bouslimani—two months in a mountain grave before his corpse was discovered—reeked of formaldehyde as it lay, wrapped in a brown and yellow blanket, in the colonial town square beneath the Atlas Mountains.

Sitting on the floor of the single-storey family home, up in the foothills above the plain of the Mitidja, his eighty-four-year-old mother, Zohra, tears gleaming on wrinkled cheeks behind old spectacles, tried to understand why her son had been murdered. "Thank God I was able to see him in the hospital and able to kiss him," she said. "I hope we will see him in paradise. He was an obedient son. It was God in his mercy who gave him to us and God in his mercy who took him away from me. I must accept this."

In Algeria, acceptance—of kidnapping, murder, head-chopping, death—is now a way of life. But who did kill Bouslimani? Who would want to kidnap and then assassinate a professor of Arabic who was leader of Algeria's "Guidance and Renewal" charity, who only a year before had travelled to Sarajevo and brought back dozens of wounded Bosnian Muslims to recover in Algeria? "The hand of traitors took him away," was the explanation of Sheikh Mahfouz Nahnah, the leader of the Hamas party of which Bouslimani was a founding member, as he preached in that small colonial square, weeping before eight thousand mourners.

So who were the "traitors" here? The murderers, certainly: the four men who took the balding, bearded sheikh from his single-storey villa on 25 November 1993, and allowed him just one brief telephone call to his family a few days later before silencing him for ever. In the study of his home, we could see the religious books he was reading when called to the front door, and the telephone line—now reconnected with black masking tape—which the kidnappers cut before they took the sheikh away in his own battered Renault car. Just for a chat, a few words, nothing to worry about, they told his wife, Goussem. He would be back soon. The usual tale.

Amid the hundreds of white-scarved women who sat below the eucalyptus trees and the ramshackle slum in which Sheikh Bouslimani lived, an old friend recounted the inevitable. "They let him make just one telephone call. His family asked: 'Who is holding you?' and he was silent. Then they heard a voice in the background saying: 'Tell them it's the GIA.' Then he said: 'You heard.' His family asked the sheikh how he was, and he replied: 'Sometimes you have to thank God, even in the worst of situations.' And that was the last anyone heard of him."

But not the last that was seen. Ten days before a hopeless "national conference" on Algeria which was supposed to resolve the country's crisis, a rumour spread that the sheikh's body had been found high in the mountains, buried beside trees near a cemetery at El-Affroun. No more was said until the conference, which Hamas briefly attended but which was boycotted by all major political groups, came to an end. At which point the Algerian authorities suddenly announced that the sheikh's remains had indeed been found on the mountainside. And, with almost the same breath, that two men suspected of his kidnapping—Guitoun Nacer and Rashid Zerani—had been arrested. Nacer and Zerani, it was said, had been ordered by Djafaar el-Afghani, a FIS member who allegedly played a leadership role in the GIA, to abduct the sheikh in order to persuade Hamas to boycott the conference.

The government was happy to blame the FIS for all the country's miseries. Tens of thousands of Islamist militants—and members of the armed groups at war with the *pouvoir*—lived in Blida. That is why its walls were covered in FIS slogans and why the town's young men watched foreigners with the deepest suspicion. That is why the paramilitary police, clad in dirty khaki and fingering their Kalashnikovs, stood in the streets around us wearing woollen hoods, sacks with slits just wide enough for eyes to observe and orders to be shouted.

But there were friends of the sheikh—schoolfriends from his days at the Blida *lycée* where he taught Arabic—who were suspicious of the story. "All of a sudden, the government finds the body and the culprits just after the conference ends," a

Hamas member said. "What am I supposed to think of this? Hamas is more moderate than the FIS, but there are sympathisers of the FIS in our party. So why should the FIS kill him? I don't know—though I'd like to hear the FIS denounce this murder; I would like to hear them say it wasn't them. But there are those who say that the government wants to kill off Hamas—he is the second leader to be murdered—so that they can have an open war between the army and the FIS. And there are other parties like the Culture and Democracy Party who don't want to see any party like Hamas because it shows that Islam can be humane and moderate. My suspicion is simple: everyone was ready to see the sheikh killed." People die when everyone finds that their death is in their interest. The FIS lost a moderate opponent, the authorities were able to blame the FIS, while those who have no truck with religion in Algerian politics no longer have the annoyingly popular Bouslimani to contend with.

And the sheikh *was* a popular man in Blida. His funeral in the shadow of the ice-sheathed mountains was a dolorous, dignified affair. Mourners in the square wept themselves into unconsciousness, swooning into the arms of their friends, as Sheikh Nahnah announced that Bouslimani "did everything for the soil of Algeria and now the soil of Algeria is taking him back." Bouslimani had no children—his brother died in the war against the French in which the sheikh himself was imprisoned for five years—but he and Goussem had been bringing up a sister's daughter as their own. Asma lay crying in front of her adopted mother, wringing her hands in grief as the body was taken for its final burial in the town below the family's poor suburb of Sidi el-Kebir. The broken-down hamlet was named after the sixteenth-century founder of Blida, Ahmed el-Kebir, who brought with him from Spain the Arabs of Andalusia—irrigators of fields and planters of orange orchards—long before the French arrived in Algeria to colonise a nation whose tragedy had still not ended.

Algeria's next president was a colourless ex-general who knew about anarchy long before this latest war. As ambassador to Romania, General Liamine Zeroual witnessed the chaos that followed the overthrow of President Ceauşescu. A former artillery commander at Sidi Bel-Abbès, commanding officer of the 6th Motorised Regiment at Tamanrasset, director of the Cherchell military academy, former minister of defence and now the country's sixth post-independence president, Zeroual was to be the latest "last chance" for Algeria. In grey suit and dark tie, he marched into the "Club des Pins," past the FLN nomenklatura, past the ranks of crimson-and-green uniformed Spahi warriors, a frozen smile on his face, nodding to the row of generals and admirals whose golden crossed swords and palm-leaf insignia twinkled under the television lights. No live coverage for this installation, I noticed. No more live television of a president after Boudiaf's live-time demise. So we all listened in pin-dropping silence on 31 January 1994 as Zeroual placed his hand on the Koran and promised "to find a way out of the country's crisis through dialogue."

Did anyone believe this? As Zeroual entered the auditorium, he must have heard what had just happened. Only three and a half hours earlier, yet another politician had walked to his front door in Algiers to be confronted by a man who, with deadly efficiency, cut his throat, left him dead upon the pavement and—like almost all Algeria's murderers—made good his escape. Rachid Tzigani, the national secretary of a minuscule right-wing party which had long called for an army takeover, was leaving his apartment block in Badjdera to drive to his office at the Ministry of Public Works when he came face to face with his assassin. There were, of course, no witnesses.

A day later, French television journalist Olivier Quemener is filming in the Casbah. A gunman assassinates him and he is found with his wounded reporter lying beside him in tears. At Zeroual's installation, I had helped to carry Quemener's camera legs. We had travelled back together on the same bus to Algiers, chatting about the difficulties of working in this "democratic" police state, of the dangers that awaited us. And now he was added to the list of murdered foreigners. "He didn't take a police escort with him," a cop said with near-contempt at the Hôtel el-Djezair. No of course not, Quemener was trying to do his job, bravely and unprotected in the heart of Algeria's war.

Within the steel-grilled office of Agence France-Presse, the French news agency, in the centre of old Algiers, the statistics are pinned to the wall. A recent total shows 243 security forces dead, along with 881 "Islamists" and 335 civilians—with an overall official death toll of 3,000 that no one, except the government "minders," believes.* Government courts have condemned hundreds of "Islamists" to death: 212 in Algiers, 64 in Oran, 37 in Constantine. Penned in each day are those individual killings that agency journalists are able to keep track of. *Assassinats*, it says in red ink. "March 16th 1993, Djillali Liabès, former minister of education . . . shot outside his home in Kouba; March 17th 1993 . . . Laadi Flici, doctor, writer, member of national consultative council . . . December 28th 1993 . . . Yousef Sebti, poet, writer, francophone, professor, killed by unknown men . . . " Even the vice president of the Algerian Judo Federation is the victim of what the papers call a "cowardly assassination."

At dinner, a woman friend hands us a letter under the table, like someone offering pornographic literature. Why not, for the contents were obscene enough. "In the name of God, the most merciful," the anonymous sender has written to her in spidery biro. "No more work. You are a whore. In the name of God, the most merciful, no more Police . . . God is great." The woman is a dentist and among her patients are policemen. "What can I do?" she asks us. "I must go on working. Maybe I will leave Algeria." The threat is in French, the Koranic verse in Arabic. I can't help noticing that the writer's French is better than his Arabic, a strange reflection on the hatred for the West so often expressed by "Islamists"—*if* they sent the letter. It has been franked at the Algiers railway station post office at a cost of 2 dinars. Terror by mail for 14 cents.

---

*By 1995, the Algerian government would officially admit that 15,000 of its citizens had been murdered, that there had been 6,000 wounded and 2,143 acts of sabotage. In fact, the true figure of deaths was thought to be closer to 75,000.

A former minister of education, a judo expert, a poet, a dentist, a journalist. One "Islamist" tract lists thirty Francophone journalists "sentenced to death"; nine have so far been murdered. In 1993, Tahar Djaout, the award-winning novelist and editor, a lover of French literature, is shot in the head outside his home and dies in a coma. In 1994, Saïd Mekbel, perhaps the finest Algerian journalist, whose column "Mesmar J'ha"—"The Rusty Nail"—appeared in the daily *Le Matin*, was assassinated by a well-dressed young man who walked into the pizzeria where he was taking lunch and shot him twice in the head. No one intercepted the killer because he was a regular client. One of the newspaper's staff ran to the pizzeria:

> In the back of the restaurant, sitting behind the table, still holding a knife and fork in his hands, his head leaning slightly forward, as if he were looking at the food on his plate, Saïd was still breathing. I told him, "Saïd, hold on. We're taking you to the hospital." I reached out to caress his hair but pulled my hand back, covered with blood.

Mekbel, whose paternal grandfather fought for France in both the First and the Second World Wars, left an unfinished article in his office in which he wrote: "I would really like to know who is going to kill me."

Even the most innocent were "sentenced." Twenty-year-old Karima Belhaj worked as a secretary at the Algiers police welfare organisation. A pretty woman who had just become engaged to a local bus-driver, she was betrayed for $18 by a boy who lived in the same block of slums in the suburb of Eucalyptus. As she was walking home one evening, a man grabbed her hair, pulled her backwards to the ground and fired a bullet into her abdomen. As she arched forward in agony, another bullet was fired into her brain. Her brother heard the shooting. Her last words to him were: "Take me to the hospital—I want to live." Then she died.

It is important to know of these terrible deeds if we are to understand the ferocity with which the army and police responded. There was now powerful evidence that police in the Belcourt and Kouba districts of Algiers selected former prisoners for execution whenever a policeman was murdered. In three separate police stations in the capital, torture was now routine. The torture chambers were set up in underground air-raid shelters originally dug beneath French police stations by the Allied armies in 1942. There were persistent rumours that bodies wrapped in plastic sheeting were brought from these buildings during the hours of curfew for secret burial. Former inmates of Sekardji prison described months of solitary confinement in total darkness in rat-infested cells. One ex-prisoner I met described an inmate en route to his trial who "looked like a caveman," with shoulder-length hair, inch-long nails, lice on his skin and pus oozing from his ears. When Sekardji prisoners went on hunger strike to protest against these conditions in the autumn of 1993, police fired tear gas into the jail, asphyxiating an inmate to death.

Human rights activists inside Algeria had more dreadful reports. On 15 January 1994, they claimed, an army *ratissage* in the town of Larba ended when soldiers read out a list of seven men—Tayeb Belarussi, Mahfoud Salami, Halim Djaidaoui, Azedin Guename, Mohamed Kader and two brothers called Medjadni—put them against a wall and shot them. Soldiers who returned to the town later in the day allegedly fired into a crowd, killing a two-year-old girl and her grandmother. On 23 January, according to the same sources, soldiers entered the town of Boudouaou, 35 kilometres from Algiers, selected four men—Mohamed Saïd Tigalmanin, Abdullah Lanaoni, Ali Borshentouf and Messaoud Boutiche—and executed them against a wall. Was it any surprise, therefore, that many Algerians now suspected the security authorities were themselves trying to create a climate of terror? And was it any surprise that the "Islamists" helped to spread such rumours?

As the years of blood went by, we would learn that the Algerian security forces were far more intimately involved in atrocities than we could have imagined, indeed had themselves instigated some of the various massacres that they blamed upon the "Islamists." I still have my notes—from a 1995 interview with Algeria's paramilitary police at the Haddad *garde mobile* station in Harrash—in which an officer who wisely asked for anonymity told me gloomily that

> a classic guerrilla war like this will never work. It didn't work for the French. It won't work for us. The only solution is by infiltrating them, dressing like them, living with them, *using their people*.

In my notebook at the time, I underscored the last three words, adding my own reflection—"Ouch!"—in the margin.

All across Algeria were the signs of collapse. In the last two weeks of January 1994 alone, 116 policemen were believed to have been murdered, far more than officially admitted. Large areas of the country were effectively under the control of the insurgents. The government now had real control only in Algiers, Oran and Annaba. Even Constantine was in the hands of gunmen in the hours of darkness. On a 250-kilometre journey through the Kabyle Mountains, I discovered that the security authorities had retreated from the roads. Army and police checkpoints lay abandoned. The only policeman I saw between Algiers and Tizi-Ouzou stood with a machine gun behind a barricade of sandbags outside a bullet-spattered police station at Isser. In Tizi-Ouzou itself, I met frightened men and women who spoke of a "terrorist invasion" of the surrounding villages each night. On the drive back to Algiers, I came across only one military patrol, two armoured vehicles manned by helmeted and masked soldiers, their machine guns pointed at passing traffic. These were precisely the same scenes I was to witness ten years later on the highways south of Baghdad: the same loss of government control, the same abandonment, the same fear.

My own reports from Algeria now had a charnel-house quality about them: girls shot dead for refusing to wear the veil, sons beheaded because their parents were policemen and policewomen, women raped to death in police dungeons.

When terrible reports came in from the Algerian countryside in November 1994—of two young women whose throats were cut because they refused to engage in "pleasure marriages" with Muslim fighters—there were many outside Algeria who refused to believe it. When I told local Hizballah officials in Beirut of this, they shook their heads in disbelief. "Truly, I think we are the most mature Islamic group," one of them said—which, coming from the Hizballah, carried its own message.

A few years earlier, he might have claimed that all Muslim forces were united in one aim. Algeria's war changed that. There was a time when the Algerian authorities would have tried to censor the atrocities being carried out by the "Islamists," but the sheer cruelty with which the innocent were being exterminated forced them to change their policy; now they wished to *médiatiser les atrocités*. The two women did have their throats cut—their heads were afterwards torn from their bodies—because they refused "pleasure marriages." One of them was twenty-five, the other twenty-one, and both had been kidnapped with other members of their family from their home in Blida. A defecting Algerian army officer spoke of 50,000 troops now engaged in the "anti-terrorist struggle" and of "secret liquidation" of many suspected "Islamists."

MOHAMED USED TO ATTEND a Koranic school, a madrassa, and was preaching in a mosque in Algiers. He sits on a sofa in an Algiers "safe" house to which Lara Marlowe of *Time* and I have been invited. It is 3 February 1994, just four months after thirty ski-masked commandos came for him at his home at two in the morning. He is aged far beyond his nineteen years. He stares at a brass table top as he talks:

> They hit my 48-year-old mother. They blindfolded me and drove me straight to a torture room. It was down three or four flights of stairs and it was very cold. They stripped me naked. There was a manhole in the floor, and they kept dunking my head in the sewage. They asked me over and over: "Where are the weapons?" I said I didn't know. They kept insisting, because I preached in the mosque on Fridays. When they took off my blindfold, I saw they were all wearing blue police jumpsuits and hoods. There were about eighteen of them. I could hear other people screaming. There were very bright lights, and bloodstains on the walls. They tied me to a concrete bench and pinched my nostrils shut, then stuffed a rag soaked in water and bleach in my mouth. They poured more of the stuff through the rag, until my stomach filled with water and bleach, then they kicked my stomach until I vomited. This went on for three hours.

This young man was then taken to the basement of the Châteauneuf police school in the El Biar district. Mohamed points to dark purple scars on his feet. He was given electric shocks on his feet, he says, "with a thing that looked like a pistol." Ten days later, he was taken to the central commissariat near the Air France building in central Algiers:

> The officers at the commissariat in charge of torture were called Kraa and Abdel-Samad . . . they tortured us in front of each other, for psychological effect. They showed us dead people hanging by handcuffs from the ceiling. These were people who had died from torture and starvation. They had been in cells with me. They were from Belcourt . . . I saw five dead people at the commissariat. Two hanging from the ceiling. The other three had been tortured and they were burned to death with blow torches. They threatened to bring my wife if I didn't tell the truth. A man called Sid-Ahmed Shabla from Baraki was in prison with me. He told me they tortured his wife. They brought his mother and tortured and raped her in front of him. I was outside the room when they did this, and when his mother came out. She was naked and covered in blood. She was about fifty-five. She told us to be brave, to hang on. Sid-Ahmed was condemned to death. At the commissariat, I was tortured so badly that I condemned my own brother as being in the resistance. They tied my hands and feet and laid me on my stomach on the floor. They smashed my head against the floor until my teeth fell out.

Mohamed breaks down in tears. We sit and wait until he wants to talk again:

> They brought my brother to the commissariat and put us face to face in a room. I told him: "It's not true, I only said it because of the torture." My brother was weeping and he said: "May God forgive you." They broke his ribs and let him go . . . Under torture, I'd said I was collecting medicine and money for the resistance. It wasn't true. I only said this because I wanted them to stop torturing me . . . I was barefoot in front of the [tribunal] judge and my body was still covered with marks. I cried in front of him and said I'd been tortured. He said: "Yes, I know. There is nothing I can do." . . . At Sekardji, they put me in a narrow, wet cell underground for forty-five days . . . There was no light, and many rats. There I was tortured again, both by beating on my feet and the chiffon. They gave me one small bowl of soup full of cockroaches and one piece of bread every day.

He names his torturers as a Lieutenant Bouamra and Saïd Haddad; the prisoners called the latter "Hitler" because of his moustache. Mohamed was taken to court again and this time acquitted. He says the guards told him: "If you come back, we'll finish you off." Now he is in hiding "because death squads are going around killing everyone who comes out of prison."

Now a first-hand account of fraternal war, given to us by a man whom I called Lyes—for his safety—in my report:

Up the hill at Duc des Cars, there were two boys who went to school together and lived in the same building. One of them was a fundamentalist, the other a policeman. The fundamentalist was sent to a prison camp in the south. When he got out, he wanted revenge so he killed his school-friend, the policeman. So the policeman's father killed the "Islamist." Everyone in our neighbourhood knew them. If you go to a policeman's funeral, the FIS say you're with the government. And if you go to an "Islamist's" funeral, the police come after you. So the people in our building paid condolences to both families.

Even ex-general Jacques Massu vouchsafed his advice to the embattled Algerian government. "The security forces have the principal responsibility for the future of their country," the former commander of the brutal French Paras pompously announced. "With the West's help, their power will inevitably be successful."* The Algerians never asked for Massu's advice, but he would have approved of the elevation to corps commander of General Mohamed Lamari, leader of the Algerian army's *éradicateur* faction. And he would have had no objection to Abderrahmane Meziane-Cherif as Algerian minister of the interior, one of that rare breed of Algerian muscle-men of whom all Algerians talk, who believe that only a military solution can bring peace to Algeria. So when he walked into his office on the second floor of the Palais du Gouvernement—well-cut blue suit, red tie, goatee beard and a massive Havana—I asked the fatal question. Who were the *éradicateurs*? And was he one of them?

*Massu was only giving advice—the French government was supplying much more serious help to the Algerian military. Throughout much of 1994, France was sending helicopters, night-sight technology for aerial surveillance of mountain hide-outs, and other equipment, much of it aboard French military flights into Algiers airport. The son of a French government minister was said to run a private security company outside Paris which legally sold millions of francs' worth of equipment to the Algerian security police. Just as the Americans sold helicopters to Saddam during the Iran–Iraq War on the grounds that they would be used for "civilian" purposes, so the French, ten years later, sold nine Ecureuil helicopters to Algeria for "civil" use—thus avoiding statutory investigation by the French inter-ministerial commission for the inspection of military exports (Cieemg); the machines, of course, had only to be fitted with rockets and night-sights to become front-line weapons. The French were also listening in to all Algerian military radio traffic from a former cargo vessel, sailing along the Algerian coastline and crewed by members of the Direction Générale de la Sécurité Extérieure (DGSE, the French secret service). Code-numbered A646 Berry, the white-painted vessel monitored Algerian forces in the Lakhdaria Mountains. Its work was augmented by radio intercepts from French air force planes, and intelligence officers inside the French embassy in Algiers. On Christmas Eve 1994, "Islamist" gunmen seized an Air France airliner at Algiers airport and, after executing three passengers, flew it to Marseille for refuelling, threatening to crash the aircraft into the Eiffel Tower. French troops stormed the plane at Marseille, killed the hijackers and rescued the passengers. The surprising thing about the hijack was not that it took place, but that the French national airline was still operating scheduled flights into a country where law and order had virtually disintegrated and where the very name of France had become a death sentence to those of its citizens who remained in Algeria. No one, of course, asked whether the gunmen seriously intended to fly into the Eiffel Tower—or whether their plan might in the future inspire other, more ambitious projects involving passenger airliners and tall buildings.

Meziane-Cherif drew heavily on his cigar for a long time—a very long time indeed—before replying. And then he said:

A farmer can be an eradicator when he pulls weeds from the fields, sometimes a man has to purify water and cleanse things of insects and bugs. There is an extreme situation of violence and terrorism in Algeria. Do you call a law-enforcement officer who does his job an eradicator? . . . People usually call those who will commit treason and escape "conciliators." If I have to choose between the two, I will do everything to ensure Algeria remains a modern society.

In other words, Meziane-Cherif was an "eradicator," prepared to fight to the end against "terrorists," "criminals," the "virus"—his word, along with the Saddamite "insects"—that threatened the country. He was one of the hard men, sentenced to death by the French in the war of independence, a former governor of Jelfa, Nijaya, Gelba, Aïn Defla and Algiers, the kind of guy whose jails would not have air conditioning. When I ask if it was fair to condemn a recent Western initiative in Rome in which Algerians—including the FIS—called for peace and condemned violence, the minister's aide, a bruiser of a man with close-cropped hair and a handshake as fierce as a lobster's claw, mutters: "It condemned violence in a philosophical way." So much for conciliation.

The Algerian war had slipped into a system of self-provocation in which every atrocity would be avenged fourfold. In January 1995 the "Islamic Salvation Army," widely regarded as the military wing of the FIS, had announced that they would launch a bloody offensive to coincide with Ramadan in which they would intensify their attacks against "apostates and their henchmen." A few days earlier, issue No. 33 of the "Islamic Salvation Army" broadsheet *El-Feth el-Moubine*—"Brilliant Victory"—promised that the group's operations would "affect the capital." Sure enough, a car bomb in the centre of Algiers killed 38 people and left 256 wounded. This was precisely what Iraq's insurgents would do a decade later, by marking Ramadan as a month of military offensive—and then assaulting their American occupiers and their Iraqi police auxiliaries without any heed to the innocents who would die. The Algiers bomb had been set off outside the police headquarters in Amrouche Street—a gaunt, four-storey building in whose dungeons many Islamists claimed to have been tortured—and exploded at a time when Algerians were buying food before the start of the month of fasting. Many of the 256 wounded lost limbs.

The most vulnerable of the innocent were, increasingly, the victims of the most ruthless attacks. In January 1995, gunmen came to the home of Salah Zoubar, an independence war veteran, near Chlef in western Algeria, kidnapped his twenty-four-year-old daughter and three sons—the youngest only thirteen—and shot all of them in the head. In February, the "Islamists" murdered Azzedine Medjoubi, the director of the Algerian national theatre. A popular film actor with a comical drooping moustache—he was well known in Algiers for his adaptation of Tennessee Williams's *A Streetcar Named Desire*—he was walking out of his theatre after organising a children's performance when two men in their twenties fired several bullets into his head.*

Events now moved so fast in Algeria that even those of us travelling regularly to the country could scarcely keep pace. In February, a prison riot at the Sekardji jail—the old French Barberousse prison in central Algiers where the guillotine once fell on the necks of FLN captives—ended with ninety-nine inmates dead, among them two senior officials of the FIS. Algerian paramilitary police had surrounded the prison after four of the guards, according to the authorities, had their throats cut. No one knew if they were trying to break out—as 900 "Islamists" did from Tazult-Lambese jail the previous year—or whether the bloodbath was, as the FIS would later claim, a deliberate massacre by the authorities. Two Algerian newspapers reported that fourteen prisoners had been murdered by their own cellmates. At first, it was said that Lembarek Boumarafi—accused of Boudiaf's murder—was among the dead. But then he suddenly surfaced on television screens with nothing more than a wounded knee, sporting a new moustache, smiling slightly and greeting viewers of his videotape with the words: "It's me, Boumarafi, and I'm alive." Then the rumour spread that it was not Boumarafi on the tape.

The Algerian war was being fought in the shadows. Both sides wished this darkness to envelop their struggle, although the results were always ghoulishly publicised. I spent several days with the Algerian *garde mobile*, transformed into paramilitary units for the duration, watching the hooded, masked cops hauling young men from the slums for interrogation. We would snake through the poverty of Algiers in a convoy of green-and-white Land Cruisers, Kalashnikovs pointing from the doors of the rear vehicles, between crowds of men who stood in the ordure and garbage that lay piled along the tracks through Château Rouge, Cher-

---

*Ramadan in 1994 had been an especially doleful one for Algerian intellectuals. The dramatist Abdelkader Alloula, director of the Oran national theatre, was shot dead on his way to give a drama lecture. Four days later, Aziz Smati, a television producer, had been seriously wounded—he was now a paraplegic—and in September of the same year, gunmen shot dead Cheb Hasni, the best-known performer of *rai* music. Only a threat by the Kabyle people to "declare war on Islam" temporarily saved the life of their own kidnapped singer Lounes Matoub; he was released after fifteen days of captivity. Accusing intellectuals of "frivolity" and of insulting the Muslim religion, the armed goups had come to regard the artistic community—not without reason—as the forefront of the intellectual battle against an Islamic republic. One of Rachid Mimouni's best-known books was *Of Barbarity in General and Fundamentalism in Particular*; the only surprising thing about his own death in February 1995 was that he died of natural causes. In Egypt, authors were also being targeted. The writer Farag Fhoda was murdered; the Gema'a Islamiya—the "Islamic Group"—knifed the Nobel prize–winning author Naguib Mahfouz in Cairo but failed to kill him. Karim Alrawi, the Egyptian writer who had done so much for the human rights movement in Cairo, explained that the "Islamic struggle" was specifically cultural in nature. "Because Islam is the religion of the Book, the Koran is the very word of God uttered in the Arabic language. Arabic is therefore both the language of everyday discourse and the Sacred Language . . . Yet to be a writer is to be a creator of texts and to claim for them a truth that does not necessarily partake of the sole truth of the one sacred text. For that reason, the target is writers, not merely their words."

arba, Gaid Gassem, Eucalyptus, Houaoura. Sometimes we broke into open country, the gendarmes in their green uniforms running into the orange orchards around Blida to search youths whose hands were held high, their faces filled with terror, the muzzles of the cops' Kalashnikovs caressing the backs of their necks. What happened, I kept asking myself, when we journalists were not travelling with the police?

Commandant Mohamed—I knew his family name but promised never to reveal it—would become an inverted tourist guide, pointing out places of dangerous attraction: two gutted supermarkets, a burned-out gas factory, a row of carbonised trucks belonging to a government cooperative, a wrecked school with shattered windows. Once we passed an entire railway train, its row of silver carriages burned and twisted in a siding. Noting their hoods and ski-masks, the people of Algiers had long ago nicknamed the cops *Ninjas*, a title they were happy to adopt. Each time we passed a road, we could see young men at the other end, running for cover into shops and laneways. The youths who did not run looked at us with such hatred that their gaze went right through us, as if they had already defeated the government which the commandant's men represented. But the facts came pouring forth from Mohamed. Almost all the armed "Islamists" carried Czech or Israeli weapons—"Skorpions or Uzis," he said—he thought they had been smuggled across Algeria's borders with Morocco, Libya, Tunisia or Mali. They were making bombs with butane gas bottles filled with explosives, glass, acetylene, sulphur and iron filings, buried in the roads and detonated with batteries.

"They are organised," he said. "There is a 'brain' behind them. These are people who evolve with the situation. They change. They used to use stolen hunting rifles. Now they use automatic weapons and explosives. They strike wherever they want and they have the initiative. They have 'spotters' and they have a method. The leaders know each other but those who make the attacks don't know each other. It's a pyramid structure." The Islamists had shaved their beards, donned djellaba robes, sometimes pretended to be fruit-pickers, rifles at their side in the orange groves, resting in the slums at night, walking out through the suburban *wadis* by the sewage overflows at dawn. "In Algiers, the GIA are much more numerous than the FIS's armed movement," Commandant Mohamed confided to us as he relaxed in his office in Harrash, an old Rolling Stones 33 rpm long-playing record track—"Street-Fighting Man"—on the turntable. "When you fight with them, they fight to the end. They never surrender." Six years later, that is what the U.S. Special Forces officers would say about the al-Qaeda men whom they fought in western Afghanistan.

In Bab el-Oued, the hardest of all the "Islamist" strongholds in any Algerian city, Commandant Mohamed and his fifteen men strung themselves along the pavement, watched by perhaps a thousand young men, so I could take photographs. "It's swarming with 'spotters,' " he murmured. "Look at the way they look at us." The cops pointed their rifles at the roofs and balconies as the crowds grew thicker, more disturbed. Then suddenly, Mohamed wanted to leave. We had been here just two minutes. "We should go," he snapped. "Now." How many new GIA recruits had his men just created? Support for authority does not come from a rifle at the neck. Almost every street through which we passed had effectively been lost to government control. There were, to be sure, no "no-go" areas in Algiers. But there were no safe areas either.

I liked travelling with these men and they liked the company of Westerners for the false sense of protection it gave them. It was false. I knew if I stuck with them long enough, I would see the war; I knew that as the days passed, there would be a shooting, an ambush which I would see with my own eyes rather than report at second hand hours or days later. But I never believed it would come so quickly.

THE PINE TREES SWAYED in the early morning light, the orange orchards gleamed gold, the fields of yellow rape seed stretched to a grey curtain of mountains. You couldn't find a more sleepy laneway, meandering through cypress trees past streams flooded by the night showers. This is how they used to illustrate paradise in children's books.

Chaibia was a one-street town, some broken old French villas and a row of cheap cement houses. The shutters were open. In fact, the windows were open on this brisk, cold morning. There were no people on the streets. And somewhere inside my head—and I was in the heated cocoon of Commandant Mohamed's Land Cruiser—part of my brain was asking another part of my brain a question. It must be cold outside. The people were at home. But why had they all opened their windows? What a very odd thing to do . . .

That's when we were ambushed. I don't like the "we." But you can't stick a journalist's flag on top of an Algerian police vehicle; besides, the bombers would have been more than happy to know that they had a foreigner as well as sixteen gendarmes as their target. And when the first bomb went off, it sounded, inside our leading armoured vehicle, like a tyre bursting behind us. The cops in their ski masks knew what it was and the second bomb went off 100 metres away as I opened the rear door, a wall of sound and a sheet of concrete and smoke behind the second police van.

I pulled up my camera and looked through the lens at the second car—to capture the smoke drifting behind it—when there was a third blast like someone bashing their hands over my ears and, through my telephoto lens, a curtain of roadway, grass, iron and muck streaming upwards in slow motion. A policeman ran in front of me, firing into the yellow-flowered field to the left, a woman came screaming out of a broken-down house—an old *pied noir* villa, I remember thinking—shrieking and imploring God and the police to stop the noise. A rain of stones and concrete thundered onto the roadway around us and the petrol cap of the third police van came bowling down the roadway and jumped past my face. That's when the fourth bomb went off.

"Get down, get down, there may be another," Commandant Mohamed shouted. I looked around. There was a sinister ditch beside me, a deserted barber's shop on the other side of the road with *Coiffeur des Jeunes* crudely painted on the glass door. So we were lying on the ground when the shrapnel came pattering down again, a mad rain on this beautiful spring morning in paradise. There was a silence broken only by the crying of the terrified woman and the sound of men breathing and coughing and a voice on the radio asking if anyone had been hurt and a policeman saying, very quietly: "God is Great." At which point, the gendarmes began spraying the trees with bullets, the rounds hissing into the leaves, firing into the fields again, their bullets thwacking through undergrowth and howling towards a railway embankment. I had been reporting Algeria's war second hand; not any more.

It was a perfect ambush. They—the GIA, no doubt, led by its new *emir* in the Blida Wilaya, Saïd Makhloufi—had set the roadside bombs 50 metres apart, four of them to hit the four vehicles of the patrol. "They were very professional," Mohamed said. "They waited till we got out of our vehicles before they set off the fourth bomb, but our vans were spread out. Then they ran. They could be there . . . " And he pointed to the oh-so-innocent village of Chaibia, deserted again, not a soul on its streets, all of its people forewarned by the GIA so that the bombs did not break the glass of their windows which is why—yes, my brain had not quite worked out the significance in time—they had opened those windows on this cold spring morning. "Or they could be there—or there," Mohamed said, his finger sweeping across the horizon where the sunshine now splashed merrily on the walls of hamlets almost buried behind the trees.

We trudged into the fields, warily, the cops firing in front of them, looking for the wires, splashing through the soggy grass and stunted orchards. A railway train clicked past, the local diesel from Blida to Algiers, the passengers with their morning papers staring at us out of drowsy carriages as if we were on a lunatic field exercise. That's when we found the electric detonator lines, four car batteries carelessly covered with earth, a series of broken lightbulbs for detonators, near the massive craters in the road. One of the police vehicles had its windscreen smashed, its door fittings ripped off, shrapnel gashes on the bodywork, no one hurt.

The electric leads ran across the fields and a police sergeant followed them, pulling them out of the mud and water like that scene in *The Bridge on the River Kwai* when Alec Guinness discovers that someone is planning to blow up his bridge. The wires sucked their way out of the mud, stretching to knot on a barbed wire fence from which a single thin green fishing line ran towards the railway. The line ended on the tracks. That's where they had waited for us, three, maybe four of them, listening on their scanners—according to Commandant Mohamed—to the police radios. An old man was cutting grass in the corner of the fields. "There were some guys here this morning with hunting guns," he said. "They were shooting birds." But in truth everyone in Chaibia must have known what was going to happen. It must have taken hours to lay the butane gas bottles of explosives, the electric lines, the batteries and detonators. They may have lain there for days, just waiting for us.

When we left Chaibia, the people did not look at us, did not even glance at the bomb-damaged Toyota van; it was as if we did not exist, the fate that the GIA had intended for us. All that was wrong was the distance between the bombs. "Distance—keep your distance from each other," Commandant Mohamed called into his radio. And then he said *Allahu akbar*—God is great—again. And the cop beside me muttered a prayer in Arabic and the words "Mohamed is the Prophet of God." All the policemen said this. It intrigued me, this praying, in a way I did not at first understand. It went on and on, for minutes, for an hour after the ambush. The police were thanking God for his mercy. And I had no doubt that, on the other side of that railway embankment, the bombers must have used the very same words, seeking God's grace and invoking the Prophet's name in their endeavour to kill us all. It was Commandant Mohamed who turned to me on the road back to Algiers and said: "We had beautiful luck today."

I had beautiful luck, too. I wanted to see the war and I had my first-hand report and I was back in the safety of the Hôtel el-Djezair, but at 5:38 next morning—I had formed the habit of checking my watch every time a bomb went off—there was a great thunderous roar and a mass of black smoke hanging over the police family residence in Kouba. Just before the explosion, the bombers had fled the scene shouting—oh, for the unity of Islam—*Allahu akbar*. God is great. And the cops would believe this doubly since the detonation that was supposed to bring down the entire building on the heads of their families only tore down the front wall. Most of the twenty-one wounded were women and children, the youngest a year-old baby. There used to be two police on guard duty outside. "But they were both assassinated last year," an off-duty gendarme told me. "Since then, there hasn't been a guard on our buildings."

It was instructive to watch the Algerian security forces as they turned up at the bomb-site. There were gendarmerie men in green uniforms and ski masks and city traffic policemen in blue uniforms and white braids and another rarely seen species dressed all in black with crimson bandoliers and black hoods with slits for the eyes and mouth, who hung around the outside of the crowds, watching us all. Who were they?

"I'LL TURN THIS ON so they can't hear us," the young man says, and places a small transistor on the windowsill, its brassy music smothering any listening equipment the Algerian security men may have rigged up near the house. The story we listen to is one of secrecy and fear, of summary execution, of clandestine government death squads, of an "Islamist" leader shot dead "while trying to escape," of mass graves and numbered corpses in plastic bags. The slaughter at Sekardji prison killed off 223 "cadres" of the FIS, according to the men in the room, all "murdered" in revenge for the bombing of the Algiers police commissariat.

There is not a hint of doubt among these men, not a moment's hesitation in their story. For them, the GIA are not "terrorists" but the "armed opposition." Ask about the claims—backed up by all-too-detailed evidence—that the GIA rape women, and one of the men replies: "This is just an attempt to discredit the resistance." Express incredulity at this answer, and the response is softened, the kind of grubby reply that governments give when called to account. "There are excesses by the GIA, of course." Which is one way of saying that the GIA rape women.

But it is government excess of which they wish to speak, brutal, consistent, carried out with the help—so they claim in Algiers—of a special "anti-terrorist brigade" based at the Châteauneuf police station, the torture centre where women are still taken, according to these same men, for systematic rape and execution. Lawyers acting on behalf of FIS men say that in many cases the Algerian police no longer bother to torture prisoners for confessions before dragging them into court. They merely execute them.

An Algiers lawyer tries to explain. "In the last month and a half, there have been no more judicial hearings in Algiers—there have been no trials—but there have been thousands of arrests. The government set up special courts in Oran, Algiers and Constantine in September 1992, but they didn't work because the lawyers wouldn't cooperate. The government abolished special courts this year—and this was said to be a good, liberal thing. But there have been no court hearings since then, just the arrests."

He mentions the cases of two "Islamist" physics teachers from Blida, Dr. Fouad Bouchlagem and Dr. Ahmed Noulaaresse. "Both were arrested by the Algiers police. One had a Ph.D. from Toulouse University, the other was trained at MIT. Then later, after their detention, the police just said that they were both 'shot while trying to escape.' What are we supposed to conclude from this?" More frightening still are the cases of Dr. Nourredine Ameur, head of the orthopaedic unit at the Harrash hospital in Algiers, and Dr. Cherif Belahrache, head of the rheumatology department at Constantine University. Taken from their hospitals by armed policemen in 1994, they have simply disappeared.

Then there is the case of Azedine Alwane, an accountant in the nationalised water company, SEDAC. "A cop had been killed last year and my client was accused of the crime," a second lawyer says. "Alwane's father was a *moudjahed*, a hero of the independence war against France. But in prison they tortured Alwane very badly and then they castrated him. His father intervened to try and get him out of prison and we got an acquittal in court—the other policemen in the courtroom were weeping when they heard the evidence of what had been done to him . . . His father even went to the minister of the interior, Meziane-Cherif, and asked for his help, but the minister told him that he couldn't help because the men responsible were not under his orders."

When I had interviewed the cigar-chomping *éradicateur* Meziane-Cherif, he had denied the existence of an "anti-terrorism brigade" but agreed that "we have organised groups within the army, the police and the gendarmerie" to counter "terrorism." According to the men in the room, these "groups" were now 6,000 strong and worked out of police stations in the Algiers suburbs of Hussein Dey, Kouba, Ben Aknoun and Fontaine Fraiche as well as Châteauneuf. One of them said that a doctor at Sekardji prison told them that 230 inmates had been killed. "It was a liquidation. Among our cadres killed was Ikhlef Sherati, an imam and a professor at

a small Koranic school . . . and Noureddin Harek, a professor of education . . . "
All the victims were buried in mass graves at the Al-Alia cemetery, thirty or forty
in holes in the ground with numbers on the graves. The Algerian government
announced an inquiry into the scandal. And who was appointed to head the investigation? Why, Meziane-Cherif, of course.

And all the while, the war becomes more atrocious, harder to report—not just
because of its physical dangers but because its horrifying details disgust even
those of us who must chronicle its bestialities. The Algerian newspapers do their
best—with the government's encouragement, of course—to terrify readers with
photographs of these crimes against humanity. An Algerian schoolgirl, only fifteen
years old, her throat slashed, lying on a mortuary slab at Blida, eyes open in accusation at the reader. Another photo shows her body, bathed in blood, hands tied
with wire behind her school uniform. Pictures in another Algerian daily show the
decapitated body of another young woman. The moment I open the papers each
morning, I feel I must look over my shoulder to see if anyone is watching me.
Merely to look at these terrible images is a criminal act. Can Algeria produce more
horror?

It can. Fatima Ghodbane was wearing a veil in her classroom in the Mohamed
Lazhar school when they came for her in March 1995, six men armed with hunting
guns and pistols. According to her classmates, she cried and pleaded with the gunmen who took her to the school gate, where they tore off her veil, tied her hands,
stabbed her in the face and then cut her throat. One witness said the gunmen placed
her severed head outside the classroom door, where many of the other children
became hysterical. Algerian police found several of them unconscious with terror.
On one of Fatima's hands, the men had scratched the letters "GIA." Fatima Ghodbane's father was a retired public works inspector, which hardly qualified him as a
government agent. The newspaper *El Watan* concluded that Fatima's crime had
been her beauty.

Two days before Fatima's death, gunmen broke into the home of a farmer's
family at Reghaia at five in the morning, locked the youngest daughter in the bathroom and lined up her two sisters, Amal, aged eighteen, and Karima Geudjali, who
was twenty-one—beside their father. Then they shot Amal in the head with two
bullets and Karima in the heart with another. Amal had been engaged to marry an
Algerian police officer. That same night, more armed men broke into a house in
Tessala el-Mardja near Blida and shot Yamina Amrani, a nine-months-pregnant
woman of twenty-six whose husband was away from the house. Three other
women—two in their twenties—were also murdered near Blida in the same week;
a few days later, two sisters aged sixteen and seventeen were taken by gunmen
from their home in the Aurès mountains; their throats were cut 200 metres from
their front door.

What primeval energy produces such sadism? Although the cost was terrible,
the Algerians won their war against the French. They are all Muslims, all of the
Sunni sect. Their huge land stands on billions of dollars' worth of oil and natural
gas deposits. Algeria is the world's eighteenth-largest exporter of petrol, the sev-

enth for gas. After France and Canada, it is the world's third francophone country. It should be as wealthy as the Arab Gulf states, its people able to buy property and invest in Europe and America like the Saudis and the Kuwaitis. Yet it suffers 25 per cent unemployment, 47 per cent illiteracy and one of the world's cruellest internal conflicts. At the Interior Ministry they now produce videotapes of the massacres, more revolting, more banal even than the government's porno-picture books of death. Up to 200 men and women are now dying every week in the towns around Algiers; Algerian journalists privately suspect that up to 100,000 were now dying every day.

In many of the recent massacres, the GIA appeared to be taking revenge on those villages that had set up government-sponsored militias to fight them— another of Meziane-Cherif's little initiatives. Trucks and buses were stopped outside these towns at the frightening *faux barrages*; their occupants—twenty or thirty at a time—had their throats cut. Near Laghaout in November 1996, an ambulance carrying a sick woman and her husband, along with a paramedic, stopped behind a bus at a "police" checkpoint. According to *Liberté*, perhaps the only reliable journalistic source left in this war, the "police"/gunmen cut the throats of the paramedic, the driver and the husband, leaving the sick woman alone in the vehicle. All the bus passengers in front are murdered in the same way. Several motorists queued up behind the ambulance until they realised what was happening, turned their cars round and drove for their lives to Laghaout.

At Sidi el-Kebir, there is no such escape. The village menfolk are in the hills above their homes on 6 November, searching for the "terrorists" against whom the government had armed them. Behind them, up to thirty GIA members enter Sidi el-Kebir and proceed, again systematically, to kill all whom they find in the village. A baby reportedly has its throat cut after a discussion among the intruders about the morality of killing children. At least ten women are *égorgées*. A newly married couple are "executed" in their home, the husband on the bed, the woman in the doorway of their bedroom, after reportedly—and inexplicably—being ordered to lay out her wedding trousseau. Their tiny baby is left tied up in the same room.

Gunmen arrive high in the Algerian mountains at the monastery of Tibherine. They take seven monks from the building. France is appalled. These kindly, spiritual men gave help even to wounded GIA men. Seven months later, I am sitting beside the little French Catholic chapel in Hydra in Algiers with the bespectacled figure of Monseigneur Henri Teissier, archbishop of Algiers, a sixty-seven-year-old French professor of Arabic who took Algerian nationality after independence. On 21 May 1996, he took a phone call which told him that all seven monks had been decapitated:

> It is true that we found only their heads. Three of their heads were hanging from a tree near a petrol station. The other four heads were lying on the grass beneath. But it is marvellous that the families of those monks maintained their friendship for us and for all Algerians. They had visited the

monastery. They had been able to accept the loss of their sons. They knew it was not all Algerians who did this thing.

So who did "this thing"? The GIA, said the Algerian government, led by a man called Sayah Attia; one of the Tibherine priests had recognised him—when he answered the door—from a newspaper photograph that identified Attia as the murderer of the Croats whose throats were slashed near the monastery.

So could the archbishop understand what happened in the minds of the killers when they took up their knives?

> They will kill a boy of two or an old man of eighty-five. I think they are out of their consciences. They work under their understanding of Islamic law—"We have to kill the enemies of the Lord"—and it is finished. We think not only of our life but of the lives of all the people in Algeria . . . The most difficult thing is to know that every day some people die, mothers cry for their sons and daughters. We ourselves are not in the same situation as we were before this crisis. When you begin celebrating the Eucharist, you cannot help remembering that Jesus was murdered by human violence—and in the name of religion. Now we have to understand the risk in this society, that we are walking in the footsteps of Jesus. We cannot look at the cross of Jesus as we have done before. Before, it was an abstract thing. Now it is a daily reality.

The archbishop had just celebrated mass for six nuns and monks in Algiers, the priest reading from St. Matthew, chapter 25, verse 13. "Watch therefore, for ye know neither the day nor the hour wherein the Son of man cometh." They had come to remember one of France's first religious martyrs in Algeria, Vicomte Charles de Foucauld, the soldier-turned-priest who was assassinated by an Islamist in Tamanrasset in 1916 and whose murder set an awful precedent for the monks and nuns who still refused to leave Algeria. Early in 1996 the bishop of Oran, Monseigneur Pierre Claverie, died in a bomb explosion on the same day he had met the French foreign minister, Hervé de Charrette. "The bomb went off in the street," Archbishop Teissier said. "He was crushed by the door of the chapel and his brains were found on the chapel floor. It was absurd, idiotic, unconscionable."

HE WAS YOUNG, well-dressed, an expensive leather jacket over his shoulders. I had already received a contact call from Britain but never expected a representative of Algeria's "Islamist" guerrilla force to turn up at my Algiers hotel with its heavy security guard, its armed cops in the front hall, its militiamen at the gates. "You can call me 'Abu Mohamed,' " the young man said as we sat on the balcony of my room, the palm trees dipping in the wind behind us. Openly acknowledging his membership of the military wing of the FIS, he stated categorically that after months of internecine war, his own Islamic Salvation Army had united with the GIA. He was the mediator, he said, of the third meeting at Chlef at the beginning of October at which the final decision had been taken to combine the two commands.

But he claimed that the GIA had been deeply infiltrated by the Algerian military intelligence service. He even alleged that the worst atrocities of the war—especially the massacre of women and children in mountain villages—were carried out at the instigation of government agents. His words were ruthless and absolute. When I asked him why the Muslim groups cut the throats of their enemies, he replied:

> It's the best way to become closer to God, the best way to kill a *taghout* [enemy of God]. If you have someone who is capable of killing five-year-old children, what do you do with him? Kill him with bullets? Bullets are precious to us—they are very expensive. Take a 9-mm Kalash[nikov] bullet—it's as if you are throwing it away. Anyone who tries to destroy Islam, to destroy the Good Lord, who takes the Lord's name in vain, is a devil. You can do anything to wipe out a devil.

There was another of those inversions at work here. "Abu Mohamed" believed the police and government agents were child-killers. The police and government believed the GIA were child-killers. Or so they said. So who was killing the children? At one point, "Abu Mohamed" handed me an Islamic tract and a key chain with "Khaled" written on the handle. Khaled, he added, was the name of his local military leader or *emir*. He repeatedly referred to the need to "exterminate with God's help" the Algerian government in order to set up a legitimate Islamic state, justifying his remarks by quoting the Koran in a state of near ecstasy.

"I've lost 200 friends, but it doesn't matter because I know that one day we'll see each other again," he said. "For the 200 who were killed, another 600 or 700 have become *moudjahedin*." He described how he had been arrested in January 1996—it was now December of the same year—and tortured by security men with electricity:

> I thank God I gave no information. The moment you give one piece of information, you are finished because they will torture you for more information until you die . . . There have been many women who have secretly worked for the Islamists . . . Sometimes they contact the *moudjahedin* and tell them that their husbands work for the state. This happened to me, a woman came to me a year ago and denounced her husband and said he worked for military security. We had to follow it up to find the proof. The GIA killed him—the real GIA which is not infiltrated. The military security have captured women and tortured and raped them and thrown them into prison. Do you know what they are asking us? They are asking us to put a bomb in their prisons. Do you know why? Because they have suffered too much. They are living a nightmare. They are all pregnant.

There had been many consistent reports, gathered by *The Independent* as well as human rights groups, of the rape of women prisoners in Algeria.

"Abu Mohamed" was equally adamant in his view of other Arab states. "Muslims are everywhere, but all their presidents are devils. All Muslims are at war with the state—in Egypt, in Tunisia, in Libya. They say Sudan is a Muslim country but there are mistakes there. Iran is Shiite—they're not really Muslim." "Abu Mohamed" did not know that a bomb had just exploded on the Paris Métro, but his response was immediate. "It's legitimate. France is the cause of everything that's going on in Algeria. It helps the Algerian state . . . So why do you think they specifically choose France? You have to ask yourself that question."

"Abu Mohamed" looked less like an "Islamist" than a playboy, with his leather jacket and his neatly shaved face and his overpowering aftershave. So his reflections on martyrdom seemed all the more bizarre. "The Koran promises us victory or martyrdom. It says real martyrs don't bleed very much. When they die, they smell of musk perfume. This is true. When a martyr dies, he is met in paradise by seventy-two beautiful women."

But I am beginning to wonder if all the beautiful women haven't been murdered, whether some of those seventy-two women won't have bloody wounds round their necks. In 1997, the holy month of Ramadan is again marked by a collective bloodbath of throat-cuttings, beheadings, car bombs and even baby-strangling. Three hundred die and even the prime minister admits 80,000 Algerians have now been killed. In Benachour, 50 kilometres from Algiers, whole families are eviscerated in revenge for the villagers' support for their local pro-government militia. The dead include a child of six, two thirteen-year-old schoolgirls and a pregnant woman who is disembowelled before being beheaded. At Harouch Trab, ten civilians—including seven women and a ten-year-old boy—have their throats cut. The first is a twenty-five-year-old woman whose head is later cut off and tied by her hair to a pike—and left by the roadside so that she can "welcome" her husband when he returns from his militia patrol. "War through war and destruction through destruction. Kouka will return," the killers spray-paint on a village wall. "Kouka" is the *nom de guerre* of a local GIA leader—real name Halilat Kouk—killed by "communal guard" militia forces a year earlier.

A young woman we know tells us in horror that her friend was on an Algiers bus, travelling to work, when the vehicle passed a street in which a policeman's head had been attached to a pole on top of a gate. Another Algiers resident describes a new GIA machine, a primitive version of Madame Guillotine, a makeshift head-cutter with an iron blade to which its victims are subjected after being dragged from their homes. According to residents, the guillotine is mounted on a truck. Those condemned to die by the GIA are taken from their apartments with their mouths stuffed full of newspaper and are guillotined on the truck.

RAÏS AND BENTALHA. Two more dirt villages in the *bled*. But this time, the sadism as well as the scale of the attacks mark a new depth of savagery, something we have never seen before, entire villages liquidated by the knife, their population slaughtered en masse like animals, cut open, axed down, hacked apart. When we are taken to these flat, poor hamlets—Bosnian-style ghost towns of crumbling walls and collapsed roofs—even the cops and soldiers fall silent. Through shame or guilt?

From the roof of Ali's house in Raïs, I can see the local army barracks just half a kilometre across the fields, yellow-painted with a green-and-white Algerian flag fluttering gaily from the roof. No, Ali says, he doesn't know why the soldiers didn't intervene when the murderers turned up—dressed in Afghan robes and hats, he says—to cut the throats of his family. Round the side of Ali's neck, there is a ferocious purple scar that slices through his skin, crudely stitched—because they cut Ali's throat too.

"There were up to a hundred men who came into our village from three directions—they were here for at least three hours," he says, his head leaning at an odd, permanent angle to the right. "There was shooting and screaming. No one helped us." Around him, in cheap brick villas and chicken yards and burned-out garages, lay still the thick scum of old blood, all that remains in the village of the 349 Algerians—mostly women and children—slaughtered in the late evening of 29 August 1997. When I ask Ali to describe the night, he stares at me in silence, fingering his left arm, which is swathed in bandages but reveals another frightful purple scar at the wrist. A neighbour whispers in my ear: "They knifed his wife in front of him." And it was this that forced Ali to talk:

> I had most of my family here. My wife, my three sons, my brother, his
> wife, sons and daughter, and many cousins. We hid in the house but they
> threw bombs through the windows and broke down the door with axes.

Ali sways against the balcony wall as he says these words. I have already crunched through the carbonised interior of the house and found, beside the begonia plants and vines on the balcony, an old tray bearing the words "There is no God but God and Mohamed is his Prophet." Beside it, as if painted onto the wall in defiance of all religion, was a darkened stream of blood. Ali draws in his breath. He is about to plunge deep into an ocean of pain:

> My baby son Mohamed was five and they cut his throat and threw him out
> of the upper window. Then they cut the throat of my eldest son Rabeh and
> then my brother's throat because he saw they were kidnapping his wife and
> tried to stop them. They took some of the other girls.

And Ali raises his hand and says: "Blood." There is more downstairs, stained brown across the living-room floor where Ali's final calvary took place:

> They cut my throat and I felt the knife in my neck but I tried to shield
> myself and the man sliced me on the arm. My wife was so brave. She tried

to help, to fight them, to save me. So they dragged her to the door where I was lying and slit her throat in front of me. There was another baby, the mother tried to hide it behind some bricks but they cut her throat and then did the same to the baby on the bricks. The man who used the knife on me—I recognised him. I had seen him on the streets of our village.

There were times in this place of atrocities when the sheer awfulness of what happened almost blinded one to the obvious questions. Why *didn't* the army venture across the fields? They must have heard the shrieks from the buildings on the main road. They must have seen the fires in the roofs. They must have heard the bombs. And who were the so-called "Islamists" performing these acts of unparalleled butchery? Why should "Islamists" murder the very same villagers who voted so faithfully for the FIS and who traditionally opposed the Algerian government?

In the neighbouring village of Bentalha—with about 240 dead—the old FIS election signs remain on walls and lamp-posts. Here, too, a fifty-four-year-old man who would only give his name as Saïd claimed to me that the village men had fled to warn the army, leaving their women and children behind. The more I walked through these desolate streets, the more I remembered. Two years before, Commandant Mohamed of the *garde mobile* drove me through these villages. In Bentalha, his squad of cops had arrested two men who tried to run away from them—just next to a sewage outflow, which I recognised as I walked through the village now. The men had been fearful of execution. The people all supported the "Islamists." The villagers, the commandant had told me in his Land Cruiser back then, were "with the terrorists." It was a "terrorist area." So why would the "terrorists" now want to kill all these people who allegedly supported them? Bentalha, far from being a village of politically uninvolved civilians, had been a stronghold of the FIS.

The big houses—for the poor fled to larger homes for protection when the gunmen and axemen arrived—were burned out, their back yards swamped with blood. "The men ran away—it was a mistake," Saïd conceded miserably. "They knew what would happen. Some tried to throw slates and bricks from the roofs of the houses. One of our men got a rifle and killed one of these savages. The dead man turned out to be from this same village." Again, the screaming had gone on long into the night. And again, soldiers from the local barracks only arrived after the murderers had fled. The "Islamists," Saïd recalled, even shouted curses as they poured through the unpaved street in turbans and gowns. "They kept crying: 'You will die and go to hell—we will kill you and go to heaven.' "

Most of the people of Bentalha fled after the massacre. A few now drifted back in the morning. I found two of them trying to repair the blackened interior of their homes, screwing half-burned light fittings back into the walls, ignoring my questions while a group of children—who had hidden on the roof during the massacres—watched them in silence. Another man refused to name his dead wife. "Her name belongs to me," he said, and began to cry.

The pathetic remnants of families evoke something more than pity. They are as frightened of the future as they are of the past. In each kitchen, cheap metal trays have been twisted out of recognition, the pots smashed, medicines thrown over the floor. In one house, a bomb has been thrown at a bird cage, hurling its dead occupants in a mass of blackened feathers around the room. What sort of men would throw a bomb into a bird cage? A pile of school books in a garage next to three huge pools of congealed blood showed how earnestly its dead owner had tried—amid the immense poverty of these Algerian slum villages—to improve his lot.

The first page of the boy's exercise book shows his name was Koreishi; he had practised his declensions and dutifully written the biography of his doomed family. "Abdelkader is my father, he is an electrician. Zhor is my mother, she is a dressmaker. Hamid is my uncle, he is a policeman. Salima is my aunt, she is a nurse . . . " And I wondered whether Hamid's job might have sent the family to their deaths. But the survivors said there was no discrimination. All the victims were treated equally: they were all killed. One man said he heard the gunmen who entered the village shouting that their enemies were "Jews."

A man who pleaded with me not to publish his name said he saw the poorer families of Bentalha seeking refuge in a large house in Hijilali Street. "It was no good for them. I stood here at the window and I could hear those poor people screaming and dying. When I looked out of my window, I could see them axeing the women on the roof." At least seventeen people died in that one house. In a corner of it, I discovered a book of European art—a coloured photograph of Michelangelo's *Pietà* lay face up on the floor—and another depicted the features of dead martyrs of the war against the French, their faces disfigured by bullets and shrapnel. How little Algeria's suffering had changed. Days later, a photograph of a distraught Bentalha woman, told that her family were dead, will become the image of this Golgotha. They will call the picture the *Pietà*.

So who killed all these poor people? On 20 August, just two days before the massacre at Raïs, President Zeroual had announced that "terrorism is living its last hours in our country." Violent acts were now to be regarded as "residual terrorism." Bentalha was the village whose destruction had been studied by the Algerian hotel concierge in Paris, the hotel in which the Australian soldier whom my father was told to execute had killed the British military policeman in 1919. That Algerian, too, noticed how the army did not enter the villages until the murderers had gone. He had used the word *pouvoir*—the authorities—and chosen to say no more.

WE ALL KNEW IT WAS HAPPENING in Algeria. For more than four years, released prisoners had been telling us of the water torture and beatings, the suffocation with rags, of nails ripped out by interrogators, of women gang-raped by policemen, of secret executions in police stations. The evidence was convincing enough, even when it came from self-declared enemies of the Algerian regime or members of the armed organisations opposed to it. But by mid-1997, even as the village massacres were taking place—blamed, of course, on the FIS, the GIA, the "terrorists," "barbarians"—I had collected hundreds of pages of evidence from Algerian lawyers and human rights workers which proved incontrovertibly that the Algerian security forces had been guilty of "disappearances," of torture and crimes against humanity. Even more sensational was that, after weeks of tentative contacts, I found members of the Algerian security forces who had sought asylum in Britain—and were themselves now prepared to talk of the terrors they had witnessed.

I travelled to London to talk to Andy Marshall, my new foreign news editor at *The Independent*. I brought with me from Algeria photographs of young women who had been "disappeared" and—from my meetings with these ex-Algerian police officers—details of torture and execution by the security forces. Andy recoiled at the obscenity of what he read in the transcripts of my interviews which I gave him. "I believe it," he said. "We need to get the editor to put this all over the front." I knew what this meant. Little chance now of those hard-sought visas to Algeria. No explanation of our impartiality would wash my reputation clean with the *pouvoir* after we presented them with this evidence of human wickedness. My reporting started in Algiers city.

Maître Mohamed Tahri puts the number of "disappeared" at 12,000, but the moment I am about to dispute this terrifying figure, a young woman in a white headscarf walks quietly through the door and whispers in Maître Tahri's ear. The forty-six-year-old lawyer listens without emotion, his eyes on the floor. He is a little moustachioed vole of a man with sharp eyes, impressive and heroic, but no match for the lanky *flics* who have arrived at his office. I catch sight of them briefly: tall, thin men staring through the front door, the noise of the Algiers suburb of Kouba behind them. Above Maître Tahri, his court robes hang on the wall: black with white fur edges, a fading symbol of the Napoleonic law that once governed Algeria. But the government now is metres away.

"She says the men have come from the commissariat of police and want to see me again," Tahri mutters. On his desk there lies a file of photographs, thousands of them, men and women, the quick and the dead, all "disappeared" by the Algerian police—the very same *flics* who are now at the door. Tahri pulls coloured snapshots out of the file to give to me; two young women, one in a patterned black pullover with a heart-shaped brooch, a fringe over her forehead, the other sitting in a photographer's studio in a long red dress, a thinner fringe but with the same open, delicate face.

Naïma and Nedjoua Boughaba are sisters, aged twenty-three and twenty-nine; both were arrested by the Algerian police on 12 April 1997. Both were court clerks, one working for an Algiers judge who by misfortune was investigating a list of suspected "Islamists" drawn up by the Swiss police—and sold by a Swiss policeman to the Algerian intelligence services. The women were kidnapped by government agents outside the tribunal. They are thought to be alive. Tahri pulls another snapshot out of his file, of a beautiful young woman with a radiant face, her tousled hair held back by a pink band, half smiling at the photographer. Amina Beuslimane is alleged to have taken photographs of cemeteries and blown-up buildings—perhaps to have proof of government violence against civilians. She was twenty-eight when she was arrested by security police on 13 December 1994, never to be seen again. Her mother has been advised by friends who have contacts in the prisons that she must not hold out any hope of seeing her daughter again. Amina, they have told her, was tortured to death.

Each time Tahri produces a photograph, I catch sight of hundreds of others; of bland, middle-aged men, of suspected "Islamists" in beards, and girls and old men. The oldest "disappeared" in the Tahri files is seventy-four-year-old Ahmed Aboud, arrested on 23 February 1997. The youngest is fifteen-year-old Brahim Maghraoui. A photocopy of a photograph shows Moussa Maddi, a paraplegic in a wheelchair arrested on 3 May 1997. No one knows why. An attractive young woman in a red dress with Princess Diana–style hair, Saïda Kheroui is—or was—the sister of a wanted member of an armed "Islamist" group. Her snapshot is smaller than the others. She was "disappeared" by intelligence agents on 7 May 1997. All that is known of her fate is that the security police, during her interrogation, broke the bones of one of her feet.

Mohamed Tahri was frightened in October 1997 that he was about to be added to the list. He had called a meeting of mothers of the "disappeared" in front of Algiers' central post office. The police broke it up. "They told me not to follow the protesters," he says to us in an ultra-quiet voice, aware that the police are still lingering at the front door. "They told me to go down a side street where there were only policemen and I was afraid I would be kidnapped. So I started shouting: 'I am a lawyer, I defend human rights—you have no right to hinder my movements.' I took out my professional card but there was a high-ranking policeman pushing me to prevent me being able to leave." Cops surrounded Tahri. "I said, 'I'm a lawyer' but the police officer said: 'You're not a lawyer—you're a traitor because you have contact with foreigners and with so-called human rights organisations.' When I said I refused to go down the street . . . the officer said: 'Take him in.'

"They took me to an office at the Cavignac police station—I know people who had died there under torture. They said to me: 'You are the one who gives information to Amnesty International and other organisations . . . you're the one who arranges the demonstrations, who causes trouble in this country.' " Before he was released, Tahri was taken to the commissariat in Amirouche Street, where he was told: "You have contacts with journalists . . . "

If Tahri's evidence was damning, the meetings I arranged with defecting Algerian police and army officers in London provided even more compelling proof of their government's involvement in crimes against humanity. All but one of my interviews with these brave, frightened men—and one woman—were conducted on a different political planet, not in an Algiers suburb but in a conference room at the Sheraton Belgravia Hotel in Knightsbridge in central London, a room that grew lung-crushingly fuggy as these lonely witnesses to savagery smoked their way through pack after pack of cigarettes.

DALILAH IS USED TO BLOOD. When she describes the prisoners, stripped half-naked and tied to ladders in the garage of the Cavignac police station, she does so with a curious detachment. Later, when I have spent more than an hour listening to her evidence of cruelty and death, she will turn to me with a terrifying admission. "I'm being treated by a psychologist because I have bad dreams," she says. "My great passion now is to go to see horror movies—it's the only thing that interests me. I want to see blood."

It is an extraordinary remark to come from this attractive woman of thirty with her abundant dark black hair tied in a bunch, dandling the child of an Algerian woman friend on her knee. She joined up as a detective in the Algerian special branch in 1985—"I'd wanted to be a policewoman to serve my people since I was twelve years old," not least because her father had been a cop—but things began to go seriously wrong for her after the cancellation of elections:

> I was moved to Cavignac police station near the post office and I hated what was happening there, what was happening to the police. They tortured people—I saw this happening. I saw innocent young people tortured like wild animals. Yes, I myself saw the torture sessions. What could I do? They executed people at 11 o'clock at night, people who had done nothing. They had been denounced by people who didn't get along with them. People just said "He's a terrorist" and the man would be executed. They tied young people to a ladder with rope. They were always shirtless, sometimes naked. They put a rag over their face. Then they forced salty water into them. There was a tap with a pipe that they stuck in the prisoner's throat and they ran the water until the prisoners' bellies had swelled right up. When I remember it, I think how it hurt to see a human being like this—it's better to murder men than see them tortured like that.

Dalilah talks about torture like an automaton, her voice a monotone. She says she saw, over a period of months, at least 1,000 men tortured at the rate of twelve a day, the police interrogators starting at 10 a.m. and working in shifts until 11 p.m. But she cries when she describes what she saw:

> The torturers would say: "You must confess that you killed so-and-so" and they made the prisoner sign a confession with their eyes blindfolded—they didn't have the right to read what they were signing. There were prisoners who wept and said: "I've done nothing—I have the right to a doctor and a lawyer." When they said that, they got a fist in the mouth. Those who died were under the water torture. Their bellies were too swollen with water. Sometimes while this happened, the torturers would put broomsticks up their anuses. They enjoyed it. Some of the prisoners had beards, some didn't. They were all poor. The top policemen gave the order to torture—I think it was given over the phone. But they didn't use the word torture— they used to call it *nakdoulou eslah*—"guest treatment." There would be screaming and crying from the prisoners. They would shout: "In the name of God, I did nothing" or "We're all the same, we're Muslims like you."

They screamed and cried a lot. I saw two men who died like that on the ladder. The two bodies hung there on the ladder. They were dead and the torturer said: "Take them to the hospital and say they died in a battle." They did the same thing with those who were executed at eleven at night—it was done after curfew when only the police and the gendarmerie could drive around. I had to fill out the death certificates so the bodies could be taken out of the hospitals. I had to sign that it was a body that had been found in the forest after it had decomposed—it was very hot then.

Dalilah says that she tried to protest to a superior officer, whose name she gives as Hamid:

I said to him: "You mustn't do these things because we are all Muslims— there should at least be evidence against these people before you kill them." He said to me: "My girl, you are not made for the police force—if you suspect someone, you must kill him. When you kill people, that's how you get promoted." Any cop would hit the prisoners with the butt of his "Kalash." Some of the prisoners went completely mad from being tortured. Everyone who was brought to the Cavignac was tortured—around 70 per cent of the cops there saw all this. They participated. Although the torture was the job of the judiciary police, the others joined in. The prisoners would be twenty or thirty to a cell and they would be brought one by one to the ladder, kicked in the ribs all the time. It was inhuman.

According to Dalilah, women prisoners were taken to a special section of the Châteauneuf police station called the "National Organisation for the Suppression of Criminality," where Algerian military security police prevented all but those with special passes from entering. "You had to be a high-ranking officer to get in there because of the way they treated women. They killed there too . . . " Dalilah's tragedy was personal. "I can't sleep in the dark because I'm afraid. It's not my fault, because my fiancé was murdered during Ramadan in 1993. The men who did this to him were dressed as policemen—and they killed him because he was a policeman." Who are "they"? I ask. And she replies: "That's the big question." But it was torture that destroyed Dalilah's life—and which proved her undoing:

There was a group of elderly people who were tortured. I couldn't stand to see it, especially one man of about fifty-five whose arm was rotting. He had gangrene and he smelled very bad. I couldn't bear it and I went and bought him some penicillin and put it on his arm because I thought it would help. There were another six people in his cell who had been tortured—it smelled like death in there. But another policeman had seen me and I asked him not to say anything. You see, we didn't have the right to talk to prisoners—only to hit them. But the policeman wrote a report to the commissioner who called me in . . . He said: "Maybe you'll go to prison for helping terrorists." The man I helped was freed afterwards—which showed me he was innocent.

Armed "Islamists"—four young men who turned up at her mother's home—had meanwhile targeted Dalilah, demanding she hand over her police pistol within fifteen days. When she asked for police protection, she was denied it. Dalilah slept in police stations at night. Then she slipped away from her home and bribed her way onto a boat for Europe, on the run from both the Algerian security services and the "Islamist" guerrillas.

REDA LEFT LONG PAUSES between his sentences. Safe in London, the soldier's memory was on a road 30 kilometres from Algiers. He had been on military service, part of a commando unit outside Blida:

> They gave us vaccinations in our backs and then told us to inject each other before we went out on sorties. It was an off-white liquid which we injected into each other's arms . . . It made us feel like Rambo . . . We were on a roadblock, stopping anyone we suspected of being a terrorist. If a man had a face like a terrorist, if he had a big beard, he was shot. There was a man with a beard walking past the petrol station. I told him to stop. He said: "Why should I stop?" The man was rude, so I killed him. It's like I was dreaming and it wasn't me. I didn't remember it till my friends told me . . . The bullets hit him in the chest. When he died, he cried: "There is no God but God." I hope that God will forgive me and that all humanity will forgive me.

Knightsbridge may be an unexpected place to seek forgiveness but from time to time, Reda wept—for the killings, for the torture he witnessed, for the soldiers he believed were murdered by his own army. He began his military service in the town of Skikda, then moved to Biskra for weapons training. "We were told that all people were against us. We were taught how to recognise terrorists—by their beards and *khamis* robes, their Islamic clothes."

On 12 May 1997, Reda was flown to Blida for active service in the anti-guerrilla war. On his first sortie into the village of Sidi Moussa on 27 May, he and his comrades ordered families from their homes and he said that, while searching their houses, they stole all the money and gold they could find:

> We took sixteen men for torture. We had been told by informers that there were terrorists there. Whatever they told us to do, we would do it. All sixteen men were bearded. There was an underground room at the Blida barracks called the *katellah*—the "killing room"—and the prisoners were all given names by the interrogators, names like Zitouni. The men were stripped and bound and tied to a chair and hosed with cold water. Two sol-

diers stood in front of each prisoner and asked questions. Then they started
with the electric drill.

Reda fidgets with his hands as he tells his awful story. The drills were used on the
prisoners' legs. He says he saw one army torturer drill open a man's stomach. It
lasted four hours with each prisoner—if they lived, they were released after a
week. At one point in his story, Reda asks his younger brother to leave the room;
he doesn't want his family to know what else he has seen:

> There was a cable about five centimetres in diameter and they put it in the
> ears or anus of the prisoners. Then they threw water at them. Two of the
> men began cursing us . . . And the torturer would shout *Yarabak*—"God
> damn you—so much for your God." The torture went on twenty-four hours
> a day. I was only a conscript. I watched but I didn't take part. The man
> whose stomach was drilled, he was drilled because he was suspected 100
> per cent of being a terrorist.

In June 1997, Reda was asked to join a protection force around Sidi Moussa
during a raid by regular troops. "We had to go in if there were flares sent up—but
there were no flares and we went home after two hours. Next day . . . we heard that
in this same village a massacre had taken place and twenty-eight villagers had
been beheaded. And that made us start thinking about who did it. I started to think
that our people had been the killers."

Two days later, Reda says, he and fellow conscripts were cleaning the barracks
and searching the clothes of regular troops for cigarettes when they found a false
beard and musk, a perfume worn by devout Muslims. "We asked ourselves, what
were the soldiers doing with this beard?" Reda concluded that this army unit must
have carried out the Sidi Moussa massacre but his alarm worsened when twenty-
six of his fellow conscripts were driven off to another barracks at Chréa. "They
later brought all their bodies back to us and said that they had been killed in an
ambush, but I am sure they were executed because they weren't trusted any more.
There had been no wounded in the 'ambush.' Maybe they talked too much. All our
soldiers knew these men had been eliminated—because earlier, before they were
taken away, we were told not to talk to them."

The end of Reda's military career was not heroic. His teeth were kicked out by
colleagues, he says, and he was imprisoned for a week after he was seen giving
bread to prisoners. Then, ambushed while on roadblock duty on the edge of Blida,
he was recognised by two armed Islamists. "They were friends of mine and they
saw me in my paratroop uniform and my green beret. One of them shouted: 'There
is plenty of time left in the year to get you. Take care of yourself and your wife and
child.' I and three other conscripts ran away with the help of locals who gave us
civilian clothes. Now I am between two fires—between the terrorists and the
Algerian government."

Reda turned up at Heathrow Airport in London a few weeks later, pleading for protection. The Algerian authorities claimed they knew him—and that he fabricated his story of military atrocities to gain asylum in Britain. But why would Reda seek asylum in Britain in the first place, along with dozens of other members of the Algerian security services? Reda's last news from Algeria when he spoke to me was horrifying enough: eight relatives in the suburb of Boufarik—not far from Blida—had just had their throats cut.

Other former Algerian security personnel were interviewed for *The Independent*. Inspector Abdessalam, who was in charge of police ordnance at the Dar el-Beïda police station near Algiers airport, also described to me how he watched suspected "Islamists" interrogated by torturers, some of whose names he also provided, names that were confirmed to be those of security operatives. "Sometimes," he said, "prisoners were forced to drink acid or a cloth was tied to their mouths and acid poured over it. Prisoners were forced to stand next to tables with their testicles on the table and their testicles would be beaten . . . A small number of the prisoners gave information. Some preferred to be killed. Some died under water torture."

*The Independent*, which was using a new page layout that projected our reports on the front page in depth and at length, published photographs of four of the missing young women—Amina Beuslimane, Naïma and Nedjoua Boughaba and Saïda Kheroui—with "DISAPPEARED" stamped over their faces. Our series started on 30 October 1997, with the page one headline: "Lost souls of the Algerian night: now their torturers tell the truth." We were not the only newspaper trying to uncover the Algerian government's role in crimes against humanity—several French journalists had nursed these suspicions for years—but our reports were treated by governments with the same disdain that had met our dispatches on Saddam's tortures in the 1980s, our investigation of Israeli killings in the same period, our inquiries into depleted uranium munitions in Iraq and our reopening of the Turkish–Armenian genocide of 1915.

The Algerian ambassador in London wrote a spiteful and abusive letter to the editor of *The Independent*, sneering at Saïda Kheroui, the young woman whose foot was broken under torture, because I referred to her "Princess Diana–style hair," and suggesting that the thousands of "disappeared"—including the other young women who had been tortured to death—had "in most cases, joined the terrorist bands."

Ambassadors are expected to lie for their country. The response of Western nations to the growing evidence of Algerian government complicity in the horrors of this war, however, was as pitiful as it was shameful. In May 1998, more than six months after *The Independent* had devoted so much space and resources to reveal the testimony of Algerian ex-security forces and human rights lawyers, the British Foreign Office published a policy statement on Algeria. It said that while there were reports of Algerian complicity in the massacres, "there is no credible, substantive evidence to support the allegations." It claimed that "large scale and brutal violence"—rather than the suspension of democratic elections—was "the genesis of the terrible events" in Algeria.

Far from recognising the courage of those former policemen who were denouncing their country's crimes, Britain had in early 1997 rejected an asylum appeal by another former Algerian ex-policeman and forcibly returned him to Algeria in handcuffs. He was arrested at Algiers airport, brutally interrogated by his former comrades-in-arms about his Algerian contacts in London and then murdered by the security police. His body was delivered to his mother for burial two weeks after he was deported from London. He had changed his address in Britain and thus failed to receive his notice of leave to appeal the initial refusal of his asylum request. Scandalously, the UK authorities furnished the Algerian government with details showing he had been a police officer—which, of course, doomed him at once.*

When Mary Robinson, the UN Human Rights Commissioner, tried to address the causes rather than the acts of violence in Algeria, the country's foreign minister, Ahmed Attaf, berated her. "What causes justify killing women and children?" he demanded to know. Mrs. Robinson then held her tongue. Far more obnoxious was the UN panel led by former Portuguese prime minister Mário Soares which embarked on an "information-gathering" mission to Algeria in the autumn of 1998. It produced a report that might have been written by the Algerian government itself. In an extraordinary act of moral cowardice, Soares allowed Algerian officials to read the UN report before it was published, entirely accepted the Algerian government's claim that it was "fighting terrorism" and concluded that "Algeria deserves the support of the international community in its efforts to combat this phenomenon." In just nineteen pages, the report used the word "terrorism" or "terror" ninety-one times without asking who these "terrorists" were or why they opposed the government. It agreed with interviewees who said that "excesses" committed by the security forces could not compare with the "Islamists' " "crimes against humanity." Although around 20,000 Algerians were still being held on "terrorism" charges, the UN panel interviewed only one of them. No wonder Attaf distributed the Soares report to the local Algerian press for publication. When Amnesty International condemned the UN report as a "whitewash," Attaf brusquely dismissed the charge.

An earlier European Union mission had behaved with even less heed to the evidence of torture and murder by the authorities. In just eighteen hours in Algiers, it never left the villas and government offices of the Algerian authorities. The vice president of the European Commission, Manuel Marin, urged the Europeans to "tread softly"; there were no questions about torture or the need for an international inquiry into the massacres. A few days earlier, the Irish foreign minister David Andrews had told radio listeners that the time had come for outsiders "to stop condemning Algeria from afar."

---

*The British were not alone in sending Algerians back to their homeland for execution. The Belgian authorities deported a junior FIS leader, Ben Othman Bousria, to Algeria on 15 July 1996, on the fraudulent grounds that he would not be in danger if he was returned. After again trying to flee Algeria, he was arrested while trying to cross the Libyan border and died in police custody at Mostaganem. A police report said he had "committed suicide" by throwing himself out of a security forces office while awaiting trial.

Much the same sentiment was being expressed by President Jacques Chirac of France. Asked what France could do to stop the massacres, he replied: "Nothing by interference. We have to find a way of acting effectively from the outside." It was a policy that suited the Algerian authorities perfectly. They were eager to accept French weaponry and military equipment to fight their civil war but refused to accept any demands for investigations on the grounds that this would constitute interference in their domestic affairs. For a time, even France's most boring intellectual, Bernard-Henri Lévy, bought the Algerian government line. He said it was "obscene" and "an affront to the memory of the victims" of the massacres to ask who was killing whom in Algeria—because it was so obviously Muslim fundamentalists who were to blame. In so obscene and shameful way did Lévy ignore the thousands of victims of government torture. Abdelhamid Brahimi, a former Algerian prime minister who accuses the military of massacring thirty-one of his relatives in Médéa, was to claim that—by rejecting an international inquiry—Lévy and other French intellectuals "defend the regime by denying the responsibility of the *junta* in these massacres."

The United States had largely kept out of Algerian affairs, save for several American diplomats in Algiers who awarded young Algerian women visas in return for their favours. Although Algeria gave financial support to the PLO during the 1982 Israeli invasion of Lebanon—it sent $20 million in arms via the Soviet Union—the country was always sympathetic to America. During the Cuban missile crisis, Ben Bella was in New York and took a secret message to Fidel Castro from President John Kennedy, warning him of the seriousness of the confrontation with the Soviets. Ben Bella had not forgotten that Kennedy was alone in Congress in calling for Algerian independence during the war with the French.

But repeated claims by the Algerians that they were fighting foreign as well as FIS "terrorists" had its effect. The U.S. Justice Department tried to deport the FIS spokesman, Anwar Haddam—who spoke of the need for peace and reconciliation at a Rome conference—by using dozens of reports from the government-controlled Algerian press and misquotations from my own articles in *The Independent*. Although the U.S. State Department had acknowledged that "there is convincing evidence that the security forces carried out dozens of extrajudicial killings and often tortured and otherwise abused detainees," the Justice Department largely relied on Algerian government supporters for its "evidence" against Haddam of "crimes against humanity," "rape" and "beheading"—for none of which was Haddam held personally responsible.*

The American press either reported the mass killings of "Muslim militants" by

---

*In its highly mendacious "evidence," the U.S. government quoted an article from *The Independent*—filed by me from Algiers on 8 March 1995—in which I wrote that photographs of murdered Algerian intellectuals were "enough to make you hate them [Islamists], despise them, deprive them of any human attribute, let alone human rights—which was, of course, the intention, provided you could forget how many people voted for the FIS in the elections which the government annulled." The U.S. Justice Department failed to see the irony in the last line—nor the clear implication that the pictures had been published as part of an Algerian government pro-

"security forces sweeping through a western region wracked by recent massacres" without questioning how so large a number might have been killed in so short a period of time—this came from the Associated Press on 11 March 1998—or persuaded readers to believe that the slaughter of civilians somehow encouraged Algerians to support the government that might have been partly responsible for the killings. Thus John Lancaster in *The Washington Post* apparently discovered in 1997 that "the violence appears to have generated a backlash against the militants, even among those who once supported their cause." Only an oblique reference was made in his dispatch to claims that the authorities might be involved in the massacres.

By the late 1990s, when the complicity of the Algerian military in the killings was already widely suspected, the U.S. Navy undertook manoeuvres with Algerian warships in the Mediterranean while American diplomats were encouraged to visit Algiers. Robert Pelletreau was a guest of the Algerian government in 1996. In 1998, the State Department sent a more prominent figure to the Algerian capital, none other than Martin Indyk, the point man for President Clinton's "peace process" team to the Israeli–Palestinian talks and a former director of research at the largest Israeli lobby group in Washington. Algerian radio heralded Indyk's arrival by announcing that American policies had changed "now that the White House has decided to support the struggle against terrorism and Congress has several times condemned the GIA."

Given this indifference to the true nature of the massacres—and who might be responsible for them—Algerian officials now felt able to dismiss security force atrocities with near abandon. "It's not impossible, in the situation in which we find ourselves, that some excesses may have occurred on the part of individuals acting outside the orders of their commander," the Algerian chief of staff and principal *éradicateur* General Mohamed Lamari blandly admitted. A further jump into the depths of insensitivity came from Algeria's former minister of higher education, Abdelhak Bererhi, who announced in 1998 that "to compare a rape in a police station to a rape by a GIA terrorist is indecent." Even Lévy could not have equalled this.

The GIA was not itself an Algerian government creation, although its Afghan origins are unclear. While thousands of Algerians did travel to join the anti-Soviet *mujahedin*, some of whom gave their support to Osama bin Laden—I had, after all, met Algerians in al-Qaeda during my own visits to bin Laden in Afghanistan, and stood beside them as that prophetic comet soared above us near his camp in 1997—recent research suggests that even here the hand of the *pouvoir* was present. Algeria's military security, it is now reported, sent their own men to Afghanistan to

---

paganda campaign. The American documentation was also very sloppy. The titles of at least two Algerian newspapers were misspelled—and no reference made to the Algerian *pouvoir*'s insistence that the Algerian press must print news of "terrorism" according to the regime's instructions. Many of the articles reported massacres that the FIS had condemned. After I wrote about the American administration's misuse of my articles in *The Independent*, all reference to them mysteriously disappeared from the U.S. Justice Department's list of "exhibits" against Haddam.

maintain surveillance over the Algerian "Afghanis" who had taken up the jihad—posing as loyal Muslim fighters while reporting back to Algiers on the aims and methods of the army of "Islamists" who would eventually filter home to seek a conflict with its own corrupt "socialist" enemies. Algeria's military penetration of its antagonists was therefore accomplished at a very early stage.

When the GIA leader Djamel Zitouni was killed, supposedly in an Algerian army ambush, the authorities triumphantly announced that they had scored a tactical victory over their "terrorist" enemies. The twenty-nine-year-old son of a chicken farmer, who had worked in his father's shop in Algiers before coming under the influence of Mustafa Bouyali, he went underground in 1991 and was allegedly given the command of the GIA's "Phalangists of Death" squad, becoming the organisation's *emir* when its earlier leader, Cherif Gousmi, died in 1994. Zitouni personally claimed responsibility for the Air France hijacking and a wave of bomb attacks in France in 1995, and even wrote a 62-page book—possibly ghost-written by his colleagues—on the "duties of holy warriors." But Zitouni, according to the GIA itself, had been banished from the movement on 15 July 1996, and would be judged for his activities It was a statement from the GIA's *majlis e-shoura* council that announced his death the following day, adding that Antar Zouabri had taken over the leadership. So was Zitouni killed by the army or executed by the GIA? Or did these two possibilities amount to one and the same thing?

The Algerian government, for example, had long accused Zitouni of responsibility for the beheading of the seven French priests from the monastery at Tibherine in 1996. But two years later, a long investigation in *Le Monde* suggested that Algerian security forces were implicated in the executions after a double-cross by French secret servicemen—an act much resented by Zitouni's lieutenant, who was a former officer in the Algerian military security apparatus. The same article alleged that French diplomats believed the bomb that killed Pierre Claverie, the bishop of Oran, might have been planted by the Algerian authorities—because he might have known of secret negotiations between the French and Algerian governments over the kidnapped monks. In 2002, by which time up to 200,000 Algerians had been killed in the war, the army killed Zitouni's successor, Antar Zouabri—this time displaying his body, complete with bullet-broken head, as proof.

But international human rights groups now performed the task that both the UN and the EU—and, of course, the United States and other Western nations—had so disgracefully evaded: they actively demanded answers to the epic "disappearances" of the war. Human Rights Watch accused the authorities of kidnapping, torture and extrajudicial executions. A year later, Amnesty International did the same, listing 3,000 victims—a small proportion of them already named in *The Independent*'s investigation—who had apparently been murdered by the authorities, including hospital workers, civil servants, schoolchildren, secretaries, farmers and lawyers. When General Khaled Nezzar, one of the leaders of the 1992 military coup and former Algerian minister of defence, was visiting France in 2001 to publicise his new book on Algeria, a French court opened an inquiry against him—at the request of relatives of victims—for torturing detainees. Nezzar left France when the inquiry was dropped.*

Successive elections in Algeria, all designed to promote the idea that the country remained "democratic" despite the control of the military, threw up in 1999 another relic of the FLN nomenklatura, Abdelaziz Bouteflika, as president. Bouteflika's policy of "working for peace and civil concord" produced a Saddamite 98.3 per cent of the vote—a statistic that went unchallenged in the West—and he survived even widespread demonstrations when a Berber revolt in Tizi-Ouzou turned into a social insurrection against poverty and corruption. He wanted Algerians to forget what they had done to each other—and, by implication, what the government had done to them—and enjoy prosperity after the military had chosen seven prime ministers and four presidents since 1992. But the evidence of Algeria's "dirty war" built up against the regime.

When former Algerian Special Forces Lieutenant Habib Souaïda published *La Sale guerre*—"The Dirty War"—in Paris in 2001, the sky should have fallen. It was the first time an officer had allowed his full name—and his photograph—to appear in the press. "I've seen colleagues burn a 15-year-old child alive," Lt. Souaïda wrote. "I've seen soldiers massacre civilians and claim their crimes were committed by terrorists. I've seen colonels murder suspects in cold blood. I've seen officers torture Islamists to death. I've seen too many things. I can no longer keep silent." He gave names, dates and locations—in the forlorn hope that there might one day be war crimes trials against those responsible. The Italian judge Ferdinando Imposimato wrote in the preface that "there has always been a hidden centre of power in Algeria . . . It has locked up society, it has liquidated opponents . . . "

There could be no more damning evidence against the regime. The French knew it was true—just as British readers of *The Independent* knew that the Algerians who bravely spoke to us had told the truth—but it was like the truth behind the 2003 Iraq War. The lies and the misinformation and the grotesque exaggerations and deliberate distortions were fully understood by those who cared to know—and in Europe, at least, they were in the majority—but the "official" world ignored the evidence. "Official" France did not respond to Lt. Souaïda's revelations. "Official" France went on supporting the Algerian regime—as the U.S. administration did, as the EU did. "Official" Britain saw no "credible or substantive evidence" of army involvement in the massacres.

In 2004, Amnesty International appealed for an investigation into the discovery of at least twelve mass graves found in Algeria since 1998, the latest of them on 29 July, "to establish the truth about these killings." The world ignored Amnesty's appeal. At the same time, U.S. Special Forces began operations in the

---

*On 16 December 2004, an investigator approved by the Algerian government admitted that Algerian security force members were believed to have killed 5,200 civilians. ". . . individually, agents of the state carried out these illegal acts," Farouk Ksentini said. "The war was terrible and there were excesses. But the state itself has not committed any crime." Two weeks later, Ksentini told Reuters that "agents of the state" had "disappeared" 6,146 civilians.

southern Algerian deserts against al-Qaeda—alongside their Algerian opposite numbers. The very men who were suspected of crimes against humanity were now working with the Americans to hunt down those responsible for crimes against humanity. This military cooperation, the Pentagon declared, was part of "the war on terror."

CHAPTER FIFTEEN

# Planet Damnation

... war began, that is, an event took place opposed to human reason and to human nature. Millions of men perpetrated against one another such innumerable crimes, frauds, treacheries, thefts ... incendiarisms, and murders, as in whole centuries are not recorded in the annals of all the law courts of the world, but which those who committed them did not at the time regard as being crimes.

—Leo Tolstoy, *War and Peace*

CURLED UP IN THE EXTRA CREW SEAT, snug in the womb-like flight deck of the 707, lights down, the night a pageant of stars, the air-conditioning hushing through the vents, I look down onto the hot, darkened desert of Saudi Arabia as the fireflies zip past us. White, yellow, streaking gold, they flick around us at almost a thousand miles an hour—their maximum speed and ours in opposite directions—or they glide below us, mimicking our own progress east. The voices in my cans are bored, tired, sometimes irritated men with the accents of Texas, of Cairo, Gloucestershire and the Hejaz.

"Mike two zero zero five." A Midwest voice from out of the great black globe, desperately seeking guidance from a Saudi ground controller. "Requesting higher level to technical area." Hushhhhhhhh, the air conditioner breathes. The Middle East Airlines pilot turns and grins at me. "He wants to climb en route to the Dhahran air base—I bet the Saudis turn him down." Hushhhhhhhh. "No higher level available." A Saudi voice, heavy accent bringing up the "b" in "available," turning information into an order. Hushhhhhhhh. The 707 crew burst into laughter. "What did you expect?" The American: "Say again? Say again?" More laughter. The stewardess, her gold MEA uniform turned to hospital white in the dim cockpit light, hands me a glass of champagne. "Thought you might need it, Robert," the Lebanese pilot says. "You're going to be here for a long time, I think."

I sip from the cold glass. Champagne. France. Paris. Boulevards. And I look to the north, up into the darkness to where—as they say—"civilisation" began, to where the ancient Euphrates and Tigris join and curdle their way to the Gulf, and towards that preposterously rich little emirate into which the descendants of all those Sumerians and Umayyads and Seljuks and Abbasids and—yes, I suppose—the Mongols had just arrived with their T-72 tanks, their ZSU-23 tracked, mobile, radar-guided anti-aircraft guns, their Scuds and 155s and their Kalashnikovs and

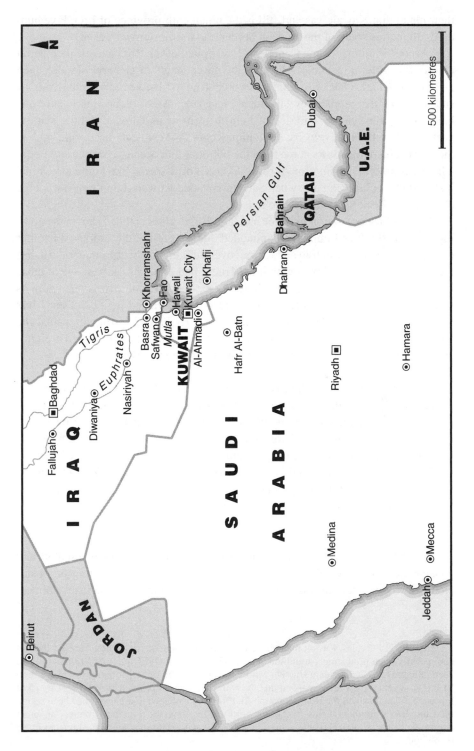

their claim that Kuwait was and still is the nineteenth province of Iraq. Five hundred kilometres south of the Kuwaiti border, the fireflies grow thicker.

"Ascot." Plummy, Home Counties. How typical of the Brits to code their aerial call to arms after a racetrack. Here are the descendants of General Maude's men and Private Charles Dickens's comrades preparing to liberate more Arabs from the successors of the people they "liberated" in 1917. "Ascot requesting twenty-one hundred." A tiny yellow pinprick of light in front of us flares, dazzling, spitting past us at Darth Vader velocity. "See him, Robert?" Yes, I saw him, and I look at the radar screen that glows at me from the bottom of an ocean-green sea and I espy a happy little blip heading for Akrotiri. Even Cyprus seems like home now. I had just started a holiday in Paris when Saddam invaded Kuwait. I don't even want the champagne. Fuck Saddam, I say to myself.

The old Fisk prediction machine had failed. The glass ball had shown me nothing back in Beirut as I impatiently pounded out my pre-holiday stories of another childish dispute between Iraq and Kuwait over oil theft and overproduction. Hadn't Kuwait funded Saddam's war with Iran? True, I had asked in 1988, in one of those interminable centre-pagers that the *Times* editors liked to consume when conflicts ended, how Saddam now intended to employ his hardened legions. Then I had moved to *The Independent* and returned to the Hizballah's struggle against the Israeli occupation of Lebanon and the first Palestinian intifada. I stuffed photocopies of my last reports into my bag before I boarded the MEA flight:

> *The Independent*, July 19th, 1990. By Robert Fisk, Beirut. Kuwait's rulers responded with alarm yesterday to Iraq's renewed threats against them, calling an emergency meeting of parliament and dispatching the Kuwaiti foreign minister to appeal for help from Saudi Arabia ... According to Tareq Aziz, the Iraqi foreign minister, Kuwait had "violated" the Kuwaiti–Iraqi frontier and stolen oil worth $2.4 billion ... Kuwait was cheating on the OPEC oil production quota system, he said, "in a premeditated and deliberate plan to weaken Iraq and undermine its economy and security."*

Premeditated. Deliberate. The Plot. The Baath party machine fed on plots and conspiracies, it wolfed them down, unforgiving, its appetite feeding on suspicion. Kuwait was committing "economic sabotage" against Iraq, Saddam claimed.

---

*Under OPEC rules, Kuwait maintained a production quota of 1.5 million barrels a day but had recently been producing 1.9 million barrels. The favoured OPEC price of $18 a barrel had been falling to $14 and Saddam Hussein was claiming that a fall of $1 per barrel would cost Iraq $1 billion a year in lost revenue—and that the collapse in world prices had so far cost Iraq $14 billion. No one disputed the overproduction. But the Iraqis alleged that Kuwait had been taking oil from Iraq's southern fields by boring northwards along their mutual frontier—in other words, Kuwait was thieving the resources of the nation whose war machine saved it from Iran's revolution.

I only have to read my own reports to see how stupid I was to set off for my Paris vacation. Fisk on 19 July, filing out of Beirut, I now note with remorse, had all the clues. "President Saddam Hussein spoke . . . of a 'last resort' against his neigh-bours, adding that 'cutting necks' was better than cutting standards of living." Iraq faced foreign debt repayments of between $30 and $40 billion. None of the Gulf states, I added, "believe that the United States would interfere militarily to protect them from Iraq. At present, there are only seven American warships in the Gulf." And that, we now know, is what Saddam believed, too. And so I flew off to Paris to be in the wrong place at the right time. Wasn't I the same guy who'd been told the Israelis would invade West Beirut in September 1982, that there would be mas-sacres in the camps—and then flown off to a holiday in Ireland? The Israelis wouldn't attack because Fisk was going on holiday to Ireland. Saddam wouldn't invade Kuwait because Lord Fisk was flying to Paris. 2 August 1990. "Iraqi forces have invaded Kuwait"—the BBC 8 a.m. news, just as I was heating the *pains au chocolat.*

Maybe we had all fallen under Saddam's spell—or Washington's spell—in those last critical days before the invasion. Even after all Saddam's threats against Kuwait, the Americans still thought of the Iraqi dictator as "their" man. Asked in an interview just four days before the invasion whether Saddam's threats were not like those of Hitler on the eve of the Second World War, Richard Murphy, the former U.S. assistant secretary of state for Near Eastern affairs, scorned such remarks as "too glib." Saddam, he said, "is a rough, direct-talking leader who has not hesitated to use force . . . I think it needs a constant dialogue with the Iraqis . . . he acted out of frustration." Murphy's interview came four days *after* America's ambassador in Baghdad, April Glaspie, held her notorious meeting with Saddam in which she remarked that the dispute was "an Iraqi–Kuwaiti matter." In later testimony to the U.S. Senate Foreign Relations Committee, Glaspie suggested that the Iraqi tran-script of this conversation had been doctored and that, after taking a call from President Mubarak of Egypt, Saddam had returned to their meeting and "promised not to use force, but to act within the diplomatic framework he had set up."

As usual, all the portents of disaster were there, had we, journalists as well as diplomats—Arab as well as Western—chosen to read them. A Bahraini minister would later admit to me that even he failed to realise the significance of the Iraqi leader's words at an Arab summit less than three months before the invasion:

> The first sign of what Saddam Hussein was going to do was shown by him at the Baghdad summit in May . . . In a closed session of the summit, Sad-dam showed a signal that he was agitated at the state of his economy. "The drop in the price of oil is crippling us," he said. He said he could not sur-vive if oil prices stayed where they were. I was there and we heard him say this, but we didn't realise what it meant. It was King Hussein [of Jordan] who said in public that *his* country was desperate for economic help and that he needed economic assistance—that is what the world remembers. But they did not hear what Saddam Hussein said.

Within twenty-four hours of Saddam's invasion, King Fahd of Saudi Arabia took the "historic decision"—this was the Saudi expression for such an unprecedented step—to invite the Americans to enter the land of Islam's two holiest cities, Mecca and Medina, to defend the kingdom. Arab Gulf ministers and businessmen believed that Fahd would, at most, ask for American air cover if his own over-equipped and under-trained forces had to defend Saudi Arabia, and that the Saudis would fund Arab guerrillas to assist Kuwaiti resistance to the Iraqi occupation, just as it had bankrolled Osama bin Laden's Arab army against the Soviets in Afghanistan. But bin Laden's offer of help was spurned—with what fateful consequences we might only imagine. After four decades of humiliation at the hands of Israel—America's greatest ally in the Middle East—the Arabs would now watch these same Americans arrive on their sacred soil to "defend" them from another Arab leader. If King Fahd was "the custodian of the holy places," the 82nd Airborne was now the custodian of "the custodian of the holy places." To many Arabs, this sounded like blasphemy.

In these early, boiling days of August, I went—as I so often did in the Gulf—to seek the wisdom of Ali Mahmoud, the Associated Press bureau chief in Bahrain, an Egyptian who had been imprisoned under Nasser* but who possessed a dark prescience when it came to human folly in the Arab world. "No matter what the outcome, the harm is done," he said. "The fact that the theocratic and nationalist regimes have invited the United States to the Middle East will long be resented and will never be condoned. When this crisis is over, the worst is yet to come." And six years later, in Afghanistan, I would remember Ali's words as bin Laden listed for me, one by one, the historical sins of the House of Saud.

Saddam's subsequent behaviour—his offer to withdraw from Kuwait if the Israelis withdrew from the occupied Palestinian territories, his seizure of thousands of foreign hostages in Iraq and Kuwait, his formal annexation of the emirate—appeared in the West to be a policy of naivety and illusion. But in the Arab world—to which Saddam was primarily addressing himself—it did not necessarily look like this. For Arabs, the Israeli occupation of Palestinian land was as great an enormity—and far longer-lasting—as Iraq's occupation of Kuwait, where the occupiers were at least Arabs.[†]

The television pictures of thousands of U.S. troops pouring from their aircraft amid the sandstorms of north-eastern Saudi Arabia would later become one of the

---

*Mahmoud was a political dissident as well as an AP reporter in Nasser's Egypt. He would always wear a broad smile when he recalled the experience of being questioned by police torturers while suspended by his feet above a vat of lukewarm human faeces in Cairo's Citadel prison.

[†]This was fully understood by Western oil analysts whose carefully argued if essentially dull studies made the same point. "Most Arabs are convinced that the U.S. intervention in the region is not motivated by a desire to uphold international law," Robert Mabro wrote in October 1990. "They would have dearly liked the U.S.A to play this role in the region, to play it in Palestine and in Lebanon as it is now claiming to do in Kuwait. But the U.S.A's consistent failure over decades to uphold international law when Israel's policies and actions are involved leaves very deep doubt in the Arab mind about the true motivations on this occasion."

most tedious images of the crisis, but in those first days of August 1990 the arrival of the 82nd Airborne and other American troops at Dhahran—about 1,100 kilometres from Mecca and over 300 kilometres from forward elements of the Iraqi invasion force—was the biggest and least-covered story in the world. A visa to the kingdom normally took weeks to obtain; in a secretive, xenophobic oligarchy like Saudi Arabia, which hid the Iraqi invasion from its own citizens for at least twenty-four hours, no state official would dream of allowing foreign journalists to witness an infidel force moving into so sacred a land.*

Which is how I came to be hunched in the cockpit of MEA's scheduled 707 flight to Dhahran. Joe Kai, one of the airline's Beirut station staff and among its smartest managers, realised that even without a visa, an MEA passenger had transit rights through Saudi Arabia—providing he held a ticket with an onward connection to another Arab Gulf state. So he booked me via Saudi Arabia to the small Gulf emirate of Bahrain—and helped *The Independent* to scoop the world. I would have exactly five hours on the ground at Dhahran. "You'll see the Americans, *habibi*," Joe announced. "They'll be all over the place."

They were. As my MEA flight touched down in Saudi Arabia, I could see dozens of American Bell/Agusta helicopter gunships clustered under the airbase arc lights, their rotor-blades tied back like fans, packed tight like a giant nest of insects, midnight black, awaiting transport north. A row of Galaxies was disgorging more helicopters and piles of white-tipped missiles. A desert-brown Hercules C-130, propellers throbbing, was loading up with missiles for its journey northwest towards the Saudi airfields near the border. Inside the terminal, the Saudis flicked through my passport, glanced without interest at my Bahrain ticket and told me to wait in the lounge.

And as Joe said, they were all over the place, all those American crews of the U.S. 3rd Airlift Squadron with shoulder flashes which said "Safe, Swift, Sure." Here we were, apparently on the brink of war, a Christian army landing in Islam's most sensitive bit of real estate, with a message that had more to do with supermarket delivery times than theology. All this was quite lost on the clean-cut young men and women who stood on the tarmac, gazing east to watch another big Lockheed C-5B howl in from the dawn sky. Every fifteen minutes, the Galaxies arrived, their wheels shrieking under their load of Cobra gunships, their sinister 30-metre wings flopping and bouncing like old birds as they touched down in the desert heat.

The Americans were cheerful, happy to talk, not at all fazed that a journalist had found them injecting their thousands of troops and choppers into Saudi Ara-

---

*As usual when we needed visas, they were not forthcoming. If the Saudis wanted to invite journalists to an Arab conference, however, their embassies were ready to issue us with entry permits within hours. When we wished to avoid these tiresome events, we merely declined to fill in the question in the visa application which asked for our religion. The Saudis would then assume that we were Jewish—and, abiding by their own outrageous and racist policy, decline to issue us with a visa.

bia. U.S. Air Force Major Curt Morris was waiting for the bus that would take him back to his Galaxy. "We stayed at a real nice hotel in town. We ate some good Arabic food last night. Yeah, we enjoyed it. And it's been cool the last couple of days." He smiled a lot. "In a couple of days, we'll be back in your country—at Mildenhall—we're looking forward to that." Tourism. Cool weather, exotic food, home to southern England. On the other side of the airbase, Egyptian troops were filing down the steps of an Egyptair 737, the kind that normally takes holidaymakers to Luxor.

The Saudis, at least, appeared to understand the ironies of the events that they were witnessing. Their airport militiamen were equipped with coal-black gas masks with little eyeholes. "America says she has come to protect us," one of them—a thin young man with a pencil moustache—said to me as we watched an RAF transport aircraft land out of the dawn, "Would America have come to protect us if we had no oil?" I knew the answer, with the same certainty that Major Morris brought to his optimism. The Saudi policemen and soldiers I would meet in the coming months were no fools; if they were not university graduates, their religion taught them enough to exercise the greatest concern—if not downright suspicion—towards the dangerous leap of imagination that the American arrival in their country represented.

American, Egyptian and Moroccan troops—from this very early stage, the U.S. forces managed to acquire religious camouflage from the most loyal of their Arab allies—were already being housed in makeshift camps far out in the desert. The border town of Khafji had been partly evacuated and turned into a barracks. So had Hafr al-Batn, the lorry-park town farther west where the territory of Saudi Arabia runs along the frontier of Iraq itself, whose airbase and residence blocks, built back in 1985 at a cost of $5 billion, could house 70,000 soldiers. So had the local Aramco oil workers' camp. Major Morris stood next to a tall, blond female soldier, her hair in a chignon, another item of American culture with which to shock the Saudis. "I sure don't want to think what will happen if our people have to wear their anti-gas clothes when the heat really gets up," Morris said. "Oh boy, I tell you, people will die of heat-stroke in those things."

When my Gulf Air flight took off for Bahrain after dawn, I could see that the whole of the Dhahran airbase had been surrounded by batteries of silver-and-white missiles. From my passenger seat, I shot several pictures of the lines of Galaxies and their brood of helicopters. History in the Middle East was moving too quickly to be grasped. Was it like this, I wondered—and these were parallels of surprise rather than scale—when the British went to war in 1914? We had no idea then what chaos the imperial powers of Europe would visit upon themselves. Who would have thought, just a fortnight ago, that Kuwait would disappear, that the British and Americans would be holding the line against Iraq in the sands upon which the Prophet Mohamed walked, that their battle, when it was joined, would lead them all the way—thirteen years later—to the most dangerous conflict the Middle East had witnessed since the fall of the Ottoman empire?

From Bahrain, I hitched a ride over the Gulf with my old mates among the

U.S. television network crews with whom, only a few years earlier, I had patrolled the hot, fish-crowded waters when Iraq was our friend, when Iraq could attack an American warship and get away with it. Only two years ago, I reflected as our little white commercial aircraft buzzed over the soft waves with their shoals of flying fish, Saddam was still our friend, still the "rough, direct-talking leader" who he was to remain until he decided to steal Kuwait. Only a few months earlier, when Mubarak had packed a bunch of senators off to see Saddam, they had agreed that the Iraqi dictator's real problem was with the press. Much laughter. Yes, Saddam needed a public relations consultant. But now the PR men were employed by the Kuwaiti royal family and by the overweight commander of the Saudi "Allied Joint Forces Commander," his Royal Highness Prince Khaled bin Sultan bin Abdul Aziz, nephew of King Fahd and son of Prince Sultan, the Saudi defence minister.

Across the gently-moving waves we flew, over motorised dhows whose symmetry and curved prows demonstrated the fragility of another age and culture. But even travelling at more than 100 miles an hour above the water, the perspiration ran in streams down our faces and backs. After five or six hours in 130 degrees of heat, the sea and the sky became a yellow-grey fog in which only the sun retained its faded gold. How could anyone contemplate a war in this natural oven? The evidence was there. One hundred kilometres out of Dubai, we found the French frigate *Commandant Ducuing* taking on supplies from a freighter, a giant tricolour heaving from her stern, her deck-crew huddled around an anti-aircraft gun. The water played sunlight off its hull number—F795—and then it was lost in the mist. Turn 180 degrees in the haze and there is the *Ducuing* again, making steam, propellers frothing the grey sea green.

Through the humidity glided other reminders of the Iraqi invasion to the northwest, empty oil tankers heading east out of the Gulf, a natural contradiction, since they should head west empty and leave east heavy with Kuwaiti crude, their Plimsoll line beneath the surface. The *T. M. Regulus* of Singapore, miserably high in the water, showing its rust-red hull, lay at anchor in the fog; even the old Kuwaiti tanker *Chesapeake City*, which—reflagged as an American tanker—had been a symbol of America's protection from Iranian "aggression" in the tanker war only two years earlier, was riding the swell off Bahrain. In the banks of mist, we even found a cargo ship, its hold and decks piled high with Toyotas, yet more luxuries for the richest emirate in the Gulf, now fleeing for Hormuz and the open seas. The good days were over.

Save for the few Western journalists marooned in Kuwait itself—Tony Walker of the *Financial Times* was among them and emerged across the desert with a powerful story of brutality and fear*—the world's reporters now filed from Bagh-

---

*Many were the brave expatriates—and Kuwaitis—who escaped their Iraqi captors. George Woodberry, the British temporary Securicor operations director in Kuwait, had approached the border in his four-by-four only to find 50 Iraqi tanks lined up in front of him. "We couldn't see them until we were on top of the dune and by then it was too late to turn round," he told us. "So

dad or from the uninvaded cities of the Arab Gulf. From there, we tried to leaven the propaganda war with question marks, little hand grenades of doubt that might prompt the reader to ask as many questions as we did in the long dry evenings of steak and orange juice in Saudi Arabia. Kidnappers in Lebanon had long demanded the release of seventeen Shia Muslims imprisoned in Kuwait in return for American hostages, including my old friend Terry Anderson, AP's bureau chief in Beirut. Two of the fifteen had been freed. All were members of the Islamic Dawa party. Had Iraq liberated the other fifteen? Answer: no, they had escaped. Thirteen years later, the Dawa would become a political party in "liberated" Iraq, demanding elections from the Americans who seemed oblivious to the fact that the Dawa members to whom they politely talked had been the "super-terrorists" of the 1980s. Diplomats said that Palestinians living in Kuwait had connived with the Iraqi intelligence service, supplying them with the home addresses of Kuwaiti officials prior to the invasion. Was the PLO helping Saddam to occupy Iraq? Answer: No, because some Palestinians even joined the slowly forming Kuwaiti resistance movement. But Iraqi-trained Palestinians had later been brought down from Baghdad and could be seen with guns on the streets of Kuwait. And what an opportunity this presented for the now-exiled Kuwaiti royal family—who could one day return to their emirate and demand the expulsion of the 300,000 Palestinian "traitors," some of whom had been born there. Which is what they did.

The Syrians sent a brigade of soldiers to join the Americans in Saudi Arabia, the "Vanguard of the Arab Nation" now aligning itself with the friends of Zionism—or so it seemed—against their Baathist enemies. And every day, the network crews and hundreds of other television teams from around the world were bussed out to the Dhahran airbase—to the same runways I had surveyed immediately after the invasion—to watch the Americans arrive, companies and battalions and regiments and brigades and divisions, tens of thousands of them to augment an army that would—by the new year of 1991—place half a million men and women against Saddam's armies. In 1991 the United States thought it needed this many soldiers to liberate Kuwait. In 2003 the Pentagon calculated they would need less than half that number to capture and occupy the whole of Iraq. But in 2003, nobody made that comparison.

If it wasn't statistics we got, it was advice. RAF officers coaxed journalists on how to don their gas masks. They advised us to use the "buddy-buddy" system, whereby you helped your fellow scribe to fit the filter onto his mask but ensured your own was fitted first—while your colleague presumably suffocated to death.

---

we drove on between them with tanks 40 yards on each side of us. We didn't wave or say anything, we just kept driving. The tank crews were just standing there, watching us . . . " Woodberry described occupied Kuwait where "the place has stopped working. The Iraqi soldiers bang on people's doors demanding money and food. Every shop has been looted. The Palestinians looted as well as the Iraqis—Palestinians who had lived there for years. There are safes and strongboxes lying in the streets where people dragged them out to break them open. There's not a shop or an office in the centre of the city which hasn't been cleaned out by the looters."

The whole wretched business involved "hunkering down"—a phrase I suspect the military got from the press—while gallons of Saddam's vile cocktail clouded around us. A visit to the French Foreign Legion—red wine in the desert seemed a lot more sensible than a British ration of lukewarm water—convinced me that there were simpler methods of avoiding chemical extinction. A British member of the Legion's Second Infantry Regiment from the East End of London told me that his unit—battle honours included the Marne—had its own unique operational instructions. "Basically," he said, "when there's a red gas alert, someone blows a whistle and we all pile on our lorries and drive like fuck out of the area."

This seemed to me eminently sensible. For more prosaic advice, we could turn to the *Saudi Gazette*, the newspaper that failed to inform its readers that 100,000 Iraqi troops had invaded Kuwait, shot the Emir's brother and were standing on the borders of Saudi Arabia. "Do's and don'ts in a gas attack," read the headline—on page 3. This was to be one of the world's most exclusive doctors' advice columns, one that turned out to say as much about Saudi Arabia as it did about chemical warfare. And those who remembered that King Fahd had that very year laid responsibility for the death of more than 1,400 Muslim pilgrims in Mecca on "God's will" would have found the initial advice faintly familiar.

"If you are outside your home and in the open, you cannot do anything except to accept your destiny," the article announced. If you were at home, on the other hand, "look out your windows for birds dropping from the trees, cats, dogs and people dropping and choking, cars crashing and general panic which are all signs of a gas attack. When you see such things happen, barricade doors and windows and let nobody in or out of the house." Other helpful hints included the advice to "dress yourself to the hilt in long sleeves, socks and hat . . . cover your entire head with a wet towel or blanket . . . get into the shower and stay there."\* But the *Saudi Gazette* was not a paper to frighten its readers. Its front page on 4 August 1990 contained a single, curious paragraph in bold type. "King Fahd and Bush exchanged views on the situation in the region in the light of current developments," it said. That was the paper's sole concession to reality. The "current development" was the Iraqi *anschluss* of Kuwait.

The Americans were given cultural assistance. Some were eminently sensible: don't drink alcohol, don't show any interest in Arab women, don't lose your temper. Others betrayed the real problems of America's Middle East policy. The American army's official guide to Saudi Arabia included a section headed "Sensitive areas" which urged U.S. personnel not to discuss "articles or stories which discuss the friendship ties between the U.S. and Israel," "anti-Arab demonstrations or sentiment in the U.S." or "support for Israeli actions and presence [!] in Lebanon." The fact that this military guide could not even refer to Israel's invasions or occupation in those words suggested that these subjects were even more "sensitive" for the Pentagon than they might have been for Arabs—who *could* dis-

---

\*Washing continuously in a shower was good advice for victims of a gas attack; the hat was an exotic addition unless it was an enclosed hood.

cuss them. An earlier volume instructed U.S. personnel to avoid discussion of the "Jewish lobby and U.S. intelligence given to Israel"—a category that was meekly deleted by the Pentagon after the World Jewish Congress wrote to U.S. defence secretary Dick Cheney to express its "sense of distress" and "deep sense of hurt and anger" that U.S. troops were being asked to "submerge entirely those values of tolerance, pluralism, and open-mindedness that have made the U.S. a unique democratic society." The Jewish lobby thus succeeded in erasing all discussion of the Jewish lobby.

American soldiers were also urged to remember that "the Prophet Mohamed, founder of the Islam [sic] religion, was born in Arabia in 570 AD . . . That fact has had a deep impact on Saudi Arabia, making it the recognized center of the Islamic religion." I came across the Saudi version of this "guidance" late one night when I was travelling back to Dhahran from a visit to the Kuwaiti border and stopped at a petrol station. A Saudi army truck pulled up and two soldiers walked over to my car. "Sir, we want you to have these," one of them said, handing me two pamphlets produced in English by the "World Assembly of Muslim Youth" and published by the "Islamic Dawa'a and Guidance Centre" in Dammam. The first document was entitled The Sword of Islam and claimed that the mere shine of this sword "eliminates falsehood just like light wipes away darkness." It included a series of quotations from Westerners who had converted to Islam, including Cat Stevens—who was to be refused entry to the United States in 2004 on the totally false suspicion that he was involved in "terrorism"—whose name was now Yusuf Islam. "It will be wrong to judge Islam in the light of the behaviour of some bad Muslims who are always shown on the media," the pamphlet quoted Stevens as saying. "It is like judging a car as a bad one if the driver of the car is drunk . . . " The second pamphlet urged foreigners—"atheist or . . . agnostic . . . or a believer in democracy and freedom"—to study the life and teachings of the Prophet.

"We give these to the Americans," the Saudi soldier told me. A tall, thin man with a goatee beard, he saluted and turned back to his lorry. It was an American truck, of course, and they were carrying American Kevlar helmets and were under American command. Indeed, it seemed to be the fate of so many Muslims to live under this Western "canopy." It is an irony that the Saudis—like the Iranians— have to live in a country of American-built expressways and toll booths, of U.S.-built airbases where the helicopters and fighter-bombers are American, that they have to live in nations whose infrastructure is American, whose princes—or, in the case of Iran, revolutionaries—were in many cases educated in the United States and speak English with American accents. So when in the days immediately following the Iraqi invasion, President George Bush explained that his military deployment in Saudi Arabia was also intended to "safeguard the American way of life"—and he presumably wasn't thinking of theocracy and Saudi head-chopping—he may have had a point.

But Saudi Arabia did not wear only American clothes. The country was awash with British hardware—including more aircraft than the Saudis had qualified pilots to fly—thanks to the 1988 $23 billion Al-Yamamah arms contract which included the sale of 132 Tornado and Hawk aircraft and commissions which were allegedly given to British middlemen as well as members of the Saudi royal family. The British National Audit Office was to launch an investigation into this folly in 1989 but its report was officially suppressed—to avoid upsetting the Saudis, according to the British government. The prime minister, Margaret Thatcher, had been personally involved in the project to prevent French and American competition.

Oil, of course, had nothing—absolutely nothing—to do with the deployment of American troops in Saudi Arabia. If General H. Norman Schwarzkopf's contention boded ill for those who feared that rhetoric and reality were parting company in the Middle East, it had to be said that the general made his claim with real imagination. As supreme United States commander in the Gulf, he used language with the subtlety of a tank.

"Absolutely not," he roared at me when I was gullible enough to suggest that America's enthusiasm to defend Saudi Arabia might have something to do with petroleum. "I don't know why people keep bringing this up. I really don't. If anyone has any question in their mind about what Iraq has done, I suggest they look for another line of work. What you've got here is a situation where not only is this a mugging—but a rape has occurred." The American television crews had switched the cameras and sound recorders back on. Here was a general who not only talked in soldiers' language—or what television crews thought was soldiers' language—but obligingly spoke in sound bites, too. "It is an international rape of the first order," he boomed on. "We all 'tsk-tsk' when some old lady is raped in New York and twenty-four people know about it and do nothing . . . it's not just a question of oil. There's not a single serviceman out there who thinks that—not any I've met."

So all that history of American support for Saddam—for his invasion of Iran, his chemical assaults on Iranians and Kurds, Washington's blind eye to the torture chambers and the mass graves, all that "tsk-tsking" in the face of atrocities which the whole world knew about and did nothing about—didn't happen. History started yesterday. It was time I looked for "another line of work." Those of us who had met scarcely a serviceman who did *not* think this was about oil would have to hold our tongues in future. When we asked the general why America had not used its troops to prevent the mugging and rape of other Middle Eastern nations, we were told not to be hypothetical.

General Schwarzkopf, a giant of a man with a barrel chest and a head the shape of an American football, loved all this. He, after all, was the general who'd served two combat tours in Vietnam, the second as 1st Battalion commander in the unhappy "Americal" Infantry Division whose units—not under Schwarzkopf's command—were responsible for the My Lai massacre, a man who held fourteen military awards including the Distinguished Service Medal, three Silver Stars, the Legion of Merit, the Distinguished Flying Cross and two Purple Hearts. No one asked about his dad, of course, the other Norman Schwarzkopf who helped to destroy Iranian democracy in 1953, along with Kermit Roosevelt and "Monty" Woodhouse. Iraqi morale? he was asked. "Jesus, I hope it's lousy! I hope they're hungry. I hope they're thirsty and I hope they're running out of ammunition . . . I think they're a bunch of thugs." Any chance he thought the Iraqis would still invade Saudi Arabia? "The difference is we're here now. If they fight, they're going to have to fight me. It's not a question of taking on some weak neighbour." Mistake. The Saudis didn't want to be regarded as a "weak neighbour." They were strong, confident, able to defend themselves. Was not Lieutenant General Prince Khaled bin Sultan bin Abdul Aziz the commander of the "joint forces"?

And indeed, as we delved through the military jungle that was entangling the Gulf, we discovered that in the month since U.S. forces started their deployment, not a single American tank crew or gunner had been permitted to test-fire their weapons. The Saudi authorities had refused to allow the Americans even to calibrate their guns—for fear that the sound might alarm the civilian population. Even the megalithic battleship USS *Wisconsin*, whose nine sixteen-inch guns could fire shells over more than 30 kilometres, was constrained to announce the time of its live-firing exercises to prevent panic on the Gulf coastline. At some points in the eastern desert, the U.S. 24th Infantry Division had to reposition its tanks lest their tracks damage camel-grazing fields.

If the Saudis could temporarily emasculate the United States military, the Iraqi army was undergoing an interesting psychological transformation of its own. When it invaded Kuwait on 2 August, it was a million-strong, "battle-hardened" army which had "polished its offensive capability," a "powerful battle force." Now, however, Saudi and American officers drew inspiration from the stories of Kuwait's wretched refugees; Iraqi troops were looting shops and homes, there had been rape and disciplinary hangings. British officers talked of the Iraqi army as a "shambles" with poor morale. "As far as we are concerned," the captain of the British destroyer *York* told us, "there's far too much hype about chemical warfare." Yet by the beginning of November, the *Desert Shield Order of Battle Handbook* prepared by the U.S. Deputy Chief of Staff for Intelligence was again describing the Iraqi army as "one of the best-equipped and most combat experienced in the world . . . distinguished by its flexibility, unity of command and high level of mobility."

Maybe it depended on the audience. When General Colin Powell, chairman of the Joint Chiefs of Staff—the same supposedly liberal, thoughtful, eloquent secretary of state in the Bush Junior administration a decade later—addressed marines aboard the *Wisconsin* on 14 September, he talked down to U.S. servicemen. Saddam was "this joker we've got up here in Baghdad," to whom the world had said: "We can't have this kind of crap any longer." If somebody wanted to fight the United States, Powell instructed his men, "kick butt." The Palestinians in Kuwait were meanwhile further denigrated by Alan Clark, the British junior minister, who claimed in Bahrain that they had created an "informal militia" in Kuwait. Many Palestinian "residents," he claimed—untruthfully as it turned out—had "helped themselves to firearms."

In Dhahran the flight line was witness to every arrival, to the thousands of young Americans who clambered down the aircraft ramps clutching plastic bottles of water, stunned by the temperatures, suddenly realising that they had just met their first enemy, right here on the tarmac. Some wound scarves over their faces, wedging Ray-Bans between the scarves and their helmets so that they looked like a hundred-strong version of the Invisible Man. The airbase howled and screamed with turbine engines, with F-15s and F-16s and Galaxies and Hawks shimmering through the dust bowl beside the still untested Patriot anti-missile missiles.

Journalists became part of this military deployment. They were brought to film these constant arrivals—initially, as Schwarzkopf admitted, to give the impression that there were more U.S. troops in Saudi Arabia than was the case—and to encourage the idea that American forces represented overwhelming strength. If war was to start, journalists would be allowed to accompany troops in "pools"—and reporters and their newspapers and television stations subsequently fought like tigers to join these "pools" in which they would be censored, restrained and deprived of all freedom of movement on the battlefield. The rest were supposed to abide by the rules of Captain Mike Sherman. Though a trifle shorter than the crusty old man who burned his way through Georgia, Sherman's eyes possessed the same kind of penetrating, weary reproach that you could discover in the monochrome portraits of his ancestor, General William Tecumseh Sherman. This was not surprising because Captain Sherman commanded one of America's most powerful weapons systems in the Gulf, a great beached whale of a vessel permanently anchored in a grotesquely decorated ballroom of dreams and expectations in the Dhahran International Hotel.

Even to say that the ballroom was in Dhahran was enough to earn one of Captain Sherman's famous "letters of admonition." For there were rules aboard his ship and the journalists who enjoyed its warlike facilities were expected to obey them. "Violations of ground rules" by any of the 1,300 newspaper and television folk who had signed up to cover the war—including the identification of military bases, even Dhahran, which Iraqi pilots used during the Iran–Iraq War (though Sherman was unaware of this)—would be "dealt with on a case-by-case basis." There was something of the schoolmaster in all this, for Captain Sherman's command—officially known as the Joint Information Bureau or "JIB"—was itself an education. It provoked, confused, infuriated and misled.

In the old days, back in mid-August when war seemed closer, Sherman ran the JIB with only six military officers, corralled behind a stable-like door of the hotel. In an identical room beside them sat two representatives of the Saudi information ministry. But as America's military goals widened—as President Bush's decision to liberate Kuwait was transformed into a decision to destroy Saddam Hussein—so Captain Sherman's ship turned into a behemoth and moved upstairs, beneath a roof of giant blue and gold eggshell design, into a bigger ballroom of high-pile carpets, telephone bells, word processors, kitbags, rifles, notebooks and more information than any sane person would ever need to obtain about the mechanics of killing fellow human beings.

On the right, behind a long wooden arras, sat the representatives of the Western military alliance, thirty uniformed officers from the U.S. Marines, Army, Navy and Air Force and—new crew members aboard Sherman's hulk—a team of British defence ministry functionaries. On the other side of the ballroom, with fewer computers and more telephones, sat eighteen Saudis, each dressed in red kuffiah and white *dishdash* robe. At an isolated desk, there also sat a representative of Kuwait's government-in-exile, dispensing coloured snapshots of torture victims. Like girls and boys at dancing class, the Westerners rarely crossed the ballroom to talk to their Saudi opposite numbers. Only the journalists moved between these two cultures, perhaps 6 metres separating the power of the West from the cradle of Islam. At opposite ends of the ballroom were two massive television sets. At the Arab end, Saudi television broadcast football matches and prayers. At the U.S. end, CNN portrayed the American way of life. The Saudis much preferred CNN.

Within this emporium of war, journalists from fifty nations could seek information about Patriot missiles, arrange an overnight visit to the 82nd Airborne, set up breakfast with fighter pilots from an RAF Tornado squadron, demand to know the range of an F-15, the explosive power of a Sidewinder or the calibre of a Challenger tank barrel. They could sign up for buses and planes to take them to U.S. battleships, Egyptian armoured brigades, Syrian commandos, the U.S. 101st Infantry Division, the American 1st Cavalry or the Puerto Rico reservists. The Saudis would even escort reporters to the Hofuf camel market.

It took a few days before one realised that while this might seem exciting, there was also something very disturbing about the JIB. All the promises of military potential, the inescapable firepower, the expressions of confidence, the superiority of technique and equipment, took on a subliminal quality. For while you might learn all you wished about the squash head of a 155-mm shell or the properties of a cluster bomb, you were not permitted to dwell upon the results of its use. What happens when the shell or the Sidewinder explodes? There was much talk of "neutralising" targets and the "loss of assets" and the way in which "enemy" units would be "negativised." You might demand a visit to the British 7th Armoured Brigade, but not to a mortuary. Requests to visit medical facilities were politely granted. Ask about the body-bags arriving in Dhahran and a reporter was quietly told that his question was "morbid." For this was war without risks, war made acceptable. It was clean war—not war as hell, but war without responsibility, in which the tide of information stopped abruptly at the moment of impact. Like sex without orgasm, the USS *Jib* was easy to view, drama and entertainment suitable for all the family. If you believed in the JIB, there was nothing X-rated about the future.

It was Saddam Hussein who had cornered the market in death. The Iraqis dispensed no information about their military machine, there were no facility trips to the Republican Guard. But over the airwaves each night, it was Saddam who talked of the desert turning into a graveyard, of bones bleaching in the sun, or corpses rotting in the heat. Iraqi radio described the putrefaction of death as the ultimate cost of war for the United States, martyrdom as the highest price for Iraqi patriotism. The Americans talked about confidence, the Iraqis about worms.

But if Captain Sherman was now marketing war, we journalists were its sales-men. Observe my colleagues in the ballroom of expectation. Several of them have taken to wearing military fatigues. The man from Gannett News Service is pur-chasing military name-tags to stitch onto his clothes. A lady from the Voice of Columbia (S.C.) Television station has turned up in the JIB kitted out entirely in U.S. combat dress. Lou Fontana of WIS TV, South Carolina, wears boots camou-flaged with paintings of dead leaves, purchased for the desert at Barron's Outfit-ters. (Anyone who has glanced at a desert—even looked at a desert in a picture—will be aware that there are no leaves in the sand, no trees, no nothing.)

Behind the arras, Captain Sherman's men and women, some of them journal-ists in civilian life, feel more at home with the press than with the military. Sher-man himself is based in California and was naval adviser to the television version of Herman Wouk's *War and Remembrance*. Naval First Lieutenant Charles Hoskinson took a college major in Middle East studies but regards his true voca-tion as journalism, reporting on education and politics for *The Daily Reflector* of Greenville, North Carolina. I keep meeting marines who want to write stories. The reporters in uniform and the soldiers with journalism in their veins suggest a sym-biotic, even osmotic relationship. Half the reporters in Saudi Arabia, it seems, want to be soldiers. Half the soldiers want to be in the news business.

The rest were mouldering away in the desert, feeding on meals-ready-to-eat and copies of *Stars and Stripes* and wondering, many of them, how they came to sign up for a college education only to find themselves on the "big beach" waiting to fight a man whom many of them had never heard of until a couple of weeks before leaving home. Every time I could, I would wheedle a ride into the desert, official or unofficial, with soldiers I made friends with in Dhahran or on official junkets run by Captain Sherman and his fellow entertainers or with the French journalists who—with an admirable freedom of spirit—refused to abide by the rules and simply drove off into the sand in search of pictures and interviews with soldiers of any description, American, British, Egyptian, Kuwaiti, Syrian, Saudi, even Pakistani. Yes, the Gulf contingents contained their own Asian expatriate sol-diers, the military version of all those millions of Pakistani, Filipino, Sri Lankan and Indian maids who slaved across the Arabian peninsula for Arab masters and mistresses.

The sand was their enemy as it was ours. The sun shone like a sword and the sand invaded us. It was the same sand, hot and dry and sticky, that had prickled its way into our lives in the Iran–Iraq War, sugar-thick or fine as ground salt, brown and white and grey, clinging to the hairs in our ears, lodged between our toes, moist and scratchy between our thighs, blasted like a viscous spray into our faces, slithering up between eyelids and eyes, a wind described in P. C. Wren's *Beau Geste*, the book my dad gave me as a boy, which is "not so much a sand-storm, but a mist or fog or dust as fine as flour, filling the eyes, the lungs, the pores of the skin, the nose and throat; getting into the locks of rifles, the works of watches, defiling water, food . . . rendering life a burden and a curse."

I looked for Wilfred Owen—even the occasional Rupert Brooke—out in the desert, forgetting that Brooke was a virgin soldier and that Owen's poetry was forged in war, not in the highway supermarkets between Dhahran and Khafji where the soldiers queued for milk shakes and Cadbury chocolates and vanilla ices and stood in the forecourt with their mobile phones talking to Cedar Rapids or Bristol and bitching about the mail and the lack of booze and women and the presence of the scorpions—big snappy things that arrived at night to replace the torment of heat with the torment of freshly torn skin—and the lack of news. We played on all this, of course, we scribes. We took newspapers with us, heaps of them, and phones so that the soldiers, if we caught them on the motorway where the mobiles were in range, could call home free of charge and—when they did so—we felt their discipline and their orders slipping away as we became their friends, to whom they could disclose their fears and their loneliness and the shocking unpreparedness of soldiers who might have to go to war. How many times was I asked by marines or infantry or ambulance drivers if they could beg, borrow or buy my maps? Soldiers without maps, soldiers with no idea where they were in this ocean of grit, the sand moving at such speed over the landscape that the gales blew it in dust across Iran and Turkmenistan, staining the Mediterranean brown, heaping it up during the *khamsin* winds on my own balcony in Beirut, drifting it over Greece and southern Italy and deep into those parts of Europe that Arab invasions never reached.

There are no poets in Bravo Company of the U.S. 24th Mechanized Infantry Division. They admit that their letters home are full of boredom and descriptions of the heat. They read a bit, sleep a bit, work a lot, mostly at night when the air cools. They live in a world of oppressive silence, so that you can hear Private Andrew Shewmaker rummaging around deep inside the hot bowels of his M-1 tank. When he climbs out of the turret, he is clutching a folded sheet of brown cardboard. He leans his right elbow on the gun barrel and scuffs the glistening, sugary sand away with his left hand before sitting on the scorched outer casing of the armour. He unfolds the cardboard with great care, as if it is a love letter.

Running across it is a set of straight lines, intersecting and dividing in a series of perfectly drawn circles. Each circle possesses a name. Saturn, Pluto, Uranus, Mercury, Earth. At the top, in biro, an almost childish hand—it is Private Shewmaker's—has underlined the words "Planet Damnation." It's his idea. All you need is a dice. "I wanted to keep the guys from being bored," he says in a shy, embarrassed way. "We each start off in a spaceship from Planet Earth and have to travel far through space. At each planet—at Mars, say—we have to take on fuel. But distances are so great that we start running short. You have to try and reach just one more planet before you run out of gas and then you can refuel. The last person to keep going, he wins. The rest lose."

Private Shewmaker does not realise, I think, that he has captured the lives of his tank crew on this creased, rectangular sheet of cardboard. Isolation, the desperate need for fuel, fear of the unknown. On the tank around him, and sitting in the sand beside its tracks, Shewmaker's friends listen intently as he explains the board-game. In the eleven days since they settled into this immense, lonely planet, they have received no letters from home, no newspapers, no hot meals. Many of them have no maps. When they talk, they do so in a monologue, having thought a lot and spoken little since they arrived. On the other side of the gun barrel, Sergeant Darrin Johnson is sitting on his haunches, eyes focused on that point in the desert where the sand is so white and the blue sky so pale that the two become one. Not once does he look at you when he speaks. He has been married for just twenty days.

"Her name's Virginia, I love her. I guess there's nothing unusual about her—except that she wears blue contact lenses." The other men laugh nervously. "I've known her for ten months. She was working in Hardee's fast food when I met her. We were going to get married on my birthday on September twenty-third. I was alerted at Fort Stewart on August seventh and we both decided then to get married right away. We had the ceremony at her mom's home. Her people were there, my mother couldn't make it. I had eight or nine days with her." Sergeant Johnson was still staring at the missing horizon, his thoughts far beyond it. "She came to say goodbye to me at the airport and I'm luckier than some. There's a guy over there"—he waves his hand across the scrubland to the west—"who only had three or four hours with his new wife. He got married at lunchtime the day we left. I've written two letters to Virginia so far. What did I tell her? That I was OK and that they probably wouldn't do anything."

The "they" was Sergeant Johnson's concession to Saddam Hussein and President Bush. But what he told his young wife was a lie. "To keep her from being upset," he says. Sergeant Johnson believes that "they" will indeed "do something." "It looks like it's going to happen," he says. "But if we do have a war, I hope it's over soon. Getting wounded comes into my mind a lot. Yes, I think about it a lot. I guess I feel safe in our tank, I feel I'll survive in there. I've been in tanks for seven years and I know what it will do."

When I climb into his tank, it does not feel very safe. On one side is a worn black plastic seat—Sergeant Johnson's position to the left of the gun breech—and on the right is Private Shewmaker's platform, with his gas mask slung over the back. It is perhaps six feet from wall to wall. The thermometer on the ammunition locker reads 125 degrees. When the tank is moving, it climbs to 135. When I haul myself back out of their fragile spaceship, the men are holding their hands to their faces to shield them from the blowtorch wind. The desert here is spiked with broken, dried-up bushes. Spread out in the sand beneath their thick camouflage netting, Bravo Company's tanks look like giant, long-dead spiders whose webs have decayed and overgrown them, congealing them into the desert floor.

But there is no protection from the sand. Its grains fly into our hair like insects, into our ears and mouths and noses. When I close my jaws, I can feel the sand crunching between my teeth. When I sweat behind the tank, the perspiration leaves sand tracks down my face. Shewmaker and Johnson and their comrades are in full battledress, most of them wearing their helmets. There are no showers.

There are thin lines between cynicism and duty, between complaint and courage, lines which are not as straight as those on Private Shewmaker's board-game. Specialist Cleveland Carter from Georgia has little heart for this adventure in the Middle East. "I like the army, don't get me wrong. But I never thought I'd come here. This is none of my business—*Ay-rabs*, you know—but since I'm told to do this job, I do it. I'm a soldier. But I'd like some of those Congressmen to come out here, with all that patriotism, to feel the heat in the desert. It doesn't seem right to me. I'd rather folks paid more for their oil, than pay for their oil with my life."

The generals may be roaring for battle, but the young American soldiers I was talking to were not gung-ho for war. Sergeant Parrott, a thin, reedy tank-loader from Texas, says he is wasting his time in the desert. He joined the army for a college scholarship, not to fight in Saudi Arabia. They talk about the chances of war in few words. Private Shewmaker also joined the army to finish a college degree. "But I always wanted to be in the army, you know. I used to love all those movies. I used to watch so many films about the Second World War. I loved *Patton*, you know? I always wanted to be in tanks after that." He is twenty years old. Most of the 24th's battalion commanders are Vietnam veterans. Most of their men were five-year-olds when the war ended in Indochina.

The politics of oil have not infected them all. Johnson thinks that "if the Saudis are our friends, then we've a duty to protect them." Sergeant Jeff Eggart believes that "the Saudis needed our help, we promised it and we've got to provide it." Two of the soldiers talk about their duty to obey the president. After a while, "duty" begins to occur in all their explanations for being in the desert. They do not demonstrate any hatred towards the Iraqis. Their enemies are a little nearer. "The scorpions come out at night," Johnson says. "Dozens of them. There are snakes, too, you can see their tracks in the sand. So we can't sleep down there. We all have to sleep up here, on blankets because the metal is so hot, curled round the turret of our tank."

Two midnight-black A-10 jets fly over us, the famous—or infamous—"Tank Buster" that is supposed to protect Private Shewmaker and his friends from the Iraqi armour; clinging to the underbelly of each of the two aircraft is a yellow-painted missile. The soldiers do not even look up. "If they're ours, I don't care," Eggart says. "I know how to recognise theirs, the MiG-23s, the Mirages. But I don't think the Iraqis would use chemical weapons. I tell my wife that in my letters to her. I say that the longer this delay lasts before a war, the less chance they'll use chemicals. It's just my logic. I don't know why."

Two years ago, Private Shewmaker got engaged to his eighteen-year-old girl-friend, Heidi. "We were going to be married soon, but I had not seen her for five months when I was sent here. All I could do was call her on the phone and say goodbye. I left straight from barracks at Fort Stewart. I've written her but have no letter back yet, nothing from my Mom. I think about them at night. I sit on the tank and look at the stars. I thought up my game about the planets that way."

The tankers have neither battle experience nor prescience. Private Shewmaker and the other members of his crew seemed dulled by the heat. Shewmaker did not even have a radio on which he could listen to the BBC. "What's happening out there?" Shewmaker and Johnson and their friends chorused when I was leaving them. I told them there had been a summit between Bush and Gorbachev, about Iraq's release of some women and child hostages, about the growing tragedy of refugees on the Iraqi–Jordanian border. Just briefly, they caught sight of the outside world and their response was immediate. "Will you call my wife?" Sergeant Johnson asked. Shewmaker wanted me to phone his mother. And the other soldiers scribbled into my notebook the numbers of their families 8,000 miles away, further than any line on Shewmaker's board-game.

A few hours later, I called them. Virginia Johnson sounded very young. "I'm writing to him this very minute. Tell him I got his first letter. I write to him every day . . . " I told Eggart's family that he sent his love and needed cigarettes. Shewmaker's mother wanted to know if he was in the front line. "Can you tell me, not exactly but roughly, if he's near Kuwait?" I told her he was more than 50 miles from the Kuwaiti border. I did not tell her there was nothing but sand between him and the frontier.

Saddam could be on one of Shewmaker's planets. He holds a grotesque meeting with British hostages, pats a British child on the face and asks if he is drinking milk regularly—Saddam's public statements show an obsession with milk—and he threatens Saudi Arabia with holy war and offers free oil to Third World countries. In Washington and London, these events are treated with contempt. In Morocco there are pro-Iraqi riots. In Algeria crowds turn up for spontaneous demonstrations—always a threat in the Arab world when they are real and not the government-sponsored variety—to support Iraq. Huge murals in Algiers depict Saddam's Hussein missiles, the ones he threatens to fire at Israel—and which he *will* fire at Israel within months. Close to the Kuwaiti border, the U.S. 21st Special Operations Squadron—a supposedly secret force which has spent its time interviewing Kuwaiti refugees and whose insignia is a dust-devil emerging from a sandstorm—finds that vast areas of Kuwait City are not shown on their maps; Kuwait's recent wealth created new streets and satellite towns far faster than any cartographer could record them.

All day and all night, the great American convoys hum up the six-lane highway towards the Kuwaiti frontier with their armour and guns, troop transporters, bridge-building equipment, tanks and ammunition lorries, jeeps and petrol bowsers. A fleet of U.S. helicopters, dark green, lizard-like against the sand, follow the roads east, their loads of artillery, missiles and generators—even prefabricated buildings—slung beneath their bellies. The sheer scale of an advancing army possesses an energy and seriousness of purpose that no Hollywood director can reproduce. By late October, the multinational army was spread across the desert, the terrain now humped and distorted by thousands of armoured vehicles, command bivouacs, missile sites, encampments, camouflage-draped artillery emplacements, by fleets of bulldozers cutting revetments and bunkers into the powdered sand. The dust of a hundred new military roads hung in the air while beneath it, in the fog, sat the tens of thousands of soldiers who were supposed to be "defending"

Saudi Arabia. How much longer can Bush and Thatcher claim that's all we're doing?

So many Arab, Muslim armies now lay across the Saudi desert to create the theological foundation of our "coalition"—proof that this was not an oil-generated U.S. operation—that no sacrifice was too much for the West. When Saudi women believe that America's presence in the kingdom represents a new freedom—and demonstrate against the country's prohibition on women motorists by driving through Riyadh in their own cars—Washington stays silent as they are punished. The BBC pulls a videotape of British soldiers in the desert commemorating Remembrance Sunday on the seventy-second anniversary of the end of the First World War—lest the Saudis take offence at the sight of a Christian religious service on their Islamic soil. U.S. troops are told not to wear crucifixes or stars of David outside their uniforms.

When Israeli police shot dead nineteen Palestinian demonstrators in Jerusalem in October, Saudi and other Arab newspapers reacted to the slaughter by speaking of a "massacre"—which it clearly was. U.S. secretary of state Baker was reduced to calling it a "tragedy." Had soldiers of an Arab nation killed nineteen Jews—and how many times must one make these comparisons?—would Baker have called it a tragedy? Would anyone? The agencies would then rightly have talked of a "massacre" while the Arabs would have been reduced to pathetic appeals for "restraint"—the very same inappropriateness of response that President Bush demonstrated towards the dreadful events at the Al-Aqsa mosque in Jerusalem. There was no link at all, Baker was reduced to saying, between the "tragedy" in Jerusalem and the crisis in the Gulf. Yet the mere fact that he felt constrained to say this proved he knew it was untrue. America's most important Middle East ally had just killed (or massacred) nineteen Palestinians in Islam's third-holiest shrine while America's second most important Middle East ally—Saudi Arabia, which contained Islam's first and second holiest shrines—was encouraging America to attack the Arab armies of President Saddam. These were the double standards of the "New World Order" which President Bush was now espousing. Bush wanted to end the Iraqi occupation of Kuwait. But he was not at all keen to end the Israeli occupation of the West Bank and Gaza. The two lands were not conquered in the same way—in 1967, Israel was under attack—but how could Washington now treat the two occupations in so different a fashion?*

And how could we so easily turn our former Iraqi "allies"—the men we had so assiduously supported in their aggression against Iran—into our enemies? I was struck by this one cold night in the desert with the Queen's Royal Irish Hussars,

---

*Simple. In June and August 1980, the UN Security Council declared Israel's annexation of Jerusalem "null and void" under international law. In December 1981, the UN Security Council declared Israel's annexation of the Syrian Golan Heights "null and void" under international law. On 9 August 1990, the UN Security Council declared Iraq's annexation of Kuwait "null and void" under international law. For the third declaration—but not for the first two—the West would insist on the strict application of "international law." Arabs already knew, of course, that there was one rule of law for the Israelis, a quite different one for non-Israelis.

whose battle honours went back to one of Britain's most flamboyant disasters.*
Trooper Kevin Stevely—who had never spoken to a Saudi but had shrewdly concluded that this was about oil rather than democracy—took me out aboard his
Challenger tank amid the dunes. I liked scrambling into these personal worlds.
Travelling with him on the turret, clinging to the hatch as the beast lunged through
the sand, I discovered that Stevely commanded an entire ship. The Challenger,
with highly-tuned suspension, dipped and yawed over the desert like a great vessel, its gun barrel the prow, the stinging sand from the tracks a substitute sea-
spray, its passage as inevitable as a straight line on any navigation map. But when
the soldiers settled down at their camp fires for the night, they liked to face west,
long after the sun had gone down. Because the Iraqis—the enemy—were in the
west.

The "them" and "us" mentality was as natural as it was infectious. Ten years
ago—almost to the very day—"they," the Iraqis, were storming into the Iranian
city of Khorramshahr, cowering in the ruins of its burning houses under mortar
fire. And I had been with those Iraqis. "We" had been together then, sharing the
same dangers, hiding in the same military positions. Jon Snow and I had placed
our trust in those Iraqi commandos and "our Major" who helped to rescue the
Britons on board the *Al-Tanin* in the Shatt al-Arab river. They had been friends,
part of "us." When Jon set off on his truly perilous night-time rescue mission to the
ship, there was no doubt who "we" were. Yes, "they" had then been "we." And
now, sitting with these British soldiers, the "we" had become "they" and Trooper
Stevely was wondering if "they" would drop chemicals on "us." And no doubt, I
thought, somewhere across that great, frightening chasm of sand in front of "us"—
which in reality could be no more than 300 kilometres—were some of the veterans
of Khorramshahr, including "our Major" whom Jon and I had so profusely thanked
those ten years ago.

If we forgot the humanity of the Iraqis, it was equally easy for us to ignore the
feelings of the Saudis and the passions which "our" presence was going to unleash
in their society. Too often, in those last months before Kuwait's liberation, the
Saudis had become bit players in our drama, attendant lords who were supposed to
mouth the right words of support and loyalty towards us, and hatred of the Iraqi
leadership. When in August 1990 the defence minister, Prince Sultan bin Abdul
Aziz, insisted that no offensive would ever be mounted from Saudi territory
against "our Iraqi brothers," President Bush summoned Prince Bandar, the Saudi
ambassador in Washington, to explain this deviation from the script. Similar consternation was caused when Prince Sultan suggested in late October that while

---

*I visited the British unit on 26 October and every soldier I spoke to reminded me that as the
Light Brigade, they charged into the valley of death at Balaclava exactly a hundred and thirty-six
years and two days earlier. "It is one of the classics of British army tradition," Lt. Col. Arthur
Denaro admitted, "that we tend to celebrate defeats." True to the statistics of imperial history, 35
per cent of the Hussars were from Ireland, which is why so many of the men preparing to fight
Saddam had accents from Belfast, Derry, Dublin and Cork. Even their tanks bore the names of
Irish towns.

Iraq must withdraw from Kuwait, Saudi Arabia would support "any rightful Iraqi territorial claims" to the emirate.

In late November 1990, I took a call in my Dhahran hotel from the sheikh of a nearby mosque whom I had, from time to time over the previous months, dropped by to talk to. When I arrived at the empty school beside his mosque, the sheikh was clearly agitated about something he had been discussing with a group of bearded, middle-aged men who were sitting in white robes around a back room. I thought he wanted to discuss the prospects for war, but what he asked was: "When are the Americans leaving?"

The sheikh was no radical. His sermons, broadcast over loudspeakers from the ugly concrete minaret beside his mosque, repeated the need for calm amid crisis. They were about the Prophet's conviction that trust in God affords protection for all true believers. Even now, fifteen years later, he must remain anonymous because—despite President Bush's contention at the time that he was defending "freedom" in the Gulf—Saudi Arabia was not and is not and never will be a democracy.

"When the Americans came here, we were frightened of Saddam," the sheikh said. "But now they have been here for more than three months, and nothing has happened. Our government has said that the Americans would leave the moment this crisis was over. We believed this. We still believe this. But I think we believe this because we *want* to believe it." The sheikh had heard all the rumours. Saudi businessmen in Jeddah were quietly boasting that they had secured five-year contracts for leasing land to the U.S. military forces stationed in the kingdom. In Dhahran, the Americans were said to have taken two-year contracts on car parks, warehouses and transport facilities. Their sea-lift ships were bringing in construction equipment as well as weapons.

To outsiders—to the Americans and British—the strains within Saudi society were not obvious. Each day, the Saudi press wearily trumpeted President Bush's resolve to evict Saddam Hussein from Kuwait. When Bush visited Saudi Arabia in November 1990, local entrepreneurs took full-page advertisements in the Riyadh newspapers to extol his decision to send American forces "to preserve, protect and defend peace and freedom in this part of the world." But other, potentially far more important, messages were now being heard in Saudi Arabia.

Religious tapes were being distributed in which preachers expressed growing concern about the presence of Westerners in Islamic lands. Government-approved shops had for years handed out audio-cassettes of sermons by Muslim scholars, but Saudi police withdrew six tapes from circulation in the first three months of the U.S. deployment for their "subversive" content. Some of these newly censored sermons reminded Saudis of their country's previous relations with Iraq, when Saddam was officially regarded as the embodiment of Arab nationalism and virtue and when his cruelty—well documented in the West if greeted with silence by Western governments—was ignored by the Saudi royal family. Other tapes were fiercely critical of Saudi Arabia's allies, especially President Hafez Assad of Syria. Many hundreds of Syrian refugees from the brutally suppressed 1982 Hama uprising—when Assad's army crushed the savage Sunni Muslim revolt—now lived in Saudi Arabia and their memories had deeply influenced members of the religious hierarchy.

One preacher, Sulieman al-Owda, produced a taped sermon known as "The Fall of Nations." While ostensibly a philosophical oration on the reasons for the decay of nation-states, it identified corruption, nepotism and lack of free expression—the lack of a *shura* consultative council—as key causes of national collapse. Listeners immediately understood that he was talking about the House of Saud. Shortly after this tape was banned, King Fahd announced—for the third time in as many years—that plans for just such a council were in "their final stages." Al-Owda, who was dean of the Mohamed bin Saud University of Qassim, gave his lecture in early September 1990 and tapes of the sermon were immediately seized.*

Against this, Saudis heard only the platitudes of their own princes, the interminable promises of freedom and protection from Western leaders, and statements by those who would define Christian philosophy as a vehicle to render any future war morally acceptable. The Archbishop of Canterbury announced that it would be a "just war" while other clerics mouthed the same nonsense that would be used to launch the illegal invasion of Iraq in 2003. In 1990 the Reverend Edward Norman, the dean of chapel of Christ Church College in Canterbury, proclaimed that Iraq needed to be destroyed as a nuclear threat while sustained as "a country whose contribution to the world and Arab society could be of immense value." Soon, he wrote:

> her nuclear weapons will be in place, and Iraq has the capability to deliver them . . . Military force now, with all the admitted suffering and loss of life it will produce, is by any standards morally preferable to the loss of life which would result from a future nuclear conflict in the Middle East . . . The loss of lives in a war now will save the loss of millions of lives in a few years' time. That, surely, is a profoundly Christian conclusion . . . A society which puts material welfare and human comfort above the pursuit of higher and more durable values is not a noble prospect, and is, anyway, one that is likely to be overrun by those who actually believe in their values.

Quite apart from its uncannily identical justifications for the next war but one against Iraq, the last third of this arrogant thesis might have been uttered by Osama bin Laden.

But there was another quaint parallel to the 2003 invasion of Iraq: the unequal relationship between Washington and London. While the support expressed by Margaret Thatcher—and later John Major—for the liberation of Kuwait bore little of the grovelling, pseudo-spiritual enthusiasm of Tony Blair for the invasion of Iraq, Britain's role as an obedient servant of Washington's military decision-making was clear long before the 1991 war began. On the ground, the Anglo-

---

*This was the same Sheikh al-Owda whose release from custody bin Laden would demand when I met him in Afghanistan seven years later.

American alliance looked impressive. A 7th Armoured Brigade liaison officer was now based inside the desert tactical headquarters of General Michael Myatt, commander of the U.S. 1st Marine Expeditionary Force. Marines and British troops performed joint defence and attack exercises under the eyes of Brigadier Patrick Cordingley, the British commander. Lieutenant General Sir Peter de la Billière, the overall British commander in the Gulf, discussed and agreed to a series of offensive scenarios with Schwarzkopf in Riyadh. British tanks would play an integral role in U.S. marine offensive operations.

But the moment a conflict began, Britain would effectively lose its decision-making capability. Planning was one thing, execution quite another; national command in time of war would turn the multinational force into a shambles. Britain's position in the command-and-control chain was put most revealingly by de la Billière during a visit to Saudi Arabia by British defence secretary Tom King on 14 November, when he acknowledged the symbolic role of the Saudis and the military role of the Americans. "The commander in chief is Prince Khaled . . . his authority and that of General Schwarzkopf meets my requirements . . . for what the British services get involved in. The British ground forces and the British air forces are under the TACON [tactical control] of the Americans."*

But my own sources within the Anglo-American command suggested that the relationship between the British and Americans was not as close—or as trusting—as the world was led to believe. This was particularly clear when word reached me during my Christmas holidays in Paris that a thief had stolen a briefcase and computer containing Gulf War briefing plans from an unmarked RAF car at Acton in West London. The documents were being carried, according to my source, in the hands of a senior RAF officer—subsequently revealed to be Wing Commander David Farquhar, the personal staff officer to Sir Patrick Hine, who was de la Billière's immediate superior—and were taken from the vehicle by a thief as Farquhar stopped to look at a second-hand car in an Acton showroom. The thief had thrown away documents—discovered a few hours later—but had kept the computer to sell, unaware that it contained military information. Far more serious, according to my source, was that the British had not told the Americans of the theft.

I called *The Independent* with this extraordinary story, only to be told that the British government had issued a "D-notice" on the information in the hope of preventing its disclosure in the press—and that our acting editor, Matthew Symonds, had agreed to abide by the request and keep the story secret. Symonds was one of the three founders of *The Independent* who had, in the most unlikely venture of its kind in the history of British journalism, set up a newspaper that would not be swayed by the power of press barons or governments. Andreas Whittam Smith

---

*The question was also raised when Marshal of the Royal Air Force Sir David Craig, the chief of the UK Defence Staff, visited the kingdom. Asked if any British officer would have a power of veto over an American decision, he replied, according to my notes at the time: "Well, I think that's a difficult sort of way to put it because there is no question when you go to war, that you're under command and you obey accordingly." Stripped of its discretion, this meant that de la Billière would have to do as he was told once the shooting started.

never bowed to pressure, but Symonds, who had begun to show an embarrassingly romantic enthusiasm for war, failed to realise that the "D-notice" had primarily been issued not for "security" reasons but to prevent the Americans' hearing of the theft. So I mentioned the affair to a colleague on the *Irish Times*, which—published in the Irish Republic and not obliged to snap to attention when the British military establishment roars—immediately published the report of the theft. "I wouldn't have let the 'D-notice' stop us," Andreas exclaimed to me when he returned to the office from his own holiday and when I was back in Saudi Arabia.

It revealed an interesting rift in the management of my paper, which Andreas himself explained in our Sunday magazine six years later. The one thing he regretted, he said:

> is being persuaded by him [Symonds], against my own views, about the Gulf war. I wish I had run the paper as being anti-war, but Matthew and everybody else persuaded me not to do this, because they didn't agree with my view.

Far more interesting was my informant's contention that the real reason for the D-notice was to conceal the theft from Britain's American allies. In his own account of the Gulf War, de la Billière admits that the Americans had indeed been left in ignorance by the British and that the *Irish Times*'s disclosure—which, under different editorship that week, would have appeared in *The Independent*—created just the political embarrassment that newspapers were normally in the business of revealing:

> This news put me in a devilishly awkward position. What was I to tell Norman Schwarzkopf? If I said nothing, he would certainly hear about the theft from somewhere else. I suggested that as the matter was of such crucial importance, Paddy [Hine] himself should fly out to brief the CinC personally and this he agreed to do. At the same time, the Vice Chief of the Defence Staff, General Sir Richard Vincent, flew to Washington to brief Colin Powell, so dangerous did the whole incident seem and so potentially destructive of Anglo-American relations.

Schwarzkopf "seemed relaxed" at the news, according to de la Billière, although the latter's contemporary notes reveal another little secret hitherto kept from Washington. "Cock-up No 2," de la Billière wrote, "is when I'm told to tell NS [Norman Schwarzkopf] we are with him all the way, whatever happens, and he finds out Brit ministers will not delegate ROE [rules of engagement] for me to release aircraft for rapid response to a pre-emptive Iraqi strike . . . "*

---

*The computer was returned by the patriotic thief, who left the following note with the machine: "Dear Sir, I am a common thief and I love my Queen and country. Whoever lost this should be bloody hung. Yours, Edwards."

It was an unsettling Christmas. My friend and colleague Terry Anderson was still a hostage in Lebanon, held by men who were demanding the release of those Dawa party prisoners in Kuwait—if, indeed, they were still in jail. Because I was able to maintain some slight contact with Terry via his kidnappers, I flew to New York to talk to Terry's boss at AP, Louis D. Boccardi—a small, dapper man with the disconcerting habit of talking to visitors while playing taped music very loudly in his office—and to Terry's close friend, Don Mell. Mell, or Donald C. Mell the Third as we were constrained to call him, had been Terry's photo editor in Beirut and took me out for a memorable turkey dinner in the Rainbow Room of the GE building in Manhattan. I say "memorable" although, like most of Mell's dinners in Beirut, it was difficult to remember the last part of it. While not as slim as he was in his nimble wartime days in Lebanon, Mell had the disconcerting ability to attract throngs of gorgeous waitresses the moment he entered the restaurant, an effect he greeted with a wicked smile.

"Fisky, there's going to be a war and the old U-S-of-A will win, as usual," he said once we'd sat down. "Remember Lebanon? Remember what a giant fuck-up that was? Well, I'm sure we'll do just as well in Iraq." He might have been talking of events thirteen years later, although, for tens of thousands of Iraqis—at least half a million if we were to include the long-term aftermath of the 1991 war—his assessment would be all too accurate. Mell was also travelling back to the Gulf for the liberation of Kuwait—we didn't doubt that this would be accomplished—and we drank champagne together over the Manhattan skyline. The Empire State Building was patriotically illuminated in red, white and blue and the World Trade Center simmered at the tip of Manhattan. Mell and I both agreed that the impact of America's actions in the Middle East would eventually come to haunt the West— we even talked about this over dinner—although we never guessed that the explosion was less than eleven years and less than four miles away.

I arrived back to a cold, damp, bleak Saudi Arabia. The three hundred thousandth Kuwaiti refugee had long ago crossed the border—the Iraqis had reduced the indigenous population of their "nineteenth province" to two-thirds of its pre-invasion level—and King Fahd and Saddam Hussein were engaged in a bitterly personal dispute in which both God and Satan were invoked. It related directly to Saudi Arabia's original support for Iraq's 1980 aggression against Iran. Saddam had complained of Fahd's meanness at this time—an extraordinary insult to any Arab, let alone a Saudi—and Fahd's response was as devastating in its exposure of their quarrel as it was revealing in its detail of just how much the Saudis had spent in their attempt to destroy Iran a decade before:

> Why did you not fulfil your promise to me and Egyptian President Hosni Moubarak that you would not launch an aggression in Kuwait? After only a few days from your pledge, you committed the most vicious crime in the history of mankind when you crept in with your army in the darkness and shed blood and expelled an entire nation [in]to the desert in violation of all norms and values . . . you have . . . insisted on continuing aggression,

claiming that Kuwait was part of Iraq. God knows that Kuwait was never under the Iraqi rule and the members of the family of Sabah were rulers of Kuwait since about 250 years.* . . . Who authorised you to kill [a] million Iranian and Iraqi Muslims? . . . Who authorised you to occupy Kuwait and kill its sons, rape its women, loot its property and destroy its landmarks? No doubt Satan and your covetousness have urged you to do so at the expense of the Arab Gulf countries which were proud of the Iraqi army.

It was instructive that King Fahd should have blamed Saddam for a million Muslim lives lost during the 1980–88 Iran–Iraq War—since Saudi Arabia had been Iraq's principal bankroller in that war—but the details of just how much money the Saudis had been prepared to spend on Saddam's behalf in that conflict were as shameful as they were revealing:

> You said in your message that we had only extended to you $11.53 million to contribute to [the] reconstruction of al-Basra in addition to one million dinar[s] worth of equipment to reconstruct Fao.
> But we would like to make [the] facts clear:
> Oh Ruler of Iraq, the Kingdom extended to your country $25,734,469,885. 80¢.

The implications of this took some time to sink in. Saudi Arabia, whose king called himself the custodian of Mecca and Medina, had given Saddam $25 billion to fight and kill fellow Muslims in Iran.[†] The Americans had supplied the intelligence and some of the chemicals (along with the Germans). The Russians gave most of the armour. But the Saudis largely supplied the cash. I mused for some seconds on the eighty cents tacked on the end of the bill, an addition which suggested that a truly eccentric mind was at work in the Saudi royal treasury.

ONE OF THE DHAHRAN AIRPORT Saudi immigration officers had invited us to dinner in his desert tent, and it seemed a good place to watch the sands of peace run out in Geneva. Mohamed poured the hot, over-sweet tea. Abdullah handed

---

*This was pushing the envelope of history a little far. Kuwait was part of the Ottoman governorate of Basra and the Turks regarded the Sabah family as Ottoman governors even after a new sheikh, Mubarak Sabah—who had killed his two half-brothers—agreed in 1899 to make Kuwait a protectorate of Britain for £15,000 a year. After the overthrow of the Iraqi monarchy in 1958, Iraq demanded a union with Kuwait and was only dissuaded from invading when British troops were rushed to the sheikhdom—much as U.S. forces flew to "save" Saudi Arabia in 1990.

[†]The breakdown of this figure was as follows: non-repayable loans, $5,843,287,671.23; soft cash loans, $9,246,575,343.46; development loans, $95,890,410.95; military equipment and logistics, $3,739,184,077.85; petroleum, $6,751,159,583; industrial products for the reconstruction of Basra, $16,772,800; payments for industrial repairs, $20,266,667; trucks, tractors, caterpillars, asphalt rollers (270 vehicles), $21,333,333.50. The Saudi calculation was out by a $1.19.

round the plates of grapes, bananas and carrots. James Baker flickered on a black-and-white screen in the corner of the Arab tent. It was a strangely comforting place to hear the news. There we were, surrounded by six Saudis in their white-and-brown robes and kuffiah headdress, lying on brightly coloured carpets, our shoulders hunched against camel saddles, munching away on spiced chicken and shish kebab as the path to war was laid out before us. When Baker suddenly looked up and began with those all important words—"Regrettably, ladies and gentlemen," dreadful, hollow words which should have frightened us all—the Saudis merely glanced at the screen with the same attention they would later apply to a videotape of a dance band.

And when the U.S. secretary of state, his image floating up and down on the big old screen, pronounced his fatal judgement—"in over six hours, I heard nothing that suggested to me any Iraqi flexibility whatsoever"—only Mohamed's younger brother paid attention. He raised his hands level with his shoulders like a man in the act of surrender. "So it will be war," he said. "What can we do?"

This must have been how the tribes regarded impending disaster hundreds of years ago, lying on their carpets, tearing the legs off a roast chicken under the protection of a cloth roof. In front of us, a charcoal brazier glowed, its iron legs buried deep in the sand. Mohamed and Abdullah passed around more tea and fruit; the others paid more attention to Baker now. Khaled, a thin youth with a pointed beard, clucked his tongue. "On the day this starts," he said, "I shall pack up and leave."

Mohamed had rigged up his television set to a home-made aerial which sucked in CNN's live broadcast from the Geneva press conference. The signal was poor but we could read the words "Intercontinental Hotel, Geneva" on the lectern in front of Baker, and listen to his explanation of why he would not accept "linkage" between the Gulf crisis and the Arab–Israeli conflict. To a Westerner, Baker made sense. He insisted that Iraq was opposed by "twenty-eight nations" rather than by the United States. "Now the choice lies with the Iraqi leadership." But when Tariq Aziz appeared on the television, his Arab accent drawing the attention of all in our little tent, Baker's words seemed somehow less convincing, not because Iraq had right on its side—everyone agreed that Saddam Hussein was a bad man—but because Baker was an American and Aziz, like the six Saudis, an Arab.

Why, I asked Mohamed, had the Saudis for so long been Saddam Hussein's closest friends? Had they really trusted him and his foreign minister, Tariq Aziz? Had they not believed the reports of Iraq's use of poison gas in the war against Iran? Or had they been friends because Saddam was an Arab or, more to the point, a strong Arab whose power was feared as well as respected? It was Abdullah who replied. "We were never told bad things about Saddam," he said. "We were told in our newspapers—by our government—that he was a good man. Governments always say what they want their people to understand. That is what happens here. We were not told the truth." Then he paused for a few seconds. "But I will do anything my government tells me."

One of the Saudis walked into the tent with a tray of whisky bottles, perhaps half a dozen of them, which Mohamed proceeded to pour into pint-size mugs. Jameson, Johnnie Walker, Jack Daniel's, I couldn't believe this. "We confiscate them from the passengers who try to smuggle alcohol into the airport," Mohamed beamed. Given the vast quantities his guests were now drinking, glugging the stuff back as if it was juice instead of liquor, I realised that Saudi Arabia's strict anti-alcohol laws had as much to do with consumption as they did with religion. Saudis didn't know how to drink.

I knew something was wrong when I asked Abdullah if he really thought the Americans would leave Saudi Arabia. At this, Khaled suddenly stood up and announced angrily: "I will not stay here in this tent if you continue this conversation." It was a dark, unnerving moment, as if the disaster presaged on that flickering screen had at last penetrated the minds of the six Saudis, creating some kind of disorder in the tent. Mohamed asked if the Kurds should have a state. "Why should they?" Khaled asked, his face flushed.

He did actually leave the tent, his robes flowing at his heels, until Mohamed went to persuade him to return. Another man arrived, along with his wife, an unprecedented breach of custom and etiquette and—many Saudis would say—morality. She was a dark-haired woman with a gentle smile who did not wear a veil but sat silently beside her husband at one side of the tent, clutching a black gown around her shoulders. The men talked vigorously, Mohamed all the time asserting that he would not leave his home if there was a war. "Where would I go?" he asked. "What is the point? The war can go anywhere."

On the screen, Dan Rather was telling us now of the probability of war. He spoke of massive bombardments of Iraqi forces, of devastating air strikes, of "neutralising" Iraq's military potential. Sitting amid these Saudis, his words seemed obscene, unnatural. He was a Westerner, talking with promiscuous ease about the possible violent death of thousands of Arab Muslims at the hands of America. The Saudis listened to this with great discomfort. So did I. Imbibing the poisoned fruits of the West, they were about to experience its killer instincts.

They might have spoken of this had there not come from behind us, through the tent's fragile green wall, a growl of sound, long, persistent, gradually increasing in depth and intensity. We all knew what it was. Its howl penetrated every corner of the tent, drowning out Rather's voice, making the picture jump nervously until our ears were swamped with the sound. We were all familiar with it. One of President Bush's great C-5 military transports on the final approach to the nearest airbase, 30 metres over our heads, filling our vulnerable tent with its decibels.

In the last days before the onslaught, it was still possible to drive up the highway to the Kuwaiti border. They were days of gales and irony. The stormclouds gusted in over the coast and fanned the white smoke that trailed in a friendly way from the chimneys of the Kuwaiti power station. You could see it all quite clearly from the Saudi frontier, the pale white generating station and its twin chimneys still providing electricity to Iraq's occupying soldiers and their captive citizens on the other side of the border. It spoke of normality, of life going on as usual.

Down the hill from the deserted customs shed, I found a Pakistani at the till of his grocery store, its shelves half empty. No point in restocking just now, he told me. Round the corner in the playpark by the sea, a man in a white robe stood with his black-veiled wife and their tiny child. Change their clothing and it could be any rainy day on the seafront at Margate or Coney Island. No sign of Iraq's half-million soldiers on the other side of the frontier. And on this side, only a fat Westerner with grey hair in a pick-up truck—Vietnam generation, unable to hide his paunch under a parka jacket—stared towards Kuwait to represent the half-million Americans and their allies.

I walked around Khafji, but the integrity of the Arab quarrel was elusive. Most of the women and children had fled but a few Saudi soldiers were phoning home from the local post office, a war film playing on the television set in the lounge of the Khafji Beach Hotel, watched intently by a policeman. I had to drive down the bypass before I found a three-vehicle U.S. army patrol, its soldiers helmeted and perched high in their armoured vehicles, obeying the speed limit, halting at the traffic lights. For months I had watched the armour streaming up this highway. Like the Kuwaiti power station, it had become a sight so familiar that it had acquired its own permanence. I could imagine that in another six months, even in a year's time, the tanks and guns would still be advancing up this road, that Bush would still be threatening to evict Iraq from Kuwait, that the power station would still be emitting its white smoke, as if the preparations for war were eternal, like the desert.

On the day before Schwarzkopf commenced his bombardment of Iraq—"I have already issued the terrible orders that will let the monster loose," he wrote to his wife on 17 January 1991—American journalists seemed almost disappointed. Like the British press, the big American papers had been telling their readers—up to the point where war really was imminent and a certain reticence became obligatory—that the fighting would be a pushover. "K" Day for the headline writers was a relief. When Baker and Tariq Aziz were still talking, there was an almost palpable sense of unease among some of the American media experts. Peace fears loomed. But once Baker admitted failure, they were happy. War hopes rose. This was not mere cynicism. One U.S. radio reporter warned his listeners in the first week of January that the Gulf crisis was "sliding" towards a settlement. Like Shewmaker's hero General Patton—who ended up admiring the beauty of war and distrusting the horrors of peace—many of the reporters had psyched themselves into a state of mind in which peace was immoral and war represented goodness.

Nor, at first, did it seem there was much place in this new war for print reporters. We all knew that the air bombardment of Iraq would begin after Saddam refused a United Nations deadline to withdraw from Kuwait. So when my phone rang in the early hours of 17 January and a young journalist on *The Independent*'s night shift snapped that "CNN are showing the first bombs dropping on Baghdad—when can you file?" I told him that I was watching the same pictures in Dhahran and that we knew the bombs would drop this morning. The real story, I said, was that the most powerful armies in Christendom were now poised to fight the largest military force in the Muslim world. "So when can you file on this?" the voice asked again. I already have, I said. The Christian–Muslim "clash of arms" had been on our front page the previous day.

But I drove across to the airbase at Dhahran and there were the American jets taking off by the squadron, bomb-heavy and leaving a trail of gold-and-purple exhaust fires across the sky. It made good television, an Eastman Color insert into the pale electric greens of CNN's Baghdad anti-aircraft fire and distant explosions. In the early hours of that same morning, twelve Saudi fighter-bombers also took off from an airbase in the Eastern Province to attack Iraq. The decision to dispatch the Tornadoes on their sorties—they were purchased as part of the Saudi–British Al-Yamamah project—was taken personally by King Fahd and warmly applauded by President Bush. No attention was paid to the fact—no reporter mentioned—that at dawn, eleven of the twelve jets returned with their bombs still attached to their wings, their pilots saying they failed to find their targets. The twelfth plane unloaded its ordnance over the western Iraqi desert. But did they really lose their way?

The following night, a further seven Saudi-piloted Tornadoes took to the air from the same base, en route for western Iraq. Of these planes, no fewer than six failed to drop their bombs. But appearances had been preserved. The pilots were duly paraded before the press. The Saudis were fighting. President Bush could claim that Arab as well as Western forces were at war with Iraq. You only had to look at the Tornadoes to see the irony involved. The tail of each fighter-bomber displayed the Saudi flag, upon which was inscribed in Arabic the first words of the Koran. "There is no God but God and Mohamed is his Prophet." Thus did the first sura of Islam's holiest book constitute the battle flag of the Arabs who had gone to war against another Muslim nation. "Yes, Iraq is Arab," one of the Saudi pilots explained to me before leaving on a third sortie. "But when a brother Arab attacks you, he is your enemy. Saddam is our enemy now."

Or so it appeared. One day after the beginning of the bombardment—calling this blitzkrieg a war was pushing the margins of reality a little far at that stage—Fahd himself announced that the battle constituted "the sword and voice of truth" and that God would "register victory for His army." The House of Saud had now committed itself irrevocably to the Western military forces. King Fahd remained overall commander of the "joint forces," another of the quaint epithets behind which America's overwhelming strength within the alliance was supposed to be hidden. The Saudis thought they had muzzled criticism of the Americans from their own religious hierarchy, allowing sheikhs to vent their anger on domestic targets—upon women drivers, for example—and generously acting as hosts to the distraught if intensely arrogant Kuwaiti royal family.

As the "war" progressed—as the pictures of bombers streaking across Saudi Arabia and the skies above Kuwait became routine—those of us who did not join the infamous "pools" discovered a conflict that did not fit so easily into the television studios, with their super-patriotic anchormen, their verbose ex-generals, their model tanks and their bloodless sandpits. Saudi military checkpoints were ordered to prohibit all journalists from travelling towards the border unless they had signed up for the military "pool" and censorship. So along with a bunch of recalcitrant French reporters and photographers, I dressed myself up in the camouflaged anti-gas kit which *The Independent* had purchased for its staff and stuck on my head a large British steel helmet. This was a gift from Major Alan Barnes, a sympathetic and highly subversive member of the British army's education corps. His selection of First World War poetry, apparently nicked from an army library, travelled with me throughout the conflict. The French contrived to dress up in the sloppy battle-dress of their own national army—Gitanes dangling from lower lips only enhanced their cover—while in my airless anti-gas cape and Barnes's commando-style helmet, I was able to pass myself off as a vaguely bored liaison officer. The key to success, we quickly discovered, was to approach each checkpoint without looking at the soldiers guarding the road. Our lack of courtesy proved we were genuine.

By the time I reached Khafji in this way, the Saudi border town had been transformed. A towering column of smoke rose 3 kilometres high over the abandoned streets. Iraqi shells—forty in all, fired from a 130-mm gun in a clump of trees on the Kuwaiti side of the frontier—had found their target. Flames bubbled around the base of the smoke inside the Arabian oil company's storage depot, crimson and yellow, taunting U.S. Marine Sergeant Bill Iiams and his nine men who stood in the sand, dismantling their long-range radio aerials and preparing, without much enthusiasm, to enter the town. A transistor radio was broadcasting from the back of his Humvee, from which came the voice of a Washington reporter extolling the track record of the U.S. Air Force. Marine Rafee Saba, a twenty-year-old from Columbus, Ohio, with a disconcerting Yorkshire accent—he had spent his child-hood in Sheffield—was more interested in the radio than in the evidence that the Iraqis just might be able to hit back. "Only one plane lost in one thousand sorties," he shouted. "Can you beat that?"

Sergeant Iiams was still watching the fires from the oil terminal and the canopy of smoke that was now spreading 15 kilometres out to sea. "No one's attending the fire, are they?" he asked. My French colleagues and I had already done the rounds of Khafji and knew more than the marines. No, we said, no one had called the fire brigade. In fact, there was not a soul in Khafji to lift a telephone. The entire popu-lation—every family, the owner of the barber's shop, the Pakistani store owner, the managers of the town's three restaurants, the staff of the local hotel, even the local Khafji constabulary—had fled.

And we had already discovered Khafji's unhappy secret. Street after street bore the evidence of panic: clothes lying in the middle of the road where they had fallen from trucks and jeeps, limousines left unlocked, a police car abandoned in the main highway, its driver's door open. When we drove right down to the Kuwaiti border, well within range of the Iraqi gun-line, we found the Saudi army's positions unmanned, their sandbagged emplacements empty, their tents deserted. Only a lone Saudi National Guard patrol—three tall young men with very long beards and red berets—was left to represent the kingdom of Saudi Arabia.

They were proud men who shook our hands because they were pleased to see friendly faces so close to the Iraqis. How many Iraqis there were beyond the trees it was impossible to say, but their shells had tracked across the town in a straight line, next to the empty customs post, through the wall of a garden, in the middle of a street, until one of the last rounds hit the oil terminal and provided this scruffy place with its landmark plume of smoke. Not long after the shelling, we watched a helicopter fly up the coast and fire two missiles into the trees and the artillery stopped firing. There were other fires, deep inside Kuwait. Perhaps 25 kilometres from us, an immense curtain of smoke, kilometres in length and height, rose magisterially into the pale winter sky. It must have been an ammunition dump or a petrol store which the Americans had set alight.

The French were good in the desert. Some of my French reporter colleagues had served in their army in Africa and used compasses to move off the highway and drive through the sand to avoid the American checkpoints that wouldn't be fooled by our outlandish military clothes. A journalist from the French military magazine *Raids* was later bombed by one of his own country's Mirage aircraft; the ordnance failed to explode, so he lifted the unexploded bomb onto the back of his jeep and took it off to a French airbase to complain.

The wet sand clung to our tyres and turned the roads into mud-rinks. The soldiers were cold. The troops of the U.S. 24th Mechanized Infantry Division sat on their vehicles in their rainproof ponchos, slapping their sides for warmth. Across the mud, the British were huddled in their trucks with blankets or sitting in tents with an oil stove sputtering between them. No one could believe that the temperature would fall to almost zero in the Saudi desert. The wind came from the southwest, blasting over the sodden mass of grey earth, filling the *sabkha* depressions with water, turning the oil-soaked supply routes into death traps. A Humvee lay almost unrecognisable in the sand after its collision with a truck. A massive American M1A1 battle tank lay upside down in the desert, its turret and barrel half buried in the mud, a lone soldier watching over its vast hulk.

Far out across the desert, we could hear the thumps and bangs of U.S. Marine batteries shelling the Iraqis. But the gathering of allied armies—how quickly we had begun to use the word "Allies" as if this was the eve of D-Day—bore little relation to the comfortable, efficient scenarios outlined by the American and British commanders in Riyadh. Construction work on supply routes was hopelessly behind schedule, six-hour traffic jams had built up in the mudpits around divisional headquarters and many junior officers were leading their units to the front lines without maps. The entire British 32nd Field Hospital drove all the way to the Kuwaiti frontier without a single map and were trying to negotiate their way through the last Saudi patrol east of Khafji—and straight into the arms of the Iraqis—until we alerted a group of U.S. Special Forces soldiers who turned them round.

They were lucky they did not turn up in the early hours of 30 January 1991, when an Iraqi mechanised column of tanks and armoured personnel carriers—alerted no doubt that their target was undefended—crossed the border and entered Khafji from the west, capturing the town and, in a separate engagement to the south-west, killing twelve U.S. marines. Exactly two weeks after the Americans announced that the liberation of Kuwait had "begun," American troops were now fighting—and dying—to liberate a corner of Saudi Arabia. It wasn't meant to be this way.

By the time I reached the edge of Khafji next morning, a blanket of dense, oily fog hung over the frontier as American 155-mm guns banged shells into the streets around the oil storage depot. I found Marine Corps Sergeant John Post, a tall man with a big bushy moustache, recording "hostile" incoming fire on his sand-sprinkled, crackling radio near the American guns as mortars exploded inside the town, a faint white wisp of smoke showing their fall of shot. A broken water tower, smashed away by shells after someone concluded that the Iraqis had put a forward observer on top, stood out against the grey backcloth of smoke. "I don't know why we let the Iraqis go into Khafji in the first place," Post said. "But this is a Saudi operation and the Iraqis are still in there—maybe two hundred of them. They're said to be Iraqi special forces. I guess the Saudis got several hundred prisoners— I've counted twelve busloads of them so far with Saudi guards at both ends of each bus. But the Iraqis are fighters."

All night, flares had hung over Khafji and its stubborn defenders. A Harrier had swooped out of the east and bombed near the seafront. We made a call to the Khafji Beach Hotel, to be greeted by an Iraqi soldier who announced his support for "Arabism" and issued a string of oaths into the receiver, deprecating "Hosni Mubarak and the so-called Custodian of the Two Holy Places." Sergeant Post, with fourteen years in the Marine Corps, shook his head and leaned against his Humvee, the squat, crablike version of the jeep which the Americans had now brought into battle for the first time, a TOW missile-launcher mounted on its back. They were to become part of American life in the decade to come. As usual, there was a transistor playing on top of the vehicle, a combination of pop music—which the marines enjoyed and which competed with the din of artillery fire—and news reports of 300 Iraqi dead in Khafji and 500 Iraqi prisoners, which the marines enjoyed even more.

The Saudis were fighting in the town, although many of their reinforcements, it quickly transpired, were Qatari—some of them Pakistani soldiers on loan to the government of Qatar—and on the highway I caught sight of a heavy transporter bearing the wreckage of a Qatari army tank, a shell hole clean through its rear-mounted engine. There was another rumble. Sergeant Post shook his head again. "Those B-52s are laying it on over there in Kuwait," he said. "Can you imagine what it must be like under that?" No, it was impossible to conceive of the carnage going on across the border, under that terrible black cloud. Hours earlier, in the night 240 kilometres away, I had heard the earthquake of the B-52s. The desert carried the sound much further, a deep, distant drum roll, a minute and a half in length.

Iraqis were dying only 25 kilometres away, in their hundreds, but the euphoria of power had already gifted the Americans with a certain jubilation which, I suggested in a report that night, "will earn them more enemies in the Middle East in the years to come." On the ground, the marines were more prosaic. Captain John Borth, Post's commanding officer, viewed it all with the eyes of a man who had seen only the few kilometres of land around him. "If Saddam can take an empty town like Khafji—big deal," he said. "He's losing a lot of men to take a town that has no significance. I'm sure if we'd been more concerned about it, we'd have done a lot more." Perhaps. But Khafji did matter a lot. It was in Saudi Arabia. It was one of the kingdom's biggest towns. Schwarzkopf contemptuously and wrongly referred to it as a "village" when he originally reported the Iraqi attack. It was a town. It was therefore essential for the Allies to announce its recapture—which British prime minister John Major, having evicted Mrs. Thatcher from Downing Street, did while Iraqi troops were still fighting in the streets.

In the end, it had to be a famous Saudi victory. The "martyrs of Khafji"—the eighteen soldiers and national guardsmen killed in its recapture—were now immortalised by Crown Prince Abdullah as "the symbol of valour and courage in the minds of generations to come. What they have gained is a great honour for this country and their families." Saudi television neglected to point out that this "honour" would have been unnecessary had Saudi and American soldiers defended Khafji in the first place; they also spared readers the videotape of the shrivelled, carbonised bodies of the kingdom's "martyrs," lying in the ash of their personnel carriers. Amid the wreckage of the town to which its population returned, I heard no rejoicing. Why, the shopkeepers asked us, were the Americans not now liberating Kuwait? Instead, they were witnessing, live on their television sets, the destruction of Iraq. When I tried to explain to a Saudi clothing importer that the liberation of Kuwait was obviously going to be preceded by bombing, his response was immediate. "But the bridges, the electricity, the oil in Iraq, the people in the hospitals . . . Why must the Americans do this?"

It was a question asked with ever-increasing frequency. It was pointless for the Americans to explain that the more they bombed those "cockroaches," the less would be the human cost to the allied forces—including the Arab armies—when they at last advanced upon Kuwait. On CNN, an ever more potent and therefore dangerous medium for the local population, Saudis heard that the killing and wounding of Iraqi civilians—of Arabs, most of them Muslims—constituted "collateral damage" in a "target-rich environment," phrases that possessed a personal as well as an obscene edge when viewers were of the same faith as the victims.

The role of journalism in the 1991 Gulf War was as cheap as it was dishonest. If the relationship between reporters and soldiers was osmotic, it was also, on the journalists' part, parasitical. We fed off war. We wanted to become part of it. An American colonel commanding the U.S. airbase in Bahrain decided to honour the "pool" reporters who had been attached to his fighter-bomber squadrons since the day war broke out. They had not flown in any aircraft. They had braved no ground fire. Save for a few false Scud alerts, they had done nothing more than repeat the clichés of the returning pilots and their commanders. But the base commander produced for each of them a small American flag which, he said, had been carried in the cockpits of the very first U.S. jets to bomb Baghdad. "You are warriors too," he told the journalists as he handed them their flags.

The incident said a lot about the new, cosy, damaging relationship between reporters and the military, one that would be honed and chiselled and polished in time for the 2003 invasion of Iraq. So thorough had been the preparation for this war, so dependent had journalists become upon information dispensed by the Western military authorities, so enamoured of their technology, that press and television reporters found themselves trapped by their own childish enthusiasm.

For most of the journalists in the Gulf—and for most of the Western soldiers—war was an unknown quantity, exciting as well as frightening, historic as well as deadly. The notion that this was a "just war"—as Archbishop Robert Runcie and President Bush would have had us believe—presented us all with a moral context for our presence. If Saddam Hussein was the Hitler of the Middle East—worse than Hitler in Bush's flawed historical analysis—then it was inevitable that our reporting of the conflict would acquire an undertow of righteousness, even romanticism.

Thus when RAF fighter pilots took off from a Gulf airbase in late January 1991, a young British reporter told her audience that "their bravery knows no bounds." When U.S. navy jets took off from the carrier USS *John F. Kennedy* at the start of the war—in a campaign which was to cause many civilian casualties—a reporter for *The Philadelphia Inquirer* filed a "pool" dispatch from the ship describing how "Thursday morning was one of those moments suspended in time . . . paving the way for a dawn of hope." Journalists were now talking of Iraq as "the enemy," as if they themselves had gone to war—which, unfortunately, they had.

Their language was often that of the 1940s, when Hitler's armies had reached the Pas de Calais and were poised to invade Britain. Journalists in army costume and helmets were attempting to adopt the *gravitas* of Edward R. Murrow and Richard Dimbleby. The "pool" reporters were not under air attack like Murrow. They were not flying on missions over "enemy" territory as Dimbleby had done on the Hamburg firestorm raid. But they were preparing the world for "the biggest tank battle since World War Two" and "the largest amphibious operation since D-Day or Korea." There was to be no major tank battle and no amphibious operation at all. But the armies constituted "the Allies," with that reassuring echo of the wartime alliance which overthrew Hitler—and in which Saddam's hero, Stalin, played arguably the leading role.

This nonsense was as dangerous as it was misleading. When the three largest Christian armies in the world were launching a war against a Muslim nation from another Muslim nation which contained Islam's two holiest shrines, this was no time to draw parallels with the Second World War. If Ed Murrow were alive today, he would have been among the few reporters in Baghdad—like my colleague Patrick Cockburn of *The Independent*—describing the effects of American air raids on civilians. This bombardment could well presage the start of renewed hatred between the West and the Arab world, but our reporting did not begin to reflect this.

It is not easy for journalists to exercise self-criticism when they are reporting history. And to cast doubt on the word of American or British officers in the Gulf was to invite almost immediate condemnation. Those of us who reported the human suffering caused by Israeli air raids on Beirut in 1982 were libelled as anti-Semitic. Any expression of real scepticism about American military claims in the Gulf thus provoked parallel accusations. Had we taken Saddam's side? Did we not realise that Iraq invaded Kuwait in August 1990?

There could not be a reporter in Saudi Arabia who did not realise that Saddam Hussein was a brutal, wicked dictator who ruled through terror. There could be no doubt about the savagery of his army in occupied Kuwait. Reporters who wandered off to investigate military affairs in Saudi Arabia risked at worst deportation. The last journalist who did that in Baghdad had been hanged. Long before Saddam Hussein invaded Kuwait, we were reporting on his atrocities—unlike the Saudi royal family who were bankrolling his dreadful regime, and the U.S. government who were supporting it.

Yet most of the journalists in military "pools" were now wearing the uniform of their Western protectors. They relied upon the soldiers around them for advice. Fearful of a conflict on land, they naturally looked to the soldiers for comfort. They dug trenches with their protectors. They lined up submissively with the soldiers for the frightful cocktail of pills and injections—against anthrax, against bubonic plague—which the Western armies wished to pump into them. I advised one close colleague to have nothing to do with this witches' brew—now widely believed to be, along with depleted uranium munitions, a cause of the debilitating and sometimes fatal "Gulf War Syndrome"—and to this day she is grateful to me. These journalists were dependent on the troops for communications, perhaps for their lives. And there was thus a profound desire to fit in, to "work the system," a frequent and growing absence of critical faculties.

This was painfully illustrated for me when the Iraqis took Khafji. The "pool" reporters were at first kept up to 25 kilometres from the fighting and—misled by their U.S. military "minders"—filed stories incorrectly stating that the town had been recaptured. But when I travelled independently to the town to investigate, an American NBC reporter who was a member of the "pool" confronted me. "You asshole," he shouted at me. "You'll prevent us from working. You're not allowed here. Get out. Go back to fucking Dhahran." He then betrayed me to an American marine "public affairs" officer who announced to me: "You're not allowed to talk to U.S. marines and they're not allowed to talk to you."

It was a very disturbing moment. By travelling to Khafji, *The Independent* discovered that the Iraqis were still fighting in the town when the British prime minister was claiming outside Downing Street that it had been liberated. For the American reporter, however, the privileges of the "pool" and the military rules attached to it were more important than the right of a journalist to do his job. I named the NBC journalist in *The Independent*—and in an interview with *The New York Times*—and he was withdrawn from the Middle East. But the American authorities had been able to set reporters against reporters, to divide journalists on the grounds that those who tried to work outside the "pool"—"freelancers," as the

U.S. military misleadingly called them—would destroy the opportunities of those who were working—under heavy censorship restrictions—within it. That is why, when an enterprising reporter from the *Sunday Times* of London managed to find the Staffordshire Regiment in the desert in late January 1991, he was met by an angry British officer who said that if he didn't leave, "you'll ruin it for the others."

The "others," however, already had problems. When American correspondents on the carrier *Saratoga* quoted the exact words of air force pilots, they found that the captain and other senior officers deleted all swearwords and changed some of the quotations before sending on their dispatches after a delay of twelve hours. On the *Kennedy*, news agency "pool" reporters recorded how U.S. pilots watched pornographic videos in order to relax—or to become aroused—before their bombing missions. This was struck from their reports.

At one of the two American airbases in Bahrain, a vast banner was suspended inside an aircraft hangar. It depicted an American "Superman" holding in his arms a limp, terrified Arab with a hooked nose. The existence of this banner, with its racist overtones, went unreported by the "pool" journalists on the base. A "pool" television crew did record Marine Lieutenant Colonel Dick White when he described what it was like to see Iraqi troops in Kuwait running for their lives. His words are worth repeating. "It was like turning on the kitchen light late at night and the cockroaches started scurrying," he said. "We finally got them out where we could find them and kill them." These astonishing remarks did not elicit a single question from the "pool" reporter, although there was certainly one that was worth putting to the colonel: What was the "New World Order" worth when an American officer, after only three weeks of bombing, compared his Arab enemies to insects?

Journalists even felt the Iraqis had not been punished enough and sought to falsify the record of the war to prove it, suggesting that the land liberation of Kuwait, which took just over four days, constituted the entire conflict. In *The Washington Post*, Jim Hoagland was to write that "except for the 100 hours of Desert Storm in 1991, the United States and its allies have treated Saddam's regime as an acceptable evil." In the same paper, Richard Cohen joined Hoagland in the amelioration of history by telling readers that "the war lasted, you will recall, just one hundred hours." As Arab-American activist Sam Husseini would point out, "forgotten were the nearly 40 days and 40 nights that the U.S. rained down 80,000 tons of explosives on Iraq—more than all the conventional bombing of Europe in World War II."

But long before this war had concluded with the wholesale slaughter of fleeing Iraqi troops—and in the disgrace of our betrayal of the hundreds of thousands of brave Iraqis who rose against Saddam at our request—journalists had become mere cyphers, mouthpieces of the generals, discreetly avoiding any moral questions, switching off their cameras—as we would later witness—when the horrors of war became too obvious. Journalists connived in the war, supported it, became part of it. Immaturity, inexperience, upbringing: you can choose any excuse you want. But they created war without death. They lied.

The questions that the Saudis asked were in many ways more relevant than those put by the tamed reporters. "What is the New World Order?" a Saudi preacher asked me. Order is something the Saudis like the sound of. The world is an entity from which many Saudis are isolated. But "new" is a word which for Gulf Arabs had a dangerous ring about it. I tried to explain what President Bush might have meant by the phrase, referring to the context in which it first appeared. The Cold War was over, Eastern Europe was free. The Americans thought that these winds should blow through the Middle East as well. Dictators were no longer going to be tolerated—certainly not dictators who opposed the wishes of the United States. In retrospect, I realise now, I was explaining the official ideology of Bush Junior; I was just a decade too soon.

Given their concerns about any "new" world order, let alone the "American way of life," it was a natural step for King Fahd to demand that Saddam Hussein should "return to God's order"—a distinctly theological version of the Bush vision—and add that "we invoke God that He might register victory for His army." In Baghdad, Saddam had himself sought God's inspiration against the forces of "Satan and his hirelings." Having adopted the persona of the twelfth-century Kurdish warrior Saladin, he tried to speak with the same voice. "Satan will be vanquished," he said three days after the start of the bombardment of Iraq. The quotation was almost word-perfect. Faced by the French crusaders at the battle of Hittin on 4 July 1187, al-Malik al-Afdal, Saladin's own son, records how his father rallied his Muslim troops with the battle cry: "Satan must not win." Bush in turn asked God to protect America's soldiers in the Gulf. But he had already placed the conflict on quasi-theological, moral grounds when he addressed a meeting of Christian religious leaders in the United States, declaring that the Gulf conflict was "between good and evil, right and wrong." The ideological foundation of the American invasion of Iraq in 2003 was thus laid down before the liberation of Kuwait in 1991.

THE SIX O'CLOCK FOLLIES on 13 February 1991 had never started so late, but no one was surprised. There was a problem to contend with, as every journalist in Riyadh knew. How would Brigadier General Richard Neal, the U.S. deputy director of operations, respond to the killing of more than four hundred innocent Iraqi civilians in the Amariya air-raid shelter in Baghdad?

Would he begin by announcing an investigation into what appeared to be a devastating tragedy, the accidental bombing of a shelter packed with civilians, an expression of regret if the Baghdad reports turned out to be true? Or would he claim that the deaths occurred in a hardened military bunker, that the target was "legitimate," and that he had no idea how civilians came to be there?

The latter reply was precisely what Neal gave, proving to millions of Arabs that the Americans were heartless as well as all-powerful. He even boasted of his pilots' prowess in firing missiles down the bunker's air shaft. The Arabs must have drawn in their breath. Indeed, the general chose to spend more than ten minutes recording the day's military activity—the number of air sorties, of Iraqi aircraft claimed to have been destroyed on the ground and of oil wells set alight—before mentioning the hundreds of deaths in Baghdad as a coda, as if it was the last thing anyone was likely to be interested in. A "bunker strike" was what he called it. "I'm here to tell you it was a military bunker—it was a command-and-control facility . . . it was a hardened shelter . . . there is no explanation at this time why there were civilians in this bunker."

Once he had finished, the general found himself—to borrow his own war-speak—in a question-rich environment. What happened? General Neal's replies were calculated to reassure the Allies that their military tactics remained as ethical as ever—and were bound to inspire indignation in much of the Arab world. Neal talked about America's "active bunker-busting campaign." The shelter/bunker was a military target—it had been on the Allies" target list for some days. Military signals had come from it. He said it had been painted with camouflage, although under later questioning he admitted that "I was only told this when I came in." The Americans had meant to hit it, he said. "These young pilots don't go out by the seat of their pants . . . this air campaign was scrupulously targeted. The folks spent a lot of time on it."

Hitherto, the general had uttered not one expression of regret. Only when asked if there might be some such gesture of sorrow did he reply: "You're damn right . . . but I would add that this was a legitimate target. But if four hundred civilians, as reported, were killed, logic would tell you that of course the American public and the coalition forces are saddened by the fact . . . if in fact . . . there were civilians, if in fact it did occur, it is a tragedy." If, if, if. It was a military target. It was "legitimate." They were great pilots. It was a "command-and-control facility." But it wasn't.

The truth—hidden at Neal's press conference—was revealed to me within twenty-four hours in a suburban villa on the outskirts of Riyadh. The Americans believed that the bunker was used by senior members of the Iraqi Baath party and their families and friends. They regularly bombed bunkers where they assumed civilians associated with the regime were sleeping. The bombing of targets where women and children were staying was routine. My source was impeccable—a former American air force general who was now the senior targeting officer for the Royal Saudi Air Force. He examined the USAF photo-reconnaissance and satellite imagery each day. He knew the Amariya bunker.

When I visited him for morning coffee, he was in a state of great distress. One of the two American laser-guided missiles had travelled down the Baghdad bunker's air-ventilation shaft, he said. The other had hit a dirt patch outside, causing damage to surrounding buildings. "All the Saudis are furious about this," he said. "The Arabs in the Coalition are saying that Iraq will be effectively destroyed if these bombings continue. The infrastructure is being deliberately degraded— infrastructure for civilians as well as military—but this bombing was a serious error."

Sipping my coffee, taking notes, watching the pain on this man's face, I could only ponder the chasm between the deliberate, brutal nature of the American bombing campaign and the soft-focus, equally deliberate perversion of the truth imbibed and swallowed and duly regurgitated by the media. Far from the "target-rich environment" that Neal and his fellow generals claimed, the Americans and British were now flying between 150 and 200 sorties every day over Baghdad alone, and pilots were reporting that they were bombing the same targets five or six times, even after the structures had been virtually destroyed. The general spoke slowly, deprecating the activities of the air force he once served—though never, of course, the pilots—and had witnessed the arguments between Lieutenant General Charles Horner, commander of allied air forces in the Gulf, and Lieutenant General Ahmed el-Baheri, commander of the Saudi air force:

> There is a great deal of feeling among Saudis in the MODA [the Saudi Ministry of Defence and Aviation] because of the Baghdad bombing. They are distraught over the continued bombing. They are very concerned that Iraq should not be destroyed—they are thinking about the postwar era—and the Saudis didn't want to go along with the Washington statement that the bunker was a "legitimate military target." "Chuck" Horner is in favour of the continuing bombing of Baghdad. He's a technology guy. He's a nice guy. General Baheri feels we should get on with the ground war. Neal talked about camouflage on the roof of the bunker. But I am not of the belief that any of the bunkers around Baghdad have camouflage on them. There is said to have been barbed wire there but that's normal in Baghdad. We've been told that wire is sometimes put up to control crowds, that there is barbed wire near bakers" shops to prevent riots. There's not a single soul in the American military who believes that this was a command-and-control bunker. Senior commanders in the field do not report to command-and-control bunkers in Baghdad. The military did believe it contained soldiers. We thought it was a military personnel bunker. Any military bunker is assumed to have some civilians in it. We have attacked bunkers where we assume there are women and children who are members of the families of military personnel who are allowed in the military bunkers. The shelters are totally worthless against LGBs [laser-guided bombs]—just think of the kinetic energy of a bomb dropped at mach speed.

I could think of that energy very easily. I would visit that bunker in the Amariya suburb of Baghdad many times in the years to come. It would become a shrine, its blackened walls smothered with photographs of the 400 and more women and children and babies who died there. It had been used as a shelter each night for local families—there were no Baath party officials among them—and the two missiles fired at the structure burned them all alive. On some parts of the walls, flesh adhered for years afterwards. Other concrete surfaces were found to be imprinted with the shapes of the human beings who were liquefied in a millisecond at the moment the American missiles exploded. Hiroshima-like, they would leave their memory as a shadow on the walls.

The general drank more coffee than I—he had seen the satellite pictures and he

must have understood the degree of superhuman pain that the victims underwent—but he remained locked into the tactical issues of the air bombardment. The
best military sources, even when they unmask military lies, do not always say what
we want to hear. If the bombs were killing the innocent in Baghdad, the general
also lamented the wastefulness of the munitions:

> We are committed to a 40 per cent reduction in Iraqi troops in the KTO
> [Kuwaiti Theatre of Operations]. We should maximise our weaponry to
> better effect. We're past the point of diminishing returns in the Baghdad
> bombings. The lucrative targets are in Kuwait. We can assume we are
> killing a lot of their frontline troops. It's a crap shoot. But we shouldn't be
> bombing in Baghdad. A bombing campaign like that tends to run itself out.
> After the bunker hit, we're going to get nervous about continuing the Bagh-
> dad bombing campaign. President Bush had a free hand until yesterday's
> hit. He doesn't have that any more. Now he's in a box. I think this acceler-
> ates a ground war . . . The pilot of the aircraft who did this will know it was
> him. But it wasn't his fault. Saddam Hussein does put children in military
> bunkers and he is to blame for this irresponsibility. But we were wrong too.
> Kelly [Lieutenant General Thomas Kelly, director of operations for the
> Joint Chiefs of Staff] is a personable guy, he's a nice person, I know him,
> but he's so intoxicated with this damned air war technology that he went on
> television and said he was "comfortable" about the targeting. We could, by
> genuinely expressing our sorrow, do something to repair this.

The Amariya bunker was only the bloodiest of civilian bombings. On 3 February, jets—believed to be British—killed 47 civilians and wounded a further 102
when they destroyed a river bridge crowded with pedestrians in Nasiriyah. Most of
the victims fell into the Euphrates. On 14 February, British bombers attacked a
motorway bridge in the western city of Fallujah—twelve years later it would be
the centre of resistance to the American occupation of Iraq—but missed the bridge
and hit an apartment block and a crowded market, killing dozens of civilians.

Reporters often justify their own unique form of self-censorship—their uncritical repetition of the statements of generals and major generals—on the grounds
that their "access" to senior military officials must be kept open, that this access
gives them information that might otherwise be denied their readers. In Northern
Ireland and in the Middle East—both among Arab or Iranian military officers and
American and British forces—I have found the opposite to be the case. The more
journalists challenge authority, the more the military whistleblowers want to talk
to them. My files contain hundreds of messages or letters from officers of almost
every army operating in the Middle East. One set came from a linguist serving
with a U.S. AWACS crew monitoring intelligence over the Gulf before and during
the 1991 conflict. His own recollections created for me an intriguing new dimension to the American military presence in Saudi Arabia. He wrote that at an official
"Commander's Call" in October 1990:

... it thoroughly sickened me that, apart from our immediate reason for being in Saudi Arabia (dubious though it was), a lot of high-ranking people had a completely separate agenda, and far reaching plans for after the war ... certain elements within the military had in mind from the very beginning the intention to keep our presence there long after the war was over.

The AWACS officer was far more sickened by the testing of a massive new bomb against Iraqi troops:

One of the most exciting times for the briefers was when, in an absolutely textbook case of overkill, the U.S. Air Force decided to drop the world's largest non-nuclear bomb right on the Republican Guard. They actually dropped four of them over two nights. It was a psychological (PSYOPS) operation, conducted by the Special Ops guys. The bomb in question is the BLU-82, commonly referred to as the "Daisy Cutter." It is a 15,000-lb. bomb that is dropped on a pallet out of a C-130 like a cargo bundle. In this case two MC-130s dropped two of them in two locations simultaneously. This was followed by another MC-130 dropping leaflets telling the Iraqis that they would get the same thing the next night and that they should all surrender. The next night they dropped two more along with more leaflets saying we told you so. Since they were dropped in twos, the briefers wasted no time in coining the term "Blues brothers" for these bombs. Touching, isn't it?*

Crews on the AWACS reconnaissance planes during the 1991 Gulf War would fly in complete darkness, the one window at the back of the aircraft covered to prevent glare on their computer screens. Each crewman or -woman sat at a "rack" that included a large graphics screen with a map of the Gulf area; the plane was equipped with data links over which crew members received radar tracks from other AWACS, E2Cs and ground radar. Crews could watch the strike "packages"—another of the military's hygienic phrases—as they entered Iraq and Kuwait, hit their targets and returned as little arrow-shaped symbols on the screen. My source was tasked "to make sure the Iraqi Air Force never had a chance" and

---

*It is instructive to compare this humane if cynical account of the BLU-82 with the gung-ho report by a Reuters correspondent on another American "super-weapon," used in 1991 to destroy hardened underground bunkers. "The bomb, called a GBU-28, was five times more powerful than any non-nuclear weapon previously built. It was just hours old when dropped on Iraq's strongest underground fortress and its designers had their fingers crossed that it would work. The new bomb, built at breakneck speed by Lockheed Missiles and Space Co. and Texas Instruments Inc. in an unprecedented team effort, was dropped from an F-111 onto a command complex at Al Taji airbase ... the 4,700-pound superbomb—a howitzer barrel filled with explosives and guided by a laser—penetrated the massive concrete walls and blew up inside the bunker ... 'It's a story of patriotism and unprecedented cooperation,' said Merl Culp of Lockheed Corp ... "

his description of this ruthless operation shows just how sophisticated American surveillance technology had become:

> If they even so much as keyed a microphone, I would know who they were, what type of aircraft they were in, where they were, where they were going, and what they were going to do. During the first three or four days of the air campaign, lots of Iraqi pilots at least tried to make a show of defending their country. As soon as they made their first radio call, I would radio the AWACS and tell them number and type of aircraft, location, direction, and altitude, and the AWACS would immediately send coalition fighters after them. The reality of what was happening came through my earphones, as the Iraqi pilots became almost immediately disoriented, confused, terrified, and finally, silent. I truly felt sorry for them. They would all be talking over one another on the same frequency to the point that their ground controller couldn't get through to them to warn them of approaching coalition fighters.*

"THEY ARE BURNING OUR OILFIELDS," the Kuwaiti official said down the phone. The evidence was incontrovertible. Only 100 kilometres north of Riyadh, we could see it along the horizon, the penumbra of a dark, forbidding cloud that stretched across the far edge of the bright desert. An hour later, 150 kilometres further north, and it towered over us, reaching out towards the sun, turning the sand into a white, pasty colour. The drivers on the highway north were all looking at it, as if from the immensity of darkness they expected some sign, unconscious of the fact that the cloud was the sign. The Iraqis were scorching the earth, just as they had promised to do. The Americans had helped, by dropping fuel-air explosives on oil wells in Kuwait as well as Iraq. Now the shadow of Kuwait's destruction was spreading over the north-east of Saudi Arabia.

It was an open secret that the Americans and the British would soon lunge deep into western Iraq—well over 250 kilometres—in the opening offensive to liberate the emirate. This preparedness was obvious on the highway now. It was almost empty. The tanks and howitzers and missile batteries were already over the skyline, beneath that great darkness. Only ammunition and fuel trucks now sped up the roads to the border. Camels grazed on the thickets between the dunes, bored policemen did not bother to check our papers.

The "pool" reporters were now marooned with "their" military units—all of them waiting to move forward in the night, north and then east into Kuwait City or

---

*The AWACS crewman noticed a profound difference between the Iraqi pilots' behaviour during the 1991 war and "the smooth polished professionalism with which I heard these same pilots conducting strikes deep inside Iran scarcely three years previously. On one such mission the Iranians even managed to shoot one of them down, but they didn't even discuss it other than to say that they didn't have a 'complete formation' on the return trip."

right on across the Iraqi frontier and up towards the Euphrates River. The straight road up the coast from Khafji—the quickest way to reach Kuwait in peacetime— was regarded as a death trap, mined and closely defended by Iraq's best troops. American planners had decided that the Kuwaiti army itself—and their Saudi allies—would have the dubious honour of taking this highway and liberating the Kuwaiti capital. So with something close to trepidation, I hitched a ride with Sky Television and a unit of Kuwaiti commandos who could not wait to drive up that unpleasant, sinister road. There would be oil-filled trenches and berms set on fire to burn us alive, kilometres of interconnected minefields to blow us to bits, enfilading rifle fire from Iraqi emplacements, dug-in T-72 tanks to blast our vehicles off the highway. Or so we were told.

In the pre-dawn darkness on the morning of 25 February, the Sky crew and I drank tea with all the enthusiasm my dad must have felt on the Somme in 1918. Then we swung in behind a Kuwaiti petrol tanker and ground through the rubble of the Saudi customs post and suddenly, as the sun struck through the wadis, we crossed the infamous berms. Half-filled with black sludge, the ditches and earthworks ran guiltily across the Kuwaiti desert, the sand dark and soggy with oil. We were supposed to have been incinerated. But there were no cremation trenches, no snipers, no activated minefields, just mile after mile of burned out Iraqi armour and ammunition trucks ripped apart by precision bombs. The Iraqis had already fled.

I breathed in the dawn air. It was as if God had given us a second life. We wound through kilometre after kilometre of Saudi and Kuwaiti convoys—Arab troops with just a few U.S. Special Forces Humvees cutting through the desert alongside us, their radio aerials adorned with the red, green, white and black flags of Kuwait. "Kuwait City," the road signs beckoned to us. By the time we stopped beneath lowering clouds of burning oil, the air pressure changing with the blast of artillery shells, the prize was only 70 kilometres away, the suburbs only 50 kilometres, half an hour's drive. In the dreary town of Azour, where the Americans were firing at the few Iraqi infantrymen who failed to join the rout, stood Colonel Fouad Haddad of the Kuwaiti army's 9th Battalion, his massive beard and shades almost obscuring his smile. "I feel I am dreaming," he said.

We felt like that, too. After so many months and so much planning—and, let us be frank, ruthlessness—the "Allied" armies had broken through the Iraqis in just a few hours and we had sped down the highway like kings. The Iraqis destroyed the telephone lines in Kuwait but my Saudi mobile still maintained a fractured signal west of Azour. I called the foreign desk of *The Independent*. Harvey Morris wasn't surprised. Richard Dowden, our most daring foreign correspondent, had long ago found himself confronted by Iraqi soldiers who asked him to take them prisoner. Reports from the west spoke of Iraqis surrendering by the thousand. After promising the "Mother of All Battles," Saddam had ordered his army to retreat out of Kuwait, like a child grown bored with a familiar game, tired of the bombing and rhetoric, anxious to start a new epic, create a new narrative of empty courage.

How long, I wondered, before Baghdad told us of the unquenchable resolve of the Iraqis never to surrender to the United States, how Iraq alone had faced the world's only superpower, how their occupation of Kuwait, however temporary, had been a historic Iraqi victory? About a week, in fact. And munching an unspeakable American military chocolate bar in the cover of a Special Forces Humvee, I remembered how Khorramshahr was going to be defended in 1984, a Stalingrad of fortitude against the Iranian hordes; until one day seven years ago Saddam had woken up and decided to withdraw his army from the city it had captured with so much blood in 1980. Kuwait was a repeat of Khorramshahr. For the second time, what was billed as one of the great battles of Iraqi history was simply erased from the history books. A new script would begin tomorrow.

Beside the Kuwait City highway were piles of unexploded anti-personnel mines and broken Iraqi trucks whose contents of unused rocket-propelled grenades and boxes of machine-gun ammunition and brass cartridges sparkled in the sand. Electricity pylons had been torn down. There were expensive cars, turned over on their roofs, wheels ripped off. Crude piping lay everywhere across the desert, reeking of fuel oil; there were liquid-filled trenches, acres of black scum. Could they not have been set alight? Or were the Americans too quick for them? Or had Saddam just given up? What had the Iraqis done? It was like a dead land.

And in Kuwait City, we asked a far more devastating question: What kind of people would do this? Day had been turned into night, so thick was the canopy of smoke, the nation's oil wells burning gold and orange along the black-fringed horizon, and so we had—again I must use the example of that most sadistic of medieval cultural images—Hieronymus Bosch; courtesy, this time, of the Iraqi army. Five years later, the Chinese would complain of the pollution and black snow on Mount Everest caused by Kuwait's oil fires.

The Iraqis had even used the modern equivalent of a torture wheel. All day, Kuwaiti men, young and old, approached our car with their terrible stories. "They twisted my son on a pole and broke his legs with pieces of wood," a stooped old man said. "They thought he was in the resistance. Now they have taken him away, with all the others, as a human shield." Then there was Heather Rennison, an Englishwoman married to a Kuwaiti. "A cousin of my mother-in-law was arrested. She was only nineteen and they found two-way radios in her bedroom. Three days later they came to her home to ask her parents for clothes and blankets. So her parents thought she would be all right. Then the Iraqis hanged her and dumped her body outside her home. There were burns from electricity on her arms and legs. Of course, the Iraqis kept the clothes and blankets."

Perhaps one needed to walk the pavements of Kuwait City to understand the extent of what the Iraqis did, that it really did amount to a war crime. "I will show you the mosque where they shot eleven men on Friday," a bearded man shouted to us from a car. The Abdullah Othman mosque stands in the Palestinian Hawali quarter. The bearded man pointed to a yellow wall. "The Iraqis said that all those at prayer would be taken away—kidnapped—and eleven men stayed in the mosque and refused to go. So they brought them here, blindfolded them, made them stand with their backs to the wall and shot them in the face." The bullets that passed through the worshippers' heads were now embedded in the yellow wall. "Don't be surprised," the man said. "I had two neighbours who the Iraqis thought were in the resistance. So they pushed them into drains, closed the grille, poured petrol on them and set them on fire. Their families buried them later—you can't leave bodies in drains."

The figure of 5,000 Kuwaiti men abducted in the last hours before Iraq's retreat seems fantastic until you find—as I did that day—that the first three families who offered me lifts to various locations in Kuwait City had all lost sons as hostages. The young men had simply been ordered into Iraqi army buses as they walked to work. Three thousand men and women were murdered here, the Kuwaitis also tell you. Who could do this?

It is comforting, in trying to record a reign of terror, to search for some logical reason; long-standing hatred perhaps, or some aberrant unit of the Iraqi secret police. But this would be fanciful. What was one to think when one walked, as I did, through the smoking embers of the National Museum, fired by the Iraqis on Tuesday? Or the gutted interior of the parliament? Or the still burning library in the Sief Palace—its magnificent golden clock tower smashed by a tank shell—when I found, lying on a chair, the remains of a book published by the government of India, *The Collected Works of Mahatma Gandhi*? What kind of people burn museums and libraries? Fast-forward. Would I not be writing these same words, 800 kilometres north of here, in Baghdad, in almost exactly twelve years from now?

Outside the museum, Kuwait's collection of antique wooden boats had been burned to cinders. The "Islamic house" lay in ruins. The walls of the emir of Kuwait's Dasman Palace were torn down with explosions and bulldozers. The Iraqis used tanks to shoot at the parliament. The great hotels had been systematically fired. The Iraqis planted explosives in the bedrooms of the Meridien. It was like a medieval army that conquered, looted and then burned even on an individual level. Boat owners found their yachts stolen or sunk in the marinas. Shopkeepers found their stores burned if they could not be looted. At an abandoned anti-aircraft gun on the coast—where the Iraqis mined the beaches against a non-existent U.S. marine amphibious landing—I came across piles of brand-new women's shoes, made in France, none of them matching, all wrapped inside Iraqi army blankets along with body-building magazines. Why did they do this, these soldiers? Why had they stolen an exhibition display of women's eye shadow? There were cartridge cases across the forecourt of the museum, bullet-holes in the cracked walls of the building that once contained Kuwait's finest—and long ago looted—national treasures. What was he thinking, this soldier, when he opened fire on a museum?

The seafront restaurants had been torn down, the high, glass-covered landmark water towers machine-gunned. At Al-Ahmadi, the Iraqis set off explosives every hour at the two oil farms, each containing twenty tanks. The fine old British "White House" there was burned down along with the control room that operated the oil pipelines.

I suppose one sensed in Kuwait that something very wicked and—here it comes—something at times very evil had visited this city. Not just an occupation army, not even the Iraqi Baath party apparatus, but something that intrinsically links dictatorship and corruption. "Down with the dirty Fahd, Sabah and Hosni," said a blood-red graffiti on the wall of one of the burned palaces. "Long live Saddam Hussein." In the little, looted museum of Kuwaiti peasant art, I found a poster of Saddam stapled to a wall. "Most victorious of all Arabs, the great leader Saddam Hussein—God bless him," the caption said.

Whoever uttered such prayers? Colonel Mustafa Awadi of the Kuwaiti resistance movement offered to show me. On a bleak housing estate in the suburb of Quwain, he took me to a school—the Iraqis used schools as interrogation centres—and in a classroom he introduced me to sixteen Iraqi soldiers. They sat on the floor, legs crossed, mustachioed, miserable, ordinary men with tired, dirty faces and grimy uniforms. "They were happy to surrender," the colonel said. "See? We even give them food and tea. I promise they will be handed over unharmed to the Kuwaiti army." Two of the men had been wounded in the face—their bandages were fresh—and they all smiled when I greeted them and when they heard me tell the colonel in Arabic that I would mention their presence to the Red Cross. One could not help but feel sorry for these defeated teenagers with their sad smiles. So what kind of men raped Kuwait?

And what—here, at last, was my opportunity—was it like under our bombardment, under the laser-guided munitions and the GBUs and the "Daisy Cutters"? What was it like to be an Iraqi soldier attacked by the Americans? "The Americans and British both bombed us," Mohamed said. "We knew all the planes—Tornado, Jaguar, B-52, F-16, F-15—and we knew what was going to happen." Mohamed was a thirty-three-year-old Iraqi reservist, one of the oldest of the men, and his fellow prisoners nodded in agreement as he described their suffering. He moved his left hand in a fast, sweeping movement from left to right. "All over the explosions went, one big bomb and lots of smaller bombs, everywhere, like this." Mohamed was describing the effect of a cluster bomb.

After all the briefings and the bomb-aimer's video films, here at last was what it was like on the Other Side, in the words of those who tried to survive in the "target-rich environment." Schwarzkopf had described the Iraqis as poorly fed, living in fear of their own execution squads. On the evidence of Mohamed and his comrades, it was true. Not one of the Iraqi soldiers I spoke to had eaten anything but rice and bad bread for months. All talked with disgust of the *kuwat al-khassa*, the "special guards."

According to Ali, a twenty-two-year-old private from Diwaniya, it was the *kuwat al-khassa* that controlled the death squads. "They came to see us at the front at Wafra [in Kuwait] and told us what they would do to us. One of them said that if we ran away, we knew what would happen to us and he invited one of us to go and look at the bodies of fifty soldiers who had been executed. None of us would go to look at them. But later—a few days ago, at the end of the war—one of my friends, Salaam Hannoun, a soldier from Amara, ran away. They caught him and brought him back and made us watch his execution. He waited for his death and cursed Saddam Hussein. Then they shot him. He was twenty-three."

Mohamed's description of the death squads was terrifying. "They were all members of the party. They change their names so they can never be identified. If a man is Mohamed, they call him Hussein. They have no emotion. They have no mercy." The executions did not deter Ali. "Ten of us tried to run away at the end, under the bombing," he said. "We were caught and our hands were tied and they put blindfolds on us. They said they would kill us. But then the order to withdraw came and they needed us to help drive the trucks out of Kuwait. So after a while, a captain came and said: 'Release them.' "

If the difference between life and death in the Iraqi lines was a matter of tactical convenience, the soldiers appreciated the dangers of the Allied bombing. "At night, during the bombing, we always hid in our shelters in the sand," Mohamed said. "We hid there all the time, waiting for the bombing to end and for the ground attack. One of my friends, Abbas, from Baghdad, was thirsty one night when they were dropping cluster bombs on us. He kept complaining that he needed water. We said to him: 'Don't go out there—it's too dangerous.' The water was kept in another shelter only ten metres from us. Abbas left despite our warnings and immediately a piece of shrapnel hit him in the head and killed him. We had to leave him there. He was not buried."

Ghassan, a thirty-year-old Iraqi reservist from Nasiriyah, complained that there had been little chance of surrendering to the Allies although, three days ago, he and his comrades had handed themselves over to the Kuwaiti resistance. "After we read the leaflets dropped on us, we wanted to run away. We kept the leaflets with us all the time and we made some white flags to wave at helicopters if they came. But there were too many mines in front of us to run—and at the start, we were forty kilometres from the border." The Iraqis said they had received only water, rice and bread "mixed with small pieces of sawdust" since they were posted to Kuwait. In Iraq, they said, their military rations had been five kilos of flour a month and three pieces of bread a day.

Several of the prisoners spoke with emotion of bereavement and suffering within their own families in Iraq. Adnan's eight-month-old baby boy was suffering from acute diarrhoea and a high temperature when he last saw him; his family could not obtain medicines from the doctor, he said, because of the UN blockade, and he did not know if the child was still alive. Ghassan's sister Nidal died two days after giving birth because two hospitals were unable to provide her with oxygen—again, he said, because of the blockade. This was the first evidence I found—even before the liberation of Kuwait—that the UN sanctions were lethal.

Shortages at home, death squads, starvation diets and twenty-four-hour bombing at the front destroyed the morale of the sixteen soldiers who spoke to me. One of them spoke bitterly of Saddam Hussein, no doubt hoping to impress his Kuwaiti captors but unafraid that his comrades might betray him later. "I want to go back to an Iraq where there is no Saddam Hussein," he said. It was a wish devoutly held by many millions of Iraqis. Just a day earlier, we—the West—had urged the people of Iraq to bring this about, to rise up and destroy the tyrant.

How easily we did this. How natural it seemed. We had, after all, gone to war in alliance with "the Arabs." Good men and true of the Christian and Islamic faiths had fought together against Saddam. This was the image portrayed when Schwarzkopf and Prince Khaled, the "commander-in-chief of all foreign forces," sat down at Safwan on 3 March 1991 to arrange the Iraqi ceasefire—and allowed Saddam to keep his helicopters and surviving Republican Guard divisions intact. In the years that followed, the memoirs of those who supposedly led this war proved that the alliance was a sham—and that our reporting of the conflict was as deeply flawed as the men who fought it.

Prince Khaled used to employ an American public relations company to manage his press conferences. Deep in the high-pile-carpeted interior of the Saudi defence ministry, an Irish-American of massive build—a certain Mr. Lynch from Chicago—would stand just behind Prince Khaled, choosing which journalists should be permitted to ask questions and suggesting to the rather portly Saudi commander how he should reply. It was, to put it mildly, an unbecoming performance. Prince Khaled would beam into the television cameras and pour out his effusive thanks to the American people for sending their sons to defend his land while Mr. Lynch nodded sagely at his shoulder. The prince's presentation was made all the more extraordinary by a hairline so thick and low that he appeared to have recently undergone a hair implant. His thin moustache added an even more surreal touch, making him look unhappily like those bewhiskered gentlemen who in silent movies used to tie ladies to railway lines in front of express trains.

King Fahd's decision to invite American troops to Saudi Arabia had been "one of the most courageous of his life," Khaled told us. He himself saw nothing wrong with this invitation to the foreign "guests." America would respect the laws of Saudi Arabia; Saudi Arabia respected the United States. "Respect" was the word the Saudis always used. The foreigners would respect Islam and would respect the Arabs. And of course, Arabs would respect America. Khaled expressed his "respect" for Schwarzkopf, and Schwarzkopf duly disclosed his own "respect" for Khaled's generalship. It sometimes seemed that there was no end to this mutual admiration, even when Saudi troops fled their posts at Khafji. After the Saudis and Qataris and their Pakistani mercenaries fought their way back into the town, there was the ever-smiling prince, now sporting a bright blue Kevlar helmet adorned with transfers of a general's four stars, declaring his pride in his army and their American allies.

Imagine, therefore, Khaled's surprise when, browsing through Schwarzkopf's autobiography a year later, he found that the American commander's "respect" for him was not quite as deeply held as he apparently thought. Khaled, according to Schwarzkopf, complained that American troops were wearing T-shirts bearing a map of Saudi Arabia (maps were "classified"), that a rabbi had boasted of blowing the Rosh Hashanah ram's horn on Islamic soil (the rabbi was in America and quoted in an Israeli newspaper), that the Americans were bringing "dancing girls" into Dhahran; Khaled wanted the Americans to launch their ground offensive from Turkey rather than Saudi Arabia and told Schwarzkopf that the Syrians didn't want to fight. Khaled was chosen for his job, Schwarzkopf wrote, by two American generals.

The Saudis should have expected such treatment. In the months that followed the liberation of Kuwait, Saudi Arabia emerged as America's main financial client in the Middle East, a vassal state supporting the finances of Washington's poorer allies in the region—Egypt, for example—and buying off the suspicions of those less enthusiastic about American policy, especially Syria. In return for American firepower and political support, Saudi Arabia became Washington's bankroller.

Predictably, an embittered Prince Khaled launched a series of attacks on the "respected" Schwarzkopf, accusing him of concocting stories and distorting facts "to give himself all the credit for the victory over Iraq while running down just about everyone else." Poor Khaled. Did he really believe that the Americans would accept him as a four-star general alongside the Schwarzkopfs and the de la Billières? Typically, he failed to object to one of the most offensive passages in Schwarzkopf's book, perhaps because he failed to understand its implications. Readers are invited to spot the insult:

Khalid [*sic*] was ideal; he'd been educated at Sandhurst, the British military school, had attended the U.S. Air War College at Maxwell Air Force Base in Alabama, held a master's degree in political science from Auburn University, and was the highest ranking prince in the Saudi Armed Forces. His military credentials were nowhere near as important as his princely blood, since almost all power in Saudi Arabia resides in an inner circle of the royal family. Simply put, unlike the other generals, Khalid had the authority to write cheques.

Cheques for transportation. Cheques for water. Cheques for fuel. This is why Prince Khaled was important. For the Gulf War, after massive arms purchases from the West had discredited George Bush's promise to reduce the level of weapons in the Middle East, ended as a net profit to the Western alliance, fought by young men from Detroit and Glasgow but paid for by Prince Khaled's uncle and king, the "Custodian of the Two Holy Places." Could two such partners show each other anything more than mercantile respect?*

---

*The Arabs spent $84 billion underwriting Operation Desert Shield and Operation Desert Storm, the two melodramatically named phases of the 1990–91 Gulf crisis and war, according to an Arab economic report published in 1992. This was more than three times what the Saudis paid for Saddam's eight-year war with Iran. Prince Khaled bin Sultan would calculate Saudi Arabia's individual contribution to the 1991 conflict at more than $27.5 billion, slightly more than it gave Saddam. In all, the Arabs sustained a loss of $620 billion because of the Iraqi invasion and subsequent conflict. Kuwait had been the first to contribute to the war coffers when it agreed to pay part of the $6 billion for America's initial military deployment in September 1991. Washington complained in August 1991 that Saudi Arabia and Kuwait still owed $7.5 billion to the United

Curiously, the commanders of the two largest Western armies in the Gulf spent a good deal of their memoirs trying to persuade us that they do "respect" the Arabs and the Muslim Middle East. Visiting the Gulf as head of the U.S. Central Command in 1989, Schwarzkopf claimed to admire the Arab way of life, hunting with Sheikh Mohamed bin Zayed al-Nahyan in the Emirates, even dressing up in Kuwaiti robes for dinner. His Arab counterparts welcomed him into their palaces and mosques, Schwarzkopf wrote, "now that they knew of my fascination with their culture."

General Sir Peter de la Billière seemed even more smitten with Arab "culture." "I liked and respected Arabs and understood their way of life," he wrote. "I came to appreciate the Arabs well, to appreciate their fine culture." A few pages later, he is boasting again of "my understanding of Arabs and their way of life." Yet a good part of de la Billière's previous service in the Middle East had involved hunting down Arabs as an officer in the SAS. In Oman, he says, he failed to "eliminate" or capture the three dissident Arab leaders but succeeded in forcing them into exile. At Wadi Rawdah, the SAS attacked two guerrilla strongholds and "effectively put them out of business." Oddly, de la Billière does not choose to mention the Iranian embassy siege in London when the SAS—of which he was then director—broke into the building, rescued the civilian captives held there and then proceeded to execute all but one of the Arab hostage-holders.

Perhaps it was necessary, so many months after the Gulf War, to romanticise the relationship between the West and the Arabs, between Christians and Muslims, unconsciously to simplify and reconstruct the reasons why the Western armies embarked on their crusade to save the biggest oil lake in the world and to prevent Saddam from becoming the largest controller of the world's oil. Schwarzkopf, who at least understood the need for America to maintain its relations with the Arab world, stated that one of the war's aims was to "eliminate Iraq's ability to threaten the Arab world." Millions of Arabs suspected that the war—and the invasion of Iraq twelve years later—was to eliminate Iraq's ability to threaten Israel, which, given the enormous effort to destroy the mobile Iraqi Scud-launchers which were firing at Israel, may not have been far from the truth.*

Neither Schwarzkopf nor de la Billière chose to mention the killing of hundreds of Palestinians in Kuwait and the "ethnic cleansing" of tens of thousands of

---

States for their share of Gulf War costs. By that stage, the two had respectively already contributed $1.7 billion and $12.5 billion. The Middle East may have proved a new economic reality in the world economy: that wars can be fought for profit as well as victory, a lesson that the invasion of Iraq might have reinforced until the occupation ended in disaster.

*Israel was constantly boasting of its superior intelligence about the Iraqi regime—as it did in 2003 when it added to the fraudulent warnings about the weapons of mass destruction that no longer existed in Saddam's arsenal. Although American officers told me in 1991 that Israel's "intelligence" on the location of Scud batteries in the Iraqi desert invariably turned out to be wrong, it is interesting that de la Billière—believing that Israel would enter the war after Saddam's provocative Scud attacks on Tel Aviv and other cities—"began to devise a plan whereby we would allocate their [Israeli] ground forces a sector of Iraq in which to operate exclusively."

others by the Kuwaitis that followed the war. Schwarzkopf has only three references to Palestinians in his book, the second of which shows an insensitivity that might well have provoked Khaled. It records a conversation between the general and the prince in October 1990, after Israeli police shot down twenty-one Palestinian civilians in Jerusalem. Schwarzkopf says he "cautioned General Khalid not to be too quick to condemn America's historic support of Israel, particularly just after the American people have absorbed ten accidental deaths incurred while defending Saudi Arabia." That Schwarzkopf could compare military accidents—however tragic—with what was, in effect, a massacre shows just how removed from reality was his "fascination with Arab culture."

Both men thunder their condemnation of Saddam's iniquities, although even here de la Billière's history is skewed. At one point, he talks of Saddam's war against "expansionist Iran" when in fact it was Saddam who was expansionist. It was Iraq that invaded Iran in 1980, not the other way round. So much for understanding "the Arab way of life." If "respect" there was for the Arabs and Muslims, however, it was squandered when de la Billière made his jubilant demand at the war's end as the corpses of tens of thousands of Iraqi Muslim soldiers lay across Kuwait and Iraq, many of them thrown unidentified into mass graves—that British people should "get out there and ring the church bells." However unconscious he may have been of its content or effect, could there have been a clearer revelation of Christian triumphalism over Islam?

But even de la Billière's outrageous self-promotion does not touch Prince Khaled. For when the latter's own memoirs duly appeared in 1995, he felt able to tell his readers that the approval of his application to enter the war college at Maxwell Air Force Base suggested that "God [was] guiding my career to prepare me for what was to come." He is "touched" when Chinese diplomats compare him to Henry Kissinger. Before the war, Khaled slept in a room beneath the Saudi defence ministry. "I suffered from loneliness," the general who called his book *Desert Warrior* tells us. " . . . To calm myself and to take my mind off the war, I developed a night-time addiction to American TV comedies. After chortling over one of these for half an hour, I would fall peacefully to sleep."

It got worse. Arguing with the French defence minister, Prince Khaled indirectly compares himself to Churchill, whose Cross of Lorraine (de Gaulle) was also hard to bear. He fusses because Schwarzkopf's chair is bigger than his, insists that Schwarzkopf must visit his office for meetings rather than the other way round, and describes the Khafji fighting as "a pivotal battle of the war." His task, Khaled solemnly informs us, was "more difficult and complicated" than Schwarzkopf's. Khaled cannot kneel when he accepts an honour from Queen Elizabeth and goes on to pick up Légions d'Honneur and other decorations from France, Bahrain, Hungary, Kuwait, Morocco, Niger, Oman, Qatar, Senegal and, of course, Saudi Arabia. This was, the general informs us, "something of a record . . . for an Arab soldier in war," adding happily that "I would like to thank those who gave me a medal." Is this really what soldiering is all about?

Khaled tells us about the need to protect Saudi Arabia's unique culture and "traditions." The latter, though he doesn't say so, include lopping off the heads of criminals—shooting in the back of the head if the condemned prisoner is a woman—and virtual apartheid for the entire female population of the kingdom. Khaled spends two pages dictating the need for loyalty to the royal family—the system by which 5,000 or so princes, including himself, dominate a land of around 9 million people after inviting the Americans to protect them. Khaled's own father, Prince Sultan, he constantly reminds us, was defence minister and played a role "as important as that of Defence Secretary Cheney in the United States." Yet it was Prince Sultan who suggested as America prepared for war that the West should perhaps do a deal with Saddam after all.

In Khaled's sahara of a book, there are occasionally revealing moments; how the Iraqi intelligence service infiltrated the postwar Iraqi refugee camps in Saudi Arabia, for example, and Schwarzkopf's stunning lapse at Safwan when he gave the Iraqis permission to use helicopter gunships after the ceasefire. "Absolutely no problem," the American told the amazed Iraqi generals. " . . . this is a very important point, and I want to make sure that's recorded, that military helicopters can fly over Iraq . . . " Thank you, the Iraqis said. And went on to slaughter the Shia of Basra and the Kurds of the north.

The good prince quotes Clausewitz, but had to take a holiday after the war "to recover my composure after the stress of the great events in which I had played a part." He often suffered, it transpires, "from nightmares about fighting, about death . . . Had I done a good job? I leave this to the judgement of my contemporaries—and to history."


As PRINCE KHALED WAS RECOVERING from the war and preparing for his holidays, the wreckage of the Iraqi army was streaming home, still under ferocious attack by the Americans. After the ceasefire, for example, General Barry McCaffrey's 24th U.S. Infantry Division staged a four-hour assault against retreating Iraqis near the Euphrates River, destroying more than 750 vehicles, including a busload of women and children, and killing thousands of soldiers. An Apache helicopter crewman was heard yelling "Say hello to Allah" as he launched a Hellfire missile at them. Not a single American was killed.* Western news agency journalists in Baghdad interviewed fleeing soldiers who described the horrific battlefield massacres. "It was dark," one Iraqi told the Associated Press. "I was stepping on bodies, arms, legs and heads of dead soldiers." Another described how "we were taken in army trucks and cars from the battlefield, and scores of dead bodies covered the 12-lane highway. We would not stop to pick up the living wounded. We ran for our lives."

---

*The most thorough investigation of this scandalous attack was conducted by the same man who revealed the Abu Ghraib torture scandal in 2004: Seymour Hersh. As usual, the "pool" journalists failed to uncover the extent of the 24th Division's killings and presented it as an Iraqi assault on the Americans.

In the years to come, I would meet many of the Iraqi soldiers who survived those terrible last days. Lieutenant Ehsan al-Safi was a junior officer in the Iraqi 15th Engineering Brigade when he and a friend found themselves under American air attack on a Kuwait bridge. "Covered in flesh" from other soldiers, they lay on the ground as two more Iraqis leaped to safety from their armoured personnel carrier. The blast of the American bomb hurled the abandoned vehicle forward towards el-Safi's friend. When he got to his feet, he grabbed his friend's arm "but there was nobody attached to it." On two wide parallel highways north of Kuwait, the Iraqis were burned alive in convoy traffic jams. Many of them were conscripts. Some survivors whom I met came from the Kurdish and Turkoman communities in Iraq, a number were Armenians, one of whom had grandparents murdered in the 1915 genocide. One Kurd to whom I spoke had endured the firestorm on the highway and escaped back to Iraq, only to find himself homeless in the mountains of the far north when the Kurdish uprising—encouraged by the Americans—was crushed by Saddam.

SADDAM'S ROAD TO RUIN stretches for 100 kilometres up the highway from Kuwait City to the Iraqi border at Safwan. It is a road of horror, destruction and shame; horror because of the hundreds of mutilated corpses lining its route, destruction because of the thousands of Iraqi tanks and armoured vehicles that lie charred or abandoned there, shame because in retreat Saddam's soldiers piled their armour with loot. Shame, too, because we punished them all with indiscriminate, unnecessary death.

The dead are strewn across the road only 8 kilometres out of Kuwait City and you see them still as you approach the Iraqi frontier where the burning oil wells are squirting fire into the sky. It is, of course, the horror that strikes you first. Scarcely 25 kilometres north of the city, the body of an Iraqi general lies half out of his stolen limousine, his lips apart, his hands suspended above the roadway. You can see his general's insignia on his stained uniform. He had driven into the back of an armoured vehicle in the great rout. Farther up the road, corpses lay across the highway beside tanks and army trucks. One Iraqi had collapsed over the carriageway, curled up, his arms beside his face, a neat moustache beneath a heavy head with its back blown away.

Only when ambulance drivers arrived and moved his body did we realise that his left leg had also gone. In a lorry which had received a direct hit from the air, two carbonised soldiers still sat in the cab, their skulls staring forward up the road towards the country they never reached. Kuwaiti civilians stood over the bodies laughing, taking pictures of the Iraqis' mortal remains.

The wholesale destruction begins another 25 kilometres on, beneath a motorway bridge that stands at the bottom of a low hill called Mutla. It was here, trapped by American and British bombing of the road at the top of the hill, that the Iraqis perished in their hundreds, probably their thousands. Panic-stricken they must have been, as they jammed themselves in their vehicles, twenty abreast, a vast column 6 kilometres long, picked off by the American and British pilots. There were tanks and stolen police cars, artillery and fire engines and looted limousines, amphibious vehicles, bulldozers and trucks. I lost count of the Iraqi corpses crammed into the smouldering wreckage or slumped face-down in the sand. In scale and humiliation, it was, I suppose, a little like Napoleon's retreat from Moscow. There must have been all of two divisions spread up this road.

Napoleon's army burned Moscow and Saddam's army tried to burn Kuwait, but the French did not carry back this much loot. Amid the guns and armour, I found heaps of embroidered carpets, worry beads, pearl necklaces, a truckload of air conditioners, new men's shirts, women's shoes, perfume, cushions, children's games, a pile of hardback Korans on top of five stolen clocks. There were crude rubber gas masks and anti-gas boots—the Iraqis had prepared themselves for chemical warfare of a kind—and thousands of rifles, rocket-propelled grenades, shells and bayonets.

My car bumped over unspent grenades and rifle barrels. I discovered several tanks and armoured vehicles abandoned in such terror that the keys were in the ignition, the engines still running. I found one that was loaded with suitcases full of matches, rugs, food mixers and lipstick. A child's musical box lay in the sand still playing "and a happy new year, and a happy new year . . . " Iraqi equipment— daggers, belts, berets and helmets—lay everywhere with their owners' names written on the straps.

On top of one armoured vehicle, its engine still idling, I found the helmets of Lieutenant Rabah Homeida and Private Jamal Abdullah. They had stood no chance, for in front of their vehicle lay another 3 kilometres of burned Iraqi military traffic, at the end of which stood a squad of American soldiers from the U.S. 2nd Armored Division whose motto—*Hell on Wheels*—appropriately summed up the fate of the thousands in the ghoulish traffic jam below. No film could do credit to this chaos. It was both surreal and pathetic. Saddam Hussein called it an "orderly withdrawal."

Around the carnage and dust drove two British Land Rovers of the 26th Field Regiment Royal Artillery, a giant Union flag floating above both of them. It was Staff Sergeant Bob Halls and Gunner Barry Baxter who showed us the track through the sand to reach the Mutla Ridge, picking their way past unexploded cluster bombs and live shells. "You can't really take in what war does till you've seen it," Baxter says to me. "Why did this happen? Saddam's forces are nothing to be reckoned with, are they? They didn't want to go to war. They just wanted to put their hands up. They are our enemy but they didn't want to be in the war in the first place. They are a sorry sight to see."

They were. The prisoners we saw—remnants of the world's fourth-largest army—were unshaven and exhausted, herded by soldiers of the 16th/5th Lancers, trudging through the desert, throwing personal arms onto a pile of weapons 4 or 5 metres high, guarded by U.S. troops. All the way to the Iraqi border, we found the detritus of the Iraqi retreat, tanks and armour across the road, on their backs in ditches, scattered over the flat desert on either side. Some were still burning. The Americans and British looked at all this with a mixture of awe and relief.

Lieutenants Andrew Nye and Roy Monk of C Company, 1st Battalion, the Staffordshire Regiment, had spent part of the morning burying the dead. They included women and children, Iraqis or Kuwaitis or Egyptian refugees fleeing the battlefront and caught in the last American and British air attacks. Lt. Nye had lost one of his own men in the fighting. "One of our blokes was killed," he said. "He was hit in the chest by a rocket-propelled grenade after some Iraqis had raised the white flag. It may be that some of the Iraqis didn't know others had surrendered. By then we had grown so used to the prisoners, we had seen so many of them and heard about the huge numbers of POWs on the radio. You have to feel this to believe it. There are booby-traps here and the Iraqis who died on this road were stripping Kuwait City. But I shudder to think what it would have been like in their position."

We did. Imagining death—the end of life—can leave one gasping with horror at the vacuum, with the nothingness to follow. But to become one with these burned creatures at the moment of immolation, the seconds of indescribable pain, the brief awareness, the *knowing* of such suffering, this was surely too much. Yet we looked into these carbonised faces. I sought something from them, I suppose, some terrible mystery which I was not entitled to search for and which they were not entitled to reveal.

My AWACS friend was flying the day after the highway of death had been bombed. "I remember," he wrote to me six years later:

> ... how absolutely ecstatic the briefer was when telling us how "the JSTARS had spotted a whole convoy up near Safwan and had called the ABCCC who called in the A-10s who just had a field day!" Apparently, after incinerating a few U.S. Marine Bradleys and at least one British APC, the A-10 pilots had finally improved their aim.

Much later, we would discover that even the pilots had been sickened—far too late—by their own vile handiwork. "Low pilot morale" was the way it was put, and the British foreign secretary said as much six months later. His words carry infinitely more meaning today than they did then, because his warnings—of what would have happened if "we" had not stopped in Kuwait, of the dangers awaiting "us" if "we" went all the way to Baghdad—connect directly with the disaster in which "our" armies now find themselves in Iraq. If ever the ghosts of the future could come to haunt us, many must have been the phantoms who came back down the years to gaze upon the Mutla Ridge on those cold and overcast days of 1991. Some people, British foreign secretary Hurd said,

> argue that the coalition should have carried the fight to Baghdad and demanded Saddam's head. In fact, once the Iraqi forces had effectively lost

their capacity to defend themselves, many pilots were reluctant to continue the fight . . . First, the coalition explicitly limited its objectives to those set out in the UN resolutions, which related to the liberation of Kuwait. Second, had we gone to Baghdad we would have found ourselves forced to choose and then sustain a new Iraqi government.

This, Hurd said, would have drawn "allied troops" into the "morass of Iraqi politics," risking "our" lives and public support for the mission.

LATE ON THE AFTERNOON of 2 March 1991, my old friend Alex Thomson of ITV and I drove from the "highway of death," north up the road to Safwan and beyond, to a place where the Iraqi dead lay in profusion over the desert floor. Packs of dogs had got among them, tearing the limbs apart, ripping at clothes to gnaw at stomachs and thighs. The dogs fought each other for this nightmare feast. Some had already run off with severed body parts. One dog had an arm in its mouth and raced across the sand, the fingers of a dead hand trailing cruelly through the muck. Thomson's crew dutifully filmed this obscenity. Alex, who was to write one of the most critical studies of the media in this war, looked at me coldly. "Never get on the air of course," he said. "Just for the archives."

And that was it. When journalists wished to film the war, they chafed at the restrictions placed upon them; but when the war was officially over and the restrictions lifted and they could film anything they wanted, they did not, after all, want to show what conflict was like. I noticed how the Iraqis who had comparatively clean deaths—those who were obliging enough to die in one piece and collapse picturesquely, lying like fallen warriors by the roadside—would turn up on television screens, briefly of course, to symbolise the "human cost" of war. But the world was not allowed to see what we saw, the burned, eviscerated souls, the chopped-off, monstrous heads, the scavenging animals. Thus did we help to make war acceptable. We connived at war, supported it, became part of it.

Back in Kuwait that night, I filed my dispatch to *The Independent*, tired and depressed and angry at my own profession. To the end of my report on the Iraqi dead, I added, almost as an afterthought, two paragraphs about Egyptian guest workers who were fleeing the chaos to the north:

As we neared the Iraqi frontier, Egyptian refugees began to straggle down the highway, some weighed down with blankets and begging for water, others pushing their surviving possessions in rusting supermarket trollies, a few asking for cigarettes. Many were too tired to talk, having walked 60 miles from Basra.

"They shoot all Egyptian people in Iraq," one of them said, but would not add to that chilling remark. A group of American soldiers said they had heard the Iraqis were shooting at refugees on the border.

I called the paper's foreign desk an hour later to ask if Harvey Morris had any questions about my report. "Ah-ha, I was interested in the last two paragraphs," he said. "I suppose you realise what you are reporting, don't you? The rising has started."

How typical that I should have failed to realise what this meant. Now that the Gulf War was officially over, the real bloodbath was about to begin.

# CHAPTER SIXTEEN

# *Betrayal*

*. . . waving our red weapons o'er our heads,*
*Let's all cry, "peace, freedom, and liberty!"*

—Shakespeare, *Julius Caesar,* III, i, 110–11

ON THE EVENING OF 24 FEBRUARY 1991, as the Sky television crew and I were preparing to set off for Kuwait from the Saudi border town of Khafji, a CIA-run radio station called The Voice of Free Iraq broadcast a call to the Iraqi people to rise up against Saddam Hussein's regime. It was explicit: the war and destruction would continue unless the Iraqi people overthrew their dictator. The radio didn't say that the moment of liberty was at hand. Iraqis were told that if they wanted to survive, they must rebel. "Hit the headquarters of the tyrant and save the homeland from destruction," the radio said. But anyone listening to the station was entitled to believe that the Western and Arab armies would come to their rescue.

The speaker was Salah Omar al-Ali, ex-member of Saddam's Revolutionary Command Council and the Regional Command of the Arab Socialist Baath Party, personally purged by Saddam in 1972. The radio was transmitting from Saudi Arabia. And al-Ali was quite specific:

> Rise to save the homeland from the clutches of dictatorship so that you can devote yourself to avoid the dangers of the continuation of the war and destruction. Honourable sons of the Tigris and the Euphrates, at these decisive moments of your life, and while facing the danger of death at the hands of foreign forces, you have no option in order to survive and defend the homeland but to put an end to the dictator and his criminal gang.

No option. No option if Iraqis were to survive. This was crude, frightening stuff. Saddam, al-Ali said, was "the criminal tyrant of Iraq" who was pushing the country's sons to a massacre because he had refused to withdraw from Kuwait:

> Prove to your people and nation that you are faithful and honourable sons of this generous country and this honourable nation. Stage a revolution now, before it is too late. He thinks of himself alone. He is not interested in what suffering you endured during the past few months of this destructive

crisis. He insists on continuing to push your faithful sons into this massacre in defence of his false glory, privileges and criminal leadership.

Saddam, according to the broadcast, had already smuggled his family and personal wealth from Iraq. "He will flee the battlefield when he becomes certain that the catastrophe has engulfed every street, every house and every family in Iraq." The Voice of Free Iraq used Iraqi state radio frequencies and the same opening music for its news broadcasts; it had begun its short- and medium-wave broadcasts at the start of the year, and the Iraqis had tried to jam the station's heretical messages almost at once, even though it only transmitted for a few hours every evening.

But it wasn't just the CIA's clandestine radio that was relaying this dangerous, apocalyptic message. Seventeen-year-old Iraqi Shiite Haidar al-Assadi listened in Basra to the call to arms over the Arabic Service of the Voice of America and expected "the allies to liberate Iraq and rid us of this criminal." He put a Kalashnikov rifle over his shoulder and walked the streets of his native city, tearing pictures of Saddam off the walls. Only days earlier, al-Assadi's home had been destroyed when a U.S. jet fired a missile into several buildings in the city, leaving his brother with shrapnel wounds to the shoulder. But like many other Iraqis who suffered under Allied bombardment, he heeded the American appeal.

"I joined in because ever since I opened my eyes, people around me hated Saddam. Both my uncles were imprisoned for twelve years for saying that the Iran–Iraq war would not end without the death of Saddam . . . I remember listening to the Arabic service of the Voice of America which told us that the uprising was large and we would be liberated." By 6 March, *The Independent*'s Richard Dowden had moved in front of the American army and reached the Iraqi city of Nasiriyah 160 kilometres north-west of Basra, already in Iraqi rebel hands. As he wrote in his extraordinary dispatch:

> The revolution, bursting out after years of oppressive Baath rule, appears confused and chaotic, united only by the hatred for Saddam Hussein of the Shia Muslims in southern Iraq. It is a nationalist revolution aimed at ridding the country of the Baath regime, according to its leaders, but it also has strong overtones of an Iranian-style Islamic fundamentalism. Abu Iman, the rebel commander of this town, said the regime would be replaced by a government of the people which would not model itself on western democracy or the Iranian revolution, but follow its own path. It would be neither Sunni nor Shia but for all Iraqis.

Where Saddam's portrait had been defaced, Dowden found posters of Ayatollah Khomeini and a leading Shiite cleric. But he was also given a printed announcement by Nasiriyah's "revolutionary committee" which said the aims of the new government

> were to finish the war, sweep away the Baath system and establish a new government based on democracy and nationalism. It ordered Baath mem-

bers to join the new government despite what they had done to Iraq. However, according to the revolutionary leaders, the governor of the town, Taha Yassin Hussein, and other leading local Baath figures have already been executed. This appears to be a revolution of the poor. All its leaders were scruffily dressed in dirty *kuffiyas* and *djellabas*; they were unshaven and argued constantly . . .

Yet another "highway of death" had greeted Dowden as he approached Nasiriyah, where the road was:

> littered with wrecked military vehicles, many of them with decomposing bodies hanging from them or lying on the ground near by. At the entrance to the town, by the rebels' roadblock (which consists of a chair, a table, two tyres and a cluster bomb casing) are two juggernauts. Inside each are the corpses of about 100 Iraqi soldiers. These refrigerated meat lorries were bringing the bodies back from the front four days ago and, we were told, their drivers refused to stop at the roadblock. The rebels fired on the drivers who fled. The bodies have not been touched since.

But Dowden finished his report with a disturbing comment from the local rebel leader, Abu Iman:

> The Americans are not helping us. They stop us on the road and take our weapons. It is they who helped build up Saddam, then they destroyed him; now the war is over they will support him again.

In the years to come, American and British leaders would deny responsibility for the mass Iraqi uprising which they encouraged. Already in northern Iraq, tens of thousands of Kurds had also risen against their oppressors and—ignoring past American betrayals—eagerly awaited allied help. The first reaction of British prime minister John Major was sarcastic. "I don't recall asking the Kurds to mount this particular revolution," he snottily remarked. And in the first days of Kuwait's liberation, the men who claimed they'd fought a "just" war got away with it. So great was the relief in the West that so few Americans and British had been killed during the conflict which had apparently ended, so appalling were the stories of individual Iraqi atrocities in Kuwait, so enormous the oil fires—though they burned at even greater temperatures across southern Iraq, where American B-52s had set the wells on fire—that the terrifying events north of the American lines went initially almost unnoticed.

War breeds a special kind of exhaustion. We all suffered from it beneath the vast clouds of burning oil that turned day into night, blanketing huge areas of Kuwait and Iraq; Western and Arab soldiers, fleeing Iraqis, liberated Kuwaitis, fearful Palestinians, Iraqi prisoners, journalists too, we moved through a cloak of half-darkness and fatigue. Slogging fourteen floors up the fire escapes of Kuwait's

Meridien Hotel, the reporters who might have been moving further north were staggering under a burden of broken phone lines, immense tiredness and statistics. The figures came at us like gunfire. General Schwarzkopf announced on 27 February that "we were 150 miles from Baghdad and there was nothing between us and Baghdad" and that his army had captured or destroyed 3,000 Iraqi tanks, 1,857 armoured vehicles and 2,140 artillery pieces. More than 50,000 Iraqis had been taken prisoner. British military figures put the number of prisoners at 175,000 and suggested that up to 4,000 Iraqi tanks might have been destroyed in the liberation and the thirty-eight-day air bombardment that preceded it.

No one questioned how Schwarzkopf could have acquired such precise statistics less than twenty-four hours after President Bush had announced the liberation of Kuwait. He had confidently announced on 30 January that all thirty Scud missile sites in Iraq had been destroyed in "almost 1,500 sorties" while on 14 February, U.S. Lieutenant General Tom Kelly said that thirty days of bombardment had destroyed about 1,300 "of the 4,280 Iraqi tanks in and around Kuwait" and that around another 500 had been severely damaged. Only a truly sceptical eye would have spotted a Reuters report on 27 February which quoted British Captain Simon Oliver of the Royal Scots Dragoon Guards as saying that Saddam's best Republican Guard troops, still equipped with their T-72 tanks, appeared to have escaped the allied forces south of Basra. "We have seen tank tracks leading north, and the Republican Guards may have withdrawn," he said. Journalists should have guessed what the military must already have known; that the Republican Guards had other, far more pressing business inside southern Iraq.

The Americans were quite specific about their casualties: 148 Americans killed. They were less forthcoming about Iraqi losses. On 14 February, Kelly said he thought "the number's very high because of the constant bombing." By 28 February the Saudis were talking about 100,000 Iraqi dead, while a former French military analyst, Colonel Jean-Louis Dufour, estimated Iraqi dead at up to 150,000. Schwarzkopf talked only of "a very, very large number." On 19 February, Saadoun Hamadi, the former Iraqi deputy defence minister, had claimed that 26,000 Iraqis—civilian and military—had been killed in 65,000 air sorties. When a Pentagon source told *Newsday* almost six months after the Kuwait liberation that 8,000 Iraqi troops had been buried alive in their trenches by the earthmovers and ploughs mounted on the tanks of the attacking U.S. Mechanized Infantry Division, the brief moment of compassion which this engendered probably had more to do with guilty consciences over Western inaction towards the Iraqi insurgents than it did with the enormous loss of human life that it represented.*

*Journalists would subject Iraqi armed forces to unprecedented metamorphoses in the quarter-century between 1980 and 2005. When they invaded Iran, many of the Iraqi army units were obsequiously referred to in the Western media as "crack troops"—they were, after all, attacking "expansionist" Iran. After the same army invaded "friendly" Kuwait ten years later, they became the "enemy," often described—not without reason—as ruthless or cruel. Once Iraqis—including many of the same "enemy" troops defeated in the Kuwait liberation—turned

Only later would we learn some less heroic truths about the liberation of Kuwait. The Americans, it transpired, dropped nearly as many tons of bombs each day as were dropped on Germany and Japan daily during the Second World War. Of the 148 U.S. servicemen killed, 35—almost one-quarter—had lost their lives to "friendly fire" from other American forces.* The non-partisan U.S. General Accounting Office would subsequently state that the Pentagon and its military contractors made claims for the precision of their Stealth fighter jets, Tomahawk cruise missiles and laser-guided "smart bombs" that were "overstated, misleading, inconsistent with the best available data or unverifiable." The supposedly "invisible" Stealth achieved only around a 40 per cent success rate on bombing runs, while only 8 per cent of the bomb tonnage dropped on Iraqi targets were "smart" or guided munitions. The much-trumpeted Patriot anti-missile missile, the GAO said, destroyed only 40 per cent of the Scud missiles aimed at Israel and 70 per cent of those fired at Saudi Arabia. In fact, as Seymour Hersh, that blessing for journalism, would reveal, an Israeli air force report later stated that "there is no clear evidence of a single successful intercept" of an Iraqi Scud by a Patriot over Israel.

Inside the city of Kuwait, we journalists were overwhelmed by stories of Kuwaiti loss and fierce revenge against the Palestinians, a phenomenon that the Americans simply ignored. Only a week after the liberation, parts of the city resembled the anarchy of wartime Beirut, with gunmen controlling streets and Palestinians kidnapped from their homes by armed Kuwaitis. Western ambassadors and relief organisations pleaded with the few Kuwaiti ministers to have arrived—the emir and his immediate family had not yet deigned to return—to restore law and order before they lost control of the capital.

Yet even the Kuwaiti army seemed set on retaliating against the Palestinian community, some of whom had undoubtedly collaborated with the Iraqi occupiers. Up to 400 young Palestinians were said to have been kidnapped from their homes in the first three days of March. When Colin Smith of *The Observer* and I drove into the Kuwait City suburb of Hawali—home to tens of thousands of Palestinians—on the morning of 3 March, we found Kuwaiti soldiers driving twelve armoured vehicles through the streets, shooting in the air, ordering shops to close and beating Palestinian civilians who fell into their hands. Incredibly—or so it seemed to us—American Special Forces troops who were present did nothing to

---

on Saddam in 1991, they became "rebels." But when the surviving ex-soldiers then rose up against the American occupation after 2003, they turned into "terrorists," "die-hards" or—incredibly—"Saddam loyalists." Later, perhaps because they attacked the world's only superpower so ferociously, we gifted them with the title of "insurgents."

*Among the many thousands of Americans who were decorated for their role in the Kuwait liberation was a young gunner on a Bradley fighting vehicle who received the Bronze Star and several other medals. Timothy McVeigh, a promising young soldier, then tried to join the U.S. Special Forces, but dropped out and left the army embittered on 31 December 1991. He was executed on 11 June 2001 for the 19 April 1995 Oklahoma City bombing, which killed 167 Americans.

stop this brutality, instead shouting obscenities at journalists who asked why they did not intervene.

When three armed Kuwaiti soldiers began to beat up a Palestinian boy on a bicycle in Hawali, Smith and I were forced to intervene, physically pulling the Kuwaitis off the young man and ordering them to lower their rifles. The fact that Smith and I were still wearing the camouflaged gas capes in which we had smuggled ourselves into Kuwait must have persuaded the Kuwaitis that we were allied personnel and they let the boy go. But when we shouted at U.S. Special Forces personnel to help us, they either stared at us or laughed. When I asked a U.S. Special Forces officer, a captain, why he would not come to our assistance, he replied: "You having a nice day? We don't want your sort around here with your rumours. This is martial law, boy. You have a big mouth. Fuck off!" Smith and I took the number of the American vehicle—IS055A—and I later visited the reopened U.S. embassy to tell them what we had seen. By chance, the BBC had filmed the incident. After some minutes, a U.S. officer emerged along with Fred Cuny, one of the most courageous American aid officials of the postwar years. But the American officer seemed little interested in what we had to tell him. "Have you people seen any sign of Palestinian terrorists in these streets?" he wanted to know.

So here we go again, I said to Smith later. Palestinians are terrorists, terrorists, terrorists. The Americans were more anxious about "terrorists" than law and order.* The two men confirmed the registration number of the Special Forces Humvee and said they would "look into the matter." The soldier admitted that "we're having problems all over the city—we've had a colonel of ours threatened by armed men. Things are getting completely out of control. Has this BBC film been shown?" Cuny, a tall, balding, heroic man who was to acquire legendary fame for his selfless work with refugees in Kurdistan and Sarajevo—and in Chechnya, where he would ultimately lose his life—seemed at first more interested in preventing the BBC from airing the tape than in persuading U.S. forces to act with discipline. "I thought we'd stopped the tape getting on air," he said, and seemed put out that he had failed.

In itself, the incident was minuscule. Compared with the crimes committed by the Iraqis in recent weeks—not to mention the uprising now burning its way across Iraq—the youth's painful experience was insignificant. But it was symbolic of a disturbing reaction among U.S. forces in the aftermath of the liberation. Weeks later, Cuny would tell me that he had filed a report on the incident and that the abu-

---

*As so often, American "intelligence sources" had contributed to this mind-set. As early as 2 February, Douglas Jehl of the *Los Angeles Times*, a "pool" journalist with American forces in Saudi Arabia, was referring to "intelligence reports issued to commanders last week warning that more than a dozen Palestinian terrorists were known to be operating in the sector now occupied by [the] 1st Armored Division." These non-existent "terrorists" were linked by "most officers" with the disappearance of fifty American military vehicles from a U.S. base. How twelve Palestinians—or anyone else—could have stolen so many vehicles went unexplained. Jehl did suggest one possibility, far down in his dispatch: that U.S. soldiers were themselves stealing the trucks and Humvees to cannibalise for spare parts for their own vehicles.

sive Special Forces team had been sent back to the United States within days. But they had been disciplined not because they allowed a Palestinian youth to be beaten in front of their eyes. They were sent home because they "submitted an incomplete report." The Special Forces officer had informed his superiors of a "confrontation" with journalists—but had chosen not to mention the reason for this "confrontation": his refusal to help the Palestinian boy.

Much worse was to follow. Death squads roamed the streets of Kuwait, one of them run by a son and nephew of a senior Kuwaiti prince. American government officials held a secret meeting with the prince later in March 1991, and, after listening to his indignant denials, handed him a list of names, dates and other details of the execution squads. Cuny was transferred to the fields of Kurdistan in northern Iraq to cope with the tide of Kurdish refugees fleeing Saddam's vengeance, and it was he who disclosed to me in late April that an undercover team of U.S. Special Forces and specially trained military reservist officers—including a U.S. federal judge and an assistant district attorney for Philadelphia—had been tasked to track down the fate of hundreds of missing Palestinians in Kuwait. The State Department, according to Cuny, learned long before the liberation that Kuwaiti authorities had drawn up secret plans to deport the entire Palestinian community into Iraq in buses painted with the logo of the Red Crescent humanitarian relief organisation. Another plan that reached American ears was for Kuwaitis to execute large numbers of Palestinians "to try to stampede the community into a mass exodus"— a variation on the method used by Israel to depopulate western Palestine in 1948, although this was not an observation the Americans made.

Cuny admitted that "things were not right at first in Kuwait. Our people on the ground didn't understand what their role was. Some of our senior officers were not reporting things up the channel. We would find that our Special Forces officers based in Kuwait police stations would know people were being tortured there but couldn't prove it. We would have American officers who would hear someone screaming but who couldn't say the man was being tortured because he wasn't witnessing it. So they wouldn't report it to us." All of this I duly reported in *The Independent*, although the inaction of Americans listening to screams of torture yet failing to report them because they couldn't actually see the torture was a truly bizarre—almost Iraqi—explanation.

But the kidnapping of Palestinians was already going on,* and, in the end, the Kuwaiti government got its way. Within months, it deported more than 200,000

---

*There was no difficulty in gathering evidence of this. In Hawali, Sara Moussa told me how she watched her two sons, Tahseen and Amin, taken from their home on 1 March 1991 by six Kuwaitis armed with G-3 rifles. "They searched the house, they tied their hands and blindfolded them," she said. "When they told the Kuwaitis not to touch their sisters, the gunmen beat them with their rifles. Then they put them both in the trunk of a car and drove them away. I have not seen them since." Tamam Salman's twenty-three-year-old son Ibrahim was taken by gunmen the same day, thrown into the trunk of a car and driven off. She said that when she asked a Kuwaiti policeman for help, he spat at her "because I am a Palestinian." Other testimony to Kuwaiti persecution appeared in numerous European newspapers.

Palestinians. Others would follow later. The only difference was that many of them travelled north to Iraq in Red Cross buses actually hired by the Red Cross—rather than in buses disguised with the insignia of the Red Crescent. The Kuwaiti resistance themselves acknowledged that 5 per cent of their comrades-in-arms against the Iraqis were Palestinians, but this did not save them.

Yet the experience of those same Kuwaitis was sometimes so terrible that other crimes faded from our tired reports. By the time of the liberation, the resistance had already compiled a list of martyrs, who included women as well as men, some of whom—arrested in the very last hours of the Iraqi occupation—suffered terrible fates. Abu Sami, Abu Ahmed and Abu Saad were among them. "The Iraqis knew who they were," a member of the Kuwaiti resistance in the suburb of Qurain told me. "They had been watching them for many days and they decided to get them at the end." Two of their comrades in Qurain were women but their fate was the same. "They penetrated their heads with drills," the resistance man, Tariq Ahmed, said. "We saw the bodies afterwards. They were murdered in this way." Such appalling accounts might be dismissed as exaggeration were it not for some of the bodies that later turned up in Kuwaiti hospitals. At least three were found to have drill holes through their arms and legs, mechanically crucified.

If nothing else, it should have given us a terrifying picture of the treatment that the Iraqi government would visit upon any Iraqi rebels who unwisely heeded the American call for insurrection further north and then fell into the hands of Saddam's security men. Still, however, reporters in Kuwait—including myself—were obsessed by the extent of the Iraqi army's defeat in Kuwait rather than by its fearful reincarnation inside Iraq. In the very early days of the liberation, I drove beyond the Kuwaiti frontier with Lara Marlowe of *Time* magazine. There was still little sign of the terrible events taking place beyond the American lines, only the distant sound of shooting further north, and an American army officer who talked of men arriving at his checkpoint to beg for weapons and being told that they could have none.

On the Iraqi highway north of Safwan, a young black tank crewman from the American 1st Armored Division offered me a cold Pepsi on top of his Abrams tank and we sat there together, staring north across the grey and dun-coloured wastes of southern Iraq. The tank was parked on a perfect clover-leaf motorway intersection whose smooth six-lane highway possessed a dangerously normal perspective, a transplanted bit of Europe or America amid the debris of war, an illusion heightened by the concrete picnic tables placed at regular intervals along the road. It was cold and damp and we could hear the roar of the oil fires whose clouds towered high into the desolate sky. "Just think of it," the American tanker said after a while. "They call this the cradle of civilisation."

And of course, he was right. Just east of here lay the great ziggurat of Ur, the 4,000-year-old Sumerian city of Mesopotamia and biblical birthplace of Abraham; a sharp-eyed U.S. artillery officer had just stopped a tank crew firing live rounds into the monument when he spotted "historic ruins" on the corner of his map. North towards Baghdad lay Babylon and Nineveh and the great primal rivers of the Tigris and Euphrates, as well as the Shiite shrines of Najaf and Kerbala.

From the north, three Iraqi soldiers in the red berets of Saddam's Republican Guards walked gingerly towards Lara and myself. They had no weapons and moved with their arms away from their sides in the familiar "walking duck" attitude we all adopted when we wanted to demonstrate that we were harmless. Cigarettes? they asked. We gave them some Marlboros, watched by the American soldier on the tank. Then the tallest of the three men pointed to an Iraqi army truck abandoned in a field to the north of the highway. Would we give him permission to drive it away? Sure, we said, but we'll just check with the Americans. Any problem with these guys taking their truck back? we asked. The soldier on the tank gave us a thumbs-up. "They're beaten—they can take their crap," he said. There were more cigarettes and the three Iraqis then walked purposefully to the Russian-built military lorry, started the engine and bumped off across the desert floor northwards. Only later did we ask ourselves why they came for the lorry. Amid all this destruction, why did they care about an abandoned truck? What would the Republican Guard want this stuff for now?

Next day, I understood. Back at Safwan, the empty clover-leaf motorway interchange had transformed itself from Western-normal to Eastern-terrible; drifting down the highway towards us came the damned. Some were Iraqi soldiers, others frightened women; many were wounded. Around us flowed a mass of huddled, shuffling figures, many crying, others throwing themselves into the motorway ditches to sleep. Hundreds of Kuwaitis kidnapped in the last hours of the occupation but newly freed by the Basra insurgents were now on the road with terrible stories of hospitals crammed with the dead and dying. One of them was a pharmacist and former Kuwaiti MP called Ahmed Baktiar. He had been taken to Basra hospital to help the wounded men and women littered across the floors, he said. "A young man just died in front of me. The tanks were coming and they were firing straight into the houses on each street, reducing the houses to ashes. There are lots of people dying of a strange sickness. Some think it's because they have to drink the water lying in the streets which is contaminated. Others say it's because the water in Basra now contains oil from the smoke over the city."*

And all the while, the tide of sick and starving and frightened people shuffled past us. Some came in hand-pushed carts, old men and babies with filthy blankets thrown over them, and I thought of the medieval carts that went from house to house when the Great Plague struck Europe, collecting the dead. Some of the peo-

---

*Unlike their government, Kuwaitis could show moving sympathy towards those who had also suffered. At Safwan stood a young Kuwaiti woman, Siham el-Marzouk, searching in vain among the wretched masses fleeing Iraq for her brother Faisal, kidnapped in the last days of the war. It was raining when she found a bedraggled Egyptian who had lived more than thirty years in Kuwait, working as a school caretaker, until abducted by the Iraqis. Now the Kuwaiti authorities would not let him return home. From bits of a shattered motorway intersection barrier, he had fashioned a hut to shield himself from the rain and pleaded for someone to tell the Egyptian ambassador in Kuwait of his plight, writing out the story of his grief on a piece of paper he had found in the sand, crying all the while. The Kuwaiti woman tried to comfort him, gave him food and money. When she saw a destitute Filipina woman, she took off her black woollen cloak and gave it to the refugee. Two days later, her kidnapped brother Faisal arrived safely at Safwan.

ple in these carts *were* dead. There were two television crews pointing their lenses at close range into the faces of the refugees, and I noticed how, for once, the faces did not react to the cameras. It was as if every face was also dead.

Two U.S. embassy officials were standing beside a station wagon along with a senior American officer. "We can't have them just all coming down here," one of the embassy men said to Staff Sergeant Nolde of the 1st Armored Division. "They can't cross the border. We have no facilities to handle this. They've got to go back." I noticed Cuny standing beside the embassy men, listening in silence. "Look, you've *got* to stop them moving down this road," the embassy man was saying. "It's tragic, I know that, but we simply don't have the facilities for them." Cuny asked if extra first-aid tents couldn't be erected for the refugees, and the embassy man sighed. It wasn't supposed to be like this. Liberation, a clean victory—and now this mess. And on television. You could see his problem. "You've got to stop them, Sergeant," the embassy man repeated. The officer joined in. "Iraqi agents could infiltrate back into Kuwait among the refugees."

But suddenly, there on this cold, damp, hellish road, all the bright sunlight of what was best about America—all the hope and compassion and humanity that Americans like to believe they possess—suddenly shone among us. For the young, tired 1st Armored staff sergeant turned angrily on the man from the U.S. embassy. "I'm sorry, sir. But if you're going to give me an order to stop these people, I can't do that. They are coming here begging, old women crying, sick children, boys begging for food. We're already giving them most of our rations. But I have to tell you, sir, that if you give me an order to stop them, I just won't do that." You could see the embassy men wince. First it was these pesky folk cluttering up the highway, then the television cameras, and now a soldier who wouldn't obey orders. But Sergeant Nolde just turned his back on the diplomat and walked over to a queue of refugee cars. "Tell these people to park at the side of the road over there," he yelled at the soldiers on his checkpoint. "Tell them to be patient but we'll try to look after them. Don't send them back."

Around Nolde, two famished Iraqi families, the women in filthy black chadors, the children barefooted, the men's faces dazed, were sitting in the dirt, tearing open the American military ration packs with their nails, scoffing the cold lumps of stew, pouring the contents of the sauce packets into their mouths. Across the cold sand, Nolde's soldiers had already helped to house an Iraqi woman and five children. Their story was simple and terrible. Their father had been executed for refusing to join the Republican Guard, their mother raped afterwards. The children were taken by their aunt southwards towards the American lines and there they all were now, squatting in an abandoned electricity shed. The Americans were feeding them, and had found four puppy dogs and a small, gentle-faced donkey which they had given to the grimy children.

Now a line of battered cars was driving steadily towards Nolde's position, packed with fearful civilians. Many had not eaten for days. The men were unshaven, the women in tears, the children had urinated in the car in the long journey across a devastated Iraq. Whole families were crying for civilian relatives killed in the allied air assault. Their convoy stank. A little girl was held out of the window of an old black Mercedes by a screaming woman. The child's body was jerking grotesquely, the convulsions about to kill her.

This was not quite what the generals in Riyadh had been thinking about when they announced their days of "battlefield preparation" and "communications inter-diction." Nolde ordered one of his men to run down the line of cars. "Where is the car with the sick child?" the soldier kept shouting in English, until someone trans-lated his question into Arabic. There was a wail from the Mercedes. "Get a medic down here, fast," the soldier ordered. Two more Americans arrived, a big, black soldier who took the little girl into his arms and touched her brow. "Oh, Jesus, she's having a fit," he said. "Tell the field hospital we're coming down with her."

The stricken child, together with her distraught mother, was taken from the car. Nolde arrived to order the vehicle out of the column. "Tell the rest of the family we need to search their vehicle then they can go and wait by the Red Cross truck," he said. Nolde and his twelve soldiers of the 1st Armored handed out more of their own rations. There would be no medals for performing these duties.

And with good reason. For a conflict of interest was becoming apparent. That is why the American officer and the U.S. diplomats had arrived to inspect Nolde's position. The newly returned and "legitimate" government of Kuwait—on whose behalf the Americans had gone to war—had no desire to see these refugees given sanctuary in Kuwait. The officer even muttered into Nolde's ear the following revealing sentence: "We had an Iraqi soldier give himself up near here the other day and a Kuwaiti soldier just took him to one side, shot him in the head and pushed his body into a ditch. If you let these people through Safwan, they could face the same danger." Nolde looked at the officer in contempt. He must have known very well what was going on. He was being ordered to send these people back to their deaths—not because of "lack of facilities" or "Iraqi infiltration" but because the Kuwaitis didn't want them cluttering up their newly liberated treasure-house emirate. And Nolde refused.

There weren't many good moments in this war—or any other—but here, just for a moment, an angel's wings brushed past us, the spirit of Raoul Wallenberg in the Budapest railyards, handing out Swedish passports to the doomed Jews of Hungary. No, this wasn't the Second World War. Let us have done with such obscene parallels. But these Iraqis would die if they were forced to turn back and the sergeant had disobeyed an order so that they might live. Just as an equally young officer on the Somme seventy-three years earlier had refused to execute another soldier. The American sergeant had refused to obey. Would that Bush and Cheney and Schwarzkopf and John Major had shown his courage now.

In Basra, the *Independent*'s correspondent, Karl Waldron—bravely clinging to his assignment until the last moment of escape on 6 March—now described the results of their betrayal with frightening simplicity:

It was almost over by 2.00 am. The T-72s of the Medina unit of the Repub-lican Guard deployed from the centre of Basra, crashing their way through barricades in the narrow streets . . . Small nests of resistance, mainly Shia groups such as the "Brothers of Atiq"—the liberated—maintained their fire until they were overrun or forced to withdraw by the advancing heavily armed infantry . . . on Nassr Street, the last remnants of a cadre, the day before proudly in uniform, red bandannas tied round sleeves and heads in the universal image of revolution, were now in mufti . . . There was ammunition aplenty here but it was the wrong calibre for their Soviet rifles; what was left that would work was now in the ammunition clips of the sentries watching for the Guard's advance. The squeak of tank tracks . . . signalled that they were closing in and the group fell back, its numbers gradually dwindling as men disappeared into the night with their treasonable loads. As we ran south, hopping the low fences round the apartment blocks, the noise of other tracks was audible, this time ahead of us . . .

The refugees who now streamed down to Safwan told in horrifying detail of what happened behind those Iraqi tanks. They had seen rebels hanged from tank barrels, tanks driving over corpses; some said that Baath party officials participated in the mass lynching of civilians. Iraqi troops who had gone across to the insurgents were now being hanged, their bodies riddled with bullets.

In Basra, Haidar al-Assadi, the seventeen-year-old who had listened to the Voice of America calling upon Iraqis to stage the uprising against Saddam, now fled the city for the Shatt al-Arab and the doubtful refuge of Iran.* Many of the surviving rebels did the same, along with Waldron:

It became clear that the only way out was back to the [river], a scramble over the rubble of recent allied air attack, where we hoped the tanks would not go, praying that the Iranian on the boat on the other side had not lost his nerve. When we found it at last, there were two others returning to Khorramshahr. One man in his late twenties, the other a little older, sat shivering in the prow of the small boat, taking cover from the wind and rain under a fish box tarpaulin. As they recovered, the muttered trickle of condemnation increased to a torrent: Saddam, Bush, Fahd, Mitterrand, formed an unholy alliance in the flow of curses. "Why didn't they come? Why did they let them come?" asked the younger man. He said the resistance groups had

*Al-Assadi's purgatory had only just begun. At first housed in unsanitary refugee camps in southern Iran, he later moved to Qom, where he was associated with the Iraqi opposition Al-Wahda party. But the Iranian authorities suspected the group was an American espionage network and al-Assadi was beaten into videotaping a false confession that he was trying to overthrow the Iranian government. In 1996—five years after his escape from Basra—he was sentenced to three years' imprisonment but briefly freed, he said, when he agreed to collaborate with the Iranians. Given fifteen days' leave from jail, he bribed his way across the border to Kurdish-held northern Iraq, received residency papers from Massoud Barzani's Kurdish Democratic Party, then set off across the Tigris River to Syria and on to Lebanon, where the author met him in 1998 as he desperately sought UN assistance to travel to Europe. He eventually left for Finland to live with his brother.

heard of the liberation of Kuwait, had expected allied support or at least that allied troops would prevent Iraq deploying its heavy armour into Basra province, much of which must have been seen by American satellites and must have passed within the range of allied guns. The spectre of the allies having won their war and now fearing the emergence of a Shia block in the northern Gulf, abandoning the people of Basra, will not go away. Even worse, the allies tolerating or encouraging the survival of the Saddam regime.

The Iraqi Shias were correct. "Better the Saddam Hussein we know than an unwieldy weak coalition, or a new strong man who is an unknown quantity," an American diplomat would later be quoted as saying. Those who survived Saddam's fury drifted semi-conscious to the American checkpoints in Iraq with further tales of mass executions—4,000 a day, they said, especially in the smaller Shia cities north-west of Basra or south of Baghdad where the population had no chance of fleeing to Iran. In many cases, the evidence of their testimony—which was all true—would not emerge for another twelve years. Only in 2003, for example, would I discover what happened in the town of Musayeb when at last—after the Anglo-American occupation—the mass graves began to be opened.

EACH NEW MASS GRAVE produces some extra helping of wickedness, some tiny incremental addition to cruelty. In the oven-grey desert west of the Tigris, it was a gleaming steel rod amid a heap of brown bones and a rag of cheap cloth that symbolised Saddam's rule: a hip replacement. A gravedigger gently tapped at the leg of the decomposing corpse beside it; there was a ghostly, hollow sound. The murdered man had a wooden leg. On the day of their death, they were hospital patients.

Body number 73—they are numbered by the diggers according to the chronology of their discovery—even had a hospital tag still tied to a bone. If they had their identity papers—and Saddam's executioners seemed to care little about such matters—their names were written in crayon onto the white shrouds in which their remains were wrapped. Thus these men's lives were revealed in a stranger's hand. "Abdul Jalil Kamel Badr" was written on a heap of bones, hair and decaying flesh. "Student at Kufa University Educational College—Arts Department." Somehow the "arts department" bit made one draw in one's breath.

They lay in their white shrouds—more than eighty of them—under the midday sun like dead sheep, just as others were lined in rows, 470 at the latest count, in the school basketball stadium back in Musayeb, the scruffy town on the Tigris where all of them—Shia Muslims to a man—obeyed the order of Hussein Kamel, Saddam's son-in-law, twelve years ago to assemble for a "meeting." Every man over seventeen had to be there and the few women who watched them gather in their thousands said that at least forty lorries were waiting for them on the first night, 5 March 1991. The Muslim Shia rebellion in this area had just been crushed. The executioners were already waiting at the desert killing fields at Joufer Safa. The name means "beach of rocks."

Many of the just-discovered dead still had their hands—or at least bits of their hand bones—tied behind their backs. Ahmed Kadum Rassoul had been bound in this way. So had Rada Mohamed Hamza from Hilla, and Ali Hassouni Alwan and Ibrahim Abdul Sadr. So had the unidentified male "wearing dark green military clothing and shoulder patches" who was obviously a deserter from the army who had taken up arms for the Shia uprising. "There are many other sites all round here," a farmer, who was helping in the excavation, told me wearily. "Some of us heard the shots at the time and saw the bulldozer. It was very 'ordered,' very routine. We were told that if anyone spoke of it, they would immediately be shot." He pointed to patches of disturbed land to the south—you could see the revetments left by the bulldozers once the deeds were done—and it was only then that the truth became obvious. There were thousands murdered here. Once a mass grave was closed, Saddam's killers simply dug another one.

You imagine a neat hole in the back of the skull. But as the Iraqi villagers in the grave pit brushed away at the grey desert soil, the heads that emerged were cracked, the bullet having broken open each skull. Nor did the earth always give up its dead so willingly. One gravedigger tugged for minutes at a great rock until it suddenly came away and a skull with dark hair and a shirt with bones spilling from it sprang towards him.

A clutch of American soldiers, a U.S. Rangers officer, two British forensic scientists and a bossy man from USAID were watching the exhumations. The soil was littered with cheap plastic sandals and sometimes—it was oddly moving—tufts of hair, like a child's on the floor of a barber's shop. Many of the bodies were in *dishdash* white domestic robes, the clothes they must have been wearing when they were ordered from their homes. Another corpse had a wristwatch whose date had stopped at 9 March; it had resolutely ticked away on its dead owner's wrist for another four days in the earth.

But mass graves are political as well as criminal affairs. Hussein Kamel Hassan, Saddam's son-in-law—the man who ordered this slaughter—is the same Hussein Kamel who fled to Jordan and gave away Iraq's chemical weapons secrets. Before he returned to Iraq—to be murdered, of course, by Saddam—Kamel Hassan talked to the CIA about Iraq's chemical weapons. Did he talk about this too, about the desert killing fields, about the fate of the men of Musayeb? In the children's stadium, the shrouds lay in military lines. Just over 170 had been positively identified. "These people are the victims of Saddam," Riad Abdul Emir—one of the mass grave investigators—said as he walked slowly along the rows of dead. "But they are also victims of the Arab regimes who cooperated with Saddam, and of the West which supported him—because our 1991 intifada could have succeeded were it not for the interference of the American administration. They let Saddam do this because it was in their interests at the time."

The presence of eight Egyptian bodies—apparently truck-drivers working in Iraq who may have tried to fight on the Shia side or merely been freed from prison in the initial days of the uprising—suggested that other foreigners might soon be found. Where, for example, were the more than 600 Kuwaiti prisoners who never returned from Iraq in 1991? Mohamed Ahmed was vainly searching through the corpses for his brother's remains. "These dead people had rights," he said. "But how can we ensure that they get their rights?"

BUT THE DEAD HAD NO RIGHTS in Iraq. Nor the living. In Beirut, twenty-three Iraqi opposition groups were brought together in mid-March 1991 under the auspices of Syria, a great mass of arguing, pleading, angry men—some of them Shia preachers, many others defectors from Saddam's regime—to demand help from the Americans so that they could set up a new and free nation amid the ruins of Iraq and the Baath party. It was pitiful. In a coffee shop opposite the Bristol Hotel, a Shia delegate looked at me with exhaustion. "What are the Americans up to?" he asked as dozens of his fellow Shias and Sunnis, Kurds and communists thronged the lobby. "The American army allowed the Republican Guards to pass down the road to Basra to attack our fighters there. Why did they do that? I thought the ceasefire agreement said there should be 'no movement of forces.' Do the Americans want Saddam to stay?"

I drank so many coffees that day. Scarcely a soul did not ask about America's intentions in Iraq, although the Beirut conference which began on 10 March—the area around the Bristol Hotel infested with Syrian troops and plain-clothes intelligence men with pistols in their belts—was supposed to agree on a common political goal for the post-Saddam era. There was even talk of a government-in-exile, although it was discreetly referred to in Baath-speak as a "joint command," an instrument of power in Baghdad after Saddam's demise which would ensure that a new nationalist and democratic Iraq would emerge from the ashes. But not a single American observer attended the conference.

It seemed to have a supreme irrelevance. I had driven from Kuwait via Saudi Arabia for Bahrain, where I picked up MEA's resumed service to the Gulf and flew home to Beirut. We travelled over Iran and at dawn over Turkey I looked east and saw the black oil clouds from Kuwait and Iraq hanging high over the frosts of Ararat, darkening even the sacred mountain of ancient Armenia and that country's own long-hidden mass graves. When I landed at Beirut and drove home and stood on my balcony in the cool morning air, I looked out over the Mediterranean and there in the distance was that same smudge of black rime on the horizon. Some of the Iraqis at the Bristol would walk down to the sea and notice the same grim mark of their country's fate.

Amid desolation, they searched for hope. They listed the Iraqi cities they claimed Saddam had lost. They insisted the mere fact that 325 Iraqis from such different faiths and factions could meet together was in itself a victory. The banner strung across their conference hall announced that "our unity is a guarantee of our salvation from dictatorship." No one, they told us, wanted to force an Islamic republic on Iraq—already they realised that this was the American and Kuwaiti and Saudi nightmare—but it was left to Ayatollah Taqi al-Mudaressi to express their fears. "Some Iraqis are beginning to think that the Americans prefer Saddam," he said. "They are wondering if America prefers Saddam without teeth to an Iraq without Saddam."

All the Iraqis in Beirut talked in code. When they proclaimed their desire for popular elections and a democracy, they were trying to assuage American fears that an Iran-style Islamic republic would be set up in a post-Saddam Iraq. When they talked of unity, they were attempting to convince each other that Iraq would not be divided into a Shia state, a Sunni state and a newly-born Kurdistan. And when they condemned the presence of foreign forces on Iraqi soil—for which read American troops—they were denying that they were Western stooges. "We will not accept foreigners on the sacred banks of the Tigris and the Euphrates," one of the delegates shouted from the platform. At which point, the Americans lost interest in this display of democracy.

This wasn't the only reason. For while the Islamic parties were largely Shia groups, the Sunnis who constituted about 40 per cent of the population were not represented by a single political organisation. Nor could Christians and communists have taken much inspiration from the start of the conference, at which delegates listened to a long reading from the Koran. Lebanese Shia leaders were closely linked to some of the Iraqi movements. Ayatollah Mohamed Bakr al-Hakim, the man believed to be behind the Basra insurrection—who would be assassinated in a massive bomb explosion in Najaf during the American occupation twelve years later—was the first cousin of Sayed Mohamed Hussein Fadlallah, regarded as the spiritual adviser to the Lebanese Hizballah movement and the secret inspiration of the Iraqi Dawa party. Hakim's mother was from the Lebanese Bazi family.

But there was one small feature of the make-up of this conference that went unmentioned. We all knew that among the Iraqi parties were the seventeen who made up the "Joint Action Committee for Iraqi Opposition" which had met in Damascus in December 1990 to seek a new and democratic Iraq. They included the Dawa, the Islamic Council—the most important of the pro-Iranian groups with close links to Ali Akbar Mohtashemi, the former Iranian minister—the Iraqi Communist Party, and at least four Kurdish parties and two groups, the "Islamic Movement" and the "Independent Nationalists," supported by Saudi Arabia. But the Saudis also insisted that Salah Omar al-Ali's "Nationalist Iraqi Constitution" and Saad Saleh Jaber's "Free Iraq Congress" participate in the conference. And Salah Omar al-Ali was the very same former Baathist who had issued that devastating, fateful call for an uprising over the CIA's radio station on 24 February.

In days to come, these American-organised appeals for an insurgency against Saddam would be compared to the Soviet demands for a Polish uprising against the Germans in Warsaw in 1944, when Russian troops reached the eastern suburbs of the city and appeared ready to liberate the Polish capital once the insurrection began. In the event, the Poles obeyed the call to rise up against the Nazis—and the Soviets waited until the Germans had annihilated the rebels, efficiently destroying the Polish nationalist forces that would have opposed communist rule. The Iraqis working for the Americans and the Saudis had now done much the same. They appealed for an insurrection and watched Saddam annihilate the rebels, thus destroying any chance of an Islamic republic—or any other kind of state—in Iraq. Later—twelve years later—they would take Baghdad and appoint their own "interim government," much as the Soviets did in postwar Poland.

In Beirut, I interviewed Ayatollah al-Mudaressi, who agreed that Basra had probably fallen but claimed that Amara, Nasiriyah, Diwaniyah, Samara, Najaf and Kerbala were still holding out against Saddam's forces. While the Americans might be tempted to support a toothless Saddam out of fear that an Islamic republic might take its place, he told me, the United States should realise that the Iraqi rebellion focused on the rebuilding of Iraq, not on revolution:

> This fear the West has is directly linked to Iran. The West does not have good relations with Iran—so it is worried about what happens now in Iraq. But this is a misjudgement. The uprising did not take place during the eight-year war between Iran and Iraq. It has happened because of what Saddam has done. You cannot copy a revolution from one country to another. I think we must ask the people what kind of republic we want. Personally, I would like an Islamic republic—but not by force. If the people choose this road, I am with them. If they choose another road, I am with them. But Iraqis will not forget America's lack of support when they overthrow Saddam.

But within twenty-four hours, the Iraqi opposition was admitting what we all knew: that the Shia insurgency was collapsing. The most convincing evidence of this came from Abdul-Aziz al-Hakim, brother of Ayatollah Mohamed Bakr al-Hakim, who acknowledged that Najaf and Kerbala were no longer "in the hands of revolutionaries." Even the communists admitted that the uprising now faced "serious difficulties." Only the Kurdish delegates were able to encourage the conference with claims that their own guerrillas were still capturing villages north of Kirkuk.*

The most dignified figure in Beirut was that of old Mohamed Mahdi Jawahiri,

---

*Among the most interesting developments at the Beirut conference—in light of America's later invasion and occupation of Iraq—was the performance of the secret anti-Saddam Dawa party. Widely regarded as the most influential Shia opposition group in the country—Saddam certainly thought so—its principal delegate from Tehran, Abu Bital al-Adib, promised to abide by a parliamentary constitution under which the party would stand in a general election. Coming from a group which—despite its own denials—had tried to kill the emir of Kuwait and had bombed the U.S. and French embassies in Kuwait in 1983, this desire for democracy was little short of extraordinary. U.S. hostages in Beirut were being held captive in return for the freeing of the Dawa men imprisoned after the attack on the emir. Yet when the United States was desperate to hold elections in Iraq in 2005, few parties were more enthusiastic to take part in the poll than the same Dawa party.

Iraq's finest living poet. Ninety years old, he sat on the dais in a crumpled jacket with a soft cap on his bald head, speaking in the language of verse. "I didn't expect to participate in this conference," he said:

> The children of Iraq are smiling at this moment, old men too. Our people under the regime of Saddam Hussein are suffering—all of us are suffering—execution, torture and deportation. But we are patient and united. My heart is with you. My hand is in yours. The intifada in Iraq needs your help . . . There is a limit to everything and for every crime there is a punishment . . .

In the end, the Iraqi opposition could only end its deliberations with an uninspiring demand for a host of "committees"—those get-out institutions so loved by Arab leaders who want to avoid serious decisions—the most important of which was supposed to be the "Committee for National Salvation," the nearest they could agree to a government-in-exile, and the most ridiculous of which was the creation of a delegation to tell the rest of the world what was happening in Iraq—as if the world did not already know. For it was now clear that when the American 1st Armored Division halted its tanks north of Safwan, the killing fields went on moving northwards into Iraq without them, consuming the land in fire and blood. As many—perhaps more—Iraqis were now perishing each day than died in the allied air assaults of the previous month. It was Ayatollah al-Mudaressi who graphically summed up his people's tragedy. "Kuwait has been liberated," he said, "at the cost of the blood of the Iraqi people."

As the truth of this was made manifest in the execution grounds of southern and central Iraq, Washington watched in cruel silence. The administration, according to *The Washington Post*, could not decide whether it wished to keep U.S. troops in Iraq to restrain "Hussein's ability to suppress the rebellions" or withdraw "so Iraqi military forces could consolidate control and then possibly challenge his claim to leadership." The chairman of the U.S. Joint Chiefs of Staff, General Colin Powell, was at his most craven. "What's the better option to get rid of Mr. Saddam Hussein?" he asked rhetorically. "I really don't know." The Bush administration had taken no position on the issue "because it really is an internal problem" within Iraq. Powell had "no instructions to do anything" that would benefit either side.

American aircraft were now flying at will over Iraq, low enough for their pilots to see the battles with their own eyes. Their reconnaissance pictures picked up the street barricades, burning buildings and Iraqi tanks—and in some cases the attacking Iraqi helicopters which Schwarzkopf and Prince Khaled had obligingly allowed them to keep flying—in the streets of Iraq's major cities. If the Americans would reluctantly move in to protect the Kurds—as they were later forced to do by public opinion—no such inclination was shown towards the Shia of southern Iraq. Despite the eyewitness evidence of terrible crimes against humanity, there would be no attempt to save the Shia population whose religious links with Iran so frightened Washington and its Arab allies in the Gulf.

On the American lines in southern Iraq, further descriptions of these atrocities were now being given by Iraqi ex-soldiers. Ibrahim Mehdi Ibrahim, a thirty-two-year-old army deserter, told how Republican Guard units lured families from their homes with promises of safe passage and then trained artillery on them. Saddam's soldiers, he said, were trying "to harvest them, the wheat with the chaff, with helicopter gunships while they hid in the fields." A U.S. Army medic told of treating terrified Shia refugees who had been "beaten with pipes, with burns and a lot of kids beaten with barbed wire. A lot had families killed off. A couple of girls, twelve and thirteen, were beaten on the face with fists or blunt objects." Several weeping men arrived at an American checkpoint at Suq as-Shuyukh with identical stories of entire families massacred together by Iraqi Republican Guard forces. Another Iraqi army deserter said that "families that wanted to leave, they were surrounded and mowed down on the street. We saw with our eyes how they brought the wounded out of hospitals and shot them along with the doctors treating them. When the Iraqi army entered one week ago, the families that had fled the fighting returned with their children. They lined them up against walls and executed them." The secrets of the mass graves outside Musayeb—revealed so many years later—proved that this man's story was no exaggeration.

In America, *The New York Times* announced that the United States had "consigned the Iraqi insurgents to their fate," quoting a "senior official"—as usual, anonymous—who said, "We never made any promises to these people. . . . There is no interest in the coalition in further military operations." This was certainly the case among America's Arab allies. For if the behaviour of the United States and Britain was both shameful and immoral, the reaction of most of the Arab regimes was humiliating. Many Arab journalists had expressed their revulsion that the Iraqi army—the largest and supposedly the most sophisticated in the Middle East—had been routed so ignominiously. In Arab newspapers, the destruction on Mutla Ridge was called a *nakhba*, a catastrophe—the same word used for the Palestinian exodus of 1948. But except in Syria, there were few words of sympathy in Arab capitals for the desperate men fighting on against Saddam in the ruins of southern Iraq or in the Kurdish mountains. The massacres in Basra and Najaf and, later, in Kirkuk elicited no expressions of horror from the Gulf kings and emirs, nor among the ageing presidents supported by the West. Almost all had their own minorities to repress—many of them Shia minorities—and were in no mood to rouse their people to indignation at the outcome of the Iraqi insurgency. To his disgrace, Yassir Arafat—a man whose own people's exile should have awoken in him an equal sympathy for the fleeing Kurds—expressed not the slightest compassion for them.

The calvary of the Shia went largely uncovered by Western reporters—certainly by television—and its dimensions could only be gathered from the desperate men and women arriving at the American checkpoints north of Kuwait. In Kurdistan, however, television and newspaper reporters were on the ground, living—and in at least four cases dying—among the fighters and refugees as Saddam's counter-attack set off a tragedy of biblical proportions. Journalists trudged alongside the tens of thousands of Kurdish men and women as they fled north into the snow-thick mountains along the Turkish border, old men dying of frostbite, women giving birth in the snow, children abandoned amid the drifts. As *The Independent* was to say with bleak accuracy, "the mightiest military machine assembled since the Second World War watches the atrocity show from the sidelines."

So, despite the anguished dispatches of their own correspondents, did the great American newspapers and the East Coast heavyweight "opinion formers." *The Washington Post* was in favour of non-intervention, while *The New York Times* columnist Leslie Gelb complained that "the logic of intervention leads on, inevitably, to capturing Baghdad . . . While Iraqi troops failed to fight in Kuwait, we cannot count on similar timidity in their citadel. And who will fight on our side? No one. And what of civilian casualties? Many more. And what do we do after we have occupied Baghdad? And for how long? And at what cost?"

Here again, the ghosts of the future might visit the past. Yes, if American forces had continued towards Baghdad, as Schwarzkopf quite soon believed they should have done, what would have happened? The Arab coalition would have fallen apart. America—probably alongside Britain—would have had no "friends." But there can be little doubt that if the Americans had pressed on to destroy Saddam's regime, they would have received the welcome from the Iraqis that they confidently expected—but did not get—in 2003. Indeed, after the betrayal of 1991, the Americans could never receive that welcome. In 1996, President George Bush Senior was to speak on television in a series of interviews that his own son would rashly ignore when he illegally invaded Iraq in 2003. If U.S. forces had pursued Saddam to Baghdad, Bush Senior said haltingly, "there would be, downtown Baghdad . . . America occupying an Arab land, searching for this brutal dictator who had the best security in the world, involved in an urban guerrilla war."

Which, of course, subsequently came to pass, even if Bush failed to realise that it was the capture of Saddam that would encourage the "urban guerrilla war" of which he presciently spoke.* The moral issue, however, is that Bush had supported the call for the Iraqi rebellion. He had enthusiastically endorsed the rising. The CIA's radio station had broadcast appeals to the Iraqi population to overthrow Saddam. These appeals, it was plain, burdened the Americans with a moral obligation to protect those they had called to arms on their side. To ignore these brave and desperate men when they responded—to leave them and their families to be exterminated—was not only an act of dishonour but a crime against humanity. Yet even after the American government was forced to offer military protection to the Kurds—albeit when their insurrection had been substantially crushed—they could still regard the Gulf War as a moral conflict, indeed an uplifting one for Ameri-

---

*There were other eerie voices within the administration at this time. A *Washington Post* report on 14 April 1991 quoted an anonymous (of course) official saying that "the thing that could make it like Vietnam was to go into Iraq and get bogged down, establishing a new government, protecting a new government against a hostile population. That would be a recipe for disaster." Ouch.

cans. By August 1991, U.S. defence secretary Dick Cheney was able to describe the war as a "catharsis" for post-Vietnam America. "It was almost a healing process for a wound that had been open for a long time," he said.

The real wounds—the tens of thousands of desperately wounded survivors of the Iraqi insurgency, the broken, decimated families of the Shias and Kurds, the even greater number of executed fighters and civilians now entombed beneath the sands of Iraq by Saddam's killers—were not part of Cheney's "healing process." Their catharsis was to die. They did our bidding. They had served their purpose. They had failed to topple Saddam. This was their fate. But "we" had been "healed." Bush had called for the overthrow of Saddam and then said he never intended to help the rebels in their struggle. An Associated Press report bluntly outlined the Bush policy in early April. The president, it said, "is betting that Americans are more concerned about getting U.S. troops back from the Gulf than helping Iraqi rebels topple Saddam Hussein."

But the yellow bunting and the church bells with which we Westerners were enjoined to celebrate the "end" of the 1991 Gulf War were now a mockery. The splintering of the fragile glass upon which the Middle East rests had now stretched 800 kilometres up the Tigris and Euphrates. More human lives—most of them civilians—were being destroyed every day inside Iraq than at any time since Saddam's invasion of Kuwait. "We warned them of this," a senior Gulf Cooperation Council official told me in Riyadh. "We told the Americans that the liberation of Kuwait might set the region on fire. We told them they might have to stay, even though our people did not want this. But they never, never learn."

You only had to talk to the Kuwaitis, let alone the Iraqi opposition or the Syrians, that dreadful spring to realise that for them the events in the Gulf represented not an isolated, dramatic moment in their history—bloody yet controllable—but a tragic continuum that began before the break-up of the Ottoman empire and which was now growing more terrible in the mountains of Kurdistan. Historically, no Western involvement in the Arab world has been without its betrayals, although treachery followed more swiftly on this occasion than anyone could have guessed. What was supposed to have started as a noble Western crusade to free Kuwait from aggression had turned into a tragedy of catastrophic proportions. "Future historians," I wrote in my paper in April 1991, "may well decide that the liberation of Kuwait marked only the first chapter of the Gulf War, the massacre of Shiites and Kurds inside Iraq the second. History itself suggests the West will not be able to avoid involvement in the forthcoming chapters."

By the first week of April, 2 million Kurdish refugees were clustered along the icy frontiers of Turkey and Iran, up to 12,000 of them dying on the borders. And America, along with its Western allies, now decided that the tragedy—far from being the logical result of their own appeals for an insurrection—was yet another of Saddam's crimes against humanity. Kurdish suffering, and the brutality of Saddam's killer-squads, *did* represent a crime against humanity by the Iraqi regime. But all Western involvement in the Iraqi insurgents' predicament would now be expunged in a welter of humanitarian aid. Guilty consciences would be drowned in meals-ready-to-eat, tents and millions of dollars' worth of aid. And in the weeks to come, as U.S. and British troops deployed in northern Iraq to protect the Kurdish refugees, dropping thousands of tons of blankets and food in hundreds of air-drops—several of which actually killed the recipients when they crashed into the mountains—a new and deeply unpleasant message would be put forth by the West. Come, see what happened to the Kurds. See what Saddam's murderers were capable of. Who could now doubt the moral case for war against Saddam? Here was final proof—amid the refugee camps in the mountains—of Saddam's viciousness. Just as we would dig up the mass graves of the insurgents and their families twelve years later as more "final proof" of Saddam's iniquities—to "prove," of course, that we were right to have invaded Iraq in 2003—here in 1991 we were displaying an equal body of evidence to display his wickedness. The Shia dead, needless to say, had already been largely forgotten.

History now had to be rewritten to take account of these less than subtle shifts of U.S. policy. "We will not countenance interference in refugee operations," Bush's national security adviser, Brent Scowcroft, ponderously warned Saddam on 14 April. Then, in the very same breath, he added, "We are not going to intervene, as we've said before, in a civil war." This was outrageous. Without anyone challenging these deceitful remarks, Scowcroft turned the insurgency that his own government had called for into a "civil war" between Iraqis. The rebels were now participants in an internal dispute. Those whom we had called upon to overthrow Saddam were taking part in a conflict that now had nothing to do with us. These Iraqis, of course, believed what we had originally told them: that they were trying to overthrow a dictator at our request.

President Bush then proceeded to expand on this new and mendacious narrative of events. In a speech in Alabama the same day, he said that Washington would "not tolerate any interference" in international relief efforts, but then said, "I do not want one single soldier or airman shoved into a civil war in Iraq that's been going on for ages." Note the semantics here. Saddam must not interfere in the distribution of international relief—but he *wasn't* interfering, or even planning to interfere, in what the Americans were to call "Operation Provide Comfort." Saddam's helicopters and murder-squads were annihilating the insurgents and their civil populations *before* they could reach the relief centres, machine-gunning and bombing the Kurds as they desperately tried to reach the shelter of the mountains. When they arrived there, they were evidence of Saddam's brutality. But while they were on their way, they were participants in a "civil war"—and therefore unworthy of intervention. Furthermore, they were—before they reached the location of our "international relief efforts"—taking part in a civil war that had been "going on for ages."

It was a mystery to most Iraqis that they were involved in a civil war in the first place, let alone one that had been going on for so long. True, Saddam's persecution of the Kurds might have been intended to ignite just such a conflict. But civil war was the one form of violence from which Iraq had been historically free. There had never been a civil war in Iraq. And this remained true when, twelve years later, the

American and British occupation forces in Iraq claimed that their enemies in the country were trying to foment a civil war—having presumably forgotten that Bush Senior thought one had already occurred in Iraq. All this, it should be recalled, was a pre-run for our refusal to save the lives of the innocent in the Bosnian war in 1992, just a year after the Iraq war was declared to be at an end. In Bosnia, as the Muslims were slaughtered by the Serbs, European and American statesmen repeated the same mantra: that this was a "civil war"—indeed, that this "civil war" had been going on for "ages."

Maybe the American line troops and the marines understood the truth, along with the aircrews who now found themselves home from Kuwait and turned round within days and sent all the way back to the country they thought they'd finished with. They were there in their thousands, another army, this time an army of conscience—of guilty conscience, I suspected—ordered to save lives rather than to kill. The Shia lives were gone, of course, the last execution pits filled north of Basra, but the Kurdish lives were still there, some of them. The Americans were smart guys. A helo ride was to plug into real small-town America, cassette in my hand as we flew over the making of a new country which one day, if the Kurds weren't betrayed yet again—as I rather thought they might be—would be a nation called Kurdistan. The first break-up of Iraq.

As usual, the Americans wanted to be tourist guides. "OK, Bob, we'll show you some of Iraq." Warrant Officer Tim Corwin meant exactly what he said. He guided the CH-47 Chinook—"Cyclone-Seven-Five"—off a mountain wall above a 600-metre chasm where the valleys and the great fertile plains of Mesopotamia spread out below us. On the aviation chart, which bounced on Corwin's knee in time to the engines, we were indeed moving deep into Iraq. In reality, we were flying over a country called Kurdistan. Woe betide the Iraqi soldier who fired on us or on the British troops snaking down the mountainsides below us.

Corwin's voice, crackling through the headphones to Chief Warrant Officer "Chuck" Lancaster, told the whole story. "Iraqi half-track on the right. Three Brits beside it. Very pretty valley, this whole place. If you see any bad guys, let me know." On the end of a rubber-coated radio wire, Sergeant James Sims swung his heavy machine-gun barrel out of the American helicopter's starboard door, traversing the valley walls that raced past us. "No one," he replied, his eyes scanning the outcrops of rock above him, feet braced against the turbulence that wafted up out of the crevasse. "Ain't no bad guys."

Outside al-Amadia, there were more "Brits," Royal Marine berets moving along a road, green flowers against the black tarmac, and a string of Land Rovers. Corwin pressed his radio button. "The Brits are all over the place." Lancaster nodded and pressed his own button. "I like to see that." More Land Rovers now on the long straight road to Zakho, and civilian cars piled high with bedding.

On the hilltops, the Iraqi bunkers lay abandoned, the muddy tracks of armour and guns slinking away towards the nearest roads. An Iraqi fortress, complete with gunslits and four stone turrets, drifted past to port, its Iraqi flag in tatters, its doors open to the wind, the last wreckage of Saddam's persecution of the Kurds. This was no longer Iraq. It had become something different, a new creation shaded onto our maps, ever deeper down the rift valleys towards the heat haze over Mosul.

Cyclone-Seven-Five thumped away beneath us as the hills receded. "Sure is *beeeoootiful* country," crowed Corwin. "This is like home in Arizona." The mountains to the north blocked the horizon, gashed with snow, a trail of fluffy white clouds clinging to the granite, "trash" in Lancaster's aviation language. The four American army flyers looked at it all intently, back-chatting like Vietnam aircrews, filling the radio lines with complaints and transponder checks and torque calculations. They were humorous, intelligent men who happily mixed politics with avionics. At the back of the helo, Sergeant Charles Nabors sat in silence most of the time. You learned a lot by flying with them and listening to them, the lines crackling, mud huts slipping beneath the hull of Cyclone-Seven-Five, another little womb-bubble in which I could crouch with my cassette recorder and feel safe, with a Cyclopean eye on the world. Far to the west, the Tigris glistened.

CORWIN: Sure I know this is history. I guess this is going to be the state of Kurdistan, whatever they say.
LANCASTER: If we have to stay here more than three months, my humour level will be going down.
CORWIN: I just hope it's not going to be a quagmire like Beirut, Lebanon. I just hope Bush knows what he's doing.
LANCASTER: He'll have to, 'cos I tell you the people won't put up with shit. This is costing a whole bunch of money. We're costing between 2,500 and 3,000 dollars here on this helo every hour in maintenance alone. Moment. Contact provider on 375, I've got a mission up to Five-Delta. Only thing I'm concerned about is the fuel pump in that altitude. Just look at that village. It looks like the Old Testament.
CORWIN: It's just like you read in the Bible. Tarsus is west of here, that's where Paul came from. And Mount Ararat's to the east. Isn't that something? I was in Izmir where they imprisoned Richard the Lionheart. I was fifteen miles from Troy earlier. Just think, Homer, the Odyssey . . . There's so much blood on this ground, it's unbelievable. All in the name of Christianity—all that blood and gore.
LANCASTER: How long do you reckon this quagmire will last?
CORWIN: I'll bet you a can of beer not a month and a half—Bitburg Pils. What about the Kurds?
LANCASTER: They don't trust us.
CORWIN: No—rightly so.
LANCASTER: Did we help them out when the rebellion happened?
NABORS (at the back of the helicopter): I had a four-year-old kid die in my arms. I guess she had dysentery. She was very dehydrated. We took her on board with all her family for Zakho to try and save her. She began breathing very bad and I held her in my arms, like. All the men in the family knelt beside me on the helo and put their hands on her. They were praying, you

see. Her father put his hand on her forehead and prayed and looked away. That's how the Kurds all prayed for her on the Chinook, for the little girl. You see, they knew she was gonna die. Then she just died. She went like that. In my arms.

I walked to the back of the Chinook. Nabors's eyes were filled with tears.

Below us drifted the remains of a medieval—perhaps neolithic—village, grass-covered circles and roads of antiquity in what was once Iraq. They were good men on Cyclone-Seven-Five. They were transporting food into Yekmal camp, high in a Turkish mountain ravine, and Lancaster took us in, cursing the ground control, swearing when he tore refugee tents out of the ground with the wash of his rotors. There were 60,000 people under canvas below us and when Corwin switched off the engines we suddenly heard the sound of 60,000 people talking. When we took off, we were back in our glassed, Olympian world, swooping over pine stands and waterfalls, victorious in flight, safe in our little existence of transponders and torques and oil pressure above Kurdistan. Perhaps it is with this detachment that we create nations.

Certainly, the operation to save lives sometimes bore an uncanny similarity to the opposite. It was the daily mission report that gave you a palpable sense of unease. "This is the twenty-eighth day of Operation Provide Comfort," it would announce. "As of six a.m. . . . a total of 1,954 missions have air-dropped 8,713 tons of supplies . . . All sorties are being flown by the U.S., the UK, France, Canada, Italy and Germany . . . total coalition forces . . . continue to grow, with over 13,146 military personnel from eight countries now participating . . . " Where had we heard this language before? Why, only two months earlier, the same literary hand was welcoming us to the twenty-eighth day of Operation Desert Storm. The number of missions and sorties, the number of coalition partners, the strength of military personnel were presented to us then with the same bravado and pride. Then, the F-16s and A-10s delivered ordnance on a target-rich environment. Now the CH-47s delivered rations and blankets on a refugee-rich environment. War-speak had become peace-speak, a unique but almost imperceptible linguistic shift. Only the uniforms had changed: instead of kitty-litter yellow, they wore mountain green.

There was nothing self-serving about these American servicemen who returned to Iraq. They had a far more acute sense of responsibility than their political masters—most guessed they would be returning long before Bush and Major said so—and an impressive desire to save life. I helicoptered into Ilikli—a ravine of grass, poplar trees and a frothing stream that the American Special Forces called "Happy Valley"—to find young soldiers opening wells and springs, installing pumps and water spigots and medical vaccination tents. Sergeant Johnny Hasselquist of the U.S. 10th Special Forces Corps, whose Kurdish interpreter had been a member of the Iraqi invasion force in Kuwait the previous August, had been administering medicine to sick refugees for two weeks, living beside them, sharing his food with them, falling sick himself with acute diarrhoea in order to stay with the civilians he was sent to rescue. There was the same infinite sadness about his account of events as Charles Nabors had experienced:

> We had a baby girl die yesterday. We knew the kid would die. She was premature. She wouldn't eat. She was dehydrated. We told the mother to boil the water she gave her baby but whatever we told her, she wouldn't boil it. She took the water from the stream, which is contaminated. She said it tasted OK. We said "Boil it." She wouldn't. So the baby died.

These men were all now seeing at first hand a kind of suffering they had rarely witnessed before in their lives. There was no doubt about their humanity when faced with this torment of the innocents. They knew they had a responsibility to these people, that they should "be here." What was lost was the narrative sequence, the missing link between Operation Desert Storm and Operation Provide Comfort. Saddam's regime had committed atrocities aplenty against the Kurds. Indeed, the Americans now encouraged journalists to travel down to the "liberated" town of Halabja, the scene of one of the monstrous gassings ordered by Chemical Ali in 1988. But all of this missed the point. These Kurds were not dying in the mountains because Saddam had suddenly decided to resume his persecution now that Kuwait was liberated. His army had turned viciously against the Kurdish people because they had responded to our demands to rise up against the Baathist regime. Their predicament now was brought about—directly—by our encouragement, our policy, our appeals. We, the West—and our "friendly" Arab dictators in the Gulf—bore responsibility for this catastrophe, yet we dressed it up to our advantage and deleted everything that happened between the liberation of Kuwait and the arrival of these hundreds of thousands of teeming masses in the mountains. Yes, we *did* have responsibility for them—but as victims of our political immorality as much as of Saddam's cruelty. Like the daily mission reports, our humanitarian "relief" was the flip-side of war.

It was scarcely surprising that the Kurds, having reached the frozen wastes of their mountains, now refused to leave them. The American and British commanders were anxious to persuade them to return south under Western protection, to live in the vast tent cities that the Americans were erecting around Zakho and the Iraqi towns to the east. The snowline was disappearing, the last frosts a dirty grey stain along the peaks. Soon the heat would be up, the water would grow fouler and there would be widespread disease. But the Kurds wouldn't budge. We put this down to fear of Saddam—they were frightened that his army would return to kill them all—but we understandably ignored the fact, which every Kurd explained with great eloquence, that they didn't trust us to protect them if they moved out of the mountains. We promised we wouldn't allow Saddam's killers to reach them, but we were the ones who had told them to destroy Saddam and then left them to their fate less than two months earlier.

This was Sergeant Frank Jordan's problem when I found him standing boot-deep in a field of poppies at Tel el-Kbir, not far from Zakho. The last time we had met, the U.S. reservist from Maine—a very kind man with spectacles and lots of lines on his face—had been up to his ankles in sand in southern Iraq, trying to cope with the thousands of Shia refugees to whom he could give no tents and little food. Now he was guarding hundreds of tents and thousands of ration packs with scarcely a refugee to take advantage of them. The American role in Iraq had come full circle.

The United States had taken just three days to transfer Jordan from Safwan to Tel el-Kbir, and now the fifty-three-year-old grandfather was waiting for the Kurds to come down from the mountains. But of course, they were not coming. It was not quite the same Sergeant Jordan whom I found now. Instead of the desolation of sand, he was surrounded by thick, ripening corn and those sad, blood-red poppies. Instead of coping with the aftermath of war, he was waiting to cope with the results of our betrayal and beginning to realise that perhaps the war was not over after all. "There was a lot of shooting up in the hills last night," he said. "And when I was in Zakho, there were lots of Iraqi soldiers and I was nervous because I kept thinking about snipers."

Under the terms of an understanding solemnly agreed between the Allies and the Iraqi authorities in Baghdad, the Iraqi army would withdraw farther south while the representatives of the Iraqi state—the police—would remain behind to ensure "law and order" and the sovereignty of the Iraqi nation. It would debase the nature—and the gravity—of the crisis in northern Iraq to mock Jordan's concerns, but Gilbert and Sullivan would have found the inspiration for a lively operetta down the road in Zakho, where hundreds of Iraqi soldiers were pretending to be policemen, while hundreds of Iraqi secret policemen pretended to be civilians. The American troops were going along with this charade, even though the policemen were carrying Kalashnikovs and the Americans M-16 rifles. A policeman's lot was not a happy one.

Only the tens of thousands of Kurds refused to abide by this theatrical code because they, at least, acknowledged that the Iraqi soldiers were not policemen and that the U.S. civil affairs officers were soldiers. If the latter would only acknowledge the reality of the former, then the Kurds might feel secure enough to come down from the mountains. In the meantime, the operetta continued. "What is your name?" I asked one of the Iraqi "policemen" outside the Zakho police station. "My name is policeman," he replied as his plain-clothes colleagues laughed. If I stopped to chat to a schoolteacher, an engineer, a stall-holder, two or three young men in civilian clothes would glide to my side to listen. Asked for their identity, they would chorus *asker* (soldier) or *taleb* (student). How earnestly Saddam Hussein must have fostered higher education in Kurdistan. So why did his people not love him?

"We want the Americans to stay," announced one city worthy. "Why they no come?" And here one had to go back to Sergeant Jordan's tents. For many of the marines constructing the massive, empty encampment at Tel el-Kbir were members of the 24th Marine Expeditionary Unit which, back in 1983, as the 24th Marine Amphibious Unit, played a somewhat different role in Beirut. In 1982 the

Israelis invaded Lebanon and the U.S. Marines turned up to evacuate the PLO guerrillas trapped in the city. "Mission accomplished," they officially announced when they left a few days later. There followed the massacre of hundreds of unprotected Palestinian civilians by Israel's Phalangist allies. America's conscience—and a public outcry not unlike the one that greeted the Kurdish exodus—sent the United States back to Beirut to "protect the civilians," a mission that quickly involved the Marines in the Lebanese civil war because they took the side of the Phalangist government installed by Israel. In October 1983, 241 American servicemen—most of them members of the 24th Marine Expeditionary Unit—were killed by one of the Middle East's first suicide bombers. In 1990 the Iraqis had invaded Kuwait; the United States drove them out and again announced, in effect, mission accomplished. Then came the uprising we had encouraged and the television pictures of the Kurdish trek into the mountains that sent the Americans back to Iraq. The parallels were not exact, of course, but they were understood. Sergeant Jordan was fearful that if the Americans stayed too long in northern Iraq, they would be suicide-bombed again. Twelve years later, his fears would prove true. But he saw it all in simpler, more human terms:

> When they told us to withdraw from Safwan, they told us not to look back. But from my armoured vehicle I saw a little Iraqi boy. He didn't wave or give V-signs like the others. He just stared at me with these fixed eyes and then he rubbed his tummy, never taking his eyes off me. He must have been so hungry . . . I was so angry . . . for two days, I couldn't talk to anybody. Now I can't stop thinking about the numbers of dead Kurds, about 1,000 dead a day.

Yet the Middle East's conflicts overlap like the tectonic plates that, every few decades, shift malignly below the region and bring down its cities and offices and apartment blocks and mosques. North of the Iraqi border one night, I was unable to find a room at any of the truck-stop hotels on the southern Turkish border road and ended up driving into the hills at night because a Christian missionary had told me of an ancient village where I would be given a bed. My Turkish taxi-driver was negotiating the potholed road when orders were suddenly screamed at us from the darkness. I opened my door, told the driver to douse the headlights and put on the inside light of the car. Running down the road towards us, rifles to shoulders, was a squad of Turkish soldiers. They wore blue berets—soldiers of Turkey's Special Forces—and shouted aggressively as they stood around the car. I didn't understand a word, but I didn't need to. My driver was now beside the car, arms in the air, torchlight full in his face. In such circumstances, I use the "outraged Brit" performance. I put my hands on my hips and bellowed: "What on earth is going on?"

An officer walked up to me and I stuck out my hand. It's a sure-fire way of reducing tension among angry soldiers. However furious or frightened or drunk, no officer wants to humiliate himself by refusing to shake hands with a perfectly friendly stranger. The soldier duly moved his rifle to his other hand and shook my hand and smiled and asked, in absolutely flawless English: "What exactly do you think you are doing here?" I told him. I was looking for a bed, I had been told of this village in the mountains and I planned to spend the night there. "Do you know there's a problem here?" he asked.

Ah yes, there was indeed a problem. The Kurds. If the Kurds of Iraq were prepared to rise up against Saddam—and then get betrayed by us—and then flee to the mountains, the Kurds of Turkey were also, some of them, prepared to rise up against Atatürk's Turkish state because they, too, would like to live in a country called Kurdistan. This was the same "Kurdistan" that President Wilson had initially agreed to protect more than seven decades ago but which, like Armenia, was simply forgotten in the wastes of American isolationism. The Turks, as we have seen, had dealt with inspirational cruelty with their "Armenian problem" seventy-six years earlier. Now a system of military repression, resettlement, "ethnic cleansing," torture and extrajudicial murder was being used by the Turkish state to deal with the current "Kurdish problem."

And of course, the Turks were now doubly fearful of Kurdish nationalism because the Kurds of Iraq were demanding their own nation and a million and a half of them wanted to flee across the Turkish border into the Turkish part of their "homeland." Since Turkey was a NATO ally and a "friend" of the United States—hence America's cowardice in addressing the Armenian Holocaust—Washington was also anxious to keep the Kurds of Iraq inside Iraq, which was an unspoken and all-important reason for sending U.S. troops to protect the Kurds inside Iraq and persuade them to leave the mountain frontier and move back towards their Iraqi homes. This was also one reason why Sergeant Jordan had been told to pitch all those tents outside Zakho. The Iraqi Kurds had to be kept away from their fellow Kurds in Turkey. The Iraqi Kurds had to be protected. But so did the Turkish state, as I would soon learn to my cost.

I had grown used to "choppering" around northern Iraq. The Americans gave us an almost Vietnam-like freedom on their helicopters, obligingly issuing us passes to travel on any machine to mountain fastnesses that would have taken days to reach by road or on foot. Our documentation and helicopters were arranged by a bald American civilian air controller with a hook instead of a right hand. Even on the most fog-bound or gale-kicked days, he would send us off into the mountains with his men to watch the Kurds surviving and dying in the snow-covered camps. I turned up at the Salopi air base on 29 April with my haversack of notebook, maps and spare clothes, a day of horizontal rain and wind when at least twelve helicopters were thumping and roaring on the apron. "Captain Hook" was soaked and scarcely looked at me as he handed me my chit and pointed through the storm. "Go! Go!" he shrieked in my ear and I ran towards the green, jerking chopper whose crew were beckoning to me through the rain. They didn't seem to have the usual laid-back panache that I was used to seeing in Corwin, Lancaster and the others. The pilot gestured impatiently at me from the cockpit as I climbed aboard, and one of the crew gave me a fierce shove from behind that had me landing on my belly on the floor.

That's when I realised that this was an Apache gunship, a big tank-killer, not one of those nice friendly Chinooks with a long snout, but a sharp, pointy, state-of-the-art piece of military aggression packed with serious-looking Americans. I sat on the spare seat, struggling into my safety harness as the machine bashed up into the sky. That's when I noticed that all the Americans were in civilian clothes. And that they were all carrying pistols or snipers' rifles. The American opposite, a big, beefy man with a lantern jaw, leaned towards me and shrieked in my ear: "Where you from?" England, I said plaintively. A journalist from *The Independent* newspaper. "Jeeesus Christ!" he shouted and turned to his neighbour and screamed in his ear. The two men frowned at me, the muscular guy shaking his head in disbelief. He leaned towards me again. "There must have been a fuck-up!"

I didn't know. I'd boarded the helicopter "Captain Hook" told me to take. Or I thought I did. It dawned on me then that I was on the wrong helicopter. Or rather— it took a few seconds in the din and rain to grasp this—that as a journalist I was clearly on the right helicopter. Whatever was happening, it had to be more exciting than another food drop. I leaned towards lantern-jaw. So where are *you* from? I asked. "U.S. embassy, Ankara, most of these guys are CIA. You aren't supposed to be here!" I stared at him. And I grinned. In fact, I positively burst into laughter, so loudly amid the cabin noise that even lantern-jaw gave me a smirk. I leaned towards his ear again because now it was my turn. "Jesus Christ!" I said. And he gave me a more friendly smile. "You," he said, "have got yourself one hell of a fucking story."

The chopper barrelled across the landscape, leapt through the cracks in the mountain chain, climbed with breath-sucking speed into the clouds and raced along the snowline, its passengers staring in front of them like men possessed. We were heading east at an astounding speed. I pulled my laminated map from my sack and traced the miles by laying my outstretched finger against the mountains. We were heading directly towards the Iranian border. Lantern-jaw took my map and turned it towards me, his own finger on a tiny name printed in italics. "Yasilova," it said. I squinted at the map as the Apache jerked between two walls of rock. If a helicopter ever came into contact with rock, Lancaster had told me, the rock "always wins." And we were moving far faster than the old Chinook.

In one moment, we had soared through dark blue skies and then sideways into a cloud bank to emerge scarcely 5 metres from the tops of pine trees. The Apache had an astounding ability to "skid" in the air, to turn corners like a car and to flatten out and swoop like a bird at a patch of rock. And I remembered all those burned-out tanks and armoured vehicles and cars across the sands of southern Iraq and realised, yet again, that the Iraqis never had a chance of surviving. This was death by computer, the same computer upon which our lives now depended in this mechanical wasp. Yasilova. It meant nothing to me. The Iranian border ran just a fingernail to the right of the name. And then we descended.

The CIA men and the embassy guards—I guessed they were all the same— checked their ammunition and held their weapons across their chests as we came whupping down a fairytale valley of soft grass and spring-leaved trees and a small river that moved in a torrent over the landscape. There were refugees below us, dirty tents and men and women looking up at our Apache and then, straight in front of us as the doors opened, the soldiers of two great armies pointing their rifles at each other, Turks to the left, British Royal Marines to the right, the Turks manning a machine gun on one side of the river and the green berets of the Brits moving through the lighter green of the grass, weapons at the ready. As the rotors cut and the CIA men sprang out of the helicopter, lantern-jaw tapped me on the knee. "Your guys and the Turks are about to go to war," he shouted. And he shot me a real big smile. "I told you you had a great fucking story!"

I was out of the chopper like a rat, running for my life with the Americans, down towards the river where a Royal Marine radio operator was struggling with his back-pack through the mud in the direction of the Americans. The Turks were running up the eastern bank of the river, shouting and pointing their guns at us. High up on an escarpment 25 kilometres to the east, along the ridge-line of a great white mountain, lay the Iranian border. What, I wondered, did the Islamic Republic make of this?

Some of the CIA men were splashing through the river towards the Turkish troops, many of whom were standing beside piles of bedding and mattresses and boxes of food. The rest were running in front of me towards the British. And then we were among the British. "What's your position?" one of the Americans shouted at a young officer. "Have you exchanged fire?" I saw the soldier shake his head. "Not yet," he said. "You're not going to," the American replied. And then a British marine with a Home Counties accent touched my sleeve. "Are you by any chance a reporter?" he asked, and when I nodded, he actually smiled. "Bloody good—we need a reporter here." I could hardly believe my ears. The British Ministry of Defence spent much of its time trying to keep journalists away from real stories like this. In fact, ever since I'd worked in Northern Ireland, the ministry had taken a particular dislike to my reporting. But this was not controllable. This was Planet Earth—albeit of a cold and mountainous variety—and something very odd was going on. Why were British soldiers about to shoot at Turkish soldiers for the first time since Gallipoli?

Surgeon Lieutenant Peter Davis of the Royal Marine Mountain and Arctic Warfare Cadre was the only doctor ministering to 3,000 refugees—some of whom were standing around us with a mixture of awe and terror—and he explained what had happened with the precision and speed of all professional soldiers. "The Turkish soldiers have been stealing the refugees' food and blankets, so we had to stop this and we've been standing off, locked and loaded ever since." I looked across the river to the huge pile of water boxes and blankets that stood guiltily next to the Turkish troops. The Kurdish refugees—many of them Assyrian Christians, some of whom had fled all the way from Baghdad—stood with the British whom they obviously regarded as their protectors. The Turks had just stolen another sixty boxes of water from these homeless refugees, and for several minutes the outnumbered British and Americans had been forced to watch the Turks stealing more blankets, bed linen and food, all of it supplied by international charities. The

British wanted to fly all 3,000 Kurdish refugees out of Yasilova to protect them from the Turks—but a Turkish officer had refused them permission to fly. Now Davis and his men were piling what was left of the Kurds' food onto an RAF Chinook parked by the trees to take it out of the Turks' reach. They were going to fly the relief supplies away from the refugee camp.

There were Americans who had been here with the British for a week and all of them, along with the marines, told a story of successive Turkish army looting throughout the entire period. A British captain was shaking with anger as he spoke. "The Turkish soldiers here are shit," he said. "They don't seem to care what happens to these Kurds—and it's the Turks who are supposed to be running this camp. They take whatever they want. One of them said to me: 'It's better to starve the Kurds—that way, we can control them.' I can't let that happen."

The scandal at Yasilova camp had gone unreported, partly because it was so remote, partly because it had only now degenerated to the verge of open military hostilities, and partly because of the natural desire of the coalition armies—who had known about this disgrace for days—to maintain good relations with Turkey. When British and American troops first arrived at Yasilova camp, the Turks were in sole charge. "The Kurds were in a pitiful state," an American said. "They were suffering from acute diarrhoea. There were no medical services given by the Turks. The place was on the verge of a cholera outbreak." It was still the most squalid of the camps. The place reeked of sewage.

At least a hundred of the refugees were begging the British and Americans to take them to Europe because, they said, they were about as frightened of the Turks as they were of the Iraqis. "We have relatives in Austria, in Sweden, in America," one young woman pleaded with me. "For God's sake, tell them we are here." There were dark stories in the camp, that the Turks were trying to divide up the families and charge them for transport to another camp to the west. The British were still piling their food supplies onto the Chinook, heaping boxes of water and blankets onto a pallet beneath the machine. "If the refugees can't have it, we're damn well not going to let the Turks take it," one of the marines said.

I flew out on the RAF helicopter along with the food, a sick child, a Kurdish woman looking for her lost son and a Kurdish man who had been wounded in the eye during the uprising. We dropped them off at Zakho and flew on to Diyarbakir, where I now had a hotel room. I called Harvey Morris in London and told him I had a story for the front page—which is where the scandal of Yasilova appeared next morning.

I knew the Turkish authorities would resent the report. With a million Kurdish refugees on their frontier, the Turkish army felt it was losing control of the relief operation—in reality, it did not have the resources to maintain it—and in Turkey, any criticism of the army can be regarded as a crime. This was part of the legacy of Atatürk, whose own military career at Gallipoli was part of the legend upon which modern, secular Turkey had been built. But Turkey also wanted to join the European Community—as it then was—and could scarcely deny the truth of what had happened at Yasilova. Or so I thought.

I spent the next day back in the air, travelling with the American Chinook crews around Zakho, but when I returned again to Diyarbakir, a British relief worker told me that "the Turks are very angry and I'd let your office know if I were you." I called Harvey. "Of course the Turks will be angry," he laughed. "You've offended their bloody army. Call me if you have any trouble." Trouble came two hours later with a knock on my bedroom door. I opened it. In front of me stood the hotel manager, a small Kurdish man, but behind him stood two tall, unsmiling men in black leather jackets. "I am sorry to bother you, Mr. Fisk, but some policemen are here to talk to you."

The police spoke no English, I no Turkish, so the diminutive Kurd assured me that they came as "friends" and would like me to visit the police station. I was to take my belongings with me. I lifted the phone, and—as the policemen protested—dialled London and got through to my foreign editor, Godfrey Hodgson. I told him in one sentence what had happened, that I suspected this might be more serious than we had imagined, and asked him to call my elderly parents in Maidstone to tell them we had a problem. Bill and Peggy would not want to hear this on the radio.* Trailed by a colleague from the *Daily Mail*, I was driven to the police station, where a portly police inspector invited me to sit in his office. "You are here as a guest of the police inspector," my luckless hotel manager explained. "You have not been arrested." In that case, I said, I would like to take tea with the police inspector. He scowled. Tea arrived after half an hour. From the wall above him, Atatürk scowled down at me too.

So did Paul O'Connor, the British embassy's second secretary in Ankara. "They want to question you about your report," he said coldly. "My advice is to say nothing." What quickly became apparent, however, was that the police were considering formal charges against me for defaming the Turkish army—I suspected that this was a military order to the police, not an instruction from the interior or foreign ministries in Ankara. One of the cops told me, with considerable pleasure, that defaming the army carried a sentence of ten years. I sat in the inspector's chair, remembering *Midnight Express* and cursing "Captain Hook." My chopper ride with the CIA was having unpleasant repercussions.

More policemen entered the room. The inspector took several telephone calls, glancing at me as he listened to the speaker. A plain-clothes cop arrived with a massive old German typewriter and began to root through my bag, slowly extracting my toothbrush, spare blanket, chocolate bars and—to my despair—a book on Armenian history. It was now one in the morning. O'Connor drooped with tiredness. He asked that I be allowed back to my hotel. The inspector said he had no power to permit this. The cop with the typewriter then announced that my interrogation would begin. O'Connor objected. But I decided that an interrogation might be just the thing to end this farce. I asked him to translate; which, to be fair, he

---

*They did. For some unaccountable reason, Hodgson—a first-rate journalist and a good friend—failed to tell them.

wearily agreed to do, struggling to stay awake. The construction of the Turkish language is such that each sentence has to be completed before it can be translated. It would be 4:45 in the morning before this nonsense was over.

When did I first enter Turkey? Had I entered the country from any place other than Habur (the border crossing from Iraq outside Zakho)? Did I come to Diyarbakir directly from Ankara? Did I work for *The Independent*? Did I write an article in *The Independent* on 30 April 1991? Is there another Robert Fisk on the paper? Did I have any other article published in *The Independent* on 30 April 1991? This was witless stuff, infantile, ridiculous. I began to realise why the Turks could not suppress the Kurdish revolt in southern Turkey. It was also quickly becoming obvious that the police version of my story came not from my own paper but from the reports of Turkish correspondents in London who had recycled my report back to Istanbul and Ankara.

Did I see Turkish soldiers stealing water? Did I take pictures of this? I understood this question. If I had photographs of the Turkish army looting, then the prosecution would collapse. So they needed to seize those pictures. But I didn't have any. I kept replying that the answer to their questions could be found in my article in *The Independent*. Did I see Turkish soldiers stealing *helvar*? O'Connor struggled to translate this exotic commodity which turned out to be a form of Turkish biscuit that I had never seen let alone tasted in my life. More cops now arrived and—despite O'Connor's presence—stood around me, each holding wooden coshes in their hands. The inspector said that I might like to spend the night in the basement of the police station. "This is getting a bit heavy," O'Connor muttered. Then came the moment I had been waiting for:

COP: In the article in the newspaper *Independent* on 30 April 1991, and which bears your name, is it true that the aid in Yasilova camp has been looted by Turkish soldiers?
FISK: My father always told me that Mustafa Kemal Atatürk was one of the titans of the twentieth century. I believe my father was right. Unfortunately, some of your soldiers at Yasilova did not obey the high standards and principles set by Mustafa Kemal Atatürk, the founder of the Turkish nation.

Suddenly, the atmosphere changed. I silently thanked Bill Fisk for all those boyhood history lessons. I'm not at all sure that Atatürk was a titan (or that Bill thought so), but I was quite prepared to become his admirer for the inspector and his friends. They began to talk to one another with great animation. Swooning with tiredness, O'Connor told me they would probably now allow me to return to my hotel. The word "deport" popped up in their conversation. And I knew why. If my argument was going to be a rousing condemnation of the way in which the Turkish army had turned its back on the father of the nation—a man whose integrity I would defend against the army—then there could be no prosecution and no court case. And so it came to pass.

A few hours later, I was solemnly informed that I would be deported, and

O'Connor trotted off to buy an air ticket. Turkish foreign ministry spokesman Murat Sungar announced Fisk's imminent departure from the homeland; "his existence in Turkey is no longer needed because of his prejudiced, biased and ill-intentioned reporting," he said. It was a bumpy flight back to Ankara and I had to comfort one of the two Turkish cops guarding me because he had never travelled in an aircraft before. But "Captain Hook" 's decision to put me on the Apache was now rippling the pond. The Turks ordered that the British Royal Marines should also be deported and claimed that they had roughed up a local Turkish official. The Ministry of Defence immediately "redeployed" them south of the border and inside Iraq. Journalists' organisations protested. The European Commission demanded an explanation from the Turkish ambassador to the EC in Brussels. One of AP's executives in New York sent me a two-liner: "Hard to imagine the quality of the meals in a jail in Diyarbakir. You're probably envying the Kurdish refugees about now."

The problem was that the Kurdish refugees had already disappeared from this ridiculous saga. It was the honour of the Turkish army that was now at stake. The Turkish army's chief of staff, General Dogan Gures—who should have been disciplining his soldiers at Yasilova and protecting the Kurds—thundered that my perfectly accurate report was "planned, programmed propaganda." But what was I supposed to have done? Declined to board the helicopter at Salopi? Ignored the evidence of my own eyes at Yasilova? Censored my own reporting in the interests of Western–Turkish relations? At Ankara, I was put aboard a Lufthansa flight to Frankfurt. "You're the man who's being deported, aren't you?" the stewardess greeted me. "You must have been telling the truth."

Which is what I wanted to go on doing in northern Iraq. But how to return there now that Turkey was closed to me? I flew back to Beirut and drove to Damascus, where the former subjects of the Ottoman empire were more than happy to oblige. I explained my predicament to Mohamed Salman, the minister of information—to be disgraced by the Assad regime eight years later—who suggested I visit a certain General Mansour, in charge of Syrian army intelligence in the border city of Kimishli. I drove the length of Syria, back to the Turkish border—I could actually see the Turkish flag outside General Mansour's window—and he arranged for a squad of Syrian troops to take me down to the Tigris River where it flowed out of Turkey and formed the border of Syria and northern Iraq. An old man in a wooden boat was waiting in the dawn light and the Syrian soldiers waved goodbye as he rowed me silently across the great expanse of pale, soft water to the other shore where three *peshmerga* Kurdish guerrillas were waiting for me. Sister Syria—as Assad's nation was called with dubious affection in Lebanon—had friends inside Kurdistan. "Mr. Robert?" one of the Kurds asked. "We are here to take you to Zakho." And so I returned to the story of the Kurdish disaster.

It was now late spring. The Americans and the British were planning to leave. The United Nations had arrived with their observers to "protect" the Kurds. Yet only by extending "free" Kurdistan farther south could the Americans close down the refugee camps in which the Kurds had eventually been induced to live after leaving the mountains. Soon the Kurds would be attacked again, usually by Turkish troops and pilots who would, in the coming years, bomb Kurdish villages where they believed guerrillas of the Kurdistan Workers Party, the PKK, were hiding. Turkish soldiers would enter Zakho in contravention of all their agreements with the Western allies. And Saddam would strike back against the Kurdish exiles in northern Iraq whose plots to assassinate the wretched dictator—it was all part of a hopeless CIA conspiracy—miserably failed. So while the Americans tried to leave northern Iraq, they had to push farther south to set up more "safe havens" for the Kurds. They approved of new Kurdish negotiations with Saddam. They were now enthusiastic to work with the Baathist regime—or "the government in Baghdad" as they preferred to call it—in order to withdraw. Suddenly, the Americans needed Saddam's cooperation.

The Kurds saw the implications of this. They could not stop the Americans leaving, but they could purge what was left of Baath party rule from the towns that were to be included in the "safe haven," and this they did with their usual ruthlessness. Many of Saddam's acolytes were murdered or driven from their homes, their police stations taken over and their torture chambers opened for the first time in more than two decades.

Deep in the underground dungeons of Dahuk secret police headquarters, the young Kurdish women who were raped and murdered by the Iraqi *mukhabarat* had left their last record on the filthy walls. One drew a portrait of herself with large eyes and long hair flowing over her shoulders, a pretty girl wearing a high-collared blouse. Another drew a rose, above it the words: "I am going to die. Please tell the others." Yet another, whose name appears to have been Nadira, wrote on her cell wall just four words: "This is my fate."

The Kurdish *peshmerga* and several hundred of the local Dahuk population had stormed the police station, almost too late to prevent the Iraqi plain-clothes men burning files containing the names of the prisoners—and their tormentors—in a concrete sentry box at the main gate. They were still smouldering when we arrived there, watched uneasily by twelve Iraqi policemen who were now, in effect, hostages of the Kurds. The last young woman to be imprisoned here had died in these foetid cells just two months earlier. The *peshmerga* said they found three of the women's bodies, naked and with their hands bound, in the cells. One of the girls was twelve years old. Another, older woman had been gang-raped and died later. Anyone who wanted to know why a million and a half Kurds fled their homes in March 1991 had only to visit the Dahuk police station.*

On the face of it you might have expected the Americans to have taken a look

---

*The existence of Iraqi "raping rooms" became the object of an unnecessary controversy when the exiled writer Kanan Makiya claimed in 1993 that he had in his possession an official document which proved that rape was used as a political weapon. The card index, issued by the Iraqi "General Security Organisation," contained the name Aziz Salih Ahmad and apparently described his activity as "Violation of Women's Honour." Several of Makiya's critics—themselves no supporters of Saddam—claimed that he had misinterpreted the card and that the activity indicated Ahmad's crime rather than his job; in other words, that this was a surveillance note written by the police rather than an employment card. The evidence suggests that Makiya's critics are right. But ex-prisoners have described how female relatives of Saddam's opponents were

at this evidence of Saddam Hussein's barbarism. The Dahuk secret police offices, housed in a large two-storey villa, stood only a few kilometres from the new U.S. military headquarters. Here at last was proof that the servants of the dictator so often compared by President Bush to Hitler really could behave like Nazis. Were not some of the Allies once demanding war crimes trials?

Not any more, it seemed. At least two of the most senior police officers in Dahuk—men who must have known of the terrible secrets beneath that villa— were now meeting daily with senior U.S. army officers to discuss the return of Kurdish refugees to the town. Colonel Moakdad and Colonel Jamal were now instrumental in ensuring there were no clashes between armed Iraqis and allied troops in Dahuk. Each morning, driven by chauffeurs in Oldsmobile limousines, they would turn up at the new hotel which the Americans took for their headquarters, occasionally saluting the U.S. troops.

How much longer could this hypocrisy continue? On 25 May, Colonel Moak-dad even arrived with a *peshmerga* representative, turning to an American colonel who greeted him and twining his two forefingers together. We are friends now, the gesture said. The Iraqi police and the Kurds were supposed to be in alliance while their leaders negotiated in Baghdad. Once those talks were complete, the Iraqis would guarantee democracy to the Kurds, or so we were supposed to believe. And then, of course, the Western allies could go home. Any price, it seemed, was worth paying for a withdrawal, even indifference to the secret police headquarters.

There was a neat perfumed garden in front of the building, rose bushes neatly planted beside the path. The portico of the headquarters had been tastefully deco-rated with small brass Arabic lamp shades. It was as pretty as the garden outside the Savak torture chamber in Tehran in 1979. But a few metres to the right were some stairs. With the local *peshmerga* leader, Tassin Kemeck, we pulled open a steel door nine inches thick and descended. Water dripped down the staircase. At the bottom were a series of narrow cells and several large rooms. They were strewn with excrement and dirty blankets. "This is where they brought the women," Kemeck said. "They were not wives of *peshmerga*, just pretty women. They tor-tured them, raped them and killed them. Some were very young. The Iraqi army used to come to the women in this cell"—here he pushed open a heavy iron door— "and rape them one after the other." On the floor was a stained mattress and some women's clothes. The walls were covered in graffiti. "Sometimes they wrote their names in blood," Kemeck said.

But America's desire to call Saddam to account had receded as its desperation to withdraw from Iraq increased. No one was more clear-cut in his determination to get out than the commander of the 15,000-strong coalition army in Kurdistan

---

raped in front of them—my own first report on this during the Iran–Iraq War was the reason for that excoriating letter to *The Times* from the Iraqi ambassador in London—and I found evidence of the Dahuk police dungeons two years before Makiya produced the card index paper. However, whenever I later referred to rape in Iraqi prisons, I was accused of using Makiya as my source. An academic feud now obscured the reality of "raping rooms"—which did really exist in Saddam's regime, however casually chosen the victims may have been.

that now controlled 13,000 square kilometres of northern Iraq, Major General Jay Garner. Twelve years later, Garner would be the first of the American proconsuls in occupied Iraq—a man who so alarmingly mismanaged the task that he was replaced within months—but in 1991, no one could have been keener to negotiate with the Iraqi authorities. "We've told the Kurds from the first day that we're here for two things," he said. "To stop the dying in the mountains and to create an environment in which they could resettle. We never signed up to be a north Iraq security force . . . We were sent here to do one thing and we've done that pretty well. I don't think the Kurds will go back to the mountains unless they're under attack. And if they are, that's a problem for the United Nations and world leaders, and they'll have a tough decision to take. That's what leaders get paid for—tough decisions."

Garner, a short, stocky man who talked in clipped, carefully punctuated sentences, was deputy commander of the U.S. Fifth Corps in Europe. But in Kurdistan, he was playing politician. "I don't think you should keep forces here. The Kurds are Iraqi citizens. I don't think you should keep forces to protect citizens from their own government. I agree this is a vicious leader [in Baghdad], a vicious regime. But if you want military forces to stay here, you've got to change the mission and got to change the rules . . . They [the Kurds] were dying at four hundred a day in the Turkish mountains. They weren't Turkish citizens so something had to happen there. Right now, their own leaders are close to signing an agreement with Saddam . . . they live here. The fact that we came here gave them a better bargaining position."

Garner was a little like an unhappy policeman who has to invent his own laws while walking the beat. If UN Security Council Resolution 688 allowed humanitarian intervention in a foreign country, it afforded few guidelines to the U.S., British, French, Spanish and Dutch staff officers who met the general each evening for their daily briefing. "My worst fear," Garner confided, "is getting our people in the middle [of a battle] and then getting hurt. The Iraqis and the *peshmerga* have been fighting ever since we got here . . . We're not an occupation army. No one's under martial law. There's no legality . . . "

In the corner of Garner's office was an old bolt-action rifle bearing on its stock the coat of arms of the Pahlavi dynasty. The bolt was rusted and the wood had cracked but the Shah's lion was plain to see on the royal insignia. For Garner, the Iranian firearm—turned in by an Iraqi soldier when the Western armies arrived in Kurdistan—was a souvenir of the "civil war" that Garner's president believed had been going on "for ages," the conflict which the two-star general intended to keep out of. It all seemed so simple. The Kurds would patch things up with Baghdad. The Kurds were Iraqi citizens, not Turkish citizens—clearly, Turkey's concerns were high on Garner's list of priorities—and if Saddam came back to persecute them, well, that was the UN's problem.

Garner did admit to a private uneasiness in talking almost daily to Iraqi officials who might well have been responsible for torturing civilians before and during the Kurdish uprising in Dahuk. But he said that his job did not involve such emotions. "In meetings with me, they are polite. You have a few who're tough. They're pretty hard. Those who come to the meetings in civilian clothes have been a bit more direct. They'll stand up and give you a long political lecture and reflections on the way you do things. We listen to them and say: 'Thank you for your comments.' "

So this is what it had come to. Thank you for your comments. The Beast of Baghdad was no longer to be feared. He was to be placated, worked with, relied upon to treat his Kurds—"Iraqi citizens"—fairly. The end was surely not far away. Summer was coming to northern Iraq in a lazy way, a warm breeze rippling the hundreds of square kilometres of wheat fields around Dahuk. Anticipating the effects of United Nations sanctions in 1990, Saddam had ordered Iraqis to plant wheat on all available land. The American humanitarian groups, the U.S. military and the UN were now encouraging the Kurds to harvest the crop that was sown to beat UN sanctions.

In the middle of the dual carriageway north of Dahuk where six hot and tired U.S. marines were waving returning Kurdish refugees through their wire chicane, there stood a sign with the words "Allied Control Zone" stencilled in black paint. To the east, a battery of marine 105-mm howitzers nestled under camouflage in the heat haze, a little ghost of all those artillery positions that once lay across the Saudi desert 800 kilometres to the south. The world's conscience was being eased. The epic tragedy of the Kurdish retreat to the mountains had now been ameliorated by return and resettlement. Instead of dying babies and sick children, the fields around Zakho were now filled with thriving families. At night, a necklace of lights moving down the mountains proved that the Kurds were returning home.

So who could be surprised when General Colin Powell, arriving at Saddam's private airport at Sirsenk on the afternoon of 30 May, said, in so many words, that there would be no guarantees for the Kurds left behind? The "international community" would be "measuring Baghdad's actions in the weeks ahead," he told us. The United States would use "every diplomatic and political means and whatever other means might be appropriate" to convince the Iraqi authorities not to use force against the Kurds.

Powell's press conference was weird. He simply wouldn't mention the name Saddam. The monster who had obsessed the world for months could no longer be spoken of. I even asked Powell about the omission. Here he was, I said, standing on the very tarmac of Saddam's personal airport—black marble tiles lining the unfinished terminal building—and within sight of Saddam's winter palaces on the surrounding mountains, yet the name of Saddam would not cross his lips. Why? And he replied with an evasiveness that was truly courageous. "It would not be in the interests of the leadership in Baghdad to return to this area in force or in an aggressive way which would threaten these people and cause them to fear for their lives again." He talked, too, about "the government in Baghdad" as if this was some vast democratic bureaucracy. And that was it. Saddam had been erased from the discourse.

When an American reporter asked Powell if the United States had really won the 1991 Gulf War despite the massive oil fires in Kuwait, the ecological damage in the Gulf, Saudi Arabia's unwillingness to assist American security plans, the Kurdish catastrophe and the deadlock in the Middle East "peace process," Powell reminded his audience that the invasion of Kuwait had been reversed and the emirate had now been restored to its legitimate (if undemocratic) government. "Our closest friends in this region are no longer threatened by the fourth-largest army in the world." This was a victory. The strategic situation in the region had entirely changed. What had not changed, of course, was the continued presence of Saddam in Baghdad. But that was a name General Powell would no longer mention.

There were times when even history could not be mentioned in Kurdistan. In Zakho there was a fine Roman bridge, and the locals would tell visitors that the low, grass-covered hills that protect the town were trodden by Xenophon's Greek thousands. Fifteen kilometres farther west, on the banks of the Habur River, history was too recent to be addressed. The locals do not mention that nine thousand Armenians were massacred here during the 1915 Armenian genocide. Because the Kurds were the murderers.

So Zakho was a town with secrets. It kept them even from the allied armies. In 1919, it was notorious for the assassination of British army officers, killed by Kurds who were demanding independence during the British Mandate. British soldiers were shot dead in the same year in the neighbouring village of Amadia—currently governed by the Royal Marines. No wonder Zakho hid its past as it hid its present. Opposite the Iraqi police station, I would be told, was the *mantaqa jehudi*—the "place of the Jews"—where Zakho's substantial Jewish community lived until they departed for the new state of Israel in 1948. The houses there were poor, single-storey, mud-and-brick affairs. The old Jewish cemetery lay beneath the foundations of the Ashawa Hotel on the other side of town. Saddam's men saw to that.

But take a walk across the river to the *kenaisi*—"church"—district and you would be among both Kurds and Armenians, grandsons and granddaughters and great-grandsons and great-granddaughters of the killers and the killed of 1915. Even now you could not ask about the massacres without arousing suspicion. The Kurds would tell you that the Turks were responsible. The Armenians would tell you, correctly, that the Kurds hereabouts were the culprits, on Turkish orders. "We have Kurdish friends," an Armenian businessman told me. "Of course we talk about what happened. My Kurdish friends and I have coffee together. We have agreed that what the Kurds did was a mistake. They were used by other people—the Turks—to do what they did against us. But, yes, most of my friends are Christian." There were only about 1,500 Armenians left in Zakho, living among 150,000 Kurds. A few hundred Assyrians and Chaldeans made up the only other Christian communities.

The Armenians obeyed the law under Saddam. When the Kurds of Zakho fled to avoid military service, the Armenians obediently went to fight for Saddam Hussein. Three Armenian soldiers from Zakho died under allied air attack in 1991—in Kuwait, Basra and Mosul. More than 130 Armenians from the town were killed in the eight-year war between Iraq and Iran. The only Kurds who fought in the 1991 war could be found in the refugee camps outside Zakho, although they were not from the town. One of them lived in a blue-and-white tent with his father and mother, a young man with a moustache who was a member of the Iraqi Rafidain Tank Regiment and survived the American and British attacks on the Mutla Ridge. "I was hiding in the sand when the planes came," he said, making the usual appeals that his name should never be printed. "I saw all the Iraqi vehicles in the traffic jam and they started blowing up. There was a military petrol lorry and I saw an American plane fire a rocket at the lorry. There was a golden fire and the lorry went to twice its size and then it disappeared. I managed to reach Basra and was given five days' leave so I travelled up to the mountains here to escape."

But the Kurdish revolt did not bring the Kurdish and Armenian communities in Zakho any closer. When the Kurds returned to the town under U.S. protection, they found that the Armenians had not left their homes. "They thought we had taken the side of the government," an Armenian teenager said. "They did not understand that we could not afford to rebel. We are too few." Several Armenian families fled to the mountains when the Kurdish rebellion collapsed. Four Armenian babies were among the hundreds who died on the Turkish frontier, sharing their graves with the descendants of those who had massacred their great-grandparents.

Now the Armenians were interested in a different crisis. "We want to go to the Motherland," an Armenian engineer said. "The Soviet Union is breaking apart and soon Soviet Armenia will be a free country, our Motherland which will protect us. I don't hear the Baghdad or the Kurdish radios. I listen to the Armenian radio every night at six-thirty, from Yerevan in the Soviet Union. They say: 'This is the broadcast of the Armenian Republic.' They tell us that the Russian soldiers and the Azeris are raping our women like the Kurds did. Will Armenia be free soon? Can we go there?"

Everyone, it seemed, wanted to leave Iraq. All except the dead. Some would say that 200,000 died in the uprising that followed the liberation of Kuwait—twice the total of Iraqis who were killed in the war according to some estimates—which would mean that well over a quarter of a million souls perished in Iraq in the first half of 1991. Among the dead were thousands of Marsh Arabs, whose fate went largely unrecorded because their homes lay in the ancient Sumerian wetlands of eastern Iraq.

Back in 1982, in the fleapit shop of one of Baghdad's seedier hotels, I bought a guidebook to the country. It was published by the Baath party or—as it pompously proclaimed on page 1—by the "State Organisation for Tourism General Establishment for Travel and Tourism Services." And where did this little booklet advise me to go for some tourism? "And now, off to a unique world, the Marshes, where nature seems to preserve its virgin aspect. Miles and miles of water, with an endless variety of birds, of fish, of plants and reeds and bulrushes, dotted as far as the eye can see with huts, each a little island unto itself." The first time I saw the Marshes, just east of the Baghdad–Basra highway, the tourist guide was true to its words. For kilometres, thousands of reed huts stood on earth and papyrus islands, each inhabited by the descendants of the ancient Sumerians, a time warp of simplicity which, according to old Arabic scripts, may have begun with a devastating flood around AD 620.

Saddam probably began to drain the marshlands in 1989, just a year before his invasion of Kuwait, and the officially stated explanation—"security reasons"—could not fail to hide its potential effect. For years, the Marsh Arabs were turning up in Kuwait and Iran with stories of dried-up riverbeds, of starvation and disease. The man who rebuilt Babylon in his own image was destroying Sumeria. Of course, it was his war with Iran that first drew Saddam's attention to the vulnerability of the marshland; it was here that the Iranian boy soldiers made their biggest penetration of Iraq and Saddam, as we have seen, swamped the marshes with gasoline, fire and death by electricity. Within a year of the end of that war, the first work began, massive walls and dams of pre-stressed concrete, initially in secret and then—once the first satellite pictures revealed what Saddam was doing—in public. After 1991, American journalists were taken to see the northern ramparts of what was described as an "irrigation" project. They were banned from the crusted lake-beds further south, for it was here that Saddam was still being assaulted, by army deserters who emerged from the wetlands at night to assault army convoys and police posts, even three years after the 1991 war.

As usual in the Arab world, everyone knew what was happening and no one said a thing. The American and British pilots flying the pointless southern "no-fly" zone could see the receding waters of the Marshes, the evaporating reedbeds and lagoons. But we did nothing. And the Arab regimes remained silent. Neither Mubarak nor Arafat nor Assad nor Fahd—none of the supposed titans of the Arab world—uttered the mildest word of criticism, any more than they did when the Kurds were gassed. The Iraqi exiled writer Kanan Makiya drew attention to an incendiary article in the Baath party's *Al-Thawra* newspaper in April 1991 while Saddam's army was still trying to crush the southern rebellion. The author attacked the Marsh Arabs for their poverty, backwardness and immorality, referring to them as vicious, slatternly and dirty. "One often hears stories of perversion that would make your mouth drop," the paper said. So the Marsh Arabs—whose brides were once carried to their weddings on convoys of reed-boats—were bestialised before their culture was destroyed. Saddam had dried up another corner of Iraq, put the people and the birds to flight, and made sure that there were no more little islands unto themselves.

# CHAPTER SEVENTEEN

# The Land of Graves

*My home is dark, the heart of my garden and the desert is dark,*
*. . . every corner of this ruined city is black.*
*The sky is tired; the sun has given up.*
*Like a prison cell, the travelling moon is dark.*

—Quhar Ausi, *Darkness* (*Tareeq*), 1990

ON THE HEIGHTS OF THE MUTLA RIDGE, a tattered, cheap bouquet of artificial roses, bleached white by the sun, thrashes in the wind, still fixed to a rusting metal pipe that stands upright in the sand. It is 2 August 1991, a year to the day after Saddam Hussein's army invaded Kuwait. The plastic rose is the only memorial to the slaughter that took place here, a lone act of gentleness by an American soldier—for it was the Americans I saw here five months ago, heaping the mangled corpses into the pit, scarves over their mouths, an army bulldozer widening the mass grave. The sand, shawling over the desert—cutting into your face and hands if you stand facing the wind—has now covered the two mounds of dirt that the bulldozer created. Only those twin piles—and those pathetic fake roses—mark the last resting place of Saddam's legions.

How many died here? Who were those Iraqis whose stiffened, shabby remains we found lying around their burned-out tanks and trucks and looted buses, guns and armoured carriers after the American and British jets had trapped them at night in their flight from Kuwait? When it comes to this particular cull, you can forget the Geneva Convention and that clause about the exchange of lists showing "the particulars of the dead interred therein." On the highway below their graves, the rusting armour and the stolen cars are still there, covered now in the graffiti of the victors, cheerful jokes for Mom and Pa, American unit slogans and interminable, grotesquely obscene remarks—not so much about Iraq and Saddam but about women, humiliating and disturbing, as if the conquerors needed to associate sex with violent death.

Just as the sand has subtly changed the landscape at each end of the mass grave, time changes our perception of such events. At the time of their death, we had just witnessed the evidence of Iraqi savagery in the newly liberated city of Kuwait. We had visited the Iraqi torture chambers, seen the mutilated bodies of Kuwaiti men and women, the destruction of Kuwait's palaces and oil wells. In among the doomed convoys at Mutla, we had found plunder on a medieval scale. I had seen hundreds of dead here; there must have been thousands. The Kuwaitis talk about 100,000 Iraqi soldiers killed in the desert. Some say 200,000. Shouldn't we have been referring back then, not to the "Highway of Death"—the popular headline around the world—but to the Massacre at Mutla Ridge?

The plunder has long since been re-looted. But there are still ghosts in the desert. Beside the wreckage of an Iraqi truck—battalion insignia, a blue square beside a white triangle, for armies are about bureaucracy as well as death—I tug at the spines of shredded files and exercise books, three-quarters buried in the sand, detritus of the defeated Iraqi army's administration, faithfully loaded in the hours before its destruction on 28 February 1991. At first, the sand will not yield these papers so I trowel with my fingers in the muck and dig and pull at these archives with my nails. In my hands, I hold a company inventory that lists the soldiers of this battalion by name, Muslim Arabs, Kurds, Christians, even Armenians. "Abdul Rida Rahim Ahmed, motorcycle dispatch rider, born 1954, primary school education, Arab Muslim, home: Basra. Mandil Ahmed Qadis Mustafa al-Koli, motorcycle dispatch rider, born 1952, Kurdish Muslim, home: Al-Ta'amim. Gunner Ali Hussein Hamza, artillery, born 1949, primary school education, Arab Muslim, home: Qadisiya . . ."

Are these the men lying now on the Mutla heights? Not only names, I find nightmares beneath the desert. I see the edge of a larger book, almost buried, and get down on my knees and seize the edge of it and tug from side to side, feeling my knees sinking into the sand until the volume suddenly slips out into my hands. I open the pages and specks of sand begin to heap up in the spine; these are the handwritten notes of an anonymous Iraqi Baath party functionary attached to an unknown military unit, recording the minutes of a meeting between Saddam Hussein and the Iraqi minister of industry on 28 February 1990, a year to the day before his army was destroyed in this very desert. I am squatting on my haunches, but when I see Saddam's name, I sit back on the sand and nurse the book in my lap. It actually quotes Saddam, hubristic but already feeling the financial constraints that led him to invade Kuwait just over five months later. "We will give the people 20 dinars each for every bomb that is manufactured inside Iraq," the tattered notebook records Saddam as saying. "Make our factories produce 5,000 bombs every day. Let our local industries compete with each other so that they can compete with the international arms industry. We have to save millions of dollars in military spending . . . so let's spend a little bit more on our local manufacturing so that we can reach the point where we will be completely independent of the international market . . ."

Militarily independent. Saddam's New World Order. From beneath the sands of the Kuwaiti desert these words came to me, and with what irony. For it was not Iraq's toiling masses but the Western world that created Saddam's military power, that furnished his republic of terror with credits and food and with the very means of his own destruction. It was Britain that was still sending nuclear substances to Baghdad, even as Saddam was planning his monumental output of domestically-produced weapons. It was America that provided funds and the Soviets who gave

Saddam the tanks and armour that were now decaying on the Mutla Ridge. No wonder Saddam still lied to the United Nations about what was left of his armoury. The more powerful he could remain, the longer he could survive President Bush's version of the New World Order, an international system in which aggression would in theory no longer pay dividends and where arms were no longer supposed to be supplied with such promiscuity to the nations of the Middle East. Perhaps— and this would be the darkest of all nightmares—Saddam might still succeed.

Who, after all, now remembered George Bush's assurance to the people of Iraq that it was not them but their leader with whom he was in conflict? "We have no argument with the people of Iraq," he insisted on 15 February 1991. "Our differences are with that brutal dictator in Baghdad." Yet while the people of Iraq were now dying of sickness and starvation caused by the war, Saddam's brutal regime had survived. Indeed, when the Iraqi people tried to destroy Saddam, the Americans and their allies permitted him to destroy his people and to emerge with his ultimate proclamation on this very week of the anniversary of his invasion, that Iraq had won a "great historical duel"—since victory should not be regarded "as a fight between one army and several others." This was not a view that would commend itself to the ghosts of Mutla Ridge.

Nor to the Saudi and Kuwaiti ruling families who also survived the conflict intact. Yet they had cause for satisfaction. Forgotten now were the hopes of the educated Saudi middle classes that America's military presence in the Gulf would liberalise their nation and make their royal family more amenable to collective leadership. In the aftermath of Saddam's humiliation, Saudi Arabia had become more, not less, conservative, its *mutawin* morality police more powerful, its military establishment stronger despite all the talk of disarmament. For the Pentagon now said that it planned to sell the Saudis laser-guided components, 2,100 cluster bombs and 770 Sparrow air-to-air missiles at a cost of $365 million. The White House had already told Congress of its plans to sell an additional $473 million of jeeps and military support services to Saudi Arabia. Since the liberation of Kuwait, Washington had disclosed plans to send a total of $4.2 billion in weapons to Saudi Arabia, Egypt, Morocco, Oman and Turkey—the latter receiving eighty F-16 fighter-bombers. So much for the disarming of the Middle East. The Saudis and their allies were now receiving the sort of largesse that Saddam obtained just over a year earlier.

We had come a long way since George Bush proposed to the post-Kuwait liberation world, on 29 May 1991, that there should be a Middle East arms control initiative that would "slow and then reverse the build-up of unnecessary and destabilising weapons" in the region. Less than three months earlier, he had vouchsafed the thought that "it would be tragic if the nations of the Middle East and Persian Gulf were now, in the wake of war, to embark on a new arms race." Yet just over two years later, Kuwait was buying 236 U.S. M1A2 Abrams tanks at a cost of $2 billion. Saudi Arabia was buying $7.5 billion worth of British Tornadoes and spending a further $3.9 billion on French frigates after the previous year's announcement of an awesome $9 billion purchase of American F-15XP fighter jets. To understand these figures, one had to remember the total Saudi financial support for the Palestinian–Israeli Gaza–Jericho accord: a mere $100 million. The United Arab Emirates, which in 1993 was buying $3.5 billion of French Leclerc tanks, had pledged just $25 million to the Palestinians. The U.S. sold well over $28 billion of arms in the two years following the 1991 Gulf War, of which the Saudis accounted for $17 billion. Sales of weapons to the Middle East in 1993 were running at $46 million a *day*.

Yet the treatment of the Iraqi dead lay heavily upon those whose duty it is to ensure that the "rules of war" are obeyed by the victors. Already, stories were coming out of Washington that 10,000 Iraqi soldiers had been buried alive near the Saudi frontier when the American army first stormed over the border into Kuwait. Faced with the alternative of fighting their way into the network of trenches and bunkers which the Iraqi forces had dug into the desert, or of bulldozing the sand over them—literally smothering them as they stood ready to fight—the United States understandably decided on the latter option. Was entombment alive any worse for the Iraqis than being annihilated by shellfire—especially when U.S. casualties would be higher in open fighting?

A semantic game was played by the Americans. Most of the Iraqi dead, claimed those inevitably anonymous "military sources"—in this case, to the Reuters news agency—would have died during the five weeks of air attacks that preceded the four-day ground conflict. They would have been buried by their comrades. The total number of Iraqi occupation troops, originally put at half a million, might have been exaggerated. Iraqi divisions, normally up to 12,000 strong, might have been 50 per cent depleted before they arrived in Kuwait. At least 62,000 Iraqis, hungry and fearful, surrendered to the Allies. All officers would say was that "large numbers" of Iraqis were killed in the war. Which meant—and was no doubt intended to mean—nothing.

For no U.S. officer saw fit to mark the vast graves into which the Americans and British had committed the Iraqi dead, or to pass on the information to the International Committee of the Red Cross as the Allies were bound to do under international law. In late May 1991, Dr. Jeannik Dami, a Swiss doctor for the ICRC in Kuwait, was called to examine the bodies of nine unburied Iraqi soldiers lying in the desert near the headquarters of the Kuwaiti army's 6th Brigade not far from the Iraqi border. She found that the remains of the dead Iraqis were badly decomposed but that a further thirteen Iraqi corpses had been buried a few yards away beneath a wooden stake, upon which was written in English the single word "Unknown."

It was highly misleading. All but one of these buried bodies were dressed in the remains of Iraqi army uniforms. And on eight of them, Dr. Dami found identification papers or "dog-tags" with their names. They were not "unknown" at all. Most of the corpses had been interred in U.S. military body bags and one of them—a twenty-seven-year-old Iraqi conscript named Jabr Elwan Qidar—had his legs tied together with rope. The only body not in uniform was that of a woman.

What was even more remarkable about Dr. Dami's discovery was that this was the first time the Red Cross had been able to inspect the graves of dead Iraqi soldiers. Three months had passed since the end of "Operation Desert Storm"—and the American estimates of Iraqi dead had already reached 100,000—yet the Red Cross had obtained access to the graves of only twenty-one Iraqis. In total violation of Article 17 of the Geneva Conventions, Allied and Arab coalition forces failed to provide even the vaguest statistics of the Iraqi death toll. The American military authorities gave neither the names of their tens of thousands of dead enemies nor the location of mass graves in which they were buried to the International Red Cross. What this true figure was—and why the Allies failed to disclose it— was to remain one of the most disturbing mysteries of the 1991 Gulf War.

Saddam Hussein, of course, was in no position to complain about breaches of the Geneva Conventions. Allied prisoners-of-war were tortured by the Iraqis; and Saddam's Baathist regime, as everyone knew, routinely tortured and executed its political opponents. Saddam's use of poison gas to kill thousands of Iranian soldiers and then Kurdish civilians and his butchering of Shiite rebels during the postwar rising in March 1991 marked one of the vilest human rights records in the world.

Yet the Geneva Conventions state that "parties to [a] conflict shall ensure that burial or cremation of the dead, carried out individually as far as circumstances permit, is preceded by a careful examination . . . of the bodies, with a view to confirming death, establishing identity and enabling a report to be made . . . They shall further ensure that the dead are honourably interred, if possible according to the rites of the religion to which they belonged, that their graves are respected . . . properly maintained and marked so that they may always be found." Under the convention, armies are required to organise a graves registration service that will exchange "lists showing the exact location and markings of the graves together with particulars of the dead interred therein."

The 1991 Gulf War Allies ignored every one of these basic rules. After the liberation of Kuwait, General Schwarzkopf brusquely dismissed questions about Iraqi fatalities with the rejoinder that he was "not in the business of body counts." Yet under the Geneva Conventions, generals—even American generals—had to ensure that bodies were indeed counted. True, Iraqi troops had committed what might well classify as war crimes during their occupation of Kuwait, but even Hitler's SS soldiers who were killed fighting the Americans around Bastogne in 1944 were identified and buried in marked graves.

As usual, we had to turn to humanitarian workers—speaking anonymously lest they lose what little moral power they had with the victorious armies—to find out what the Red Cross felt. "They are bloody angry and I don't blame them," a British doctor told me. "What's really puzzling is that the Americans know where a lot of mass graves are and must have files on how many Iraqis they buried in each grave. They are hiding the figures. The Red Cross knows this, but they can't get the allied powers to come up with a single figure. Why not? Well, either the Americans killed far fewer than they claim—maybe only ten or twenty thousand; in which case people are going to ask if their victory was as big as they claimed. Low casualty figures would explain why Saddam had enough soldiers left to crush two big uprisings in Iraq the moment the allied advance stopped. Or maybe the Americans killed too many, say more than two hundred thousand—and they're worried the Arabs would be disgusted at, say, the slaughter of a quarter of a million fellow Arabs."

Christophe Girod, the senior ICRC delegate in Kuwait, confirmed to me on 4 August 1991 that the Red Cross had twice asked the U.S. embassy for details of the Iraqi dead without receiving any information. The Red Cross was told to seek details directly from the Pentagon. But the Pentagon proved equally unhelpful. "We are still waiting for a reply from the allies about the location of mass graves, the numbers of dead and, hopefully, names and details," Girod said. "It is their obligation to give us this information under Article 17 of the Geneva Conventions and we hope they will provide it." Some hope. The Americans never supplied any of these locations, statistics or names.* It was to become a habit. In 2003, the United States and Britain showed equally little interest in recording details of enemy dead—or, for that matter, the civilians killed in their invasion—although they were rigorous, as they were in the 1991 Gulf War, in listing the American, British and other Western, or "coalition," soldiers killed in action.

"Our" dead—the heroes, the Westerners who died for "freedom," "democracy" or whatever other benefit we planned to impose on the losers—were sacrosanct. In 1991, the Americans lost 125 soldiers, their allies around 70. Their names would live for evermore, just like those on the Lutyens memorials along the old Western Front in France in Bill Fisk's war. There would be religious services to honour them, interviews with wives and children, parents and fiancées. There would be—in both wars—controversy about the accidental killing of British troops by trigger-happy Americans. But we would know who they were. Our dead would have identities, families, public mourning. They were individuals, even in death. The Iraqi dead were an amorphous mass, as nondescript as the graves into which they were shovelled. They were the occupiers of Kuwait—or, later, the "remnants" or "terrorists" who insisted on fighting the invaders of their country in 2003—and they did not deserve a memorial. In this, the Americans were ably assisted by Saddam's regime. For the Baath party in Baghdad had no desire to reveal to the world the extent of the country's military defeat and would give no indication of the scale of their own casualties. As the Americans had pointed out, many hundreds of Iraqi soldiers died under allied air bombardment before the land offensive. Saddam was happy for their names and numbers to remain unknown, just as he was indifferent to the rest of his "martyrs" in the Kuwait war. The Americans and the Iraqis thus shared a happy coincidence of intention. Both sides wanted to keep the Iraqi dead a secret.

Towards the end of the first week of August 1991, Christophe Girod drove me

---

*This indifference to the Geneva Convention did not apply, however, when Iraq paraded captured British pilots on television during the war, some of whom appeared to have been beaten. American and British officials then insisted on absolute observance by the Baghdad regime of the Geneva Conventions on prisoners-of-war. Some pilots bore the marks of their emergency ejection from their aircraft, although RAF crews later gave graphic accounts of their mistreatment at the hands of Iraq's security goons.

up to the Mutla Ridge so that I could identify for him the mass grave I had come across the previous February. The artificial rose was there and Girod immediately noted the ramparts of sand thrown up by the bulldozer when it covered over the bodies. Dozens of corpses were subsequently exhumed there and returned to Iraq. But it was the only grave I could still find. At other locations I had jotted into my notebook back in February, the wind had changed the landscape. Flat terrain beside the highway to Iraq had been turned into sand dunes, the hump of individual graves in the soil had been smoothed into the desert floor by the spring gales.

But American and British units had participated in thousands of hasty burials in this desert in February 1991. I saw at least seven of them myself, young soldiers staggering under the weight of soggy, corpse-filled blankets, digging into the sand and dumping their burden in the holes they had made. All over the land north of Kuwait City, this ritual took place. Kuwaiti Red Crescent workers, some of whom helped to clear the dead from the Mutla Ridge and the other largely unexplored "highway of death" to the east of it, were involved in the same process. The Kuwaitis later told Western aid workers that dozens of victims of these allied air attacks were innocent Kuwaiti civilians being taken to Iraq as hostages by the retreating Iraqi army.

As for the Red Cross, they repatriated the twenty-one dead Iraqi soldiers to Baghdad. Dr. Dami found that the corpses had not been buried—as they should have been according to their religious rites—facing Mecca. They had been interred two at a time with identity papers between the body bags. In several of their uniforms, she found personal papers and diaries which, under the Geneva Conventions, should have been returned to their next-of-kin. On one page of a diary belonging to Burhan Ahmed Faraj was the name Burhan Hamad Faraj—the nephew of the buried soldier—through whom the Iraqis were able to inform the dead man's closest relatives. Other names found on the bodies and handed to the Iraqis by the Red Cross included Mussair Jabr Hamdi, Musalam Ismail Ibrahim, Ahmed Fahd Malalla and Hassan Daoud Salman. One of the bodies had a bottle of perfume in a pocket, probably looted in Kuwait. Why Jabr Elwan Qidar's legs were tied together was never explained.

Had the Red Cross not exhumed their remains, these soldiers would have been, as British world war headstones used to record, "known unto God." Yet they did not even have known graves. As for the dead woman, her body was taken to Kuwait City, where the authorities said they could identify her from her fingerprints. She was a former resident of Kuwait. When I asked a Kuwaiti aid official for her identity, his voice filled with contempt. "They said she was an Iraqi whore," he replied.

The only serious attempt to estimate overall casualties was made by Beth Osborne Daponte, the U.S. Census Bureau demographer assigned to gather statistics on the number of Iraqis killed during the war. Her figures suggested that 86,000 men, 40,000 women and 32,000 children died at the hands of American-led coalition forces, during the American-inspired insurgencies that followed and from immediate postwar deprivation. Daponte was fired. The bureau then rescinded her dismissal but rewrote her report, lowering the death toll and deleting the fatalities of women and children. A subsequent Pentagon official history omitted a chapter on casualties and made no mention of Iraqi deaths.

Needless to say, the massive bloodletting that these military operations involved was never allowed to spoil the "big picture," the war aims that Western leaders and editorial writers could point to as proof that this had been a "good" war with God on their side—though which God was invoked was a moot point. Kuwait's royal family was restored to power, just as President Bush had promised it would be. And no one who entered the Kuwaiti capital on the day of its liberation—as I and my colleagues did—could doubt that its freedom was devoutly to be wished. Had Saddam succeeded in holding on to his "nineteenth province," it would have been a disaster for the region and for the international system of nation-states.

Yet in Kuwait, as in Saudi Arabia—and in Iraq, for that matter—the aftermath of the ground fighting was not participation in a New World Order but a restoration of the status quo. The Arab rulers were back within their respective, British-drawn borders. Those Kuwaitis who refused to leave during the occupation and who had endured horrifying personal risk for their country found that those who had fled Kuwait, including the royal family, were brought back to rule them. The emir and his entourage, who suffered exile in the most luxurious hotel in Taif, had returned to tell the Kuwaitis who stayed—and who sometimes resisted with great courage—that they could not have democracy just yet.

Most scandalous of all in Kuwaiti domestic politics was to be the expulsion of 360,000 Palestinians over the next two years, an act of "ethnic cleansing" unparalleled in the Middle East since the massacres that accompanied the Palestinian flight from Israeli forces in 1948. The UN Security Council did not even bother to discuss this outrage, nor to question the Kuwaitis about their miserable excuse for such treatment of their fellow Arabs: that some Palestinians had collaborated with Iraq during the occupation. Up the long road towards Basra each day, I would watch the overloaded trucks and pick-ups carrying the Palestinians into yet another exile—through Iraq to Jordan—without even the luxury of selling the homes and property which they had owned for decades in Kuwait. "They will throw me out before you return," Sulieman Khalidi, a Palestinian friend in Kuwait, told me in 1992. "Give me a call if you like, but I don't think I'll be here to answer the phone." In January 1993, I called Khalidi as I had promised. And as he had promised, he was not there. "Yes, he was living in this house but he left for Jordan," a woman answered irritably. "No, he is not coming back. Yes, I am Kuwaiti."

Less epic in scale but almost equally scandalous was the plight of the Kuwaiti Bedouin troops who refused to run away on 2 August 1990, who chose to fight the Iraqi invaders and who were taken prisoners-of-war by Saddam's army. These thousands of young men did not hold Kuwaiti citizenship, yet they fought for the emirate. But now, while most of the Kuwaiti officers who fled were reinstalled in their posts, Kuwait refused to allow these loyal Bedouin soldiers to return from their Iraqi imprisonment. Hundreds more were held in an internment camp at Abdali on the Kuwaiti–Iraqi border, having been freed from their Iraqi jails during the Shiite uprising but rejected by the nation for which they fought, Kuwaiti patriots now held prisoner by the Kuwaiti soldiers who took to their heels in their country's hour of need.

One broiling morning, I drove up to Abdali. It was a disgrace. It wasn't the latrines, whose stench pervaded the place. Nor the sandstorms that howled across its wastes, turning its occupants into white and grey shadows. Nor even the shacks of cloth and corrugated iron and old tin sheets whose constant demented rattle turned a conversation into a shouting match. It was the fact that the inhabitants of this awful place—all 1,173 of them—appeared to be decent and honest Kuwaitis who had been left to rot here because they were never given citizenship and happened to be on the wrong side of the Gulf War front line when President Bush announced his ceasefire the previous February.

Many of them were Kuwaiti policemen with years of service to the emir, who were arrested during the occupation and taken hostage to Iraq by Saddam Hussein's secret police. Others were the wives and children of Kuwaiti policemen who were searching for missing relatives in Iraq when the Americans arrived at the border town of Abdali five months earlier and who were then refused permission to return to their homes in Kuwait—even though their families were waiting for them there. A few were Kuwaitis without citizenship who made the mistake of trying to buy food with Iraqi currency after the liberation—and who were shipped up to this desolate place by the emir's security police.

The prisoners' fate was to belong to the *bidoon*—the "withouts"—the quarter of a million Kuwaitis whose failure to register as citizens, or whose parents' failure to register, after the emirate's independence in 1920 left them loyal but stateless citizens of a country that would not give them a passport. Now that Kuwait was liberated and now that the Sabah family wanted to reduce the number of non-Kuwaiti citizens, the *bidoon*—along with Kuwaiti-born Palestinians, and large numbers of other Arabs who made their homes in the emirate decades ago—were being accused of collaboration with the Iraqi occupiers.

And so, choking in the gales of sand in the south-eastern corner of Abdali camp, I found—behind a protective sheet of rusting iron—the bearded figure of Saba Abu Nasr al-Kaldi, clerk at the interior ministry and well-known Kuwaiti artist until 2 August 1990. "I never tried to go to my office when the Iraqis came, because I knew they were arresting government officials," he told me. "But I did draw posters for the Kuwaiti resistance and someone informed on me and the Iraqis took me from my home. I was taken to the Salahiyeh police station where I was beaten but I refused to tell them anything. So they let me go home. But a month later, they took me again and put me on a convoy of buses with four hundred other *bidoon* to a military barracks at Amara, inside Iraq. We were held prisoner there for three months. When the Americans began to bomb, we were moved to Diwaniya. We had little food. We were filthy. I wondered if I would see my home again."

Al-Kaldi and his fellow "withouts" were freed during the Shiite uprising in southern Iraq, awoken to their imminent freedom when shoals of bullets smashed through the windows of their cells. From his prison, al-Kaldi said, he walked with forty other Kuwaitis for ten days over desert and scrubland, eating tomatoes and dates, sleeping at night in wrecked Iraqi mosques, empty dugouts or in the shadow of abandoned Iraqi tanks. His narrative—of rotting Iraqi corpses along the road-sides and the constant explosion of underground munitions as he made his way south—was as frightening as it was convincing. "One night, we slept on a hill called Tell el-Lahm and there were terrible explosions," he said. "The ground moved beneath us all the time and shells went over us. God saved us. Can you know how we felt to reach Kuwait, to know that we would see our families again? But the Kuwaiti government were here and they stopped us. They said 'You are *bidoon*.' So we stayed here, and stayed and stayed."

The Kuwaiti authorities claimed that many *bidoon* joined the Iraqi "Popular Army" after the occupation. And when the Kuwaiti government announced in July 1991 that it would hang anyone who had joined Iraq's "voluntary" units, more than 3,000 "withouts"—including women and children—abandoned the Abdali camp and walked back to Iraq. More than 1,000, however, stayed put, arguing that they had never helped the Iraqis, and that those who signed up with the occupiers did so through coercion and never turned up for work. "It was a lie by the Iraqis to call these people a 'volunteer' army," one of the *bidoon* at Abdali said. "They were no more members of the Iraqi army than the foreign hostages in Iraq were 'guests.'"

The *bidoon* of Abdali all carried their official Kuwaiti papers—the policemen showed me laminated government cards with photographs in which they were dressed in smart blue police uniforms—and the Red Cross workers who ran the camp, mostly from America and Europe, did not doubt their authenticity. It was of little use. "All of us want to return to our homes where we were born, where we lived and worked before this terrible war," al-Kaldi said. "What is our crime? What is the crime of the children here? Nobody cares about us." In his captivity, al-Kaldi drew a series of sad and beautiful sketches of life during the war. The most moving showed a *bidoon* family burying their policeman son, murdered by the Iraqis dur-ing the occupation. A boy near the grave is waving goodbye towards the distant city of Kuwait, identifiable by its water towers. "You see what is happening?" al-Kaldi asked me. "The *bidoon* can die here, but they will not be allowed to live here."

But if the geographical restoration of Kuwait to its rulers was a measure of the war's worth, its oil fires cast more than a physical shadow over the land. The destruction of the wells remained Saddam's greatest crime in the emirate, their continued burning proof that the war had not yet ended. I had to fly over them to realise the enormity of what had happened. From the air, it was possible to see lakes of oil, hundreds of square kilometres of sludge, the white of the sands turned to blackness. In a hundred years, the evidence will still be there to see. The desert has changed colour for generations to come. Arriving in Kuwait on one of MEA's elderly Boeing 707 airliners, I could physically *feel* the extent of the damage. Sit-ting on the plane's flight deck, I watched the pilot twisting his aircraft around the oil clouds as if he were performing at an air display. But when we actually hit one of the black columns of smoke on final approach, the old airliner bucked in the sky, juddering and shaking as it smashed into the haze of sulphur.

Standing next to the fires, the very ground vibrated beneath my feet, their roar awesome and elemental. The Kuwaitis were more than willing to take reporters to these scenes of Saddam's environmental and economic crimes. We would drive in our own cars out of Kuwait City that dazzling, cooking August to be confronted by fires so bright they hurt our eyes, the heat so powerful that every few seconds we would instinctively turn round to cool the left or right side of our faces and arms. "The Iraqi who did this arrived about three months after the invasion," Mahmoud Somali told us as we stood beside one of these thundering, squirting torches of oil, the smoke above us so thick that I could not have seen my own notebook but for the golden fires. "He was a very ordinary sort of guy, I've even forgotten his name. He was very friendly to us, not hostile at all. He chatted a lot, had coffee with us in the Ahmadi canteen each day. He said he was a good Muslim and every Friday he went to the mosque. But then he put the mines down the wells and he told us this was his duty, that he had to do his duty."

Was this the banality of evil, this man with the forgettable name—an official from the Iraqi oil company, most of the Kuwaitis at Ahmadi now believed—who dutifully, efficiently, committed what must qualify as a war crime as well as an environmental catastrophe? For let us not deny his professionalism. Of Kuwait's 940 or so producing oil wells, he set off mines in 732, turning 640 of them into basins of fire. Stand beside the burning lagoons of the Burgan oil field even now— more than five months after the coffee-drinking Iraqi with his religious obser- vances had left—and you could only wonder at the implications of his act.

The clichés were long ago exhausted: the fires of hell, darkness at high noon. All had an element of truth about them. Across the black lakes, reflecting the fine, brown-gold light of the fires, the curtains of smoke that smothered the sun—a but- ton of pale yellow light immediately above us—were almost as frightening as the thunder of the burning wells. At Burgan, I scribbled these observations into my notebook until I realised that the pages were becoming spotty and then soaked in a slippery brown substance that was settling on our clothes, our shoes, faces and hair. We were breathing crude oil. We coughed for hours afterwards. It was then that it dawned on me: Saddam Hussein did use chemical warfare.

What, after all, were a few mustard gas shells compared to the 2 million tons of carbon dioxide and 5,000 tons of soot spurting into the sky over Kuwait every day, drifting as gently as any sarin or tabun across the Gulf? Everyone was a witness. Mr. Somali's daughter was asthmatic, and he had to move accommodation to pro- tect her lungs every time the wind changed. Down at the al-Ahmadi headquarters, an Iranian drilling team had arrived to help the Kuwaitis put out their fires, serious, inevitably bearded, genuinely shocked men who had never seen anything on this scale, not even in the eight years of Iraqi destruction in their own country.

"Of course it is an environmental disaster, and not just here," Homayoun Motier, the drilling engineer from the National Iranian Oil Company, said to me. "I come from Ahwaz and this smoke has covered us there—there is pollution from these fires all across southern Iran. Do you realise that there is soot all over our Zagros mountains a thousand kilometres away? I have seen it there. It lies in layers beneath the snow, frozen in layer after layer." Later, as the Iraqi invasion receded, the Americans and the British would paint Iran in the same dangerous colours as Iraq—partly to persuade the Arabs to buy more weapons—and Iran would be touted as the next aggressor, the next threat to the Arab Gulf states, just as it had been in the aftermath of the 1979 Islamic revolution. And the work of Homayoun Motier and his men would be forgotten.

Watching the fountains of burning oil and the fires spreading across the lagoons, you could not avoid the conviction that the Gulf War had not ended. And that Saddam Hussein did not intend it to end when he was driven from Kuwait. The statistics changed each day, but by 5 August three American teams and a Canadian unit of firefighters had capped and controlled 274 of the 640 burning wells, most of them in the biggest fields of Burgan (total wells: 426), Maqwa (total wells: 148) and Ahmadi (total wells: 89). They were spraying tons of sea water onto the fires—using the original oil pipelines to pump the salt water back into the fields—to cool the superheated coking that had built up around the flames. The 115,000 barrels of oil that the Kuwaitis were now able to export each day almost all came from the Maqwa field. Yet more than 60 million barrels of oil and gas a day—from an original loss of more than 110 million each day—were still being burned away, transformed into the chemicals that were now poisoning the land and seas as far east as the Himalayas.

Mahmoud Somali had been twenty-two years in the Kuwait Oil Company's drilling department and had no illusions about what happened. "When the Iraqis came here in the first week of the occupation, soldiers and a lot of Iraqi civilian technicians arrived," he said. "The soldiers did not allow us to go into the fields. The technicians, they wanted to start up the oil exportation again. They told us we must increase production. They wanted to export Kuwaiti oil. This was before the sanctions. Then one day, after the UN decided on sanctions, we had an accidental gas cut-out and the soldiers took me out to the field to repair it. When I got there, I saw at once a series of white wires running to the wells. They were very professional. The wires went down below the master valves so that if they wanted to blow them up, we couldn't turn them off. And that's what happened. Three months later, the Iraqi came who was in charge of the mines and he was the one who put the explosives down the wells . . . from the start, the Iraqis were thinking of destroying our oil." Somali had few doubts that innocents were going to die from all this—of chemical poisoning, of cancer—not only in Kuwait but in Iran, Afghanistan, Pakistan. "Probably yes, they will die," he said amid the darkness of Burgan. "But who is going to take responsibility? Saddam?"

The Kuwaitis claimed they were now exporting 115,000 barrels a day, a total that rose to 200,000 if you included the oil from the Neutral Zone. If the fires in the al-Maqwa and al-Ahmadi fields could be extinguished by the end of August, the emirate could be producing half a million barrels by the New Year of 1992, a victory of sorts, but nothing like Kuwait's pre-invasion OPEC quota of 1.5 million barrels a day—and much less than its actual oil overproduction of 2 million barrels that provoked Saddam to invade. To defend this reconstituted source of wealth, the United States was now forced to maintain a combat brigade in Kuwait, which is why, at the Mutla Ridge, the same American M1A1 tanks I saw five months earlier were still patrolling the highway to Iraq.

However strong the U.S. Air Force might remain in the Gulf, there was not much else on land to defend Kuwait. When the Saudis decided they no longer wanted Egyptian and Syrian troops on their soil, the whole projected edifice of an Arab Gulf security force collapsed. And the Kuwaitis could no more mount a defence of their emirate now than they could a year earlier. On this mournful anniversary, however, we were encouraged to look elsewhere, to the peace conference in Madrid that would end the Middle East conflict for ever. Here at last, it was suggested, we would see the real fruits of war, provided we could forget what war actually meant, if we could ignore the tens of thousands of Iraqi dead bulldozed into their mass graves by the allies, the thousands of Shiites who were put before Saddam's mass execution squads, the epic tragedy of the Kurds. If we could accept that the New World Order was merely the Old World Order put on good behaviour, then maybe we could believe in the impossible.

In one sense, a peace conference—or, more to the point and far more difficult, a peace settlement—would be a restoration of the integrity of the frontiers drawn up after the 1914–18 war, with the creation of the original 1948 Israel grafted onto it. It would be about a return to accepted borders. It was about the Old World Order. For that is what lay at the roots of Western policies in the Middle East. We should have realised this when the Americans allowed Saddam's domestic opponents to be massacred. Faced with the alternative of allowing Iraq to disintegrate, or of permitting the people of Iraq to remake their own map of their part of the Middle East, the West opted for Saddam on good—or at least internationally harmless—behaviour.

This is what the 1991 Gulf War should have taught us: that it was the West that was going to decide the future of the region, in however benign or disastrous a fashion, just as the Western superpowers had done for more than seventy years. Those regional leaders who stepped out of line—including Saddam—would pay the price, even if it was individually less terrible than the fate of those in the mass graves on Mutla Ridge.

Against this frightening horizon, Kuwait's own continuing pain—its demand for the return of 850 "missing" citizens who remained captive in Iraq—might have seemed diminutive, even irrelevant. But missing they were, and the "sighting" of these men and women—in many cases, seized by the Iraqis in the last hours of their occupation—was to be a bruising experience for thousands of Kuwaitis in the years to come. You only had to visit the gymnasium-size hall in which the Kuwaiti "National Committee for Missing Persons and POW Affairs" had installed itself in the suburb of Sabaha Salman to understand; it was filled with silence and photographs. Some were studio portraits of young men in white or brown robes, others of grinning students in black gowns nursing American college degrees. Around the walls there were pictures of officers in police uniforms, soldiers and doctors, children and women in scarves, re-photographed snapshots and cutaways of Kuwaitis at parties and weddings and anniversaries, smiling with all the wealthy, carefree confidence of pre-invasion Kuwait. No one wished to divide these pictures into the quick and the dead—although most were, already, in mass graves.

As the years went by, these 850 souls became part of Kuwait's *raison d'être*, its proof of victimhood, the vital statistic that would help to distract the world's attention from the new life of misery that Iraqis were now entering north of the border. Their plight was emblazoned like an Olympics advertisement on the fuselage of Kuwait's restored national airline. "Return our 850 POWs" was painted next to every aircraft passenger door. What were 850 missing Kuwaitis compared to 100,000 Iraqi dead? The Kuwaitis would politely reply that the Iraqis were the invaders while the 850 were innocent victims of that aggression.

But by the mid-1990s, the horrors of Bosnia, the slaughter and mass rape of Muslims in the old Yugoslavia had also long surpassed the sufferings of Kuwait under Iraqi occupation. And Kuwait's own act of "ethnic cleansing"—the expulsion of the 360,000 Palestinians from their homes after the liberation—had squandered much of the international sympathy that might have been forthcoming for the families of those Kuwaitis who were trucked off to prison in Basra and Baghdad, Nasiriyah and Samawa. In his autobiography, General Schwarzkopf admits that the return of Kuwaiti civilian prisoners from Iraq was the one ceasefire condition that Saddam Hussein's generals refused to discuss—perhaps because they knew that most of them were already dead.

In retrospect, General Schwarzkopf's account of these hundreds of civilians is a story of painfully weak diplomacy on the part of the victorious allies. "We settled for his [an Iraqi general's] assurance that anyone who had come to Iraq since the invasion of Kuwait would be free to approach the Red Cross and leave if he wanted," Schwarzkopf wrote in his account of the February 1991 ceasefire negotiations. In fact, the ICRC did not receive a single communication from Kuwaitis, either in Baghdad or in their sub-office in Basra. Greatest concern was expressed for the 650 or so civilians—30 of them women—who were known to have been arrested in Kuwait during the occupation and who were later seen in prisons inside Iraq. Many of the Kuwaitis taken hostage in the last days of Iraqi rule saw these civilians in their Iraqi jails shortly before they themselves were freed, returning to Kuwait with first-hand evidence that the missing men and women were alive. But since February 1991, there had been no direct word from them, no handwritten messages, no access to their prisons for the Red Cross and only the occasional, months-old evidence that Kuwaitis remained alive in Iraq's prisons.

Two Egyptians, for instance, supposedly saw "Samira"—for the sake of her security, her family name was not given—on 1 August 1991, working alongside other female POWs in Baghdad. She had asked them to tell her mother she was still alive, that she was a cleaner in the Saadi hospital, living in the al-Qadimiya prison, ruled over by Uday Hussein, son of the president. That was all she told the two Egyptians, a message they faithfully delivered to the authorities in Kuwait. The twenty-nine-year-old—the snapshot in her file showed an attractive woman with bright brown hair and sparkling eyes—had been seen only once before, on 15 March 1991, when her message had been the same. Then there had been silence.

Kuwaitis drew strength from the 2,000 Iranian POWs whom Iran had thought dead but who emerged alive from Saddam's prisons after the end of the Iran–Iraq War in 1988. Saddam liked hostages, they reasoned. He knew how to use them. He had held thousands of Westerners captive after his invasion of Kuwait in 1990. But Kuwaiti prisoners held no interest for him. None of the 850 men and women—not even Samira—were ever seen alive again. Only after the Anglo-American invasion in 2003 did Kuwaitis know why. Amid the thousands of corpses dug up from the execution pits in the desert west of Hilla were dozens of men still carrying their Kuwaiti citizenship papers. So now Kuwait would have yet more names to add to their list of "martyrs" from the war, a small figure perhaps, but further proof that Arabs die at the hands of Arabs.

North of the Kuwaiti border, however, there now lay a barren land of misery, fear and defeat, its power stations bombed out, its water purification systems shattered by allied explosives, its sewers overflowing into streets and houses. Western journalists taken on a UN helicopter across southern Iraq saw thousands of tank revetments and trenches, all now covered with grass and sand; the Iraqi army had spent its energies in destroying the uprising and preserving the regime—threatening its neighbours was no longer an option. Iraq was prostrate and its people, under the burden of UN sanctions that were first intended to persuade Saddam to withdraw from Kuwait without a fight and then to destroy his regime—neither of which was accomplished—were about to embark on a slow mass death, made more terrible and more immoral because those sanctions were imposed by nations that regarded themselves as the most civilised on earth.

Across southern Iraq, the Shiites lived in mortal peril of their lives, their sons and husbands and brothers already filling the execution grounds around Hilla and Nasiriyah. The great golden-domed mosque of the Imam Ali in Najaf was in partial ruins, its centuries-old blue marble tiles lying in heaps around the shrine, souvenirs for passing journalists and for Saddam's Republican Guards who had blasted their way into the sacred buildings of Shiite Islam to kill the Iraqi insurgents seeking sanctuary there. Twelve years later, Shiite insurgents—in some cases the very men who had fought Saddam's killers in 1991—were hiding in the very same shrine, this time from American army tank fire. In the north, the Kurds—now under American and British protection—lived amid the hundreds of villages that had been gassed and then systematically destroyed on Saddam's orders. We had betrayed the Shiite rebellion. We had betrayed the Kurdish rebellion. Later—much later—when we came to destroy Saddam himself, we would expect them to be grateful to us. But they would remember.

The sanctions that smothered Iraq for almost thirteen years have largely dropped from the story of our Middle East adventures. Our invasion of Iraq in March 2003 closed the page—or so we hoped—on our treatment of the Iraqi people before that date, removed the stigma attached to the imprisonment of an entire nation and their steady debilitation and death under the UN sanctions regime. When the Anglo-American occupiers settled into their palaces in Baghdad, they would blame the collapse of electrical power, water-pumping stations, factories and commercial life on Saddam Hussein, as if he alone had engineered the impoverishment of Iraq. Sanctions were never mentioned. They were "ghosted" out of the story. First there had been Saddam, and then there was "freedom."

And indeed, when sanctions were first imposed after Iraq's invasion of Kuwait, there was little outcry; if they could induce Saddam to withdraw from Kuwait without the need for war, then few would criticise them. Besides, before the liberation of Kuwait, Iraq's power stations were still operating at full capacity and its economy, while crippled by the eight years of war with Iran, was capable of providing Iraqis with one of the highest standards of living in the Arab world. Rationing was introduced in Iraq in September 1990, but most Westerners—and most Arabs—assumed that once Saddam had withdrawn from Kuwait, hopefully before any hostilities took place, these sanctions would be lifted. As so often in the Middle East, a decision that initially appeared benign was to be quickly transformed into a weapon far more deadly than missiles or shells.

UN Security Council Resolution 661 was passed on 6 August 1990, scarcely four days after Saddam's army had crossed the Kuwaiti border, calling upon all states to prevent the import of "all commodities and products originating in Iraq or Kuwait" and to prohibit the supply of all goods except "supplies intended strictly for medical purposes, and, in humanitarian circumstances, foodstuffs." In retrospect, it is clear that the United States never had any faith that these sanctions—mild by comparison with the postwar restrictions—would persuade Saddam to order his forces out of Kuwait. Just as America and Britain would claim, twelve years later, that the UN arms inspectors could not be given the time to finish their work before the 2003 invasion, so the Americans gave up on the sanctions regime by the time their troops were in place for the liberation of Kuwait. The Washington Institute for Near East Policy concluded before the end of 1990 that "sanctions cannot be counted on to produce a sure result." By 15 January 1991, British foreign secretary Douglas Hurd was announcing that Britain was resigned to fight for Kuwait because UN sanctions had had no "decisive effect" on Saddam's capacity to wage war.

Only after the war did the United States make it clear that there would be no lifting of sanctions until Saddam Hussein was gone. Sanctions would remain, White House spokesman Marlin Fitzwater said, "until there was a change of government in Iraq." But the effect of sanctions was now catastrophic. In 1991 the Allies had crippled power stations and deliberately bombed water and sewage facilities—a decision that was bound to cause a humanitarian catastrophe among the civilians of Iraq. A Harvard team of lawyers and public health specialists, after visiting forty-six Iraqi hospitals and twenty-eight water and sewage facilities, stated in 1991 that deaths among children under five in Iraq had nearly quintupled, that almost a million were undernourished and 100,000 were starving to death. Their research found that 46,700 children under five had died from the combined effects of war and trade sanctions in the first seven months of 1991.

As more and more Iraqis started to die—not only ravaged by the foul water they were forced to drink from bomb-damaged water-cleansing plants but increasingly prevented from acquiring the medicines they might need to recover—a UN commission redrew the country's southern border to deprive it of part of the Rumeila oilfield and the naval base at Um Qasr, Iraq's only access to the waters of the Gulf. The confiscated territory was given to Kuwait. Western leaders insisted that Saddam Hussein could use Iraq's own resources to pay for humanitarian supplies, wilfully ignoring the fact that Iraqi financial assets had been blocked and oil sales prohibited. By the end of 1994, Iraqi inflation was running at 24,000 per cent a year and much of the population was destitute. On the streets of Baghdad, even the middle classes were selling their libraries for money to buy food. Volumes of Islamic theology, English editions of Shakespeare, medical treatises and academic theses on Arab architecture ended up on the pavements of Mutanabi Street in Baghdad: paper for bread.

By 1996, half a million Iraqi children were estimated to have died as a result of sanctions. Madeleine Albright, who was then U.S. ambassador to the United Nations, gave an infamous reply on 12 May that year when asked about sanctions on the CBS news programme *60 Minutes*. Anchor Leslie Stahl put it to Albright: "We have heard that half a million children have died. I mean, that's more children than died in Hiroshima. Is the price worth it?" Albright's reply: "I think this is a very hard choice, but the price—we think the price is worth it." In March 1997, Albright—now U.S. secretary of state—emphasised the impossibility of ending sanctions. "We do not agree with the nations who argue that if Iraq complies with its obligations concerning weapons of mass destruction, sanctions should be lifted. Our view, which is unshakable, is that Iraq must prove its peaceful intentions . . . And the evidence is overwhelming that Saddam Hussein's intentions will never be peaceful."

In October 1996, Philippe Heffinck, the representative in Iraq for the United Nations Children's Fund (UNICEF), estimated that "around 4,500 children under the age of five are dying here every month from hunger and disease." A year later, a joint study between the UN and the World Food Programme concluded that sanctions "significantly constrained Iraq's ability to earn foreign currency needed to import sufficient quantities of food to meet needs." On 26 November 1997, UNICEF was reporting that "32 per cent of children under the age of five, some 960,000 children, [are] chronically malnourished—a rise of 72 per cent since 1991. Almost one quarter . . . are underweight—twice as high as the levels found in neighbouring Jordan or Turkey."

And all this while, the reasons for sanctions—or the conditions upon which they might be lifted—changed and extended. Saddam must allow the United Nations Special Commission on Monitoring (UNSCOM) arms inspectors to do their work freely, must end human rights abuses, free Kuwaiti POWs, end the torture of his own people, recognise Kuwaiti sovereignty, pay wartime reparations and withdraw missile batteries from the (non-UN) "no-fly" zones. Individually, there was nothing immoral about any of these demands. Collectively, they were intended to ensure that the sanctions regime continued indefinitely. By January 1998, the Pope was talking of the "pitiless embargo" visited upon Iraqis, adding that "the weak and innocent cannot pay for mistakes for which they are not responsible." U.S. officials began to warn that sanctions would stay "for ever" unless Saddam complied with American demands.

American spokesmen and spokeswomen repeatedly pointed out that Saddam Hussein was escaping the effect of sanctions. Albright appeared before the United Nations with satellite photographs of vast building complexes in Iraq, pictures, she said, of further palace-building by Saddam Hussein. She was correct in what she said, but wrong in her conclusions. For if Saddam had managed to avoid the effects of the UN sanctions on his regime, then those sanctions had clearly failed in their objective. In 1998, British foreign secretary Robin Cook became obsessed with the Iraqi regime's purchase of liposuction equipment which, if true, was merely further proof of the failure of sanctions. He repeatedly stated that Iraq could sell $10 billion of oil a year to pay for food, medicine and other humanitarian goods—but since more than 30 per cent of these oil revenues were diverted to the UN compensation fund and UN expenses in Iraq, his statement was wrong.

And Saddam Hussein yet again found a common cause with the Americans. Just as the latter needed to prove that Saddam had permitted the further suffering of his people while building temples to his greatness, so Saddam needed to show the world—especially the Arabs—how cruel were the Americans and their allies in decimating the innocent people of Iraq. It was a calculation that found a constant response in one of his own Arab enemies, Osama bin Laden, who regularly expressed his sympathy—he did so in an interview with me—for the Iraqis suffering under the U.S.-inspired sanctions.

Those of us who visited the grey and dying world of Iraq during these ghastly years were sometimes almost as angered by the Iraqi government's manipulation as we were by the suffering we witnessed. Each morning, Ministry of Information "minders" would encourage foreign journalists to witness the "spontaneous" demonstrations by Iraqi civilians against the sanctions. Men and women would parade through the streets carrying coffins, allegedly containing the bodies of children who had just died of disease and malnutrition. Only when we asked to see inside the wooden boxes were we told that the protest was symbolic, that the coffins only represented the dead. Yet the dead were real enough. The rivers of sewage that now moved inexorably through even the most residential of Baghdad suburbs were evidence of the breakdown of the most basic social services. From the countryside came credible reports that Iraqis were eating weeds to stay alive.

So why did the Americans and the British and their other friends at the United Nations impose this hateful sanctions regime on Iraq? Many of the Western humanitarian workers and UN officials in Baghdad had come to their own conclusions. Margaret Hassan, a British woman married to an Iraqi, a brave, tough, honourable lady who ran CARE's office in the Iraqi capital, was outraged by the tragedy with which she was striving to cope. "They want us to rebel against Saddam," she said. "They think that we will be so broken, so shattered by this suffering that we will do anything—even give our own lives—to get rid of Saddam. The uprising against the Baath party failed in 1991 so now they are using cruder methods. But they are wrong. These people have been reduced to penury. They live in shit. And when you have no money and no food, you don't worry about democracy or who your leaders are."

Margaret Hassan was right. "Big picture," an air force planner told the *Washington Post* in 1991. "We wanted to let people know, 'Get rid of this guy and we'll be more than happy to assist in rebuilding. We're not going to tolerate Saddam Hussein or his regime. Fix that and we'll fix your electricity.'" Just before the 1991 liberation of Kuwait, a U.S. Defense Intelligence Agency document described the probable results of the destruction of power stations and continued economic sanctions. "With no domestic sources of both water treatment replacement parts and some essential chemicals, Iraq will continue attempts to circumvent United Nations sanctions to import these vital commodities. Failing to secure supplies will result in a shortage of pure drinking water for much of the population." In other words, the United States and Britain and other members of the Security Council were well aware that the principal result of the bombing campaign—and of sanctions—would be the physical degradation and sickening and deaths of Iraqi civilians. Biological warfare might prove to be a better description. The ultimate nature of the 1991 Gulf War for Iraqi civilians now became clear. Bomb now: die later.

Not long before Christmas 1997, Dennis Halliday, the bearded and balding Irishman who was heading the UN's Oil-for-Food programme in Iraq, received personal and deeply distressing evidence of what this meant. He had a paid a visit to four small Iraqi children suffering from leukaemia in the Saddam Hussein Medical Centre. "The doctors told me they couldn't get the drugs to treat them and I got involved with them," Halliday told me in his cramped Baghdad office, the walls hung with cheap Arab rugs. "With a World Health Organisation colleague, I managed to get the drugs they required—some from Jordan, one from northern Iraq, which means it was probably smuggled in from Turkey. Then I dropped in on Christmas Eve to see the children in their ward. Two were already dead."

Halliday was already palpably torn by his task of distributing food and medicine to 23 million Iraqis, all of whom were being punished and some of whom were dying in appalling hospital conditions because of Saddam's crimes. At the same time as he was seeking drugs for the children, Halliday—who was clearly close to resigning—wrote an impassioned letter to UN secretary general Kofi Annan, complaining that what the UN was doing in Iraq was causing untold suffering to innocent people. "I wrote that what we were doing was undermining the moral credibility of the UN," he said. "I found myself in a moral dilemma. It seemed to me that what we were doing was in contradiction to the human rights provision in the UN's own charter." Halliday, a Quaker who worked in Kenya and Iran before joining the UN's bureaucracy in New York, was looking for some alternative to sanctions—vainly, because the United States and Britain had no intention of ending Iraq's misery.

His desk was piled with statistics the UN didn't want to know; that Iraq's electrical power stations were producing less than 40 per cent of capacity, that water and sanitation systems were on the point of breakdown. Doctors were forced to reuse rubber gloves during operations, their wards were without air-conditioning or clean water. Without electrical pumps, water pressure was falling in the pipes and sewage was being sucked into the vacuum. "The government here used to encourage the use of infant formula—and infant formula with contaminated water is a real killer." But Halliday was worried by other, long-term effects of this suffering. "There are men and women now in their twenties and thirties and forties who have known little more than the Iran–Iraq War, the Gulf War and the sanctions. They see themselves as surrounded by unfriendly people, and a very unsympathetic America and Britain. They are out of touch with technology and communications. They have no access to Western television. And these are the people who are going to have to run this country in the future. They are feeling alienated and very Iraqi-introverted. Their next-door neighbours are going to have a tough time dealing with these people."

Halliday's colleague in the Baghdad UNICEF office was no more optimistic. Outside, feral children prowled through street-corner garbage. Inside, Philippe Heffinck's files showed that chronic malnutrition for children under five stood at 31 per cent. "That accounts, in the whole of Iraq, for 1.1 million children, including the Kurdish areas. This is a serious problem—particularly serious when you have chronic malnutrition up to two years old, because that is the period when the brain is formed. You become stunted. There is a lack of physical and mental growth that will afflict the child—his schooling, his job opportunities, his chances of founding a family and quite possibly his or her offspring as well."

Patrick Cockburn, reporting from Baghdad for *The Independent* in April 1998, described the way in which the Tigris River had changed colour to "a rich *café au lait* brown" because raw sewage from 3.5 million people in Baghdad and other towns upstream was pouring into the river. Contamination of drinking water, he wrote, was the main reason why the proportion of Iraqi children who died before they reached twelve months had risen from 3.5 per cent in the year before sanctions to 12 per cent nine years later. Lack of spare parts for electrical equipment, absence of staff and the subsequent reduced power supply had cut off clean water in many areas.*

Western humanitarian workers sometimes felt their own contribution was near-useless. Judy Morgan, who worked for CARE in Baghdad, described how she felt like a poor relative of King Canute. "The water is lapping round our feet before

---

*The evidence of massive human suffering was now overwhelming. A UN humanitarian panel on sanctions reported in 1999 that "the gravity of the humanitarian situation of the Iraqi people is indisputable and cannot be overstated. Irrespective of alleged attempts by the Iraq authorities to exaggerate the significance of certain facts for political propaganda purposes, the data from different sources as well as qualitative assessments of bona fide observers and sheer common sense analysis of economic variables converge and corroborate this evaluation." UNICEF reported in August 1999 that "if the substantial reduction in child mortality throughout Iraq during the 1980s had continued through the 1990s, *there would have been half a million fewer deaths* of children under five in the country as a whole during the eight-year period 1991 to 1998" (emphasis in original).

we've even had the chance to order the tide to turn back," she told me one afternoon in 1998. Her colleague Margaret Hassan had a thick file of examples to prove that she was telling the truth. "If this was a Third-World country, we could bring in some water pumps at a cost of a few hundred pounds and they could save thousands of lives," she said. "But Iraq was not a Third-World country before the [1991] war—and you can't run a developed society on aid. What is wrong with the water system here is a result of breakdown and damage to complex and very expensive water purification plants. And this eats up hundreds of thousands of pounds in repairs—for just one region of the country. The doctors here are excellent—many were trained in Europe as well as Iraq—but because of sanctions, they haven't had access to a medical journal for eight years. And in the sciences, what does that mean?"

A mere glance at the list of the items prohibited by the UN sanctions committee revealed the infantile but vindictive nature of the campaign now being waged against Iraq. Included in the list were pencils, pencil-sharpeners, shoe laces, material for shrouds, sanitary towels, shampoo, water purification chemicals, medical swabs, gauze, medical syringes, medical journals, cobalt sources for X-ray machines, disposable surgical gloves, medication for epilepsy, surgical instruments, dialysis equipment, drugs for angina, granite shipments, textile plant equipment, toothpaste, toothbrushes and toilet paper, tennis balls, children's clothes, nail polish and lipstick.*

The campaigning journalist John Pilger, one of the few reporters who had the courage to condemn the sanctions at the time as wicked and immoral, recorded how, just before Christmas 1999, the British Department of Trade and Industry—a government department which tried to defend the sale of two mustard gas components to Iraq prior to Saddam's invasion of Kuwait on the grounds that one of them could be used to make ink for ballpoint pens—blocked a shipment of vaccines meant to protect Iraqi children against diphtheria and yellow fever. "Dr. Kim Howells told parliament why. His title of under secretary of state for competition and consumer affairs, eminently suited his Orwellian reply. The children's vaccines were banned, he said, 'because they are capable of being used in weapons of mass destruction.' That his finger was on the trigger of a proven weapon of mass destruction—sanctions—seemed not to occur to him."

By 2000, up to 70 per cent of Iraqi civilian industrial enterprises were closed or operating at a much reduced level. Unemployment had reached at least 60 per cent. Halliday and his successor Hans von Sponeck, the top UN humanitarian officers in Iraq, had both resigned their posts in Baghdad—Halliday in September 1998, and von Sponeck on 14 February 2000—and were now speaking out in the press, on television and at public meetings, von Sponeck pointing out that 167 Iraqi children were dying every day. "In all my years at the UN," he said, "I had never been

---

*For example, the Iraqi National Spinal Cord Injuries Centre—set up with the help of a Danish team during the Iran–Iraq War to look after seriously wounded soldiers—lacked medicine and supplies throughout the period of sanctions. Staff were forced to re-sterilise gauze and catheters and were not permitted to receive new medical textbooks and journals.

exposed to the kind of political manoeuvring and pressure that I saw at work in this programme. We're treating Iraq as if it were made up of 23 million Saddam Husseins, which is rubbish."

Halliday was far more outspoken. "The World Health Organisation confirmed to me only ten days ago," he said in October 1998, "that the monthly rate of sanctions-related child mortality for children under five years of age is from five to six thousand per month. They believe this is an underestimate, since in rural parts of Iraq children are not registered at birth, and if they die within six weeks of birth, they are never registered . . . I recently met with trade union leaders [in Iraq] who asked me why the United Nations does not simply bomb the Iraqi people, and do it efficiently, rather than extending sanctions which kill Iraqis incrementally over a long period . . . Sanctions are undermining the cultural and educational recovery of Iraq, and will not change its system of governance. Sanctions encourage isolation, alienation and fanaticism . . . Sanctions constitute a serious breach of the United Nations charter on human rights and children's rights." In 2000, Halliday wrote that "here we are in the middle of the millennium year and we are responsible for genocide in Iraq. Today the prime minister, Tony Blair, is on the defensive on a range of largely domestic issues. His unending endorsement of the Clinton/Albright programme for killing the children of Iraq is seldom mentioned. What does that say about us all?"

The British Foreign Office—and especially Peter Hain, who was now minister of state with responsibility for the Middle East—tried to trash the UN officials who had resigned. "We know that some have raised concerns about the resignations of Hans von Sponeck and, before him, Dennis Halliday, as UN Humanitarian Coordinator in Iraq," a sleekly worded letter from the Foreign Office's Middle East Department told a medical doctor who was an *Independent* reader.

> Managing a unique and complex programme worth billions of pounds is a job for an experienced and dedicated administrator committed to making the most of the "oil for food" programme for the Iraqi people. Unfortunately neither Halliday nor von Sponeck was the right man for it. It was clear from very early on that they disagreed with the decisions of the Security Council and the purposes of the UN resolutions. It was not therefore in their interests to make "oil for food" work.

This was ridiculous. Halliday, a compassionate and decent man, and the earnest von Sponeck were both experienced humanitarian workers. To claim that two UN coordinators, one after another, were both "wrong men" for the job was beyond credibility.

The same letter claimed that a new Security Council Resolution, 1284, would make the "oil for food" programme more effective because it removed the ceiling on Iraqi oil exports, failing to add that Iraq's broken oil facilities and a sudden lowering of the price of oil—which was not the UN's fault—largely neutered the effects of the initiative. What Iraq needed was not the sudden relaxation of restrictions on personal items but serious reinvestment in industry, infrastructure and commercial life—something that UN sanctions did not permit. Toothpaste and toilet rolls were no use if Iraqis could no longer afford them.

And every few months, as the UN inspectors sent to disarm the Baathist regime of chemical, biological and nuclear weapons—often faced with the obtuseness and threats of Iraq's security police—sought to discover the extent of Saddam's armoury, the Americans would announce another "threat" by the Iraqi dictator to invade Kuwait, to ignore the U.S.-imposed "no-fly" zones in southern and northern Iraq—supposedly set up to "protect" the Shiites and Kurds—or to retrieve ground-to-ground missiles that had been left behind in the UN-administered zone along the Iraqi–Kuwaiti border. Repeatedly, in the early nineties, I would race to Beirut airport for yet another flight to Kuwait, just in case Saddam was about to repeat his messianic blunder of 1990—even though network news shows were filming Iraqi soldiers milling around rusting troop trains, some of them barefoot, many of them clearly emaciated, their uniforms torn and discoloured.

Almost two years after they celebrated victory in the 1991 Gulf War, the conflict's three principal Western allies—the United States, Britain and France—launched a series of air strikes against Iraq's supposed violation of the southern no-fly zone and its seizure of Silkworm anti-ship missiles from the United Nations. On 12 January 1993, six British Tornado bombers and a squadron of French Mirage jets based in Saudi Arabia joined a much larger force of American planes from the carrier *Kitty Hawk* in attacking targets inside Iraq, most of them missile sites and radar bases. For more than a week, the United States had protested at Iraq's positioning of SAM anti-aircraft missile batteries inside the "no-fly" zones.

Yet if the Americans needed a regular crisis in the Gulf, Saddam also wanted to provoke tension. Saddam's spokesman had claimed once more that very day that Kuwait was "an integral part of Iraq that will be restored." The United Nations had escorted a troop of journalists up to the new Iraq–Kuwaiti frontier—the one that the UN revised in favour of Kuwait but that Iraq did not accept—and happily displayed the wooden boxes (stamped "Ministry of Defence, Jordan") from which the Iraqis had indeed seized their old Silkworm missiles the previous weekend, weapons that were taken before the eyes of the UN guards.

That same morning, the Iraqis had made their third foray across the new frontier—the one they didn't recognise—saying they had an agreement with the UN to remove their equipment from warehouses up to 15 January. But they had not asked permission from the UN or the Kuwaiti government to do so. Why not? And why, for that matter, had we not hitherto been told that the Iraqi forays into the Um Qasr naval base began *eight months* previously? In May 1991, it emerged, Iraq took eleven Silkworm missiles from the base and then another four less than a month later. It subsequently gave the four back—at the request of the UN Iraq–Kuwait Observer Mission—but kept the other eleven. The weekend's foray allowed them to "recapture" those four missiles yet again.

Saddam was acting, it seemed, according to an American script. It wasn't the first time that this odd continuity operated between Washington and Baghdad. Just as both sides found it expedient to ignore the mass Iraqi casualties of the 1991 war, so now Saddam was playing his appointed role as aggressor. "Saddam is mad, but you know why he's done this?" an old Kuwaiti friend—one of the lucky ones to escape captivity inside Iraq in the last days of the war—asked me. He was laughing, a trifle contemptuously, I thought. "Saddam doesn't care about Bush. He wants the *Arabs* to care. The UN fails in Bosnia . . . More important, the UN fails to get Israel to take back the Palestinian detainees in Lebanon [deported illegally by the Israelis as 'terrorists']. But the UN lets America use the big stick on Iraq. Saddam wants the Arabs to think about that difference. He thinks that way the Arabs will turn to him."

Saddam was doing this in an increasingly self-delusional way. His half-hour television broadcast to Iraqis on 17 January 1993 was a masterpiece of Arab nationalist bombast. He cursed the Arab "traitors" who had opposed him and the Iraqis who had rebelled against his rule two years earlier. The UN he branded a mere satrapy of the United States—this, at least, was an allegation of some merit—and insisted that the "Mother of all Battles" had not ended, nor had the struggle for "victorious Iraq." Nor for a "liberated Palestine." And Kuwait and Iraq were part of "one nation." It was a Gulf War anniversary speech aimed at "the children of Arabism everywhere."

In some ways, the unsmiling Saddam was the same dictator whom the West had learned to loathe during the occupation of Kuwait. His olive-green uniform, with the inevitable brigadier-general's crossed-swords insignia on its shoulders, was crudely offset by a bowl of red-and-white flowers. Iraq was glorious, its people steadfast, acting only on behalf of the "Arab nation." America and its partners were "criminals," bent only on the division of a powerful Arab nation prepared to stand alone and on the acquisition of Kuwait as a "rented oil well." But he then embarked on a striking personal attack on the ruling Sabah family of Kuwait, talking to the Kuwaiti population in an eerie combination of threat, entreaty and apology.

He urged Kuwaitis to "learn the lessons," to "absorb the circumstances" and "understand" the period of Iraqi occupation. Iraqis who had committed any acts against Kuwaitis had been punished, he announced. "Those Kuwaitis who remained in their country will remember that one of the [Iraqi] officers remained hanging for everyone to see because of the bad things he did to Kuwaitis. This is the real face of Baghdad. These are the principles of Baghdad . . . if there were any bad acts they took place through traitors, directed by the enemies of Iraq."

There was no mention of the torture chambers, the rape of foreign women, the doorstep execution of resistance men and women (in front of their families, of course); merely a reference to the unfortunate necessity that faced Iraqi armoured forces to "return fire" when they were attacked. Kuwaitis should therefore feel "brotherhood and love in God and in the nation which holds them in its heart in Baghdad." Kuwaitis did not remember history quite so romantically, though few would forget the hanging Iraqi colonel—truly "the real face of Baghdad"—who was indeed suspended from a crane in a central square, allegedly, so it was said at the time, for helping the Kuwaiti resistance.

But the culprit for all this suffering, according to Saddam, was the Kuwaiti emir. He had invested $60 billion in Western banks while Arabs endured "poverty and starvation."* He had failed to heed Baghdad's warnings not to seek Iran–Iraq War debt repayments and to end oil overproduction, warnings made by Saddam at the Arab summit on 27 May 1990, repeated on 17 July and again in an Iraqi foreign ministry memorandum to the Arab League that same day. Saad Abdullah al-Sabah, the Kuwaiti negotiator at the Jeddah summit with the Iraqis—the meeting whose breakdown led immediately to Iraq's invasion—had received, so Saddam's tale went, secret orders from the emir not to settle the dispute. The people of Kuwait should learn their lesson and take control of their country from a family which allowed foreigners to run Kuwait but who fled from the Iraqi army "like leaseholders, without saying goodbye."

As for the "infidels" whose forces still stood "on sacred Muslim land," they had changed their objectives, from the defence of Saudi Arabia to the destruction of "the Iraqi regime." Why else had the "no-fly" zones been instituted? These zones, along with the refusal to allow Iraqi planes to fly, were "an act of war despite the ceasefire." The West was anxious to destroy the nation which "from Zakho [in Kurdistan] to Fao [in the far south of Iraq] remains a bastion of freedom." With just a hint of emotion, he predicted that "the infidels will ultimately know who is victorious . . . if the aggressors continue, they will fail. God help you!" Here, without any doubt, was the old Saddam.

And within hours of their January 1993 air strikes against Iraq, the Americans decided to make an issue of further Iraqi "provocations" along the Iraq–Kuwait border, demanding that Baghdad close down six of its police posts in the UN-controlled demilitarised zone by midnight on 14 January—or face the consequences. The U.S. threat came on the eve of the arrival in Kuwait for "operational reasons" of 1,250 American soldiers from the U.S. 1st Armored Cavalry Division. The six Iraqi positions—all containing armed Iraqi border policemen—had actually been in existence for almost a year, during which the frontier had been withdrawn—although Washington had made no issue about their presence then.

In all of this, journalists played a special role: to run the American story. And sure enough, the U.S. military reinforcements sent into Kuwait were attended by the usual camera crews and hair-perfect reporters and agency men who wanted those equally perfect shots of the men who were going to defend Kuwaiti freedom. So it was that Captain Lackey drew his line on the tarmac of an Iraqi airbase. "If you come over this line, I'm going to remove you from the airfield," he bawled at the reporters. "I'm going to tell the security people to move you out of here if you don't obey this instruction. Is there anybody who doesn't understand what I've

---

*There was to be a macabre return to this personal abuse against the Kuwaiti royal family at Saddam's own macabre and American-arranged first trial hearing in Baghdad in 2004 when he accused the "animals" in the Kuwaiti government of trying to impoverish Iraqi women to become "whores."

told you?" The camera crews dutifully assembled like schoolchildren, toes and tripods on the white-painted strip. The U.S. 1st Cavalry Division was about to arrive.

Maybe it was the American army's revenge for the media debacle on the beaches of Mogadishu—the collapse of the UN mission to Somalia was still to come—but Captain Lackey knew what he wanted. While long lenses whirred at the miniature figures climbing down the steps of the 747, we craned over the necks of the photographers to catch sight of this latest symbol of America's "resolve" in the Gulf as the soldiers, many of them carrying "comfort bags," straggled across the apron to a line of old American school buses parked 300 metres from the jumbo.

Instead of talking to the soldiers who were about to perform—if President Bush's words about his bomber pilots applied to them—"God's work," we were instead encouraged to talk to the civilian crew of the chartered Northwest Airlines 747. So journalists surrounded the prettiest crimson-uniformed stewardess as the plane's captain—in a splendidly staged advertisement for his airline—regaled us with the soldiers' in-flight meal services. The men and women drawing yet another line in the sand had spent their sixteen hours in the air munching their way through barbecued chicken, rice and eggs. No questions here—no thought for what the Iraqis were eating 100 kilometres to the north of us. Just the usual network men performing their usual duties, breathlessly and urgently. I pulled out my notebook to capture some of their gems. "Just sixty miles from the Iraqi border . . ." ". . . six weeks, but they could be here much longer." ". . . and for the Kuwaitis, this is another reassuring sign . . ." ". . . a deterrent against retaliation Saddam Hussein might try across the Kuwaiti border."

The quotations were real, but was the mission? Were these young men and women with their pre-positioned company of Bradley Fighting Vehicles, of M1A1 tanks and their artillery battery anything more than a symbol? Not really. In the end, President Bush fired off another set of cruise missiles towards Baghdad—and within minutes of their arrival, the Iraqi policemen began dismantling their posts in Um Qasr, one of them being shot dead by a Kuwaiti policeman. "It was just an ordinary night," Captain Mike Maugham of the 1st Cavalry's Alpha company described it to me later. "We stayed up half the night watching the football game—we got the whole match with the Bills. But the first sergeant would come in from time to time switching the channel and during breaks in the game, we'd go over to CNN in Baghdad."

Breaks in the game. Captain Maugham confessed that watching the anti-aircraft fire over Baghdad on CNN was "a sobering experience," but there were plenty of well-worn clichés to be had along the line of Bradleys next morning. Saddam was "going to get his ass kicked" and it was "time to finish the job." CNN had uncomfortably proved that an explosion in the lobby of the Rashid Hotel which killed a female receptionist was caused by an American missile—Brent Sadler popped up with a hunk of cruise missile, complete with computer codings—and this produced the usual scepticism. "Nobody likes to see civilian casualties"—this from Second Lieutenant Bernard Ethridge—"but that's kind of a function [*sic*] of war. It just happens. But if a cruise missile hit that hotel, I don't think the hotel would have so little damage. Our soldiers talked about this; they thought that maybe a dud anti-aircraft round came back on the Iraqis." As usual. When Palestinians died under Israeli bombing in Beirut in 1982, they were killed by their own gunfire. When the Americans bombed Libya, the civilian casualties were killed by stray Libyan anti-aircraft missiles. When the Americans blasted civilians to bits in the streets of Baghdad in 2003, the Iraqis were killed, once more, by their own anti-aircraft rockets—or by pieces of old shrapnel cunningly planted in the ruins by Saddam's secret policemen. It was never us. Or if it was, we didn't mean it.

Thus when President Clinton loosed off another twenty-three Tomahawk cruise missiles against Baghdad on 27 June 1993 in retaliation for Iraq's alleged involvement in the attempted murder of George Bush in Kuwait more than two months earlier—the case against the accused Iraqis, still to be heard, would be riddled with inconsistencies and the court hearing deeply flawed—little interest was shown by journalists when eight civilians were found to be among the victims. One of them was Leila Attar, a distinguished Iraqi painter who had exhibited her work in Kuwait, Cairo and New York. It would be almost five years before I heard the full story of her tragedy.

For in 1998, in an art gallery behind the Meridien Hotel in Baghdad, there worked an old man, Abu Khaled—"a guest in this life with perhaps three or four more years to live"—who told me of that hot June night when he said farewell to Attar, who was the joint director of the gallery. "She left at nine p.m. and it was only in the morning that the man who made tea here said: 'Abu Khaled, Madame Attar is in the hospital.' But she was not. I found her daughter and her son in the hospital. But they said she was still under her house." When Abu Khaled reached the artist's home in the Mansour district of Baghdad, he found Leila Attar's husband dead under the rubble. "No one could find her," he said. "But then I saw her long hair between the bricks of the house and I knew she was there. We found her with her handbag still gripped in her hand. She was trying to get away when the missile struck."

There was neither apology nor remorse in Washington. It was Saddam who was being attacked, his regime and his murderous apparatus of secret policemen. And when I visited the rubble of Leila Attar's home in Baghdad in 1998, sure enough, there was, just behind her house, a large *mukhabarat* security service compound of high brick walls and barbed wire. The cruise missile had not quite cleared her house on the way to its target. So again, it wasn't our fault. Collateral damage. We didn't mean it. President Clinton told Americans they could "feel good" about the attack.

And all this was apparently provoked by an Iraqi plot to kill ex-President Bush. In October of 1994—well over a year after the Clinton air raids—I went along to the Kuwait appeal "trial" of the thirteen men convicted of planning to kill Bush. The accused, grey-uniformed and grey-faced, many of them bearded and several apparently praying, listened without emotion as Judge Abdullah al-Issa started his judicial review. But given the chance to talk, at least one of the condemned men had plenty to say. And for a man who had been convicted by President Clinton—who had launched his retaliatory air raids before the initial court hearings had been concluded—and sentenced to the gallows by the state of Kuwait, Wasli al-Ghazali looked understandably angry as he fingered the brown-painted bars of the cage in Court No. 15. "Every Arab child is worth all of America," he shouted at us. "I am an Iraqi citizen. Bush killed sixteen members of my family. I have lost all of my feelings." Al-Ghazali and the twelve other men, one of them a Kuwaiti, were all allegedly involved in the plot.

According to the Kuwaiti authorities, Iraqi intelligence ordered the defendants to kill Mr. Bush in a plot that was uncovered by the Kuwaiti security services just a day before the former president arrived in the country. One of the defendants was said to have been found in possession of a car loaded with 180 pounds of explosives, while al-Ghazali was accused of planning to assassinate Bush with a belt-bomb strapped to his waist. However, he later retracted his confession, while others in the original trial claimed they had been beaten into making false confessions or had crossed the border on a smuggling expedition.

And although the earlier court had sentenced all of the men—six to death, the rest to prison terms—there was a host of reasons why Kuwaiti and foreign lawyers should have doubted the fairness of this particular trial. There had been plea retraction, other evidence of beatings by the security police, a scandalous lack of pre-trial access to the defendants by local lawyers and, most extraordinary of all, of course, a missile attack on Baghdad—based on the defendants' guilt but staged before their conviction. It was little wonder that Najib al-Wougayan, the small and persistent lawyer for the only Kuwaiti condemned to death, Badr al-Shaamari, claimed that the Clinton attack prejudiced the fairness of his client's trial.

"Clinton's missile attack on Baghdad placed the hearing in a political context," he said. "Before the trial finished, Clinton said that he had evidence that Iraq was behind the bomb attack on Bush. How could he do this before the trial had been concluded? There are defendants who have admitted their guilt and I do not quarrel with this—they made confessions. But Badr did not. He is innocent and the Americans condemned him." In fact, the White House had said that it had "certain proof" of Iraqi guilt in the plot, a claim that Amnesty International would later condemn as undermining the defendants' presumption of innocence. Eight years later, George Bush's son, during a speech intended to garner support for his invasion of Iraq, would recall how Saddam "tried to kill my dad."

The explanation that the men were involved in routine smuggling rather than political assassination was given further credibility when Salim al-Shaamari, the brother of the accused Kuwaiti, began giggling during a court appearance after being asked by the judge why his face appeared familiar. He replied that he had been imprisoned on fifteen previous occasions for smuggling whisky into Kuwait. Further doubt was cast on the court's fairness when a public prosecutor referred to the accused as "this rotten group of defendants."

For all this, Leila Attar died.

CHAPTER EIGHTEEN

# The Plague

> There is such a thing as legitimate warfare: war has its laws; there are
> things which may fairly be done, and things which may not be done. He
> has attempted (as I may call it) *to poison the wells.*
>
> —John Henry, Cardinal Newman, *Apologia pro Vita Sua,* 1864

IN OCTOBER 1994, we had another "Crisis in the Gulf," as CNN liked to bill each
would-be re-invasion of Kuwait. This time, according to the Pentagon, Saddam
had "massed" 60,000 troops in southern Iraq, along with 900 tanks and even more
armoured vehicles. None of the journalists sent off to report this latest drama
apparently remembered how confidently they had described the routing of the
Iraqi army in 1991, how Saddam's soldiers had been in "disarray," his Republican
Guards "decimated" by U.S. bombing, his logistics "annihilated." But after being
assured by the world's leaders that Saddam had been totally defeated, his "decimated" Republican Guard divisions were now supposedly returning to haunt the
battlefields again. And those television pundits and reporters for the satellite channels were bombarding Middle East capitals with visa requests and booking themselves on to any aircraft that could reach the Gulf faster than President Clinton's
carrier group. "Were they manipulating us or falling into the trap of believing their
own reports?" I asked in my paper.

A Kuwaiti journalist probably got it right when he pointed out that Saddam
was trying to force the UN to lift sanctions—as well as redeploy his own Iraqi
army after a rumoured coup attempt in Baghdad—while Clinton wanted to distract
attention from his indolence in Bosnia before congressional elections. But our pre-
programmed response seemed to be unstoppable.* As usual, no one bothered to
assess the civilian casualties that would follow yet another strike on Iraq.

And sure enough, journalists who were transported up to Kuwait's border with
Iraq found it hard to meet the demands of their editors. Many of us could discover
only a solitary Kuwaiti tank in the desert, a vehicle that was subsequently used to

---

*Even on *The Independent on Sunday*, where a nervous night sub-editor—seeing yet another
"crisis" story on the agency wires on the night of 9 October—"pulled" my own sceptical report
from the paper after the first edition for fear that war would have started by breakfast-time. It was
the only occasion on which this happened to a report of mine in the paper, whose editors agreed
next day that there wasn't much point in asking a journalist to reflect his doubts about exaggerated reporting if those same exaggerations were to cause us to suppress the story.

tow our own press bus out of the sand. On the other side of the border, there were equally slim pickings. United Nations officers disclosed that their reconnaissance aircraft, whose flight path gave them a view over 20 kilometres north of the frontier, had not observed a single Iraqi tank or personnel carrier. The few Iraqi policemen beyond the border—now abiding by the line of the new border—could hardly be called aggressive; several of them, it transpired, regularly begged for food from the UN, pleading for clothes to replace their ragged uniforms. "We're not supposed to give them anything," a UN officer admitted. "But it's hard to turn someone away when they're hungry."

Yet by 12 October there were reported to be 39,783 U.S. troops back in the Gulf, along with 659 aircraft and 28 ships. The RAF was flying a Hercules C-130 into Kuwait every two hours through the night, some of them carrying 155-mm artillery, and the first elements of 45 Royal Marine Commando had just walked off a Tristar. We had seen it all before: the sultry night, the C-130s' propellers still racing on the tarmac, the accents of Sheffield and Oxford and Liverpool under the Gulf skies. Instead of "Operation Granby"—the 1990 British deployment to the Gulf—we now had Operation Driver, but the soldiers all carried the same little nuclear–chemical–biological warfare kits.

And when the U.S. 15th Marine Expeditionary Unit arrived to start live-fire training exercises, which location did they choose? The Mutla Ridge, of course. Many of the marines knew very well that this was the top of the "highway of death" where Iraq's fleeing convoys had been roasted out of existence just over three and a half years earlier. The men of the 15th MEU, 130 of them, weighed down with heavy machine guns and anti-armour weapons, set up their tripods and blasted thousands of rounds of ammunition into the dunes just below the hill where the anonymous mass graves still lay beneath the sand. "A lot of our marines were here at the time and some of the men here know what happened," Lieutenant Colonel Rick Barry said, enthusiastically adding that marine units helped to trap the retreating Iraqi convoys in 1991. In the new, ever more contagious language of marine-speak, Colonel Barry's men talked of their amphibious helicopter-borne landings as an "evolution"—note the positive, progressive nature of that word—as a "sustainment exercise," an "adventure" and, of course, a "photo-opportunity."

The television camera crews scrummed around the marines, cursing and pushing each other—though taking care to avoid any frames that showed that the marine "evolution" was a journalistic circus. And so the machine-gun cartridges skipped across the concrete revetments below Mutla Ridge as the marines charged through smoke grenades across the sand, whooping and shrieking at Saddam's imaginary legions. Captain Stephen Sullivan, eyes turning into cracks against the piercing midday sun, tried to put it into a historical perspective which turned into a weird combination of morality and more marine-speak.

"Since this country was basically raped and plundered just a couple [*sic*] of years ago," he said, "and there's a massive troop build-up on the border, that is a distinctive threat to this country and all the nations that represented the [allied] coalition. We are a forward deployed presence that's routine. We think this yields stability with power projection to show our presence . . ." But did he not ask himself why his marine unit's "power projection" didn't get focused on Bosnia, where rape was now on a somewhat larger scale than it had been in Kuwait? Captain Sullivan didn't hesitate for a moment. Bosnia came under the U.S. Mediterranean Command and the 15th Marine Expeditionary Unit was not tasked to cover the Mediterranean area. And that was that.

There were times, reporting all this, when one wondered if insanity was not an advantage in reporting the Middle East. A day after the marines deployed at Mutla Ridge, U.S. defence secretary William Perry, a chunky, short figure in a pale brown uniform, marched across the tarmac at Kuwait airport to threaten Saddam with war if he did not withdraw his soldiers from southern Iraq. Then, just half an hour later, Russian foreign minister Andrei Kozyrev, tall and dapper in a pale blue suit and tie, walked into the airport's VIP lounge and threatened peace. Whom were we to believe? Mr. Perry, who bellowed that further American troop reinforcements would be sent to the Gulf, or Mr. Kozyrev, who said he'd just been told by Saddam that he would at last recognise the new frontiers of Kuwait? "I have brought good news to the people of Kuwait and to the whole Middle East," Kozyrev whispered into the microphone. "Good news that this day the independence of Kuwait is reinforced."

Perhaps it was as well that the Cold War was over. Back in the days of Jimmy Carter, the U.S. defence secretary would have been urging peace while Leonid Brezhnev's men would have been warning of war if America bombed Iraq. To add to this transformation came the assertion from Senator John H. Warner, the former chief of the U.S. Navy who was standing next to Perry. "The lessons learned from the Gulf War," he said, "really made it possible for this swift deterrence to be put in place." The real lesson of the Gulf War for more conservative Americans, of course, was that if Saddam Hussein's regime had been toppled at the time, it wouldn't be necessary to send all this "deterrence" back to the Middle East now.

The growing regularity of attacks on Iraq did more than dull the senses of journalists; it gave a continuity to their story, so when the United States and Britain, the sole surviving allies of the 1991 war—the French had wisely pulled out of the "no-fly" zone bombardments—attacked Iraqi "military positions" over the next decade, their actions became routine, part of a pattern, a habit which, as the years went by, ceased to be a "news story" at all. The southern "no-fly" zone was supposed to protect the Shiites from Saddam, even though the Shiite insurgents of 1991 were long in their mass graves or still hiding in their refugee camps over the border in Iran. In the north, the "no-fly" zone was supposed to protect the Kurds from similar aggression; but the "safe haven" created by the allies of 1991 at least still existed there, even if it was not enough to save the Kurds of Irbil when Saddam sent his tanks into the city to break up a CIA-run operation in 1996.

Nor did it save the Kurds from the Turks, as John Pilger was to reveal. In March 2001, RAF pilots flying out of the Turkish airbase at Batman complained that, far from protecting the Kurds, they were frequently ordered to return to their airfields to allow the Turkish air force to bomb the very people they were supposed to be protecting. British pilots returning to patrol the skies over northern Iraq—having been ordered to turn off their radar so they could not identify the Turkish targets—would see the devastation in Kurdish villages after the Turkish raids. U.S. pilots, also ordered back to base, would pass American-made "Turkish F-14s and F-16s inbound, loaded to the gills with munitions," one pilot was to recall. "Then they'd come out half an hour later with their munitions expended." On returning to their mission, the Americans would see "burning villages, lots of smoke and fire." In 1995 and 1997, up to 50,000 Turkish troops with tanks, fighter-bombers and helicopter gunships attacked alleged Kurdistan Workers' Party bases in the "safe haven."

Despite much obfuscation by the Americans and the British—to the effect that the "no-fly" zones were part of, or supported by, UN Security Council Resolution 688—they had no UN legitimacy, nor were the zones ever discussed or approved by the United Nations. But they were to become the excuse for a continuing air war against Iraq, undeclared and largely unreported by the journalists who were so keen to focus on Saddam's own provocations, especially when they involved his refusal to help—or his deliberate misleading of—the UNSCOM arms inspectors. The UN team had entered Iraq immediately after the 1991 ceasefire and was engaged in seeking out and destroying the chemical, biological and potentially nuclear weapons that Saddam had long sought and in some cases acquired. This was the same Saddam who had used gas against the Kurds of Halabja and hundreds of other villages—his equally ruthless gassing of the Iranian army was recalled less emotionally, if at all, in the West—and he had to be "defanged." Within three years, the inspectors had achieved considerable success.

Their operation, which was eventually to be compromised by the Americans themselves, has been catalogued in detail many times; but it is fascinating to compare these efforts with later attempts by the U.S. and British administrations to send UN inspectors back into Iraq in 2002—and then to persuade the world that Saddam was continuing to produce and hide weapons of mass destruction. By the end of April 1992, the al-Atheer nuclear weapons establishment in Iraq had been destroyed and the explosives-testing bunker filled with concrete, a process in which a thousand Iraqi workers were forced to help. In 1994, Rolf Ekeus, the head of UNSCOM, reported that most of the information demanded of the Iraqis had been given and that weapons-monitoring systems were being set up. While Iraq was still trying to avoid handing material to the UN inspectors, U-2 reconnaissance aircraft—borrowed from the United States—had flown 201 missions over Iraq and UN helicopters had flown 273 missions to 395 suspected sites.

Iraq claimed all the while that the inspectors were working not for the UN but for the CIA; UNSCOM, according to Saddam, was "an advertising agency" for Washington. He could hardly be blamed for this contention. The CIA had asked Congress for $12 million for covert operations in Iraq and the Iraqi authorities feared that the UN's information would be used not just for further inspections but for missile-targeting next time the U.S. president wanted to fire cruise missiles at Baghdad. In May 1995, Ekeus expressed concern about 17 tons of missing material that could be used to manufacture biological weapons, but in August 1995, Lieutenant General Hussein Kamel Hassan and Lieutenant Colonel Saddam Kamel Hassan, two sons-in-law of Saddam Hussein, defected to Jordan, where they told UN inspectors—though this was not divulged until 2003—that all weapons of mass-destruction programmes in Iraq had been abandoned.

Yet the Americans never accepted the UN's assurances. While Saddam's *mukhabarat* did frequently try to impede the work of the inspectors—UN inspector Scott Ritter's Hollywood appearances at the most sensitive of Saddam's security headquarters were proof enough of that—the U.S. government was constantly raising "evidence" from Iraqi defectors that nuclear production continued, that the Iraqis were burying biological bombs in the desert, that Saddam's refusal to comply with all requests for information on chemical materials was proof of his dishonesty. Iraqi claims that many archives on such weapons had been destroyed in the 1991 uprising were dismissed—not always without reason—as obfuscation. But as the UN hunt for Iraq's libraries of scientific research continued, Saddam came to the conclusion that the UN was now spying—on behalf of Iraq's enemies—into the country's military future as well as its past.

Ritter's experiences as a U.S. Marine Corps officer who had dismissed Schwarzkopf's claims about Scud missile destruction while serving in Riyadh during the 1991 war were important. Even after promising that it had no interest in germ warfare in its first submission to the UN, Iraq had 90 gallons of a microorganism that causes gas gangrene, more than 2,000 gallons of anthrax, 5,125 gallons of botulinum toxin (which paralyses and strangles its victims) and 2.7 gallons of the toxin ricin. Iraq reluctantly admitted that it had produced VX nerve gas and up to 150 tons of sarin gas.

Ritter's own dramatic, successful and sometimes farcical confrontations with Saddam's security men provide a chilling portrait of the regime, as well as a remarkable insight into the mind of an American weapons inspector.* "The Iraqis, they're like sharks," he once famously remarked. "Fear is like blood. They smell it and they'll come in at you. Once that game of intimidation starts, you're never going to win . . . I am the alpha dog. I'm going in tail held high. If they growl at me, I'm gonna jump on 'em . . . When we go to a site, they're gonna know we're there, we're gonna raise our tails and we're gonna spray urine all over their walls . . ." Yet after six years, Ekeus had forced Saddam's regime to destroy 40,000 chemical shells and other munitions, 700 tons of chemical agents, 48 long-range missiles, an anthrax factory, a nuclear centrifuge programme and 30 missile warheads. Journalists were invited to photograph a vast fleet of Scud missiles as they lay, broken-backed, on the desert floor.

But like so many long-term operations of its kind, UNSCOM became contam-

*The two best independent accounts of Ritter's work and of the CIA's infiltration of UNSCOM were published by *The New Yorker*: Peter J. Boyer's "Scott Ritter's Private War," on 9 November 1998, from which the above quotation is taken, and Seymour M. Hersh's "Saddam's Best Friend: How the CIA made it a lot easier for the Iraqi leader to rearm," on 5 April 1999.

inated. Ritter, who in 2002 would bravely and consistently—and correctly—claim that Iraq no longer possessed any weapons of mass destruction, had taken his information to the Israelis, proof positive for the Arabs that the UN was sharing its military secrets with Iraq's only enemy in the Middle East. Ritter went so far as to tell the Israeli newspaper *Ha'aretz* that Israel had been helping the UN inspectors in Iraq from 1994 to 1998. "I can honestly say that if it weren't for Israel, the commission wouldn't have been able to carry out the anti-concealment effort," he said. On 5 August 1998, Baghdad had suspended all cooperation with UNSCOM, claiming that it was being used by American intelligence agents. It said it would continue to cooperate with UN officials in Baghdad—but not with its U.S. members.

The UN, without revealing the truth of Iraq's claims, decided on 13 November to withdraw its entire seventy-eight-strong team from Baghdad. Saddam, the Western media announced, had "defied" the UN Security Council—which was true only if the Iraqi allegations were false. President Clinton did not wait to explain. "Operation Desert Fox"—the nickname of Hitler's General Erwin Rommel, though that apparently didn't occur to U.S. military planners—involved another bombardment of 200 cruise missiles against Iraq, killing 62 Iraqi soldiers and 82 civilians. U.S. jets carried out 622 sorties against 100 targets, dropping around 540 bombs. The British flew 28 Tornado sorties against 11 targets. The Iraqis were not the only ones to note that many of the bombed facilities—including two buildings where Saddam was believed to meet his mistresses—had recently been visited by the American inspectors of UNSCOM. In early January, UNICEF and the World Food Programme reported that the attack also flattened an agricultural school, damaged at least another dozen schools and hospitals and knocked out water supplies for 300,000 people in Baghdad.

It was the endgame, the final bankruptcy of Western policy towards Iraq, the very last throw of the dice. As the missiles were launched, President Clinton announced that Saddam had "disarmed the inspectors," which was a lie, and Tony Blair, agonising about the lives of the "British forces" involved—all eighteen pilots—told us that "we act because we must." In so infantile a manner did we go to war, although the semantics of its presentation bore some intriguing clues about our future military aggression in the region. There were no policies, no perspective and not the slightest hint as to what might happen after the bombardment ended. With no UN inspectors back in Iraq, what were we going to do? Declare eternal war on Iraq? In fact, that's pretty much what we had already done—and would do for the next three years—though we didn't say so at the time.

We were "punishing" Saddam—or so Blair would have us believe at the time. Was there a computer that churned out this stuff? Maybe there was a cliché department at Downing Street that also provided British foreign secretary Robin Cook with Madeleine Albright's tired phrase about how Saddam used gas "even against his own people." For little had we cared when he used that gas against the Kurds of Halabja—because, at the time, those Kurds were allied to Iran and we, the West, were supporting Saddam's invasion of Iran.

The giveaway was the lack of any sane, long-term policy towards Iraq. Our patience, according to Messrs. Clinton and Blair, was exhausted. Saddam could not be trusted to keep his word—they had just realised! And so Saddam's ability to "threaten his neighbours"—neighbours who didn't actually want us to bomb Iraq—had to be "degraded." We were now, presumably, bombing the weapons facilities that the inspectors could not find. But how? For if the inspectors couldn't find the weapons, how come we knew where to fire the cruise missiles?

There seemed to be no end to the fantasies in which we had to believe. Again, they appear, in retrospect, to be a dry-run for the phantom threat that Saddam represented in advance of the 2003 Anglo–American invasion. Saddam, we were told, could destroy the whole world, or—I enjoyed this particular conceit—could do so "twice over." U.S. defence secretary William Cohen announced that there would be "serious consequences" for Iraq if it attacked Israel. Mr. Cohen, who was the American—not the Israeli—defence minister, did not explain what "consequences" there could be when we had already fired 200 missiles into Iraq. Then on 16 December 1998—and this was almost three years before the assaults on the United States—the Americans claimed that Osama bin Laden had been chatting on the phone to Saddam Hussein. In truth, bin Laden—who always referred to Saddam with contempt in his conversations with me—was as likely to call up the Beast of Baghdad as he was President Clinton. Clinton said he wanted "democracy" in Iraq. But no questions were asked, no lies contradicted.

Vice President Al Gore told Americans that this was a time for "national resolve and unity." You might have thought the Japanese had bombed Pearl Harbor or that General MacArthur had just abandoned Bataan. When President Clinton faced the worst of the Monica Lewinsky scandal, he bombed Afghanistan and Sudan. Faced with impeachment, he was now bombing Iraq. How far could a coincidence go? No wonder some of the UN inspectors called this "the War of Monica's Skirt." So two Christian armies—America's and Britain's—went to war with a Muslim nation, Iraq. With no goals but with an army of platitudes, they had abandoned the UN's weapons control system and opened the door to an unlimited military offensive against Iraq. And nobody asked the obvious question: What happens next?

In Washington, we were informed that the impeachment hearings against Clinton—for it was he, rather than Saddam, who was in danger of being "degraded"—were delayed because "American forces were in harm's way." In reality, the men firing missiles at Iraq from the safety of warships in the Gulf were about as much "in harm's way" as a CNN newsreader. The only people in danger were the Iraqis. Yet when the RAF joined in the bombardment, we were treated to an excited newsreader on the BBC World Service announcing that British aircraft had been "in action" over Iraq—as if this was the Battle of Britain rather than the bombing of an Arab country already crushed by near-genocidal sanctions.

When I called up a Saudi journalist friend and told him that Downing Street was claiming the attack on Iraq was intended to protect the Arab Gulf, he shouted one word down the phone to me: *Zbeili! Zbeili* is Arabic for "garbage." "Why do you want to kill more of those poor people?" he asked. The British were trying to present this bombing offensive on Iraq in all its old 1991 Gulf War purity. Iraq's neighbours were under threat and must be safeguarded from its weapons of mass destruction. But with the exception of Kuwait—some of whose citizens had repeated their now familiar routine of fleeing over the Saudi border—the Arab Gulf states wanted none of the West's protection, especially when this "protection" involved even further destruction of Iraq's infrastructure.

For the Basra oil refinery was one of the Anglo–American targets. Clinton and Blair had promised that only military targets would be hit, but the refinery had allegedly been used to smuggle oil and thus became a "military target." Maybe we would soon be told that oil refineries were weapons of mass destruction. What they most certainly were, of course, was a means of producing oil income to pay for the Oil-for-Food programme that was supposed to lessen the effect of UN sanctions. But it was not this blatant manipulation of words that angered the Arabs. What infuriated them—and non-Arab Muslims—was the hopelessly one-sided and hypocritical way in which we tried to justify the attack on Iraq.

Just going through the 1998 list of excuses for belligerency was enough. According to Clinton and Blair, Saddam Hussein (1) was refusing to abide by countless United Nations Security Council resolutions; (2) continued to build weapons of mass destruction; (3) blocked the work of UNSCOM arms inspectors; (4) abused human rights; (5) had used poison gas "on his own people." Now we all knew that Saddam Hussein was awful; not as bad as Hitler and Stalin but probably worse than Laurent Kabila and certainly worse than Muammar Ghadafi and quite possibly worse than Slobodan Milošević.

But who else qualified in 1998 for the first crime? Israel and Serbia. Who qualified for the second? Iran, Israel, Syria, Pakistan, India and North Korea. Crime number 3 was exclusive because there was no UNSCOM to inspect other countries' weapons of mass destruction. But qualifying for crime number 4? Algeria, Egypt, Iran, Israel, Libya, Palestine, Syria, Saudi Arabia, Turkey . . . Crime number 5? Only Iraq—with a caveat: for still no Western leader would admit that Saddam killed far more Iranians than he did Iraqi Kurds at a time when the State Department and the British Foreign Office were supporting Iraq.

So what were we doing bombing Iraq? Back in February 1998, we wanted to bomb Iraq when Saddam prevented UN arms inspectors from entering his palaces. UN Secretary General Kofi Annan produced a "memorandum of understanding" to allow the UN to make a one-time inspection, in the company of foreign diplomats, of these supposed symbols of Iraqi sovereignty. But once Saddam objected to the American UN inspectors, it was "chocks away": he now almost certainly wished to be bombed—because he had given up any hope of sanctions being lifted and knew that the Arab world would sympathise with Iraq. Journalists became frightened of the figure of half a million children dead under sanctions; it was safer to debate the rights and wrongs of killing eighty-two civilians in the December air raids. Arabs did not see events in so distorted a way. However deplorable their regimes, they were possessed of an overwhelming sense of fury and humiliation;

the conviction that the raids on Baghdad were all staged to avoid Clinton's impeachment seemed to place events beyond the immoral.

Then—and only then, in the New Year, in the first week of January 1999, less than three weeks after the attacks were staged on Iraq because Saddam had "blocked" the UNSCOM teams—came the revelation. American arms inspectors *were* spies. CIA men had been planted among the UN teams—along with MI6 agents from Britain, if a report in *The Independent* was correct—and the UN was forced to admit that "UNSCOM directly facilitated the creation of an intelligence collection system for the United States in violation of its mandate." U.S. agents had installed a "black box" eavesdropping system into UNSCOM's Baghdad headquarters that intercepted Saddam Hussein's presidential communications network. Operation Shake the Tree was supposed to uncover the regime's weapons concealment system, but UN officials quickly realised that the SIGINT operation run by the CIA's Near East Division—which was led by Ritter's nemesis Steve Richter—was not sharing its intelligence information with UNSCOM. The UN arms mission to Iraq had become a U.S. spying operation against the regime. Few bothered to recall that Saddam's reasons for expelling the U.S. inspectors—the official cause of the December bombardment—had now been proved true. But UNSCOM was finished.

The military assault on Iraq was not. For with little publicity—and amid virtual indifference in Western capitals—U.S. and British aircraft staged well over seventy air strikes against Iraq in just five weeks during January and February 1999, inflicting more damage than the pre-Christmas Anglo–American bombardment. Pilots flying out of Saudi Arabia and Kuwait were now given new rules of engagement that allowed them to open fire on Iraqi installations even if their aircraft were not directly threatened. The air offensive was carefully calibrated to avoid criticism or public debate, although it coincided with further attempts by Washington to overthrow Saddam Hussein's regime.

At my home in Beirut that great rain-washed winter, I spent hours searching through back copies of the Arab and British press for details of these raids. I visited Tewfiq Mishlawi, a veteran Palestinian-Lebanese journalist whose daily *Middle East Reporter* was meticulous in recording each Western air attack on Iraq—and its political consequences in the Arab world—and found that his own archives were filled with small, often apparently inconsequential quotations from Western military spokesmen. Yet, sitting in his cold drab offices near the centre of Beirut, I placed these paragraphs of copy next to one another and found myself reading a coherent and all too disturbing account of a near-secret war. One-inch news items—*nibs,* as we call them in the trade—would turn into longer stories as I photocopied them and pinned them, one after the other, into my file. The file began to thicken. Every hour, I would have to open a new folder for the next stack of cuttings.

Iraqi missile sites were being attacked without warning and radar stations targeted solely because their presence—rather than any offensive activity—was said to menace American forces in the Gulf. In early February, for example, U.S. aircraft bombed a CSSC-3 "Seersucker" anti-ship missile battery on the Fao peninsula which, according to a spokesman, "could [*sic*] have threatened shipping in the Gulf." Military sources said that there was no evidence the missiles were about to be fired, although American and British government officials continued to maintain for more than a year afterwards that pilots responded only to specific threats against their aircraft. In an article in *The Independent* on 7 August 2000, for instance, Foreign Office minister Peter Hain—the same Peter Hain who had condemned Halliday and von Sponeck for their outspoken criticism of UN sanctions—wrote that "there have been about 850 direct threats against our aircrew in the past year and a half, including missile attacks and heavy anti-aircraft fire. Our pilots have taken action *only to defend themselves against this kind of attack*" (my emphasis).

This was obviously untrue. But by attacking Iraq every day while issuing only routine information about the targets, American and British officials had also ensured that their salami bombardment attracted little or no interest in the press; newspapers now frequently carried little more than four lines about air-strikes that would have captured front-page headlines a year earlier. Only when U.S. missiles hit civilian areas was the mildest criticism heard. Often, these attacks turned out to be even more bloody than the Iraqis admitted at the time. When an American AGM-130 missile exploded in a Basra housing complex, initial reports spoke of eleven civilian casualties, although a total of sixteen died on that day and almost a hundred were wounded. Von Sponeck, who was still the UN humanitarian coordinator in Baghdad at the time, stated that two missiles hit civilian areas 30 kilometres apart, the first in Basra—where a woman and five children were among the dead—and the second in the village of Abu Khassib, where five women and five children were killed. In other words, most of the victims were children; a Pentagon spokesman later admitted the Basra attack, responding to the casualties with the words: "I want to repeat that we are not targeting civilians."

The 1999 air offensive had begun at the New Year with five American attacks in two weeks and was followed on 11 January when U.S. aircraft attacked Iraqi missile sites from air bases in Turkey. Almost daily air raids continued to the end of January, by which time British fighter-bombers were joining U.S. planes in the attacks. On 31 January, eight British and American jets were bombing "communications facilities" in southern Iraq. A statement from the Americans on 4 February that U.S. and British planes had by then destroyed forty missile batteries—adding that this alone caused greater damage than was caused to Iraq in the whole December air bombardment—passed without comment. Neither Washington nor London explained whether the attacks had UN backing—they did not—and a warning by Britain's socialist elder statesman, Tony Benn, went unheeded.

On 11 February, General Sir Michael Rose, Britain's former UN force commander in Bosnia, condemned the offensive in a speech at the Royal United Services Institute. "The continual TV images of the West's high-technology systems causing death and destruction to people in the Third World will not be tolerated for ever by civilised people," he said. But his remarks were largely ignored. Instead, U.S. officials continued their fruitless attempts to form a united Iraqi opposition to Saddam and to seek Arab support for their plans. By declaring the Western "no-fly" zones invalid—which they were in international law—Saddam could encourage his air defences to fire at U.S. and British aircraft. He even offered a reward of $14,000 for ground-to-air missile crews who shot down raiding aircraft. It went unclaimed; Iraq's air defence batteries were hopelessly inferior to American and British technology.

Yet still this near-secret war went on. In Baghdad, six more civilian deaths were announced—one in an air raid near Najaf on 10 February 1999, and five more, with twenty-two wounded, in southern Iraq five days later. After *The Independent* published the details of this war-by-disinterest, I continued my trawl through the daily Arab press. On 22 February, for example, it was reported that U.S. and British jets had attacked an Iraqi missile site and two communications bases near Amara and Tallil. On 1 March, American jets dropped more than thirty 2,000-pound and 500-pound laser-guided bombs on radio relay sites, "communications targets and air defence guns" in northern Iraq. Defence Secretary Cohen said the same day that U.S. pilots had been given "greater flexibility" in their attacks. When an air raid disrupted Iraqi oil exports to Turkey, the executive director of the UN's Oil-for-Food programme, Benon Sevan, complained that there was already a $900 million shortfall between expected revenues and what was needed to fund the humanitarian programme under sanctions, and that continued raids could frustrate efforts to supply food and medicines to Iraqi civilians. Like Benn and Rose, he was ignored.

But Arab press reports on the U.S. and British attacks proved that Rose's warnings were accurate. Even Qatar, a long-standing ally of Washington, opposed the campaign. "We do not wish to see Iraq bombed daily or these attacks which are being made on the no-fly zones," Qatar's foreign minister, Sheikh Hamad bin Jassim al-Thani, told Cohen on 9 March. Esmat Abdul-Meguid, the Arab League secretary general, demanded an end to the air raids. The Kosovo war—in which both the Americans and the British could take on the role of protector of Muslims—further helped to smother the Iraq war. On 2 April, the Iraqis stated that aircraft had destroyed a control centre at the oil-pumping station at Mina al-Bakr.

There was no end to this. On 6 April, the Pentagon announced a joint Anglo-American attack on a surface-to-air missile battery near Faysaliyah. Three civilians were reported killed in raids in Iraqi Kurdistan on 8 May, another twelve killed in Mosul five days later. And so it went on. By August 1999, even *The New York Times* had noticed that an Iraqi shooting war was continuing behind the backs of the American public, reporting on 13 August that American and British pilots had fired more than 1,100 missiles against 359 targets in the previous eight months, flying about two-thirds as many missions as NATO pilots conducted over Yugoslavia during the seventy-eight-day bombardment that spring. And the response to all this from the State Department? Spokesman James Rubin said that "ultimately responsibility for these events . . . lies with Saddam Hussein."

Throughout the year, the Americans and British continued to nibble away at Iraq's infrastructure and what was left of its defences, a war of attrition whose regularity had reduced the almost daily raids to a non-story. But not in the Arab world. Newspapers throughout the Gulf damned the assault with equal regularity;

Saudi officials privately noted that the air bombardment was causing increasing fury among the young and more religious citizens of the kingdom. General Rose had warned that this violence would not be "tolerated for ever." Yet how would the Arabs respond? What weapons did they have in their arsenal to redress the imbalance of power between East and West, save for the planes and tanks we sold their dictators to increase our own wealth?

THERE WAS ONE FINAL SCOURGE to be visited upon the Iraqi people, however, a foul cocktail in which both our gunfire and our sanctions played an intimate, horrific role, one that would contaminate Iraqis for years to come, perhaps for generations. In historical terms, it may one day be identified as our most callous crime against the Middle East, against Arabs, against children. It manifested itself in abscesses, in massive tumours, in gangrene, internal bleeding and child mastectomies and shrunken heads and deformities and thousands of tiny graves.

I first heard that Iraqis might be suffering from a strange new cancer "epidemic" while visiting the Syrian capital of Damascus in the summer of 1997. An Iraqi opposition leader, a Shiite cleric who made his way to Iran after the failed Shiite uprising of 1991 and had then travelled to Syria, told me that Iraqi ex-soldiers seeking refuge in camps in southern Iran were being diagnosed with an unusual number of cancers; most had fought in the 1991 tank battles south-west of Basra, their armour struck repeatedly by American depleted-uranium shells. The cleric spoke, too, of Iraqi children in the Iranian camps who had also fallen ill. If this was true—and these children would also have come from southern Iraq—then what was the state of health of children in Basra today? What were these mysterious cancers?

When I arrived in Baghdad in early 1998, I was confronted almost at once by unexpected cases of cancer. An Iraqi family I had known for years had lost three of its members to leukaemia in two years. The family had a history of smoking. But the middle-aged lady who greeted me at the door was, unusually for her, wearing a scarf over her head. She had just been diagnosed with cancer—and she had never smoked. Then there was the government official whose two children had just been sent to hospital with an unknown lung complaint—which subsequently turned out to be cancer. Another Iraqi acquaintance told me of a neighbour's baby that developed a "shining" in one of her eyes. Doctors had taken the eye out so that the cancer should not spread.

It took several days before I grasped what this meant: that something terrible might have happened towards the end of the 1991 Gulf War. Some Iraqis blamed the oil fires which had burned during and after the war, releasing curtains of smoke that hung over the country for weeks, producing a carcinogenic smog over Baghdad and other large cities. Others suspected that Saddam's bomb-blasted chemical weapons factories might be to blame. But increasingly, we found that those most at risk came from areas where allied aircraft—and in the far south, tanks—had used large quantities of depleted-uranium munitions. DU shells are made from the waste product of the nuclear industry, a hard alloy that is tougher than tungsten and that ignites into an aerosol uranium "spray" after punching through the armour of tanks and personnel carriers. As I expected, the Americans and the British maintained that these munitions could not be the cause of cancer.

This was not an easy story to investigate. Unlike bomb fragments with their tell-tale computerised codes, DU munitions—while easy to identify because they left a penetrator "head" in or near their target—could not be physically linked to the leukaemias afflicting so many thousands of Iraqis, other than by a careful analysis of the location of these cancer "explosions" and interviews with dozens of patients. Some of the children I spoke to, for example, were not even born in 1991; but invariably, I would find that their fathers or mothers had been close to allied air or tank attacks. There was another difficulty in reporting this story which I and my colleagues, Lara Marlowe, now of the *Irish Times*, and Alex Thomson of Britain's Channel 4 television—who worked with me on my first investigation—encountered the moment we visited Iraq's dilapidated and often dirty hospitals.

Cancer wards are shocking, child cancer wards more so, places that should not—if life and youth have meaning—exist on this earth. But child cancer wards for those who die from the diseases of war are an abomination. For what slowly became evident was that an unknown chemical plague was spreading across southern Mesopotamia, a nightmare trail of leukaemia and stomach cancer that was claiming the lives of thousands of Iraqi children as well as adults living near the war zones of the 1991 Gulf conflict.

They smiled as they were dying, these children. Ali Hillal was eight when I met him in the Mansour hospital in Baghdad. He lived next to a television station and several factories at Diyala, repeatedly bombed by allied aircraft. He was the fifth child of a family that had no history of cancers. Now he had a tumour in his brain. Dr. Ali Ismael recalled how malnourished the little boy was when he first arrived at the hospital. "First he had the mumps, then he had swelling in his chest and abdomen," he said. "Now the tumour has reached his brain. When the condition reaches this point, the prognosis is very poor." Ali Hillal's mother, Fatima, recalled the bombings. "There was a strange smell, a burning, choking smell, something like insecticide," she told me. "Yesterday, he had a very severe headache," Dr. Ismael said, smiling at the child. "He was screaming. When I gave him an injection between his vertebrae, he told me he knew the pain of the needle, but that he would be very quiet because he knows I want what is best for him."

Latif Abdul Sattar was playing with a small electric car when I first caught sight of him. His smile, beneath the dome of his baldness, suggested life. But he would die.*

---

*Diagnosed with non-Hodgkin's lymphoma three months earlier, he had received two cycles of cytotoxins. "But the third cycle is partial because he's getting only cyclophosphamide adriamycin as a substitute for vincristine," Dr. Ismael said. What Latif needed is produced by a company in Germany called Astra Medica. "We received twenty vials of this ten days ago. Before that, the patients' families were buying it for 160,000 dinars—more than two years' salary for many Iraqis. But still we can't get enough. Latif needs the treatment as long as his malignancy continues."

I walked with Dr. Ismael on his morning rounds. Youssef Abdul Raouf Mohamed from Kerbala—close to military bases bombed in 1991—has gastrointestinal bleeding. He still has his curly hair and can talk to his parents but has small blood spots on his cheeks, a sure sign of internal bleeding. And Dr. Ismael is bothered by a memory. "Since the UN embargo, patients often die before they can even receive induction treatment," he says, looking at the floor because he knows his story is going to be a terrible one. "They get thrombocytopenia, a severe reduction of blood platelets. They start bleeding everywhere. We had another child like Youssef. He was called Ahmed Fleah. And after we started the cytotoxin treatment, he started bleeding freely from everywhere—from his mouth, eyes, ears, nose, rectum. He bled to death in two weeks."

Dr. Ismael, who is resident doctor in the cancer ward, sat down in his office, staring in front of him. "When Faisal Abbas died two days ago, I came here, closed the door, sat down and cried," he said. "I gave drugs to him from my own hands. He was like a brother to me. He was only ten years old. He was diagnosed with leukaemia three years ago and we treated him with drugs—he received treatment, but it was only partial because we lack so many drugs."

Dr. Ismael blamed the sanctions, of course, for blocking the medicines; and he blamed the 1991 war for turning his paediatric cancer ward into a way-station for dying children, for the infants who—given their first medicines—bleed to death in front of the doctors. "In three years, I have seen hundreds of children with leukaemia and last year there was a dramatic increase," Dr. Ismael said. "This month we diagnosed twenty new cases, mostly from the south—from Basra, Nasiriyah, Kerbala and Najaf. It's mainly caused by radiation." The doctors here had an odd way of expressing themselves, in a kind of scientific-emotional grammar. "We have palliative treatment but not curative treatment," one of them said.

When I walk into the child cancer ward across the hall, I understand what this means. Little Samar Khdair lies in what the doctors quite casually call the "ward of death." She is only five years old but looks much younger, lying shrivelled on her bed, her eyes squeezed shut with pain, her large, unwieldy father—massive in his grey *galabiya* robe amid such frailty and pain—gently placing a damp yellow compress on her face. She comes from al-Yussfiya on the road to Babylon, the target of regular allied raids in February 1991.

Samar's father, Jaber, looks poor because he is. He spent 15,000 dinars to buy cytotoxins for his dying daughter—more than three months' wages for Jaber. "I sold my car to buy the medicine for her," he tells me quietly. And how would he pay for the next dose? we ask. "I will borrow the money." Dr. Ismael listens in silence, then he says to me in English: "I've seen these patients' families so many times. They sell everything in their house, even their beds—and then their child dies anyway."

You could not move through Baghdad's "ward of death" without two emotions—a deep sense of unease, even shame, that "our" 1991 military victory over the cruel Saddam might well have created this purgatory of the innocent by poisoning both the air they breathe and the land they try to grow up in; and a profound admiration for the dignity of the poor Iraqis who sometimes sell their own clothes in a vain effort to save the children who die in their arms. And no one could remain unaffected by the bravery of the victims.

Dr. Selma al-Haddad is the kind of doctor whom you would select for your own terminal illness. My notes, scribbled in near-incredulity into my pocketbook that year, fill dozens of pages. In the Saddam Hussein Medical Centre in Baghdad—it is necessary to adopt a semantic amnesia with the names of so many institutions in Iraq—Dr. al-Haddad cuddles the children who she knows will soon die. She jokes with thirteen-year-old Karrar Abdul-Emir, who is frightened of his own leukaemia but too frightened to take the drugs which may save him. She introduces me to each child by name without ever looking at the chart at the bottom of the beds to check their identity. "Now here is Cherou Jassem and she has put on a party dress for you to take her picture," Dr. al-Haddad laughs.

And the beautiful girl in the sun bonnet—her name means "budding rose" and she has acute myloblastic leukaemia—smiles with delight. Amna Ahmed sits, bald, radiant, a kind of tranquillity about her baby face, framed in my camera lens by the electric fan that cools her fever. The machine, fighting the heat of the Baghdad afternoon, becomes a kind of halo round her head, an angel from Babylon who is dying of an abdominal mass. "Yes, of course I'm depressed and frustrated," Dr. al-Haddad says. "I can't save many of these children—but what can I do? I have a sense of responsibility towards these poor children. Most times, I feel helpless." She asks if I will send the copies of my photographs of the children to Baghdad as soon as I can. In a month or two, Amna may well be dead. Cherou too. Dr. al-Haddad wants them to see my photographs before they die.

What was one to make of the words of mothers and fathers standing by the beds of their dying children? Seven-year-old Youssef Mohamed, a handsome little boy in a blue-and-white pyjama top—unrelated to the child from Kerbala—has acute leukaemia and his mother, Hassiba, thinks she knows why. "There was a military base near our home in Baghdad," she says. "It was bombed heavily by the Americans, also the local telephone exchange. We felt ill with the choking smoke at the time. I already had a healthy child, born before the war. But when I became pregnant after the war, I had a miscarriage. Then I had Youssef, who has leukaemia, then another miscarriage. Why should this have happened to me? My brother-in-law, Abdul-Kadem Mooushed, died of leukaemia two years after the war. He had been a soldier; he was only thirty-six. How could my family—which never had a history of cancer—suddenly suffer like this?"

Ashwark Hamid is thirteen, with acute leukaemia, a quiet, gentle-faced girl in a yellow patterned scarf. She needs a bone marrow transplant—for which there is no hope in Iraq. Her grandmother Jasmiya sits on her bed. "We are from Diyala in eastern Iraq," she says. "The bombing was very near to us—the airport and the agricultural factory was heavily bombed. We smelled strange fumes, like the smell of gas." What, one wondered, was the "agricultural" factory making? Pesticides or gas? Or what were the American or British bombs made of?

Oulah Falah is four, born four years after the Gulf conflict, and has a kidney tumour; her father was a soldier in the 1991 war—there are many rumours in Baghdad that Iraqi veterans are dying in large numbers from cancer—and her mother, Fatin, still shakes her head at her daughter's fate. "Still I am surprised why my child got cancer," she says. A few feet away, Dhamia Qassem is in critical condition after suffering heart failure during recent treatment for acute leukaemia. She is thirteen. Mysteriously, her aunt died of cancer only forty days ago. The aunt was just thirty-six years old. Ahmed Walid's case is much more disturbing.

He was diagnosed as having chronic myeloid leukaemia just three years ago and was only a baby during the bombing of his home town in Diyala. But his mother tells a frightening story. "We all smelled the strange fumes after the bombing and then the children round about started bringing in pieces of rockets and shells as souvenirs. They were very bright—a light, bright silver colour—and they played with them in our house. A neighbour of ours was killed when a rocket hit his farm and the children brought big iron pieces of the rocket into our home."

One evening, after spending ten hours in the children's "ward of death" in Baghdad, I visit the Iraqi government's press centre where the Western agency journalists are filing their latest reports on the negotiations between Kofi Annan and Saddam. I walk through the shabby hall to the AP office, a rectangular booth with hardboard walls, and tell a long-standing American colleague and friend what I have been discovering. He listens patiently, recalls the Iraqi "empty coffin propaganda" and gives me his slightly irritated response. "Robert," he says. "I am *not* writing Iraqi *baby* stories!" But what I am hearing is unending, consistent and undoubtedly true, since the often uneducated parents do not know I am going to visit their children, let alone ask about the 1991 war. Again and again, I hear the same thing.

Tareq Abdullah is thirteen, again with acute leukaemia. He himself tells me how neighbours "brought bright pieces of bombs into our home. They were very heavy, like iron." Tareq was diagnosed just a year ago. Karrar Abdul-Emir, the boy even more frightened of the drugs that may save him than he is of his own leukaemia, comes from Kerbala in southern Iraq. His mother, Ihlass, remembers the bombs falling close to their home. "Some scattered pieces fell nearby. I tried to find them and they were very sharp, like razor blades. I didn't allow the children to touch them in case they cut themselves. There was a very harsh smell; it made our eyes swell." Rasha Abbas from Basra has leukaemia, fifteen years old with a fever and a declining blood count, with mouth lesions, unable to talk, her father a fatality in the earlier Iran–Iraq War. "In 1991," her mother, Hasna, tells me—slowly, wondering what happened to her family—"our house was bombed. It burned and the explosion ruptured Rasha's ears. Pieces of rocket came right into our house. All the children were running to touch these pieces . . ."

Of course, children were not the only victims, in Baghdad or in the south of Iraq. In the corner of the cancer ward at the Basra teaching hospital, the wreckage of Matar Abbas's emaciated body seems to mock the broad, blue Shatt al-Arab outside the window. He has already lost an eye and is hawking mucus into a handkerchief, his scarf slipping from his head to reveal the baldness of chemotherapy treatment, part of his face horribly deformed by the cancer that is now eating into his brain. He comes from Nasiriyah, the city whose outskirts were shelled and bombed by the allied forces in the last days of the 1991 war.

His wife, Ghaniyeh, is a peasant woman with tattoos on her face, and stayed throughout the war with Matar—a sixty-year-old former taxi-driver with nine children—on the road between Amara and Misan. "We saw the flashes of the bombs but nothing was bombed near us," she recalls for me, speaking carefully, as if her memory might somehow save her doomed husband. "We were safe." But Dr. Jawad Khadim al-Ali, a member of the Royal College of Physicians, begs to disagree. "We rarely saw these types of tumours before the war," he says, gently touching Matar's right ear. Dr. al-Ali smiles a lot, although—from time to time— you notice tears in his eyes and realise that he might also be a spiritually broken man. He looks a little like Peter Sellers, physically small with thinning hair and a drooping moustache. But there is nothing funny about his commentary.

"Because of the tumour in his ear, Matar Abbas is now unable to talk or take food and is deaf," he said. "He came for his first treatment only on January sixteenth, with a swelling and an inability to talk or drink. The biopsy showed cancer. I am giving him cytotoxic chemotherapy—but later on, the cancer will go to his brain and lungs. He will probably live one year, not more." The doctor leads me across the room to where Zubeida Mohamed Ali lies, chadored, on her bed. She comes from Zubayr—close to the Iraqi air base that was saturated with allied bombs in a series of raids that started on the night of 13 February 1991. "She has tumours of the lymph nodes and they have infiltrated her chest," Dr. al-Ali says. "She is suffering shortness of breath." Zubeida is seventy.

Opposite lies fifty-five-year-old Jawad Hassan, diagnosed with cancer of the stomach two years ago. He lived very close to the Basra television station that was the target of allied bombing. "He was exposed to fumes and bombs at his home," Dr. al-Ali continues. "He was also close to the river bridges that were bombed. He is losing weight despite our treatment, which makes his prognosis very bad." The man, prematurely aged, looks at me with a blank expression. "Ever since I was exposed to the fumes of the bombings," he says, "I complained about pains in my abdomen."

The implications of what these cancer victims were saying were so terrible that I almost wished my visit had been the result of a feeble attempt by the authorities to set up a visiting journalist with an easy-to-expose lie, a crude attempt by Saddam's regime to raise a grave moral question over the entire 1991 war. But again, Dr. al-Ali had no idea I was visiting him until the moment I walked into his Basra office. His patients did not expect visitors. And if some of them were—like so many cancer victims elsewhere in the world—elderly, what was to be made of the flock of men and women, young and old, who were waiting outside his oncology department when I arrived? "It's a tragedy for me," Dr. al-Ali said, pointing to a tall, handsome youth standing amid a group of women. "I'm losing friends every day—this boy has Hodgkin's lymphoma. This girl is suffering lung cancer." She was small, petite, with a big, smiling, moon-like face. Another, Fawzia Abdul-

Nabi al Bader, was a fifty-one-year-old English teacher who walked into the department office and pulled her collar down to show a suture on her neck and then opened her blouse to show the scar where her right breast should have been. "Why should this have happened to me?" she asked. "My first operation was in 1993. Until then, my health was very good."

In his office, Dr. al-Ali's maps tell their own story: "Number of cancer patients of all kinds in the Basra area," it says over a map of the Basra governorate, sliced up into yellow, red and green segments. The yellow, mainly to the west of the city, represents the rural and desert areas that were battlefields in 1991. A green area to the north indicates an average incidence of cancer. But a large blood-red rectangle in the centre stands for the almost 400 cancer patients whom Dr. al-Ali had to treat in 1997. It is his thesis that the old Gulf War battlefields in the yellow area to the west contaminated the water, the fields, even the fish with depleted uranium and nitrate, contaminating the land not only for survivors of the war but for those still unborn.

Back in the last days of the conflict, U.S. strategists were debating whether the damage to Iraq's infrastructure—the bombing of water pipes, power plants and oil refineries—would take the lives of Iraqis in the months or years to come. But never did they publicly suggest that a policy of bomb now, die later would ever involve cancer. Many of the hundreds of children in Baghdad who have died of leukaemia and stomach cancer since the war came from the south and were sent north by Dr. al-Ali. "Every one of us is in despair," he said. "It is a great burden on me—I am losing many of these patients every day. They need bone marrow transplants but we cannot give these to them. I cannot sleep at night for thinking about them."

Armed with one of Dr. al-Ali's cancer cluster maps, Lara, Alex and I drive south of Basra, back to those fields in which the last tank battles of the 1991 war were fought. We travel with a goon from the Ministry of Information, a "minder," but a man who has long ago been suborned by us, who is now paid more by us in a day than he earns from the ministry in a month. When we need to travel somewhere that might not be permitted—or when we wish to ask something that might not meet with the ministry's approval—he suffers a cold and returns to his hotel or moves to the other side of the room. But we need him south of Basra, an Iraqi military area which overlaps with the operational area of the UN's frontier peacekeeping force.

I had always thought that the last battles of the 1991 Gulf conflict were fought in the desert, in the thick sand of northern Iraq which tormented us in February 1991. But the countryside through which we are driving is pasture-land. There are streams and cows grazing, fields of vegetables and—scattered amid this bucolic landscape—the burned-out hulks of Iraqi tanks. Some had exploded into pieces, bent iron that was now lying in ditches or half buried in the earth. Others are remarkably intact, their gun barrels still pointing south and west towards the American enemies that destroyed them.

We drive on for another 15 kilometres. At first glance, the Adwan family's tomato plantation doesn't look like a killing field. The polythene covers reflect the high, bright winter sun. And when I ask sixteen-year-old Imad Adwan what happened here during the Gulf War, he glances at the man from the Ministry of Information beside me and says he cannot remember. It pays, you see, to have a short memory in Iraq—and to lie. As water trickles through the ditches between the rows of pale green bushes, a sharp wind blows out of the desert to the west, just as it did in February 1991 when Major General Tom Rhame's U.S. 1st Infantry Division—the "Big Red One"—swept up the highway to Safwan, shelling the retreating columns of the Iraqi Republican Guard with DU rounds. Imad Adwan is watching me to see if I have understood his amnesia.

"Don't worry," the ministry man says, and produces an identity card. The boy grins. "The battles were all around us here—we didn't even stay in the house because we knew it would not give us cover. But we didn't leave. The wrecked tanks are over there." Far beyond the barbed wire surrounding the farm, beyond a stand of trees and another plantation, the rusting victims of General Rhame's attack are settled deep in the damp earth. Imad's mother has appeared beside us, a scarf around her head, a black dress tugged by the breeze. She is holding a pale green tomato in her hand. "Please," she says. "It is for you."

The tomato is small, plucked from the bush in front of us, a poisoned fruit—according to the Basra doctors—from a poisonous war, grown on a dangerous stem, bathed in foetid water. "The soldiers died on this road," she says, gesturing towards the highway behind us which leads south-west towards Safwan and the new Kuwaiti frontier. "The battles went on for hours. People still get killed—two boys were blown up by mines over there last July." The outline of a collapsed trench shows the fatal spot. But it is other deaths that we have come about. Are the Adwans worried about their land? Do they know what the doctors say about it? Imad's mother has heard of cancer cases in the farmlands but none in her family.

It is then that Hassan Salman walks up to us. He grows tomatoes and onions on the other side of the road. He has a distinguished face, brown from the sun, and is wearing a gold-fringed robe. When we mention cancer, he frowns. "Yes, we have had many cancer cases here," he says. "I think it happened because of the fires and what happened during the battles. The tanks were just down the road." He pauses. "My daughter-in-law died of cancer around fifty days ago. She was ill in the stomach. Her name was Amal Hassan Saleh. She was very young—she was just twenty-one years old."

Official Western government reaction to the growing signs of DU contamination was pitiful. When I first reported from Iraq's child cancer wards in February and March 1998, the British government went to great lengths to discredit what I wrote. I still treasure a sarcastic letter from Lord Gilbert at the Ministry of Defence, who told *Independent* readers that my account of a possible link between DU ammunition and increased Iraqi child cancer cases would—"coming from anyone other than Robert Fisk"—be regarded as "a wilful perversion of reality." According to his Lordship, particles from the DU-hardened warheads—used against tank armour—are extremely small, rapidly diluted and dispersed by the weather and "become difficult to detect, even with the most sophisticated monitoring equipment." Now I have to say that over the months, I had gathered enough evidence to suggest that—had this letter come from anyone other than his Lordship—its implications would be mendacious as well as misleading.

So let's start with a far more eloquent—and accurate—letter sent to the Royal Ordnance in London on 21 April 1991 by Paddy Bartholomew, business development manager of AEA Technology, the trading name for the UK Atomic Energy Authority. Mr. Bartholomew's letter, of which I obtained a copy—I called him later and he confirmed he was the author, but would make no other comment—refers to a telephone conversation with a Royal Ordnance official called J. Y. Sanders on the dangers of the possible contamination of Kuwait by depleted-uranium ammunition. In an accompanying "threat paper," Mr. Bartholomew notes that while the hazards caused by the spread of radioactivity and toxic contamination of these weapons "are small when compared to those during a war," they nonetheless "can become a long-term problem if not dealt with in peacetime and are *a risk to both the military and the civilian population*" (my emphasis). The document, marked "UK Restricted," goes on to say that "U.S. tanks fired 5,000 DU rounds, U.S. aircraft many 10s of thousands and UK tanks a small number of DU rounds. The tank ammunition alone will amount to greater than 50,000 lbs of DU . . . if the tank inventory of DU was inhaled, the latest International Committee of Radiological Protection risk factor . . . calculates *500,000 potential deaths*" (again, my emphasis).

Mr. Bartholomew added in his 1991 paper that while "this theoretical figure is not realistic, however it does indicate a significant problem." And he continues:

The DU will spread around the battlefield and target vehicles in various sizes and quantities . . . it would be unwise for people to stay close to large quantities of DU for long periods and this would obviously be of concern to the local population if they collect this heavy metal and keep it. There will be specific areas in which many rounds will have been fired where localised contamination of vehicles and the soil may exceed permissible limits and these could be hazardous to both clean up teams and the local population.

Mr. Bartholomew's covering letter says that the contamination of Kuwait is "emotive and thus must be dealt with in a sensitive manner," adding that the AEA's regional marketing director (Alastair Parker) might send a copy of the "threat paper" to the UK ambassador in Kuwait. AEA Technology could "clean up" the depleted uranium under a contract with the Kuwait government. Needless to say, no one had bothered to suggest a clean-up in Iraq, where so many children were dying of unexplained cancers. Why not? And why did Lord Gilbert write his extraordinary and deeply misleading letter to *The Independent* in March of 1998? Here's a clue. It comes in a letter dated 21 March 1991, from a U.S. lieutenant colonel at the Los Alamos National Laboratory to a Major Larson at the organisation's "Studies and Analysis Branch" and states that:

There has been and continues to be a concern regarding the impact of DU on the environment. Therefore, if no one makes a case for the effectiveness of DU on the battlefield, DU rounds may become politically unacceptable and thus be deleted from the arsenal. If DU penetrators proved their worth during our recent combat activities, then we should assure their future existence (until something better is developed) through Service/DOD [Department of Defense] proponency. If proponency is not garnered, it is possible that we stand to lose a valuable combat capability.

So there it is. Shorn of the colonel's execrable English, the message is simple: the health risks of DU ammunition are acceptable until we—the West—invent something even more lethal to take its place. No wonder, then, that an official British government review of the UK's Ministry of Defence radioactive waste management at the British firing range for DU ammunition in the Lake District in December 1997 detailed the extraordinary lengths taken to protect local British villages. They included firing shells into tunnels with a filtered extract system, pressure-washing the surfaces and sealing up the contaminated residues in cemented drums. Lord Gilbert did not tell *Independent* readers about that in his letter to the paper. So much for the "wilful perversion of reality."*

If governments did not care about the Iraqi children, however, British people did. *The Independent* launched an appeal for the medicines these children so desperately needed, and within weeks our generous readers had donated more than $250,000 for us to buy cancer drugs and medical equipment to take to Iraq. At last, it seemed, we could *do* something, rather than just write angry articles about the plight of these pariah children. But could we? Were we going to save lives, or merely prolong suffering?

It was mundane work. In October 1998 we employed refuse carts and a squad of sweating Iraqis to heave our boxes of medicinal supplies from a refrigerated truck that we had backed into the broken loading bay of a Baghdad hospital; across town at the Mansour hospital, we had to use a stretcher to transport the 5,185 kilograms of medicine, stuffing the painfully expensive vincristine into the director's personal fridge. It was a bit of an anticlimax, until I saw the children in the wards upstairs. Weeping with pain or smiling in innocence of their fate, the cancer children of Iraq—in Mosul and Basra as well as Baghdad—were at last receiving help. "Have you brought something for me?" a little girl asked as a doctor told her that all the drugs must be shared equally.

In one corner of the Mansour cancer ward, Hebba Mortaba lay in a patterned blue dress, a hideous tumour distorting her tiny figure. When her mother lifted the dress, her terribly swollen abdomen displayed numerous abscesses. Doctors had already surgically removed an earlier abdominal mass—only to find, alien-like,

---

*Readers wishing to learn more about DU munitions should refer to the voluminous reports of Swords into Ploughshares and—on the effect of pre-2003 sanctions as well as DU—to the regular bulletins of *Voices in the Wilderness UK* of 16b Cherwell Road, Oxford OX4 1BG.

that another grew in its place. During the 1991 war, Hebba's suburb of Basra was bombed so heavily that her family fled to Baghdad. She was now just nine years old and, so her doctors told me gently, would not live to see her tenth birthday.

Given UN sanctions and then Saddam Hussein's own ban on medicine imports, it was in truth something of a miracle that our truck made it across the Iraqi desert, finally shepherded around the country's hospitals by CARE's two indomitable Iraqi representatives, Margaret Hassan and Judy Morgan. The UN at first fulminated about the length of time that it might take to clear our medicines through the sanctions commission—until we told them that we would take the medicines whether they liked it or not, at which point, on 15 June, clearance was given in twenty-four hours. The office of the Iraqi president was almost equally obtuse, delaying and prevaricating and ignoring our shipment request until September, when Saddam Hussein gave his personal approval—another example of that disturbing coincidence of intention between the West and the dictator in Baghdad.

"The members of the [Security Council] Committee have no objection to the sending of the specified items . . ." the UN's pompous letter had concluded, as if they were doing us a favour. The documentation at the UN accurately referred to the medical payment as "readers donations from *Independent* newspaper." But the fifty-eight cartons and boxes, flown from Heathrow to Amman by Royal Jordanian Airlines and then trucked the 800 kilometres to Baghdad by Iraqi driver Rahman Jassem Mohamed—cloxacillin and ampicillin vials, cytarabine and vincristine, methotrexate and dexamethasone ampoules and syringes and gloves and blood solutions—were successfully distributed to children's hospitals across Iraq.

But were we in time? The truth should be told. Most of the children whose suffering I had recounted were already dead—even the boy whose portrait became the symbol and logo of *The Independent*'s appeal. I had taken a photograph of Latif Sattar from Babylon, the five-year-old with non-Hodgkin's lymphoma who was playing with a toy car and smiling beneath the bald dome of his head when I met him the previous February. I took his picture close-up as he lay on his bed in a knitted pullover, his eyes staring at me. But the records of the paediatric hospital in Baghdad show that he died on 7 April 1998. Then there was leukaemia victim Samar Khdair, the beautiful girl whose photograph appeared in my paper the day after Latif's. She was the child who lay in her nightie, her father pressing a yellow compress to her forehead, her eyes squeezed shut with pain. Again, the hospital file provided no comfort. It recorded how Samar suffered a relapse through lack of drugs and blood products. But she fought on—only to die on 20 September 1998, just days before the drugs paid for by our readers arrived in Baghdad.

Most of the tiny children I was now seeing in Iraq would die too. "When the cancers reach this stage, there is not much we can do," Dr. al-Ali told me frankly when I reached Basra and talked to him again. "But you must understand what your people have done—they have helped to prolong these small lives, and to improve the quality of life of these children. They are going to die in one month, two months, two years . . . Yes, perhaps a few will live . . . believe me, it is worth bringing your drugs here." I go on scribbling the names of the soon-to-be-dead in my notebook. Nour Shehab and Halah Saleh are ten and Haitham Ahmed is eight. Tiba Favel is only eighteen months old. Moustapha Jaber is eight and Dhamia Qassem is thirteen. All have acute leukaemia except for Moustapha, who has lymphoma.

It was impossible to visit these cancer wards again without a feeling of great indignation. Even now, when the children had the drugs they needed for leukaemia, blood platelets for them were not being made fast enough in Iraq because the machine that separated the blood needed maintenance. UN sanctions had broken the back of the hospital system. We in the West—we, in the most literal sense of the word—were responsible for all this, we who accepted the UN sanctions against Iraq, the sanctions that were clearly killing these children and that, equally clearly, were not harming Saddam Hussein. But there was also reason for exasperation.

For although the U.S. and British administrations understandably tried to keep the two groups of victims separate, the American and British soldiers suffering from what had become known as Gulf War Syndrome appeared to be suffering from almost identical cancers and leukaemia and internal bleeding as the children of Iraq. The explosion of cancers in Iraq largely affected the Shiite community, and it was therefore no surprise that, seven years after the war, Saddam Hussein's regime had made no mention of it—yet again, Clinton, Blair and Saddam had made common cause in a total failure to explain the calamity. But even as I was touring the cancer wards of Basra and Baghdad, Tony Flint, the acting chairman of the British Gulf Veterans' and Families' Association, was warning that the very same DU shells could be responsible for cancers that had so far killed at least thirty British veterans. A day later, the American National Gulf War Resource Center, a coalition of U.S. veterans' groups, announced that as many as 40,000 American servicemen might have been exposed to depleted uranium dust on the battlefield.

In October 1998, Phil Garner telephoned me to ask how he could make contact with the doctors treating Iraq's child cancer victims. He had been reading my reports on the growing evidence of links between cancers and depleted uranium shells. During the 1991 Gulf War, Garner was in the British Royal Army Medical Corps. He wasn't in the front lines, but he handled the uniforms of Britain's "friendly fire" casualties, men who were accidentally attacked by U.S. aircraft that were using depleted-uranium rounds. And now he was suffering from asthma, incontinence, pain in the intestines, and had a lump on the right side of his neck. What does this mean? I knew all about these lumps. I had seen them on the necks of the Iraqi children.

In Basra again, I watch the anguish of a parent. "Oxygen, for God's sake get some oxygen—my son is dying." It is an almost animal wail from the man on the staircase of the paediatric hospital, tears running from his eyes, shaking uncontrollably. In the small room at the top of the stairs, his son, Yahyia Salman, is crying with fear, desperate to breathe. A leukaemia relapse—especially in the sulphurous heat of southern Iraq—is a thing of panic. "Stop shouting, we have another oxygen bottle," Dr. Jenane Khaleb admonishes the father, pursing her lips with a mixture of irritation and concern. But the man will not be consoled. "My God, what am I going to do?" he cries as a technician with a ratchet begins to unscrew the top of another massive, dented black oxygen bottle. The little boy's eyes move across the room, towards the doctor, towards me and his father. This is not the moment to tell the child that his hospital now has all the drugs it needs for leukaemia. The boxes of vincristine and vials of cefuroxine, ampoules of metoclopramide, of surgical gloves and syringes arrived less than twenty-four hours ago. But Yahyia Salman has gone a long way down the road towards death.

So has two-year-old Youssef Qassem in the next room and Halah Saleh who, just ten years old, is suffering from acute lymphoblastic leukaemia. The doctors show me these children with infinite weariness, and I can understand why. They have received so many visitors and so many promises of help. At least ours was honoured. Dr. Khaleb asks, very carefully, if the Basra hospital received the same amount of drugs as other hospitals in Baghdad and Mosul. I understand the purpose of her question: it was the Shiites here in the south who rose against the Iraqi government in 1991 and there are those in Baghdad who have never forgiven them.

Dr. Khaleb says nothing of this. Yes, I insist, *The Independent*'s medicines were pre-packed before leaving Heathrow to ensure that every area of Iraq received an equal share. And she smiles as she reads through the drug manifest which I have brought with me. It is the first smile I have seen on this trip to Basra. For the doctors here are overwhelmed as much by the implications of their discoveries as they are by lack of medicine. The increase in child cancer in these southern provinces—it is now October 1998—is in places reaching ferocious heights.

While in some areas an average of only 3.9 children in every 100,000 are suffering from cancer, the districts of Harthe and Gurne now produce statistics of 71.8 and 41.8 respectively. There was heavy bombing in these suburbs in 1991 and the words "depleted uranium" are heard in every ward; even the parents now know the meaning of the phrase. Dr. Jawad al-Ali is stupefied. "I don't know how to explain the implications of this to you but I am now seeing terrible things," he said. "One of our medical students who has just graduated, Zeineddin Kadam, has cancer and he will die in a few days. The wife of one of our orthopaedic surgeons died just a week after a diagnosis of acute leukaemia—she died less than a month ago when she thought she merely had an appendix problem. They found part of her small intestine was gangrenous."

Dr. al-Ali opens another thick file of notes. "Of fifteen cancer patients from one area, I have only two left. I am receiving children with cancer of the bone—this is incredible. I have just received a fifteen-year-old girl, Zeinab Manwar, with leukaemia—she will live only a year. My God, I have performed mastectomies on two girls with cancer of the breast—one of them was only fourteen years old—this is unheard of!"

Dr. Akram Hammoud, director of the paediatric hospital, is no less appalled. "Almost all the children here will die in a few months," he says. "We have one family with three children, all of whom have Hodgkin's lymphoma. What can have done this? Before the war, we received in this hospital about one cancer patient a week—now I am getting an average of forty a week. This is crazy. We are getting patients with carcinoma cancer below the age of twenty—one of my patients is twenty-two, another eighteen. One of the symptoms of leukaemia is bleeding from the nose—now every child that has a nosebleed is brought here by panic-stricken parents." The doctors are careful in talking about depleted uranium. They do not want their patients—or their own observations—to be used for propaganda, however justifiably, but they know of the 1990 American military report which states that cancers, kidney problems and birth defects are among the health effects of uranium particle contamination.

"Even the common cold in Basra is changing its features," Dr. al-Ali says. "It takes longer to cure here now and we get advanced cases, sometimes associated with encephalitis." He reopens his file. "In 1989, we received 116 cancer patients in the whole area; last year, the figure was 270. Already in the first ten months of this year, it's 331. No one will give us the equipment to test the soil. Probably we are all polluted."

The British government responded to the new evidence of child cancers in Iraq with the same lethargy and indifference as Lord Gilbert. "The Government is aware of suggestions in the Press, particularly by Robert Fisk of the *Independent*, that there has been an increase in ill-health—including alleged deformities, cancers and birth defects—in southern Iraq, which some have attributed to the use of depleted uranium (DU) based ammunition by UK and U.S. forces during the 1990/91 Gulf conflict," the British minister for the armed forces, Doug Henderson, wrote in December 1998. "However, the Government has not seen any peer-reviewed epidemiological research data on this population to support these claims and it would therefore be premature to comment on this matter." I liked the bit about "peer-reviewed epidemiological research data" because, of course, there weren't any—nor would there be. Even when the Royal Society was asked to investigate the effects of depleted uranium, its researchers didn't visit Iraq.* The evidence, as shameful as it was shocking, had little effect. At a Christian service in 2000 to mark the fifty-fifth anniversary of the wartime RAF and American fire-

---

*This same scandalous indifference towards the effects of DU was to be repeated just over two years later when, in January 2001, reports began to emerge from Bosnia that hundreds of Serbs—living close to the site of U.S. Air Force depleted-uranium bombings in 1995—were suffering and dying from unexplained cancers. When I travelled to Bosnia to investigate these deaths, I found that up to 300 Serbian men, women and children living close to the site of a 1995 DU bombing of a military base in the Sarajevo suburb of Hadjici had died of cancers and leukaemias over the following five years—they lay next to each other in an extended graveyard at Bratunac in eastern Bosnia, the town to which they had travelled as refugees.

One frozen winter's morning in Bratunac, I interviewed twelve-year-old Sladjana Sarenac, who had picked up a bomb fragment outside her home in Hadjici. Her story was eerily and painfully familiar. "It glittered and I did what all children do," she said. "I was six years old and I pretended to make cookies out of the bits of metal and soil in the garden. Within two months I got a kind of yellow sand under my fingernails and then the nails started to fall out." Sladjana had been seriously ill ever since. Her nails had repeatedly fallen out of her fingers and toes, she had

bombing of Dresden, the bishop of Coventry, Colin Bennetts, declared that Britain had to accept responsibility for the death and deformity of children in Iraq as a result of allied bombing during and after the 1991 Gulf War. While criticising Saddam Hussein's "evil," the bishop said that the child victims of Iraq "were conceived and born around the time of the Gulf War. They were born with hideous physical deformities. Many are also suffering from infantile leukaemia. There is very strong evidence to suggest that all this was caused by the depleted uranium in our weapons." Yet still the Americans and British refused to acknowledge any such guilt. In just three years' time, they were to use depleted uranium yet again—once more, against Iraq.

What did all this say about our pretensions for the future, about our desperate, fantasy hope—if we ever did invade Iraq and destroy Saddam's regime—that these people would greet us as liberators? Iraqis might take satisfaction at the overthrow of their dictator. But punished by twelve years of brutal sanctions, bombed repeatedly by allied aircraft over the same period under the spurious notion that enforcement of the "no-fly" zones would protect them, dusted over by the poison of our depleted-uranium munitions, twice in just over a decade, would they really come to greet and love us—the new occupiers who had so punished them, who had humiliated them and persecuted them over so many years?

By the late Nineties, my reports from Iraq have now become a diary. I am overwhelmed by what we are doing—what we have done—to this country. How can Iraqis in Baghdad contemplate the future when they have to live by selling their last possessions in the Soukh Midan? One day in February 1998, I found at least a hundred ill-kempt men and a few women standing in the drizzle below the magnificent magenta cupola of the Jama'a al-Qushla mosque. At their feet lay the most pitiable things on display at any of the world's bazaars: a collection of rusting bath fittings and old car parts, some torn leather shoes, nuts and bolts and moth-eaten rugs, used shirts, second-hand socks and a broken television set lying forlornly in a puddle, its massive brown wooden fittings and tiny screen mindful of a pre-Baathist age. A woman in a soiled black chador looked up at me. Her name was Leila, she said. "Our money is worthless—only God can help us."

Sohad still had money, the middle-class wife of a former diplomat whose home

---

suffered internal bleeding, constant diarrhoea and vomiting, enduring a thirty-hour coma and a calvary of Yugoslav hospitals. It was the same old story. NATO said they had no evidence of the ill-effects of DU munitions in Bosnia but wanted to know if any existed; yet when offered the opportunity to investigate such reports, they showed no interest in doing so. On 17 January 2001, I appealed in *The Independent* for any NATO doctors in Bosnia to get in touch with me on my temporary Sarajevo telephone number, offering to take them to Bratunac and to introduce them to Sladjana. The phone never rang. The Iraqis were Muslims and the Serbs were Orthodox Christians—most of them hostile to Bosnia's Muslim community—but they shared one characteristic: in 1991 and 1995, they were both, respectively, our "enemy" and thus could be ignored. Similarly, the UN was left to carry out an inconclusive survey of DU use during the 1999 Kosovo war after which the American military admitted that it had "lost count" of the number of DU rounds used during the NATO bombardment of Serbia. (See the author's reports in *The Independent*, 4 October and 22 November 1999.)

overlooked the banks of the great brown greasy Tigris River. She was eighty-one, and a long stay in India taught her the Hindu virtue of sublime patience. "All of us have changed these past seven years," she said with an air of finality. "We are accepting life as it is. If we can't get proper medicine, we will go back to old medicine. I had a knee problem. This friend of ours produced a medicine for me from an old herbal formula that the Chinese invented two thousand years ago and I drank a cup of it every morning and now my knee is better."

Sohad's sister was eighty-five. "We live from day to day, from hour to hour. This is part of our changed life—for us, planning is now a luxury. I am not in control, so why bother about it? Now I just want to have a flower in my life, a flower from our garden to look at during the day." In the hall of their old home is a spread of sepia photographs of Turkish grandfathers, some of them dressed in the tunics and scabbards of the Ottoman army—the army that Private Charles Dickens of the Cheshire Regiment fought in Mesopotamia and that the doomed Australian Gunner Frank Wills fought at Gallipoli. "This is how we get our strength," Sohad said. "It comes from our Arab and Georgian and Kurdish and Turkish origins." I met another old lady of great dignity that same day, a woman who had just sold almost all her baccarat glasses. "I bought these glasses on my first visit to Paris in 1947," she said. "But now I needed the money, so I said 'to hell with it'—we had it for a great time and enjoyed it, so I let it go. For 'peanuts' I sold it. I have only a jug and a carafe left."

Yes, Iraqis are a proud people, but the poor have a special, demented vacuum in which they must live. Across the estuary calm of the Tigris, Baghdad continued to moulder away, its pavements veined with weeds, bushes growing in the cracks of the city underpasses, its great railway yards packed with rusting, empty carriages. Even the portraits of Saddam Hussein had become bleached by seven summer suns. As the sanctions ate into the fabric of every soul—except the soulless centre of the regime itself—an army of beggars deployed across the streets.

The children and women who came beating on the doors and windscreen of my car in the centre of Baghdad were pleading for money and food. One small boy, tears coursing through the mud on his face, no more than four years old, barefoot and dressed in a worn, oversize leather jacket with a dozen holes ripped into it, banged his hands against the car passenger window. "Give me money!" he shrieked, kicking the door, staring at me through the glass and wrinkling his eyes to imitate tears. Or was it imitation? On the pavement an hour later, three more children attacked Lara Marlowe of the *Irish Times* and myself, older this time, grabbing at our coats, screaming "money" until we gave them a dollar. They grabbed our bags for more until we pushed them from us, cursing them for their assault. Would Madeleine Albright have given them a dollar? Or would she have lectured them on the iniquities of their leader and the need for UN sanctions, the Iraqi invasion of Kuwait and the immorality of weapons of mass destruction? In the only decent coffee shop near my hotel, they were playing a scratched tape of Doris Day. "*Que sera sera*," she sang, as the beggars watched through the windows. "Whatever will be, will be—the future's not ours to see . . ."

On my way to Basra from Baghdad with Lara, I hand a beggar girl a 250-dinar note—scarcely 14 cents—only to see her thrown to the road by her friends, the money torn from her dirty fist. Basra is now a pit of desolation. In front of Fatima Hassan's house, a tide of pale blue and creamy-white liquid streams gently through an open sewer. Her iron front door cannot hide the stench, nor the sound of the screaming, shoeless children in the street. Jumping the sewer—leaping across this little canyon of filth—is a pastime for the kids of the suburb of Dour Sheoun. Stand outside Fatima's door and they run towards you, blistered, whey-faced, with large eyeballs, the irises ivory-white with malnutrition. A woman—a bright, pretty woman in a black robe with a white headband—introduces us to her eight-year-old daughter Roula, then suddenly says: "Please take her with you." Sundus Abdel-Kader is just thirty-three—and she is ready to give away her own child.

Fatima has five children. Her husband was a car-painter in Kuwait before Saddam invaded the emirate; he stayed on for eight months after its liberation, still working but unpaid by his Kuwaiti employers. Now he sells sandwiches. "We don't eat eggs or milk," she says. "We can't afford to eat meat. We drink the tap-water—we don't boil it. This little boy of mine has trouble breathing, this one has a swollen stomach because of the water. We go to the hospitals but the doctors say there is no medicine. Wherever we go, they say there is no medicine."

Outside, an older woman in black pushes her way through the street urchins. "I have two crippled people in my family," she pleads. "They have fever and sore throats. Can you take them with you to Europe?" We explain that we are not doctors, but she thrusts into our faces a thick piece of yellow paper with a history of muscular dystrophy from which her relatives are suffering. After half an hour, my writing hand grows numb listing the sicknesses and starvation. A child has anaemia, another has severe respiratory problems, a third cannot control its bowels; it appears to be dying. "When are you going to lift the sanctions?" yet another woman shouts at me. "Our children need food and clothes."

At the end of the street, there is a tootling trumpet, a fat man with a drum and a stooped old soldier marking time for a squad of thirty-three middle-aged, half-bearded men, all carrying Kalashnikovs but most of them in shoddy uniforms. These are the local Dad's Army, Saddam's heroic volunteers, preparing to withstand the might of America. They march round a traffic island while the children chant the Iraqi national anthem:

> *A country that stretches its wings over the horizon*
> *And clothes itself in the glory of civilisations . . .*
> *This land is a flame and a light,*
> *Like a mountain that overlooks the world . . .*
> *We have the anger of the sword*
> *And the patience of the Prophet.*

Then the kids go back to sewer-jumping. And this, I remind myself, is the country which, according to Messrs. Clinton and Blair, threatens the whole world.

We drive across to Basra's old port, the harbour that the British invested in 1914, once visited in the late eighteenth century by the young Horatio Nelson. "Five Englishmen ran this port until 1958," Ali al-Imara proudly announces. "The first chairman was John Ward, from 1919 until 1942, and then we had William Bennett until 1947. They were very good men. In 1958, Mr. Shaawi took over; he was a very good man too." There is no mention of the 1958 Iraqi revolution that ended British stewardship of Basra's old harbour and of Iraq itself. But why be churlish in a place of such decrepitude? Today, the gates to the wharf are still adorned with well-polished Tudor roses, but the slates have cascaded off the roofs of the old colonial offices. The railway lines, laid down when Basra was an international terminal, are corroded.

The wide, sluggish waterway of the Shatt al-Arab, so fateful and laden with death in Iraq's recent history, drifts past the hulks tied up on the quays. Here is the *Yasmine*, a trawler under whose black paint it is still possible to read the words *Lord Shackleton, Port Stanley, F.I.* (Falkland Islands); and there the *Wisteria*, all 6,742 blackened tons of her, her mentors slowly dismembering the burned-out tanker. Who set fire to her? I ask three Iraqi officials on the quay. "An Iranian missile hit it in 1981," one of them replies. But his friend mutters in Arabic: "Tell him it was the Americans." Then they all chorus: "It was the Americans!"

Basra lives on lies: if only the Iranians hadn't attacked Iraq and closed the river in 1980, they tell you—but it was the Iraqis who invaded Iran; if only the UN had not slapped sanctions on Iraq after the Iran–Iraq War—and we are supposed to forget the little matter of Iraq's invasion of Kuwait in 1990. Even the ships have changed their names in embarrassment. The supply ship *Atco Sara*, according to a half-erased name, used to be the *Pacific Prospector* of Illinois and, before that, the *Northern Builder*. There is a Krupps hoist and a set of rusting cranes bearing the name "Thomas Smith and Sons of Leeds" on a black iron plate.

And I cannot but remember how I arrived at this city and its port eighteen years before. I had watched these ships burn. Just downriver was the island from which Jon Snow had embarked to rescue the crew of the trapped freighter *Al-Tanin* as I cowered on the riverbank waiting for him, the Iranian tracer fire zipping towards us across the darkened Shatt al-Arab River. It was on this very quayside, aboard a Yugoslav freighter, that I filched the maps of the waterway for Jon and the Iraqi frogmen who were to rescue the crew. From Basra each morning, Gavin Hewitt of the BBC and I would set out to watch the "Whirlwind War" that would destroy the Islamic Republic. And now the Iraqis had reaped the whirlwind.

Behind us now, the marshalling yards are filled with long freight trains, massive grey wagons hooked up to leave on a journey that should have started in 1980, the trucks now entangled with weeds and bushes. Mr. al-Imara strides along the docks. "Take as many pictures as you want," he says. "If it wasn't for the sanctions, we would have this port dredged and running." An old dog falls asleep on the tracks below the stern of the *Wisteria*, its steel ladders twisted against the hull to which they were welded eighteen years ago.

It is an odd affliction that now besets Iraq's Baathist bureaucracy. Tutored to boast of all that is best about Iraq, they now have to publicise all that is worst. It must be an awfully difficult transition. For who knows when the orders might come down from Baghdad to reverse the process yet again? Mr. al-Imara tells us he is a poet as well as being "foreign relations adviser" to Basra port. And he quotes, as we walk beside his decaying, marooned ships, a work of his which he calls "Confrontation":

> *When you shoot with a bullet from anywhere,*
> *The bullet will head straight for my chest;*
> *Because the events through which we have passed*
> *Have made my chest round.*

And we look at Mr. al-Imara's diminutive chest and laugh politely. Whose bullets is the poet referring to? Surely not those that scar the façade of Basra's central police station, still a gutted marble shell beside one of the city's foetid canals. Certainly not those that smashed into the burning governorate building during the same 1991 uprising by Basra's Shiite majority, now replaced with masses of pre-stressed concrete. And not the bullets that were fired into the city's police cars, now replaced—as they have been throughout Iraq—with gleaming new Hyundai saloons, a final mockery to the starvation of the people the police are supposed to "control." On the grainy old television in my Basra hotel room, Saddam is seated before his Revolutionary Command Council, making a joke at which his uniformed courtiers guffaw. "When he laughed, respectable senators burst into laughter."

The Corniche of Martyrs corrects any misapprehension about the enemy. For along the west bank of the Shatt al-Arab, below the dank portals of the Basra Sheraton Hotel, stand the dead heroes of Saddam's "Whirlwind War." For these three dozen Iraqi soldiers—out of perhaps half a million—death will not have been in vain. Each man, modelled in bronze from photographs, points across the muddy waterway towards the precise location of the war front, inside Iran, at which he died. "Corporals and Sergeants and Captains and Majors and Colonels—all martyrs of the *Qadisiya* war," it says in brass on each pedestal.

The soldiers, three times life-size, are identified by name, along with a colossus down the bank representing Saddam's cousin General Adnan Khairallah, one of the greatest and most popular of Iraq's military leaders—too popular for Saddam perhaps. He stands facing his cannon-fodder, right arm raised in honour of their courage; he was to die—"tragically," as the Iraqi press obediently announced at the time—in a helicopter crash not long after the Iran–Iraq War ended. Below these statues, the street urchins hawk nuts parcelled in old newspapers at 12 cents a package.

They are as far as they can get from the food chain, at the furthest corner of Iraq, clamped between Iran's suspicions to the east, and Kuwait's hatred to the south, and the West's contempt, dominated by rusting ships and the towering giants of the dead. Each night in Iraq, I pound away on my heat-cracked laptop with its partially damaged screen, writing about the suffering and the volcanic anger of Iraqis. It is 16 October 1998. This is the report I send to my paper that night from Baghdad, one that I will read again in 2003, after we have occupied Iraq and found ourselves facing a ferocious insurgency:

Fairy lights illuminate the Babeesh Grill Restaurant in President Street. Mock stained glass windows discreetly protect the clientele. For this is an up-market bistro for up-market eaters, most of them UN officials. The hungry Iraqis who are not dazzled by the fairy lights outside can just make out the candlelit tables and the foreigners inside as they wolf their way through beef and roast chicken, side-plates heaped with fruits and vegetables or—the Babeesh's speciality—shrimp salad. Soft music plays as white-jacketed waiters serve the UN's finest, the sanctions boys and the arms inspectors and the men and women who try desperately to undo the suffering caused by the gentlemen in the glass building on the East River 5,990 miles away.

But despite the white-liveried waiters, whatever you do, don't mention the *Titanic*. Iraqi state television has shown James Cameron's film three times (he can forget about the royalties) as a balm for hardship, the Baghdad equivalent of bread and circuses. But unlike the *Titanic*, the Babeesh has no third class diners. This is a restaurant for those who measure money by the kilo rather than the Iraqi dinar note. Now that the dinar is worth 0.0006 of a dollar (thanks to the employers of the Babeesh's clientele), my own meal for three needed a stack of 488 one hundred dinar notes, a wad of cash a foot thick. No wonder some cafes have given up counting their takings—they check the bills by stacking the dinar notes on a weighing machine.

So you can forget the Weimar Republic in a land where an average villager can expect to earn a mere 3,400 dinars a month. Let me repeat that: 3,400 dinars—*two dollars*—a month. Which means that our little snack at the Babeesh—and there was no wine because alcohol is banned in restaurants on orders from the man whose name no one says too loudly—cost fourteen times the monthly salary of an Iraqi. So why no food riots? Why no revolution?

Take a stroll off Rashid Street in the old part of town and you can see why. The sewage stretches in lakes, wall-to-wall, a viscous mass of liquid so pale green in colour that it possesses its own awful beauty. This is what happens when the electricity cuts out and the water treatment plants and sewage facilities go unrepaired. Electrical appliance vendors—for Rashid Street is where you go for a light-bulb, an adapter, a piece of wire—hug the walls like nuns to keep the mess from their plastic shoes. "You have done this to us," a thin, bearded man said to me as I asked (heaven spare me) for an electric kettle. The kettle could only be obtained at a foreign goods shop in the suburbs for just over $20—around nine and a half times the monthly salary of the Iraqi villager.

Grind down the people to this abject level and survival is more important than revolution. Unless you choose highway robbery. I'm not talking
of the kind practised at the Babeesh, but on the long motorways west to
Jordan or south to Basra. "That's where they shot the Jordanian," my driver
said to me 100 kilometres out of Baghdad on the Amman road, a carefree
reference to the diplomat who chose to travel after dark and paid the price.
You don't drive to Basra overnight for fear of deserting soldiers, so the
rumour goes, who've turned to banditry to keep their families alive. By
night, the gunmen lurk, by day the village women who sell themselves for
"temporary marriage" and a few more dinars. The latter I didn't believe.

Until I left Basra one hot afternoon and drove out through the slums
with their own lakes of sewage—warmer than the Baghdad variety, for the
Gulf temperatures drive up the heat of every liquid—and saw a crazed
mass of men and women, tearing at their faces with their nails, carrying in
front of them the body of a child, pushing it into a battered orange and
white taxi on the main road. And a young man, maybe only 16, suddenly
jumped into the sewage lake beside the highway and plastered his body in
filth, screaming and raging and smacking his hands into the green water so
that it splattered all the mourners with filth.

To what does poverty and hunger drive a people? I soon found out. Seventy miles north of Basra, where the road mirages in the heat between the
endless encampments of Saddam's legions who are suppressing the Marsh
Arabs, a group of girls could be seen, dressed in red turbans and black
dresses, their faces cowled like Touaregs, dancing—actually twirling
themselves round and round—in the fast lane of the motorway until we
drew to a halt. One of them approached the driver's window, her eyes soft,
her voice rasping. "Come buy our fish," she whispered. "Come see our fish
and you will want to buy them."

She pronounced the Arab word for fish—*sumak*—with a hiss, and the
driver giggled in a cruel, lascivious way. She was maybe 16 and she was
selling not fish but herself. And when they realised we were not customers,
the fish girls of Iraq twirled back into the motorway lane to offer themselves in front of a speeding Jordanian truck. Yes, you can forget the overthrow of Saddam Hussein, let alone the destruction of his magnificent
palaces and ornamental lakes and colonnaded halls. But I do wonder how
the Iraqis in President Street can resist the temptation of breaking through
the windows of the Babeesh restaurant and tearing its customers to pieces,
perhaps even choosing the odd remaining foreign limb to supplement their
diet.

# CHAPTER NINETEEN

## *Now Thrive the Armourers . . .*

LADY BRITOMART: There is no moral question in the matter at all, Adolphus. You must simply sell cannons and weapons to people whose cause is right and just, and refuse them to foreigners and criminals.

UNDERSHAFT (determinedly): No: none of that. You must keep the true faith of an armourer . . . To give arms to all men who offer an honest price for them, without respect of persons or principles: to aristocrat and republican, to Nihilist and Tsar, to Capitalist and Socialist, to Protestant and Catholic, to burglar and policeman, to black man, white man and yellow man, to all sorts and conditions, all nationalities, all faiths, all follies, all causes and all crimes . . .

—George Bernard Shaw, *Major Barbara,* Act III

JUST BEFORE I ENTER the 24,000-square-foot exhibition centre close to Abu Dhabi airport, I receive an elaborate invitation on vellum parchment. "Under the patronage of His Highness Lt. General Sheikh Mohamed Bin Zayed al Nahyan," it says, "it is the pleasure of His Highness Sheikh Falah Bin Zayed al Nahyan, Chairman of Ghantout Racing and Polo Club, to cordially invite you for The Final of the Idex Al Basti Polo Tournament at 7.30pm followed by dinner . . . Formal Dress." A few minutes after I have cleared the security gates, I am offered a fine Persian silk carpet—from Qom, I recall—and, at a mercifully smaller price, a set of Arab brass cooking utensils and coffee pots. There are tea stands and flowers, purple and gold and green in the early spring heat. The Arabs wear their white robes with dignity, the Western visitors dark blue suits and ties, their wives, bright, tight-fitting dresses, often with those slightly silly racing hats that come with purple stalks and fake blooms on top. Several of the ladies drop off to look at the jewellery shop with its gold bangles and rings. One of Sheikh Mohamed's military pipe bands plays English and Scottish marches. Smartly attired Indian and Pakistani workers labour to erect Arab tents before the midday sun reaches its height.

What was it George Bernard Shaw's armourer, Andrew Undershaft, told his daughter in *Major Barbara* when she visited his massive arms factory at Perivale St. Andrews? "Cleanliness and respectability do not need justification . . . they justify themselves. I see no darkness here, no dreadfulness." And he was right. Polo, silk carpets, coffee pots, flowers, a highlander's lament and tea and jewellery while the natives protect pink faces from the oriental sun. It is as civilised as fine art; which is what the sale of weapons has become for the world's armourers.

For behind the tents and trinket shops and the pipe band in this vast compound in the emirate of Abu Dhabi, there lay on display some of the most sophisticated and most lethal ordnance ever made by man, so new you could smell the fresh paint gleaming in the sun, so clean, so artistically bold in their design that you might never guess their purpose. And each time I wandered over to examine a French missile, a German tank, an American Hellfire rocket, a British armoured vehicle, a Dutch self-propelled gun, a shelf of Italian pistols, a Russian automatic rifle, a South African army video-screen of crimson explosions, up would come a charming gentleman in another of those dark blue suits, a merchant of death brandishing a file of glossy, expensively produced brochures, offering a powerful handshake and another cup of tea.

Occasionally, they were a bit portly—selling death on a large scale means a lot of hospitality—and often they carried a small purple or blue flower in their button hole. Ballistics was their fascination. "As the day warms up, a bullet flies faster," a cheerful Australian confided to me. "In the evening, the air grows heavier and the bullet goes more slowly." Smiling field marshals and jolly generals from across the Arab world drifted through the arms pavilions, peering through sniper rifles, clambering like schoolchildren onto howitzers and tanks, running their hands repeatedly along the sleek missile tubes, masturbating the instruments of death.

I have to admit a grim fascination of my own in all this, a professional interest. It is the spring of 2001. For twenty-five years now, the crudest and most fabulously designed bullets, rockets, missiles, tank shells, artillery rounds and grenades have been hurled in my direction by some of the nastiest and most "moral" armies on earth. Israelis with American Hellfire air-to-ground missiles, Syrians with Russian T-72 tanks, RAF pilots with American cluster bombs, Afghan mujahedin with Russian AK-47 rifles, Russians with Hind helicopter gunships, Iraqis and Azerbaijanis with Russian-manufactured Scud rockets and Iranians with U.S.-made sniper rifles and Americans with Boeing fighter-bombers and battleships whose shells were the size of Volkswagens: they have all sent their produce swishing in my direction. Even as I walk between the immaculate stands of this exhibition, the tinnitus hisses viciously in my ears from that Iraqi 155-mm gun that so seriously damaged my hearing back in 1980. In a quarter of a century, I've seen thousands of corpses—women and children as well as men—blasted, shredded, eviscerated, disembowelled, beheaded, lobotomised, castrated and otherwise annihilated by the multi-billion-dollar arms industry. Almost all of them were Muslims. This is a symbol of our triumph over the Middle East in Abu Dhabi this hot March day of 2001, our ability to kill Muslims—and to help Muslims kill other Muslims—with our weapons. They have no weapons that can touch us. Not yet. Not for another six months.

I regularly prowled the arms bazaars of the Middle East, seeking an answer to the same old questions. Who are the men who produce this vile equipment? How can they justify their trade? How will the victims respond to this pulverisation of their lives? What language can compass science and death and capital gains on such a scale? For there is, I was to discover in Abu Dhabi, an integral, frightening correlation between linguistics and guns, between grammar and rockets. It's all about words. Thus I circle the arms-sellers' pavilions with a large canvas bag and a kleptomaniac's desire to hoard every brochure, pamphlet, book and magazine from Americans, Russians, British, Chinese, French, Swedes, Dutch, Italians, Jordanians and Iranians, squirrelling away thousands of pages of the stuff. "Take some more," a Pakistani arms technician shouts to me as I scoop cardboard cut-outs of general-purpose bombs and ship-borne missiles into my bag. And back in my tiny hotel room, I rifle through the lot.

The Russians are the mildest in their language. "You will feel protected by our smart weapons' shield," promises Russia's KEP Instrument Design Bureau. Uralvagoncavod's latest T-90 tank—the descendant of all those old Warsaw Pact T-55 clunkers—is advertised simply as "the Best." The State Enterprise Ulyanovsk Mechanical Plant's anti-aircraft missiles give an "awesome punch" to their buyers. The British are smoother. Vickers Defence Systems are trying to flog the new Challenger 2E, "optimised to represent the best balance of fightability, firepower and mobility . . . its ability to deliver combat effectiveness . . . has been proven . . ." Well yes, I recall. The earlier Challenger 2 was used by our chaps in the Gulf. And the Challengers fired, I remember, depleted uranium munitions. "Proven" indeed.

Australian Defence Industries—by a bizarre arms globalisation, they are now part of the French manufacturer Thales—are selling a "live fire defence training system" which includes "a ruggedised portable unit." This is taken right to the battlefield so that soldiers can practise shooting computerised human beings in between killing real ones. "Target movers"—a real favourite of mine, these—were "able to respond to programmable functions, including 'appear on command' . . . 'fall when hit,' 'reappear after hit,' 'hold up to accept and count automatic fire' and 'bob'"—to "cycle up and down as desired until hit." A huge Australian later demonstrates this fearful little toy for me. The computerised dead on the screen are obliging. They really do pop up when I ask them to. I kill them. Then they are resurrected so that I can shoot them again and again, cycling up and down as desired.

The Italians like their verbal trumpets. Beretta firearms provide "quality without compromise," "experience, innovation, respect for tradition . . . the Beretta tradition of excellence." The compact size and "potent calibres" of Beretta's new 9000 S-TYPE F pistols are "developed to deserve your trust." Benelli, which like Beretta makes hunting guns, promotes its animal killer as "black, aggressive, highly technological." Benelli's pump-action shotgun is described as "gutsy in character." Finland's Sako 75 hunting gun manufacturers boast that their designers have been asked a simple question: "What would you do if given the resources to design the rifle of your dreams, the new ultimate rifle for the new millennium?" And later, of course, just a few months later, I will look at this question again and wonder what Osama bin Laden would have said—or did say—if or when he was asked to design the weapon of his dreams, the new ultimate weapon for the new millennium.

"Excellence" crops up again and again in the brochures. Oshkosh of Wilmington manufactures military trucks with "a tradition of excellence," the company's produce "grounded in history, focused on another century . . ." Then comes Boeing's Apache Longbow attack helicopter. "It's easy to talk about performance," their ad runs. "Only Apache Longbow delivers." The European Aeronautic Defence and Space Company are among the few to let the cat out of the bag. "True respect," their advertising brags, "can only be earned by making superior weapons systems. Only by owning them."

In 1905, Shaw's Andrew Undershaft said exactly that. Asked whether he would choose honour, justice, truth, love and mercy, or money and gunpowder, Undershaft replies: "Money and gunpowder; for without enough of both, you cannot afford the others." After a while, I begin to feel a little sick. There is something infinitely sad and impotent about the frightful language of the merchants of death, their circumlocutions and macho words balanced by the qualities the weapons are designed to eliminate, their admission that guns mean power, the final definition of "excellence." But worse is to come.

Bofors (from peace-loving, Nobel-awarding Sweden) is a "provider of technologies for a safer future . . . reliable and innovative." Pakistan Ordnance Factories make ammunition "chiselled to perfection." Mowag (from peace-loving, cuckoo-clock Switzerland) manufactures a Piranha III armoured personnel carrier with a "family concept for many mission role variants." But Lockheed Martin of Dallas scoops them all with a "winning portfolio" of missiles and bombers; the "timeless" F-16 Fighting Falcon fighter; new target-acquisition systems that are "the brains and brawn" of Lockheed's Apache helicopters; the F-22 Raptor, "a new breed of superfighter" that will "dominate the skies" and bring "unequalled capability" to U.S. fighter pilots; the Javelin "fire-and-forget" missile that will give "maximum gunner survivability"; and the new multiple-launch rocket system that the Iraqis, in their terror, called "steel rain" in 1991—Lockheed actually quotes the Iraqis—and which gives its users a "shoot and scoot" capability. "Shoot and scoot" was General Norman Schwarzkopf's sneering description of the supposedly cowardly Iraqi Scud missile gunners—no reminder of that here.

And so the glossy magazines pile up on my bedroom floor. It is a linguistic journey into a fantasy world. Half the words used by the arms-sellers—protection, reliability, optimisation, excellence, family, history, respect, trust, timelessness and perfection—invoked human virtues, even the achievements of the spirit. The other half—punch, gutsy, performance, experience, potency, fightability, brawn and breed—were words of naked aggression, a hopelessly infantile male sexuality to prove that might is right. The Americans named their weapons—the Apache helicopter, the Arrowhead navigation system, the Kiowa multiple launch platform, the Hawkeye infrared sensors—after a Native American population that their nation had laid waste. Or the Western manufacturers called them raptors or piranhas. The only thing they didn't mention was death.

Perhaps amnesia has something to do with it. At an arms fair in Dubai on 12 November 1993, I spent three hours watching guests—European ladies in gowns and miniskirts along with government agents and Arab potentates—passing the Hughes missile stand where a photograph showed an American

Ticonderoga-class warship firing a missile into the sky. It was an identical missile, fired by a Ticonderoga-class anti-air warfare cruiser equipped with a "combat-proven" Aegis "battle management" system—the USS *Vincennes*, equipped with that very same Aegis system—that brought down the Iranian Airbus on 3 July 1988, killing all 290 passengers and crew. No mention of that at the pavilion, of course. I still have my notes of my brief conversation at the stand with Bruce Fields of Hughes International Programme Development. "Yes, it was one of our standard missiles," he said. "I didn't want them to use any photographs of a Ticonderoga-class ship in our publicity this week. It was only when I got here that I saw this picture on our wall. Fortunately, we're not passing it out with our publicity." I watched a trail of smiling dignitaries, thoughtful Arab defence ministry officials and U.S. defence attachés inspecting the hardware, and finally—threading his way between British fighter-bombers and Royal Navy missiles—our very own Charles, Prince of Wales.

There were flowers everywhere, as if this were a wedding rather than an arms bazaar. Roses, lilies, birds of paradise, chrysanthemums, all potted neatly between the missiles. But the brightest flower to be seen in Dubai was as artificial as it was ironic; the blood-red poppy of Flanders. Did the captains of British aviation industry, the British ambassador and consuls—did Prince Charles himself, who wore a poppy on the lapel of his grey suit—grasp this paradox?

> *In Flanders fields the poppies blow*
> *Between the crosses, row on row,*
> *That mark our place . . .*

When he wrote those lines during the second battle of Ypres in 1915, the Canadian doctor John McCrae could not have known the use to which those Flanders poppies would be put more than seventy years later. For a week in Dubai that November of 1993, those red poppies could be seen dancing on the breasts of men as they admired the latest in "Combat Support Weapons," Apaches, Pumas, Harriers, Lynxes, F-18s and the new Mirage 2000.

Even the Honoured Dead didn't get a look in at Abu Dhabi eight years later. Save for that brief, fearful mention of "steel rain," the extinction of life did not exist. Talk about "kill factors" referred only to the killing of machines, of tanks and ships. Even "war" is a banned word. It's defence. As in Ministry of Defence. As in "International Defence Exhibition" (Idex), which is what the whole Abu Dhabi jamboree was called. There was one odd moment when, at the arms fair's opening press conference in the compound, I asked Sultan Suwaidi, the Idex director, why the United Arab Emirates—a peaceful, small but wealthy Muslim country—was running an arms bazaar for weapons that might be used to kill fellow Muslims. There was a long, meaningful pause, during which Sultan Suwaidi looked intently at me. "These equipments are not in any way the creators of wars or the decision-makers of the wars," he said. "It is the strategy of countries which decide whether to use these equipments against Muslims or others. In no way are we here provoking or supporting wars or offensive actions . . . We are a peaceful country. Our boss [the ruler of the Emirates] is known as one of the most peaceful leaders in the world."

And when I went off to talk to the men who were in Abu Dhabi to turn a dollar on all these "equipments," they were as innocent, as squeaky clean, as nice a bunch of middle-class family men as you could meet. You have to be polite, of course. They know all the arguments. Some of them have seen *Major Barbara* and smile bleakly when I mention Andrew Undershaft. At the Vickers pavilion stands Derek Turnbull from Blyth in Northumberland, watching a scale model of the Challenger 2E tank moving eternally round and round on a plastic stand. Ask him if he ever thinks about what all these weapons do to human beings and his response is immediate. "Anyone who says 'no' is a liar. Any civilised person who works in this business knows what the purposes are. But we're more hidebound that anyone else. Large exports like this are strictly controlled by the British government. If we sat down with a map of the world in front of us and blanked out the countries we can't sell to, there's not much left . . ." The British government—and Vickers and Mr. Turnbull—was, it seems, following the advice of Shaw's Lady Britomart, to "sell cannons and weapons to people whose cause is right and just, and refuse them to foreigners and criminals."

But then Mr. Turnbull added a strange remark. "You have to remember that a tank is to kill tanks, not people," he said. "That's the purpose of it." Now Derek Turnbull is an intelligent as well as a friendly man. Is he really satisfied with a comment like that? Aren't there humans—some mothers' sons—inside the tank when it is "killed"? Does he really think they survive when a British shell chews its way through the armour? Turnbull has two children: Stephen, who is sixteen and studying sound engineering, and fourteen-year-old Craig, "who would probably make a good journalist." And Blyth, where the Turnbulls have their home, is by chance the town in which I first worked as a reporter—for the *Newcastle Evening Chronicle*—and where I first saw the body of a murder victim, shot dead by a friend, so far as I remember, with a German or Italian pistol.

Turnbull thinks about my question for a bit. He talks about the detachment that comes with military information technology. "Everyone comes to terms with it in their own way," he says. "Most people talk about the engineering and the technology. It is mentioned from time to time." The "it," of course, is the infliction of death; although at no point does he use the word. Then it turns out that he was in Saudi Arabia for Vickers during the 1991 Gulf War, and that although he was not a soldier, he arrived at the infamous "Road of Death" south of Basra within two days of the mass slaughter of fleeing Iraqis by American and British pilots, looking down upon the killing fields—in which fleeing women also died—from the Mutla Ridge.

Turnbull is thoughtful when he talks about this, reflecting upon his own reactions at the time, an armaments man looking at the end result of all his technology. "It was horrendous. But in a funny sort of way, I didn't have the reaction I'd expected. You see, we'd driven up through Kuwait, and we'd driven through all the oil wells that had been set alight by the Iraqis. It was the most awful thing I'd ever seen. And by the time I'd gone through all this awful devastation, I wasn't too shocked by the damage at Mutla." We were silent for a while. The damage at Mutla was human as well as material. I remembered the Iraqi soldier I found squashed flat in the sand, his whole body just an inch thick. The burning oilfields were awesome; but human death was surely something different. Turnbull—and it must be said that he seemed to enjoy my questions—then turned into the archetypal arms salesman. "Look, Robert," he said. "If the world was full of nice human beings who did civilised things, we wouldn't need all this kit."

A few feet away—and this shows just how entangled armies and salesmen have become—was a British soldier, thirty-one-year-old tank crewman Sergeant Ashley Franks, a man who had driven, armed and commanded the Challenger but who missed the Gulf War. "I was in Northern Ireland," he admits. "My tank went to the Gulf, but I didn't. Shame, really." But then his little lecture on the Challenger improvements—how Vickers must love this military assistance, I thought— begins to sound like the publicity manuals back in my hotel room. "The 2E has a different, upgraded power-pack; Challenger 2 was 1,200 horse-power but 2E is 1,500 horse-power. For a desert scenario, the extra horse-power is a must. Challenger 2 is lovely if you've never driven 2E. The other enhancement is that when Challenger 2 was in production, we were very limited in our thermal sighting system. Challenger 2E has independent thermal sightings for the gunner. With the battle management system, if one vehicle is laser-targeted, everyone knows that an enemy vehicle is targeting a tank. The battle-group commander also has at his disposal the same system. The beauty of it is that . . . another vehicle can take it [the enemy tank] on . . ." The British army sergeant's language was now so familiar. "Power-pack," "lovely," "enhancement," "independent," "beauty." It was as if Sergeant Franks was trying to sell me a new sports car—which in a sense I suppose he was.

As he talked, the model tank twisted on its plastic axis and I could see, with all the clarity of a defence attaché, the commander of the new 2E pushing through the desert at speed—I'd sat atop a Challenger 2 in Saudi Arabia, doing just that, only days before the Gulf War—and I could understand the confidence of Sergeant Franks and his mates as their tank came under fire. But then I also recalled how Britain sold Chieftain tanks to the Shah of Iran and how, after his overthrow in 1979, the Islamic Republic used those same Chieftains against Iraq; and I could never shake off the vivid memory of climbing inside that Chieftain captured by the Iraqis in 1980, of turning my head to the right to find the skeletal remains of its Iranian gunner sitting in the seat beside me. He might have been Sergeant Franks's age. The British government had approved the Chieftains' sale to Iran. They ended up in the hands of Ayatollah Khomeini's soldiers—and then in Saddam's.

But arms fairs are about buying, not dying. A few metres from Turnbull and Franks, I come across two handsome female Ukrainian army students brandishing their new diplomas in front of some nonplussed Arabs. Maria Verenis and Julia Bartashova were the very model of a modern major publicity campaign—Ukraine was selling tanks—while over in the American pavilion, an even more startling figure was making her way past the Winchester rifle stand. Ramona Doll was advertising body armour in a skin-tight, thigh-clutching steel blouse and trousers, complete with handgun and far too much lipstick. Not the flip side, but the very embodiment of all that macho rubbish in the missile brochures.

Lieutenant General Mustafa Tlass would have appreciated her. I discovered Syria's long-standing minister of defence being escorted around the Jordanian military pavilion by young King Abdullah of Jordan, the son of Britain's late friend (and British arms purchaser), Plucky Little King Hussein. Tlass, peering into armoured vehicles and guns with still a bit of room left on his tunic for more medals, once declared his love for Gina Lollobrigida and wrote a poem in her honour. If only his soldiers on parade, he wrote to her in verse, could hold missiles that turned into tulips of love. But Syria's SAM-6 missiles gathered rust and went the way of all munitions. The Americans drained their old M-48 tanks of oil and dumped them into the sea off Florida to form a coral reef. The Czechs used their T-55 tank barrels to make lamp-posts. Undershaft's Salvation Army daughter Barbara would have approved.

But the weapon that had long haunted my imagination—and that will come to be the villain of this chapter—is called Hellfire, an anti-armour weapon used for years by the Israelis in Lebanon and, more recently, in the occupied West Bank and Gaza. It was a Hellfire I, fired by an American-made Israeli Apache, which was targeted into a Lebanese ambulance in 1996, killing four children and two women on board. It was the remains of the improved Hellfire II that I found in a partially destroyed civilian home in the Christian village of Beit Jalla in the Israeli-occupied West Bank the previous November, fired at Palestinians by the Israelis after Palestinian gunmen shot at the Jewish settlement of Gilo—partly built on land seized from the Palestinians of Beit Jalla. The Hellfire occupied pride of place on the Lockheed Martin stand and sixty-nine-year-old Vice President John Hurst was its expert. He said he hadn't heard about the ambulance. Nor the houses of Beit Jalla. Lockheed's top men in Israel, it turned out, were sometimes Israelis. Nettie Johnson—who admitted her company had omitted Israel from its clients in the official list handed out to the Arabs in Abu Dhabi—expressed her unease at all the talk about Israel.

But about Hellfire, John Hurst sounded like a proud father. Rockwell had won the competition for the Hellfire air-to-ground missile in the Seventies but Hughes beat them on the Maverick programme. There was a whole history of the Hellfire, its succession to the TOW, Lockheed Martin's development of a low-cost laser-seeker, the F-model ("a quick fix for reactive armour"), joint production between Lockheed (80 per cent) and Boeing (20 per cent) and now Lockheed's 100 per cent production and the sale of Hellfire II to Israel, Saudi Arabia, the Emirates, Egypt . . . The U.S. government had to approve the buyer. This is history as arms manufacturers like to tell it, stripped of politics and death, full of percentages and development costs and deals.

But Hurst had read *Major Barbara*—he mentioned Undershaft's name before I did—and when I insisted on talking about the morality (or immorality) of his work, he had a "mission statement" all his own. On reflection, I think it was a creed. He wanted me to understand. "I've had great debates," he said. "On a religious basis, too. Before this, I was the development director of Pershing II. I had the responsibility of selling Pershing II to the U.S. forces as well as other countries such as Germany which bought Pershing 1A." He pauses here to see if I understand the implications; selling Pershing was selling nuclear war. There was a moral code, Hurst said. It was about "arming other countries to fight their own wars rather than sending our own soldiers to do it for them."

But he wanted to go further than that; so I sat in the Lockheed pavilion as John Hurst, forty-five years with Lockheed, outshafted Undershaft. "From a religious point of view, I'm a very strong Christian. I'm Episcopalian. You can look through the entire New Testament and you won't find anything on defending yourself by zapping the other guy." Yes, he acknowledged, there was a reference in Saint Paul to putting on "the armour of God." But the Old Testament, that was something different. "There's plenty there that says God wants us to defend ourselves against those that will strike us down. In the New Testament, it says the Lord wants us to preach His gospel—and we can't very well do that if we're dead. That's not an aggressive posture . . . the guy that wants to hurt me has to think twice . . . the Lord wants us to defend ourselves and arm ourselves so that we can spread His Word."

This sounded less like morality than the Crusades, the exegesis of an armed missionary. Yes, Hurst is a family man, married to Letitia with four kids. His first son, John, quit his job at Marriott hotels, fell in love with a Budapest girl and married her; William is a marketing manager for Marriott in Orlando with two daughters; Byron is working on navy programmes for a consultancy company in Washington, D.C.; Carol is a schoolteacher with kids of her own. And of course I ask again. Children? Weapons? Death? "You have to think it through," Hurst replies. "I knew people in the Pershing programme who quit the company. They couldn't even think about nuclear warfare. You have to look at it from a strategic planner's point of view—better Pershings in your backyard than an SS-20 on your roof. That's what Alexander Haig said back then. And the Russians didn't fire their SS-20s."

But death? I ask again. Death? "Right or wrong, I never associate it with what I'm doing. If I see a bomb go off and legs flying off, I never say to myself, 'I could have been the cause of that.' Because we're trying to prevent that. Sometimes some 'wacko' wants to torch something . . . When a guy like [Saddam] Hussein pulls the plug like that, we have no recourse . . . [we say] 'Here's what happens when you do that—don't do it again!' "

But while the armourers peddled the linguistics of power, beauty, excellence, protection, reliability, potency and brawn, the gospel preached at Abu Dhabi had nothing to do with John Hurst's god. It was ultimately about fear and threats: the fear of Iraq and Iran, the threat of Saddamite aggression, the constant, reiterated warnings that these gentle, soft, sandy, unspeakably wealthy Arab Gulf oil states must arm and rearm to defend themselves against chemical, biological or nuclear attack. This grim and entirely false scenario, of course, was to become wearily familiar eighteen months later when President Bush and Prime Minister Blair used exactly the same demons to propel us to war. But in Abu Dhabi in March 2001 they were introduced for entirely commercial gain: to terrify "our friends" in the Gulf, to persuade them that only by purchasing billions of dollars of weaponry could they be safe. In retrospect, these tactics were a dress rehearsal for the reuse of the same inaccurate material to justify our invasion of Iraq in 2003.

How this gospel was defined—and preached—was all too evident in the large, air-conditioned hall on the other side of the arms bazaar. The "Gulf Defence Conference" was the place to learn about threats. On the very first day, there was Neil Patrick of the Royal United Services Institute, lecturing his audience about "countries of concern in the Gulf." We heard all about Iran's medium-range ballistic missile capability, Iraq's potential capability to reconstruct mobile missile-launchers. "So what happens . . . when Iran goes nuclear?" the Arabs were asked.

Mr. Patrick's offerings were hedged with conditional clauses. But the message was clear enough. "The important thing is building a coalition with Gulf Arabs . . . building a coalition with the Americans and the European allies . . ." Osama bin Laden—"not by any means a one-man operator"—was a threat, along with criminals in the former Soviet Union and Russia's possible transfer of high-tech weaponry to Iran.* Across the Abu Dhabi arms bazaar, the warnings were pursued more crudely. At the British Aerospace stand ("BAE Systems provide you with the total package, tailored to your needs"), a massive video-production demonstrated how British military know-how could end a border dispute. The warring parties in this absurd film were "Orange" (the aggressor) and "Blue" (the victim), whose territory—and here was the clue—contained "oil and gas reserves in the border area." Which of course meant Kuwait and Saudi Arabia and Bahrain and the Emirates. The only power sharing a common border with Kuwait and Saudi Arabia was Iraq. So colour Saddam orange. Handed out to Arab visitors to the fair, Western military journals carried a parallel theme. "Now is the time for the Persian Gulf States to get serious about their collective security," thundered Gannett's *Defense News* of Springfield, Virginia. Threats to the area "underscore the importance of bolstering defensive systems across the Middle East's soft underbelly, the Arabian peninsula . . . in the absence of greater cooperation, their security situation grows more tenuous by the day."

In vain did the Kuwait deputy chief of staff, Major General Fahad Ahmad al-Amir, tell delegates that Israel remained a threat to the Arabs, that "the security sit-

---

*Only six months before the attacks on the United States, it is fascinating to see that bin Laden was regarded as a secondary threat, lumped in with Russian criminals and nuclear expertise from the former Soviet Union. Saddam's regime—which had no weapons of mass destruction at all—was still touted as the greatest danger. Once Afghanistan was bombarded and Osama had escaped, the same scenario was reintroduced by Messrs. Bush and Blair in 2002. But then again, Osama bin Laden's existence was not likely to generate the obscene profits in weapons sales procured at Abu Dhabi and other arms fairs in the Middle East.

uation in the Gulf and the security situation in the Arab–Israeli conflict are linked." Hopeless was his plea that "if we want to create a paradigm of peace in the Gulf region, we must have a paradigm of peace in Palestine." Pointless was his warning that the fate of Jerusalem lay close to every Arab heart. The Emirates arms bazaar organisers had ignored the faxed appeals from Israeli arms manufacturers to exhibit in Abu Dhabi. But free copies of *Jane's Intelligence Review* handed out to the arms boys contained an article with all the usual myths about the Arab–Israeli dispute. The illegal Jewish settlement built on Arab land at Har Homa was referred to only as a "disputed . . . project" (its Arab name of Jebel abu Ghoneim was omitted), the occupied Palestinian West Bank was given its Israeli name of Judaea and Samaria, while the latest death toll of 450 in the latest intifada failed to add that the vast majority of these victims were Palestinian Arabs. The article was written by David Eshel, a "defence analyst" who just happened to be a former Israeli army officer.

Yes, what was being preached at Abu Dhabi was the new George W. Bush doctrine: the threat comes from war criminal Saddam Hussein, not from peace-loving Israel. The Arabs need to defend themselves—quickly; a policy that necessitates the wholesale milking of the Arab Gulf's wealth, the Arab squandering of billions of dollars on Western arms to protect the Gulf from the wreckage of Iraq and the chaos of Iran. The statistics told it all. In 1998 and 1999 alone, Gulf Arab military spending came to $92 billion. Since 1997, the Emirates alone had signed contracts worth more than $11 billion, adding 112 aircraft to their arsenal, comprising 80 F-16s from Lockheed Martin and 32 French Mirage 2000-9s. The figures are staggering, revolting. Between 1991 and 1993, the United States Military Training Mission was administering more than $31 billion in Saudi arms procurements from Washington and $27 billion in new U.S. acquisitions. The Saudi air force already possessed 72 American F-15 fighter-bombers, 114 British Tornadoes, 80 F-5s and 167 Boeing F-15s. At Idex, 800 exhibitors from forty-two countries displayed their weapons. The Russian military pavilion contained fifty Russian military enterprises selling tanks, armoured vehicles, surface-to-air missiles and warships. Incredibly, Philippe Roger, the French armament directorate's international relations director, announced in Abu Dhabi that "while [Gulf] governments could consider using the higher receipts [from oil] for servicing their debt, we believe that higher allocations could go for defence-related spending . . ."

And if the Arab people—as opposed to their rulers—objected to this insanity, there was even available, at the arms bazaar, the means to end their protest. South Africa's Swartklip Products was advertising smoke generators for "large scale clearance operations," a 37-mm baton round that "neutralises a rioter by delivering a hefty, non-lethal punch," a smoke round to fire into buildings, and a 12-gauge shotgun baton to provide an "accurate means of disabling selected activists."

In despair, I walked to the Russian pavilion. And it was here that I met him. Indeed, I could scarcely believe that a name so notorious in all the world's wars and atrocities, so redolent of insurgency and revolution, so frequently used in battle dispatches that the very word has become a cliché of war reporting, really bore corporeal form—other than that of the AK-47, the most famous rifle in the world. This was the rifle I had seen in Lebanon, Palestine, Syria, Iraq, Egypt, Libya, Algeria, Armenia, Azerbaijan, Bosnia, Serbia. This was the rifle I had held in my hands on that frozen Soviet army convoy to Kabul when we came under attack from the Afghan mujahedin twenty-one years ago. It was a sign of Russian times that to sell their tanks and MiGs, they had enlisted the help of the eighty-one-year-old inventor of that most iconic of weapons and freighted him all the way here to Abu Dhabi.

I found him sitting in a small room, Mikhail Kalashnikov himself, a small, squat man with grey, coiffed hair and quite a few gold teeth, hands unsteady but Siberian eyes alert as a wolf, still wearing his two Hero of Socialist Labour medals. "Hasn't it ever occurred to you that you should change your faith?" a Saudi army major had asked him a few years earlier. "By Christian standards, you are a great sinner. You are responsible for thousands, even tens of thousands, of deaths around the globe. They've long prepared a place for you in hell." But, said the major, Kalashnikov was a true Muslim. "And when the time of your earthly existence is over, Allah will welcome you as a hero . . . Allah's mercy is limitless."

At least, that's how Mikhail Kalashnikov tells the story. And he is at least one of the very few arms-sellers to have experienced war. Born in November 1919, he was one of eighteen children of whom only six survived, a Soviet T-38 tank commander in 1941, wounded in the shoulder and back when a German shell smashed part of the tank's armour into his body. "I was in hospital and a soldier in the bed beside me asked: 'Why do our soldiers have only one rifle for two or three of our men when the Germans have automatics?' So I designed one. I was a soldier and I created a machine gun for a soldier. It was called an Automat Kalashnikova—the automatic weapon of Kalashnikov—AK—and it carried the date of its first manufacture, 1947."

The AK-47, the battle rifle of the Warsaw Pact, became the symbol of revolution—Palestinian, Angolan, Vietnamese, Algerian, Afghan, Hizballah. And I asked old Mikhail Kalashnikov how he could justify all this blood, all those corpses torn to bits by his invention. He had been asked before. "You see, all these feelings come about because one side wants to liberate itself with arms. But in my opinion it is good that prevails. You may live to see the day when good prevails—it will be after I am dead. But the time will come when my weapons will be no more used or necessary."

This was incredible, preposterous. The AK-47 has mythic status. Kalashnikov admits this. "When I met the Mozambique minister of defence, he presented me with his country's national banner which carries the image of a Kalashnikov submachine gun. And he told me that when all the liberation soldiers went home to their villages, they named their sons 'Kalash.' I think this is an honour, not just a military success. It's a success in life when people are named after me, after Mikhail Kalashnikov." Even the Lebanese Hizballah have included the AK-47 on their Islamic banner—the rifle forms the "l" of "Allah" in the Arabic script. There was no point in asking the old man what his children thought of him. His fifty-seven-year-old son Viktor is a small-arms designer and was part of the Russian delegation to Abu Dhabi.

So we embarked down the Russian version of a familiar moral track. "My aim was to protect the borders of my motherland," Kalashnikov tells me. "It is not my fault that the Kalashnikov became very well known in the world, that it was used in many troubled places. I think the policies of these countries are to blame, not the weapons designers. Man is born to protect his family, his children, his wife. But I want you to know that apart from armaments, I have written three books in which I try to educate our youth to show respect for their families, for old people, for history . . ."

He was now in nostalgic mode. "I lived at a time when we all wanted to be of benefit to our [Soviet] state. To some extent, the state took care of its heroes and designers . . . In the village where I was born, according to a special decree, a monument was erected to me, twice my height. In the city of Ishevsk where I live, there is now a Kalashnikov museum with a section dedicated to my life—and this was erected in my lifetime!" No, Mikhail Kalashnikov tells me, he is not rich, he has little money. "I would have made good use of this money if I had it. But there are some qualities which may be more important. President Putin called me on my birthday the other day. No other president would telephone an arms designer. And these things are very important for me." And God? I asked. What would God say of Mikhail Kalashnikov? "We were educated in such a way that I am probably an atheist," he replied. "But something exists . . ."

There was only one other place to seek an answer. I walked over to a small stand hidden away in the corner of one of the farthest pavilions, where brown-painted models of mobile-launched rockets lay on a shelf. This was the Iranian arms bazaar. Their missiles were called "Dawn" or "Morning Sunrise," although one caught my eye, a big V-2-look-alike 125-kilometre-range monster produced by the S. B. Industrial Group of Tehran, called the *Nazeat*. It's a Persian word meaning "Horror of Death." Yes, Iran—the only nation in all of the world's arms market to tell the true purpose of a weapon—had actually named a missile after the extinction of life. Did the answer to all my questions, I wondered, lie here?

These missiles were not for sale, I was solemnly informed by Morteza Khosravi. They were only to show Iran's "capabilities"—although in the year 2000, Iran had sold $31 million worth of "defence" products to Asia and Africa. Khosravi, a young man from the Iranian Ministry of Defence with a small beard and an intense expression and a family that lost its own "martyrs" in the 1980–88 Iran–Iraq War, explained carefully—he took half a minute to reflect on each question before replying—that "the defence equipment in our production lines belongs to all Islamic nations—we are here to establish a joint cooperation with them." But, he swiftly added, Iran sold only according to strict rules, under the UN's Export Control Act. Once more, Lady Britomart had come to the rescue. In any case, more than 60 per cent of Iran's military capacity had been switched to civilian production.

I knew all this. What I wanted to hear about was the immorality of arms production. Morteza Khosravi seemed puzzled. Was it not perfectly clear? "There are two main purposes for the production of weapons," he said. "Some provide them for aggression, others for self-defence. The latter is the case for our country; we produce weapons only for self-defence and for the protective policy of our government. We have had a peaceful state but others have invaded us—we had the eight years 'Imposed War.' The only policy of our troops at that time was to defend their borders and their country. We always had a policy of defending ourselves." There was another long pause. Then Khosravi uttered the mantra of every arms-seller. "It is a fact that each human being must defend himself."

I had heard this from Derek Turnbull, from Mikhail Kalashnikov, from John Hurst. If only the world was full of nice human beings who did civilised things. The Lord wants us to defend ourselves. Man is born to protect his family. Protection, respect, trust, history, timelessness. It seemed useless to listen to these words any more. They were unstoppable, unarguable, impossible. Now thrive the armourers indeed. The merchants of death sell death in the form of protection, killing as defence, as God's will, human destiny, patriotic duty. The bills—human and financial—come later. And we poor humans are the "target movers," frightened folk to fleece with talk of threats and aggression. The threat is inside ourselves, of course, as we travel through the world. It is our task to "cycle up and down as desired until hit."


THUS FEEL THE PALESTINIANS. Scarcely a month after my conversation with John Hurst, I was in Bethlehem in the Israeli-occupied West Bank, where Lockheed Martin of Florida and the Federal Laboratories of Pennsylvania had made quite a contribution to life in the local municipality. Or—in the case of Lockheed—death. I found that pieces of Hellfire missile were stored in sacks in the civil defence headquarters as evidence of eighteen-year-old Osama Khorabi's violent death. The Hellfire had exploded in his living room, killing him instantly, less than two months earlier. The missile engine, fuel pipe and shreds of the wiring system had been sorted into plastic bags by ambulance-drivers and paramedics, alongside shrapnel from dozens of U.S.-made fuses for shells fired by Israeli tanks into Beit Jalla, in the attack on the Palestinian Christian village that Jim Hurst said he hadn't heard about. The Palestinians could read the evidence of the weapons' American origin but were unable to identify the actual missiles and shells that were used. "We are humanitarian workers," one of the ambulance-drivers said to me one rainy Saturday morning as I trawled through a bag of iron missile parts and shrapnel in his Bethlehem office. "We are not scientists."

The use of American armaments against Arabs by Israel has been one of the most provocative sources of anger in the Middle East, and the narrative of their use is almost as important as the political conflict between Israel and its enemies. For it is one thing to know that Washington claims to be a "neutral partner" in Middle East peace negotiations while supporting one side—Israel—in all its demands; it is quite another when the armaments Israel employs to enforce its will—weapons that kill and tear apart Arabs—carry the engraved evidence of their manufacture in the United States. Even the CS gas cartridges fired by Israelis at Palestinians in Bethlehem are American-made. Palestinians claimed—with good reason—that the gas has caused serious breathing difficulties among children after the rounds were fired at stone-throwing children near Rachel's tomb. The cartridges and gas canisters are labelled "Federal Laboratories, Saltsburg, Pennsylvania 15681" and are stated on the metal to be "long range projectiles 150 yards." The rounds, according to the U.S. manufacturers' instructions I read on the side, contain "tear gas which is highly irritating to eyes, nose, skin and respiratory system . . . If exposed, do not rub eyes, seek medical assistance immediately."*

Throughout early 2001, Israeli tank crews routinely aimed shells at Beit Jalla when Palestinian gunmen fired Kalashnikov rifles—yes, the invention of cheerful eighty-one-year-old Hero of Socialist Labour Mikhail Kalashnikov—from the village of Beit Jalla at the neighbouring Jewish settlement of Gilo, and most of these tank rounds carried U.S. fuses. All were coded: "FUZE P18D M549ACo914H014 014" (in some cases the last digit read "5"). One of these shells killed Dr. Harald Fischer, a German citizen living in Beit Jalla, in November 2000.

The engine of the Lockheed Hellfire missile that struck Osama Khorabi's home in February 2001 carried the coding "189 761334987 DMW90E003007" and its "Lot" number—the batch of missiles from which it came—was 481. On a small steel tube at the top of the missile engine was written the code "12903 9225158 MFR-5S443." A small, heavy, cylindrical dome which appears to come from the same projectile was labelled "Battery Thermal" and carried the code "P/N 10217556 E-W62, Lot No. EPH-2111, Date of MFR [manufacture] 08776, MFG Code 81855." The codes are followed by the initials "U.S." Other missile parts include damaged fragments of a hinged fin and a mass of wiring. The missile attack, according to the Israelis, was a "pre-emptive strike" against the village, although Mr. Khorabi was no militant and his only ambition was to join the Beit Jalla theatre project. The Israelis used Apache helicopters to fire their missiles into Beit Jalla on at least six occasions—including the one on which Mr. Khorabi was killed—and the Apaches are made by Lockheed at their massive arms plant at Orlando, Florida, home of the Hellfire I and II missiles. U.S. manufacturers routinely refuse to accept any blame for the bloody consequences of their weapons' use. I found that the Pennsylvania gas cartridges used by the Israelis in Bethlehem actually carried an official disclaimer. "Federal Laboratories," it said on the cartridge, "will assume no responsibility for the misuse of this device."

The world arms market, immoral and deceitful and murderous as it is, is nonetheless a beast that clamours for both publicity and secrecy. It needs to sell

---

*Palestinians were still trying to discover the nature of a gas canister now regularly used by Israelis, containing what they called "brown smoke." Obviously feared by Palestinian protesters, it was described as having a far more potent effect even than the Federal Laboratories Pennsylvania-made gas. At least one "brown smoke" gas canister which I examined in Bethlehem was covered in Hebrew markings and carried the code 323 1-99. It did not appear to be of U.S. manufacture.

just as much as it needs to conceal, to make its billions from the Arabs while at the same time avoiding any mention of the blood and brains that will be splashed upon the sand as a result. The French arms conglomerates Giat and Dassault, along with Lockheed Martin, all have local headquarters in gleaming office blocks in Abu Dhabi. And the middlemen—the Arabs and Israelis and Germans and Americans and Britons who negotiate between manufacturers and buyers—also have a strange inclination to court the press, to reveal their more sinister characteristics, to boast of their ruthlessness, of their necessity in an immoral world. I sometimes think they want to use journalists as confessionals.

Perhaps for this reason, I have spent years, collectively, investigating the ways in which we—the Americans, the Europeans (including the Russians), the "West" in the most generous definition of the word—have produced the instruments of death for those who live in the Middle East. Never once did we reflect upon how Arab Muslims might respond to this extraordinary, wicked trade in arms, how they might attempt to revenge themselves upon us—not in their own lands but in ours. During the Lebanese civil war, I tried hard to connect the victim with the killer, sometimes travelling across Beirut to seek out the sniper or the gunner who had blown a man or woman to pieces. Once, in East Beirut, I confronted the Christian Phalangist militiaman who, I am sure, fired the mortar shell that killed a young woman in a West Beirut street. He refused to talk to me. So I searched for the arms-dealers who made these killings possible. More than anything, I sought to confront the arms-makers with the total and inescapable proof that their particular weapon had slaughtered the innocent. It was a journey that was to take me tens of thousands of kilometres over ten years—to the Gulf, Iran, Palestine, Israel, to Germany, Austria and to the United States. It was a woeful, depressing assignment, for the more I learned, the more profoundly hopeless did the Middle East's tragedy appear to be. To have venal Western nations peddling their lethal products to the Muslim world and Israel was one thing; to watch those same Middle East nations pleading and whining and squandering their wealth to purchase those same weapons, quite another.

One cold late winter's day in 1987, as Iran's terrible war with Iraq was entering its final, most apocalyptic stage, I arrived at the railway station at Cologne in Germany to meet a dealer who knew far too much about that most costly of Middle East conflicts. He was a plump, bespectacled arms-merchant who had many times acted as a conduit between the U.S. government and Saddam Hussein's regime in Iraq. He sat in his office with a broad smile, insisting that he must remain anonymous lest I wished to be responsible for his assassination. So was it true, I asked him, that he had given the CIA's intelligence on the Iranian army to the Iraqi government? He laughed—so long, so deeply, perhaps for more than thirty seconds—before he admitted all. "Mr. Fisk, I will tell you this. At the very beginning of the war, in September of 1980, I was invited to go to the Pentagon. And there I was handed the very latest U.S. satellite photographs of the Iranian front lines. You could see everything on the pictures. There were the Iranian gun emplacements in Abadan and behind Khorramshahr, the lines of trenches on the eastern side of the Karun River, the tank revetments—thousands of them—all the way up the Iranian side of the border towards Kurdistan. No army could want more than this. And I travelled with these maps from Washington by air to Frankfurt and from Frankfurt on Iraqi Airways straight to Baghdad. The Iraqis were very grateful—*very* grateful!"

The Germans seem to have a penchant for playing these treacherous games. For months in the mid- to late Eighties, I investigated the Middle East arms trade and often I found myself back in that place of Europe's dark past, trailing through snow-covered valleys in Germany's great trains, my bag stuffed with notebooks and files containing Iran's entire weapons procurement demands for 1987, 1988 and beyond—into uncounted years of warfare against Iraq that would be foreshortened in just twelve months" time.

In the frost of 1987, one of these long trains carries me into Königswinter, a chauffeur with a well-heated limousine waiting for me at the station to take me to the *Schloss* in which the "Spider of Bonn" helps to change the military map of the Middle East. Gerhard Mertins smokes long, fat Cuban cigars and looks like an arms-dealer, a part that is played to perfection because it is real. There are no doubts, no lack of confidence, no moral ambiguities as he walks into the study of his Königswinter office, the snow falling heavily and comfortably outside the window. "I love this kind of weather, don't you?" he asks, brushing the flakes from his jacket.

The telephone rings and Herr Mertins speaks intently into the receiver. "We have to know the needs of your generals," he says impatiently. Then he replaces the receiver with an indulgent chuckle. He makes a great appearance of being candid. "That was the Greek Cypriot army. They are interested in new anti-aircraft guns and mines for their harbours. Mark my words, something is cooking in the island of Cyprus." He laughs again, a man-in-the-know, unshocked by the iniquities of war. When I ask Herr Mertins to whom he sells guns, he almost coughs at the indignity I have cast upon him. "I think, if you will forgive me, that this is a very naive question."

He puffs heavily on his cigar and then moves his arm forward and uses it to describe an elliptical, almost aerobatic circle in front of him. "Let me tell you frankly, I am on the Arab horse. Why not? You know, I have principles. I do not do this for profit. Yes, things are said about me—in Mexico, the paper *Excelsior* said I was a Nazi, an SS man, a friend of Klaus Barbie, the 'Butcher of Lyon.' I have never met this man. But they felt they had to deport me from Mexico." Herr Mertins maintains offices in Jeddah and Riyadh—he needs no visa to travel to Saudi Arabia—and he shows me a snapshot of himself standing next to long-robed Gulf sheikhs. He mourns the old Beirut, the city destroyed in the civil war that is still scissoring Lebanon to pieces, with the special melancholy of the rich. "I have such fond memories of the Lucullus restaurant. It is destroyed? That is too bad. A beautiful city, so sad." Beirut was destroyed by weapons—by bombs and mines and artillery fire and fighter-bombers and bullets—but no hint of this damages Herr Mertins's memories.

He is warming to his theme. "I never in my life made business just to make profit. We have a lot of problems just at the moment—they think I am like Adnan Kashoggi." Iran-Contra dogs the weapons-dealers of Europe, unfairly so in their eyes because America's arms entanglement with Iran was comparatively trivial, a small-scale business deal handled without professional advice or discretion, using dubious Iranian middlemen who real arms suppliers would never invite to their offices, let alone to their homes. The distinction between arms-dealer and middleman is not an easy one to make. In some cases—where the dealer's own country imposes strict rules on weapons exports—the dealer becomes a middleman, passing on procurement lists to dealers in other nations with less scrupulous codes of arms-exporting conduct. When other nationals are brought in as financiers, the system becomes more complicated. When Lieutenant Colonel Oliver North was setting up his arms-for-hostages deal with the Iranians, for example, the middleman was Manucher Ghorbanifar, playing the official role of "Iranian intermediary," who arranged Robert McFarlane's secret visit to Tehran in May 1986. Adnan Kashoggi, a Saudi, was the financier whose cash set the arms transfer into motion. The dealer (and supplier) was in this case the U.S. government—or Colonel North, depending on your point of view.

Dealers like to be close to their national government and Herr Mertins is no different. German cabinet ministers play on his private tennis courts and U.S. customs agents in Bonn refer to him, not entirely sympathetically, as the "Spider of Bonn." In his immaculate works canteen, Mertins is greeted with affection by his employees—a true Andrew Undershaft, although he does not like the comparison—and he is immensely proud of his family, especially his new American daughter-in-law. "Mr. Fisk, you should take tea as it should be taken," he announces at a family lunch in the company canteen. "With rum." He sips for a long time at his *apéritif.* "Why do people say these stupid things about me? You know I have read all the books: the Talmud, the Bible, the Koran . . ." Later he asks rhetorically: "You know the trouble with Germany today? It has lost its nationalist sentiments." I cringe.

Back in 1965, Herr Mertins sprang a surprise on several nations after the outbreak of the India–Pakistan war. The Americans embargoed arms supplies, although John Kenneth Galbraith, the former U.S. ambassador to India, later claimed that American weapons shipments had "caused the war." Herr Mertins is still proud of his role in the affair. He had acted as middleman for the export of ninety American F-86 jet fighters to Pakistan under the guise of sending them to Iran. "We put Iranian transfers on the wings and they flew over Tehran in an air display and I was standing next to the Western ambassadors and I said: 'See, these are the planes you claimed I had sent to Pakistan.' But then the planes flew back to their Iranian air base and we changed their markings back to Pakistan again." Herr Mertins slaps his right fist into his left hand. "You see? A case of pure German plastic science."

But all this is a theatrical prelude to the real and current war. For in his office on this cold German mountainside, Herr Mertins—like his colleagues elsewhere in Germany and Austria—has a very shrewd idea of what is going on in the Iranian

Ministry of Defence. The Iranians had become enamoured of cheap Soviet arms supplies after they signed an agreement with Moscow for the export of Iranian gas. "They bought a lot of Russian stuff—122-mm and 130-mm artillery and 12.7 and 14.5-mm anti-aircraft guns. They tried to get a lot of the same things from China—the Iranians were flying to Peking to discuss this—but China wants to be a 'middle' country. It doesn't want to be up front. Then the Iranian armed forces became unhappy with the material they were getting."

The story of the arms trade to Iran is both complex and fearful—and involves Israel as well as the West. One of Herr Mertins's colleagues, a young man in a smart suit with excellent English, agreed to explain it, albeit anonymously. He brought into Mertins's office a heavy file which he handed to me. I opened the blue-backed folder and there lay thousands of appeals for weapons from the Iranian government, for mortar tubes, gun sleeves, artillery ammunition and spare parts for American-made fighters. "The Russians were selling better equipment to the Iraqis than to the Iranians—and the Iranians knew it," the man said. "That's why the Iranians turned to the Israelis for help. The first Israeli plane to fly to Iran landed in Shiraz with 1,250 TOW missiles at $2,700 each. It was very expensive and it was old material, so the Iranians went to other countries. They were looking for 155-mm guns and approached the Voest-Canonen Company of Austria. They liked the 105-mm and 155-mm artillery that was produced in New York. The U.S. administration—Richard Perle, in fact—stopped this deal. So the Iranians became interested in a Helsinki company that was selling 60-mm, 81-mm and 120-mm mortars.

Mertins regards the whole Iran-Contra scandal with scorn. "It is easy to understand the Iranians," he says. "The Iraqis had Russian MiG-25 'Foxbat' aircraft that were dropping bombs from a high level on Tehran. And it was highly embarrassing for the mullahs in Iran to have nothing which could shoot down the 'Foxbat.' So they needed air-to-air missiles for their F-14s. You have to understand their need and the way in which others will deliver to them—they will deliver to the Devil—no morals, no ethics. As for the Iranians, every Iranian with a letter of credit begins with the words: 'I am a relative of Khomeini.' " The Americans, who used the Israelis for their first arms shipment to Iran, thought they had managed to combine weapons and ethics—were they not, after all, seeking the liberation of innocent U.S. citizens held captive in Lebanon?—although it is instructive to note that the American administration believed, according to the Tower Commission report, that the Iranians needed Hawk ground-to-air missiles to shoot down high-level reconnaissance aircraft being flown by Soviet pilots 65 kilometres into Iranian airspace from Russia. Herr Mertins had no such illusions. The Iranians wanted to shoot down Iraqis.

Yet the Iran-Contra transactions—2,086 TOW anti-tank missiles and a plane-load of F-14 spare parts sold to Iran at a cost of $30 million—only placed in perspective the colossal international arms deals concluded with the public consent or private connivance of America's friends and enemies. In his congressional testimony, McFarlane struggled to hide the identity of a Middle East country which agreed to place its name on an end-user certificate for arms sales. But arms-dealers working out of Germany were in 1987 paying $100,000 for Third World end-user certificates, the documentary "evidence" that is coldly obtained by weapons manufacturers to prove to their own governments that they possess a legal export contract. For somewhere between the international ordnance factories, the bureaucracy of export documentation and the human wound, there is a certain moral—or immoral—ambiguity.* Undershaft boasted that he was not "one of those men who keep their morals and their business in watertight compartments." But diplomats do not share this comfortable sincerity. By 1987, American and Soviet officials were weekly bemoaning the human cost of the Iran–Iraq War as their own weapons continued to flow towards the battlefronts. European governments repeatedly emphasised their neutrality in the conflict, their earnest if unbusinesslike desire to see it speedily and fairly concluded.

But Iran, its military establishment supposedly boycotted by this outraged world, was currently spending $250 million a month on weapons. German and Austrian arms-dealers had no illusions about what this meant. They claimed that this money was spent with the active or passive assistance of the governments of the Soviet Union, China, the United Kingdom, Italy, Spain, Greece, North Korea, South Korea, Taiwan, Pakistan, Dubai, Syria, Libya, Czechoslovakia, East Germany, Japan, Brazil, Argentina, Holland, Israel, Portugal, India and Saudi Arabia. They added Belgium as a "late joiner" to the club, with four shipments of arms from Antwerp to Bandar Abbas in 1986.

As the war entered its final year, the Iranians desperately tried to restructure their procurement effort. They had inherited more than 1,000 helicopters from the Shah, but when the war began only 250 Cobra gunships were operational. By 1987, only 30 of them could still fly. More inventive than the Iraqis, the Iranians tried to improvise, ordering spare parts for American-made helicopters and fighter aircraft—exact copies of the U.S. originals that sanctions prevented Iran from obtaining—from local metalworkers in the bazaars. But there was too much sulphur in Iranian steel and they used the wrong metallurgy; the metal broke up under the strain of powered flight and Iran lost several pilots as their aircraft disintegrated in the air.

The Iranians also possessed detailed lists of foreign arms shipments to Iraq, an equally extraordinary tribute to the mercantile abilities of the world's arms manufacturers. A selection of Iraqi purchases gives something of the flavour of these lists: battle-tank armour from the UK (1983), six Super-Etendard fighter-bombers from France (October 1983), SS-12 missiles from the Soviet Union (May 1984), multiple rocket-launchers from Brazil (June 1984), 500-pound cluster bombs from Chile (flown out of Santiago aboard an Iraqi Airways 747 in 1984). On 25 September 1985, Dassault announced the sale of 24 Mirage F-1 jet fighters to Iraq, the delivery to begin within eighteen months. Some of these weapons systems were

---

*During my investigations, I was given a genuine end-user certificate from the state of Oman in the Gulf, already signed by the authorities. If I had wished to transport arms to the Middle East, I had only to write in the weapons of my choice for the shipment to be "legal."

sold under "existing arms contracts"—Moscow's favourite phrase for a continuation of shipments to a lucrative buyer like Iraq—on the grounds that the credibility
of the vendor nation would be damaged if they reneged on a signed agreement just
because their client had later invaded someone else's country. Other deals carried
that special dog-tag that ensured innocence on the part of the vendor.

In 1986, for example, the British Plessey company agreed to a $388 million
deal to supply radar to Iran, equipment that would—so the British were promised—
be used on Iran's frontier with Russian-occupied Afghanistan and the Soviet
Union. Asked how the British government could be sure that the radar would not be
used on Iran's western front—in military operations against Iraq—an official of the
Ministry of Defence in London told me that "we have diplomats in Tehran who can
go out and check these things." But this was untrue. Britain's diplomatic presence
in Iran was confined to an "interests" section of the Swedish embassy; when I
enquired in Tehran about the freedom of movement of British officials in Iran, I
discovered that the Iranians were so restrictive that they had just refused a senior
diplomat's request to visit the Caspian Sea—a non-military area—for a holiday
weekend.

It was as if there was an understanding in such matters, an unspoken commitment by all sides not to pry into the personal affairs of arms-dealers or their buyers, or into the weapons empire which needs secrecy in order to create demand,
war in order to stimulate growth. The modern-day Undershafts will talk only of
their competitors' markets and mistakes. They will disclose only their rivals' bids.
It is a droll world of paper and procurement lists, forwarded by largely anonymous
officials in ministries of defence—always defence—whose spelling is sometimes
as deplorable as their handwriting.

A ten-page Iranian wartime procurement list handed to Austrian dealers and
subsequently passed on to me demands specific spare parts for Soviet-made tanks,
from grid frames to "third and fourth inversing glued lenses in frame," from telescopic sights to headlights, from range-finders to turret motors. Yet the ordnance
officer spelled "second" as "secound," "circuit-breaker" as "dirduit-breaker," "bottle" as "bottel." It is a shabby document, with the column listing the quantity of
required spare parts mistakenly filled into the unit number column, then crudely
crossed out afterwards.

Broken down into the literal nuts and bolts of weaponry, there is an innocuous
quality about such lists, as if Middle Eastern wars are fought through procurement
agencies or manufacturers rather than by angry nations and frightened killer-
soldiers. During my inquiries, I saw hundreds of such documents emanating from
Iran, sometimes bearing the letterhead of the Iranian Armed Forces Headquarters
in Tehran, at other times—when the broker acting for the Iranians wished to
remain secret—typed anonymously, if imperfectly, on plain paper. In this way,
tank tracks and gun barrels and McDonnell–Douglas spare parts become, quite literally, the liquid assets of big business or a source of international barter; you can
exchange guns for money or oil or military favours—or even hostages. There is
nothing exclusive about this. Long before President Reagan agreed to trade mis-

siles for captives, Syria was funnelling weapons to Iran in return for shipments of cheap and sometimes free oil. Chancellor Helmut Schmidt was only just restrained from selling German tanks to Saudi Arabia under an oil barter deal which, with falling oil prices, would have cost Germany more than it normally paid for oil.

War, too, throws up its own special barters. When in the first months of Saddam Hussein's invasion of Iran in 1980 his forces captured dozens of British-built Chieftain tanks—often undamaged—from their enemy, they not unnaturally wished to reuse them against Iran. But they were unable to operate or maintain such sophisticated armour. So the tanks were transported to Jordan where, officially belonging to the Jordanian armed forces, they were repaired and overhauled by British technicians. At least one British arms manufacturer believes the tanks were then secretly returned to Baghdad for use in the Iraqi war effort, but Israeli military specialists later concluded that they remained in Jordan—as part payment for King Hussein's generosity in allowing Iraq to ship its Soviet weapons supplies through the Jordanian port of Aqaba.

For their part, the British authorities maintain a special discretion about arms sales, dutifully issuing lists of annual military exports under armoured fighting vehicles, tanks, artillery, side-arms, revolvers, bombs and gun barrels. But unlike other export details, the British lists fail to specify to which countries the weapons have been sold. The Department of Trade and Industry refuses to discuss the individual applications of arms companies for export licences.*

In July 1991, four years after my inquiries into the Middle East arms trade began, the same British Department of Trade and Industry was expressing its confidence that there was a "reasonable and legitimate" explanation for export licences—listed in a House of Commons committee report—for the shipment to Iraq of raw materials for chemical weapons. The exports—some of which continued until 5 August 1990, three days after Saddam Hussein had invaded yet another Muslim nation, Kuwait—included two chemicals which, mixed together, formed mustard gas. During Iraq's war with Iran, Britain had exported more than $200,000 worth of thiodiglycol, one of two components for mustard gas, to Baghdad in 1988, another $50,000 worth the following year. Thionyl chloride, the other component, was also sent to Iraq in 1988 and 1989 at a price of only $26,000. Government officials anxious to avoid the obvious truth—that Britain was partly responsible for providing Saddam with weapons of mass destruction—hastily pointed out that the chemical had civilian uses. It could be used, they said, in the making of ink for ballpoint pens and fabric dyes. This was the same government department that would, eight years later, prohibit the sale of diphtheria vaccine to Iraqi children on the grounds that it could be used for "weapons of mass destruction."

The same House of Commons report stated that Britain had also exported small quantities of uranium and plutonium as well as military and communications

---

*Michael Hitchcock, a press officer for the Department of Trade and Industry, told me in 1987 that "our policy is we don't discuss whether a company has applied and been granted a licence because it was for civil use. We would consult the Ministry of Defence and the Foreign Office if we thought it necessary."

equipment to Iraq. Included on the list were artillery fire control systems, armoured vehicles and decoders and encryption devices. Also on the list was zirconium, which has nuclear weapons applications. Ministry guidelines, the DTI insisted in all seriousness, "prevent the export of lethal weapons or equipment that would significantly enhance the military capacity of either country [Iraq or Iran]." The ministry was "absolutely confident" that all the goods sold to Iraq fitted this description.

With such dishonesty—with such malfeasance—how can the obscene trade in arms to the Middle East ever be halted? Note how the British government had been "absolutely confident" that the exports of mustard gas chemicals, armour and secret communications equipment could not "enhance" Iraq's military "capacity." This was a truth containing a very substantial sliver of glass. If it was not going to "enhance" Iraq's military capacity, this British equipment was most surely intended to restore its military capability after the substantial losses in Iraqi materiel during the eight-year war with Iran—just in time for Saddam's next act of aggression, against Kuwait.

Note, too, how the dual-use excuse for weapons exports was, within a matter of months, turned on its head as a means to deprive Iraqis of basic social needs. Just as in 1988 and 1989 a chemical used for mustard gas could be exported to Iraq since it could also be used in ballpoint ink, so—once UN sanctions were imposed after Iraq's invasion of Kuwait—school pencils could not be exported to Iraq because the graphite in the pencils had dual military use. For the same reason, we would refuse to allow the Iraqis to import vital equipment for the repairing of oil wells, sewage plants and water-treatment facilities.

This kind of cynicism was reflected among the arms-traders. There is little honour among some of them, as Hamilton Spence, the managing director of Interarms of Manchester, a real home-grown British arms-supplier, discovered when he travelled to Beirut in 1980, at the height of the civil war, to sell M-16 rifles—legally—to the Lebanese government army in the company of Jim Davis of Colt firearms. "We sat down in a room to speak to the commander of the army, General Khoury," he said. "Then when the tenders were being opened, we found three other men there, a West German, a Lebanese and a man of unknown nationality. All three of them then produced false cards representing them as 'Colt' agents. So we jumped up, pointed at them and shouted: 'These people are imposters.' "

Two years later, just after the massacre of Palestinians by Israeli-supported Phalangist militiamen, Spence was watching Israeli troops unearthing PLO arms supplies from tunnels beneath the Palestinian camps in West Beirut. "There were our own 'Interarms' markings on some of the boxes," Spence claimed. "They were all fake. Someone had been using our name." Like Mertins, Spence was scornful of the American arms deal with Iran. "The CIA have a unique ability to get everything screwed up," he said. Yet Spence's boss, Sam Cummings, the chairman and principal shareholder in Interarms, had himself worked for the CIA. He described the arms business as "founded on human folly," a trade in which all weapons are defensive and all spare parts non-lethal.

Yet Spence displayed contempt for those who would attack him as a merchant of death. "I was at a party some time ago and a young girl came up to me and accused me of selling weapons for people to kill each other. I said: 'Nonsense. You're paying taxes, you are paying part of your salary every month to pay for nuclear weapons. How can you accuse me?' " Spence did not feel ashamed. He and Cummings had as their company motto *"Esse quam videri"*—"To be, rather than to seem to be"—and their Manchester workshops stood next to a fine, grey-stone Victorian church, the gods of love and war in intimate relationship with each other. "Not quite," Spence told me. "The church was built to commemorate the battle of Waterloo." He might also have added that while Interarms remained open for business, the church had been closed down some years before.

Israel's own arms industry could be forgiven for adopting Cummings's company motto for its own role in the Middle East arms market—although its attempts at secrecy are often as serious as a strip-tease artist's attempts at modesty. Companies that produce the Merkava tank and have become masters of upgrading and transforming outdated munitions need to advertise themselves as much as they need to maintain their privacy. Glossy Israeli military magazines have extolled the virtues of battlefield surveillance radar, towed assault bridges, tank-fire control systems, aircraft bomb-ejection racks and the mini-Uzi sub-machine gun.

By the mid-Eighties, the Israeli electronics manufacturer Tadiran had moved into electronic warfare technology with the development of a frequency-hopping VHF radio system. Elbit Computers was advertising its weapons delivery and navigation systems. Israeli Military Industries—its weapons "subjected to the extensive operational testing of actual combat"—employed 14,000 workers and exported to the United States and several NATO countries. Israel even began buying, quite legally, avionics systems from the United States, upgrading them, installing them on Israeli aircraft and then sharing the newly modernised equipment and new technical knowledge with the Americans. In this way, Israeli technology turned up in U.S. equipment sold to Saudi Arabia, a country whose American arms imports are always opposed by Israel's lobby in Washington and—usually—by the Israeli government.

Much less legal, however, was a secret operation—much of it still undisclosed in Israel itself—in which Israeli military technicians were sent to Beijing throughout the mid-Eighties to re-fit and modernise hundreds of Soviet-made tanks and heavy artillery for the Chinese People's Army. The Israeli personnel, many of them working for commercial weapons companies inside Israel, flew to Beijing with the tacit permission of the Israeli government, upgrading the Russian tanks with new fire-control systems, laser range-finders and—in some cases—new guns, many of which contained sensitive instruments of American manufacture. Israeli technicians flew to Beijing via Copenhagen and Bangkok—always using Scandinavian Airlines and choosing the one route to China which passed over friendly territory all the way. They worked in three-month shifts in Chinese ordnance depots, their equipment sent by sea from the Israeli port of Eilat.

Although I wrote extensively about this illicit trade in *The Times* in May 1987, only the Associated Press followed up the story. Neither the Pentagon nor the White House would make any comment, working on the assumption that American journalists would not touch so sensitive a subject without "confirmation" from U.S. authorities—confirmation they were not prepared to give. Their assumption was correct. Only when the CIA informed the Senate Government Affairs Committee in October 1993 that Israel had been providing China for over a decade with "several billion dollars' " worth of advanced military technology did the story become kosher for U.S. journalists. Yitzhak Rabin, the Israeli prime minister, then admitted that Israel had sold arms to China.

Israel's ability to upgrade Soviet military hardware was well established. Israeli technicians revolutionised a process to "Westernise" T-54 and T-55 battle tanks after capturing hundreds of them in wars with the Russian-equipped Arab armies. The Israelis replace the tank's 100-mm cannon with 105-mm guns and add their own fire-control system, which enables the gun to remain pointed at its target in rough country. Thermal sleeves were fitted to tank barrels to prevent heat warp while other innovations allowed tank commanders to predict weather conditions.*

Israel was also exporting hardware to Latin America, to the Somoza regime and then to the Contras in Nicaragua,† to apartheid South Africa and to Pinochet's Chile. But what infuriated the Americans was that the Chinese were receiving U.S. technology for their tanks via Israel—technology that was specifically banned from export to communist countries, including China. More critical still was the arrival of some of these same upgraded Russian tanks in Iran, purchased by Iranian arms-buyers while on extended visits to Beijing. Israel could not have been unaware of these deals—Iran operated a daily flight to Beijing during the eight-year war with Iraq, specifically to gain access to the Chinese arms market. The U.S. authorities only realised that the Israelis had been using U.S. instruments during the Beijing operations when a visiting Egyptian arms delegation inspected a newly modernised Russian T-62 tank, only to find U.S. and Israeli technology—with instructions in both English and Hebrew—inside.

The guerrilla armies of the Middle East—particularly in Lebanon during the county's 1975–90 civil war—sought arms in less ambitious ways. The Hizballah in Lebanon acquired their Katyusha and anti-tank rockets from Iran via Syria—a spectacularly successful alliance, since it used low-grade weaponry ultimately to drive Israel's occupation army and its Lebanese surrogates from southern Lebanon

---

*The Israelis learned how to sell weapons by learning how to change their shape. Their first conflict—their war of independence, which drove 750,000 Palestinians from their homes in what is now Israel—was fought with the help of two Sherman tanks, two elderly Cromwells and ten French tanks made around 1935. The Israelis modified the gun barrels to lengthen their range and fitted pieces of new armour to the structure. By the 1950s, they were still buying up battlefield junk from the wreckage of the Second World War, including tanks from Italy and even the Far East. Many were simply cannibalised to re-create whole working tanks for the country's new army. Some of the Shermans, painstakingly upgraded, later fought in the 1967 Middle East war and even the 1973 conflict. They were then discarded—as gifts to Israel's brutal proxy "South Lebanon Army" militia, and to Uganda.

†Israel, according to former army officers in Tel Aviv, shipped 2,000 Kalashnikov rifles and hundreds of RPG-7 anti-tank rockets to Nicaragua in 1983, all captured from PLO guerrillas during Israel's invasion of Lebanon the previous year.

in May 2000. The Christian Phalangists acquired weapons, including wire-guided missiles, from Israel and from South Africa, the latter provoking a government inquiry in Johannesburg after the end of the apartheid regime.*

IT WAS INEVITABLE, I suppose, that Lebanon, the land in which I have lived for half my life, should eventually provide me with that one unique and terrible connection which I had sought for so long to understand, between the armourers and their ultimate victims, between the respectable weapons manufacturers and the innocents whom their weapons kill. For many years in the Middle East, I had pondered the morality of those who made the guns that killed the people around me. What long-dead Soviet worker in Stalin's or Khrushchev's Russia had manufactured the Katyusha rocket to be fired, decades later, by the Palestinians and the Hizballah at the Israelis—either inside Israel or against Israel's occupation troops in southern Lebanon? What technician in the United States had put together the cluster bombs that Israel rained down on civilian areas of West Beirut in 1982?

What manufacturer, what developers—decent, patriotic, God-fearing Americans, no doubt—had built the Hellfire missile which an Israeli pilot fired into a Lebanese ambulance on 13 April 1996, killing two women and four children? Five years later, in Abu Dhabi, John Hurst of Lockheed would tell me he had no knowledge of this frightful little bloodbath. But then Mikhail Kalashnikov told me he felt no regrets about the carnage caused by the rifle he had designed; he had invented the AK-47 not to kill the innocent but to protect his country—the refrain of every armourer.

Yet the events of 13 April 1996 would allow me to challenge this mantra, to take the evidence of savagery back to the men in the United States who created the instrument of death for six poor Lebanese civilians whose only guilt lay in their nationality, in the location of their dirt-poor village and in the cynicism of the conflict which had been fought in that part of their country for twenty-one years. In all, 150,000 men, women and children were killed in the Lebanese civil war, tens of thousands of them victims of American munitions. These six civilians were to die long after that war had officially ended—victims of a constantly renewable conflict between Israel's occupation army and the Lebanese Hizballah guerrillas who eventually drove their enemies out of almost all of Lebanon.† In the months to

---

*In 1994, the Cameron Commission of Inquiry was appointed to look into alleged arms transactions between Armscor, the South African state weapons procurement body, and Christian militia groups between 1983 and 1993. After the Lebanese war ended in 1990, the Phalange were accused of sending surplus arms to Croatia and Slovenia at the height of the Balkans conflict, an accusation that became all too credible when the Yugoslav navy, which was in Serbian hands, seized a vessel carrying the weapons through the Adriatic, stored them in a warehouse in the port of Bar and then sent a bill to the Phalange for storage charges. According to the Lebanese government, the weapons included four French-made Gazelle helicopter gunships, several patrol boats, artillery shells and multi-barrelled rocket-launchers.

†I have referred readers in the Preface to my own book on the Lebanese conflict, *Pity the Nation*; those who want to understand the wider context to the Israeli killing of almost 200 Lebanese civilians in April 1996, including the massacre at Qana, can turn to the new British and American editions of the book, especially pp. 669–89.

come, I would interview all the survivors, all the witnesses—UN soldiers and Lebanese civilians—and the American arms manufacturers involved in this dreadful affair, which I still regard as a crime against humanity.

The Lebanese Shia Muslim village of Mansouri lay scarcely 8 kilometres from the Lebanese–Israeli frontier, and all that morning of Saturday, 13 April, the Israelis had shelled the area. Thirty-two-year-old Fadila al-Oglah had spent the night with her aunt Nowkal, cowering in the barn close to the villagers' donkeys and cows. But that Saturday she came out of hiding because there was no more bread in the village and the Israeli artillery rounds were now landing between the grimy concrete houses. Abbas Jiha, a farmer who acted as volunteer ambulance-driver for the Shia Muslim village, had spent the night with his twenty-seven-year-old wife, Mona, their three small daughters—Zeinab, Hanin and baby Mariam—and their six-year-old son, Mehdi, in the family's one-room hut above an olive grove, listening to the threats broadcast by the Voice of Hope radio station which was run by Israel in the 10 per cent of Lebanese territory it occupied north of its border. "The Israelis kept saying over the radio that the people of the villages must flee their homes," Abbas Jiha recalled for me. "They named Mansouri as one of those villages. They were telling us to escape. They were saying that they wouldn't attack the cars that were leaving the villages. And when I opened the door, I saw that the shelling was coming into Mansouri."

Across all of southern Lebanon on that spring morning, towering clouds of black and grey smoke drifted towards the Mediterranean as thousands of Israeli shells poured into the hill villages. The sky was alive with the sound of supersonic F-16 fighter-bombers, while several hundred metres above the hamlets and laneways hovered the latest and most ferocious addition to Israel's armoury—the American-made Apache helicopters whose firepower had proved so deadly to the retreating Iraqi army in Kuwait five years before. Just four days earlier, a fourteen-year-old Lebanese boy had been torn to pieces by a booby-trap bomb disguised as a rock near the village of Bradchit; the pro-Iranian Hizballah militia, accusing Israel of responsibility, sought revenge by firing Katyusha rockets across the border into Israel, wounding several civilians. In response, Israeli prime minister Shimon Peres—vainly seeking re-election by portraying himself as a soldier-statesman at war with Hizballah "terrorism"—ordered the mass bombardment of southern Lebanon from the air, sea and land.*

The United States meekly called for both sides to "exercise restraint" but publicly sympathised with Israel. The Hizballah, according to the U.S. State Department, were ultimately to blame for the death of all those civilians—there were to be almost 200 within the next three weeks—killed by Israeli fire. Although Washington was—as usual—officially neutral, the Lebanese found it difficult to dissoci-

---

*Irish UN troops in Bradchit concluded that the booby-trap had been laid by the Israelis to kill Hizballah guerrillas attempting to infiltrate the Israeli-occupied zone. The Israelis denied planting the bomb and—given the impossibility of *proving* that it was Israel's handiwork—the guerrillas committed an act of folly by retaliating when they must have known this would unleash an Israeli bombardment of civilians in southern Lebanon.

ate their latest war from the United States. The Voice of Hope radio station ordering them to flee their homes was partly funded by right-wing American evange-
lists. The 155-mm artillery shells hissing over their villages were made in
America. So were the F-16 jets and the Apache helicopters hovering like wasps in
the pale blue skies above them. Even the name chosen by Shimon Peres for Israel's
latest adventure in Lebanon—"Operation Grapes of Wrath"—appeared to be
influenced by America. If it did not come from the Book of Deuteronomy, then it
was inspired by Julia Ward Howe's nineteenth-century "Battle Hymn of the
Republic"—where the Lord is seen "trampling out the vintage where the grapes of
wrath are stored"—or by the best-selling novel of the American writer John Steinbeck, who once described Arabs as "the dirtiest people in the world and among the
smelliest."

The fruits of the operation could already be seen in Mansouri. Shortly after
dawn on 13 April, a shell had struck a house on the edge of the village, wounding
Abdulaziz Mohsen, a twenty-three-year-old farmer and former Lebanese army
conscript. Despite the gunfire, Abbas Jiha ran from his home to ask for the keys of
the Mansouri ambulance from the village *mukhtar*, or mayor. The battered, white-
painted Volvo—a gift to the people of Mansouri from villagers who had made
money after emigrating to West Africa—had two empty stretchers lying on the
back floor and Jiha pushed Mohsen into the vehicle, setting off through the shellfire to the city of Tyre, up the Mediterranean coast to the north-west. There he
bought sacks of flat Arabic bread for the marooned villagers of Mansouri. He
arrived back by nine in the morning, and was handing out the bread when another
shell hit a laneway, wounding a two-month-old baby called Ali Modehi. Back
drove Abbas Jiha once more in the old village ambulance, its blue light flashing on
the roof, until he had safely delivered Ali to the Tyre hospital. He bought yet more
bread for the families of Mansouri, then set off again for the village.

As he did so, Najla Abujahjah, a young Reuters camerawoman, was on an
equally dangerous mission, driving through the foothills east of Mansouri in an
attempt to film the Israeli air attacks for the British news agency. Unwilling to
leave the battlezone, Abujahjah—a resourceful and brave woman who would
never forget the terrible event she was shortly to witness—headed west to a road
near Mansouri where she caught sight of two more Apaches that appeared to be
watching something, "almost stationary in the sky but moving a few metres backwards and then a few metres forwards."

Abbas Jiha was now back in the centre of Mansouri, enveloped in a scene of
mass panic. "Many people had already fled their homes but a few were left, including my own family, and the shells were falling all over the place. A jet came and
dropped a bomb on the edge of the village. So I said the people could get into the
ambulance and I'd take them to safety. I got Mona and our children." Abbas Jiha
said that just as he put nine-year-old Zeinab, five-year-old Hanin and two-month-
old Mariam, along with their brother Mehdi, into the back of the ambulance, he
saw two helicopters. "They were low and the pilots seemed to be watching us," he
told me.

Fadila al-Oglah bought two bags of bread from Abbas but was herself now fearful of the planes. "Although the Israelis said we would not be attacked if we fled our houses, the Apaches were strafing the roads with bullets, and shells were bursting around our homes," she was to tell me later. "My brothers had left in a pick-up and other people had escaped in farm tractors. My parents told me: 'Leave and follow your brothers.' I went down to the village to look for another pick-up but then I saw Abbas Jiha driving the village ambulance with his wife and family inside. I asked if he would take me and he said: 'No problem.'"

By the time Abbas Jiha left Mansouri, he had thirteen terrified passengers crammed into the vehicle. There was his wife, Mona, and their four children, Fadila and her aunt Nowkal, Mohamed Hisham, a window repairman, and five members of the al-Khaled family—twenty-two-year-old Nadia, who was Nowkal's daughter, and her four nieces, Sahar, aged three, Aida, seven, Huda, eleven, and thirteen-year-old Manar. Abbas and Mohamed Hisham, the only male adults, sat in the front of the ambulance along with six-year-old Mehdi; the rest sat pressed together in the back. "Can you imagine what it was like with fourteen people in the vehicle?" Fadila asked me when I interviewed her later. Abbas Jiha remembers that part of the village was now on fire, the smoke curling over the fields. "We left in a convoy of tractors and cars and headed for Amriyeh where there was a UN post with Fijian soldiers on the main coast road to Tyre. The shells were falling all round us in the fields."

Najla Abujahjah was herself now standing in front of the Fijian position—UN Checkpoint 123—taking still pictures of refugee traffic on the road, her friend holding her video-camera. "There were two helicopters in the sky, watching the checkpoint," she told me. "I was worried about those helicopters, about what they were doing there. I saw an ambulance coming down the road and thought it must have wounded on board but then I saw it was full of women and children. There was another car moving in the opposite direction and the ambulance driver was waving with his hand, telling it to turn back." The videotape record of those moments shows the ambulance passing the unmanned UN checkpoint—the Fijian soldiers were not on the road, but in their protective bunkers—and Abbas Jiha's hand appears at the window of his vehicle, urging the other car to stop.

It was then that Abbas Jiha heard the women in the back of his ambulance shouting at him. "One of them was crying out to me: 'The helicopter is coming close to us—it's chasing us.' I looked out of the window and I could see the Apache getting closer. I told them all: 'Don't be afraid—just say *Allahu akbar*, God is Great, and the name of the Imam Ali.' I had told them not to be afraid but I was very frightened."

Najla Abujahjah saw the same helicopter. "It was getting lower and nearer, and I've learnt that this means the pilot is going to fire. I felt he was going to fire a missile but I didn't imagine the target would be so close to me. I heard a sound like 'puff-puff,' a very small sound. And I saw a missile flying from the Apache with a trail of smoke behind it." In fact, the Israeli helicopter pilot fired two missiles; one was later discovered unexploded beside a neighbouring mosque, its steel cylinder, fins and nameplate still intact. Najla Abujahjah's videotape recorded what happened to the other rocket. Milliseconds after the ambulance cleared UN Checkpoint 123, the missile exploded through the back door, engulfing the vehicle in fire and smoke and hurling it 20 metres through the air into the living room of a house.

All Fadila al-Oglah could remember was "a great heat in my face, like a blazing fire. Somehow I was outside the ambulance and I found a big barrel of water and started to wash my face from the heat. It was all I could think of, despite the screaming and smoke, this terrible heat. It was as if someone was holding a flame in front of my eyes."

Abbas Jiha was to recall how he hurled himself from the door of the ambulance just before it crashed into the house. "I was terrified. I couldn't believe it. It was the end of my world. I knew what must have happened to my family." Najla Abujahjah, trembling with fear, was now videotaping the terrible aftermath of the Israeli missile attack. Her tape shows Abbas Jiha, wounded in the head and foot, standing in the road beside one of his dead daughters, weeping and shrieking "God is Great" up into the sky, towards the helicopter. "I raised my fists to the pilot and cried out: 'My God, my God, my family has gone.'"

Abbas found his son Mehdi alive. Then he saw two-month-old Mariam lying 3 metres from the ambulance. "All her body had holes through it. Her head was full of metal." Najla saw women and children "coming out of the back of the ambulance, cowering and screaming and hiding. One man threw himself into the orchard then came out holding two children by the arms. One was a little girl who was wounded and barefoot but she was still trying to put her scarf back on. I saw a girl lying on the road with blood coming out of the top of her head. The driver was crying out: 'My children have died, God have mercy on us.' I saw another girl— she was Manar—and she had blood all over her, and she kept saying: 'My sister's head has exploded.' "

Still fearful that the helicopter would fire again—the pilot had clearly seen that his target was an ambulance—Najla Abujahjah ran towards the house to find a scene which she has said will torment her for the rest of her life. "I couldn't get the doors open because the vehicle was wedged in the room. But there were three children inside who were clearly in the last seconds of their life. It was as if they were entombed. One of them—she was Hanin—collapsed on the broken window frame, her blood running in streams down the outside of the vehicle. In her last seconds she tried to look at me but she couldn't because dust covered her face. Another little girl was sitting in the lap of a dead woman, wailing and crying 'Aunty, Aunty.' There was a third girl who had her face covered in blood; she was sitting up, turning her head from side to side. Another had a terrible wound to her head and neck and she collapsed." As the children died one by one in front of her, Najla Abujahjah heard a strange scraping sound. "The missile had set off the windscreen wipers and they were going back and forth against the broken glass, making this terrible noise. It will haunt me for the rest of my days."

Abbas Jiha, overwhelmed with grief, was tearing at the ambulance with his bare hands, along with UN Fijian troops from the checkpoint. "I could see Hanin's back—she was cut through with holes like a mosquito net," he recalled. "Then I found my wife Mona. She was so terribly wounded, I couldn't recognise her face. I had lost her and three of my children." Mona Jiha, nine-year-old Zeinab, five-year-old Hanin and the two-month-old baby, Mariam, were all dead. So was sixty-year-old Nawkal and her eleven-year-old niece Huda. The Israeli helicopter remained in the sky over UN Checkpoint 123 for another five minutes. Then it flew away.

Within hours, the Israelis admitted they had targeted the ambulance but made two claims: that the vehicle was owned by a Hizballah member—which was untrue—and that it was destroyed because it had been carrying a Hizballah guerrilla—likewise untrue. "If other individuals in the vehicle were hit during the attack," an Israeli spokesman said, "they had been used by the Hizballah as a cover for Hizballah activities." There were no apologies. Yet international law demands the safeguarding of civilian lives even in the presence of "individuals who do not come within the definition of civilians," and the claim that the vehicle had been targeted because it was believed to be owned by the Hizballah was in some ways even more outrageous. How, the survivors asked themselves, could it be justifiable for the Israelis to slaughter the occupants of an ambulance just because they didn't like the suspected owner of the vehicle? And what kind of missile, they also asked, could home in on an ambulance, blasting it 20 metres through the air? If the Apache helicopter was American—as it most certainly was—who made the rocket that killed Nowkal, Mona and the four children, Zeinab, Hanin, Mariam and Huda?

For days after the killing, the smashed ambulance lay in the wreckage of the house into which it had been blasted on 13 April. I passed it myself each day as I drove the frightening coast road south of Tyre, two Apache helicopters watching my movements as they did all vehicles on the highway. Within a week, the bloodbath at Qana, in which 109 Lebanese civilian refugees were massacred by Israeli artillery, had eclipsed this particular horror, eventually bringing "Operation Grapes of Wrath" to an ignominious end—and failing to win Shimon Peres's election. But there were many other incidents during the Israeli bombardment which bore a remarkable similarity to the ambulance attack. Close to the Jiyeh power station, south of Beirut, for example, another Israeli helicopter pilot had fired a missile at a car, killing a young woman who had just bought a sandwich from a local café. In West Beirut on 16 April, a missile decapitated a two-year-old girl. Two days later, yet another helicopter-fired missile was targeted at a block of apartments at Nabatieh, killing a family of nine, including a two-day-old baby.

What were these terrible weapons that were now being used so promiscuously in Lebanon? Who sold them to the Israelis? And—if it was an American company which had manufactured the missile—what conditions were attached to its sale? In the village of Mansouri, Abbas Jiha spent months ruminating upon this same question. "How would the people who made this missile feel if their children were killed as mine were?" he asked me. "These things are meant to be used against armies, not civilians." Fadila al-Oglah was more resigned. "The Americans will keep giving these weapons to the Israelis whatever we say," she remarked to me one day in the same draughty two-room house she had fled a year before. "They don't care about us. We will continue to suffer." Which was perfectly true.

Shortly after the bombardment ended, however, UN ordnance officers searching through the wreckage of the ambulance found an intriguing clue to the missile's identity. Among fragments of shrapnel and twisted steel, a young UN liaison officer—Captain Mikael Lindval of the Swedish army—discovered a hunk of metal bearing most of a coded nameplate. It had come to rest a few inches from the bloodstained window frame where Hanin had died, and contained the logo "AGM 114C" and a manufacturer's number, "04939." There was also an intriguing single letter, "M." Lindval knew AGM stood for "Air-to-Ground Missile," and the 114C coding identified the 1.6-metre projectile as a Hellfire anti-armour missile, jointly manufactured by Rockwell International and Martin Marietta. Rockwell—now taken over by Boeing—had its missile headquarters, according to *Jane's Defence Weekly*, at Satellite Boulevard, Duluth, in Georgia, about thirty minutes' drive from Atlanta. Martin Marietta, now part of Lockheed, was making missles in Orlando, Florida. Those who made the missile that killed four Lebanese children and two women now had an address.

I even found the manufacturer's advertisement for the Hellfire. "All for One and One for All," it said in the publicity literature. Could ever Alexandre Dumas' reputation have been so traduced? What did the rallying cry of the Three Musketeers have to do with this weapon? But there was a far more important question. Now that I had identified them, how would the missile manufacturers respond to the bloodbath inside the Mansouri ambulance?

Lindval duly handed over to me the fragment containing the codes. They were scratched and in some cases illegible, but they included a National Stock Number in a 42-34 digit sequence, "141001-1920293." The second section of the sequence—"01"—would prove to be of vital importance. The missile's Lot No. was "MG188J315534." Then the Fijians found the second, unexploded Hellfire missile almost totally buried beside the mosque. On the undamaged fuselage, the codings were complete and it was thus possible to reconstruct some of the missing figures on the projectile which had exploded inside the ambulance.*

Somehow, I had to get the coded missile part to America, to present it to the makers. The first question was how to get this piece of shrapnel—the vital and only proof that the ambulance had been hit by a Hellfire—from Lebanon to the United States. There were no direct flights. It was not difficult to get it aboard an

---

*Even tragedy can contain its own dark humour. Some days after the destruction of the ambulance, Lindval called me in Beirut to say that the Fijians had unearthed the second, unexploded Hellfire. "What on earth did you ask the Fijians to do with it?" he asked me. I had asked them to send me the metal code sheet from the fuselage. Lindval was not amused. "Seems they didn't understand you, Robert," he said. "They thought you wanted the entire missile—I found them loading it onto a truck to bring to you in Beirut." I had a brief image of my landlord's horrified face as the entire projectile was delivered by UN soldiers to my apartment door. Hopefully defused.

international flight from Lebanon to France. Sympathetic officials at Beirut airport and in the airline brought the missile part on board my Air France flight to Paris. But explaining to American security men that I wanted to carry it all the way to Washington was going to end in journalistic disaster. I consulted the Paris station manager of another European airline. "Don't think about hand-carrying it, Bob," he told me, fondling the jagged metal fragment containing the Hellfire codes. "They'll pick up explosive traces on your hands, let alone the stuff you'd be carrying in your bag." I could see what he meant. And I could imagine the headline: "British reporter found with missile part on flight to Washington . . ." I could even guess the reporter's by-line beneath the headline.

The hunks of shrapnel were now no more a rocket than a piece of broken china constituted a plate, but the very word "missile" would cause palpitations to any U.S. agent in the aftermath of the recent TWA disaster off New York; in five years' time, the whole exercise would have been impossible. In the end, Amnesty International—well aware of the ambulance killings in Lebanon—agreed to airfreight the missile parts from Paris to their Washington office. A few days later, I flew Air France to the United States; I can remember my sense of excitement as my aircraft stopped over briefly in New York. I stood with the French crew on the steps of the plane in the early afternoon, looking towards the distant skyscrapers and the tall grey towers of the World Trade Center on the warm horizon. Now at last I could confront the armourers with the consequences of their profession.

In Washington, I picked up the Hellfire fragment in the heart of the capital whose alliance with Israel allows neither criticism not restraint. I wasn't going to take a local flight and get caught on the metal detectors at Washington's Ronald Reagan airport, so the Crescent, a railroad train en route to New Orleans, would take me through the night down to Georgia, where Bob Algarotti of Boeing had agreed to meet me to discuss the Hellfire at the very home of the missile. He wanted to explain its advantages, its combat-proven abilities, to a reporter who— he wrongly assumed—wanted to write a puff piece about the missile's accuracy.

Washington, that late spring day, was beautiful. The Capitol and the great government buildings looked like ancient Rome. And when I awoke the next bright morning in my sleeping car heading south, the neat little American towns looked like they were on a Hollywood set. The soft green countryside and the clapboard houses sailed past the window of my carriage. How neat those little gardens were with their flowers and children's swings. Was I only 6,000 miles away from Lebanon—or on a different planet? There were Episcopalian churches and smart Georgian courthouses and towns called Cornelia and Magnolia Acres flicking past, and a gunstore—in a land where every man and woman has the right to bear arms—called Lock, Stock and Barrel. And so many flagstaffs that dawn morning I could see from my carriage window. And so many red, white and blue American flags snapping proudly from them. There hadn't been a war in these parts, I thought, for 130 years.

I climbed down at Gainesville station, where a taxi man with one surviving tooth took me down Interstate 85 to the Old Peachtree Road exit. We passed a sign saying Duluth and then Satellite Boulevard and then, less than 3 miles further on, we turned into a campus of discreet two-storey buildings hidden behind tall trees and manicured lawns. "Boeing Defense and Space Group," it said on the sign at the gate.

It was to be a disturbing afternoon. A tiny, green-painted model of the Hellfire stood on a shelf of the room in which Bob Algarotti of Boeing introduced me to two executives intimately involved in the production of the missile. They were highly intelligent men; both were former serving officers in Vietnam and both would later request anonymity—for their security, it seemed, although their concern about Boeing's reaction to the interview appeared to outweigh any fear of Hizballah or "terrorism."

I explained that I was interested in writing about the abilities of the Hellfire—but also about its specific use in the Middle East. The executive to my right—whom I shall call the Colonel, for that was his rank in Vietnam—produced a glossy brochure that detailed the evolution of the Hellfire modular missile system, and placed it on the table between us. Page 2 carried a series of small illustrated cross-sections of the rocket and, following the dates 1982–89, a coding of AGM 114A, B, C. The piece of shrapnel—which, unbeknown to the Boeing men, was in my camera bag—was marked AGM 114C. So the missile that killed Abbas Jiha's family, Nowkal and her niece was at least seven years old.

The Colonel listed the countries which had purchased either an early or later, improved, category of the Hellfire. First on the list was Israel with both categories—"they take soldiering pretty seriously," the Colonel said admiringly, a remark I decided to let go for the moment—but Egypt, South Africa and the United Arab Emirates were also included. Sweden and Norway had purchased an anti-ship version of the Hellfire. The British had category two. It was a popular product and the Colonel was keen to explain why. "It's probably the most precise anti-armour weapon in the world," he said. "You can fire it through a basketball hoop at five miles and it would do it every time." So the women and children in the ambulance, I thought to myself, had stood no chance.

I understood at once what this meant. The Boeing men were promoting the accuracy of their weapons as part of their humanitarian pitch: the more accurate the Hellfire, the less chance civilians would be killed by it. The problem came when the weapon was specifically aimed at a civilian target—as it had been by the Israelis in Lebanon—when the very precision of the missile ensured that civilians would be killed. So I asked what checks Boeing carried out on the use to which the Hellfire had been put by the nations that purchased it. They read the papers, both executives said. I asked about Israel. "We do not get information from the Israelis about what they've done," one of the men replied. "They don't give much information."

It was time to produce the missile fragment. And as I knelt to extract it from my camera bag, I felt the electricity in the air behind me. I turned round and laid the shard of iron which had helped to kill the Lebanese in the centre of the table. I told all three men the date of its use, the location, the appalling results and Israel's explanation. The Colonel picked it up, turning it in his hand and muttering something about how it might be too small a fragment to identify. This was absurd. He could read the codes on the metal from the missile. He understood what they meant better than I did. His colleague to my left said nothing, stared at the fragment and looked at me. Bob Algarotti, the public relations man, picked it up, glanced at his colleagues, and said quietly: "Yeah, well, it's a Hellfire, we all know that."

Then he said: "I'm getting a little uncomfortable." But the Colonel was angry. "This is so far off base, it's ridiculous," he said. I begged to disagree. These men manufactured this missile. Did they not bear some responsibility for its use—at least to ensure that it was used responsibly by their clients? Was reading about its use in the newspapers enough? Was that the extent of their interest or care? There then followed some very uncomfortable minutes. Algarotti complained that you couldn't blame a knife-maker if someone used the knife to murder someone else. Yes, I said, but this was not a knife. The Hellfire was an anti-personnel weapon. "It's not!" the Colonel replied angrily. "It's an anti-armour weapon." And then there was silence—because, of course, if the missile was an anti-armour weapon, it most surely was not an anti-ambulance weapon.

"Are you on some kind of crusade?" one of the executives asked. I said I thought this an unfortunate remark.* Algarotti interrupted quietly to agree with me. We were dealing with the death of innocent people, I repeated, including children. What was I looking for? one of the men asked. For some sign of compassion from them, I replied. One of the men in the room said: "I, as a person—sure I have feelings, but as a Boeing company employee, all we do is make missiles." I then agreed to lay down my pen while the three men discussed how they could frame some statement of their feelings. Both executives clearly felt deeply troubled about the events that I described; they were family men and wanted to express their horror at the deaths of innocents. But they didn't want Boeing involved and—equally obviously—they were frightened of criticising Israel. During the afternoon, one man at Boeing would be heard to say twice—in identical words, I observed in my notebook—"Whatever you do, I don't want you to quote me as saying anything critical of Israel's policies."

And here was the nub. These men, these armourers—so powerful, so overwhelmingly part of America's defence system, so patriotic in their motives, so immutably part of the history of the U.S. armed forces in Vietnam—were frightened of offending Israel, fearful that a mere word of criticism would damage or end their careers or send them careening off into a political crisis within the aerospace company so serious that their careers would be for ever ravaged. "Whatever you do . . ." the man had said.

Then one of the executives made up his mind. "Let me speak as a soldier, not as an employee of Boeing. No professional soldier is going to condone the killing

*Doubly so for Boeing. The executive's question was used as one of the headlines on my report in *The Independent on Sunday* on 18 May 1997.

of innocent people as targets. We're trained to preserve the peace . . . of course, the Boeing company is troubled if its weapons are misused or targeted against, you know, innocent people. But we build weapons systems to U.S. requirements, we get permission to sell to many different countries . . . we don't sell missiles that are intended for non-military targets . . ."

I pulled from my bag the photographs that Najla Abujahjah had taken of the victims. I laid them on the table, images of blood and torn limbs. The executive on my left looked through them with distaste. Then he said: "I don't want these." And he slid the pictures of the dead and wounded members of the Jiha family across the heavily polished tabletop. The Colonel looked at them and gently returned them to me. We parted with handshakes; and I felt oddly sad for these men. They were decent, hard-working, loyal employees of Rockwell—now Boeing—and they had been shocked by the story of the ambulance. They wanted to show their compassion—and did so, up to a point—but were desperately anxious to avoid any offence to Boeing or to Israel. I told them to keep the Hellfire missile fragment. I was returning it to them. And as I left the room, I heard a voice behind me say: "I don't think we'll put this one in the trophy room."

And there my story might have ended. The *Review* section of the London *Independent on Sunday* published my detailed account of the Israeli attack on the ambulance and the long journey to the south of the United States to find the men who made it. On the front cover, the paper ran a coloured photograph of the missile fragment, showing in minute detail the codings that had survived the explosion. But two days later, I received a letter from a European missile technician. He wanted anonymity. He said he wanted "some focusing of Human Rights for these people" killed in the ambulance. Then he went on:

> The vital piece of evidence, the missile fragment, says a lot more than you revealed . . . The NATO Stock Number is partially obliterated, but does give a vital clue. The NSN is made up of a 42-34 digit sequence . . . the two digit part is the Nation Code. Each NATO country . . . has an identifying nationality code—in this case, the "01" for the U.S.A is clearly visible. This shows that the weapon was originally supplied to U.S. forces . . . The Lot No. is the most significant. This would tell you exactly where and when it was made, and more importantly, where it was delivered . . . you will see that the first part of the Lot No. has been obliterated . . . It also appears to have been made by a chisel-like instrument . . . being pushed down on the plate; the other damage is all of a glancing/scraping nature. So who cut out the Lot No.? Israeli forces upon receipt of "illegally exported" U.S. weaponry? U.S. forces before delivery? . . . It is quite clear that this missile . . . was exported from U.S. government stocks and given to the Israelis covertly.

The writer ended with a warning, telling me that I should be careful what I said on the telephone about my missile inquiries, because "all satellite transmissions are monitored by the U.S. National Security Agency at Menwith near Harrogate . . . 'Compromising NATO Security' would be the charge [against me] so please be discreet in your handling of this letter."

Discreet I was. I messaged a friend in France and asked her to call the anonymous letter-writer. Minutes later she was on the line. "He called me back from a pay phone. He wants to meet you tomorrow for lunch at the Lutetia Hotel in Paris." Next morning I boarded the first flight to Paris, the 8:05 from Beirut—the same plane I had flown with the missile fragment only a few days earlier. At Charles de Gaulle airport, I took a taxi to the *6ème arrondissement*. This was an assignment, it seemed, that would turn me into the ancient mariner, the Hellfire missile my personal albatross.

The technician had arrived in Paris with his wife. He went straight to the point. "Mr. Fisk, that missile was *never* sold to the Israelis. The '01' shows it was sold to the U.S. armed forces. And the 'M' proves it was sold to the U.S. Marine Corps." Was he sure? He pulled from his pocket NATO's entire arms coding list. Israel's imported NATO weapons, for example, would carry the numerals "31." Britain's NATO coding is "99," Italy "15." But the nationality code for the United States was—suitably enough—"01." Which was the code on the missile fragment. And "M" stood for the U.S. Marines. So how, in heaven's name, did a Marine Corps missile come to be fired by the Israelis into an ambulance in southern Lebanon? I called my then editor, Andrew Marr. "Bob," he said, "looks like you'll be adding up some more air miles—get back to Washington."

I did. I made a formal request to the Pentagon, giving them full details of the missile's codes, asking them for "the exact provenance of this missile . . . did it pass through U.S. military hands and, if so, how did it find its way to the Israel Defence Forces? . . . What follow-up action was taken by the U.S. government after the April 13 attack?" I received no reply. Indeed, after more than thirty calls from me to the U.S. Defense Department and the State Department—faxing and hand-delivering not only the coding of this missile but the coding on the unexploded missile which had also been fired at the ambulance, from which we had established some of the figures scratched off the exploded rocket—not a single official American government spokesman, either at Defense or State, was prepared to give me any information. "Some questions come to us with a kind of jinx attached," a Defense Department official told me during another vain call to his office. "Yours seems to have a jinx."

But the U.S. Marines took a different view. When I faxed them details of the missile codings and the ambulance attack, I was immediately called back by a spokeswoman for the office of the Marine Corps Commandant. "We don't like our missiles being used to attack kids," she told me. "Where are you staying?" I waited next day at my hotel near Dupont Circle and at 5:30 a car arrived for me. It took me to a marine base outside Washington where seven men in civilian clothes were waiting to talk to me. We sat in the officers' mess and they examined my photographs of the missile parts and told me—at last—the story of Hellfire No. MG188J315534.

It had been one of up to 300 shipped to the Gulf by the U.S. Marines in 1990 to be used against Saddam Hussein's occupation army in Kuwait. Of these, 159 were fired at Iraqi forces—although the marines reported at the time that some of the Hellfires were hitting Iraqi vehicles but failing to explode on impact; just as the second missile which the Israeli pilot fired at the Lebanese ambulance failed to explode in 1996. But when the conflict was over, the marine officers told me, around 150 unused Hellfires—along with other ordnance—were dropped off at the Haifa munitions pier in Israel by a U.S. warship as part of a secret quid pro quo— a gift to Israel—for keeping out of the 1991 Gulf War when it was under Iraqi Scud missile attack.

I called up General Gus Pagonis, who was head of U.S. military logistics during the 1991 war against Iraq; he insisted to me that "everything we took off the ships [in Saudi Arabia] I put back aboard them en route to America." But Pagonis—who was now head of logistics for the Sears Roebuck chain of department stores—added meaningfully that "I don't know if the ships stopped anywhere on the way." They did. After passing through the Suez Canal, the U.S. Navy put the Hellfires and other missiles ashore in northern Israel.*

If the missile had been *sold* to Israel, conditions on its use would have been attached. But this was a military transfer, straight from American stocks. The missile had been paid for by the marines but ultimately handed over to the Israelis, no questions asked, and—five years later—fired into the back of an ambulance. Thus did a U.S. Marine missile kill seven people in southern Lebanon.†

And there in Washington my journey might have ended were it not for a message from Bob Algarotti of Boeing. It was, to say the least, confusing. His people,

---

*The Defense Department's inspector general later found that 188 Stinger missiles had "gone missing" from U.S. armouries during the 1991 Gulf conflict. In the same year, the U.S. military's General Accounting Office admitted that another 2,185 missiles—Stingers, Dragons and Redeyes—had disappeared from European U.S. weapons storage sites. Where did they go?

†For the U.S. military, this was just a small provocation. It was the virtually unchallenged ability of Israel to rifle through U.S. military stocks that so upset serving and retired officers in the U.S. armed forces who, in the course of a two-week investigation by *The Independent* into arms transfers to Israel, spoke of their fury at watching thousands of tanks and armour taken from U.S. inventories over a period of twenty years, and transferred to Israel despite objections from the Department of Defense. In the late 1970s, according to one officer who was serving in northern Europe, senior U.S. military personnel objected to a vast quantity of armour being withdrawn from Germany for transfer to Israel. "I was in the headquarters in Germany with the Chairman of the Joint Chiefs and he went through the roof," he told me. "We were ordered to hand over hundreds of tanks at very short notice—and this was at the height of the Cold War. We were opposite the Fulda Gap and the Warsaw Pact was on the other side and we were screaming that we were depleting our assets at a moment of high European tension. The general was saying 'fuck them'—he used those words—but he was excluded from the decision. The Department of Defense was directed under orders to turn over the tanks. We didn't do it voluntarily."

An air force officer recalled for me how, around the same period, he returned from leave to his naval air station in the United States to discover that half his squadron of aircraft were being repainted with Israeli markings. "We only had fifty per cent of our squadron left—I was flabbergasted," he said. "I wasn't consulted. I was told 'They've got to go to Israel—we're out of business for a while.'"

he said, had been studying the missile fragment which I had left with them. They thought it had been made at the Orlando factory in Florida, by Lockheed Martin—at that time a rival company. But the story wasn't that simple. The "Fed Log" number, partly damaged in the explosion, showed the figures to be 04939. "And that—at least the last four [digits]—definitely indicated it's either got to be us or it's got to be Martin Marietta then." This hardly seemed conclusive. If it was either Rockwell (now Boeing) or Martin Marietta (now Lockheed Martin), which of them made this killer missile? The Hellfire that the Israelis fired into the ambulance had obviously been designed and developed by Boeing in Duluth. Now it seemed that the missile itself might have been put together by Lockheed. There was a lot of buck-passing going on here.

Boeing—whose headquarters in Seattle refused to add to what I'd been told in Duluth—said it had not contacted Lockheed Martin about my inquiry. But when I called Al Kamhi, Lockheed's director of communications—who, by chance, was on a business trip to London—he knew exactly what I was investigating. "You talking about what you discussed with Rockwell?" he asked sharply. ". . . I mean, I have no way of knowing what missile that was. I have no way of knowing if that missile ever came from where you say it came from . . . They [Boeing] can be as convinced as they want to be . . . as far as I'm concerned, I'm not going to start looking at missile fragments from . . . Their origin is totally unknown—I'm just not going to do that."

"Can I let you have them anyway?" I asked. And our conversation became almost surreal:

---

Officially, arms transfers to Israel have to undergo a period of thirty days' formal notice. Major U.S. defence equipment with a value of more than $14 million requires congressional notification—amounts of less than $14 million do not. "Anyone on the Hill knows that challenging any transfers to Israel is not going to help their political career," a former American army officer commented to me. "The Israeli lobby is very, very powerful. It's not going to be criticised." In fact, after it used U.S. Navy anti-tank cluster bombs on civilian areas of west Beirut in 1982, Israel *was* taken to task in Washington. President Reagan briefly held up deliveries from Dover Air Force Base of U.S. F-15 and F-16 fighter-bombers to Israel while congressional hearings investigated the use of the cluster bombs in Lebanon. But even after classified material was edited out of their final report, the State Department refused to publish the full findings on the grounds that the entire sessions were "classified."

"Classified" was a word that occurred fairly often in Washington when I asked about weapons transfers. The congressional branch of the National Archives contains numerous references to classified "legally approved transfers" to Israel. But they are not open to public inspection. No one in Washington was able to explain to me in June 1997, for example, why Israel needed—and had been given—98,000 new artillery shells from U.S. stocks. An American defence "analyst"—a breed that would normally court publicity but in this case did not—remarked to me that "an awful lot of shells are transferred to Israel and nobody knows a hell of a lot about it. The military here is downsizing and wants to get rid of some ordnance because it's old. But an equal amount of good material just leaves our stocks for Israel without a by-your-leave. It goes through the legal channels but no one reports it, no one questions it, no one asks where it's used or how it's used. And if it kills innocent folk, do you think the Clinton administration is going to make a song and dance about it? They'll say that criticising Israel may 'damage the peace process.' Every assurance has been given to Israel that it will not be touched."

KAMHI: No, I won't accept them.

FISK: You won't accept them?

KAMHI: No.

FISK: Can you tell me why not, sir? . . . I mean, this involves the death of four children and two women in an ambulance.

KAMHI: I don't know that that missile has anything to do with it . . . I mean, I can't comment on something I have no information on.

FISK: Well, I'm offering you the information so that you can check on it, sir. Boeing does seem convinced that it was made by your people.

KAMHI: And I'm not sure I understand—if it was or if it wasn't—what the point is.

I told Kamhi that I wanted to know the response of the company that manufactured the Hellfire to the events that took place when its missile was used. "I have no comment on what took place," he replied. "I'm not even going to get into that arena . . . Our sales are made through foreign military sales . . . that's the way it's done, through the Pentagon." I repeated that UN officers had found the missile in the ambulance, along with another Hellfire close by which had failed to explode. There was no doubt about their provenance. But our conversation continued in an even more bizarre manner.

KAMHI: Well, frankly, the missile has nothing to do with the manufacturer.

FISK: But you made it.

KAMHI: Well, we make a lot of things, too . . . our products are sold to allied nations.

FISK: Does that include Israel?

KAMHI: I presume if Israel has Hellfire, then they purchase the Hellfires through legal channels and through legal means.

FISK: But I mean, do you care about the use to which your missiles are put by those people to whom you sell them? I mean, this is a very important point, sir.

KAMHI: I'm sorry—I'm not going to dignify that question with a response. It's a no-win question . . . I'm just not going to respond to that . . . the question you have asked is a "Have-you-stopped-beating-your-wife?" question. No matter how I respond to that question, we all of a sudden are the bad missile manufacturer. We make missiles. We make electronics systems. We make a variety of defence systems. And it is our hope that they're never used . . . We don't know that the missile was misused. A missile can miss . . .

I explained to Kamhi that the Israelis agreed the ambulance was the target. They should respond to it, he said. But then, when I suggested that the U.S. government was itself concerned about the use to which its country's weaponry was put by clients, Kamhi changed his tone, though only fractionally. "We're always concerned when someone is hurt," he said. "As far as why the missile was used . . . there's no way we can control or understand why . . . We don't have any say in that . . . you know, every day over six hundred people are shot in America. Not once do I know that anyone has gone back and questioned the bullet-maker."

And so it went on, Kamhi ever more irritated. He repeated he didn't know if the ambulance was the intended target—and again I offered him my documentation with photographs of the missile part. "I can't make the determination," he replied impatiently. "I wasn't the one pulling the trigger. Lockheed Martin was not the one that was there, firing the missile. Ultimately it has to come down to the responsibility of the user . . . It is not for us, the manufacturer, to go ahead and take action in a case like this."

Kamhi's replies were hopeless, pathetic. But their message was clear. If an American missile was fired into an ambulance, those who made it would fiercely deny any blame. It was for Israel to explain. And when it did—agreeing that against all the rules of war, the Hellfire had been deliberately fired into an ambulance—America was silent. The equation was complete. Israel, it seemed, could do what it wanted. And Lockheed had no intention of cooperating with our inquiry—not least, I suspect, because Lockheed was now a joint partner in missile development with the Israeli aeronautics company Raphael.

Al Kamhi agreed to let me drop off at his London hotel a packet of news reports on the ambulance killings, along with the missile codings and my photographs of the Hellfire fragment that I had left with Boeing. So the next day, I took the Channel tunnel train from Paris to London with my package. It travelled with me through the fresh spring countryside of Kent, through my own home town of Maidstone—it had been a long journey since I left the south Lebanese village of Mansouri—and to the Britannia Hotel in London where Al Kamhi was staying. He was not in his room, so I left the package with reception, receiving a promise that it would be handed to Mr. Kamhi the moment he came back to the hotel.

Three days later, the same package—opened but then resealed—arrived at *The Independent*'s foreign desk in London.

Returned to Sender.

CHAPTER TWENTY

# Even to Kings, He Comes . . .

*How shall I go in peace and without sorrow?*
*Nay, not without a wound in the spirit shall I leave this city.*
*Long were the days of pain I have spent within its walls, and*
*long were the nights of aloneness; and who can depart from his*
*pain and his aloneness without regret?*
*Too many fragments of the spirit have I scattered in these streets . . .*
*It is not a garment I cast off this day,*
*but a skin that I tear with my own hands.*

Kahlil Gibran, *The Prophet*

MY HOME IN BEIRUT has been a time-box for almost thirty years, a place where time has stood still. I have sat on my balcony over the Mediterranean in the sticky, sweating summer heat and in the tornadoes of winter, watching the midnight horizon lit by a hellfire of forked lightning, the waves suddenly glistening gold as they slide menacingly below my apartment. I have woken in my bed to hear the blades of the palm trees outside slapping each other in the night, the rain smashing against the shutters until a tide of water moves beneath the French windows and into my room. I came to Lebanon in 1976, when I was just twenty-nine years old, and because I have lived here ever since—because I have been doing the same job ever since, chronicling the betrayals and treachery and deceit of Middle East history for all those years—I am still twenty-nine.

Abed, my driver, has grown older. I notice his stoop in the mornings when he brings the newspapers, the morning dailies in Beirut and *The Independent*, a day late, from London. My landlord, Mustafa, who lives downstairs, is now in his seventies, lithe as an athlete and shrewder, but sometimes a little more tired than he used to be. The journalists I knew back in 1976 have moved on to become associate editors or executive editors or managing editors. They have settled into Manhattan apartments or homes in upstate New York or in Islington in London. They have married, had children; some of them have died. Sometimes, reading the newspaper obituaries—for there is nothing so satisfying as the narrative of a life that has an end as well as a beginning—I notice how the years of birth are beginning to creep nearer to my own. When I came to Beirut, the obituary columns were still recording the lives of Great War veterans like my dad. Then the years would encompass the 1920s, the 1930s, at least a comfortable ten years from my own first decade. And now the hitherto friendly "1946" is appearing at the bottom of the page. Sometimes I know these newly dead men and women, spies and soldiers and statesmen and thugs and murderers whom I have met over the past three decades in the Middle East, Yugoslavia and Northern Ireland. Sometimes I write these obituaries myself. One cold spring day, I wrote of the life of my old friend and journalist colleague Juan Carlos Gumucio, a man of inspiring courage and deep depressions—who saved my life in war and who had sat on my own balcony so many times, dispensing wisdom and cynicism and fine wines—and who took his life, shooting himself at his home in Bolivia because the world no longer seemed a kind or gentle or worthy place for him.

And still I am twenty-nine. I can look back over the years with nightmare memories but without dreams or pain. Lebanon has a brutal history but it has been a place of great kindness to me. It has taught me to stay alive. And amid all the memories of war, of friendships and beautiful women and books read past midnight—long into the early hours, when dawn shows the crack between the curtains—there has always been the idea that Beirut was the place one came home to. How many times have I sat on the flight deck of MEA's old 707s—from the Gulf, from Egypt or from the Balkans or Europe—and watched the promontory of Beirut lunging out into the Mediterranean "like the head of an old sailor" and heard a metallic voice asking for permission to make a final approach on runway 18 and known that in half an hour I would be ordering a gin and tonic and smoked salmon at the Spaghetteria restaurant in Ein el-Mreisse, so close to my home that I could send Abed home and walk back to my apartment along the seafront to the smell of cardamom and coffee and corn on the cob.

Of course, I know the truth. Sometimes when I get out of bed in the morning, I hear the bones cracking in my feet. I notice that the hair on my pillow is almost all silver. And when I go to shave, I look into the mirror and, now more than ever, the face of old Bill Fisk stares back at me. The night he died, a car collided with an iron rubbish skip outside my Beirut flat. The impact made a gong-like sound, followed by the scraping of the skip's iron wheels on the tarmac. The car drove away without stopping, so I padded downstairs in my dressing gown and helped Mustafa push the heavy cart back to the side of the road so that no other motorists would be hurt, and then, at around 8:15 a.m., Peggy called to tell me that Bill had died in his nursing home. She wouldn't be attending his funeral, she said. I had to arrange that. And I told her—it was the first thing that came into my head—that he was a man of his generation; it was an allusion to his infuriating Victorian obtuseness but I added that he had taught me to love books, which is true and which Peggy found herself able to agree with. So I went downstairs and told Mustafa and his family that my father was dead, and, according to Arab custom, each in turn shook hands with me—an affecting and somehow appropriate way of expressing sorrow, far more honourable than the clutching and happy-clappy hugging of so many Westerners. But I couldn't say I was sorry. Maybe Bill had lived too long—or maybe Lebanon and the war crimes I had reported had made me somehow atavistic, as if the backlog of history that always seemed to hang over the events I witnessed had driven into me a cold and heartless regard for the present.

The knights of the First Crusade, after massacring the entire population of Beirut, had moved along the very edge of the Mediterranean towards Jerusalem to avoid the arrows of Arab archers; and I often reflected that they must have travelled over the very Lebanese rocks around which the sea frothed and gurgled opposite my balcony. I have photographs on my apartment walls of the French fleet off Beirut in 1918 and the arrival of General Henri Gouraud, the first French mandate governor, who travelled to Damascus and stood at that most green-draped of tombs in the Umayyad mosque and, in what must be one of the most inflammatory statements in modern Middle East history, told the tomb: "Saladin, we have returned." Lara Marlowe gave me an antique pair of French naval binoculars of the mandate period—they may well have hung around the neck of a French officer serving in Lebanon—and in the evenings I would use them to watch the Israeli gunboats silhouetted on the horizon or the NATO warships sliding into Beirut port. When the multinational force had arrived here in 1982 to escort Yassir Arafat's Palestinian fighters from Lebanon—and then returned to protect the Palestinian survivors of the Sabra and Chatila camps massacre—I counted twenty-eight NATO vessels off my apartment. From one of them, the Americans fired their first shells into Lebanon. And one night, I saw a strange white luminosity moving above the neighbouring apartment blocks and only after a minute realised that they were the lights of an American battleship towering over the city.

Iranians I meet often believe that Beirut is populated by CIA agents; Americans are convinced that Beirut is packed with bearded Iranian intelligence men. Sometimes I suspect they are both right. For in a sense, Beirut continues the tradition of postwar Vienna, an axis for the world's opponents to look at each other and wonder what common bond or hatred keeps them on this earth together. I recall that an American ambassador in Beirut once described how Lebanon was a beacon of democracy in the Arab world—in the very same week that Sayed Mohamed Hussein Fadlallah announced that Lebanon was "a lung through which Iran breathes."

Those were the days, in October 1983, when Vice President George Bush could announce—after the killing of 241 U.S. servicemen at the Beirut U.S. Marine barracks—that "we are not going to let a bunch of insidious terrorist cowards shake the foreign policy of the United States. Foreign policy is not going to be dictated or changed by terror." How archaic those words seem now, how lost in time. By 1998, we had found a new focus for what was to become "war on terror." Al-Qaeda's bombs were striking at the American jugular, at embassies and barracks. President Bill Clinton bombed Sudan—an innocent pharmaceuticals factory, despite Washington's initial lies to the contrary—and then sent a swarm of cruise missiles into Osama bin Laden's camps in Afghanistan. Where was this going to end?

Against such history, what did Bill's death matter? It was easy to forget, sitting on my Beirut balcony, that General Gouraud had arrived in Lebanon as a result of the Sykes–Picot agreement and the Anglo–French victory in the 1914–18 war, that even before the official collapse of the Ottoman empire, the French were deposing the Arab king, Feisal, who had taken Damascus. France would rule Syria and carve Lebanon out of its body and give it to a thin Christian Maronite majority that would soon be a minority amid the Muslims of the new and artificial French-created Lebanese state. Lebanon's existence, like much of the future Middle East, was contingent upon the victory of the British, French and Americans, and was made possible by the peace that followed the armistice of 11 November 1918—on the evening of which Second Lieutenant Bill Fisk had marched to his billets in Louvencourt.

I have in my Beirut home volumes of works on the French Mandate—most of them published in Paris in 1921, recording the reconstruction of the country, the restructuring of the Ottoman system of justice, the new currency and banks and railway renovation, all part of France's supposed mission of civilisation to the Middle East. The French brought to the Lebanese–Syrian railway system a set of modern steam locomotives for use between Tripoli and Homs, big 08-0s which had been awarded to them under the Treaty of Versailles as wartime reparations from the Kaiser's Germany.

With a schoolboy enthusiasm for steam locos that my father understood all too well, I went up to look at them in the aftermath of Lebanon's civil war. They still stood on their tracks, these great steamers, their boilers cut open by shells, their eight driving wheels chipped by bullet holes—they had formed part of the Palestinian front line against Syrian troops around Tripoli's port in 1983—and their oil continuing to bleed from their gaskets, a railway junkyard of early nineteenth-century state-of-the-art technology. For when I wrote down the engine serial numbers and returned to Beirut and called that renowned expert of Middle East steam, Rabbi Walter Rothschild of Leeds, he informed me that they had indeed belonged to the Reich railway system. These behemoths, it transpired, had once pulled the middle classes of Germany from Berlin to Danzig. And I remembered how once, long ago or so it seems to me now—it was in 1991—a woman friend whom I treasured wrote me a poem in which she said that she loved "the little boy in you who wanted to drive steam trains."

And I did. I loved railways. Peggy's French holiday scrapbook shows me loco-spotting at Creil, and one of Peggy's first colour films shows me watching the red-and-cream Trans-Europe express pulling into Freiburg station in Germany. Once in Lebanon, I found that the government had temporarily restored the old track between Beirut and Byblos, and I sat with the driver as he steered his massive Polish diesel loco and its single, tiny wooden carriage—brought across from British India after the First World War—so slowly that Abed would travel alongside the train and wave at me as the engine-driver tooted cars out of our way.

And then there came a day, of course, when it was my mother's turn to die. Peggy had suffered from Parkinson's disease since before Bill's death, but she had carried on living in the home I grew up in at Maidstone, where three kindly ladies looked after her. She wanted to die at home and so in September 1998 there was another call from Maidstone and this time one of the women who cared for Peggy said she thought my mother had only a few more days to live. I still had time to reach England. Years before her death, Peggy told me there must be no black ties at her funeral. "Everyone must wear bright clothes," she said. And so in the beau-tiful little Anglo-Saxon church at Barming outside Maidstone, she had the funeral she asked for. There were mountains of flowers, not a black tie in sight—even the bearers wore casual suits—and the congregation sang "All things bright and beau-tiful." But my mother's death was not as she would have wished. And it was cer-tainly not a death she deserved.

Like Bill, she was a patriotic soul, though with none of Bill's bombast. In the Second World War, during the Battle of Britain, she joined the Royal Air Force, repairing radio sets in war-damaged Spitfires; her sister Bibby trained air gunners in radio navigation. Peggy became a flame of optimism over my young life. "Everything will work out all right in the end," she used to say to me. And when I once asked what was the point of struggling with my homework when we were all going to die one day, she replied: "By the time you grow up, they may have found a cure for that." In a way, my mother did believe in immortality, and I took her incurable optimism with me thousands of miles from Kent—to Afghanistan, through the terrible battles of the Iran–Iraq War and to the conflict in Lebanon.

But there was another side to Peggy. As Father fretted in retirement, she became a magistrate. I recall how one day, gently arguing with my father—whose views on criminal justice might have commended themselves to Judge Jeffreys—Peggy said, quite sharply: "The accused often tell the truth—and I don't always trust policemen." When I was a small boy, the first book she urged me to read on my own was *The Diary of Anne Frank*—because she wanted me to understand the nature of good and evil. During the Israeli siege of Beirut in 1982, she discovered a rare telephone line into the Lebanese capital and used it to tell me how she deplored the cruelty visited upon the Palestinians. She asked me repeatedly why governments spent so much money on guns.

She took up painting, watercolours and oils, still life and portraits. Her diary testifies to the difficulties of living with Bill in his old age but she would talk qui-etly about the life of independence she would lead afterwards. She wanted to travel, to visit Lebanon, to go to Ireland. She saw a lifetime of painting in front of her. But after the onset of Parkinson's, she steadily lost the physical ability to live a dignified life—as surely as she maintained the will to survive. Within four years, she could scarcely speak or walk. So she communicated by pointing with a stick to letters on a piece of cardboard. Then she could no longer point. She insisted on being pushed about the garden of her home in a wheelchair. Then Peggy became too ill to move. Her last attempt to paint ended when she threw her brush onto the floor in frustration. Almost to the end, she believed they would find a cure for Parkinson's—the same "they" who might one day find a cure for mortality.

In her last days, Peggy lost the power to swallow or eat and caught pneumonia. Bibby visited her and told her that she had been "the apple in your mother's eye" and Peggy had managed a smile. When I arrived home, she was desperately trying to cough, apparently drowning in her own lungs, weeping with pain. And as I watched her dying, I remembered the cost of Bill Clinton's latest adventure in the Middle East. In all, the U.S. government spent $100 million in five minutes firing those cruise missiles into Afghanistan and Sudan. How much had it spent on investigating Parkinson's disease? How much, for that matter, had the British government spent?

On 11 September 1998, the day after Peggy died—there was no glimmer of recognition or emotion, Peggy just stopped breathing—I called the Parkinson's Disease Society in London. Each year, they put up between $1.5 and $2 million on research. So did the British government. But in 1997, an official for the society told me, the Medical Research Council stopped funding neurological research. I called New York to talk to one of the top Parkinson's groups in the United States. Around $45 million was spent by the U.S. government on neurological research (not all on Parkinson's), another $10 million by private organisations, just over $3 million by the U.S. Defense Department (for veterans), and pharmaceutical companies spent about $35 million. So we—the West—were spending less on Parkinson's research in a year than we spent in five minutes on weapons.

It was the kind of human folly that would have angered Peggy. And at her flowered funeral, I decided to point this out. I suggested to her friends who came to Barming church that we spent far too much time accepting cruel deaths, uncomplaining when money that might have cured cancer or Alzheimer's or Parkinson's was spent on weapons or military adventures. "Why do we not rage against those who accept the shameful idea that sickness must be 'incurable,' that our betters know what they are doing when they prefer missiles to medicine?" I asked. If resources had been better spent, I said, Peggy would not have been in that coffin in front of the altar.

All this had an odd effect. You could have heard a flower petal drop when I was speaking. But the rector, a kindly, intelligent man though evidently not from the Church Militant, responded with a prayer, saying he would "commit this anger to God"—which, of course, entirely missed the point. Unless there is a Heavenly Post Office which redirects packages of anger to our presidents and prime ministers, there wasn't much point in bothering the Almighty. It was Peggy's friends I was addressing. Some of them had told me of their own relatives who were dying of supposedly incurable diseases; yet I felt afterwards that I had failed to make them understand as surely as I had the rector.

They talked about Peggy being "at rest" now that she was no longer suffering. Letters arrived that spoke of Peggy's "release"—as if my mother wanted to die. I heard from one old lady about "God's will," which would suggest, if taken to its logical conclusion, that God was a sadist. If the message of Peggy's life was optimism and joy for others, the manner of her death—courtesy of our society's inverted values—was totally unnecessary. My father, an old-fashioned man, would have condemned my remarks in the church. It was also, I suppose, the first time Osama bin Laden's name had been mentioned in the sanctuary of the Church of England. Peggy might have objected to the vehemence of my words. But she would have wanted me to tell the truth.

She missed September 11, 2001, by three years and a day. Would her love of life, her optimism, have been tarnished by the international crimes against humanity in New York, Washington and Pennsylvania? Or would the sense of right and wrong which had provoked her anguished phone call to besieged Beirut in 1982 have surfaced? She had a sense of proportion that was quite lacking in the aftermath of 2001. I think it was because she had lived through the Second World War. She always complained when politicians used parallels with that Golgotha of a struggle. She knew that perhaps 50 million perished in those years, that thousands were slaughtered around the world every day between 1939 and 1945. Hardhearted though it may be to ask, what are 3,000 dead compared with such a testament of blood? Certainly, Peggy—and, it has to be said, in old age my father too—would curse at the mendacity of our presidents and prime ministers. Peggy had finely tuned political antennae and—in the way that the dead come back to us and talk in our imaginations—I could hear her anger in the years to come, in Afghanistan, in Iraq, just as I could feel her confidence in life. And now that this life was becoming more dangerous—especially to journalists, especially for us—I could remember with ever greater clarity the words I had muttered to myself as Peggy lay dead in bed in the front room of her home. I suppose every child without brothers and sisters says the same thing: I'm next.

I flew back to Beirut that wet September. I had known the Lebanese airline crews for years and I sat as so often behind the pilot's seat. A journalist has a magpie's instinct for the collection of useless facts, a rag-bag of inane details conjured from a thousand flights, visits to a hundred hospitals. The Lebanese pilots were political beasts, mines of gossip and information. They would soak up every story I told them and—by way of return, I suppose—they would try to interest me in their job. They would teach me to read the aircraft instruments, help me to understand the principles of powered flight, the purpose of the engine reverse thrust, the system of communication with ground control. Could it really be this easy to learn to fly?

"I am lucky to be alive," a local taxi-man said to me when I climbed into his car on the Beirut Corniche four years ago. "And you are also lucky to be alive." And it was my companion who noted the significance of these words—and then I thought yes, I was lucky, very lucky to be alive. I had travelled so far over those years, I had criss-crossed the Middle East month after month, and by the mid-Nineties I was lecturing across Europe and America, flying to the United States from Beirut, often twice a month. One evening I would be lecturing in Los Angeles, next morning I would be in Paris and twenty-four hours later Abed would be driving me through southern Lebanon. I would wake up on airliners, perspiring, quite forgetting where I was travelling, anxiously peering through the windows. Was it morning or dusk? Had I arranged to call the office from Paris? Should I have filed a report from California last night—"last night" being mid-morning in London? My parents could never have imagined such a life.

I was still Northern Ireland correspondent when I first visited New York in 1975. I was flying to see a girl from Clonmel who worked in Wall Street and I arrived in a snowstorm, bashed my hire-car against the side of a bus on the Verrazano bridge and then—with my date sitting beside me, impatient for dinner—I misread the route to our restaurant and got lost beside the East River. I brushed the ice off a phone booth and dialled the restaurant. They'd keep open for us, the waiter said, just follow the direction of the new World Trade Center towers and I'd drive past the restaurant. It was blizzarding across New York but we watched those two towers far across Manhattan for more than an hour until we drove right up to them and there was the waiter standing in the snow with an umbrella.

The United States did not seem so aggressive then. The British were angry that the IRA could raise funds in America—since these were the years before the "war on terror," the RAF did not choose to take the conflict to the enemy and bomb Boston—and the United Nations seemed able to handle "peace" in the aftermath of the 1973 Middle East war. I had visited pre–civil war Beirut on holiday from Belfast and noticed that there were too many Lebanese soldiers in the streets, that the Palestinians lived, armed and resentful, in the slums of Lebanon's refugee camps. But I was too involved then with the conflict in Britain's own dependency of Northern Ireland to comprehend the fires that were being lit so far away.

Sometimes the beauty of the sea off Beirut would discourage me from travelling. I would be due to leave on a 6 p.m. flight for Jordan but then, halfway through the afternoon, seduced by the sun and the bright green of the trees against the waves, I would call Ahmed Shebaro, my travel agent, and plead with him to find an early morning flight next day. And so I would sleep early and wake to the cooing of doves in the palms and then head off to that little sandpit that Winston Churchill created for the Hashemites, whose ruling family was still represented by the man we called the "PLK," the Plucky Little King.

Dinner with the PLK. That's how the news would go the rounds of the Middle East press corps. Informal, the royal court would insist. Off the record, we would assume. And when we turned up for dinner at the palace—this was in September 1993—and saw the candlelit table, more candles nestling amid the bookshelves, the *mezze* laid out along the flower-smothered marble table, it seemed that informality meant confidential. So when King Hussein ibn Talal of Jordan said "on the record," the notebooks fluttered like doves into our laps, the pocket cassette recorders clacking onto the marble table top. If invited, the king might visit Arafat in Jericho. The Israeli government was "courageous and far-sighted" in recognising the PLO. The world should support this historic initiative. It was "a last chance."

How often had we heard those words "last chance"? Camp David had been a "last chance." Now the Arafat–Rabin accord was a last chance. And it was inevitable that an American reporter should enquire after the king's health. Of course, he told us, he had returned from the United States minus one kidney. "But the last check-up did not show any trace of cancer." There would be a check-up every six months. "I'm trying to exercise as much as I can—and I'm still trying to give up smoking." And we all looked at the packet of Marlboro Lights that appeared in the king's left hand at the end of the meal. Not a frail man, but the PLK was aware of his mortality, an elder statesman now with nothing to lose by speaking his mind in public. Though when the lady from the *Washington Post* dared to question his right to postpone elections, he quoted the Jordanian constitution—and the king's prerogatives—in a faintly irritated way. Not a man to be crossed, one thought, not a man to brook opposition. But it was often difficult to fault the PLK.

He promised equality for those Palestinians in Jordan who chose to remain Jordanians after Arafat's self-autonomy elections. And after acknowledging in Rabat back in 1974 that the PLO was the sole representative of the Palestinian people, he remained the only Middle East leader in half a century to formally relinquish his claim to Arab lands rather than demand more.

We sat round the table and listened to all this, the half-American Queen Noor supervising the pourers of orange juice and the purveyors of spiced chicken and fruit, we scribes almost too respectful to raise, Banquo-like, the ghost of Saddam Hussein. But he had to appear at the feast. What, we asked the king, would be Saddam's role in a Middle East peace? And out it tumbled. Jordan had suffered for its humanitarian concern for the Iraqi people during the 1991 Gulf War. Aqaba, Jordan's only artery to the rest of the world, was moving towards desuetude. "It's no secret that I've not seen eye-to-eye with the Iraqi leadership for a very long period of time, since before the war . . . my whole concern was . . . for every country in this region." Jordan had tried and failed to persuade the Iraqis to withdraw from Kuwait. But had we read the report by UNICEF that by the end of 1993, a million Iraqi children would die as a result of UN sanctions? Yes, "in a context of peace and if Iraq can pull itself together—a democratic, pluralist Iraq, respecting human rights—the country has a tremendous part to play." That seemed to exclude Saddam, although the king did not say so. And the PLK talked about democracy, that unique phenomenon which he claimed could save the Middle East from extremism.

Were we taken in by this? The king may not have wanted to run his country without a parliament, as he told us, but Jordan was not exactly a Western-style democracy. "More democracy, more participation, more human rights," he said at one point. What did this mean? He hoped, he said, to live to see Jerusalem again. The candlelight gleamed off the king's balding head. He hoped nothing would happen to "Chairman Arafat." Mortality had made its appearance at the dinner table. King Hussein had just over five more years to live.

The PLK was a tough man and his refusal to oppose Saddam Hussein after Iraq's 1990 invasion of Kuwait kept the Jordanians and their half population of Palestinians loyal. He had the disarming—and disconcerting—habit of calling everyone "Sir," which must have been a hangover from his days at Sandhurst, but which led us journalists into the trap of thinking that he felt respect for his interlocutors. He had been damned by the usual American media for not supporting America's war against Saddam; newspaper readers were then forced to make their way through endless analyses of the king's likely fate. Was this the end of the Hashemites? Would Jordan cease to exist? The same outcome had already been predicted for Arafat. Was this the end of the PLO? But of course, the same international isolation that made Arafat weak enough to make peace with Israel also made King Hussein friendless enough to make peace with Israel.

It was a peace that froze very quickly and one that King Hussein might have preferred to wait longer to find. But Arafat's own blundering deal at Oslo made Jordan's treaty with Israel on 26 October 1994 inevitable. We went there, needless to say, to watch the next "last chance." It needed a lot of signatures. Down in the heat of Araba, even the statesmen found it hard to comprehend. There were four volumes of documents, each to be signed by six hands, and pages of annexes. No wonder Bill Clinton, the desert light reflecting off the papers, kept rubbing his face, asking for sunglasses and dabbing his pained eyes with a black cloth. Then soldiers brought the maps.

Six feet in length, they were opened for more signatures. Maps of Baqura-Naharayim, of Zofar, of ground-water tables, of Yarmouk, of saltpans in the Dead Sea. Abdul Salam Majalli, the Jordanian prime minister, raised one arm in astonishment as more volumes were thumped onto the table. Clinton, overwhelmed by the light off the sheets, turned his back on his guests as an aide provided him with an eye-bath, right there in the middle of the desert. Andrei Kozyrev, the Russian foreign minister, wore a sun-cap and sunglasses that made him look—as he scribbled his name again and again—like a football manager signing up a new star.

Thus did the men of Araba firmly divide Jordan from Israel, and Jordan from the land that was Palestine. Thus did King Hussein allow Israelis to go on living on strips of Jordanian territory. Thus did Jordan and Israel end their forty-six years of war, witnessed by just a single, junior PLO official from Amman, the sole representative of the people—the Palestinians—over whom they had fought each other. A minute's silence honoured the thousands of Israelis and Jordanians—some of whom must have been Palestinians—killed in those forty-six years. "I believe they are with us on this occasion," King Hussein said.

It was the noblest remark of the day by an ageing and tired king, a man who now thought much of death and one whose own people had the gravest reservations about this peace. Not many kilometres over the grey-brown mountains to the north-west of the seats upon which the dignitaries perched lay the city of Jerusalem, its eastern side—and the West Bank—still under the occupation of the very Israeli army that stood to attention before us. The Jordanian journalists stood unsmiling in the heat. "There's no real jubilation on our side," one of them said as Bill Clinton's stretch limo swept between the old minefields of the Jordanian–Israeli frontline. "The people are looking at this like surgery—something they have to go through. For the Israelis, this is a victory. For us, it's defeat."

That was not how the statesmen of Araba put it. It was "a peace of the brave" (Clinton), a "source of pride," the "dawn of a new era" and "a day like no other" (King Hussein), "the peace of soldiers and the peace of friends" (Israeli prime minister Yitzhak Rabin). The king came across as the most dignified of men and ended with a remark that left an unanswered question: "This [treaty] is not just a piece of paper . . . it will be real, as we open our hearts and minds to each other." Rabin touched on the same thought when he said that "peace between states is peace between people." Yet both men knew that in much of the Middle East, peace between states did *not* necessarily mean peace between people.

An Israeli journalist threw his arms around a Jordanian bureaucrat while scores of Israeli girls distributed cold water, each bottle labelled "Israeli–Jordanian peace October 1994" in Arabic and Hebrew, but with its provenance—the Israeli-occupied Golan Heights—printed only in Hebrew. The hundreds of chairs were tied together with thin plastic handcuffs, the same handcuffs used by the Israeli army. The twenty-one-gun salute by artillery crews who could have been shooting at each other, the rumbustious Jordanian anthem played before the haunting beauty of the "Hatikvah," the two granddaughters of Jordanian and Israeli soldiers killed in the 1967 war; they touched the elderly warriors standing next to the American president. But it needed Bill Clinton's stock of clichés—"Turn no-man's-land into every man's home"—and his ritual threats against "terrorism" to remind the 5,500 guests that this was an American peace, engineered by the United States and guaranteed by the United States—whose closest Middle East ally is Israel. Only when the annexes were published later did we discover that the border between Jordan and the occupied West Bank had been marked as the frontier between Jordan and Israel.

Nor did Hussein have any reason to feel that Jordan was safer for the peace treaty. Only weeks before his death, he was particularly vexed when an Israeli journalist, Israel Harel, disinterred an idea that had long appealed to Ariel Sharon. Writing in *Ha'aretz*, Harel claimed that "Jordan was founded on part of the Jewish homeland . . . It will ultimately become apparent . . . that two nations [i.e., Israel and Palestine] cannot live on the small piece of land to the west of the Jordan and that two states cannot live there. If nations with vast stretches of land that have no need for additional acreage are feasting their eyes on Jordan, Israel must also stake its claim to Jordan . . . With that territory—even part of it—we could solve in cooperation with our peace process partners, many territorial disputes we have with the Palestinians."

Israeli prime minister Rabin was to be assassinated by an Israeli—an "extremist," according to Western journalists, of course, not a "terrorist"—just over a year after the Araba treaty was signed, and King Hussein would survive for only another four and a half years. He had never given up the Marlboro Lights and his death from cancer followed gruelling chemotherapy treatment in the United States and an ill-advised, rain-soaked motorcade through Amman to celebrate his supposed recovery.

It was on this initial return to Jordan that a scandal of royal proportions broke over the Hashemites. Hussein disgraced the cosy, avuncular figure of his brother Hassan by taking away his role as crown prince. Hassan knew the game of kings had ended the moment Hussein arrived at Queen Alia airport. There was a formal embrace from the man who thought he had won his battle with cancer. But he ignored Hassan's son Rashid and then showed what he thought of his crown prince by choosing to travel into the city not with Hassan—his normal routine—but alongside Queen Noor. Hassan was left behind. The man who had waited thirty-four years to be king of Jordan was stunned.

In his American clinic, Hussein had been told that Hassan had tried to fire the chief of staff of the Jordanian army, that Hassan's Pakistani-born wife Princess Sarvath had changed the carpets in the royal palace in anticipation of becoming queen. Both stories appear to have been untrue. Hassan had told Walid bin Talal, a Saudi billionaire, that he could not purchase the home of the chief of staff because it belonged to the field marshal. And Sarvath had been redecorating her own home—a period villa once owned by the former British ambassador Sir Alec

Kirkbride—not the king's. But far too many portraits of Crown Prince Hassan had begun to appear across Jordan and—a dangerous precedent, this—pictures of his own son as well. Hussein publicly accused Hassan of plotting little less than a coup d'état.

When word of the king's suspicions first reached Hassan, he presented himself before his brother and asked Hussein bluntly: "How have I offended you? Here is my gun. If I have been disloyal to you, please shoot me—but do not disgrace me." The king ordered Hassan to take his gun back and reassured him that he was still regent. The sequel to this was far more extraordinary. The king called Hassan to the royal palace at half-past midnight on 20 January 1999, to present him with his letter of dismissal. A photographer was waiting to snap Hassan handing over his insignia to the new crown prince, Hussein's son Abdullah. Hassan returned to his car without time to read the document; driving away, he turned on the radio only to hear the contents of the unopened letter on the national news. Uneasy lies the head that wears a crown.

Many Jordanians felt that the manner of his dismissal was unnecessarily cruel. As crown prince, Hassan had been ordered by the king to handle Jordan's development projects—a role that inevitably brought him into conflict with the government of Prime Minister Abdul Karim Kabariti, who was said to dislike Hassan personally. Ministers believed that Hassan was trespassing on their prerogatives— something he had no right to do, since in Jordan the right of succession is the crown prince's only constitutional power.

But had Hassan cast his mind back to the day nearly forty-three years earlier when another trusted servant of the Jordanian monarchy believed he was secure in his job, he might have known his fate. King Hussein was only twenty-one at the time but he had already argued with Lieutenant General Sir John Bagot Glubb, British commander of his Arab Legion and principal military adviser to his majesty. Glubb had disagreed with Hussein over strategy—the young king wanted to retaliate against the Israelis for raids on his border—and Glubb also presented Hussein with a list of Arab Legion officers who he claimed were "subversives" and should be dismissed.

Convinced that London was trying to control Jordan's armed forces, the king fired the fifty-nine-year-old British general, along with his two top officers, the chief of staff and director of intelligence. In a tantrum, Hussein told his cabinet that his orders should be "executed" at once. Glubb Pasha was taken to the airport next morning in Hussein's own car. The king's anger subsided. Everything had been done in the interests of his nation. But to the sick king in the Mayo clinic in 1999, the crown prince was trying to take over the army—just as Glubb Pasha had been accused of trying to accomplish in 1956.

There was therefore nothing surprising about the dismissal of Crown Prince Hassan. The Hashemites had always lived on the edge, provoking disaster and recovery with a drama and nerve that still astonish other Arab leaders. They have a tendency to move rapidly between rage and contemplation, political folly and eternal friendship, that might be a characteristic of the Gulf Arabs rather than the Levant. But of course, Hussein's family did indeed come from the Gulf, from the province of Hejaz, and it was his great-grandfather, also Hussein, whom the Ottomans named as emir, sherif of the holy Muslim city of Mecca. An austere religious group faithful to the al-Saud family—the "Islamic fundamentalists" of their time—were to drive the Hashemites from what was to become Saudi Arabia and Winston Churchill was to appoint King Hussein's grandfather Abdullah as emir of Transjordan. Abdullah had wanted to be king of Palestine—for which the British had other plans. Abdullah's brother Feisal would become king of Iraq, the consolation prize for losing the monarchy of Syria—for which the French had other plans. King Abdullah tried to make peace with the Zionists who were planning their new state on Palestinian land—and after the Palestinian catastrophe of 1948, the monarch's life was forfeit. He had annexed the West Bank of the Jordan River; almost all the rest of Palestine had become Israel. The fifteen-year-old Hussein personally witnessed Abdullah's assassination in Jerusalem, a killing organised by Palestinians.

The Hashemites were thus a family of loss, a dynasty used to suspicion as well as resolution. They lost the Hejaz, they lost the west of Palestine. In Baghdad ten years later, King Feisal the Second—grandson of old Abdullah's brother who had been appointed by the British—was murdered in a Baathist coup which, twenty years later, would bring Saddam Hussein to power. In 1967, King Hussein, in the greatest disaster of his career, chose to join Egypt and Syria in their war against Israel, and was driven out of East Jerusalem and the West Bank. In less than half a century, therefore, the Hashemites had lost the Hejaz, Iraq and all of Palestine.

Inevitably the story of the family became the story of the PLK. His English schooling naturally endeared him to the British, who admire courage in adversity and, even more, plucky losers. When Hussein married Antoinette Avril Gardiner, daughter of a Royal Engineers lieutenant colonel, in 1961, it felt as though Jordan had become a British protectorate once again. "Toni," who became Princess Muna, gave birth to two sons, Abdullah—now the king—and Feisal. She was the second of four wives for a king whose marriages could be as turbulent as his nation's politics.* He had divorced his first and older wife Dina within eighteen months; the Jordanian ambassador to Egypt delivered the king's goodbye letter to the queen when she was visiting a sick relative in Cairo. The marriage to "Toni" foundered when his roving eye settled on the beautiful Alia Toukan, an employee of Royal Jordanian Airlines, whose love for the king might have given him lasting peace of

---

*A British diplomat would remark in 1983 that to witness the king's unhappy personal life was "a deeply saddening experience." Even then, he regarded Hussein as a sick man, suffering a heart condition and exhausted after nine hours of negotiations with Yassir Arafat. The king's fear at the time was that the Israelis would annex the West Bank and drive tens of thousands of Palestinians eastwards across the Jordan River. The same diplomat told me that "the Israelis would prefer a radical Palestinian state in Jordan to a friendly Western state under the Hashemites on the grounds that no one would expect them to make concessions to an extremist PLO nation on the east bank but that America would constantly be demanding negotiations with Hussein if Jordan survived in its present form." He was constantly at a loss, he said, to know why the Americans failed to understand what was going on in the Middle East. "They have enormous resources for tapping information, but they never seem to interpret it correctly." Not much was to change in the next twenty years.

mind—they married in 1972—had she not been killed in a helicopter crash just over four years later. Amman's Alia international airport is thus the only international airport in the world to be named after the victim of an air crash. Then in 1978, the king married Elizabeth Halaby, who became Queen Noor, an equally beautiful but forceful woman who physically towered over the king and who developed a strong distrust of his introverted, over-intellectualising brother Hassan. If the latter had become king, it was said in Amman, Noor would have left the country.

Having lost the West Bank, the king had to face the consequences: Palestinian contempt and what amounted to an attempted coup d'état by Palestinian guerrillas. With a ruthlessness that has still not been fully acknowledged, Hussein's Bedouin troops slaughtered their way through the Palestinian camps of Jordan and crushed guerrilla power. Having learned from his rash decision to go to war in 1967, the king sat out the 1973 Middle East conflict in near silence, maintaining semi-secret contacts with Israeli leaders, just as his grandfather had done. What he had, he would hold. The preservation of Jordan—as artificial a country as Britain ever invented—became the be-all and end-all for the Hashemites. The PLK would be a friend of the West. When a Washington newspaper claimed that the king had received millions of dollars from the CIA, the stories were suppressed in Amman.

In the West, we tend to divide the Arabs into three fictitious groups that prove our own racism as much as our ignorance: the scheming, hook-nosed greedy Gulf businessmen who appear in feature films and anti-Semitic cartoons in the American press—the Arabs, like the Jews, being Semites; "fundamentalist terrorists"; and thirdly—a throwback to the original Hollywood portrayal of the Bedouin desert leader immortalised by Rudolph Valentino—as "hardy warriors of the desert." The Hashemites were definitely in the "hardy warrior" bracket, or at least King Hussein was. A friend of the king once compared Hassan to Cecil Rhodes, a difficult personality to follow.

As for the king, he not only enjoyed sport and flying; he had a keen eye on the sport of the bedroom. Only months before his cancer was diagnosed, he was courting a Jordanian in her early twenties. Queen Noor was not amused. But it did his reputation no harm. Saudi Arabia's princes do not lack women and the emir of Kuwait has endured a series of revolving-door marriages with tribal ladies. Yet it was impossible to separate King Hussein's prolific love life from political gambles. Long regarded as a pliable "friend" of the West, he astonished his American allies by embracing Saddam Hussein—quite literally—after Iraq's 1990 invasion of Kuwait.* Did he really believe that Saddam would "liberate" Jerusalem? Or that

---

*There was nothing new in Hussein's propensity to shock. In 1987, just after the revelation that Dr. Kurt Waldheim, the former UN Secretary General and then president of Austria, had been an intelligence officer in the Wehrmacht's brutal Army Group "E" in Bosnia during the Second World War—a role he had hitherto carefully concealed—the king invited Waldheim on a state visit to Jordan. Hussein took his guest by helicopter to the heights of Um Quiess to overlook the Israeli-occupied West Bank, awarded him the Hussein bin Ali medal—named

Jordan could survive without the Gulf Arabs? He grew a beard; in Amman he was called Sherif of Mecca. The Saudis were enraged. He appeared to be looking towards lost lands. He knew the Palestinians would support Iraq. He became the most popular monarch in the Arab world at the very moment he became the most unpopular monarch in the West.

The Americans were ready to roll up the Hashemite carpet. But then in 1993 came Arafat's peace "deal" and his own treaty with Israel and overnight, the treacherous ally of the beastly Saddam had become again the Plucky Little King. Jordan was "ours" again. The Americans built a new, massive, fortified embassy on the outskirts of Amman. "Is this the new CIA headquarters?" Hussein joked to Jordanian friends one night as he looked across their gardens at the floodlit compound. He may have been right. The Hashemites may trace their ancestry back to the Prophet Mohamed—as they do—but they are Tudors rather than democrats, an oligarchy rather than a modern monarchy, however liberal and decent they are as individuals.

The wraithlike king was finally taken to hospital in Amman to die, and the storms that embraced the Middle East that first week in February 1999 seemed to presage something, the dark night that strangled the travelling lamp after Duncan's murder. Whirlwinds moved in from the sea off Beirut; one hit my balcony just after I saw it coming and escaped indoors, hurling my glass dining table to the wall and smashing the plates. In Amman, a dark fog covered the city, wrapping itself around the thousands of shrouded figures outside the King Hussein Medical Centre. Such wind, such very thick fog, but I could hear their voices from a kilometre away. "With our blood, with our soul, we sacrifice ourselves for you." Always the same words, the same desire for martyrdom. We had heard it from Palestinians, from Iraqis, now from Jordanians. Did they mean this when they said it?

Inside the hospital, royal courtiers struggled with a unique problem: when to turn off the king's life-support system which was all that kept him alive. Dialysis machines and intravenous drips were still pumping life into a king who, as a deeply religious man, believed that he should die when God—not man—decided. But the science of prolonging the life of the desperately sick took no account of the Koran any more than it did of the Bible. No Muslim prelate had yet succeeded in defining Islam's response to a development which had taken the moment of death out of the hands of Allah. In the end, he died, as a friend of the royal family told me, "in an orderly way and without any sense of shock." Even to kings, he comes . . .

Outside the hospital, the crowd's posters portrayed the dead king who lay only

---

after his grandfather—and praised Waldheim for his patriotism, integrity, wisdom and "noble human values." Watching him inspect a Jordanian guard of honour at Amman airport, I couldn't help noticing Waldheim's heels snapping smartly to attention, arms straight and head bowed, when saluted by the commander of the Royal Guard. German army discipline obviously ran deep.

a few hundred metres from us: fighter pilot Hussein, Bedouin warrior Hussein, Field Marshal Hussein. But not a single photograph of the king and his son together. The new King Abdullah—how strange the name sounded that day—was not in the thoughts of the screaming men or of the old woman who prostrated herself in a torrent of freezing water streaming down the roadway.

King Abdullah. It had a strange resonance; of another king almost half a century earlier at the Al-Aqsa mosque in Jerusalem, Abdullah's great-grandfather, with a bullet in his head and his turban rolling away from him, while a teenage boy—now the bald corpse inside the hospital behind us—collapses in horror. Jerusalem still lay only 70 kilometres away through the suffocating, frozen fog, as lost to the Jordanians today as it was when King Hussein's army retreated more than three decades ago.

So now this odd, fragile, brave little land had another British military graduate to run its affairs. Sandhurst, Oxford, Georgetown, tank commander and general with his very own Praetorian Guard. His special forces—one of those supposedly "crack" units that breed all over the Middle East—had put down a riot or two over the past few years. You only had to watch those people outside the hospital—and the uncontrollable nature of their grief—to understand how heavy would be the burden for King Abdullah. The people pushed at the police lines and sobbed into their hands and collapsed fainting into the mud around the gates. To a Westerner, to a tourist, Jordan is a friendly sandpit of Roman ruins, rock palaces, camels and an old railway line blown up by Colonel Lawrence. But its people had been wounded; 65 per cent of them could count Palestinian dispossession in their family tree. All day, the rain fell out of those cold, lowering clouds. And there was something about Hussein's funeral that betrayed a fearful reality for those who saw it.

Two Jordans buried their king. There was the formal, Westernised nation with its Scottish-style bagpipers and new, English-accented monarch who invited the world's statesmen to bury the "fallen warrior" on his polished gun carriage, Hussein's Arab steed—empty boots reversed in the stirrups—clopping obediently behind the coffin. And what the world saw—indeed, what the world was supposed to see—was the adoration of kings, presidents, prime ministers and princes: Clinton, Bush Senior, Blair, Assad, Yeltsin, Chirac, Shamir, Netanyahu, Mubarak, Weizman, Arafat, Sharon, Carter, Ford, the Prince of Wales . . . After all, had not President Clinton already consigned this man to paradise in his latest pronouncement on Jordan's loss?

Then there was the other Jordan. Outside the gate, sweating and shrieking to God, smashed back by gun butts, sworn at by the descendants of Glubb Pasha's Arab Legion as they clawed their way towards King Hussein's coffin, the other Jordan did not quite fit in with the pageantry on the other side of the palace wall. When the Jordanians broke through the troops and charged in their thousands towards the gates, they were confronted by hundreds more armed soldiers. "In the name of God, help me!" an old woman moaned as the crowd stamped her into the mud.

So which was the real Jordan? Was it the nation enshrined just above the marble floor of the Rhagadan Palace, where the coffin of the "little king" was honoured, prayed to, watched and nodded at by all the dangerous, untrustworthy allies who had variously loved, hated or plotted against him? Such sincerity, such affection, they all showed. There was Israel's prime minister, Benjamin Netanyahu, who had sent his killer squad into Jordan only a few months earlier to assassinate a Hamas official, bowing stiffly before the coffin. There was former president George Bush, who only eight years earlier had regarded Hussein as little more than an enemy agent. Yassir Arafat, whose gunmen once sought to destroy Hussein's kingdom, snapped to attention in his olive fatigues, twice saluting the flag-draped coffin in front of him.

And behind the coffin, scarcely moving, was the studied, often frowning face of King Abdullah the Second and his two half-brothers, Crown Prince Hamzah and Prince Hashem. They stood there, hands out in prayer from time to time, all dressed in immaculate suits and ties and wearing the same kind of chequered red-and-white kuffiah as Arafat. It was as if they were acting out some kind of unusual ritual, more like English public schoolboys in an unfamiliar play than Arab warrior princes, trying to cut a dash among the tall men of the old Arab Legion—Hussein had renamed them the Jordan Arab Army after dismissing Glubb—who guarded the coffin and its royal standard.

"Vulnerable" was the word that came to mind. The princes did not look old enough, or hard enough, or cynical enough, to handle the sleek men who passed before them to honour their father, some of them gentlemen, others venal dictators, quite a few with an awful lot of blood on their hands, the harmless and the harmful, one after the other, parading before the coffin as if waiting for passport pictures. I suppose it was not surprising that history was being rewritten for the watching world. On satellite television, the cancer-dead king was being eulogised as the man who freely made peace with Israel, whose country was praised—this from CNN—because it was now closer to Israel than to many Arab states. So we had to forget that the king once privately talked of the "manacles" of the Oslo agreement, which forced Jordan into so unpopular a peace treaty with Israel, and remember what Clinton had told us two days earlier: King Hussein was now in paradise. Which is where we were told Egyptian president Anwar Sadat had gone after his death—that being the destiny, it seems, of all Arab leaders who make peace with Israel at our behest.

The television boys—in some cases, the very same "experts" who had predicted the fall of Hussein when he refused to support America's 1991 war—were in full flow. "Unassailable moral integrity," "a visionary for peace," "a man of great charisma" with an "unquestioned" legacy, a man who "always wanted to give his people the rights that they deserved." These are, unfortunately, authentic quotations. What was that legacy again? And what political rights did Jordanians receive, save for a vote in a rubber-stamp parliament and the knowledge that if they stepped out of line in their "man-in-the-street" interviews with Western television reporters on the future of King Abdullah—just like his father, a soldier king, a chip off the old block, in fact—they would be taken off to His Majesty's constabulary for a thumping.

As for those crowds whose voices could be heard baying beyond the palace gates by the beautifully groomed kings and presidents inside, they loved the king, some of them. But there was less enthusiasm for the new king and much less for Prince Hamzah, Hussein's son by his last wife, Queen Noor. "Hamzah was chosen as new crown prince by the United States," a girl insisted.* She was a Palestinian Jordanian.

"Rubbish," I snorted at her. "You shouldn't believe in the *moamara*, '*The plot*,'" I said. But then, an hour later, I saw the full list of dignitaries at the palace and was struck by the number of State Department men, the boys from the Washington peacemaking department led by Martin Indyk, the ex-research director at the largest Israeli lobby group, who could not manage to persuade Netanyahu to stop building Jewish settlements on Arab land but who insisted Arafat must "crack down on terrorism." So was the real Jordan, then, among the swaying mass of shabbily dressed, shouting youths on the highway to the palace, many of them poorly educated, some pathetically adorned with crinkled pictures of the dead king glued to their shirts and scarves?

For when the coffin approached, a kind of ripple, half sound and half movement, spread through the lines of tired, somehow broken faces, as if a stone had been thrown into a human pond. There was no signal from them in advance, no instruction or indication save for a line of children who suddenly moved from the trees into the road. Then en masse the people swarmed towards the coffin and its jeepload of headscarved Jordanian guards, tears streaming down their faces, hands outstretched to touch, even to seize, the flag or perhaps the coffin itself.

I remembered thinking, before a panicking soldier struck two men with his rifle and punched me in the chest as the crowd fell on us, that it was like throwing petrol onto a kitchen stove. It was a strange, frightening kind of hysteria because it combined both love and fury in almost exactly equal measure, intense loyalty married to absolute rage. When I rolled over, I found the soldier lying beside me. At the funeral of Ayatollah Khomeini almost ten years earlier, the crowds tore at his shroud. And if the Arab Legion's descendants had not shouted in the name of their dead king and if the other soldiers had not laid into the first of the young Jordanians who tried to clamber onto the carriage, it might have happened again.

Violence is portrayed so differently when its progenitors are outside palace walls. How, one wondered, did these masses feel about the large presence of the Israeli foreign minister, Ariel Sharon, in front of their king's coffin, the very man who sent Israel's Lebanese Phalangist allies into the Sabra and Chatila Palestinian refugee camps in 1982? What did they make of the arrival of President Assad of Syria, who ordered his soldiers to "eliminate" an Islamic uprising in Hama in 1982, an operation that left the dead in their thousands? Or of the former Israeli prime minister Shimon Peres, whose 1996 offensive against Lebanon culminated

---

*In 2004, King Abdullah would in turn dismiss Hamzah as crown prince.

in the Israeli massacre of 109 Lebanese civilians in a United Nations camp at Qana, not to mention the dead of that ambulance in Mansouri? In every case, the victims had been Muslims, just as they had been in the war unleashed by the man who most astonished the world by turning up in Amman, whose butchery in Chechnya was still scarcely mentioned in the West. Boris Yeltsin waved to the cameras—I am alive, I am alive, he was trying to tell us—and walked falteringly into the palace. Close to him, Hussein's favourite white stallion, Amr, briefly reared up on her hind legs behind the coffin. As a remark of respect, it was said, she would never be ridden again.

And so we had to listen to more public adulation. Arafat claimed that Hussein had been a Saladin, the warrior knight who had driven the Crusaders from Palestine. In truth, it was the Israelis who drove the Hashemites from Palestine. But Hussein was a courtly man. What king would ever have turned up at his own state security jail to drive his most vociferous political opponent home? Leith Shubeilath had infuriated the monarch and was slapped into prison for asking why Queen Noor wept at the funeral of Yitzhak Rabin when the widow of a Palestinian radical leader murdered by the Israelis in Malta "did not receive any official condolences, nor was a single teardrop shed by a princess or the wife of any official." When the king arrived at the jail, Shubeilath delayed him for ten minutes while he said goodbye to his fellow inmates. Hussein waited patiently for him. Would Saddam have done that? Or King Fahd? Or President Mubarak? Or would Benjamin Netanyahu?

Perhaps it is this which distinguished the king: among the monsters of the Middle East, he appeared such a reasonable man. He believed that if he trusted enough in another person, his good faith would be returned; he was cruelly rewarded. He believed in Benjamin Netanyahu until the Israeli prime minister refused him permission to fly Arafat from Amman to Gaza in his private aircraft. "My distress is genuine and deep over the accumulating tragic actions which you have initiated at the head of the government of Israel, making peace—the worthiest objective of my life—appear more and more like a distant elusive mirage," he wrote to the Israeli premier in March 1997. Netanyahu announced that he was "baffled by the personal attacks against me." This was the same Netanyahu who turned up, bareheaded and black-coated, to mourn the king's passing.

What is it about dictators—kings or "strongmen" if they're on our side—that somehow infantilises all the people who live under them? Across the Middle East I would watch this process of dictator–people love, its extreme form made manifest in Iraq, but present in the Gulf states and in that brew of Arab nationalism and Soviet friendship which produced the Baathist regime of Syria. Always derided and scorned and often hated by America's right-wing friends of Israel, President Hafez Assad's Syria was throughout the Eighties and Nineties an unusual mixture of paternalism and ruthlessness, a mixture of childish "adoration" for the Baathist president and fear of the state security police, an understandable and cringing respect for authority made partly genuine by the fear of all those Arab states set up by the colonial powers: of chaos, anarchy and civil destruction should the whole architecture of the one-party state suddenly fall to bits. In Assad's case, his crown prince was his son Basil. The problem was that Basil was dead.

Syria was the only country I could reach by car from Beirut, and I travelled there when I could, always allowed a visa, my barbs and my condemnation and my occasional cynicism permitted, so a Syrian minister of information once explained to me with cloying *politesse*, because I wrote from "a good heart" and was not a foreign agent and because the government was prepared to forgive my "mis- takes"—a charitable policy that was not extended to Arab journalists. This created inevitably missing heartbeats among the middle-aged men who worked for the minister, who knew very well that they would have to smooth my way for inter- views that could—and sometimes did—go terribly wrong. "Oh God, Fisk is back again!" one of them would always shout when I put my head into his office in Damascus.

You could see his point. Under the door of every foreign guest in the three big hotels in Damascus would arrive each morning a symbol of the regime: the *Syria Times*. This was no flagship of new Arab democracy, no investigative organ trying to open up Baathism to the world as a free society. It was a paper with which min- isters and civil servants could feel safe, at home, even bored—because life in a dic- tatorship is essentially boring. That is the nature of dictatorial power. Nothing ever changes. Assad's ministers would outlast those of any other country—especially Iraq—and their loyalty was rewarded by Assad's loyalty.

So page 1 of the *Syria Times* would invariably contain a large photograph of President Assad, often seen reading a newspaper—though never, I noticed, the *Syria Times*—and even more frequently pictured as he addressed crowds of sup- porters or denigrated "Zionist expansionism." The *Syria Times* was one of those papers—brave in a perverse way, I suppose—that risked sending its few readers to sleep with front-page stories of five-year industrial plans, agricultural overproduc- tion and long telegrams from flour-mill workers in northern Syria congratulating President Assad on the anniversary of his "correctionist movement." Its inside pages would be filled with dull poetry, anti-Israeli tracts of inordinate length and, occasionally, articles by me which the paper had cribbed—without permission— from *The Independent*. I took the charitable view that this was obviously a mistake made with a "good heart." It was surprising how easy it was to adopt Syria's poli- cies for oneself.

The Syrian ministry man who always greeted me with an invocation was the same luckless official who would sit by my side one day when I asked the editor of the *Syria Times* if I could buy his newspaper, printing press and all. Why would I want to do that? the editor asked me. Because, I replied, I could close it down and would never have to read it again. The editor looked at me down his nose and said he didn't understand my reply. I smiled. He smiled. That's how it was done in Syria. Another "mistake" by me. The Syrian ministry official remains anonymous in this book because he still works for the present minister. That is the nature of Syria: obedience, faithfulness and continuity, the qualities every father-figure desires from his family. But Syria was a "middle" dictatorship. If you flew in from

London—or drove from Beirut—Damascus was the capital of a police state. If you arrived from Baghdad, it felt like a liberal democracy.

Every journalist would seek to find out something new about Syria. Was there any hope of political reform, a new purge on corruption perhaps? A new banking system that would ease the economy out of the hands of the old Baathists that surrounded the president? But Syria was not a country that lived on its future. It was in many ways devoted to its past, and its people—however much they might freeze politically in the sparse Baathist drawing rooms of Damascus—understood their country's history in a way that few Westerners did, or even tried to do.

One cold day in November 1996, I set out for the village from which President Assad came, high in the Alawi Mountains of western Syria, to Qardaha where his son lay in a mosque of grey concrete under an equally leaden sky. They were still building the shrine over Basil Assad, *chevalier* of Syria, leader of men, enemy of corruption, favourite son of Hafez, the president of Syria. At the gates of the unfinished mosque at Qardaha, a paratrooper in a red beret and a young man greeted me.

The civilian was dressed in black and I noticed at once that he was wearing a black tie bearing the image of Basil, in which the president's dead son wears black sunglasses. Another young man approached me, the guardian of the shrine, unwilling to give his name because "Basil outshone all of us who remain alive." I gesture towards the monument to my right, a tall concrete spire upon which an artist's impression of Basil, in the uniform of the Syrian army, is riding his show-jumping horse upwards towards the stars of heaven while his father Hafez, in presidential blue suit, holds out his arms in farewell, his face a mask of sorrow and pride. Tell me about Basil, I ask the anonymous guardian. Is Basil not now more present in death—in all his portraits—than he ever was in life?

The guardian of the shrine smells of musk. He smiles and clutches my hand. "The late Basil had no peers—as a leader, no one could match him," he says. "He won a gold medal as a horse-rider in the tenth Mediterranean games. He had no rival in sportsmanship. As a free-fall paratrooper, he was one of our heroes." I try to ask another question but the guardian politely raises his hands in protest. "Thanks to the late Basil, the government has computers—he was the founder of the Syrian Data Processing Society. He was a staff major in the army, winning all his military courses, and he graduated with a Ph.D. in military science from the Khrushchev University in Russia as well as a civil engineering degree at Damascus University." I wanted to talk about the monument but the admonishing hand rose again. "The late Basil spoke French and English fluently. He was modest. He talked to all the people in an ordinary way. He embodied the modesty of our president but you would never think the late Basil was the son of so important a man. He was against corruption and encouraged the youth to turn to sports in order to avoid the evils of drugs. He symbolised the morality of the younger generation."

There was here, I thought, the faintest ghost of Tom Graham, V.C., the fictional British soldier who went to fight in Afghanistan and whose "life" appeared to inspire young Bill Fisk. The man was perfect. It was as simple as that. Basil could do no wrong. He was the *sans pareil*. It was an oral version of the words carved on the shrines of great Arab nobles, but unstoppable—at least until I ask the dates of Basil's birth and death. "He was born on 23 April 1962. He died on 21 January 1994." Died, it should be added, on a foggy morning on the Damascus airport highway when his car overturned as he rushed to catch a flight to Germany.

The guardian invited me to enter the shrine. A cloud of incense funnelled towards the roof and, beyond a glass door, there stood the catafalque of Basil Assad, draped in green silk and embroidered with gold Koranic script: "God is Great and his Prophet is Mohamed." The tomb is that of a nobleman, faintly modelled on that of the horseback warrior who drove the Crusaders from the Holy Land and who rests today under an equally green canopy scarcely 135 miles away in Damascus, the same Saladin whom General Gouraud had mocked in 1921. Behind the catafalque, two bright sodium lamps illuminated a startling oil painting of Basil: unsmiling, bearded, handsome, hair tossed carelessly over his forehead, a look of grim determination on his face, a man—like his father—not to be crossed, in life or in death. The young mourners in black were there to ensure respect and watched me carefully for a minute, but then—with a sudden flourish of open arms—told me I could take photographs. "Because it is darker here, I suppose you'll be using 800 film," the guardian said softly. It was like the end of a religious service, that moment when the priest warns his congregation that it is raining outside, that they will most certainly need their umbrellas. Yes, I needed 800 film.

Assad means "lion," and the roadside outside Qardaha greeted me with the words: "Welcome to Qardaha, the Lion's Den." The lion's den turned out to be an unremarkable village—save for its luxury hotel and modern highway—buried in a fold of hills below the mountains east of Lattakia in north-west Syria where the minority Alawite people, to whom President Assad belongs, form a majority of the population. The Lion of Qardaha became the Lion of Damascus on 16 November 1970, when, as minister of defence in the Baath socialist government, Hafez Assad toppled his rivals in a bloodless coup—this was the "correctionist movement" of which the *Syria Times* so often wrote—opening up his country to economic and political liberalisation but ensuring that his rule remained—with the help of an efficient secret police apparatus—unchallenged.

But now that his favourite son was gone, could Assad's regime survive his own death? It was a question that every Syrian asked. Assad gave his country stability and unity, crushed his internal "Islamist" enemies and fought the Israelis, in a vain attempt to recapture the Golan Heights in 1973 and in a successful battle to prevent Israel from subduing Lebanon in 1982. He had wanted to bequeath to his favourite son a Syria that had regained its lost lands, that stood unchallenged as the vanguard of the Arab world. The son had now died; but Assad's Syria was still demanding the return of the Golan Heights from Israel. There could thus be no Middle East peace without Syria—this became Baathist shorthand for many months of negotiations—but it was Basil's ghost that now stood sentinel over Syria's future. "He is with us still," the guardian of the shrine tells me in the frozen wind outside the mosque. "He will always inspire us." And he holds my hands in both of his, looking into my face.

As I drive out of Qardaha, the smell of musk comes from my hands—it will remain with me all day. On the right of the road, towering over the trees and embankment, a massive statue of Basil and his horse stares down at me. Basil will follow me all over Syria, on banners and flags and posters, in the camouflage uniform of the Syrian army, in khaki dress on horseback or, in bronze, striding towards me beside the international highway north of Damascus. And so will his father, the sixty-six-year-old man whose giant statues and busts appeared at the gates of Syria's great cities. From some of his plinths, he holds out his arms towards me. From others, he stares at my passing car, eyes fixed, presidential sash over his shoulders. At the village of Deir Attiah, the home of Assad's *chef de cabinet* and close personal friend, Abu Selim Daabul, his statue dominates a cliff-face, waving down at me cheerfully through the winter rains. "We cannot stop the people from erecting his statues out of gratitude," a Damascus newspaper editor insisted when I raised with him what could easily be mistaken for a personality cult. "The president did not ask for these statues. They were not his doing." And the editor watched me for a long time after saying this, to see if I believed him.

It was certainly true that the cult of presidential adoration with which Saddam Hussein had surrounded himself in Iraq—a Saddam City, Saddam International Airport, Saddam hospital and a Saddam art gallery—was quite absent in Syria. While Basil's name had been given to hospitals and provincial airports, there is only one Syrian institution which is dedicated in the name of the father. In Damascus, he sits today on a mighty iron chair—open book in his right hand—outside the Assad Library, a vast institution whose 22,000 square metres of pre-stressed concrete galleries contain the very continuity of Syrian history: 19,300 original manuscripts dating back to the eleventh century, 300,000 volumes, an audio-visual and computer centre, a series of state-of-the-art halls for ancient manuscript repairs and preservation. When I meet Dr. Mazin Arafi, director of the library's "cultural activities," he speaks in near-reverence, in a whisper, of the mass of information now being placed on computer, including every Syrian law enacted since 1918—when the Syrians briefly enjoyed freedom from the Ottoman empire before French colonial rule was clamped upon them. Every Syrian-produced film, including Palestinian documentaries of the 1948 war with Israel, has been videotaped. Even those books banned by the regime are available for student research, including the later works of Michel Aflaq, who co-founded the secular, socialist Baath party in 1940, but who subsequently exiled himself to Iraq when the party divided between Syrian and Iraqi factions.

Dr. Nihad Jord opens the cabinet at the entrance to the manuscripts department and there, six inches from my face without a sheet of glass to separate us, lie pages of gold-and-blue Farsi script, a work of Islamic philosophy by Bin al-Marzouban al-Azerbaijani, handwritten in western Iran in 1066. As Harold of England was preparing to fight William of Normandy at Hastings, al-Azerbaijani was completing a text that would, nine centuries later, be photographed and placed on a database at the Assad Library. Dr. Jord walks through a narrow passageway. Lying beside us are a 1649 French translation of the Koran, a 1671 Bible in Latin and Arabic, a 500-year-old Arabic dictionary, the collected speeches of the Caliph

Ali—dated 1308—and a 1466 study of how an Arab warrior should ride his horse while fighting with sword and spear. All have been transferred to the computer where Syria's modern history is also carefully recorded for posterity.

It is like a brain, this library; I understand this when Hasna Askihita takes me into the computer room. "Here we have put on our database every speech made by our president since 1970," she says. And how many speeches has the president made since he came to power? I ask. Quick as a flash, she replies: "He has made 544 speeches. Would you like to call for one?" And she trawls through the computer memory. Up on the screen comes an angry denunciation of fundamentalist violence in 1982, a presidential meeting with British journalists on 30 January 1992, a conversation between Assad and *Time* magazine editors the same year, a 1994 press conference with President Clinton. Here is immortality indeed—and, I reflected, a demonstration of just how formidable must be the capacity of Syria's other computerised institutions; its intelligence services, for example. But it has greater relevance than this.

For the Assad Library is clearly intended to provide a continuity that connects the caliphate with the Baath, the ancient Islamic philosophers with Hafez Assad, as carefully as the women in the archive repair rooms bind together the torn pages of fifteenth-century books. Indeed, the president's latest speech is that very day being entered into the database, Assad's address to mark the twenty-sixth anniversary of the "correctionist movement." "With adamant resolve," it begins, "we continue our march for victory, working with all strength for increased immunity of the homeland." Which, come to think of it, must have been what Harold of England was telling his troops on his way to do battle with William of Normandy in 1066.

What Syria tells its soldiers today is inscribed in a Koranic quotation around the top of the Memorial to the Unknown Soldier opposite Assad's hilltop palace above Damascus. "Don't think that those who have been killed for the cause of God are dead now. They are alive and are now enjoying the gifts of God." In the crypt, a flurry of Syrian officers walk over to me, small moustaches above grey and brown uniforms. "Do you know what this is?" one of them asks, pointing to an oil painting of a brown-walled building with smoke pouring from its windows. Like all Syrians, he wants to test the foreigner's knowledge of history, to see where he should start his narrative. I know that the building is the Syrian parliament in 1946, under fire from troops of a French government that refused to abandon its old League of Nations mandate after the Second World War—twenty-five Syrian MPs and soldiers died in the bombardment. In showcases in the wall, there are three-dimensional tableaux depicting a similar continuity to that established at the library. In one large showcase, Saladin is depicted slaying Crusader occupation forces at the battle of Hittin north of Jerusalem. Another shows Syrian Special Forces retaking the hilltop Al-Shaikh observatory from the Israelis in 1973 before the Israelis stormed back onto the heights of Golan. A third display shows Syrian infantry destroying Israeli tanks at the battle of Sultan Yacoub in southern Lebanon after Israel's invasion of 1982.

A fourth tableau displays a struggle about which every Syrian learns at school but about which almost every Westerner is ignorant: the 1920 battle of Maysaloun. In the aftermath of the 1914–18 war, France was given the League of Nations mandate for Syria, an obligation that it honoured by chopping part of the Mediterranean coast off from Syria—to create the Christian-dominated Lebanon which was to collapse in civil war fifty-five years later—and destroying the Syrian army which had trusted the British promise of Arab independence in return for its help against the Turks. The Syrian minister of defence, Youssef Azmi, led his cavalry against French tanks in the narrow valley at Maysaloun, on the border between present-day Lebanon and Syria—there was, of course, no border then because "Lebanon" was part of Syria—on 24 July 1920. General Henri Gouraud's mechanised armour—in a largely unrecorded historical precedent to the German tank attack on Polish cavalry nineteen years later—annihilated the warrior horsemen from Damascus and left them to rot in the summer heat.

The road to Maysaloun today is a six-lane motorway; Azmi's tomb lies almost hidden in a grove of trees to the south. When I arrived there on a cold evening, I found only his grave and a group of broken houses on the main road that appeared to have been destroyed by shells. Up on the hillside, however, was an old man who had vague memories of the battle: Hamzi Abdullah could not remember his own age but he had a clear recollection of a boyhood in which he spent weeks picking up the cartridge cases and shell fragments after the hopeless, doomed Arab cavalry charge of 1920. Hamzi was unshaven but wore an old kuffiah headdress. "The French came down from Wadi Nemsi with their Algerian and Senegalese troops," he said. "There were aircraft too and we didn't have any chance."

Hamzi held his right hand and wobbled it from side to side like a biplane caught in an updraught of air. "It was all over in hours and the French killed almost everyone they found. My mother was taken prisoner and put in a house just over there. Youssef Azmi and another of our leaders were tied up and the French decided to execute them. My mother has been dead twenty-seven years but I remember her telling me how she saw Azmi led to a telegraph pole to be executed. He threw his kuffiah at her and the other women and said: 'This is for you to remember me.' My mother said the women were crying but they threw it back to him, saying: 'You are the hero and you are the only one worthy of wearing these clothes.' He was tied to a post over there and the French told the French Algerians to shoot him. But they refused. They were good Muslims. So the French told their Senegalese colonial troops to do it. And the Senegalese shot him as he was tied to the telegraph pole."

Hamzi Abdullah's family produced the obligatory hot, sticky coffee, and a younger man joined us, a soldier who had fought in Lebanon. "I'll show you the place where they kept the women and Youssef Azmi," he said, and led me down the dirt hillside to one of the smashed Ottoman houses by the road. "This is where the French imprisoned them. But the house was mostly destroyed in 1967 when the Israelis shelled this area." So what the French had left undone, it seemed, the Israelis had finished. But not quite. For the ex-soldier's story was not complete.

"This has always been my home. In 1982, I fought across the border in the battle of Sultan Yacoub—we captured the Israeli tanks there—and the next year, when I was at home here, the American navy shelled us right across Lebanon and the shells of the battleship *New Jersey* fell on the hills up here." There was a silence while I scribbled this powerful example of historical continuity into my notebook. In 1920, the French had destroyed the Arab army at Maysaloun. In 1967, at the end of the Six Day War, the Israelis had shelled Maysaloun. Another sixteen years later, the U.S. 6th Fleet, supporting President Ronald Reagan's collapsing NATO force in Beirut, had shelled the Syrian army's supply route through this very same valley of Maysaloun. And the man who was telling me this had himself fought in the tank battle commemorated in the Memorial to the Unknown Soldier. France, Israel, America. If the Syrians were xenophobic, it was easy—here in this valley where the bodies of men and horses were once left to decay—to see why.

Syria's soldiers would fight to oppose the nascent Israeli state in 1948, and then to confront Israel in 1967, in 1973, in Lebanon in 1982. And they fought, also in 1982, at a city in central Syria called Hama—a name that is remembered with as much fear as it is left unspoken. When I began the long drive up the international highway, the cold, grey anti-Lebanon mountain range scudded with snow to my left, I found the very name of Hama oppressive. I had driven this same road many times as a reporter during the "Muslim Brotherhood" uprising of 1982, as the rebels of Hama assaulted the city's Baath party officials. They had cut the throats of the families of government workers, murdered policemen, beheaded school-teachers who insisted on secular education—as the GIA had done in Algeria, just as the Afghan rebels had hanged the schoolteacher and his wife outside Jalalabad in 1980; I still remembered the piece of blackened meat on the tree, twisting in the wind. Back in 1982 I had, for an extraordinary—and, I now realise, dangerous—eighteen minutes, succeeded in entering Hama as the army's special forces under Hafez Assad's brother Rifaat crushed the uprising with great savagery. I stood by the river Orontes as Syrian battle-tanks shelled the ancient city; I saw the wounded, covered in blood, lying beside their armoured vehicles, the starving civilians scavenging for old bread. Up to 20,000, it was said, died in the underground tunnels and detonated buildings. The real figure may have been nearer 10,000, but most of the old city was destroyed.* Now I was going back and I had some uneasy thoughts. Only a week earlier, I had been to Algeria, reporting the massacre of civilians by the armed Islamic opposition, the throat-cuttings and beheadings, the death squads and torture rooms of the government. Back in 1982, the world condemned Syria for the cruelty of its suppression of Hama; now it was largely silent as the Algerian government bloodily eradicated its own "Islamist" enemies. Was there not, I asked myself as my car hissed up the rain-soaked highway, an awful parallel here? We demand respect for human rights in the Middle East—rather more loudly among the Arab states than in Israel, to be sure—but we also warn of the dangers of fundamentalism, of "Islamic terror."

---

*For an account of the killings and destruction of Hama, see the author's *Pity the Nation*, pp. 181–87.

The roadblocks of plain-clothes intelligence men who had stopped me in and around Hama in 1982 had gone, but their presence could still be felt in a society in which any opposition to Assad's rule was regarded by the authorities as treachery. There is no doubt about who rules Hama today—nor about the need to erase its past. Over the wreckage of much of the old Hama now stand gardens, an Olympic-size swimming pool, a luxury hotel and a magnificent new mosque under construction. The latest British guidebook to Syria made not a single mention of the events of 1982, save for acknowledging the mysterious—and unexplained—absence of the original Great Mosque. Only when I walked across a small bridge in the Keylani suburb did I find reminders of the past: eighteenth-century buildings scarred by bullets, a palace of black-and-white stone lying gutted behind one of the city's famous noria water-wheels, a modern villa with a shell-hole where the window should have been. A few local painters were keeping alive what had been lost, in fragile watercolours that can be bought as postcards in the market.

And a few bold souls were prepared to recall what happened. Mohamed—it was the name he chose—stood in a narrow street in Keylani, speaking slowly and with great circumspection. "I lived here throughout the battle," he said. "My home was on the front line between the army and the rebels. I lived in the basement with my family of six for eighteen days. You cannot imagine how we felt when we ran out of food. I crawled out and found some old bread by an oil drum—it had been soaked in oil but we ate it. At the end, on the last day of the battle, we were able to leave."

The fact that Mohamed spoke at all to me was almost as extraordinary as his story. Was the climate of fear evaporating in Syria—or was the bloodbath at Hama now seen in a new perspective? A junior government employee—necessarily anonymous but genuinely loyal to Assad—tried to explain this to me as we lunched at the Sahara restaurant in Damascus. It is an expensive café of white linen tablecloths and bow-tied waiters, owned—ironically—by the man who oversaw the suppression of the Hama rebellion, the president's brother Rifaat. "I know you disapprove of what happened at Hama, Robert, the killings and the executions," he said. "But you must also realise that if our president had not crushed that uprising, Syria would have been like Algeria today. We tried to talk to the Brothers at first, to negotiate with them. We didn't want this bloodbath. We asked them: 'What do you want?' They said: 'The head of the president.' And, of course, that was the end. We were not going to have an Islamic fundamentalist state in Syria. You in the West should be grateful to us. We crushed Islamic fanaticism here. We are the only country in the Middle East to have totally suppressed fundamentalism." And over our plates of chickpeas and tomatoes and garlic-pressed yoghurt, the local arak burning our mouths, one could only reflect upon the devastating truth of the man's last statement.

Assad's own hatred of the Muslim Brotherhood comes through in a speech he made a month after the Hama bloodbath, his words now dutifully preserved in Hasna Askihita's computer memory in the Assad Library under the date of 7 March 1982. Assad's comments are astonishing, even frightening, for he might have been talking about Algeria. "Nothing is more dangerous to Islam than distorting its meanings and concepts while you are posing as a Muslim. This is what the criminal Brothers are doing . . . They are killing in the name of Islam. They are butchering children, women and old people in the name of Islam. They are wiping out entire families in the name of Islam . . . Death a thousand times to the Muslim Brothers, the criminal Brothers, the corrupt Brothers."

And so it came to pass, just as President Assad said; death did find them, a thousand times and more.

Two years after Hama, Rifaat would try to seize power from his brother, trundling his T-72 tanks through the streets of Damascus, and would be exiled to Spain and would, even when Hafez died, speak of the "farce" of the presidential succession—which was not to be his. The restaurateur and nightclub owner and sword of vengeance against the Muslim Brothers of Hama would never come to power. Like Prince Hassan of Jordan, he had mightily—though more violently—displeased his brother.

Other enemies, meanwhile, remained at Syria's gates. After agreeing to the land-for-peace formula of the old Bush administration, Assad was now being told by the Israelis that he must make peace without the return of Golan. Six times in 1996, the Israeli military talked of a possible war with Syria. When Assad transferred some of his 21,000 troops out of Lebanon and positioned an armoured brigade south of the Damascus–Beirut highway to prevent a possible Israeli assault that autumn, he was accused of preparing an attack on Israel. In reality, he was the only Arab leader to warn of the dangers of the "peace process" and to speak publicly of his suspicions that the Israelis would decide—after obtaining concessions from the Arabs—to hold on to most of the land they seized in 1967.

It is not difficult to see just how much land this involves. I sped down the long straight road to Quneitra, the Syrian city that the Israelis systematically destroyed when they retreated from the initial 1973 postwar ceasefire lines under the Kissinger agreement. To my right, the Golan Heights, occupied by Israel since 1967—and the very fulcrum of the "peace process"—grew purple through the winter haze, capped by a line of snow. Israel's refusal to return this territory—contrary to the pledges given by the United States before the 1991 Madrid Arab–Israeli summit—remains, outside the occupied Palestinian lands, the one outstanding *casus belli* in the original Arab–Israeli conflict.

I drove past the old front lines of the 1967 war, the abandoned, overgrown gun-pits of the 1973 war, the new revetments of the Syrian army's forward units, sprouting with radio aerials, defended with armoured vehicles and troop trucks. And far down the road, inside the UN ceasefire zone, I came to the ghost-town of old Quneitra, greeted as usual by an Assad statue and a string of banners above a ruined house, each portraying a smiling Assad and his son Basil. In the name of the father and of the dead son, the land beyond this town—the heights of Mount Hermon and the string of hills boasting Israel's high-tech radar stations—is all supposed to be liberated one day, whether by peace or by war. On the Syrian front line—so close that I could see the Israeli soldiers looking at me through binoculars—a Syrian lieutenant pointed to a group of tourists across the fields. "You see those three cars? They are probably Jews, foreigners, being told that Syria is their country, that everything they see should belong to them, Damascus and beyond." This, I am sure, is what the lieutenant believed. And I was almost equally certain that the tourists in those three cars were being told that Golan was part of Israel and that Syria was only waiting to seize it.

A hundred metres away, neatly maintained amid yew trees and grass plots, I found the graves of the Syrian soldiers who fought across this ground over almost half a century. Most lay beneath Islamic headstones, though some were beneath Christian crosses. Here lay twenty-nine-year-old Major Ismail Bin Khalaf al-Shahadat, a Muslim who "fell martyr on October 9th, 1973." Beside him lay Sergeant Mikael Srour bin Wahebi, a Christian from northern Syria, who was killed in action just one day earlier. There were twenty-one-year-old corporals from Latakia and Aleppo and, behind them, older remains. Here was Private Kamel Mohamed Yassin of the 2nd Infantry Regiment, killed in action "for the Pan-Arab cause"—the attempt to destroy the infant state of Israel—on 13 July 1948; and Corporal Salah Brmawi of the 2nd Cavalry Regiment, and a hundred others.

At the edge of the cemetery, I found former Syrian air force Private Assad Badr, now the grave-keeper of Quneitra, tending his roses in the bright midday sun. How did he feel about the dead? "The feeling of any live man for the dead," he replied. "We take pride in martyrdom." But when I asked if *he* had seen death in war, the man's smile clouded. Yes, he said, at the Dumair air base during the 1973 war. "We were sitting in a slit-trench eating our lunch out of tin cans when an Israeli Phantom jet suddenly came at us, firing its cannon. The bullets ripped right through the trench and just missed me. But my friend, Morem es-Sair, was next to me and the bullets cut him in half—right in half beside me." Then two explosions changed the air pressure around us and, far above the front line to the west, two Israeli jets sonic-boomed their way northwards, their silver contrails hanging like ropes behind the war memorial and the white gravestones.

But Golan was not the only "lost land" the Syrians desired. The map of Syria that you can buy in Damascus bookstalls contains an intriguing anomaly. To the south, the Golan Heights are shown as Syrian—which they are, though under Israeli occupation—but in the north, the national territory is drawn up the Mediterranean coastline, way beyond Latakia. Yet drive up the coastal highway and the map seems to be a little ambitious. Even before I reached the town of Sweidiyeh, I found, beyond a Syrian customs post, the Turkish flag. And above the frozen mountain road inland to Aleppo, alongside the wood-smoked valleys and frosted orange orchards, Turkish flags stood upon the heights—100 kilometres south of the border printed on my map. Only on closer inspection did I notice a thin, almost invisible broken line on the paper, marking the modern-day Turkish frontier and another piece of lost Syria. The cartography told that largely forgotten story of France's 1939 "gift" to Turkey of the Syrian city of Alexandretta in the hope of persuading the Turks to join the Allied side in the forthcoming war against Germany.

It was astonishing to realise how much Syria—as a land rather than a nation—

had lost in the twentieth century. Portrayed as an expansionist state only awaiting the opportunity to seize all of Lebanon, Palestine, even Israel, Syria has contracted rather than expanded, losing northern Palestine, Lebanon and Transjordan after the First World War. Alexandretta in 1939, Golan in 1967—the first three through Western trickery and the last through war. If the Hashemites had spent their modern life losing land, so had Syria.

Just over a year after King Hussein departed, another caliph was to die, the Lion of Damascus himself, and in circumstances of some irony for Syria's enemies. For almost a quarter of a century, Assad's army had been present in Lebanon—to oppose Israel's invasion, it is true, but also to ensure obedience. At noon on Saturday, 10 June 2000, Hafez Assad was talking on the telephone to his Lebanese protégé, President Emile Lahoud, telling him—and this was the way Assad spoke—that "our destiny is to construct for our children a future which reassures them." At this point, Lahoud heard the telephone drop and the line cut. Ten minutes later, Lahoud was reconnected to the presidential palace in Damascus, to find another voice on the phone. It was Bashar Assad, the president's ophthalmologist son. "My father has just passed away," he said.

Another king, another funeral. Yet when at last it reached us, Assad's coffin seemed ridiculously small, a narrow, polished wooden box under a Syrian flag, dwarfed by the truckload of sweating troops in front and the pale green field gun behind. The Lion of Damascus had also compared himself to Saladin, whose own twelfth-century remains lay little more than a kilometre from us. But then a few metres away—a shock in the heat and dust and xenophobia of Damascus—walked the tall figure of his son Bashar, black-suited, black sunglasses above a tiny moustache and prominent nose, ramrod-straight, brisk and businesslike behind the gun carriage that bore his father. If his uncle Rifaat, Assad's brother, really wanted to dethrone him, as many in Syria believed—if there was anyone here amid the tens of thousands, a single person who wanted to destroy the life of the heir apparent—Bashar did not seem to care. In Amman, the leaders and the people had been kept apart. In Damascus, they walked together.

Bashar Assad, a computer enthusiast who never expected to be the crown prince of Baathism, was flanked by his braided generals, as all Middle East leaders must be, and I had seen most of them before, over the years: General Ali Aslan, the chief of staff whose 5th Division almost recaptured the Golan Heights in the 1973 Middle East war and who ordered Syria's helicopter units to prevent Israel's advance up the Lebanese mountains in 1982; General Mustafa Tlass, Assad's faithful retainer and minister of defence, who almost died in an Israeli air raid on Lebanon. And there was Bashar Assad's younger brother, Maher. And his uncle Jamil, who once, pleading for Rifaat after he had opposed Hafez Assad, was told by the old man now lying in the coffin: "I am your elder brother to whom you owe obedience—don't forget that I am the one who made you all." Thus the creation of the dead president followed him on his last journey through Damascus. "How can we bring Assad back?" the crowds thundered. And their reply was the beat of a funeral drum.

It was an orderly affair as such things go in the Middle East, less of the shriek-ing chaos of King Hussein's funeral, more of the regimented mourning learned in ministries and police stations. The Republican Guard with their automatic rifles faced away from the cortège, towards the Syrian "masses" who so often gave— and here we take a sublime leap into the mysteries of Assad's electoral system— 98 per cent of their votes for the now dead president. The two police cars in front had the word "PROTOCOL" in capital letters painted in white on their bonnets— which is the way this regime liked to conduct its affairs: ordered, measured, ruth-lessly uncompromising.

So it was surprising, amid the dust rising from the feet of the running crowds and the soldiers screaming at the young men in black to stand back from the gun carriage, to hear a youth turn on a policeman. "*Lesh amtet fauni?*" he bawled. "Why are you pushing me?" And equality, I suppose, is what Baathism was sup-posed to be about. Thousands of teenagers in cheap shirts and jeans—smelling of sweat and cigarettes and, some of them, crying—ran level with the coffin, and there was indeed an equality of hysteria and desperation. But at the People's Palace, we learned what equality was really about. U.S. secretary of state Made-leine Albright marched like a Georgetown teacher into the state rooms in blue hat and white scarf, ahead of President Mohamed Khatami of Iran. But there she stayed while the Syrians brought the dignified, robed Iranian leader at once to the coffin.

Where was Clinton? How come Hussein of Jordan deserved an American pres-ident but not Assad of Syria? Was this bureaucracy? Or was it because Hussein did what the Americans wanted and Assad did not? Khatami prayed before the flag-draped casket, lips moving, just as President Mubarak of Egypt had done a few minutes earlier, the Egyptian president's eyes all the while moving fishlike across the diplomats in the same room. Did Mubarak reflect on the two stars that still adorned the flag on the coffin, the almost forgotten symbol of union between Syria and Egypt, the very last vain attempt at Arab unity?

Arafat was given his moments at the coffin, but merely coffee beside Bashar, his left, Parkinson's-quivering hand clutching the side of a chair. How Hafez had raged at this little man in his ill-fitting uniform and kuffiah, once expressing his irritation that Arafat's Arab slobbering kisses lasted far too long. For once, there were few mourners with blood on their hands—barring, I suppose, the long-congealed blood of those tens of thousands of Iraqi children who had died under the sanctions that Madeleine Albright had so sternly supported. Vladimir Putin, the killer of Grozny, sent the old Russian prime minister, Primakov. Sharon could never have come. Rifaat, the butcher of Hama, faced arrest if he turned up for the funeral. But there were guerrilla fighters aplenty: as well as Arafat, the chairman of Hizballah, Sayed Hassan Nasrallah, and a clutch of minor, soon-to-die Palestin-ian fighters from the old, beaten days of Fatahland in southern Lebanon.

On Syrian television, they back-clothed the whole affair with Beethoven while a commentator swooned over the dead president. "You are our teacher and our method and we have learnt from your example—we will learn from your thoughts and ideas. Our hearts are broken and our eyes are weeping—we were stunned by your death and we cannot really wake up . . . and we cannot believe that you have left us." Here again was that essential infantilism of every dictatorial regime. This was not adoration. This was, you might say, more than adoring; a systematic, god-like transformation of Syria's leadership into Titans.

It was no different at Qardaha, where Assad was now ceremonially laid in the ground, in the same mosque as his son Basil, beneath a bed of white flowers. "Oh God!" an old man shrieked beside the grave, hurling himself to the marble floor, writhing and groaning, his words more and more distorted by the cavernous interior of the building. "My God! My God!" he kept crying. "He has lost his senses," the head of protocol muttered. Maan Ibrahim was a tall man in midnight-black clothes. "This often happens here. The people loved him so much, you see. But we see these things all the time now." The middle-aged man was dragged past us by three officials, the back of his head reflected off the marble floor, thick clouds of incense drifting past us in the smoky interior.

Idolatry or love? Affection or insanity? They passed through the mosque at the rate of 5,000 an hour, Shiite prelates and Catholic priests and Syrian generals, the sunlight splashing off their golden lapels, and elderly women and girls in tight black trousers and village men, unshaven and weeping, and an entire passenger aircraft crew, all in their neatly pressed Syrian Arab Airlines uniforms. There was only so much of this that a visitor could take. Critical obituaries were not to be had in Syria; references to past "mistakes" are only acceptable because Assad himself once referred to them.

But there were lessons to be learned. Qardaha was the very centre of the Alawi Syrian minority which has controlled so much of Syria's destiny, indeed so much of Syria, over the past thirty years. Which also helped to explain why a convoy of Hizballah coaches turned up at Assad's tomb, their black-shirted occupants, bearded and funeral-faced, longing to pay reverence to the greatest of all modern Alawites. The black flags and a fascination for the meaning of death seemed quite natural for these young men, the guerrillas who had just driven the last Israeli soldiers out of southern Lebanon, many of whose colleagues had been torn to pieces by Israeli rockets and bombs over the past eighteen years of guerrilla warfare.

For the Alawis themselves are a Shiite sect, a remnant of the Shiite Muslim upsurge that swept Islam a thousand years ago. Like the Shiites, the Alawites believe that the Prophet's cousin and son-in-law Ali—hence "Alawite"—was robbed of his inheritance by the three caliphs. Like the Christian Maronites of Lebanon, they took refuge in mountain valleys, safe from the torments of their Sunni Muslim cousins. Most Alawites belong to four tribes—the Matawira, the Haddadin, the Khaiyatin and the Kalbiya. Assad's grandfather Sulieman belonged to the Kalbiya.

Officially, Baathism, the great equaliser, could not accept the concepts of Alawite leadership—certainly no discussion of it—and Assad was a Syrian first and a Syrian last. Forget the Qardaha motorway, the luxury hotel, the local airport. "I'm just a Syrian Arab citizen," Maan Ibrahim had told me when I asked him where he was from. The Alawites comprised perhaps 12 per cent of Syria's 15 million people. So under Assad's rule, any questioning of the apparent disproportion of Alawites to the majority Sunnis in positions of power could cost you your freedom or your job. Yet close analysis proved how many senior positions in the military and government had been given to Alawites. Assad and his family were Alawites, so was the head of Syrian military intelligence in Lebanon, Brigadier General Ghazi Kenaan, and the then information minister, Adnan Omran. So were many of the most powerful intelligence and special forces officers in Syria.

During the French Mandate, some—though by no means all—Alawites gave their support to Paris, helping to repress Sunni insurgency. And during the Sunni "Islamist" insurgency against Assad's rule, exploding from the cities of Aleppo and Hama, Alawites were the primary target. More than fifty Alawite officer cadets were massacred at the Aleppo artillery school in 1979; the initial Hama atrocities by fundamentalists were directed against Alawite officials and their families.

While Assad ensured a large Sunni participation in government—including the defence and foreign ministers—the ethnic origins of Syria's political power have been used by the country's enemies. Israel's constant predictions of civil war between Alawites and Sunnis have not been fulfilled. But Alawite power explains many things. It explains why Iran—the very vanguard of the Shiite Muslim revolution—should have become so close an ally of a country ruled by a man whose own faith sprang from Shiism. It explains why the Hizballah, a Shiite organisation though it claims to be interfaith, should be so enamoured of the regime in Damascus. Though the Baath is secular, the women of Qardaha cover their faces even more assiduously than the women of Tehran.

Yet not since the days of Haroun al-Rashid had we seen a non-monarchical Arab potentate pass on his inheritance to his son. The Syrian parliament lowered the age of future presidents to thirty-four to accommodate Bashar Assad's new inheritance. In private, he echoed his father: a strategic decision of land-for-peace, no peace treaty with Israel until all of Golan was returned, a final agreement based not on Arafat-style piecemeal bargaining but on UN Security Council Resolution 242: an Israeli withdrawal from occupied territory in return for the security of all states in the area. And good relations with the Christians of Lebanon—providing they do not scream for the withdrawal of Syria's 21,000 soldiers. If Syria ever leaves her little "sister" Lebanon, it would not be at the behest of the Christian minority that first invited her there.

From the place of Assad's burial, I returned briefly to Hama. Outside a state school in this haunted city hung a black banner. "Oh master of our nation, to Paradise eternal gone!" it proclaimed. But from the homes of Hama's survivors, there hung only washing and tattered sun awnings. In the paper shop across the road from the great, creaking noria water-wheel, three piles of unsold posters lay on the counter: Hafez, Basil and Bashar. Fear remained. "What happened, happened," an old Hama friend remarked sadly as the sun cut through the broken glass of an old store and the cats hissed at each other in the light. "The past is gone. We are children of the present—'eighty-two is over with. Let's say no more." The water-wheel outside his home creaked on, a screaming complaint of ancient iron axles and soaked wood and weight as the water of the Orontes splashed onto the disused aqueducts.

But still no one will tell the truth: of the slaughter in the underground tunnels of Hama, of the Muslim "suicide girls" who hurled themselves into the arms of soldiers and blew them up with grenades held to their breasts, the original "black widows" whom we would later see in the occupied West Bank and Gaza and Israel and in Chechnya and Russia. The party men and Rifaat's lads went round the smoking ruins afterwards, summarily executing the wounded and the suspicious and those who could not explain their presence.

Which raised a familiar question. Can a regime survive without some form of acknowledgement of sins past, a truth-accountancy test for the inheritors of Baathism as well as the survivors of the murderous Muslim Brotherhood? Would a time come when Bashar Assad could—would—say that terrible things were done in the name of the party? Given his need for the support of some of the same dark forces that were responsible for Hama, I doubt it. Truth and reconciliation may work in South Africa or in Northern Ireland, but in the Middle East, history lies too deep. Too deep in Algeria, too deep in Iraq—where no Baathist regime survives to resist such admissions—too deep in Palestine, too deep in Israel, too deep in Lebanon.

In Beirut, true, there is a "garden of forgiveness," but the only physical memorial to the civil war—save for a concrete block impregnated with guns and armour outside the defence ministry and the thousands of Lebanese houses still peppered with bullet holes—is the old statue commemorating the Christians and Muslims who were hanged by the Turks in 1915 and 1916 for daring to oppose Ottoman rule. "Martyrs' Square," as it was called, acquired a different meaning during the fifteen-year Lebanese civil war, for it lay on the front line between Christian and Muslim militias, its very significance demeaned by those who used its geographical location in the centre of Beirut to destroy their capital city. The statue's protecting angel was perforated with hundreds of bullets; but it has been preserved for the future with the bullet holes still clearly visible—a permanent rebuke to those who would destroy the brotherly love that this long-ago martyrdom supposedly represented.

Before the First World War, Arab intellectuals had argued publicly for a new relationship between the Arab world and Constantinople, seeking a form of "home rule" for the Arab lands inside the Ottoman empire, either through a federal system of government—under which the sultan would be crowned king of the Arabs as well as king of the Turks—or, more mischievously in Turkish eyes, with an autonomy guaranteed by Western powers, especially France. At this time, a similar though not identical crisis afflicted the proponents of Home Rule in Ireland, some advocating a "free" Ireland within the British empire, others complete independence from Britain.

Syrian notables met in Paris before the war and discussed what form of autonomy they might be given; among other demands, they asked that Arabic should be taught in schools alongside Turkish and used with Turkish in all government affairs. But although the Turks appeared initially well disposed towards these ideas, the deliberately vague nature of the instructions sent out to Turkish governors in the Arab provinces quickly proved that the Sublime Porte had no intention of dividing power within the Ottoman empire. There would be no "Austro-Hungarian" solutions in the Middle East. Thus by the time they declared war on the Allies in 1914—arguably the greatest mistake the Ottoman authorities had made since the fourteenth century—the Turks had maintained the unity of their empire but allowed sufficient debate for this same unity to be threatened.

No one can dispute the suffering of the Lebanese during the First World War. The British and French navies blockaded the Ottoman Mediterranean coastline from 1914, preventing food entering the Levant. So Turkish Ottoman forces impounded all the grain in Lebanon for their troops and commandeered farm animals; a plague of locusts that set about the country in 1915 destroyed what crops were left. The land could not be tilled and there was a famine of biblical proportions. In northern Syria, 300,000 are estimated to have perished, 120,000 of them Lebanese; in Beirut alone, civilians were dying at the rate of a hundred a day. Abriza Kerbej was still alive in 1998 to give her own account of this semi-genocide. "We had become like animals. We took to eating rotten fruit off the ground. But that didn't last long and we were soon digging up wild roots and grass." Her family lived on boiled weeds. Neighbours were discovered dead only because of the stench from their homes.

Turkey's fears were not for the lives of its Arab Ottoman citizens in the Levant—Lebanon being part of Syria—but for the Arab lands that it ruled. Ahmed Jemal Pasha was commander of the Turkish 4th Army in Syria as well as one of the triumvirate of Young Turks who now effectively governed the Ottoman empire. Just as the Turks feared that their Armenian population would assist the Russians, French or British, so they suspected that their Arab Ottoman troops might defect to the Allies or join a pro–Allied Arab revolt. Jemal Pasha dispatched Arab units of his army to Gallipoli and then turned with venom upon the handful of civilians under his rule against whom any evidence of treachery could be produced. Upon these men, Jemal Pasha's fury would now be administered with Saddam-like cruelty.

When Turkey entered the war, the French abandoned their consulate in Beirut, and it was in this building—officially under the protection of the United States, which remained a neutral power until 1917—that the Ottoman secret service discovered letters and documents signed by thirty-three Arabs—most of them Lebanese—who had failed to leave the Levant before the war but who had been foolish enough to trust French diplomats with their written opinions on the future of Syria. These unfortunate men, both Muslim and Christian, were dragged for interrogation to the Lebanese hill-town of Aley, brutally tortured and then placed before drumhead courts for inevitable death sentences. Twenty-seven were Muslims, six were Christians, and their suffering was ever afterwards to be extolled by the Lebanese as proof that both religions could fight and die together for the independence of their country.

They were to die, most of them, on gallows set up scarcely a mile from where my Beirut home would later stand and—each time I rooted through Beirut's old bookshops or travelled around the Middle East—I would seek some contemporary account of their life and death. Here, after all, were Arab "martyrs" who died that others should live free—and who went to their deaths for their nation rather than for sectarian regimes or armies. After many years, in a small antiquarian shop in Kasr el-Nil Street in Cairo, I came across a heavily stained pamphlet published in Egypt in 1922 and written by a Lebanese Christian Maronite priest, Father Antoine Yammine. It was littered with poorly reproduced photographs of stick-boned children and corpses lying beside laneways. But it also carried a compelling account of the last days—and last speeches—of the condemned men.

The first eleven were taken to the Beirut central police station in the Place des Canons—later, of course, to be Martyrs' Square—where, at three in the morning, they were given white smocks to wear as shrouds for their hanging. Eleven gallows had been set up on the square and, before their execution, the Turks permitted each of the doomed men to speak to the crowds who had gathered in the darkness, along with the Turkish governor, the Turkish chief of police and members of the court martial "tribunal" who had condemned the victims.

With the rope around his neck, Abdul-Karim al-Khalil shouted down from the scaffold: "My dear fellow countrymen, the Turks want to suffocate our voice in our lungs! They want to prevent us from speaking and from claiming our right to independence and our liberation from the hateful slavery of Turkey . . . But . . . we will ask all the civilised nations of the world for our independence and freedom. My beloved country, remember always these eleven martyrs! O paradise of my country, carry our feelings of brotherly love to every Lebanese, to every Syrian, to every Arab, tell them of our tragic end and tell them: 'For your freedom, we have lived and for your independence we are dying!' "

At this point, according to the Maronite author, al-Khalil himself pushed away the stepladder to the gallows, effectively hanging himself. Next to die were two brothers, Mohamed and Mahmoud Mahmessani. For a quarter of an hour, Mohamed held his brother in his arms and tried to comfort him. "I have never betrayed my country," he told the crowd. "I swear this before God and all men. The Turks judged me guilty, but this is a lie. I don't believe it's a crime to love freedom and to want the liberation of my country." Turning to the executioner, he pleaded that he and his brother should be hanged at the same moment—so that neither should see the other die. Mohamed's wish was granted.

Other condemned men cursed Jemal Pasha for his cruelty. Joseph Bechara Hani went to the gallows, like so many others, denying any treachery. "I am innocent, completely innocent—I swear this before God . . . I have lived a blameless life and I die without fear . . ." Then the hangman kicked the ladder from beneath Hani's feet. Within months, another fourteen men would be hanged in Beirut, two of them colonels on the general staff of the Ottoman army who went to the scaffold in full military uniform. One of them, Selim Djezairi, said that he died "with love for my fellow Arabs, love for my country and hatred for the Turks." Of two brothers—both Christians—one wrote a last letter to his wife, saving her the knowledge of his impending execution by pretending that they would soon meet again at their home in Jounié.

Despite the natural desire to dress their words in courage, even the Turks were said to have been impressed by the heroism of the victims, who included at least one Arab from Palestine. The Ottoman authorities decreed that their bodies should be thrown into a mass grave on the beach at Ras-Beirut. In those days, the area now covered by Beirut airport had not been reclaimed and the sea shore ran along the edge of what is today Corniche Mazraa. In this red earth, the Muslim and Christian dead were buried without ceremony.

But how were they betrayed? A French scholar, researching his country's foreign affairs archives at Nantes, has provided the most detailed account of this miserable affair. The interpreter at the French consulate in Beirut, Philippe Zalzal, himself a Christian, had been imprisoned by the Turks in Damascus and, in order to secure his return to his native Lebanese town of Bikfaya, had told Jemal Pasha of the letters, which French diplomats had concealed behind a false wall and a table in the consulate. The consul who left the documents—including signed letters that specifically requested French military intervention in Lebanon and Syria—was none other than François Georges Picot, the very same Picot who, with Sir Mark Sykes, reached the secret agreement in 1916 that France should form its own administration in Syria and Lebanon after the war was over, no matter what "independence" the Arabs were demanding. As a direct result of this foreign accord, the French carved Lebanon out of Syria and deposed the Arab king Feisal in Damascus. The slaughter at the battle of Maysaloun was a direct result of the same Sykes–Picot agreement which was concluded, in a letter from the French ambassador in London, on 9 May 1916—exactly two days after the Turks hanged the second group of Lebanese patriots in Beirut. Picot's reaction to the discovery of the incriminating letters he so shamefully left behind was never recorded.

When the French army reached Beirut in 1918, the Lebanese martyrs were exhumed from their common grave, but the very faiths which they had placed second to their patriotism now prevented their joint re-interment. The Christians would not allow the Muslim martyrs of Beirut to be buried in their cemeteries. Nor would the Muslim authorities permit the executed Christians to lie in their holy ground. In the end, the Lebanese Druze, whose mystical Sunni beliefs permit a more liberal view of life and death, offered the martyrs a small quarter-acre of Lebanon in which these courageous men of different religions who died together could remain alongside one another into eternity. Unknown to most Lebanese, their remains lie today beside the Druze parliament in the Hamra district of Beirut.

Yet perhaps even their common role as martyrs was an illusion. Both Christians and Muslims opposed Turkish tyranny in Syria, but the Christian Maronites of Lebanon were hoping for French tutelage after the war—and were to give their loyalty to the French Mandate for more than two decades. The Muslims were Arab nationalists who wished to establish an independent Arab nation, one in which the Christians would obviously constitute a small minority. Close examination of the martyrs' last words on the scaffold shows that even in death, their aims were not in unison. A Maronite priest, Joseph Hayek, was among the first to be executed and his last words were: "Vive le Liban! Vive la France!" These were not the sentiments of those who, in their last breath, addressed themselves to their "fellow Arabs."

But their deaths were probably the final catalyst of the Arab Revolt. Emir Feisal—the future "king" of Syria who would become Britain's first king of Iraq—was staying outside Damascus in the spring of 1916 and had repeatedly begged Jemal Pasha to spare the second group of condemned men, who belonged to some of the most illustrious families in Syria and Lebanon. The scholar and historian George Antonius records how the emir and his hosts, the Bakri family, were breakfasting in the garden when a runner brought them a special edition of the pro-Turkish *Al-Sharq* newspaper which carried a full report of the hangings. One of the Bakris read out the names of the hanged men, which "lingered like the notes of a dirge on the still air of that spring morning in the orchards of Damascus." Someone recited the opening verse of the Koran. Then Feisal leapt to his feet, tore his kuffiah from his head and trampled it beneath his feet. The Arab Revolt had begun. "Arabs!" he cried. "Death now will be a pleasure for us."

# CHAPTER TWENTY-ONE

# Why?

*Out of a fired ship, which, by no way*
*But drowning, could be rescued from the flame,*
*Some men leap'd forth, and ever as they came*
*Near the foes' ships, did by their shot decay;*
*So all were lost, which in the ship were found,*
*They in the sea being burnt, they in the burnt ship drown'd.*

—John Donne, "A Burnt Ship"

I HAD FORGOTTEN to turn off my mobile phone. I felt its vibration in my pocket only seconds after I had sat down on the Sabena transatlantic flight and my first thought—though we had not yet finished boarding—was that I had broken the rules. We believe in laws instinctively, without question, secular rules that govern our lives rather than religious dictates. So I left my seat and returned to the air-bridge on which passengers were still waiting to board the Airbus.

"Robert?" It was the features editor. "Look, I think you should know that after all this, we're probably going to have to hold your Sabra and Chatila piece again. A light aircraft has just flown into the World Trade Center in New York and the building's on fire." Damn. Damn! DAMN! This was the third time. Does it really matter that much? I asked. A light aircraft? "Well, it seems quite serious and I think it would look rather odd having a big story like this in New York and us carrying a nineteen-year-old story on the front of the features section." I gave up. It was as if our new investigation of the Israeli role in the Beirut Palestinian massacres of 1982 would never be published. All through the first week of September 2001, I had been pushing for space. Then on Thursday, 6 September, Simon Kelner decided it could run on Monday, 10 September. Then Kelner went on holiday and Ian Birrell, the deputy editor, took over Simon's seat and postponed my report until the morning of the 12th. That meant the final proofs would go away on the afternoon of 11 September. From Brussels airport that morning—tired after my overnight flight from Beirut—I called *The Independent*. Leonard Doyle, my foreign editor, talked about the suicide assassination of Ahmed Shah Massoud, the Afghan Northern Alliance militia leader who had fought with such bravery against the Russians but showed only contempt for Osama bin Laden. Two Arabs posing as journalists had killed him with a bomb in their camera. Did I think bin Laden was behind it? I didn't know. In our first edition, Leonard had called Massoud by his powerful Afghan title, "the Lion of Panjshir." Some idiot on the back-bench had changed it in the night, paring Massoud down to that darling of sub-editors, a "guerrilla leader." Overnight, American cruise missiles had hit Kabul.

When I had first spoken to the features editors from the Brussels departure lounge, they confirmed that my Sabra and Chatila report would run at last. It was to be on the cover of that night's review section—there was a news story for the front—and the design showed blood across the photographs of the dead Palestinians. I didn't plan to call the office again. I would be out of touch for the six-and-a-half-hour flight over the Atlantic. I pulled out the copy of the text for a last check.

Sana Sersawi speaks carefully, loudly but slowly, as she recalls the chaotic, dangerous, desperately tragic events that overwhelmed her almost exactly 19 years ago, on 18 September 1982. As one of the survivors prepared to testify against the Israeli prime minister Ariel Sharon—who was then Israel's defence minister—she stops to search her memory when she confronts the most terrible moments of her life. "The Lebanese Forces militia had taken us from our homes and marched us up to the entrance to the camp where a large hole had been dug in the earth. The men were told to get into it. Then the militiamen shot a Palestinian. The women and children had climbed over bodies to reach this spot, but we were truly shocked by seeing this man killed in front of us and there was a roar of shouting and screams from the women. That's when we heard the Israelis on loudspeakers shouting, 'Give us the men, give us the men.' We thought, 'Thank God, they will save us.' " It was to prove a cruelly false hope.

Mrs. Sersawi, three months pregnant, saw her 30-year-old husband Hassan, and her Egyptian brother-in-law Faraj el-Sayed Ahmed standing in the crowd of men. "We were all told to walk up the road towards the Kuwaiti embassy, the women and children in front, the men behind. We had been separated. There were Phalangist militiamen and Israeli soldiers walking alongside us. I could still see Hassan and Faraj. It was like a parade. There were several hundred of us. When we got to the Cité Sportive, the Israelis put us women in a big concrete room and the men were taken to another side of the stadium. There were a lot of men from the camp and I could no longer see my husband. The Israelis went round saying 'Sit, sit.' It was 11 o'clock. An hour later, we were told to leave. But we stood around outside amid the Israeli soldiers, waiting for our men."

Sana Sersawi waited in the bright, sweltering sun for Hassan and Faraj to emerge. "Some men came out, none of them younger than 40, and they told us to be patient, that hundreds of men were still inside. Then about 4 in the afternoon, an Israeli officer came out. He was wearing dark glasses and said in Arabic: 'What are you all waiting for?' He said there was nobody left, that everyone had gone. There were Israeli trucks moving out with tarpaulin over them. We couldn't see inside. And there were jeeps and tanks and a bulldozer making a lot of noise. We stayed there as it got dark and the

Israelis appeared to be leaving and we were very nervous. But then when the Israelis had moved away, we went inside. And there was no one there. Nobody. I had been only three years married. I never saw my husband again."

The smashed Camille Chamoun Sports Stadium—the "Cité Sportive"—was a natural "holding centre" for prisoners. Only two miles from Beirut airport, it had been an ammunition dump for Yassir Arafat's PLO and repeatedly bombed by Israeli jets during the 1982 siege of Beirut so that its giant, smashed exterior looked like a nightmare denture. The Palestinians had earlier mined its cavernous interior, but its vast, underground storage space and athletics changing-rooms remained intact.

It was a familiar landmark to all of us who lived in Beirut. At mid-morning on 18 September 1982—around the time Sana Sersawi says she was brought to the stadium—I saw hundreds of Palestinian and Lebanese prisoners, perhaps well over 1,000 in all, sitting in its gloomy, cavernous interior, squatting in the dust, watched over by Israeli soldiers and plain-clothes Shin Beth agents and a group of men who I suspected, correctly, were Lebanese collaborators. The men sat in silence, obviously in fear. From time to time, I noted, a few were taken away. They were put into Israeli army trucks or jeeps or Phalangist vehicles—for further "interrogation."

Nor did I doubt this. A few hundred metres away, up to 600 massacre victims of the Sabra and Chatila Palestinian refugee camps rotted in the sun, the stench of decomposition drifting over the prisoners and their captors alike. It was suffocatingly hot. Loren Jenkins of *The Washington Post*, Paul Eedle of Reuters and I had only got into the cells because the Israelis assumed—given our Western appearance—that we must have been members of Shin Beth. Many of the prisoners had their heads bowed. Arab prisoners usually adopted this pose of humiliation. But Israel's Phalangist militiamen had been withdrawn from the camps, their slaughter over, and at least the Israeli army was now in charge. So what did these men have to fear?

Looking back—and listening to Sana Sersawi today—I shudder now at our innocence. My notes of the time . . . contain some ominous clues. We found a Lebanese employee of Reuters, Abdullah Mattar, among the prisoners and obtained his release, Paul leading him away with his arm around the man's shoulders. "They take us away, one by one, for interrogation," one of the prisoners muttered to me. "They are Haddad militiamen. Usually they bring the people back after interrogation, but not always. Sometimes the people do not return." Then an Israeli officer ordered me to leave. Why couldn't the prisoners talk to me? I asked. "They can talk if they want," he replied. "But they have nothing to say."

All the Israelis knew what had happened inside the camps. The smell of the corpses was now overpowering. Outside, a Phalangist jeep with the words "Military Police" painted on it—if so exotic an institution could be associated with this gang of murderers—drove by. A few television crews had turned up. One filmed the Lebanese Christian militiamen outside the Cité Sportive. He also filmed a woman pleading to an Israeli army colonel called "Yahya" for the release of her husband. The colonel has now been positively identified by *The Independent*. Today, he is a general in the Israeli army.

Along the main road opposite the stadium there was a line of Israeli Merkava tanks, their crews sitting on the turrets, smoking, watching the men being led from the stadium in ones or twos, some being set free, others being led away by Shin Beth men or by Lebanese men in drab khaki overalls. All these soldiers knew what had happened inside the camps. One of the tank crews, Lt Avi Grabovsky—he was later to testify to the Israeli Kahan commission—had even witnessed the murder of several civilians the previous day and had been told not to "interfere."

And in the days that followed, strange reports reached us. A girl had been dragged from a car in Damour by Phalangist militiamen and taken away, despite her appeals to a nearby Israeli soldier. Then the cleaning lady of a Lebanese woman who worked for a U.S. television chain complained bitterly that Israelis had arrested her husband. He was never seen again. There were other vague rumours of "disappeared" people.

I wrote in my notes at the time that "even after Chatila, Israel's 'terrorist' enemies were being liquidated in West Beirut." But I had not directly associated this dark conviction with the Cité Sportive. I had not even reflected on the fearful precedents of a sports stadium in time of war. Hadn't there been a sports stadium in Santiago a few years before, packed with prisoners after Pinochet's coup d'état, a stadium from which many prisoners never returned?

Among the testimonies gathered by lawyers seeking to indict Ariel Sharon for war crimes is that of Wadha al-Sabeq. On Friday, September 17th, 1982, she said, while the massacre was still—unknown to her—under way inside Sabra and Chatila, she was in her home with her family in Bir Hassan, just opposite the camps. "Neighbours came and said the Israelis wanted to stamp our ID cards, so we went downstairs and we saw both Israelis and Lebanese Forces on the road. The men were separated from the women." This separation—with its awful shadow of similar separations at Srebrenica during the Bosnian war—was a common feature of these mass arrests. "We were told to go to the Cité Sportive. The men stayed put." Among the men were Wadha's two sons, 19-year-old Mohamed and 16-year-old Ali and her brother Mohamed. "We went to the Cité Sportive, as the Israelis told us," she says. "I never saw my sons or brother again."

The survivors tell distressingly similar stories. Bahija Zrein says she was ordered by an Israeli patrol to go to the Cité Sportive and the men with her, including her 22-year-old brother, were taken away. Some militiamen—watched by the Israelis—loaded him into a car, blindfolded, she says. "That's how he disappeared," she says in her official testimony, "and I have never seen him again since." It was only a few days afterwards that we journalists began to notice a discrepancy in the figures of dead. While up to 600 bodies had been found inside Sabra and Chatila, 1,800 civilians had been reported as "missing." We assumed—how easy assumptions are in war—that they had been killed in the three days between September 16th, 1982, and the withdrawal of the Phalangist killers on the 18th, that their corpses had been secretly buried outside the camp. Beneath the golf course, we suspected. The idea that many of these young people had been murdered outside the camps or *after* the 18th, that the killings were still going on while we walked through the camps, never occurred to us.

Why did we journalists at the time not think of this? The following year, the Israeli Kahan commission published its report, condemning Sharon but ending its own inquiry of the atrocity on September 18th, with just a one-line hint—unexplained—that several hundred people may have "disappeared around the same time." The commission interviewed no Palestinian survivors but it was allowed to become the narrative of history. The idea that the Israelis went on handing over prisoners to their blood-thirsty militia allies never occurred to us. The Palestinians of Sabra and Chatila are now giving evidence that this is exactly what happened. One man, Abdel Nasser Alameh, believes his brother Ali was handed to the Phalange on the morning of the 18th. A Palestinian Christian woman called Milaneh Boutros has recorded how, in a truck-load of women and children, she was taken from the camps to the Christian town of Bikfaya, the home of the newly assassinated Christian president-elect Bashir Gemayel, where a grief-stricken Christian woman ordered the execution of a 13-year-old boy in the truck. He was shot. The truck must have passed at least four Israeli checkpoints on its way to Bikfaya. And heaven spare me, I had even met the woman who ordered the boy's execution.

Even before the slaughter inside the camps had ended, Shahira Abu Rudeina says she was taken to the Cité Sportive where, in one of the under-ground "holding centres," she saw a retarded man, watched by Israeli sol-diers, burying bodies in a pit. Her evidence might be rejected were it not for the fact that she also expressed her gratitude for an Israeli soldier—inside the Chatila camp, against all the evidence given by the Israelis—who prevented the murder of her daughters by the Phalange.

Long after the war, the ruins of the Cité Sportive were torn down and a brand new marble stadium was built in its place, partly by the British. Pavarotti has sung there. But the testimony of what may lie beneath its foundations—and its frightful implications—will give Ariel Sharon further reason to fear an indictment.

I had been in the Sabra and Chatila camps when these crimes took place. I had returned to the camps, year after year, to try to discover what happened to the missing thousand men. Karsten Tveit of Norwegian television had been with me in 1982 and he had returned to Beirut many times with the same purpose. Lawyers weren't the only people investigating these crimes against humanity. In 2001, Tveit arrived in Lebanon with the original 1982 tapes of those women pleading for their menfolk at the gates of the Cité Sportive. He visited the poky little video shops in the present-day camp and showed and reshowed the tapes until local Palestinians identified them; then Tveit set off to find the women—nineteen years older now—who were on the tape, who had asked for their sons and brothers and fathers and husbands outside the Cité Sportive. He traced them all. None had ever seen their loved ones again.*

In the months to come, I would reflect on the personal irony of those last minutes at Brussels airport. I was reading through the minutiae of a crime against humanity which had been committed almost exactly nineteen years earlier—while on the other side of the Atlantic at that very moment, an international crime against humanity was on the point of being committed. At Sabra and Chatila and in the mass murders afterwards, we estimated that at least 1,700 Palestinian men, women and children were slaughtered. In New York, Washington and Pennsylvania, more than twice that number of human lives were about to be extinguished.

After the call from the features editor, I returned to my seat on the Airbus. Then my phone rang again. Anne Penketh was calling from the foreign desk. "It seems a helicopter has hit the Pentagon, Robert. Don't know any more yet but I think we need you to write today." I was sitting in business class and there was an airline satellite phone tucked into the arm-rest beside me. I ran my credit card through the side-swipe and the screen showed positive. I would be able to go on talking to London and to send my copy in-flight. The last passengers were boarding and I walked across to the chief purser. I told him about the helicopter. I kept referring to the "Free Trade Building" rather than the World Trade Center, although I had a vivid image of the twin towers in my mind, sentinels above Manhattan to the left of my taxi when I returned to JFK after giving a lecture at Princeton a few months before.

I made one more call to the office on my mobile. "Robert," Ann had just enough time to say before I was forced to close down. "It was an airliner—a passenger aircraft that flew into the World Trade Center. And now there's another!" I closed down the phone. The horror of this was obvious but my journalist's brain, the professional computer that calculates event, reaction and deadline, was now moving fast. What was happening in the United States was deliberate. It was, in

---

*Tveit even found an ex-Phalangist militiaman who took him up a hillside east of Beirut and pointed to a former Christian Phalangist barracks, describing how 300 Palestinians whom the Israelis handed over to them after the camp massacre had been imprisoned in the barracks in a series of containers. The Phalangists had tried to use their Israeli-provided prisoners as hostages for Christians whom they believed to be in Muslim militia hands. But there had been no prisoner swap, so three weeks after the Sabra and Chatila mass murder, these 300 Palestinians were taken from the containers and machine-gunned to death in a mass grave. The grave, the Phalangist told Tveit, was beside a chapel in the barracks of what was now a Lebanese army base.

that most classic of clichés, a "terrorist attack." The American East Coast was six hours behind Brussels. Thousands would be arriving in the Twin Towers for work. And in the Pentagon.

The Airbus was moving across the apron for take-off but the purser came to my seat. Did I know any more? I told him about the second plane and he went straight to the flight-deck. He came back a few seconds later, even as the engines were rising for take-off. "There's been a passenger aircraft crashed in Pennsylvania too." I just looked at him. Bin Laden. Who else? I pulled out my notebook and tried to remember everything bin Laden had ever said to me: his hatred for the Saudi royal family, his experience fighting the Russians, his determination to drive the Americans from the Gulf.

We were over the Irish Sea when I made my first satellite call to London. Leonard took the call. He sounded over-serious, his "Father Doyle" voice as I always called it, but I realised he was just shocked. "Two planes into the World Trade Center, an airliner into the Pentagon, another airliner crashed in Pennsylvania. You should see the pictures." On board the Airbus, they brought round the pre-lunch drinks. The gin-and-tonic tasted like tonic. Twenty—thirty—thousand dead? That's how I thought. This was on a still unimaginable scale. And what would be America's revenge? I recalled the old newsreels after Pearl Harbor, the "day of infamy," when the sound-tracks filled with racist demands to crush the "sneaky Japs." Bin Laden. I kept coming back to bin Laden. This day represented not just a terrible crime but a terrible failure, the collapse of decades of maimed, hopeless, selfish policies in the Middle East which we would at last recognise—if we were wise—or which, more likely, we would now bury beneath the rubble of New York, an undiscussible subject whose mere mention would indicate support for America's enemies.

I walked to the galley and asked the cabin crew what they thought. All four planes must have been hijacked. There must have been many hijackers. "They wanted to die," the young stewardess said without thinking, and we all agreed, and then the purser looked at me very hard. I knew what he was thinking. We too were bound for America. Those four planes had taken off like ours, heading off into the bright morning with friendly crews and law-abiding passengers . . . I walked round the plane with the purser. I didn't like it. I guess I came back with the images of thirteen passengers in my mind, thirteen I didn't like because they had beards or stared at me in what I could easily translate as hostility or because they were fiddling with worry beads or reading Korans. Of course, they were all Muslims. In just a few minutes, the so-called liberal Fisk who had worked in the Middle East for a quarter of a century—who had lived among Arabs for almost half his life, whose own life had been saved by Muslims on countless occasions in Lebanon, Iraq and Iran—yes, that nice, friendly Fisk had turned into a racist, profiling the innocent on board his aircraft because they had beards or brown eyes or dark skin. I felt dirty. But this, I already suspected, was one of the purposes of this day. To make us feel dirty, to make us so fearful—or so angry—that we no longer behaved rationally.

I called Leonard again. There had been phone calls from the passengers on the four planes. The hijackers had cut the throats of some of the crews and passengers. Men and women were throwing themselves from the upper floors of the Twin Towers. There had been some television pictures of Palestinians celebrating. Leonard, I said, I'm going to have to write about history. We've got to have a context, some explanation. I said that this was so epic a crime that I would do something I had not tried since my reporting days in Northern Ireland when the IRA–British war had to be filed against deadline, from notes and memory rather than from written script. In the old days, before computers and mobiles, we dictated our reports to copy-takers, men and women wearing earphones who would type out our stories as we shouted them down the line from Irish villages or—in my early days in the Middle East—from Cairo or Damascus hotels. Now I would do the same again. I would "talk" my story over the phone so as to match the hour with the spontaneity that journalism should possess. Or so I arrogantly thought.

Even as I was talking, the Belgian Airbus captain was on the public address system. There had been terrorist attacks on New York and Washington, he said, the United States had closed its air-space to all commercial aircraft. We were dumping fuel over the sea far to the west of Ireland before returning to Europe. We started to fly in big concentric circles, sunlight bursting through the starboard then through the port windows of the plane as if the sun was perpetually rising and setting, the desolation of the north Atlantic mocking our warm isolation. They served lunch as we described these spheres in the sky, foie gras and steak with glasses of Médoc. I looked at my notebook. I wrote down the names of Balfour, Lawrence of Arabia, bin Laden. Then I scribbled them out. I picked up the satellite phone, swiped the card and dialled *The Independent*. Leonard put me through to one of the paper's copy-takers, a woman in Leeds with a Yorkshire accent. I told her where I was, that I was filing from my head, asked her to be patient. "Take your time, love," she said. But it came quite easily. I knew what I wanted to say. It was like reading a letter to a friend:

> So it has come to this. The entire modern history of the Middle East—the collapse of the Ottoman empire, the Balfour declaration, Lawrence of Arabia's lies, the Arab revolt, the foundation of the state of Israel, four Arab–Israeli wars and the 34 years of Israel's brutal occupation of Arab land—all erased within hours as those who claim to represent a crushed, humiliated population struck back with the wickedness and awesome cruelty of a doomed people. Is it fair—is it moral—to write this so soon, without proof, when the last act of barbarism, in Oklahoma, turned out to be the work of home-grown Americans? I fear it is. America is at war and, unless I am mistaken, many thousands more are now scheduled to die in the Middle East, perhaps in America too. Some of us warned of "the explosion to come." But we never dreamt this nightmare.
>
> And yes, Osama bin Laden comes to mind, his money, his theology, his frightening dedication to destroy American power. I have sat in front of bin

Laden as he described how his men helped to destroy the Russian army in Afghanistan and thus the Soviet Union. Their boundless confidence allowed them to declare war on America. But this is not the war of democracy versus terror that the world will be asked to believe in the coming days. It is also about American missiles smashing into Palestinian homes and U.S. helicopters firing missiles into a Lebanese ambulance in 1996 and American shells crashing into a village called Qana and about a Lebanese militia—paid and uniformed by America's Israeli ally—hacking and raping and murdering their way through refugee camps.

No, there is no doubting the utter, indescribable evil of what has happened in the United States. That Palestinians could celebrate the massacre of 20,000, perhaps 35,000 innocent people* is not only a symbol of their despair but of their political immaturity, of their failure to grasp what they had always been accusing their Israeli enemies of doing: acting disproportionately. All the years of rhetoric, all the promises to strike at the heart of America, to cut off the head of "the American snake" we took for empty threats. How could a backward, conservative, undemocratic and corrupt group of regimes and small, violent organisations fulfil such preposterous promises? Now we know.

And in the hours that followed yesterday's annihilation, I began to remember those other extraordinary assaults upon the U.S. and its allies, miniature now by comparison with yesterday's casualties. Did not the suicide bombers who killed 241 American servicemen and 100 French paratroops in Beirut on 23 October 1983 time their attacks with unthinkable precision?

There were just seven seconds between the Marine bombing and the destruction of the French three miles away. Then there were the attacks on U.S. bases in Saudi Arabia, and last year's attempt—almost successful it now turns out—to sink the USS *Cole* in Aden. And then how easy was our failure to recognise the new weapon of the Middle East which neither Americans nor any other Westerners could equal: the despair-driven, desperate suicide bomber.

And there will be, inevitably, and quite immorally, an attempt to obscure the historical wrongs and the injustices that lie behind yesterday's firestorms. We will be told about "mindless terrorism," the "mindless" bit being essential if we are not to realise how hated America has become in the land of the birth of three great religions.

Ask an Arab how he responds to 20,000 or 30,000 innocent deaths and he or she will respond as decent people should, that it is an unspeakable crime. But they will ask why we did not use such words about the sanctions that have destroyed the lives of perhaps half a million children in Iraq, why we did not rage about the 17,500 civilians killed in Israel's 1982 invasion

*In the hours after the attacks, these were the first, highly exaggerated, casualty figures.

of Lebanon. And those basic reasons why the Middle East caught fire last September—the Israeli occupation of Arab land, the dispossession of Palestinians, the bombardments and state-sponsored executions . . . all these must be obscured lest they provide the smallest fractional reason for yesterday's mass savagery.

No, Israel was not to blame—though we can be sure that Saddam Hussein and the other grotesque dictators will claim so—but the malign influence of history and our share in its burden must surely stand in the dark with the suicide bombers. Our broken promises, perhaps even our destruction of the Ottoman empire, led inevitably to this tragedy. America has bankrolled Israel's wars for so many years that it believed this would be cost-free. No longer so. But, of course, the U.S. will want to strike back against "world terror," and last night's bombardment of Kabul may have been the opening salvo. Indeed, who could ever point the finger at Americans now for using that pejorative and sometimes racist word "terrorism"?

Eight years ago, I helped to make a television series that tried to explain why so many Muslims had come to hate the West. Last night, I remembered some of those Muslims in that film, their families burnt by American-made bombs and weapons. They talked about how no one would help them but God. Theology versus technology, the suicide bomber against the nuclear power. Now we have learnt what this means.

September 11, 2001, was not the genesis of this book. But it proved to me that history's power is inescapable. Rereading that story I filed over the telephone from 37,000 feet over the Atlantic, I am appalled; not so much by its conclusions but by the repercussions that those conclusions—painfully accurate as they would turn out to be—would provoke. I was right about the way in which the world would be told that this was a war of "democracy versus terrorism," about the attempt to obscure the historical injustices that lay behind this terrible act. I never imagined how brutal, how dangerous and how bloody would be the attempts to suppress all but the most sublime acceptance of this naive, infantile version of history.

As we flew back to Belgium in the dusk, I asked myself if we could really—at this early stage—name the guilty party, however strong our suspicions. I knew that with so awesome a crime, there would be those who would argue that the ordinary rules of journalism must be suspended. That we should all be "onside." That if we stopped for a moment to ask the question "Why," we would count as supporters of "world terror." The Israelis had already perfected this outrageous logic. Merely to be called "pro-Palestinian" was to associate you with suicide bombing and "world terror." You were with us or against us. George Bush Junior would use just that simplistic, dishonest argument—an argument much favoured, of course, by bin Laden himself—to shut us up, to keep us silent, to close down any debate about the Middle East or America's role there or—an even more taboo subject—America's relationship with Israel.

I wrote a second article on the plane that night. "Is the world's favourite hate figure to blame?" the headline on this story would read in next day's *Independent*. "If bin Laden was really guilty of all the things for which he has been blamed, he would need an army of 10,000," I wrote:

> And there is something deeply disturbing about the world's habit of turning to the latest hate figure whenever blood is shed. But when events of this momentous scale take place, there is a new legitimacy in casting one's eyes at those who have constantly threatened America . . . If . . . the shadow of the Middle East falls over yesterday's destruction, then who else could produce such meticulously timed assaults? The rag-tag and corrupt Palestinian groups that used to favour hijacking are unlikely to be able to produce a single suicide bomber . . . The bombing of the U.S. Marines in 1983 needed precision, timing and infinite planning. But Iran, which supported these groups, is more involved in its internal struggles. Iraq lies broken, its agents more intent on torturing their own people than striking at the the U.S. So the mountains of Afghanistan will be photographed from satellite and high-altitude aircraft in the coming days, bin Laden's old training camps . . . highlighted on the overhead projectors in the Pentagon. But to what end? . . . For if this is a war between the Saudi millionaire and President Bush's America, it cannot be fought like other wars. Indeed, can it be fought at all without some costly military adventure overseas? Or is that what bin Laden seeks above all else?

The moment my Airbus touched down in Brussels, my mobile began to ring like a grasshopper. The office, radio stations in America, Britain, Ireland, France. I was in the taxi to my hotel when Karsten Tveit came on the line. "Robert, have you seen the pictures?" No, I said. "You must see the pictures. They are in-cred-ible." Karsten, I said, I'm still in the taxi. I can't watch television in a bloody taxi. "Look at the pictures!" he said again. "You've got to see the pictures. The moment you reach your room, look at the pictures—then you'll understand." When I reached my room, I turned on the television. The Twin Towers were smoking, incandescent. Figures floated like feathers, fast, upside down, with a terrible grace. The United passenger jet slid into the side of the south tower again and again, as if some scientific achievement was being demonstrated, as if this airliner was supposed to knife so effortlessly into the thin skin of the tower. And then there was the golden spray of fire. CNN put the edited sequences together so that the United plane crashed into the building while its burning fuel splashed out the other side, the second tape spliced in a millisecond after the collision. Hollywood could not compete with this—because it *was* Hollywood. The disaster movie of September 11th would never be made. It has already *been* made. Al-Qaeda productions got there first. This was "shock and awe" before America invented the expression for its invasion of Iraq.

All the dreams and nightmares of tinsel-town—all the racist movies depicting venal, murderous Muslims—had finally reached the screen *en vérité*. "Never before in the history of motion pictures . . ." If we have come to model ourselves on our film heroes, to mimic their language, their simplistic ideas, their robust, ultimately savage morality, now at last we could believe in those heroes and villains. Instead of reality turned into fiction, fiction had become reality. Still the United plane went on sliding into the tower, obsessively, obscenely, its passage so well known that one looked elsewhere on the screen. Did the tower shake, just a little, with the impact? Was that a bird that flicked across the screen just before the plane hit the building, innocence fleeing the darkness to come? And when the French crew produced their unique film of the aircraft that hit the other tower, that man on the sidewalk who looked up at the sound of the ramped-up jet engines—at what point exactly did he realise what he was watching? Or was he too seduced by the neatness, the ease with which an airplane could fly into a building?

On the Airbus, I had been connected via Irish radio to Conor O'Clery, the *Irish Times*'s man in New York, who had reported the Soviet invasion of Afghanistan with me almost a quarter of a century earlier. His office was next to the World Trade Center. He had described with his usual devastating clarity how he had seen the second plane come in, how he saw the aircraft flaps moving up and down at speed as the hijacker at the controls fought desperately to bring the aircraft into the centre of the tower. The pilot's act of mass murder was to be as perfect as possible. In Brussels I called Chibli Mallat, the young Lebanese lawyer who was trying to arraign Ariel Sharon in a Belgian court for his role in Sabra and Chatila. Only a few hours earlier, I had assured him that my report on the new massacre evidence would be published next day. No more. "Of course, Robert, this changes everything," he said. "I think that legally and morally we must regard what happened today as an international crime against humanity."

The calls kept coming. Italian radio, CBS, BBC World, BBC Cardiff, BBC Belfast, Pacifica, NPR, Radio France International. They all wanted to know what no one could yet know. Who did it? How did they do it? No one—but no one—wanted to know *why* "they" might have wanted to do it, for this was the forbidden question. Eamon Dunphy put me on his show out of Dublin with Alan Dershowitz, the leftist, pro-Israeli academic at Harvard. I tried to explain that there must have been reasons for this atrocity, that crimes are not committed just because men are bad and don't like democracy. Dershowitz was—I tried to think of the right word as I listened to his uncontrollable, hysterical anger—frenzied. Fisk was a bad man, a patronising man, a dangerous man; Fisk was anti-American and "anti-Americanism is the same as anti-Semitism . . ." Dershowitz shouted at me and shouted at Dunphy who eventually switched him off the air. But I got the message. Only one line was going to be allowed after these massacres in America. Any opposition to U.S. policy—especially in the Middle East—was criminal and "pro-terrorist." Anyone who criticised America now was an anti-Semite. Anti-Semites are Nazis, fascists. So America was sacrosanct—so was Israel, of course—and those of us who asked the question "Why" were the supporters of "terrorism." We had to shut up. On the night of September 11th, the BBC's 24-hour news channel, reviewing the next morning's British newspapers, produced a pro-Israeli American commentator who remarked of my article that "Robert Fisk has won the prize for bad taste."

I sat on my hotel bed, flicking channels, watching the towers burn and their biblical descent in dust and ash. Our New York correspondent, David Usborne, had been called by the office with the story of the light aircraft hitting one of the towers and took the subway downtown, only to find the south tower falling at his feet. Again and again, the towers fell. Then the planes came in again. Only ash and smoke were taped at the Pentagon, and in that pit in the Pennsylvania field, but New York remained the iconic image that would now justify the "war on terror." September 11th, I suspected, was to become a law, a piece of legislation that would be used to close down any conversation, lock up any suspect, invade any country. Opposition? Why, just show those bodies hurtling once more towards the streets of Manhattan.

I lay on my pillow, watching them again on the television at the foot of my bed. They moved at such speed, they had a kind of symmetry to them until you realised that their legs were kicking, that this was the moment of awfulness, the moment I had tried to understand when I looked into those monstrous, carbonised faces of the dead at Mutla Ridge. Those figures cascaded out of the sky and they fell, over and over at the bottom of my bed, plummeting into the blankets.

And then I realised what Karsten had meant when he urged me to concentrate on the pictures. The message was the act. Even if the casualties had not been so appalling, this wickedness so awesome, the attacks themselves so professional, this was not a routine act of "terror." There would be no claims of responsibility, I was sure of that. There would be no statements from bin Laden or al-Qaeda, no explanations. The message—the statement—was the act itself. The claim was contained in the pictures. Our own television cameras were the claim of responsibility. I remembered again what bin Laden had said to me about his wishes for America. And looking at those pictures of the thunderous, concrete-thick clouds that surrounded Manhattan, I had to admit that New York was now "a shadow of itself."

But why? I was right about the reaction to this question. Next morning, a blizzard of emails began to descend on *The Independent*, mostly in support of my article, many demanding my resignation. The attacks on America were caused by "hate itself, of precisely the obsessive and dehumanising kind that Fisk and bin Laden have been spreading," said one. According to the same message from Judea Pearl of UCLA, I was "drooling venom" and a professional "hate peddler." Another missive, signed Ellen Popper, announced that I was "in cahoots with the archterrorist" bin Laden. Mark Guon labelled me "a total nut-case." I was "psychotic," according to Lilly and Barry Weiss. Brandon Heller of San Diego informed me that "you are actually supporting evil itself . . ." How quickly the pattern formed. Merely to suggest that Washington's policies in the Middle East, its unconditional support for Israel, its support for Arab dictators, its approval of UN sanctions that cost the lives of so many Iraqi children, might lie behind the venomous attacks of September 11th was an act of evil.

This harsh and unrelenting shower of emails came in by the thousand, many of them—as the days went by—using identical phrases and, in some cases, identical sentences. Clearly this was turning into an orchestrated campaign—the kind that is taken far too seriously by American papers but treated with the scorn it deserves in Britain—and when a "reader" in San Antonio announced that he would "no longer take your magazine" because of my article, it was clear that something was amiss. *The Independent* does not (alas) circulate in Texas—and it definitely isn't a magazine.

But reporters continued to avoid the "whys." We could examine the "hows"— the hijackers had learned to fly, taken business class seats, used box-cutters—and the "whos." The fact that the hijackers proved to be all Arabs—and that most of them came from Saudi Arabia—posed no problem to reporters or readers. This fell into the "where-and-what" slot. "Arab terrorists" are, after all, familiar characters. The sin was to connect the Arabs with the problems of the lands they came from, to ask the "why" question. All of the mass murderers came from the Middle East. Was there a problem out there? In articles and lectures in the United States, I was to raise this issue repeatedly. If a crime is committed in Los Angeles or London, the first thing the cops do is look for a motive. But when an international crime against humanity in the United States was committed on this unprecedented scale, the one thing we were *not* allowed to do was seek a motive.

George Bush Junior now talked about a "crusade" against evil. The "why" question was quickly disposed of by the U.S. administration—and left unvisited by American journalists—with a one-liner: "They hate our democracy." You were with us or against us. "We are good people." And in the national grief that clutched every American town and city, the latter made sense. The idea that the United States somehow "deserved" such an assault—that more than three thousand innocents should pay some kind of death-price for America's sins abroad—was immoral. But without any serious examination of what had caused these acts of mass murder—political, historical reasons—then the United States and the world might set themselves on a warpath without end, a "war on terror" which, by its very nature, had no finite aim, no foreseeable conclusion, no direction except further war and fire and blood. The credo now set up by the United States and obsequiously embraced by the world's statesmen and media—that September 11th, 2001, "changed the world for ever"—was a lie. Countless massacres of far greater dimensions had occurred in the Middle East over previous decades without anyone suggesting that the world would never be the same again. The million and a half dead of the Iran–Iraq War—a bloodbath set in train by Saddam, with our active military support—elicited no such Manichaean observation.

Nineteen years earlier, the greatest act of terrorism—using Israel's own definition of that much misused word—in modern Middle Eastern history began. Typically, on 16 September 2001, no one remembered the anniversary in the West. I took a risk and wrote in the *Independent* that no other British newspaper— certainly no American newspaper—would recall the fact that on that date in 1982, Israel's Phalangist militia allies started their three-day orgy of rape and knifing and murder in the Palestinian refugee camps of Sabra and Chatila. It followed an

Israeli invasion of Lebanon—designed to drive the PLO out of the country and given the green light by the then U.S. secretary of state, Alexander Haig—which cost the lives of 17,500 Lebanese and Palestinians, almost all of them civilians. That was more than five times the death toll in the September 11th, 2001, attacks. Yet I could not remember any vigils or memorial services or candle-lighting in America or the West for the innocent dead of Lebanon—no stirring speeches about democracy or liberty or "evil." In fact, the United States spent most of the bloody months of July and August 1982 calling for "restraint."

No, Israel was not to blame for what happened on September 11th, 2001. The culprits were Arabs, not Israelis. But America's failure to act with honour in the Middle East, its promiscuous sale of missiles to those who use them against civilians, its blithe disregard for the deaths of tens of thousands of Iraqi children under sanctions of which Washington was the principal supporter—all these were intimately related to the society that produced the Arabs who plunged New York into an apocalypse of fire. And I began to regard the response of the United States administration and the British government as a form of cowardice. If September 11th, 2001, really did "change the world," then bin Laden had won the moment the hijackers boarded their four airliners. In the days that followed the attacks, I felt it ever more necessary to oppose this chicanery. Bush wanted to persuade the world that it had changed for ever so that he could advance a neo-conservative war—cloaked in honourable aspirations of freedom, democracy and liberty—that would plunge the Middle East into further chaos and death. But why must I let nineteen Arab murderers change *my* world?

While Bush and Tony Blair prepared their forces for an inevitable attack on Afghanistan—whose Taliban priests predictably declined to surrender their "guest" bin Laden—they went on explaining that this was a war for "democracy and liberty," that it was about men who were "attacking civilisation." Bush informed us that "America was targeted for attack because we are the brightest beacon for freedom and opportunity in the world." But this was not why America was attacked. If this was an Arab–Muslim apocalypse, then it was intimately associated with events in the Middle East and with America's stewardship of the area. Arabs, it might be added, would rather like some of the democracy and liberty and freedom that Mr. Bush was telling them about. Instead, they got a president who had just won a Saddam-like 98 per cent in Egyptian elections*—Washington's friend, Hosni Mubarak—and a Palestinian police force, trained by the CIA, that tortured and sometimes killed its people in prison. The Syrians would like a little

---

*Arab elections are among the quaintest of the Middle East's attempts to reproduce the Western-style "democracy" they claim they already possess. In 1993, for example, Mubarak "won" 96.3 per cent of the vote for his third six-year term in office (his fourth six-year victory in 1999 brought him a measly 93.79 per cent). His predecessor, Anwar Sadat, claimed a thumping 99.95 per cent victory for political reform in a 1974 referendum. Saddam Hussein supposedly gained 99.96 per cent for his presidency in 1993—the identity of the errant 0.04 per cent of disloyal voters was not disclosed, although they had obviously thought better by 2002 when Saddam's minions announced a clear 100 per cent vote. In 1999, Hafez Assad of Syria scored what

of that democracy. So would the Saudis. But their effete princes are all friends of America—in many cases, educated at U.S. universities. No, it was "our" democracy and "our" liberty and freedom that Bush and Blair were talking about, our Western sanctuary that was under attack, not the vast site of terror and injustice that the Middle East had become.

Yes, it was shameful of Arabs to rejoice at the horrors in New York and Washington. Not only did Palestinians express their satisfaction in the streets of Ramallah, they handed out celebratory sweets to motorists in the Lebanese city of Sidon. Arab friends told me later that these comparatively small demonstrations were not the only manifestations of their kind. On a bus carrying officials to the Egyptian opera in Cairo, there was cheering and hand-clapping when news of the carnage was broadcast over the bus radio. "We didn't believe that Americans deserved this, no," one of those present told me later. "But we were thinking to ourselves: 'Now *they* know what it's like.'" And as Palestinians would point out, America's name is literally stamped on the missiles fired by Israel into Palestinian buildings in Gaza and the West Bank. In August 2001, I had identified one of them as an AGM 114-D air-to-ground rocket made by Boeing and Lockheed-Martin at their factory in—of all places—Florida, the state where some of the September 11th suiciders trained to fly.

Now at last, the suicide bomber had made his way west. Partly because of the suicide bomber, the Israelis had retreated from Lebanon in 2000. Specifically because of a suicide bomber in 1983, the Americans fled Lebanon. Now the suicide bomber was here to stay. It was an exclusive weapon—it belonged to "them," not us—and no military power appeared able to deal with this phenomenon. As long as "our" side will risk but not "give" their lives—cost-free war, after all, was partly an American invention—the suicide bomber is now the other side's nuclear weapon. The suicider did not conform to a set of identical characteristics. Many of the callow Palestinian youths blowing themselves to bits—and, more often than not, the most innocent of Israelis—had little or no formal education, a poor knowledge of the Koran but a powerful sense of fury, despair and self-righteousness to propel them. The Hizballah suiciders were more deeply versed in the Koran, older, often with years of imprisonment to steel them in the hours before their immolation.

The September 11th suicide bombers created a precedent. There were nineteen of them. Did they all know each other? Did they all know they were going to die? They must have had a good working knowledge of the fly-by-wire instrument panel of the world's most sophisticated aircraft. It was the number that kept recur-

the official Syrian news agency called a "slashing victory" of 99.987 per cent for a new seven-year term in office—a mere 219 citizens voted against him—though he did not live to complete it. After this, Abdelaziz Bouteflika's 73.8 per cent victory in Algeria in 1999 and Mahmoud Abbas's 62.3 per cent as Palestinian president in 2005 were persuasive enough to believe. In 1992, a popular joke in Damascus had it that George Bush Senior, facing defeat at the polls in the United States, asked the Syrian security services to arrange an Assad-style victory for the Republicans; they did, and Americans duly voted 99 per cent—for Assad.

ring to me in my exhaustion. If only four of them knew they were going to die, we had never seen this kind of suicide-cooperation before. In the Middle East, the suicide bomber is admired by millions of Arabs. Not because he is a mass killer—which he is—but because something invincible, something untouchable, something that has always dictated the rules without taking responsibility for the results, has now proved vulnerable. What if the numbers went on increasing? What if the school of self-immolation could produce a suicider a day, or two or three a day, calling them up Wal-Mart-style and deploying them against Western targets? It would take just twenty-two years from the first suicide bombing in Lebanon in 1982 for this fearful possibility to become reality. Iraq proved that suiciders could be summoned off-the-shelf, constantly replaced, repeatedly activated.

I studied the notes which Mohamed Atta, the Egyptian leader of the September 11th killers, supposedly left behind. They were fearful, grotesque—but also very, very odd. If the handwritten five-page document that the FBI said it found in Atta's baggage was genuine, then the murderers believed in a very exclusive version of Islam—or were surprisingly unfamiliar with their religion. "The time of fun and waste is gone," Atta, or one of his associates, is reported to have written in the notes. "Be optimistic . . . Check all your items—your bag, your clothes, your knives, your will, your IDs, your passport . . . In the morning, try to pray the morning prayer with an open heart."

Part theological, part mission statement, the document raised more questions than it answered. Under the heading of "Last Night"—presumably the night of 10 September—the writer tells his fellow hijackers to "remind yourself that in this night you will face many challenges. But you have to face them and understand it 100 per cent . . . Obey God, his messenger, and don't fight among yourselves where [*sic*] you become weak . . . Everybody hates death, fears death . . ." The document begins with the words: "In the name of God, the most merciful, the most compassionate . . . In the name of God, of myself, and of my family."

The problem was that no Muslim—however ill-taught—would be likely to include his family in such a prayer. He would mention the Prophet Mohamed immediately after he mentioned God in the first line. Lebanese and Palestinian suicide bombers have never been known to refer to "the time of fun and waste"—because a Muslim would not have "wasted" his time and would regard pleasure as a reward of the afterlife.* And what Muslim would urge his fellow believers to recite the morning prayer—and then go on to quote from it? A devout Muslim should not need to be reminded of his duty to say the first of the five prayers of the day—and would certainly not need to be reminded of the text. It was as if a Christian, urging his followers to recite the Lord's Prayer, felt it necessary to read the whole prayer in case they didn't remember it.

However, the full and original Arabic text was not released by the FBI. The

---

*This may, however, be a poor translation from the Koran, in which we find in Sura 6, ayah 32: "And this world's life is not but a play and an idle sport, and certainly the abode of the hereafter is better than those who guard [against evil]." Sura 6, ayah 70 advises: "And leave those who have taken their religion for a play and an idle sport and whom this world's life has deceived . . ."

translation, as it stood, suggested an almost Christian view of what the hijackers might have felt—asking to be forgiven their sins, explaining that fear of death is natural, that "a believer is always plagued with problems." A Muslim is encouraged not to fear death—it is, after all, the moment when he or she believes they will start a new life—and a believer in the Islamic world is one who is certain of his path, not "plagued with problems." There were no references to any of Osama bin Laden's demands—for an American withdrawal from the Gulf, an end to Israeli occupation, the overthrow of pro-American Arab regimes—nor any narrative context for the atrocities about to be committed. If the men had an aspiration—and if the document was above suspicion—then they were sending their message direct to their God.

The prayer/instructions may have been distributed to other hijackers before the massacres occurred—*The Washington Post* reported that the FBI found another copy of "essentially the same document" in the wreckage of the plane that crashed in Pennsylvania. No text of this document was released. In the past, CIA translators have turned out to be Lebanese Maronite Christians whose understanding of Islam and its prayers may have led to serious textual errors. Could this be to blame for the weird references in the notes found in Atta's baggage? Or was there something more mysterious about the background of those who committed these crimes against humanity? American scholars had already raised questions about the use of "100 per cent"—hardly a theological term to be found in a religious exhortation—and the use of the word "optimistic" with reference to the Prophet was a decidedly modern concept.

From the start, the hole in the story was the reported behaviour of the hijackers. Atta was said to have been a near-alcoholic, while Ziad Jarrah, the Lebanese hijacker of the plane that crashed in Pennsylvania, had a Turkish girlfriend in Hamburg and enjoyed nightclubs and drinking. Was this why the published text referred to the "forgiveness" of sin? The final instruction, "to make sure that you are clean, your clothes are clean, including your shoes," may have been intended as a call to purify a "martyr" before death. Equally, it may reflect the thoughts of a truly eccentric—and wicked—mind. The document found in Atta's baggage ended with a heading: "When you enter the plane." It then urged the hijackers to recite: "Oh God, open all doors for me . . . I am asking for your help. I am asking you for forgiveness. I am asking you to lighten my way. I am asking you to lift the burden I feel . . ." Was this an attempt to smother latent feelings of compassion towards the passengers on the hijacked planes—especially the children—or towards the thousands who would die when the aircraft crashed? Did the nineteen suicide bombers say these words to themselves in their last moments? Or didn't they need to?

And how did these perverse men—and perhaps "perverse" was the very opposite of their persona—fly these aircraft with such painless accuracy into three of their four targets? Within days, we would learn of their flight-training programmes, their desire to learn only how to fly an airliner once it had taken off. I was travelling from Beirut to Paris in late September and sought the reflections of my friends on the flight deck, by chance the same crew with whom I'd flown into Dhahran in 1990 when the United States sent its soldiers to Saudi Arabia. "Eighteen months? You think it takes eighteen months to learn how to fly a Boeing 757 once it's in the air?" the pilot asked. Far below us, the clouds of central Europe passed like a white screen, faint ripples of emerging cumulus climbing from the plateau of mist in the afternoon sun. "I can teach you how to fly this in two minutes. At least, I can teach you all you need to know in order to become a hijacker." As evening drew in, the instruments began to shine green in front of us. The co-pilot had laid his maps across his lap. His colleagues tut-tutted. "A hijacker doesn't need these maps," he said. "All he needed to do was code in the exact location of the World Trade Center Twin Towers. On automatic pilot, the plane will follow these instructions. He switches off the transponder [identifying aircraft for ground control]—this knob—and the plane will head for his chosen destination."

The pilot leaned forward. The code word for the setting was punched in as "FISK" along with a series of numbers, in this case 123456789, so that the plane would fly itself to its "target." "The hijacker probably couldn't put an airliner through a take-off—but he doesn't have to," the pilot said. "The hijackers in America let the flight-deck crew do that. They wait until the 757 is at its cruising altitude, say 35,000 feet, then they burst into the cabin, murder the pilot and take over. Most of their work has already been done for them." It dawned on me then that faith, however perverted, had now connected with modern technology—in just the same way as the volumes in those Algerian bookshops, works on Islam and works on science, had been placed next to one another.

A pattern of towns emerged like white and yellow blood vessels in the body of darkness below us. "Your hijacker has now reached the area west of New York, and he lets the plane take him to within sight of the city," the pilot says. "Then he just presses this button to cut the automatic pilot and flies the plane himself. He can see the Twin Towers. In broad daylight, it's easy—every pilot into New York would see the Trade Center. Then he pushes the wheel forward and starts his dive." Middle East pilots had already discussed the last moments of the two aircraft to hit the Twin Towers. They had studied the photographs in the news magazines, watched and listened to the videotapes. On our flight deck, the crew had a set of press photographs of the last moments of the American Airlines and United Airlines jets.

"On the videotape that was made of the first plane to hit, you can clearly hear the twin engines," the pilot says. "They are so loud that someone in the street looks up. The engines are over-powered, they were never meant to be flying the plane that fast, they are under immense pressure." And he makes a noise like a jet through his teeth. "The way the plane is plunging—he's pushing it down with the wheel [control stick], remember, it's now flying way forward of its permitted speed. I reckon that first aircraft hit the tower at maybe nine hundred—even one thousand—kilometres an hour."

We all digest this thought as a bubble of air gently rocks the wings of our own jet, aware of just how easily this secure cocoon of warmth, our air coming pressured into the cabin from the engines, our flight-path directed and watched from central and northern Europe, can turn into a tomb. "You know why those people jumped from the windows of the building?" the co-pilot suddenly asks. "That wasn't gasoline that had burned into the buildings, the kind you use in a car. That jet was carrying"—and here he glances at a fuel manual—"around twenty thousand gallons of aviation fuel, which is the same as kerosene. Ordinary gasoline will burn you, but kerosene burns ferociously, it's much hotter. The people burning in that tower were, in effect, being tortured to death. They jumped because of the pain."

U.S. secretary of state Colin Powell laid out the ground rules for the first war against "evil" within three days of September 11th. His message to the Taliban was simple: they had to take responsibility for sheltering bin Laden. "You cannot separate your activities from the activity of these perpetrators," he warned.* But the Americans absolutely refused to associate their own response to their predicament with their activities in the Middle East. And we were supposed to go on holding our tongues even when Ariel Sharon—a man whose name will always be associated with the massacre at Sabra and Chatila—announced that Israel also wished to join the battle against "world terror." No wonder the Palestinians were fearful. In the four days following September 11th, twenty-three Palestinians were killed in the West Bank and Gaza, an astonishing figure that would have been front-page news had America not been blitzed. But if Israel was allowed to join the new conflict, then the Palestinians—by fighting the Israelis—would, by extension, become part of the "world terror" against which Bush was supposedly going to war. Not for nothing did Sharon now claim that Yassir Arafat had connections with Osama bin Laden—a statement as empty of truth as Bush's later attempt to persuade the world that Saddam Hussein had links with bin Laden.

It took a while to grasp what was now going on, the extraordinary, almost unbelievable preparations under way for the most powerful nation ever to have existed on God's earth to bomb the most devastated, ravaged, starvation-haunted and tragic country in the world. Afghanistan, raped and eviscerated by the Russian

---

*The plans for an assault on Afghanistan had bitter historical precedents. *Tom Graham, V.C.*, the novel that so influenced Bill Fisk just before the First World War, was about the Great Game, which was supposed to be about frontiers—about keeping a British-controlled Afghanistan between the Indian empire and the Russian border—but it was a history of betrayals. Those we thought were on our side turned out to be against us. Until 1878, we had thought the Amir Sher Ali Khan of Kabul was our friend, ready to fight for the British empire—just as a man called Osama bin Laden would later fight the Russians on "our" behalf—but he forbade passage to British troops and encouraged the robbery of British merchants. He had "openly and assiduously endeavoured . . . to stir up religious hatred against the English," our declaration of war had announced on 21 November 1878. The Amir's aiding and abetting of the murder of the British Embassy staff was "a treacherous and cowardly crime, which has brought indelible disgrace upon the Afghan people," Sir Frederick Roberts announced in 1879 when the British occupied Kabul. The Amir's followers "should not escape . . . penalty and . . . the punishment inflicted should be such as will be felt and remembered . . . All persons convicted of bearing a part [in the murders] will be dealt with according to their deserts." This truly Victorian warning was a preamble to the words we were now hearing from Bush.

army for ten years, abandoned by its friends—us, of course—once the Russians had retreated, was about to be attacked by the surviving superpower. President Bush was now threatening the obscurantist, ignorant, super-conservative Taliban with the same punishment he intended to mete out to bin Laden. Bush had originally talked about "justice and punishment" and about "bringing to justice" the perpetrators of the atrocities of September 11th. But he was not sending policemen to the Middle East; he was sending B-52s. And F-18s and AWACS planes and Apache helicopters. We were not going to arrest bin Laden. We were going to destroy him. And B-52s don't discriminate between men wearing turbans, or between men and women or women and children.

None deserved this fate, but after twenty-one years of continuous conflict, the Afghans merited it least of all. The Saudis and the Pakistanis had, on America's behalf, helped to arm the militias of Afghanistan against the Soviet Union, and then—disgusted by the victors' feuding—supported Mullah Omar's Wahhabi army of self-righteous peasant clerics, the Taliban. Saudi Arabia had poured millions of dollars into the madrassas—religious colleges—in Pakistan throughout the Afghan–Soviet conflict and the Taliban was an authentic product of Wahhabism, the strict, pseudo-reformist Islamist state faith of Saudi Arabia founded by the eighteenth-century cleric Mohamed Ibn Abdul-Wahab. Western scholars like to refer to Abdul-Wahab's beliefs—such as they were—as extremist, but to Muslims they had a quite different connotation. For waging war on fellow Muslims who had "erred" was an obligatory part of his philosophy, whether they be the "deviant" Shias of Basra—whom he vainly attempted to convert to Sunni Islam— or Arabians who did not follow his own exclusive interpretation of Muslim "unity." He also proscribed rebellion against rulers. His orthodoxy therefore both threatened the modern-day House of Saud because of its corruption, yet secured its future by forbidding any revolution. The Saudi ruling family thus embraced the one faith that could both protect and destroy it.

SAUDI ARABIA'S ROLE in the September 11th, 2001 attacks has still not been fully explored. While senior members of the royal family expressed the shock and horror that was expected of them, no attempt was made to examine the nature of Wahhabism and its inherent contempt for all representation of human activity or death. Abdul-Wahab ordered all tombs and mosques built over tombs to be destroyed, including the tomb of Zayd bin al-Khattab, a companion of the Prophet. The destruction of the two giant Buddhas of Bamiyan by the Taliban in 2000— along with the vandalism in the Kabul museum—fitted perfectly into this theocratic wisdom. So, too, it might be argued, did the Twin Towers of the World Trade Center.

Saudi Muslim legal iconoclasm led directly to the detonation of the Buddhas. In 1820, the much-worshipped statues of Dhu Khalasa, dating from the twelfth century, were destroyed by Wahhabis. Only weeks after Lebanese professor Kamal Salibi suggested in the late 1990s that once-Jewish villages in what is now

Saudi Arabia may have been locations in the Bible, the Saudi authorities sent bull-dozers to destroy the ancient buildings there. Saudi organisations have destroyed hundreds of historic structures in the name of religion in Mecca and Medina, and former UN officials have condemned the destruction of Ottoman buildings in Bosnia by a Saudi aid agency which decided they were "idolatrous." When the Saudis built the massive Faisal mosque in the Pakistani capital of Islamabad—originally destined for Kabul—its construction was followed almost at once by the smashing of a large number of early Islamic figure shrines in the city. Graffiti appeared beside graveyard shrines saying they must be destroyed because "there can be no sainthood in Islam." Of the many Islamic countries to have condemned the destruction of the Bamiyan Buddhas, one Muslim nation was noticeable by its silence: Saudi Arabia, where even private Christian worship at Christmas is for-bidden and where kings and emirs are buried without gravestones.

In 1998, a Saudi student at Harvard produced a remarkable thesis—based upon first-hand research in his country—which argued convincingly that U.S. forces had suffered casualties in bombing attacks in Saudi Arabia because American intelligence did not understand Wahhabism and had underestimated the extent of the dissatisfaction among senior ulema towards the U.S. presence in the kingdom. Nawaf Obaid, who drew up his report at the request of a senior State Department official, named the two most vocal clerics opposed to King Fahd as Sheikh Sulie-man al-Owda and Sheikh Safar al-Hawali. Al-Awdah had distributed tapes of ser-mons that compared members of the royal family to the last sultans of the Ottoman empire and the Americans to an occupying force. He drew his support, Obaid pointed out, from a town called Buraiydah, where his followers attempted to pre-vent his arrest in 1994.

Obaid quoted a senior officer in the Saudi army as telling him that "I was amazed at the 'secret' agreement that the king and the minister of defence had made with the Bush administration agreeing to U.S. troop retention after the war. I knew then and there that the society . . . would never understand or accept this sit-uation." More ominously, a Saudi National Guard officer told Obaid that "the more visible the Americans became, the darker I saw the future of the country."

Wahhabi puritanism meant that Saudi Arabia was always likely to throw up men who believed they had been chosen to "cleanse" their society from corrup-tion—the royal family usually being fingered as the centre of this Satanic cancer—and it was a former National Guard officer, Juhayman Ibn Mohamed al-Utaybi, who led the siege of the Great Mosque at Mecca in November 1979, along with his friend Mohamed Ibn Abdullah al-Qahtani. Al-Utaybi proclaimed al-Qahtani the mahdi, the divinely inspired figure foretold by the Prophet who would restore jus-tice to a corrupt world. The Saudis deployed 10,000 troops to take back the mosque from the two hundred gunmen who had seized the building. But the Great Mosque was a veritable Afghanistan of underground caves and hiding places. Only after French riot police were brought to Mecca two weeks later—undergoing a brief but formal conversion to Islam to legitimise their presence in a city that only Muslims may visit—was the siege brought to a bloody end. The French flooded the basements of the mosque and inserted cables into the water, electrocuting Saddam-style many of the rebels "like kippers." On 9 January 1980, in towns across Saudi Arabia, sixty-three men were beheaded in public.

Yet still the Saudis could not confront the duality of protection-and-threat that Wahhabism represented for them. Both Saudis and their Western allies have tried to bury this in obfuscations and metaphors that prevent any serious inquiry into this "puritanism." Prince Bandar ibn Sultan, Saudi Arabia's long-time ambassador to the United States, once characterised his country's religion as part of a "timeless culture" whose people lived according to Islam "and our other basic ways." A former British ambassador advised Westerners to "adapt" in Saudi Arabia and "to act with the grain of Saudi traditions and culture." This "grain" is all too evident in the libraries of Amnesty International appeals for the hundreds of men—and occasionally women—who are beheaded each year in the kingdom, often after torture and grossly unfair trials.

With considerable prescience, the Saudi scholar Obaid concluded in 1998 that "in the Taliban, the U.S. will have a chance to witness a Wahhabi government without the moderating presence of the al Saud, and perhaps a glimpse into what Saudi Arabia could become if the traditional balance of power is disrupted in favour of the religious establishment." It was to prove a fearful experience. The Taliban made no secret of their intolerance, their merciless punishments, the hanging of thieves—along with videotapes and television sets—their amputations and beheading and beating and execution of women.* But when faced with Shia Muslim opponents, they were capable of applying Abdul-Wahab's concept of waging war on "deviant" Muslims with a ferocity that quite matched their Afghan militia opponents. In August 1998, they succeeded in breaking into the last stronghold of Ahmed Shah Massoud's Northern Alliance, the city of Mazar-e-Sharif. The first eyewitness accounts of the ferocious massacre—kept secret for two months in a series of confidential United Nations files—provided horrific evidence of rape, throat-slitting and mass suffocation of Shia Muslim men and women by the Saudi-funded army. The reports, compiled by officials of the UN Commissioner for Human Rights in Pakistan, were sent to New York but kept secret because the UN was still trying to negotiate with the Taliban. Outraged by what he read in the documents, however, a Swedish diplomat passed on their contents to me.

An Afghan man, a Tajik father of three, described to UN officials how he had "never before witnessed such scenes of bestial violence" until the day the Taliban entered Mazar to find the unsuspecting men and women of the city going about

---

*The ritual of head-chopping was most graphically described by an expatriate Irishman who witnessed a triple execution in Jeddah in 1997. "Standing to the left of the first prisoner, and a little behind him, the executioner focused on his quarry . . . I watched as the sword was drawn back with the right hand. A one-handed back-swing of a golf club came to mind . . . The down-swing begins. How can he do it from that angle? . . . the blade met the neck and cut through it like . . . a heavy cleaver cutting through a melon . . . a crisp, moist smack. The head fell and rolled a little. The torso slumped neatly. I see now why they tied wrists to feet . . . the brain had no time to tell the heart to stop, and the final beat pumped a gush of blood out of the headless torso onto the plinth."

their daily shopping. "They were shooting without warning at everybody who happened to be on the street, without discriminating between men, women and children," he said. "Soon the streets were covered with dead bodies and with blood. No one was allowed to bury the corpses for . . . six days. Dogs were eating human flesh and going mad and soon the smell became intolerable." The same witness said that on the second day of their victory, the Taliban began house-to-house searches in a hunt for Shia Muslim families who were identified by their facial features. "Almost all who were found were either shot three times on the spot (one bullet in the head, one in the chest and one in the testicles), slaughtered in the Halal way (with a knife to the throat) or stuffed into containers after being badly beaten."

Up to twelve of these containers were parked all day long in the sun with sealed doors, and the witness "saw a container that had its doors opened after all the males inside had died of suffocation. Some of the containers were filled with children (boys and girls) who were taken to an unknown destination after their parents were killed." Women, the UN report said, "were usually abused and many rape cases were reported . . ." One witness fleeing through Mazar heard the calls of the muezzins in the mosques "asking all Shias to convert to Sunni [Islam] and attend the daily prayers for their own sake." A woman whose husband and two brothers were executed—shot twice and then their throats cut—described how the Taliban, as they left the house, shouted "that they had more serious executions to carry out, but that they would be coming back."

Ten Iranian diplomats and an Iranian journalist were killed when Taliban men entered their consulate. Their bodies were left lying in the building for two days until they were buried in a mass grave in the compound of the Sultan Razia Girls' High School. The murder of the Iranians almost provoked Tehran to stage a military incursion into Afghanistan in September 1998. Of the thousands of Shia Muslims taken from Mazar, not one returned.

In the early spring of 2000, I visited a Taliban production line, a school of committed, earnest young men whose Koranic learning was aided by the modern science that captivates so many Islamists. Its pupils—*talib* means "student"—were of many nationalities, all seeking the divine revolution which they believed would occur in their lifetime. Arriving at the college at Akora Khattak in Pakistan's North West Frontier province with film-makers Nelofer Pazira and Siddiq Barmak, I found Tajikistan's Islamic "liberators" more than willing to talk to us. Down a narrow passageway, the young men were gathered, bearded, smiling, crying *Allahu akbar*, posing before posters that showed the Russian bear skewered with a green Muslim flag. Abdul-Raouf—there were no student family names for us as at the great mosque and its religious school opposite the railway track from Peshawar—grasped my arm. "We would like to make an Islamic revolution in Tajikistan and we believe in the rebirth of Islam in Tajikistan," he shouted in Russian, which Siddiq—who trained in the Soviet Union—could translate. "The great light of Islam will shine upon our country. It is the promise of God for us." His face was thin, his beard pointed, his eyes alight with conviction. Abdul-Raouf and his fellow students in the madrassa founded by Mullanah Abdul al-Haq had only recently taken leave of their Chechen colleagues, young men who—after a year of Koranic teaching at Akora Khattak—had returned to their country to fight the Russians.

The al-Haq college stood for everything the Americans and Russians most feared: a Taliban factory, an ideological school run by seventy teachers from Pakistan and Afghanistan for thousands of international Islamists eager to struggle for a united Muslim nation in south-west Asia. And if that Muslim nation was to include most of the former southern Soviet republics, Afghanistan and even Pakistan, then the *Haqqania* will have played its role. As twenty-two-year-old Abdul-Raouf put it when I asked about his former Chechen classmates, "they are our brothers and if they need help, we can give it to them."

The madrassa, founded by Rashed al-Haq's grandfather in 1974, was school to all of the Taliban leadership now ruling in Kabul, and a new four-storey boarding hostel for 3,000 students proved that this was an expanding project rather than a dying ideal. If President-General Pervez Musharraf and his Pakistani authorities liked to assure Western leaders that such institutions were a thing of the past, it was instructive to note that eight black uniformed and armed Pakistani policemen lived within the complex, guarding Mullanah Sami al-Haq—Rashed's father—and his students. They arrived here in 1998, on the orders of the now-deposed prime minister Nawaz Sharif, for "security reasons." Nor was this huge college steeped in the past. If its Koranic volumes were studied with exceptional reverence, the madrassa ran its own publishing house and had gone high-tech, its computer room next to the library and managed by Sajjat Khan, who was already constructing a website. Rashed al-Haq, walking me round the campus in his robe and soft Pashtun hat, insisted that the college cost only a million rupees to run—a mere $20,000 a year—but agreed that its funding came from around the world. "Not from countries, just from individuals." I thought, of course, of Saudi Arabia.

"All the major Islamic leaders in this area were students of my grandfather and father," al-Haq said. "Especially the Taliban. The Islamic revolution is very near, *Inshallah*, God willing." Rashed al-Haq's grandfather, whose bound works have an honoured place in the college library, is buried in a plot beside the college, along with his wife and sister. The soft pebble-rush of pouring concrete emerged from the hostel next door where workmen were completing a new fourth floor. The military takeover of Pakistan in October 1999 had left the college untouched. "In fact, we were happy [at this] because the majority of members of the assembly were dishonest people," Rashed al-Haq said. "This was not a real democracy—and a real democracy is what we are struggling for in Islam. For fifty years since the foundation of Pakistan, we have been waiting for real Islamic law to be introduced." And suddenly, the voice of Rashed al-Haq sounded like that of General Musharraf, the military ruler of Pakistan. For were not their aims similar? Did they not both demand an end to corruption? Did they not both denounce Nawaz Sharif's rule as a fake democracy? So why should Pakistan heed Washington's demand by closing down the Taliban factory in Akora Khattak?

Yet other remarks showed how far the college had gone in espousing everything the Americans—and Russians—hate. As we walked past the madrassa's delicate blue-and-white tiled mosque, Rashed al-Haq, who spent a year at the Islamic university of Al-Azhar in Cairo and spoke Arabic with a thick Egyptian accent, became emotional. "There is, believe me, going to be an Islamic revolution. The more the United States and the Western world and the nations that murder Muslims oppress us, the sooner there will be an Islamic republic. Our morale is high and it's possible to have an Islamic Union all over this area and we want to create such a union—like the EU and NATO."

NATO, I asked? NATO? Rashed al-Haq was thinking in military as well as ideological terms. "If India and other Western countries make a nuclear bomb, everyone accepts this, it's OK. But if one poor Muslim nation like Pakistan makes a bomb, then everyone is against it and it becomes an Islamic bomb. If the Hindus make a bomb, it's not a Hindu bomb. But the Muslims who make a bomb are called fundamentalist terrorists." And so I found another point of contact between the al-Haq college and General Musharraf. For Rashed al-Haq and his students and for the Pakistani general, the bomb was a symbol of pride that was there to stay.

ZIAD JARRAH'S FATHER sat beside me and opened his palms in that gesture of innocence that is also a form of special pleading. "He called just two days before the planes crashed to tell me he'd received the two thousand dollars I'd sent him." Still recovering from open-heart surgery, Samir Jarrah sat, half slumped, sick and traumatised in a green plastic chair beneath the vines of his Lebanese garden. "Ziad said it was for his aeronautical course. He had told me last year that he had a choice of courses—in France or in America—and it was me who told him to go to the States. But there are lots of Ziads. Maybe it wasn't him? He was a good, kind boy . . ." At which point, Samir Jarrah leaned forward, brought his hands to his face and broke down in tears. Ziad Jarrah was the pilot of United Airlines flight 93 from Newark to San Francisco, the plane that crashed in Pennsylvania when its passengers apparently tried to storm the flight deck, wrestling with the hijackers, perhaps with Ziad Jarrah as he gripped the aircraft controls.

Everyone knew. Around us, a bunch of middle-aged men sat on identical chairs, all Sunni Muslims, all appalled that a crime against humanity should have stained the tiny but wealthy village of Almarj in the Lebanese Bekaa Valley. A massive new village mosque—I'd never seen so big a mosque in so small a town— stood scarcely 200 metres from the front door, but both friends of the family and Ziad Jarrah's uncle insisted that he was neither religious nor political. "He was a normal person," Jamal Jarrah said. "He drank alcohol, he had girlfriends. Only last August, his Turkish girlfriend Aysel came to meet our family here because she wanted to meet her future in-laws. He wasn't able to come with her because he said he was too busy with his studies." It is now 15 September 2001, four days after the attacks on the World Trade Center and the Pentagon and the suicide hijackers' plane crash in Pennsylvania.

Too busy to bring his fiancée to meet his family? Busy doing what? And what was the $2,000 for? To continue studies at his Miami aeronautical school? Or to buy air tickets for the Boeing 757 flight to California, for him perhaps, and maybe for the other hijackers on the flight. Aysel was in Germany, freely giving evidence to the Bochum city police who had just searched her apartment, discovering "aircraft-related documents" in a suitcase belonging to one of three men named by Washington as hijackers. All of them—something the Jarrah family could not explain or would not believe—lived together in Hamburg. Aysel had already reported Ziad missing—just as she had eighteen months before when Ziad Jarrah disappeared for up to five weeks. And what she told the Jarrah family over the telephone then gave them their first suspicion that something was terribly wrong with their only son.

For according to a family friend, Aysel told the Jarrahs that her fiancé, who would visit her each weekend from his university in Hamburg, might have gone to Afghanistan. Jamal Jarrah told me that this is what Aysel had feared. "But it turned out that he had been moving from his first university in Greifswald to his new courses in Hamburg and had not been in contact with Aysel during that time." Five weeks to change universities? Without telling his fiancée?

The details of Ziad Jarrah's life were as simple—or so the family said—as his death was obscure to them. He was twenty-six, born—according to his Lebanese identity documents—on 11 May 1975, a village boy from a wealthy family. His father was a civil servant in the Beirut Department of Social Security, his mother a schoolteacher. Ziad Jarrah attended the Evangelical School in the Christian town of Zahle, about 20 kilometres from his home, and his father paid thousands to put his son through university. He travelled to Hamburg on a student visa in 1997, later attending the city's Technical University. He briefly went missing in 1999, just before setting off for the United States on his father's advice. "Whenever he asked for money, I would send it," Samir Jarrah said. "He needed money—he had a private home in Germany and a girlfriend to look after. He had to fund his studies."

In February, Ziad Jarrah returned to Lebanon for the last time to be present during his father's open-heart surgery. "He looked after his dad and went to the hospital every day to see him," Jamal, the uncle, told me. "He was so normal. His personality and his life bore no relation to the kind of things that happened . . . He had girlfriends, he went to nightclubs, he went dancing sometimes." Everyone I spoke to in Almarj said the same thing: Ziad Jarrah was a happy, secular youth, he never showed any interest in religion and never visited the mosque for prayers, he liked women even if he was at times reserved and shy. Mohamed Atta, who lived in Hamburg with him and flew the American Airlines plane into the World Trade Center, was known to knock back five or six stiff drinks in an evening. Surely such behaviour would lead to banishment from the ranks of bin Laden's al-Qaeda movement. Or was this an attempt to blind any American intelligence agencies that might be watching the men? Who would believe that a young man drinking in a bar—with a Turkish girlfriend back in Germany with whom he'd been living— would be planning to crash an airliner with thirty-three innocent passengers aboard into—where? Congress? The White House?

But Samir Jarrah's son did board the plane with a knife and a box-cutter—

a woman's last phone call from the flight revealed that these were the hijackers' only weapons—and the intention to kill himself, along with the passengers, crew and, quite possibly, President George Bush and his staff. What, then, did he learn at his Zahle school and the Christian Patriarchate college where he also studied in Beirut? He was only seven when the Israeli army surrounded him and tens of thousands of other Lebanese civilians in the siege of Beirut in 1982. He was never involved in the civil war, his neighbours told me. He was never interested in militias. "We are ready to cooperate with the authorities," Jamal Jarrah said to me wearily. "We all regard what happened in America as a terrorist act. It's a tragedy for Americans, for us, for all people in the world . . ." Samir kept shaking his head, going through a creed of refusal. "My boy was just a normal person. He would never do this. Why, there may have been another 'Ziad Jarrah' on the plane." But the men and women gathering at the family home that morning understood and had come dressed in black.

WHEN THE AIR BOMBARDMENT of Afghanistan began on 7 October 2001, there were no Western journalists inside the Taliban's three-quarters of Afghanistan, only in the sliver of north-eastern territory held by Massoud's Northern Alliance. The sole picture of life—and death—inside Kabul was Qatar's Al-Jazeera satellite channel, which not only broadcast the statements of bin Laden but showed a tape of bomb damage to civilian areas of the capital. A few months earlier, my old friend Tom Friedman had set off for the small Gulf emirate, from where, in one of his imperial columns for *The New York Times*, he informed the world that the tiny state's television channel was a welcome sign that democracy might be coming to the Middle East. Al-Jazeera had been upsetting some of the local Arab dictators— Mubarak of Egypt for one—and Tom thought this a good idea. So did I. But by early October the story was being rewritten. Colin Powell was now rapping the emir of Qatar over the knuckles because—so he claimed—Al-Jazeera was "inciting anti-Americanism."

The Americans wanted the emir to close down the channel's office in Kabul, which was scooping the world with its tape of the U.S. bombardments and bin Laden's televised statements. The most wanted man in the whole world had been suggesting that he was angry about the deaths of Iraqi children under sanctions, about the corruption of pro-Western Arab regimes, about Israel's attacks on Palestinian territory, about the need for U.S. forces to leave the Middle East. And after insisting that bin Laden was a "mindless terrorist"—that there was no connection between U.S. policy in the Middle East and the crimes against humanity in New York and Washington—the Americans needed to close down Al-Jazeera's coverage.

Needless to say, this tomfoolery was given little coverage in the Western media, whose editors knew they did not have a single correspondent in the Taliban area of Afghanistan. Al-Jazeera did. Bin Laden's propaganda was pretty basic. He taped his own statements and sent one of his henchmen off to the Al-Jazeera office in Kabul. No cross-questioning, of course, just a sermon. We didn't see any video clips of destroyed Taliban equipment, the ancient MiGs and even older Warsaw Pact tanks that had been rusting across Afghanistan for years. Only a sequence of pictures—apparently real—of bomb damage in a civilian area of Kabul.

As usual, the first reports of the U.S. missile attacks were covered without the slightest suggestion that innocents were about to die in the country we planned to "save." Whether the Taliban were lying or telling the truth about thirty civilians dead in Kabul, did we reporters really think that all our bombs fell on the guilty and not the innocent? To be sure, we were given Second World War commentaries about Western military morale. On the BBC we had to listen to an account of "a perfect moonless night for the air armada" to bomb Afghanistan. We were told on one satellite channel of the "air combat" over Afghanistan. A lie. The Taliban had none of their ageing MiGs aloft. There was no combat.

Of course, there was a moral question here. After the atrocities in New York and Washington, how could we be expected to "play fair" between the ruthless bin Laden and the West? We couldn't make an equivalence between the mass-murderer's diatribes and the American and British forces who were trying to destroy the Taliban. But that was not the point. It was our viewers and readers with whom we had to "play fair." Because of our rage at the massacre of the innocents in America, and because of our desire to kowtow to the elderly "terrorism experts," did we have to lose all our critical faculties? Why at least not tell us how these "terrorism experts" came to be so expert? And what were their connections with dubious intelligence services?

In some cases, in America, the men giving us their advice on screen were the very same operatives who steered the CIA and the FBI into the greatest intelligence failure in modern history: the inability to uncover the plot, four years in the making, to destroy the lives of nearly 3,000 people. President Bush said this was a war between good and evil. But that was exactly what bin Laden was saying. Wasn't it worthwhile to point this out and to ask where such theories might lead?

In the Middle East, Osama bin Laden was already gaining mythic status among Arabs; his voice, repeatedly beamed into millions of homes, articulated the demands and grievances—and fury—of Middle Eastern Muslims who had observed how their pro-Western presidents and kings and princes wriggled out of any serious criticism of the Anglo–American bombardment of Afghanistan. Viewing bin Laden's latest videotape, Western nations concentrated—if they listened at all—on his remarks about the atrocities in the United States. If he expressed his approval, though denied any personal responsibility, didn't this mean that he was really behind the mass slaughter of September 11th? Arabs listened with different ears. They heard a voice that accused the West of double standards and "arrogance" towards the Middle East, a voice that addressed the central issue in the lives of so many Arabs: the Palestinian–Israeli conflict and the continuation of Israeli occupation. Now, as a long-time resident of Cairo put it to me, Arabs believed that America was "trying to kill the one man ready to tell the truth."

But the response of Arab leaders to both the atrocities in America and the

American bombing of Afghanistan was truly pathetic. Listening to the speeches of the Muslim leaders at the Organisation of the Islamic Conference emergency summit on 10 October, it *was* possible to believe that bin Laden represented Arabs more faithfully than their tinpot dictators and kings. Please give us more evidence about September 11, besought the emir of Qatar. Please don't forget the Palestinians, pleaded Yassir Arafat. Islam is innocent, insisted the Moroccan foreign minister. Everyone—but everyone—wished to condemn the September 11 atrocities in the United States. No one—absolutely no one—wanted to explain why nineteen Arabs decided to fly planeloads of innocent people into buildings full of civilians.

The very name "bin Laden" did not sully the Qatar conference hall. Not once. Not even the name "Taliban." Had a Martian landed in the Gulf—which looks not unlike Mars—he might have concluded that the World Trade Center in New York was destroyed by an earthquake or a typhoon. Was it not President Hosni Mubarak of Egypt who said, back in 1990, that the Iraqi invasion of Kuwait would blow over "like a summer's breeze"? Delegates condemned to a man the slaughter in America without for a moment examining why it might have come about. Like the Americans, the Arabs didn't want to look for causes. Indeed, the conference hall was a miraculous place, in which introspection included neither guilt nor responsibility.

Arafat demanded an international force—a good idea for a new Afghanistan—but it quickly turned out that he was talking about an international force to protect Palestinians in the West Bank and Gaza which, according to the map, was about 3,000 kilometres from Kabul. Of course, he condemned the World Trade Center massacre. So did Sheikh Hamad al-Thani, the emir of Qatar, and Mohamed bin Issa, the Moroccan foreign minister, and Abdelouahed Belkeziz, the Islamic Conference's secretary-general. But that was about it. Indeed, the collected speeches amounted to a chorus: please don't kill innocent Afghans, but—whatever happens—don't bomb Arab countries. For much of the day, Afghanistan appeared a faraway country of which they knew little—a mendacious thought, given that Saudi Arabia and Pakistan were midwives to the Taliban—and wanted to know even less.

Only Farouq al-Sharaa, the Syrian foreign minister, stated frankly that attacking Muslim states was "forbidden." This meant, he said, "that all Arabs and Muslims will stand with the country that is attacked." Which must have made them shiver in their boots on board the U.S. carriers in the Gulf. There was the usual rhetoric bath from other conference delegates. The communiqué from the fifty-six conference members claimed that they rejected "the linking of terrorism to the Arab and Muslim people's rights, including the Palestinian and Lebanese people's right to self-determination, self-defence and resisting Israeli and foreign occupation and aggression." Translation: Please, America, don't take the Israeli side and bomb Hamas, Islamic Jihad, the Lebanese Hizballah, Damascus, Tehran et al. "Resistance is not terrorism" had become as familiar a slogan in the Arab world as "war against terrorism" had in the Western world.

There was little that George Bush or Tony Blair would have disagreed with.

Retaliation "should not extend to any but those who carried out those attacks [which] requires conclusive evidence against the culprits," Sheikh Hamad pronounced. "The Islamic world was the first to call for the dialogue of civilisation." This might have been scripted for the British prime minister. But the Qatari emir got off one quick biff at the Americans. The world should not, he said, fall "into conflicting sects, camps and clashing dichotomies based on the principle of 'If you are not on my side, then you are against me.'"

Wasn't Israel the real problem? the delegates tried to ask. Principal among them, of course, was our old friend Y. Arafat, Esq. Of course he condemned the attacks in America. Of course he felt "solidarity" with the American people—the old socialist "solidarity" put to an original new use. Money was to be had in a good cause. Qatar opened a fund for the Afghans and the Saudis put in $10 million, the United Arab Emirates $3 million, Oman $1 million. But what the delegates wanted was evidence—"conclusive evidence," according to Sheikh Hamad—that Washington had identified the culprits of September 11th. This at least allowed him to avoid the fatal words "bin Laden." Indeed, it allowed everyone to duck this annoying, dangerous, frightening man who was calling for the overthrow of almost every single one of the Islamic delegates. We're sorry about September 11th, they said. Please don't bomb Afghanistan more than you have to. Please don't kill the innocent. And please don't bomb us.

For journalists, it was a frustrating war to cover. Around the Taliban's embassy in Islamabad and its consulate in Peshawar, we gathered in our hundreds. Names were scribbled onto visa applications and scooped up at the end of the morning by a scowling man with a long, pointed beard—and, I had no doubt, deposited in a large rubbish bin. In Quetta, I arrived at the consulate with a letter from a prominent supporter of the Taliban, insisting that I should be given a visa. I handed it to a Taliban "diplomat" in a dirty white robe. "Get out," he screamed at me. Once outside, I saw the letter—screwed up into a ball—sail over the consulate wall onto the pavement in front of me. Hamid Mir, a Pakistani journalist, managed to enter Afghanistan and interview bin Laden and emerged to tell me that bin Laden himself had asked why I was not in the country to see him. Months later, I learned that the Taliban had sought to find me, that I could have travelled to Afghanistan and talked to bin Laden—but that the message never reached me. The Scoop that never was.

Unaware of all this, I went on vainly pestering the Taliban's men for a visa. I settled into a villa in Peshawar, working my contacts in Islamabad for that all-important, hopeless document. I would take tea on the lawn. Perhaps only in the old British empire do they make black tea and milk in the same scalding pot, poured with lashings of sugar into fragile cups. The bougainvillea blasted crimson and purple down the brick wall beside me while big, aggressive black birds pursued one another over the cut grass. At the end of my road lay the British cemetery I had first explored twenty-one years earlier wherein memorials recorded the assassination of the Raj's good men from Surrey and Yorkshire, murdered by what were called *ghazis*, the Afghan fundamentalists of their age, who were often accompanied into battle—and I quote Captain Mainwaring who was in the Second Afghan War—"by religious men called *talibs*." In those days, we made promises. We promised Afghan governments our support if they kept out the Russians. We promised our Indian empire wealth, communications and education in return for its loyalty. Little had changed.

As day turned into sweaty evening, fighter-bombers pulsed through the yellow sky above my lawn, grey supersonic streaks that rose like hawks from Peshawar's mighty runway and headed west towards the mountains of Afghanistan. Their jet engines must have vibrated among the English bones in the cemetery at the end of the road, as Hardy's Channel firing once disturbed Parson Thirdly's remains. And on the big black television in my bedroom, the broken, veined screen proved that imperial history did indeed repeat itself. General Colin Powell stood at the right hand of General Pervez Musharraf after promising a serious look at the problems of Kashmir and Pashtun representation in a future Afghan government. The U.S. secretary of state and the general spent much of their time on 15 October chatting about the overnight artillery bombardment by that other old empire relic, the Indian army. General Musharraf wanted a "short" campaign against Afghanistan, General Powell a promise of continued Pakistani support in the United States's "war on terror." Musharraf wanted a solution to the problem of Kashmir. Powell, promising that the United States was now a close friend of Pakistan, headed off to India to oblige.

Scarcely three days before Powell acquired his sudden interest in the problems of Kashmir, Yassir Arafat, the discredited old man of Gaza—"our bin Laden," as ex-General Ariel Sharon indecently called him—was invited to Downing Street, where Tony Blair, hitherto a cautious supporter of Palestinian independence, declared the need for a "viable Palestinian state," including Jerusalem—"viable" being a gloss for a less mangled version of the Bantustan originally proposed for Arafat. Blair had no need to fear American wrath since President Bush Junior had already discovered that even before September 11th—or so he told us—he had a "vision" of a Palestinian state that accepted the existence of Israel. Arafat—speaking English at length for the first time in years—instantly supported the air bombardment of Afghanistan. The Afghans were not on hand to remind the world that the same Yassir Arafat had once enthusiastically supported the Soviet invasion of Afghanistan. Why did we always make quick-fix promises to vulnerable allies of convenience after years of accepting, even creating, the injustices of the Middle East and South-West Asia?

It was intriguing, that sweltering autumn in Pakistan, to read the full text of what bin Laden demanded in his first post–World Trade Center attack videotape. He said in Arabic, in a section largely excised in English translations, that "our [Muslim] nation has undergone more than eighty years of this humiliation . . ." and referred to "when the sword reached America after eighty years." Bin Laden might be cruel, wicked, ruthless or evil personified, but he was intelligent. He was obviously referring to the 1920 Treaty of Sèvres, written by the victorious allied powers, which broke the Ottoman empire and did away—after 600 years of sultanates and caliphates—with the last dream of Arab unity. Bin Laden's lieutenant, Ayman Zawahri—shouting into the video recorder from his Afghan cave on 6 October 2001—stated that the al-Qaeda movement "will not tolerate a recurrence of the Andalusia tragedy in Palestine." Andalusia? Yes, the debacle of Andalusia marked the end of Muslim rule in Spain in the fifteenth century. We may sprinkle quick-fix promises around, but the people of the Middle East have longer memories.

However one approaches this Arab sense of humiliation—whether we regard it as a form of self-pity or a fully justified response to injustice—it is nonetheless real. The Arabs were among the first scientists at the start of the second millennium, while the Crusaders—another of bin Laden's fixations—were riding in technological ignorance into the Muslim world. So while in the past few decades our popular conception of the Arabs vaguely embraced an oil-rich, venal and largely backward people, awaiting our annual handouts and their virgins in heaven, many of them were asking pertinent questions about their past and future, about religion and science, about—so I suspect—how God and technology might be part of the same universe. No such long-term questions for us. We just went on supporting our Muslim dictators around the world—especially in the Middle East—in return for their friendship and our false promises to rectify injustice.

We allowed our dictators to snuff out their socialist and communist parties; we left their population little place to exercise their political opposition except through religion. We went in for demonisation—Messrs. Khomeini, Abu Nidal, Ghadafi, Arafat, Saddam, bin Laden—rather than historical questioning. And we made more promises. Presidents Carter and Reagan made pledges to the Afghan mujahedin: fight the Russians and we will help you. We would assist the recovery of the Afghan economy. A rebuilding of the country, even—this from innocent Jimmy Carter—"democracy," not a concept to be sure that we would now be bequeathing to the Pakistanis, Uzbeks or Saudis. Of course, once the Russians were gone in 1989, there was no economic assistance.

The problem, it seemed, was that without any sense of history, we failed to understand injustice. Instead we compounded it, after years of indolence, when we wanted to bribe our would-be allies with promises of vast historical importance— a resolution to Palestine, Kashmir, an arms-free Middle East, Arab independence, an economic Nirvana—because we were at war. Tell Muslims what they want to hear, promise them what they want—anything, so long as we can get our armadas into the air in our latest "war against evil." And up they flew. In the sand-blasted mud villages along the border of Afghanistan, we could watch their contrails, white gashes cut into the deep blue skies that would suddenly turn into circles and—from far away across the Kandahar desert—we would hear a distant, imperial thunder. With binoculars, we could even make out the sleek, four-engined bombers, the sunlight flashing off their wings. Then the planes would turn southwest and begin their long haul back to Diego Garcia.

There was a children's doctor I met in Peshawar, who provided considerable insight into the Taliban's mentality at war. "After the Taliban radio went off the air . . . the next day I saw them assembling a new antenna. The Taliban always did this. Every time something was destroyed, they replaced it at once. They would go round and collect up all the wrecked equipment. This was very fast action. The Taliban were very relaxed about this. I'm trying to describe the Taliban reaction to the bombing. You know? They weren't *interested* in the attacks. It was very intriguing—and strange—for me to see this." But the doctor was no disinterested observer. "Most people, neutral people who're not connected with political groups, they hate the American policy—and if the Taliban would change just 20 per cent of their policy against the people, then the people would stand shoulder-to-shoulder with them. We are waiting for an end to the Taliban policy against women and against education. People will never forget what Pakistan has done to undermine Afghanistan—they see Pakistan as the eternal enemy. Among educated people, September 11th created a new situation. We knew that America helped to create the Taliban and Osama and we call them the 'kids' of America and Pakistan." And, he might have added, Saudi Arabia.

On 22 October, the Americans killed Saifullah of Turungzai, MA in Arabic and MA in Islamic Studies (Peshawar University), BSc. (Islamia College), B.Ed. and Certificate of Teaching, M. Phil. student and scholarship winner to Al-Azhar in Cairo, the oldest university in the Arab world. He spoke fluent English as well as Persian and his native Pushtu and loved poetry and history and was, so his family said, preparing a little reluctantly to get married. His father, Hedayatullah, was a medical doctor, his younger brother a student of chartered accountancy. No one outside Pakistan—and few inside—had ever heard of Saifullah. In these Pashtun villages of the North West Frontier, many families do not even have proper names. Saifullah was not a political leader; his fifty-year-old father said that his son was a humanitarian, not a warrior. His brother Mahazullah said the same. "He was always a peaceful person, quiet and calm, he just wanted to protect people in Afghanistan who he believed were the victims of terrorism." But everyone agreed how Saifullah died. He was killed when five American cruise missiles detonated against the walls of a building in the Darulaman suburb of Kabul where he and thirty-five other men were meeting.

His family now called him a "martyr." Hedayatullah embraced each visitor to their home of cement and mud walls—including me—and offered roast chicken and *mitha* sweets and pots of milk and tea and insisted that he be "congratulated" on being the proud father of a man who died for his beliefs. I dutifully ate the vast mounds of chicken that Hedayatullah tugged from the braziers of food on the floor. Hens clucked in the yard outside; an old coloured poster, depicting a Kalashnikov rifle with the word "jihad" above it, was pasted on the wall. But "peace" is the word the family uttered most. Saifullah had only gone to take money to Kabul for the suffering Afghans, said Mahazullah, perhaps no more than 20,000 rupees—a mere $350—which he had raised among his student friends.

That wasn't the way the Americans told the story. Blundering through their target maps and killing innocent civilians by the day, the Pentagon boasted that the Darulaman killings targeted the Taliban's "foreign" fighters, of whom a few were

Pakistanis, Saifullah among them. In Pushtu, his name means "Sword of God." Mahazullah dismissed the American claims. Only when I suggest that it might not be unusual for a young Muslim with Saifullah's views to have taken a weapon to defend Afghanistan does Mahazullah say, very quickly, that his brother "may have been a fighter." He never imagined his brother's death. A phone call prepared the family for the news, a friend with information that some Pakistanis had been killed in Kabul. "It has left a terrible vacuum in our life," Mahazullah said. "You cannot imagine what it is like without him. He was a person who respected life, who was a reformer. There was no justification for the war in Afghanistan. These people are poor. There is no evidence, no proof. Every human being has the right to the basic necessities of life. The family—all of us, including Saifullah—were appalled by the carnage in New York and Washington on September 11th. Saifullah was very regretful about this—we all watched it on television." At no point did the family mention the name of Osama bin Laden.

Turungzai was a village of resistance. During the Third Afghan War in 1919, the British hunted down Hadji Turungzai, one of the leaders of the revolt, and burned the village bazaar in revenge for its insurgency. Disconcertingly, a young man entered Saifullah's home, greeted me with a large smile and introduced himself as the grandson of the Hadji, scourge of the English. But this was no centre of Muslim extremism. Though the family prayed five times a day, they intended their daughters to be educated at university. Saifullah spent hours on his personal computer and apparently loved the poetry of the secular Pakistani national poet Allam Mohamed Iqbal of Surkhot (Sir Mohamed Iqbal after he had accepted a British knighthood), and, according to Mahazullah, was interested in the world's religions. When Saifullah left for Afghanistan, "Trust me" were the last words he spoke to his father. Perhaps he was remembering one of Iqbal's most famous verses:

> *Of God's command, the inner meaning do you know?*
> *To live in constant anger is a life indeed.*

To children, death also came. Mullah Mohamed Omar's ten-year-old son died in the third week of October. He was, according to Afghan refugees fleeing Kandahar, taken to one of the city's broken hospitals by his father, the Taliban leader and "Emir of the Faithful," but the boy—apparently travelling in Omar's car when it was attacked by U.S. aircraft—died of his wounds. No regrets, of course. Back in 1986, when American aircraft bombed Libya, they also destroyed the life of Colonel Muammar Ghadafi's six-year-old adopted daughter. No regrets on our part then, either. In 1992, when an Israeli pilot flying an American-made Apache helicopter fired an American-made missile into the car of Said Abbas Moussawi, head of the Hizballah guerrilla army in Lebanon, the Israeli pilot also killed Moussawi's ten-year-old. Again, no regrets.

And so the casualties in Afghanistan began to mount. From Kandahar came ever more frightful stories of civilians buried under ruins, of children torn to pieces by American bombs. When a few television crews were able to find eighteen fresh graves in the devastated village of Khorum outside Jalalabad, the U.S. defence secretary Donald Rumsfeld ridiculed the deaths as "ridiculous." If each of our wars for infinite justice and eternal freedom had a familiar trademark—the military claptrap about air superiority, suppression of "command and control centres," radar capabilities—each had an awkward, highly exclusive little twist to it. For the Afghan refugees who were turning up in their thousands at the border, it was palpably evident that they were fleeing not the Taliban but our bombs and missiles. The refugees spoke vividly of their fear and terror as our bombs fell on their cities. These people were terrified of our "war on terror," victims as innocent as those who were slaughtered in the World Trade Center on September 11th.

Despite the slavish use of the phrase on the BBC and CNN, this was not a "war on terror." We were not planning to attack Tamil Tiger suicide bombers or ETA killers or Real IRA murderers or Kurdish PKK guerrillas. Indeed, the United States had spent a lot of time supporting "terrorists" in Latin America—the Contras sprang to mind—not to mention the very same Taliban whom we were now bombing in Afghanistan. This was a war on America's enemies. Increasingly, as the date of September 11th acquired epic status, we were retaliating for the crimes against humanity in New York and Washington. But we were not setting up any tribunals to try those responsible.

And what was going to happen when the deaths for which we were responsible in Afghanistan approached the same figure as September 11th? Once the UN agencies gave us details of the starving and the destitute who were dying in their flight from our bombs, it wouldn't take long to reach 3,000. Would that be enough? Would 12,000 dead Afghans appease us, albeit that they had nothing to do with the Taliban or Osama bin Laden? Or 24,000? Sure, we would blame the Taliban for future tragedies, just as we had been blaming them for drug exports from Afghanistan. Tony Blair was at the forefront of the Taliban–drug linkage. And all we had to do to believe this was to forget the UN Drug Control Programme's announcement in October 2001 that opium production in Afghanistan had *fallen* by 94 per cent, chiefly due to Mullah Omar's prohibition of drug production in Taliban-controlled areas of the country. Most of Afghanistan's current output came from our allies in the Northern Alliance.

And what of Pakistan? By allying himself with America's "War on Terror," General Musharraf had secured de facto international acceptance of his 1999 coup. Suddenly, all he had wished for—the lifting of sanctions, massive funding for Pakistan's crumbling industry, IMF loans, a $375 million debt rescheduling and humanitarian aid—had been given him. Of course, we had to forget that it was Pakistan's Inter-services Intelligence (ISI) outfits—the highest ranks of the country's security agencies—that set up the Taliban, funnelled weapons into Afghanistan and grew rich on the narcotics trade. Ever since the Soviet invasion of Afghanistan in 1979, the ISI had worked alongside the CIA, funding the mullahs and *mawlawis* now condemned as the architects of "world terror." Most Pakistanis now realised that the ISI—sanctioned by Washington rather than Pakistan's own rulers—had turned into a well-armed and dangerous mafia, and while money was pouring into its smuggling activities, Pakistan's people lacked education, security and a health service. No wonder they turned to Islam and the madrassa schools for food and teaching. Pakistan's military was now more important than ever, an iron hand to maintain order within the state while its superpower ally bombed the ruins of Afghanistan.

Meanwhile, the United States—unable to bomb the Taliban into submission—cosied up to the murderers and rapists of the Northern Alliance. The Alliance's bloodiest commander, Rashid Dostum, who first visited Washington in 1996, was now a good friend of the Bush administration. Here for example is how Pakistani journalist Ahmed Rashid met the man:

> The first time I arrived at the fort to meet Dostum there were bloodstains and pieces of flesh in the muddy courtyard . . . the guards . . . told me that an hour earlier Dostum had punished a soldier for stealing. The man had been tied to the tracks of a Russian-made tank, which then drove around the courtyard crushing his body into mincemeat, as the garrison and Dostum watched.

Surely now the Americans would send in ground troops. First came the hopeless U.S. raid on Mullah Omar's office in Kandahar. They didn't find him. Then came the dispatch of U.S. Special Forces to the ruthless thugs of the Northern Alliance. If the Taliban had anyone to fear, it was the Alliance's Shah Massoud. But he had been murdered by the two Arab suicide bombers on 9 September. Then Abdul Haq—a U.S. favourite who opposed the Taliban—was hanged while trying to arrange a regional coup in Pashtun areas of southern Afghanistan. So what did our new "friends" in the Northern Alliance have in store for us?

The capture of Kabul, of course. They arrived to liberate the capital on 12 November 2001 after originally promising not to enter it. The Alliance was supposed to enter, at most, Mazar-e-Sharif and perhaps Herat, to demonstrate the weakness of the Taliban, to show the West that its war aims—the destruction of the Taliban and thus of Osama bin Laden's al-Qaeda movement—were going to be accomplished. Captured Taliban men were executed or beaten in front of television cameras. Was it not Colin Powell who had assured General Musharraf that the Alliance would be kept under control? In the end, it did not matter to the Americans. The pictures of jubilation, of a single Afghan woman unveiled among her still burqa-ed sisters, were enough. Kabul had been freed. Western democracy was at hand. The misogynist Taliban had been crushed.

We so idolised the Northern Alliance, were so infatuated with them, supported them so unquestioningly, pictured them on television so deferentially, that now we were immune to their history. Nor would you have thought, listening to the reports from Afghanistan after the fall of Kabul, that the Northern Alliance was responsible for more than 80 per cent of the drug exports from the country in the aftermath of the Taliban's prohibition of drug cultivation. Why, I wondered, did we always have this ambiguous, dangerous relationship with our allies? For decades, we accepted the received wisdom that the "B" Specials were a vital security arm of the Northern Ireland authorities against the IRA on the grounds that they "knew the territory"—just as we now relied upon the Northern Alliance because it "knew the land." The Israelis relied upon their Phalangist militia thugs in Lebanon because the Christian Maronites hated the Palestinians. The Nazis approved of their Croatian Ustashi murderers in 1941 because the Ustashi hated the Serbs.

There were brave men in the Alliance. Its murdered leader, Ahmed Shah Massoud, was an honourable man. But it remained a fact that from 1992 to 1996, the Northern Alliance was a symbol of massacre, systematic rape, and pillage. Which is why we—and I include the U.S. State Department—welcomed the Taliban when they originally arrived in Kabul. The Northern Alliance left the city in 1996 with 50,000 dead behind it. Now its members were our foot-soldiers. Better than bin Laden, to be sure. But what—in God's name—were they going to do in our name? We were soon to discover.

As soon as the U.S. Air Force bombed Mazar-e-Sharif, our Afghan allies moved into the city and executed up to 300 Taliban fighters. The report was a footnote on the television satellite channels, a nib in journalistic parlance, perfectly normal, it seemed. The Afghans have a "tradition" of revenge. So, with the strategic assistance of the USAF, a war crime is committed. Journalists watched the Mazar-e-Sharif prison "revolt" in the third week of November, in which Taliban inmates opened fire on their Alliance jailers. U.S. Special Forces—and, it quickly emerged, British troops—helped the Alliance to overcome the uprising and, sure enough, CNN told us that some prisoners were "executed" while trying to escape. It was an atrocity. British troops were now stained with war crimes. Within days, *The Independent*'s Justin Huggler had found more executed Taliban members in Kunduz.

The Americans had even less excuse for this massacre. For U.S. defence secretary Donald Rumsfeld stated quite specifically during the siege of the city that U.S. air raids on the Taliban defenders would stop "if the Northern Alliance requested it." Leaving aside the revelation that the killers of the Alliance were now acting as air controllers to the USAF in its battle with the killers of the Taliban, Rumsfeld's incriminating remark meant that the United States was acting in full military cooperation with the militia. Most television journalists showed a minimal interest in these crimes. Cosying up to the Northern Alliance, chatting to the American troops, most had done little more than mention the war crimes against prisoners in the midst of their reports.

One of the untold stories of this conflict was the huge amount of money handed out to militia leaders to persuade them to fight for the United States. When Taliban members changed sides for an Alliance payment of $250,000 and then attacked their benefactors, we all dwelt on their treachery. None of us asked how the Alliance—which didn't have enough money to pay for bullets a few weeks earlier—could throw a quarter of a million bucks at the Taliban in the middle of a firefight. Nor how the Pashtun tribal leaders of Kandahar province were now riding around

in brand-new four-wheel-drives with thousands of dollars to hand out to their gunmen. In December 2001, a new atrocity was revealed: up to 1,000 Taliban survivors of Kunduz who had been taken away towards Sherberghan prison by the
Alliance in sealed containers; almost all were suffocated to death—or were later
shot—in the desert. Human rights officials and reporters found the mass grave at
Dasht-e Leili in which they were buried. U.S. Special Forces officers were said to
have known of the killings—even been present—but declined to intervene. The
UN called for an international inquiry. The Americans were silent.

What had gone wrong with our moral bearings since September 11th? I feared
I knew the answer. After both the First and Second World Wars, we—the West—
planted a forest of legislation to prevent further war crimes. The very first
Anglo–French–Russian attempt to formulate such laws was provoked by the
Armenian Holocaust at the hands of the Turks in 1915; the Entente said it would
hold personally responsible "all members of the Ottoman government and *those of
their agents who are implicated in such massacres.*" After the Jewish Holocaust
and the collapse of Germany in 1945, article 6 (c) of the Nuremberg Charter and
the Preamble of the UN Convention on Genocide referred to "crimes against
humanity." Each new post-1945 war produced a raft of legislation and the creation
of ever more human rights groups to lobby the world on liberal, humanistic Western values. Over the previous fifty years, we stood on our moral pedestal and lectured the Chinese and the Soviets, the Arabs and the Africans, about human rights.
We pronounced on the human-rights crimes of Bosnians and Croatians and Serbs.
We put many of them in the dock, just as we did the Nazis at Nuremberg. Thousands of dossiers were produced, describing—in nauseous detail—the secret
courts and death squads and torture and extra-judicial executions carried out by
rogue states and pathological dictators. Quite right too.

Yet suddenly, after September 11th, we abandoned everything we claimed to
stand for. We bombed Afghan villages into rubble, along with their inhabitants—
blaming the insane Taliban and Osama bin Laden for this slaughter—and then we
allowed our ruthless militia allies to execute their prisoners. President George
Bush signed into law a set of secret military courts to try and then liquidate anyone
believed to be a "terrorist murderer" in the eyes of America's awesomely inefficient intelligence services. They were created so that Osama bin Laden and his
men, should they be caught rather than killed, would have no public defence; just
a pseudo-trial and a firing squad. What had happened was quite clear. When people with yellow or black or brownish skin, with Communist or Islamic or nationalist credentials, murder their prisoners or carpet-bomb villages to kill their enemies
or set up death-squad courts, they must be condemned by the United States, the
European Union, the United Nations and the "civilised" world. We were the masters of human rights, the liberals, the great and the good who could preach to the
impoverished masses. But when *our* people are murdered—when our glittering
buildings are destroyed—then we shred every piece of human rights legislation,
send off the B-52s in the direction of the impoverished masses and set out to murder our enemies.

Winston Churchill took the Bush view of his enemies. In 1945 he preferred the straightforward execution of the Nazi leadership. Yet despite the fact that Hitler's monsters were responsible for at least 50 million deaths—more than 17,000 times greater than the victims of September 11th—the Nazi murderers were given a trial at Nuremberg because Chief Justice Robert H. Jackson made a remarkable decision. "Undiscriminating [sic] executions or punishments," he said, "without definite findings of guilt fairly arrived at, would . . . not sit easily on the American conscience or be remembered by our children with pride." No one should have been surprised that George W. Bush—a small-time Texas governor–executioner— should fail to understand the morality of a statesman in the White House. What was so shocking was that the Blairs, Schröders, Chiracs and all the television boys should stay silent in the face of the Afghan executions and east European–style laws sanctified by September 11th.

Yet bin Laden was allowed to get away. He retreated with his hundreds of Arab fighters to the Tora Bora mountains outside Jalalabad. Under intense U.S. bombardment, he was reluctant to leave but—so his associates let me know later—he was eventually prevailed upon to flee into the Pakistani tribal territories, at one point physically forced by his own followers to retreat below the mountain chain after U.S.-paid Afghan tribal fighters were suborned for a higher price by bin Laden's own men. Yet America was not quite the "paper tiger" he had boasted to me about on a neighbouring mountain just over four years earlier. Defeat for the Russians did not mean defeat for the Americans.

By 25 November, the Taliban controlled only a small area around the city of Kandahar. Kabul, Herat, Jalalabad—all the other great cities of Afghanistan—had been lost to them. And at the moment of their downfall, they decided to give me a visa. The Pakistani government had already ordered the Taliban's embassy in Islamabad closed, but with the help of contacts, several bearded Taliban diplomats were finally prevailed upon to reopen the building for ten minutes, just long enough to stamp a pre-dated visa into my passport, the very last ever to be issued for Taliban Afghanistan. One of them wrote on the side of page 34 of my passport: "The Visa Valid Only for Kandahar." I had no problem with that. Kandahar was the only place I wanted to go. Would I be able to watch its fall? Was bin Laden still in Afghanistan? Could there be, perhaps, a Last Interview?

At the Chaman border station, the Pakistani immigration officer offered me a cup of tea. "Perhaps your last?" he asked me with a sorrowful smile. A few metres past a chain that lay in the dust along the Durand Line, a young Taliban whose black turban glistened like birds' feathers stamped "Entry" over my visa and, less encouragingly, "Exit." I would have less than a day in Afghanistan. But the Taliban, I informed him with all the authority of a Roman emperor, had specifically arranged for my journey to Kandahar. The young man looked at me with pity. There was a dark conversation about me with two other men in the corner of the mud hut that was the Taliban immigration office in Spin Boldak. Far away across the Kandahar desert, I could hear that drumroll again, the thunder of B-52 bombs. Then a more senior man stepped forward. He had large, slightly amused eyes. "We will give you some men who will take you down the Kandahar road," he said. "Then they will decide what to do when you get to Takhta-Pul." It was the same old James Cameron predicament that I had experienced in the Iran–Iraq War. The doughty war correspondent wished to forge onwards towards the fray, to witness the last theocratic struggle for Afghanistan. The sane fifty-five-year-old Englishman with increasingly greying hair wanted to return to Beirut, to live on into happy old age and write books and sip cocoa by the fire.

I climbed into the front of a beat-up Japanese truck and we shot off down the dust-covered road towards Kandahar. The driver was a big Pashtun man, a plump face beneath his turban, who talked about his father and his grandfather and his family. A good sign, I thought. Family men don't want to die. I was right. "You'll never get through," he told me. "The Northern Alliance have taken Takhta-Pul and the Americans are bombing the centre of the town." Impossible, I said. Takhta-Pul is only 40 kilometres away, a few minutes' ride from the Afghan border. But then a refugee with a cracked face and white hair matting the brow below his brown turban—he looked seventy but said he was only thirty-six—stumbled up to our truck. "The Americans just destroyed our homes," he cried. "I saw my house disappear. It was a big plane that spat smoke and soaked the ground with fire."

For a man who couldn't read and had never left Kandahar province in all his long-short life, this was a chilling enough description of the Spectre, the American converted AC-130 "Bumble-Bee" aircraft that picks off militiamen and civilians with equal ferocity. And down the tree-lined roads poured hundreds more refugees—old women with dark faces and babies carried in the arms of young women in blue burqas and boys with tears on their faces—all telling the same stories. I climbed from the truck to watch this trail of misery. Mullah Abdul Rahman slumped down beside me, passed his hand over the sweat on his face, and told me how his brother, a fighter in the same town, had just escaped. "There was a plane that shot rockets out of its side," he said, shaking his head. "It almost killed my brother today. It hit many people."

Suddenly, being the last reporter in Taliban-controlled Afghanistan didn't seem quite as romantic as it sounded. So this is what it was like to be on the losing side in the American–Afghan bloodbath. Everywhere was the same story of desperation and terror. "You'll never get to Kandahar, they've cut the road," another Taliban gunman shouted at me. An American F-18 soared through the imperial blue heaven above us as a middle-aged man approached with angry eyes. "This is what you wanted, isn't it?" he screamed. "Sheikh Osama is an excuse to do this to the Islamic people." I pleaded with yet another Taliban fighter—a thirty-five-year-old father of five called Jamaldan—to honour his government's promise to get me to Kandahar. He looked at me with irritation. "How can I get you there," he asked, "when we can hardly protect ourselves?"

The implications were astonishing. The road from the Iranian border town of Zabol to Kandahar had been cut by Afghan gunmen and U.S. Special Forces. The Americans were bombing the civilian traffic—and the Taliban—on the road to Spin Boldak, and the Northern Alliance were firing across the highway. Takhta-

Pul was under fire from American gunships and being invested by the Alliance. Kandahar was surrounded. No wonder I came across the local Taliban commander, the thoughtful and intelligent Mullah Haqqani, racing for the Pakistani border to Quetta—for "medical reasons."

Out of a dust-storm came a woman cowled in a grey shawl. "I lost my daughter two days ago," she said. "The Americans bombed our home in Kandahar and the roof fell on her." Amid the chaos and shouting, I did what reporters do. Out came my notebook and pen. Name of the daughter? "Muzlifa." Age? "She was two." I turn away. "Then there was my other daughter." She nods when I ask if this girl died too. "At the same moment. Her name was Farigha. She was three." I turn away. "There wasn't much left of my son." I turn back to her. Notebook out again, for the third time. "When the roof hit him, he was turned to meat and all I could see were bones. His name was Sheriff. He was a year and a half old."

They came out of a blizzard of sand, these people, each with their story of blood. Shukria Gul told her story more calmly. Beneath her burqa, she sounded like a teenager. "My husband, Mazjid, was a labourer. We have two children, our daughter, Rahima, and our son, Talib. Five days ago, the Americans hit an ammunition dump in Kandahar and the bullets came through our house. My husband was killed by them in the bedroom. He was twenty-five."

U.S. Marines landed at Kandahar's sporting club, the airport at which Saudi princes once arrived to hunt animals with the Taliban. The end was coming. At the border, you could see it already. About Chaman, they say nothing good. The muck moved across the Afghan plain in whirlwinds, great grey tunnels of the stuff, the sand and grit settling as usual into our ears and teeth and noses and behind our lips. Beyond, black mountains rose from the ocean of sand, and from way out across the Afghan moonscape, below the bomber contrails, came those changes in air pressure to remind us that the War for Civilisation was only a few miles away. The river of Afghan men, women and children that flooded through Chaman's border wire was a CinemaScope obscenity. First, they needed to state their reasons for entering Pakistan to a soldier sitting atop a concrete bunker. Then they had to produce documents at the border gate. Then they had to face the press.

The television cameras moved like beetles through the mob of refugees, selecting a man who dares to speak, who saw a body hanging in the main square of Kandahar, a man who—in a second—becomes the centre of an ever-growing amoeba of wires and lenses and notebooks and video-cassettes. The man wears an old brown shawl around his shoulders and a sparkling Pashtun hat. Other young men appear from the gate amid a crowd of boys. There were two bodies twisting in the breeze in Kandahar, not just one, they say. A Pakistan government official with a stick lashes out at the kids with a kind of swagger. Yet a third man is cornered by television crews from Japan, France 2 and Catalan television. He doesn't speak Japanese or French or Catalan—indeed, the Catalan reporter turns out to be a Basque—but their Pakistani translator bellows questions about the body in the Kandahar square. "He was a young man," the Afghan replies warily. "He was tortured and killed before they hung him up. He was a friend of Mullah Khaksar." The story gets clearer. Mullah Khaksar was the Taliban interior minister in Kabul before he changed sides. His friend—the hanged man—was allegedly found with a GPS device, enough to condemn him as an American spy.

His fate, of course, is important to us. It is further proof of the ruthlessness of the Taliban, our enemy in the War for Civilisation, of their cruelty and their despair. A truck-driver who has lost two family members in American bombing attracts fewer cameras. Not a single photographer bothers with an old Afghan man I find resting in the broken metal chair of the immigration officer. He is wearing an odd pair of shoes, the toes of the right shoe pointing to the sky. The reason is simple: only a wooden stump emerges from his right trouser leg. It somehow adheres to the shoe but upends it the moment the weight of his body is applied. The left shoe is flat on the ground. Above it stands a bright pink plastic leg with a wooden foot which fits the shoe, a hairless, feminine prosthesis.

I try to talk to the sweating, bearded, legless man but he will not respond. He is gritting his teeth with pain but he could talk if he chose. How did he lose his legs? His eyes move towards the dustbowl of Chaman with its packed, filthy, Dickensian streets and he stands up, swaying, and begins to stump off down the road between lines of barbed wire. The cameramen ignore him. They know he is the victim of another war of landmines—there are millions in Afghanistan—laid by the Russians who are our new allies in the War for Civilisation. He knows that too. He will not talk to me and, after a few moments, I realise he is right not to talk.

The crowds still gather on the other side of the wire. We stand there, three at a time, to take pictures, focusing on the tractor-load of children, the elderly man lying on sacks on a truck, the Afghan girl, perhaps five years old, who is begging from a soldier. But we cannot absorb the sheer mass of people. They came like this when the Russians invaded in 1979, but somehow they have become too familiar—*banalisés*, as my colleagues from France 2 would say—in history. Vietnam 1972, Palestine 1948, Poland and Germany 1945, France 1940. The poor and the dispossessed and the terrified are background material, wallpaper to our drama.

An old couple arrive in wheelbarrows, the man hunched in one, the woman—head lolling out of the bucket—in the one behind, each pushed by two grinning, laughing youths who shout to the journalists and point cruelly to their charges. Had the couple been able to walk, we would have ignored them. But an elderly man and woman in wheelbarrows is too good a picture to miss. Not so the white-haired man who stared at me with his left eye until I was forced to look at his right eye, a nightmare socket, a tissue of skin criss-crossed with tiny red scars. No photos of this Cyclops in rags.

Down the road at Takhta-Pul, they are talking about another massacre—of 160 Taliban prisoners by tribal rulers—and from all over the countryside come stories of villages crushed by American bombs; an entire hamlet destroyed by B-52s at Kili Sarnad, fifty dead near Tora Bora, eight civilians killed in cars bombed by USAF jets on the road to Kandahar, another forty-six in Lashkargah, twelve more in Bibi Mahru. We are not supposed to know the details of these deaths. "Investigation?" U.S. defence secretary Rumsfeld roared at a press conference at the beginning of October 2001, claiming he knew nothing of Amnesty International's call for an inquiry into the Mazar prison massacre. "I can think of a dozen things there that people could inquire into."

So could we. There's the hanged man in Kandahar, a local poet, we later learned. Then there's the sweating man with no legs. And the begging five-year-old. And the old couple in the wheelbarrows and the awful Cyclops with the purulent right eye and the dead of Takhta-Pul and Kili Sarnad and Lashkargah and Bibi Mahru and the whole swelling mass of humanity standing in the squalor of Chaman. Not to mention the slaughter at Mazar. And the War for Civilisation.

I am invited to meet a senior Taliban official who has just fled to his family home across the Pakistani border, in the wind-whipped village of Pishin. He sits on the floor of a large, cold, wooden-ceilinged room, back against the wall, an embroidered grey shawl wound over his black turban, large eyes wearily surveying me. "An adviser to the Taliban Elders of Kandahar" is how he asks to be described. He asks to be called "Mullah Abdullah"—which is his real first name—although the thirty-two-year-old graduate of Sheikh Hassanjan's madrassa in Kohat held a different identity and a far more important post in the Taliban hierarchy. The great mud-walled *hujra* family home below the mountains is blasted by a vicious little wind that has given the mullah a bout of flu. Defeat is hard.

So are words in this cold climate. "The people think we are defeated because we have lost many of our men," Mullah Abdullah concedes. "But our men lost their lives in martyrdom and therefore they were successful. So we don't think we have been defeated . . . When the Americans go home, we'll have the land back. The Americans didn't come here for Osama bin Laden—that's not their main reason. They are here because they don't want a country run under an Islamic system of law. They want a government that will do what they want." It is the authentic voice of Taliban Kandahar. The mullah, it emerges, has just arrived from the Taliban's besieged little caliphate, trekking six hours into the desert to avoid the American air raids round Takhta-Pul, resting here before returning to Kandahar, a man in denial or a man who has already decided to go into the mountains. He seems almost uninterested in the strategy of war. He has held a post in the Taliban defence ministry in Kabul—Arabs, he says, were employed to maintain his vehicles—but every military question brings a theological reply. "Even now the Americans have not succeeded in finding Sheikh Osama bin Laden and his al-Qaeda. They haven't achieved this mission of theirs. For us, Osama is a Muslim and a Muslim from another country is a brother. As for us, we will fight on in the mountains as guerrillas if we lose Kandahar—and if we achieve martyrdom, this is victory."

I am growing tired of all this but I am beginning to understand. Victory comes with success and victory comes with defeat. Two years later there would be a Bush version of this same nonsensical ideology as he tried to explain why Iraq was descending into chaos: the better things were, the worse the violence would become—because life was improving. "The Afghans," Lieutenant Colonel Alexander Burnes pompously observed in 1841, "are not deficient in the imaginative faculties, and they may be quoted as a proof that invention precedes judgement." Yet for Mullah Abdullah, history and politics and defeat appear part of a religious text. "A hadith of the Holy Prophet says that it is the right of Muslims to perform jihad. It was not necessary for us to rule the whole of Afghanistan when the Taliban started its existence in a tiny village. There were only a few Talibans who began all this. At the start, we stated that this was enough. We never cared that we succeeded in gaining 95 per cent of the land of Afghanistan. So we don't care about the land we've lost. The Taliban doesn't want the land as such—our main purpose is to convey Islam to the people. If our people return and take back this lost land, it's a success. If we are killed trying to do so, we have received martyrdom and this will be a great success for us too."

Only occasionally does the worm of doubt creep into the mullah's conversation. "Only time can tell if we will hold Kandahar or not—we are doing our best." It might be an editorial from a Taliban newspaper—if, that is, they hadn't banned newspapers. "If we are thrown out of Kandahar, we will go to the mountains and start the guerrilla war as we did with the Russians." I try to argue that the Americans are not the Russians, that this is not a simple repeat performance, that the Taliban have for the most part been fighting other Afghans, that the Americans have only attacked them from the air. It is no use. He will go to the mountains. The Taliban will ambush the Americans. They will fight on. And they did.

The Americans are entering Kandahar. I will make just one last effort to reach the city. It is 8 December. If I can drive to Chaman, I have the opportunity to pick up a lift with a CNN crew all the way to Mullah Omar's caliphate. All I have to do is hook up with Justin Huggler—fresh from covering the Mazar massacre—and travel in a jeep with our Pashtun driver, Amanullah, and our translator, Fayyez Ahmed, from Quetta to Chaman. It must have been around 4:30 p.m. that we reached Kila Abdulla, about halfway through our journey, when our jeep stopped in the middle of a narrow, crowded street. A film of white steam was rising from the bonnet, a constant shriek of car horns and buses and trucks and rickshaws protesting the roadblock we had created. All four of us got out of the car and pushed it to the side of the road. I muttered something to Justin about this being "a bad place to break down."

Kila Abdulla was home to thousands of Afghan refugees, the poor and huddled masses that the war had created in Pakistan. Many of these Afghans, so we were to learn later, were outraged by what they had seen on television of the Mazar massacres, of prisoners killed with their hands tied behind their backs. A villager later told Amanullah that they had seen the videotape of two CIA officers threatening death to a kneeling prisoner at Mazar. Some of the Afghans had been in the little village for years. Others had arrived—desperate and angry and mourning their newly slaughtered loved ones—over the past two weeks. Sure it was a bad place to break down, a bad time too, just before the *Iftar*, the end of the daily fast of Ramadan. These people were uneducated—I doubt if many could read—but you don't have to have schooling to respond to the death of loved ones under a B-52's bombs.

Amanullah went off to find another car—there is only one thing worse than a crowd of angry men and that's a crowd of angry men after dark—and Justin and I smiled at the initially friendly crowd that had already gathered around our steaming vehicle. I shook a lot of hands and we said *Salaam aleikum* many times. Peace be upon you. I knew what could happen if the smiling stopped. The crowd grew larger and I suggested to Justin that we move away from the jeep, walk into the open road. A child flicked his finger hard against my wrist and I persuaded myself it was an accident, a childish moment of contempt. Then a pebble whisked past my head and bounced off Justin's shoulder. Justin turned round. His eyes spoke of concern and I breathed in. Please, I thought, it was just a prank. Then another kid tried to grab my bag. It contained my passport, credit cards, money, diary, contacts book, mobile phone. I yanked it back and put the strap round my shoulder. Justin and I crossed the road and someone punched me on the back.

How do you walk out of a dream when the characters suddenly turn hostile? I saw one of the men who had been all smiles when we shook hands. He wasn't smiling now. Some of the smaller boys were still laughing but their grins were transforming into something else. The respected foreigner—the man who had been all *Salaam aleikum* a few minutes ago—was upset, frightened, on the run. At one point, I later discovered, a screaming teenager had turned to Amanullah and asked, quite seriously: "Is that Mr. Bush?" The West was being brought low. Justin was being pushed around and, in the middle of the road, we noticed a bus-driver waving us to his vehicle. Fayyez, still by the car, unable to understand why we had walked away, could no longer see us. Justin reached the bus and climbed aboard. But as I put my foot on the step, three men grabbed the strap of my bag and wrenched me back onto the road. Justin's hand shot out. "Hold on!" he shouted. I did.

That's when the first mighty crack descended on my head. I almost fell down under the blow, my ears singing with the impact. I had expected this, though not so painful or hard, not so immediate. Its message was awful. Someone hated me enough to hurt me. There were two more blows, one on the back of my shoulder, a powerful fist that sent me crashing against the side of the bus while clutching Justin's hand. The passengers were looking out at me and then at Justin. But they did not move. No one wanted to help. I cried out "Help me, Justin!" and Justin, who was doing more than any human could do by clinging to my ever-loosening grip, asked me—over the screams of the crowd—what I wanted him to do. Then I realised I could only just hear him. They were shouting at me and about me. Did I catch the word *kaffir*—infidel? That's when I was dragged away from Justin's grasp.

There were two more cracks on my head, one on each side, and for some odd reason part of my memory—some back street in my brain—registered a moment at school, at my primary school called the Cedars in Maidstone more than fifty years before, when a tall boy building sandcastles in the playground hit me on the head. I had a memory of the blow *smelling*, as if it had affected my nose. The next shock came from a man I saw carrying a big stone in his right hand. He brought it down on my forehead with tremendous force and something hot and liquid splashed down my face and lips and chin. I was kicked. On the back, on my shins, on my right thigh. Another teenager grabbed my bag yet again and I was left clinging to the strap, looking up and realising there must have been sixty men in front of me, howling at me; they had, I now noticed, big, wolfish smiles. Oddly, it wasn't fear I felt but a kind of wonderment. So this is how it happens. I knew that I had to respond. Or, so I reasoned in my stunned state, I had to die.

In a place of peace and clarity, I might have remembered that baleful morning in the Afghan city of Ghazni more than two decades earlier when Gavin Hewitt and I and his crew had been urged to leave before the crowd attacked us with stones. I could have recalled all those tales of Afghan cruelty from British officers of the Raj, even in Bill Fisk's gift from his mother, *Tom Graham, V.C.* Yet the only thing that shocked me was my own physical sense of collapse, my growing awareness of the liquid beginning to cover me. I don't think I'd ever seen so much blood before. For a second, I caught a glimpse of something ghastly, a nightmare face— my own—reflected in the window of the bus, streaked in blood, my hands drenched in the stuff like Lady Macbeth, slopping over the collar of my shirt and down my pullover until my back was wet and my bag dripping with crimson and vague splashes suddenly appearing on my trousers. I was swamped in it. Who would have thought the old man had so much blood in him? That was the quotation as I remembered it, right there, at that moment. The more I bled, the more the crowd gathered and beat me with their fists. Pebbles and small stones bounced off my head and shoulders. How long, I remember thinking, could this go on? How long does it last?

My head was struck by stones on both sides at the same time—not thrown stones but stones in the palms of stout men who were using them to try and break my skull. Then a fist punched me in the face, splintering my glasses on my nose, another hand grabbed at the spare pair of spectacles round my neck and ripped the leather container from the cord. And here I have to thank Lebanon. For twenty-five years, I had covered Lebanon's wars and the Lebanese used to teach me, over and over again, how to stay alive. Take a decision—any decision—but don't do nothing. So I wrenched the bag back from the hands of the young man who was holding it. He stepped back. Then I turned on the man on my right, the one holding the bloody stone in his hand, and I bashed my fist into his mouth. I couldn't see very much—my eyes were not only short-sighted without my glasses but were misting over with a red haze—but I saw the man cough and a tooth fall from his lip and then he fell back on the road. For a second, the crowd stopped. Then I went for the other man, clutching my bag under my arm and banging my fist into his nose. He roared in anger and it suddenly turned all red. I missed another man with a punch, hit more, and ran.

I was back in the middle of the road but could not see. I brought my hands to my eyes and with my fingers I tried to scrape the gooey stuff out. It made a kind of sucking sound but I began to see again and realised that I was crying and weeping and that the tears were cleaning my eyes of blood. What had I done? I kept asking myself. I had been hurting and punching and attacking Afghan refugees, the very people I had been writing about for so long, the very dispossessed, mutilated people whom my own country—among others—was killing, along with the Taliban, just across the border. God spare me, I thought. I think I actually said it. The men whose families our bombers were killing were now my enemies too.

Then something quite remarkable happened. A man walked up to me, very calmly, and took me by the arm. I couldn't see him too well for all the blood that was running into my eyes again, but he was dressed in a kind of robe and wore a turban and had a white-grey beard. And he led me away from the crowd. I looked over my shoulder. There were now a hundred men behind me and a few stones skittered along the road, but they were not aimed at me—presumably to avoid hitting the stranger. He was like an Old Testament figure or some Bible story, the Good Samaritan, a Muslim man—perhaps a mullah in the village—who was trying to save my life. He pushed me into the back of a police truck. But the policemen didn't move. They were terrifed. "Help me," I kept shouting through the tiny window at the back of their cab, my hands leaving streams of blood down the glass. They drove a few metres and stopped until the tall man spoke to them again. Then they drove another 300 metres.

And there, beside the road, was a Red Cross–Red Crescent convoy. The crowd were still behind us, but two of the medical attendants pulled me behind one of their vehicles, poured water over my hands and face and began pushing bandages onto my head and face and the back of my head. "Lie down and we'll cover you with a blanket so they can't see you," one of them said. They were both Muslims, Bangladeshis, and their names should be recorded because they were good men: Mohamed Abdul Halim and Sikder Mokaddes Ahmed. I lay on the floor, groaning, aware that I might live.

Within minutes, Justin arrived. He had been protected by a massive soldier from the Baluchistan Levies—a true ghost of the British empire who, with a single rifle, kept the crowds away from the car in which Justin was now sitting. I fumbled with my bag. They never got the bag, I kept saying to myself, as if my passport and credit cards were a kind of Holy Grail. But they had snatched my final pair of spare glasses—I was blind without all three—and my mobile telephone was missing and so was my leather-covered contacts book, containing twenty-five years of telephone numbers throughout the Middle East.* God dammit, I said, and tried to bang my fist on my side until I realised it was bleeding from a big gash on the wrist—the mark of the tooth I had just knocked out of a man's jaw, a man who was truly innocent of any crime except that of being the victim of the world.

So why record my few minutes of terror and self-disgust near the Afghan border, bleeding and crying like an animal, when thousands of innocent civilians were dying under American air strikes in Afghanistan, when the War for Civilisation

---

*I later reflected on the odd fact that while my passport and credit cards and money—of obvious use to refugees—had been left in my bag, my contacts book had been among the items taken. Two days later I returned to Kila Abdulla, met the sheikh of the village and offered $100— a very large amount for anyone in that region of Baluchistan—for the return of my all-valuable journalist's book of names and numbers. It was never produced. Had it been thrown away? Or had someone else bought it?

was burning and maiming the people of Kandahar and other cities because "good" must triumph over "evil"? I had spent more than a quarter of a century reporting the humiliation and misery of the Muslim world and now their anger had embraced me too. Or had it? There were the Red Crescent men, and Fayyez, who came panting back to the car incandescent at our treatment, and Amanullah, who invited us to his own home for medical treatment. And there was the Muslim saint who had taken me by the arm. And—I realised—there were all the Afghan men and boys who had attacked me, who should never have done so but whose brutality was entirely the product of others, of us—of us who had armed their struggle against the Russians and ignored their pain and laughed at their civil war and then armed and paid them again for the War for Civilisation just a few miles away and then bombed their homes and ripped up their families and called them "collateral damage."

So I thought I should write about what happened to Justin and me in this fearful, silly, bloody, tiny incident. I feared other versions produce a different narrative, of how a British journalist was "beaten up by a mob of Afghan refugees." The *Mail on Sunday* won the prize for just such a distortion. Fisk, it reported—apparently aged sixty-three, not fifty-five—was, yes, "beaten up by a mob of Afghan refugees." And I was supposed to have said—but didn't—that "I'm going to bear the scars for the rest of my life." All reference to my repeated assertion that the Afghans were justified in their anger—that I didn't blame them for what they had done—was omitted. The Afghans had become, like the Palestinians, generically violent. And of course, that was the point. The people who bore the scars were the Afghans, the scars being inflicted by us—by our B-52s—not by them. And I wrote in *The Independent* that "if I was an Afghan refugee in Kila Abdulla, I would have done just what they did. I would have attacked Robert Fisk. Or any other Westerner I could find."

Among a mass of letters that arrived from readers of my paper, most of them expressing their sympathy, came a few Christmas cards, all but one of them unsigned, expressing the writers' disappointment that the Afghans hadn't "finished the job." *The Wall Street Journal* published an article that said more or less the same thing under the subhead "A self-loathing multiculturalist gets his due." In it, columnist Mark Steyn wrote of my reaction that "you'd have to have a heart of stone not to weep with laughter." The "Fisk doctrine," he went on, "taken to its logical conclusion, absolves of responsibility not only the perpetrators of September 11 but also Taliban supporters who attacked several of Mr. Fisk's fellow journalists in Afghanistan all of whom, alas, died before being able to file a final column explaining why their murderers are blameless."*

*Quite apart from the fact that most of the journalists who died in Afghanistan during the bombardment and immediately afterwards—three correspondents, one of them a woman, killed in the Kabul Gorge after the fall of the capital, for example—were killed by thieves who had taken advantage of the Taliban's defeat, Steyn's article was interesting for two reasons. It insinuated that I in some way approved of the crimes of 11 September 2001—or, at least, would "absolve" the mass murderers. More importantly, the article would not have been written had I

In Quetta, two Pakistani doctors washed and bandaged my face but missed a gash on my head, so that I woke in the night stuck to my pillow with blood and had to stand in the shower and drench myself with water to detach the material from the wound. Back in Islamabad, I was befriended—ironically, in view of Steyn's forthcoming abuse—by the *Journal*'s new South-West Asia correspondent, Daniel Pearl, and his wife, Marianne. They made me bottomless cups of coffee, supplied me the contents of their own contacts books, assured me that I looked as full of energy as ever. I wasn't so sure. I asked Daniel if he was travelling to Afghanistan. "No," he said. "My wife is pregnant and we're not going to take that kind of risk."

Within two months, Daniel Pearl would be dead, beheaded by his Muslim captors after being kidnapped on assignment in Karachi, forced to speak of his Jewish family in the videotape of his vile execution. His murder was as horrifying as it was gruesome.* It raised again not just the cruelty of al-Qaeda and its satellites but the degree to which we as journalists had lost our immunity. In Lebanon in the mid-1980s, in Algeria and then in Bosnia, our protection as neutral correspondents had disintegrated. We were abducted, murdered because we were Westerners or because we were regarded as combatants. Two months before I was beaten at Kila Abdulla, I had attempted to interview a Muslim cleric in a village mosque outside Peshawar. "Why are you taking this *kaffir* into our mosque?" a bearded man had shouted at the mullah. I conducted the interview outside the building. But I was a *kaffir*. So was Pearl. So, it seemed, were we all. Where did it go wrong?

I have always thought the rot started in Vietnam. For decades, reporters have identified themselves with armies. In the Crimean War, William Howard Russell of *The Times* wore his own self-designed uniform. In both twentieth-century world wars, journalists worked in uniform. Dropping behind enemy lines with U.S. commandos did not spare an AP reporter from a Nazi firing squad. But these were countries in open conflict, reporters whose nations had officially declared war. It was in Vietnam that journalists started wearing combat fatigues and carrying weapons—and sometimes shooting those weapons at America's enemies—even though their countries were not officially at war and when they could have carried out their duties without wearing a soldier's clothes. In Vietnam, reporters were murdered because they were reporters.

---

ignored the context of the assault that was made on me. Had I merely reported an attack by a mob, the story would have fitted neatly into the general American media presentation of the Afghan war; no reference to civilian deaths from U.S. B-52 bombers and no suggestion that the widespread casualties caused in the American raids would turn Afghans to fury against the West. We were, after all, supposed to be "liberating" these people, not killing their relatives. Of course, yet again my crime—the *Journal* actually gave Steyn's column the headline "Hate-Me Crimes"—was to report the "why" as well as the "what-and-where."

    *After Pearl's abduction, a *Wall Street Journal* correspondent called to ask if I would sign a petition pleading for his release—this from a paper whose headline said that I deserved to have faced death by beating in December 2001. I preferred to go one better and made a personal appeal to bin Laden—in an article in *The Independent*—for his intercession to save the life of Daniel Pearl, whom I referred to as "my friend." I suspected—correctly as it turned out—that bin Laden, although on the run from the Americans, continued to read my reports. Tragically, Pearl had already been murdered.

This tendency of journalists to be part of the story, to play their own theatrical role, took hold only slowly. When the Palestinians evacuated Beirut in 1982, I noticed that several French reporters wore Palestinian headscarves. Israeli reporters turned up in southern Lebanon carrying pistols. In the 1991 Gulf War, as we have seen, many correspondents dressed up in army costumes—complete with helmets—as if they were members of the 82nd Airborne. In Pakistan and Afghanistan in 2001, something similar happened. Reporters in Peshawar could be seen wearing soft Pashtun hats. Geraldo Rivera of Fox News claimed on television that while in Jalalabad he was carrying a gun. He fully intended to use it, he said on another occasion, to kill Osama bin Laden. "I'm feeling more patriotic than at any time in my life, itching for justice, or maybe just revenge," he vouchsafed to the world. "And this cartharsis I've gone through has caused me to reassess what I do for a living." It was the last straw. The reporter had become combatant.

Of course, I had held a gun in a Soviet convoy to Kabul in 1980.* But I had little choice. And I avoided rhetoric of the kind that Rivera sought to employ, even the unfortunate and sinister phrases used by my CNN colleagues. Like several of my colleagues, I did not like hearing CNN's Walter Rodgers quoting a Marine major on 2 December 2001 that U.S. troops and "opposition groups" might be squeezing Kandahar "like a snake." The moment that cities or people become snakes or vermin, they can be crushed, liquidated, eliminated like animals. And every journalist's integrity was placed at risk by the obnoxious remark of CNN boss Walter Isaacson, who instructed staff during the Afghan bombardment that "it seems perverse to focus too much on the casualties or hardship in Afghanistan" because such reporting ran the risk of helping the Taliban. In the next stage of the "war on terror"—the invasion of Iraq—many more journalists would pay with their lives because their role as correspondents simply no longer guaranteed them protection.†

Yet there was another way in which our good faith was damaged, indeed fatally undermined: the unwillingness of major television channels to relay the reality of the Middle East and to support their reporters when confronted by powerful lobby groups. Back in 1993, I had worked on a three-part television series for Britain's Channel 4 and America's Discovery Channel called *From Beirut to Bosnia* which attempted, in the words of our first episode, to show "how Muslims were coming to hate the West." We were filming exactly eight years before the attacks of 11 September 2001, and, rewatching the series today—it was made on real film, not videotape, and cost more than a million dollars—I am ever more astonished at what it told viewers. For it turns out to have been a ghastly, unintended but all too accurate warning of September 11th. In one segment, I walk into a burned-out mosque in Bosnia and ask "what the Muslim world has in store for

---

*See pp. 67–68.

†This applied to both sides. Just before the fall of Kabul, an American cruise missile exploded inside the local office of Al-Jazeera, the Arab satellite channel which had so infuriated the U.S. government with its bin Laden transmissions. No explanation was forthcoming, a particularly ominous precedent, since the station's offices in Baghdad would be attacked by the U.S. Air Force only seventeen months later.

us," adding that I should perhaps end each of my reports from the Middle East with the words "Watch out!" There are other similar premonitions of terrors to come, which were included in our coverage of the Israeli occupation of Gaza and the West Bank. We were trying to answer the question "why?"—before it needed to be asked.

It was not an easy series to make. We filmed in Lebanon, Gaza, Israel, Egypt, Bosnia and Croatia, questioning Hizballah guerrillas about their war against Israeli occupation troops, and filming women in Lebanese hospitals who were covered in burns from Israeli phosphorus shells. During curfews in Gaza we were repeatedly ordered off the streets by Israeli soldiers—several of whom put their hands over our camera lens to stop us working. We filmed an Israeli officer who told us that a pregnant Palestinian woman had been allowed to break the curfew to go to hospital—then found the woman still trapped in her home. Outside the walls of Jerusalem, we talked to a Jewish settler about why an elderly Palestinian was being evicted from his land—because Jews would be living there and because, in the settler's words, "he's an Arab. He's not Jewish." In Israel we traced the home of a Palestinian refugee now living in Beirut, talked to the elderly Israeli who moved into the house after 1948—and took our cameras to the Polish town from which he fled and from which his parents and brother were taken by the Nazis to be murdered in the Jewish Holocaust. In Egypt we talked to armed opponents of Mubarak's regime and in Sarajevo to the Bosnian soldiers defending the city, and to the Muslim imam who believed his people were being persecuted "solely because we are Muslims."

Michael Dutfield, the director, and I knew this would be easy for a British audience to watch. Europeans are used to free if sometimes bitter debates on the Middle East, where the old canard of "anti-Semitism" flung at anyone who dares to criticise Israel has largely lost its power. There are, as I always say, plenty of real anti-Semites in the world whom we must fight without inventing more in order to smother all serious discourse on Israel and the Arabs. But in the United States we knew things would be different. Our film would be a challenge not for American audiences—who were perfectly mature enough to understand our film if given the chance to watch it—but for the U.S. lobby groups which regularly set out to prevent the showing of any documentary that presents Americans with an alternative to the pro-Israeli "news" regularly served up on U.S. networks. Initial reports in the American media were faintly critical and often inaccurate.*

Then, only days after Discovery showed the three films coast-to-coast, the letter-writing campaign began. Discovery first reported that some of its advertisers were being pestered with telephone calls from supposedly outraged viewers.

---

*On 27 April 1994, for example, *The New York Times* carried a prominent review of our series which included some apparently wilful distortions. In his review, Walter Goodman claimed that "most of the three-hour report concentrates on Palestinians," and that I had made only what he called "references" to the Jewish Holocaust. This was untrue. Less than a third of the series dealt with Palestinians, and we had fully covered the story of the Israeli family's suffering in the Shoah, filming not only their original Polish home town but at the site of the Treblinka extermination camp. These sequences were not mere "references," I wrote in a letter to the editor

American Express, one of the channel's sponsors, received credit cards back from customers; the cards had been cut in half. An outfit calling itself "Promoting Responsibility in Middle East Reporting" (Primer) wrote to Discovery with a sinister warning. Robert Fisk had "impeccable English diction," wrote Joseph I. Ungar, the group's vice president, in June 1994. Fisk projected "the essence of refinement and respectability . . . He could easily play the stage role of Henry Higgins. But he could be a Higgins with fangs." In journalism, you have to laugh at this sort of nonsense. But the campaign against *Beirut to Bosnia* was not funny at all. The president of the same lobby group, Sidney Laibson, wrote a letter to John Hendriks, chairman of Discovery, the same month. "By airing *From Beirut to Bosnia*," he wrote, "the Discovery Channel has provided the purveyors of insidious propaganda an opportunity to spread their venom into the living-rooms of America."

Ungar's letter claimed that for us to say that Israel "confiscates," "occupies" and "builds huge Jewish settlements on Arab land"—all facts acknowledged by Israeli human rights groups, Israeli journalists and foreign correspondents as well as by the U.S. government for more than twenty years—was "twisted" history. A reference in my commentary to the "Christian gunmen" that the Israelis sent into the Sabra and Chatila camps—a course of action described in Israel's own Kahan commission of inquiry—was condemned by Ungar as "an egregious falsehood." Alex Safian of the "Camera Media Resource Center" wrote to Clark Bunting, senior vice president of Discovery, to claim that we had edited an interview with the Jewish settler Mickey Molad in such a way as to cut out a remark by him that Jews originally owned most of the land for the future settlement. We diligently searched back through all the rough-cuts—an hour of them—of the Molad interview only to find that he made no such comment in any of them. Safian's claims, Dutfield wrote back, were "absurd and demonstrably wrong." There were further meretricious statements: that the Palestinian woman refused permission to go to hospital was a fraud, that she was not even pregnant. She gave birth to her child three months after we filmed her.

Then an *Independent* reader informed me that "American friends" had told her a scheduled re-airing of our series had been cancelled by Discovery because of the complaints. Dutfield wrote to the channel asking for an explanation. Bunting sent back the most preposterous denial I have ever heard from a television executive. ". . . given the reaction to the series upon its initial airing," he wrote, "we never scheduled a subsequent airing, so there is not really an issue as to any re-airing being cancelled." When I read those gutless words, I was ashamed to be a foreign correspondent.

Here we were, trying to explain a grim reality of our age to an audience that

---

of *The New York Times*, asking them to correct these errors of fact. "Mr. Goodman accuses our camera of 'lingering' . . . on [wounded] women and children. But why does he object to this?" I asked. "Because he feels these scenes are distasteful? Or because the wounded women and children were Arabs who had been bombed and shelled by Israel? Mr. Goodman may find the facts unpalatable, but that is no excuse for impugning the reputation of a working journalist in so unprofessional a manner." I forwarded my letter through *The New York Times*'s London bureau to ensure it reached its head office in the United States. Of course, it was not published.

deserved to hear another side to the Middle East conflict, that needed to hear the voices of those deeply aggrieved, increasingly angry people upon whom great injustice was being visited. Yet those who claimed to speak for truth—and for Israel—had effectively censored us off the air, with the cringing assistance of a major television channel. Here, long in advance of the international crimes against humanity of 2001, were answers to the "whys" that we would be told not to ask *after* the attacks on New York, Washington and Pennsylvania. In advance, we were not supposed to explain the explosion to come—even if this warning might have helped us to prevent it. Afterwards, we would be ordered to remain silent. This, for me, remains one of the most frightening and distressing elements to the "war on terror": the suppression of a truth without which no free judgement could be made, before or after the event.

Is there, I ask myself, a key to all this, some incident, some lone truth that will illuminate all that we have done to the Middle East, the anger we have created, the terror we have inflicted upon those we now regard as our enemies? Is there some way in which to communicate this without reiterating the demands of the self-righteous, some way in which the death of innocence can be portrayed outside the framework of hatred? Osama bin Laden does not have to be the voice of those who have suffered. He has no monopoly over their grief and pain. He was never appointed their representative on earth. So I am drawn to the story of a young woman who died needlessly and tragically, who could never have countenanced the crimes against humanity of 11 September 2001, but whose terrible end was ignored by the nation that killed her and whose reporters showed no interest in her fate.


THE AMERICANS KILLED RAAFAT AL-GHOSSAIN just after two o'clock on the morning of 15 April 1986. In the days that followed her death, U.S. officials claimed that Libyan anti-aircraft fire might have hit her home not far from the French embassy in the suburbs of Tripoli. But three weeks later, the Pentagon admitted that three bombs dropped by an F-111 aircraft in the U.S. attack on Colonel Ghadafi had "impacted in the vicinity of the French embassy" and had caused—to use the usual callous euphemism—"collateral damage." Raafat was eighteen years old, a graduate of an English school on holiday from London, a promising and beautiful artist whose individual death went unrecorded in the country that killed her nineteen years ago.

She lives on only in the seventh-floor Beirut apartment of her parents and her younger sister where a half-hour videotape of Raafat's 1985 graduation day at Marymount International college at Kingston-on-Thames brings her briefly back to this world. "Raafat Bassam Fawzi al-Ghossain from Palestine," the English principal announces, and a tall, striking young woman in a white ball gown can be seen walking self-consciously to receive her graduation certificate to the tinkling of Elgar's "Land of Hope and Glory" on a school piano. She listens attentively to a graduation speech from an American teacher who tells the girls that "with the gift of youth, nothing is too daunting." On the left side of the stage on which she sits is the Stars and Stripes, on the right the Union flag of Britain.

In the college gardens, Raafat stands next to her American-educated Palestinian father Bassam. "Here we are," he says when he spots the video camera, and Raafat dutifully kisses her father on the cheek. Her mother watches proudly through sunglasses while a six-year-old girl—Raafat's younger sister, Kinda—primps in front of the camera. As Raafat leaves the college hall with its American and British flags, the same high-pitched piano plays Thomas Arne's "Trumpet Voluntary." On this English summer afternoon, Raafat al-Ghossain has less than a year to live. The men who will kill her are American, flying—with special permission of Margaret Thatcher—from RAF Lakenheath, scarcely 75 miles from Marymount International College in Kingston.

Palestine, Britain, Libya, America. It is as if the Western conflict in the Middle East hovered over Raafat al-Ghossain all her short life. Bassam always wanted her to have an English education—Kinda was born in London and holds a British passport—and still feels that Britain represents something intrinsically good in the world. His father, Fawzi, was a graduate of Balliol College, Oxford, a lawyer in the British Mandate government in Jerusalem, an adviser to Sir Herbert Samuel, the first High Commissioner to Palestine. A slightly blurred photograph shows Fawzi al-Ghossain and Samuel, who was Jewish, walking through a tree-lined avenue in Jerusalem together, deep in conversation. Even after the family was forced to flee Palestine in 1946 to settle for several years in Cairo, the al-Ghossains never lost their faith in the West. Bassam was given a scholarship to study in America by a Quaker couple who noticed his fascination with model aircraft. He graduated in chemical engineering from the Drexel Institute of Technology in Philadelphia and started work as a petroleum engineer for the national oil company in British-administered Kuwait in 1957. "My family always admired the British," Bassam says. Rarely was a family to be so cruelly betrayed by the society and culture in which they had put their trust.

Bassam met his future wife, Saniya, half-Lebanese, half-Turkish—a daughter of the Beirut city treasurer—in 1963, but they left Kuwait during the 1967 Arab–Israeli War and moved to Algiers, where Bassam took a job in the country's oil production company. A French doctor delivered Raafat, weighing 3.8 kilos, at an Algiers hospital; when she was only five months old the family moved to Libya, where Bassam took a job with ESSO, and later with American Occidental. Colonel Ghadafi's revolution was only fifteen months away.

"We would take Raafat out to picnics with us, visiting the [Roman] cities of Leptis Magna and Sabratha," Bassam remembers. "There were parties every week and swimming. When Raafat was four, we enrolled her at the Lycée Français in Tripoli. She was a very pretty little girl. She loved doll's houses, she liked putting all the members of a family in one house. Always she wanted our family to live together . . ." Raafat—"Fafo" was her nickname in the family—spoke French fluently but transferred to the American school in Tripoli when she was twelve. "She was there for two years but I thought the educational standards were not good enough. So we sent her to Marymount in Kingston-on-Thames." And Bassam pulls from his file a thick bunch of school reports.

Raafat's sister Kinda had been born three years earlier, on 1 January 1979. At fifteen, Raafat now found herself alone at boarding school, with neither her parents nor her baby sister to comfort her. Racked by home-sickness, and schoolwork which she initially found too advanced, she begged to return to Libya, to the family villa not far from the sea, to the house in which all the al-Ghossains could live together. "A pleasant character," a philosophy teacher noted coldly, "but quite ill-disciplined—will not work." At maths, there were complaints of Raafat "misusing her ability" while a singing teacher reported that Raafat "would be an excellent choral member if she were not so chatty and giggly." But in art, she excelled. Mr. McFarland, her art teacher, wrote to her parents in 1984 that "Raafat has worked really well this quarter & I am very pleased with her progress."

The anguish that lay behind Raafat's unhappiness at school comes through painfully in a letter she wrote to herself in English on lined notepaper on 17 November 1981, addressed to "God" and headed with three words in capital letters: "PLEASE—PLEASE—PLEASE":

> Dear God, I love you very much. God, I have a few things I would like to ask you about and asking [*sic*] if you could help me. First, of course, is that you give us a long life for about 200 years (you know what I mean), I and my whole FAMILY and friends . . . Second, keep your blessings on us and help us through life . . . Third, please let my parents leave [Libya] on Friday 27th . . . or even Tuesday or Wednesday but please after this weekend . . . Fifth, please please a thousand times let it be my last year at Marymount or even if it is possible—half year . . . Don't separate our small family [in] Libya. Let the conditions in Libya push them to leave on [*sic*] January and make ME leave Marymount although it is a nice school but I get homesick too much. Let me go to a day-student school this year. PLEASE. Or make my parents come here and live . . .

Raafat's reference to "conditions" in Libya was not without reason. A self-declared enemy of Israel and America, Libya was already being accused of "international terrorism" by the United States and Britain. The British condemned Colonel Ghadafi's support for the IRA—he sent at least one shipload of weapons to Ireland—and in 1984 a British policewoman was shot dead by a Libyan "diplomat" outside the country's London embassy. Ghadafi had sent hit men to eliminate his domestic opponents abroad. The West was already treating Libya as a pariah state, although Raafat al-Ghossain—conscious of her father's birthplace and of her grandfather Fawzi's stories of life in Jerusalem—thought of a country that no longer existed, nearly 1,300 miles to the east of Tripoli.

"Return our holy land PALESTINE, soon and let my whole family enjoy it and live there for a long time—if it is possible, next year," Raafat wrote in her letter to "God." In 1982, enraged by the Sabra and Chatila massacre, she joined a peaceful protest march on the streets of London. A poorly focused photograph of Raafat shows her in a raincoat in Knightsbridge, a green, red, black and white Palestinian flag curling above her head. "She went on several demonstrations," Bassam recalls. "They were all peaceful and she would come back from all of them drenched in rain." In her last note in the Marymount school magazine in 1985, Raafat was to write that "I would like to say a final sentence and that is May Peace and Hope come from Palestine, my homeland."

Bassam admits that Raafat found life very difficult. "She did not want to be away from us. She cried a lot. But she had no chance of education in Libya. In London, she had stomach upsets. It was psychological. She suffered a lot from hay fever." But Raafat was to overcome her homesickness after four long years, winning a gold medal for her painting and for drama. The 1985 video of her graduation shows her pride in triumphing over loneliness, aware that she was to follow a career in painting at the Heatherley School of Fine Art in London. Her parents came to London in December of the same year, the last Christmas of Raafat's life. "We went that night to San Lorenzo's in Beauchamp Place but Kinda was too young to go out so Raafat asked to stay home with her sister," their mother, Saniya, remembers. "It was as if that Christmas was very special to her." Just over a month later, on 8 February 1986, Raafat wrote in her diary: "My life is changing. I'm slowly, at last, finding myself. It feels great to at last meet my real self. Freedom!!"

Bassam al-Ghossain played no part in politics but his collection of newspaper clippings shows the growing crisis over Libya. Ghadafi was accused of organising the bombing of a TWA passenger jet over Greece. President Reagan's administration announced that it had unequivocal proof that the Libyan embassy had arranged the bombing of a Berlin discothèque on 5 April 1986, in which an American serviceman and a Turkish woman were killed. The Berlin police were later to dispute the nature of this evidence—some Western journalists suggested Syria rather than Libya might have been behind the bombing—but by then Reagan was in the Gulf, calling Ghadafi "the Mad Dog of the Middle East" and promising unspecified retaliation.

"We thought about what all this meant, that there might be an attack, but we thought the Americans would only hit military targets," Bassam says now. "It just didn't occur to us that they would hit civilians. The patio of our home was wall-to-wall with the French embassy." Raafat was due home for the Easter holiday from her new art college and wrote an excited postcard, full of humour and maturity and affection—it was illustrated with a French painting of a black ladies' hat—from London. It was to be her last written message to her parents:

Dearest Mummy and Daddy,
I'm sending this card 'cause it has a touch of class just like you! I miss you *so* much! I can't wait, soon I'm going to be with you! How is my baby sister, send her all my love and kisses. How are my grandparents, send them also all my love and tell them that I miss them *a lot*. Well, I'll have to love you and leave you. Till the 23rd March—god willing—take care! Lots of love [from] your daughter that love [*sic*] you the most . . .

Raafat's Lebanese passport shows that she cleared Gatwick Airport immigration on the 23rd, exactly twenty-two days before the American crew of the F-111 that was to kill her took off from Lakenheath. She arrived in Tripoli with an attack of spring hay fever. Raafat was to return to London in the third week of April and was nearing the end of her holidays when, on 13 April, she spent the night at the home of the Ghandour family, Lebanese friends of long standing. There were already reports of a possible American bombing raid against Ghadafi's headquarters in Tripoli and against the offices of Libyan intelligence. Western journalists—myself among them—had gathered at the largest hotel in the city and noticed the hurried departure of a Soviet destroyer from the waterfront on the morning of 14 April. "Raafat was in her dressing gown at breakfast in the morning and all we talked about was the possible raid and what would be the targets and if the Americans would hit civilians," Moutassim Ghandour remembers. "She kept roaming around this point. She felt that someone close would be killed. She was fully convinced that there was going to be a raid. I tried to talk politics with her. But she kept going round and round, talking about the planes that might come. She went on about this for three hours. I think that somehow she knew she was going to be killed that day."

On the evening of the 14th, Raafat was so overcome with hay fever that Saniya called in the doctor. "He told her to sleep well and gave her antihistamine and nose drops," her mother recalls. "She immediately said she felt better. We talked about the art college. And she said she was happy because she had kept herself for the man she would one day marry. She looked very beautiful, like a girl standing on the stage. Bassam and Kinda came in and we had a light meal—of cheese and tomatoes and a plate of sweets from the Syrian ambassador's wife. We let Raafat sleep in the TV room because there was a machine there that controls pollen. I went to bed in the girls' room and Kinda slept beside her father in our bed." At almost the same moment the al-Ghossain family went to bed, twenty-four American F-111s from the U.S. 48th Tactical Fighter Wing, based at RAF Lakenheath, were taking off for Libya. One of the aircraft was crewed by Captain Fernando Ribas-Dominicci of Puerto Rico and Captain Paul Lorence of San Francisco.

It was just after two in the morning that Saniya awoke with a start. "There was a tremendous roaring noise and I got out of bed and shouted: 'Wake up, Bassam, the Americans are here!' I looked into the TV room and saw Raafat sleeping peacefully there and I thought I'd better not wake her up. I went back to bed." Bassam woke again moments later. "I heard anti-aircraft fire and the next thing I knew my feet were buried in rubble. I couldn't move. Kinda was in the bed next to me. She was screaming. Her body was covered by a door. I held her hand to quieten her down. The door had protected her when the ceiling came down."

Saniya reawoke to hear Bassam's voice shouting "as if from another planet—it was a voice I had never heard before. He was shouting 'My God! My God!' and calling our names. I was choking on the smoke and dust. I stood up and it was all darkness. I couldn't see anything. I was walking on glass on my bare feet. I put my hand on the bedroom wall and found there was no door there. I asked Bassam what happened to Kinda. He said: 'I am touching her. She is alive.' I went to Raafat's room and the side wall was down. I shouted her name many times. She didn't answer. A feeling came over me that Raafat had died. I shouted: 'Bassam—Raafat has gone.' Then I walked out of the house to get help, on my bare feet. Tripoli was like a haunted city. I saw all the water of the city coming out of the pipes. I looked back at the wreckage of our home and there was nobody to be seen, it was as if it had been like this for a hundred years. Eventually, I found a young man who went to what was left of our home to help." To Saniya's amazement—it registers on her face when she recalls the fact years later—the rescuer was a Palestinian who had survived the 1982 Sabra and Chatila massacre, the atrocity which had so horrified the homesick Raafat in London.

Badly cut and bruised, Bassam and Kinda were taken to hospital. Neither can remember the following hours. Saniya was taken to a friend's house. A 2,000-pound bomb had destroyed the home of the al-Ghossains' Libyan neighbours, killing all five of them. The blast had blown down the wall of the TV room onto Raafat. Moutassim Ghandour, the family's Lebanese friend, found a team of Libyan civil defence workers with a bulldozer at the neighbours' ruined house and pleaded with them to find Raafat. It was already mid-morning on 15 April. He later wrote a legal testimony of what he saw:

> The bulldozer tried to lift the roof slab which was on top of the couch where "Fafo" had been lying and it was then that her face appeared for the first time, she was lying on her back with the head turned on the right cheek, she was intact, her hair undisturbed and a small streak of blood coming from the top side of her head, flowing down her left cheek. When she appeared, the bulldozer stopped and rescue workers got close to her to find out if she was still alive. I was led away about 10 metres, and then somebody screamed "Every soul will have the taste of death . . ." together with other verses relevant to death and martyrdom from the Holy Koran. At this stage I realised that "Fafo" was dead.

Kinda scarcely recalls the bombing and was too young to understand what Raafat's death meant. "I remember a door on top of me and a rock near my head and shouting 'Dad! Dad! Dad!' My father had lots of blood on him. I couldn't move my legs." Bassam was distraught. In the hours to come, he would hear journalists claim that his home had been hit not by an American bomb but by Libyan anti-aircraft missiles. The United States dismissed the death of at least thirty civilians in the raid on Tripoli as "collateral damage," adding—in the Pentagon's words—that "only 1 or 2 per cent of the bombs impacted in civilian areas." America's targets—including Ghadafi's headquarters and intelligence offices—had been hit, they claimed. A security office not far from the al-Ghossains" home had been touched, but the French embassy had suffered far worse damage and the al-Ghossain home was virtually destroyed. Not a word of regret came from Washington.

A U.S. official admitted that Ghadafi had been one of the targets of "Operation El Dorado Canyon"—this was the raid in which Ghadafi's adopted daughter had

been killed—and a Pentagon report later stated that "in terms of equipment performance, the strike was a success." A Pentagon official told *The Washington Post*
that the air force F-111s from Britain had been included in the raid because their
pilots wanted "a piece of the action." This may have been true. "It was the greatest
thrill of my life to have been involved," one of the pilots later told the *Chicago Tribune*. "It is what we are trained for." Defence Secretary Caspar Weinberger later
agreed that the Americans had killed the civilians and that an F-111 lost in the raid
might have dropped the bombs that killed Raafat al-Ghossain and her neighbours
when it was shot down. Captain Fernando Ribas-Dominicci and Captain Paul
Lorence were flying the doomed plane. Over Tripoli, the former was heard shouting: "I'm hit!" and another, anonymous pilot was recorded replying: "Sorry about
that." The body of Ribas-Dominicci was later recovered from the Mediterranean
by the Libyans and returned to the United States.

Bassam still carries a file of newspaper articles on the American raid. *The New
York Times* wrote that "even the most scrupulous citizen can only approve and
applaud the American attacks on Libya . . . the United States has prosecuted
[Ghadafi] carefully, proportionately—and justly." Israeli prime minister Shimon
Peres claimed that the Americans had been taking their revenge for the slaughter
of 241 U.S. servicemen in the Beirut truck-bombing three years earlier. But
Ghadafi had no more to do with that mass killing than Saddam Hussein was to
have with the mass slaughter of 11 September 2001. Bassam al-Ghossain's file
also includes a headline from *The Times* of London—"Raid destroyed terrorist
nerve-centre." Underneath, the by-line says: "From Robert Fisk, Tripoli." My
report did not mention "terrorists"—that had been a sub-editor's work in the headline, and it was only a little over two years later that *The Times* would censor my
report on the Iranian Airbus slaughter—but Bassam al-Ghossain was unforgiving.
"It gives the impression we are terrorists, it says that Raafat was a terrorist."

At the mass funeral three days later, I noticed Raafat's coffin because—living
in Lebanon—I had straight away caught sight of the Lebanese flag and the Palestinian flag lying on her casket. It had been Saniya's idea. I knew nothing of the
family but had found Raafat's shocked and badly wounded mother. "We are Muslims but we have one God," she had told me then. "We are one people. I hope Mr.
Reagan understands that." A stone was placed upon Raafat's grave which quoted
the Koran: "Thou causest the night to pass into the day, and thou causest the day to
pass into the night. And thou bringest forth the living from the dead, and thou
bringest forth the dead from the living . . ."

Saniya wanted the flags of every Arab nation on the coffins of those killed in
the American raid—"because it was their fault, because they did not unite and
because, for this reason, Raafat was killed by all the Arab world." A year later,
eight-year-old Kinda would write a letter to her dead sister:

Dear Fafo,
I will see you one day. I miss you very much. I wish I was with you all the
time. I love you. When you died, everything changed it was ever [*sic*]

worse. I shout at my Mom and Dad . . . Please come back one day or I go to you. You come and take me in the night and take me to see you. And then bring me back. I just wish. I love you. Your sister Kinda.

Bassam refused to visit his daughter's grave. In 1994 he resigned from the nationalised Libyan oil company and returned to Beirut with his family, leaving Raafat's remains behind in Tripoli. "Once the soul leaves the body, it doesn't matter where the body is," he remarked years later. "It says this in the Koran. I don't believe in visiting graves. I am a strong believer. I believe that one day you're going to meet that person again. Visiting a grave means that you're attached to a body and that is wrong." Saniya is not so strict. "Raafat always wanted to be with us. Sometimes I feel 'at least let our bones be together.' " Nineteen years after her death, on a visit to Libya in 2005, Bassam did visit the cemetery where his daughter was buried and stood and wept before Raafat's grave.

But Bassam's anger never died, not least because Kinda suffered deeply from her sister's death. Still feeling leg pains from injuries to her spinal cord, it was nine more years before she realised Raafat was dead, when she at last visited her sister's grave in 1995. "I had to grow up without her, without having a big sister," she says. "I have a lot of friends and they sometimes ask what it's like to be an only child, sometimes I tell them how Fafo died in the air raid . . ." Today, Kinda, a remarkably pretty young woman of twenty-six, teaches in the educational studies department at the Deutsche Schule in Beirut. Bassam, who believes in the law as he believes in justice, wrote to ex-President Reagan's daughter Patti, to ex-President Carter, to lawyers in Britain and America to seek redress. In the United States he was warned that any legal action for damages for Raafat's death might be treated as a "frivolous suit" in the courts. "If you don't follow up an injustice and let the world know what happened to you, then injustice wins," he says. "I want the world to know what happened to our family . . . People say that it is a tragedy Kinda doesn't have an elder sister. But she *did* have a sister—and she was taken from us."

Among the family snapshots, Saniya treasures two crumpled sheets of paper that she found in the rubble of the villa. Both are covered in Raafat's handwriting. Apparently written to herself only days before her death, the letter is an expression of Raafat's fear and suspicion of the world but also of her hopes of a future happiness, a sombre and moving tribute to her own life:

People are only faces, images, masks worn by each one of them to deceive each other . . . Meanwhile, here I am watching, trying to survive, among a group of actors who try to show as if they understood it all but really have understood nothing, [the] hypocrites. Life is a game, a gamble, and people are its victims, its players . . . I hope that one day I shall find that stream of light, that breath of life which will open my soul up and let [me] go FREE, FREE, FREE to eternity.

At the bottom of the letter, Raafat has drawn the wings of four great white birds.

# CHAPTER TWENTY-TWO

# The Die Is Cast

*Oh, what a tangled web we weave,*
*When first we practise to deceive!*

—Walter Scott, *Marmion,* VI,
introduction, st. 17

HOW SMALL HE LOOKED in the high-backed chair. You had to sit in the auditorium of the UN General Assembly to realise that George Bush Junior—threatening war in what was built as a house of peace—could appear such a little man. But then again Julius Caesar was a little man, and so was Napoleon Bonaparte. So were other more modern, less mentionable world leaders. Come to think of it so was General Douglas MacArthur, who had his own axis of evil, which took him all the way to the Yalu River. But on 12 September 2002, two-thirds of the way through George W. Bush's virtual declaration of war against Iraq, there came a dangerous, tell-tale code which suggested that he really did intend to send his tanks across the Tigris River. "The United States has no quarrel with the Iraqi people," he told us in the UN General Assembly. In the press gallery, nobody stirred. Below us, not a diplomat shifted in his seat. The speech had already rambled on for twenty minutes but the speechwriters must have known what this meant when they cobbled it together.

Before President Reagan bombed Libya in 1986, he announced that America "has no quarrel with the Libyan people." Before he bombed Iraq in 1991, Bush the Father told the world that the United States "has no quarrel with the Iraqi people." In 2001, Bush the Son, about to strike at the Taliban and al-Qaeda, told us he "has no quarrel with the people of Afghanistan." And now that frightening mantra was repeated. There was no quarrel, Mr. Bush said—absolutely none—with the Iraqi people. So, I thought to myself as I scribbled my notes in the UN press gallery, it's flak jackets on.

Perhaps it was the right place to understand just how far the Bush administration's obsession with Iraq might take us. The green marble fittings, the backcloth wall of burnished gold and the symbol of that dangerous world shielded by the UN's olive branches gave Mr. Bush the furnishings of an emperor, albeit a diminutive one. Television flattens faces, gives false familiarity to expressions that ought to be studied. In the flesh, Bush had none of the idealised, polished integrity that he believed he showed on the screen. I watched the angry—pugnacious—way in which he spoke. "The people"—here he looked up to his right, eyes narrowed—"of the United States"—up to the left now, eyes still narrowed—"of America." There are two prompters at the UN, on the left and on the right of the speaker. But now Bush looked straight ahead, eyes wider, challenging, almost desperate, a mixture of innocence and arrogance. Just a day earlier, he told us, America had commemorated an attack that had "brought grief to my country." But he didn't mention Osama bin Laden, not once. It was Saddam Hussein to whom we had to be reintroduced—he used Saddam's name eight times in his address, with fifteen references to the "Iraqi regime."

Surfing that veil of American tears which bin Laden's killers had created, it was also clear that the Bush plans for the Middle East were on a far greater scale than the mere overthrow of the Iraqi leader who once regarded himself as America's best friend in the Gulf. There must be a democratic Afghanistan—President Hamid Karzai vigorously nodded his approval down among the General Assembly dictators—and there must be democracy in Palestine; and this would lead to "reforms throughout the Muslim world." Reforms? In Saudi Arabia? In Jordan? In Iran? We were not told. The Bush theme, of course, was an all too familiar one; of Saddamite evil, laced with the usual caveats, conditional clauses and historical distortions. We all knew Saddam Hussein was a vicious, cruel dictator—we knew that when he was our friend—but the president insisted on telling us again. Saddam had repeatedly flouted UN Security Council resolutions; no mention here, of course, of Israel's flouting of resolutions 242 and 338 demanding an end to the occupation of Palestinian land.

Bush spoke of the tens of thousands of opponents of Saddam Hussein who had been arrested and imprisoned and summarily executed and tortured—"all of these horrors concealed from the world by the apparatus of a totalitarian state"—but there was no mention that these same beatings and burnings and electric shocks and mutilations and rapes were being readily perpetrated when America was on very good terms with Iraq before 1990, when the Pentagon was sending intelligence information to Saddam to help him kill more Iranians. Indeed, one of the most telling aspects of the Bush speech was that all the sins of which he specifically accused the Iraqis—a good many undoubtedly true—began in the crucial year of 1991. There was no reference to Saddam's flouting of UN resolutions when the Americans were helping him. There were a few reminders by Bush of the gas attacks against Iran—without mentioning that this very same Iran was now supposed to be part of the "axis of evil."

Then there were the grammatical problems, the sleight of hand historians use when they cannot find the evidence to prove that Richard III really did kill the princes in the tower. If it wasn't for the 1991 Gulf War, Iraq "would likely" have possessed a nuclear weapon by 1993. Iraq "retains the physical infrastructure needed to build" a nuclear weapon—which is not quite the same thing as actually building it. The phrase "should Iraq acquire fissile material" didn't mean it had acquired it. And being told that Iraq's enthusiasm for nuclear scientists "leaves little doubt" about its appetite for nuclear weapons wasn't quite the same as having proved it had obtained these weapons. Was this the evidence upon which America would go to war?

The UN—for this was the emperor's message to the delegates sitting before him—could take it or leave it, join America in war or end up like that old donkey, the League of Nations. Bush mentioned the League, dismissing it as a talking shop without adding that the United States had refused to join.* But it was clear how he intended to sell the war on the back of 11 September 2001. "Our greatest fear is that terrorists will find a shortcut to their mad ambitions when an outlaw regime supplies them with the technologies to kill on a massive scale," he said. And there we had it. Osama bin Laden equalled Saddam Hussein and—who knows?—Iran or Syria or anyone else.

If al-Qaeda productions had outdone Hollywood on 11 September 2001, Bush productions were now the makeover artists, turning Osama bin Laden into Saddam Hussein, al-Qaeda's Saudi hijacker-killers into Iraqis. The creative centre of America, as one columnist was to point out after the Iraqi invasion, was no longer New York or Los Angeles. For the moment, it was Washington, "where every day, more fiction is spun by the yard." Who would have believed, a year ago, that it would be the shaven features of Saddam Hussein we'd have to hate rather than the unshaven features of Osama bin Laden? As usual, our newspaper and television journalists connived at it all. Wasn't it the task of reporters to have asked why the picture suddenly changed? When did the transition take place? I asked during a lecture in New York. I owe it to Professor Robert Alford of the City University of New York Graduate Center to have enlightened me—it happened about the time of the Enron scandal.[†]

For months, I had not believed in this future war. Simon Kelner, my editor at *The Independent*, agreed with me. "I doubt if there's going to be a war over Iraq," he said. Leonard Doyle, my foreign editor was not so sure. But when Bush stopped speaking on 12 September 2002, I walked out of the General Assembly, picked up a pay phone and dialled London. "Leonard, I was wrong," I said. "I've never seen a man of such arrogance before—and he means what he says. There's going to be a war."

---

*President Woodrow Wilson, who had demanded a new international order in the wake of the 1914–18 war, was one of the midwives of the League that gave birth to Poland, Yugoslavia, Czechoslovakia, a reshaped Europe and, of course, a new Middle East. The modern state of Iraq also owed its creation to the League. But Wilson fell ill, the U.S. Congress declined to join the world body and America turned to isolationism. The future superpower, whose influence for peace would have been so beneficial to the world—and whose growing economic and military power might have made Hitler revise his plans—turned its back on the League. George W. Bush was perhaps not the right man to be giving lectures on this subject.

[†]A series of tables that Alford sent me showed that the "Iraq" story started growing—and the Osama saga, by extension, diminishing—just as the Enron scandal broke. Back in January 2002, Enron was receiving 1,137 "mentions" in *The New York Times*, *The Washington Post* and the *Los Angeles Times*, Iraq only 200. The Iraq stories grew by almost 100 per cent by early spring as Enron "mentions" declined by 50 per cent to 618. After a slight dip in early summer, Iraq soared up to 1,529 "mentions," with Enron down to a mere 310.

Looking back on those extraordinary months, it is as if we lived in a dream—Bush, his earnest, obedient partner, the British prime minister Tony Blair, and all those of us who thought this future conflict a madness. We drifted towards the abyss, knowingly, awake yet asleep, aware that we could protest at this folly—we did, in words, in the streets—yet watching mesmerised as sleepwalkers led our countries to war. Hitler once remarked that he "walked the path that destiny dictates." Saddam Hussein had always done this. So, presumably, did Osama bin Laden think of himself. But now Bush and Blair were walking the same omniscient, vain road.

We had seen the nature of the new America that Bush was growing on the ruins of the World Trade Center, the cruel, extrajudicial world that was to be nurtured with the blood and souls of all who died on 11 September 2001. Prisoners shackled, hooded, sedated. Taken to a remote corner of the world where they may be executed, where the laws of human rights are suspended. It took time to realise that Guantanamo was a mirror of the treatment that every Middle East dictatorship meted out to its opponents. Shackled, hooded, threatened with death by "courts" that would give no leeway to defence or innocence: this was how every Arab secret police force dealt with enemies of the regime. This was what the Western hostages of Beirut faced in the 1980s; this was the "justice" that Iran's hanging judges bestowed upon their enemies, what Iraq's insurgents would do with their captives. In this project, we journalists were complicit. Had not Roger Ailes, the chairman of the Fox News Channel, personally advised Bush to take the "harshest measures possible" against those who had attacked America?

And in the coming months, all that we most feared about this new form of "justice" came to pass: torture, sexual humiliation, murder under interrogation, rape, extrajudicial killings—by American and British troops, by our vicious allies in the "war on terror," by all who were convinced that our cause—democracy, freedom, liberty—should be defended with any means, even if those means destroyed the democracy, freedom and liberty that we claimed to be defending. As we prepared ourselves for the next stage of our "war on terror"—the invasion of Iraq—we let slip the collective memory of Afghanistan's betrayal. Even more seriously, we ignored the lessons that post-Taliban Afghanistan might hold for us. We chose not to dwell too much on the way in which we—the victors, the liberators, the bringers of freedom—treated the Afghans with whom, of course, we had "no quarrel."

THE "WAR ON TERROR" reached the Afghan village of Hajibirgit at midnight on 22 May 2002. Haji Birgit Khan, the bearded, eighty-five-year-old Pashtun village leader and head of 12,000 local tribal families, was lying on a patch of grass outside his home. Faqir Mohamedin was sleeping among his sheep and goats in a patch of sand to the south when he heard "big planes moving in the sky." Even at night, it is so hot that many villagers spend the hours of darkness outside their homes, although Mohamedin and his family were in their mud-walled house. There were 105 families in Hajibirgit, and all were woken by the thunder of helicopter engines and the thwack of rotor blades and the screaming voices of the Americans.

Haji Birgit Khan was seen running stiffly from his lawn towards the white-walled village mosque, a rectangular cement building with a single loudspeaker and a few threadbare carpets. Several armed men were seen running after him. Hakim, one of the animal-herders, saw the men from the helicopters chase the old man into the mosque and heard a burst of gunfire. "When our people found him, he had been killed with a bullet, in the head," he says, pointing downwards. There is a single bullet hole in the concrete floor of the mosque and a dried bloodstain beside it. "We found bits of his brain on the wall."

Across the village, sharp explosions were detonating in the courtyards and doorways. "The Americans were throwing stun grenades at us and smoke grenades," Mohamedin recalls. "They were throwing dozens of them at us and they were shouting and screaming all the time. We didn't understand their language, but there were Afghan gunmen with them, too, Afghans with blackened faces. Several began to tie up our women—our own women—and the Americans were lifting their burqas, their covering, to look at their faces. That's when the little girl was seen running away." Abdul Satar says that she was three years old, that she ran shrieking in fear from her home, that her name was Zarguna, the daughter of a man called Abdul-Shakour—many Afghans, as we have seen, have only one name—and that someone saw her topple into the village's 18-metre well on the other side of the mosque. During the night, she was to drown there, alone, her back apparently broken by the fall. Other children would find her body in the morning. The Americans paid no attention. From the description of their clothes given by the villagers, they appeared to include Special Forces and also units of Afghan Special Forces, the brutish and ill-disciplined units run from Kabul's former Khad secret police headquarters. There were also 150 soldiers from the U.S. 101st Airborne, whose home base is at Fort Campbell in Kentucky. But Fort Campbell is a long way from Hajibirgit, which is 80 kilometres into the desert from the south-western city of Kandahar. And the Americans were obsessed with one idea: that the village contained leaders from the Taliban and Osama bin Laden's al-Qaeda movement.

A former member of a Special Forces unit from one of America's coalition partners supplied his own explanation for the American behaviour when I met him in Kandahar a few days later. "When we go into a village and see a farmer with a beard, we see an Afghan farmer with a beard," he said. "But when the Americans go into a village and see a farmer with a beard, they see Osama bin Laden."

The women and children were ordered to gather at one end of Hajibirgit. "They were pushing us and shoving us out of our homes," Mohamedin says. "Some of the Afghan gunmen were shouting abuse at us. All the while, they were throwing grenades at our homes." The few villagers who managed to run away collected the stun grenades next day with the help of children. There are dozens of them, small cylindrical green pots with names and codes stamped on the side. One says "7 BANG Delay: 1.5 secs NIC-01/06-07," another "1 BANG, 170 dB Delay:

1.5s." Another cylinder is marked: "DELAY Verzogerung ca. 1,5s." These were the grenades that terrified Zarguna and ultimately caused her death. A regular part of U.S. Special Forces equipment, they are manufactured in Germany by the Hamburg firm of Nico-Pyrotechnik—hence the "NIC" on several of the cylinders; "dB" stands for decibels. Several date stamps show that the grenades were made as recently as March 2002. The German company refers to them officially as "40mm by 46mm sound and flash (stun) cartridges." But the Americans were also firing bullets. Several peppered a wrecked car in which another villager, a taxi-driver called Abdullah, had been sleeping. He was badly wounded. So was Haji Birgit Khan's son.

A U.S. military spokesman would claim later that American soldiers had "come under fire" in the village and had killed one man and wounded two "suspected Taliban or al-Qaeda members." The implication—that eighty-five-year-old Haji Birgit Khan was the gunman—is clearly preposterous. The two wounded were presumably Khan's son and Abdullah, the taxi-driver. The U.S. claim that they were Taliban or al-Qaeda members was a palpable lie, since both of them were subsequently released. "Some of the Afghans whom the Americans brought with them were shouting 'Shut up!' to the children who were crying," Faqir Mohamedin remembers. "They made us lie down and put cuffs on our wrists, sort of plastic cuffs. The more we pulled on them, the tighter they got and the more they hurt. Then they blindfolded us. Then they started pushing us towards the planes, punching us as we tried to walk." In all, the Americans herded fifty-five of the village men, blindfolded and with their hands tied, on to their helicopters. Mohamedin was among them. So was Abdul-Shakour, still unaware that his daughter was dying in the well. The fifty-sixth Afghan prisoner to be loaded on to a helicopter was already dead: the Americans had decided to take the body of eighty-five-year-old Haji Birgit Khan with them.

When the helicopters landed at Kandahar airport—headquarters to the 101st Airborne—the villagers were, by their own accounts, herded together into a container. Their legs were tied and then their handcuffs and the manacle of one leg of each prisoner were separately attached to stakes driven into the floor of the container. Thick sacks were put over their heads. Abdul Satar was among the first to be taken from this hot little prison. "Two Americans walked in and tore my clothes off," he said. "If the clothes would not tear, they cut them off with scissors. They took me out naked to have my beard shaved and to have my photograph taken. Why did they shave off my beard? I had my beard all my life."

Mohamedin was led naked from his own beard-shaving into an interrogation tent, where his blindfold was removed. "There was an Afghan translator, a Pashtun man with a Kandahar accent, in the room, along with American soldiers, both men and women soldiers," he says. "I was standing there naked in front of them with my hands tied. Some of them were standing, some were sitting at desks. They asked me: 'What do you do?' I told them: 'I am a shepherd—why don't you ask your soldiers what I was doing?' They said: 'Tell us yourself.' Then they asked: 'What kind of weapons have you used?' I told them I hadn't used any weapon.

One of them asked: 'Did you use a weapon during the Russian [occupation] period, the civil war period or the Taliban period?' I told them that for a lot of the time I was a refugee."

From the villagers' testimony, it is impossible to identify which American units were engaged in the interrogations. Some U.S. soldiers were wearing berets with yellow or brown badges, others were in civilian clothes but apparently wearing bush hats. The Afghan interpreter was dressed in his traditional shalwar khameez. Hakim underwent a slightly longer period of questioning; like Mohamedin, he says he was naked before his interrogators. "They wanted my age and my job. I said I was sixty, that I was a farmer. They asked: 'Are there any Arabs or Talibans or Iranians or foreigners in your village?' I said 'No.' They asked: 'How many rooms are there in your house, and do you have a satellite phone?' I told them: 'I don't have a phone. I don't even have electricity.' They asked: 'Were the Taliban good or bad?' I replied that the Taliban never came to our village so I had no information about them. Then they asked: 'What about Americans? What kind of people are Americans?' I replied: 'We heard that they liberated us with [President Hamid] Karzai and helped us—but we don't know our crime that we should be treated like this.' What was I supposed to say?"

A few hours later, the villagers of Hajibirgit were issued with bright-yellow clothes and taken to a series of wire cages laid out over the sand of the airbase—a miniature version of Guantanamo Bay—where they were given bread, biscuits, rice, beans and bottled water. The younger boys were kept in separate cages from the older men. There was no more questioning, but they were held in the cages for another five days. All the while, the Americans were trying to discover the identity of the eighty-five-year-old man. They did not ask their prisoners—who could have identified him at once—although the U.S. interrogators may not have wished them to know he was dead. In the end, the Americans gave a photograph of the face of the corpse to the International Red Cross. The organisation was immediately told by Kandahar officials that the elderly man was perhaps the most important tribal leader west of the city.

"When we were eventually taken out of the cages, there were five American advisers waiting to talk to us," Mohamedin says. "They used an interpreter and told us they wanted us to accept their apologies for being mistreated. They said they were sorry. What could we say? We were prisoners. One of the advisers said: 'We will help you.' What does that mean?" A fleet of U.S. helicopters flew the fifty-five men to the Kandahar football stadium—once the scene of Taliban executions—where all were freed, still dressed in prison clothes and each with a plastic ID bracelet round the wrist bearing a number. "Ident-A-Band Bracelet made by Hollister" was written on each one. Only then did the men learn that old Haji Birgit Khan had been killed during the raid a week earlier. And only then did Abdul-Shakour learn that his daughter Zarguna was dead.

The Pentagon initially said that it found it "difficult to believe" that the village women had their hands tied. But given identical descriptions of the treatment of Afghan women after the U.S. bombing of an Uruzgan wedding party, which followed the Hajibirgit raid, it seems that the Americans—or thcir Afghan allies—did just that. A U.S. military spokesman claimed that American forces had found "items of intelligence value," weapons and a large amount of cash in the village. What the "items" were was never clarified. The guns were almost certainly for personal protection against robbers. The cash remains a sore point for the villagers. Abdul Satar said that he had 10,000 Pakistani rupees taken from him—about $167 (£114). Hakim says he lost his savings of 150,000 rupees—$2,500 (£1,700). "When they freed us, the Americans gave us two thousand rupees each," Mohamedin says. "That's just forty dollars [£27]. We'd like the rest of our money."

But there was a far greater tragedy to confront the men when they reached Hajibirgit. In their absence—without guns to defend the homes, and with the village elder dead and many of the menfolk prisoners of the Americans—thieves had descended on Hajibirgit. A group of men from Helmand province, whose leader was once a brutal and rapacious mujahedin fighter against the Russians, raided the village once the Americans had taken away so many of the men. Ninety-five of the 105 families had fled into the hills, leaving their mud homes to be pillaged.

The disturbing, frightful questions that creep into the mind of anyone driving across the desert to Hajibirgit today are obvious. Who told the United States to raid the village? Who told them that the Taliban leadership and the al-Qaeda leadership were there? For today, Hajibirgit is a virtual ghost town, most of its houses abandoned. The U.S. raid was worthless. There are scarcely forty villagers left. They all gathered at the stone grave of Zarguna some days later, to pay their respects to the memory of the little girl. "We are poor people—what can we do?" Mohamedin asked me. I had no reply. President Bush's "war on terror," his struggle of "good against evil," descended on the innocent village of Hajibirgit.

And now Hajibirgit is dead.

I SPENT PART OF THE VAPID hot summer of 2002 in Afghanistan, trying to learn what "liberation" meant. If the experience of Hajibirgit was typical—and it quickly turned out that it was—then what would happen to the people of Iraq if we decided to "liberate" them from Saddam Hussein? And how would Iraqis react to the same treatment?

I was at my small hotel in Kandahar when the U.S. Special Forces boys barged into it one day. One of them wore kitty-litter camouflage fatigues and a bush hat, another was in civilian clothes, paunchy with jeans. The interiors of their four-wheel-drives glittered with guns. They wanted to know if a man called Hazrat was staying at the guest house. They didn't say why, didn't say who Hazrat was. The concierge had never heard the name. The five men left, unsmiling, driving at speed back on to the main road. "Why did they talk to me like that?" the concierge asked me. "Who do they think they are?" It was best not to reply.

"The Afghan people will wait a little longer for all the help they have been promised," the local district officer in Maiwand muttered to me a few hours later. "We believe the Americans want to help us. They promised us help. They have a little longer to prove they mean this. After that . . ." He didn't need to say more. Out at Maiwand, in the ovenlike grey desert west of Kandahar where the teenage heroine Malalai charged the British guns in the Second Afghan War, the Americans were doing raids, not aid.

But even when the U.S. military tried to turn its hand to humanitarian work, the Western NGOs—the non-governmental organisations working with the UN— preferred to keep their distance. As a British NGO worker put it with devastating frankness in Kandahar: "When there is a backlash against the Americans, we want a clear definition between us and them." I heard that phrase all the time in Afghanistan. "When the backlash comes . . ." It was coming already. The Americans were being attacked almost every night. There had been three shootings in Kandahar, with an American officer wounded in the neck near the airport in mid-July of 2002. American troops could no longer dine out in Kandahar's cafés. Now U.S. forces were under attack in Khost province. Two Afghan auxiliaries were killed and five American soldiers wounded near the Pakistan border at the end of July.

For the NGOs in Kabul, the danger lay in the grey area—a deliberate grey area, they said—which the Americans created between military operations and humanitarian aid. "Up in Kunduz, they've got what they call a 'humanitarian liaison team' that has repaired a ward in a local hospital and been involved in rebuilding destroyed bridges," the Briton said. "Some of the men with them have been in civilian clothes but carrying guns. We took this up with them, because Afghans began to think that our aid organisation also carried guns. The U.S. told us their men didn't carry weapons openly or wear full uniforms out of deference to the feelings of local tribal leaders. Eventually, we all had to raise this matter in Washington."

It wasn't hard to see the dangers. In Kabul, the Americans were operating an organisation called the CJCMOTF, the Coalition Joint Civil–Military Operations Task Force, whose mission, an official U.S. document said, included "expertise in supply, transportation, medical, legal, engineering and civil affairs." Headquartered in Kabul, it had "daily contact with [the] U.S. embassy." Their personnel definitions included "physician, veterinarian, attorney, civil engineer, teacher, firefighter, construction, management," but their military experience was listed as "Desert Storm, Operation Provide Comfort, Panama, Haiti, Somalia, Bosnia, Kosovo." Then there's the CHLC, the Coalition Humanitarian Liaison Center, at Mazar-e-Sharif, whose objective was liaison between "assistance [*sic*] community and military coalition" and which was "rebuilding public facilities, 14 schools, providing a generator for the airport terminal and providing a medical clinic, a veterinarian clinic and a library." But its tasks also included "security information," a "channel of communication to coalition commanders, U.S. embassy and USAID" and—an interesting one, this—"miscellaneous supplies, e.g. concertina wire." Somehow, rebuilding schools had got mixed up with the provision of barbed wire.

It made the aid agencies shudder. "I have banned all coalition forces from my compound and will not meet with them in public," an Australian humanitarian official told me in Kabul. "If they want to contact me, I tell them to send me emails. I will meet them only in certain public authority offices. Yes, of course we are worried that people will mistake us for the military . . . They simply have no idea how to deal with the social, cultural, political complex of life here. They are really not interested. They just want to fight a 'war on terror.' I don't think they care."

This was no minor official but a Western coordinator handling millions of dollars of international aid. He knew, as did his staff, how angry Afghans were becoming at the growing U.S. presence in their country. As long as Washington went on paying the private salaries of local warlords, including some who opposed President Hamid Karzai, a kind of truce would continue to exist, but Afghans took a shrewd interest in America's activities in their country and their anger was only stoked by U.S. bombing raids that left hundreds of innocent Afghans dead.

After the Americans bombed a wedding party in Uruzgan on 30 June 2002—the death toll eventually came to fifty-five—Pashtuns were outraged at eyewitness accounts of U.S. troops preventing survivors helping the wounded. They were especially infuriated by a report that the Americans had taken photographs of the naked bodies of dead Afghan women. An explanation was not difficult to find. For their own investigation, U.S. forces might well have taken pictures of the dead after the Uruzgan raid and, since bombs generally blast the clothes off their victims, dead female Afghans would be naked. But the story had become legend. Americans took pictures of naked Afghan women. It was easy to see how this could turn potential Afghan friends into enemies. Now guerrilla attacks were increasingly targeting Afghan forces loyal to the government, or to local drug-dealers who were friendly with the Americans. Just as the first mujahedin assaults on the Russians after the 1980 Soviet invasion tended to focus on Moscow's Afghan Communist allies, so the new attacks were being directed at America's Afghan allies. If America invaded Iraq, who would the insurgents there attack?

An Australian Special Forces man had his own thoughts on the subject. The Kandahar garden in which we met was overgrown, the roses scrawny after a day of heat, the dust in our eyes, noses, mouth, fingernails. But the message was straightforward. "This is a secret war," the Special Forces man told me. "And this is a dirty war. You don't know what is happening." And of course, we were not supposed to know. In a "war against terror," journalists are supposed to keep silent and rely on the good guys to sort out the bad guys without worrying too much about human rights.

How many human rights did the mass killers of September 11 allow their victims? You are either with us or against us. Whose side are you on? But the man in the Kandahar garden was worried. He was one of the "coalition allies," as the Americans liked to call the patsies who have trotted after them into the Afghan midden. "The Americans don't know what to do here now," he went on. "Even their interrogations went wrong." Brutally so, it seems. In the early weeks of 2002, the Americans raided two Afghan villages, killed ten policemen belonging to the U.S.-supported government of Hamid Karzai and started mistreating the survivors. American reporters—in a rare show of mouselike courage amid the self-censorship of their usual reporting—quoted the prisoners as saying they had been beaten by U.S. troops. According to Western officials in Kandahar, the U.S. troops "gave the prisoners a thrashing."

On 17 March U.S. soldiers arrested at least thirty Northern Alliance gunmen at Hauzimated in Kandahar province: according to eighteen of the prisoners, the Americans refused to listen to their explanation that they were allies and—believing they were Taliban members—punched, kicked and kneed their captives before holding them in cages for four days. They then released them with an apology.

Now things had changed. The American forces were leaving the beatings to their Afghan allies, especially members of the so-called Afghan Special Forces, the Washington-supported thugs at the former Khad torture centre in Kabul. "It's the Afghan Special Forces who beat the Pashtun prisoners for information now—not the Americans," the Australian Special Forces man said. "But the CIA are there during the beatings, so the Americans are culpable, they let it happen."

This is just how the Americans began in Vietnam. They went in squeaky-clean with advisers, there were some incidents of "termination with extreme prejudice," after which it was the Vietnamese intelligence boys who did the torture. The same with the Russians. When their soldiers poured across the border in 1979, they quickly left it to their Afghan allies in the Parcham and Khad secret police to carry out the "serious" interrogations. And if this was what the Americans were now up to in Afghanistan, what was happening to their prisoners at Guantanamo? Or, for that matter, at Bagram, the airbase north of Kabul to which all prisoners in Kandahar were now sent for investigation if local interrogators believed their captives had more to say? And what about civilian casualties of the Americans" increasingly promiscuous air raids? If so many hundreds of civilians were dying in these bombing attacks across Afghanistan, how many would die in Iraq if Washington redirected its forces to Mesopotamia?*

---

*A broad count of civilian deaths in Afghanistan, taken from journalists, aid workers and government authorities since October 2001, included the following details: four UN employees killed by a missile in Kabul on 9 October 2001; between 160 and 200 dead when U.S. bombs destroyed the village of Karam on 11 October; up to 190 dead when the Sultanpour mosque in Jalalabad was bombed twice on 17 October, between 40 and 47 dead in Kandahar bombings the same day; on 18 October, at least 10 killed when the bazaar near Kepten was bombed, 40 killed in Kabul on the same day, several dozen killed in Tarin Kot on 19 October; 60–70 killed in Herat and 50 in Kandahar on 20 October; on 21 October, bombs accidentally hit a 300-bed hospital in Herat, killing approximately 100 civilians, another 20 (including 9 children) killed the same day when their tractor-trailor was bombed at Tarin Kut. Within twenty-four hours, 61 more civilians were killed—including an eight-year-old girl—mostly in Kabul and Kandahar. On 21 October, during bombing of roads and fuel trucks by U.S. forces, another hundred civilians were reported killed; at least 28 dead in the bombing of the villages of Darunta, Torghar and Farmada on 23 October, and at least 52 more the same day at the village of Chowkar Kariz. On 29 October, 25 more civilians were killed in Kabul. On 5 November, 36 civilians were killed by stray U.S. bombs in Ogopruk village, near Mazar. On 10 November, 125 civilians were killed in three villages near Khakrez. On 17 November, 62 were killed when a religious school was bombed in Khost, 42 nomads lost their lives near Maiwand, 30 people were killed in Charikar, 28 in Zani Khel and 13 elsewhere. The following day, scores of gypsies were killed by U.S. bombs in Kun-

Of course, it was possible to take a step back from this frightening corner of America's Afghan adventure. In the aftermath of the Taliban's defeat, humanitarian workers achieved some miracles. UNICEF reported 486 female teachers at work in the five south-western provinces of the country, with 16,674 girls now at school. Only in Uruzgan, where the Taliban were strongest, had not a single female teacher been employed. UN officials could boast that in these same poverty-belt provinces, polio had now been almost eradicated. But the UN was fighting polio before the Taliban collapsed, and the drugs whose production the Taliban banned were now back on the market. The poppy fields were growing in Helmand province again, and in Uruzgan local warlords were trying to avoid government control in order to cultivate their own new poppy production centres. In Kabul, where two government ministers had been murdered in seven months, President Karzai was now protected—at his own request—by American bodyguards. And you didn't have to be a political analyst to know what kind of message this sent to Afghans.

The Australian Special Forces man saw things more globally. "Perhaps the Americans can start withdrawing if there's another war—if they go to war in Iraq. But the U.S. can't handle two wars at the same time. They would be overstretched." Prescient words for July 2002. So, it seemed, to end America's "war against terror" in Afghanistan—a war that has left the drug-dealers of the Northern Alliance in disproportionate control of the Afghan government, many al-Qaeda

---

dar, up to 150 people in villages near Khanabad, 35 in Shamshad and 24 in Garikee Kha. On 20 November, 40 civilians were killed when their mud huts were hit by stray bombs near Kunduz. On 25 November, 92 people, including 18 women and 7 children, were killed by bombing in Kandahar, another 70 by cluster bombs in Kunduz. On 1 December, about 100 were killed by 25 bombs in the village of Kama Ado. At least 30 died when bombs hit trucks and buses outside Kandahar the same day. Another 20 died in the Agam district, 15 in refugee vehicles in Arhisan, over 30 near Herat. On 2 December, 150 civilians died across Afghanistan and in the same week over 300 villagers were killed during the Tora Bora offensive. False intelligence about a Taliban base led the Americans to bomb Mashikhel in Paktia, killing 10 in the city's mosque. On 20 December, U.S. AC-130 gunships attacked a convoy—thought to belong to the Taliban but in fact containing tribal elders en route to Hamid Karzai's inauguration—killing up to 65 people. That same night, between 25 and 40 people were killed in Naka. On 31 December, a B-52 bomber and two helicopters killed over 100 civilians in a village near Gardez. One woman lost 24 members of her family. On 24 January 2002, U.S. commandos accidentally killed 16 government soldiers— the Pentagon's own figure—in Uruzgan. On 30 June 2002, 48 civilians at a wedding party at Del Rawad in Uruzgan were killed and another 117 wounded when they were bombed by U.S. aircraft; celebratory gunfire was mistaken for hostile fire by the Americans. President Bush later expressed "deep condolences" for this loss of life. On 30 October 2003, 6 civilians, including 3 children and an old woman, died in the home of a provincial governor. On 6 December, U.S. Special Forces killed 6 children and 2 adults in Gardez. Seven boys, two girls and a twenty-five-year-old man were killed when A10 aircraft attacked them with other villagers sitting under a tree at Hutala. Many of the above attacks were carried out near front lines or on villages which were wrongly thought to contain wanted Taliban commanders, or because of sloppy intelligence. Professor Marc Herold of the University of New Hampshire was to calculate that between 3,000 and 3,400 civilians were killed in Afghanistan between 7 October and 7 December 2001, more than were murdered on September 11th. The "mantra" of the "U.S. mainstream corporate media" over each bombing, he wrote, was: "The report cannot be independently verified."

men on the loose and little peace in the country—we had to have another war in
Iraq.

All that year of 2002, I criss-crossed the Atlantic, reporting from the Middle
East, lecturing in the United States, sometimes arriving in New York on a Friday
evening only to be filing dispatches from Cairo the following Monday. Perhaps no
one was travelling between East and West so often that year, and it was a paradox-
ical experience, the polemic of one continent about another—the American about
the Arab or Middle Eastern—bearing as little relation to reality as the solecisms of
Arab Muslims towards the world's sole superpower. Both sides of the world
appeared to have retreated into their own illusions and fears. It produced weird
results.

In Washington, before dawn on 11 September 2002, the first anniversary of the
attacks, I flicked through six American television channels and saw the Twin Towers fall to the ground eighteen times. The few references to the suicide killers who
committed the crime made not a single mention of the fact that they were Arabs.
The previous week, *The Washington Post* and *The New York Times* went to agonising lengths to separate their Middle East coverage from the September 11th commemorations, as if they might be committing some form of sacrilege or be acting
in bad taste if they did not. "The challenge for the administration is to offer a
coherent and persuasive explanation of how the Iraq danger is connected to the
9/11 attacks" was about as far as the *Washington Post* got in smelling a rat—and
this was only dropped into the seventh paragraph of an eight-paragraph editorial.
All references to Palestine or illegal Jewish settlements or Israeli occupation of
Arab land were simply erased from the public conscience that week. When Hanan
Ashrawi, that most humane of Palestinian women, tried to speak at the University
of Colorado during the week of September 11th, Jewish groups organised a massive demonstration against her. U.S. television simply did not acknowledge the
Palestinian tragedy. But maybe all this no longer mattered. When Defence Secretary Donald Rumsfeld could claim—as he did when asked for proof of Iraq's
nuclear potential—that the "absence of evidence is not evidence of absence," we
might as well have ended all moral debate. But when Rumsfeld referred to the "so-
called occupied territories," he revealed himself to be a very disreputable man.

Strange events were now going on in the Middle East. Arab military intelligence reported the shifting of massive U.S. arms shipments around the region—
not just to Qatar and Kuwait, but to the Arabian Sea, the Red Sea and the eastern
Mediterranean. American and Israeli military planners and intelligence analysts
were said to have met twice in Tel Aviv to discuss the potential outcome of the next
Middle East war. The destruction of Saddam and the break-up of Saudi Arabia—a
likely scenario if Iraq crumbled, so the "experts" claimed—had long been two
Israeli dreams. As the United States discovered during its fruitful period of neutrality between 1939 and 1941, war primes the pumps of the economy. Was that
what was going on today—the preparation of a war to refloat the U.S. economy?

Then in one brisk, neat letter to Kofi Annan, Saddam Hussein pulled the rug
from right under George W. Bush's feet. At the United Nations, Bush had been

playing the unlikely role of the multilateralist, warning the world that Iraq had one last chance—through the UN—to avoid Armageddon. "If the Iraqi regime wishes peace," he had told us all in the General Assembly, "it will immediately and unconditionally forswear, disclose and remove or destroy all weapons of mass destruction, long-range missiles and all related material." So now Saddam welcomed the UN arms inspectors. No conditions. Just as Bush had demanded. Saddam would do everything he could to avoid war. Bush, it seemed, was doing everything he could to avoid peace.

No wonder that the United States immediately began to speak of "false hopes." No wonder, I wrote in *The Independent*, that the Americans were searching desperately for another *casus belli* "in an attempt to make sure that their next war keeps to its timetable." But for now, the Americans had been stymied. It would take at least twenty-five days to put the UN inspection team together, another sixty for their preliminary assessment, then another sixty days for further inspections. Bush's latest war had been delayed by more than five months. But a careful examination of the Bush UN speech showed that a free inspection of Saddam Hussein's supposed weapons of mass destruction was just one of six conditions which Iraq would have to meet if it "wishes peace." The other Bush demands included an "end of all support for terrorism." Did this mean the UN would now be urged to send inspectors to hunt for evidence inside Iraq for Saddam's previous—or current—liaisons with guns-for-hire? Bush had also demanded that Iraq "cease persecution of its civilian population, including Shias, Sunnis, Kurds, Turkomans and others." Notwithstanding the inclusion of Turkomans—worthy of protection indeed, though no doubt because they sat on very lucrative oil deposits—did this mean that the UN could demand human rights monitors inside Iraq? In reality, such a proposal would be both moral and highly ethical, but America's Arab allies would profoundly hope that such monitors were not also dispatched to Riyadh, Cairo, Amman and other centres of gentle interrogation.

Yet even if Saddam was prepared to accede to all these demands with a sincerity he had not shown in response to other UN resolutions, the Americans had made clear that sanctions would only be lifted—that Iraq's isolation would only end—with "regime change." For Bush's sudden passion for international adherence to UN Security Council resolutions—an enthusiasm that never, of course, extended to Israel's flouting of UN resolutions of equal importance—was in reality a manoeuvre to provide legitimacy for Washington's planned invasion of Iraq.

Tony Blair's adherence to this cynical policy must remain one of the more mystifying elements in this chapter of Middle East tragedy. The coalescence of Bush's born-again Christianity with Blair's High Church pronouncements—and the unique combination of Blair's own self-righteousness and legal casuistry—was to produce one of the strangest alliances of our times. The hollowness of the British political contribution—symbolised by the Downing Street "dossier" of 24 September 2002—should have made this obvious months before its warning of a "45-minute" WMD attack came to be debated in Parliament and in the later Hutton Report.

I first read this document in Beirut and—as always in the Middle East—its contents appeared quite different to a reader 3,000 kilometres from London than they did to an MP in Westminster or an editor in what used to be called Fleet Street. I found it truly shocking—but not for any 45-minute warnings. Reading it, I wrote, "can only fill a decent human being with shame and outrage. Its pages are final proof—if the contents are true—that a massive crime against humanity has been committed in Iraq. For if the details of Saddam's building of weapons of mass destruction are correct—and I will come to the 'ifs' and 'buts' and 'coulds' later—it means that our massive, obstructive, brutal policy of UN sanctions has totally failed. In other words, half a million Iraqi children were killed by us—for nothing." In May 1996, as we know, Madeleine Albright had told us that sanctions worked and prevented Saddam from rebuilding weapons of mass destruction. Our then Tory government agreed, and Tony Blair toed the line. But when asked by an interviewer if the "price"—the death of half a million children—was worth it, she had replied to the world's astonishment: "I think this is a very hard choice, but the price, we think the price is worth it."

Now we were being told—if Blair was telling us the truth—that the price was *not* worth it. The purchase bought with the lives of hundreds of thousands of children wasn't worth a dime. For the Blair "dossier" was telling us that, despite sanctions, Saddam was able to go on building weapons of mass destruction. All that nonsense about dual-use technology, the ban on children's pencils—graphite could have a military use—and our refusal to allow Iraq to import equipment to restore the water-treatment plants that we bombed in the Gulf War, was a sham. This grievous conclusion was the only moral one to be drawn from the sixteen pages that supposedly detailed the chemical, biological and nuclear horrors that the Beast of Baghdad had in store for us. It was difficult, reading the full report, to know whether to laugh or cry. The degree of deceit and duplicity in its production spoke of the trickery that informed the Blair government and its treatment of MPs.

Let us take just one example of the document's dishonesty. On page 45, we were told—in a long chapter about Saddam's human rights abuses—that "on March 1st, 1991, in the wake of the Gulf War, riots broke out in the southern city of Basra, spreading quickly to other cities in Shia-dominated southern Iraq. The regime responded by killing thousands." What's wrong with this paragraph is the lie in the use of the word "riots." These were not "riots." They were part of a mass rebellion specifically called for by President Bush Junior's father and by that CIA-run radio station in Saudi Arabia. The Shia Muslims of Iraq obeyed Bush Senior's appeal. And were then left to their fate by the Americans and British, who they had been given every reason to believe would come to their aid. No wonder they died in their thousands. But all this was cut out from the Blair "dossier."

Indeed, anyone reading the weasel words of doubt that were insinuated throughout this text could only have profound concern about the basis on which Britain was to go to war. The Iraqi weapon programme was "almost certainly" seeking to enrich uranium. It "appears" that Iraq was attempting to acquire a magnet production line. There was evidence that Iraq had tried to acquire specialised aluminium tubes (used in the enrichment of uranium) but there was "no definitive intelligence" that it was destined for a nuclear programme. "If" Iraq obtained fissile material, it could produce nuclear weapons in one or two years. It was "difficult to judge" whether al-Hussein missiles could be available for use. Efforts to regenerate the Iraqi missile programme "probably" began in 1995. And so the "dossier" went on. Yes, Saddam—we had to say this in every radio interview, every lecture, write it in every article in order to be heard—was a brutal, wicked tyrant. But were "almost certainly," "appears," "probably" and "if" really the rallying call to send our Grenadiers off to the deserts of Kut-al-Amara?

There was high praise in the document for UN weapons inspectors. And there was more trickery in the relevant chapter about them. It quoted Dr. Hans Blix, the executive chairman of the UN inspection commission, as saying that in the absence of (post-1998) inspections it was impossible to verify Iraqi disarmament compliance. But on 18 August 2002—scarcely a month before the Blair "dossier"—Blix had told the Associated Press that he couldn't say with certainty that Baghdad possessed WMDs. This quotation, of course, was excised from the British government document. So there it was. If these pages of trickery were based on "probably" and "if," we had no business going to war. If they were all true, we murdered half a million Iraqi children for nothing. How was that for a war crime?

Yet each day, someone said something even more incredible—even more unimaginable—about President Bush's obsession with war. In October, Bush was himself talking to an audience in Cincinnati about "nuclear holy warriors." Forget for a moment that we still couldn't prove Saddam Hussein had nuclear weapons. Forget that the latest Bush speech was just a rehash of all the "ifs" and "mays" and "coulds" in Tony Blair's flimsy sixteen pages of allegations in his plainly dishonest "dossier." We now had to fight "nuclear holy warriors." That's what we had to do to justify the whole charade through which we were being taken by the White House, by Downing Street, by all the decaying "experts" on terrorism and, alas, far too many journalists. Forget the fourteen Palestinians, including the twelve-year-old child, killed by Israel a few hours before Bush spoke in Cincinnati, forget that when American-made aircraft killed nine Palestinian children in July, along with one militant, the Israeli prime minister Ariel Sharon—a "man of peace" in Bush's words—described the slaughter as "a great success." Israel was on our side in the "war on terror." We had to remember to use the word "terror"—about Saddam Hussein, Osama bin Laden, Yassir Arafat, in fact about anyone who opposed Israel or America. Bush used the word in his Cincinnati speech thirty times in half an hour—that was one "terrorism" a minute.

What we had to forget if we were to support this madness, needless to say, was that President Ronald Reagan dispatched a special envoy to meet Saddam Hussein in December 1983. It was essential to forget this for three reasons. First, because the awful Saddam was already using gas against the Iranians—which was one of the reasons we were now supposed to go to war with him. Second, because the envoy was sent to Iraq to arrange the re-opening of the U.S. embassy—in order to secure better trade and economic relations with the Butcher of Baghdad. And third, because the envoy was Donald Rumsfeld. One might have thought it strange, in the course of one of his folksy press conferences, that Rumsfeld hadn't chatted to us about this interesting tit-bit. You might think he would wish to enlighten us about the evil nature of the criminal with whom he so warmly shook hands. But no. Until questioned much later about whether he warned Saddam against the use of gas—he claimed he did, but this proved to be untrue—Rumsfeld was silent. As he was about his subsequent and equally friendly meeting with Tariq Aziz—which just happened to take place on the day in March 1984 that the UN released its damning report on Saddam's use of poison gas against Iran.

We had to forget, too, that in 1988, as Saddam destroyed the people of Halabja with gas, along with tens of thousands of other Kurds—when he "used gas against his own people" in the words of Messrs. Bush/Cheney/Blair/Cook/Straw et al.—President Bush Senior provided Saddam with $500 million in U.S. government subsidies to buy American farm products. We had to forget that in the following year, after Saddam's genocide was complete, the elder Bush doubled this subsidy to $1 billion, along with germ seed for anthrax, helicopters, and the notorious "dual-use" material that could be used for chemical and biological weapons. And of course, we had to forget about oil. Indeed, oil is the one commodity—and one of the few things that George Bush Junior knew something about, along with his ex-oil cronies Cheney and Condoleezza Rice and countless others in the administration—which was never mentioned. In all of Bush's thirty minutes of anti-Iraq war talk in Cincinnati—leavened with just two minutes of how "I hope this will not require military action"—there wasn't a single reference to the fact that Iraq might hold oil reserves larger than those of Saudi Arabia, that American oil companies stood to gain billions of dollars in the event of a U.S. invasion, that, once out of power, Bush and his friends could become multi-billionaires on the spoils of this war. We had to ignore all this before we went to war. And that's pretty much what we did.

In the continuing war against al-Qaeda, Washington trumpeted its victories, even when they set new records in extrajudicial executions. A "Clean shot" was *The Washington Post*'s description of the murder of the al-Qaeda leaders in Yemen by a U.S. Predator unmanned aircraft in November 2002. The U.S. press used Israel's own definition of such deaths as "targeted killing"—the BBC parroted the same words on 5 November. No one explained why these important al-Qaeda leaders could not have been arrested. Or tried before an open court. Or, at the least, taken to Guantanamo Bay for interrogation. Instead, the Americans released a clutch of Guantanamo "suspects," one of whom—having been held for eleven months in solitary confinement and then returned to Afghanistan—turned out to be around one-hundred years old, and so senile that he couldn't string a sentence together. Unsurprisingly, American intelligence never seemed aware of just how many of bin Laden's associates it had been fighting in Afghanistan.*

---

*Ahmed Zeidan, a Syrian Al-Jazeera correspondent who met bin Laden several times and attended the wedding feast of bin Laden's son Abdullah, gave a remarkable account of al-Qaeda's order of battle in his Arabic-language book *Al-Qaeda Unmasked*. This 215-page trea-

The very expression "targeted killing" had now become part of the lexicon of the "war on terror." Ariel Sharon of Israel used the term. So too did the Russians in their renewed war on Chechnya. After the disastrous "rescue" of Moscow theatre hostages held by rebel Chechens in Moscow, Putin was supported by Bush and Tony Blair in his renewed onslaught against the broken Muslim people of Chechnya. In October 2002, *Newsweek* ran a brave and brilliant and terrifying report on the Chechen war. In a deeply moving account of Russian cruelty there, it told of a Russian army raid on an unprotected Muslim village. Russian soldiers broke into a civilian home and shot all inside. One of the victims was a Chechen girl. As she lay dying of her wounds, a Russian soldier began to rape her. "Hurry up, Kolya," his friend shouted, "while she's still warm." But no matter. The "war on terror" meant that Kolya and the boys would be back in action soon, courtesy of Messrs. Putin, Bush and Blair.

That very brave Israeli, Mordechai Vanunu, the man who tried to warn the West of Israel's massive nuclear war technology, imprisoned for twelve years of solitary confinement—and betrayed, so it appears, by Robert Maxwell—wrote a poem in his confinement. "I am the clerk, the technician, the mechanic, the driver," Vanunu wrote. "They said, 'Do this, do that, don't look left or right, don't read the text. Don't look at the whole machine. You are only responsible for this one bolt, this one rubber stamp.'"

Kolya would have understood that. So would the U.S. Air Force officer "flying" the drone that killed the al-Qaeda men in Yemen. So would the Israeli pilot who bombed the apartment block in Gaza, killing nine small children as well as well as his Hamas target, the "operation" described by Sharon as "a great success." Was this not part of the arrogance of colonial power? Here, for example, is the last French executioner in Algeria during the 1956–52 war of independence, Fernand Meysonnier, boasting in October 2002 of his prowess at the guillotine. "You must never give the guy the time to think. Because if you do he starts moving his head around and that's when you have the mess-ups. The blade comes through his jaw, and you have to use a butcher's knife to finish it off. It is an exorbitant power—to kill one's fellow man." So perished the brave Muslims of the Algerian fight for freedom.

When Julius Caesar crossed the Rubicon, he wrote, in his *Gallic Wars: "Alea iacta est."* The die is cast. Just after 11 a.m. on 8 November, when the United Nations Security Council voted 15–0 to disarm Iraq, President George W. Bush

---

sure trove revealed that there were 2,742 Afghan "Arabs" from al-Qaeda—in other words, Muslims who fought for bin Laden—in Afghanistan during the Taliban era: they included 62 Britons, 30 Americans, 8 Frenchmen, 1,660 North Africans, 680 Saudis, 480 Yemenis, 430 Palestinians, 270 Egyptians, 520 Sudanese, 80 Iraqis, 33 Turks and 180 Filipinos. During the Taliban rule, Arab fighters were dispersed across Afghanistan as follows: 260 Arabs in four bases around Kandahar, 145 Arabs in Uruzgan in two bases, 1,870 fighters in Kabul in seven bases, 404 around Mazar-e-Sharif, 400 in three bases around Kunduz, 300 in Laghman province, 1,700 in 12 bases in Nangahar opposite Pakistan's North-West Frontier province, 160 in Kunar, 600 in Khost and 740 in Paktia.

crossed the Rubicon. "The world must insist that that judgement must be enforced," he told us. The Rubicon is a wide river. It was deep for Caesar's legions. The Tigris would be more shallow—my guess was that the first American tanks would be across it within one week of war—but what lay beyond? "Cheat and retreat . . . will no longer be tolerated," Bush told the UN. And after eight weeks of debate in the Security Council, no one any longer mentioned the crimes against humanity of 11 September 2001, because, of course, Iraq had absolutely nothing to do with September 11th. "Should we have to use troops," Bush told a 7 November press conference, ". . . the United States, with friends, will move swiftly—with force—to do the job." In other words, he would invade Iraq, the "friends," presumably, being British.

The United Nations could debate any Iraqi non-compliance with weapons inspectors, but the United States would decide whether Iraq had breached UN resolutions. In other words, America could declare war without UN permission. The BBC, with CNN and all the other television networks, billed Resolution 1441 as "the last chance" for Saddam Hussein. In fact, it was a "last chance" for the United Nations. It was easy to identify the traps. America's UN ambassador, John Negroponte—later to be his country's ambassador in Iraq—insisted that the Security Council resolution "contains no hidden triggers." But it did. It allowed the Security Council to discuss non-compliance without restraining the United States from attacking Baghdad. "One way or another," Negroponte said, ". . . Iraq will be disarmed." Sir Jeremy Greenstock, Britain's nightmare headmaster at the UN, performed appropriately. "Crystal clear," "unequivocal choice," "serious consequences," no more "ambiguous modalities." You could almost feel the cane. No mention, of course, of the CIA's manipulation of the last team of UN weapons inspectors in Iraq. Washington wanted a UN fig leaf for a war on Iraq and was willing to go through an inspection process in the hope that Iraq obstructed it.

I AM IN ST. LOUIS, MISSOURI, preparing to give a lecture to university students on the coming war in Iraq. It is mid-November, and in my hotel room I am dusting off my description of bin Laden, of how I met him in Sudan and Afghanistan. Not since the battle of Tora Bora in Afghanistan have we heard his voice, although my contacts have insisted to me that he is alive. I turn on CNN. And there, sitting in my room above the Mississippi, I hear his voice. He is alive. It takes only a brief round of phone calls to the Middle East and South-West Asia for my sources to confirm that it is Osama bin Laden's gravelly voice that is threatening the West in the short monologue transmitted by the Al-Jazeera television channel. So the Saudi billionaire, the man in the cave, the "Evil One"—I quote a *Newsweek* headline—the bearded, ascetic man whom the greatest army on earth has sought in vain, is with us still.

"U.S. intelligence"—the heroes of September 11th who heard about Arabs learning to fly but didn't quite manage to tell us in time—come up with the usual rubbish for the American media. It may be him. It's probably him. The gravelly voice may mean he's been hurt. He is speaking fast because he could have been wounded by the Americans. Untrue. The United States was finally forced to acknowledge on 18 November that the man some of them had claimed to be dead was still very much in the land of the living—and uttering the kind of threat that confirms the darkest fears of Western leaders. "Just like you kill us, we will kill you," bin Laden said.

When he was recorded, bin Laden was not talking into a tape-recorder. He was talking into a telephone. The man on the other end of the line—quite possibly in Pakistan—held the recorder. Bin Laden may not have been in the same city as the man with the recorder. He may well not have been in the same country. Osama bin Laden always speaks slowly. His voice is rapid, and the reason for this is apparently quite simple: the recorder's battery was low. When replayed by Al-Jazeera at real-time speed, the voice goes up an octave.

Writing about bin Laden now is one of the most difficult journalistic tasks on earth. I have to say what I know. I have to say what I think must be true. I have to ask why he made this tape. I start to tap out my report for *The Independent*. My story moves deeper into questions. Why? What for? Why now? It requires a new, harsh way of writing to tell the truth, the use of brackets and colons. Knowledge and suspicion, probability and speculation, keep grinding up against each other. Bin Laden survived the bombing of Tora Bora. Fact. Bin Laden escaped via Pakistan. Probability. Bin Laden is now in Saudi Arabia. A growing conviction.

So here, with all its imperfections and conditional clauses, is what I suspect this tape recording means. The story is a deeply disturbing one for the West. I am frightened of the implications of this tape. One of its messages to Britain—above all others after the United States—is: Watch out. Tony Blair was right (for once) to warn of further attacks, though the bin Laden phone call was not (I suspect) monitored. But it was bin Laden. We must start with Tora Bora in the autumn of 2001. Under heavy bombardment by the U.S. Air Force, bin Laden's al-Qaeda fighters realised they could not hold out indefinitely in the cave complex of the White Mountains above Jalalabad. Bin Laden was with them. Al-Qaeda men volunteered to fight on to certain death against the Afghan warlords paid by the Americans, and bin Laden at first refused to go. He argued that he wished to die with them. His most loyal bodyguards and senior advisers insisted he must leave. In the end, he abandoned Tora Bora in a state of anguish, his protectors hustling him down one mountainside with much the same panic as Dick Cheney's security men carried the U.S. vice president to the White House basement when al-Qaeda's killer-hijackers closed in on Washington on September 11th. All of the above comes under the label of "impeccable source."

Bin Laden went either to Kashmir (possible, though unlikely) or Karachi (most probable). I say this because bin Laden boasted to me once of the many admirers he had among the Sunni clergy of this great, hot and dangerous Pakistani city. He always talked of them as his "brothers." He had given me those posters in Urdu which these clerics had produced and pasted on the walls of Karachi. He liked to quote their sermons to me. So I'll go for Karachi. But I may be wrong. In the months that followed, there were little, tiny hints that he remained alive, like the smell of tobacco in a room days after a smoker has left. An admirer of the man insisted to me that he was alive (fact, but not an impeccable source). He was trying to find a way of communicating with the outside world without meeting any Westerner. Absolute fact. His most recent videotape—which was dismissed as old by those famous "U.S. intelligence sources" because he didn't mention any events since November 2001—was new. (Strong possibility, backed up by a good—though not impeccable—source.)

So why now? The Middle East was entering a new and ever more tragic phase of its history, torn apart by the war between Israelis and Palestinians and facing the incendiary effects of a possible Anglo–American invasion of Iraq. Bin Laden must have realised the need to once more address the Arab world—and his audiotape, despite the threats to Britain and other Western countries, was primarily directed towards his most important audience, Arab Muslims. His silence at this moment in Middle East history would have been inexcusable in bin Laden's own eyes. And just to counter the predictable counter-claims that his tape could be old, he energetically listed the blows struck at Western powers since his presumed "death." The bombings of French submarine technicians in Karachi, a synagogue in Tunisia, the massacre in Bali, the Chechen theatre siege in Moscow, even the killing of a U.S. diplomat in Jordan. Yes, he was saying, "I know about all these things." He was saying he approved. He was telling us he was still here. Arabs might deplore this violence, but few would not feel some pull of emotion. Amid Israel's brutality towards Palestinians and America's threats towards Iraq, at least one Arab was prepared to hit back. That was his message to Arabs.

Bin Laden always loathed Saddam Hussein. He hated the Iraqi leader's un-Islamic behaviour, his secularism, his use of religion to encourage loyalty to a Baath party that was co-founded by a Christian. America's attempt to link al-Qaeda to the Baghdad regime has always been one of the most preposterous of Washington's claims. Bin Laden used to tell me how much he hated Saddam. So his two references to "the sons of Iraq" are intriguing. He makes no mention of the Baghdad government or of Saddam. But with UN sanctions still killing thousands of children—and with Iraq the target of a probable American invasion—he cannot possibly ignore it. So he talks about "Iraq's children" and about "our sons in Iraq," indicating Arab Muslim men who happened to be Iraqi, rather than Iraqi nationalists. But not Saddam. It's easy to see how the U.S. administration may try to use these two references to make another false link between Baghdad and al-Qaeda, but bin Laden—who is intelligent enough to be able to predict this—clearly felt that an expression of sympathy for the Arabs of Iraq outweighed any misuse Washington could make of his remarks. This has to come under the label of speculation (although near-certainty might be nearer the mark). Washington does indeed use these phrases to prop up its false contention that there are bin Laden–Saddam links. Back in 1996, bin Laden told me that British and French troops in Saudi Arabia were as much at risk of being attacked by his followers as American forces. In 1997 he changed this target list. The British and French he now dissociated from any proposed attacks. But in the new audiotape they are back on the hit list along with Canada, Italy, Germany and Australia. And Britain is at the top.

The message to us—the West—is simple and repeated three times. If we want to back George W. Bush, the "pharaoh of the age"—and "pharaoh" is what Anwar Sadat's killers called the Egyptian president after his murder more than two decades ago—we will pay a price. "What business do your governments have in allying themselves with the gang of criminals in the White House against Muslims . . . ?" I have heard bin Laden use that Arabic expression *ifarbatu al-ijran* twice before in conversation with me. "Gang of criminals." Which is what the West has called al-Qaeda.

A few days earlier, after I gave a lecture in North Carolina, a woman in the audience had asked me when America would go to war in Iraq. I told her to watch the front page of *The New York Times* and *The Washington Post* for the first smear campaigns against the UN inspectors. And, right on time, the smears began in early December. One of the UN inspectors, it was now stated—a man appointed at the behest of the State Department—was involved with pornography. Another senior official, we were told—a man who again was appointed at the urging of the State Department—was previously fired from his job as head of a nuclear safety agency. Why, I wonder, did the Americans want these men on the inspection team? So they could trash it later? The official drubbing of the UN inspectors began way back in September when *The New York Times* announced, over Judith Miller's byline, that the original inspections team might, according to former inspector David Kay, be on a "mission impossible." The source was "some officials and former inspectors."

President George W. Bush was banging on again about Iraqi anti-aircraft defences firing at American and British pilots—even though the "no-fly zones" had nothing to do with the UN inspections nor, indeed, anything to do with the UN at all. The inspections appeared to be going unhindered in Baghdad. But what was George Bush now telling us? "So far the signs are not encouraging." What did this mean? Simply that America planned to go to war whatever the UN inspectors found. *The New York Times*—now a virtual mouthpiece for scores of anonymous U.S. "officials"—had persuaded itself that Iraq's Arab neighbours "seem prepared to support an American military campaign." Despite all the warnings from Arab leaders, repeated over and over again, month after month, urging America not to go to war, this was the nonsense being peddled in the United States.

And suddenly, the British government came up with another of its famous "dossiers" on Saddam's human rights abuses. Yes, again, we knew about his raping rooms and his executions and his torture when we eagerly supported his invasion of Iran in 1980. So why regurgitate it yet again? I noticed at once a little point in the latest British "dossier." It revealed that a certain Aziz Saleh Ahmed, a "fighter in the popular army," held a position as "violator of women's honour." Now I happened to remember that name. This was the same Aziz Saleh Ahmed who turned up on page 287 of the book published back in 1993 by Kanan Makiya, who formerly called himself Samir al-Khalil. Even ignoring the controversy about this "revelation" at the time, what was the British government doing rehashing the Aziz Saleh Ahmad story all over again as if we'd just discovered it, when it was at least eight years old and—according to Makiya—was first seen more than a decade ago?

In the meantime, Bush's foreign policy advisers were busy hatching up the conflict of civilisations. Kenneth Adelman, who was on the Pentagon's Defense Policy Board, was saying that for Bush to call Islam a peaceful religion was "an increasingly hard argument to make." Islam was "militaristic" in Adelman's eyes. "After all, its founder, Mohammed, was a warrior, not a peace advocate like Jesus." Then there was Eliot Cohen of the Johns Hopkins School of Advanced International Studies, who was also on the Pentagon board. He now argued that the "enemy" of the United States was not terrorism but "militant Islam." Adelman and Cohen did not vouchsafe their own religion, but Islam was clearly their target. Pat Robertson, the religious broadcaster—who used to run a radio station in southern Lebanon which uttered threats against Muslim villagers and UN troops—said that "Adolf Hitler was bad but what the Muslims want to do to Jews is worse." Jerry Falwell, one of the pit bulls of the religious right, called the Prophet a "terrorist," while Franklin Graham, son of the same Billy Graham who made anti-Semitic remarks on the Nixon tapes, called Islam "evil." Graham had spoken at Bush's inauguration.

We ignored this dangerous rhetoric at our peril. Did Blair ignore it? Wasn't he aware that there were some very sinister people hovering around Bush? Did he really think Britons were going to be cheer-led into war by "dossiers" and the constant reheating of Saddam's crimes? Didn't we want the UN inspectors to do their work? If a reporter's job is to describe the lies of statesmen, then at least *The Independent* also thought it a journalist's duty to condemn them. "I rather think that we are being set up for war," I wrote in my paper on 4 December, "that Britain will join America in invading Iraq, whatever the inspectors discover. In fact, we are being prepared for the awful, incredible, unspeakable possibility that the UN inspectors will find absolutely no weapons of mass destruction in Iraq. That will leave us with only one conclusion: they were no good at their job. They should have been in the oil business."*

After a lecture in New York, I am approached by a young American, a member

---

*For a long time, British tabloid newspapers had been setting up their readers for war. During the critical first anniversary of the New York and Washington attacks, *Express* newspapers slavishly followed the Blair–Bush line and their bogus "intelligence." On 8 September 2002, the *Sunday Express* announced that a "senior Washington intelligence source" had revealed to it "the chilling extent of Saddam Hussein's weapons of mass destruction." Under the headline "Saddam: We Have the Evidence," the paper listed Saddam's weapons as "Enough germ weapons to kill everyone in London and New York, 30,000 litres of deadly botulism and six tons of nerve gas, Six nuclear plants run by Russian and Korean scientists" and, incredibly, "Kidney machines adapted to trigger atom bombs." On the following day, the *Daily Express*, under the headline "Nuclear Attack in Just Months," claimed that Blair was warning that a "devastating assault by the Butcher of Baghdad against Britain could 'explode' in a matter of months." All of this later proved to be fiction.

of a U.S. Special Forces intelligence team newly returned from Afghanistan. He shows me photographs of al-Qaeda suspects, hooded and shackled as they are put aboard an American transport aircraft to Kandahar. They live in pens of eight or ten men. They are given cots with blankets but no privacy. They are forced to urinate and defecate publicly because the Americans watch their prisoners at all times. We agree to meet at a coffee shop in lower Manhattan next morning. He turns up on time but nervous, looking over his shoulder, worried that someone might be following us, starting from his seat when my mobile phone rings.

U.S. forces, he says, have not only failed to hunt down Osama bin Laden while they are preparing for war in Iraq; they are finding it almost impossible to crack the al-Qaeda network because bin Laden's men have resorted to primitive methods of communication that cut off individual members of al-Qaeda from all information. This man's prognoses were totally at variance with the upbeat briefings of U.S. defence secretary Donald Rumsfeld. Even in Pakistan, the man tells me, middle-ranking Pakistani army officers are tipping off members of al-Qaeda to avoid American-organised raids. "We didn't catch whom we were supposed to catch," he says. "There was an over-expectation by us that technology could do more than it did. Al-Qaeda are very smart. They basically found out how we track them. They realised that if they communicated electronically, our Rangers would swoop on them. So they started using couriers to hand-carry notes on paper or to repeat messages from their memory, and this confused our system. Our intelligence is high-tech—they went back to primitive methods that the Americans cannot adapt to."

There were originally "a lot of high-profile arrests." But the al-Qaeda cells didn't know what other members were doing. "They were very adaptive and became much more decentralised. We caught a couple of really high-profile, serious al-Qaeda leaders but they couldn't tell us what specific operations were going to take place. They would know that something big was being planned but they would have no idea what it was." The intelligence officer, who had spent more than six months in Afghanistan in 2002, was scathing in his denunciation of Rashid Dostum, the Uzbek warlord implicated in the suffocation of up to 3,000 Taliban prisoners in container trucks. "Dostum is totally culpable and the U.S. believes he's guilty but he's our guy and so we won't say so . . . one of the things we failed to do was create a real government. We let the warlords firmly entrench themselves and now they can't be dislodged."

American security agents in Karachi were looking for Daniel Pearl's murderers, but they would find their arrest targets had fled because of secret support within middle ranks of the Pakistani army. "We would go with the Pakistanis to a location but there would be no one there because once the middle level of the Pakistani military knew of our plans, they would leak the information. In the North-West Frontier province, the frontier corps is a second-rate army—they are a lot more anti-Western in sentiment than the main Pakistani army. In the end we had to coordinate everything through Islamabad."

When I asked about prisoners, the Special Forces officer became worried, withdrawn. He asked for another coffee. "In Kandahar, in what we call their living areas, the prisoners are given cots with blankets and Adidas suits and runners, but they have no privacy. There are no sides to their living areas because we have to see them all the time. They have no privacy in the bathroom. Some of them masturbate when they are looking at the female guards. Our guards had no reaction to this. They are soldiers. When the interrogations take place, the prisoners are allowed to sit. I don't want to get into specifics about the questions we ask them." As for the Western journalists he met at Bagram, the American intelligence officer had a low opinion. "They just hung around our base all day. Whenever we had some special operation, we'd offer the journalists some facility to go on patrol with our Special Forces and off they'd go—you know, 'We're on patrol with the Special Forces'—and they wouldn't realise we were stringing them along to get them out of the way."

IF JOURNALISTS COULD BE FOOLED by the Americans, Afghans made their own judgements on recent history. For while U.S. Special Forces cruised the streets of Kandahar in their four-by-fours, the people of this brooding, hot city were now visiting a bleak graveyard with the reverence of worshippers. Beneath grey, parched mounds of dust and dried mud lay the "martyrs" of al-Qaeda. Here, among the 150 graves, lay the men who held out to the end in the city's Mirweis hospital, shooting at the Americans and their Afghan allies until they died amid sewage and their own excrement. They were honoured now as saints. Other earth hid the bodies of the followers of Osama bin Laden who fought at Kandahar airport in the last battle before the fall of the Taliban. They are Arabs and Pakistanis and Chechens and Kazakhs and Kashmiris and all—if you believe the propaganda—are hated and loathed by the native Pashtun population of Kandahar.

Not true. The people of the Taliban's former caliphate tended the graves in their hundreds. On Fridays, they came in their thousands, travelling hundreds of miles. They brought their sick and dying. Word had it that a visit to the graveyard of bin Laden's dead would cure disease and pestilence. As if kneeling at the graves of saints, old women gently washed the baked mud sepulchres, kissing the dust upon them, looking up in prayer to the spindly flags that snapped in the dust storms. The Kandahar *kabristan*—the place of graves—was a political as well as a religious lesson for all who came there.

"Foreigners are advised to stay away from the al-Qaeda graveyard," a Western aid worker solemnly announced. "You may be in danger there." But when I visited the last resting place of bin Laden's men, there were only the fine, gritty winds of sand to fear. Many of the men around the graves kept their scarves around their faces, dark eyes staring at the foreigner in their midst. Two soldiers of the "new" Afghan army, stationed here by the supposedly pro-American authorities, watched the visitors as they put bowls of salt on the graves and took pieces of mud to touch with their tongues. An old man from Helmand was there. He had put stones and salt and mud on the tombs—he shook hands with me with salt on his fingers—and he had come because he was sick. "I have pain in my knee and I have polio and I heard that if I came here I would be cured," he said. "I put salt and grain on the graves then later I will collect the grain and eat the salt and take the mud from the grave home." *Khurda*, the Pashtuns call this, bringing salt to the tomb of saints.

A second, even older man had travelled from Uruzgan with his mother. "My mother had leg and back pains and I brought her to Kandahar so she could see the doctors. But when I heard the stories about these martyrs' graves—and that they might cure her—I also brought my mother here. She is happier here than going to the doctors." I watched his aged mother on her knees, scraping dust from the mud tombs, praying and crying. The government soldiers appeared to have succumbed to the same visionary trance. "I've seen for myself people who get healed here," a young, unbearded man with a Kalashnikov on his shoulder told me. "People get well after visiting the graves. I've seen deaf men who could hear again and I've seen the dumb speak. They were cured."

This was not the time—and definitely not the place—to contradict such conviction. The sand blasted over the graveyard with a ruthlessness worthy of bin Laden. The city cemetery is much larger—there are square miles of tribal graveyards within its perimeter. But it was the al-Qaeda dead who attracted the mourners. Attracted by what? The rumours and legend of healing? By the idea that these men resisted the foreigners to the end, preferred to die rather than surrender, that the non-Afghan "martyrs" had fought like Afghans?

So there was secret collusion, a fraudulent attempt to use the United Nations as a fig leaf for war, a largely unsympathetic British public, journalists used as propagandists and our enemy—an Arab dictator previously regarded as a friend of the West—compared to the worst criminals of the Second World War. This was our world in the winter of 2002.

But it also happened to be our world almost half a century earlier, a conflict not about oil but over a narrow man-made canal linking the Mediterranean with the Red Sea. The Suez crisis has haunted British governments ever since 1956—it hung over Margaret Thatcher during the 1982 Falklands War, and its memory now moved between the Foreign Office and Downing Street, Jack Straw and Tony Blair. For Suez destroyed a British prime minister—along, almost, with the Anglo-American alliance—and symbolised the end of the British empire. It killed many civilians—all Egyptian, of course—and brought shame upon the allies when they turned out to have committed war crimes. It rested on a lie—that British and French troops should land in Egypt to "separate" the Egyptian and Israeli armies, even though the British and French had earlier connived at Israel's invasion. Colonel Gamal Abdel Nasser was described by the British prime minister, Anthony Eden, as "the Mussolini of the Nile" even though, scarcely a year earlier, Eden had warmly shaken Nasser's hand in an exchange of congratulations over a new Anglo-Egyptian treaty—shades of Donald Rumsfeld's chummy meeting with the "Hitler of Baghdad" in 1983. In the end, British troops—poorly equipped and treating their Egyptian foes with racial disdain—left in humiliation, digging up their dead comrades from their graves to freight back home lest the Egyptians defile their bodies.

I have always been fascinated by the "other side," by how the losers thought and fought and—occasionally—turned out not to be the losers after all. When I was with the Iraqi army during the 1980–88 war with Iran, I always wanted to talk to the Iranian soldiers on the other side of the front lines. When I was with the Iranians, I was determined to talk to their Iraqi opponents. When the Hizballah fought the Israeli occupation army in southern Lebanon, I longed to listen to the Israeli army's analysis of the Hizballah—far from the usual "terrorist" rhetoric produced by their politicians, Israeli junior officers often showed respect for the Hizballah's guerrilla tactics. In Baghdad in 2003, I lived among Iraqis as they were bombed and attacked by the Anglo–American invasion force. I was too young to cover Suez—my mother, as I have recalled, was relieved I was too young to be a British soldier in the invasion of Egypt—but on the thirtieth anniversary of the crisis, I did set out to talk to the Egyptians who took over the Suez Canal and fought the British, spending weeks in Cairo listening to those who dared to oppose the British empire and the French nation and the invading Israelis.

The Egyptians do not call it the "Suez Crisis" or even the "Suez War." They refer to it, always, as "the Tripartite Aggression," so that their countrymen may never forget that two European superpowers colluded with Israel to invade the new republic of Gamal Abdel Nasser. Suez was a complex crisis, but it revolved around Nasser's decision—against international agreements—to nationalise the canal and take over the Suez Canal Company. British banks and businesses had long dominated investment in Egypt and held a 44 per cent stake in the company, originally negotiated by Benjamin Disraeli. Nasser's takeover was greeted with delirium by Egyptian crowds who had been aghast at America's earlier withdrawal from the Aswan High Dam project. The code word for the takeover was "de Lesseps," who had built the canal when Egypt was part of the Ottoman empire, and the moment Nasser uttered the Frenchman's name in a radio speech from Alexandria on 26 July 1956, twelve of Nasser's collaborators stormed the company's great wooden-framed headquarters.

Among them was Captain Ali Nasr, a shy twenty-six-year-old Suez Canal pilot with a thin moustache who walked up the steps of the building in Ismailia and calmly told the French employees inside that they were now working for the Egyptian Canal Company. Nasr was the only seaman of the group. "We all knew it was a job we had to do for our country—we were ready to lay down our lives for this," he was to tell me thirty years later. "We had the feeling of being soldiers awaiting instructions. We were led inside by Engineer Mahmoud Younis, who had been given his sealed orders by Nasser himself. Engineer Younis had a pistol. I was unarmed—I have never believed in carrying a weapon. But inside, we found the French and British and Greeks were very friendly. We told them: 'The canal is nationalised. It belongs to Egypt now. We want your cooperation. The ships must go on moving in the canal.' Then we exchanged cigarettes with them. We slept in the offices, usually slumped on the desks of the French officials. That is how we came to run the canal."

As Captain Nasr was turning in to sleep in Ismailia, Anthony Eden was concluding a dinner at Downing Street with the Iraqi king and his prime minister, Nuri es-Said. Both would be assassinated in Baghdad two years later. But on that night in 1956, es-Said's venom was directed at the Egyptian leader. "Hit him," he advised Eden. "Hit, hit hard and hit now." In London, Eden summoned his chiefs of staff. He wanted to topple Nasser—"regime change" is a new version of the same idea—and free the canal. But the British military informed him it couldn't be done. Troops were out of training, landing craft out of commission. "It was only when we eventually dropped outside Port Said," a Parachute Regiment officer told me more than forty years later, "that we suddenly realised how far our army's readiness had declined since the Second World War. Our transport aircraft could only unload from the side, our jeeps broke down and they couldn't even drop artillery to support us."

The first test of Nasser's strength came on 15 September 1956, when almost all the foreign pilots in the Suez Canal Authority withdrew their labour. Eden and Guy Mollet, the French prime minister, had devised the walkout in London five days earlier. The world would be shown that the Egyptians were not competent to run the canal. Of the 205 pilots capable of steering convoys through the 101-mile ditch between the Mediterranean and the Red Sea, only forty were Egyptian—and five of them were on holiday. "Younis realised this was going to happen and he called us Egyptian pilots together to ask what we should do," Captain Nasr recalled. "I told him we must train extra pilots but that we did not have time to teach them the navigation of the whole canal. I told him we should teach the men four sectors of the canal—one lot would learn how to pilot vessels southbound on the first half of the canal to Ismailia, the next would be taught the second stage southbound to Suez, the other two would learn the canal northbound in the same stages."

On the night of 15 September, Nasr found himself aboard a 14,000-ton German ship at Port Said. "The foreign pilots had left and I was so anxious about my job and my responsibility for the new scheme that I found I couldn't distinguish the green buoy lights from the red buoy lights at the mouth of the canal. But the German captain was very kind and gave me encouragement. We moved down the canal at night, and at dawn I saw the lights of a car on the road beside us. It was Younis with a megaphone, shouting encouragement to me and to the pilots of each ship as they steamed past him."

In Britain, the days and weeks and months that followed Nasser's seizure of the Suez Canal were taken up with prevarication, parliamentary lies, desperate attempts to form a coalition army and—most damaging of all—a secret meeting at Sèvres, outside Paris, in which the Israelis, the British and the French agreed that the Israeli army should invade Egypt and that Britain and France would then intervene, instruct the Israeli and Egyptian armies to withdraw their forces either side of the canal, and then place an Anglo-French intervention force in the Canal Zone around Port Said. "Operation Musketeer," it would be called, and the British people were duly summoned from their postwar lethargy by newspaper editorials that condemned those who questioned Eden's right to use military force.

*The Times* led the way. "Of course, it [public opinion] wants to avoid the use of force," the paper's editorial—written personally by its editor, William Haley— thundered. "So does everyone and we hope no one does so more than the British

Government. But that is a far cry from saying that because there seems little we can do about it, the best thing is to find excuses for, and forget, the whole business. Nations live by the vigorous defence of their interests . . . The people, in their silent way, know this better than the critics. They still want Britain great." The *Manchester Guardian* claimed that *The Times*'s editorial was an attack on the right to speak out against government in times of crisis—a similar debate restarted when the Iraqi war grew closer in early 2003—and Eden's press secretary, William Clark, played a role not unlike Alastair Campbell's in Downing Street under Blair.

"Clark worked in unison with *The Times*," Tony Shaw recalled in his brilliant and sometimes outrageously funny history of the crisis. Clark's job—and here there is a deeply uncomfortable parallel with George Bush and the UN—was "to prepare the ground for the government's brief referral of the dispute to the United Nations . . . This required a certain amount of ingenuity since Eden and the paper had hitherto dismissed the organisation as unwieldy and incapable of producing swift results." Eden had told Haley that he wanted to use the UN as an instrument solely to prove Nasser's guilt and justify force—which is pretty much what George W. Bush wanted the UN arms inspectors to do in Iraq in 2002.

And there was another 1956 *Times* editorial that could have been reprinted in late 2002 with the word "Iraq" substituted for "the canal":

> The objection to the matter being simply referred to the UN and left there has all along been, and remains, that the UN is likely to be dilatory and certain to be ineffective as a means of freeing the canal. But whatever international control is eventually brought about by negotiation or otherwise should certainly be under the aegis of the UN and the sooner the UN is officially informed of what has happened the better.

"Collusion," according to Kennett Love's monumental study of the Suez War, "was born of a marriage between Eden's anti-Nasser policy and the unwritten anti-Nasser alliance of France and Israel." Israel was to invade Sinai on 29 October, stating that its forces had attacked Palestinian Fedayeen bases and that their military operations had been necessitated "by the continuous Egyptian military attacks on citizens and on Israeli land and sea communications." Britain and France would call for a ceasefire between Israeli and Egyptian forces, a truce which—as had already been decided in advance—the Israelis would accept. Nasser, who had long convinced himself—correctly—that the three powers were conniving on the war, would refuse.

The Egyptian army retreated with some acts of bravery but much chaos across Sinai to the banks of the canal.* On 31 October the British and French air forces

---

*The Egyptian retreat may have been hastened by the Israeli execution of at least forty-nine Egyptian soldiers who had been taken prisoner in the Sinai Desert. According to Arye Biro, the Israeli officer who ordered the killings, he and his men had been stranded with the prisoners behind Egyptian lines. "I didn't have the troops to guard them," he said years later. "We had to

commenced their own long-planned operations against Egypt. Reserve Major Mustafa Kamal Murad of the Egyptian army's eastern command drove down the desert road from Cairo that afternoon. "It was a nightmare," he was to recall for me thirty years later. "There was mile after mile of Egyptian armour on the road and every truck and armoured vehicle was burning after the air attacks. I was terribly shocked. The poor farmers were walking onto the road and screaming at us: 'You have brought this destruction on our land, you devils.'" Murad found Ismailia calm but milling with frightened and disillusioned troops from Sinai. "Morale was very bad, our soldiers had swollen feet from walking in the desert and were putting fear into the army defenders and our home guard, the 'National Guard.' All withdrawing armies tell lies to their friends. We had to send them down to Cairo quickly."

Murad found himself in the old British consulate in Ismailia, which now served as emergency Egyptian military headquarters, an institution, Murad was to remember, "which was a great pleasure to our officers as the British had left behind them crates of whisky, champagne, beer and cognac." Egyptian troops were looting civilian homes in the city—until their commander, Kamaledin Hussein, ordered all thieves to be shot on sight. Under the strain of command, some Egyptian officers went to pieces. "Colonel Abdul Aziz Selim was told to defend the outskirts of Ismailia and he shouted at Hussein: 'My battalion will be completely annihilated by the British air force,'" Murad recalled. "I urged Hussein to send him back to Cairo. But in the morning, Selim's batman came to us and said there was blood seeping from beneath the colonel's door. When we opened the door, we found Selim had shot himself on my desk."

Murad's recollection of the RAF bombing at Ismailia was still so vivid when I met him in 1986 that as he recalled the violence his hand repeatedly swooped through the air to illustrate the raids on the airfields around Ismailia. "I was astonished that they attacked no civilians. They were very accurate. When I got to the airfields after the raids, I found that our young soldiers had disobeyed their orders to retreat to the slit trenches under air attack. Instead, they had stayed at their anti-aircraft guns and kept on firing. The RAF rockets were so accurate that they always hit the guns. The rockets cut our men in half. I would find their legs and the trunks of their bodies on the guns: their top half would be missing."

On 5 November 1956, the Anglo-French force landed around Port Said, many of them carried in a fleet of ageing warships from Cyprus. At Gamil airfield 780 British paratroopers were dropped, and 470 French paratroopers landed at two bridges on the canal at Raswa. In the early hours, Murad was sleeping fitfully on a sofa at his Ismailia headquarters when he was awoken by a tall man standing

---

move on to Ras Sudar. So I decided to liquidate them." The murders only came to light in 1995 after the publication of an internal Israeli army research paper, *Political and Military Aspects of the 1956 Sinai War.* The soldiers responsible for the executions were members of Israeli Parachute Battalion 890, commanded by Rafael Eytan, who was later to become chief of staff of the Israeli army and a Knesset member for the right-wing Tsomet party. The Egyptians initially censored the revelations from Cairo newspapers but later demanded an explanation from the Israeli government.

beside him. "I stood up and was astonished to find it was Gamal Abdel Nasser. He was in a very nicely fitted civilian suit. I said to him: 'Welcome, Mr. President— but what are you doing here? You should be in Cairo. The roads are very danger- ous because the British are bombing them.' He said he was going to Port Said. I said: 'Forget about it, sir, you must return to Cairo at once because the British paratroopers are expected to land at Port Said in a few hours.' Nasser asked for a room to rest in and I put him in the British consul's bedroom. A few hours later, the British were already in Port Said, fighting for the Gamil airbase."

Major Murad may thus have prevented Anthony Eden capturing the Egyptian he so hated. Nasser, wearing fresh clothes and smelling of eau de cologne, did return to Cairo—but not before Murad had put an important question to him. "I asked Nasser: 'Is there an agreement with the Russians for military aid?' He said there was not. I asked: 'Not even a gentleman's agreement?' He said: 'No.' I was furious. I thought that this man must be mad in challenging all three forces at once. I said: 'Sir, we shall do our best but it will be a miracle if we can stand up against the British, the French and Israel.' He just replied: '*Rabina ma'ana*'—May God be with us. Then he left."

Captain Nasr was living in his apartment in Jumhuriya Street in Port Said when the British landed. "We heard the firing—everyone was told to stay in their homes for twenty-four hours. The first thing I saw when I went outside was a neighbour of mine, Adel Mandour, lying dead in the street. He was a member of the National Guard. He had been shot by a British soldier and he was lying face-down in the gutter with his arms spread out. I remember his mother walked out of her house and just silently lifted him up and took him into her home." At first the dead were buried privately, but dozens of bodies, most of them civilians, were placed in a mass grave near the airfield. The British stormed an Egyptian police station that held out under intense fire and killed almost all the policemen inside. A British general estimated that almost a thousand Egyptians died in the city, a figure at vari- ance with Major Murad's high opinion of RAF bomb-aiming. Several civilians were massacred by French paratroopers, one of whom was to write later that he and his colleagues shot dead a group of innocent fishermen because the French had been ordered to take no prisoners. The paratroopers shot others in the face at point- blank range when they pleaded for mercy in the canal.

"The British were well behaved—they did not steal anything when they bil- leted men in my apartment," Captain Nasr said. "But the French behaviour was very different. They treated people very badly. Maybe it was their experience of Algeria but I think they were angry because they thought the canal belonged to them and that they had a right to take it back." Nasser was publicly supporting the FLN struggle in Algeria.

At Gamil airport, a young Egyptian guerrilla, Mohamed Mahran Othman, was seized by the British, who wanted to know the whereabouts of Egyptian arms stores. He later claimed that his eyes were cut out by British military doctors in Cyprus when he refused to divulge information about arms dumps or broadcast propaganda for the allies from a radio station in Cyprus. There is no independent testimony to this, although in 1997 I met Othman, whose eyes had clearly been taken from their sockets. He claimed then that the British were also taking revenge for the wounding of a military doctor during his descent onto Gamil airfield. A Parachute Regiment doctor, Lieutenant A. J. M. "Sandy" Cavenagh, the 3rd Parachute Regiment battalion medical officer, was hit in the left eye by shrapnel during his descent on Gamil, although he told me forty years later that he knew nothing of the blind Egyptian's claims; ironically, Cavenagh had many years later noticed Othman working as a guide in the Port Said military museum, but did not speak to him. A gentle and kindly man, Cavenagh, who was to write a graphic account of the landings, was praised by his commander for continuing, while seriously wounded, to treat his comrades for five more hours.*

The archives contain evidence of the racism that marked the former imperial army. The poorest area of Port Said was marked on British maps as "Wog-Town," while a note about propaganda from "Allied Forces Headquarters" on 1 December 1956 refers to the "malicious mentality" of Arabs. The British prevented reporters from reaching Port Said until days after the battle, but a week after the ceasefire, reporter Alex Efthyvoulos was to see bodies still unburied in Port Said.

The Egyptian commander of Ismailia, Kamaledin Hussein, was outraged when his opposite number in Port Said, Brigadier General Salahedin Moguy, came through on a surviving telephone line. "He told us he had agreed on a six-hour ceasefire with a British general to collect the dead and wounded," Murad recalled. "Hussein shouted back: 'How dare you meet an English general without my orders?' I heard Moguy replying: 'I am the commanding officer in Port Said and it is my decision.' Then he hung up."

Early on the morning of 7 November, Murad was plodding gingerly up a narrow canal road north of Ismailia with his sub-machine gun on his back. He had just passed a fishing village called Jisr el-Hind when he saw what he thought were two red poppies moving in the long grass to his right. "Then I could see these two boys, both British paratroopers in red berets, lying in the long grass watching me. They were pointing their guns towards me from about seventy yards away. They pulled

---

*British military papers of the time—many others, like Eden's records of the secret Sèvres meeting, were deliberately destroyed in the months after Suez—make no reference to Othman's allegation, although I spent three weeks at the Public Record Office in London trying to find some record of the interrogation of prisoners. One file showed that intelligence officers of the British 2nd Corps reported after the Port Said battle that "interrogation of Prisoners of War in Port Said has not produced the full result which was hoped for. No HQs have been located . . ." Oddly, the files from Port Said contain no entries for the dates 6 to 8 November 1956. PRO archives did show that the International Red Cross in Egypt asked if any prisoners had been transferred to Cyprus. The War Office was also questioned as to whether Egyptians had been asked to speak over a British propaganda radio station in Cyprus. "We have not extended our enquiries to the radio station which operated from Cyprus under the name of the Voice of Britain during the Suez landings," a British official responded unhelpfully, "but although you may like to ask the Ministry of Defence to follow this line of enquiry I do not think it is likely to be fruitful." Sefton Delmer, who was the *Daily Express* correspondent in prewar Berlin and the director of a wartime "black" German propaganda station during the Second World War, was flown to Cyprus to help operate this mysterious radio station.

out white handkerchiefs and tied them on their bayonets and one of them shouted: 'Hallo.' I kept my hand away from my gun and said 'Hallo' back to him. In front of me, I could see British tanks and some soldiers pulling barbed wire across the road . . . These two boys could have shot me so I had this feeling that there must have been a ceasefire. I kept thinking: 'How stupid the British commander was to have stopped here, only thirty-eight kilometres south of Port Said. There is nothing in front of him—he could be in Cairo in only a few hours.'"

But the British moved no farther. Murad had just stumbled into the very end of the British army's very last imperial adventure. It took him some time to realise that the Americans had intervened and that an era had also come to an end. President Eisenhower had been furious when he learned that Israel's invasion had been set up by the Allies—mainly by the French—and, contrary to the Bush doctrine of 2003, reserved America's right to condemn the whole invasion. Eisenhower's famous remark to Foster Dulles—that his job was to go to London and tell Eden: "Whoa, boy"—showed just how close he was to cutting off all support for Britain. By 28 November, the British foreign secretary, Selwyn Lloyd, was telling the Cabinet that "if we withdrew the Anglo–French troops as rapidly as was practicable, we should regain the sympathy of the U.S. government."

Questioned by the 1922 Committee about the collusion of Israel, Britain and France, Eden said that "some [half-truths]—and if they existed at all, they were not serious or many in number—were necessary, and always are in this sort of operation which demands extreme secrecy." On 20 December he lied to the House of Commons. "I want to say this on the question of foreknowledge and to say it quite bluntly to the House, that there was not foreknowledge that Israel would attack Egypt—there was not. But there was something else. There was—we knew it perfectly well—a risk of it, and, in the event of the risk of it, certain discussions and conversations took place, as, I think, was absolutely right, and as, I think, anybody would do." In the aftermath of the illegal 2003 invasion of Iraq, Tony Blair could not have bettered that. Eden was a sick man—he had just suffered an operation in which a surgeon had accidentally left a medical instrument inside him—and began, as W. Scott Lucas recalls in his account of the drama, to sound out colleagues about his future. On 9 January 1957 he told Harold Macmillan that his doctors had warned him his health was in danger if he stayed in office and that "there was no way out." Macmillan was stunned. "I could hardly believe that this was to be the end of the public life of a man so comparatively young, and with so much still to give," he wrote. "We sat for some little time together. We spoke a few words about the First War, in which we had both served and suffered . . . I can see him now on that sad winter afternoon, still looking so youthful, so gay, so debonair—the representation of all that was best of the youth that had served in the 1914–18 war."

Eden's resignation marked the end of the last attempt Britain would ever make to establish, as Scott Lucas writes, "that Britain did not require Washington's endorsement to defend her interests." Henceforth, Britain would be the servant of U.S. policy. It would be American policy to act unilaterally to "defend" the Middle

East. The 1957 Eisenhower doctrine led inexorably to the hegemony the United States now exercises over the world. Now Washington might need Britain's endorsement to defend her interests—at least in an invasion of Iraq, although even that was doubtful.

In Egypt, Nasser ruled to ever greater acclaim, even surviving his appalling defeat at Israel's hands in the 1967 Arab–Israeli war, suppressing all domestic opposition with executions and torture. Suez distracted the world's attention as Russian troops stormed into Budapest on 30 October 1956 and crushed its revolution. Some never forgave the Labour leader Hugh Gaitskell for his November broadcast in which he labelled British troops as aggressors—unlike in 2003, there was at least a serious political opposition to the government in the House of Commons—while *The Observer* lost readers it never recovered for opposing the war.

"It was all a gamble," ex-Major Murad was to say thirty years later. "Nasser was very lucky that the Americans intervened and asked the British to cease fire and evacuate—the Americans wanted to replace the Europeans as the big power in the Middle East. But it was luck. If I had been in Nasser's place, I would not have done this because there was no agreement with Russia. The war was not an equal match—it was not even a war. It was an action taken against the nationalisation of the canal to destroy Nasser's power. We realised this at the time."

But the last word should go to Eden just after the British landed at Suez. "If we had allowed things to drift," he said, "everything would have gone from bad to worse. Nasser would have become a kind of Muslim Mussolini, and our friends in Iraq, Jordan, Saudi Arabia and even Iran would gradually have been brought down. His efforts would have spread westwards, and Libya and North Africa would have been brought under his control." We would hear all this again in 2002 and 2003, even if Eden's hatred for Nasser had some limits. "I have never thought Nasser a Hitler," Eden was to write. ". . . But the parallel with Mussolini is close." Guy Mollet, the French premier, referred to Nasser as an "apprentice dictator." He and Eden were both possessed by what Mollet himself called "the anti-Munich complex."


IN BRITAIN IN 2003, newspapers screamed their arguments for war. In America they argued with books, heaps of them, coffee-table books recalling the attacks of 11 September 2001, paperbacks pleading for peace in Iraq, great tomes weighed down with footnotes extolling the virtues of "regime change" in the Middle East. In New York, the publishers as well as the media went to war. You only had to read the titles of the 9/11 books—many of them massive photo-memorial volumes—on America's news-stands: *Above Hallowed Ground, So Others Might Live, Strong of Heart, What We Saw, The Final Frontier, A Fury for God, The Shadow of Swords* . . . No wonder American television networks could take the next war for granted. "Showdown in Iraq," CNN announced. "Prepared for War." No one questioned its certainty. I protested during a live radio show in the United States in January that the participants—including an Israeli academic, a former Irish UN officer, a Vietnam veteran, Tony Benn and others—were asked to debate not whether there should be a war in Iraq, but what the consequences of that war would be. The inevitability of conflict had been written into the script.

The most recent and most meretricious contribution to this utterly fraudulent "debate" in the United States had been *The Threatening Storm: The Case for Invading Iraq,* by Kenneth Pollack, a former CIA spook and an ex-director for "Gulf affairs" at the National Security Council. It was the book that all America was supposed to be talking about and its title—*The Threatening Storm* was, of course, a copy-cat version of *The Gathering Storm,* the first volume of Winston Churchill's Second World War history—told you all you needed to know about the contents. Just as in 2002 George W. Bush tried to dress himself up as Churchill fighting appeasement, so Pollack twice pretended that the world was confronting the same dilemma that faced Britain and France in 1938. The Allies could have won in a year, he claimed, if they had gone to war against Hitler then. The fact that Britain and France, though numerically stronger in troops, were weaker in modern armaments—whereas the United States could now crush Saddam's forces in less than a month—was not allowed to interfere with this specious argument. Pollack accepted that Saddam was not Hitler, but once more Saddam was dressed in Hitler's clothes—just as Nasser was the Mussolini of the Nile during the Suez crisis of 1956—and anyone who opposed war was, by quiet extension, a Nazi sympathiser.

Before and immediately after the start of the Second World War—the real Second World War, that is—British publishers deployed their authors to support the conflict. Victor Gollancz was a tireless defender of British freedoms. By 1941, we were publishing the bestselling *Last Train from Berlin* by Howard K. Smith, the brilliant American foreign correspondent's desperate account of life in Nazi Germany before the United States entered the conflict. But these were often works of literature as well as ideology. What happened in the United States in the weeks before the invasion of Iraq was something quite different: a mawkish, cheapskate attempt to push Americans into war on the back of the hushed, reverent, unimpeachable sacrifice of September 11th.

Removing Saddam "would sever the 'linkage' between the Iraq issue and the Arab–Israeli conflict," Pollack wrote. In the long term, "it would remove an important source of anti-Americanism" and produce a positive outcome "if the United States were to build a strong, prosperous, and inclusive new Iraqi state . . . a model of what a modern Arab state could be." Pollack's argument for war was breathtakingly amoral. War would be the right decision, it seemed, not because it was morally necessary but because we would win. War was now a viable and potentially successful policy option. It would free up Washington's "foreign policy agenda," presumably allowing it to invade another country or two where American vital interests could be discovered. And that all-important "linkage" between Iraq and the Palestinian–Israeli war would be over. This theme recurs several times in Pollack's text, and the narrative—in essence an Israeli one—is quite simple: deprived of the support of one of the Arab world's most powerful nations, the

Palestinians would be further weakened in their struggle against Israeli occupation. Pollack referred to the Palestinians' "vicious terrorist campaign" without the slightest criticism of Israel. He talked about "weekly terrorist attacks followed by Israeli responses," the standard Israeli version of the conflict. The author regarded America's bias in favour of Israel as nothing more than an Arab "belief." Needless to say, there was no mention of former UN weapons inspector and ex-Marine Major Scott Ritter, whose own tiny volume opposing the war—*War on Iraq: What Team Bush Doesn't Want You to Know*—was a mere ninety-six-page flea-bite on the back of the pro-war literature churned out in Washington.

As this material came off the presses, the latest fantasies were seeping out of Washington and London. Stories of further attacks—on the Lincoln Tunnel and the Golden Gate bridge in the States—were mixed with all the scare stories Britons had been fed over previous weeks: smallpox, dirty bombs, attacks on hotels and shopping malls, a chemical attack on the Tube, the poisoning of water supplies, "postcard target" attacks on Big Ben and Canary Wharf, the procurement of 5,000 body bags, 120,000 decontamination suits, survival classes for seven-year-old schoolchildren, new laws to quarantine Britons in the event of a biological attack. There seemed no end to this government terrorism. Did they want Osama bin Laden to win? Or was this merely part of the countdown to war on Iraq, the essential drug of fear that we all needed to support Messrs. Bush and Blair?

For these stories provided a vital underpinning to pro-war literature. In the United States, the intellectuals' support for war in fact went far further than Kenneth Pollack's insipid book. In *Foreign Affairs* magazine, for example, Johns Hopkins University Professor Fouad Ajami, constantly disparaging the Arab world for its backwardness, its lack of democracy, its supposed use of the Israeli–Palestinian conflict "as an alibi for yet more self-pity and rage," announced, "with sobering caution . . . that a war will have to be waged." And—here was the line for fantasy-lovers to remember—"any fallout of war is certain to be dwarfed by the terrible consequences of America's walking right up to the edge of war and then stepping back, letting the Iraqi dictator work out the terms of another reprieve."

The logic of this was truly awesome. America had to go to war because it had threatened to do so. Its own threat was now to become the cause of war; peace would therefore be more terrible than war. As New York St. Lawrence University Professor Laura Rediehs remarked in a perceptive essay in *Collateral Language*, one of the best books on the linguistics of this conflict, in a Cosmic Battle between Good and Evil of the kind Bush imagined, the taking of innocent lives by us would be justified because we were good. But when the other side killed innocents, it was unjustified because the other side was evil. "What makes the deaths of innocent people bad, then, is not their actual deaths, but the attitudes and feelings of those who killed them." By far the most moving contribution towards the anti-war campaign in the same book was that of Amber Amundson, whose husband Craig of the U.S. Army was killed in the attack on the Pentagon on 11 September 2001. "Will the invasion of Iraq really bring us to a more peaceful global community?" she asked her nation's leaders. ". . . If you choose to respond to this incomprehensible brutality [of September 11] by perpetuating violence against other human beings, you may not do so in the name of justice for my husband."

Obsessed with their own demonisation of Saddam Hussein, both Bush and Blair now constantly reminded us of the price of appeasement. Bush thought he was the Churchill of America, refusing the appeasement of Saddam. It seemed as if the Second World War would be for ever the excuse, the warning, the justification, the utterly dishonest paradigm for every folly, for every bloodbath we initiated. The Second World War was an obscenity. It ended in 1945. Yet you might have thought, in early 2003, that Hitler was alive in his Berlin bunker. The Luftwaffe, if you listened to Bush and Blair, was still taking off from Cap Gris Nez, ready to bombard London after years of appeasement of Nazi Germany. Yet it was our air forces that were about to strike from Iraq's "Cap Gris Nez"—Kuwait and Qatar and Saudi Arabia and Turkey and assorted aircraft carriers—to pulverise not London but Baghdad. What was it about our Lilliputian leaders that they dared to trivialise the massive sacrifice of the Second World War for their squalid conflict against Iraq, elevating Saddam's tinpot dictatorship into the epic historical tragedy of the 1939–45 war?*

---

*By mid-January of 2003, the U.S. ambassador to the European Union, Rockwell Schnabel, was also comparing Saddam to Hitler. "You had Hitler in Europe and no one really did anything about him," Schnabel lectured the Europeans in Brussels. "We knew he could be dangerous but nothing was done. The same type of person [is in Baghdad] and it's there that our concern lies." Mr. Schnabel ended this infantile speech by adding that "this has nothing to do with oil."

History, said Blair—who had never seen a war in his life—had important lessons for this crisis. Neville Chamberlain's efforts to appease Hitler were the work of "a good man who made the wrong decision," he told us. President Jacques Chirac, defending France from charges of political cowardice, recalled that when his country wanted to take action in the Balkans, it found itself alone, recalling "the West's appeasement of Hitler." Provoked by a promised French veto at the UN Security Council, the *New York Post* printed a photograph of American soldiers' graves in Normandy. "They died for France but France has forgotten," the paper announced—as if liberation from the Nazis in 1944 involved France's surrender of free speech fifty-eight years later. "Where are the French now, as Americans prepare to put their soldiers on the line to fight today's Hitler, Saddam Hussein?" the *Post* asked.

Saddam himself joined in these contemptible parallels. In an interview with the British elder statesman Tony Benn, the "Hitler of Baghdad" advised his British visitor that "if the Iraqis are subjected to aggression or humiliation, they would fight bravely—just as the British in the Second World War had defended their country in their own way." Saddam's prime minister, Tariq Aziz, later told the Italian newspaper *Corriere della Sera* that "the truth is that Bush is dismantling the United Nations, like the Third Reich in the 1930s nullified the League of Nations."

And so it went, on and on. Barbara Amiel, wife of the former *Daily Telegraph* owner Conrad Black, told readers of the Canadian *Maclean's* magazine that "destroying Saddam's regime will genuinely be a liberation for the people of Iraq, and when it happens the liberators will be greeted with the same extraordinary joy that met the Allies in France in 1945 . . ." The "liberators" of Iraq were not, of course, greeted with such joy—and France was liberated in 1944, not 1945. But no matter. We had to forget that one of those nations that wanted to use its veto in the UN Security Council—Russia—lost up to 30 million citizens in its battle against the Nazis. Yet even the BBC was by early 2003 talking about the "Allies" who would invade Iraq. When Bush, Blair and Spanish prime minister Aznar met in the Azores on 16 March, the Second World War symbolism reached its apogee. The Big Three—Churchill, Roosevelt and Stalin—met in Yalta to decide the future of the post-Nazi world. Now the Little Three were meeting on an obscure Portuguese island to decide the future of the Middle East.

How could a sane human being react to this pitiful stuff? One of the principal nations that "did nothing about Hitler" was the United States, which enjoyed a profitable period of neutrality in 1939 and 1940 and most of 1941 until it was attacked by the Japanese at Pearl Harbor. And when the Churchill–Roosevelt alliance decided that it would only accept Germany's unconditional surrender— a demand that shocked even Churchill when Roosevelt suddenly announced the terms at Casablanca—Hitler was doomed.

Not so Saddam, it seemed. For Donald Rumsfeld offered the Hitler of Baghdad a way out: exile, with a suitcase full of cash and an armful of family members, if that is what he wished. I couldn't recall Churchill or Roosevelt ever suggesting that the Führer should receive a golden handshake. Saddam is Hitler—but then suddenly he's not. He is—said *The New York Times*—to be put before a war crimes tribunal. But then he's not. He could scoot off to Saudi Arabia or Latin America, if he took Rumsfeld at his word. In other words, he wasn't Hitler after all.

What, I kept asking, happens after the invasion? On 26 January I asked our *Independent on Sunday* readers what we planned to do when Iraqis demanded our withdrawal from their country. "For we will be in occupation of a foreign land. We will be in occupation of Iraq as surely as Israel is in occupation of the West Bank and Gaza. And with Saddam gone, the way is open for Osama bin Laden to demand the liberation of Iraq as another of his objectives. How easily he will be able to slot Iraq into the fabric of American occupation across the Gulf. Are we then ready to fight al-Qaeda in Iraq as well as in Afghanistan and Pakistan and countless other countries? It seems that the peoples of the Middle East—and the West—realise these dangers, but that their leaders do not, or do not want to."

Travelling to the United States more than once a month, visiting Britain on the penultimate weekend of January 2003, moving around the Middle East, I had never been so struck by the absolute, unwavering determination of so many Arabs and Europeans and Americans to oppose a war. Did Tony Blair really need that gloriously pertinacious student at the British Labour party meeting on 24 January to prove to him what so many Britons felt: that this proposed Iraqi war was a lie, that the reasons for this conflict had nothing to do with weapons of mass destruction, that Blair had no business following Bush into the war? Never before had I received so many readers' letters expressing exactly the same sentiment: that somehow—because of Labour's huge majority, because of the Tory party's effective disappearance as an opposition, because of parliamentary cynicism—British democracy was not permitting British people to stop a war for which most of them had nothing but contempt. From Washington's pathetic attempt to link Saddam to al-Qaeda, to Blair's childish "dossier" on weapons of mass destruction, to the whole tragic farce of UN inspections, people were no longer fooled. The denials that this war had anything to do with oil were as unconvincing as Colin Powell's claim in January 2003 that Iraq's oil would be held in "trusteeship" for the Iraqi

---

Everyone, it seemed, suffered under Second World War delusions. In his second interview with me, in 1996, bin Laden himself drew a parallel between the French resistance to German occupation and Muslim resistance to U.S. "occupation" in the Gulf.

people. "Trusteeship" was exactly what the League of Nations offered the Levant when it allowed Britain and France to adopt mandates in Palestine and Transjordan and Syria and Lebanon after the First World War. Who will run the oil wells and explore Iraqi oil reserves during this generous period of "trusteeship"? I asked in my paper. American companies, perhaps?

Take the inspectors. George W. Bush and Dick Cheney and Donald Rumsfeld and now, alas, Colin Powell didn't want to give the inspectors more time. But why not, for God's sake? On 12 September 2002, when Bush, wallowing in the nostalgia of the 11 September 2001 crimes against humanity, demanded that the UN act, he insisted that it send its inspectors back to Iraq. They should resume and complete their work. Bush, of course, was hoping that Iraq would refuse to let the inspectors return. Horrifically, Iraq welcomed the UN. Bush was waiting for the inspectors to find hidden weapons. Terrifyingly, they found none. Now they were still looking. And that was the last thing Bush wanted. Bush said he was "sick and tired" of Saddam's trickery—when what he meant was that he was sick and tired of waiting for the UN inspectors to find the weapons that would allow America to go to war. He who wanted so much in September 2002 to get the inspectors back to work, now, in January 2003, didn't want them to work at all. "Time is running out," Bush said. He was talking about Saddam but he was actually referring to the UN inspectors, in fact to the whole UN institution so laboriously established after the Second World War on the initiative of his own country.

The only other nation pushing for war—save for the ever-grateful Kuwait—was Israel. Here are the words of Zalman Shoval, Israeli prime minister Ariel Sharon's foreign affairs adviser, in January 2003. Israel, he said, would "pay dearly" for a "long deferral" of an American strike on Iraq. "If the attack were to be postponed on political rather than military grounds, we will have every reason in Israel to fear that Saddam Hussein uses this delay to develop non-conventional weapons." As long as Saddam was not sidelined, Shoval said, it would be difficult to convince the Palestinian leadership that violence didn't pay and that it should be replaced by a new administration. Arafat would use such a delay "to intensify terrorist attacks." So now the savage Israeli–Palestinian war could only—according to the Shoval thesis—be resolved if America invaded Iraq; terrorism could not be ended in Israel until the United States destroyed Saddam. There could be no regime change for the Palestinians until there was regime change in Baghdad. And by going along with the Bush drive to war, Blair was, indirectly, supporting Israel's occupation of the West Bank and Gaza (since Israel still claimed to be fighting America's "war on terror" against Arafat).

Saddam was not unlike the Dear Leader of North Korea, Kim Jong Il, the nuclear megalomaniac with whom the Americans had just been having "excellent" discussions but who didn't have oil. How typical of Saddam to send Ali "Chemical" Majid—the war criminal who gassed the Kurds of Halabja—to tour Arab capitals, to sit with President Bashar Assad of Syria and President Emile Lahoud of Lebanon as if he never ordered the slaughter of women and children. But Bush and Blair said nothing about Majid's tour—either because they did not want to offend the Arab leaders who met him or because the link between gas, war crimes and Washington's original support for Saddam was still a sensitive issue.*

On 4 February 2003 I was in Austin, Texas, waiting to fly up to New York to watch Colin Powell convince the UN Security Council that Washington's lies about weapons of mass destruction were not lies at all but honest-to-God truth. But there was one sure bet about the Powell statement, I wrote that day: he wouldn't be talking about Afghanistan. For since the Afghan war was the "successful" role model for America's forthcoming imperial adventure across the Middle East, the near-collapse of peace in this savage land and the steady erosion of U.S. forces in Afghanistan—the nightly attacks on American and other international troops, the anarchy in the cities outside Kabul, the warlordism and drug trafficking and steadily increasing toll of murders—were unmentionables, a narrative constantly erased from the consciousness of Americans who were now sending their young men and women by the tens of thousands to stage another "success" story. This article, I wrote:

> is written in President George Bush's home state of Texas, where the flags fly at half-staff for the *Columbia* crew, where the dispatch to the Middle East of further troops of the 108th Air Defence Artillery Brigade from Fort Bliss and the imminent deployment from Holloman Air Force Base in neighbouring New Mexico of undisclosed numbers of F-117 Nighthawk stealth bombers earned a mere 78-word down-page inside "nib" report in the local Austin newspaper.
>
> Only in New York and Washington do the neo-conservative pundits suggest—obscenely—that the death of the *Columbia* crew may well have heightened America's resolve and "unity" to support the Bush adventure in Iraq. A few months ago, we would still have been asked to believe that the post-war "success" in Afghanistan augured well for the post-war success in Iraq.
>
> So let's break through the curtain for a while and peer into the fastness of the land that both President Bush and Prime Minister Blair promised not to forget. Hands up those who know that al-Qaeda has a radio station operating *inside* Afghanistan which calls for a holy war against America? It's true. Hands up again anyone who can guess how many of the daily weapons caches discovered by U.S. troops in the country have been brought into Afghanistan *since* America's "successful" war? Answer: up to 25 per cent.

---

*And all the while, the American media continued their servile support for the Bush administration. As I reported in my own paper on 26 January, we were now being deluged with yet more threats from Washington about "states that sponsor terror." "Take Eric Schmitt in *The New York Times* a week ago. He wrote a story about America's decision to 'confront countries that sponsor terrorism.' And his sources? 'Senior defence officials,' 'administration officials,' 'some American intelligence officials,' 'the officials,' 'officials,' 'military officials,' 'terrorist experts' and 'defence officials.'" Why not, I asked, "just let the Pentagon write its own reports in *The New York Times*?"

Have any U.S. troops retreated from their positions along the Afghan–Pakistan border? None, you may say. And you would be wrong. At least five positions, according to Pakistani sources on the other side of the frontier, only one of which has been admitted by U.S. forces. On December 11th, U.S. troops abandoned their military outpost at Lwara after nightly rocket attacks which destroyed several American military vehicles. Their Afghan allies were driven out only days later and al-Qaeda fighters then stormed the U.S. compound and burned it to the ground.

It's a sign of just how seriously America's mission in Afghanistan is collapsing that the majestically conservative *Wall Street Journal*— normally a beacon of imperial and Israeli policy in the Middle East and South-west Asia—has devoted a long and intriguing article to the American retreat, though of course that's not what the paper calls it.

"Soldiers still confront an invisible enemy," is the title of Marc Kaufman's first-class investigation, a headline almost identical to one which appeared over a Fisk story a year or so after Russia's invasion of Afghanistan in 1979–80. The soldiers in my dispatch, of course, were Russian. Indeed, just as I recall the Soviet officer who told us all at Bagram air base that the *"mujahedin* terrorism remnants" were all that was left of the West's conspiracy against peace-loving (and Communist) Afghans, so I observed the American spokesmen—yes, at the very same Bagram air base—who today cheerfully assert that al-Qaeda "remnants" are all that are left of bin Laden's legions.

Training camps have been set up inside Afghanistan again, not—as the Americans think—by the recalcitrant forces of Gulbuddin Hekmatyar's anti-American Afghans, but by Arabs. The latest battle between U.S. forces and enemy "remnants" near Spin Boldak in Kandahar province involved further Arab fighters, as my colleague Phil Reeves reported. Hekmatyar's Hezb-i-Islami forces have been "forging ties" with al-Qaeda and the Taliban; which is exactly what the *mujahedin* "terrorist remnants" did among themselves in the winter of 1980, a year after the Soviet invasion.

An American killed by a newly placed landmine in Khost; 16 civilians blown up by another newly placed mine outside Kandahar; grenades tossed at Americans or international troops in Kabul; further reports of rape and female classroom burnings in the north of Afghanistan—all these events are now acquiring the stale status of yesterday's war.

So be sure that Colin Powell will not be boasting to the Security Council today of America's success in the intelligence war in Afghanistan. It's one thing to claim that satellite pictures show chemicals being transported around Iraq, or that telephone intercepts prove Iraqi scientists are still at their dirty work; quite another to explain how all the "communications chatter" intercepts which the U.S. supposedly picked up in Afghanistan proved nothing. As far as Afghanistan is concerned, you can quote Basil Fawlty: "Whatever you do, don't mention the war."

The 5th of February 2003 was a snow-blasted day in New York, the steam whirling out of the road covers, the U.S. Secret Servicemen—helpfully wearing jackets with "Secret Service" printed on them—hugging themselves outside the fustian, asbestos-packed UN headquarters on the East River. Exhausted though I was after travelling thousands of miles around the United States, the idea of watching Secretary of State Colin Powell—or General Powell, as he was now being reverently re-dubbed in some American newspapers—make his last pitch for war before the Security Council was an experience not to be missed. In a few days, I would be in Baghdad to watch the start of this frivolous, demented conflict. Powell's appearance at the Security Council was the essential prologue to the tragedy—or tragicomedy if one could contain one's anger—the appearance of the Attendant Lord who would explain the story of the drama, the Horatio to the increasingly unstable Hamlet in the White House.

There was an almost macabre opening to the play when General Powell arrived at the Security Council, cheek-kissing the delegates and winding his great arms around them. CIA director George Tenet stood behind Powell, chunky, aggressive but obedient, just a little bit lip-biting, an Edward G. Robinson who must have convinced himself that the more dubious of his information was buried beneath an adequate depth of moral fury and fear to be safely concealed. Just like Bush's appearance at the General Assembly the previous September, you needed to be in the Security Council to see what the television cameras missed. There was a wonderful moment when the little British home secretary Jack Straw entered the chamber through the far right-hand door in a massive power suit, his double-breasted jacket apparently wrapping itself twice around Britain's most famous ex-Trot. He stood for a moment with a kind of semi-benign smile on his uplifted face, his nose in the air as if sniffing for power. Then he saw Powell and his smile opened like an umbrella as his small feet, scuttling beneath him, propelled him across the stage and into the arms of Powell for his big American hug.

You might have thought that the whole chamber, with its toothy smiles and constant handshakes, contained a room full of men celebrating peace rather than war. Alas, not so. These elegantly dressed statesmen were constructing the framework that would allow them to kill quite a lot of people—some of them Saddam's little monsters no doubt, but most of them innocent. When Powell rose to give his terror-talk, he did so with a slow athleticism, the world-weary warrior whose patience had at last reached its end.

But it was an old movie. I should have guessed. Sources, foreign intelligence sources, "our sources," defectors, sources, sources, sources. Ah, to be so well-sourced when you have already taken the decision to go to war. The Powell presentation sounded like one of those government-inspired reports on the front page of *The New York Times*—where it was, of course, treated with due reverence next day. It was a bit like heating up old soup. Hadn't we heard most of this stuff before? Should one trust the man? General Powell, I mean, not Saddam. Certainly we didn't trust Saddam, but Powell's speech was a mixture of awesomely funny recordings of Iraqi Republican Guard telephone intercepts à la Samuel Beckett that just might have been some terrifying proof that Saddam really was conning the UN inspectors again, and ancient material on the Monster of Baghdad's all too well known record of beastliness.

If only we could have heard the Arabic for the State Department's translation of "OK buddy"—"Consider it done, sir"—this from the Republican Guard's "Captain Ibrahim," for heaven's sake. The dinky illustrations of mobile Iraqi bio-labs whose lorries and railway trucks were in such perfect condition suggested the Pentagon didn't have much idea of the dilapidated state of Saddam's railway system, let alone his army. It was when we went back to Halabja and human rights abuses and all Saddam's indubitable sins, as recorded by the discredited UNSCOM team, that we started eating the old soup again. Jack Straw may have thought all this "the most powerful and authoritative case" for war—his ill-considered opinion afterwards—but when we were forced to listen to the Iraqi officer corps communicating by phone—"Yeah," "Yeah," "Yeah?," "Yeah . . ."—it was impossible not to ask oneself if Colin Powell had really considered the effect this would have on the outside world. From time to time, the words "Iraq: Failing to Disarm—Denial and Deception" appeared on the giant video screen behind General Powell. Was this a CNN logo? some of us wondered. But no, it was the work of CNN's sister channel, the U.S. Department of State.

Because Colin Powell was supposed to be the good cop to the Bush–Rumsfeld bad cop routine, one wanted to believe him. The Iraqi officer's telephone-tapped order to his subordinate—"Remove 'nerve agents' whenever it comes up in the wireless instructions"—seemed to indicate that the Americans had indeed spotted a nasty new line in Iraqi deception. But a dramatic picture of a pilotless Iraqi aircraft capable of spraying poison chemicals turned out to be the imaginative work of a Pentagon artist. And when Secretary Powell started talking about "decades" of contact between Saddam and al-Qaeda, things went wrong for the "General." Al-Qaeda only came into existence in 2000, since bin Laden—"decades" ago— was working against the Russians for the CIA, whose present-day director was sitting grave-faced behind Mr. Powell. It was the United States which had enjoyed at least a "decade" of contacts with Saddam.

Powell's new version of his President's State of the Union lie—that the "scientists" interviewed by UN inspectors had been Iraqi intelligence agents in disguise—was singularly unimpressive. The UN talked to Iraqi scientists during their inspection tours, the new version went, but the Iraqis were posing for the real nuclear and bio boys whom the UN wanted to talk to. General Powell said America was sharing its information with the UN inspectors, but it was clear already that much of what he had to say about alleged new weapons development—the decontamination truck at the Taji chemical munitions factory, for example, the "cleaning" of the Ibn al-Haythem ballistic missile factory on 25 November—had not been given to the UN at the time. Why wasn't this intelligence information given to the inspectors months ago? Didn't General Powell's beloved UN Resolution 1441 demand that all such intelligence information should be given to Hans Blix and his lads immediately? Were the Americans, perhaps, not being "proactive" enough? Or did they realise that if the UN inspectors had chased these particular hares, they would have turned out to be as bogus as indeed they later proved to be?

The worst moment came when General Powell dscussed anthrax and the 2001 anthrax attacks in Washington and New York, pathetically holding up a teaspoon of the imaginary spores and—while not precisely saying so—fraudulently suggesting a connection between Saddam Hussein and the anthrax scare. But when the secretary of state held up Iraq's support for the Palestinian Hamas organisation, which has an office in Baghdad, as proof of Saddam's support for "terror"— he of course made no mention of America's support for Israel and its occupation of Palestinian land—the whole theatre began to collapse. There were Hamas offices in Beirut, Damascus and Iran. Was the 82nd Airborne supposed to grind on to Lebanon, Syria and Iran?

How many lies had been told in this auditorium? How many British excuses for the Suez invasion, or Russian excuses—the same year—for the suppression of the Hungarian uprising? One recalled, of course, this same room four decades earlier when General Powell's predecessor Adlai Stevenson showed photographs of the ships carrying Soviet missiles to Cuba. Alas, Powell's pictures carried no such authority. And Colin Powell was no Adlai Stevenson.

IF POWELL'S ADDRESS merited front-page treatment, the American media had never chosen to give the same attention to the men driving Bush to war, most of whom were former or still active pro-Israeli lobbyists. For years they had advocated destroying the most powerful Arab nation. Richard Perle, one of Bush's most influential advisers, Douglas Feith, Paul Wolfowitz, John Bolton and Donald Rumsfeld were all campaigning for the overthrow of Iraq long before George W. Bush was elected U.S. president. And they weren't doing so for the benefit of Americans or Britons. A 1996 report, *A Clean Break: A New Strategy for Securing the Realm*, called for war on Iraq. It was written not for the United States but for the incoming Israeli Likud prime minister Benjamin Netanyahu and produced by a group headed by Perle. The destruction of Iraq would, of course, protect Israel's monopoly of nuclear weapons—always supposing Saddam also possessed them— and allow it to defeat the Palestinians and impose whatever colonial settlement Sharon had in store for them. Although Bush and Blair dared not discuss this aspect of the coming war—a conflict for Israel was not going to have Americans or Britons lining up at recruiting offices—Jewish–American leaders talked about the advantages of an Iraqi war with enthusiasm. Indeed, those very courageous Jewish–American groups who opposed this madness were the first to point out how pro-Israeli organisations foresaw Iraq not only as a new source of oil but of water, too; why should canals not link the Tigris River to the parched Levant? No wonder, then, that any discussion of this topic had to be censored, as Professor Eliot Cohen of Johns Hopkins University tried to do in *The Wall Street Journal* the day after Powell's UN speech. Cohen suggested that European nations' objections to the war might—yet again—be ascribed to "anti-Semitism of a type long thought dead in the West, a loathing that ascribes to Jews a malignant intent." This nonsense was opposed by many Israeli intellectuals who, like Uri Avnery, argued that an Iraq war would leave Israel with even more Arab enemies.

The slur of "anti-Semitism" also lay behind Rumsfeld's insulting remarks about "old Europe." He was talking about the "old" Germany of Nazism and the "old" France of collaboration. But the France and Germany that opposed this war were the "new" Europe, the continent that refused, ever again, to slaughter the innocent. It was Rumsfeld and Bush who represented the "old" America; not the "new" America of freedom, the America of F. D. Roosevelt. Rumsfeld and Bush symbolised the old America that killed its native inhabitants and embarked on imperial adventures. It was "old" America we were being asked to fight for— linked to a new form of colonialism—an America that first threatened the United Nations with irrelevancy and then did the same to NATO. This was not the last chance for the UN, nor for NATO. But it might well have been the last chance for America to be taken seriously by her friends as well as her enemies.

Israeli and U.S. ambitions in the region were now entwined, almost synonymous. This war, about oil and regional control, was being cheer-led by a president who was treacherously telling us that this was part of an eternal war against "terror." The British and most Europeans didn't believe him. It's not that Britons wouldn't fight for America. They just didn't want to fight for Bush or his friends. And if that included the prime minister, they didn't want to fight for Blair either. Still less did they wish to embark on endless wars with a Texas governor–executioner who dodged the Vietnam draft and who, with his oil buddies, was now sending America's poor to destroy a Muslim nation that had nothing at all to do with the crimes against humanity of 11 September 2001.

Those who opposed the war were not cowards. Brits rather like fighting; they've biffed Arabs, Afghans, Muslims, Nazis, Italian Fascists and Japanese imperialists for generations, Iraqis included. But when the British are asked to go to war, patriotism is not enough. Faced with the horror stories, Britons and many Americans were a lot braver than Blair and Bush. They do not like, as Thomas More told Cromwell in *A Man for All Seasons*, tales to frighten children. Perhaps Henry VIII's exasperation in that play better expresses the British view of Blair and Bush: "Do they take me for a simpleton?" The British, like other Europeans, are an educated people. Ironically, their opposition to this war might ultimately have made them feel more, not less, European.

Palestine had much to do with it. Brits have no special love for Arabs, but they smell injustice fast enough and were outraged at the colonial war being used to crush the Palestinians by a nation that is now in effect running U.S. policy in the Middle East. We were told that our invasion of Iraq had nothing to do with the Israeli–Palestinian conflict—a burning, fearsome wound to which Bush devoted just eighteen words in his 2003 State of the Union address. Even Blair could not dismiss it this easily, hence his "conference" for Palestinian reform, at which the Palestinians had to take part via video-link because Israel's prime minister, Ariel Sharon, refused to let them travel to London.

Across the Middle East, thousands of journalists now gathered for the latest war-by-media. There would be no more "pools"; henceforth, journalists travelling with the military would be "embedded." It was a sign of the complacency of the press and television that they willingly adopted this supine word as part of their own vocabulary. Fox and CNN and the big American networks now spoke as one. Part Two of the "War on Terror" was about to begin, complete with its golden logos and theme music. American journalism had developed its own special controls over the years, the use of "controversial" words—"occupied" being one of those most necessary to avoid, unless used about Saddam's 1991 invasion of Kuwait—deleted in favour of a set of "safe" definitions. I even listed some of the phrases and clauses that would become de rigueur in the Iraqi war: "liberated" for American-occupied, "terrorists" for Iraqis who resisted American occupation, "die-hards" for insurgents, "now at last it can be told" for reporters at the site of Saddam's mass graves. They were all used. "Collateral damage" was reheated for further use. Television journalists based in Baghdad were told that their reports would carry a caveat: that their dispatches had been "monitored by the Iraqi authorities." "Monitored" meant "censored," although in many cases this was not true. Whenever I was interviewed on air from Baghdad in the coming weeks, I would always protest that no one listened to my calls—and that if they did, I would tell the truth whether they liked it or not. But television and radio stations like rules. They feel safer that way.*

---

*A 27 January 2003 CNN instruction—*Reminder of Script Approval Policy*—fairly took the breath away. "All reporters preparing package scripts must submit the scripts for approval," it said. "Packages may not be edited until the scripts are approved . . . All packages originating outside Washington, LA [Los Angeles] or NY [New York], including all international bureaus, must come to the ROW in Atlanta for approval." The "ROW" was the row of script editors in Atlanta who could insist on changes or "balances" in the reporter's dispatch. "A script is not approved for air unless it is properly marked approved by an authorised manager and duped [duplicated] to burcopy [bureau copy] . . . When a script is updated it must be re-approved, preferably by the originating approving authority." I noted the key words: "approved" and "authorised." CNN's man or woman in Kuwait or Baghdad—or Jerusalem or Ramallah—may know the background to his or her story; indeed, they would know far more about it than the "authorised manager" in Atlanta. But CNN's chiefs would decide the spin of the story.

The results of this system were evident from an intriguing exchange in 2002 between CNN's reporter in the occupied Palestinian West Bank town of Ramallah, and Eason Jordan, one of CNN's top men in Atlanta, who resigned in 2005 over a remark about the American military shooting of journalists in Iraq. The correspondent's first complaint was about a story by reporter Michael Holmes on the Red Crescent ambulance-drivers who were repeatedly shot at by Israeli troops. "We risked our lives and went out with ambulance drivers . . . for a whole day," Holmes complained. "We have also witnessed ambulances from our window being shot at by Israeli soldiers . . . The story received approval from Mike Shoulder. The story ran twice and then Rick Davis [a CNN executive] killed it. The reason was we did not have an Israeli army response, even though we stated in our story that Israel believes that Palestinians are smuggling weapons and wanted people in the ambulances." The Israelis refused to give CNN an interview, only a written statement. This statement was then written into the CNN script. But again it was rejected by Davis in Atlanta. Only when, after three days, the Israeli army gave CNN an interview did Holmes's story run—but then with the dishonest inclusion of a line that said the ambulances were shot in "crossfire" (i.e., that Palestinians also shot at their own ambulances). The reporter's complaint was all too obvious. "Since when do we hold a story hostage to the whims of governments

On 15 March, I took the last commercial flight into Saddam's Iraq—the very last plane whose baggage would be tagged to "Saddam International Airport"—a Royal Jordanian Airbus containing a few journalists, some eastern European contract workers and a flood of Iraqis who preferred to spend the coming terrible weeks with their families—perhaps to die with them—rather than exile themselves in the third-class hotels of Amman. We were heading for a country about to be invaded by more than a 100,000 American and British troops, but the crew went about their business as if there was no crisis and no war. We ate the usual cake and sandwich in-flight meal, were told to put our seats in the upright position before landing, to keep our seatbelts fastened until the aircraft had come to a complete halt. Our safety was their first concern.

For Baghdad, it was night number one thousand and one, the very last hours of fantasy. As UN inspectors prepared to leave the city in the early hours of 17 March, Saddam Hussein appointed his own corrupted son Qusay to lead the defence of the city of the caliphs against the American invasion. Yet at the Armed Forces Club, I found the defenders playing football. Iraqi television prepared Baghdad's people for the bombardment to come with music from *Gladiator*. Until the last moment, the UN—only hours from packing—diligently continued its work by disarming the soon-to-be-invaded nation, observing the destruction of two more al-Soummoud missiles. It was a disarmament which the Americans had so fervently demanded and in which they had now totally lost interest. With the inspectors gone, there would be nothing to stop the Anglo-American air forces commencing their bombardment of the cities of Iraq.

So was Baghdad to be Stalingrad, as Saddam told us in those last hours of peace? It didn't feel like it. The roads were open, the checkpoints often unmanned, the city's soldiery dragging on cigarettes outside the UN headquarters. From the banks of the Tigris—a muddy, warm-sewage-swamped version of Stalingrad's Volga—I watched the evening fishermen casting their lines for the *masgouf* that Baghdadis eat after sunset. The Security Council Resolution withdrawn? Blair calls an emergency meeting of the Cabinet? Bush to address the American people? Baghdad, it seemed, was sleepwalking its way into history almost as soundly as America and Britain.

How come I found a queue of Iraqis waiting outside the Sindbad Cinema in Saadun Street that night queuing for that ancient Egyptian clunker *Private Lives*,

---

and armies? We were told by Rick that if we do not get an Israeli on-camera we would not air the package. This means that governments and armies are indirectly censoring us and we are playing directly into their own hands."

All this was relevant to the coming war in Iraq. Clearly a U.S. Army officer would have to be ready to deny anything contentious stated by the Iraqis if Baghdad reports were going to get on air. In fact, a 31 January 2003 memo ensured that CNN's system of "script approval" became stricter. CNN staff were now told that a new computerised system of script approval would allow "authorised script approvers to mark scripts [i.e., reports] in a clear and standard manner. Script EPs [executive producers] will click on the coloured APPROVED button to turn it from red (unapproved) to green (approved). When someone makes a change in the script after approval, the button will turn yellow." Yellow indeed.

its posters displaying the ample thighs of its heroine? True, the local Baathist papers regaled us with reports of peace marches and peace protests around the world—as if Bush was going to call back his 140,000 men because Jordanians burned American flags in Amman.

The detachment was quite extraordinary, as if we were breathing in Baghdad a different kind of air, existing on a planet quite removed from the B-52s and Stealths and cruise missiles and Mothers of All Bombs that would soon make the ground tremble beneath our feet. The very history and culture of the Arab world were about to be visited by a Western-made earthquake, the like of which had never been seen before. Even the aftermath of the First World War and the collapse of the Ottoman empire would be made redundant in the next few hours. Yet on the banks of the Tigris stood a massive statue, bound up in sacking and gauze, a monolith of epic proportions, waiting for its unveiling: another bronze likeness of Saddam Hussein.

In the fumes of Baghdad's traffic, among its old yellow taxis, brand-new red double-decker buses and trucks, I searched for signs of the tempest to come. There were a few. Queues of cars outside gas stations, filling up for the last time, a clutch of antique shops closing down for the duration, a gang of workers removing the computers from a ministry, just as the Serbs did before NATO visited Belgrade in the spring of 1999. Didn't the Iraqis know what was about to happen? Did Saddam?

I could only be reminded of that remarkable and very recent account by a former Cuban ambassador. He had been part of a 1990 delegation sent by Castro to persuade Saddam of the overwhelming American firepower that would be sent against him if he did not withdraw from Kuwait. "I've received several reports like that," Saddam replied. "It's our ambassador to the UN who sends them to me and most of the time, they finish down there." And here Saddam gestured to a marble rubbish bin on the floor.

Was the marble bin still being filled with similar reports? Iraqi state television told us yet again on 16 March that Saddam had said, personally, once more, that although Iraq had weapons of mass destruction in the past, they no longer existed today. Now we know he was telling the truth. It was America's own weapons of mass destruction and its sponsorship of Israel, Saddam said, that threatened the world. All day, a UN C-130 aircraft baked on the tarmac at Saddam International Airport—there were two more UN transport aircraft in Cyprus—ready to bring the 140 inspectors out of Iraq before Bush and Blair launched their blitz. No one questioned the obvious: why had the inspectors bothered to come in the first place? If the British, as the attorney general in London claimed on 16 March, didn't need UN Security Council Resolution 1441 to wage war because they were justified under earlier resolutions, why on earth did they vote for it? Because they hoped Saddam would refuse to accept them back. Or, as Saddam put it rather neatly in his latest address, "the inspectors came to find nothing."

A group of foreign "peace activists" stood hand-in-hand along the parapet of Baghdad's largest bridge, old men and young American Muslims and a Buddhist in a prayer shawl, smiling at the passing traffic, largely ignored by Iraqi motorists. It was as if Iraqis were less caught up in this demonstration than the foreigners, as if their years of suffering had left them complacent to the terrible reality about to fall upon them. What did this portend for the Americans? Or the Iraqis?

So I went at dusk on this last night of peace to the great eggshell monument that Saddam erected to the Iraqi dead of his 1980–88 war against Iran, whose cavernous marble basements are inscribed with the names of every lost Iraqi. "Hope comes from life and brings fire to the heart," one of the lines of Arabic poetry says round the base. But the couples sitting on the grass beside the monument had not come to remember loved ones. They were courting students whose only political comment—aware of that "minder" hovering over my shoulder—was that "we have endured war so many times, we are used to it."

So I am left with a heretical thought. Might Baghdad ultimately become an open city, its defenders moved north to protect Saddam's heartland, the capital's people left to discover the joys and betrayals of an American occupation on their own? I suppose it all depends on the next few hours and days, on how many civilians the Americans and the British manage to kill in their supposedly moral war. Would Iraqis have to construct another monument to the dead? I asked in my report to *The Independent* that night. Or would we?

# CHAPTER TWENTY-THREE

# Atomic Dog, Annihilator, Arsonist, Anthrax, Anguish and Agamemnon

You ask me about the sack of Baghdad? It was so horrible there are no words to describe it. I wish I had died earlier and had not seen how the fools destroyed these treasures of knowledge and learning. I thought I understood the world, but this holocaust is so strange and pointless that I am struck dumb. The revolutions of time and its decisions have defeated all reason and knowledge.

The Persian poet Saadi of Shiraz describing the sack of
Baghdad by Hulagu, grandson of Genghis Khan, 1258
(translation: Michael Wood)

A PULSATING, MINUTE-LONG ROAR of sound brought President George W. Bush's crusade against "terrorism" to Baghdad. There was a thrashing of tracer on the horizon from the Baghdad air defences and then a series of tremendous vibrations that had the ground shaking under us, the walls moving, the sound waves clapping against our ears. Tubes of fire tore into the sky around the Iraqi capital, dark red at the base, golden at the top. Looking out across the Tigris from the riverbank, I could see pin-pricks of fire reaching high into the sky as America's bombs and missiles exploded on to Iraq's military and communication centres and, no doubt, upon the innocent as well. Valhalla, I said to myself. This needed Wagner, the Twilight of the Gods, *Götterdämmerung*.

No one in Iraq doubted that the dead would include civilians. Tony Blair had said just that in the House of Commons debate that very same week. But I wondered, listening to this storm of fire across Baghdad, if he had any conception of what it looks like, what it feels like, or of the fear of those innocent Iraqis who were, as I wrote my report an hour later, cowering in their homes and basements. Just before the missiles arrived, I talked to an old Shia Muslim woman in a poor area of Baghdad, dressed in traditional black with a white veil over her head. I pressed her for what she felt. In the end, she just said: "I am afraid." The explosions now gave expression to her words.

That this was the start of something that would change the face of the Middle East was in little doubt; whether it would be successful in the long term was quite another matter. It was a strange sensation to be on the ground, in at the start of this imperial adventure. The sheer violence of it, the howl of air-raid sirens and the air-cutting fall of the missiles, carried its own political message; not just to Saddam but to the rest of the world. We are the superpower, those explosions announced. This is how we do business. This is how we take our revenge for 11 September 2001.

Not even President Bush had made any pretence in the last days of peace to link Iraq with those international crimes against humanity in New York, Washington and Pennsylvania. Yet the Americans were—without the permission of the United Nations, with most of the world against them—acting out their rage with a fiery consummation. Iraq, of course, could not withstand this for long. Saddam might claim, as he did, that his soldiers could defeat technology with courage. Nonsense. What fell upon Iraq on 19 March—and I witnessed in Baghdad just an infinitesimally small part of this festival of violence—was as militarily overwhelming as it was politically terrifying. The crowds outside my hotel stood and stared into the sky at the flashing anti-aircraft bursts, awed by their power. Did the British, I wondered as I later stood on my hotel balcony near the Tigris, know where this will lead? Did we British not walk down this same arrogant path against the petty tyrants of Mesopotamia almost a hundred years ago? And look what happened to the British empire. Now, listening to those great explosions around Baghdad, I wondered what time had in store for the American empire.

Baghdad had always been a harsh place for me. Over the years, I had made many friends in the city—businessmen and their families, artists, retainers from the old regime, and, yes, Baathists and their families and at least one minister, Naji al-Hadithi, first the information minister then the foreign minister, a man whose first response to pointed questions would be to look at the ceiling of his office. Up there, he would be telling us. Up there, in the ceiling, was the microphone. But in the homes of Iraqis, I felt safe. Old photographs would show grandfathers in British army uniform, young women shopping at Harrods in the 1950s and—much later—the same women, middle-aged, enjoying the oil wealth of Saddam's Iraq, walking in Knightsbridge in the late 1970s and 1980s. But the insufferable heat of Baghdad in summer and the constant "minders" whom the information ministry would attach to reporters on the most innocent of stories would have a claustrophobic effect. After a while the minders took our money and worked for us rather than the regime. We could "buy" them, and during this last Saddamite war they would move imperceptibly from being servants of the regime to servants of the television networks. In the weeks following the "liberation" of Baghdad, they would become our employees, and a few months later we would find them working as employees of the U.S. occupying power.

When we could shake off the minders, persuade them we were only taking a taxi to the grocery store when in fact we were heading to the slums of Saddam City, we could hear the men of the Shiite opposition, the rage of the Dawa party, the courageous voices of families who lived amid filth, who rose up at our bidding in 1991 and were betrayed but who still waited for their moment of freedom. The senior ministry men knew we were making these illicit visits, but for $100 or $200 they would disregard them. The regime was as corrupting as it was corrupt. Standing on the world's greatest wealth, it had given its people war and more war and yet more war. I had been in Baghdad as the Iranian Scud missiles had crashed into the nighttime city, on the front lines in the assault on Khorramshahr in 1980; I had seen the Iraqi dead inside Iran in 1982 and inside Kuwait in 1991; and now I would see the Iraqi dead again. Inside my brain was a memories box in which I would see as many Iraqis dead as alive, their bodies as vivid as the living.

And it dawned on me over a long period that Iraqis must have seen themselves this way. They were both dead and alive. War had become not just part of their lives, but the very fabric of their existence. To fight and die—for Saddam, for Iraq, for Arab nationalism, for patriotism, out of fear—was a natural phenomenon. Between 1980 and 1988 they fought the Iranians to prevent the occupation of their country. Occupation, for Iraqis, for Arabs—for anyone of any race or religion— was not just humiliation. It was a form of rape. The enemy came into your country, your city, your street, your home, your bedroom. They would tie you up, insult your family, torture you, kill you. Saddam's own secret policemen did that. They, too, were occupiers. Woe betide anyone who tried to take their place.

The night before the first raids, I had walked around the Jadriya suburb of Baghdad, mixed Sunni–Shia middle class, watching soldiers with their children on their shoulders, hugging their wives goodbye, kitbags over their shoulders, rifles in hand. Snapshot. Paris and Berlin and London 1914. Berlin 1939. Warsaw 1939. London 1939. The Soviet Union 1941. The United States 1941. And before Korea and during Vietnam and among all the armies of the world as they set off on their wars to defend or promote civilisation or fascism or communism. Second Lieutenant Bill Fisk, perhaps, in Birkenhead, 1918? And now. I called at a pharmacy to buy bandages and plaster and lavatory paper. The chemist was a thoughtful man, explaining to the other glowering customers that the foreign journalist was going to share their dangers, that they should treat him with kindness. I told the man that he was especially generous since I thought my own air force, the RAF, would soon be bombing Baghdad. "Yes," he said with a sad smile, "I rather think they will."

So at the start of this new and one-sided war, we reporters would be recording two different conflicts: the suffering of Iraqis and the death throes of the regime. The latter wanted us to view the two as identical. The Americans and British insisted that they were destroying the regime in order to end the suffering. In fact, the suffering and the dying struggle of Iraqi Baathism could no more be separated than you could tear the bandages off a wound without causing the patient to shriek in pain. It was easy to argue that Saddam's wickedness was the cause of all their woes, but wounded and dying Iraqis did not see their fate in quite those terms. They were being attacked by Americans, not by Iraqis. American missiles and bombs were destroying their homes. Had they fought and died on the Iran front, only to be attacked and occupied by another foreign power? The Pentagon clearly understood this equation. Why else would the American military refuse to do what any professional army—or occupying power—would do: to count the number of civilian deaths during and after the war?

Donald Rumsfeld was to assert that the American attack on Baghdad was "as targeted an air campaign as has ever existed." But he could not have told that to five-year-old Doha Suheil. She looks at me on the first morning of the war, drip-feed attached to her nose, a deep frown over her small face as she tries vainly to move the left side of her body. The cruise missile that exploded close to her home in the Radwaniyeh suburb of Baghdad blasted shrapnel into her legs—they were bound up with gauze—and, far more seriously, into her spine. Now she has lost all movement in her left leg. Her mother bends over the bed and straightens her right leg, which the little girl thrashes around outside the blanket. Somehow, Doha's mother thinks that if her child's two legs lie straight beside each other, her daughter will recover from her paralysis. She was the first of the patients brought to the Mustansariya University Hospital after America's blitz on the city began.

There is something sick, obscene, about these hospital visits. We bomb. They suffer. Then we reporters turn up and take pictures of their wounded children. The Iraqi minister of health decides to hold an insufferable press conference outside the wards to emphasise the "bestial" nature of the American attack. The Americans say that they don't intend to hurt children. And Doha Suheil looks at me and the doctors for reassurance, as if she will awake from this nightmare and move her left leg and feel no more pain. So let's forget, for a moment, the cheap propaganda of the regime and the cocky moralising of Messrs. Rumsfeld and Bush, and take a trip—this bright morning in March 2003—around the Mustansariya College Hospital. For the reality of war—and here I unashamedly make my point again—is ultimately not about military victory and defeat, or the lies about "coalition forces" which our "embedded" journalists were already telling about an invasion involving only the Americans, the British and a handful of Australians. War, even when it has international legitimacy—which this war does not—is primarily about suffering and death.

Take fifty-year-old Amel Hassan, a peasant woman with tattoos on her arms and legs, but who now lies on her hospital bed with massive purple bruises on her shoulders—they are now twice their original size. She was on her way to visit her daughter when the first American missiles struck Baghdad. "I was just getting out of the taxi when there was a big explosion and I fell down and found my blood everywhere," she told me. "It was on my arms, my legs, my chest." Amel Hassan still has multiple shrapnel wounds in her chest. Her five-year-old daughter Wahed lies in the next bed, whimpering with pain. She had climbed out of the taxi first and was almost at her aunt's front door when the explosion cut her down. Her feet are still bleeding, although the blood has clotted around her toes and is stanched by the bandages on her ankles and lower legs. Two boys are in the next room. Saad Selim is eleven, his brother Omar fourteen. Both have shrapnel wounds to their legs and chest.

Isra Riad is in the third room with almost identical injuries, in her case shrapnel wounds to the legs, sustained when she ran in terror from her house into her garden as the blitz began. Imam Ali is twenty-three and has multiple shrapnel wounds in her abdomen and lower bowel. Najla Hussein Abbas still tries to cover her head with a black scarf but she cannot hide the purple wounds to her legs. Multiple shrapnel wounds. After a while, "multiple shrapnel wounds" sounds like a natural disease, which I suppose—among a people who have suffered more than twenty years of war—it is.

So was all this, I asked myself, for 11 September 2001? All this was to "strike back" at our attackers, albeit that Doha Suheil, Wahed Hassan and Imam Ali had nothing—absolutely nothing—to do with those crimes against humanity, any more than had the awful Saddam? Who decided, I wondered, that these children, these young women, should suffer for September 11th? Wars repeat themselves. Always, when "we" come to visit those we have bombed, we have the same question. In Libya in 1986, American reporters would repeatedly cross-question the wounded: had they perhaps been hit by shrapnel from their own anti-aircraft fire? Again, in 1991, "we" asked the Iraqi wounded the same question. And now a doctor found himself asked by a British radio reporter—yes, you've guessed it—"Do you think, Doctor, that some of these people could have been hit by Iraqi anti-aircraft fire?"

Should we laugh or cry at this? Must we always blame "them" for their own wounds? Certainly we should ask why those cruise missiles exploded where they did, at least 320 in Baghdad alone, courtesy of the USS *Kitty Hawk*. Isra Riad came from Sayadiyeh, where there is a big military barracks. Najla Abbas's home was in Risalleh, where there were villas belonging to Saddam's family. The two Selim brothers lived in Shirta Khamse, where there was a storehouse for military vehicles. But that's the whole problem. Targets are scattered across the city. The poor—and all the wounded I saw were poor—live in cheap, sometimes wooden houses that collapse under blast damage.

It's the same old story. If we make war, we are going to kill and maim the innocent. Dr. Habib al-Hezai, whose FRCS was gained at Edinburgh University, counted 101 patients of the total 207 wounded in the raids in his hospital alone, of whom 85 were civilians—20 of them women and 6 of them children—and 16 soldiers. A young man and a child of twelve died under surgery. No one will say how many soldiers were killed during the attacks.

Driving across Baghdad was an eerie experience. The targets were indeed carefully selected, even though their destruction inevitably struck the innocent. There was a presidential palace with four 10-metres-high statues of the Arab warrior Saladin on each corner—the face of each, of course, was Saddam's—and, neatly in between, a great black hole gouged into the façade of the building. The Ministry of Air Weapons Production was pulverised, a massive heap of prestressed concrete and rubble. But outside, at the gate, there were two sandbag emplacements with smartly dressed Iraqi soldiers, rifles over the parapet, ready to defend their ministry from the enemy which had already destroyed it.

The morning traffic built up on the roads beside the Tigris. No driver looked too hard at the Republican Palace on the other side of the river or the Ministry of Armaments Procurement beside it. They burned for twelve hours after the first missile strikes. It was as if burning palaces and blazing ministries and piles of smoking rubble were a normal part of daily Baghdad life. But then again, no one under Saddam's regime would spend too long looking at such things, would they?

Iraqis were puzzled as to what all this meant. In 1991, the Americans struck the refineries, the electricity grid, the water pipes, communications. But on day two of this war, Baghdad could still function. The land-line telephones worked, the Internet operated, the electrical power was at full capacity, the bridges over the Tigris remained unbombed. My guess was that when—"if" was still a sensitive phrase—the Americans arrived in Baghdad, they would need a working communications system, electricity, transport. What had been spared was not a gift to the Iraqi people, I concluded; it was for the benefit of Iraq's supposed new masters. How wrong I was.

The *Iraq Daily* emerged with an edition of just four pages, a clutch of articles on the "steadfastness" of the nation—steadfastness in Arabic is *soummoud*, the same name as the missiles Iraq partially destroyed before Bush forced the UN inspectors to leave by going to war—and a headline that read: "President: Victory Will Come in Iraqi Hands." During the bombing on Friday night, Iraqi television—again, there had been no attempt by the United States to destroy the television facilities—showed an Iraqi general, appearing live, to reassure the nation of victory. As he spoke, the blast waves from cruise missile explosions blew in the curtains behind him and shook the television camera.

So where did all this lead us? In the early hours next day, I looked once more across the Tigris at the funeral pyre of the Republican Palace and the colonnaded ministry beside it. There were beacons of fire across Baghdad and the sky was lowering with smoke. The buttressed, rampart-like palace—sheets of flame soaring from its walls—looked like a medieval castle ablaze; Ctesiphon destroyed, Mesopotamia at the moment of its destruction, as it had been seen so many times, over so many thousands of years. Xenophon struck south of here, Alexander to the north. The Mongols sacked Baghdad. The caliphs came. And then the Ottomans and then the British. All departed. Now come the Americans. It was not about legitimacy. It was about something much more seductive, something Saddam himself understood all too well, a special kind of power, the same power that every conqueror of Iraq wished to demonstrate as he smashed his way across this ancient civilisation.

That second afternoon, the Iraqis lit massive fires of oil around Baghdad in the hope of misleading the guidance system of the cruise missiles. Smoke against computers. The air-raid sirens began to howl again just after 6:20 p.m. on 22 March, when Saddam's biggest military office block, a great rampart of a building twenty storeys high beside his palace, simply exploded in front of me, a cauldron of fire, a 100-foot sheet of flame and a sound that had my ears singing for an hour afterwards. The entire buttressed edifice shuddered under the impact. Then four more cruise missiles came in. It was the heaviest bombing Baghdad had suffered in more than twenty years of war. To my right, a long colonnaded building looking much like the façade of the Pentagon coughed fire as five missiles crashed into the concrete. In an operation officially intended to create "shock and awe"—Rumsfeld's latest slogan—shock was hardly the word for it. The few Iraqis in the streets around me—no friends of Saddam, I would suspect—cursed under their breath.

From high-rise buildings, shops and homes came the thunder of crashing glass as the shock waves swept across the Tigris in both directions. Minute after minute the missiles came in. Many Iraqis had watched—as I had—the television tape of those ominous B-52 bombers taking off from Britain only six hours earlier. Like me, they had noted the time, added three hours for Iraqi time ahead of London and guessed that, at around 9 p.m., the terror would begin. The B-52s, almost certainly firing from outside Iraqi airspace, were dead on time. Policemen drove at speed through the streets, their loudspeakers ordering pedestrians to take shelter or hide under cover of tall buildings. Much good did it do. Crouching next to a block of shops, I narrowly missed the shower of glass that came cascading down from the upper windows as the shock waves slammed into them.

A few Iraqis—husbands and wives, older children—could be seen staring from balconies, shards of broken glass around them. Each time one of the great golden bubbles of fire burst across the city, they ducked inside before the blast wave reached them. As I stood beneath the trees on the corniche, a wave of cruise missiles passed low overhead, the shriek of their passage almost as devastating as the explosions that were to follow. How, I asked myself, does one describe this outside the language of a military report, the definition of the colour, the decibels of the explosions? The flight of the missiles sounded as if someone was ripping to pieces huge canopies of silk across the sky.

There is something anarchic about all human beings, about their reaction to violence. The Iraqis around me stood and watched, as I did, the tongues of flame bursting from the upper stories of the building beside Saddam's palace, reaching high into the sky. Strangely, the electricity grid continued to operate and around us the traffic lights continued to move between red and green. Billboards moved in the breeze of the shock waves; floodlights continued to blaze on public buildings. Above us, curtains of smoke were moving over Baghdad, white from the explosions, black from the burning targets. How could one resist this? How could the Iraqis ever believe—with their broken technology, their debilitating twelve years of sanctions—that they could defeat the computers of these missiles and of these aircraft? It was the same old story: irresistible, unquestionable power.

Well, yes, we said to ourselves, could one attack a more appropriate regime? But that was not the point. For the message of this new raid was the same as that of the previous night's raid, and of all the raids in the hours to come: the United States must be obeyed; the EU, UN, NATO—nothing must stand in its way. Many Iraqis were already asking me: How many days? Not because they wanted the Americans or the British in Baghdad, but because they wanted this violence to end: which, when you think of it, is exactly why these raids took place.

It is the morning of 25 March 2003. Let us now praise famous men. Saddam Hussein is doing just that. Today he proceeds to list the Iraqi army and navy officers who are leading the "resistance" against the Anglo–American army in Um Qasr, Basra and Nasiriyah. Major-General Mustafa Mahmoud Umran, commanding officer of the 11th Division, Brigadier Bashir Ahmed Othman, commander of the Iraqi 45th Brigade, Brigadier-Colonel Ali Khalil Ibrahim, commander of the 11th Battalion of the 45th Brigade, Colonel Mohamed Khallaf al-Jabawi, commander of the 45th Brigade's 2nd Battalion, Lieutenant-Colonel Fathi Rani Majid of the Iraqi army's III Corps . . . And so it goes on. "Be patient," Saddam keeps saying. Be patient. Fourteen times in all, he tells the army and the people of Iraq to be patient. "We will win . . . we will be victorious against Evil." Patient but confident in victory. Fighting Evil.

Wasn't that how President Bush was encouraging his people a few hours earlier? At other times, Saddam sounds like his hero, Josef Stalin. "They have come to destroy our country and we must stand and destroy them and defend our people and our country . . . Cut their throats . . . They are coming to take our land. But when they try to enter our cities, they try to avoid a battle with our forces and to stay outside the range of our weapons." Was this modelled on the Great Patriotic War, the defence of Mother Russia under Uncle Joe? And if not, how to account for those hundreds of Iraqi soldiers still holding out under American air and tank attacks? People, party, patriotism. The three Ps run like a theme through the Saddam speech, along with a bitter warning: as the American and British forces make less headway on the ground, Saddam says, they will use their air power against Iraq ever more brutally. So what does it feel like to live these days in President Saddam's future Stalingrad?

A few hours later, the cruise missiles and the planes came back. The great explosions blanketed Baghdad in the darkness. One of the Tomahawks smashed into the grounds of the Mustansariya University—twenty-five students wounded and one dead, so they claimed. There were other sounds in the early hours. A blaze of automatic gunfire on the Tigris corniche—attempts to capture two escaping U.S. airmen, the authorities insisted—and then a full-scale gun battle not far from the city centre at 2:30 a.m. There were rumours. Armed men had come from Saddam City, the Shia slums on the edge of Baghdad, and had been intercepted by state security men. No "independent confirmation." A story that the railway line north of Baghdad has been cut. Denied.

On Sunday, the Iraqi minister of defence, General Sultan Hashem, gave a remarkable briefing on the war, naming the units involved in front-line fighting— the 3rd Battalion of the Iraqi army's 27th Brigade was still holding out at Suq ash-Shuyukh south of Nasiriyah, the 3rd Battalion of the Third Iraqi Army was holding Basra. And I remembered how these generals gave identical briefings during the 1980–88 war against Iran. When we checked on their stories back then, they almost always turned out to be true. Did the same apply today? General Hashem insisted that his men were destroying U.S. tanks and armour and helicopters. This was easy to dismiss—until videotape of two burning U.S. armoured personnel carriers popped up on the television screen. Vice-President Taha Yassin Ramadan had been obliging enough to explain the Iraqi army's tactics. It was Iraqi policy to let the Anglo–American armies "roam around" in the desert as long as they wanted, and to attack them when they tried to enter the cities. Which seemed to be pretty much what they were doing.

From Baghdad, with its canopy of sinister black oil smoke and air-raid sirens, the American plan appeared to be rather similar: to barnstorm up the desert parallel to the Tigris and Euphrates valley and try to turn right at every available city on the way. If there's trouble at Um Qasr, try Basra. If Basra is blocked, have a go through Nasiriyah. If that's dangerous, try to turn right through Najaf. But the open road—the long highway to Baghdad lined with adoring Iraqis throwing roses at GIs and Tommys—was proving to be an illusion.* Yet we could not travel. No Western journalist—even with permission to take a street taxi—could leave the Baghdad city limits. On 27 March, I went to see my old friends at the Al-Jazeera channel whose local offices stood on the west bank of the Tigris. They had a crew in Basra which was under British ground and air attack. I begged them to show me the roughcuts of the videotape they had received from Basra. If I could not go there, I could at least look through the lens of their cameraman before the Iraqis—or, after transmission, the Americans and the British—got their hands on it.

I sit in their editing studio, the sound of anti-aircraft guns pummelling away outside the walls. The video-camera is hand-held, unsteady, the cameraman nervous. Two British soldiers lie dead on a Basra roadway, an Iraqi girl—victim of an Anglo–American air strike—is brought to hospital with her intestines spilling out of her stomach, a dreadfully wounded woman screams in agony as doctors try to take off her black dress. An Iraqi general, surrounded by hundreds of his armed troops, stands in central Basra and announces that Iraq's second city remains firmly in Iraqi hands. The unedited Al-Jazeera tape—filmed over the past thirty-six hours and newly arrived in Baghdad—is raw, painful, devastating.

It is also proof that Basra—reportedly "captured" and "secured" by British troops—is still under the control of Saddam Hussein's forces. Despite claims by British officers that some form of uprising has broken out there, cars and buses continue to move through the streets while Iraqis queue patiently for gas bottles as they are unloaded from a government truck. A remarkable part of the tape shows fireballs blooming over western Basra and the explosion of incoming—presumably British—shells.

The short sequence of the dead British soldiers—for the public showing of which Tony Blair was to express such horror a day later—was little different from dozens of similar clips of dead Iraqi soldiers shown on British television over the past twelve years, pictures that never drew any expressions of condemnation from the British prime minister. The two Britons, still in uniform, are lying on a roadway, arms and legs apart, one of them apparently hit in the head, the other shot in the chest and abdomen. Another sequence from the same tape shows crowds of

---

*You could observe this cockiness when Mohamed Saeed al-Sahaf, the jovial but far from funny information minister, spoke of Tony Blair. "I think the British nation has never been faced with a tragedy like this fellow." Fellow. Ah yes, Sahaf knew how to mock the Brits. He would read out daily casualty reports which—given the years of controversy to come about the number of Iraqi civilian dead—now have an archival importance they did not possess at the time. On this, the third day of the invasion, he gave the following figures for dead and wounded: in Baghdad, 194 wounded; in Nineveh, 8 wounded; in Karbala 10 killed and 32 wounded; in Salahuddin, 2 killed and 22 wounded. In Najaf, the figures were 2 and 36; in Qadisiya, 4 and 13; in Basra, 14 and 122. In Babylon, the Iraqi government claimed 30 killed and 63 wounded. In all, 62 civilians had been killed so far.

Basra civilians and armed men in civilian clothes, kicking the soldiers' British army jeep—registration number HP5AA—and dancing on top of the vehicle. Other men can be seen kicking the overturned Ministry of Defence trailer, registration number 91KC98, which the jeep was towing when it was presumably ambushed. Also to be observed on the unedited tape is an RAF pilotless drone photo-reconnaissance aircraft, its red-and-blue roundels visible on one wing, shot down and lying overturned on a roadway. Marked "ARMY" in capital letters, it carries the code sign ZJ300 on its tail and is attached to a large cylindrical pod that probably contains the plane's camera.

Far more harrowing than the pictures of the dead British soldiers, however, is the tape from Basra's largest hospital as victims of the bombardment are brought to the operating rooms, shrieking in pain. A middle-aged man is carried into the hospital in pyjamas, soaked head to foot in blood. A girl of perhaps four is brought into the operating room on a trolley, staring at a heap of her own intestines protruding from the left side of her stomach. A blue-uniformed doctor pours water over the little girl's guts and then gently applies a bandage before beginning surgery. A woman in black with what appears to be a stomach wound cries out as doctors try to strip her for surgery. In another sequence, a trail of blood leads from the impact of an incoming—presumably British—shell. Next to the crater is a pair of plastic slippers.

The Al-Jazeera tapes—most of which will never be seen—are the first vivid proof that Basra remains totally outside British control. Not only is one of the city's main roads to Baghdad still open—this is how the tapes reached the Iraqi capital—but Iraqi General Khaled Hatem is interviewed in a Basra street, surrounded by hundreds of his uniformed and armed troops, telling Al-Jazeera's reporter that his men will "never" surrender to Iraq's enemies. Armed Baath party militiamen can also be seen in the streets, where traffic cops are directing lorries and buses near the city's Sheraton Hotel.

Mohamed al-Abdullah, Al-Jazeera's correspondent in Basra, must be the bravest journalist in Iraq right now. In the sequence of three tapes, he can be seen interviewing families under fire and calmly reporting the incoming British artillery bombardments. One tape shows that the Sheraton Hotel on the banks of the Shatt al-Arab has sustained shell damage. On the edge of the river—beside one of the huge statues of Iraq's 1980–88 war "martyrs," each pointing an accusing finger across the waterway towards Iran—Basra residents can be seen filling jerrycans from the sewage-polluted river.

On 22 March the Iraqi government said that 30 civilians had been killed in Basra and another 63 wounded. On 27 March it claimed that more than 4,000 civilians had been wounded in Iraq since the war began and more than 350 killed. But Mr. al-Abdullah's tape shows at least seven more bodies brought to the Basra hospital mortuary over the past thirty-six hours. (One of them, his head still gushing blood onto the mortuary floor, was identified as an Arab correspondent for a Western news agency.) Other grisly scenes show the partially decapitated body of a little girl, her red scarf still wound round her neck. Another girl lies on a stretcher with her brain and left ear missing. Another dead child has its feet blown away. There is no indication whether American or British ordnance killed these children. The tapes give no indication of Iraqi military casualties.

But at a time when the Iraqi authorities will not allow Western reporters to visit Basra, this is the nearest to independent evidence we have of continued fighting in the city and the cost of resisting the British army. For days, the Iraqis have been denying optimistic reports from "embedded" reporters—especially from the BBC—who give the impression that Basra is "secured" or otherwise effectively under British control. This the tapes conclusively prove to be untrue. There is also a sequence showing two men, both black, who are claimed by Iraqi troops to be U.S. prisoners-of-war. No questions are asked of the men, who are dressed in identical black shirts and jackets. Both appear on the tape nervous and looking at the camera crew and at the Iraqi troops who are crowded behind them.

The dead civilians, however, will soon be erased from the story of war. They are among the statistics that will be for ever kept from us. They will become unknown, the undead, the "collateral damage" that will simply not end up in the Pentagon or British Ministry of Defence archives—or at least, not in any file that the public will be allowed to see. Thus the little girl will not have lost her head. Her companion will not have lost her brain. The third child's feet will remain firmly attached to her body. At least for the historical record—for there will be no historical record. That is part of our new war.

On 28 March we realised that the Americans—perhaps because they were not advancing as fast as they planned—did not want to keep Baghdad's communications intact. It was difficult to weep over a telephone exchange. True, the destruction of the local phone system in Baghdad was a miserable experience for tens of thousands of Iraqi families who wanted to keep in contact with their relatives during the long dark hours of bombing. But the shattered exchanges and umbilical wires and broken concrete of the Mimoun International Communications Centre scarcely equalled the exposed bones and intestines and torn flesh of the civilian wounded of Iraq. "Command and control centres" is how the CENTCOM boys described the targets they zapped in the early hours of the 28th. It represents another of those little degradations that we—as in "we, the West"—routinely undertake when things aren't going our way in a war. Back in "our" 1991 blitz on Baghdad, we started off on the presidential palaces and barracks, then moved on to communications, then electricity and then water treatment plants. In Serbia in 1999, it was the same story. First went the Yugoslav army barracks and arms factories, then the road bridges, phone system, the electricity. Now the same old story has begun in Baghdad. The presidential palaces and barracks have been hit. Time to smash the phones once again.

Obviously, "we" hoped it wouldn't come to this. The Anglo–American armies wanted to maintain the infrastructure of Baghdad for themselves—after they had "liberated" the city under a hail of roses from its rejoicing people—because they would need working phone lines on their arrival. But after a night of massive explosions across the city, communications had been sacrificed. The huge Rashid telecommunications centre—destroyed in the 1991 bombardment—was struck by a cruise missile that penetrated the basement of the building. The exchange in Karada—where Baghdadis pay their phone bills—was ripped open.

Outside each of these blocks—as outside every government institution here—can be found a giant billboard of Saddam, doing whatever is appropriate to the relevant ministry or department. In front of Baghdad Central Station, for example, a Saddam in a felt hat is acting as signalman to speed an express on its way to Basra—services to the city, by the way, are now officially "suspended" because of the British military siege. At the Mimoun exchange, Saddam is standing in front of the telecommunications mast. At the Rashid offices, he is talking on an old-fashioned Bakelite black telephone while taking notes on a pad with a large brown biro.

No more. Because "we" have decided to destroy the phones and all those "command and control" systems that may be included, dual use, into the network. So now most Baghdadis have to drive across town to get news of each other; there is more traffic on the roads than at any time since the start of the war. Down, too, went Baghdad's Internet system. Iraqi television, whose studios were bombed by the Americans on 26 March, can only be watched between a growing number of power cuts.

So what's next? Electricity or water? Or, since power runs the water pumps, both? Each day brings news of events which—on their own—have no great import but which together add a grim new dimension to the invasion and its aftermath. At the end of March, hundreds of tribesmen from across Iraq met at the Baghdad Hotel before meeting Saddam. The Iraqi tribes—ignored by the military planners and Washington pundits who think that Iraq is held together only by the Baath party and the army—are a powerful force, their unity cemented by marriage and a network of families who provide a force as cohesive as the Baath party itself. Tribesmen guard the grain silos and some of the electricity generating stations around Baghdad. Two of them were credited with disabling an Apache helicopter captured a week earlier. And now tribal leaders arrived from all over Iraq, from Fallujah and Ramadi and Nineveh and Babylon and Basra and Nasiriyah and all the cities of Mesopotamia. So much for Defence Minister Geoffrey Hoon's contention that Saddam has "lost control" of southern Iraq. They will return today and tomorrow to their cities and villages with instructions on how to oppose the American and British armies. Saddam has already issued one set of orders that tells the tribesmen "to fight [the Americans and British] in groups and attack their advance and rear lines to block the way of their progress . . . If the enemy settles into a position, start to harass them at night . . ."

I am puzzled about this. Guerrilla forces may harass an occupying army but will do little harm during an invasion when the overwhelming firepower and movement of the invaders can suppress any opposition. Only when the occupying soldiers settle into barracks and routine patrols do they become vulnerable. So is Saddam giving these tribesmen their marching orders for the war—or their instructions for the postwar occupation? Could it be that Saddam is confronting the possibility of military defeat in the field? Is there a future insurrection being planned here in Baghdad as the Americans storm up the road towards Nasiriyah?

On the tenth floor of the Palestine Hotel where I live amid the cell-like rooms of more than a hundred other journalists, I have squirrelled away a library of books to read in the long, loud nights. William Shirer's *The Rise and Fall of the Third Reich* and J. F. C. Fuller's *The Second World War*, to remind me of what *real* war is like, and Tolstoy's *War and Peace* to recall for me how conflict can be described with sensitivity and grace and horror—I can heartily recommend the Battle of Borodino to anyone—and some volumes of poetry and a big, disorderly pile of newspaper and magazine articles which I tore from my Beirut archives before leaving for Amman and Baghdad. Tonight, I pull out a long rant by Pat Buchanan, written well over five months earlier, and almost without thinking, I pull my pen from my pocket and start scribbling harsh lines in the margin of this prophetic article:

> If Providence does not intrude, we will soon launch an imperial war on Iraq with all the "On to Berlin!" bravado with which French poilus and British Tommies marched in August 1914. But this invasion will not be the cakewalk neoconservatives predict . . . To destroy Saddam's weapons, to democratise, defend and hold Iraq together, U.S. troops will be tied down for decades. Yet, terrorist attacks in liberated Iraq seem as certain as in liberated Afghanistan. For a militant Islam that holds in thrall scores of millions of true believers will never accept George Bush dictating the destiny of the Islamic world. With our MacArthur Regency in Baghdad, Pax Americana will reach apogee. But then the tide recedes, for the one endeavour at which Islamic peoples excel is expelling imperial powers by terror and guerrilla war. They drove the Brits out of Palestine and Aden, the French out of Algeria, the Russians out of Afghanistan, the Americans out of Somalia and Beirut, the Israelis out of Lebanon . . . We have started up the road to empire and over the next hill we will meet those who went before. The only lesson we learn from history is that we do not learn from history.

IT WAS AN OUTRAGE, AN OBSCENITY. The severed hand on the metal door, the swamp of blood and mud across the road, the human brains inside a garage, the incinerated, skeletal remains of an Iraqi mother and her three children in their still-smouldering car. Two missiles from an American jet killed them all—twenty-one Iraqi civilians—torn to pieces on 27 March before they could be "liberated" by the nation that destroyed their lives. Who dares, I ask myself at the scene, to call this "collateral damage"? Abu Taleb Street was packed with pedestrians and motorists when the American pilot approached through the dense sandstorm that covered northern Baghdad in a cloak of red-and-yellow dust and rain that morning.

It was a dirt-poor neighbourhood, of mostly Shia Muslims, the same people whom Messrs. Bush and Blair still fondly hoped would rise up against President

Saddam Hussein, a place of oil-sodden car-repair shops, overcrowded apartments and cheap cafés. Everyone I spoke to heard the plane. One man, shocked by the headless corpses he had just seen, could say only two words. "Roar, flash," he kept saying and then closed his eyes so tight that the muscles rippled between them. I am faced by the same old question: How to record so terrible an event? Iraqis are now witnessing these awful things each day; so there is no reason why the truth, all the truth, of what they see should not be told. For another question occurred to me as I walked through this place of massacre. If this is what we are seeing in Baghdad, what is happening in Basra and Nasiriyah and Kerbala? How many civilians are dying there too, anonymously, indeed unrecorded, because there are no reporters to be witness to their suffering?

Abu Hassan and Malek Hammoud were preparing lunch for customers at the Nasser restaurant on the north side of Abu Taleb Street. The missile that killed them landed next to the westbound carriageway, its blast tearing away the front of the café and cutting the two men—the first forty-eight, the second only eighteen—to pieces. A fellow worker led me through the rubble. "This is all that is left of them now," he said, holding out before me an oven pan dripping with blood. At least fifteen cars burst into flames, burning many of their occupants to death. Several men tore at the doors of another flame-shrouded car in the centre of the street that had been flipped upside down by the same missile. They were forced to watch helplessly as the woman and her three children inside were cremated alive in front of them. The second missile hit on the eastbound carriageway, sending shards of metal into three men standing outside a concrete apartment block with the words "This is God's possession" written in marble on the outside wall.

The building's manager, Hishem Danoon, ran to the doorway as soon as he heard the massive explosion. "I found Ta'ar in pieces over there," he told me. His head was blown off. "That's his hand." A group of young men and a woman took me into the street and there, a scene from any horror film, was Ta'ar's hand, cut off at the wrist, his four fingers and thumb grasping a piece of iron roofing. His colleague, Sermed, died the same instant. His brains lay piled a few feet away, a pale red-and-grey mess behind a burnt car. Both men worked for Danoon. So did a doorman who was also killed.

As each survivor talked, the dead regained their identities. There was the electrical shop owner killed behind his counter by the same missile that cut down Ta'ar and Sermed and the doorman, and the young girl standing on the central reservation, trying to cross the road, and the truck-driver who was only feet from the point of impact and the beggar who regularly called to see Mr. Danoon for bread and who was just leaving when the missiles came screaming through the sandstorm to destroy him.

In Qatar, the Anglo-American forces announced an inquiry. The Iraqi government, who are the only ones to benefit from the propaganda value of such a bloodbath, naturally denounced the slaughter, which they initially put at fourteen dead. So what was the real target? Some Iraqis said there was a military encampment less than a mile from the street, though I couldn't find it. Others talked about a local fire brigade headquarters, but the fire brigade can hardly be described as a military target. Certainly, there had been an attack less than an hour earlier on a military camp further north. I was driving past the base when two rockets exploded and I saw Iraqi soldiers running for their lives out of the gates and along the side of the highway. Then I heard two more explosions; these were the missiles that hit Abu Taleb Street.

Of course, the pilot who killed the innocent could not see his victims. Pilots fire through computer-aligned coordinates, and the sandstorm would have hidden the street from his vision. But when one of Malek Hammoud's friends asked me how the Americans could so blithely kill those they claimed to want to liberate, he didn't want to learn about the science of avionics or weapons delivery systems. And why should he? For this is happening almost every day in Baghdad. On 24 March an entire family of nine was wiped out in their home near the centre of the city. On 25 March a busload of civilian passengers was reportedly killed on a road south of Baghdad. On the 26th, Iraqis were learning the identity of five civilian passengers slaughtered on a Syrian bus that was attacked by American aircraft close to the Iraqi border.

We may put on the hairshirt of morality in explaining why these people should die. They died because of September 11th, we may say, because of the "weapons of mass destruction"—which do not exist—because of our desperate desire to "liberate" all these people. Let us not confuse the issue with oil. Either way, I wrote that night, I'll bet we are told that Saddam is ultimately responsible for their deaths. We shan't mention the pilot, of course. And we didn't. Faulty Iraqi anti-aircraft missiles—the same old excuse—had probably killed them all, the Americans said. It was not possible. The two missiles had exploded equidistant from each other on both carriageways. No guidance system could fail on two anti-aircraft missiles at exactly the same time, causing them to land so neatly on the same road.

There is no end to this. Just a day later—on 28 March—the atrocity is repeated. The evidence this time is a piece of metal only a foot high, but the numbers on it hold the clue. At least sixty-two civilians have died by the afternoon of 29 March and the coding on that hunk of metal contains the identity of the culprit. The Americans and British were doing their best to suggest—here we go again— that yet one more Iraqi anti-aircraft missile destroyed those dozens of lives, adding that they were "still investigating" the carnage. But the coding on the missile fragment is in groups of numerals and Latin letters, not in Arabic. And many of the survivors heard the plane.

In the al-Noor hospital, there were appalling scenes of pain and suffering. A two-year-old girl, Saida Jaffar, swaddled in bandages and tubes, a tube into her nose, another into her stomach. All I could see of her was her forehead, two small eyes and a chin. Beside her, blood and flies covered a heap of old bandages and swabs. Not far away, lying on a dirty bed, was three-year-old Mohamed Amaid, his face, stomach, hands and feet all tied tightly in bandages. A great black mass of congealed blood lay at the bottom of his bed.

This is a hospital without computers, with only the most primitive of X-ray machines. But the missile was guided by computers and that vital shard of fuse-lage was computer-coded. It can be easily verified and checked by the Ameri-cans—if they choose to do so. It reads: 30003-704ASB7492. The letter "B" is scratched and could be an "H." This is believed to be the serial number. It is fol-lowed by a further code which arms manufacturers usually refer to as the weapon's "Lot" number. It reads: MFR 95214 09. The piece of metal bearing the codings was retrieved minutes after the missile exploded on the evening of the 28th, by an old man whose home is only a hundred metres away from the 2-metre crater. Even the Iraqi authorities do not know that it exists. The missile sprayed hunks of metal through the crowds—mainly women and children—and through the cheap brick walls of local homes, amputating limbs and heads. Three brothers, the eldest twenty-one and the youngest twelve, were cut down inside the living room of their brick hut on the main road opposite the market. Two doors away, two sisters were killed in an identical manner.

"We have never seen anything like these wounds before," Dr. Ahmed, an anaesthetist at the al-Noor hospital, told me later. "These people have been punc-tured by dozens of bits of metal." He was right. One old man I visited in a hospital ward had twenty-four holes in the back of his legs and buttocks, some as big as pound coins. An X-ray photograph handed to me by one of his doctors clearly showed at least thirty-five slivers of metal still embedded in his body.

As with the Abu Taleb Street massacre, Shu'ale is a poor Shia Muslim neigh-bourhood of single-storey corrugated iron and cement food stores and two-room brick homes. Again, these are the very people whom Messrs. Bush and Blair expected to rise in insurrection against Saddam. But the anger in the slums was directed at the Americans and British, by old women and bereaved fathers and brothers who spoke without hesitation—and without the presence of the ubiqui-tous government "minders." "This is a crime," a woman muttered at me angrily. "Yes, I know they say they are targeting the military. But can you see soldiers here? Can you see missiles?"

The answer has to be in the negative. A few journalists did report seeing a Scud missile on a transporter near the Sha'ab area on Thursday and there were anti-aircraft guns around Shu'ale. I heard an American jet race over the scene of the massacre and just caught sight of a ground-to-air missile that was vainly chasing it, its contrail soaring over the slum houses in the dark blue sky. An anti-aircraft battery—manufactured around 1942—also began firing into the air a few blocks away. But even if the Iraqis do position or move their munitions close to the sub-urbs, does that justify the Americans firing into those packed civilian neighbour-hoods, into areas that they know contain crowded main roads and markets—and during the hours of daylight? The 27 March attack on Abu Taleb Street was carried out on a main road at midday during a sandstorm—when dozens of civilians are bound to be killed, whatever the pilot thought he was aiming at.

"I had five sons and now I have only two—and how do I know that even they will survive?" a bespectacled middle-aged man asked in the bare concrete back room of his home. "One of my boys was hit in the kidneys and heart. His chest was full of shrapnel; it came right through the windows. Now all I can say is that I am sad that I am alive." A neighbour interrupted to say that he saw the plane with his own eyes. "I saw the side of the aircraft and I noticed it changed course after it fired the missile."

Plane-spotting has become an all-embracing part of life in Baghdad. I respond in my paper to a reader who thoughtfully asks if I can see with my own eyes the American aircraft over the city; I have to reply that in at least sixty-five raids by aircraft, I have not—despite my tiger-like eyes—actually seen one plane. I hear them, especially at night, but they are flying at supersonic speed; during the day, they are usually above the clouds of black smoke that wash over the city. I have, just once, spotted a cruise missile—the cruise or "Tomahawk" rockets fly at only around 400 mph—and I saw it passing down a boulevard towards the Tigris River. But the grey smoke that shoots out of the city like the fingers of a dead hand is unmistakeable, along with the concussion of sound. And when they can be found, the computer codings on the bomb fragments reveal their own story. As the codes on the Shu'ale missile surely must.

All morning, the Americans were at it again, blasting away at targets on the perimeter of Baghdad—where the outer defences are being dug by Iraqi troops—and in the centre of the city. An air-fired rocket exploded on the roof of the Iraqi Ministry of Information, destroying a clutch of satellite dishes. One office building from which I was watching the bombardment swayed for several seconds during a long raid. Even in the al-Noor hospital, the walls were shaking as the survivors of the market slaughter struggled for survival. Hussein Mnati is fifty-two and just stared at me—his face pitted with metal fragments—as bombs blasted the city. A twenty-year-old man was sitting up in the next bed, the blood-soaked stump of his left arm plastered over with bandages. Only twelve hours ago, he had a left arm, a left hand, fingers. Now he blankly recorded his memories. "I was in the market and I didn't feel anything," he told me. "The rocket came and I was to the right of it and then an ambulance took me to hospital." Whether or not his amputation was dulled by pain-killers, he wanted to talk. When I asked him his name, he sat upright in bed and shouted at me: "My name is Saddam Hussein Jassem."

AT THE END OF MARCH 2003, Sergeant Ali Jaffar Moussa Hamadi al-Nomani drove a car laden with explosives into a U.S. Marine checkpoint in southern Iraq and blew himself up. He was the first Iraqi combatant known to stage a suicide attack. During the uprising against British rule not one Iraqi killed himself like this to destroy his enemies. Nomani was also a Shia Muslim—a member of the sect the Americans faithfully believed to be their secret ally in their invasion of Iraq. Even the Iraqi government initially wondered how to deal with his extraordinary action, caught between its desire to dissociate itself from an event that might remind the world of Osama bin Laden, and its determination to threaten the Americans with more such attacks.

The details of the fifty-year-old sergeant's life were few but intriguing. He was a soldier in the 1980–88 Iran–Iraq War and volunteered to fight in the 1991 Gulf War, the "Mother of All Battles" according to Saddam Hussein. Then, though he was over-age for further fighting, Nomani volunteered to fight the Anglo–American invasion. And so it was, without telling his commander and in his own car, that he drove into a U.S. Marine checkpoint outside Najaf. Saddam awarded him the Military Medal (1st Class) and the "Mother of All Battles" medal. The dead man left five children, a widow and a new place in the 2,000-year history of Iraqi resistance to invasions. A U.S. spokesman said that the attack "looks and feels like terrorism," although, since Nomani was attacking an occupation army and his target was a military one, no Arab would ever believe this.

Within hours al-Homani's death, Taha Yassin Ramadan, the Iraqi vice president, was talking like a Palestinian or Hizballah leader, emphasising the inequality of arms between the Iraqis and the Americans. "The U.S. administration is going to turn the whole world into people prepared to die for their nations," he said. "All they can do now is turn themselves into bombs. If the B-52 bombs can now kill 500 or more in our war, then I'm sure that some operations by our freedom fighters will be able to kill 5,000." It was clear what this meant; the Iraqi leadership was just as surprised at Nomani's attack as were his American victims.

This made no sense to us. Iraqis were not suiciders. As the Americans might say, this did not "compute." I wrote a half-hearted dispatch to *The Independent* on 30 March, trying to make sense of what had happened. Of course, I had forgotten the Iran–Iraq War—the conflict in which Nomani had participated—and the suicidal battles in which the Iraqis fought and died. Suicide bombers, I wrote:

> whether they be the Shia Muslim Lebanese successfully evicting Israel's army of occupation or the Palestinians destroying Israel's sense of security, are the ultimate weapon of the Arabs. The U.S. first understood its power when suicide bombers struck the American embassy in Beirut in 1983 and the marine barracks in Beirut on 23 October the same year, when 241 American servicemen died. Only when Arabs bent on a far more devastating suicide mission launched their attacks on September 11th, 2001, did Washington finally realise that there was no effective defence against such tactics. In a strange way, therefore, September 11th at last finds a symbolic connection with Iraq. While the attempts to link President Saddam's regime with Osama bin Laden turned out to be fraudulent, the anger that the U.S. has unleashed is real, and has met the weapon the Americans fear most. Most suicide bombers are younger than Nomani and unmarried. But someone must have helped him to rig the explosives in his car, must have taught him how to set off the detonator. And if this was not the Iraqis, as they claim, then was there an organisation involved of which both the Americans and the Iraqis know nothing?

There was some talk by Vice President Ramadan of "the martyr's moment of sublimity," an expression hitherto unheard of in the Baathist lexicon. General

Hazim al-Rawi of the Ministry of Defence recalled that the dead man bore the same name as "the Imam Ali" and announced that the new "martyr Ali has opened the door to jihad." He said that more than 4,000 volunteers from Arab countries were now in the country and that "martyrdom operations will continue not only by Iraqis but by thousands of Arabs who came to Baghdad." In my report that night, I wrote that "suddenly, it seems, Islam has intruded into this very nationalistic war of liberation—for that is what it is called here—against the Americans."

In retrospect, Nomani's suicide was one of the most important moments in this war. It shocked the Americans—whose superficial reaction about "terrorism" hopelessly underplayed the meaning of the attack—and it surprised the Iraqis. But the language of the Baathists—the talk of "martyrdom operations" and the international Arab legion that would supposedly continue them—should have set those old cliché "alarm bells" ringing loud. Something had started outside Najaf, a precedent most serious for any invading army; in a land without any such tradition, a match had been lit.

A vicious dark storm has smashed into Baghdad, leaving my hotel room yellow with sand. The dust and muck of the city now lies like a shroud over the carpets and bed linen and tables. The cleaning staff have long ago fled. My files are covered in fine grains of sand so that the pages slither out of their boxes with the sound of a knife leaving a sheath. I work my way with dirty fingers through the section that I have marked with the word "Islam." Mostly, the pages are about Shiite resistance. But I have some handwritten notes—never used in a report, since I did not understand their meaning—to the effect that Saddam had, in 2000, allowed the creation of "Islamic committees," groups of Sunni Muslim religious scholars and their followers who would be permitted to discuss Islamic law and Koranic teaching provided they never mentioned politics, never combined their beliefs with the secular world of the Baath. These committees now existed in Mosul and Baquba, Fallujah and Ramadi, and in Baghdad.

Another sand-engrained page emerged from my file, a single flimsy page from a five-year-old copy of *The Economist*. "Iraqis, saddened by misfortune, are turning for comfort to their religion," the report says. "So, in his own manipulative way, is their leader." Saddam was building in Baghdad the largest mosque in the world, with room for 45,000 worshippers and minarets 600 feet in height. The Iraqi flag now had the words *Allahu akbar*—God is great—inscribed in the white rectangle between the red and black of the national banner, the eagle of Iraq between the *Allahu* and the *akbar*. In 1997 Saddam had given Abdul Monim Abu Zant, a Jordanian calling for an Islamist state in his own country, a weekly half-hour programme on Iraqi television.

"Mosque attendance is rising fast, particularly among the young," the *Economist* reporter writes. He quotes a Baghdad resident who says: "Before the [Kuwait] war about 90 men would come to the mosque in my neighbourhood for Friday prayers. Now, more than 1,000 worshippers turn up, mostly young people. There is not enough space, so they pour into the streets." There had been increased observance during the Ramadan month of fasting. *The Economist* regarded Saddam's involvement in this reawakening of Islam as "manipulative" but, listening to the government's response to the suicide bombing—not to mention the news of Nomani's "martyrdom"—I began to wonder if Saddam was being compliant rather than manipulative, whether he had discovered a power that would have to be appeased rather than suppressed, one that embraced his own Sunni Muslim people as well as the Shia. Within a week, two women—an even more unheard-of precedent—would blow themselves up at another American checkpoint.

At dusk, the ground around the Baghdad North Gate Cemetery shook with the vibration of the bombs. The oil-grey sky was peppered with anti-aircraft fire. And below the clouds of smoke and the tiny star-like explosion of the shells, Sergeant Frederick William Price of the Royal Garrison Artillery, Corporal A. D. Adsetts of the York and Lancaster Regiment and Aircraftman First Class P. Magee of the Royal Air Force slept on. An eerie place to visit, perhaps, as the first of the night's raids closed in on the capital of Iraq. Not so. For Iraqi foreign minister Naji Sabri had spoken earlier of these graves of colonisers past. For No. 1401979 Sergeant Price and No. 4736364 Corporal Adsetts and No. 210493 Aircraftman Magee all died in Britain's first colonial war in Iraq, in 1921.

And what was it that Mr. Sabri, dressed in his Baath party uniform, said? "British soldiers already have their graveyards in Iraq, from the 1920s and from 1941 . . . Now they will have other graveyards where they will be joined by their friends, the Americans." Which is why I took a street taxi that very same hour of dusk to the North Gate Cemetery on the old Mosul road from Baghdad to have a look at the men about whom Naji Sabri spoke. Private Nicholson of the York and Lancaster Regiment was only twenty-three when he died on 12 August 1921, Private Clark of the Royal Army Service Corps was thirty-eight when he was killed six days later. This first guerrilla war against Western occupation is now to be refought, according to the Iraqi Baath party. But when? Against this huge invading force? Or afterwards?

"We shall turn our desert into a big graveyard for the American and British soldiers," Sabri said. As the missiles criss-crossed Baghdad—one swept over the Tigris at only 200 feet above the ground to explode with a roar and a plume of grey smoke in a presidential compound—the temperature of the language rose proportionately. The new colonisers, according to the foreign minister, were using the old British "golden rule" of "divide and conquer"—forget for a moment that "divide et impera" was originally a Roman rule—and he promised they would never break the unity of the Iraqi people. How much of this rhetoric would be abandoned if there was a way out of this war? "Real diplomacy," the fantastical Sahaf announced, "is to kill them [the Americans and British] on the battlefield so that they feel that their dreams have been foiled. We are not going to allow these dirty lackeys to remain on the land of Iraq." Lackeys? Didn't it use to be "lackeys and running dogs" when the Soviet Union existed? Are we really reverting to colonialism? Since the Americans have not reneged on their pledge of occupation and military government, it's hard to avoid the question. Nor was it difficult to imagine what Aircraftman First Class Magee might think as his grave vibrated to the explosion of bombs from the very same Royal Air Force he long ago died for in Iraq.

It is growing hotter in Baghdad—in every sense of the word—and in a month the temperature will rise to 35 degrees Celsius. The dense black shroud of oil smoke that covers the city is now creating a fog that makes even the mildest of air raids into a thing of mystery. At 4:45 p.m. next day comes the sound of jets yet again, followed by a series of short, sharp explosions that last for up to a minute. They sound all too familiar to my ears: the rumble of cluster bombs—legal against armour but decidedly illegal if used against civilians. I peer for ten minutes through the smoke from a high-rise apartment block, to no avail. Whether the bombs are dropped in the suburbs, on a military barracks or in a built-up area is impossible to discover. Nor is the status of Baghdad in this war. Far from being besieged, its main roads north and south are still open—a few trains are still leaving for northern cities—and although U.S. troops are reported to have set up a checkpoint on the road west to Amman, they appear to have been a "flying column," stopping trucks and cars for a few hours and then vanishing into the desert at night.

By evening, Vice President Ramadan turns up at the pseudo-Greek villa assigned to government spokesmen beside the Ministry of Information—he has the intriguing habit of never looking at anyone who asks him a question—to insist that 6,000 Arab volunteers have arrived in Iraq to fight the Americans and British, half of them anxious for "martyrdom." Ramadan repeats yet again that Iraq has no weapons of mass destruction and spends some time—rather a lot of time, in fact—claiming that the Americans and British might plant such weapons in Iraq in order to fool the world and justify their invasion. And then comes a lecture which, I couldn't help suspecting, reflected all too faithfully the current anger of Saddam Hussein.

The Saudi foreign minister, Prince Saud al-Feisal, was Ramadan's—and thus Saddam's—target. "He has offered advice—which is something he is in the habit of doing—and his advice is that he would like to see our leader leave his post . . ." Ramadan thunders. "Let me tell this lackey, this stooge, this small entity—they know full well who his cousin is, the so-called Prince [Ambassador] Bandar in Washington, and who he works for. Let them [the Saudis] say to him: 'Go to hell. All we wish for is that you do not have an Arab name . . .' Let me tell you—you are too small, too small, too much of a nothing, to say a word to the leader of Iraq. Those who give up will be swept away from the land of the Arabs." Which didn't do a lot for Iraqi–Saudi relations.

Then we in Baghdad hear that Secretary of State Colin Powell is announcing— to the American–Israel Public Affairs Committee, the largest Israeli lobby group in the United States, who of course support the invasion—that Syria and Iran are "supporting terror groups" and will have to "face the consequences." What, we all asked, was happening now? Are we going to forget Baghdad for a few months and wheel our young soldiers west to surround Damascus? George W. Bush now tells us the war may be "long and difficult"—he didn't tell us that before, did he?—and according to Tony Blair, this is "only the beginning." Strange how all that fuss about chemical and biological warfare had been forgotten. The "secret" weapons, the gas masks, the anti-anthrax injections, the pills and chemical suits and all the rest have now been erased from the story—because bullets and rocket-propelled grenades are now the real danger to British and American forces in Iraq. Even the "siege of Baghdad"—a city that is 30 miles wide and might need a quarter of a million men to surround it—is fading from the diary. Secretary of Defence Donald Rumsfeld, according to *The New Yorker*, interfered with the generals' plans. This was going to be—I quote Rumsfeld—"war of a kind we have never seen before."

Sitting in a Baghdad café, listening to the god-awful propaganda rhetoric of the Iraqis but watching the often promiscuous American and British air attacks—targeting an alleged missile battery near a marketplace in a capital city at midday during a sandstorm *is* going to kill civilians—I have a suspicion that this war's foundations were based not on military planning but on ideology. Long ago, as we knew, the right-wing pro-Israeli lobbyists around Mr. Bush planned the overthrow of Saddam. This would destroy the most powerful Arab state in the Middle East— Israel's chief of staff, Shoal Mofaz, demanded that the war should start even earlier than it did—and allow the map of the region to be changed for ever. Powell stated just this a month ago.

Illusions were given credibility by a superpower moral overdrive. Any kind of mendacity could be used to fuel this ideological project. September 11th (oddly unmentioned now), links between Saddam and Osama bin Laden (unproven), weapons of mass destruction (unfound), human rights abuses (at which we originally connived when Saddam was our friend), and then, finally, the most heroic project of all—the "liberation" of the people of Iraq. Oil was not mentioned, although it is the all-important and dominating factor in this illegitimate conflict. No wonder General Tommy Franks, the American commander, admitted that his first concern, prior to the war, was the "protection" of the southern Iraqi oilfields. So it was to be "liberation" and "democracy." How boldly we crossed the border. With what lordly aims had we invaded Iraq.

Few Iraqis doubted—even the ministers in Baghdad spoke about this—that the Americans could, ultimately, occupy the country. "They have the force," I wrote on 2 April, "and they have the weapons to smash their way into every city and impose a curfew and rule the land by martial law. But can they make Iraqis submit to that rule? Unless the masses rise up as Mr. Bush and Mr. Blair hope, this is now a nationalist war against the most obvious kind of imperial power. Without Iraqi support, how can General Franks run a military dictatorship or find Iraqis willing to serve him or run the oil fields? The Americans can win the war. But if their project fails, they will have lost." I read these words today with some mystification. There they are, printed in *The Independent*. But I cannot remember writing them. Perhaps the suicide bombing had jogged my reporter's hand, maybe that rhetoric about "martyrdom." War produces infinite fatigue. All day we would travel and write and try to stay alive and then at night, curled up in our beds in the Palestine Hotel in the belief—vain as it was to turn out—that this guaranteed our safety, we would lie awake as giant explosions tore across the city. War is also about insomnia.

At last, the Iraqis decide to truck us out of Baghdad. To Mussayib and to Hilla. The road to the front in central Iraq is a place of fast-moving vehicles, blazing Iraqi anti-aircraft guns, tanks and trucks hidden in palm groves, a train of armoured vehicles bombed from the air and hundreds of artillery positions dug into revetments to defend the capital. Anyone who doubts that the Iraqi army is prepared to defend its capital, I wrote in my notebook, should take the highway south of Baghdad. How, I kept asking myself, could the Americans batter their way through these defences? Looking back, I wonder if that is why we were taken, to view the earthworks and ditches and gun embrasures that would, in a few days, be abandoned by their defenders.

For mile after mile they go on, slit trenches, ditches, earthen underground bunkers, palm groves of heavy artillery and truckloads of combat troops in battle fatigues and steel helmets. Not since the 1980–88 Iran–Iraq War have I seen the Iraqi army deployed like this. The Americans may say they are "degrading" the country's defences but there was little sign of that here. That a Western journalist could see more of Iraq's military preparedness than many of the reporters "embedded" with British and American forces said as much for the Iraqi government's self-confidence as it did for the need of Saddam's regime to make propaganda against its enemies.

True, there are signs of the Americans and British striking at the Iraqi military. Two gun pits have been turned to ashes by direct air strikes, and a military barracks—empty like all the large installations that were likely to be on the Anglo-American target list—has been pulverised by missiles. A clutch of telephone exchanges in the towns around Hilla have been destroyed; along with the bombing of six communications centres in Baghdad, the country's phone system appears to have been shut down.

On a rail track further south, a train carrying military transport has been bombed from the air, the detonations blasting two entire armoured vehicles off their flat-bed trucks and hurling them in bits down an embankment. But other APCs, including an old American M-113 vehicle—presumably a captured relic from the Iranian army—remained intact. If that was the extent of the Americans' success south of Baghdad, there are literally hundreds of military vehicles untouched for 150 kilometres south of the capital, carefully camouflaged to avoid air attack. Like the Serb army in Kosovo, the Iraqis have proved masters of concealment. An innocent wheat field fringed by tall palm trees turned out, on closer scrutiny, to be traversed with bunkers and hidden anti-aircraft guns. Vehicles were hidden under motorway bridges—which the Americans and British very definitely do not wish to destroy because they want to use them if they succeed in occupying Iraq—and fuel trucks dug in behind deep earth revetments. At a major traffic intersection, an anti-aircraft gun was mounted on a flat-bed truck and manned by two soldiers scanning the pale blue early summer skies.

As well they might. Contrails hung across the skies between Baghdad, Kerbala and Hilla. Above the centre of Hilla, home to the ancient Sumerian Babylon, a distant American AWACS plane could be seen circling high in the heavens, a tiny white dot indicating the giant scanner above the aircraft, its path followed by the eyes of scores of militiamen and soldiers. Driving the long highway south by bus, I could see troops pointing skywards. If hanging concentrates a man's mind wonderfully, fear of an air strike has almost the same effect. An Iraqi journalist beside me insisted that an American or British aircraft whose course we had been fearfully tracking from our vehicle was turning back towards the south, ignoring traffic on the main road. A few minutes later, it reappeared in front of us, flying in the opposite direction.

Driving the highway south, a lot of illusions are blown from the mind. There are markets in the small towns en route to Babylon, stalls with heaps of oranges and apples and vegetables. The roads are crowded with buses, trucks and private cars—far outnumbering the military traffic, the truckloads of troops and, just occasionally, the sleek outline of a missile transporter with canvas covers wrapped tightly over the truck it is hauling. In the town of Iskandariyah, cafés and restaurants were open, shops were selling take-away *kofta* meat balls and potatoes and the tall new television aerials that Iraqis now need to watch their state television channel, whose own transmitters have been so constantly attacked by American and British aircraft. This was not a population on the edge of starvation; nor indeed did it appear to be a frightened people. If the Americans were about to launch an assault through this farmland of canals and massive forests of palm trees and wheat fields, it looked at first glance like a country at peace.

But the large factories and government institutions seemed deserted, many of the industrial workers and employees standing outside the main gates. Only 30 kilometres south of Baghdad, there came the thump of bombs and our bus shook with the impact of anti-aircraft rounds. A series of artillery pieces to our right were firing at an elevation over our heads, the gun muzzles blossoming gold, the shells exploding above the canopy of grey smoke from Baghdad's oil fires which now spread 80 kilometres south of the city.

The images sometimes stretched the limits of comprehension. Children jumping over a farm wall beside a concealed military radio shack; herds of big-humped camels moving like biblical animals past a Soviet-made T-82 battle tank hidden under palm branches; fields of yellow flowers beside fuel bowsers and soldiers standing amid brick kilns; an incoming American missile explosion that scarcely prompts the farmers to turn their heads. On one pile of rubble north of Hilla someone had fixed the red, white and black flag of Iraq, just as the Palestinians tie their banners to the wreckage of their buildings after Israeli attacks.

Was there a lesson in all this? I had perhaps two hours to take it all in, to wonder how the Americans could batter their way up this long, hot highway—you can feel the temperature rise as you drive south—with its dug-in tanks and APCs and its endless waterlogged fields and palm plantations. The black-uniformed men of the Saddam Fedayeen with red and black kuffiah scarves round their heads, whom I saw 150 kilometres south of Baghdad, were kitted out with ammunition pouches and rocket-propelled grenades. And they did not look to me like a "degraded" army on the verge of surrender.

All this, I wrote that night, may be an illusion. The combat troops I saw may have no heart for battle. The tanks may be abandoned when the Americans come down the highway towards Baghdad. The fuel bowsers may be towed back to the capital and the slit trenches deserted. Saddam may flee Baghdad when the first American and British shells come hissing into the suburbs and the statues of the Great Leader that stand outside so many villages along the highway may be ritually sundered. This would prove to be very much the case. But it didn't feel that way in early April. It looked like an Iraqi army and a Baath party militia that were prepared to fight for their leadership, just as they had at Um Qasr and in Basra and Nasiriyah and Suq al-Shuyukh. Or was it something else they might be fighting for? An Iraq, however dictatorial in its leadership, that simply rejected the idea of foreign conquerors? Or Iraqis who cared more about Iraq than Saddam and who identified the Americans as their enemies without obeying Saddam's orders?

THE WOUNDS ARE VICIOUS AND DEEP, a rash of scarlet spots on the back and thighs or face, the shards of shrapnel from the cluster bombs buried an inch or more in the flesh. The wards of the Hilla teaching hospital some 50 kilometres south of Baghdad are proof that something illegal—something quite outside the Geneva Conventions—occurred in the villages around the city once known as Babylon. The wailing children, the young women with breast and leg wounds, the ten patients upon whom doctors had to perform brain surgery to remove metal from their heads, talk of the days and nights when the explosives fell "like grapes" from the sky. Cluster bombs, the doctors say—and the detritus of the air raids around the hamlets of Nadr and Djifil and Akramin and Mahawil and Mohandesin and Hail Askeri shows that they are right.

Were they American or British aircraft that showered these villages with one of the most lethal weapons of modern warfare on 29, 30 and 31 March? The sixty-one dead who have passed through the Hilla hospital cannot tell us. Nor can the survivors who, in many cases, were sitting in their homes when the white canisters opened high above their village, spilling thousands of bomblets that explode in the air, or swoop through windows and doorways to burst indoors, or skip off the roofs of the concrete huts to blow up later in the roadways.

Rahed Hakem remembers that it was 10:30 that Sunday morning, when she was sitting in her home in Nadr, that she heard "the voice of explosions" and looked out of the door to see "the sky raining fire." She said the bomblets were a black-grey colour. Mohamed Moussa described the clusters of "little boxes" that fell out of the sky in the same village and thought they were silver-coloured. They fell like "small grapefruit," he said. "If it hadn't exploded and you touched it, it went off immediately. They exploded in the air and on the ground and we still have some in our home, unexploded."

Karima Mizler thought the bomblets had some kind of wires attached to them—perhaps the metal "butterfly" which contains sets of the tiny cluster bombs and which springs open to release them in showers above the ground. Some died at once, mostly women and children, some of whose blackened, decomposing remains lay in the tiny charnel-house mortuary at the back of the Hilla hospital. The teaching college had received more than 200 wounded since the night of Saturday, 29 March—the sixty-one dead are only those who were brought to the hospital or who died during or after surgery, and many others are believed to have been buried in their home villages—and of these doctors say about 80 per cent were civilians.

Soldiers there certainly were, at least forty if these statistics are to be believed, and amid the foul clothing of the dead outside the mortuary door I found a khaki military belt and a combat jacket. But village men can also be soldiers and both they and their wives and daughters insisted there were no military installations around their homes. True or false? Who is to know if a tank or a missile-launcher was positioned in a nearby field—as they were along the highway north to Baghdad yesterday? But the Geneva Conventions demand protection for civilians even if they are intermingled with military personnel, and the use of cluster bombs in these villages—even if aimed at military targets—thus transgresses international law.

So it was that twenty-seven-year-old Asil Yamin came to receive those awful round wounds in her back. And so Zaman Abbais, five years old, was hit in the legs and forty-eight-year-old Samira Abdul-Hamza in the eyes, chest and legs. Her son Haidar, a thirty-two-year-old soldier, said that the containers which fell to the ground were white with some red and green sometimes painted on them. "It is like a grenade and they came into the houses," he said. "Some stayed on the land, others exploded."

Heartbreaking is the only word to describe ten-year-old Maryam Nasr and her five-year-old sister Hoda. Maryam has a patch over her right eye where a piece of bomblet embedded itself, and wounds to the stomach and thighs. I didn't realise that Hoda, standing by her sister's bed, was wounded until her mother carefully lifted the younger girl's scarf and long hair to show a deep puncture in the right side of her head, just above her ear, congealed blood sticking to her hair but the wound still gently bleeding. Their mother described how she had been inside her home and heard an explosion and found her daughters in a pool of blood near the door. The girls alternately smiled and hid when I took their pictures. In other wards, the hideously wounded would try to laugh, to show their bravery. It was a humbling experience.

The Iraqi authorities, of course, were all too ready to allow us journalists access to these patients. But there was no way these children and their often uneducated parents could manufacture these stories of tragedy and pain. Nor could the Iraqis have faked the scene in Nadr village where the remains of the tiny bomblets littered the ground beside the scorch marks of the explosions, as well as the shreds of the tiny parachutes upon which the bomb clusters float to the ground once their containers have broken open. A crew from Sky Television even managed to bring a set of bomblet shrapnel back to Baghdad from Nadr with them, the wicked metal balls that are intended to puncture the human body still locked into their frame like cough sweets in a metal sheath. They were of a black colour which glinted silver when held against the light.

The deputy administrator of the Hilla hospital and one of his doctors told a confused tale of military action around the city in recent days, of Apache helicopters that would disgorge Special Forces troops on the road to Kerbala. One of their operations—if the hospital personnel are to be believed—went spectacularly wrong one night when militiamen forced them to retreat. Shortly afterwards, the cluster-bomb raids began—artillery rather than aircraft might have been used to deliver the bomblets—although the villages that were targeted appear to have been on the other side of Hilla to the abortive American attack. The most recent raid occurred on Tuesday, when eleven civilians were killed—two women and three children among them—in a village called Hindiyeh. A man sent to collect the corpses reported to the hospital that the only living thing he found in the area of the bodies was a hen. Not till four days later were Iraqi bomb disposal officers ordered into the villages to clear the unexploded ordnance.

Needless to say, it was not the first time that cluster bombs had been used against civilians. During Israel's 1982 siege of West Beirut, its air force dropped cluster bomblets manufactured for the U.S. Navy across several areas of the city, especially in the Fakhani and Ouzai districts, causing civilians ferocious and deep wounds identical to those I saw in Hilla. Vexed at the misuse of their weapons, which are designed for use against exclusively military targets, the Reagan administration withheld a shipment of fighter-bombers for Israel—then relented a few weeks later and sent the aircraft anyway. Nor is it easy to listen to Iraqi officials condemning the use of illegal weapons by the USAF and RAF when the Iraqi air force itself dropped poison gas on the Iranian army and on pro-Iranian Kurdish villages during the 1980–88 war against Iran. Outraged claims from Iraqi officials at the abuse of human rights by American and British invaders sound like a bell with a very hollow ring. But something grievous happened around Hilla at the end of March, something unforgivable, and contrary to international law.

CONCEIT RULED BAGHDAD. Information Minister Sahaf promised that the Americans would perish like snakes in the desert—even as those same Americans were massed on the outskirts of Baghdad. Almost encircled by his enemies, Saddam now appeared on state television to urge Iraqis to fight to the death against the Anglo-American invasion force, because "victory is in reach." He appeared in military uniform and black beret beside an Iraqi flag with a white cloth as background. Accusing the Americans of fighting by stealth, he told Iraqis they could fight with "whatever weapons they have." The enemy, he said, "is trying in vain to undermine our heroic resistance by bypassing the defences of our armed forces around Baghdad. The enemy avoids fighting our forces when they find out that our troops are steadfast and strong. Instead, the enemy drops some troops here and there in small numbers, as we had expected. You can fight these soldiers with whatever weapons you have." The phrase "as we expected" suggested that the Iraqis had in fact been taken by surprise by the mobility of the American tactics which had, in effect, erased the very notion of the "front line" upon which Iraqi troops were traditionally taught to fight. "Remember that brave old farmer who shot an Apache helicopter with his rifle," Saddam remarked. The chopper had been brought down on 24 March, and conspiracy theorists immediately suggested that the president's television address might have been recorded more than a week ago in anticipation of a siege of Baghdad. They need not have bothered. In the last days of his rule, Saddam had become the repository of his own myth, a man who—even as Bush threatened him with war—had preferred to write romantic novels in his palaces.

And now his soldiers—and the civilians of Iraq—were paying the price. I ventured out on 5 April, in a fast car with a government driver who had already been "bought" by *The Independent* and was now loyal to Fisk rather than Saddam. It was just as well. We drove at speed towards the airport, then turned back towards the city as we heard the power-diving of jets. These were glimpses of fear and death, mere sketches to take back with me to fill out the front page of our Sunday on this last weekend of the invasion. Beside the highway, a squad of troops was stacking grenades as the ground beneath us vibrated with the impact of U.S. air strikes. The area was called Qadisiya. It was Iraq's last front line. An Iraqi armoured vehicle was still smouldering, a cloud of blue-grey smoke rising above the plane trees under which its crew had been sheltering. Two trucks were burnt out on the other side of the road. The American Apache helicopters had left just a few minutes before we arrived. A squad of soldiers, flat on their stomachs, were setting up an anti-armour weapon on the weed-strewn pavement, aiming at the empty airport motorway for the first American tanks to come thrashing down the highway.

A truck crammed with more than a hundred Iraqi troops, many in blue uniforms, all of them carrying rifles that gleamed in the morning sunlight, sped past me towards the airport. A few made victory signs in the direction of my car—my driver was touching 145 kilometres an hour on the speedometer—but of course one had to ask what their hearts were telling them. "Up the line to death" was the phrase that came to mind. Two miles away, at the Yarmouk hospital, the surgeons stood in the car park in bloodstained overalls; they had already handled their first intake of military casualties.

A few hours later, an Iraqi minister was to tell the world that the Republican Guard had just retaken the airport from the Americans, that they were under fire but had won "a great victory." Around Qadisiya it didn't look that way. Tank crews were gunning their T-72s down the highway past the main Baghdad railway yards in a convoy of armoured personnel carriers and jeeps and clouds of thick blue exhaust fumes. The more modern T-82s, the last of the Soviet-made fleet of battle tanks, sat hull-down around Jordan Square with a clutch of armoured vehicles. Across vast fields of sand and dirt and palm groves, I saw batteries of Sam-6 anti-aircraft missiles and multiple Katyusha rocket-launchers awaiting the American advance. The soldiers around them looked relaxed, some smoking cigarettes in the shade of the palm trees or sipping fruit juice brought to them by the residents of Qadisiya whose homes—heaven help them—were now in the firing line.

But then a white-painted Japanese pick-up truck pulled out in front of our car. At first, I thought the soldiers on the back were sleeping, covered in blankets to keep them warm. Yet I had opened my car window to keep cool this early summer morning and I realised that all the soldiers—there must have been fifteen of them in the little truck—were lying on top of each other, all with their heavy black military boots dangling over the tailboard. The two living soldiers on the vehicles sat with their feet wedged between the corpses. So did America's first victims of the day go to their eternal rest.

Dawn on 6 April started with a series of massive vibrations, a great "stomping" sound that physically shook my room. Stomp, Stomp, Stomp, it went. I lay in bed trying to fathom the cause. It was like the moment in *Jurassic Park* when the tourists first hear the footfalls of the tyrannosaur, an ever-increasing, ever more frightening thunder of regular, monstrous heartbeats. From my window on the east bank of the Tigris, I saw an Iraqi anti-aircraft gun firing from the roof of a white four-storey building half a mile away, shooting straight across the river at something on the opposite bank. Stomp, Stomp, it went again, the sound so enormous that it set off the burglar alarms in a thousand cars along the riverbank.

And it was only when I stood on the roadway a few minutes later that I knew what had happened. Not since the last Gulf War in 1991 had I heard the sound of American artillery fire. And there, only a few hundred metres away on the far bank of the Tigris, I saw them. At first they looked like tiny armoured centipedes, stopping and starting, dappled brown and grey, weird little creatures that had come to inspect an alien land and search for water.

You had to keep your eye on the centipedes to interpret reality, to realise that each creature was a Bradley Fighting Vehicle, that its tail was a cluster of U.S. Marines hiding for cover behind the armour, moving forward together each time their protection revved its engines and manoeuvred closer to the Tigris. There was a burst of gunfire from the Americans, a smart clatter of rocket-propelled grenades and puffs of white smoke from the Iraqi soldiers and militiamen dug into their foxholes and trenches on the same riverbank further south. It was that quick and that simple and that awesome.

Indeed, the sight was so extraordinary, so unexpected—despite all the Pentagon boasts and Bush promises—that one somehow forgot the precedents that it was setting for the future history of the Middle East. Amid the crack of gunfire, the tracer streaking across the river and the huge oil fires that the Iraqis lit to give them cover to retreat, one had to look away—to the great river bridges farther north, into the pale green waters of that most ancient of rivers—to realise that a Western army on a moral crusade had broken through to the heart of an Arab city for the first time since Maude marched into this same city of Baghdad in 1917 and Allenby into

Jerusalem in 1918. But Allenby entered Jerusalem on foot, in reverence for Christ's birthplace, and yesterday's American thrust into Baghdad had neither humility nor honour about it.

The marines and Special Forces who spread out along the west bank of the river broke into Saddam Hussein's largest palace, filmed its lavatories and bathrooms and lay resting on its lawns before moving down towards the Rashid Hotel and sniping at both soldiers and civilians. Hundreds of Iraqi men, women and children were brought in agony to Baghdad's hospitals in the hours that followed, victims of bullets, shrapnel and cluster bombs. We could see the twin-engined American A-10s firing their depleted-uranium rounds into the far shore of the river.

From the eastern bank, I watched the marines run towards a ditch with rifles to their shoulders to search for Iraqi troops. But their enemies went on firing from the mudflats to the south until, one after another, I saw them running for their lives. The Iraqis clambered out of their foxholes amid the American shellfire and began an Olympics of terror along the waterside; most kept their weapons, some fell back to an exhausted walk, others splashed right into the waters of the Tigris, up to their knees, even their necks. Three soldiers climbed from a trench with their hands in the air, in front of a group of marines. But others fought on. The Stomp, Stomp, Stomp of the American guns went on for more than an hour. Then the A-10s came back, and an F-18 fighter-bomber that sent a ripple of fire along the trenches, after which the shooting died away.

It seemed as if Baghdad would fall within hours. But the day was to be characterised with that most curious of war's attributes, a crazed mixture of normality, death and high farce. For even as the Americans were fighting their way north up the river and the F-18s were returning to bombard the bank, Sahaf, the Iraqi minister of information, turned up to give a press conference on the roof of the Palestine Hotel, scarcely half a mile from the battle. As shells exploded to his left and the air was shredded by the power-diving American jets, Mohamed Sahaf announced to perhaps a hundred journalists that the whole thing was a propaganda exercise, the Americans were no longer in possession of Baghdad airport, reporters must "check their facts and re-check their facts—that's all I ask you to do." Mercifully, the oil fires, bomb explosions and cordite smoke now obscured the western bank of the river so that fact-checking could no longer be accomplished by looking past Sahaf's shoulder.

What the world wanted to know, of course, was if Baghdad was about to be occupied, whether the Iraqi government would surrender and—the Mother of All Questions—where was Saddam? But Sahaf used his time to condemn Al-Jazeera for its bias towards the United States and to excoriate the Americans for using "the lounges and halls" of Saddam Hussein to make "cheap propaganda." The Americans "will be buried here," he shouted above the battle. "Don't believe these invaders. They will be defeated." Only a week ago, Sahaf had informed us that the Americans would acquire graves in the desert. Now their place of interment had moved to the city. And the more he spoke, the more we wanted to interrupt Sahaf, to say, "But hang on, Mr. Minister, take a look over your right shoulder." But of course, there was only smoke over his right shoulder. Why didn't we all take a drive around town, he suggested.

So I did. The corporation's double-decker buses were running and, if the shops were shut, stallholders were open, and near Yassir Arafat Street, men had gathered in cheap tea-houses to discuss the war. I went off to buy fruit, and the shopkeeper didn't stop counting my dinars—all 11,500 of them—when a low-flying American jet crossed the street and dropped its payload 1,000 metres away in an explosion that changed the air pressure in our ears. But every street corner had its clutch of militiamen, and when I reached the side of the Foreign Ministry on the western bank of the river upstream from the marines, an Iraqi artillery crew was firing a 120-mm gun at the Americans from the middle of a dual carriageway, its tongue of fire bright against the grey-black fog that was drifting over Baghdad.

Within an hour and a half, the Americans had moved up the southern waterfront and were in danger of overrunning the old Ministry of Information. Outside the Rashid Hotel, they opened fire on civilians and militiamen alike, blasting a passing motorcyclist onto the road and shooting at a Reuters photographer who escaped with only bullet holes in his car. All across Baghdad, hospitals were inundated with wounded, many of them women and children hit by fragments of cluster bombs. By dusk, the Americans were flying F-18s in close air support to the marines, so confident of their destruction of Iraq's anti-aircraft gunners that they could clearly be seen cruising the brown and grey skies in pairs over central Baghdad, turning lazily southwards and west while the cross-river shellfire continued.

At mid-afternoon, the Americans had located an ammunition dump on the western bank of the river not far from the presidential palace—one of three they occupied—and blew up the lot in a sheet of flame several hundred feet high. For hours afterwards, shells could be heard whizzing from the conflagration, sometimes exploding in the sky. Even as they did so, the Americans—clearly intending to enrage Saddam and his ministers—transmitted live pictures of their exploration of the Republican Palace on the banks of the Tigris, videotape that showed the presidential lavatory seat, Saddam's marble-walled bathroom and gold-plated taps and chandeliers, and Special Forces soldiers sun-bathing—though there was no sun—on the presidential lawn.

As night fell, I came across a small rampart of concrete at the eastern end of the great Rashid Bridge over the Tigris. Its three Iraqi defenders had propped their Soviet-made rocket-propelled grenade launchers neatly in line along the top of the parapet. Hundreds of American tanks and armoured vehicles were pouring towards the Tigris from the south-west of Baghdad and these three Iraqis—two Baathist militiaman and a policeman—were standing there ready to defend the eastern shore from the greatest army ever known to man. That in itself, I thought, said something about both the courage and the hopelessness of the Arabs. The pain was still to come.

It was a scene from the Crimean War, a hospital of screaming wounded and floors running with blood. I stepped in the stuff, it stuck to my shoes, to the clothes of all the doctors in the packed emergency room, it swamped the passage-ways and the blankets and sheets. The Iraqi civilians and soldiers brought to the Adnan Khairallah Martyr Hospital in the last hours of Saddam's regime—some-times still clinging to severed limbs—are the dark side of victory and defeat, final proof, like the dead who are buried within hours, that war is indeed about the total failure of the human spirit.

As I wandered amid the beds and the groaning men and women on them—Dante's visit to the circles of Hell should have included these visions—the same old questions recurred. Was this for September 11th? For human rights? For weapons of mass destruction? In a jammed corridor, I came across a middle-aged man on a soaked hospital trolley. He had a head wound that was almost indescrib-able. From his right eye socket, hung a handkerchief that was streaming blood on to the floor. A little girl lay on a filthy bed, one leg broken, the other so badly gouged out by shrapnel during an American air attack that the only way doctors could prevent her moving it was to tie her foot to a rope weighed down with con-crete blocks. Her name was Rawa Sabri.

And as I walked through this place of horror, the American shelling began to bracket the Tigris River outside, bringing back to the wounded the terror of death they had suffered only hours before. The road bridge I had just crossed to reach the hospital came under fire and clouds of cordite smoke drifted over the medical cen-tre. Tremendous explosions shook the wards and corridors as doctors pushed shrieking children away from the windows.

Florence Nightingale never reached this part of the old Ottoman empire. But her equivalent is Dr. Khaldoun al-Baeri, the director and chief surgeon, a gently-spoken man who has slept an hour a day for six days and who is trying to save the lives of more than a hundred souls a day with one generator and half his operating theatres out of use—you cannot carry patients in your arms to the sixteenth floor when they are coughing blood. Dr. al-Baeri speaks like a sleepwalker, trying to describe how difficult it is to stop a wounded man or woman from suffocating when they have been injured in the thorax, explaining that after four operations to extract metal from the brains of his patients, he is almost too tired to think, let alone in English.

As I leave him, he tells me that he does not know where his family is. "Our house was hit and my neighbours sent a message to tell me they sent them away somewhere. I do not know where. I have two little girls, they are twins, and I told them they must be brave because their father had to work night and day at the hos-pital and they mustn't cry because I have to work for humanity. And now I have no idea where they are." Then Dr. al-Baeri choked on his words and began to cry and could not say goodbye.

There was a man on the second floor with a fearful wound to the neck. It seemed the doctors could not stanch his blood and he was dribbling his life away all over the floor. Something wicked and sharp had cut into his stomach and six inches of bandages could not stop the blood from pumping out of him. His brother stood beside him and raised his hand to me and asked: "Why? Why?" A small child with a drip-feed in its nose lay on a blanket. It had had to wait four days for an operation. Its eyes looked dead. I didn't have the heart to ask its mother if this was a boy or a girl. There was an air strike perhaps half a mile away and the hospital corridors echoed with the blast, long and low and powerful; it was followed by a rising chorus of moans and cries from the children outside the wards.

Below them, in that worst of all emergency rooms, they had brought in three men who had been burned across their faces and arms and chests and legs, naked men with a skin of blood and tissues whom the doctors pasted with white cream, who sat on their beds with their skinless arms held upwards, each beseeching an absent saviour to rescue him from his pain. "No! No! No!" another young man screamed as doctors tried to cut open his pants. He shrieked and cried and whinnied like a horse. I thought he was a soldier. He looked tough and strong and well fed but now he was a child again and he cried "Ummi, Ummi." Mummy, mummy.

I left this awful hospital to find the American shells falling in the river outside. I noticed, too, some military tents on a small patch of grass near the hospital's administration building and—God damn it, I said under my breath—an armoured vehicle with a gun mounted on it, hidden under branches and foliage. It was only a few metres inside the hospital grounds. But the hospital was being used to conceal it. And I couldn't help reminding myself of the name of the hospital. Adnan Khairallah had been Saddam's minister of defence, a man who allegedly fell out with his leader and died in a helicopter crash whose cause was never explained. Even in the last hours of the Battle of Baghdad, its victims had to lie in a building named in honour of a murdered man.


I AM DRIVING BACK to the Palestine Hotel. The noise of the shelling has receded. There are American tanks on the Jumhuriya Bridge over the Tigris but there is no fighting here. When we slow to turn into Saadun Street, I hear birds. Then the crack of a cannon and the hiss of a shell and we arrived at the Palestine to see a puff of grey smoke drifting from an upper floor. Sahaf and Naji Sabri are on the lawn below, still holding court, but then from the hotel entrance journalists and staff come shrieking into the dull sunlight carrying a sheet with something heavy inside, the material sopping with blood. Not for the first time that day, the Americans are killing journalists.

That single tank shell, fired at the Palestine, hit the Reuters television bureau, killing one of the agency's cameramen, father of an eight-year-old son, and wounding four other members of staff along with a cameraman for the Spanish Telé 5 channel. He was to die later. Was it possible to believe this was an accident? This was our first question on that awful day.

These were not, of course, the first journalists to die in the Anglo–American invasion of Iraq. Terry Lloyd of ITN was shot dead by American troops in southern Iraq who apparently mistook his car for an Iraqi vehicle. Most of his crew were still missing. Michael Kelly of *The Washington Post* tragically drowned in a canal. Two reporters died in Kurdistan. Two journalists—a German and a Spaniard—

were killed at a U.S. base on the edge of Baghdad, along with two Americans, when an Iraqi missile exploded among them. Nor could we forget the Iraqi civilians who were being killed and maimed by the hundreds and who—unlike their journalist guests—could not, as I have said before, leave the war and fly home Business Class. So the facts should speak for themselves. Unfortunately for the Americans, they made it look bad. For a U.S. pilot had already that day killed Al-Jazeera's reporter and badly wounded his colleague.

The U.S. jet turned to rocket Al-Jazeera's office on the banks of the Tigris at 7:45 a.m. Their chief correspondent in Baghdad, a Jordanian–Palestinian called Tareq Ayoub, was on the roof with his second cameraman, an Iraqi called Zuheir, reporting a pitched battle near the bureau between American and Iraqi troops. As Ayoub's colleague Maher Abdullah recalled afterwards, both men saw the plane fire the rocket as it swooped toward their building, which is close to the Jumhuriya Bridge upon which two American tanks had just appeared. "On the screen, there was this battle and we could see bullets flying and then we heard the aircraft," Maher Abdullah said. "The plane was flying so low that those of us downstairs thought it would land on the roof—that's how close it was. We actually heard the rocket being launched. It was a direct hit—the missile actually exploded against our electrical generator. Tareq died almost at once. Zuheir was injured."

Now for America's problems in explaining this little saga. Back in 2001, the United States fired a cruise missile at Al-Jazeera's office in Kabul—from which tapes of Osama bin Laden had been broadcast around the world. No explanation was ever given for this extraordinary attack on the night before the city's "liberation"; the Kabul correspondent, Taiseer Alouni, was unhurt. By the strange coincidence of journalism, Alouni was in the Baghdad office to endure the USAF's second attack on Al-Jazeera. Far more disturbing, however, was the fact that the Al-Jazeera network—the freest Arab television station, which had incurred the fury of not just the Americans but, as we have seen, Saddam, for its live coverage of the war—gave the Pentagon the coordinates of its Baghdad office in February and received its assurances that the bureau in Iraq would not be attacked. Then on 6 April a State Department spokesman visited Al-Jazeera's offices in Doha and, according to a source within the Qatari satellite channel, repeated the Pentagon's assurances. Within twenty-four hours, the Americans had fired their missile into the Baghdad office.

The next assault—on Reuters—came just before midday after the Abrams tank on the Jumhuriya Bridge pointed its gun barrel towards the Palestine Hotel where more than 200 foreign journalists were staying. Sky Television's David Chater noticed the barrel moving. The French television channel France 3 actually had a crew in a room below Reuters and videotaped the tank on the bridge. After a long period of silence on the sound track, their tape shows a bubble of fire emerging from the tank's barrel, the sound of a massive detonation and then pieces of paintwork falling past the camera as it vibrates with the impact.

In the Reuters bureau on the fifteenth floor, the shell exploded among the staff. It mortally wounded their Ukrainian cameraman Taras "Sasha" Protsjuk—

who was also filming the tanks—seriously wounded another member of the staff, Briton Paul Pasquale, and two other journalists, including Reuters' Lebanese–Palestinian reporter Samia Nakhoul. On the next floor, Telé 5's Spanish cameraman Jose Couso was also badly hurt. Protsjuk died shortly afterwards. His television camera and its "legs" were left in the office, which was swamped with the crew's blood.

The American response ignored all the evidence. Major General Buford Blount of the U.S. 3rd Infantry Division—whose tanks were on the bridge—announced that his vehicles had come under rocket and rifle fire from snipers in the Palestine Hotel, that his tank had fired a single round at the hotel and that the gunfire had then ceased. But I had been driving on that road between the tank and the hotel at the moment the shell was fired—and heard no small-arms fire. The French videotape of the attack runs for more than four minutes and records utter silence before the tank's armament is fired. It is my absolute belief that there were no snipers in the building. Indeed, the dozens of journalists and crews living there—myself included—watched like hawks to make sure that no armed men should ever use the hotel as an assault point. This is, one should add, the same General Blount who boasted back in March that his crews would be using depleted-uranium munitions—the kind many believe to be responsible for an explosion of cancers after the 1991 Gulf War—in their tanks. For General Blount to suggest—as he clearly did by saying that the sniper fire stopped once the Reuters camera crew were hit—that the crew were in some way involved in shooting at Americans merely turned an unbelievable statement into a libellous one.

Again, we should remember that three dead and five wounded journalists do not constitute a massacre—or even the equivalent of the hundreds of civilians being maimed by the invasion force. And it was a truth that needed to be remembered that the Iraqi regime has killed a few journalists of its own over the years, along with tens of thousands of its own people. The name of Farzad Bazoft came to mind. But something very dangerous appeared to be getting loose. Blount's explanation was the kind employed by the Israelis after they have killed the innocent. Was there therefore some message that we reporters were supposed to learn from all this? Was there some element in the American military that had come to hate the press and wanted to take out journalists based in Baghdad, to hurt those whom Britain's home secretary, David Blunkett, had claimed to be working behind enemy lines? Could it be that this claim—that international correspondents were in effect collaborating with Mr. Blunkett's enemy (most Britons having never supported this war in the first place)—was turning into some kind of a death sentence?

I knew Tareq Ayoub. I broadcast to Doha during the war from the same Baghdad rooftop on which he died. I told Ayoub then how easy a target his Baghdad office would make if the Americans wanted to destroy its coverage—seen across the entire Arab world—of the civilian victims of the Anglo–American bombing. Sasha Protsjuk of Reuters often shared the Palestine Hotel's insupportably slow elevator with me. Samia Nakhoul had been a friend and colleague since the 1975–90

Lebanese civil war. She is married to the *Financial Times*'s correspondent David Gardner. And now she lay covered in blood in a Baghdad hospital. And Major General Buford Blount dared to imply that this innocent woman and her brave colleagues were snipers. What, I wonder, did this tell us about the war in Iraq?*

Earlier, the U.S. Air Force bombed a civilian housing complex in the Mansour district of Baghdad because American intelligence officers believed Saddam was staying there. Their four 2,000-pound bombs dismembered thirteen Iraqi civilians—by chance, they were mostly Christians—but Saddam was not there. Days later, a fourteenth Iraqi—a baby—would be discovered under the pile of rubble thrown up by the bombs. From Qatar, the BBC reported that U.S. intelligence knew it was not a "risk-free" operation. No risk to the Americans, mark you, only a risk that Iraqi civilians would die for nothing—which they did—and there was, as expected, no apology.

Yet still civilians were being cut down. America's "probing" raids, their advance up one street, their retreat down another—always covered by the massive use of firepower—were cutting down the innocent in a way that, so we all thought, must have its effect on the post-invasion psychology of the Iraqis. Could all this be forgiven in the name of "liberation"?

We always went to the hospitals. They lay in lines, the car salesman who'd just lost his eye but whose feet were still dribbling blood, the motorcyclist who was hit by bullets from American troops near the Rashid Hotel, the fifty-year-old female civil servant, her long dark hair spread over the towel she was lying on, her body pockmarked with shrapnel from an American cluster bomb. For the civilians of Baghdad, this was the direct result of America's "probing missions" into Baghdad. It looked very neat on television, the American marines on the banks of the Tigris, the oh-so-funny visit to the presidential palace, the videotape of Saddam's golden loo. But the innocent were bleeding and screaming with pain to bring us our exciting television pictures and to provide Bush and Blair with their boastful talk of victory. I saw one boy in the Kindi Hospital, his mother and father and three brothers all shot dead when they approached an American checkpoint outside Baghdad. I watched two-and-a-half-year-old Ali Najour lying in agony on the bed, his clothes soaked with blood, a tube through his nose, until a relative walked up to me. "I want to talk to you," he shouted, his voice rising in fury. "Why do you

---

*A Pentagon investigation showed that U.S. soldiers on the Jumhuriya Bridge thought they had identified an "enemy hunter/killer team on the balcony of a room on the upper floors of a large tan-colored building." Reporters Without Borders carried out its own investigation into the Palestine Hotel deaths on 8 April 2003, interviewing both journalists and U.S. forces involved in the incident. It concluded that while the killings were not deliberate, the failure of U.S. commanders to inform their forces that the Palestine Hotel was a base of hundreds of journalists was "criminal" and that the U.S. Army had lied when it continued to insist that "direct firing" had come from the hotel when this was clearly untrue. The headquarters of Major General Blount "bore a heavy responsibility" for not providing information "that would have prevented the death of the journalists." The question, the report said, "is whether this information was withheld deliberately, because of misunderstanding or by criminal negligence." Regrettably, Reporters Without Borders did not investigate the attack on the Al-Jazeera office the same day.

British want to kill this little boy? Why do you even want to look at him? You did this—*you* did it!" The young man seized my arm, shaking it violently. "Are you going to make his mother and father come back? Can you bring them back to life for him? Get out! Get out!"

In the yard outside, where the ambulance drivers deposit the dead, a middle-aged Shiite woman in black was thumping her fists against her breasts and shrieking at me. "Help me," she cried. "Help me. My son is a martyr and all I want is a banner to cover him. I want a flag, an Iraqi flag, to put over his body. Dear God, help me!" It's becoming harder and harder to visit these places of pain and grief and anger. And I'm not surprised. The International Red Cross is reporting civilian victims of America's three-day offensive against Baghdad arriving at the hospitals now by the hundreds. The Kindi alone had taken fifty civilian wounded and three dead in the previous twenty-four hours. Most of the dead—the little boy's family, the family of six torn to pieces by an aerial bomb in front of Ali Abdulrazek, the car salesman, the next-door neighbours of Safa Karim—were simply buried within hours of their being torn to bits. There was no point in bringing corpses to a hospital.

On television, it looked so clean. On the previous Sunday evening the BBC showed burning civilian cars, its reporter—my old friend and colleague Gavin Hewitt, with whom I had travelled across Afghanistan almost a quarter of a century ago but now "embedded" with American forces—saying that he saw some of their passengers lying dead beside their vehicles. That was all. No pictures of the charred corpses, no close-ups of the shrivelled children. So perhaps there should be another warning here for those of a "nervous" disposition. Read no further unless you want to know what America and Britain did to the innocents of Baghdad.

I'll leave out the description of the flies that have been clustering round the wounds in the Kindi emergency rooms, of the blood caked on the sheets and the dirty pillow cases, the streaks of blood on the floor, the blood still dripping from the wounds of those I talked to. All were civilians. All wanted to know why they had to suffer. All—save for the incandescent youth who ordered me to leave the little boy's bed—talked gently and quietly about their pain. No Iraqi government bus took me to the Kindi Hospital. No doctor knew I was coming.

Let's start with Ali Abdulrazek. He's forty years old, the car salesman who was walking yesterday morning through a narrow street in the Shaab district of Baghdad—that's where the two American missiles killed twenty-one civilians in Abu Taleb Street—when he heard the jet engines of an aircraft. "I was going to see my family because the phone exchanges have been bombed and I wanted to make sure they were OK," he said. "There was a family, a husband and wife and kids, in front of me. Then I heard this terrible noise and there was a light and I knew something had happened to me. I went to try to help the family in front of me but they were all gone, in pieces. Then I realised I couldn't see properly."

Over Abdulrazek's left eye is a wad of thick bandages, tied to his face. His doctor, Osama al-Rahimi, tells me "we did not operate on the eye, we have taken care of his other wounds." Then he leans towards my ear and says softly: "He has lost his eye. There was nothing we could do. It was taken out of his head by the shrapnel." Abdulrazek smiles—of course, he does not know that he will be for ever half-blind—and suddenly breaks into near-perfect English, a language he learned at high school in Baghdad. "Why did this happen to me?" he asks.

Mohamed Abdullah Alwani was a victim of America's little excursion to the banks of the Tigris, the operation that provided such exciting television footage. He was travelling home on his motorcycle from the Rashid Hotel on the western side of the Tigris when he passed a road in which an American armoured vehicle was parked. "I only saw the Americans at the last moment. They opened fire and hit me and I managed to stay on the cycle. Then their second shell sent bits of shrapnel into the bike and I fell off." Dr. al-Rahimi peels the bandage back from Alwani's side. Next to his liver is a vicious, bloody, weeping gash, perhaps half an inch deep. Blood is still running down his legs and off his toes. "Why do they shoot civilians?" he asked me. Yes, I know the lines. Saddam would have killed more Iraqis than us if we hadn't invaded—not a very smart argument in the Kindi Hospital—and we're doing all this for Alwani and his friends. Didn't Paul Wolfowitz tell us all a couple of weeks ago that he was praying for both the American troops and for the Iraqi people? Aren't we coming here to save them—let's not mention the oil—and isn't Saddam a cruel and brutal man? But amid these people, you'd have to have a sick mind to utter such words.

Saadia Hussein al-Shomari is pin-cushioned with bloody holes. She is a civil servant from the Iraqi Ministry of Trade and she lies asleep, exhausted by pain, another doctor swiping the flies off her wounds with a piece of cardboard, asking me—as if I knew—whether a human can recover from a severe wound to the liver. A relative tells slowly how Saadia was leaving her home in the Baghdad Jdeidi district when an American plane dropped a cluster bomb on the estate. "There were some neighbours of hers. They were all hit. From one of them, a leg flew off, from another, an arm and a leg went flying into the air."

Then there was Safa Karim, eleven years old and dying. An American bomb fragment struck her in the stomach and she is bleeding internally, writhing on the bed with a massive bandage on her stomach and a tube down her nose and—somehow most terrible of all—a series of four cheap and dirty scarves that tie each of her wrists and ankles to the bed. She moans and thrashes where she lies, fighting pain and imprisonment at the same time. A relative—her black-shrouded mother sits by the bed in silence—says that she is too ill to understand her fate. "She has been given ten bottles of drugs and she has vomited them all up," he says. Through the mask that the drip tube makes of her face, Safa moves her eyes toward her mother, then the doctor, then the journalist, then back to her mother.

The man opens the palms of his hands, the way Arabs do when they want to express impotence. "What can we do?" they always say, but the man is silent, and I'm glad. How, after all, could I ever tell him that Safa Karim must die for September 11th, for George W. Bush and Tony Blair's religious certainty, Paul Wolfowitz's dreams of "liberation," and for the "democracy" that we are blasting these people's lives to create?

. . .

BUT THE DAY MUST DAWN. It is 9 April and the Americans have "liberated" Baghdad. They have destroyed the centre of Saddam Hussein's quarter-century of brutal dictatorial power but brought behind them an army of looters who have unleashed upon the ancient city a reign of pillage and anarchy. It was a day that had begun with shellfire and blood-spattered hospitals and ended with the ritual destruction of the dictator's statues. The mobs shrieked their delight. Men who, for twenty-five years, had grovelled to Saddam's most humble secret policemen turned into giants, bellowing their hatred of the Iraqi leader as his vast and monstrous statues thundered to the ground.

"It is the beginning of our new freedom," an Iraqi shopkeeper shouted at me. Then he paused, and asked: "What do the Americans want from us now?" The great Lebanese poet Kahlil Gibran once wrote that he pitied the nation that welcomed its tyrants with trumpetings and dismissed them with hootings of derision. And now the people of Baghdad performed this same deadly ritual, forgetting that they—or their parents—had behaved in identical fashion when the Arab Socialist Baath party destroyed the previous dictatorship of Iraq's generals and princes. Forgetting, too, that the "liberators" were a new and alien and all-powerful occupying force with neither culture nor language nor race nor religion in common with Iraq.

When tens of thousands of Shia Muslim poor from the vast slums of Saddam City poured into the centre of Baghdad to smash their way into shops, offices and government ministries—an epic version of the orgy of theft and mass destruction that the British did so little to prevent in Basra two weeks earlier—U.S. Marines watched from only a few hundred yards away as looters made off with cars, rugs, hoards of money, computers, desks, sofas, even door-frames.

In Fardus Square, U.S. Marines pulled down the gaunt and massive statue of Saddam by roping it to an armoured personnel carrier. It toppled menacingly forward from its plinth to hang lengthways above the ground, right arm still raised in fraternal greetings to the Iraqi people. It was a symbolic moment in more ways than one. I stood behind the first man to seize a hatchet and smash at the imposing grey marble plinth, but within seconds, the marble had fallen away to reveal a foundation of cheap bricks and badly cracked cement. That's what the Americans always guessed Saddam's regime was made of, although they did their best—in the late Seventies and early Eighties—to arm him and service his economy and offer him political support, to turn him into the very dictator he became.

In one sense, therefore, America—occupying the capital of an Arab nation for the first time in its history—was helping to destroy what it had spent so much time and money creating. Saddam had been "our" man and now we were annihilating him. Hence the importance of all those statue-bashing mobs, all that looting and theft. At Fardus Square I had seen a small group of young men arriving with a rope and pick-axes. They came as one, not spontaneously, and I have often wondered who organised their little melodrama. But they could not pull the statue down. As so often, the Arabs needed American help. So the marines obliged and it was left to the United States to tear down the dictator's likeness. A hundred cameras whirred and whined and sucked in this fraudulent scene for posterity. The Iraqi people tear down the image of their oppressor. Only they didn't. The Americans destroyed the statue of Saddam in front of those too impotent to do the job themselves.

The man's rule, of course, was effectively over. The torture chambers and the prisons, I wrote in my paper that night, should now be turned into memorials, the true story of Iraq's use of gas warfare revealed at last. "But history suggests otherwise. Prisons usually pass over to new management, torture cells too . . . And indeed they did."

Not that the nightmare was over. For though the Americans would mark 9 April as their first day of occupation—they would call it "liberation"—vast areas of Baghdad still remained outside the control of the United States. Just before darkness curled over the land, I crossed through the American lines, back to the little bit of Saddam's regime that remained intact within the vast, flat city of Baghdad. Down grey, carless streets, I drove to the great bridges over the Tigris that the Americans had still not crossed from the west. And there, on the corner of Bab al-Moazzam Street, was a small group of mujahedin fighters, firing Kalashnikov rifles at the American tanks on the other side of the waterway. It was brave and utterly pathetic and painfully instructive.

For the men turned out to be Arabs from Algeria, Morocco, Syria, Jordan, Palestine. Not an Iraqi was among them. The Baathist militiamen, the Republican Guard, the greasy Iraqi intelligence men, the so-called Saddam Fedayeen, had all left their posts and crept home. Only the foreign Arabs, like the Frenchmen of the Nazi Charlemagne Division in 1945 Berlin, fought on. At the end, many Iraqis had shunned these men; a group of them turned up to sit outside the lobby of the Palestine Hotel, pleading to journalists for help in returning home.

"We left our wives and children and came here to die for these people and then they told us to go," one of them said. But at the end of the Bab al-Moazzam Bridge they fought on into the night, and when I left them I could hear the American jets flying in from the west. Hurtling back through those empty streets, I could hear, too, the American tank fire as it smashed into their building. If there was to be a resistance in the future, here were willing recruits for the insurgency—if they survived.

Tanks come in two forms: the dangerous, deadly kind that spit fire and the "liberating" kind from which smart young soldiers with tanned faces look down with smiles at Iraqis who are obliging enough to wave at them, tanks with cute names stencilled on their gun barrels, names like "Kitten Rescue" and "Nightmare Witness"—this with a human skull painted underneath—and "Pearl." And there has to be a first soldier—of the occupying or liberating kind—who stands at the very front of the first column of every vast and powerful army. So I walked up to Corporal David Breeze of the 3rd Battalion, 4th Marine Regiment, from Michigan. He hadn't spoken to his parents for two months, so I called his mother on my satellite phone and from the other side of the world, Mrs. Breeze came on the line and I handed the phone to her son. And this is what the very first American soldier to enter the centre of Baghdad told his family: "Hi you guys. I'm in Baghdad. I'm ringing to say 'Hi! I love you. I'm doing fine. I love you guys.' The war will be over in a few days. I'll see you all soon."

Yes, I wrote that evening:

They all say the war will be over soon. There would be a homecoming no doubt for Corporal Breeze and I suppose I admired his innocence despite the deadly realities that await America in this dangerous, cruel land. For even as the marine tanks thrashed and ground down the highway, there were men and women who saw them and stood, the women scarved, the men observing the soldiers with the most acute attention, who spoke of their fear for the future, who talked of how Iraq could never be ruled by foreigners.

"You'll see the celebrations and we will be happy Saddam has gone," one of them said to me. "But we will then want to rid ourselves of the Americans and we will want to keep our oil and there will be resistance and then they will call us 'terrorists.' " Nor did the Americans look happy "liberators." They pointed their rifles at the pavements and screamed at motorists to stop—one who did not, an old man in an old car, was shot in the head in front of two French journalists.

Of course, the Americans knew they would get a good press by "liberating" the foreign journalists at the Palestine Hotel. They lay in the long grass of the nearest square and pretended to aim their rifles at the rooftops as cameras hissed at them, and they flew a huge American flag from one of their tanks and grinned at the reporters, not one of whom reminded them that just 24 hours earlier, their army had killed two Western journalists with tank fire in that same hotel and then lied about it.

But it was the looters who marked the day as something sinister rather than joyful. In Saddam City, they had welcomed the Americans with "V" signs and cries of "Up America" and the usual trumpetings, but then they had set off downtown for a more important appointment. At the Ministry of Economy, they stole the entire records of Iraq's exports and imports on computer discs, with desk-top computers, with armchairs and fridges and paintings. When I tried to enter the building, the looters swore at me. A French reporter had his money and camera seized by the mob.

At the Olympic sports offices, run by Uday Hussein, they did the same, one old man staggering from the building with a massive portrait of Saddam which he proceeded to attack with his fists, another tottering out of the building bearing a vast ornamental Chinese pot. True, these were regime targets. But many of the crowds went for shops, smashing their way into furniture stores and professional offices. They came with trucks and pickups and trailers pulled by scruffy, underfed donkeys to carry their loot away. I saw a boy making off with an X-ray machine, a woman with a dentist's chair. At the Ministry of Oil, the minister's black Mercedes limousine was discovered by the looters. Unable to find the keys, they tore the car apart, ripping off its doors, tyres and seats, leaving just the carcass and chassis in front of the huge front entrance. At the Palestine Hotel, they smashed Saddam's portrait on the lobby floor and set light to the hoarding of the same wretched man over the front door. They cried *Allahu akbar* . . . And there was a message there, too, for the watching Marines if they had understood it.

And so last night, as the explosion of tank shells still crashed over the city, Baghdad lay at the feet of a new master. They have come and gone in the city's history, Abbasids and Ummayads and Mongols and Turks and British and now the Americans. The United States embassy reopened yesterday and soon, no doubt, when the Iraqis have learned to whom they must now be obedient friends, President Bush will come here and there will be new "friends" of America to open a new relationship with the world, new economic fortunes for those who "liberated" them, and—equally no doubt—relations with Israel and a real Israeli embassy in Baghdad.

But winning a war is one thing. Succeeding in the ideological and economic project that lies behind this whole war is quite another. The "real" story for America's mastery over the Arab World starts now.

If 9 April was the day of "liberation," 10 April was the day of the looter. They trashed the German embassy and threw the ambassador's desk into the yard. I rescued the European Union flag—flung into a puddle of water outside the visa section—as a mob of middle-aged men, chadored women and screaming children rifled through the consul's office and hurled Mozart records and German history books from an upper window. The Slovakian embassy was broken into a few hours later. At the headquarters of UNICEF, which had been trying to save the lives of millions of Iraqi children since the 1980s, an army of thieves stormed the building, throwing brand-new photocopiers on top of one another down the stairs and sending cascades of UN files on child diseases, pregnancy death rates and nutrition across the floors.

The Americans might have thought they had "liberated" Baghdad after the most stage-managed photo-opportunity since Iwo Jima, but the tens of thousands of thieves—they came in families and cruised the city in trucks and cars searching for booty—seemed to have a different idea of what "liberation" meant. It also represented a serious breach of the Geneva Conventions. As the occupying power, the United States was responsible for protecting embassies and UN offices in their area of control, but their troops drove past the German embassy even as looters carted desks and chairs out of the front gate. It was a scandal, a kind of disease, a mass form of kleptomania which American troops simply ignored. At one intersection of the city, I saw U.S. Marine snipers on the rooftops of high-rise building, scanning the streets for possible suicide bombers while a traffic jam of looters—two of them driving stolen double-decker buses crammed with refrigerators—crammed the highway beneath them. Outside the UN offices, a car slowed down beside me and one of the unshaven, sweating men inside told me in Arabic that it wasn't worth visiting because "we've already taken everything."

Understandably, the poor and the oppressed took their revenge on the homes of the men of Saddam's regime who impoverished and destroyed their lives—sometimes quite literally—for more than two decades. I watched whole families search through the Tigris bank home of Ibrahim al-Hassan, Saddam's half-brother and a former interior minister, of a former defence minister, of Saadoun Shakr, one of Saddam's closest security advisers, of Ali Hassan al-Majid—"Chemical" Ali—and of Abed Hmoud, Saddam's private secretary. They came with lorries, container trucks, buses and donkey-drawn carts to make off with the contents of these massive villas.

It also provided a glimpse of the shocking taste in furnishings that senior Baath party members obviously cultivated: cheap pink sofas and richly embroidered chairs, plastic drink trolleys and priceless Iranian carpets so heavy that it took three muscular thieves to carry them, standard lamps concealed inside brass palm trees, inlaid wooden tables, mother-of-pearl chests of drawers and huge American fridges, so many fridges for so much booze to be drunk by so many of Saddam's acolytes. Outside the gutted home of one former interior minister, a fat man was parading in a stolen top hat, a Dickensian figure who tried to direct the traffic jam of looters outside.

City buses passed me driven by leering young men while trucks backed up to living-room windows to load furnishings directly from the rooms. On the Saddam Bridge over the Tigris, a thief had driven his lorry of stolen goods at such speed that he had crashed into the central concrete reservation and still lay dead at the wheel. But there seemed to be a kind of looter's law. Once a thief had placed his hand on a chair or a chandelier or a door-frame, it belonged to him. I saw no arguments, no fist-fights. The dozens of thieves in the German embassy worked in silence, assisted by an army of small children. Wives pointed out the furnishings they wanted, husbands carried them down the stairs while children were employed to unscrew door hinges and—in the UN offices—to remove light fittings. One stood on the ambassador's desk to take a light bulb from its socket in the ceiling.

On the other side of the Saddam Bridge, an even more surreal sight could be observed. A truck loaded down with chairs but with two white hunting dogs—the property of Saddam's son Qusay—tethered by two white ropes, galloping along beside the vehicle. Across the city, I even caught a glimpse of four of Saddam's horses—including the white stallion he used in presidential portraits—being loaded onto a trailer. Every government ministry in the city had now been denuded of its files, computers, reference books, furnishings and cars. To all this, the Americans turned a blind eye, indeed stated specifically that they had no intention of preventing the "liberation" of this property. One could hardly be moralistic about the spoils of Saddam's henchmen, but how was the government of America's so-called "New Iraq" supposed to operate now that the state's property has been so comprehensively looted?

And what was one to make of the scene on the Hilla road, where I found the owner of a grain silo and factory ordering his armed guards to fire on the looters who were trying to steal his lorries. This desperate armed attempt to preserve the very basis of Baghdad's bread supply was being observed from just 100 metres away by eight soldiers of the U.S. 3rd Infantry Division, who were sitting on their tanks—and doing nothing. The UN offices that were looted downtown were just 200 metres from a U.S. Marine checkpoint.

And already America's army of "liberation" was beginning to look like an army of occupation. The previous morning I had watched hundreds of Iraqi civilians queuing to cross a motorway bridge at Doura, each man ordered by U.S. soldiers to raise his shirt and lower his trousers—in front of other civilians, including women—to prove that they were not suicide bombers. Following a gun battle in the Adamiya area during the morning, an American marine sniper sitting atop the palace gate wounded three civilians, including a little girl, in a car that failed to halt—then shot and killed a man who had walked onto his balcony to discover the source of the firing. Within minutes, the sniper shot dead the driver of another car and wounded two more passengers in his vehicle, including a young woman. A crew from Channel 4 Television was present when the killings took place. In the suburb of Doura, the bodies of Iraqi civilians—many of them killed by U.S. troops in a clash with Iraqi forces earlier in the week—still lay rotting in their smouldering cars.

And this was just Day 2 of the "liberation" of Baghdad.

AND SO TO DOURA. Something terrible—how many times have I written those words—happened there, on Highway 8, in the last hours of the "liberation" of Baghdad. Some say a hundred civilians died there. Others believe that only forty or fifty men and women and children were cut to pieces by American tank fire when members of the U.S. 3rd Infantry Division's Task Force 315 were ambushed by the Republican Guard. Many of their corpses lie rotting in their incinerated cars, a young woman, burned naked, slumped face-down over the rear seat on the Hilla flyover bridge next to half of a male corpse which is hanging out of the driver's door. Blankets cover a pile of dead civilian bodies, including that of a cremated child, a few metres away. A red car, shot in half by an American tank shell, lies on its side with the lower half of a human leg, still in a black shoe, beside the left front wheel.

No one disputes that the American troops were ambushed here—nor that the battle only ended thirty-six hours later. On the flyover I found a dead Iraqi Republican Guard in uniform, his blood drained into the gutter, one foot over the other, shot in the head. A hundred metres away lay a car with an elderly civilian man dead under the chassis. Two fuel trucks—one of them still burning—lay in a field. A burned-out passenger bus stood beside the main motorway. Hundreds of Iraqis stared at the corpses in horror, most of them holding handkerchiefs to their faces and swatting the flies that buzzed between the living and the dead.

Captain Dan Hubbard, commanding the 315th's Bravo Company whose ten tanks and four Bradley Fighting Vehicles hold the flyover bridge, described to me how his men came under fire "from 360 degrees" with rocket-propelled grenades and AK-47 rifles at 7 a.m. on the morning of 6 April when civilian traffic was moving along the motorway. "We're here to fight the Iraqi regime, not the civilians," he said. "There were cars on the road when we were ambushed and we fired over their heads two or three times to get them to stop. Ninety per cent of the vehicles turned away after a warning shot." And here the captain paused for a moment. "A lot of things go on in people's heads at such times," he said. "A lot of people speed up . . . I had to protect my men. We tried our very best to minimise any kind of injuries and death to civilians . . . I have got to protect my soldiers because we don't know if it's a carload of explosives or RPGs [rocket-propelled grenades]. We'll have the cars removed. The bodies will be taken care of."

Captain Hubbard was a thoughtful man, a thirty-four-year-old from Tennessee who named his tank "Rhonda Denise" after his wife who is "the toughest woman I've ever met"—though what she would make of the civilian horror on Highway 8 doesn't bear thinking about. Hubbard's M1A1 Abrams tank took five direct hits from RPGs—one on the engine—and it was his tank that opened fire on a motorcycle carrying two soldiers at dusk on the first day of the fighting. "In the morning, I went to look at the bodies. There was the Republican Guard whom you saw, who was hit in the head and chest. But his friend was wounded and still alive—he had survived the whole night on the flyover  so I carried him back to our tank, placed him on top and gave him medical aid. Then we got him to our medics and he survived." Clearly the Iraqi Republican Guard also have a responsibility for this carnage, since they started their ambush, knowing full well that civilians would be on the motorway.

On the front of the incinerated bus, for example, I found part of a Kalashnikov rifle, its wooden butt in cinders but its ammunition clip still intact. There were crude slit trenches beneath the flyover and the wreckage of a military truck. In all, two American soldiers were killed in the battle and up to thirty wounded. Special Forces were involved in the shooting and six U.S. vehicles destroyed, including two tanks. Captain Hubbard said he had been fired at from a row of civilian houses beside the road and had shot a tank round on to one of the roofs. Its impact was clearly visible.

Many families had come to find their dead relatives and bury them, but I counted at least sixteen civilian bodies—and parts of bodies—still on the highway, several of them women. And of course, this killing field raised a now familiar question. Americans fired tank shells at civilian motorists. Still their bodies lay mouldering beside the road—along with the dead soldier—and still no one had buried them. Sure, the Americans tried not to kill civilians. But all would have been alive today had President Bush not ordered his army to invade their country.*

There would be no inquiry. Nor would there be any inquiry into any of the dreadful events that occurred during the *Gone With the Wind* epic of looting and

---

*This appalling incident is recalled in David Zucchino's *Thunder Run: Three Days in the Battle for Baghdad* (Atlantic Books, London, 2004), which covers the journey of the U.S. 3rd Infantry Division's 2nd Brigade from southern Iraq to Baghdad during the invasion. In this account of the motorway killings (pp. 231–46), Hubbard and his comrades are confronted by "suicide vehicles" on Highway 8 that were "relentless" and "kept speeding north." Hubbard, the book says, "couldn't comprehend the repeated, futile forays—each one ending in an eruption of

anarchy with which the Iraqi population chose to celebrate our gift to them of "liberation" and "democracy." It started in Basra, with our own shameful British response to the orgy of theft that took hold of the city. The British defence minister, Geoffrey Hoon, made some especially childish remarks about this disgraceful state of affairs, suggesting in the House of Commons that the people of Basra were merely "liberating"—that word again—their property from the Baath party. And the British army enthusiastically endorsed this nonsense. Even as tape of the pillage in Basra was being beamed around the world, there was Lieutenant Colonel Hugh Blackman of the Royal Scots Dragoon Guards cheerfully telling the BBC that "it's absolutely not my business to get in the way." But of course it *was* Colonel Blackman's business. Pillage merits a specific prevention clause in the Geneva Conventions, just as it did in the 1907 Hague Convention upon which the Geneva delegates based their "rules of war." "Pillage is prohibited," the 1949 Geneva Conventions say, and Colonel Blackman and Mr. Hoon should have glanced at *Crimes of War*, published in 2002 in conjunction with the London City University Journalism Department, to understand what this means.

When an occupying power takes over another country's territory, it automatically becomes responsible for the protection of its civilians, their property and institutions. Thus the American troops in Nasiriyah became automatically responsible for the driver who was murdered for his car in the first day of that city's "liberation." The Americans in Baghdad were responsible for the German and the Slovak embassies that were looted by hundreds of Iraqis, and for the French Cultural Centre that was attacked, and for the Central Bank of Iraq that was torched on 11 April and which, however contaminated it may be by the previous regime—Arab nations tend to deposit their most odious creatures in the role of central bank governor—is the core financial power in Iraq, the new version of Iraq just as much as the old.

But the British and Americans discarded this notion, based though it is upon conventions and international law. And yet again, we journalists allowed them to

---

flames and flying metal as one vehicle after another was destroyed by high-explosive rounds." Zucchino quotes a young army private complaining that "Damn, we're killing a lot of people here." Another private "saw one of the first vehicles get hammered . . . He saw the car explode, and he saw human beings explode, too." A few hours later, according to Zucchino, "from the west and north came suicide cars, nearly twenty of them by mid-afternoon." Yet the book makes no reference to the large number of civilians who died under U.S. tank fire, many of whose bodies I had seen with my own eyes. If so large a number of suicide bombers were really deployed against the Americans on Highway 8, then this was a major turning point in the war—and a key to the forthcoming insurgency. But my own evidence as an eyewitness to the aftermath suggests that, while there clearly was a military ambush, most of the dead were civilians and that American fear of suicide bombers led them to fire at any vehicle which did not clear the road. As Hubbard told me, "a lot of people sped up . . . I had to protect my men." Zucchino's book, incidentally, gives a fairly convincing account of the military confusion surrounding the killing of the journalists at the Palestine Hotel (pp. 296–307), although it repeats the canard that gunmen were firing from the building. It is worth adding that if it is true, as Zucchino's book says, that the 3rd Infantry Division endured "one of the most brutal and decisive battles in combat history" in Baghdad, then the Pentagon's contention that Iraqi forces simply declined to fight and "melted away" in the capital is untrue.

do so. We clapped our hands like children when the Americans "assisted" the Iraqis in bringing down the statue of Saddam Hussein in front of the television cameras, and yet we went on talking about the "liberation" of Baghdad as if the majority of civilians there were garlanding the soldiers with flowers instead of queuing with anxiety at checkpoints and watching the looting of their capital. We journalists cooperated, too, with a further collapse of morality in this war. Take, for example, the ruthless bombing of the residential Mansour area of Baghdad in the attempt to kill Saddam. The Anglo–American armies claimed they believed Saddam and his two evil sons Qusay and Uday were present. So they bombed the civilians of Mansour and killed at least fourteen decent, innocent people, almost all of them—and this would obviously be of interest to the religious feelings of Messrs. Bush and Blair—Christians.

Now one might have expected the BBC World Service Radio next morning to question whether the bombing of civilians did not constitute a bit of an immoral act, a war crime perhaps, however much we wanted to kill Saddam. Forget it. The presenter in London described the slaughter of these innocent civilians as "a new twist" in the war to target Saddam—as if it was quite in order to kill civilians, knowingly and in cold blood, in order to murder our most hated tyrant. The BBC's correspondent in Qatar—where the Centcom boys pompously boasted that they had "real-time" intelligence that Saddam was present—used all the usual military jargon to justify the unjustifiable. The "Coalition," he announced, knew it had "time-sensitive material"—i.e., that they wouldn't have time to know whether they were killing innocent human beings in the furtherance of their cause or not—and that this "actionable material" (again I quote this revolting BBC dispatch) was not "risk-free."

And then he went on to describe, without a moment of reflection on the moral issues involved, how the Americans had used their four 2,000-pound "bunker-buster" bombs to level the civilian homes. These were the very same pieces of ordnance that the same U.S. Air Force used in their vain effort to kill Osama bin Laden in the Tora Bora mountains in 2001. So now we were using them, knowingly, on the flimsy homes of civilians of Baghdad—folk who would otherwise be worthy of the "liberation" we wished to bestow upon them—in the hope that a gamble, a bit of "intelligence" about Saddam, would pay off.*

The Geneva Conventions have a lot to say about all this. They specifically refer to civilians as protected persons, who must have the protection of a warring power even if they find themselves in the presence of armed antagonists. The same protection was demanded for southern Lebanese civilians when Israel launched its brutal "Grapes of Wrath" operation in 1996. When that Israeli pilot, for example, fired his U.S.-made Hellfire missile into the Mansouri ambulance in Lebanon, killing three children and two women, the Israelis claimed that a Hizballah fighter

---

*A report on the military assessment of "the lessons of the war with Iraq" in *The New York Times* on 20 July 2003 stated that the approval of Donald Rumsfeld was required if "any planned airstrike was thought likely to result in deaths of more than 30 civilians. More than 50 such strikes were proposed and all of them were approved." So the Christian families of Mansour stood no chance.

had been in the vehicle. The statement proved to be untrue. But Israel was rightly condemned for killing civilians in the hope of killing an enemy combatant. Now we were doing exactly the same. So no more namby-pamby Western criticism of Israel after the bunker-busters have been dropped on Mansour.

More and more, we were committing these crimes. The mass slaughter of more than 400 civilians in the Amariya air-raid shelter in Baghdad in the 1991 Gulf War was carried out in the hope that it would kill Saddam. In the 1999 bombardment of Serbia we repeatedly bombed civilian areas—after realising that the Yugoslav army had abandoned their barracks—and in one of the most vicious incidents towards the end of that war, an American jet bombed a narrow road bridge over a river. NATO said the bridge could carry tanks even if there was no tank on it at the time. In fact, the bridge was far too narrow to carry a tank. But another pilot returned to bomb the bridge again, just as the rescuers were trying to save the wounded. Victims of the second bomb included schoolgirls. Again, we forgot about this in our euphoria at winning the war.

Why? Why cannot we abide by the rules of war that we rightly demand that others should obey? And why do we journalists—yet again, war after war— collude in this immorality by turning a ruthless and cruel and illegal act into a "new twist" or into "time-sensitive material"? Wars have a habit of turning nor- mally sane people into cheerleaders, of transforming rational journalists into nasty little puffed-up fantasy colonels. But surely we should all carry the Geneva Con- ventions into war with us, along with the history books. For the only people to ben- efit from our own war crimes will be the next generation of Saddam Husseins. Isn't that what the insurgents were to learn within weeks and months of the occupation?

BUT WE COULD ALWAYS FALL BACK on the argument that would become our sine qua non in the months and years to come, the most quotable quote, the easiest line in the book, the very last resort of the scoundrel in Iraq: Saddam was worse. We weren't as bad as Saddam. We didn't kill and torture in the Abu Ghraib prison— these qualifications would be dropped later for obvious reasons—because we were civilised, liberators, democrats who believed in freedom. We were the good guys.

So in those first hours after the "liberation" of Baghdad, I did go and take a peek into the heart of darkness. I waded through the cartridge cases of the Jumhuriya Bridge battle that lay like winter leaves across the highway—the tank whose shell had killed my two colleagues was still there, hatches down—and walked through the great Raj-gate of Saddam's Presidential Palace. Inside was the holiest of holies, the ark of Saddam's Baathist covenant, his very own throne. The seat was covered in blue velvet and was soft, comfortable in an upright, sensible sort of way, with big gold arm-rests upon which his hands—for Saddam was obsessed with his hands—could rest, and with no door behind it through which assassins could enter the room. There was no footstool, but the sofas and seats around the vast internal conference chamber of Saddam's palace placed every offi- cial on a slightly lower level than the caliph himself.

Did I sit on Saddam's throne? Of course I did. There is something dark in all our souls which demands an understanding of evil rather than good, because—I suppose—we are more fascinated by the machinery of cruelty and power than we are by angels. So I sat on the blue throne and put my hands over the golden arm-rests and surveyed the darkened, gold-glistening chamber in which men of great power sat in terror of the man who used to sit where I was now sitting. "He knew human folly like the back of his hand," Auden wrote of his eponymous dictator. Ah yes, the hands.

Behind the throne was a vast canvas of the al-Aqsa mosque in Jerusalem—minus the Jewish settlements—so that the third-holiest city of Islam hung above the head of the mightiest of Iraqi warriors. And opposite Saddam's chair—there was no electricity and the room was in darkness and the torchlight that illuminated the opposite canvas could only produce a gasp of astonishment and horrible clarity—was a different work of Baathist art. It depicted a clutch of huge missiles, white-hot flames burning at their tails, soaring towards a cloud-fringed, sinister heaven, each rocket wreathed in an Iraqi flag and the words "God is Great."

The godly and the ungodly faced each other in this central edifice of Baathist power. The American 3rd Infantry Division who were camped in the marble halls and the servants' bedrooms had been searching in vain for the underground tunnels that were supposed to link this complex with the bomb-smashed Ministry of Defence next door. They had kept the looters at bay—though I found some of them thieving televisions and computers in the smaller villas of the palace grounds—because, so they said, General Tommy Franks would probably set up his procon-sulship here and, if the Americans could create a compliant Iraqi government, a new U.S.-appointed administration might be running the country from this vast pseudo-Sumerian complex within a few months.

They would find Saddam's swimming pool intact, along with his spacious palm groves and rose gardens. Indeed—how often are brutal men surrounded by beauty—the scent of roses drifted even now through the colossal marble halls and chambers and underground corridors of the Republican Palace. There were peonies and nasturtiums and the roses were red and pink and white and crimson and covered in white butterflies, and water—though the 3rd Infantry Division had not yet found the pumps—gurgled from taps into the flower beds. There was even a miniature zoo with a cuddly old bear and lion cubs to which the Americans were feeding a live sheep per day. In Saddam's pool-side washing room, piles of books had been tied up for removal—Iraqi poetry and, would you believe it, volumes of Islamic jurisprudence—while exercise machines waited across the floor to keep the second Saladin in moderate physical shape. His sixty-sixth birthday would fall in two weeks' time. Over the door were the initials "S.H."

Walking the miles of corridors—after walking the 2-mile road to the palace itself, through yet more fields of roses and palms and piles of spent ammunition and the smell of something awful and dead beyond the flower beds—one was struck by the obsessive mixture of glory and banality. The 15-foot chandeliers inspire admiration, but the solid gold bathroom fittings—the solid gold loo holder and the solid gold loo handle—created a kind of cultural aggression. If one was supposed to be intimidated by Saddam's power—as the Coliseum and the triumphal arches were meant to impress the people of Rome—what was one to make of the narrow unpolished marble staircases or the great marble walls of the antechamber with their gold-leaf ceilings, walls into which were cut quotations from the interminably dull speeches and thoughts of "His Excellency President Saddam Hussein."

Fascist is the word that sprang to mind, but fascism with a touch of Don Corleone thrown in. In that great conference room would sit the attendant lords—the senior masters of the Baath party, the security apparatchiks upon whom the regime depended—desperately attempting to keep awake as their leader embarked on his four-hour explanations of the state of the world and of Iraq's place within it. As he talked of Zionism, they could admire the Al-Aqsa mosque. When he became angry, they could glance at the fiery missiles streaking towards that glowering sky with the clouds hanging oppressively low in the heavens.

His words were even cut into the stonework of the outer palace walls where four 20-foot-high busts of the great warrior Hammurabi, clad in medieval helmet and neck-covering, stare at one another across the courtyard. Hammurabi, however, had a moustache and—amazing to perceive—bore an uncommon likeness to Saddam Hussein. Could the government of the "New Iraq" really hold its cabinet meetings here while these four monsters stared at their American-supplied Mercedes? Answer: no. The statues were removed by crane within six months.

The gold leaf, the marble, the chandeliers, the sheer height and depth of the chambers took the breath away. In one hall, a Pantheon-like dome soared golden above the walls, and when I shouted "Saddam" I listened to the repeated echo of "Saddam" for almost a minute. And I had an absolute conviction that Saddam did just that. If he could instruct his masons to carve his name upon the walls, surely he wanted to hear it repeated in the heights of his palace.

Far below was the Saddam private cinema, with its blue patent leather seats and two rolls of film—one French, one Russian—still waiting for the final picture show. Outside, beyond the great lawns and the fountains, stood the American Abrams tanks of the 3rd Infantry Division, their names containing the banality and power of another nation. On their barrels I could read how the crews have dubbed their armoured behemoths. *Atomic Dog. Annihilator. Arsonist. Anthrax. Anguish. Agamemnon.* Saddam would have approved.


BAGHDAD WAS BURNING. I counted sixteen columns of smoke rising over the city on the aftenoon of 11 April. At the beginning, there was the Ministry of Trade. I watched the looters throw petrol through the smashed windows of the ground floor and the fire burst from them within two seconds. Then there was a clutch of offices at the bottom of the Jumhuriya Bridge which emitted clouds of black, sulphurous smoke. By mid-afternoon, I was standing outside the Central Bank of Iraq as each window flamed like a candle, a mile-long curtain of ash and burning papers drifting over the Tigris.

As the pickings got smaller, the looters grew tired and—the history of Baghdad insists that anarchy takes this form—the symbols of government power were cremated. The Americans talked of a "new posture" but did nothing. They pushed armoured patrols through the east of the city, Abrams tanks and Humvees and Bradley Fighting Vehicles, but their soldiers did no more than wave at the arsonists. I found a woman weeping beside her husband in the old Arab market. "We are destroying what we now have for ourselves," she said to him. "We are destroying our own future."

The flames spread. By mid-afternoon, the al-Sadeer Hotel was burning—the army of child thieves sent into the building had already stolen the bed-linen and the mattresses, the beds and tables, even the reception desk and its mass of iron keys. Then from the towering Ministry of Industry, a concrete pile of Third Reich conception, came trails of black smoke. Every central street was strewn with papers, discarded furniture, stolen, wrecked cars and the contents of the small shops whose owners had not bothered to buy armoured doors. At last, the banks were also looted. Since the collapse of the Iraqi dinar—it stood at more than 4,000 to the dollar—no one had bothered to bash their way into the banks before. But in the morning, I saw a mob storming the Rafidain Bank near the Baghdad governorate, dragging a massive iron safe to the door and crowbarring it open. Given the worth of the dinar, they would have done better to leave the cash inside and steal the safe.

Iraq's scavengers thieved and destroyed what they were allowed to loot and burn by the Americans—but a two-hour drive around Baghdad showed clearly what the United States intended to protect, presumably for its own use. After days of arson and pillage, I compiled a short but revealing scorecard. U.S. troops had sat back and allowed mobs to wreck and then burn the ministries of Planning, Education, Irrigation, Trade, Industry, Foreign Affairs, Culture and Information. They did nothing to prevent looters from destroying priceless treasures of Iraq's history in the Baghdad Archaeological Museum and in the museum in the northern city of Mosul, nor from looting three hospitals.

However, the Americans put hundreds of troops inside two Iraqi ministries that remained untouched—and untouchable—with tanks and armoured personnel carriers and Humvee jeeps surrounding both institutions. So which particular ministries proved to be so important for the Americans? Why, the Ministry of the Interior, of course—with its vast wealth of intelligence information on Iraq—and the Ministry of Oil. The archives and files of Iraq's most valuable asset—its oilfields and, even more important, its massive reserves, perhaps the world's largest—were safe and sound, sealed off from the mobs and looters, and safe to be shared—as Washington almost certainly intended—with U.S. oil companies.

It cast an interesting reflection on America's supposed war aims. Anxious to "liberate" Iraq, it allowed its people to destroy the infrastructure of government as well as the private property of Saddam's henchmen. The Bush administration insisted that the oil ministry was a vital part of Iraq's inheritance, that the oil fields were to be held in trust "for the Iraqi people." But was the Ministry of Trade—relit on 14 April by an enterprising arsonist—not vital to the future of the Iraqi people?

Were the ministries of Education and Irrigation—still burning fiercely—not of critical importance to the next Iraqi government? The Americans, as we now knew, could spare 2,000 soldiers to protect the Kirkuk oilfields, containing probably the largest reserves in the world, but couldn't even invest 200 soldiers to protect the Mosul museum from attack.

There was much talk of that "new posture" from the Americans. Armoured and infantry patrols suddenly appeared on the middle-class streets of the capital, ordering young men hauling fridges, furniture and television sets to deposit their loot on the pavement if they could not prove ownership. It was pitiful. After billions of dollars' worth of government buildings, computers and archives had been destroyed, the Americans were stopping teenagers driving mule-drawn carts loaded with worthless second-hand chairs. There was a special anger now to the crowd that gathered every afternoon opposite the American lines outside the Palestine Hotel. On 12 April, they chanted "Peace-peace-peace—we want a new Iraqi government to give us security." Two days later, some of them shouted "Bush–Saddam, they are the same."

But there was worse—far worse—to come. Never, in all my dreams of destruction, could I have imagined the day I would enter the Iraqi National Archaeological Museum to find its treasures defiled. They lay across the floor in tens of thousands of pieces, the priceless antiquities of Iraq's history. The looters had gone from shelf to shelf, systematically pulling down the statues and pots and amphorae of the Assyrians and the Babylonians, the Sumerians, the Medes, the Persians and the Greeks and hurling them on to the concrete floor. My feet crunched on the wreckage of 5,000-year-old marble plinths and stone statuary and pots that had endured every siege of Baghdad, every invasion of Iraq throughout history—only to be destroyed when America came to "liberate" the city. The Iraqis did it. They did it to their own history, physically destroying the evidence of their own nation's thousands of years of civilisation.

Not since the Taliban embarked on their orgy of destruction against the Buddhas of Bamiyan and the statues in the museum of Kabul—perhaps not since the Second World War or earlier—have so many archaeological treasures been wantonly and systematically smashed to pieces. "This is what our own people did to their history," the man in the grey gown said as we flicked our torches across the piles of once perfect Sumerian pots and Greek statues, now headless, armless, in the storeroom of Iraq's National Archaeological Museum.

"We need the American soldiers to guard what we have left. We need the Americans here. We need policemen." But all the museum guard, Abdul-Setar Abdul-Jaber, experienced on 12 April 2003 were gun battles between looters and local residents, the bullets hissing over our heads outside the museum and skittering up the walls of neighbouring apartment blocks. "Look at this," he said, picking up a massive hunk of pottery, its delicate patterns and beautifully decorated lips coming to a sudden end where the jar—perhaps two feet high in its original form—had been smashed into four pieces. "This was Assyrian." The Assyrians ruled almost two thousand years before Christ.

And what were the Americans doing as the new rulers of Baghdad? Why, that morning they were recruiting Saddam's hated former policemen to restore law and order on their behalf. The last army to do anything like this was Mountbatten's force in South-East Asia which employed the defeated Japanese army to control the streets of Vietnamese cities—bayonets fixed—after the recapture of Indo-China in 1945. A queue of respectably dressed Baghdad ex-cops formed outside the Palestine Hotel in Baghdad after they heard a radio broadcast calling for them to resume their "duties" on the streets. In the late afternoon, at least eight former and very portly senior police officers, all wearing green uniforms—the same colour as the uniforms of the Iraqi Baath party—turned up to offer their services to the Americans, accompanied by a U.S. Marine.

But there was no sign that any of them would be sent down to the Archaeological Museum. There was no electricity in Baghdad—as there was no water and no law and no order—and so we stumbled in the darkness of the museum basement, tripping over toppled statues and blundering into broken-winged bulls. When I shone my torch over one far shelf, I drew in my breath. Every pot and jar—"3500 BC," it said on one shelf corner   had been bashed to pieces. Why? How could they do this? Why, when the city was already burning, when anarchy had been let loose—and less than three months after U.S. archaeologists and Pentagon officials met to discuss the country's treasures and put the museum on a military database—did the Americans allow the mobs to destroy so much of the priceless heritage of ancient Mesopotamia? And all this happened while U.S. Secretary of Defence Donald Rumsfeld was sneering at the press for claiming that anarchy had broken out in Baghdad. "Stuff happens," he said. Could there really be so many vases in Iraq?

For well over 200 years, Western and local archaeologists have gathered up the remnants of this centre of early civilisation from palaces, ziggurats and 3,000-year-old graves. Their tens of thousands of handwritten card index files—often in English and in graceful nineteenth-century handwriting—now lay strewn amid the broken statuary. I picked up a tiny shard. "Late 2nd century, no. 1680" was written in pencil on the inside. To reach the storeroom, the mobs had broken through massive steel doors, entering from a back courtyard and heaving statues and treasures past a generator to cars and trucks.

The looters had left only a few hours before I arrived and no one—not even the museum guard in the grey gown—had any idea how much they had taken. A glass case that had once held 40,000-year-old stone and flint objects had been smashed open. It lay empty. No one knows what happened to the Assyrian reliefs from the royal palace of Khorsabad, nor the 5,000-year-old seals nor the 4,500-year-old gold-leaf earrings once buried with Sumerian princesses. In the vast museum library, only a few books—mostly mid-nineteenth-century archaeological works—appeared to have been stolen or destroyed. Looters set little value on books. I found a complete set of *The Geographical Journal* from 1893 to 1936 still intact—lying next to them was a paperback entitled: *Baghdad, The City of Peace*—but thousands of card-index sheets had been flung from their boxes over stairwells and banisters.

British, French and German archaeologists played a leading role in the discovery of some of Iraq's finest ancient treasures—that great British Arabist, diplomatic schemer and spy Gertrude Bell, the "uncrowned queen of Iraq," whose tomb lay not far from the museum, was an enthusiastic supporter of their work. The Germans built the modern-day museum beside the Tigris and only in 2000 was it reopened to the public after nine years of closure following the first Gulf War.

But even as the Americans encircled Baghdad, Saddam's soldiers showed almost the same contempt for its treasures as the looters. Their slit trenches and empty artillery positions were still clearly visible in the museum lawns, one of them dug beside a huge stone statue of a winged bull. Only a few weeks before, Jabir Khalil Ibrahim, the director of Iraq's State Board of Antiquities, had referred to the museum's contents as "the heritage of the nation." They were, he said, "not just things to see and enjoy—we get strength from them to look to the future. They represent the glory of Iraq." Ibrahim had temporarily vanished, like so many government employees in Baghdad, and Abdul-Jaber and his colleagues were now trying to defend what was left of the country's history with a collection of Kalashnikov rifles. "We don't want to have guns—but everyone must have them now," he said. "We have to defend ourselves because the Americans have let this happen. They made a war against one man—so why do they abandon us to this war and these criminals?" Half an hour later, I contacted the Civil Affairs unit of the U.S. Marines in Saadoun Street and gave them the exact location of the museum and the condition of its contents. A captain told me that "we're probably going to get down there." Too late. Iraq's history had already been trashed by the looters whom the Americans unleashed on the city during their "liberation."

But "liberation" had already turned into occupation. Faced by a crowd of angry Iraqis in Fardus Square demanding a new Iraqi government "for our protection and security and peace," U.S. Marines, who should have been providing that protection, stood shoulder to shoulder facing them, guns at the ready. The reality, which the Americans—and of course, Mr. Rumsfeld—failed to understand, was that under Saddam, the poor and deprived were always the Shia Muslims, the middle classes always the Sunnis—just as Saddam himself was a Sunni. So it was the Sunnis who were now suffering plunder at the hands of the Shia. And so the gun battles that broke out between property-owners and looters were, in effect, a conflict between Sunni and Shia Muslims. "By failing to end this violence—by stoking ethnic hatred through their inactivity—the Americans are now provoking a civil war in Baghdad," I wrote that night in *The Independent*:

I drove through the city for more than an hour. Hundreds of streets are now barricaded off with breeze blocks, burned cars and tree trunks, watched over by armed men who are ready to kill strangers who threaten their homes or shops . . . A few Marine patrols did dare to venture into the suburbs yesterday—positioning themselves next to hospitals which had already been looted—but fires burned across the city at dusk for the third consecutive day. The municipality building was blazing away last night and on the horizon other great fires were sending columns of smoke miles high into the air. Too little too late. Yesterday, a group of chemical engineers and water purification workers turned up at the Marine headquarters, pleading for protection so they could return to their jobs. Electrical supply workers came along, too. But Baghdad is already a city at war with itself, at the mercy of gunmen and thieves . . . "You are American!" a woman shouted at me in English . . . "Go back to your country. Get out of here. You are not wanted here. We hated Saddam and now we are hating Bush because he is destroying our city." It was a mercy she could not visit the Museum of Antiquity to see for herself that the very heritage of her country—as well as her city—has been destroyed.

And so, on 14 April, it was the burning of books. First came the looters, then came the arsonists. It was the final chapter in the sack of Baghdad. The National Library and Archives—a priceless treasure of Ottoman documents including the old royal archives of Iraq—were turned to ashes in 3,000 degrees of heat. Then the library of Korans at the Ministry of Religious Endowment was set ablaze. I saw the looters. One of them cursed me when I tried to reclaim a book of Islamic law from a boy who could have been no more than ten years old. Amid the ashes of hundreds of years of Iraqi history, I found just one file blowing in the wind outside: pages and pages of handwritten letters between the court of Sherif Hussein of Mecca—who started the Arab revolt against the Turks for Lawrence of Arabia—and the Ottoman rulers of Baghdad.

And the Americans did nothing. All over the filthy yard they blew, letters of recommendation to the courts of Arabia, demands for ammunition for Ottoman troops, reports on the theft of camels and attacks on pilgrims, all of them in delicate handwritten Arabic script. I was holding in my hands the last Baghdad vestiges of Iraq's written history. But for Iraq, this was Year Zero; with the destruction of the antiquities in the Archaeological Museum and the burning of the National Archives and then the Koranic library of the ministry 500 metres away, the cultural identity of Iraq was being erased. Why? Who set these fires? For what insane purpose was this heritage being destroyed?

When I caught sight of the Koranic library burning—there were flames 30 metres high bursting from the windows—I raced to the offices of the occupying power, the U.S. Marines' Civil Affairs bureau, to report what I had seen. An officer shouted to a colleague that "This guy says some biblical library is on fire." I gave the map location, the precise name—in Arabic and English—of the building, I said that the smoke could be seen from three miles away and it would take only five minutes to drive there. Half an hour later, there wasn't an American at the scene—and the flames were now shooting 60 metres into the air.

There was a time when the Arabs said that their books were written in Cairo, printed in Beirut and read in Baghdad. Now they burned libraries in Baghdad. In the National Archives were not just the Ottoman records of the caliphate, but even the dark years of the country's modern history, handwritten accounts of the

1980–88 Iran–Iraq War, with personal photographs and military diaries, an entire library of Western newspapers—bound volumes of the *Financial Times* were lying on the pavement opposite the old Defence Ministry—and microfiche copies of Arabic newspapers going back to the early 1900s. The microfiche machines were burned too.

Palestinian newspapers from the early years of the PLO—even the journals of the "Kashmir Liberation Cell"—were lying on the floor. But the older files and archives were on the upper floors of the library opposite the Ministry of Defence, where petrol must have been used to set fire so expertly to the building. The heat was of such strength that the marble flooring had buckled upwards and the concrete stairs which I climbed through the acres of smouldering documents had been cracked by the furnace. The papers on the floor were almost too hot to touch, bore no print or writing, and crumbled into ash the moment I picked them up. And again, standing in this shroud of blue smoke and embers, I asked the same question: Why?

So, as an all too painful reflection on what this means, let me quote from the shreds of paper that I found on the road outside, blowing in the wind, written by long-dead men who wrote to the Sublime Porte in Constantinople or to the Court of the Sherif of Mecca with expressions of loyalty and who signed themselves "your slave." There was a request to protect a camel convoy of tea, rice and sugar, signed by Husni Attiya al-Hijazi (recommending Abdul Ghani-Naim and Ahmed Kindi as honest merchants), a request for perfume and a warning from Jaber al-Ayashi of the royal court of the Sherif Hussein to Baghdad to warn of robbers in the desert. "This is just to give you our advice for which you will be highly rewarded," al-Ayashi says. "If you don't take our advice, then we have warned you." A touch of Saddam there, I thought. The date was 1912.

Some of the documents list the cost of bullets, military horses and artillery for the Ottoman armies in Baghdad and Arabia, others record the opening of the first telephone exchange in the Hejaz—soon to be Saudi Arabia—while one recounts, from the village of Azrak in modern-day Jordan, the theft of clothes from a camel train by Ali bin Kassem, who attacked his interrogators "with a knife and tried to stab them but was restrained and later bought off." There is a nineteenth-century letter of recommendation for a merchant, Yahyia Messoudi, "a man of the highest morals, of good conduct and who works with the [Ottoman] government."

This, in other words, was the tapestry of Arab history—all that was left of it, which I picked off the road*—as the mass of documents of centuries still crackled in the immense heat of the ruins of the National Archives. Sherif Hussein of the Hejaz, the ruler of Mecca—whose court personnel are the authors of many of the letters I saved—was later deposed by the Saudis. It was his son Feisal who became king of Iraq and Feisal's brother Abdullah who became the first king of Jordan, the grandfather of King Hussein and the great-grandfather of the present Jordanian monarch, King Abdullah the Second.

---

*This one file of letters and court documents is now deposited—appropriately enough and courtesy of *The Independent*—in the royal Hashemite archives in Amman.

For almost a thousand years, Baghdad was the cultural capital of the Arab world, the most literate population in the Middle East. Genghis Khan's grandson burned the city in the thirteenth century and, so it was said, the Tigris ran black with the ink of books. Now the black ashes of thousands of ancient documents filled the skies of Iraq. Why? Who sent the looters? Who sent the arsonists? Were they paid? Who wanted to destroy the identity of this country?

America's project in Iraq was going wrong faster than anyone could have imagined. "The army of 'liberation' has already turned into the army of occupation," I wrote in my paper on 17 April:

> . . . Even the individual U.S. Marines in Baghdad are talking of the insults being flung at them. "Go away! Get out of my face!" an American soldier screamed at an Iraqi trying to push towards the wire surrounding an infantry unit in the capital yesterday. I watched the man's face suffuse with rage. "God is Great! God is Great!" the Iraqi retorted. "Fuck you!"
>
> It is much worse than that. The Americans have now issued a "Message to the Citizens of Baghdad," a document that is as colonial in spirit as it is insensitive in tone. "Please avoid leaving your homes during the night hours after evening prayers and before the call to morning prayers," it tells the people of the city. "During this time, terrorist forces associated with the former regime of Saddam Hussein, as well as various criminal elements, are known to move through the area . . . please do not leave your homes during this time. During all hours, please approach Coalition military positions with extreme caution . . ." So now—with neither electricity nor running water—the millions of Iraqis here are ordered to stay in their homes from dusk to dawn. Lockdown. It's a form of imprisonment. In their own country.
>
> Written by the commanding officer of the 1st U.S. Marine Division, it's a curfew in all but name. "If I was an Iraqi and I read that," an Arab woman shouted at me yesterday, "I would become a suicide bomber." And all across Baghdad, you hear the same thing, from Shia Muslim clerics to Sunni businessmen, that the Americans have come only for oil, and that soon—very soon—a guerrilla resistance must start. No doubt the Americans will claim that these attacks are "remnants" of Saddam's regime or "criminal elements." But that will not be the case.
>
> Marine officers in Baghdad were yesterday holding desperate talks with a Shia militant cleric from Najaf to avert an outbreak of fighting around the holy city—I met the prelate just before the negotiations began. He told me that "history is being repeated." He was talking about the British invasion of Iraq in 1917, which ended in disaster for the British. To gain entrance to the desert town of al-Anbar, U.S. intelligence officers yesterday had to negotiate with tribal leaders in the best restaurant in Baghdad.
>
> Everywhere are the signs of collapse. And everywhere the signs that America's promises of "freedom" and "democracy" are not to be hon-

oured . . . Here's what Baghdadis are noticing—and what Iraqis are noticing in all the major cities of the country. Take the vast security apparatus
with which Saddam surrounded himself, the torture chambers and the huge
bureaucracy which was its foundation. President Bush promised that
America was campaigning for human rights in Iraq, that the guilty, the war
criminals, would be tracked down and brought to trial. Now the 60 secret
police headquarters in Baghdad are empty; even the three-square-mile
compound headquarters of the Iraqi Intelligence Service. I have been to
many of them. But not a single British or American officer has visited the
sites to sift through the wealth of documents lying there or talk to the ex-
prisoners who are themselves visiting their former places of torment. Is
this through idleness. Or is this wilful?

Take the Qasimiyeh security station beside the Tigris River. It's a pleasant villa—once owned by an Iranian-born Iraqi who was deported to Iran
in the 1980s—and there's a little lawn outside and a shrubbery and at first
you don't notice the three big hooks in the ceiling of each room nor the fact
that big sheets of red paper, decorated with footballers, have been pasted
over the windows to conceal the rooms from outsiders. But across the
floors, in the garden, on the roof, are the files of this place of suffering.
They show, for example, that the head of the torture centre was Hashem al-
Tikrit, that his deputy was called Rashid al-Nakib. Ex-prisoner Mohamed
Aish Jassem showed me how he was suspended from the ceiling by his torturer, Captain Amar al-Isawi, who believed Jassem was a member of the
religious Dawa party.

"They put my hands behind my back like this and tied them and then
pulled me into the air by my tied wrists," he told me. "They used a little
generator to lift me up, right up to the ceiling, then they'd release the rope
in the hope of breaking my shoulder when I fell." The hooks in the ceiling
are just in front of Captain al-Isawi's desk. I understood what this meant.
There wasn't a separate torture chamber and elsewhere an office for documentation. The torture chamber was the office. While the man or woman
shrieked in agony above him, Captain al-Isawi would sign papers, take
telephone calls and—given the contents of his rubbish bin—smoke many
cigarettes while he waited for the information he sought from his prisoners.

Were they monsters, these men? Yes. Are they sought by the Americans? No. Are they now working for the Americans? Yes, quite possibly—
indeed some of them may well be in the long line of ex-security thugs who
queue every morning outside the Palestine Hotel in the hope of being re-
hired by the U.S. Marines' Civil Affairs unit. The names of the guards at
the Qasimiyeh torture centre in Baghdad—pedestrians were forbidden to
walk down the road outside lest they heard the screams—are all named on
the documents lying on the floor. They were Ahmed Hassan Alawi, Akil
Shaheed, Noaman Abbas and Mohamed Fayad. But the Americans haven't
bothered to find this out. So Messrs. Alawai, Shaheed, Abbas and Fayad
are welcome to apply for work from the Americans.

There are prisoner identification papers on the desks and in the cupboards. What happened to Wahid Mohamed, Majid Taha, Saddam Ali or Lazim Hmoud? We shall not know. A lady in a black chador approached the old torture centre. Four of her brothers had been taken there and, later, when she went to ask what happened, she was told all four had been executed. She was ordered to leave the building. She never saw or buried their bodies . . . One man told me his brother had been brought to this awful place 22 years ago—and never seen again.

And the men who suffered under Saddam? What did they have to say? "We committed no sin," one of them said to me, a 40-year-old whose prison duties had included the cleaning of the hangman's trap of blood and faeces after each execution. "We are not guilty of anything. Why did they do this to us? America, yes, it got rid of Saddam. But Iraq belongs to us. Our oil belongs to us. We will keep our nationality. It will stay Iraq. The Americans must go."

If the Americans and the British want to understand the nature of the religious opposition here, they have only to consult the files of Saddam's secret service archives. I found one, Report No 7481, dated 24th February this year—for the Iraqi "mukhabarat" security men were still working hard on their Shia enemies less than a month before the American invasion—on the conflict between Sheikh Mohamed al-Yacoubi and Mukhtada Sadr, the 22-year-old grandson of Mohamed Sadr, who was executed on Saddam's orders more than two decades ago, a dispute which showed both the passion and the determination with which the Shia religious leaders fight even each other. But of course, no-one has bothered to read this material or even look for it.

At the end of the Second World War, German-speaking British and American intelligence officers moved into the defeated Reich to hoover up every document in the thousands of Gestapo and Abwehr bureaus across western Germany. The Russians did the same in their zone. In Iraq, however, the British and Americans have simply ignored the evidence that lies everywhere to be read. For there's an even more terrible place for the Americans to visit in Baghdad, the headquarters of the whole intelligence apparatus, a massive grey-painted block that was bombed by the Americans and a series of villas and office buildings which are stashed with files, papers and card indexes.

It was here that Saddam's special political prisoners were brought for vicious interrogation—electricity being an essential part of this—and it was here that Farzad Bazoft, the *Observer* correspondent, was brought for questioning before his dispatch to the hangman. It's also graced with delicately shaded laneways, a children's creche—for the families of the torturers—and a school in which one pupil had written an essay in English on (suitably perhaps) Beckett's *Waiting for Godot*. There's also a miniature hospital and a road named "Freedom Street" and flower beds and bougainvillea. It's the creepiest place in all of Iraq. I met—extraordinarily—an Iraqi nuclear scientist walking in fear around the compound, a colleague of the former head of Iraqi nuclear physics, Dr. Shahristani. "This is the last place I ever wanted to see and I will never return to it," he said to me. "This was the place of greatest evil in all the world."

But the Americans should pay a visit. The top security men in Saddam's regime were busy in the last hours of their rule, shredding millions of documents. I found a great pile of black plastic rubbish bags at the back of one villa, each stuffed with the shreds of thousands of papers. Shouldn't they be taken to Washington or London and re-constituted to learn their secrets? That's what the Iranians did with the shredded U.S. embassy files in Tehran in 1980.

But again, the Americans have not bothered—or do not want—to search through these papers. If they did, they would also find the names of dozens of senior Iraqi intelligence men, many of them identified by the files of congratulatory letters which Saddam's secret policemen insisted on sending each other every time they were promoted. Where now, for example, is Colonel Abdulaziz Saadi, Captain Abdulsalam Salawi, Captain Saad Ahmed al-Ayash, Colonel Saad Mohamed, Captain Majid Ahmed and scores of others? We may never know. Or perhaps we are not supposed to know.

. . . Then there's the fires that have consumed every one of the city's ministries—save, of course, for the Ministry of Interior and the Ministry of Oil—along with UN offices, embassies and shopping malls. I have counted a total of 35 ministries now gutted by fire and the number goes on rising. Take the scene played out on Wednesday. I was driving through Baghdad when I saw a vast column of black smoke staining the horizon. So I headed to see which ministry was left to burn. I found myself at the Ministry of Oil, assiduously guarded by U.S. troops, some of whom were holding clothes over their mouths because of the clouds of smoke swirling down on them from the neighbouring Ministry of Agricultural Irrigation. Hard to believe, isn't it, that they were unaware that someone was setting fire to the next building?

Then I spotted another fire, just lit, three kilometres away. I drove to the scene to find flames curling out of all the windows of the Ministry of Higher Education's Department of Computer Science. And right next to it, perched on a wall, was a U.S. Marine, who said he was guarding a neighbouring hospital and didn't know who had lit the next door fire because "you can't look everywhere at once." Now I'm sure the marine was not being facetious or dishonest—should the Americans not believe this story, he was Corporal Ted Nyholm of the 3rd Regiment, 4th Marines and, yes, I called his fiancée Jessica in the States for him to pass on his love—but something is terribly wrong when American soldiers are ordered to simply watch vast government ministries being burned by mobs and do nothing about it.

Because there is also something very dangerous—and deeply disturbing—about the crowds setting light to the buildings of Baghdad, including the great libraries and state archives. For they are not the looters. The looters come first. The arsonists turn up afterwards, often in blue and white single-decker buses. I actually followed one of them after its passengers had set the Ministry of Trade on fire and it sped out of town. Now the official American line on all this is that the looting is revenge—an explanation that is growing very thin—and that the fires are started by "remnants of Saddam's regime," the same "criminal elements," no doubt, who feature in the Marines' curfew orders to the people of Baghdad.

But people in Baghdad don't believe Saddam's former supporters are starting these fires. And neither do I. True, Saddam might have liked Baghdad to end in Götterdämmerung—and might have been tempted to turn it into a city of fire before the Americans entered. But afterwards? The looters make money from their rampages. But the arsonists don't make money by burning. They have to be paid. The passengers in those buses are clearly being directed to their targets. If Saddam had pre-paid them, they wouldn't have started the fires. The moment Saddam disappeared, they would have pocketed the money and forgotten the whole project, not wasted their time earning their cash post-payment.

So who are they, this army of arsonists? Again, we don't know. I recognised one the other day, a middle-aged, unshaven man in a red T-shirt—you can't change clothes too often when you have no water to wash in—and the second time he saw me he pointed a Kalashnikov rifle at me. Looters don't carry guns. So what was he frightened of? Who was he working for? In whose interest is it—now, after the American occupation of Baghdad—to destroy the entire physical infrastructure of the state, along with its cultural heritage? Why didn't the Americans stop this?

As I said, something is going terribly wrong here in Baghdad and something is going on which demands that serious questions be asked of the United States government. Why, for example, did Secretary of Defence Rumsfeld claim last week that there was no widespread looting or destruction in Baghdad? His statement was a lie. But why did he make it? The Americans say they don't have enough troops to control the fires. This is also untrue. If they don't, what are the hundreds of troops deployed in the gardens of the old Iran–Iraq war memorial doing all day? Or the hundreds camped in the rose gardens of the Presidential Palace near the Jumhuriya Bridge?

So the people of Baghdad are asking who is behind the destruction of their cultural heritage—their very cultural identity—in the looting of the archaeological treasures from the national museum, the burning of the entire Ottoman, Royal and State archives and the Koranic library and the vast infrastructure of the nation we claim we are going to create for them. Why, they ask, do they still have no electricity and no water? In whose interest is it for Iraq to be deconstructed, divided, burned, de-historied, destroyed? Why are they issued with orders for a curfew of millions of people by their so-called liberators? . . . It's easy for a reporter to predict doom, especially after a brutal war which lacked all international legitimacy. But catastrophe usually waits for optimists in the Middle East, especially for those who are false optimists and invade oil-rich nations with ideological excuses and high-flown moral claims and accusations like weapons of mass destruction which have still been unproved. So I'll make an awful prediction. That America's war of "liberation" is over. Iraq's war of liberation from the Americans is about to begin. In other words, the real and frightening story starts now.

CHAPTER TWENTY-FOUR

# Into the Wilderness

*Far-called, our navies melt away;*
*On dune and headland sinks the fire:*
*Lo, all our pomp of yesterday*
*Is one with Nineveh and Tyre!*

—Rudyard Kipling, from "Recessional"

HIGHWAY 8 is the most dangerous road in Iraq. It is littered with smashed and burned-out American trucks and police cars blown up by rocket-propelled grenades. Every government checkpoint has been abandoned. Insurgents swarm through the villages to the east. This is kidnap country, throat-slitting country. Highway 8 is a symbol of the collapse of all our dreams. But as I am standing by the road talking to an Iraqi family, searching for the location of a Red Cross car whose driver has just been murdered, the ground begins to move and a long, roaring beast of sound swamps us.

From far to the south, a cloud of grey smoke is powering up into the sky, a thousand exhausts turning the sun dark, the biggest convoy I have ever seen in my life. The Americans are changing their brigades, the largest military movement since the Second World War, a 40-mile trail of armour and men moving up Highway 8 towards me. With the Iraqis, I sit in the muck at the side of the road. This I must watch. This I must absorb if I am to understand this war. Abrams tanks and Bradley fighting vehicles and Humvees and hundreds of trucks with thousands of lean young men in battledress, wearing shades, pointing their rifles at the dangerous countryside, porcupine quills along the sides of each lorry, hour after hour of them. Six Apache helicopters come thrashing over the trees, riding shotgun, turning like aerial rodents and sweeping back down the highway at speed. The soldiers don't bother to look up. They glance at us, a few of them, at the Englishman and the Iraqis sitting in the dirt as these twentieth-century Crusaders drive up to their great concrete-walled fortresses on the Tigris, deep into the wilderness of occupation.

And I do begin to understand. Two thousand years ago, a little to the west of here, we would have sat by the roadside as the ground shook to the tramp of Rome's legions. Now we live in the American empire. Yes, this war was about oil. Yes, it was fuelled by folly and arrogance and lies. But it was also about the desire—the visceral need—to project power on a massive scale, based on neo-conservative fantasies, no doubt, but unstoppable, inexorable. Our army can go to

Baghdad. So it *will* go to Baghdad. It will pour over Sumeria and Babylon and all the caliphates and across the land where civilisation supposedly began.

BUT NO FOREIGN ARMIES come here and escape unpunished. It is now a broiling 5 June 2003. High over Iraq, President George W. Bush is casting his Olympian eye over ancient Mesopotamia after praising the Americans who had "managed" the war against Saddam Hussein, and far below him, on a dirty street corner in a dirty town called Fallujah that Mr. Bush would prefer not to hear about, is a story of American blood and American power and American boots smashing down the front gates of Iraqi homes. "She's got a gun," an American soldier shouts when he catches sight of a woman in her back yard holding a Kalashnikov rifle. "Get to the other side of the road," he bellows at me, "or we'll hit you when we open fire." I scamper to the other side of the road and I see the woman with the Kalashnikov. "Put it down!—Put the gun down!" he screams at her again. The soldiers are hot and tired and angry. They've been up since 3 a.m., ever since someone fired a grenade at a truckload of troops from the 101st Airborne. You could see why Bush chose to avoid any triumphal visits to Iraq.

Survivors of the ambush were among the soldiers, remembering the early hours as only soldiers can. "They fired a grenade at a two-and-a-half-ton truck full of the 101st Airborne and then strafed it with AK fire and then just disappeared into the night," one of them said. "The guys were in a terrible state. One of our soldiers was dead with his brains hanging out of his head and his stomach hanging out, and there were eight others in the back shouting and pulling bits of shrapnel out of their legs." Before dawn, the Americans came back to wash their comrades' blood off the street. Then they returned once more to deal with the people who live in this scruffy corner of the old Baathist city of Fallujah.

In Qatar—before his hour-and-a-quarter flight through Iraqi airspace—Mr. Bush had done his best to lay down an appropriately optimistic narrative of the Iraq war. Iraq was a better place now that Saddam had gone—"a great evil has been ended," he said, and praised the "humanitarian work of U.S. troops" in the country. On weapons of mass destruction, he was a little more circumspect. "We are on the look. We will reveal the truth . . . But one thing is certain. No terrorist network will gain weapons of mass destruction from the Iraqi regime, because the Iraqi regime is no more." But of course, no weapons of mass destruction had been found. Nor would they ever be found here.

If President Bush thought his soldiers should be proud of what they had done in Iraq—that is what he told his men and women commanders—in Fallujah it was all sweat and fear and loudspeakers ordering civilians from the streets. Would the gunmen who "disappeared into the night" have really hidden in the nearest houses to the main road, right next to the scene of their ambush? Not unless they were mad. But someone in the 3rd Infantry Division decided to send the American 115th Military Police Company to capture a few guns and round up the usual suspects. It didn't make for happy viewing.

Ever deeper into their occupation, these soldiers were confused about the people they had just "liberated." Some were good men. Take Sergeant Seth Cole, who once lived in the English city of Northampton, and who worked out that if just 10 per cent of the people of Fallujah didn't like Americans, "that is an awful lot of people." Take Sergeant Phil Cummings, a cop from Rhode Island, a big cheerful man who talked to the Iraqis glowering at him from the pavement. "Some of these people don't like us even though we came to save them. But I always smile at them. At the schools, the kids throw rocks at us and I give them candy. I give them candy—they give me rocks."

But it didn't take long to see why children might throw rocks. There was another American soldier 40 metres away who was busy losing hearts and minds. "Tell them to get the fuck out of here," he ordered a private soldier, pointing at a group of teenagers. Then he turned to a middle-aged man sitting on a chair on the pavement. "You stand up and I'll break your neck," he screamed.

That's when they saw the woman with the AK. "She's got a gun! There's a woman with a gun." The cry rippled down the lines of American troops. A few hours with soldiers who are as likely to be victims as they are victors, and you realise why they have to shout information to each other like street vendors. "She's got a gun!" "She's got a gun!" "She's got a gun!" went up and down the street again.

Three soldiers pushed their rifles through the iron latticework of the back gate, all shouting "Put the gun down!" until a tall, sweating MP smashed his boot into the door and it swung open. "She's put the gun down—we've got the gun!" Three soldiers ran into the yard and came back with a Kalashnikov. Then two female officers brought out the woman, a teacher in the local high school, veiled and dressed all in black. "Why did you hold the gun?" one of the women soldiers asked her. The woman's eyes stared back through the slit in her veil. Then she folded her arms in a gesture of defiance and refused to speak.

"Please, sir, you're taking my son away—he's done nothing wrong." There had been the crashing of another door down the street, and I just caught sight of a young man in a brown shirt being driven away in a Humvee between two American MPs. An elderly man was pleading with a medical officer. "Why my son? Why my son?" Things were no better 2 metres away. A tall soldier from Massachusetts—how eerie the name sounded here in this heat-blasted town—was listening to a man who spoke good English, who wanted to help. Over the road, three soldiers were hammering on a metal screen. "It's an old, sick man who lives there, it's only his shop, he sells candies to kids," the Iraqi was telling the soldier. He did not reply.

So we stood in the ovenlike sun until the shop-front door opened. Three soldiers pointed their weapons at the slowly widening crack in the door. And then behind it we saw a very old man with a massive, long white beard and white hair in all directions, a frail creature—"ancient" was the word I wrote in my notebook— who had to lean on his refrigerator of ice-creams to steady himself, dressed in a long white gown. He looked like a prophet and for a few moments the Americans paused. "I'm sorry, sir, we have to search your shop," one of them said. And the three went inside while the old man stood in the street and looked at us and at the shop and then hobbled back into the darkness.

There was some shooting a few hundred metres away and the soldiers ran for cover behind walls and gardens. Then a black-and-gold painted gate was booted open and a man in a grey *dishdash* came out and sat by the gatepost with his hands on his head and his family sitting on the porch beneath the bougainvillea while the Americans went through their home. Another AK was produced—almost every family in Iraq has two or three guns. These Iraqis were, for the most part, what we would call middle-class people, educated and with homes that might pass for villas in this run-down city with its broken munitions factories and its Baath party apparatus so deep that it's hard to find an official uncontaminated by the stain of Saddam. Here it was, all of twenty-three years ago, that I came to see the great Iranian POW camps of the Gulf War, here and in the neighbouring town of Ramadi. These were tough people. Smashing down their doors would carry a penalty.

And so the Americans made a hundred more enemies among those they had "liberated." One young man in Fallujah told me that a few nights earlier, gunmen had arrived at his family home and asked them to join a new resistance movement. "We turned them down," he said. "I don't know what I'd say if they came again."

In Fallujah, one of the American MPs turned to me as his search operation was called off. "The Third Infantry Division are coming in here to go through this place tomorrow," he said. And on the motorway east to Baghdad, I saw the American armour moving towards the city. There they all were again, Bradleys and Abrams and Humvees and transporters and trucks. And on their armour and gun barrels the soldiers had painted names. "Armed Response" was on one, with a picture of a naked girl astride a tank shell. "Another Round Anyone?" was on another. There was "Deadly Commemoration" and "Any Last Words" and, incredibly, "Abusive Father"—with a Christian cross beside the name. Fallujah was going to be "gone through." And as the months passed, it was going to inflict its own "deadly commemoration" on the Americans.

As I write these words today, in the summer of 2005, back briefly in what I still like to think of as the safety of Beirut, as I go through my notebooks of the last two and a half years, the Iraqi insurrection takes on a savage, epic quality. In Baghdad now, many reporters practise "hotel journalism," hiding in their rooms, ordered by their own security men to avoid the swimming pool, using Iraq's deteriorating mobile phone system to talk to the Americans and British marooned in their own fortress across the Tigris, behind the concrete and machine-gun embrasures they have erected around Saddam's old republican palace. Patrick Cockburn of *The Independent* and myself and several other journalists still move around Baghdad, even travelling the murderous airport road, but we do so with Iraqis in private cars, often hiding behind an Arabic-language newspaper, peeking out of the window, stopping only for a minute to see the carnage the suicide bombers have left. Mouse journalism. Now the military and political rulers of "new" Iraq have to be helicoptered from their compound to the airport—the airport road is already deemed by the authorities too unsafe for Westerners to use—and from their castle all they can see of the country they rule is through the gunslits of their own defences. Visit any Crusader castle in Lebanon and you will find out that all the Christian warriors of Europe could see from their own twelfth-century battlements was through the arrow slits built into their walls. Yes, we are the Crusaders now. But we are Crusaders who are blind to reality. George W. Bush and Tony Blair still claim their war is going well. Tens of thousands of Iraqis have been killed and are still being killed. Wal-Mart suicide bombers—produced, it seems, from some hidden assembly line—blow themselves up at the rate of two or three a day. Corpses are found by the dozen on the banks of the Tigris or dumped on Baghdad garbage tips. Foreigners are kidnapped and decapitated on tape. No weapons of mass destruction were ever discovered. Nor any link between Saddam and the massacres of 11 September 2001.

Yet the war is going well, we are told. A second war—against "terror," of course—was now being fought in Iraq, Blair announces to an astonished audience of journalists. Iraq is on the road to democracy after national elections, albeit that the Sunni population largely failed to vote. That is the story. Saddam is imprisoned and awaiting trial—actually Iraq is now so insecure that the Americans are holding him in secret at their airbase in the emirate of Qatar. Democracy is blossoming across the Middle East. Or so we are supposed to believe. And I remember those who have died. Margaret Hassan, the gentle, tough lady who distributed medicines to the dying children of Iraq, kidnapped, videotaped in tears, mistreated and then shot in the face, executed for television screens. Marla Ruzicka, who would sit by the pool at the Hamra Hotel collating the number of Iraqis who have been killed since the invasion. Fifty thousand? A hundred thousand, as one report suggested? Marla was roasted alive as a suicide bomber exploded himself against a convoy of U.S. mercenaries on the airport road. I have watched many times Ken Bigley's face as he pleads and repleads on the videotapes to Tony Blair. Then comes his inevitable decapitation.

Each morning in Baghdad, I would visit the city morgue. There would be twenty—sometimes thirty—fresh bodies arriving each day, sometimes whole families shot down or torn apart by suicide bombers or knifed to death or killed at American checkpoints. When the Americans brought bodies to the morgue, the staff were told not to perform autopsies. What did this mean? Outside, the relatives of the dead would shriek and weep and swoon with sorrow and curse the Americans, even if their loved ones were killed in family feuds or revenge attacks. The Americans and British keep no lists of the Iraqi dead, only of their own much-mourned soldiers—well over 1,700 Americans by the summer of 2005—so we can talk about "our" sacrifice and ignore the fate of those tens of thousands we came to "liberate."

How did it start, the beginning of the end? In Fallujah, only days after the occupation began, soldiers of the 82nd Airborne opened fire on a crowd of Iraqi Sunni demonstrators, killing seventeen of them. They said they had come under fire. But reporters who reached the school in which the troops were billeted could find no bullet holes. Fallujah never forgave them. The insurgency started within hours. The city would later be taken over by Iraq's ferocious resistance, along with Ramadi. Whole provinces of Iraq would fall under their control. So the Americans invaded Fallujah again—and then a second time—and fought their way over the rubble of the ruined city. We have won. Victory. After Paul Bremer arrived as America's first proconsul—he it was who was to appoint the former CIA agent Iyad Allawi as "interim" prime minister—he would call the insurgents "dead-enders," "diehards," Saddam's "remnants." All it would need was the capture of Saddam himself and the rebellion would end.

He was wrong. I remember a young, angry Iraqi in Ramadi whose family had just been shot at an American checkpoint. "I won't join the resistance as long as Saddam and his family are free because if we drive the Americans out, we'll get Saddam back again. But if they eliminate Uday and Qusay and Saddam, I will kill Americans myself." And the Americans did kill Saddam's awful sons Uday and Qusay—along with Qusay's own fourteen-year-old son, about whom they didn't talk very much—in a pseudo-Palladian villa in Mosul, shot down by Task Force 20, a mix of Special Forces and CIA operatives who didn't bother to try and capture them when they resisted. And then, inevitably, they found Saddam.

In a hole in the ground. "Ladies and gentlemen—we got him!" Bremer crowed. "This is a great day in Iraq's history." The 13th of December 2003 was supposed to be the end of the insurrection. After this, why would anyone bother to fight the occupiers of Iraq? Unkempt, Saddam's tired eyes betraying defeat; even the $750,000 in cash found in his hole in the ground demeaned him. Soon Saddam would be produced in a secret court in chains. He looked in that first extraordinary videotape which the Americans produced like a prisoner of ancient Rome, the barbarian cornered at last, the hand caressing the scraggy beard. All those ghosts—of gassed Iranians and Kurds, of Shiites shot and dumped in the mass graves of Kerbala, of the prisoners dying under excruciating torture in the villas of Saddam's secret police—must surely have witnessed something of this.

It took just 600 American soldiers to capture the man who was for twelve years one of the West's best friends in the Middle East and for twelve more years the West's greatest enemy in the Middle East. In a miserable 8-foot hole in the mud of a Tigris farm near the village of Al-Dawr, the president of the Iraqi Arab Republic, leader of the Arab Socialist Baath party, ex-guerrilla fighter, invader of two nations, a former friend of Jacques Chirac and a man once courted by President Reagan, was found. And it was difficult, looking at those pictures of the Lion of Iraq—for so he called himself—to remember how royally he had been toasted in the past. This was the man who was the honoured guest of the city of Paris when Chirac was mayor and when the French could see the Jacobins in his bloody regime. This was the man who negotiated with UN Secretary Generals Perez de Cuellar and Kofi Annan, who chatted over coffee to none other than the man who was to become U.S. secretary of defence Donald Rumsfeld, who met Ted Heath and Tony Benn and a host of European statesmen.

And there was a kind of satisfaction, driving up to al-Dawr on the Tigris River in northern Iraq, to arrive at the orange orchard where he was discovered and climb into his very hole in the ground. I lay down inside it. Seven months earlier, I had sat on his red velvet presidential throne in the greatest of all his marble palaces. Now here I was, lowering myself into the damp, dark and grey concrete interior of his final retreat, the midget bunker buried beside the Tigris—all of 8 feet by 5— and as near to an underground prison as any of his victims might imagine. Instead of chandeliers, there was just a cheap plastic fan attached to an air vent. Ozymandias came to mind. This, after all, was where his hopes finally crumbled to dust. And it was cold.

I FOUND SADDAM'S LAST BOOKS in a hut nearby: the philosophical works of Ibn Khaldun, the religious—and pro-Shiite—doctrines of the Abbasid theorist Imam al-Shafei and a heap of volumes of Arab poetry. There were cassettes of Arabic songs and some tatty pictures, of sheep at sunset and Noah's Ark crowded with animals. But this was no resistance headquarters, no place from which to run a war or start an insurgency, no Führer-bunker with SS guards and switchboards and secretaries taking down last words for posterity.

To climb inside this most famous of all bolt-holes, I had to sit on the wooden entrance ledge and swing my legs into a narrow aperture and find my footing on four stairs made of earth. You used your arms to lower yourself into this last remnant of Iraqi Baathist history. Then you were sitting on the floor. There was no light, no water, only the concrete walls, the vent and a ceiling of wooden boards. Above the boards was earth and then a thick concrete floor which—up above— was covered by the equally thick concrete yard of a dilapidated farm hut. Yet above this sullen underground cell was a kind of paradise, of thick palm fronds and orange trees dripping gold with mandarins, of thickets of tall reeds, the sound of birds buried in the treetops. There was even an old blue-painted boat tucked away behind a wall of fronds, the last chance of escape across the silver Tigris if the Americans closed in.

Of course, they closed in from two directions, both from the river and down the muddy laneway along which soldiers of the American 4th Infantry Division led me. Saddam must have rushed from the hut where he ate his food—spilling a plate of beans and Turkish Delight onto the mud floor, I noticed—and squirrelled his portly self down the hole. When the Americans searched the hut, they found nothing suspicious—except a pot plant oddly positioned on top of some dried palm fronds, placed there presumably by two men who were later seized while trying to escape. Underneath, they found the entrance to the hole.

The soldiers mooching around the "site"—their word, as if it was a Sumerian city rather than a fraudulent, muddy Baathist playpen—were indifferent to the point of tiredness. They asked me to translate the Arabic inscription over Saddam's bedroom—it began with the Koranic words "In the name of God, the compassionate, the merciful . . ."—and they lent me their torches to prowl round the Saddam kitchen.

So what could we learn of Saddam in this, his very last private residence in

Iraq? Well, he had chosen to hide only 200 metres from a shrine marking his own famous retreat across the Tigris River in 1959, on the run as a wounded young guerrilla after trying to assassinate an earlier president of Iraq. Here it was that he dug the bullet out of his body, and on a low hill within eyesight of this palm-grove is the mosque that marks the spot where, in a coffee shop, Saddam vainly pleaded with his fellow Iraqi tribesmen to help him escape. Saddam, in his last days as a free man, had retreated into his past, back to the days of glory that preceded his butcheries.

He had the use of a tiny generator, which I found wired up to a miniature fridge. There were two old beds and some filthy blankets. In the little kitchen constructed next door, there were sausages hanging to dry, bananas, oranges and— near a washing-up bowl—tins of Jordanian chicken and beef luncheon meat, heaps of "Happy Tuna." Only the Mars Bars looked fresh.

So what did Saddam discover here in the last days? Peace of mind after the years of madness and barbarity? A place to reflect on his awesome sins, how he took his country from prosperity through foreign invasion and isolation and years of torture and suppression into a world of humiliation and occupation? The birds must have sung in the evening, the palm fronds above him must have clustered against each other in the night. But then there must have been the fear, the constant knowledge that betrayal was only an orchard away. It must have been cold in that hole. And no colder than when the hands of Washington-the-all-Powerful reached out across oceans and continents and came to rest on that odd-looking pot plant and hauled the would-be caliph from his tiny cell.

But there was one other conclusion upon which every Iraqi I spoke to agreed. This bedraggled, pathetic man with his matted, dirty hair, living in a hole in the ground with three guns and cash as his cave-companions—this man was not leading the Iraqi insurgency against the Americans. If more and more Iraqis were saying before Saddam's capture, like the man in Ramadi, that the one reason they would not join the resistance to U.S. occupation was the fear that—if the Americans withdrew—Saddam would return to power, well, that fear had now been removed. So the nightmare was over—and the nightmare was about to begin. Both for the Iraqis and for us.

I remember an American search operation in Baghdad just after Saddam's capture, all door-kicking and screaming and fuck-this and fuck-that and, just a few metres away, finding a message newly spray-painted on a wall. Not by hand but with a stencil, in poor English perhaps, but there were dozens of identical messages stencilled onto the walls for the occupiers. "American Soldiers," it said. "Run away to your home before you will be a body in [sic] black bag, then be dropped in a river or valley."

While Washington and London were still congratulating themselves on the capture of Saddam Hussein, U.S. troops shot dead at least eighteen Iraqis in the streets of three major cities in the country. Dramatic videotape from the city of Ramadi 75 miles west of Baghdad showed unarmed supporters of Saddam Hussein being shot down in semi-darkness as they fled from American troops. Eleven of the eighteen dead were killed by the Americans in Samara to the north of Baghdad. All the killings occurred during demonstrations by Sunni Muslims against the American seizure of Saddam, protests that started near Samara. The first demonstrators blocked roads north of Baghdad when armed men appeared alongside civilians who believed—initially—that U.S. forces had arrested one of Saddam's doubles rather than the ex-dictator of Iraq. But their jubilation turned to fury when the Americans opened fire in Samara a few hours later. As usual, the American military claimed that all eighteen dead were "insurgents" and that U.S. forces had come under fire in all three cities. But this is what they also claimed in Samara just two weeks earlier when they boasted they had shot fifty-four "terrorists." Journalists investigating the killings concluded then that while U.S. forces in the city had been ambushed while taking new currency notes to two banks, the only victims of American gunfire that could be confirmed were nine civilians, one of them a child, another an Iranian pilgrim.

A disturbing new phenomenon in this environment of growing military violence was the appearance of hooded and masked Iraqi gunmen—working for the Americans—on road checkpoints north of Baghdad. Five of them now checked cars on the Tigris River bridge outside Samara, apparently fearing that their identities would be discovered if their faces were not concealed. They wore militia uniforms and—although they said they were part of the new American-backed "Iraqi Civil Defence Corps" (ICDC)—they had neither badges of rank nor unit markings. The same hooded men were now appearing on the streets of Baghdad. Just before the Samara killings, several policemen stopped my car outside the city to warn that the Americans were "involved in a big battle with the holy warriors"—ominously for U.S. forces, they used the word "mujahedin"—and soon we were to discover that some—perhaps many—of these men were also insurgents, cops by day, killers by night; which was exactly what happened in Algeria. Families of the dead adopted the tradition of all tribal groups, just as they did at Fallujah: the dead must be avenged. And so their retaliation also turned inexorably into a resistance war that now embraced the entire Sunni Muslim area of Iraq.

JUST BEFORE CHRISTMAS 2003. The thump of air pressure on my Baghdad window wakes me up, a blast of sound that gently shakes the walls; the sound of seventeen lives disappearing. The aftermath of bombs in Baghdad is a kind of obscene theatre. I reach the crossroads minutes later. There's a shattered minibus with the pulverised remains of its passengers inside, a screaming fireman, pieces of a lorry—blown apart with such impact that the engine block is shorn in half—and two burning cars, the flames licking at their wheels and something terrible below the driver's seat. The bomb was in the truck. But the bus, why would anyone bomb a busload of Iraqi civilians? There is flesh on the road, and vast shards of iron and metal and sandals and women's handbags around the bus where several of the dead passengers—or what is left of them—are still sitting pitifully in their seats. Shrapnel has cascaded into the slums of Al-Bayaa, a pathetic warren of brick houses and sewage-filled laneways whose broken windows now sparkle in the streets.

A group of U.S. soldiers has just arrived, three of them prowling through the muck and the oil-splattered road for the detonator. Sergeant Joel Henshon of the 11th/65th U.S. military police guards what might have been part of the mechanism, a grenade that glistens grey and sinister on the mud of a traffic island. There must be 1,000 shouting people standing in the dawn of smoke and flames, men, kuffiahed in Arab scarves, many of them in black leather jackets. I find some cops by the burning cars, friendly, American-paid policemen with smart little yellow identification badges and pale blue uniforms. A brand-new fire brigade truck arrives and a torrent of water swamps what's left of the truck and the bus. "New Iraq" responds efficiently to its growing violence. A policeman—for this is the flip side of every constabulary in the world—walks up and, incredibly, asks me if I'd like to know what he's discovered.

"The truck belonged to the Ministry of Oil, it was a tanker without a trailer, registration number 5002, and we found this in what was left of the cab." He gives me a golden sticker with "Allah" written in Arabic on one side and "Mohamed" on the other. God and his Prophet withstood the blast. Nothing else did. A dozen men have clustered ghoulishly around the nearest car and there is a mass of glistening bones beneath the blackened steering shaft, femurs and bits of a backbone. The Mercedes minibus had come from the province of Dyala, east of Baghdad, ten men and women and a driver who must have woken before dawn for a routine journey to the capital. But surely the bomber was en route to another target. Premature explosion. Was there a police station near here? Sergeant Henshon gives a Baghdad reply. "There was," he says with a beautiful Alabama twang in this grim dawn. "But it's already *been* bombed." Then a shopkeeper says he saw an American convoy driving down the road and the truck trying to catch up with it and colliding with one of the cars beside the minibus. Was this the target? A few hours later, the occupation powers announce that the bombing was a traffic accident, a petrol tanker that exploded when it collided with a bus. It is a lie. What about the grenade in the road? The chopped-up engine block? The missing trailer? But we must now live on lies. Anything to keep another suicide bombing out of the papers.

Believe we are winning. Believe that we always kill insurgents. I am in Samara again, December 2003, and schoolboy Issam Naim Hamid is the latest of America's famous "insurgents." He was shot in the back as he tried to protect himself and his parents in his home in the Al-Jeheriya district of the ancient Abbasid city. It was three in the morning, according to his mother, Manal, when soldiers of the 4th Infantry Division came to the house, firing bullets through the gate. One of the rounds pierced the door, punched through a window and entered his back, speeding on through an outer wall. His father was hit in the ankle and was taken to Tikrit hospital in serious condition. Issam cries in pain in the emergency hospital ward, a drip-tube sticking into his stomach through a wad of bloody bandages.

Then there is the case of thirty-one-year-old farmer Maouloud Hussein, who was trying to push his five young daughters and son into the back room of his two-room slum home a few hours earlier when yet another bullet came whizzing through the gate and the outer wall of the house, and smashed into Maouloud's back. His son, Mustafa, bleary-eyed with tears beside his father's bed, and his four daughters, Bushra, Hoda, Issra and Hassa, were untouched. But the bullet tore into Maouloud's body and exited through his chest. Doctors had just removed his spleen. His forty-one-year-old brother, Hamed, winces as he sees Maouloud cringing in agony—the wounded man tries to wave a hand at me but lapses into unconsciousness—and says that twenty-three bullets hit the house in their Al-Muthanna quarter of the city. Like Issam Hamid, he lay bleeding for several hours before help came. Issam's mother, Manal, tells a terrible story. "The Americans had an Iraqi interpreter and he told us to stay in our home," she says. "But we had no telephone, we couldn't call an ambulance and both my husband and son were bleeding. The interpreter for the Americans just told us we were not allowed to leave the house."

Hamed Hussein stands by his brother's bed in a state of suppressed fury. "You said you would bring us freedom and democracy but what are we supposed to think?" he asks. "My neighbour, the Americans took him in front of his wife and two children and tied his hands behind his back and then, a few hours later, after all this humiliation, they came and said his wife should take all her most expensive things and they put explosives in their house and blew it up. He is a farmer. He is innocent. What have we done to deserve this?"

What will people do when you treat them like this? I ask myself. If we can shoot down the innocent like this, how soon before we torture them as well? Soon, soon. Now the city of Samara has become, like Fallujah, a centre of resistance to the American 4th Infantry Division. "We wanted the Americans to help us," another man said to me in a street of American-vandalised homes. "This was Saddam's Sunni area, but many of us disliked Saddam. But the Americans are doing this to humiliate us, to take their revenge on the attacks against them by the resistance." Three times, I am taken into broken houses where young men tell me that they intend to join the *muqawama*—the resistance—after the humiliation and shame visited upon their homes. "We are a tribal people and I am from the al-Said family," one says to me. "I have a university degree and I am a peaceful man, so why are the Americans attacking my home and filling my wife and children with fear?"

I go back and forth through my notes. It was in May 2003, only a month after the Americans entered Baghdad, that I first asked in *The Independent*: Isn't it time we called this a resistance war? I predicted the insurgency when U.S. forces first entered Baghdad; but the speed with which the Americans found themselves fighting off a growing army of fighters was astonishing. In five, six months, a guerrilla war might have started. But one month? Two Americans shot dead and another nine wounded by unidentified gunmen in Fallujah, two U.S. military policemen badly wounded by a rocket-propelled grenade at a north Baghdad police station, a grenade thrown at American soldiers near Abu Ghraib. That was the little toll of violence for just one day after the "liberation," 27 May 2003—not counting the Muslim woman who approached U.S. troops with a hand grenade in each hand, was shot down before she could throw one of them and then, as she tried to hurl her second grenade from the ground, was finally killed by the Americans.

Even then, most people in Baghdad were receiving only two hours' electricity a day. The petrol queues—in a country whose oilfields had already been corralled by the U.S. military, along with the lucrative clean-up and reconstruction contracts for American companies—stretch for up to 2 miles. Children are being withdrawn from newly opened schools after widespread child kidnapping and rape. The police stations now guarded by U.S. troops have been turned into blockhouses, surrounded by armour and guards with heavy machine guns, in lookout posts draped in camouflage netting and surrounded by concrete walls. Baghdad is becoming a city of walls, 20 feet high, running for miles along highways and shopping streets. We Westerners are on the run. Caged inside the marble halls of Saddam's finest palace, thousands of American officers and civil servants—utterly cut off from the 5 million Iraqis in Baghdad around them—are now battling over their laptops to create the neo-conservative "democracy" dreamed up by Messrs. Rumsfeld, Perle and the rest. When they venture outside, they do so in flak jackets, perched inside armoured vehicles with escorts of heavily-armed troops.

Already, U.S. forces were driving through Baghdad much as the Israelis once did in southern Lebanon, ordering motorists to stay away from their vehicles, threatening them with death. "Stay 50 yards away from this vehicle or deadly force will be used" was the printed warning in Arabic on the back of the American Humvees. Bremer banned a small-circulation Shiite magazine—run by Muqtada Sadr's equally small party—for provoking sectarian tension and for comparing him to Saddam Hussein. So Sadr's militia rose up against the Americans. Najaf was besieged, just as the British had besieged it more than eighty years earlier. Apache gunships fired into the Baghdad Shia slums of Shuala. Iraq's cities were now hunting grounds for thieves and rapists. Its even older cities—the great archaeological treasures of Sumeria—were left unguarded, so an army of robbers had moved in to smash their way through their buried treasures to 3,000-year-old pots, turning the ancient sites into a land of craters, as if a B-52 had carpet-bombed the desert. After an international outcry following the theft of treasures from the Baghdad Museum, Washington sent an FBI–CIA team to investigate the robberies.* But the postwar tearing apart of the Sumerian cities is on an infinitely greater scale. Historians may one day conclude that this mass destruction of mankind's inheritance is among the most lasting tragedies of the Anglo–American "liberation" of Iraq.

Watching America's awesome control over this part of the world, its massive firepower, its bases and personnel across Europe, the Balkans, Turkey, Jordan, Kuwait, Afghanistan, Uzbekistan, Turkmenistan, Bahrain, Doha, Oman, Yemen,

---

*In all, 15,000 objects were looted from the Baghdad Museum. Despite much fanfare by the Western authorities when some treasures were later recovered, 11,000 were still missing in June 2005, including the famous 3,500-year-old "Mona Lisa" ivory depicting the head of an Assyrian woman. Of the 4,000 artifacts discovered, 1,000 were found in the United States, 1,067 in Jordan, 600 in Italy and the remainder in countries neighbouring Iraq.

Israel of course, and now Iraq, you can see how the Iraqis thought it through. A generation of teenagers, crucified in the eight-year war with Iran, had grown up knowing nothing but suffering and death. What did their lives count for now? And if the Sunnis among that generation should ever become allied with Osama bin Laden's al-Qaeda, what destruction might they sow among the Americans and any who chose to help them? A reborn Iraqi army of the shadows, forged in the greatest of all Middle East wars, and an army of suicide bombers; this would be an enemy to challenge any superpower.

Yet still the fantasy had to continue. Faced with ever greater armed resistance to their occupation, the Americans, it transpired, were admitting only a fraction of the attacks against their forces. Although the U.S. occupation authorities acknowledged ambushes in which their troops died, they were failing to report a mass of attacks and assaults against their patrols and bases in and around Baghdad. Yet the reality—largely unreported by the media—was that the Americans were no longer safe anywhere in Iraq: not at Baghdad airport, which they captured with so much fanfare in early April 2003, not at their military bases nor in the streets of central Baghdad nor in their vulnerable helicopters nor on the country roads. Helicopters were shot down over Fallujah, C-130s blasted out of the sky by missiles.

And the United States responded in the way of all occupation armies. Its prison camps became places of shame. Prisoners—there were 11,300 by May 2003 in Iraq alone—were routinely beaten during interrogation. Thirty had died in custody in Iraq and Afghanistan by 2005, often after brutal interrogations. We like to think we only began to discover this when the vile photographs of Abu Ghraib were revealed to the world in 2004, but in my files I discover that my colleague Patrick Cockburn and I had been writing about torture and prison abuse in the late summer of 2003. "Sources" may be a dubious word in journalism right now, but my sources for the beatings in Iraq were impeccable. Now it was happening at U.S. military bases around Iraq. "Torture works," an American Special Forces colonel boasted to a friend of mine.

He was wrong. Torture creates resistance. Torture creates suicide bombers. Torture ends up by destroying the torturers. I remember the village of Khan Dari, where the first American to be blown up by a roadside bomb was killed in July 2003. His blood was still across the highway and the crowd was gloating over his death. And a man walked up to me who wanted to talk politics of a very violent kind. He had, he said, been a prisoner of the Americans and savagely beaten. "This is the way we deal with occupiers," he said. "They came and said they were liberators but when we realised they were occupiers, we had to fight. We are people of steel. The Americans and all the other occupiers will burn." Then came something as frightening as it was terrible. "I have a one-year-old daughter," he said. "And I would happily put a bomb in her clothes and send her to the Americans to kill them."

Already, by late July 2003, Amnesty International's investigators had amassed a damning file of evidence that Iraq's Anglo–American occupiers were ill-treating or torturing prisoners, refusing to obey Iraqi court orders to release detainees, using excessive force on demonstrators, killing innocent civilians and passing their own laws to prevent newly constituted Iraqi courts from trying American or British soldiers for crimes committed in the country. Amnesty also discovered that large sums of money had gone missing after house raids by American troops, in one case receiving from the U.S. authorities an acceptance that an officer in the U.S. 101st Division had "removed" 3 million Iraqi dinars—$2,000—from an Iraqi family's home. In another case, Amnesty found that an Iraqi labourer and father of three children, Radi Numa, died in British custody only hours after his arrest in the south of the country. On 10 May, British soldiers delivered a written note to the family's home stating that he "suffered a heart attack while we were asking questions about his son. We took him to the military hospital, go to the hospital." Unaware that he was dead, the Numa family went to the hospital only to be told he wasn't there. They later found him in the mortuary where his unidentified corpse had been brought by Royal Military Police two days earlier. Baha Moussa, a young Basra hotel waiter, died in British military custody, reportedly beaten to death.

On at least two occasions arrests were made in Iraq not by soldiers but by "U.S. nationals in plain clothes"—presumably CIA agents. Nasser Abdul Latif, a twenty-three-year-old physics student, for example, was shot on 12 June in a raid on his home "by armed men in plain clothes, who were apparently U.S. nationals." Searching for a senior member of the Baath party, U.S. troops raided the home of Khreisan Aballey on 30 April and arrested him and his eighty-year-old father. His brother was shot—the family didn't know if he was alive or dead—and Aballey, who claimed not to know the whereabouts of the Baathist official, was taken for interrogation. He said he was made to stand or kneel facing a wall for seven and a half days, hooded and handcuffed tightly with plastic strips. He reported that a U.S. soldier stamped on his foot and tore off one of his toenails.*

Paul Bremer's "Coalition Provisional Authority" (CPA)—a name that just reeked of apologies for its own existence—issued edicts like a Roman emperor with the Goths, Visigoths and Ostrogoths at the gates of the capital. The Iraqi army would be disbanded, putting tens of thousands of armed men out of work. What did Bremer now think they were going to do in their spare time? Tons of razor wire now surrounded the marble Saddamite palace from which Bremer's whiz-kids and anti-terror advisers tried to govern Iraq. The "coalition"—essentially America and its British ally during the war—seemed less and less provisional and equally less an authority as the weeks went by.

The "Interim Council" and its twenty-five members, representing a dutiful balance between Iraq's Shia, Sunni, Kurdish and secular population, was already the subject of the deepest cynicism. Its first act—at the behest of the Pentagon's Shia

---

*By far the most damning document on U.S. treatment of prisoners—including their "rendition" to countries where they would also be tortured—is Amnesty International's 200-page report published on 27 October 2004, *United States of America: Human Dignity Denied; Torture and Accountability in the "War on Terror"* (AMR51/145/2004).

accolyte Ahmed Chalabi—was to declare a national holiday for 9 April, marking the downfall of Saddam Hussein. Or at least, that is how it looked in the West. For Iraqis, their first new national holiday marked the first day of foreign occupation of their land. In the conference hall that now served as press centre for the occupation authorities in Baghdad, sets of handouts were laid carefully on a table for journalists to peruse. They read like a schizophrenic nightmare. "Al Saydia Public Health Clinic Grand Opening," one would say. "Soldier Killed in Explosion" said the next. "Iraq National Vaccination Day for Children" said a third, just an inch from another flyer recording the killing of two more U.S. troops.

The Americans were buying time, making decisions on the hoof, failing to assess the effects of their every action. First it was Jay "pull-your-stomach-in-and-say-you're-proud-to-be-an-American" Garner—the man I'd last met in Kurdistan in 1991—and then the famous "anti-terrorism" expert Paul Bremer who washed up in Baghdad to fire and then rehire Baath party university professors, and then, faced with one dead American a day, to rehire the murderous thugs of Saddam's torture centres to help in the battle against "terrorism." Sixteen of America's thirty-three combat brigades were now in the cauldron of Iraq—five others were also deployed overseas—and the 82nd Airborne, only just out of Afghanistan, was about to be redeployed north of Baghdad. "Bring 'em on," Bush had taunted America's guerrilla enemies in June 2003. They took him at his word. There was so far not a shred of evidence that the latest Bush administration fantasy—"thousands" of foreign Islamist "jihadi" fighters streaming into Iraq to kill Americans—was true.

But soon that fantasy would be made manifest. What would we be told then? Wasn't Iraq invaded to destroy "terrorism" rather than to re-create it? We were told that Iraq was going to be transformed into a "democracy," and suddenly it's to be a battleground for another "war against terror." America, Bush was now telling his people, "is confronting terrorists in Iraq and Afghanistan . . . so our people will not have to confront terrorist violence in New York or . . . Los Angeles." So that was it, then. Draw all these nasty "terrorists" into our much-loved, "liberated" Iraq, and they would obligingly leave the "homeland" alone.

When the Twin Towers collapsed in New York, who had ever heard of Fallujah? When the killers of 11 September 2001 flew their plane into the Pentagon, who had heard of Ramadi? When the Lebanese hijacker flew his plane into the ground in Pennsylvania, who would ever have believed that President George W. Bush would be announcing, in August 2003, a "new front line in the war on terror" as his troops embarked on a hopeless campaign against the guerrillas of Iraq? Who could ever have conceived of an American president calling the world to arms against "terrorism" in "Afghanistan, Iraq and Gaza"?

Gaza? What did the miserable, crushed, cruelly imprisoned Palestinians of Gaza have to do with the international crimes against humanity in New York, Washington and Pennsylvania? Nothing, of course. Nor did Iraq have anything whatever to do with 11 September 2001. Nor did September 11 change the world. President Bush cruelly manipulated the grief of the American people—and the sympathy of the rest of the world—to introduce a "world order" dreamed up by a clutch of fantasists advising Secretary of Defence Donald Rumsfeld. The Iraqi "regime change," as we now all knew, was planned as part of a Richard Perle/Paul Wolfowitz campaign document to would-be Israeli prime minister Benjamin Netanyahu years before Bush came to power. That Tony Blair should have signed up to this nonsense without realising what it represented—a project invented by a group of pro-Israeli American neo-conservatives and right-wing Christian fundamentalists—truly beggared belief.

But even now, we are fed more fantasy. Afghanistan—its American-paid warlords raping and murdering their enemies, its women still shrouded for the most part in their burqas, its opium production now making Afghanistan the world's number one exporter, and its people sometimes killed at the rate of up to a hundred a week—was a "success," something that Messrs. Bush and Rumsfeld still boasted about. By 2005, the Taliban were back and so was al-Qaeda, killing American soldiers rather than Russians. Iraq—a midden of guerrilla hatred, popular resentment and incipient civil war—was also a "success." Now Bush wanted $87 billion to keep Iraq running, he wanted to go back to the same United Nations he condemned as a "talking shop" in 2002, he wanted scores of foreign armies to go to Iraq to die in America's occupation war, to share the burdens of occupation—though not, of course, the decision-making, which must remain Washington's exclusive imperial preserve.

What's more, the world was supposed to accept the insane notion that the Israeli–Palestinian conflict was part of this monstrous battle. It was the planet's last war of colonisation, although all mention of the illegal Jewish colonies in the West Bank and Gaza had been erased from the Middle East narrative in U.S. statements about the "war on terror," the cosmic clash of religious extremism that President Bush invented after 11 September 2001. Could Israel's interests be better served by so infantile a gesture from Bush? The vicious Palestinian suicide bombers and the grotesque implantation of Jews and Jews only in the colonies had now been set into this colossal struggle of "good" against "evil," in which even Ariel Sharon was "a man of peace," according to Mr. Bush.

In the Pentagon, there was some sanity. They were re-showing Gillo Pontecorvo's film of the French war in Algeria. *The Battle of Algiers* showed what happened both to the guerrillas of the FLN and to the French army when their war turned dirty. The flyers sent out to the Pentagon brass to watch this magnificent, painful film began with the words: "How to win a battle against terrorism and lose the war of ideas . . ." And, they might have added, give encouragement to every resistance force in the Middle East. "If Israel's superpower ally can be humbled by Arabs in Iraq," a Palestinian official explained to me in one of the Beirut camps in 2003, "why should we give up our struggle against the Israelis, who cannot be as efficient soldiers as the Americans?"

That's the lesson the Algerians drew when they saw France's mighty army surrendering at Dien Bien Phu. The French, like the Americans in Afghanistan and Iraq, had succeeded in murdering or "liquidating" many of the Algerians who might have negotiated a ceasefire with them. The search for an *interlocuteur valable* was one of de Gaulle's most difficult tasks when he decided to leave Algeria. But what could the Americans do? Their *interlocuteur* might have been the United Nations. But the UN had been struck off as a negotiator by the suicide bombing of its headquarters in Baghdad. So had the International Red Cross, also suicide-bombed. The insurgents were not interested in negotiations of any kind. Bush had declared "war without end." And it looked as though Iraqis—along with ourselves—were going to be its principal victims.

To Abu Ghraib prison. It is September 2003. It will be another seven months before the torture and abuse perpetrated by the Americans in Saddam's old murder house are revealed. No talking to the prisoners, we are told. We can see them beyond the dirt lot, standing in the heat beside their sand-brown tents, the razor wire wrapped in sheaths around their compound. No pictures of the prisoners, we are told. Do not enter the compound. Do not go inside the wire. Of the up to 800 Iraqis held here, only a handful are "security detainees"—the rest are "criminal detainees"—but until now almost all of them have lived out here in the heat and dust and muck. Which is why the Americans were so pleased to see us at Saddam's vile old prison. Their message? Things are getting better.

Brigadier General Janis Karpinski, commander of the U.S. 800th Military Police Brigade, has cleaned up the burned and looted jail cells for hundreds of prisoners. A new medical section with stocks of medicines, X-ray machines and even a defibrillator has been installed for the prisoners. In the newly painted cells, there are blankets and toothpaste, toothbrush, soap and shampoo for every man, neatly placed for them—and for us, I suspect—on top of their prison blankets. These are the same cells in which the prisoners will later be held naked, or forced to wear women's underclothes or bitten by dogs. This is the corridor in which a young American military policewoman will hold a naked prisoner on a dog leash, where Iraqi prisoners will be piled naked on top of each other on the floor. General Karpinski will later be the Pentagon's fall-gal for what is happening here.

General Karpinski was obviously a tough lady—she was an intelligence officer in 7th Special Forces at Fort Bragg and served as a "targeting officer" in Saudi Arabia after Saddam invaded Kuwait in 1990—but back in September 2003 she had a little difficulty at first in recalling that there was a riot at the jail four months earlier in which U.S. troops used "lethal force" when protesting prisoners threw stones and tent-poles at American military policemen. The troops killed a teenage inmate. Most of the "security detainees"—the 800th MP Brigade's publicity said that they have the responsibility of "caring" for prisoners rather than guarding them—were across at Baghdad airport where, General Karpinski said, there were men who "may be part of a resistance force." Note the word "resistance," rather than terrorist. Then when I asked if there were any Western prisoners being held, she said that she thought there were "six claiming to be American and two claiming to be from the UK." General Ricardo Sanchez, the U.S. commander in Iraq, who would also be blamed for the mistreatment of prisoners at Abu Ghraib in 2005, will deny this within twenty-four hours. No explanation given.

Then came the head doctor of Abu Ghraib prison, a Dr. Majid. When I asked him what his job was when Saddam used the place as a torture and execution centre, he replied that he had been—er—the head doctor of Abu Ghraib prison. Indeed, half his staff were running the medical centre at Abu Ghraib under the Saddam regime. "No, I didn't ever attend the executions," he said. "I couldn't stand that. I sent my junior doctors to do the death certificates." Except at night, of course, when the security services brought in political prisoners for hanging. Then Dr. Majid would receive an instruction saying "no death certificates." The politicals were hanged at night. During the day, the doctor said, it was the "killers" who were hanged. Killers? Killers? What did his use of that word imply?

The new Iraqi prison guards at Abu Ghraib, we were informed, had been trained in human rights—including two, it turned out, who had been police officers under the Saddam regime. No wonder General Karpinski said that the Americans hadn't chosen the doctors—that had been the work of the new Iraqi Ministry of Health. There were U.S. intelligence officers in Abu Ghraib but no, the military police were not present during interrogations. Yes, General Karpinski had visited Guantánamo Bay for "a few days," but she had not brought any lessons learned there to Baghdad.*

Of course, we were taken on a statutory visit to Abu Ghraib's old death chamber, the double hanging room in which poor Farzad Bazoft of *The Observer* and thousands of Iraqis were put to death. General Karpinski gave the lever a tug and the great iron trapdoors clanged open, their echo vibrating through the walls. Dr. Majid said he had never heard them before, that he was never even a member of the Baath party. So let this be written in history: the chief medical officer at Saddam's nastiest prison—who was now the chief medical officer at America's cleanest Iraqi prison—was never a member of the Baath party and never saw an execution.

Of course, there are things which only a heart of stone cannot be moved by, the last words written and carved on the walls of the filthy death row cells, just a few yards from the gallows. "Ahmed Qambal, 8/9/2000," "Ahmed Aziz from Al-Najaf governorate, with Jabah, 2/9/01," "Abbad Abu Mohamed." Sometimes they had added verses from the Koran. "Death is better than shame." "Death is life for a believer and a high honour." What courage it must have taken to write such words, their very last on Earth.

But there was something just a little too neat about all this. Against Saddam's cruelty, any institution looks squeaky clean. Yet there was a lot about Abu Ghraib

*In a 21 May 2005 email to *The Independent*, Karpinski wrote that she had visited Guantánamo for "less than an entire day and I was there to resolve some issues between two officers, nothing related to the detention operations at all. I had access to all cellblocks at Abu Ghraib. When the prison compound was transferred to the Military Intelligence Commander in November 2003, my access remained unimpeded. The limitation was in the hours I was allowed to visit Abu Ghraib. I was not allowed to go out to Abu Ghraib during the hours of darkness . . . due to the increased danger of travelling at night . . ." Most of the mistreatment and torture at Abu Ghraib appears to occur at night.

which didn't look as clean as the new kitchens. There was still no clear judicial process for the supposed killers, thieves and looters behind the razor wire. The military admitted that the transcription of Arabic names—with all the Ellis Island mistakes that can lead to—meant that families often could not find their loved ones. There was no mention—until we brought it up—of the guerrilla mortar attack that killed six prisoners in their tents. The Americans had sent psychologists to talk to the inmates afterwards and found that they believed—surprise, surprise—that the Americans were using them as human shields. And, as we know, much, much worse was to come.

OWEID POINTS ACROSS the dry earth and sweeps his hand across the grey desolation of sand, dust and broken homes to the north. "I knew all these villages," he says. "Take this down in your notebook—you should remember the names of these dead villages: Mahamar, Manzan, Meshal, Daoudi, Djezeran Nakbia, Zalal, Abu Talfa, Jdedah, Ghalivah, Um al-Hamadi, Al-Gufas, Al-Khor, Al-Hammseen . . ." It is too much. I cannot keep up with Abbas Oweid. The sheer scope of Saddam's destruction of the Marsh Arabs has outpaced the speed of my handwriting. But then, far across the rubble of bricks and broken doorframes and dried mud, there comes the cry of a bird.

Oweid's face breaks into a smile. "Where the birds are, there is the water," he says, and rests on his heels, a man—the Arabs like this—who has found the right aphorism for the right moment. But it is true. The birds are returning because the water is trickling back into the thousands of square miles that Saddam drained for ten long years. You can literally hear it, gurgling, frothing, sucking its way into old ditches and dried-up streams and round the low dirt hills upon which the Shia Muslim Marsh Arabs built their homes before Saddam decided to destroy them. This is the same estuary where my friend and colleague Mohamed Salam of AP saw the charred corpses of the Marsh Arabs twenty years ago, burned and electrocuted by Saddam's army, people who'd lived among ducks and buffaloes and fished with spears, gutted open like fish, where the innocent had to die along with the invader.

I sit on a little boat, puttering up the broad Salal River, and see an old mud and concrete house with a new roof and new palm trees planted around it and a small, green-painted boat pulled onto the dirt embankment. The bulrushes and reeds are gone and there is no tree higher than 3 feet. But one family has come back. Even Mohsen Bahedh, whose family fled to the safety of Iran during the long and terrible man-made drought that Saddam inflicted on his people, is thinking of returning.

He sat beside me in our boat, his left hand holding a Kalashnikov rifle, his right resting on the head of his five-year-old son, Mehdi. "There were 12,000 families here and they all left," he said. "We had fish and fruit and vegetables and birds and water buffalo and our homes, and Saddam dried us out, took all our water away, left us with nothing."

Our boat slowed at one point because the water level rose 6 inches in front of us, a literal ridge of higher water that fell back to the river's normal level on the other side. "Underneath us are the remains of a Saddam dam," Mohsen said. "It makes the water run over the top of it. So we can still see the dams, even when they are no longer here."

You have to come here to appreciate Saddam's ruthlessness of purpose. After the Americans and British encouraged the Shia Muslims of Iraq to rise up against Saddam in 1991—and, of course, betrayed them by doing nothing when he wiped out his opponents—deserting Iraqi soldiers and rebels who wanted to keep on fighting retreated into the swamps of Howeiza and Amara and Hamar where the Marsh Arabs, immortalised in Wilfrid Thesiger's great work so many decades ago, gave them sanctuary. Iraqi helicopters and tanks could not winkle them out. So Saddam embarked on a strategy of counter-guerrilla warfare that puts Israel's political assassinations and property destruction—and America's Vietnam Agent Orange—into the shade. He constructed his set of dams—hundreds of them—to block the waters flowing into the marshes from the Tigris and Euphrates rivers. He diverted the water through new and wide canals—one of them was called the Mother of All Battles River—which irrigated the towns and cities that remained loyal to him. The only water allowed into the marshes was from the runoffs of fertilised fields, so the Marsh Arabs' cattle walked into the centre of the streams to find fresh water. In the end, there was almost no water left.

But when the Anglo–American invasion force crashed into Iraq in March 2003 there were still some hundreds of square miles of marshes left; and in the first hours after the British reached Basra, the people of Hamar dug through the earth and concrete dams that Saddam had erected to destroy them and breached his ramparts. One old man in Nasiriyah told me his wife woke him after the first night of bombing to tell him she could hear water trickling in the old ditch behind their house. The man didn't believe her. "Then I got up and walked outside in the moonlight," he said. "And I saw water."

It is a story of hope. Faisal Khayoun's father was murdered by Saddam's secret police in 1993 while driving on the Basra Road. "They shot him in the forehead and neck," he said. "My cousin and my uncle were arrested in 1997 and hanged at Abu Ghraib. The *mukhabarat* used to come here on raids at four in the morning and I would always spend the nights on the roof, waiting in case they came. Now, for the first time in my life, I stay asleep in my home until the sun wakes me in the morning."

Mohsen Bahedh jumped ashore 4 miles north of the Hamar Bridge and we sloshed together through deep, black mud that pulled at our shoes, to the four broken walls of a house. "This was my home," he said. "I came back and knocked some of the bricks and window-frames out to build a new home south of Saddam's dam. See, that's where we kept the geese—and my cattle were where the dust is. And my boat was down there." He and Mehdi paddled through the wreckage. "Maybe we will come back now," he said. "Yes, we helped Saddam's opponents. And when the soldiers deserted and came here, we fed them and gave them places to sleep and fuel to keep them warm. We are a kind people."

Mohsen is forty-eight, but has two young wives and five children and says he can scarcely afford to finish building his new house. And the Marsh Arabs cannot just walk back to their land. Many long ago exchanged the water buffalo for a Mercedes and became traders. Other tribes moved into the area and planted crops in newly irrigated land. But Thesiger's people survived and Saddam's regime did not, and a small tide of dark blue water was now seeping back into the desert, creeping around Mahamar, Manzan, Meshal and all the lost villages of the marshes.

How hope and horror nestled against each other. As the Americans slaughtered a wedding party in an air strike—and called the guests "insurgents"—another of Saddam's mass graves would be opened. No sooner had I returned from the land of the Marsh Arabs than I would learn of the "Documentation Centre for the Female Martyrs of the Islamic Movement," whose study of Saddam's young female victims—most were subjected to vicious torture and deliberately cruel executions—is not for the faint-hearted.

Wives were forced to watch their husbands hanged before being placed in the electric chair, were burned with acid, tied naked to ceiling fans, sexually abused. In several cases, women were poisoned or used as guinea pigs for chemical substances at a plant near Samara believed to be making chemical weapons. Their names—along with the names of their torturers and executioners—are at last known. One man, Abu Widad, once boasted that he had hanged seventy female prisoners in one night at the Abu Ghraib prison. In many cases, women were put to death for the crime of being the sisters or wives of a wanted man. Most were associated with the forbidden Dawa party whose members were routinely tortured and killed by the Baathist government.

A typical entry in "Imprisoned Memories: Red Pages from a Forgotten History"—compiled by Ali al-Iraq in the Iranian city of Qum—reads as follows:

> Samira Awdah al-Mansouri (Um Iman), birthdate 1951, Basra, teacher at Haritha Intermediate School . . . married to the martyr Abdul Ameer, a cadre of the Islamic movement military wing . . . member of Islamic Dawa party . . . Torturers: Major Mehdi al-Dulaymi who tortured while drunk, Lieutenant Hussain al-Tikriti, who specialised in breaking the rib cages of his victims by stamping on them . . . Lieutenant Ibrahim al-Lamee who beat victims on their feet . . . Um Iman was beaten . . . hung by her hair from a ceiling fan and suffered torture by electricity. Having spent two months in the prison cells in Basra without giving way, al-Dulaymi recommended she be executed for carrying unlicensed arms and belonging to the al-Dawa party.

In fact, Um Iman was transferred to the Public Security Division in Baghdad, where further torture took place over eleven months. She subsequently appeared before the Revolutionary Military Security Court, which sentenced her to death by hanging. She spent another six months in the Rashid prison west of Baghdad until—when she might have hoped that her life would be spared—she was, on a Sunday evening, transferred to Abu Ghraib and executed by Abu Widad.

There are frequent accounts of women and children tortured in front of their husbands and fathers. In 1982, for instance, a Lieutenant Kareem in Basra reportedly brought the wife of an insurgent to the prison, stripped and tortured her in front of her husband, then threatened to kill their infant child. When both refused to talk, the security man "threw the baby against the wall and killed him."

Ahlam al-Ayashi was arrested in 1982 at the age of twenty because she was married to Imad al-Kirawee, a senior Dawa member. When he refused to give information to the security police, two professional torturers—named in the report as Fadil Hamidi al-Zarakani and Faysal al-Hilali—attacked Ahlam in front of the prisoner and his child, torturing her—the account spares readers the details—to death. Her body was buried in the desert outside Basra and has no known grave. Three of Ahlam's five brothers were executed along with her husband, and another brother was killed in the insurrection that followed the liberation of Kuwait in 1991. But her child Ala, who witnessed her mother's torture, was taken to Iran, where she married and was now about to enter university.

Many of the stories are painfully tragic. Twenty-one-year-old Awatif Nour al-Hamadani, for example, was betrayed by her own husband, who—under extreme torture—named his wife and several colleagues as gun-runners. Awatif was pregnant but was set on by a man called Major Amer who beat her with a metal chair and then sexually abused her. At her trial, Judge Mussalam al-Jabouri suggested that "a miniature gallows should be found for her baby daughter because she had sucked on her mother's hate-filled milk."

Awatif was first taken to be executed with two female colleagues and forced to watch the hanging of 150 men, 10 at a time; as their corpses were taken away, she recognised one of them as her husband. She was then returned to her cell. She was later executed in an electric chair. Many inmates were also killed in the same chair at Abu Ghraib, including two other women, Fadilah al-Haddad in 1982 and Rida al-Ouwaynati the following year.

Maysoon al-Assadi was an eighteen-year-old university student when she was arrested for membership in a banned Islamic organisation. During her interrogation she was hanged by her hair and beaten on the soles of her feet, and then she was sentenced to hang by Judge Awad Mohamed Amin al-Bandar. Her last wish—to say goodbye to her fiancé—was granted and the two married in the prison. But while saying goodbye to other prisoners, she made speeches condemning the leadership of the Iraqi regime and the prison governor decided that she should be put to death slowly. She was strapped into the jail's electric chair and took two hours to die.

Salwa al-Bahrani, the mother of a small boy, had been caught distributing weapons to Islamic fighters in 1980. She was allegedly administered poisoned yoghurt during interrogation by a Dr. Fahid al-Dannouk, who experimented in poisons that could be used against Iranian troops. Hundreds of mujahedin fighters of Dawa were, according to the report, used as guinea pigs for experiments with toxic chemicals at Salman Pak just south of Baghdad. Salwa died at home forty-five days after being forced to eat the yoghurt. Fatimah al-Hussaini, aged twenty, was accused of concealing weapons for al-Dawa and arrested in Baghdad in 1982. She was beaten with plastic cables, hung from the ceiling by her hands, which were tied behind her back, tortured with electricity and had acid poured on her thighs. She refused to talk and her torturer recommended execution. She was hanged at Abu Ghraib in 1982 and buried by her family in Najaf.

The 550-page report which records the dreadful suffering of Saddam's female Shiite prisoners was no literary work. Some of its prose is florid and occasionally appears to describe women's martyrdom as a fate to be emulated. Nor was this a volume that would make easy reading for Americans anxious to use it as evidence against Saddam. At the time these crimes were being committed, the United States regarded Saddam as an ally—and the book repeatedly stated that the chemicals used on women prisoners were originally purchased from Western countries. But the detail is compelling—the names and fates of at least fifty women are recorded, along with the names of their torturers—and the activities of the "Monster of Abu Ghraib," Abu Widad, have been confirmed by the few prisoners who survived the jail. He carried out executions between 8 p.m. and 4 a.m. and would hit condemned men and women on the back of the head with a hatchet if they praised a murdered imam before they were hanged. In the end, forty-one-year-old Abu Widad was caught after accepting a bribe to put a reprieved prisoner to death instead of the condemned man; he was hanged on his own gallows in 1985.

The Americans and British benefitted from these accounts of terror under Saddam. Would you rather he was still here in Iraq, torturing and gassing his own people? they would ask. Don't you think we did a good thing by getting rid of him? All this because the original reasons for the invasion—Saddam's possession of weapons of mass destruction, his links with the outrages of September 11th, Blair's 45-minute warning—turned out to be lies. But it was a dark comparison that Bush and Blair were making. If Saddam's immorality and wickedness had to be the yardstick against which all of our own iniquities were judged, what did that say about us? If Saddam's regime was to be the moral compass to define *our* actions, how bad—how iniquitous—did that allow us to be? Saddam tortured and executed women in Abu Ghraib. We only sexually abused prisoners and killed a few of them and murdered some suspects in Bagram and subjected them to inhuman treatment in Guantánamo.* Saddam was much worse. And thus it became inevitable that the symbol of Saddam's shame—the prison at Abu Ghraib—subsequently became the symbol of our shame too.

---

*By midsummer 2005, disclosures of torture by U.S. armed forces in Iraq and Afghanistan were being made almost weekly. In *The New York Times* on 23 May, Bob Herbert described the military torturers as "sadists, perverts and criminals," quoting the *Times*'s own report of 20 May of a U.S. Army document on torture in Afghanistan: "In sworn testimony to army investigators, soldiers describe one female interrogator with a taste for humiliation stepping on the neck of one prostrate detainee and kicking another in the genitals. They tell of a shackled prisoner being forced to roll back and forth on the floor of a cell, kissing the boots of his two interrogators as he went. Yet another prisoner is made to pick plastic bottle caps out of a drum mixed with excrement and water as part of a strategy to soften him up for questioning." This original report, by Tim Golden, described how an innocent man was kicked a hundred times on the leg by guards and later died in his cell, handcuffed to the ceiling.

What was interesting was the vastly different reaction in East and West to our abuses at Abu Ghraib. We "civilised" Westerners were shocked at the dog-biting and humiliations and torture "our" men and women administered to the inmates. Iraqis were outraged, but not shocked. Their friends and relatives—some of whom had been locked up by the Americans—had long ago told them of the revolting behaviour of the American guards. They weren't surprised by those iconic photographs. They already knew.

By early 2004, an army of thousands of mercenaries had appeared on the streets of Iraq's major cities, many of them former British and American soldiers hired by the occupying Anglo-American authorities and by dozens of companies who feared for the lives of their employees in Baghdad. The heavily armed Britons working for well over 300 security firms in Iraq now outnumbered Britain's 8,000-strong army in the south of the country. Although major U.S. and British security companies were operating in Iraq, dozens of small firms also set up shop with little vetting of their employees and few rules of engagement. Many of the Britons were former SAS soldiers—hundreds of former American Special Forces men were also in the country—while armed South Africans were also working for the occupation authorities.

The presence in Iraq of so many thousands of Western mercenaries—or "security contractors," as the American press coyly referred to them—said as much about America's fear of taking military casualties as it did about the multi-million-pound security industry now milking the coffers of the U.S. and British governments. Security firms were escorting convoys on the highways of Iraq. Armed plain-clothes men from an American company were guarding U.S. troops at night inside the former presidential palace where Paul Bremer had his headquarters. In other words, security companies were now guarding occupation troops. When a U.S. helicopter crashed near Fallujah in 2003, it was an American security firm that took control of the area and began rescue operations. Needless to say, casualties among the mercenaries were not included in the regular body count put out by the occupation authorities.

Nor were the names of prisoners included in their lists. When fifty-five-year-old Mohamed Abul Abbas died mysteriously in a U.S. prison camp in Iraq, nobody bothered to call his family. His American captors had given no indication to the International Red Cross that the man behind the hijacking of the *Achille Lauro* cruise liner in 1985 had been unwell; his wife, Reem, first heard that he was dead when she watched an Arab television news show. Yet in his last letter to his family, written just seven weeks earlier, the Palestinian militant wrote, "I am in good form and in good health," adding that he hoped to be freed soon. So what happened to Mohamed Abul Abbas?

Although he was a prominent colleague of Yassir Arafat for more than three decades, the world will for ever link his name with the *Achille Lauro*, when members of his small "Palestine Liberation Front" commandeered the vessel in the Mediterranean and, in a cruel killing that was to cause international outrage, shot dead an elderly Jewish American, Leon Klinghoffer. Yet within ten years the

Israelis themselves would allow Abul Abbas, now a member of the Palestine National Council, to enter the occupied territories to participate in elections in the Gaza Strip. He even visited his old family home in Haifa in Israel. He supported Israeli–Palestinian peace agreements and favoured the annulment of the anti-Israeli articles in the PLO's charter. Like so many of Arafat's colleagues, he had undergone that mystical Middle East transformation from "super-terrorist" to peacenik.

So why was he ever incarcerated in the harsh confines of America's airport prison camp outside Baghdad? He was never charged with any crime, never offered a lawyer, never allowed direct contact with his wife and family, able to communicate with the outside world only via the Red Cross. It was they who finally telephoned his wife, Reem, in Beirut to confirm that her husband was dead.

"I know nothing about this—nothing," she wailed down the telephone to me. "How did he die? Why were we told nothing?" Mohamed Abul Abbas remains the most prominent prisoner to die in U.S. custody in Iraq and joined a growing list of unexplained deaths among the 15,000 Iraqis and Palestinians held by U.S. military forces. The occupation authorities in Iraq would say only that they were to hold a post-mortem on Abul Abbas's remains. The Palestine Liberation Front had long had offices in Baghdad, along with Arafat's PLO; the head of the PLF's "political bureau," Mohamed Sobhi, said that Mohamed Abul Abbas's arrest by U.S. troops on 14 April the previous year had "no reason in law other than the need of the American soldiers at that time to look for false victories. We all knew that Abul Abbas had been to Palestine in 1995 and that the United States and Israel both allowed this. After that, he travelled to Palestinian areas and to other Arab states many times. We had told all this to the Americans here and demanded that he be released. In his last letter home, he said he hoped to be freed soon. So what happened to him?"

Reem Abul Abbas, who has a child by her husband and two by an earlier marriage, said that he was still living in Baghdad when American troops entered the city on 9 April last year. "He was trying to keep away from them because many people—Iraqis and Palestinians—were being arrested, people who had done nothing. Then American troops raided our home. Mohamed wasn't there but I saw it all on Fox Television. Would you believe I saw my own home on television and they had moved things around and draped a Palestinian flag over a mirror and then invited Fox Television to film it. On the evening of April 14th, Mohamed called me from a Thuraya satellite phone from a friend's home. It was a big mistake. I think that's how they tracked him down and found him. Not long afterwards, American soldiers came up the stairs."

The U.S. occupation authorities initially announced the capture of the "important terrorist Abul Abbas," making no mention of his return to the occupied territories or that the Israelis themselves—who might have been more anxious than the Americans to see him in prison—had freely allowed the PLF leader to enter their territory as a peace negotiator. "First he was a 'terrorist,' " his wife, Reem, said. "Then he was a man of peace. Then when the Americans arrested him, they made him a 'terrorist' again. What is this nonsense?" Within months, the same transformation was to be undergone by Yassir Arafat. Abul Abbas's last letter to his family, dated 19 January and written in neat Arabic on one side of a sheet of Red Cross paper, gave no indication of his fate. Addressed to his brother Khaled in Holland, it is a prisoner's familiar appeal for letters and news, of expressions of affection and hope. "Dear Khaled," it begins, ". . . first I present my kisses to the head of your dear mother and I hope she's ready to prepare the 'dolma' and the red chicken that I love, because my first lunch (in freedom) will be at her home. What is the news about my family and my dearest Issa? . . . Very special greetings to him, his wife and children and for your brothers and sisters and their families because they are my family, too, and my dearest ones . . . I hope you can send me a *dishdash* . . . I am in good form and in good health and I really need to know news of my family and friends. I have great hopes of being released soon—with God's will." Mohamed Abul Abbas appears to have had no premonition of his imminent death. But forty-nine days after he wrote his letter of hope, he was dead.

Iraq allowed the world to forget Palestine, where Yassir Arafat was now living in the foetid, unwashed offices in which he had been held under effective house arrest by the Israeli army in Ramallah. The Israelis broke off all contact with him. So did the Americans. Palestinian suicide bombers blew themselves up across Israel until Ariel Sharon began building a vast wall across the West Bank, cutting off hundreds of Palestinian villages, carving a de facto annexation into the land which was supposed to be a Palestinian state. The wall, it should be said at once, could not be called a wall by most journalists—even though it was far longer than the old Berlin Wall. "Wall" has ugly connotations of ghettoes and apartheid. So it became a "security barrier" in *The New York Times* and on the BBC or else, even more fancifully, a "fence." The International Court at The Hague—to which the broken Palestinian Authority sent its spokesmen—ruled the construction illegal. Israel ignored the ruling.*

And it continued its policy of murdering its opponents. These "targeted killings"—another example of Israel's semantic inventions which the BBC and others obediently adopted—went for the top, even though the innocent were inevitably killed in the same attacks. On 21 March 2004 an Israeli helicopter fired a missile at the elderly and crippled head of Hamas, Sheikh Ahmed Yassin, as he left a mosque in Gaza. It didn't take much courage to murder a paraplegic in a wheelchair. Likewise, it took only a few moments to absorb the implications of the assassination. Yes, he enthusiastically endorsed suicide bombings—including the murder of Israeli children. Yes, if you live by the sword, you die by the sword, in a wheelchair or not. But something infinitely dangerous—another sinister precedent—was being set for our brave new world.

---

*For years, Americans—not least Tom Friedman—had been lecturing the Palestinians on the principles of non-violence, suggesting that a Gandhi-like approach to occupation might yield benefits. Arab pleading at The Hague proved, of course, that such peaceful protest did not amount to the proverbial hill of beans.

Take the old man himself. From the start, the Israeli line was simple. Sheik Yassin was the "head of the snake"—to use the words of the Israeli ambassador to London—the head of Hamas, "one of the world's most dangerous terrorist organisations." But then came obfuscation from the world's media. Yassin, the BBC World Service Television told us on the day of the murder, was originally freed by the Israelis in a "prisoner exchange." It sounded like one of those familiar swaps—a Palestinian released in exchange for captured Israeli soldiers—and then, later the same day, the BBC told us that he had been freed "following a deal brokered by King Hussein."

Which was all very strange. He was a prisoner of the Israelis. This "head of the snake" was in an Israeli prison. And then—bingo—this supposed monster was let go because of a "deal." So let's remember what the "deal" was. Sheikh Yassin was set free by no less than that law-and-order right-wing Likudist Benjamin Netanyahu when he was prime minister of Israel. The now dead King Hussein hadn't been a "broker" between two sides. Two Israeli Mossad secret agents had tried to murder a Hamas official in Amman, the capital of an Arab nation which had a full peace agreement with Israel. They had injected the Hamas man with poison and the late King Hussein of Jordan called the U.S. president in fury and threatened to put the captured Mossad men on trial if he wasn't given the antidote to the poison and if Yassin wasn't released.

Netanyahu immediately gave in. Yassin was freed and the Mossad lads went safely home to Israel. So the "head of the snake" was let loose by Israel itself, courtesy of the then Israeli prime minister—a chapter in the narrative of history which was conveniently forgotten when Yassin was killed. Which was all very odd. For if the elderly cleric really was worthy of state murder, why did Netanyahu let him go in the first place? Much more dangerous, however, were the implications. Yet another Arab—another leader, however vengeful and ruthless—had been assassinated. The Americans want to kill bin Laden. They want to kill Mullah Omar. They killed Saddam's two sons. Just as they killed three al-Qaeda men in Yemen with a remotely piloted drone and rocket. The Israelis repeatedly threatened to murder Yassir Arafat. And shortly after Yassin's death, the Israelis struck again, firing another missile at the new Hamas leader, Abdul-Aziz Rantissi. It was Rantissi who had been illegally deported to Lebanon with hundreds of other Palestinians more than a decade before, who had lived out the long months of heat and snow in the "Field of Flowers" close to the Israeli border. It was the same bearded Rantissi I had last interviewed in Gaza, who had told me then, "the preferred way of ending my life would be martyrdom." I had looked out of the window then, searching for an Apache helicopter. Now it had come for him.

No one had begun to work out the implications of all this. For years, there had been an unwritten rule in the cruel war of government versus guerrilla. You can kill the men on the street, the bomb-makers and gunmen. But the leadership on both sides—government ministers, spiritual leaders, possible future *interlocuteurs valables* as the French used to call them when in 1962 they discovered they had murdered most of the Algerian leadership—were allowed to survive.

True, these rules were sometimes broken. The IRA tried to kill Mrs. Thatcher. They murdered her friend Airey Neave. Islamic Jihad murdered an Israeli minister in his hotel room. But these were exceptions. Now all was changed utterly. Anyone who advocated violence—even if palpably incapable of committing it—was now on a death list. So who could be surprised if the rules were broken by the other side?

Is President Bush now safe? Or Tony Blair? Or their ambassadors and fellow ministers? How soon before "our" leaders are "fair game"? We will not say this. If—or when—our own political leaders are assassinated, shot down or blown up, we shall vilify the murderers and argue that a new stage in "terrorism" has been reached. We shall forget that we are now encouraging this all-out assassination spree. The Americans failed to condemn Sheikh Yassin's assassination just as they did Rantissi's. So we took another step down a sinister road.

Then death came to the old man. Arafat had long shown the symptoms of Parkinson's disease but in the filth of his smashed Ramallah compound his health was bound to deteriorate further. He had fallen into the habit, even in the company of diplomatic visitors, of pulling off his socks and rubbing the sores on his feet. He had difficulty concentrating, lost his appetite. To the same visitors, he would ramble on about his 1982 battle against the Israelis in besieged Beirut. Some of his entourage realised that his mind was wandering, that he was losing his grip on the real world, that he was dying. They were right. The Israelis at last allowed the desperately sick Arafat to leave his ruined headquarters and the French transported the elderly man to the Percy military hospital outside Paris. Here, on 11 November 2004, on the eighty-sixth anniversary of the end of the First World War—the war which had produced the Balfour Declaration and Britain's support for a Jewish homeland in Palestine, the conflict which ultimately caused his people's dispossession and exile—Yassir Arafat died.

I watched his funeral in Cairo, a grim, short journey on a horse-drawn gun carriage down a boulevard in which not a single Egyptian or Palestinian civilian was allowed to walk, before a phalanx of Arab dictators, some with blood on their hands. They had been chatting beside a mosque when a far gate in a palace wall opened and six black horses clip-clopped onto the road with the coffin, still bearing the Palestinian flag which the French had laid over it. And for almost a minute, no one noticed the horses or the coffin. It was like a train that steamed unnoticed into a country station on a hot afternoon. Yet when the body arrived in Ramallah, the Palestinians gave Arafat a more familiar funeral, shrieking and wailing—tens of thousands of them—fighting to touch the coffin and shooting cascades of bullets into the air. Arafat would have enjoyed it, for it was as chaotic, as dramatic, as genuine and as frightening as his own flawed character. And of course, the world was happy. Now that Arafat had gone, there was hope. That was our reaction. While the Palestinians grieved, they were told that life would now improve.

So, after democratic elections—something that Arafat never approved of—the colourless Mahmoud Abbas became president, a man whom the Americans and British thoroughly approved of. Abbas had written Palestinian documents for the

Oslo accord, 600 pages in which he did not once use the word "occupation," in which he referred only to the "redeployment" of the Israeli army rather than its withdrawal. Yet while he promised to end "terrorism"—Abbas's ability to use America's and Israel's lexicon was among his many accomplishments—the land of Palestine slipped from under him. Hamas and Israel broke ceasefires and then President George W. Bush announced, after a meeting in the United States with Ariel Sharon, that new realities had to be faced, that while he wanted a democratic Palestinian state "side by side" with Israel, the larger Jewish settlements built illegally on Palestinian land would have to stay. He had said this first in April 2004, when Arafat was still alive. It amounted to the destruction of UN Security Council Resolution 242, which said that land could not be acquired by war. Ariel Sharon was prepared to close down the puny little settlements in Gaza—housing just 8,000 Israelis—and this was a "historic and courageous act." And the result? Vast areas of the Palestinian West Bank would now become Israeli, courtesy of President Bush. Land that belonged to people other than Israelis could now be appropriated with America's permission because it was "unrealistic" to accept otherwise. The Palestinians were appalled. This was just the sort of deceit and dishonesty that Osama bin Laden enjoyed talking about. Indeed, if George W. Bush thought he could define what was "unrealistic" in the Middle East, one was entitled to ask another question. Did he actually *work* for al-Qaeda?

We all have lands that "God" or our fathers gave us. Didn't Queen Mary Tudor of England die with "Calais" engraved on her heart? Doesn't Spain have a legitimate right to the Netherlands? Or Sweden the right to Norway and Denmark? Or Britain the right to India? Didn't the Muslims—and the Jews—have a right to fifteenth-century Andalusia? Every colonial power, including Israel, could put forward these preposterous demands. Every claim by Osama bin Laden, every statement that the United States represents Zionism and supports the theft of Arab lands, had now been proved true to millions of Arabs, even those who had no time for bin Laden. What better recruiting sergeant could bin Laden have than George W. Bush? Didn't he realise what this meant for young American soldiers in Iraq? Or were Israelis more important than American lives in Mesopotamia?

IN HIS LAST HOURS as U.S. proconsul in Baghdad in the summer of 2004, Paul Bremer decided to tighten up some of the laws that his occupation authority had placed across the land of Iraq. He drafted a new piece of legislation, forbidding Iraqi motorists to drive with only one hand on the wheel. Another document solemnly announced that it would henceforth be a crime for Iraqis to sound their car horns except in an emergency. That same day, while Bremer fretted about the standards of Iraqi driving, three American soldiers were torn apart by a roadside bomb north of Baghdad, one of more than sixty attacks on U.S. forces over the same weekend.

It would be difficult to find a more preposterous—and distressing—symbol of Bremer's failures, his hopeless inability to understand the nature of the debacle which he and his hopeless occupation authority had brought about. It was not that the old Coalition Provisional Authority—now transmogrified into a 3,000-strong U.S. embassy, the largest in the world—was out of touch. It didn't even live on planet Earth. Bremer's last starring moment came when he departed Baghdad on a U.S. military aircraft, two U.S.-paid mercenaries—rifles pointed menacingly at camera crews and walking backwards—protecting him until the cabin door closed. And Bremer, remember, was appointed to his job because he was an "anti-terrorist" expert.

It was a terrible summer. If they could not always strike at the Americans, the insurgents would produce their Wal-Mart suicide bombers and destroy those they deemed collaborators. On 28 July, for example, hordes of impoverished would-be police recruits were massacred, up to a hundred of them in the Sunni city of Baquba, as they lined up unprotected along a boulevard in the hope of finding work. The bomber—identity, as usual, unknown—drove his Renault car into a mass of 600 unemployed young men looking for jobs in the police force, deto-nated his explosives and cut them to pieces. The bomb left a 7-foot hole in the road and wounded at least another 150 men and women, many of them shopping in a neighbouring market.

It would be the last summer when it was still possible to move on the roads of Iraq with some hope of not being killed or kidnapped and decapitated. I took a boat out on the Tigris, where the boatman, a former Iraqi soldier called Saleh, who was wounded in the Iran–Iraq War, offered to take me to Basra. A bit far, I thought, a full week's journey on Saleh's barge. So I settled for a trip out of Baghdad, past Saddam's old school and the wreckage of the defence ministry and the armies of squatters in the ruined apartment blocks. And as we drifted down the pea-green waters of the Tigris, I asked Saleh, who was a Shia, if there was any hope for the Middle East, for Iraq, for us. "Our Imam Ali said that a man is either our brother in religion or our brother in humanity and we believe this," he said. "You must live with all men in perfect peace. You don't need to fight him or kill him. You know something—Islam is a very easy religion, but some radicals make it difficult. We are against anyone who is killing or kidnapping foreigners. This is not the Mus-lim way."

I call on Sheikh Jouwad Mehdi al-Khalasi, one of the most impressive Shia leaders in Baghdad. A tall, distinguished man who speaks with both eloquence and humour, he has the forehead and piercing eyes of his grandfather—the man who led the Shia Muslim insurrection against British occupation in 1920. He brings out a portrait of the grand old revolutionary, who has a fluffy but carefully combed white beard. One of the most eminent scholars of his day, he ended his life in exile, negotiating with Lenin's Bolshevik government and dying mysteriously—poisoned, his supporters believed, by British intelligence.

Sheikh Jouwad's shoulders shake with laughter when I suggest that there are more than a few parallels between the Iraqi insurrections of 1920 and 2004. "Exactly," he says. "In 1920, the British tried to introduce an Iraqi government in name only—it looks like a copy of UN Security Council Resolution 1546. Sheikh

Mehdi al-Khalasi had become the grand 'marja' [the leading Shiite scholar] after the death of Mohamed al-Shiazi and he issued a fatwa telling his followers and all Shiites in Iraq not to participate in elections, not to give legitimacy to a government established by occupation forces.

"Not only the Shiites responded to it but the Sunnis and the Jewish, Christian and other minorities as well. The elections failed and so the British forced my grandfather to leave Iraq. They arrested him at his home on the other side of this religious school where we are today—a home which many years later Saddam Hussein deliberately destroyed."

It was a familiar colonial pattern. The Brits were exiling troublesome clerics—Archbishop Makarios came to mind—throughout the twentieth century, but Sheikh Mehdi turned out to be as dangerous to the British abroad as he had been at home. He was transported to Bombay, but so great was the crowd of angry Indian Muslims who arrived at the port that British troops kept him on board ship and then transported him to the hot, volcanic port of Aden.

"He said to the British: 'You don't know where to send me—but since the pilgrimage season is close, I want to go on the haj to Mecca.' Now when Sherif Hussein, the ruler, heard this, he sent an invitation for my grandfather to attend the haj. He met Sherif Hussein on Arafat Mountain at Mecca. And then he received an invitation to go to Iran, signed by the minister of foreign affairs, Mohamed Mossadeq. And in Iran, waiting for him, were many religious leaders from Najaf." Thirty years later, the Americans would topple Mossadeq's Iranian government—with help from Colonel "Monty" Woodhouse of MI6.

Sheikh Jouwad uses his hands when he talks—Shia prelates are far more expressive with their hands than Anglican clergymen—and each new episode in his grandfather's life produces a pointed finger. "When Sheikh Mehdi al-Khalasi arrived at the Iranian port of Bushehr, he received a big welcome but an official of the Iranian Oil Company fired ten bullets at him. Many people said at the time that this was a plot by Colonel Arnold Wilson, who had been the head of the British occupation in Iraq in 1920. All the great religious leaders from Qom in Iran were waiting for him—Al-Naini and al-Asfahani, Sheikh Abdulhalim al-Hoeri al-Yezdi, who was the professor of the future Ayatollah Khomeini—and then King Feisal, whom the British had set up in Baghdad, announced that exiled religious leaders could return to Iraq—providing they promised not to interfere in politics."

Sheikh Mehdi angrily dismissed the invitation as "an attack on our role as religious leaders and on the independence of Iraq." Instead, he travelled to the northeastern Iranian city of Mashad and established there an assembly "to protect the holy places of Iraq," publishing treatises in Arabic, Persian, Urdu, Russian and Turkish.

"There was even an indirect dialogue between my grandfather and the Bolshevik revolutionaries of Lenin," Sheikh Jouwad says. "They wanted to use difficulties in the international situation to help Iraq to become a really independent country. There would be a revolution in Iraq. That was the idea. But then in 1925, my grandfather suddenly died. They claimed he had a disease. But my father always believed that the British consul in Mashad had Sheikh Mehdi poisoned. On the afternoon that he died, the consul had invited all the doctors in Mashad to a reception outside the city and so when my grandfather became ill, no one could find a doctor and there was no one to care for him."

And now? I ask Sheikh Jouwad. What of Iraq now? He chairs the Iraqi Islamic Conference—which combines both Shia and Sunni intellectuals, and which is demanding independence for Iraq, just as Sheikh Jouwad's grandfather did more than eighty years ago. "The Shia will not separate and they will not isolate themselves from the Sunni. They will have their rights when all the people of Iraq have rights. We have the right also to resist occupation in different ways and we do so politically . . . The Americans want civil war—but they will fail, because the Iraqi people will refuse to fall into civil war."

But there are Arabs who might also like to provoke a civil war and who want to portray Islam as a religion of revenge and fear. I start to look at the videotapes, the kidnap tapes, of men and women pleading for their lives. The pictures are grainy, the voices sometimes unclear. But when Kim Sun-il from South Korea shrieks "Don't kill me" over and over again, his fear is palpable. As the heads of the kidnap victims are sawn off, Koranic recitations—usually by a well-known Saudi imam—are played on the soundtrack. At the beheading of an American, the murderer ritually wipes his bloody knife twice on the clothes of his victim, just as Saudi officials clean their blades after public executions in the kingdom. Terror by video is now a well-established part of the Iraq war. The "resistance" or the "terrorists" or the "armed Iraqi fighters"—as U.S. forces now referred to their enemies—began with a set of poorly made videos showing attacks on American troops in Iraq. Roadside bombs would be filmed from a passing car as they exploded beside U.S. convoys. Guerrillas could be seen firing mortars at American bases outside Fallujah. But once the kidnappings began, the videos moved into a macabre new world. More than sixty foreigners had been abducted in Iraq by July 2004; most were freed, but many were videotaped in captivity while their kidnappers read their demands. Angelo de la Cruz's wasted face was enough to provoke street demonstrations in Manila and the early withdrawal of the small Filipino military contingent in Iraq.

But the scenario has become horribly routine. The potential victim kneels in front of three hooded men holding Kalashnikov rifles. Sometimes he pleads for his life. Sometimes he is silent, apparently unaware of whether he is to be murdered or spared. The viewer, however, will notice something quite terrible which the victim is unaware of. When the hostage is to be beheaded, the gunmen behind him are wearing gloves. They do not intend to stain their hands with an infidel's blood. There is a reading of his death sentence and then—inevitably—the victim is pulled to the right and one man bends over to saw through his throat. The latest victim had been Bulgarian. Just as Ken Bigley from Liverpool was to turn up, trussed like a Guantánamo prisoner, crying out for help from Tony Blair, so Romanian, French, Japanese, Korean, Turkish and other foreign nationals are paraded before the cameras.

The videos, usually delivered to one of two Arabic-language television channels, are rarely shown in full. But in an outrageous spin-off, websites—especially one that appeared to be in California—were now posting their full and gory contents. One American website, for example, had posted the beheading of the American Frank Berg and a South Korean hostage in full and bloody detail. "Kim Sun-il Beheading Video Short Version, Long Version," the website offered. The "short version" showed a man severing the hostage's neck. The long version included his screaming appeal for mercy—which lasted for at least two minutes and is followed by his slaughter. On the same screen and at the same time, there are advertisements for "Porn" and "Horse Girls."

The Iraqi police had watched all the execution tapes and believed that they followed an essentially Saudi routine of beheading. In many cases, the captors speak with Saudi or Yemeni accents. But a video produced of eight foreign truck-drivers—including Kenyans, Indians and an Egyptian—showed gunmen speaking in Iraqi accents. They demanded that the companies employing the drivers should end their contracts with the U.S. military in Iraq—just as a Saudi company abandoned its work after another Egyptian employee was taken captive. Clearly, the "resistance" was also trying to starve the Americans of foreign workers and force more U.S. troops back onto the dangerous highways to drive the supply convoys that traversed Iraq each day.

And where did the inspiration for all these ghoulish videos come from? In January 2004, a colleague had discovered a video on sale in the insurgents' capital of Fallujah allegedly showing the throat-cutting of an American soldier. In fact, the tape showed a Russian soldier being led into a room by armed men in Chechnya. He is forced to lie down—apparently unaware of his fate—and at first tries to cope with the pain as a man takes a knife to his throat. His head is then cut off. It takes me several months before I realise why this tape was circulated. It was intended to be a training manual for Iraq's new executioners, how to butcher your fellow man, be he a brother in religion or a brother in humanity.

But behind all this—above all this—the shadow that appeared at the back of the historical cave remained that of Osama bin Laden. Every few months, a tape or video of bin Laden himself would turn up on Al-Jazeera, often hand-delivered to the station's correspondent in Islamabad. A routine would then be adopted by reporters. Was it really him? When was the tape made? The Pentagon would say it was "studying the tape" and journalists would then point out any threat that bin Laden had made. What they rarely did was listen to the whole speech, make a full translation and find out what bin Laden was actually saying. After all, if you want to know what goes on in his mind, you have to listen to the voice, even if the rhetorical flourishes about charging horses and flashing lances become a little tedious. On 27 December 2001, for example, he read a poem supposedly dedicated to the murderers of September 11th which included a "frowning sword," "shields," "bolts of lightning," "drums" and "tempest."

What is also clear from his tapes, however, is bin Laden's almost obsessive interest in history. There are references to the Balfour Declaration and the Sykes–

Picot agreement—on 20 February 2003 he suggested that the Bush–Blair friend-ship was a modern version of the latter—and, of course, to the Treaty of Sèvres. "Our nation [the Islamic world] has been tasting this humiliation and this degrada-tion for more than eighty years," he says on 7 October 2001. In the same tape, he blames the United Nations for the partition of Palestine in 1947: ". . . we shall never accept that the tragedy of Andalusia will be repeated in Palestine," he says. Andalusia was perhaps the greatest act of ethnic cleansing perpetrated against Arabs, when Ferdinand and Isabella of Spain ejected the Moors—and the Jews, although bin Laden showed no sympathy for them, even though they are the "Peo-ple of the Book"—from south-western Europe in 1492.*

In the tape which was allegedly found by a British intelligence agent in a house in Jalalabad after the fall of the Taliban, bin Laden appears to admit his responsi-bility for the attacks of 11 September 2001. Since much of the tape is inaudible, I was initially suspicious of the Pentagon's claim that it could make a translation of bin Laden's remarks—until I read this extract:

> We were at a camp of one of the brother's guards in Kandahar. This brother belonged to the majority of the group. He came close and told me that he saw, in a dream, a tall building in America . . . At that point I was worried that maybe the secret [of the proposed 11 September assault] would be revealed if everyone starts seeing it in their dream . . . So I closed the sub-ject. I told him if he sees another dream, not to tell anybody . . .

How could I forget that frightening moment more than four years earlier when bin Laden smiled at me on a cold mountain in Afghanistan and told me that "one of our brothers had a dream," that the "brother" had seen me on a horse, wearing a beard and a robe "like us" and that I must therefore be a Muslim? Dreams occur in the words of other bin Laden followers, and their influence on al-Qaeda is proba-bly far greater than we imagine. The Taliban leader Mullah Omar claimed that in a dream he had been called by the Prophet Mohamed to save Afghanistan. Dream theories have a long history in Islam; as early as AD 866, the Islamic philosopher Ibn Ishaq al-Kindi argued that while asleep, the psyche is liberated from the senses and has direct access to "the form-creating faculty." The basis of such a belief must have been founded on the experience of the Prophet himself, who received the word of God in a series of dream-visions, many of them presented to him as he sat in a cave on Mount Hira. Bin Laden's followers would have known that their own leader dreamed in Afghan caves.

By 2004, bin Laden did not attempt to hide al-Qaeda's involvement in the 11

---

*This terrible period of Muslim–Christian history brought an end to a miniature caliphate during which scholars—Christians as well as Arabs and Jews—translated from Arabic some of the greatest works of classical literature which had been stored in Baghdad. The Edict of Expul-sion was signed on 31 March 1492, and marked, for the Jews, their greatest disaster since the destruction of the Temple of Jerusalem. It also gave rise to a long tradition of near-pornographic anti-Islamic tracts which presented the Prophet as the Antichrist.

September 2001 attacks, and especially with the leading hijacker. "We had agreed with Mohamed Atta—may God rest his soul—to conduct all operations within twenty minutes, before Bush and his administration realised what was happening," he said on 30 October. In his tape, timed to coincide with the imminent U.S. presidential elections, bin Laden specifically addressed Americans—most of his messages were primarily for a domestic Arab audience—and responded to Bush's "they hate freedom" speech about al-Qaeda. ". . . we fight you because we are free men who don't sleep under oppression," he said. "We want to restore freedom to our nation—and just as you lay waste to our nation, so shall we lay waste to yours."* Now he attributed the attacks on the Twin Towers of the World Trade Center to the memory of seeing Beirut's "towers" bombed to the ground during the Israeli siege of Beirut in 1982, adding that "I couldn't forget those moving scenes, blood and severed limbs, women and children sprawled everywhere." Bin Laden was not in Beirut in 1982—he was fighting the Soviet army in Afghanistan—and could only have seen the bombardment of Beirut in video footage. There were high-rise buildings destroyed during the siege, but Beirut had no "towers" of the kind bin Laden spoke about. But Ziad Jarrah, the Lebanese hijacker, had been in Beirut as a child in 1982. Did he, much later, recount his memories to bin Laden?

But the al-Qaeda leader's most devastating remarks—the warning that America and Britain totally ignored, indeed probably never even read—came in an audio-message broadcast by Al-Jazeera on 13 February 2003. This was five weeks *before* the invasion of Iraq. Had they studied what bin Laden was saying—had they concentrated on his message rather than spent their time feeding his tape through computers for voice identification—the Pentagon might have grasped the extent of the ruthless insurgency that was to break out less than a month after America's invasion of Iraq.

Bin Laden always expressed his hatred of Saddam Hussein, referring to him as just another American-created "agent" of the Arab world along with the House of Saud and sundry Gulf princes and emirs. But in that all-important 13 February tape, he made a clear offer to ally his forces with those of Saddam's Arab Socialist Baath Party:

---

*Bin Laden's self-righteousness was such that he clearly could not grasp the response of Americans to his long address; the nation that was the victim of the 11 September 2001 crimes against humanity was not going to open a discussion on the al-Qaeda leader's theories of bankrupting the United States by forcing them into wars. Bin Laden also named reporters on CNN and *Time* magazine who had quoted him as saying that if "defending oneself and punishing the aggressor" is terrorism, "then it is unavoidable for us." He added—and this is the kind of advertising a foreign correspondent doesn't need—that "you can read it in . . . my interviews with Robert Fisk. The latter is one of your compatriots and co-religionists and I consider him to be neutral. So are the pretenders of freedom at the White House . . . able to run an interview with him so that he may relay to the American people what he has understood from us to be the reasons for our fight against you?" Quite apart from bin Laden's erroneous belief that I was a "compatriot" American—and I'm not sure I want to be a "co-religionist" of anyone—I could have done without bin Laden's imprimatur on my work. And I certainly wasn't going to play patsy by agreeing to act as al-Qaeda's new *interlocuteur valable*.

It is beyond doubt that this Crusader war is first and foremost directed against the family of Islam irrespective of whether the Socialist party and Saddam survive or not. It is incumbent on Muslims in general and specifically those in Iraq—seriously and in the manner of jihad—to roll up their sleeves against this tyrannical campaign. Furthermore they are duty-bound to accumulate stocks of ammunition and weapons. Despite our belief and our proclamation concerning the infidelity of socialists, in present-day circumstances there is a coincidence of interests between Muslims and socialists in their battles against the Crusaders . . . Socialists are unbelievers wherever they may be, be it in Baghdad or Aden. This fight that is taking place today is to a great extent similar to the Muslims' previous fight against the Christians. The coincidence of interests is beneficial. The Muslims' fight against the Christians coincided with the interests of the Persians and did not in any way harm the companions of the Prophet.

Bin Laden's "coincidence of interests"—albeit accompanied by the reminder that socialists are "infidels"—was a call to his followers to fight alongside an Iraqi force which included Saddam's Baathists, not for Saddam, who bin Laden rightly appeared to believe might be doomed, but for the Muslim land of Iraq. Had the West read this message, then the catastrophe that would befall the Americans in Iraq might have been anticipated. Those words proved quite openly that al-Qaeda planned to involve itself in the battle against the United States in Iraq, even if this meant cooperating with those who had fought for Saddam. This was the moment when the future guerrilla army fused with the future suicide bombers, the detonation that would engulf the West in Iraq. And we didn't even notice.

FROM THE EVER MORE dangerous streets of Baghdad, I would fly a tiny twin-prop aircraft back to Beirut, to breathe, to relax by the sea, to sit on my lovely balcony and watch the Mediterranean or swim in the pool of the old and broken St. Georges Hotel. Yet each morning, I would awake early, uneasy, fearful of what was to come. Never had the Middle East been so fearful a place in which to live. Where will today's explosion be? I used to ask myself. On 14 February 2005 I was walking along the seafront corniche, opposite my favourite restaurant, the Spaghetteria, talking on my mobile phone to my old friend Patrick Cockburn, my replacement in Baghdad, when a white band of light approached at fearsome speed, like a giant bandage. The palm trees all dipped towards me as if hit by a tornado and I saw people—other strollers on the pavement in front of me—fall to the ground. A window of the restaurant splintered and disappeared inside. And in front of me, perhaps only 400 metres away, dark brown fingers of smoke streaked towards the sky. The blast wave was followed by an explosion so thunderous that it partially deafened me. I could just hear Patrick. "Is that here or there?" he asked. I'm afraid it's here, Patrick, I said. I could have wept. Beirut was now my home-from-home, my safe haven, and now all the corpses of the Lebanese civil war were climbing out of their graves.

I ran down the street towards the bombing. There were no cops, no ambulances yet, no soldiers, just a sea of flames in front of the St. Georges Hotel. There were men and women round me, covered in blood, crying and shaking with fear. Twenty-two cars were burning, and in one of them I saw three men cowled in fire. A woman's hand, a hand with painted fingernails, lay on the road. Why? Not bin Laden, I said to myself. Not here in Beirut. I was staggered by the heat, the flames that crept across the road, the petrol tanks of vehicles that would explode and spray fire around me every few seconds. On the ground was a very large man, lying on his back, his socks on fire, unrecognisable. For some reason, I thought he might have been a *kaak*-seller, one of the army of men who provide the toasted Arabic bread that the corniche pedestrians love to eat. The first medics had arrived and another blackened figure was pulled from a car that was burning like a torch.

Then through the smoke, I found the crater. It was hot and I climbed gingerly into it. Two plain-clothes cops were already there, picking up small shards of metal. Fast work for detectives, I thought. And it was several days before I realised that—far from collecting evidence—they were hiding it, taking it from the scene of the crime. I came across an AP reporter, an old Lebanese friend. "I think it's Hariri's convoy," he said. I couldn't believe it. Rafiq Hariri had been Lebanon's billionaire prime minister until the previous year. He had been "Mr. Lebanon," who had rebuilt Beirut, the symbol of its future economy, the man who had turned a city of ruins into a city of light, of fine new restaurants and shops and pedestrian malls. But the Syrians believed that he was secretly leading Lebanese opposition to their military and intelligence presence in Lebanon. They suspected that his hand lay behind an American–French UN Security Council resolution, number 1559, demanding the withdrawal of Syria's remaining 40,000 troops in the country.

Hariri had been a friend to me. He would call me from time to time when he was prime minister and invite me for coffee and warn me of the dangers of the Middle East. He would ask me what was really happening in Iraq, whether the insurgency had popular support. I reported after the civil war that I doubted if his ambitious reconstruction plans would ever work and whenever we saw each other in public he would bellow: "Ah, here's the reporter who thought I couldn't rebuild Beirut!" After I was beaten on the Afghan border in December 2001, he was the second person to call me as I lay bleeding in bed. "Robert! What happened? I will send my jet to get you from Quetta. Pervez Musharraf is my friend and we can get landing permission and have you in the AUH [American University Hospital] here tomorrow." And I had thanked him and politely declined the offer. Journalists don't take gifts from prime ministers.

And now, half an hour after the bombing, his family knew he had gone; Hariri's mobile had stopped working, along with those of all his bodyguards. The convoy's anti-bomb neutralisers—a cluster of scanners on the roofs of the armoured four-by-fours—had failed to protect him. And next day, when I opened the Lebanese papers, there was a photograph of a large man lying on his back with his socks burning and he was identified as "the martyr prime minister Rafiq Hariri."

The Syrian army did leave—faster than expected, almost certainly because of the fury with which the Lebanese greeted Hariri's assassination. A million

Lebanese—almost a third of the country's population—stood around Martyr's Square to demand their withdrawal and the truth about Hariri's murder. This would be another Hariri legacy. An initial UN investigation team, led by a senior Irish police officer, would discover that pro-Syrian Lebanese security officers had not only removed evidence from the crime scene—including all those burned vehicles which had formed part of Hariri's convoy, which were taken away during the hours of darkness—but had also planted evidence in the crater.

In the days that followed, I could only feel depressed. Death seemed to possess the Middle East and haunt my own life. Page after page of my contacts book would have little notes beside names. "Died, 2004," I had written next to Margaret Hassan's Baghdad telephone number. "Murdered 14/2/05" I now wrote beside Hariri's name. Edward Said, that majestic Palestinian scholar—he who had once sworn to me that he would stay alive "because so many people want me dead"—had died of leukaemia in 2004, depriving Palestinians of their most eloquent voice. In March 2003, Rachel Corrie, a young American woman who had travelled to Gaza to try to prevent the Israelis from destroying Palestinian homes, stood in front of an Israeli Caterpillar bulldozer to force the driver to stop. But he drove over her. And then he drove over her again. When her friends ran to her help, she said: "My back is broken." And she died.

Did we react to these constant tragedies of life and death? No, I would say, journalism should be a vocation. One could be angry at death, but we were not here to weep. Doctors—and I'm not comparing journalism to the medical profession—don't cry while they're operating on the desperately sick. Our job is to record, to point the finger when we can, to challenge those "centres of power" about which Amira Hass had so courageously spoken. But I felt exhausted. There were times when I wondered how long I would continue flying across the Atlantic, escaping the kidnappers of Baghdad, increasingly stunned by the growing tragedy of the Middle East.

In Baghdad in 2005, I walked to the voting booths with whole Iraqi families, men with babies in their arms, children with their mothers, as the air pulsated to the sound of the day's first suicide bombers. It was a moving experience. Rarely do you see collective courage on this scale. And an Iraqi government was formed, of sorts, dominated for the first time by the country's Shia Muslims but broken by the one phenomenon that undermined their legitimacy: the continued American occupation. In the polling stations, many of the families told us they were voting for power but also for an end to the occupation. And the occupation was not going to end. The Americans must leave, I used to say to myself. And they will leave. But they *can't* leave. This was the terrible equation that now turned sand into blood. The Americans insisted that they wanted democracy across the Middle East. Iraq would be the start. But what Arab nation wanted to join the hell-disaster that Iraq had now become?

Yes, Arabs and other Muslims wanted some of that bright, shiny democracy which we liked to brandish in front of them. But they wanted something else. They wanted justice, a setting-to-rights, a peaceful but an honourable, fair end to the decades of occupation and deceit and corruption and dictator-creation. The Iraqis wanted an end to our presence as well as to Saddam's regime. They wanted to control their own land and own their own oil. The Syrians wanted Golan back. The Palestinians wanted a state, even if it was built on less than 22 per cent of mandate Palestine, not a 20-foot wall and occupation. The Iranians had freed themselves from the Shah, America's brutal policeman in the Gulf, only to find themselves living in a graveyard of theocracy, their democratic elections betrayed by men who feed off the hatred for America that now lies like a blanket over the Middle East. The Afghans resisted the Soviet Union and wanted help to restore their country. They were betrayed—and finished in the hands of the Taliban. And then another great army came into their land.* However much the newly installed rulers and the old, surviving dictators whom we had helped to power over past decades might praise the West or thank us for our financial loans or for our political support or for invading their countries, there were millions of Muslims who wanted something more: they wanted freedom from *us*.

Israelis have a country—built on someone else's land, which is their tragedy as well as that of the Arabs—but its right-wing governments, happily encouraged by that most right-wing of American governments, are destroying all hope of the peace Israel's people deserve. When President Bush tells Israel that it can keep its major colonies on Palestinian land, he is helping to kill Israelis as well as Palestinians, because that colonial war will continue. And the Armenians. When will they receive their acknowledgement of loss and the admission of responsibility by the descendants of those who committed this holocaust?

*We* might be able to escape history. We can draw lines in our lives. The years of 1918 and 1945 created our new lives in the West. We could start again. We think we can recommend the same to the peoples of the Middle East. But we can't. History—a history of injustice—cloaks them too deeply. Albert Camus, the *pied noir* who understood colonial oppression in Algeria all too vividly, wrote after the Second World War:

> It is true that we cannot "escape History," since we are in it up to our necks. But one may propose to fight within History to preserve from History that part of man which is not its proper province . . . Modern nations are driven by powerful forces along the roads of power and domination . . . They

---

*The flourishing new democracy that President George W. Bush identified in Afghanistan began to fragment as the old drug barons also took power in the government while the Taliban and al-Qaeda gradually returned to the country from which they had been ejected, attacking U.S. troops and pro-government Afghan soldiers. The elected president, Hamid Karzai, had been a paid consultant of Unocal, the Calfornian oil company which once negotiated with the Taliban for a trans-Afghan oil pipeline to Pakistan. America's special envoy to Afghanistan was Zalmay Khalilzad, a former employee of Unocal. Once in power, Karzai and President Musharraf of Pakistan agreed to restart the pipeline project. It was the Israeli newspaper *Ma'ariv* which shrewdly noted that "if one looks at the map of the big American bases created [in Afghanistan], one is struck by the fact that they are completely identical to the route of the projected pipeline to the Indian Ocean." By 2005, Afghanistan was exporting more opium than it had ever produced before. Even Karzai was forced to complain bitterly after revelations in 2005 that the Americans had treated their Afghan prisoners just as cruelly as their Iraqi victims.

hardly need our help and, for the moment, they laugh at attempts to hinder them. They will, then, continue. But I will ask only this simple question: what if these forces wind up in a dead end, what if that logic of History on which so many now rely turns out to be a will o' the wisp?

T. S. Eliot, writing in the same year, 1946, addressed history with equal cynicism:

> Justice itself tends to be corrupted by political passion; and that meddling in other people's affairs which was formerly conducted by the most discreet intrigue is now openly advocated under the name of intervention. Nations which once shrank from condemning the most flagitious violation of human rights in Germany, are now exhorted to interfere in other countries' government—and always in the name of peace and concord. Respect for the culture, the pattern of life, of other people . . . is respect for history; and by history we set no great store.

Have they all died for history, then, those thousands of dead—let me be frank with myself—whom I have seen with my own eyes across the Middle East? The dead soldier with the bright wedding ring on his finger, the slaughtered masses of Sabra and Chatila, the Iranians putrefying in the desert, the corpses of Palestinians and Israelis and Lebanese and Syrians and Afghans, the unspeakable suffering of the Iraqi, Iranian, Syrian, Lebanese, Afghan, Israeli—and, yes, American—torture chambers; was this for history? Or for justice? Or for us? We know that the Balfour Declaration was made eighty-eight years ago. But for Palestinian refugees, in the slums of their camps, Balfour spoke yesterday, last night, only an hour ago. In the Middle East, the people live their past history, again and again, every day.

And so, as I write these words, I prepare for my next fraught journey back to Baghdad, back to the suicide bombers and the throat-cutters and the fast-firing Americans. And through the veil of Iraqi tears, I will draw more portraits of suffering and pain and greed and occasional courage and I wonder if, when I eventually leave this vast chamber of horrors, I will try to emulate the advice of the only poem that always moves me to tears, Christina Rossetti's "Birthday":

> *Better by far you should forget and smile*
> *Than that you should remember and be sad.*

I think in the end we have to accept that our tragedy lies always in our past, that we have to live with our ancestors' folly and suffer for it, just as they, in their turn, suffered, and as we, through our vanity and arrogance, ensure the pain and suffering of our own children. How to correct history, that's the thing. Which is why, as I have written this book, I have heard repeatedly and painfully and in a dreamlike reality the footfall of 2nd Lieutenant Bill Fisk and his comrades of the 12th Battalion, the King's Liverpool Regiment, marching on the evening of 11 November 1918 into the tiny French village of Louvencourt, on the Somme.

# Notes

## Chapter Two: "They Shoot Russians"

page 35   gave my father William a 360-page book: William Johnston, *Tom Graham, V.C., A Tale of the Afghan War* (London: Thomas Nelson & Sons, 1900).

38   An account of life in Kabul: Burnes, *Cabool*.

38   *Imperial Gazetteer of India: Afghanistan and Nepal*, pp. 26–7.

39   "It seemed to me so utterly wrong": Sykes, *Durand*, p. 96.

39   Yet Durand sent a letter: Ibid., p. 117, facsimile of handwritten letter from Durand to Ella Sykes, 26 January 1895. Durand included a poem he had composed on the death of one of the British cavalrymen in suitably Victorian verse: *"Aye, we have found him, the fair young face/Turned to the pitiless Afghan skies . . . Lying above there, out on the plain/Where the desperate charge of our horsemen broke,/Foremost fighting, and foremost slain,/Gashed by many a murderous stroke."*

39   an inquisitive and generous man: Ibid., p. 207.

40   "unless you drive me into enmity": Ibid., pp. 216–17.

44   report from *The Guardian*: "Russia's Pounds 350 Million back door" by Simon Winchester, 8 May 1978.

45   some evidence that it was Amin: Griffiths, *Afghanistan*, p. 174.

61   "it is a garden": See Micheline Centreslivres-Demont, *Popular Art in Afghanistan: Paintings on Trucks, Mosques and Tea-Houses* (Graz, Austria: Akademische Druck-u. Verlagsanstalt, 1976).

62   Within days of the Soviet invasion: Statement of Iranian foreign ministry, Tehran, 30 December 1979.

62   he hoped his country would give: Interview with the author, Tehran, 9 July 1980.

(n.) 68   From his executive office: *The Times*, 22 January 1980.

69–70   "A weird, uncanny place": Mills, *Pathan Revolts*, pp. 108–9.

## Chapter Three: The Choirs of Kandahar

(n.) 71   As usual, Churchill: See Winston Churchill, *My Early Life: A Roving Commission* (London: Thornton Butterworth, 1930), p. 156.

(n.) 84   It was instructive: See, for example, *Literaturnaya Gazeta*, 20 February 1980, p. 9.

88   had "for some reason" removed: I wrote exactly the same in my dispatch to my paper, as if this extraordinary event was scarcely worth recording. See *The Times*, 18 February 1980.

90   around $35 billion—$2.5 billion: Griffiths, *Afghanistan*, pp. 182–3.

90   Saudi Arabia, on its own admission: Anthony Hyman, "Arab Involvement in the Afghan War," in *The Beirut Review: A Journal on Lebanon and the Middle East*, No. 7, Spring 1994, p. 78.

90   25,000 Arabs saw service: Ibid., p. 79.

(n.) 90   "Now that we have . . . ": Letter from Douglas-Home to the author, 26 March 1980.

## Chapter Four: The Carpet-Weavers

(n.) 95   "we are confronted": Roosevelt, *Countercoup*, p. 18.

97   "The outcome was inevitable": Woodhouse, *Something Ventured*, p. 45.

98   "democracy of Islam . . . popular eloquence": Bill, *The Eagle and the Lion*, pp. 69–70, quoting L. P. Elwell-Sutton, *Persian Oil: A Study in Power Politics* (London: Laurence and Wishart, 1955), p. 195.

(n.) 98 Not that the future Ayatollah: Bill, p. 69.
   98 "began a new era": Ibid., p. 96.
   98 "That was a nice": Woodhouse, p. 132.
(n.) 99 One of its victims: Halliday, *Iran*, p. 87.
  101 the population of the city of Kerman: Kapuscinski, *Shah of Shahs*, pp. 36–7.
  101 The Red Cross report: *Rapport de synthèse faisant suite à la première série de visites des délégués du Comité International de la Croix Rouge à 3,087 détenus de sécurité dans 18 prisons Iraniennes*, 1977.
  101 "we have no lessons to learn": *Sunday Times*, 16 April 1978, interview with the Shah by Frank Giles, "Why Iran feels it needs no advice from the West on human rights."
  103 "are a genuine popular revolution": Edward Mortimer, "Iran: The greatest revolution since 1917," *Spectator*, 17 February 1979.
  104 "my doctor has given me": The longest English-language account in Tehran of Hoveyda's initial court appearance appeared in *Kayhan's* international edition of 17 March 1979.
  105 "The first bullets": Shawcross, *Shah's Last Ride*, p. 218.
  105 "I found that this": Letter from author to Ivan Barnes, 30 March 1979.
  109 "This is what happens": Shawcross, p. 317.
  113 U.S. diplomatic correspondence: These and subsequent quotations come from the 85 volumes of reconstructed American embassy traffic published in Tehran between 1979 and 1985. A summary of the involvement of Entezam and Bazargan can be found in Bill, pp. 290–3.
  114 "The CIA apparently believed": Ebtekar, *Takeover*, p. 98.
  125 "the anti-Koranic ideas": *The Last Message: The Political and Divine Will of His Holiness Imam Khomeini* (Tehran: The Imam Khomeini Cultural Institute, 1992). Khomeini wrote his will on 15 February 1983, six years before his death.
  127 "He was a study in concentration": Ebtekar, p. 110.

## Chapter Five: The Path to War

  139 the "grim battle" for Baghdad: Letter to the author from Charles Dickens's daughter Hilda Maddock, 28 October 2003.
  142 "we should be received": Attiyah, *Iraq*, p. 108, quoting Sir Percy Cox in a letter to the Viceroy of India on 23 November 1914. For this and subsequent details of the British occupation of Iraq, I am indebted to Ghassan Attiyah's magnificent work of research in both British and Iraqi archives of the period, a volume that should be read by all Western "statesmen" planning to invade Arab countries.
  142 "gaped emptily": Attiyah, pp. 95–6, quoting Alois Musil, *The Middle Euphrates: A Topographical Itinerary* (New York: American Geographical Society, 1927), pp. 128–9.
  142 "There is no doubt": *The Sphere*, London, 15 May 1915.
  144 "always entertained": Attiyah, p. 104, quoting correspondence in British National Archives (NA) FO371/2775/187454.
  144 "some of the Holy": Ibid., p. 105, quoting NA CAB 21/60.
  144 "clearly it is our right": Ibid., p. 130, quoting a British Admiralty memorandum of 17 March 1915.
  144 "taking Mesopotamia": Ibid., p. 130n, quoting Earl Asquith's *Memories and Reflections, 1852–1927*, vol. II, p. 69 (London: Cassell, 1928).
  144 Iraq would be governed: Ibid., p. 165, quoting NA FO371/3387/142404 (Cox).
  144 "a cabinet half of natives": Ibid., p. 168, quoting NA FO371/4148/13298.
  144 "The stronger the hold": Ibid., p. 166, quoting E. Burgoyne's *Gertrude Bell, from Her Personal Papers, 1914–1926* (London: E. Benn, 1961), pp. 78–9.
  144 "Is it not for the benefit": Hansard, Commons, vol. 127, cols. 662–4, 25 March 1920.
  145 "local political agitation": Attiyah, p. 203.
  145 "We cannot maintain": Ibid., p. 211, quoting NA FO371/5227/E6509.
  145 The authorities demanded: Ibid., p. 230.
  145 "Badr must be killed": Ibid., p. 249, quoting Iraqi Ministry of Interior document, Nasiriyah, April and May 1919.

145 "anarchy plus fanaticism": John Darwin, *Britain, Egypt and the Middle East: Imperial Policy in the Aftermath of War, 1918–1922* (New York: St. Martin's Press, 1981), quoted by Fromkin, *A Peace to End All Peace*, p. 453.

145 "heavy punishment": Attiyah, p. 343.

145 "to complete the façade": Ibid., p. 362.

145 "How much longer": Quoted in Fromkin, p. 452.

145 "about ten thousand Arabs": *The Letters of T. E. Lawrence*, ed. David Garnett (London: Jonathan Cape, 1938), p. 316, quoted in Fromkin, p. 497.

(n.) 145 "in Irak the Arabs": T. E. Laurence [*sic*], memorandum *Reconstruction of Arabia* to the Eastern Committee of the War Cabinet, 5 November 1918, National Archives CAB 27/36.

146 at least eight pilots: Clive Semple, unpublished MS, "Eight Graves to Cairo: Calamity and Cover-up," 2004, p. 4.

146 "you should certainly proceed": Churchill note to Trenchard, 29 August 1920. *Winston S. Churchill 1917–1922 Companion Volume IV* by Martin Gilbert (London: Heinemann, 1977), p. 1190.

146 "that by burning down": Dudley Saward, *"Bomber" Harris: The Authorised Biography* (London: Cassell, 1984), p. 31.

146 "they [the Arabs and Kurds] now know": A. and P. Cockburn, *Out of the Ashes*, p. 65, quoting David McDowall, *A Modern History of the Kurds* (London: I. B. Tauris, 1997), p. 180.

146 "these risings take": *Observer*, 8 August 1920.

146 But Lawrence had: Letter to the author from Peter Metcalfe, 22 June 2004.

146 "The Arabs rebelled": Garnett, *Letters of T. E. Lawrence*, op. cit., pp. 306–8, letter to *The Times* of 22 July 1920.

147 "The people of England": *Sunday Times*, 22 August 1920.

147 "maintain the policy": *Observer*, 10 February 1991, by David Omissi, "RAF officer who resigned rather than bomb Iraq."

148 British forces paused: Warner, *Iraq and Syria*, p. 117.

(n.) 148 "The *Arab liberation movement*": Quoted in Warner, p. 113.

(n.) 153 Mesopotamia had been the seat: Popovic, *Revolt of African Slaves*, p. 124.

159 And there he suddenly ended: A poor English translation of Saddam's Baghdad press conference of 20/21 July 1980 was carried in the *Baghdad Observer* of 23 and 24 July 1980—but without his remarks on the expulsions.

160 It was one of Stalin's biographers: Simon Sebag Montefiore in *International Herald Tribune*, 3 July 2004, "A disciple of Stalin in the dock."

160 "the perfume of Iraq": Quoted by David Hirst in the *Guardian*, 24 September 1980, "The megalomaniac pitted against the zealot."

166 "Iraqis who fail": *8 Days*, 1 March 1980, "Iraq drive to eradicate illiteracy" by Marion Woolfson.

166 "An enormous potential market": *Sunday Press*, Dublin, 27 March 1977, "Land of the leftist sheikhs," by Sean Cryan.

(n.) 167 "think we have to assume": Author's message to Barnes, 7 May 1980.

168 "justify their action": Hansard, Lords, 14 December 1989, cols. 1397–8.

168 "I doubt if there is any": Waldegrave memo quoted in the *Guardian*, 13 September 1993, "Sell arms to Iraq—but keep it quiet: The Scott inquiry is exposing a system corrupted by secrecy," by Richard Norton-Taylor.

169 "it would look very cynical": Norton-Taylor report in the *Guardian*, 13 March 1993.

169 "Tell Dee I'm sorry": Daphne Parish, *Prisoner in Baghdad* (London: Chapmans, 1992), pp. 124–31.

170 "another visit by Mr. Fisk": Letter from Dr. Abdul Amir Al-Anbari, Iraqi ambassador in London, 21 February 1986, to Pat Davis, assistant managing editor of *The Times*.

(n.) 170 "were extremely upset": Alloway message from Tehran to Barnes, 7 August 1980.

(n.) 172 "tried to attack Bakhtiar's": Author's interview with Anis Naccache, Tehran, 22 October 1991.

(n.) 172–3 "setting the scene": Abul-Fazl Ezzati, *The Revolutionary Islam and the Islamic Revolution* (Tehran: Ministry of Islamic Guidance, 1981), p. 195.

173 "It would be strange": The full text of Khomeini's message can be found in the English-language *Tehran Times* of 8 April 1982.

173 Among them were ten young women: *Observer*, 26 June 1983, "Bahai women die for their faith," by Colin Smith.

174 On one night, 150 women: *Observer*, 6 May 1984, "Inside Khomeini's slaughterhouse," by Colin Smith.

174 Iranian state radio recorded: *Iran Monitor* (news translations from Iran radio and the Persian Press), 4 July 1980. The *Times* stringer Tony Alloway produced this invaluable daily digest of revolutionary activities for well over a year after the overthrow of the Shah.

174 Amnesty recorded the evidence: Amnesty International's written statement on human rights in Iran to the Political Affairs Committee of the European Parliament, 28 November 1985.

174 A frightening nine-page pamphlet: The English-language booklet was handed out by Ministry of Islamic Guidance officials in 1979 under the title *The People and the Revolutionary Courts*. The author has a copy.

174 Khomeini raged: Khomeini, *Last Message*.

175 Human Rights Watch was reporting: Human Rights Watch, *Tears, Blood and Cries: Human Rights in Afghanistan 1979–1984*, a Helsinki Watch Report, December 1984, pp. 5, 9, and 35.

176 As long ago as October 1979: This assessment and the Yazdi remarks and U.S. assessment of Saddam's intentions come from vols. 10 and 12 of the U.S. embassy traffic published in Tehran.

176 Back in 1978, the Shah: *Sunday Times*, 16 April 1978, interview with Frank Giles.

178 The Iraqi Foreign Ministry: *The Iraqi–Iranian Dispute: Facts versus Allegations* (Baghdad: Iraqi Ministry of Foreign Affairs, 1981).

178 "null and void": An unconvincing explanation for Iraq's decision was contained in Iraqi prime minister Tariq Aziz's speech to the UN General Assembly on 25 September 1987.

178 "When we arrived": Interview with Fathi Daoud Mouffak, Baghdad, 30 July 2004.

## Chapter Six: "The Whirlwind War"

198 "knew something was happening": Author's conversation at home of U.S. ambassador to Jordan Richard Viets with former U.S. chargé in Tehran Bruce Laingen (then head of U.S. War College), Amman, 17 April 1983.

199 "Suppose you were an inveterate enemy": Ayatollah Khomeini, 1 July 1981, quoted in full in *Mahjoubah: The Magazine for Muslim Women*, Tehran: Ministry of Islamic Guidance, July 1981.

199 One estimate—that 10,000 suspects were hanged or shot: Bullock & Morris, *Gulf War*, p. 67, quoting Iranian sociologist Ehsan Naraghi.

206 An official history of the Guard Corps: Although carrying no publisher's imprint, the 8-page brochure was distributed by the Ministry of Islamic Guidance in Tehran around 1984 under the title *Islamic Revolution Guard Corps; A Brief Analysis*.

207 " . . . doors suddenly opened": Frederic Manning (Private 19022), *Her Privates We*, introduction by Edmund Blunden (London: Peter Davies, 1964), p. 154.

207 Egyptian-made heavy artillery shells: Author's interview with retired General Mohamed Abdul Moneim, military affairs correspondent of *Al-Ahram*, Cairo, 2 June 1982.

207 the Iraqis held an arms fair: Author's interview with Mohamed Salam, Sidon, Lebanon, 1 November 2003.

207 a U.S. military delegation: Author's interview with Mohamed Salam, Baghdad, 21 July 1985.

208 "There had been a major battle": Salam interview, 1 November 2003.

209 Iran's own official history: *The Imposed War* (Tehran: War Information Headquarters), vol. 2, pp. 163–94. A misprint on p. 164 gives the date of the first gas attack as 1980 rather than 1981.

210 "United States intelligence analysts": *New York Times*, 27 March 1985, quoted in *The Times* of London of the same date, "Iraq's use of mustard gas confirmed."

211 "I was invited": Salam interview, 1 November 2003.

213 More than sixty officers: *International Herald Tribune*, 19 August 2002, quoting *The New York Times*, report by Patrick Tyler, "U.S. aided Iraq in '80s despite gas use, officials say."

214 "By any measure, the American record": *International Herald Tribune*, 17 January 2003, "America didn't seem to mind poison gas," by Joost R. Hilterman.

214 Halabja was mentioned in 188 news stories: Rampton and Stauber, *Weapons of Mass Deception*, p. 76.

214 "is a person who has gassed": George W. Bush address, Denver, Colorado, 28 October 2002.

214 "We have had such a malicious": Rafsanjani press conference, Tehran, 25 May 1997 (author's notes).

## Chapter Seven: "War against War" and the Fast Train to Paradise

219 the first Exocet spewed 120 pounds: *Navy Times*, 26 October 1987, "Inferno The Like of Which Had Never Been Experienced," by William Matthews.

220 "Rest assured": Associated Press report from Washington, 22 May 1987.

(n.) 220 "we never before had reason": Author's interview with Ambassador Zakhem, U.S. embassy, Bahrain, 26 May 1987.

221 "this barbarous country": Reagan press conference, 27 May 1987.

222 227 ships had been attacked: Gulf shipping agents could never agree on exact figures, but these statistics, which appear the most accurate, are from Intertanko of Oslo.

222 Between May 1981: Lloyd's Intelligence, London, May 1987.

222 "The incident provided": Dispatch to *The Times* from Bahrain, sent 28 May 1987.

228 By 1986 alone, a million: Associated Press, 12 March 1986, "Up to a Million Dead, No End in Sight," by G. G. Labelle.

230 In July, Iraq began: *Washington Post*, 13 September 1985, quoted in Reuters Washington datelined report of the same date.

(n.) 234 James Cameron, one of my great: Cameron, *Point of Departure*, p. 139.

## Chapter Eight: Drinking the Poisoned Chalice

264 "marked the horrifying climax": See *Proceedings*, journal of the U.S. Naval Institute, August 1993, vol. 119/8/1,086, pp. 49–56, "Vincennes: A Case Study," by Lieutenant Colonel David Evans.

264 "Why do you want an Aegis cruiser": Evans in *Proceedings*, op. cit., p. 52, quoting a personal interview with Captain David Carlson on 23 June 1992.

264 "was on a normal commercial": *Formal Investigation into the Circumstances Surrounding the Downing of a Commercial Airliner by the USS Vincennes* by Rear Admiral William M. Fogarty, USN, 28 July 1988.

264 *Newsweek* magazine would carry out: *Newsweek*, 13 July 1992, "Sea of Lies," by John Barry and Roger Charles.

267 "He was turned into the powder": Will and Sharon Rogers, *Storm Center: The USS* Vincennes *and Iran Air Flight 655* (Annapolis, Maryland: Naval Institute Press, 1992), pp. 184–6.

271 Half the next issue: *Sunday Tribune* (Dublin), 10 July 1988.

272 Captain Rogers saw the film again: Rogers, *Storm Center*, op. cit., p. 188.

274 "As to your order to execute the hypocrites": Quoted in *Iran Bulletin* (London),Winter 1996, pp. 26–9, "The Great Massacre," by Naser Mohajer.

274 "When [they] are taken to the Hosseinieh": Quoted in *Iran Bulletin*, Winter 1996, op. cit., p. 28.

274 A former female prisoner: *Iran Bulletin*, Autumn/Winter 1998, interview with Monireh Baradaran, "Witness to Massacre." Baradaran's account of her nine years in the regime's prisons was published in Farsi as *Haghighat-e sadeh*—"Simple truth"—and in German as *Erwachen aus dem Alptraum* (Unionsverlag, 1998).

274 This was Fariba's description: *Iran Bulletin*, Summer 2000, p. 62, from an abridged translation of *Here Virgins Do Not Die* by "Shahrzad" (Paris: Khavaran, 1998).

275 Of 1,533 Iranian female prisoners: *Iran Bulletin*, Spring/Summer 1999, pp. 40–3, "The life and death of women in Islamic prisons," by Dr. Rehza Ghaffari. His *Khaterateh Yek Zendani As Zendanhaye Jumhouriye Islam*—"Memories of a prisoner of prisons of the Islamic Republic"—was published in Farsi (Stockholm: Arshag Forlag, 1998).

275 Amnesty was able to list: Amnesty International report on Iraqi executions, 25 February 1988.

276 at least 700 prisoners: Committee against Repression and for Democratic Rights in Iraq (CARDRI), press release, 2 March 1988.

276 When Khadum Fadel returned: Agence France-Presse report by Tanya Wilmer, published in *Jordan Times*, 6 February 1999.

281 "I doubt whether I would be inaccurate": Letter from Zainab Kazim, 1996 (otherwise undated), following the author's article in the *Independent on Sunday Review*, 25 June 1995, "Oh What a Lovely Holy War."

289 "Some magnificent men": Letter to author from Robert Parry, 4 October 2004.

290 "One of our soldiers": Interview with Haidar al-Safi, Baghdad, 28 July 2004.

291 "We would go to the headquarters": Mouffak interview, Baghdad, 30 July 2004.

## Chapter Nine: "Sentenced to Suffer Death"

300 the war diaries: National Archives, Kew, WO95/2126.

304 I had spent more than two years: See Fisk, *Pity the Nation*, pp. 632–49.

(n.) 307 The politics of partition: These statistics come from Henry Harris, *The Irish Regiments of the First World War* (Cork: Mercier, 1968), pp. 219–21. In all: see "*The Irish Times*, An Irishman's Diary," by Oliver Fannon, *Irish Times*, 6 September 2004.

308 "He was like one of those revolving lighthouses": *War Memoirs of David Lloyd George* (London: Odhams, 1936), vol. I, p. 450.

## Chapter Ten: The First Holocaust

320 "it may well be that the British attack": Winston Churchill, *The World Crisis: The Aftermath* (London: Thornton Butterworth, 1927), p. 405.

322 "Reports from widely scattered districts": Cipher telegram from Morgenthau to the U.S. State Department, 10 July 1915, reprinted in *United States Official Records on the Armenian Genocide 1915–1917* (compiled with introduction by Ara Sarafian, Princeton: Gomidas Institute, 2004), p. 51.

324 Armenian scholars have compiled: See, for example, the Armenian National Institute's annual report for 1998, pp. 9–10.

325 "machinery of violence": Mark Mazower in the *London Review of Books*, 8 February 2001, p. 20, "The G-Word."

325 700 pages of eyewitness accounts: *The Treatment of Armenians in the Ottoman Empire: Documents Presented to Viscount Grey of Fallodon by Viscount Bryce* (London: House of Lords, 2004). This new edition contains names and other identifying details that were omitted from the original publication to protect eyewitnesses from Turkish reprisals.

325 Leslie Davis, the thirty-eight-year-old former lawyer: Balakian, *Burning Tigris*, pp. 241–9.

326 The Germans were also involved in building: Ibid., p. 191.

326 From the start, the *New York Times*: See *The Armenian Genocide: News Accounts from the American Press 1915–1922*, ed. Richard D. Kloian (American Genocide Resource Center of Northern California, 2000).

327 Even in the Canadian city of Halifax: See *Heralding of the Armenian Genocide: Reports in The Halifax Herald 1894–1922*, compiled by Katia Minas Pettekian (Armenian Cultural Association of the Atlantic Provinces, 2000).

327 In the former Ottoman city of Basra: H. V. F. Winstone, *Gertrude Bell* (London: Barzon Publishing, 2004), pp. 276–7.

327 a group of more than 1,000 women: *United States Official Records of the Armenian Genocide*, p. 587.

328 a long account written by Cyril Barter: Barter's "account of experiences during the war, written from Baghdad in 1919" was sent to me by his son Antony, 23 June 2004.

328 "The butchery had taken place": E. H. Jones, *The Road to En-Dor* (London: White Lion Publishers, 1973; originally published London: Bodley Head, 1920), p. 83.

328 "My father, Sarkis": Letter to the author from Ellen Sarkisian Chesnut of San Francisco, 23 February 2000.

329 The first writer to call the Armenian genocide: Churchill, *The World Crisis: The Aftermath*, op. cit., p. 157.

329 "Acknowledging that British and American": Churchill, *Great War*, vol. 4, p. 1570.

329 Franz von Papen, for example: See Vahakn Dadrian, "The Historical and Legal Interconnections Between the Armenian Genocide and the Jewish Holocaust: From Impunity to Retributive Justice," in *The Yale Journal of International Law*, Summer 1998, vol. 23, no. 2, pp. 504–59. Dadrian erroneously refers to Rudolf Hoess as "Rudolf Hess."

330 And there came another fateful reference: Gilbert, *Holocaust*, p. 556, quoting German notes of Hitler's discussion with Horthy on 17 April 1943 (document D-736 in the files of the Nuremberg International Military Tribunal).

330 Some Armenian slave labourers: See Mark Levene's *The Experience of Genocide* in *Lightning Strikes Twice: The World War 1914–1945* (London: HarperCollins, 2000). Levene's note on the Baghdad railway appears on p. 16 of his original manuscript.

(n.) 330 At a conference in Beirut: A series of talks on *The First World War as Remembered in the Countries of the Eastern Mediterranean* was held in the Lebanese capital from 27 April to 1 May 2001; see *Daily Star*, Beirut, 4 May 2001.

331 A Turkish military tribunal: See *AIM· Armenian International Magazine*, January/February 2001, pp. 26–33, "A Century of Genocide," by Matthew Karanian.

331 He lectured across Germany in 1933: See Dadrian, *History of the Armenian Genocide*, p. 410.

331 In 1933, the same year: Churchill, *Great War*, vol. 4, p. 1570.

332 Of the Treaty of Lausanne: Ibid., p. 1571.

333 Lord Bryce, whose report: James Bryce, *International Relations: Eight lectures delivered in the United States in August, 1921* (London: Macmillan, 1922), pp. 65–71.

336 Mark Levene has written extensively: See Levene's "A Moving Target, the Usual Suspects and (Maybe) a Smoking Gun: The Problem of Pinning Blame in Modern Genocide," in *Patterns of Prejudice*, vol. 33, no. 4, 1999, citing R. S. Stafford, *The Tragedy of the Assyrians* (London: Allen and Unwin, 1935), pp. 168–77.

336 After writing about the Armenian Holocaust: Letter to the author from A. V. Ozoliņš, 2 February 2000.

336 "part of Europe's own forgotten past": Mazower in *London Review of Books*, op. cit.

336 When the historian Norman Davis: Letter to the author from Davis, 12 April 1998.

336 But sure enough, there was a book: Author anonymous, *The Dark Side of the Moon* (London: Faber, 1946).

337 Armenians "had defected *en masse*": Koknar email letter to the editor, 5 February 2000.

338 "purely fabricated": Cakir letter to the author, 15 April 1992.

338 The Hitler quotation was "fabricated": Tat email letter to the editor, 3 February 2000.

338 "100-year-old unfortunate victims": Zorba letter to editor, 1 February 2001.

338 "many members of my family": Haktanir letter to editor, 21 March 2001.

338 "The myth of 'Armenian Holocaust'": Letter from Ozener to the *Jerusalem Post Magazine*, 18 June 1999, citing "A Genocide Denied" by Marilyn Henry, 28 May 1999.

339 In an interview with the Anatolia News Agency: Quoted in the *Turkish Daily News*, 10 April 2001.

339 "It seems to me": Charny letter to Peres, 11 April 2001.

339 Nor did Charny flinch: Charny, *Encyclopedia of Genocide*, vol. 1, pp. 61–105.

339 "the aim of *Ittihad*": Ibid., p. 94.

339 "the Turks had let it be known": From the published proceedings of the conference by Israel Charny, *The Armenians, the Turks and the Jews* (Jerusalem: Institute on the Holocaust and Genocide, 1983).

340 "how can the destruction": Jonathan Eric Lewis, "Genocide and the Modern World," published in the *Armenian-Mirror Spectator*, April 2001.

340 "The Pope has been struck": *Milliyet*, 11 November 2000.

340 tried to disconnect it from the Nazi genocide: Dr. Salâhi R. Sonyel, *Turco-Armenian Relations in the Context of the Jewish Holocaust* (Ankara: Turk Tarih Kurumu Basimevi, 1990).

340 "Turkey firmly denies": See, for example, the *International Herald Tribune*, 27 September 2001, "Pope Prays for Armenians."

340 "more than a million Armenians": BBC World Service radio news, 26 September 2001.

342 Peter Balakian and the historian Robert Jay Lifton: Balakian, op. cit., pp. 383–5.

343 150 Holocaust scholars and historians: Fifty-three of them signed an ad in *The Washington Post*, on 23 April 1999.

343 In 1997, for example, the Ellis Island Museum: See *New York Times*, 11 September 1997.

344 Holocaust denial is alive: See Norman Finkelstein in *Index on Censorship*, Issue 2, 2000.

344 Lewis was convicted: See *Le Monde*, 23 June 1995; also, for a discussion on Lewis's original references to the Armenian killings as a "holocaust," see *Le Monde*, 26 April 1994, "Un entretien avec Anahide Ter-Minassian et Claude Mutafian."

344 French foreign ministry secretary-general: Ankara Anatolia news agency report, 18 September 2000.

(n.) 344 Strangely enough, the French national airline: *Air France Magazine*, October 1999, p. 144.

345 "after full and careful consideration": Frater letter to Joan Ablett of the Armenian Assembly of America, 21 November 2000.

345 "the Crusades, slavery, colonialism": Frater letter to Armen Lucas, 15 December 2000.

345 "any serious commemoration": Zaven Messerlian letter to Frater, 21 December 2000.

345 "Our historical frame of reference": Brittain-Catlin letter to Lucas, 16 January 2001.

346 "in the absence of unequivocal evidence": Answer by Baroness Ramsay of Cartvale to Baroness Cox in the House of Lords, 14 April 1999, Hansard, Lords, cols. 826–30, cited in Ruper Boyadjian, *Great Britain's Denial of the Genocide Against the Armenians*, proceedings of the Kigali conference, 25–30 November 2001.

348 "a messy and painful affair": Atak letter to exhibition photographer Simon Norfolk, 27 June 2000.

348 "it almost beggars belief": *Independent*, 31 August 2000, editorial "Turkey should face up to an ugly episode in its history."

348 "What is shocking": Letter to author from Toby Saul, 5 August 2000.

348 New York Life Insurance: See the Armenian National Institute, Washington, D.C., annual report for 2002.

349 "allowed pressure by a foreign government": Aram Hamparian, director of the Armenian National Committee of America, 24 April 2004.

349 "forcefully remembered": Letter to author from Sir Michael Mayne, 31 January 2000.

350 Three Turks were prosecuted: Ayshe Nur Zarakaglu, Ragip Zarakoglu and Emirhan Oguz were prosecuted for publishing *Les Armeniens, histoire d'un genocide* by Yves Ternon (Paris: Editions du Seuil, 1977) as *Ermeni tabusu* (The Armenian Taboo) (Istanbul: Belge Yayinlari, 1994); see statement from the Armenian Rights Group, London, 30 March 1994.

351 "There the Armenians had been forced to undress": *The Kevorkian Newsletter*, Paris, 9 September 2002.

354 "Bunches and bunches of roses": Verjine Svazlian, *The Armenian Genocide in the Memoirs and Turkish-Language Songs of the Eyewitness Survivors* (Yerevan: Gitutiun Publishing House, 1999), p. 12.

*Chapter Eleven: Fifty Thousand Miles from Palestine*

356 Those who knew him: Interview with former PLO ambassador to Lebanon Chafiq al-Hout, Beirut, 18 July 1994.

359 "golden opportunity": See Elpeleg, *Grand Mufti*, p. 53.

360 "world Jewry, this dangerous enemy": Ibid., p. 59, full text of Haj Amin letter to Hitler of 20 January 1941 is in Appendix B (pp. 202–5) of Elpeleg's book.

360 "I suppose it was a great mistake": Interview with Dr. Nadim al-Dimeshkieh, Beirut, 24 July 1994.

360 "Most of the Palestinians": Interview with Wassef Kamal, Beirut, 13 August 1994.

361 Haj Amin had as much right to collaborate: See Taysir Jbara, *Palestinian Leader Hajj Amin al-Husayni: Mufti of Jerusalem* (Princeton, N.J.: Kingston Press, 1985).

362 "his frequent, close contacts": Elpeleg, p. 73.

362 "If there are reasons": Ibid., p. 72, citing Mohamed Amin al-Husseini, *Zikhronot, Filastin* ("Memoirs, Palestine") (Beirut).

363 "He was of course involved": Kamal interview, 13 August 1994.

363 "Haj Amin believed": Elpeleg, p. 178, citing a Hebrew edition of Abu Iyad's *Without a Homeland (Le-Lo Moledet)* (Jerusalem, 1979), pp. 64–6.

363 "He said that after the Jews": Interview with Alia al-Husseini, granddaughter of Haj Amin, 20 July 1994.

364 "Haj Amin should have accepted the UN partition plan": Interview with Habib abu Fadel, Beirut, 26 July 1994.

364 later beaten up by Haj Amin's thugs: Bayan al-Hout interview, 18 July 1994.

364 "a very stupid act": Interview with al-Hout, Beirut, 18 July 1994.

364 "To my surprise": al-Hout interview, 18 July 1994.

365 "it has to be used with care": Antonius, *Arab Awakening*, p. 387.

366 "the capture by British troops": David Lloyd George, *War Memoirs of David Lloyd George*, vol. II (London: Odhams, 1936), p. 1092.

366 scarcely any reference to the Balfour Declaration: Ibid., vol. I, pp. 349–50.

366 "It was at one of the darkest periods": Lloyd George in the House of Commons, 19 June 1936, reported in *The Times*, 20 June 1936.

367 "the establishment of a Jewish state": Antonius, pp. 410–11.

368 "the wealthy, crowded, progressive Jewish State": Winston Churchill, *Step by Step: 1936–1939* (London: Odhams, 1947), "Palestine Partition," 23 July 1937.

368 "the Jewish tragedy owed its origin": Brigadier John Bagot Glubb, *The Story of the Arab Legion* (London: Hodder, 1948), p. 231.

368 prewar Zionist committees were contemplating the "transfer": see Mark Levene, *The Limits of Tolerance: Nation-State Building and What It Means for Minority Groups* in *Patterns of Prejudice* (Institute of Jewish Policy Research), vol. 34, no. 2, 2000, citing Nur Masalha, *Expulsion of the Palestinians: The Concept of "Transfer" in Zionist Political Thought 1882–1948* (Washington, D.C.: Institute of Palestine Studies, 1992), p. 128.

369 "I will show you my museum": Interview with Josef Kleinman, Givat Shaul, Jerusalem, 6 April 2002.

372 ninety-four of the villagers were blown up: Khalidi (ed.), *All That Remains*, p. 492 (where the village is spelled "al-Salihiyya"), citing Morris, *The Birth of the Palestinian Refugee Problem*.

373 reads like an account of the first year's Iraqi uprising: *Palestine: Statement of Information Relating to Acts of Violence*, Cmd. 6873 (London: HMSO, July 1946).

374 "They were hanging": Copy of official British "Report on the Murder of Sgt PAICE and Sgt MARTIN" sent to the author by Nadeem El Issa on 21 June 2004.

374 "we usually had a gangers' trolley": *Harakavet: A Quarterly Journal on the Railways of the Middle East* (ed. Rabbi Walter Rothschild), Issue 25, June 1994, quoting letter from Charles S. Eadon-Clarke of Western Australia.

374 "the Arabs, who have lived and buried their dead": Quoted in Gilbert, *Israel*, p. 113.

374 "if our dreams for Zionism": Quoted in Bethell, *The Palestine Triangle*, p. 183, citing Churchill in the Commons, 17 November 1944.

375 "Why then did your people murder my father?": See *The Times*, 5 July 1975, "Ex-Haganah man criticizes assassins' state funeral."

375 a day-by-day account of events in Palestine: Compiled from *The Scotsman, The Times*, from Khalidi, *All That Remains*, and from Morris, *The Birth of the Palestinian Refugee Problem*, by "Scottish Friends of Palestine" under Hugh Humphries.

379 "I will not be away from my freedom fighters": Interview with Yassir Arafat, Tripoli, Lebanon, 21 June 1983.

386 Syria, for example, had drawn up an eleven-point plan: See *Independent*, 31 October 1991.

389 "Hence Syria is worried that Jordan": See *Independent*, 26 November 1992.

394 "with the prime minister of the Jewish state": Hirst, *The Gun and the Olive Branch*, p. 21.

399 "He has changed the charter of the PLO": Interview with Chafiq al-Hout, Beirut, 10 September 1993.

## Chapter Twelve: The Last Colonial War

410 "Israeli troops shot and killed at least another twenty-five": The Israeli B'Tselem human rights group would later name twelve of twenty-one Palestinians they say were killed by Israeli troops in the six days following the Hebron massacre. See B'Tselem Case Study Number 4, 3 March 1994, *Lethal Gunfire and Collective Punishment in the Wake of the Massacre at the Tomb of the Patriarchs.*

420 as Edward Said was the first to point out: See Edward Said, *London Review of Books*, 14 December 2000.

420 Indeed, a detailed investigation in 2000: Professor Alain Joxe, director of the Interdisciplinary Centre for Research on Peace and Strategic Studies at the Ecole des Hautes Etudes en Sciences Sociales, interviewed by Lara Marlowe, *Irish Times*, 4 November 2000, "Israel accused of turning peace process into a sham, backed by U.S."

421 "the Pétain of the Palestinians": Edward Said interview in *Irish Times*, 3 July 1999, "The Powerful Voice of the Outsider."

426 As long ago as 1978: See *The Times*, 2 February 1978, "Begin moves baffle Washington."

426 "housing 16,000 Israeli families": See *Guardian*, 30 November 1978, "Jewish plan to settle 16,000 families," by Eric Silver.

426 the last Arab family: See *The Times*, 6 March 1980, "Last Arab forced out of Jewish quarter," by Christopher Walker.

427 the Israeli authorities proceeded to seize land: See *The Times*, 19 March 1989, "100,000 Jews to live on seized Jerusalem land," by Christopher Walker.

427 "past leaders of our movement": See *Guardian*, 20 November 1990, "Arab land for Soviet Jews, says Shamir," by Ian Black.

427 "these Israeli islands": Benjamin Netanyahu in *New York Times*, reprinted in *Jerusalem Post*, 5 September 1993.

427 86.5 per cent of East Jerusalem: See *Jerusalem File* (The International Campaign for Jerusalem, PO Box 11592, London SE26 6WZ), February 1996, p. 5.

427 another 70,000 new housing units: See *Jerusalem File*, November 1996, p. 2.

427 with 3,546 houses: See *Jerusalem File*, May 1997, p. 6.

427 the sale of land for 5,000 new Jewish homes: See Associated Press report from Jerusalem, 4 February 1997—which refers to the occupied territories as "disputed lands"—and the *Independent*, 19 February 1997, "Jewish settlement rekindles danger of West Bank uprising," by Patrick Cockburn.

427 was denounced as "disinformation": See *Independent*, 28 February 1997, "Netanyahu accused over Jerusalem homes pledge," by Patrick Cockburn.

428 Between the signing of the Oslo accord: Edward Said, *Al-Ahram Weekly* (Cairo), 23–29 July 1998, "After the Final Acre."

428 an additional 116,000 houses: See *Jerusalem File*, June 1999, p. 4.

428 ten times as fast: *Peace Now* press statement, 20 August 1999.

428–9 "we will not remove a settlement": Agence France-Presse report from Jerusalem, 17 September 1999.

429 The final, damning statistics: Hirst, p. 24.

429 "The day after the second bloodbath": See *Independent*, 22 August 1995, "Rabin says bus atrocity will not halt peace talks," by Patrick Cockburn.

(n.) 429 "your challenge is not one of geographical turf": *Jerusalem Post*, 2 November 2000, "Peace must be painstakingly rebuilt," by John Hume.

430 "inflicted more punishment and pain": Avi Shlaim, *London Review of Books*, 30 November 1995, "Overtaken by Events."

430 "there is no moral problem": See *Independent*, 24 January 1996, "Amir tells court he shot Rabin 'for God,'" by Patrick Cockburn.

432 "The marriage is over": see *Independent*, 5 June 1996.

433 the report that Amnesty International published: Amnesty International, *Five Years After the Oslo Agreement: Human rights sacrificed for "security,"* 9 September 1998.

(n.) 433 A Scottish pathologist confirmed . . . detainee called Youssef Baba: See *International Herald Tribune*, 2 May 1995, "Palestinian Prisoner Shaken to Death by Israelis, Doctor Says," citing report in *The New York Times* by Joel Greenberg; *The Nation*, 27 September 1999, "Israel's Torture Ban," by Alexander Cockburn; *Independent*, 21 February 1997, "Torture deaths that shame Palestine: Horrific pictures show depravity of security force interrogators," by Patrick Cockburn.

437 fired dozens of bullets into a car: See *Independent*, 21 July 2001, "Killing of baby by Jewish vigilantes ignites rural town," by Phil Reeves.

438 When the Ross delegation came to Jerusalem: See *Ha'aretz*, 15 July 1993, citing Shahak, *Open Secrets*, p. 130.

(n.) 439 This "threat" was thrown into doubt: See *International Herald Tribune*, 12 May 1997, "General Dayan Speaks from the Grave," by Serge Schmemann, originally published in *The New York Times*.

441 "Everything was pre-planned": See *Jerusalem Post*, 2 November 2000, "Sharon says his Temple Mount visit was an excuse for violence," by Greer Fay Cashman.

443 "Child Sacrifice Is Palestinian Paganism": *Jerusalem Post*, 27 October 2000, article by Gerald M. Steinberg.

(n.) 448 "One gets the impression": See *Ha'aretz*, 8 November 2000, "Mofaz: al-Dura probe was initiated by Southern Command," by Anat Cygielman.

451 "All I possess in the presence of death": "Pride and Fury" by Mahmoud Darwish, translated by Mouna Khouri and Hamid Algar in *New Writing from the Middle East* (ed. Leo Hamalian and John Yohannan) (New York: Mentor, 1978), pp. 67–8.

451 "It's not just 'the dark night of the soul' when you have the resurgence": interview with Hanan Ashrawi, Ramallah, 7 November 2000.

452 In the first month of the new intifada: Amnesty International, *Israel and the Occupied Territories: Excessive use of lethal force*, 19 October 2000.

## Chapter Thirteen: The Girl and the Child and Love

453 "She and the other women": Interview with Amira Hass, Jerusalem, 18 August 2001.

457 "A Polish prisoner warned him": Interview with Shifra Stern, New York, 29 April 1997.

460 But I wrote an article: *Independent*, 28 July 1998.

460 "I thought it may be good": Letter to author from Nezar Hindawi, 2 December 1998.

461 "another nation may take retribution": See *Independent*, 25 January 1999, obituary of Sir William Mars-Jones.

462 "That man is pure unadulterated evil": See *Evening Herald*, Dublin, 14 October 2004, interview by Sarah Glynn, "Let My Evil Ex Lover Rot in Jail."

464 "First they killed the bodyguard": Interview with Jihad al-Wazzir, Gaza, 12 April 2001.

(n.) 466 two of four Palestinian bus hijackers: See *The Times*, 5 May 1984, "Palestinian deaths after bus hijack 'a mishap,'" by Lynne Richardson; re-examination of dozens of cases: see *Independent*, 25 June 1991, "Hit squads omission fuels rights inquiries," by Michael Sheridan; *"Jewish religious law"*: see *Daily Star* (Beirut), quoting agency reports, "Chief rabbi blesses 'targeted killings'"; "immoral and illegal practice": *Independent*, 4 June 1992, "Israeli army tactics 'immoral'," by Sarah Helm; 120 Palestinians had been killed: *Guardian*, 30 June 1993, "Israeli covert units ordered to shoot to kill, says report," by Derek Brown; even President Mubarak of Egypt: *Egyptian Gazette*, 9 October 1997, "Moubarak denounces Israeli assassination attempt as 'immoral'"; Israel had already been shocked: Associated Press report from Jerusalem, 21 August 1995, by Diana Cahn; Arab murdered by a Jewish "terrorist": Agence France-Presse report from Jerusalem, 19 May 1998.

468 "Jerusalem looks like a Bosnia": *Ha'aretz*, 2 August 2001.

469 It praises Sharon's "subtlety" because: *Wall Street Journal*, 2 August 2001.

(n.) 470 "these people who were shot": Interview with Bassam Abu Sharif, Ramallah, 8 August 2001.

474 "What should the residents": *Ha'aretz*, 12 August 2001.

477 "There are qualities": Sayed Hassan Nasrallah, interviewed by the author, *Beirut to Bosnia: Muslims and the West, a Personal Journey by Robert Fisk of* The Independent, dir. Michael Dutfield (Baraclough Carey/Chameleon), 1993, Episode 1, "The Martyr's Smile."

(n.) 478 "as an Israeli": Hass interview, 18 August 2001.

(n.) 479 The most shameful explanation: See *International Herald Tribune*, 1 April 2002, "Suicide Bombers Threaten Us All," by Thomas L. Friedman, reprinted from *New York Times*.

(n.) 479 "we have been disturbed to find": *The Friend* (London), 26 July 2002, also quoting Amnesty report from Gaza.

489 Some of Israel's "targeted killing": *Vanity Fair*, January 2003, "Israel's Payback Principle," by David Margolick.

489 "there is no language known": *Mail on Sunday* (London), 23 September 2001, "You know the problem, now hear the facts," by Stewart Steven.

489 "culture that glorifies depravity": *Irish Times*, 6 October 2003, "Palestinian regime's murky terror links," by Mark Steyn.

490 called for the execution of family members: See *Forward*, 7 June 2002, "Top Lawyer Urges Death For Families of Bombers," by Ami Eden.

(n.) 490 "it is likely the misfortune": John Feffer, *North Korea, South Korea: U.S. Policy at a Time of Crisis* (New York: Seven Stories Press, 2003), pp. 20–1.

496 "there were indeed wide-scale, ugly phenomena": See *Ha'aretz*, 20 April 2002, "IDF admits 'ugly vandalism' against Palestinian property," by Amos Harel, *Ha'aretz* military correspondent.

(n.) 496 Amnesty International's statistics: 4 November 2002, *Israel and the Occupied Territories, Shielded from Scrutiny: IDF violations in Jenin and Nablus.*

497 "apparently hundreds": See *Los Angeles Times*, 13 April 2002, "Controversy over Israeli Plan to Bury Camp Dead," by Richard Boudreaux.

498 their own meticulous investigation: *Independent Review*, 25 April 2002, "Once upon a time in Jenin," by Justin Huggler and Phil Reeves.

499 "Okay, so there wasn't a massacre.": *Ha'aretz Magazine*, 26 April 2002, "The power of the word," by Arie Caspi.

499–500 Major Avner Foxman, said of the Adora killings: *National Post*, 29 April 2002, "Now I know what is a massacre," by Stewart Bell.

500 "Israel needs to deliver a military blow": See Friedman, *International Herald Tribune*, 1 April 2002, "Suicide Bombers Threaten Us All."

506 who gave the order for the expulsion: See *Daily Telegraph* (London), 28 August 1995, "Peace process fails to obscure Rabin's past," by Michael Adams.

506 "We walked outside": See *Journal of Palestine Studies*, Summer 1980, pp. 96–118, "The Palestinian Exodus," by Steven Glazer, citing a portion of Rabin's memoirs which was censored in the official edition but published in the *New York Times*, 23 October 1979.

507 bore "personal responsibility": *The Commission of Enquiry into the Events at the Refugee Camps in Beirut 1983*, Final Report (Authorized Translation) by Yitzhak Kahan, Aharon Barak, and Yona Efrat, p. 105.

507 So fearful were the Israeli authorities: See *Independent*, 27 July 2001, "Israel tells officials to avoid threat of arrest in Europe," by Phil Reeves.

507 Belgian judges: *Plainte avec Constitution de Partie Civile*, Brussels, 18 June 2001, testimony of 52 pages on the murders, rapes, disappearances and other crimes committed in the Sabra and Chatila camps in Beirut on 16th, 17th and 18th September, 1982, signed by Chibli Mallat, Luc Walleyn and Michaël Verhaeghe; see also *Ha'aretz Magazine*, 10 August 2001, "A Lawsuit Sprouts in Brussels," by Sara Leibovich-Dar, although this article erroneously claims that the author of this book had joined the plaintiffs in their suit.

507 described the Palestinians as a "cancerous manifestation": see open letter from Israeli academics, 23 September 2002, on http://www.middleeast.org.

507 "chopping off limbs": *Playboy* magazine, May 1995, "General Ariel Sharon," interview with Ranan R. Lurie.

(n.) 507 Yaron was in Washington: *Ha'aretz*, 8 January 2003, "In Washington, Israel makes its case for massive U.S. aid," by Moti Bassok.

508    "we stand together with you": Cited by James Zogby, president of the Arab American Institute, 19 April 1999 on http://www.aaiusa.org/wwatch_archives/041999.htm.

508    "Sharon's racist imagination": *Ma'ariv*, 12 April 1999, "Birds of a feather (or: The starling and the raven)," by Uri Avnery.

(n.) 508    The principal Allied excuses: See Martin Gilbert, *Auschwitz and the Allies: How the allies responded to the news of Hitler's Final Solution* (London: Michael Joseph, 1981), pp. 299–323; also Gilbert's *Winston S. Churchill*, vol. VII, *Road to Victory, 1941–1945* (London: Heinemann, 1986), pp. 846–7, for Churchill's reaction to bombing proposals.

509    Prominent American Jewish leaders: *Forward*, 10 May 2002, "Lobbyists Urge Bush to Ease Up on Sharon—Elie Wiesel: 'Trust Him,'" by Ami Eden.

509    Only a month earlier, the Americans rolled out: *Independent on Sunday*, 7 April 2002.

(n.) 509    ". . . there is something to the question": *Ha'aretz*, 5 April 1999, "Neither Auschwitz nor 1948," by Dan Margalit.

510    "fighting for the spoils": *Ha'aretz*, 5 May 2002.

510    Amid what the Palestinian writer Jean Makdisi: See *Daily Star*, Beirut, "Jean Makdisi: Our strength lies in the simplicity of truth," by Marianne Stigset.

510    "if our job is to seize": *Ha'aretz* article by Haim Hanebi, cited in *Courrier International*, no. 589, 14–20 February 2002.

510    trapped and desperate Jews of the Warsaw ghetto: One of the most harrowing accounts of the ghetto rising can be found in Gilbert's *The Holocaust*, pp. 557–67.

510–11    B'Tselem estimated that between 1987 and May 2003: B'Tselem, http://www.btselem.org/English/Statistics/

511    By 1993, 232 Palestinian children: B'Tselem, *The Killing of Palestinian Children and the Open-Fire Regulations*, June 1993.

511    In one of its most shocking reports: Amnesty International, 1 October 2002.

(n.) 511    Yet just over two years later: *Independent on Sunday*, 31 October 2004, "A critical friend is not an enemy," by Michael Williams. Readers requiring details of other human rights abuses should consult B'Tselem's voluminous and detailed reports, including *The Closure of the West Bank and Gaza Strip: Human Rights Violations Against Residents of the Occupied Territories*, April 1993; *House Demolition During Operations Against Wanted Persons*, May 1993; *Deportation of Palestinians from the Occupied Territories and the Mass Deportation of December 1992*, June 1993; *Firing at Vehicles by the Security Forces in the Occupied Territories*, February 1994. Amnesty International's *Israel and the Occupied Territories, Demolition and Dispossession: The destruction of Palestinian homes*, December 1999, is also essential reading. For Israeli army mistreatment of Palestinian civilians, see also the work of former Israeli soldier James Ron, now Assistant Professor of Sociology at Johns Hopkins, especially "Rabin's Two Legacies," published in *al-Mustaqbal al-Arabi* (Beirut), 1996, shortened version in *Index on Censorship* (London), September 1996.

512    "I was at that time reading a terrible book": *L'Express*, 27 December 2001, "C'est comme vous en Algérie, mais nous, nous resterons," interview with Ariel Sharon by Alain Louyot. The book Sharon was referring to was, of course, Alistair Horne's *A Savage War of Peace: Algeria 1954–1962*.

## Chapter Fourteen: "Anything to Wipe Out a Devil . . ."

(n.) 515    Theories abound on the origin: Horne, *A Savage War of Peace*, p. 30n.

516    A magnificent photograph: See *Archives de l'Algérie*, pp. 28–9.

517    "Soldiers, civilised nations": See Galibert, *Algérie*, p. 172.

518    its troops had asphyxiated 500: Ibid., p. 30.

518    "The country is without commerce": le Baron Baude, Conseiller d'Etat, ex-Commissaire du Roi en Afrique, *L'Algérie* (Paris, 1841), cited in *The Dublin Review*, August 1842, p. 32.

518    "On December 24th 1832": Galibert, pp. 554–6.

518    "Wherever there is fresh water": Cited in Horne, p. 30.

519    "Despite the [1914] victory of the Marne": Octave Depont, *L'Algérie du Centenaire: l'oeuvre française de libération, de conquête morale et d'évolution sociale des indigènes. Les Berbères en France. La représentation parlementaire des indigènes* (Paris: Recueil Sirey, 1930), p. 113.

519    "There's no doubt that to give everyone": Ibid., p. 186.

521    published a 320-page guide: *La France en guerre d'Algérie*.

521    Amnesty International demanded an investigation: Amnesty International, *France/Algeria: France must now face up to its judicial obligations*, 3 May 2001.

521    "a cowardly silence": Rachid Mokhtari in *Le Matin* (Algiers), cited in *Courrier International*, 10–15 May 2001.

521    "Middle Eastern Islamic fanaticism": See *Daily Star* (Beirut), 27 March 2004, "The public relations war: Algeria, France and imperial America," by Arun Kapil.

523    "we really contaminated the Algerians": *L'Express*, 14–20 March 2002, p. 105, interview with Annie Rey-Goldzeiguer.

527    "They will not talk about the future": interview with Hassan Tourabi, Khartoum, 1 December 1993.

546    "we watched the bitter struggle": See *Jerusalem Post*, 5 December 1995, "Rabin always calm, obstinate, in control of the facts," by Chaim Herzog.

547    vile dossier of decapitated corpses: *La barbarie du terrorisme: Victimes civiles de la barbarie terroriste catégories socio-professionelles touchées 1990–1994*, Algiers 1994.

548    FIS front organisation publishes: *The Atrocities in Algeria: A Photographic Testimony*, 1994, published by "Human Services," PO Box 198, Southall, Middlesex UB1 3PR, UK.

(n.) 552    By 1995, the Algerian government: *Livre Blanc du Terrorisme en Algérie*, Ministère de l'Intérieur, des Collectives Locales de l'Environnement et de la Réforme Administrative, Algiers 1995.

553    "In the back of the restaurant": See *Irish Times*, 2 May 1998, "Killed for a column," by Lara Marlowe. The translation of Mekbel's last column below the chapter-head was also by Marlowe.

558    So much for conciliation: For the full interview with Meziane-Cherif, see *Independent on Sunday*, 12 March 1995, "Whatever you do, just don't mention torture to the genial 'eradicator,'" by Robert Fisk.

(n.) 559    "Because Islam is the religion of the Book": *Index on Censorship* (London), May/June 1994, pp. 112–16, "Goodbye to the Enlightenment," by Karim Alrawi.

565    Fatima's crime had been her beauty: See *El Watan* (Algiers), 14 March 1995, "Des femmes atrocement assassinées," by Slima Tlemcani; see also *Liberté* (Algiers), 14 March 1995, "Une Fille et trois femmes assassinées en 48 heures: Egorgée devant l'Ecole," by Ilham Djanine.

575    "I was moved to Cavignac police station": Interview with Dalilah (full name known to author), Archway, London, 15 October 1997.

577    "They gave us vaccinations": Interview with Reda (full name known to author), Knightsbridge, London, 14 October 1997.

579    he watched suspected "Islamists" interrogated: Interview with Abdessalam (full name known to author), Knightsbridge, London, 14 October 1997.

579    "in most cases, joined the terrorist bands": Letter from Ahmed Benyamina, Algerian ambassador in London, to *The Independent*, 1 November 1997.

579    "there is no credible, substantive evidence": Foreign and Commonwealth Office Policy Statement on Algeria, May 1998.

580    forcibly returned him to Algeria: See *Independent*, 10 May 1997, "Refugee sent back home to his death," by Patricia Wynn Davies.

580    When Mary Robinson: See *Independent*, 10 December 1996.

580    It produced a report that might have been written: UN, *Report of the panel appointed by the Secretary-General of the United Nations to gather information on the situation in Algeria in order to provide the international community with greater clarity on that situation*, 16 September 1998.

580    When Amnesty International condemned: Amnesty, 16 September 1998, *Algeria: UN Panel report a whitewash on human rights*.

580    An earlier European Union mission: See *Irish Times*, 21 January 1998, "EU troika 'treads softly' and avoids embarrassing its hosts," by Lara Marlowe.

580    "to stop condemning Algeria from afar": See *Irish Times*, 5 January 1998, "Hand-wringing by EU over Algerian massacres will no longer be enough," by Lara Marlowe.

(n.) 580 The Belgian authorities deported: See *Independent*, 10 December 1996; see also *The Enlightenment: The Algerian Community in London*, vol. 5, no. 31, 2 August 1996, "Communiqué on the murder by torture of a FIS member deported from Belgium to Algeria."

581 "defend the regime by denying": Abdelhamid Brahimi, "Algeria's Tragedy: The Necessity for a Peaceful Commitment," address to the Foreign Affairs Committee of the Irish Parliament, Dublin, 8 April 1998.

581 Although Algeria . . . sent $20 million in arms: See *The Times*, 17 January 1983, "Algeria gave PLO $20m for arms to fight Israel," by Christopher Mosey.

581 During the Cuban missile crisis: Interview with Algerian foreign minister Lakhdar Brahimi, Algiers, 23 March 1992.

582 "the violence appears to have generated": *Washington Post*, 13 June 1997, "A Ray of Hope in Bloody Algeria: Atrocities Turning the Public Against Islamic Terrorists," by John Lancaster.

582 "now that the White House has decided": Agence France-Presse report from Algiers, cited in *Le Monde*, 14 March 1998.

582 "It's not impossible": Interview with General Mohamed Lamari by the Algerian Press Service, 28 October 1997.

582 "to compare a rape in a police station": Quoted in *Le Monde*, 20 March 1998, "Des intellectuels français dénoncent les violations des droits de l'homme en Algérie."

582 recent research suggests: See Aggoun and Rivoire, *Françalgérie*.

(n.) 582 misuse of my articles in *The Independent*: Letter to author from Mary Mourra Ramadan, lawyer for Anwar Haddam, "president of FIS parliamentary delegation abroad," including U.S. Department of Justice Executive Office of Immigration Review, Office of the Immigration Judge, Arlington, Virginia, Comprehensive Submission of Government's Exhibits and Witness List, File No. A22 751 813 of 3 February 1997.

583 Algerian security forces were implicated: See *Le Monde*, 7–8 June 1998, "La sécurité algérienne pourrait être impliquée dans le drame de Tibehirine," by Henri Tincq.

583 But international human rights groups: See *Human Rights Watch*, vol. 10, no. 1, February 1998, "Neither Among the Living nor the Dead: State-sponsored 'Disappearances' in Algeria"; also Amnesty International, 3 March 1999, *Algeria: "Disappearances": The wall of silence begins to crumble*.

584 Nezzar left France when: See *Le Monde*, 28 April 2001, "Le départ précipité du général Nezzar provoque les protestations des défenseurs des droits de l'homme," by Florence Beaugé.

584 He wanted Algerians to forget: See *Irish Times*, 18 September 1999, whose correspondent Lara Marlowe cynically—and accurately—reported that "optimistic economists believe the generals have now accumulated enough sports cars and Paris apartments to be willing to share Algeria's wealth with its people."

584 Amnesty International appealed: Amnesty International, 30 July 2004, "Algeria: Newly discovered mass grave must be fully investigated."

## Chapter Fifteen: Planet Damnation

589 "a rough, direct-talking leader": Richard Murphy interview, *International Herald Tribune*, 29 July 1990.

589 "promised not to use force": See *Independent*, 21 March 1991, "U.S. warned Iraq against invasion," by Rupert Cornwell.

(n.) 590 "Most Arabs are convinced": Oxford Institute for Energy Studies, 3 October 1990, *Political Dimensions of the Gulf Crisis*, by Robert Mabro, p. 13.

595 "Sensitive areas": See *A Soldier's Guide: Saudi Arabia* (Washington, D.C.: U.S. Army, Chief of Public Affairs, Command Information Division, 1990), p. 29.

596 "sense of distress": Associated Press, 26 October 1990, "Pentagon Lists Taboo Subjects for Troops in Saudi Arabia," by Ruth Sinai.

596 thanks to the 1988 $23 billion Al-Yamamah arms contract: see *Guardian*, 13 March 1992, "Report on Saudi arms deal suppressed," by David Hencke and Richard Norton Taylor.

598 "powerful battle force": Brig. Gen. James M. Lyle, *Winning in the Desert II* (Leavenworth, Kans.: Fort Leavenworth Media Support Center, September 1990).

609 "her nuclear weapons": *Sunday Telegraph*, 2 December 1990, "When war-war is better than 'just war' jaw," by Edward Norman.

611 The one thing he regretted: See *Independent on Sunday Magazine*, 18 February 1996, "How We Met: Matthew Symonds and Andreas Whittam Smith," interviews by Isabel Wolff.

611 "This news put me": De la Billière, *Storm Command*, p. 181.

(n.) 611 The computer was returned: See *Independent*, 26 June 1991, "Gulf war plans returned by a 'patriotic thief,' " by Tim Kelsey.

612 "Why did you not fulfil": Saudi Press Agency, 15 January 1991, "Custodian of the Two Holy Mosques in reply to the message of Saddam Hussein."

616 "I have already issued the terrible orders": Schwarzkopf, *It Doesn't Take a Hero*, p. 412.

622 "Thursday morning was one of those moments": *Philadelphia Inquirer* "pool" dispatch from USS *John F. Kennedy*, 17 January 1991 ("Combat Pool Three," navy carrier, ref RUFRSGG7170).

624 "except for the 100 hours of Desert Storm": See *Washington Post*, 5 November 1997 (Hoagland article) and *Washington Post*, 6 November 1997 (Cohen article), cited in *Middle East Report* (Washington, D.C.), Fall 1998, no. 208: 35, "Short-Circuiting the Media-Policy Machine," by Sam Husseini.

628 they destroyed a river bridge crowded with pedestrians: See *Independent*, 8 February 1991, "Allied raid on bridge kills 47 civilians," by Patrick Cockburn; *Guardian*, 18 February 1991, "Death comes to a town almost forgotten by war," by Alfonso Rojo.

(n.) 629 "The bomb, called a GBU-28": Reuters, 4 July 1991.

632 Chinese would complain: Agence France-Presse, quoted in *International Herald Tribune*, 14 June 1996, "Everest Pollution Laid to Gulf War."

(n.) 637 Arabs spent $84 billion: Arab economic report for 1992, prepared by the Arab League, the Arab Monetary Fund, the Arab Fund for Economic and Social Development and the Organisation of Arab Petroleum Exporting Countries; bin Sultan, *Desert Warrior*, pp. 292–3; see *Middle East Reporter* (Beirut), 12 September 1992, p. 17; see also *Financial Times*, 2 August 1991, "Arab countries still owe $7 billion for Gulf war costs," by Peter Riddell.

638 "began to devise a plan": de la Billière, p. 222.

(n.) 640 "I was stepping on bodies": Associated Press report from Baghdad, 21 March 1991.

(n.) 640 The most thorough investigation: *New Yorker*, 22 May 2000, pp. 48–82, "Overwhelming Force: What happened in the final days of the Gulf War?," by Seymour M. Hersh.

643 Some people, Hurd said: Hurd interview in *The Times* (London), 2 August 1991.

## Chapter Sixteen: Betrayal

646 "Rise to save the homeland": See *Middle East Reporter* (Beirut), 25 February 1991, p. 4, "Iraqis Urged to Revolt, Save Country from Dictatorship, War."

647 the Iraqis had tried to jam: See *Middle East Reporter* (Beirut), 4 January 1991, "Anti-Saddam Radio Believed Jammed."

647 "the allies to liberate Iraq": Interview with Haidar al-Assadi, Beirut, 3 May 1998.

649 Iraqi dead at up to 150,000: *Middle East Reporter* (Beirut), 1 March 1991.

649 had claimed that 26,000 Iraqis: *Jumhouri-y Islami* (Tehran), 19 February 1991, cited by Dilip Hiro in letter to *The Independent*, 8 February 1992.

649 When a Pentagon source: *Newsday*, 12 September 1991, cited by Hiro, as above.

650 dropped nearly as many tons: *International Herald Tribune*, 10 July 1996, quoting *New York Times* article by Tim Weiner, "Smart Arms in Gulf War Are Found Overrated."

650 "35—almost one-quarter": Associated Press report from Washington, 13 August 1991, "Gulf Friendly Fire Casualties Rise," by Susanne M. Chafer.

650 The independent U.S. General Accounting Office: See *International Herald Tribune*, 10 July 1996, op. cit.

650 In fact, as Seymour Hersh: *New Yorker*, 26 September 1994, pp. 86–99, "Missile Wars," by Seymour Hersh, esp. p. 92.

(n.) 650 Timothy McVeigh, a promising young soldier: Reuters report in *Irish Times*, 3 June 1997.

652 All of this I duly reported: See *Independent*, 27 March 1991.

(n.) 652    Other testimony to Kuwaiti persecution: See, for example, *Libération*, 20 March 1991, "La grande peur des Palestiniens du Kuweit," by Jean Michel Thénard.

657    The refugees who now streamed: See *Guardian*, 14 March 1991, "Rebels 'hanged from tank gun barrels' by Saddam's men," by Sharif Imam-Jomeh (Reuters) and Nora Boustany (*Washington Post*).

658    "Better the Saddam Hussein": *Guardian*, 13 March 1991, "Britain and U.S. part over Iraqi rebels," by Hella Pick.

661    would be compared to the Soviet demands: See, for example, *Independent*, 28 March 1991, "Fiddling while Basra burns," by Godfrey Hodgson.

663    "What's the better option": *International Herald Tribune*, 23 March 1991, quoting *Washington Post* report by Dan Balz and Al Kamen, "U.S. Fears of a Divided Iraq Muddle Policy on Hussein."

664    "to harvest them, the wheat with the chaff": *Guardian*, 27 March 1991, quoting *Washington Post* report by Nora Boustany, "Republican Guard reaps harvest of death."

664    "consigned the Iraqi insurgents": *Independent*, 28 March 1991, "White House leaves Iraqi rebels to their fate," by Edward Lucas, quoting *The New York Times*.

665    "the mightiest military machine": *Independent*, 2 April 1991.

665    "the logic of intervention": *New York Times*, 31 March 1991.

665    "there would be, downtown Baghdad": *International Herald Tribune*, 16 January 1991, quoting *Los Angeles Times* report by James Gertstenzang, "Bush's Gulf War Regrets: 'Could Have Done More' Against Saddam." The Bush interviews were broadcast on PBS in January 1996.

666    "It was almost a healing process": Associated Press report, Washington, 2 August 1991.

666    "is betting that Americans": Associated Press report, Houston, 8 April 1991.

680    "Hard to imagine the quality": Note to the author from Larry Heinzerling, 5 March 1991.

(n.) 681    the object of an unnecessary controversy: See Makiya, *Cruelty and Silence*; also review by Mouin Rabbani in *Middle East Report*, March–June 1993; review by Eqbal Ahmad in *The Nation*, 9–16 August 1993; Makiya's response to Ahmad in *The Nation*, 8 November 1993; review by As'ad Abu Khalil in *Middle East Journal*, Autumn 1993; *The Independent*, 27 May 1991 (containing the author's original report from Dahuk), and *The Independent*, 13 September 1994, "Showering Platitudes on Islam's Suffering Women," by Robert Fisk; typical of the mis-sourcing of the reports was a letter to the author from Mouin Rabbani, 13 November 1994, referring to the 13 September 1994 *Independent* article which mentioned "raping rooms," and claiming inaccurately: "I believe I am right in stating that it [Makiya's book] is the source of your . . . statement."

686    Some would say that 200,000 died: See, for example, statement by the Islamic Union for Iraqi Students and Youth (London), 1992, "Saddam Launches Ruthless Campaign to Wipe Out Marsh Arabs," which refers to the crushed uprising as "a betrayal that will be forever engraved on the minds of Iraqi civilians."

## Chapter Seventeen: The Land of Graves

701    the return of Kuwaiti civilian prisoners: Schwarzkopf, *Autobiography*, p. 485.

701    "We settled for": Ibid., pp. 485, 488.

703    A Harvard team of lawyers: *Public Health in Iraq After the Gulf War*, Harvard Study Team report, May 1991.

706    "Big picture": *Washington Post*, 23 June 1991.

706    "With no domestic sources": *Iraq Water Treatment Vulnerabilities*, U.S. Defense Intelligence Agency, 22 January 1991, cited in *The Progressive*, September 2001.

707    the Tigris River had changed colour: *Independent*, 25 April 1998, "Poisoned Tigris spreads tide of death in Iraq."

(n.) 707    The evidence of massive human suffering: UN Humanitarian Panel's Report on Sanctions, 30 March 1999; "if the substantial reduction": UNICEF Iraq, *Child and Maternal Mortality Surveys, Executive Summary*, August 1999.

708    A mere glance at the list: Simons, *Scourging of Iraq*, p. 118, table 3.1.

708    just before Christmas 1999: *Guardian*, 4 March 2000.

708 167 Iraqi children were dying: *Toronto Star*, 25 June 2000.
(n.) 708 For example, the Iraqi: K. M. Al-Chalabi, "Spinal Cord," *Journal of the International Spinal Cord Society,* 2004, pp. 447–9.
709 "The World Health Organisation": From a speech by Dennis Halliday on Capitol Hill, Washington, 6 October 1998.
709 "here we are": *Guardian*, 2 August 2000.
709 "We know that": Letter from Arvin Sumoondur of the Foreign Office's Middle East Department to Dr. Stephen Goldby, 19 October 2000.

## Chapter Eighteen: The Plague

718 RAF pilots flying out of: See John Pilger, "The Cost of Conflict," in *The Saddam Hussein Reader: Selections from Leading Writers on Iraq* (ed. Turi Munthe) (New York: Thunder's Mouth Press, 2002), pp. 363–4, citing a study by Dr. Eric Herring, Iraqi sanctions specialist at Bristol University, UK, and the *Washington Post*, October 2002.
721 "I can honestly say": *Ha'aretz*, 28 September 1998.
724 "UNSCOM directly facilitated": *Washington Post*, 6 January 1999, report by Barton Gellman.
734 I still treasure a sarcastic letter: Lord Gilbert to the editor, the *Independent*, 30 May 1988.
740 "The Government is aware": Letter from Ministry of Defence Secretary of State Doug Henderson, dated 22 December 1998, to Dr. Evan Harris, MP, answering a letter from his constituent, Dr. Mercy Heatley of Oxford.
(n.) 740 When I travelled to Bosnia: See the author's reports in the *Independent* between 11 and 16 January 2001.

## Chapter Nineteen: Now Thrive the Armourers . . .

769 expressing its confidence: see *Financial Times*, 29 July 1991, "Government licensed gas chemical sales."
778 "individuals who do not come within the definition of civilians": Article 50, paragraph 3, of the Geneva Conventions' Protocol 1.
784 I made a formal request: Fisk letter to Lt. Col. Byars of U.S. Defense Department, Washington, 6 May 1997.
785 Thus did a U.S. marine missile: My detailed account of the missile attack on the ambulance, "Return to Sender," was published in the *Sunday Review* of the *Independent on Sunday*, 18 May 1997.
(n.) 785 In the late 1970s: *Independent*, 24 June 1997, "A Rocket Is Returned to Sender."

## Chapter Twenty: Even to Kings, He Comes . . .

791 "we are not going to let": George Bush in Beirut, 26 October 1983.
796 Dinner with the PLK: Author's notes of dinner with King Hussein at the Royal Palace, Amman, 25 September 1993.
(n.) 801 A British diplomat: Author's notes of conversation with Alan Urwick, British ambassador in Amman, 17 April 1983.
807 why Queen Noor wept: Speech given by Leith Shubeilath in Irbid, Jordan, 7 November 1995.
818 "I am your elder brother": See Seale, *Asad*, p. 430.
820 For the Alawis: See ibid., p. 8.
822 Before the First World War: For a discussion of Arab demands on the Ottomans at this time, see especially Antonius, *Arab Awakening*, pp. 101–25, and Kamal Salibi, *The Modern History of Lebanon* (New York: Caravan, 1977), pp. 156–9.
823 "We had become like animals": See *Daily Star* (Beirut), 14 December 1998, "When life was worth a radish," by Carl Gibeily.
824 a heavily stained pamphlet: Antoine Yammine, *Quatre ans de misère: Le Liban et la Syrie pendant la guerre* (Cairo: Imprimerie Emin Hindi, 1922).
825 A French scholar: See Khoury, *La France et l'Orient Arabe*, pp. 68–71.
826 The scholar and historian: See Antonius, pp. 190–1.

## Chapter Twenty-one: Why?

828 "Sana Sersawi speaks carefully": This article was finally published in the *Independent* on 28 November 2001 under the headline "New evidence indicates Palestinians died hours after surviving camp massacres."

834 "So it has come to this": *Independent*, 12 September 2001, "The Wickedness and Awesome Cruelty of a Crushed and Humiliated People."

(n.) 841 Arab elections: See *Keysing's Record of World Events, 1993*, pp. 39711, 40797; SANA (Damascus), 2 February 1999; AP, Algiers, 16 April 1999. See also *Independent*, 8 October 1999.

(n.) 846 "a treacherous and cowardly crime": *The Second Afghan War 1878–80*, Appendix XII, pp. 656–7.

847 Wahhabism, the strict, pseudo-reformist: for a modern critique of Wahhabism, see Abu Khalil, *Battle for Saudi Arabia*, pp. 52–75.

848 In 1998, a Saudi student: Nawaf Obaid, *Improving U.S. Intelligence Analysis on the Saudi Arabian Decision-Making Process*, John F. Kennedy School of Government, Harvard University, 1998, submitted to Ambassador Ronald Neumann, deputy assistant secretary for Near East affairs; see especially pp. 18–19, 21–25, 27, and 36.

848 The Saudis deployed 10,000 troops: See *The Times*, 5 December 1979, "Last of the Great Mosque rebels rooted out by Saudi forces"; also *Guardian*, 6 December 1979, "Saudis identify disfigured body of Muslim rebel who led siege in Grand Mosque," by John Andrews.

849 sixty-three men were beheaded in public: See *Le Monde*, 20–21 November 1994, "Il y a quinze ans: La prise de la Grande Mosquée de La Mecque," by Olivier Da Lage.

849 "timeless culture": *International Herald Tribune*, 6 July 1994 (reprinted from the *Washington Post*), "Saudi Arabia's Solid Foundations Assure a Durable Kingdom," by Bandar ibn Sultan.

849 "to act with the grain": *Focus on Saudi Arabia* (Jeddah), 23 September 1994, "My Sojourn," by Sir Alun Munro, British ambassador to Saudi Arabia 1989–93.

849 Amnesty International appeals: See, for example, Amnesty's *Saudi Arabia: A Secret State of Suffering*, 28 March 2000, and *Saudi Arabia: A Justice System Without Justice*, 10 May 2000.

(n.) 849 "Standing to the left": *Irish Times*, 19 June 1997, "An Irishman at a beheading," by Gary Keenan.

863 "The first time I arrived": Rashid, *Taliban*, p. 56.

865 reporters found the mass grave: See especially *Newsweek*, 26 August 2002, "The Death Convoy of Afghanistan."

875 "beaten up by a mob": *Mail on Sunday*, 9 December 2001.

875 "if I was an Afghan refugee": *Independent*, 10 December 2001.

875 "A self-loathing multiculturalist": *Wall Street Journal*, 15 December 2001.

877 "how Muslims were coming to hate the West": Film *From Beirut to Bosnia*, 1983, op. cit.

879 "impeccable English diction": Joseph I. Ungar of "Primer," *Beyond Bias* 1994.

879 "By airing *Beirut to Bosnia*": Laibson to Hendriks, 16 June 1994.

879 to claim that we had edited an interview: Safian to Bunting, 9 June 1994.

879 "absurd and demonstrably wrong": Dutfield to Tomi Landis, Discovery executive producer, 19 June 1994.

879 "given the reaction to the series": Bunting to Chrissie Smith of Baraclough Carey Productions, 28 March 1995.

886 "in terms of equipment": *Los Angeles Times*, 9 May 1986, "Strike a Success."

886 "a piece of the action": *Washington Post*, 16 April 1986.

886 "It was the greatest thrill": *Chicago Tribune*, 16 April 1986, "Missing Jet Reportedly Fell in Sea."

## Chapter Twenty-two: The Die Is Cast

890 "where every day, fiction is spun": *International Herald Tribune*, 4 October 2003, "When the Politicians Outdo the Artists," by Frank Rich, reprinted from the *New York Times*.

898 according to eighteen of the prisoners: See *International Herald Tribune*, 27 March 2002, "Failure to communicate: 30 captive Afghans turn out to be U.S. allies," by John Ward Anderson, reprinted from the *Washington Post*.

(n.) 899 between 3,000 and 3,400 civilians were killed in Afghanistan: Professor Marc W. Herold, *A Dossier on Civilian Victims of United States Aerial Bombing of Afghanistan: A Comprehensive Accounting (Revised)*, March 2002 (http://www.cursor.org/stories/civilian_deaths .htm); for specific reports in the American media, see, for example, *International Herald Tribune*, 2 July 2002, "Errant U.S. bomb said to kill scores" (drawing on AP and Reuters dispatches) on the Uruzgan wedding bombing and, more typically, *International Herald Tribune*, 11 February 2002, "Afghan toll of civilians is lost in the fog of war: Families demand a reckoning for hundreds killed," by Barry Bearak, Eric Schmitt and Craig S. Smith, originally published in the *New York Times*.

(n.) 904 a remarkable account of al-Qaeda's order of battle: Ahmed Zeidan *Bin Laden Blaqna (Bin Laden Unmasked)* (Beirut: World Book Publishing, 2003).

914 "We all knew it was a job we had to do": Interview with Captain Ali Nasr, Port Said, Egypt, 22 October 1986.

915 "Hit, hit hard and hit now": Scott Lucas, *Divided We Stand*, p. 142.

915 The *Times* led the way: Shaw, *Eden, Suez and the Mass Media*, p. 57, quoting The *Times*, 27 August 1956, "Escapers" Club."

916 an attack on the right to speak out: Shaw, *Eden*, p. 58, quoting *Manchester Guardian*, 28 August 1956.

916 "Clark worked in unison with the *Times*": Shaw, *Eden*, p. 59.

916 "The objection to the matter": Ibid., quoting *The Times*, 1 September 1956, "Widening the Circle."

916 "was born of a marriage": Love, *Suez*, p. 433.

(n.) 916 According to Arye Biro: See *Irish Times*, 7 August 1995, "Egypt angry at admission of POW killings," by David Horowitz; also *L'Orient Le Jour* (Beirut), 22 July 1995, "L'Armée Israelienne aurait abattu des prisonniers Egyptiens en 1956."

917 "It was a nightmare": Interview with Mustafa Kamal Murad, Cairo, 18 October 1986.

918 Several civilians were massacred: Love, *Suez*, p. 601.

919 He claimed then that the British: Interview with Mohamed Mahran Othman, Port Said, Egypt, 21 July 1997.

919 to treat his comrades for five more hours: NA AIR20/9577.

919 "malicious mentality": NA AIR20/10369.

919 was to see bodies still unburied: Interview with Alex Eftyvoulos of Associated Press, Nicosia, 26 July 1997.

(n.) 919 "interrogation of Prisoners of War": NA WO288/51; "We have not extended our enquiries": NA WO32/16345.

921 "If we had allowed things to drift": Love, *Suez*, p. 578.

931 It was written not for the United States: For full text, see http://www.israeleconomy.org/ strat1.htm

## Chapter Twenty-three: Atomic Dog, Annihilator, Arsonist, Anthrax, Anguish and Agamemnon

949 "If Providence does not intrude": Pat Buchanan; see http://amconmag.com/2002_10_7/ after_the_war.html

955 "Mosque attendance is rising": *Economist*, 31 January 1998, "Iraq discovers religion: Battered by seven years of sanctions, Iraqis are turning to Islam. For his own reasons, Saddam is doing the same."

(n.) 972 It concluded that while the killings: Reporters Without Borders, *Two Murders and a Lie: An Investigation by Jean-Paul Mari*, January 2004.

## Chapter Twenty-four: Into the Wilderness

1,032 bin Laden appears to admit: A privately made videotape disclosed by the Pentagon, 13 December 2001.

1,032 Dream theories: See Iain R. Edgar's "The Dream Will Tell: Militant Muslim Dreaming in the Context of Traditional and Contemporary Islamic Dream Theory and Practice," published in *Dreaming* 14, no. 1, 2004.

(n.) 1,032 anti-Islamic tracts: see Dr. Grace Heney, "Distorted Images: Anti-Islamic Propaganda at the time of the expulsion of the Moriscos," published in *Images des Morisques dans La Littérature et les Arts* (Zaghoun, Tunisia: Fondation Termini pour la Recherche Scientifique et l'Information, April 1999).

1,037 "It is true that we cannot": Albert Camus, "Neither Victims nor Executioners" (New York: Liberation, 1960), p. 22. Camus's essay was originally serialized in the French newspaper *Combat* in the autumn of 1946; the New York *Liberation* edition was subsequently reprinted by Ourside, Gloucestershire, 2005, in its original format.

(n.) 1,037 It was the Israeli newspaper: *Ma'ariv,* 14 February 2002.

1,038 "Justice itself tends": T. S. Eliot writing on 28 January 1946 in the preface to *The Dark Side of the Moon* (London: Faber, 1946), p. 8.

# Select Bibliography

THE FOLLOWING BOOKS AND DOCUMENTS are listed here as a guide for readers who want to follow up the story of Palestine, Israel, the Armenian Holocaust, Saddam's regime, the Iranian revolution and its eight-year war with Iraq, the Algerian conflict, past and present, and the history of the modern Middle East—if indeed there is a "modern" Middle East. They are by no means comprehensive, and I disagree with some of their conclusions. Martin Gilbert's volume on modern Israel, for example, lacks the unflinching academic impartiality of his magisterial history of the Jewish Holocaust. Details of Kanan Makiya's work on the cruelty of Saddam's Iraq have been questioned by several prominent scholars. David Fromkin's wonderful analysis of the Middle East and the results of the 1914–18 war is marred by an exceptionally prejudiced section (Chapter 58) on the Palestinians. Moammar Ghadafi's ghastly novel is included to represent the delusion of dictators—I have spared the reader Saddam's own romantic epics. General Sir Peter de la Billière's account of the 1991 Gulf War is pompous and frustrating—he won't even tell his readers that his SAS men escaped via Syria—but there are some grim and disturbing references to the "anti-terrorist" war in the Gulf. The history of the 2003 Anglo-American invasion and occupation of Iraq has dealt cruelly with Kenneth Pollack's moralistic arguments for war; I've included *The Threatening Storm* to show just how specific—and misleading—were the efforts to persuade Americans to invade.

Bibliographies, like dictatorships, lack perfection. Does a biography of Haj Amin al-Husseini, the Grand Mufti of Jerusalem, fall under "Palestine" or "Middle East History"? Do books on the Iran–Iraq War come under Iran or Iraq? I have included one work on the execution of deserters in the 1914–18 war and another on the Chinese labour force in the same conflict—both of which are relevant to the chapter on my soldier father. Clearly, they fall under no Middle East category. I have tried, therefore, to list books and documents under subjects as well as countries so that the reader can search for them more easily.

## General

Charney, Israel. *Encyclopaedia of Genocide,* 2 vols. Santa Barbara: ABC-Clio, 1999.
Chomsky, Noam. *Hegemony or Survival: America's Quest for Global Dominance.* London: Hamish Hamilton, 2003.
——. *9/11.* New York: Seven Stories Press, 2001.
——. *Rogue States: The Rule of Force in World Affairs.* London: Pluto Press, 2000.
——. *World Orders, Old and New.* London: Pluto Press, 1994.
Dallas, Roland. *King Hussein: A Life on the Edge.* London: Profile Books, 1999.
Ghadaffi, Moammar. *Escape to Hell and Other Stories.* London: Blake, 1999.
Gilbert, Martin. *The Holocaust: The Jewish Tragedy.* London: Collins, 1986.
Halliday, Fred. *Two Hours That Shook the World: September 11, 2001: Causes and Consequences.* London: Saqi Books, 2002.
Kalashnikov, Mikhail. *From a Stranger's Doorstep to the Kremlin Gates: A Word from the AK Man.* Moscow: Military Parade Ltd., 1997.
Makiya, Kanan. *Cruelty and Silence: War, Tyranny, Uprising and the Arab World.* London: Jonathan Cape, 1993.
Meissonnier, Martin, Frédéric Loore, and Roger Trilling. *Uranium Appauvri: La Guerre Invisible.* Paris: Laffont, 2001.
Minghella, Anthony. *The English Patient* (screenplay). London: Methuen, 1997.
Morris, James. *The Market of Seleukia.* London: Faber & Faber, 1957.
Rodinson, Maxime. *Mohammed.* London: Penguin, 1971.

Ruthven, Malise. *Islam in the World.* London: Penguin, 1984.
Said, Edward. *Orientalism.* New York: Vintage Books, 1979.
Steinbeck, John. *Once There Was a War.* London: William Heinemann, 1959.
Summerskill, Michael. *China on the Western Front: Britain's Chinese Work Force in the First World War.* London: Michael Summerskill, 1982.
Woodhouse, C. M. *Something Ventured.* London: Granada, 1982.
Yallop, David. *To the Ends of the Earth: The Hunt for the Jackal.* London: Corgi, 1994.

## Middle East History

Antonius, George. *The Arab Awakening: The Story of the Arab National Movement.* London: Hamish Hamilton, 1969.
Armstrong, Karen. *Holy War: The Crusades and Their Impact on Today's World.* London: Papermac Macmillan, 1991.
Chomsky, Noam. *Middle East Illusions.* Lanham, Md.: Rowman and Littlefield, 2003.
———. *Peace in the Middle East? Reflections on Justice and Nationhood.* London: Fontana/Collins, 1974.
Cohen, Michael J. *Palestine: Retreat from the Mandate, The Making of British Police 1936–1945.* London: Paul Elek, 1978.
Cooper, Artemis. *Cairo in the War 1939–1945.* London: Hamish Hamilton, 1989.
Cragg, Kenneth. *The Arab Christian: A History in the Middle East.* London: Mowbray/Cassell, 1992.
Fournie, Pierre, and Jena-Louis Riccioli. *La France et le Proche-Orient 1916–1946: Une chronique photographique de la présence française en Syrie et au Liban, en Palestine, au Hedjaz et en Cilicie.* Tournai, Belgium: Department Beaux-Livres/Voyage des Editions Casterman, 1996.
Fromkin, David. *A Peace to End All Peace: Creating the Modern Middle East 1914–1922.* London: André Deutsch, 1989.
Gouraud, Philippe. *Le General Henri Gouraud au Liban et en Syrie 1919–1923.* Paris: l'Harmattan, 1993.
Green, Stephen. *Living by the Sword: America and Israel in the Middle East 1968–1987.* London: Faber & Faber, 1988.
Heikal, Mohamed. *Sphinx and Commissar: The Rise and Fall of Soviet Influence in the Middle East.* London: Collins, 1978.
Hirst, David. *The Gun and the Olive Branch: The Roots of Violence in the Middle East.* London: Faber & Faber, 1984; and New York: Thunder's Mouth Press, Nation Books, 2003.
Housepian, Marjorie. *Smyrna 1922: The Destruction of a City.* London: Faber & Faber, 1972.
Howard, Harry N. *The King-Crane Commission: An American Enquiry into the Middle East.* Beirut: Khayats, 1963.
Maalouf, Amin. *The Crusades Through Arab Eyes.* New York: Schocken Books, 1984.
Menocal, Maria Rosa. *The Ornament of the World: How Muslims, Jews, and Christians Created a Culture of Tolerance in Medieval Spain.* New York: Little, Brown, 2002.
Runciman, Steven. *A History of the Crusades,* 3 vols. Cambridge: Cambridge University Press, 1951, 1952, 1954.
Shlaim, Avi. *The Politics of Partition: King Abdullah, the Zionists and Palestine 1921–1951.* Oxford University Press, 1990.
———. *War and Peace in the Middle East: A Concise History.* London: Penguin, 1995.
Warner, Geoffrey. *Iraq and Syria 1941.* London: Davis-Poynter, 1974.
Wheatcroft, Andrew. *Infidels: A History of the Conflict between Christendom and Islam.* New York: Random House, 2004.
Zadka, Saul. *Blood in Zion: How the Jewish Guerrillas Drove the British out of Palestine.* London: Brassey's, 1995.

## Afghanistan

Borovik, Artyom. *The Hidden War: A Russian Journalist's Account of the Soviet War in Afghanistan.* London: Faber & Faber, 1990.

Burnes, Lt. Col. Sir Alexander. *Cabool: A Personal Narrative of a Journey To, and Residence In that City, in the Years 1836, 7 and 8.* Original publisher unknown, 1841; reprinted Karachi: Indus Publications, 1986.

Cooley, John K. *Unholy Wars: Afghanistan, America and International Terrorism.* London: Pluto Press, 1999.

Fullerton, John. *The Soviet Occupation of Afghanistan.* Hong Kong: Far Eastern Economic Review, 1986.

Griffiths, John C. *Afghanistan: A History of Conflict.* London: André Deutsch, 1981.

Macrory, Patrick. *Signal Catastrophe: The Story of the Disastrous Retreat from Kabul 1842.* London: Hodder & Stoughton, 1966.

Miller, Charles. *Khyber: The Story of the North West Frontier.* London: Macdonald & Jane's, 1977.

Mills, H. Woosnam. *The Pathan Revolt in North West India.* Lahore: Civil and Military Gazette Press, 1897, reprinted Lahore: Sang-e-Meel Publications, 1979.

Newell, Nancy Peabody and Richard S. *The Struggle for Afghanistan.* London: Cornell University Press, 1981.

Rashid, Ahmed. *Taliban: Islam, Oil and the New Great Game in Central Asia.* London: I. B. Tauris, 2001.

Sykes, Brig. Gen. Sir Percy. *The Right Honourable Sir Mortimer Durand, P.C., G.C.M.G., K.C.S.I., K.C.I.E.* London: Cassell, 1926; reprinted Lahore: Al Biruni, 1977.

Warburton, Sir Robert. *Eighteen Years in the Khyber 1879–1898.* London: John Murray, 1900, reprinted Karachi: Oxford University Press, 1975.

## Algeria

Aggoun, Lounis, and Jean-Baptiste Rivoire. *Francealgérie, crimes et mensonges d'Etats: Histoire Secrète, de la guerre d'indépendance à la "troisième guerre" d'Algérie.* Paris: La Découverte, 2004.

Behr, Edward. *The Algerian Problem.* London: Penguin, 1961.

Borge, Jacques, and Nicolas Viasnoff. *Archives de l'Algérie.* Paris: Michele Trinckvel, 1995.

Connelly, Matthew. *A Diplomatic Revolution: Algeria's Fight for Independence and the Origins of the Post–Cold War Era.* Oxford: Oxford University Press, 2002.

Galibert, Léon. *L'Algérie: Ancienne et Moderne depuis les premiers établissements des Carthaginois jusqu'à la prise de la smalah d'Abd-El-Kader.* Paris: Furne, 1844.

Horne, Alistair. *A Savage War of Peace: Algeria 1954–1962.* London: Pan Books, 2002.

Soouaidia, Habib. *La Sale Guerre.* Paris: La Découverte, 2001.

## Armenia

Balakian, Peter. *The Burning Tigris: The Armenian Genocide and America's Response.* London: Heinemann, 2004; New York: HarperCollins, 2003.

——. *Black Dog of Fate: A Memoir.* New York: HarperCollins, 1997.

Dadrian, Vahakn N. *The History of the Armenian Genocide: Ethnic Conflict from the Balkans to Anatolia to the Caucasus.* Oxford and Providence: Berghahn Books, 1995.

Lang, David Marshall. *The Armenians: A People in Exile.* London: Unwin, 1988.

Walker, Christopher J. *Armenia: The Survival of a Nation.* New York: St. Martin's Press, 1980.

## Egypt

Heikal, Mohamed. *Cutting the Lion's Tail: Suez Through Egyptian Eyes.* London: André Deutsch, 1986.

——. *Autumn of Fury: The Assassination of Sadat.* London: André Deutsch, 1983.

——. *The Road to Ramadan.* New York: Ballantine, 1975.

Hirst, David, with Irene Beeson. *Sadat.* London: Faber & Faber, 1982.

Love, Kennett. *Suez: The Twice Fought War.* London: Longman, 1969.

Lucas, W. Scott. W. *Divided We Stand: Britain, the U.S. and the Suez Crisis.* London: Hodder & Stoughton, 1991.

Shaw, Tony. *Eden, Suez and the Mass Media: Propaganda and Persuasion During the Suez Crisis.* London: I. B. Tauris, 1996.

El-Shazly, Saad. *The Crossing of Suez: The October War (1973)*. London: Third World Centre for Research and Publishing, 1980.
Vatikiotis, P. J. *The History of Modern Egypt: From Muhammad Ali to Mubarak*. London: Weidenfeld & Nicolson, 1991.

## The Gulf

Abukhalil, As'ad. *The Battle for Saudi Arabia: Royalty, Fundamentalism, and Global Power.* New York: Seven Stories Press, 2004.
Aburish, Said K. *A Brutal Friendship: The West and the Arab Elite*. London: Indigo, 1998.
Holden, David, and Richard Johns. *The House of Saud*. London: Sidgwick & Jackson, 1981.

## Iran

Bill, James A. *The Eagle and the Lion: The Tragedy of American–Iranian Relations*. New Haven and London: Yale University Press, 1988.
Bullock, John, and Harvey Morris. *The Gulf War: Its Origins, History and Consequences*. London: Methuen, 1989.
Ebtekar, Massoumeh, as told to Fred A. Reed. *Takeover in Tehran: The Inside Story of the 1979 U.S. Embassy Capture.* Vancouver: Talonbooks, 2000.
Graham, Robert. *Iran: The Illusion of Power.* London: Croom Helm, 1978.
Halliday, Fred. *Iran: Dictatorship and Development*. London: Penguin, 1979.
——. *The Imposed War: Defence versus Aggression,* 5 vols. Tehran: War Information Headquarters, Supreme Defence Council, 1983–87.
Kapuscinski, Ryszard. *Shah of Shahs*. London: Pan, 1986.
Al-Khomeini, Imam Ruhallah al-Musawi. *The Greatest Jihad: Combat with the Self.* Tehran: Islamic Thought Foundation, 1995.
——. *The Last Message: The Political and Divine Will of His Holiness*. Tehran: Imam Khomeini Cultural Institute, 1992.
——. *Manifest of the Islamic Revolution*. Tehran: Ali Akbar Ashtiani, 1987.
Rogers, Will and Sharon. *Storm Center: The USS* Vincennes *and Iran Air Flight 655.* Annapolis, Md.: Naval Institute Press, 1992.
Roosevelt, Kermit. *Countercoup: The Struggle for the Control of Iran*. New York: McGraw-Hill, 1979.
Shawcross, William. *The Shah's Last Ride: The Story of the Exile, Misadventures and Death of The Emperor.* London: Chatto & Windus, 1989.

## Iraq

Attiyah, Ghassan R. *Iraq: 1908–1921. A Socio-Political Study*. Beirut: Arab Institute for Research and Publishing, 1973.
Aziz, HRH Gen. Khaled bin Sultan bin Abdul, with Patrick Seale. *Desert Warrior: A Personal View of the Gulf War by the Joint Forces Commander*. London: HarperCollins, 1995.
Bellamy, Christopher. *Expert Witness: A Defence Correspondent's Gulf War 1990–1991*. London: Brassey's, 1993.
de la Billière, Gen. Sir Peter. *Storm Command: A Personal Account of the Gulf War.* London: HarperCollins, 1992.
Cockburn, Andrew, and Patrick Cockburn. *Out of the Ashes: The Resurrection of Saddam Hussein*. New York: HarperCollins, 1999.
Heikal, Mohamed. *Illusions of Triumph: An Arab View of the Gulf War*. London: HarperCollins, 1992.
Hussein, Saddam. *Social and Foreign Affairs in Iraq*. London: Croom Helm, 1979.
Kelly, Michael. *Martyr's Day: Chronicle of a Small War.* London: Macmillan, 1993.
Makiya, Kanan. *Republic of Fear: The Politics of Modern Iraq* (written under the name of Samir al-Khalil). London: Hutchinson, 1989.
Parish, Daphne, with Pat Lancaster. *Prisoner in Baghdad*. London: Chapmans, 1992.
Pollack, Kenneth M. *The Threatening Storm: The Case for Invading Iraq*. New York: Random House, 2002.

Popovic, Alexandre. *The Revolt of African Slaves in Iraq in the 3rd/9th Century.* Princeton, N.J.: Markus Wiener, 1999.

Rampton, Sheldon and John Stauber. *Weapons of Mass Deception: The Uses of Propaganda in Bush's War on Iraq.* London: Constable & Robinson, 2003.

Ritter, Scott (and William Rivers Pitt). *War on Iraq: What Team Bush Doesn't Want You to Know.* London: Profile Books, 2002.

Schwarzkopf, Gen. H. Norman, with Peter Petrie. *The Autobiography: It Doesn't Take a Hero.* London: Bantam Press, 1992.

Simons, Geoff. *The Scourging of Iraq: Sanctions, Law and Natural Justice.* London: Macmillan Press, 1998; New York: St. Martin's Press, 1998.

Timmerman, Kenneth R. *The Death Lobby: How the West Armed Iraq.* London: Fourth Estate, 1992.

Winstone, H. V. F. *Gertrude Bell.* London: Barzan Publishing, 2004.

Woodward, Bob. *The Commanders.* London: Simon & Schuster, 1991.

Zucchino, David. *Thunder Run: Three Days in the Battle for Baghdad.* London: Atlantic Books, 2004.

## Lebanon and Syria

Fisk, Robert. *Pity the Nation: Lebanon at War.* London: André Deutsch, 1990; updated editions from Oxford University Press, 2003, and New York: Nation Books, 2003.

Khoury, Gérard D. *La France et l'Orient Arabe. Naissance du Liban Moderne 1914–1920.* Paris: Armand Colin, 1993.

Longrigg, Stephen Hemsley. *Syria and Lebanon under French Mandate.* London: Royal Institute of International Affairs, 1958; reprinted Beirut: Librairie du Liban, 1968.

Saad-Ghorayeb, Amal. *Hizbullah: Politics and Religion.* London: Pluto Press, 2002.

Salibi, Kamal. *A House of Many Mansions: The History of Lebanon Reconsidered.* London: I. B. Tauris, 1988.

Seale, Patrick. *Asad: The Struggle for the Middle East.* London: I. B. Tauris, 1988.

Van Dam, Nikolaos. *The Struggle for Power in Syria: Politics and Society under Asad and the Ba'th Party.* London: I. B. Tauris, 1996.

Yammine, Antoine. *Quatre Ans de Misère: Le Liban et la Syrie Pendant la Guerre.* Cairo: Imprimerie Emin Hindie, 1922.

## Israel and Palestine

Abbas, Mahmoud (Abu Mazen). *Through Secret Channels.* London: Garnet, 1995.

Aburish, Said K. *Arafat: From Defender to Dictator.* London: Bloomsbury, 1998.

Ashrawi, Hanan. *This Side of Peace: A Personal Account.* New York: Simon & Schuster, 1995.

Bethell, Nicholas. *The Palestine Triangle: The Struggle between the British, the Jews and the Arabs, 1935–48.* London: André Deutsch, 1979.

Chomsky, Noam. *The Fateful Triangle: The United States, Israel and the Palestinians.* London: Pluto Press, 1983.

Elpeleg, Zvi. *The Grand Mufti: Haj Amin al-Husseini, Founder of the Palestinian National Movement.* London: Frank Cass, 1993.

Gilbert, Martin. *Israel: A History.* London: Doubleday, 1988.

Gilmour, David. *Dispossessed: The Ordeal of the Palestinians 1917–1980.* London: Sidgwick & Jackson, 1980.

Hass, Amira. *Drinking the Sea at Gaza: Days and Nights in a Land Under Siege.* New York: Henry Holt, 1996.

Heikal, Mohamed. *The Secret Channels: The Inside Story of Arab–Israeli Peace Negotiations.* London: HarperCollins, 1986.

Hersh, Seymour. *The Samson Option: Israel, America and the Bomb.* London: Faber & Faber, 1991.

Hirst, David. *The Gun and the Olive Branch: The Roots of Violence in the Middle East.* New York: Nation Books, 2003.

Khalidi, Walid, ed. *All That Remains: The Palestinian Villages Occupied and Depopulated by Israel in 1948.* Washington, D.C.: Institute for Palestine Studies, 1992.

Morris, Benny. *The Birth of the Palestinian Refugee Problem, 1945–49*. Cambridge: Cambridge University Press, 1987.

——. *Righteous Victims: A History of the Zionist–Arab Conflict 1881–1999*. London: John Murray, 1999.

Nazzal, Nafez. *The Palestinian Exodus from Galilee 1948*. Beirut: Institute for Palestine Studies, 1978.

Said, Edward. *The Politics of Dispossession: The Struggle for Palestinian Self-Determination 1969–1994*. London: Chatto & Windus, 1994.

——. *The Question of Palestine*. New York: Times Books, 1979.

Schleifer, Abdullah. *The Fall of Jerusalem*. New York: Monthly Review Press, 1972.

Shahak, Israel. *Jewish History, Jewish Religion: The Weight of Three Thousand Years*. London: Pluto Press, 1994.

——. *Open Secrets: Israeli Nuclear and Foreign Policies*. London: Pluto Press, 1997.

Sharon, Ariel, with David Chanoff. *Warrior: An Autobiography*. London: Macdonald, 1989.

## Journalism

Arnett, Peter. *Live from the Battlefield: From Vietnam to Baghdad. 35 Years in the World's War Zones*. London: Bloomsbury, 1994.

Cameron, James. *Point of Departure: Experiment in Biography*. London: Granada, 1980.

Ferro, Marc. *L'Information en uniforme: Propagande, désinformation, censure, et manipulation*. Paris: Editions Ramsay, 1991.

Said, Edward. *Covering Islam*. New York: Pantheon Books, 1981.

Thomson, Alex. *Smokescreen: The Media, the Censors, the Gulf*. London: Spellmount, 1992.

Zaidan, Ahmad Muaffaq. *The "Afghan Arabs": Media at Jihad*. Islamabad: Pakistan Futuristics Foundation and Institute, 1999.

## 1914–1918 War

Churchill, Winston. *The Great War*, 4 vols. London: George Newnes, The Home Library Book Company, 1933.

Moore, William. *The Thin Yellow Line*. London: Leo Cooper, 1974.

Oram, Gerard. *Worthless Men: Race, Eugenics and the Death Penalty in the British Army During the First World War*. London: Francis Boutle, 1998.

Summerskill, Michael. *China on the Western Front: Britain's Chinese Work Force in the First World War*. London: Michael Summerskill, 1982.

## Select Documents

Arnove, Anthony, ed. *Iraq Under Siege: The Deadly Impact of Sanctions and War*. Cambridge, Massachusetts: South End Press, 2000.

Aruri, Naser, ed. *Palestinian Refugees: The Right of Return*. London: Pluto Press, 2001.

Asfour, John Mikhail, trans. and ed. *When the Words Burn: An Anthology of Modern Arabic Poetry, 1945–1987*. Dunvegan, Ontario: Cormorant Books, 1988.

B'Tselem. *Activity of the Undercover Units in the Occupied Territories*. Jerusalem: B'Tselem, 1992.

Byrne, Malcolm, and Peter Kornbluh, eds. *The Iran–Contra Scandal: A National Security Archive Documents Reader*. New York: Norton & Co., 1993.

Catalinotto, John, and Sara Flounders, eds. *Metal of Dishonor: How the Pentagon Radiates Soldiers and Civilians with DU Weapons*. New York: International Action Center, 1999.

Dadrian, Vahakn N. "The Historical and Legal Interconnections Between the Armenian Genocide and the Jewish Holocaust: From Impunity to Retributive Justice." *Yale Journal of International Law*, Vol. 23, Number 2, Summer 1998.

*Documents from the U.S. Espionage Den*, compiled by Muslim Students Following the Line of the Imam. Tehran: The Centre for the Publication of the U.S. Espionage Den's Documents, 1987.

The Egyptian Organisation for Human Rights. *The Condition of Human Rights in Egypt*. Cairo: EOHR, 1993; *Recurrent Detention: Prisoners without Trial*. Cairo: EOHR, 1993–94; *Free-*

*dom of Opinion and Belief: Restrictions and Dilemmas.* Cairo: EOHR, 1994; *Democracy Jeopardized: Nobody "Passed" the Elections.* Cairo: EOHR, 1995.

*The Geneva Conventions of August 12 1949.* Geneva: ICRC Publications, permanently reprinted; *Protocols Additional to the Geneva Conventions of 12 August 1949.* Geneva: ICRC Publications, 1996.

*La France en Guerre d'Algérie,* sous la direction de Laurent Gervereau, Jean-Pierre Rioux, and Benjamin Stora. Paris: BDIC, 1992.

Girardet, Edward and Jonathan Walter, ed. *Afghanistan.* Geneva and Dublin: International Centre for Humanitarian Reporting, 1998.

*Human Rights in Iraq.* Yale University Press, Middle East Watch Books, 1990.

*Imperial Gazetteer of India: Afghanistan and Nepal.* Oxford: Clarendon Press, *c.*1910, reprinted Lahore: Sang-e-Meel Publications, 1979.

*Iraq's Weapons of Mass Destruction: The Assessment of the British Government.* London: The Stationery Office, 2002.

*Libya Under Gaddafi.* Chicago, Illinois: National Front for the Salvation of Libya, 1992.

MacArthur, Brian, ed. *Despatches from the Gulf War.* London: Bloomsbury, 1991.

Magnier, Grace. *Images des Morisques dans la Littérature et les Arts* ("Distorted Images: Anti-Islamic Propaganda at the Time of the Expulsion of the Moriscos"). Zaghouan, Tunisia: Fondation Temimi pour la Recherche Scientifique et l'Information, 1999.

*Les Mensonges du Golfe.* Montpellier: Arlea-Reporters sans frontières, 1992.

*Needless Deaths in the Gulf War: Civilian Casualties During the Air Campaign and Violation of the Laws of War.* New York: Middle East Watch Report, 1991.

Peltekian, Katia Minas, comp. *Heralding of the Armenian Genocide: Reports in the Halifax Herald 1894–1922.* Halifax, NS, Canada: Armenian Cultural Association of the Atlantic Provinces, 2000.

Reshtia, Sayed Qassem. *The Price of Liberty: The Tragedy of Afghanistan* (no publisher listed, 1982).

Sarafian, Ara, comp. *United States Official Records of the Armenian Genocide.* London: Gomidas Institute, 2004.

*The Second Afghan War 1878–80: Official Account.* Produced in the Intelligence Branch, Army Headquarters, India. London: John Murray, 1908.

Sifry, Micah L. and Christopher Cerf, eds. *The Gulf War Reader: History, Documents, Opinions.* London: Times Books/Random House, 1991.

*Tears, Blood and Cries: Human Rights in Afghanistan Since the Invasion 1979–1984.* New York: Helsinki Watch, 1984.

*The Tower Commission Report: The Full Text of the President's Special Review Board.* New York: Bantam Books & Times Books, 1987.

# Chronology

570    Birth of Prophet Mohammed

790    Islam will become the dominant religion in the Middle East

1095    First Crusade to "liberate" the Holy Land; there will be seven more over the next 186 years

1187    Salahedin's victory over the Crusaders at the Battle of Hittin; fall of Jerusalem to Muslim forces; henceforth the Middle East will be ruled by caliphates, including the Fatimids, Mamelukes and Ottomans

1798–1801    Napoleon's Egyptian expedition

1914    4 August, outbreak of the First World War

1915    British and Commonwealth troops land at Gallipoli

Start of the Armenian Holocaust; murder of 1.5 million Armenians by Ottoman Turks

British forces besieged at Kut al-Amara, Mesopotamia by the Ottoman Turkish army

Turks begin hanging Arabs in Beirut for demanding independence

1916    Sykes–Picot Agreement between France and Britain to share Syria, Jordan, Iraq and most of the Arabian peninsula

1917    Balfour Declaration giving British support for "establishment in Palestine of a national home for the Jewish people"

General Sir Stanley Maude enters Baghdad after British invasion of Mesopotamia (Iraq); a subsequent Iraqi insurgency against British rule costs thousands of lives

General Sir Edmund Allenby enters Jerusalem, routing Ottoman Turkish forces

1918    President Woodrow Wilson's Fourteen Points

Damascus falls to the Allies; King Faisal in Damascus

11 November armistice ends the First World War

1919    Treaty of Versailles

Britain awarded Mandates for Palestine and Iraq; France awarded Syria

1920    French General Henri Gouraud creates Lebanon from Syrian territory

Treaty of Sèvres negotiated between the Ottoman empire and the Allies (with the exception of Russia and the United States) agreed to the autonomy of Kurdistan, but was neither ratified nor implemented

Ottoman empire collapses

French eject Faisal from Damascus

1921    Hashemites become kings in Transjordan and Iraq

1936   Arab revolt in Palestine

1939   3 September, outbreak of the Second World War

1941   Overthrow of Rashid Ali's pro-German regime in Baghdad

       Grand Mufti of Jerusalem Haj Amin al-Husseini travels to Berlin

1942   Arab and Jews fight together in Palestine Brigade at el-Alamein

1945   8 May, end of the Second World War in Europe and Nazi Holocaust of six million Jews

1948   Creation of State of Israel; 750,000 Palestinian Arabs ejected from their land

1954   Start of Algerian war of independence against France

1956   Suez crisis; Britain, France and Israel invade Egypt after Nasser nationalises the Suez Canal

1962   Monarchy overthrown in Iraq

       Algeria wins independence from France

1967   Six Day War; Israel occupies Gaza, West Bank, Golan and Sinai

1968   UN Security Council Resolution 242 demands withdrawal of Israeli forces from occupied territory in return for security of all states in the region

1973   Yom Kippur War; Israel defeats Egyptian–Syrian forces

1975   Start of Lebanese civil war

1977   President Sadat of Egypt makes peace with Israel

1978   First Israeli invasion of Lebanon

       Saddam Hussein takes over Baath Party in Iraq

1979   Shah of Iran overthrown by Ayatollah Khomeini's Islamic Revolution

       Soviet Union invades Afghanistan; the start of a ten-year occupation by Russian troops

       Assassination of Egyptian President Anwar Sadat

1980   Osama bin Laden raises an Arab legion to fight the Soviet Army

       With America's tacit support, Iraq invades Iran at the start of an eight-year war in which gas will be used in mass attacks for the first time since the First World War

1982   Second Israeli invasion of Lebanon

       16 to 18 September, massacre of up to 1,700 Palestinian civilians after Israeli defence minister Ariel Sharon sends Israel's Lebanese militia allies into the refugee camps of Sabra and Shatila to destroy "terrorists"

1983   23 October, suicide bombing of U.S. Marine Headquarters in Beirut, killing 241 U.S. personnel

1986   First Palestinian intifada against Israeli occupation

1988   USS *Vincennes* shoots down Iranian Airbus passenger airliner over Gulf with the loss of 290 Lives

       Iran sues for peace with Iraq

       December, a bomb destroys U.S. airliner over Lockerbie, Scotland, with the loss of 270 lives

1990 Saddam Hussein invades Kuwait; start of UN sanctions against Iraq which in the next eight years will cause the deaths of 500,000 children

1991 U.S.-led Western and Arab forces liberate Kuwait

1992 Algerian army demands suspension of democratic elections in advance of Islamic party victory; start of eight-year "civil" war in which at least 150,000 Algerians will die

Outbreak of the Bosnian war

1993 September, Oslo Agreement between Israel and the PLO

1995 Yassir Arafat enters Gaza

1996 Osama bin Laden moves from Sudan to Afghanistan

1998 In Afghanistan, Osama bin Laden announces the creation of al-Qaeda, dedicated to the expulsion of Western forces from Muslim lands

2000 Israeli forces retreat from southern Lebanon after 22-year occupation

September, second Palestinian Intifada

2001 11 September, suicide pilots destroy the World Trade Center and part of the Pentagon at a loss of nearly 3,000 lives; President Bush and Prime Minister Blair announce they are fighting a "war on terror"

October, United States begins bombardment of Afghanistan and Osama bin Laden forces, culminating in the overthrow of the Taliban regime

2003 March, Anglo–U.S. invasion of Iraq

9 April, U.S. occupation of Baghdad

28 April, U.S. troops kill 14 protesters in Fallujah; start of the insurrection against U.S. occupying forces

12 December, capture of Saddam Hussein in Iraq

2004 U.S. forces twice lay siege to the Iraqi city of Fallujah; war between U.S. forces and Iraqi Shia militia of Muqtada al-Sadr

2005 Up to 100,000 Iraqi civilians have died since the start of the invasion and by mid-Summer more than 1,700 American troops; Iraq elects its first government in 30 years but descends into anarchy with U.S. forces repeatedly bombing Iraqi insurgents. Thousands of civilians—Iraqis, Western journalists, aid workers and Western mercenaries—are held hostage and many are murdered.

Yassir Arafat dies; Mahmoud Abbas appointed president in Palestinian elections; Israeli prime minister Ariel Sharon announces an Israeli withdrawal from Gaza but Jewish colonies on the occupied Palestinian West Bank continue to expand

Lebanon's former prime minister Rafiq Hariri is murdered in Beirut

Syria withdraws the last of its troops from Lebanon under UN Security Council Resolution 1559; UN Security Council Resolution 242 of 1968—calling for Israeli withdrawal from occupied land—remains unfulfilled

# Index

Abadan, Iran, 104, 181–3, 185–6, 199, 226, 284
Abadi, Parvis Habib, 285
Abayat, Hussein, 470*4*
Abbais, Zaman, 962
Abbas, Faisal, 729
Abbas, Mahmoud, 842*n,* 1026–7
Abbas, Matar and Ghaniyeh, 731–2
Abbas, Mohamed Abul, *see* Abul Abbas, Mohamed
Abbas, Lieut. Colonel Mohamed Reza Jaffar, 256*n*
Abbas, Najla, 940
Abbas, Noaman, 994
Abbas, Rasha, 731
Abda, Sami, 502
Abdali, 695–7
Abdel-Kader, Sundus, 743
Abdelkader (Algerian resistance leader), 517, 547
Abdessalam, Inspector (Algeria), 579
Abdesselam, Belaïd, 541
Abdul-Emir, Karrar, 730, 731
Abdul Hamid, Ottoman Sultan, 320
Abdul-Jaber, Abdul-Setar, 988, 990
Abdullah, Crown Prince of Saudi Arabia, 621
Abdullah, Hamzi, 813
Abdullah, Private Jamal, 642
Abdullah, Maher, 970
al-Abdullah, Mohamed, 946
Abdullah, Mullah, 870–1
Abdullah, Tareq, 731
Abdullah I, King of Transjordan (*earlier* Emir), 148, 801, 804
Abdullah II, King of Jordan, 755, 801, 803–4, 805–6
Abdul-Malikian, Mohamed Reza, 280–1, 290
Abdul-Meguid, Esmat, 726
Abdul-Nabi, Fawzia, 732–3
Abdulrazek, Ali, 973–4
Abdul-Shakour, 892, 893, 894
Abdul-Wahab, Mohamed Ibn, 847, 849
Abdur Rahman, Afghan king, 39–40
Abed, Hani, 433
Aboud, Ahmed, 574
Abu Aidi, Samir, 490
Abu Arrar, Mohamed, 487
Abu Dhabi: arms bazaar, 748–50, 751–3, 755, 757*n*

Abu Ghraib prison, Baghdad, 156–8, 169, 276, 640*n*, 985, 1011, 1015–17, 1019–22
Abujahjah, Najla, 775–7, 783
Abul Abbas, Mohamed (Mohamed Zeidan), 380–1, 1022–4
Abul Abbas, Reem, 1022–4
Abu-Nadi, Ismail, 503–4
Abu-Nadi, Mohamed, 503–4
abu-Rajab, Samir, 492–3
Abu Srur, Judge Fathi, 490–1
Abu Zeid, Inas, 482–3
*Achille Lauro* (cruise liner), 380–1, 1022
Ackerman, Piers, 269, 271
*Active,* HMS, 250
Adams, Major Robert Roy, 71
Adelman, Kenneth, 910
Aden: USS *Cole* attacked in, 225, 443
al-Adib, Abu Bital, 662*n*
Adnan Khairallah Martyr Hospital, Baghdad, 968–9
Adora, 499–500
Adsetts, Corporal A.D., 956
Adwan, Imad, 734
Afghanistan: Afghan casualties, 90; Afghan soldiers in, 49–50, 62, 74, 77–8; Algerian fighters in, 28–9, 33, 526, 535, 582–3; Arab training camps in, 928; attacks on Americans, 896, 927; author departs from, 90–1; author reports from, 46–52; author travels in, 62–9; bandit groups and dissidents in, 77; bin Laden attacked by U.S. in, 791; bin Laden finds refuge in, 23–4, 25; border with British India agreed, 39–40, 43–4; British wars with, 3, 37–40, 44, 857–8; casualties, 861–3; civilian deaths, 898*n*-9*n*; Clinton bombs, 722; conditions, 3; discussed at Qatar conference (October 2001), 857; hostility to strangers, 52–3; humanitarian work in, 896–7, 899; local allies of U.S.A. (Afghan Special Forces), 897; lorry art, 61; monarchy in, 79–80; oil pipeline, 28; opium production and exports, 15–16, 862, 863, 1014, 1037*n*; political upheavals (1970s), 44–5; President Carter's pledge to, 859; prisoners interrogated, 911–12; reforms under Amanullah, 44*n*; refugees leave, 868–71; religious leadership in, 79–80;

Afghanistan: *(continued)*
    resentment at U.S. presence, 897;
    revolutionary reforms resented, 77–8;
    Russian mines in, 18; Soviet army
    invades, 5, 7–8, 17, 40–2, 173; Soviet
    atrocities in, 175; Soviet enforced
    policies in, 58; Soviet forces and
    equipment in, 40, 45–50, 52; Soviet road
    building in, 44, 60; Taliban regime in,
    25–7, 849–50, 851, 859–60; *Times*
    withdraws correspondents from, 90*n*;
    U.S. actions in, 891–8, 928; U.S.
    casualties in, 1014; U.S. claims success
    in, 1014; U.S. journalists expelled, 69;
    U.S. post-9/11 attacks on, 841, 846–7,
    854–5, 857, 858, 859–60, 863–4, 867,
    869; U.S. Special Forces in, 892, 895,
    911–12; war crimes in, 864–5; wish for
    independence, 1037
Aflaq, Michel, 149, 811
Afri, Monique, 545
Afula, Israel, 419
Aghajanian, Astrid, 352–4
Aghajanian, Gaspar, 353
Agnew, Spiro, 100
Ahmad, Aziz Salih, 681*n,* 909–10
Ahmadzadeh, Massoud, 99*n*
Ahmed, Dr. (Baghdad anaesthetist), 952
Ahmed, Amna, 730
Ahmed, Faraj el-Sayed, 828
Ahmed, Fayyez, 871, 872, 875
Ahmed, Haitham, 738
Ahmed, Hocine Aït, 524
Ahmed, Captain Majid, 996
Ahmed, Mohamed, 660
Ahmed, Sikder Mokaddes, 874
Ahmed, Tariq, 653
Ahmed, Zulaika Mustafa, 215–16
Ahmmadvande, Shojae, 283–4
Ahwaz, 234–5, 240–1
Aideed, Mohamed, 10
Aïn Defla, Algeria, 546, 547–8
Air France: airliner hijacked by Algerian
    Islamists (1994), 557*n*, 583; on
    Armenian massacres, 344*n*
Aïssa, Amari, 537
Ajami, Fouad, 923
"Ajax, Operation," 94–5, 114, 117
AK-47 rifle, 759, 773
Akat, Mehmet, 348
Akbazadeh, Sergeant, 257
Akçam, Taner, 350, 351
Akora Khattak, Pakistan, 850
Alaf, Mouaffaq, 388
*Al-Ahram* (newspaper), 207*n*
Alameh, Abdel Nasser, 831
Alamyar, Sidaq, 86
Alawi, Ahmed Hassan, 994
Alawite sect (Shiite), 204, 820–1
Al-Bakr, 181
Albala, Nuri, 99*n*

Albright, Madeleine: at Assad's funeral, 819;
    on effect of UN sanctions in Iraq, 704–5,
    709, 742, 902; meets Netanyahu in
    London, 434–6; offers Arafat "sense of
    sovereignty" over Jerusalem sites, 440;
    on Saddam's use of gas against Kurds,
    721; urges restraint on Israel, 428, 435
Alexander the Great, 37*n*
Alexandretta province and city, 334–5, 818
Alfei Menache, Israel, 427
Alford, Robert, 890
Algarotti, Bob, 780–2, 785–6
Algeria: Algerians killed in war of
    independence, 519–20; assassinations in,
    542–4; atrocities in, 524, 895; Berbers
    in, 536, 584; detention in, 540; disorder
    and repression in, 537–9; economic
    difficulties, 536, 566; elections, 536,
    584; fighters in Afghanistan, 28–9, 33,
    526, 535, 582–3; French colonise (*pieds
    noirs*), 515–20; French war in, 9, 513,
    515, 519–22, 526–7, 1014–15;
    independence, 399; Islamic movement
    in, 529–33, 535–6, 539, 554–5, 558–60,
    562–4, 566–72; martial law imposed
    (1992), 528; massacres, 29, 312, 344,
    468, 506; mutual Muslim betrayals, 520;
    post-independence civil war in, 522–4,
    526–9, 544–6, 557–8
Algiers: barbers in, 539; car bomb in, 558;
    Casbah, 537–9; conditions, 534; police
    actions in, 559–60; Sekardji jail riot,
    559, 563, 564–5
al-Halawi, Sheikh Safar, 848
*Al-Hoot* (tanker), 225
Ali, Imam, 940–1
Ali, Major (Iraqi prison commandant), 232–3
al-Ali, Dr. Jawad Khadim, 732–3, 737–8,
    739–40
Ali, Rashid, 289
al-Ali, Salah Omar, 646–7, 661
Ali, Zubeida Mohamed, 732
Ali (Afghan bus conductor), 51, 69–70, 73–4,
    78*n*, 80, 82–4
Alia Toukan, Queen of Jordan, 802
Ali Khan, Amir Sher, 846*n*
Alipoor, Hamid Kurdi, 212
Al-Jazeera (Qatar TV station): Baghdad
    office hit by U.S. rocket, 970, 972*n*;
    bin Laden broadcasts on, 854–5, 906–7,
    1031–4; Colin Powell accuses of anti-
    Americanism, 854; condemned for pro-
    U.S. bias, 966; inside Kabul, 854; in
    Iraq, 945–7; Kabul office hit by U.S.
    missile, 877*n*; reports Israeli
    reoccupation of Jenin, 503; upsets
    Mubarak, 854
Allawi, Iyad, 1004
Allenby, General Edmund Henry Hynman, 1st
    Viscount, 366, 965–6
Allon, Yigal, 506

Alloula, Abdelkader, 559*n*
Alloway, Tony, 170*n*, 177, 240
Almarj, Lebanon, 852
Almog, Brigadier General Doron, 409
Alomari, Abdul Aziz, 33
Alouni, Taiseer, 970
al-Owda, Sheikh Sulieman, 24, 609, 848
al-Qaeda: in Afghanistan, 19, 1014;
    communications methods, 911;
    composition and order of battle, 905*n*;
    dead in Kandahar, 912–13; demands,
    858–9; and insurgency in Iraq, 1033–4;
    and murder of Daniel Pearl, 876; and
    9/11 attacks, 839, 1032–3; resistance in
    Afghanistan, 928; suicide bombers,
    443; U.S. actions against, 904; U.S.
    intelligence fails to penetrate, 911–12
Alrawi, Karim, 559*n*
*Al-Shiraa* (Beirut magazine), 243
*Al-Tanin* (ship), 194–7, 607, 744
*Al-Thawra* (Baathist newspaper), 193
Alwane, Azedine, 564
Alwani, Mohamed Abdullah, 974
Amaid, Mohamed, 951
Amal movement (Lebanon), 163, 242, 365
Amanullah, Afghan king, 44, 61
Amanullah (driver), 871–2, 875
al-Amari, Lieut. Colonel Jaber Hassan, 256*n*
Amariya air raid shelter, Baghdad, 625–8, 984
Al-Amaya, 181
Amer, Major, 1020
Amer, Ibrahim, 463–4
American-Israeli Public Affairs Committee
    (AIPAC), 438
Amiel, Barbara (Lady Black), 924*n*
Amin, Hafizullah, President of Afghanistan,
    8, 44–5, 53, 56, 60, 62, 76, 121
Amin al-Husseini, Haj, Grand Mufti of
    Jerusalem, 148, 356, 358–65, 368,
    385–6, 399
al-Amir, Major General Fahad, 757–8
Amir, Yigal, 430, 462
Amnesty International: on Anglo-American
    torture in Iraq, 1012*n*; appeals for
    investigation on Algerian mass graves,
    584; on Bahai killings, 173; calls for
    investigation into Mazar prison
    massacre, 870; on civilian targets of
    suicide bombers, 479; condemns pre-
    judging of Iraqi murder attempt on Bush,
    715; condemns UN report on Algeria,
    580; demands investigation of French
    executions in Algeria, 521; on executions
    in Iraq, 152, 162, 174, 275–6; and Iran
    executions, 199, 228–9; on Israeli
    assassinations, 466*n*; on Khiam prison
    torture, 268; on killing of children in
    Israel-Palestinian conflict, 511; lists
    Algerian murder victims, 583; on
    Palestinian-Israeli conflict, 433, 496*n*
Amouzegar, Jamshid, 131

Amrani, Yamina, 565
Amundsen, Amber and Craig, 923
Analley, Khreisan, 1012
Andalusia: Moors and Jews expelled (1492),
    1032*n*
Anderson, Robert, 152
Anderson, Terry, 242, 594, 612
Andrews, David, 580
*Anfal* campaign (against Kurds), 215–17, 336
Anglo-Armenian Association, 325*n*
Anglo-Iranian Oil Company (AIOC *later*
    British Petroleum), 94–7
Annan, Kofi, 706, 723, 731, 900, 1004
Ansari, Hushang, 131
anthrax attacks: in U.S.A., 931
Antonius, George, 365, 367, 368, 826
Aoun, Nimr, 371–2
Apollinaire, Guillaume, 294
Araba, 797–9
Arab-Israeli war (1967), 921
Arab League, 409
Arab Revolt, 825–6
Arabs: condemn bombing of Iraq, 726–7;
    elections, 841*n*-2*n*; fearlessness, 481;
    financial cost of First Gulf War, 637*n*;
    fury at West's double standards, 411–12;
    incomers resist Americans in Baghdad,
    976; and Israeli threat, 757–8; leaders
    condemn 9/11 attack, 856; at Madrid
    Middle East Peace, 383–8; in 9/11
    attacks, 840–2; in Palestine, 356, 358–9,
    365, 366–73, 374–5; seek autonomy
    under Ottomans, 822–5; sense of
    historical injustice, 858–9; suspicions of
    U.S.A., 590*n*; warn U.S.A. against war
    with Iraq, 908–9; in wars with Israel,
    377; in Washington talks (1992),
    389–90; in West Bank and Gaza, 403–4;
    Western views of, 802; *see also*
    Palestinians
Arafat, Moussa, 475
Arafat, Yassir: accepts Palestine partition,
    381–2, 394; accused of being Israel's
    man, 425; accused of supporting bin
    Laden, 846; accused of taking time out
    from diplomacy, 441; on Afghanistan,
    858; aims, 380–2; anti-press measures,
    423–4; appearance, 356, 414, 421; Arab
    opponents, 419; at Assad's funeral, 819;
    attends Qatar conference (October
    2001), 856–7; author meets, 123; birth
    and background, 398; blamed for war,
    507; calls for Palestinian state, 443;
    condemned by Arabs for treachery,
    396–7; condemns 9/11 attack, 857; at
    Confrontation Front Summit, 150;
    decline and death, 1026; emotionalism,
    381–2, 397–8; eulogises King Hussein,
    807; excludes 1984 refugees from peace
    plan, 400–1; fate predicted, 487; in Gaza,
    414–18, 419, 421–3; and Haj Amin, 358;

Arafat, Yassir: *(continued)*
  Hamas opposes, 408–9; health decline,
  435; and Hebron agreement, 436;
  intransigence, 359; Israeli opinion of,
  397–8; in Jericho, 418–19; justifies
  Washington negotiations to Arab
  League, 409–10; leadership questioned,
  442–3; leaves Lebanon (1982), 791;
  loses control of guerrilla organisations,
  510; loses popular support, 483; and
  Madrid Middle East Conference, 387–8;
  marriage and child, 398, 483; meets
  Barak at Camp David (2000), 440;
  meets Blair, 434; meets Blair in London,
  858; meets Mubarak, 394; and
  Netanyahu, 434–5; non-condemnation of
  Soviet invasion of Afghanistan, 90, 173;
  Oslo agreement with Rabin, 393, 399,
  407–9, 413–14, 429–30, 436–7, 797;
  purges Palestinians suspected of spying
  for Israel, 470n; in Ramallah, 494,
  501–2, 1024; and rival Islamic
  organisations, 390; secret negotiations
  with Israel, 389–90; security
  organisations, 422–3; shares Nobel
  Peace Prize with Rabin, 424; Sharon
  disparages, 483–4, 490; Sharon offers to
  fly out of Ramallah, 501; short-term
  decision making, 510; sixty-sixth
  birthday celebrations, 421–2; support
  for, 10, 21; supports Saddam, 358, 382;
  and Syrian claims to Golan, 440; Tenet
  threatens, 449–50; as "terrorist,"
  379–80, 390; threatened with
  assassination, 1025; torture practices,
  433; trail (political corridor), 395–7; and
  Wye agreement, 436–8
Arafat, Zahwa (Yassir's daughter), 421–2,
  423
Arafi, Mazin, 811
Arair, Nabil, 442
Ardebili, Ayatollah Musavi, 273
Arjoub, Moussa, 492
Armed Islamic Movement (Algeria), *see*
  Groupe Islamique Armé
Armenia, Soviet Republic of, 333, 686
Armenians: fight for Saddam Hussein, 685–6;
  massacred (1915–22), 308, 316–31, 333,
  336–55, 509n, 685, 865, 1037; in post-
  1919 peace settlement, 332–5, 383
arms supply: international trade, 226–7,
  748–71; by U.S.A., 689–91
Asadapur, Captain (Iranian pilot), 265–6
Ashour, Algeria, 522, 528
Ashrawi, Hanan, 387, 451–2, 489, 900
Askihita, Hasna, 812, 815–16
Aslan, General Ali, 818
Assad, Bashar: Ali al-Majid meets, 926; and
  father's death, 818–19; succeeds to
  father's presidency of Syria, 821
Assad, Basil, 808, 809–11, 821

Assad, Hafez el: appearance, 123; Arafat
  meets in Damascus, 410; attitude to
  Jewish settlements, 386–8; Clinton
  meets, 440; at Confrontational Front
  Summit, Baghdad, 150; crushes Hama
  rising (1982), 608; death and funeral,
  818–21; defences against Israel, 816;
  Hindawi's devotion to, 461; meets
  Saddam and King Hussein in Jordan,
  247; and PLO's claim to part of Golan,
  425, 440; presidential succession on
  death of, 816, 818, 821; rule, 806–8,
  810–12; suppresses Muslim
  Brotherhood, 814–16
Assad, Maher, 818
Assad, Rifat el, 814, 816, 818
al-Assadi, Haidar, 647, 657n
al-Assadi, Maysoon, 1020
Assyrians: massacred by Iraq, 336
al-Atheer nuclear weapons establishment
  (Iraq), 719
atrocities: Israeli, 457–8; against Kurds, 215,
  246; by mujahedin, 155–6; in post-First
  Gulf War Iraq, 663–4; by Russians in
  Afghanistan, 175; against Russians in
  Herat, 53; in Sudan, 11; *see also*
  massacres; torture
Atta, Mohamed, 32–3, 843, 844, 853, 1033
Attaf, Ahmed, 580
Attapour, Faribourz, 110–11
Attar, Leila, 714, 715
Attia, Sayah, 567
Auden, W.H., 139, 259, 985
Auschwitz, 370, 456–7
Ausi, Quhar, 688
Aussaresses, General Paul, 521
Australia: arms dealing, 750; Special Forces
  and humanitarians in Afghanistan, 897,
  899
Austria: arms sales, 766
Avnery, Uri, 508, 932
AWACS planes, 628–30, 643
Awadi, Colonel Mustafa, 634
al-Ayash, Captain Saad Ahmed, 996
Ayash, Yahya, 433, 505
al-Ayashi, Ahlam, 1020
Ayat, Hassan, 199
Ayoub, Tareq, 970, 971
Aysle (Ziad Jarrah's Turkish girlfriend),
  852–3
Azadi, Mustafa, 289
al-Azerbaijani, Bin al-Marzouban, 811
Aziz, Abdul, 20
Aziz, Anwar, 406
Aziz, Tariq: on Bush's dismantling UN, 924n;
  and First Gulf War, 614, 616; and
  invasion of Kuwait, 588; Rumsfeld
  meets, 170, 904; Shultz meets, 210
Azmi, Youssef, 813
Aznar Lopez, José María, 924n
Azzam, Abdullah, 526

Baath party: and acknowledgment of past sins, 821–2; and Alawites, 820; counters "conspiracies," 151; crushed in Iraq, 939; founded, 149, 811; organises 1963 coup, 148–9; regime in Iraq, 166, 167, 481; represses Shias, 162–3, 164–5; Saddam and, 908; secular nature, 821; and suicide bombing, 954–5

Baba, Youssef, 433*n*

Babchohi, Ali, 282–3

Bachari, Abdul Hadi, 152

Badr, Private Assad, 817

al-Baeri, Dr. Khaldoun, 968

Baghdad: Abu Taleb Street massacre, 952, 973; anti-Americanism, 993; and British First War campaign, 139, 141, 142; car bombs, 218; civilians killed and injured in U.S. attacks, 625–8, 937, 940–1, 949–53, 968–9, 972–4, 981, 983–4; communications system destroyed, 947–8; conditions before U.S. attack, 934–6, 939; conditions in, 746–7; conditions under U.S. control, 1010; Confrontation Front Summit, 149–50; elections (2005), 1036; falls to Americans, 965–6, 975–8; fires and arsonists, 986–8, 991, 996–7; intelligence headquarters and files, 995–6; under Iranian missile attack, 229–30, 246; Iranian Scud missiles fall on, 939; Iraqi defences, 958–9; libraries and books burned, 991–3, 997; looting and pillage, 975, 977–80, 982, 985, 986–8, 990, 996–8; Mansour area bombed, 983–4; monument to Iran war, 276–8; National Archaeological Museum treasures defiled and looted, 988–90, 1010; sacked by Hulagu (1258), 937; U.S. actions on liberation of, 977–83; under U.S. attack, 713–15, 937, 941–4, 947–53, 957, 966–7

Bagram, Afghanistan, 85, 898, 912, 1021

Bahadori, Lieutenant Ahmed, 104

Bahai faith: repressed in Iran, 173–4

Bahedh, Mohsen, 1017–18

Bahonar, Mohamed Javad, 199

Bahrain, 176, 224–6, 251, 591, 592

al-Bahrani, Salwa, 1020

Baker, James, 385–8, 412, 606, 614, 616

Bakhtiar, Shapour, 120, 131, 171–2

al-Bakr, Ahmed Hassan, 149–50, 151, 169

Bakri family, 826

Bakr Sadr, Ayatollah Sayed Mohamed, 161–3, 173

Baktiar, Ahmed, 654

Balakian, Peter, 342

Balfour, Arthur James, 1st Earl, 306, 359, 363, 366, 377, 383, 1031

Balouoch, Mehdi, 257

Bamiyan: Buddha statues, 85, 847, 988

al-Bandar, Judge Awad Mohamed, 1020

Bandar Abbas, 259–60, 262–6

Bandar ibn Sultan, Prince of Saudi Arabia, 607, 849, 957

Bani-Sadr, President (of Iran), 198

Banja Luka, Bosnia, 94*n*

Barak, Ehud, 421*n*, 428–9, 437*n*, 439–43, 450, 465, 507

Baraq, Fadel, 155

Bar Ilan, David, 428, 435

Barmak, Siddiq, 850

Barnes, Ivan, 50, 70*n*, 90, 94*n*, 105, 167*n*, 170*n*, 261*n*

Barry, Lieutenant Colonel Rick, 717

Bartashova, Julia, 754

Barter, Cyril, 328

Bartholomew, Paddy, 735

Barzani, Massoud, 657*n*

Basari, Hojatolislam Sheikh Aref, 162

Bashir, General Omar, 9

Basra: civilians killed and injured in, 945–7; conditions in, 742–5; in Iran-Iraq war, 178, 179 84, 187, 189, 191, 194–5, 252–5, 256; looting and pillage, 975, 982; massacres in, 664; missile attack on, 725; occupied by British in First World War, 141; oil refinery bombed by U.S.A., 723; resists U.S.-British attack, 945; Shia rebellion in, 902

*Battle of Algiers, The* (film), 520–1, 539, 1014

Bauer, Yehuda, 343

Baxter, Gunner Barry, 642

Bayle, Pierre, 185, 186–7, 195, 246

al-Bayoudi, Brigadier General Jamal, 256

Bayrou, François, 344

Bazargan, Mehdi, 103–4, 108, 113–14, 120–1

Bazoft, Farzad, 168–9, 240, 971, 995, 1016

Bazzaz, Abdul Rahman, 151

Bazzaz, Saad, 179

Begin, Menachim: on Arafat, 397; derides Palestinians, 507; escapes punishment, 461; invades Lebanon (1982), 509; as Irgun leader, 373, 449; and Jewish settlements, 426

Behbahani, Leila, 259

Beheshti, Ayatollah Mohamed, 198–9

Behesht-i-Zahra, Iran, 288

Beirut: Arafat and PLO in, 379; author in, 42, 789–90, 795–6, 1034–5; Cité Sportive, 828–32; garden of forgiveness, 822; Hariri assassinated by bomb (2005), 1034–6; hostages in, 242, 244, 245; Iraqi opposition group conference (1991), 660–1, 662*n*; Israeli air attacks on, 412–13; Israeli siege of (1982), 398, 1033; as NATO base, 478; pro-Iranian battles with pro-Iraqis, 177; as spy centre, 791; U.S. servicemen killed by suicide bomb in, 226, 478, 791, 835, 886, 954; *see also* Lebanon

Beit Jalla, 442–4, 469, 762

Belahrache, Cherif, 564
Belgium: considers complaint against Sharon for massacre, 507; deports Algerian asylum seeker, 580n
Belhaj, Ali, 525–6, 537
Belhaj, Karima, 553
Belkacem, Krim, 524, 543–4
Belkaïd, Abu Bakr, 543–4
Belkeziz, Abdulouahad, 856
Belkheir, General Larbi, 541
Bell, Gertrude, 144, 327, 990
Beloucif, Major-General Mustafa, 542
Benamadi, Zouaoui, 534–5
Benamara, Yamina, 548
Ben Bella, Ahmed, 523–4, 534, 581
Bendjedid, Chadli, 525, 526, 529, 530, 532, 534, 541–3
Ben Gurion, David, 506
Benn, Tony, 725, 924n, 1004
Bennett, William, 744
Bennetts, Colin, Bishop of Coventry, 741
Bentalha, Algeria, 312, 569–72
Benvenisti, Meron, 438–9
Benyahyia, Mohamed, 543
Berberian, Zakar, 318–19
Berbers: in Algeria, 536, 584
Berehri, Abdelhak, 582
Berg, Frank, 1031
Bernadotte, Count Folke, 376, 386
Bernsen, Rear Admiral Harold J., USN, 248, 251
Berri, Nabih, 243
Bethlehem: attacked by Israelis, 501–2
Beuslimane, Amina, 573–4, 579
Bhutto, Zulfikar Ali, 69
Bigley, Ken, 1003, 1030
Bill, James A., 98
bin Laden, Abdullah (Osama's son), 904n
bin Laden, Omar (Osama's son), 19, 24
bin Laden, Osama: addresses United States, 1033n; anti-Americanism, 23–4, 32; appearance and manner, 6–7, 19, 22, 29, 124; assassination attempts on, 12, 1025; associates U.S.A. and Israel, 31; attacked by U.S. in Afghanistan, 791, 983; attempts to recruit author, 29–30; author meets and interviews in Afghanistan, 12–13, 15, 16–17, 19–25, 29–33, 582, 1032; author meets in Sudan, 5–9; author pleads to for Daniel Pearl's release, 876n; and author's exclusion from Afghanistan, 857; avoids detection and capture, 866, 870, 892, 906–7, 911; blamed by Muslim governments for insurgencies, 12; broadcasts on al-Jazeera, 854–5, 906–7, 1031–4; builds roads in Afghanistan, 4–5, 8; demands, 844, 858–9; denounces Saudis, 20–2, 24, 590; followers, 19; George W. Bush condemns, 890; heroic image for Arabs, 5–6, 13; hostility to Saddam, 22–3, 722,

908, 1033–4; ideal weapon, 750; interest in history, 1031–2; on Iraqi insurgency, 1033–4; justifies Muslim resistance to U.S.A., 925n; and liberation of Iraq, 925; and 9/11 attacks, 833, 834–5, 836–7, 839, 841, 844, 855–6; as representative voice, 880; reputation, 855; Saudis support against Soviets in Afghanistan, 590; self-conviction, 22, 24; supposed links with Saddam, 958; sympathy for Iraqi suffering, 705; tape recording interpreted, 908; threatens West, 906–9; underestimated as threat, 757n; on U.S. support for Israel, 1027; war against Russians in Afghanistan, 4, 5, 7–8, 48, 90, 846n; on war between good and evil, 855; warns U.S. to leave Saudi Arabia, 19–20, 31; wives, 25
bin Laden, Saad (Osama's son), 19, 24
Binyon, Michael, 42–3
Biro, Arye, 916n
Birrell, Ian, 827
Black, Conrad, Baron, 924n
Black, Ian, 253–4, 255
Blackman, Lieutenant Colonel Hugh, 982
Blair, Tony: and air attacks on Iraq, 723; al-Sahaf mocks, 945n; Arafat meets in London, 858; and attacks on Afghanistan, 841; bin Laden inquires about, 23; bin Laden on relations with Bush, 1031–2; claims success in Iraq, 1003; claims to have no quarrel with Iraqi people, 721; on conduct of Iraq war, 958; and demands for Israeli withdrawal from West Bank, 500; and effect of sanctions in Iraq, 709; follows U.S. policy over Iraq, 98, 609, 901–2, 932, 1014; and Iraqi civilian victims, 937, 974; issues "dossier" on Iraq, 902–3; justifies war, 757; meets Netanyahu, 434; and Palestinian reform, 932; and popular opposition to Iraq war, 925; as potential assassination victim, 1026; preparations for war with Iraq, 924; proclaims annual Holocaust Memorial Day, 345; on "progress" in Middle East, 436; on Saddam's use of chemical weapons, 214; self-conviction, 22; silence on Armenian massacres, 345–7, 349–50; supports Putin against Chechens, 905; and Taliban-drug connection, 862; warns of al-Qaeda attacks, 907, 910n; on weapons inspection in Iraq, 721–2
Blida, Algeria, 549–51
Blix, Hans, 903, 930
Blood, Sir Bindon, 71
Blount, Major General Buford, 971–2
Blunkett, David, 971
Boccardi, Louis D., 612
Bodossian, Anig, 349

Bogan, Franz, 380
Bolton, John, 931
*Boone,* USS, 226
Borth, Captain John, 621
Bosnia: author forecasts civil war in, 94*n*;
    cancer cases in, 740*n*-1*n*; Muslims in,
    8–9, 11; U.S. inaction in, 718
Bouamra, Lieutenant, 556
Bouchlagem, Fouad, 564
Boudaoud, Omar, 543
Boudiaf, Madame, 543–4
Boudiaf, Mohamed: killed, 541–4; returns to
    Algeria, 529, 531, 533, 536, 537, 539–41
Boughaba, Naima and Nedjoua, 573, 579
Bouiez, Farez, 384
Boumarafi, Second Lieutenant Lembarek,
    541–2, 559
Boumedienne, Houari, 524–5, 527, 530, 540,
    544
Bourmont, Comte de, 517
Bouslimani, Sheikh Mohamed, 549–51
Bousria, Ben Othman, 580*n*
Bouteflika, Abdelaziz, 584, 842*n*
Boutros, Milaneh, 831
Boutros Ghali, Boutros, 439
Bouyali, Mohamed, 522–6, 528
Bouyali, Mustafa, 522–8, 531–2, 583
Bowie, Robert R., 127–8
Boyer, Peter J., 720*n*
boy-soldiers: Iranian, 202–4, 207, 230–3, 241,
    253–5
Bradchit, Lebanon, 774
Brahimi, Abdel-Hamid, 543, 581
Bramia, Amar, 530–1
Breeze, Corporal David, 976–7
Bremer, Paul, 100*n*, 1004, 1010, 1012,
    1027–8
Brezhnev, Leonid, 17, 31, 40–1, 45, 66, 69,
    718
*Bridgeton* (U.S. tanker), 247–8
Brindel, Captain Glenn, 219, 221
Britain: in air strikes against Iraq, 710, 724–7;
    arms sales, 750, 753–4, 757, 768–71; bin
    Laden's attitude to, 23; bin Laden
    threatens, 908–9; casualties from 1921
    war with Iraq, 956; cooperates with
    Iranian Savak, 112; dead soldiers filmed
    in Basra, 945; dossiers on Iraq, 901–2,
    909–10, 925; in First World War
    Mesopotamian campaign, 139–44, 993;
    forms and occupies Iraq (1919–20),
    144–8, 1028–9; guarantees credits to
    Iraq, 168; ill-treatment by troops in Iraq,
    1012; invades Iraq with U.S.A. (2003),
    722–3; and Iranian embassy siege in
    London, 167–8; mandate in Palestine,
    365, 367, 372–3; Palestine policy, 359;
    poets of First World War, 280–1;
    relations with U.S.A., 609–11;
    reluctance to go to war with Iraq, 932;
    returns Algerian asylum-seekers, 580;

scare-stories of terrorist attacks, 907,
    910*n*; in Suez crisis and war, 913–21;
    supplies arms and equipment to Saudi
    Arabia, 596–7; supplies nuclear material
    to Iraq, 769–70; supports Jewish
    Palestine state, 148; view of Armenian
    massacres, 345–7, 349–50, 353–4; wars
    with Afghanistan, 3, 37–40, 44
British Broadcasting Corporation (BBC): on
    attempts to kill Saddam, 983; and
    Holocaust Day commemoration, 345–6;
    restricted in Iran, 135; World Service,
    439, 480
British Gulf Veterans' and Families'
    Association, 738
Brittain, Vera: *Testament of Youth,* 314
Brittain-Catlin, Daniel, 345–6
*Broadsword,* HMS, 223–4, 261
Brooke, Rupert, 601–2
Browne, Vincent, 271
Bryce, James, Viscount, 325, 326, 328, 333,
    345, 346, 350–1
B'Tselem (Israeli human rights group), 466*n*,
    510–11
Bubiyan (island), 239
Buchanan, Pat, 949
Buddha: statues destroyed, 85, 847, 988
Bugeaud, Saïd, 518–19
Bulloch, Jim, 207
Burnes, Lt. Col. Sir Alexander, 38, 870–1
al-Burujirdi, Ayatollah Sheikh Murtada, 165
Burujirdi, Ayatollah Sayed Mohamed
    Hussein, 98*n*
Bush, George (Senior): and Al-Aqsa mosque
    killings, 606; announces liberation of
    Kuwait, 649; and arms supply to Middle
    East, 637; bin Laden disparages, 909;
    conditions U.S. loan guarantees to Israel,
    403; declares hostility to Saddam not
    Iraqis, 690; and defence of Kuwait, 606,
    607, 616; defends *Vincennes* actions,
    265; denounces Iran, 227; electoral
    defeat (1992), 388; and First Gulf War,
    617, 622, 888; and Israeli occupation of
    Arab lands, 383, 403; on killing of U.S.
    servicemen in Beirut, 791; and Madrid
    Middle East peace conference, 382–4,
    388; and New World Order, 625; and
    non-intervention in Iraqi affairs, 667; on
    non-pursuit of Saddam (1991), 665;
    promises to withdraw U.S. troops from
    Saudi Arabia, 19; and Saudi attitudes to
    war, 607–8; subsidises Saddam, 904
Bush, George W.: accepts Jewish settlements,
    1027; addresses UN General Assembly,
    888–90, 929; and administration of Iraq,
    1014; aggressiveness, 932; bin Laden on,
    1031–2; condemns dictatorship, 95; on
    crusade against "evil," 366, 840, 923;
    declares no quarrel with Iraqi people,
    888; demands on Iraq, 901; demands

Bush, George W.: *(continued)*
    withdrawal of Israel from West Bank,
    500, 509; foresees long war in Iraq, 957;
    Iraqi attempted murder plot against,
    714–15; and Iraqi civilian victims, 974;
    and Iraqi non-involvement in 9/11
    attacks, 938; justifies war, 757; at King
    Hussein's funeral, 805; meets Sharon,
    509–10; mocks "Comical Ali," 153; and
    9/11 attack, 490, 1033; nullifies UN
    Security Council Resolution 242, 501;
    on Palestinian state, 858; plans action
    against Iraq, 888, 903, 905–6, 909, 922,
    924; post-9/11 attacks on Afghanistan,
    841, 847; as potential assassination
    victim, 1026; and promise of Afghan
    democracy, 1037*n*; promises human
    rights in Iraq, 994; on Saddam as threat,
    758; on "Saddam remnants" as enemies,
    109*n*; on Saddam's use of chemical
    weapons, 214; self-conviction, 22; signs
    law on "terrorist murderers," 865;
    stature, 888; supports Putin against
    Chechens, 905; and UN weapons
    inspectors, 926; and U.S. presence in
    Iraq, 1000, 1003, 1013; view on
    Armenian massacres, 348–9; and war
    against terror, 932, 1013–14; warns
    Arafat to curb violence, 463; on world
    dichotomy, 836, 855
Butson, Mathew, 348

Çakir, Suna, 338
Çakmakoglu, Sabahattin, 343
Cameron, James, 234*n*
Cameron Commission of Inquiry, 773*n*
Campbell, Alastair, 916
Camp David: agreement (1977), 149, 150,
    426; Arafat-Barak talks (2000), 440
Camus, Albert, 1037–8
Canadian Broadcasting Corporation, 43, 102,
    188–9
cancer: post-war incidence in Iraq, 727–33,
    734, 736–41
*Capriella* (Italian freighter), 191
Carlson, Captain David, USN, 264
Carter, Jimmy: and Cold War, 718; condemns
    Jewish settlements, 426; demands Soviet
    withdrawal from Afghanistan, 76;
    freezes Iranian funds in U.S.A., 120;
    Iranians demonstrate against, 119–20;
    Khomeini accuses of breaking
    international law, 124–5; Moscow press
    disparages, 65–6; pledges to Afghan
    mujahedin, 859; and Soviet U.S.-
    licensed lorries, 65; supports Shah, 100,
    109; and Tehran embassy crisis, 118;
    urges boycott of Moscow Olympics, 86
Carter, Specialist Cleveland, 604
Caspi, Arie, 499
Castro, Fidel, 581, 935

casualties: in Afghanistan, 861–3, 890;
    British in 1921 Iraq campaign, 956;
    civilians in Iraq, 625–8, 937, 940–1,
    949–53, 958, 961–3, 968–9, 972–4, 981,
    983–4, 1007; in First Gulf War, 649–50,
    688–9, 691–4; French, 513–15, 518,
    521; in Iran-Iraq war, 193–4, 197–8, 201,
    228, 250, 255–7, 277–8, 279–80, 284,
    288–90; Russian in Afghanistan, 50, 60,
    86; U.S. in Afghanistan, 1014; U.S. in
    First Gulf War, 693; U.S. in Iraq, 1003
Cave, George, 114
Cavenagh, Lieutenant A.J.M. ("Sandy"), 919
Central Intelligence Agency (CIA): activities
    in Iran, 114; activities in post-
    "liberation" Iraq, 1012; and arms deals
    in Middle East, 770; collaborates with
    Saudis, 24; covert operations in Iraq,
    719; and Gaza killings, 449; instructs
    Savak agents, 112; and Iranian torture
    methods, 99; Iraq claims interference by,
    152; and Mossadeq coup files, 97*n*;
    papers reconstituted in Iran, 128; radio
    calls for overthrow of Saddam, 646–7;
    and reinstatement of Shah of Iran, 95;
    supports mujahedin in Afghanistan, 12,
    83; supposed assassination attempt on
    bin Laden, 12; and UN weapons
    inspectors in Iraq, 724, 906; and Wye
    agreement, 437
Cerić, Mustafa, Imam of Bosnia, 11–12
Chaibia, Algeria, 561–2
Chair-Zarrin, Hossein, 286
Chalabi, Ahmed, 243, 1013
Chaman, 868–9, 871
Chamberlain, Neville, 924*n*
Chamran, Mustafa, 198
Charles, Prince of Wales, 752
Charlton, Air Commodore Lionel, 147
Charny, Israel, 339, 343, 346
Charrette, Hervé de, 567
Chebouti, Abdelkader, 526, 528
Chechnya: war in, 175, 905, 1031
"Chemical Ali," *see* Majid, Ali Hassan
chemical weapons: in First World War, 308;
    in Iran-Iraq war, 209–14, 216–17, 228,
    252; Iraq employs against Kurds,
    214–15, 230
Chemilah, Mohamed, 153*n*
Cheney, Dick, 666, 904, 926
*Chicago Tribune,* 886
children: affected by cancer in Iraq, 727–31,
    736–41; illness in Kabul, 86; injured and
    killed in Iraq, 22, 940–1, 946–7, 951–2,
    962, 972–4, 1008, 1020; kidnappings
    and rape in Iraq, 1010; killed in Algeria,
    568; killed in bombing of Afghanistan,
    861–3, 868; killed in Israeli helicopter
    attack in Lebanon, 777; killed in Israeli-
    Palestinian conflict, 482–3, 499–501,
    503–4, 505, 511, 905; mortality from

sanctions in Iraq, 703–9, 723; provoked to marytrdom, 504; *see also* boy-soldiers; United Nations Children's Fund

Chile: Israeli arms in, 772

China: and arms supply, 766; Iraeli military technicians and arms in, 771–2

Chirac, Jacques: and Algerian atrocities, 521, 581; in Algerian conflict, 512; and Armenian massacres, 344; on French non-involvement in Iraq war, 924n; welcomes Saddam to Paris, 166, 1004

Chomsky, Noam, 458

Christopher, Warren, 19, 408

Churchill, Sir Winston: *The Aftermath,* 320; alliance with Stalin, 362; ambushed in Malakand, 71; appoints Abdullah as emir of Transjordan, 801; on Armenian massacres, 329, 331, 337, 346; and British intervention in Iraq (1920), 145–6; favours execution of Nazi leadership, 866; on Irish in Second World War, 224; on murder of Lord Moyne, 374; on proposed partition of Palestine, 368; and Roosevelt's unconditional surrender demand, 925

Çiçek, Hikmet, 350

Cilicia, 332

Clark, Alan, 598

Clark, William, 916

clash: as term, 444–5, 448–9

Claverie, Mgr. Pierre, Bishop of Oran, 567, 583

*Clean Break: A New Strategy for Securing the Realm, A* (report, 1966), 931

Clifton, Tony, 160

Clinton, Bill: absent from Assad's funeral, 819; air attacks on Iraq, 722–3; appeals to Israeli-Palestinian youth, 446; at Araba meeting on Jordan-Israel agreement, 797–9; and Arafat-Barak Camp David talks, 440; and Armenian commemoration address, 343; attacks Baghdad with missiles, 714–15; bombs Sudan, 722, 791; employs Jewish diplomats, 439; on Hebron killings, 411; invites Arafat and PLO to Washington, 435; and Iraq sanctions, 709; and Iraq's supposed weapons, 721–2; and Israeli bombardment of southern Lebanon, 413; meets Assad, 440; and Middle East peace process, 388, 394, 446; open letter from Hanan Ashrawi, 451n; policy on Iraq, 722; and Saddam's supposed aggression, 716; at Sharm el-Sheikh conference, 20; silence on Israel's violence against Palestinians, 464; and Somalia, 32; and Wye agreement, 437–8

cluster bombs: in Iraq, 961–3, 974; Israelis use, 963

CNN (U.S. television network), 933n

Coalition Humanitarian Liaison Center, Mazar-e-Sharif, 896

Coalition Joint Civil-Military Operations Task Force (CJCMOTF), 896

Coalition Provisional Authority, Iraq (CPA), 1012, 1028

Cockburn, Patrick, 142, 622, 707, 1002, 1011, 1034

Cohen, Eliot, 910, 931–2

Cohen, Rivka, 347n

Cohen, William, 722, 726

Cole, Michael, 150

Cole, Sergeant Seth, 1001

*Cole,* USS, 225, 443, 835

Collins, Michael, 394

*Columbia,* USS, 927

"Comical Ali," *see* Sahaf, Mohamed Saeed

*Commandant Ducuing* (French frigate), 593

Committee of Advice and Reform (Saudi), 13

Congo: Belgian atrocities in, 336

Connolly, James, 307

Contra scandal, *see* Iran-Contra scandal

Cook, Robin, 705, 721

Cordingley, Brigadier Patrick, 610

Corrie, Rachel, 1036

corruption: in Pakistani ISI, 13; and Saudi royal family, 13; and Shah, 104

Corwin, Warrant Officer Tim, 668–9

Couso, Jose, 971

Coxon, Lance Corporal, 310–11

Craig, James, 306

Craig, Marshal of the RAF Sir David, 610n

Croatia, 362; bans mujahedin entry into Bosnia, 9

Crusade, First, 791

Cruz, Angelo de la, 1030

CS gas cartridges, 762

Culp, Merl, 629n

Culture and Democracy Pary (Algeria), 551

Cummings, Sam, 770–1

Cummings, Sergeant Phil, 1001

Cuny, Fred, 651–2, 655

Cyprus, 242

Daabul, Abu Selim, 811

Dachau, 369, 370

Dadrian, Vahakn, 329–30, 343

Dahab, Abdul Razzak, 152

Dahlan, Colonel Mohamed, 423, 465

Dahuk, Iraq, 681–2, 683–4

*Daily Express,* 910n

Dakessian, Boghos, 318, 323–4

Dalilah (Algerian policewoman), 574–7

Dalvand, Shirin, 173–4

Damaj, Rufaida, 498

Dami, Dr. Jeannik, 691–2, 694

al-Dannouk, Dr. Fahid, 1020

Danoon, Hishem, 950

Daoud, Mohamed, 44–5, 44n

Daponte, Beth Osborne, 694

Dardanelles, 320–1

Darwish, Mahmoud, 451
Dassault, Marcel, 767
Davios, Rick, 933n-4n
Davis, Jim, 770
Davis, Leslie, 325–6
Davis, Norman, 336
Davis, Surgeon Lieutenant Peter, 676–7
Dawa party (Iraq), 156, 199, 594, 661, 662n, 1019–20
Dayan, Moshe, 439n
Debebsi, Mohamed, 492, 493
Defensive Shield, Operation (2002), 493, 500
Dehqani, Ashraf, 99n
Deir Yassin (*later* Givat Shaul), 369–71, 412, 448
de la Billière, Lieutenant General Sir Peter, 610–11, 637–9
Delmer, Sefton, 919n
Denaro, Lt. Col. Arthur, 607n
depleted-uranium: as cause of cancer, 727–8, 734–7, 738–40; used in U.S. war on Iraq, 971
Dershowitz, Alan, 490, 509, 838
de Valera, Eamon, 307
Dezful, Iraq, 197–8, 200, 202, 204, 208, 231, 252
Dhahran, Saudi Arabia, 6, 591, 594, 598–9, 601, 608
Dhari, Sheikh, 145
Dhu Khalasa, 847
Dickens, Hilda, 139, 141
Dickens, Private Charles, 139, 141, 311, 321, 742
dictators: appeal of, 807, 820; Churchill on, 172
Dien Bien Phu, 1014
Dimbleby, Richard, 622
Dimeshkieh, Nadim, 360
Dina, Queen of Jordan, 801
Dinka people (Sudan), 11
Dirya, Marwan, 469
Disraeli, Benjamin, 914
Djaout, Tahar, 553
Djezairi, Selim, 825
Djilas, Milovan, 454
Documentation Centre for the Female Martyrs of the Islamic Movement, 1019
Doll, Ramona, 755
Donne, John, 827
Dost Mohamed, King of Afghanistan, 37
Dostum, Rashid, 863, 911
Douai, France, 298, 301–5
Doudi, Abdul-Hadi, 525
Douglas-Home, Charles, 90n, 171, 261n, 268
Dowden, Richard, 631, 647–8
Doyle, Leonard, 827, 833–4, 890
Drew, Richard, 151
drugs: in Afghanistan, 15–16, 862, 863, 1037n; in Iran, 133–4
Druzes, 825
Dubai, 751–2

Dubs, Adolph, 84
Dufour, Colonel Jean-Louis, 649
al-Dulaymi, Major Mehdi, 1019
Dulles, Alan, 92, 98
Dulles, John Foster, 920
Dunphy, Eamon, 838
al-Dura, Mohamed, 447–8
Durand, Edward, 39–40
Durand, Sir Henry Mortimer, 39–40, 44, 74
Dutfield, Michael, 878, 879
Dyke, Captain (of *Al-Tanin*), 195–6

Easter Rising (Ireland, 1916), 307
Ebtekar, Massoumeh, 114
Eden, Anthony (*later* 1st Earl of Avon), 913–16, 918, 919n, 920–1
Eedle, Paul, 829
Efthyvoulos, Alex, 135, 919
Eggart, Sergeant Jeff, 604–5
Egypt: Arab economic boycott of, 150; and Jewish settlements in occupied territories, 426; refugees flee Iraq, 644; Saudi financial support for, 637; and Suez crisis (1956), 913–20; supports Iraq against Iran, 207n, 252; torture in, 411; wars with Israel, 377
Eid, Imad, 395
8 Days (magazine), 166
Ein el-Helweh camp, Sidon, 400
Eisenhower, Dwight D., 95, 98, 920–1
Ekeus, Rolf, 719–20
el-Afghani, Djafaar, 550
El Al aircraft: Hindawi attempts to blow up, 459
el-Baheri, Lieutenant General Ahmed, 627
el-Hoss, Selim, 150
Elias, Riad, 463
Eliot, T. S., 336, 1038
el-Islambouli, Shawki, 526
el-Kebir, Ahmed, 551
el-Khouly, General Mohamed, 460n
Ellsen, Isabel, 316, 318, 323–4, 369
el-Musri, Colonel Mohamed, 423
el-Nimr, Rifaat, 363
Elon, Amos, 427
Elpeleg, Zvi, 362, 364
Elphinstone, Major-General William, 3, 48
Emami, Sharif, 131
Emir, Riad Abdul, 659
Enron scandal (2002), 890
Entezam, Amir Abbas, 110, 113–15
Enver Pasha, 324, 331, 333
Erekat, Saeb, 388
Erlandsen, Hans-Gunnar, 40
Eshel, David, 758
es-Said, Nuri, 148, 360, 914–15
ethnic cleansing, *see* massacres
Ethridge, Second Lieutenant Bernard, 714
Ettehad, Enayat, 135
Euomar Tchaoush, 351
European Union: and Algerian atrocities, 580

executions: of Ayatollah's opponents in Iran, 199, 228, 274–6; by beheading, 849*n*, 1030–1; in Iraq, 151–3, 162–3, 165–6, 169, 275–6, 1019–22; by Palestinians on compatriots, 490–1; by Shah of opposition leaders, 121; of Shah's supporters in Iran, 103–8, 109, 131, 174–5; *see also* torture
Eytan, Rafael, 507, 917*n*

Fadel, Khadum, 276
Fadlallah, Sayed Mohamed Hussein, 661, 791
Fahd, Crown Prince of Saudi Arabia, 150
Fahd, King of Saudi Arabia: allows U.S. military forces in Saudi Arabia, 6, 19, 590, 636; authorises sorties by Saudi planes against Iraqis, 617; and bin Laden's struggle against U.S.A., 32; opposition to, 848; plans consultative council, 609; quarrel with Saddam, 612–13, 625
Fahd, Abdul Ali Mohamed, 256*n*
Faidazaida, Fatima, 260, 263
Faili, Habib, 174
al-Faisal, Turki, 24
Faithful to the Promise (Algerian group), 541
al-Fakhry, Major General Hisham Sabah, 208
Falah, Oulah, 730–1
Fallujah: bombed in First Gulf War, 628; British advance on (1920), 145; insurgency in, 1003–4, 1007, 1009; mortuary, 278; prisoner-of-war camp at, 232; U.S. forces in, 999–1002, 1003–4
al-Falouji, Imad, 423, 424
Falwell, Jerry, 428, 910
Fao port and peninsula, Iraq, 181–2, 213–14, 233–4, 235–40, 247, 252, 256
Farabi, Afsaneh, 275
Farah, Empress of Iran, 109, 131
Farouk, Hussein, 290
Farquhar, Wing Commander David, 610
Fatah, 507–8
Favel, Tiba, 738
Fayad, Mohamed, 994
Feinberg, Ilan, 391
Feisal I, King of Iraq, 145, 148, 336, 383, 791, 801, 826, 992
Feisal II, King of Iraq, 148, 801
Feith, Douglas, 931
Feyed, Jemel, 498
Feyed, Saeb, 498
Fhoda, Farag, 559*n*
Fields, Bruce, 752
Finland: arms sales, 750, 766
Firouz, Mariam, 122
First Afghan War (1842), 3, 37
First World War (1914–18), 294–306, 307–10, 314
Fischer, Dr. Harald, 762
Fish Lake, battle of, 253–6, 277, 280

Fisk, Edward (author's grandfather), 37, 195, 298, 301
Fisk, Margaret (author's grandmother), 35, 301
Fisk, Matilda (William's first wife), 297
Fisk, Peggy (author's mother), 295–300, 302, 314–15, 790, 793; illness and death, 792–5
Fisk, William (author's father): background and career, 294–6; death, 790; military service, 141, 294, 297–305, 313–15, 321, 477, 939, 1038; owns Churchill's books, 305–6; patriotism, 793; reads Johnston's *Tom Graham V.C.*, 35, 37; and son's upbringing, 295–6, 314–15
Fitzwater, Marlin, 703
Fleah, Ahmed, 729
Fleming, Gerald, 94
Flici, Laadi, 552
Flint, Tony, 738
FLN, *see* National Liberation Front
Fontana, Lou, 601
*Foreign Affairs* (journal), 923
*Foreign Correspondent* (Hitchcock film), 90
Foucauld, Vicomte Charles de, 567
Fourchaud, Colonel Alexandre Edouard Constant, 513, 515
*Fox*, USS, 249
France: abandons no-fly zone bombardments over Iraq, 718; aids Israeli government against insurgents, 546; air strikes against Iraq, 710; and Algerian killings, 344, 1014; and Algerian war of independence, 519–20, 583; and Arab hopes for autonomy under Ottomans, 823–4, 825; and Armenians, 334–5, 344; arms sales, 758, 763; casualties of war, 513–15, 521; colonises Algeria, 513–18; defeats Syrians at Maysaloun (1920), 813; in First Gulf War, 618–19; forbids genocide denial, 344; gives sanctuary to Ayatollah Khomeini, 120; mandate in Lebanon, 372, 791–2; military casualties in Algeria, 518, 521; monitors Algerian military radio traffic, 557*n*; non-involvement in Iraq war, 924*n*; in Suez crisis and war, 913–18, 920; supplies missiles to Iraq, 227; supports Algerian regime, 546, 584; Syrian mandate, 145, 306, 334, 792, 812–13
Franco, General Francisco, 336
Francona, Lieutenant Colonel Rick, 213–14, 240
Franjieh, Sulieman, 304
Franks, Sergeant Ashley, 754
Franks, General Tommy, 958, 985
Frater, Neil, 345
Freih, Mahmoud, 510*n*
Freisler, Roland, 108
Frej, Ali, 483
French Foreign Legion: in First Gulf War, 595

Friedman, Tom, 479n, 500, 504, 854, 1024n
*From Beirut to Bosnia* (TV series), 877–9
*Front des Forces Socialistes* (FFS, Algeria), 524
*Front Islamique du Salut* (FIS, Algeria): in Algerian civil war, 529–32, 535–8, 540–1, 545, 550–1, 560, 567; banned, 525; condemns massacres, 582n; demands Islamic republic, 530, 535, 536; fighters in Afghanistan, 535–6; founded, 526; and killing of Boudiaf, 541, 543; leaders tried, 542; in 1990 elections, 536; principles, 534–5; shaving of beards, 539
Fuzi, Yahya, 287

Gaitskell, Hugh, 921
Galbraith, Kenneth, 765
Galibert, Léon, 518
Gallipoli, 308, 311
Gamucio, Juan Carlos, 790
Gandamak, Treaty of (1879), 37
Gardner, David, 972
Garner, Major General Jay, 683–4, 1013
Garner, Phil, 738
gas (poison): Britain supplies components to Iraq, 769; proposed for use against Iraq (1920), 146; Saddam employs against Iranians, 209–14, 216–17, 233, 692; used against Kurds in Halabja, 214–15
Gaulle, Charles de, 399, 513, 516, 520, 523, 542, 1015
al-Gaylani, Rashid Ali, 148, 360
Gaza: Amira Hass in, 453, 455; Arafat in, 414–18; under Arafat's control, 419, 421; conditions, 484; Haj Amin's Palestine government in, 363–4; Hamas in, 391–2, 442; Israelis fight in and raid, 374, 390–2, 413, 419, 442, 462–4, 484, 487–8; Jewish settlements in, 427, 429, 1014; occupied by Israel, 377, 425; Palestinian Authority in, 393, 398; Palestinians in, 425; as refuge for Palestinians, 449; Sharon proposes abandoning, 506, 1027; violence in, 388; wall paintings, 483
Gelb, Leslie, 665
Gemayel, Bashir, 410, 484, 489, 831
Geneva Conventions, 691–3, 694, 982, 983
genocide: UN Convention on, 865; *see also* massacres
Germany: and Armenian massacres, 329–30; and arms trade, 763–7; Haj Amin collaborates with, 360–4, 368; plans Arab revolt, 148; supports Turkey, 326, 329–31
Ghadafi, Muammar, 163, 861, 880, 882–3, 885–6
Ghali, Hussein, 433
Ghandour, Moutassim, 884, 885
Ghapanchi, Hojatolislam Sayed Azizeddin, 162

Ghattas, Samir, 230, 246
Ghavami, Colonel Nasser, 103–4
al-Ghazali, Wasli, 715
Ghazni, Afghanistan, 51–3, 87, 873
Ghodbane, Fatima, 565
Gholamreza (Iranian taxi driver), 279–80, 282, 285, 286
Gholivand, Aresteh, 275
Ghorbanifar, Manuchehr, 765
al-Ghossain, Fawzi, 881
al-Ghossain, Kinda, 881, 884–5, 887
al-Ghossain, Raafat: killed in U.S. bombing of Tripoli, 880–3
al-Ghossain, Saniya, 881, 883, 884–7
Ghozali, Sid-Ahmed, 537
Ghulam Hyder, 39
Gibran, Kahlil, 789, 975
Gilani, Darude, 137
Gilbert, William, Baron, 734, 740
Gilo (settlement), Israel, 443–4
Ginat, Captain, 11
Girod, Christophe, 693–4
Givat Shaul, *see* Deir Yassin
Gladstone, Herbert John, Viscount, 325n
Glaspie, April, 589
Glenn, John, 221
Glubb (Pasha), Sir John Bagot, 368, 800, 805
Goiran, Roger, 96
Golan Heights, 425, 439–40, 606n, 798, 810–11, 812, 816–17, 818, 1037
Gold, Dore, 474
Golden, Tim, 1021n
Goldstein, Baruch, 410–11, 412–13, 414, 430
Gollancz, Sir Victor, 922
Goltz, Field Marshal Colmar, Freiherr von der, 326
Goodman, Walter, 878n-9n
Gorbachev, Mikhail, 382–3, 386
Gordon, General Charles George, 9
Gore, Al, 722
Gouraud, General Henri, 306, 791, 813
Gousmi, Cherif, 583
Grabovsky, Lieutenant Avi, 830
Graham, Billy, 910
Graham, Franklin, 910
Grand Mufti of Jerusalem, *see* Amin al-Husseini, Haj Mohamed
Graves, Keith, 135
Gray, Gilbert, 461
Greenberg, Joel, 434
Greenberg, Katya and Vladimir, 499
Greenberger, Ben, 402–4, 406
Greenstock, Sir Jeremy, 906
Grey, Sir Edward (*later* Viscount), 144
Grigg, John, 260–1
Gross, Kathy, 125
Groupe Islamique Armé (GIA): ambushes author and police, 562–4; and Bouyali, 522; killed by army, 546; and killing of Bouslimani, 550; killings by, 548,

566–9, 583; numbers, 560; supposed link with Middle East organisations, 528; unites with FIS, 568; U.S.A. condemns, 582

Group of Values (*al-kiam,* Algerian movement), 525

Guantánamo, 891, 898, 904, 1016

*Guardian, The* (newspaper), 426

*Guardian of Islam* (Iranian magazine), 286

Guidicelli, René and Edgar, 515

Gul, Shukria, 868

Gulabzoi, Saed Mohamed, 84

Gulf, the: heat, 223–4; mines in, 251; Royal Navy ships in, 223–4; shipping attacked in, 222, 224–5, 251; U.S. naval presence in, 221–3, 225–6, 248–51

Gulf Cooperation Council, 226

Gulf War, First (1991): casualties, 649–50, 688–9, 691–4; conditions, 601–3; conduct of, 618–21; consequences, 666, 700; ideological justification, 624–5; military deployment, 605–6; outbreak, 616–18; reporting of, 599 601, 605, 621–4, 628, 644–5, 651

Gulf War Syndrome, 623, 738

Gunther, Franz, 326

Guon, Mark, 839

Gures, General Dogan, 680

*Ha'aretz* (newspaper), 454–5, 474, 510, 721, 799

Habash, George, 113

Hachani, Sheikh Abdelkader, 529–30, 532–3, 536–7

Hacohen, David, 375

Haddad, Ahmed, 548

al-Haddad, Fadilah, 1020

Haddad, Colonel Fouad, 631

Haddad, Raymond, 304

Haddad, Saïd, 556

al-Haddad, Dr. Selma, 730

Haddam, Anwar, 546, 581, 582*n*

Hadi, Bouznad, 537–8

al-Hadithi, Naji, 938

Hadj, Messali, 537

Hafnawi, Munzer, 490–2

Hag, Shamsul, 16

Hague, The, *see* International Court

Haig, Alexander, 509, 756, 841

Haig, Field Marshal Douglas, 1st Earl, 294

Hain, Peter, 709, 725

Haji, Moussa Issa, 215–16

Hajibirgit, Afghanistan, 891–5

Hakem, Rahed, 961

al-Hakim, Abdul Aziz, 662

Hakim, Eliyahu, 374–5

al-Hakim, Ayatollah Mohamed Bakr, 661

al-Hakim, Ayatollah Sahib, 165

al-Hakim, Taghi, 165

Hakim (Afghan animal-herder), 892, 894

Haktanır, Korkmaz, 338

Halabja, Iraq, 165, 169, 214–15, 671, 719, 721, 904

Hale, Geoff, 46–7, 50–1, 60

Hale-Bopp comet, 32–3

Haley, Sir William, 915–16

Halim, Mohamed Abdul, 874

Halliday, Dennis, 706–7, 708–9, 725

Halls, Staff Sergeant Bob, 642

Hama, Syria, 173, 411, 546, 608, 806, 814–16, 821–2

al-Hamadani, Awatif Nour, 1020

Hamadi, Saadoun, 649

Hamadi, Lieut. Colonel Walid Alwan, 256*n*

Hamar, Iraq, 1018

Hamas (militia): Arafat on, 415, 422; attacks on Israel, 437; breaks ceasefire, 1027; death squads, 505; dialogue with Israelis, 409; in Gaza, 391–2, 422, 442; hatred of Jews, 485; killed by Israelis, 466*n*, 468; members deported by Rabin, 430–1; offices, 931; strength, 390, 406; and suicide bombing, 406–7, 422, 493, 495, 499; violence and killing, 465; violent protests by, 419

Hamas party (Algeria), 524, 550–1

Hamdan, Adnam, 158

Hamdona, Adel and Anwar, 504

Hamid, Ashwark, 730

Hamid, Hamdi, 406–7

Hamid, Issam Naim, 1008–9

Hamid, Naqib, 156

Hamid, Osama, 406–7

Hammoud, Dr. Akram, 739–40

Hamzah, Crown Prince of Jordan, 805–6

Hancock, Teresa, 197

Hani, Joseph Bechara, 824

Haq, Abdul, 863

al-Haq, Mullanah Abdul, 850–1

al-Haq, Rashed, 851, 852

Haqqani, Mullah, 868

Hardan, Iyad, 475–6

Harek, Noureddin, 565

Harel, Israel, 799

Hariri, Rafiq, 1035–6

Harkis (Algeria), 517

Harris, Air Chief Marshal (Sir) Arthur, 146, 479

Hart, John, 122, 124

Hashem, General Sultan, 944

Hashem, Prince of Jordan, 805

Hashemite dynasty (Jordan), 799–804

al-Hashimi, Abdul-Razak, 157

Hasni, Cheb, 559*n*

Hass, Amira, 453–6, 478*n*; *Drinking the Sea at Gaza,* 453

Hass, Avraham, 454

Hass, Hannah, 453, 454–6

Hassan, Crown Prince of Jordan, 799–802

Hassan, King of Morocco, 109

Hassan, Abu, 950

Hassan, Amel, 940

Hassan, Durar, 498–9
Hassan, Fatima, 743
Hassan, Lieutenant General Hussein Kamel, 720
al-Hassan, Ibrahim, 979
Hassan, Jawad, 732
Hassan, Margaret, 705–6, 708, 737, 1003, 1036
Hassan, Lieutenant Colonel Saddam Kamel, 720
Hassan, Wahed, 940
Hassanjabn, Sheikh, 870
Hasselquist, Sergeant Johnny, 670–1
Hatem, General Khaled, 946
Haughey, Charles, 166–7
Hawatir, Wail, 464
Hazarate Ali, 80
Hazboun, Norma, 501–2
Heath, Sir Edward, 1004
Hebron: agreement (1997), 436; Israel remains in, 432; massacre of Palestinians in, 410–12, 414
Hedayatullah, Dr., 860
Heffinck, Philippe, 704, 707
Heikal, Mohamed, 99, 153–4, 399
Hekmatyar, Gulbuddin, 14, 535, 928
Heller, Brandon, 839
Hellfire (anti-armour weapon), 755, 761, 773, 779–88
Helm, Sarah, 414–15
Helms, Richard, 129
Henderson, Doug, 740
Henderson, Loy, 95n
Hendriks, John, 879
Hennekinne, Loïc, 344
Henry, Marilyn, 338
Henshon, Segeant Joel, 1008
Herat, 53
Herbert, Bob, 1021n
Heren, Louis, 50
heroin, 15
Hersh, Aaron, 456–7
Hersh, Seymour M., 640n, 650, 720n
Herzog, Chaim, 546
Hess, Rudolf, 111
Hewitt, Gavin: in Afghanistan, 46–9, 50–3, 56–7, 60, 61, 63, 69, 70n, 73, 78, 83, 873; in Iran-Iraq war, 179, 188, 190, 192n, 744; in Iraq during U.S. invasion, 973
Al-Hezai, Dr. Habib, 941
Hezb Islami (Algeria), 535
Hezb Islami (Pakistan), 175
Hickey, Sue, 43, 57–8, 188
Hijazi, Fawzi, 206
al-Hilali, Faysal, 1020
Hilla, Iraq, 961–3
Hillal, Ali, 728
Hilterman, Joost, 214
Himmler, Heinrich, 358, 362, 386
Hindawi, Nezar, 459–62

Hine, Sir Patrick, 610
Hirst, David, 394
Hitchcock, Michael, 769n
Hitler, Adolf: and Armenian massacres, 330, 336–7, 340; Bakhtiar on, 172; "diaries," 261; Haj Amin and, 358–60, 361, 363, 368, 386; persecution of Jews, 338, 347
Hizballah: arms supply to, 772–3; at Assad's funeral, 820; attacks Israel, 774; holds Anderson hostage, 242; incredulity at Algerian Islamist actions, 555; and Iran-Contra scandal, 243; Israeli estimate of, 914; at Khartoum conference, 10, 11–12; prevails against Israel, 377; Shiite faith, 821; and suicide bombing, 406, 476–7, 479, 842; supports Marj al-Zahour Palestinians, 431
Hmoud, Abed, 979
Hoagland, Jim, 624
Hodgson, Godfrey, 678
Hodgson, W. N., 280–1
Hoess, Rudolf, 329
Holma, Colonel Heikki, 228
Holmes, Michael, 933n
Holocaust Memorial Day: in Britain, 345, 349–50
Homeida, Lieutenant Rabah, 642
homosexuality: punished in Iran, 174
Hoon, Geoff, 948, 982
Hormuz, Strait of, 223, 227, 246, 249
Horne, Alistair, 515n
Horner, Lieutenant General Charles, 627
Horthy, Admiral Miklós, 330
Hoskinson, First Lieutenant Charles, USN, 601
Hosseini, Agha, 104
hostages: in Lebanon, 242, 244, 245; in U.S. Tehran embassy siege, 118–19, 120, 124–5, 177
al-Hout, Chafiq, 356, 359, 364–5, 399, 411
Hoveyda, Amir Abbas, 104–5, 131
Howard, Dan, 220
Howe, Julia Ward, 775
Howe, Sir Geoffrey (*later* Baron), 169
Howeiza, Iran, 200, 208, 214, 277
Howeiza marshes, Iraq, 246
Howells, Kim, 708
Hoxha, Enver, 324n
Hreizat, Abed Samed, 433n
Hubbard, Captain Dan, 981
Huggler, Justin, 498, 864, 871–2, 874
Hulagu, grandson of Genghis Khan, 937, 993
human rights: Bush promises in Iraq, 994; and Iranian executions, 275; in Israel, 466n, 510–11; violated in Afghanistan, 864–5; violated in Iran-Iraq war, 233
Human Rights Watch, 466n, 583
Hume, John, 429n
Hungary: Soviets invade (1956), 921
Hurd, Douglas, Baron, 169, 643–4, 703
Hurst, John, 755–6, 761, 773

al-Hussaini, Fatimah, 1020
Hussein, King of Jordan: agreement with
    Israel, 797–8, 803; appearance, 123;
    arranges secret meeting between Saddam
    and Assad, 247; attends Shah's
    celebrations, 100; character, 807; death
    and funeral, 799, 803–7, 818–20;
    dismisses Hassan, 799–800; and downfall
    of Shah, 109; and freeing of Sheikh
    Yassin, 1025; friendship with Saddam
    Hussein, 802–3; interviewed by press,
    796–7; on Jordan's economic weakness,
    589; loses West Bank, 802; marriages,
    801–2; as PLK ("Plucky Little King"),
    796; private life, 802; pro-Western
    stance, 802; and restoration of Dome of
    the Rock, 359; suppresses Palestinian
    rising, 802; visits Baghdad, 150, 207;
    weakness, 382; welcomes Waldheim,
    802n–3n; witnesses assassination of
    grandfather Abdullah, 801, 804
Hussein, Sherif of the Hejaz, 144, 801, 992,
    1029
Hussein, Hamed, 1009
Hussein, Imam, 100
Hussein, General Kamaledin, 917, 919
Hussein, Maoulud, 1008–9
Hussein, Taha Yassin, 648
Hussein al-Tikriti, Qusay (Saddam's son),
    934, 979, 983, 1004, 1025
Hussein al-Tikriti, Saddam, *see* Saddam
    Hussein
Hussein al-Tikriti, Uday (Saddam's son), 701,
    977, 983, 1004, 1025
al-Husseini, Abdul Raouf al-Qudwa (Arafat's
    father), 398
al-Husseini, Alia, 363–4
Husseini, Sam, 624
Hutton Report (2004), 901–2
Hylton, Raymond Jolliffe, 5th Baron, 168

Ibarim, Maan, 820
Ibn al-Haythem missile factory, Iraq, 930
Ibrahim, Brigadier-Colonel Ali Khalil, 943
Ibrahim, Ibrahim Mehdi, 664
Ibrahim, Jabir Khalil, 990
Iman, Abu, 648
al-Imara, Ali, 744–5
Imasalni, Bassam, 432
Imperial War Museum, London: *Crimes
    against Humanity* exhibition, 348
Imposimato, Ferdinando, 584
*Independent, The*: on Armenian massacres,
    336–8, 347–8; author joins, 270, 281,
    397, 588; and "D-Notice" on security
    breach, 610–11; and effects of depleted-
    uranium weapons, 735–6, 739; exposes
    Algerian atrocities, 573, 579, 584
*Independent on Sunday,* 716n, 783
India: war with Pakistan (1965), 765
Indyk, Martin, 582, 806

International Court, The Hague, 1024
International Red Cross: on Iraqi civilian
    victims, 973; and Iraqi dead, 691–4; and
    Jenin killings, 497; and Kuwaiti missing
    citizens, 701; not informed of death of
    Mohamed Abul Abbas, 1022; reports
    torture in Shah's prisons, 101; suicide-
    bombed in Iraq, 1015; visits Iraqi
    prisoners in Iran, 205
intifada, 431, 441–2, 452, 468, 487
Iqbal, Lieutenant Mohamed, 76
Iqbal, Sir Mohamed, 861
Iran: access to China for arms, 772; and air
    attack on USS *Stark,* 218–22; anti-
    Americanism, 98; anti-Shah riots, 100;
    arms and defence capabilities, 760–1,
    765–9; attacked by chemical weapons,
    209–14; attacked by Mujahedin-e-Qalq's
    National Liberation Army, 273; attacks
    shipping in Gulf, 224, 226, 227; attitude
    to war, 939; Ayatollah Khomeini's
    Islamic revolution, 102–3, 105–6, 110,
    112–13, 115, 126, 136, 171–3, 226;
    Bahais killed in, 173–4; border agreed
    with Iraq, 101, 161, 178; boy-soldiers in
    war against Iraq, 202–4, 207, 230–3,
    253–5; casualties in war with Iraq, 228,
    255, 256–7, 279–80, 284, 288–90;
    ceasefire (1988), 273, 276, 280;
    communist party (Tudeh) in, 121–2;
    denies U.S. accusation of acquiring
    chemical weapons, 214–15; denounces
    Soviet intervention in Afghanistan, 62;
    drugs suppressed, 133–4; effect and
    memories of Iraq war in, 280–90;
    executions and trials in, 103–8,
    110–11, 131–4, 162–3, 174–5, 199,
    228–9, 274–6; food shortages and
    unemployment, 113n; foreign journalists
    expelled, 135; government under
    Khomeini, 228–9; hostility to USSR,
    201; internal dissent, 198–9; Israel
    supplies arms to, 227, 242–3; judicial
    system, 891; Kurds rebel in, 130, 176–7;
    left opposition in, 110–11, 113; life
    under Ayatollah's regime, 117–18;
    marshlands and marsh Arabs, 246,
    686–7, 747, 1017–19; military strength,
    176–7, 252; missile strikes against
    Baghdad, 229–30, 246; opposition
    eliminated, 228–9; pilgrims killed in
    Mecca (1987), 250n; prisoners-of-war in
    Iraqi hands, 192–3, 228, 232, 285, 291;
    public reaction to shooting down of
    Airbus, 269; quality of Iranians, 105;
    reacts to U.S. Navy presence in Gulf,
    249–50; Revolutionary Guard Corps in,
    206, 208; Revolutionary Guards in
    Lebanon, 161; Saddam attacks oil-
    exporting capability, 246; Saddam
    condemns, 159; Saudis back Saddam

Iran: *(continued)*
against, 613–14; Shah deposed, 102;
Shah reinstated by anti-Mossadeq coup
(1953), 92, 95–9, 121; Soviet agents in,
122; theocracy, 1037; torture in, 99, 101,
112; U.S. casualties in, 1003, 1009,
1011, 1027; U.S. embassy assessment of,
128–9; U.S. intelligence cooperation
with, 112–14; U.S. intelligence on, 763;
village life and opinion in, 136–8; war
poetry, 280–3, 285, 287, 290; war with
Iraq, 21, 41, 114, 170–1, 177–8, 179–98,
199–214, 216–17, 226, 227–31, 233–42,
246, 248, 251–8, 279–80, 613, 614, 769;
weapons procurement programme, 247;
"White Revolution," 100; *see also*
Khomeini, Ayatollah Ruhollah; Tehran
Iran Air IR655 (Airbus): shot down by U.S.
ship, 259–67, 269–73
*Iran Ajr* (Iranian naval vessel), 251
Iran-Contra scandal (1985), 114, 227, 242,
765, 766
Iranian Embassy siege, London, 638
Iranian National Defence Industry
Organisation (INDIO), 247
Iraq: agrees to withdraw army from north,
672; air offensive against (1998–9),
724–7, 732–4; air raids on Tehran,
229–30; air strikes for violations of
conditions, 710, 712–14; Anglo-U.S.
invasion (2003), 22–3, 434, 517, 722–3;
anti-occupation insurgency, 218; arms
supplies to, 227, 767; atrocities and
depradations in Kuwait, 632–4, 648, 653,
688, 692; attacks Kuwait (1991), 588–9,
593, 595, 612–13; attacks shipping in
Gulf, 224–5; beggars and poverty in,
741–3; bombed in First Gulf War, 621,
624, 625–9; border agreed with Iran,
101, 161, 178; Britain guarantees credits
to, 168; Britain invades (1941), 360;
British casualties from 1921 campaign,
956; British Mesopotamian campaign
(1917), 139–44, 517, 993; burns Kuwaiti
oilfields, 630; cancer cases, 727–33, 734,
736–41; casualties and prisoners in
First Gulf War, 649, 688–9, 691–5;
casualties in war with Iran, 255, 278,
284; ceasefire (1988), 273, 276;
children's deaths in, 22; civilian
casualties, 961–3, 1028; conditions after
First Gulf War, 652–7; conditions before
U.S. attack, 934–6; conditions during
war, 959–60; deaths in uprising, 686;
defences against coalition, 958–60,
964–5; demonised in U.S. press, 890*n*,
922; deserters shot, 292–3; destroys
weapons, 721; detains British subjects,
168; development as independent state,
148–9; effect and memories of war with
Iran, 276–7, 290–1; elections (2005),

1003, 1036; exclusion zone around
Kharg Island, 222, 223–4; executions,
151–3, 162–3, 165–6, 169, 275–6;
foments Kurdish rebellion in Iran, 176–7;
foreign debts, 250; genocide against
Assyrians, 336; George W. Bush
condemns, 889–90; guerrilla actions
against invaders, 948; Gulf states support
against Iran, 226–7; Highway 8, 999;
hostages murdered and videoed, 1030–1;
hostility to Khomeini, 170–1; illegitimate
forays into Kuwait and Um Qasr, 710;
imports military material from Britain,
769–70; insurgency in, 1003–4, 1007,
1009–10, 1015, 1033–4; insurrection
against British (1920), 145–7, 1028–9;
internal dissent in, 198; Islamic revival,
955; killings in, 1003–4, 1006–7;
Kuwaiti prisoners in, 700–2; literacy
drive, 166; living standards, 703; low
army morale, 634–5; maltreatment of
prisoners-of-war, 693*n*; mass graves
uncovered, 658–60, 664; mercenaries and
security contractors in, 1022; military
strength, 176, 252; monarchy established
(1922), 148; Morocco and Algeria
support, 605; mortality and illnesses
from sanctions, 703–9; no-fly zones, 710,
718–19; non-involvement in 9/11 attacks
on U.S.A., 1013; oil reserves, 904, 988;
opposition groups meet in Beirut (1991),
660–1; plans to develop nuclear
weapons, 157–9, 171; post-First Gulf
War Shia uprising and repression, 647–8,
656–9, 661–2, 666–7; post-First Gulf
War U.S. policy on, 660–1, 680–1,
682–4; prisoners of war in Iran, 205–6,
228, 256, 276; produces nerve gas and
sarin, 720; regime under Saddam, 150–1;
repression and torture in, 151–7, 166,
170, 994–5; repression of Kurds, 681–2;
retreating army massacred by coalition
troops, 640–4, 648; retreats from Kuwait,
631, 640; sanctions imposed, 703–9, 723,
901–2; Saudis support in war against
Iran, 613–14; south ruined, 702–3;
suicide bombers in, 480*n*, 953–6, 981*n*–
2*n*, 1003, 1008, 1028, 1034, 1036;
supposed possession of nuclear weapons,
609, 902–3; tactics against U.S.-British
forces, 944–5; UN weapons inspectors
in, 719–20, 723–4, 909, 910, 925–6;
U.S.A. continues attacks on, 718; U.S.
administration in, 1012–14, 1027–8;
U.S.A. supports against Iran, 207–8,
213–14, 220, 230; U.S./coalition relief
operations in, 667, 670–1; uses chemical
weapons against Iran and Kurds, 209–15,
228, 230, 252, 659, 963; uses rape as
political weapon, 681*n*, 682; U.S.
military presence and actions in,

999–1012, 1036–7; U.S. reconnaissance
flights over, 663; war memorial, 745,
936; war with Iran, 21, 41, 114, 170–1,
177–8, 179–98, 199–214, 216, 226,
227–31, 233–42, 246, 248, 251–8, 613,
614; *see also* Baghdad; Saddam Hussein
al-Iraq, Ali (compiler): "Imprisoned
Memoirs," 1019
*Iraq Daily,* 942
Iraqi Civil Defence Corps (ICDC), 1007
Iraqi Intelligence Service, 994–5
Iraqi Islamic Conference, 1030
Irbil, Iraq, 718
Ireland, John de Courcy, 328
Ireland: partitioned (1921), 306
Irgun Zvai Leumi, 369, 373–4, 412
Irish Republican Army (IRA): assassination
attempt on Mrs. Thatcher, 1025–6; raises
money in U.S.A., 796
*Irish Times,* 611
Isaacson, Walter, 877
Isahakian, Levon, 320
al-Isawi, Captain Amar, 994
Islam, Yusuf (Cat Stevens), 596
Islamic Afghan Front, 59
Islamic committees, 955
Islamic Conference: emergency summit,
Qatar (10 October 2001), 855–7
Islamic Dawa party, *see* Dawa Party
Islamic Jihad: murders by, 1026; opposes
Algerian government, 541; in Palestinian
conflict, 390, 419, 422, 430–1, 442, 465,
466*n*, 472
Islamic Salvation Army (Algeria), 558
Ismael, Dr. Ali, 728–9
Ismaili, Mohamed, 233
Ismailia, 917
Israel: agreement with Jordan (1994), 797–9,
805; Arafat accepts state of, 381–2; and
Arafat's return to Gaza, 414–16, 417–18;
arms and defence industry, 771–2; army
behaviour, 378; army looting, 496, 510;
attacks Ramallah, 442, 444–5, 456, 467,
473, 494–6; Basic Law declares
Jerusalem capital, 426–7; bombards
Lebanon (1996), 773–4, 983–4;
bombards southern Lebanon (1993),
413; bombs Osirak nuclear reactor in
Iraq, 171; breaks ceasefire, 1027; builds
settlements in occupied territories,
425–9, 435; and Bush's Middle East
policy, 1014; Civil Rights Movement,
404; clandestine flights to Iran, 242–3;
closure policy against Palestinians,
455–6, 473–4; colonists remain armed
under Wye agreement, 437; conflicts
with Syria, 812, 814, 816–17; continuing
unrest in, 1037; delivers arms to Iran,
227, 766; demonisation of Palestinians,
441, 443; destroys Kuneitra, 200;
destroys Lebanese ambulance with U.S.

missile, 776–7, 781–2, 787; dialogue
with Hamas, 409; double-standard in
reporting on Palestinians, 448; fanatics
oppose agreement with Palestinians,
409; flouts UN Resolutions, 889, 901;
Gulf sheikhdoms oppose, 227; invades
Lebanon (1982), 268, 509, 672–3, 812,
841; Jewish claims to land and
settlements in, 402–6, 438; joins battle
against "world terror," 846; and killing
and abuse of Palestinians, 433, 464–6,
467–9, 486, 488–9, 503; leaders visit
Iran, 100, 103; at Madrid Middle East
Conference, 382–7; military technicians
in Beijing, 771–2; misrepresents Arafat's
archives, 510; and 9/11 attacks, 841;
nuclear weapons, 931; occupies West
Bank and Gaza, 377, 425; and
Palestinian housing requests, 427;
Palestinian suicide bombers in, 22,
406–7, 422, 429, 433, 442, 471–6,
479–80, 502–3, 509; policy in Gaza,
390–2; practises torture, 268, 433;
proposed re-partition, 404–5; and
proposed war on Iraq, 926, 931–2, 958;
Ritter informs of Iraq weapons searches,
721; and Sabra/Chatila killings, 828–31,
840–1; Saddam attacks with missiles,
605; Saddam demands withdrawal from
occupied territories, 590; shoots
Palestinian demonstrators, 606; state
established, 365, 374, 425; in Suez war
(1956), 914, 916, 917–18, 917*n*, 920;
"targeted killings," 1024–5; and
territoriality, 389; as threat to Arabs,
757–8; and "transfer" of Palestinians,
479*n*; unauthorised acquisition of U.S.
ordnance, 785*n*-6*n*; upgrades military
equipment, 771; U.S. arms supply to,
755, 762, 779, 783; U.S. denies criticism
of, 878; U.S. strategic cooperation with,
227; U.S. support for, 333; view of
Armenian massacres, 338–9, 347; wall
built, 479*n*, 1024; War of Independence
(1948), 364, 375–6; wars with Egypt,
377, 921; in Washington talks (1992),
389–90; withdrawal from occupied
territories, 407; *see also* Palestine
al-Issa, Judge Abdullah, 714–15
Issa, Mohamed bin, 856
Italy: arms sales, 750
Ive, Derek, 111–12
Iyad, Abu, 363
Izetbegovic, Alija, 398
Izmir (Smyrna): Armenians massacred in,
328, 337

Jaafar, Ziad, 154–5, 157
Jaafarian, Mahmoud, 104
al-Jabawi, Colonel Mohamed Khallaf, 943
Jaber, Abu, 384

Jaber, Moustapha, 738
Jaber, Saad Saleh, 661
al-Jabouri, Muslim, 156
al-Jabouri, Judge Mussalam, 1020
Jackson, J. B., 327
Jadour, Aida, 396
Jahani, Nafiseh Ashraf, 275
Jahanpanar, Captain Qassem, 104
Jalalabad, 3–4, 12–17, 25, 33, 42, 49–50, 73–80, 84
Jalali, Dr. Naser, 210
Jaloukhan, Hussain, 162
Jamal, Colonel, 682
Jamma, Fadwa, 498
*Jane's Intelligence Review,* 758
Jarrah, Jamal, 853–4
Jarrah, Samir, 852–4
Jarrah, Ziad, 844, 852–4, 1033
Jarrar, Sheikh Bassam, 431–2
*Jarrett,* USS, 251
Jassem, Cherou, 730
Jassem, Mohamed Aish, 994
Javidan Guards (Iran), 102
Jawad (Iraqi market seller), 216–17
Jawahiri, Mohamed Mahdi, 662–3
Jebel Abu Ghoneim (Har Homa), 427
Jehl, Douglas, 651n
Jelal Pasha, 351
Jemaa Islamiya (Egyptian underground movement), 123
Jemal Pasha, Ahmed, 331, 823–6
Jenin: killings in, 496–500, 505
Jenkins, Loren, 829
Jennings, Peter, 122, 124, 125n
Jericho, 393, 395–6, 398, 418–19
Jerusalem: Arab claims on, 359; captured by Allenby (1917), 366, 965–6; conditions, 468–9; declared Israeli capital under Basic Law, 426–7, 442, 606n; Israel demands as permanent unified capital, 389, 438–9; Israeli killings of Palestinians in, 440–1, 606; King David Hotel bombed (1946), 373; Orient House, 473–4, 486; proposed settlement under Oslo agreement, 394; Russian Compound, 485–6
*Jerusalem Post,* 443, 484, 502
Jewish Agency, 426
Jibril, Ahmed, 272–3
Jiha, Abbas, 774–8, 781
Jihad, Abu (Khaled al-Wazzir), 415, 464
jihad: Osama bin Laden conducts, 4
*John F. Kennedy,* USS, 622, 624
John Paul II, Pope, 340
Johnson, Nettie, 755
Johnson, Sergeant Darrin, 603–5
Johnston, William: *Tom Graham, V.C.,* 35, 37–9, 846n, 873
Jones, Lieutenant E.H., 328
Jord, Nihad, 811
Jordan: agreement with Israel (1994), 797–9,

805; allows shipment of Soviet weapons to Iraq, 769; annexes West Bank, 364; economic weakness, 589; fears separate Syrian agreement with Israel, 389–90; kills Palestinians, 411; loses West Bank, 802; relations with Iraq, 797; royal succession, 799–801, 804; *see also* Hussein, King
Jordan, Eason, 933n
Jordan, Sergeant Frank, 671–3, 674
Jordan Arab Army (*formerly* Arab Legion), 805
Jouhaud, General Edmond, 516
journalists: censored, 933n; embedded, 933; in First Gulf War, 599–601, 605, 628, 644–5, 651; involvement in conflicts, 876–7; killed and wounded in Iraq, 969–72, 982n; in "liberated" Iraq, 1002–3; pools, 599, 651n; vocation, 1036

Kabariti, Abdul Karim, 800
Kabul: al-Jazeera office in, 854; Al-Jazeera offices attacked by U.S. missile, 970; conditions, 3, 45–6, 60–1, 80, 83, 85; mass anti-Soviet demonstration suppressed, 90; mosques, 79; museums destroyed, 988; Northern Alliance captures, 863; Russian officials and military in, 85; Russian troops flown to, 78, 84, 86; U.S. actions in, 896; U.S. missiles strike, 827, 860; zoo, 61
Kach movement (Jewish), 411
Kadam, Zeineddin, 739
Kadir, Omer, 166
Kahak, Iran, 136–8
Kahan commission (Israel, 1993), 412, 507, 831, 879
Kai, Joe, 591
Kalashnikov, Mikhail, 759, 773
Kalashnikov, Viktor, 759–60, 761
al-Kaldi, Saba Abu Nasr, 696–7
Kaloustian, Mayreni, 321–2
Kamal, Wassef, 360–1, 363
Kamdemir, Nuhzet, 343
Kamel, Hassan Hussein, 658–9
Kamhi, Al, 786–8
kamikaze airmen, 478
Kanafani, Ghassan, 423
Kanafani, Marwan, 423–4
Kandahar, 87–9, 866–8, 870–1, 877, 893, 912
Kanellopoulos, Panayotis, 97
Kapuscinski, Ryszard, 101
Karakashian, Father Ashod, 334–5
Karapegian, Levon, 352
Kareem, Lieutenant, 1020
Karim, Safa, 973–4
Karmal, Babrak: appeals for Afghan army support, 62–3; and deaths of Russian soldiers, 60; holds press conference,

55–7; installed as Afghan President, 40, 45, 55; on mujahedin, 83; opposition to, 58–9; orders killing of Khalq officials, 86; regime, 78–80; and rising food prices, 89; and Soviet invasion of Afghanistan, 43, 53–5, 57–8

Karni, 449–50

Karpinski, Brigadier General Janis, 1015–16

Karzai, Hamid: collaborates with Americans, 894; complains of U.S. treatment of Afghan prisoners, 1037*n*; inauguration, 899*n*; opponents, 897; protected by U.S. bodyguards, 899; reinstates pipeline project, 1037*n*; signs death sentence, 55*n*; in United Nations, 889; works for Unocal, 28, 1037*n*

Kashani, Ayatollah Abul Qassim, 97–8

Kashmir, 858

Kashoggi, Adnan, 765

Kashoggi, Jamal, 5, 6–7, 12

Kattouf, Ted, 207

Kaufman, Marc, 928

Kazim, Zainab, 281–2

Kealy, Robin, 169

Kebedjian, Haroutioun, 354–5

Kedjedjian, Maritza, 351

Kelly, Michael, 969

Kelly, Lieutenant General Thomas, 628, 649

Kelner, Simon, 337, 827

Kemal (Atatürk), Mustafa, 44*n*, 350, 677, 679

Kemeck, Tassin, 682

Kenaan, Brigadier General Ghazi, 821

Kennedy, John F., 581

Kerbala, 100, 252, 257

Kerbej, Abriza, 823

Kerman, Iran, 132

Kevorkian, Andrew, 348

Kevorkian, Aram, 351

Khaddam, Abdul Khalim, 410

Khadi, Misban, 162, 164

Khad secret police (Afghanistan), 57–8, 85, 86

Khafji, Saudi Arabia, 618–21, 623, 639

Khail, Abdul Saheb, 156

Khairallah, General Adnan, 190, 745, 969

Khairallah, Ismail, 152

Khakzar, Mullah, 868–9

Khalaj, Karim, 138

al-Khalasi, Sheikh Jouwad Mehdi, 1028–30

al-Khalasi, Sheikh Mehdi, 1028–9

Khaleb, Dr. Jenane, 739

Khaled, King of Saudi Arabia, 109

Khaled, Abu, 714

Khaled, Hassan (Lebanese Grand Mufti), 356

Khaled bin Sultan bin Abdul Aziz, Prince, 593, 598, 610, 636–7, 639–40, 663

Khalidi, Sulieman, 695

al-Khalifa, Sheikh Khalifa Sulman, 226–7

al-Khalil, Abdul-Karim, 824

Khalil, Ashraf, 407

Khalilzad, Zalmay, 28, 1037*n*

Khalkali, Ayatollah Hojatolislam Sadeq ("the Cat"), 105, 109, 118, 130–4, 168, 174

Khalq agents, 86

al-Khaltum, Um, 364

Khamenei, Ali, President of Iran, 227, 250*n*, 272

Khan, Haji Birgit, 891–3, 894

Khan, Mohamed Selim, 91

Khan, Sajjat, 851

Khani, Ali, 258

Khan Younis Palestinian refugee camp, 462, 488

Kharg Island, 222, 228, 246

Khartoum, 5–7, 9–10

Khatami, Mohamed, 284, 290, 819

Khayoun, Faisal, 1018

Khdair, Samar, 729, 737

Kheroui, Saïda, 574, 579

Khiam prison, Lebanon, 268, 269, 377

Khleef, Kassem, 470*n*

al-Khobar, Dhahran, 19–22, 31

Khodr, Mohamed, 400

al-Khoi, Grand Ayatollah Abulqassem, 163–5

al-Khoi, Youssef, 165

Khomeini, Ayatollah Ruhollah: accepts ceasefire (1988), 273; assumes power, 41; author interviews, 122–6, 136; authority, 228–9; and bin Laden, 125; calls for overthrow of Saddam, 173, 201, 229; condemns Shah's rule, 100, 120; and control of Iraq, 204–5; criticisms of, 228, 233; death and funeral, 199, 235, 806; declines ceasefire (1982), 286; defends executions, 174–5; defends Islam, 125–6; early support for Shah, 98*n*; exile, 100, 101–2, 120, 161, 162–5; and Iran-Contra affair, 245; Iraqi hostility to, 170–1; Iraqi prisoners acknowledge, 205–6; Islamic revolution on return to Iran, 102–3, 110, 171–3; "Last Message," 125–6; letter from Karmal, 62; and "martyrdom," 285; orders good treatment for Iraqi prisoners, 205; orders liquidation of political prisoners, 274; pictures defaced in war with Iraq, 182; popular appeal, 125–6, 137–8; posters in Herat, 79; protected against air attacks, 229; and revolutionary courts, 104; rule and regime, 105–6, 117–18, 120–1; Saddam Hussein condemns, 159; Saddam's treatment of, 161–2; and Tudeh party, 121–2; and war with Iraq, 187, 193, 200–1, 204, 226, 241, 273, 286; as western bogeyman, 170; wishes death of Shah, 109; and Woodhouse's coup, 94, 98

Khorabi, Osama, 761–2

Khorramshahr ("al-Mohammorah"), 168, 182–3, 185, 186–7, 189–91, 192, 199, 216, 253, 284–6, 607, 632

Khorum, Afghanistan, 862
Khosravi, Morteza, 760–1
Khourshid, Warrant Officer Najat Kazem, 152
Khoury, General (Lebanon), 770
Khrushchev, Nikita S., 153n-4n
Khudeiri, Amr Hassan, 469–71
Khuzestan, 167–8, 200
Khyber Pass, 69–70; railway, 90–1
Kianouri, Nouredin, 121–2
*Kidd*, USS, 248–9
Kider, Mohamed, 543
Kifner, John, 201, 202, 204, 234
Kila Abdulla, 871, 876
Kim Jong Il, 926
Kim Sun-il, 1030
al-Kindi, Ibn Ishaq, 1032
Kindi Hospital, Baghdad, 972–4
King, Tom, 610
King-Crane commission (U.S.), 333
Kinzer, Stephen, 341–2
Kipling, Rudyard, 35, 70, 999
al-Kirawee, Imad, 1020
Kirkuk oilfields, 988
Kissinger, Henry, 102, 120, 639
Kitchener, Field Marshal Horatio Herbert, 1st Earl, 308
Kitrey, Brigadier General Ron, 497
*Kitty Hawk*, USS, 710, 941
Kleinman, Josef and Haya, 369–71
Kleinman, Shlomo, 370
Klinghoffer, Leon, 380, 1022
Köknar, Güler, 337–8
Korea, 490n
Kosimik, René, 429
Kosovo, 508, 726, 741n
Kouk, Halilat ("Kouka"), 569
Kozyrev, Andrei, 718, 798
*Krasica* (Yugoslav freighter), 191
Kufa, 252
Kuneitra, Syria, 200
Kurdish Workers party (PKK), 335, 681, 719
Kurdistan: Iraqi vengeance in, 666; Kurdish demands for, 674; proposed purging, 206n; U.S. presence in, 668–70
Kurds: bombed by Turks, 718–19; coalition relief operations for, 670–1; deported in Iraq, 165–6; and independence from Turkey, 332; insurrections in Iraq, 102, 148–9, 152, 662, 671, 681, 683, 686; massacre Armenians, 322, 324, 327, 332, 351, 685; murdered in *Anfal* campaign, 215; purge Baathists, 681; rebel in Iran, 130, 176–7; refugees flee from Saddam, 651, 664–5, 666–7; remain in north, 671–2; Saddam's genocide and repression against, 215–17, 246, 336, 667–8, 681–2, 702; Saddam uses chemical weapons against, 214–15, 230; Shah withdraws support for, 161; and Turks, 674; Turks steal relief supplies

from, 676–7; U.S. disclaims, 683–4; U.S. protection for, 663, 665, 674
Kurtz, Stanley, 510
Kut-al-Amara, 142, 308
Kuwait: arms for Iraq pass through, 222; backs Saddam against Iran, 207, 588; Bedouin troops, 695; bombed by U.S.A. in First Gulf War, 650; capital liberated, 630–2, 649–50; citizens flee to Saudi Arabia, 723; and defence of Gulf, 227; and financing of First Gulf War, 637n-8n; in First Gulf War, 619–20, 624; given confiscated Iraqi territory, 783; imprisons non-citizens, 696–7; in Iran-Iraq war, 239; Iraqi atrocities and depradations in, 632–4, 648, 653, 688, 692; Iraqi claims to, 613n; Iraqis refuel at air base, 256n; missing citizens, 700–2; oilfields burned, 630, 648, 697–9; oil production, 588n, 699; oil revenues, 250; Palestinians killed and persecuted in, 638–9, 650–3, 695, 701; post-war conditions, 652–6; rule and rulers after war, 695; Saddam attacks royal family, 711–12; Saddam invades (1990), 5, 7, 21, 272–3, 382, 588–90, 593, 595, 597, 612–13, 769; Saddam recognises new frontiers, 718–19; Saddam repeats Iraqi claims to, 710–12; U.S. offers protection to, 247–8
Kuzichkin, Vladimir, 123

Labelle, Gerry ("G.G."), 211, 234–41
Lackey, Captain, 712–13
Laden, Osama bin, *see* bin Laden, Osama
Ladjevardi, Hojatolislam Ali, 228
Lahoud, Emile, 818, 926
Laibson, Sidney, 879
Laingen, Bruce, 114, 198
Lamari, General Mohamed, 557, 582
Lambrakis, George, 128–9
al-Lamee, Lieutenant Ibrahim, 1019
Lancaster, John, 582
Lancaster, Warrant Officer "Chuck," 668–70, 674–5
Landau, Moshe, 433n
Landi Kotal, 91
Lang, Bob, 403–4
Lang, Colonel Walter, 214
language, manipulation of, 62–3, 378–9, 411–12, 425, 436, 444–5, 448–9, 452, 453–4, 540n, 649n-50n, 718, 933
Larak Island, 246
Larson, Major (U.S. Army), 735
Latif, Nasser Abdul, 1012
Lau, Rabbi Israel Meir, 466n
Lausanne, Treaty of (1923), 332
Lavigerie, Mgr. Charles, Bishop of Algiers, 517
Lawrence, T. E., 145–7, 306
Leachman, Colonel Gerald, 145

League of Nations, 890
Lebanon: arms supply in, 772–3; author's life in, 790; bombarded by Israelis, 413, 774–8, 983–4; border with Palestine altered, 372–3; Christian conflicts in, 304; fear of Israeli invasion, 481; French mandate in, 372, 791–2; hardships in First World War, 823; hostages in, 242, 244, 245; Iranian Revolutionary Guards in, 161; Israel invades (1982), 268, 509, 672–3, 812, 841; Israel withdraws from (2000), 377, 442; martyrs for autonomy under Turks, 824–6; Palestinian refugees in, 400; railways, 792; state created, 306–7, 813, 825; suicide bombers in, 476–7; Syrian army leaves (2005), 1035–6; Syrian troops in, 150, 821; *see also* Beirut
Lederman, Major, 498
Leibowitz, Yeshayahu, 405–6
Leighton, Bandsman Charles, 71
Leighton, Roland, 314
Leila, Princess of Iran, 116 17
Lemkin, Raphael, 337, 340
Leopold II, King of the Belgians, 336
Leroy, Michel, 305
leukaemia, *see* cancer
Levene, Mark, 336
Levy, Gideon, 474
Lévy, Jules Roger, 515
Lévy, William, 515
Lewin, Nathan, 490
Lewinsky, George, 188
Lewinsky, Monica, 438, 722
Lewis, Bernard, 344
Lewis, "Chuck," 243
Lewis, Jonathan Eric, 339–40
Lewis, Martyn, 56
Liabès, Djillali, 552
Libya: accused of "international terrorism," 882–3; bombed by U.S.A., 861, 880, 881, 884–6, 888
Lifton, Robert Jay, 342–3
Lindval, Captain Mikael, 779, 779n
Lipstadt, Deborah, 343
Lloyd, Selwyn Brooke (*later* Baron Selwyn-Lloyd), 920
Lloyd, Terry, 969
Lloyd George, David, 144–5, 308, 346, 366–7
Lochner, Louis, 336
Lockerbie, 271–2
Lockheed, 629n
London: Iranian embassy siege (1980), 167–8
Long, Gerald, 68n
looting: in Baghdad, 975, 977–80, 982
Lorence, Captain Paul, 884, 886
Louvencourt, France, 296, 309, 314, 1038
Louzoum, Raymond, 545
Love, Kennett, 916
Lucas, Armen, 345–6
Lucas, W. Scott, 920

*Luce,* USS, 225
Lustig, Commander Scott, 267
Lynch (Prince Khaled's public relations adviser), 636

Ma'ale Adumim (Israeli settlement), 402–3, 428–9
*Ma'ariv* (Israeli newspaper), 438, 510, 1037n
Mabro, Robert, 590n
MacArthur, General Douglas, 888
McBride, John, 307
McBride, Sean, 120
McCaffrey, General Barry, 640
McCrae, John: "In Flanders Fields," 289, 752
MacDonald, Malcolm, 359
McFarlane, Robert, 243–5, 765, 766
Macmillan, Harold (*later* 1st Earl of Stockton), 920
McVeigh, Timothy, 650n
Madani, Abassi, 523, 525–6, 527, 537
Madani, Ayatollah Asadollah, 199
Madani, Mahmoud, 491–2
Maddi, Moussa, 574
Madrid: Middle East Conference (1991), 383–8, 420, 473, 816
"mafia," 543–4; believes in conspiracy ("the Plot"), 546–7; deaths and killings in civil war, 544–6, 547–54, 566–72, 577; "disappeared" in, 572–4, 579, 583; "eradicators" in, 557–8; friendship towards U.S.A., 581–2; international indifference to atrocities, 579–81; operations against al-Qaeda in, 584–5; police ambushed in, 560–3; police death squads and "anti-terrorist" actions, 545, 553–5, 556–7, 564–5; public support for Iraq, 605; security forces and police in, 563–4, 572–8
Magee, Aircraftman First Class P., 956
Maghraoui, Brahim, 574
Mahawi, Abdul Jalil, 152
Mahazullah of Turangzai, 860–1
Mahdi, the (Mohamed Ahmed ibn as-Sayyid), 10
Mahfouz, Naguib, 559n
Mahmessani, Mohamed and Mahmoud, 824
Mahmoud, Ali, 590
Mahmoud, Engineer, 15–17
Mahmoud, Malek, 950
Mahmoudi, Aziz, 137
Majalli, Abdul Salam, 798
Majid, Dr. (of Abu Ghraib prison), 1016
al-Majid, Ali Hassan ("Chemical Ali"), 246, 671, 926–7, 979
Majid, Lieutenant-Colonel Fathi Rani, 944
Major, John, 609, 621, 648
Makdisi, Jean, 510
Makhloufi, Saïd, 562
Makiya, Kanan, 681n, 687, 910
Mallat, Chibli, 838
Manar television station, 442

*Manchester Guardian,* 916
Mandour, Adel, 918
Manning, Frederic: *Her Privates We,* 206–7
Mansour, General, 680
Mansouri, Lebanon, 774–6, 778, 983–4
al-Mansouri, Samira Awdah (Um Imam), 1019
Manwar, Zeinab, 739
Maples, Sergeant Ladell, 125
Marcos, Imelda, 100
Margada, 316, 323–4
Margalit, Dan, 509n
Margolick, David, 489
Marin, Manuel, 580
Marj al-Zahour, 430–2, 505–6
Marlowe, Lara, 261, 549, 555, 653–4, 728, 733, 742–3, 791
Marr, Andrew, 784
Marshall, Andy, 573
Marsh Arabs (Iraq), 246, 686–7, 747, 1017–19
Mars-Jones, Sir William, 462
Martin, Samuel, 141
Martin, Sergeant Clifford, 373
martyrdom: and heavenly rewards, 477; by Iranian soldiers, 202–4, 231, 256–8; by Palestinians, 450, 504; Shias and, 281–2; *see also* suicide bombers
el-Marzouk, Siham and Faisal, 654n
Mashaal, Khaled, 466n
massacres: of Algerians, 29, 518, 519–21; by Arabs, 411–12; Armenian, 308, 316–31, 334–6, 337–50, 509n; of Assyrians by Iraq, 336; in Belgian Congo, 336; Israeli against Palestinian demonstrators, 606; by Israelis in Jenin, 497–9; of Jews (Holocaust), 331, 337, 338–9, 342, 347, 362–3; against Kurds, 246; of Palestinians in Hebron, 410–12; of Palestinians in Sabra and Chatila, 20, 412, 449, 458–9, 461, 484, 488–9, 507, 673, 791, 806, 827–32, 840–1; at Qana (Lebanon), 20, 439, 456–8; by Taliban, 849–50; of Taliban in Afghanistan, 864–5, 869–70, 871
Massoud, Ahmed Shah, 827, 849, 854, 863
Massu, General Jacques, 520, 557
Matoub, Lounes, 559n
Mattar, Abdullah, 829
Maude, Francis, 353–4
Maude, Lieutenant General Sir Stanley, 139, 141, 144, 147, 517, 965
Maugham, Captain Mike, 713
Mayne, Sir Michael, 349
Maysaloun, battle of (1920), 813–14, 825
Mazar-e-Sharif, 63, 849, 864, 870–1, 896
Mazinan, Ali, 236, 252, 254–6
Mecca, 5; Great Mosque siege (1979), 848–9; pilgrims killed (1987), 250n
Medina, 5–6
Medjoubi, Azzedine, 558–9

Megalli, Nabila, 230
Mekbel, Saïd, 513, 553
Meliani, Mansouri, 528
Mell, Donald C. III, 612
Menad, Halima, 548
Mengele, Dr. Josef, 370
Mertins, Gerhard, 764–6
Mesopotamia, *see* Iraq
Meysonnier, Fernand, 905
Meziad, Mohamed, 471
Meziane-Cherif, Abderrahmane, 557–8, 564–6
Miller, Judith, 909
Mills, Woosnam, 71
Milosevic, Slobodan, 449, 508
al-Mimar, Yussef, 152
Mimouni, Rachid, 534, 559n
Mir, Hamid, 857
Mishlawi, Tewfiq, 724
Mislet, Jamil, 443
*Missouri,* USS, 249
Mitterrand, François, 521
Mizler, Karima, 961–2
Mnati, Hussein, 953
Moakdad, Colonel, 682
Modehi, Ali, 775
Mofaz, Shoal, 500, 510, 958
Mogadishu, 713
Moghni, Abdelkader, 540
Moghrabi, Abed, 307, 789, 792, 795
Moguy, Brigadier General Salahedin, 919
Mohamed, Commandant (Algiers), 560–3, 571
Mohamed, Rahman Jassem, 737
Mohamed, Colonel Saad, 996
Mohamed, Youssef, 730
Mohamed, Youssef Abdul Raouf, 729
Mohamedin, Faqir, 891, 892–3
Mohamed the Prophet, 88, 100
Mohsen, Abduaziz, 775
Mohtashemi, Hojatolislam Ali Akbar, 161, 661
Molad, Mickey, 879
Mollet, Guy, 915, 921
Monk, Lieutenant Roy, 643
Montazeri, Ayatollah Hossein Ali, 121, 245, 273–4
Moore, William: *The Thin Yellow Line,* 297
Mooushed, Abdul-Kadem, 730
Morgan, Judy, 707–8, 737
Morgenthau, Henry, 322, 324, 326, 337
Morocco: public support for Iraq, 605
Morris, Benny, 372, 376
Morris, Major Curt, 592
Morris, Harvey, 117–18, 126, 134–6, 261, 397, 501–2, 541, 631, 645, 677–8
Morris, Steve, 46–7, 60
Mortaba, Hebba, 736–7
Mortimer, Edward, 103, 111
Mosalem, Kemal, 483
Moskowitz, Irving, 427

Mossad: CIA file on in Iran, 128; information gathering, 465; killings by, 466n, 1025
Mossadeq, Mohamed, 92, 94–8, 103, 121, 1029
Motier, Homayoun, 698–9
Mouffak, Ahmed, 292
Mouffak, Fathi Daoud, 178, 291–3
Mousbah, Sheikh, 525
Moussa, Amr, 386
Moussa, Baha, 1012
Moussa, Mohamed, 9, 961
Moussa, Sara, 652n
Moussavi, Mir-Hossein, 248
Moussawi, Said Abbas, 861
Moutaded, Caliph, 153n
Moyne, Walter Edward Guinness, 1st Baron, 374–5
Mozdooryar, Shah Jan, 59
Mubarak, Hosni: advises Saddam against invading Kuwait, 589; Arafat visits, 394; on attempted assassination of Hamas official, 466n; attends Assad's funeral, 819; condemns U.S. hijacking of Abul Abbas plane, 381; election majority, 841; offended by Al-Jazeera, 854; sends senators to meet Saddam, 593; on transience of Iraqi invasion of Kuwait, 856
al-Mudaressi, Ayatollah Taqi, 661, 662–3
Mufti of Jerusalem, *see* Amin al-Husseini, Haj
mujahedin: actions and atrocities, 74–5, 82–3; in Afghanistan, 8, 14, 19, 29, 32, 49; conflict with Taliban, 90; enforce behaviour on women and girls, 82; Karmal attempts to appease, 61; mine roads, 85; recruited from villages, 80; relations with Afghan army, 74–5, 77
Mujahedin-e-Qalq (People's Mujahedin), 174, 198–9, 273–4
al-Mukhtaseb, Zuheir, 492–3
Muna, Queen of Jordan (*née* Antoinette Avril Gardiner "Toni"), 801–2
Munro, General Sir Charles, 141
Muqimi, Zarrin, 173–4
Murad, Major Mustafa Kamal, 917–21
Murdoch, Rupert, 260–1, 268, 269–70
Murphy, Anne Marie, 459, 460n, 462
Murphy, Richard, 220, 589
Murrow, Edward R., 622
Musa Dagh, Turkey, 334–5
Musayeb, Iraq, 658, 659, 664
Musharraf, General Pervez, 851, 858, 862, 1035
Musleh, Rashid, 152
Muslim Brotherhood, 528, 814, 815–16, 822
Mustafa (Beirut landlord), 789, 790
Mutla Ridge, 640–4, 688–90, 694, 700, 717, 753–4
Myatt, General Michael, 610

Nablus, 426; attacked by Israelis, 442, 505, 509, 510
Nabors, Sergeant Charles, 669–71
Naccache, Anis, 171, 172n
Nacer, Guitoun, 550
Nadir Khan, Mohamed, 44n
Nahnah, Sheikh Mahfouz, 524–5, 529, 550, 551
Najaf, Iraq, 161–5, 252, 993, 1010; massacres in, 664
Najibullah, Mohamed, 14, 59n
Najour, Ali, 972–3
Nakhoul, Samia, 971–2
al-Nakib, Rashid, 994
Narkiss, Uzi, 546
al-Nashashibi, Raghib, 359
Nasiriyah, 647–8, 949, 982
Nasr, Captain Ali, 914
Nasr, Haj Mahmoud, 475–6
Nasr, Maryam and Hoda, 962
Nasr, Mohamed, 474–6, 478
Nasrallah, Sayed Hassan, 476–8, 819
Nasser, Captain (of Iran Air), 265
Nasser, Gamal Abdel, 159, 364, 377, 913–14, 916, 918, 921
Nasser, Nasser Ahmed, 167–8
Nasser, General Youssef, 423, 424–5
Nassiri, Mehrdrodi, 257
Nassiri, Colonel Nimatullah, 96, 99, 103, 131
National Gulf Resource Center (U.S.A.), 738
National Liberation Front (FLN), Algeria, 519–20, 522–4, 526–7, 543, 546
*National Post* (Canada), 500
NATO (North Atlantic Treaty Organisation): war against Serbia, 508
Natour, Suheil, 411
al-Nayef, Abdul Razzak, 150–1
Nazis: copy Armenian massacres, 329–30; persecution of Jews, 367
Neal, Brigadier General Richard, 625–8
Neave, Airey, 1026
Negroponte, John, 906
Netanya, Israel, 493
Netanyahu, Benjamin: Clinton's exasperation with, 437; denies massacre at Jenin, 497; denounces Rabin, 429; elected Prime Minister, 432; frees Sheikh Yassin, 1025; and Jewish colonisation of Palestinian land, 427–8, 434–5, 438, 806; at King Hussein's funeral, 805; manner, 807; negotiates Wye River agreement, 420n–1n, 437; and Perle-Wolfowitz strategic plan, 1013; *A Place Among the Nations*, 436; and proposed war against Iraq, 931; refuses establishment of Palestinian state, 438; rejects agreements with Palestinians, 432; sends assassination squad for Hamas official, 805; visits Blair in London, 434
*New Jersey*, USS, 814
Newman, John Henry, Cardinal, 716

*Newsweek* (magazine), 264–5, 266–7, 905
New World Order, 624–5, 700, 1014
New York: author visits, 795–6; World Trade
    Center destroyed (9/11 2003), 794–5,
    827, 832–4, 837, 841, 1013, 1032–3
*New Yorker, The* (magazine), 720*n*
*New York Times*, 326, 340–2, 503, 664, 726,
    878*n*-9*n*, 886, 900, 909, 927, 929, 983,
    1021*n*
Nezzar, General Khaled, 529, 536, 541, 583–4
Nicaragua: and Iran-Contra scandal, 243, 245;
    Israeli arms supply to, 772
Nidal, Abu, 150
Nikkah, Parviz, 104
Nikolai, Lieutenant, 64–5
*Nimitz,* USS (carrier), 130*n*
no-fly zones (Iraq), 710, 718–19
Nolde, Staff Sergeant, 655–6
al-Nomani, Sergeant Ali Jaffar Moussa
    Hamadi, 953–4
Noor, Queen of Jordan (*née* Elizabeth
    Halaby), 797, 799, 802, 806
Norman, Revd Edward, 609
North, Lieutenant Colonel Oliver, 243–5, 253,
    381, 765
North African Star (Algerian independence
    group), 537
Northern Alliance (Afghanistan), 854, 862–5,
    867–8, 898, 899
Northern Ireland: formed, 306, 308; territorial
    conflict in, 429*n*
North Korea: aids Iran, 227, 229–30
Noulaaresse, Ahmed, 564
Nouri, Djillali, 547–8
nuclear weapons: Britain exports components
    to Iraq, 769–70; Iraqi plans to develop,
    157–9, 171, 719; Israeli, 931; supposed
    Iraqi possession of, 609, 900, 902–3
Numa, Radi, 1012
Numbers, Book of, 402
Nuremberg trials, 866
Nuriel, Menashe, 468
Nye, Lieutenant Andrew, 643
Nyholm, Corporal Ted, 996

Obaid, Nawaf, 848–9
al-Obbeydi, Lieut. Colonel Madjid, 256*n*
*Observer* (newspaper), 168, 921
O'Clery, Conor, 46, 54–5, 838
O'Connor, Paul, 678–80
O'Donovan, Patrick, 375–6
al-Oglah, Fadila, 774, 776, 780
oil: as motive for Iraq war, 925–6; reserves in
    Iraq, 904
Oklahoma City bombing (1995), 650*n*
O'Leary, Anne, 220*n*
Oliver, Captain Simon, 649
Oman, Gulf of, 250
Omar, Mullah Mohamed, 861–3, 1025, 1032
Omar Ibn Khattab, Caliph, 191
Omran, Adnan, 821

O'Neil, Steve, 250–1
OPEC: rules on oil production, 588*n,* 699
opium: in Afghanistan, 15–16; in Iran, 133
Osirak nuclear reactor (Iraq), 159, 171
Oslo agreement (1983): and Abul Abbas, 381;
    Arafat on dissatisfactions with, 416;
    collapse of, 481; disfavours Palestinians,
    390, 441–2; divides West Bank into
    zones, 420; Hanan Ashrawi on, 451; and
    Israeli settlements on Palestinian lands,
    399, 407, 413, 420–1, 427–8, 429, 435,
    436–7; and Jordan's treaty with Israel,
    797; Khaddam denounces, 410;
    Mahmoud Abbas helps draft, 1026–7;
    promised benefits, 393–4, 395, 436–7,
    440, 456; and transitional Palestinian
    rule, 426
Othman, Brigadier Bashir Ahmed, 943
Othman, Mohamed Mahran, 918–19, 919*n*
Ottawa: 1992 talks, 388
Ottoman Empire, *see* Turkey
Oul-Hadj, Mohand, 524
al-Ouwaynati, Rida, 1020
Oveissi, Gholamali, 131
Oweid, Abbas, 1017
Owen, Robert, 245
Owen, Wilfred, 179, 183, 218, 257, 294,
    601–2
Özal, Semra, 350
Özener, Barlas, 338
Özkök, Ertugrul, 350

Pagonis, General Gus, 785
Pahlavi, Ashraf (Shah's sister), 96, 131
Paice, Sergeant Mervyn, 373
Pakistan: closes borders with Afghanistan,
    44*n*; collusion with Afghan rebels, 80;
    cooperates with U.S.A. in war on
    Afghanistan, 862–3; covert support for
    al-Qaeda, 911; as enemy of Afghanistan,
    860; Interservices Intelligence
    Organisation (ISI), 13, 862; maintains
    Khyber Pass railway, 91; and Soviet
    invasion of Afghanistan, 69–70; Taliban
    college in, 851; in war with India (1965),
    765
Palestine: Arab-Jewish struggle for, 365–73,
    375–7; Arafat accepts partition, 381–2,
    394; border with Lebanon altered,
    372–3; British mandate in, 365, 367,
    372–3; Haj Amin and, 356, 358–62;
    Jewish and Arab "terrorist" actions in,
    373–9; Jewish home and state in, 148,
    306, 359, 365–9; Jewish immigrants,
    370–1; partition, 368, 375, 384*n*, 1032;
    *see also* Israel
*Palestine* (magazine), 356, 358
Palestine Hotel, Baghdad, 969, 970, 978, 982*n*
Palestine Liberation Front, 380
Palestine Liberation Organisation (PLO):
    Arafat changes charter, 399; Hamas's

rivalry with, 390; and Iraqi invasion of Kuwait, 594; and Oslo agreement, 413, 429, 432; Soviet support for, 173

Palestinian Authority, 393, 419, 437, 473, 482, 494

Palestinians: aim to reclaim whole of Palestine, 481–2; Amira Hass reports on, 453–4; Arafat's aims for, 381; attempted coup in Jordan suppressed, 802; and Bush's Middle East policy, 1014; demonised by Israelis, 441, 443, 449, 507; disarmed under Wye agreement, 437–8; dispossessed, 364, 368–9, 370–1, 376–8, 400–1; execute collaborators, 490–3; in Gaza, 391–3; housing refused and destroyed by Israelis, 427–8; identity and culture, 489; killed and abused by Israelis, 433, 452, 457–8, 464–6, 467–9, 488–9, 497–8, 504–5, 510–11, 932; killed and persecuted in Kuwait, 638–9, 650–3, 695, 701; killed following 9/11 attacks, 846; kill Jewish settler families, 499–500; at Madrid Middle East Conference, 387; massacred at Hebron, 410–12, 414; militias, 390; and Oslo agreement, 393–4, 420–1; purged by Arafat, 470n; refugees, 400–1; refugees massacred by Phalangists in Sabra and Chatila, 20, 412, 449, 458–9, 461, 484, 488–9, 507, 673, 791, 806, 827–32, 840–1, 879, 1038; suicide bombers, 22, 406–7, 420, 471–6, 479–80, 502–3, 509, 1014, 1024; and territoriality, 389; and "terrorism," 375, 378, 489–90, 499–500; towns attacked by Israelis, 442; U.S. arms used against, 761–2; in Washington talks (1992), 389–90; welcome 9/11 attacks, 842; wish for state, 1037

Palizban, General, 131

Palme, Jens, 471

Pan Am airliner: blown up over Lockerbie, 271–2

Papazian, Serpouhi, 323

Papen, Franz von, 329

Paputin, General Viktor, 45

Parandak, Iran, 205

Paris: Iranian assassins in, 171, 172n; Iraqi gunmen in, 166; Peace Conference (1919), 383

Parish, Daphne, 168–9

Parker, Alastair, 735

Parrott, Sergeant, 604

Parry, Robert, 289

Partick, Neil, 757

Pasqua, Charles, 546

Pasquale, Paul, 971

Pathans, 44, 49, 52–3

Patriotic Union of Kurdistan (PUK), 165–6

Patton, General George S., 616

Pavelic, Ante, 362

Pazira, Nelofer, 850

Peace Now (Israeli pressure group), 429

Pearl, Daniel and Marianne, 876, 911

Pearl, Judea, 839

Pearl Harbor (1941), 925

Pearse, Padraig, 307

Pelletreau, Robert, 582

Penketh, Anne, 832

Pennsylvania: suicide plane crashes in, 832, 839, 852, 1013

Peres, Shimon, 339, 431, 465, 774–5, 778

Perez de Cuellar, Javier, 1004

Perle, Richard, 169, 766, 931, 1010, 1014

Perry, William, 718

Persepolis, 100–1

Peshavar, Ibrahim, 128

Peshawar, 70–4, 91

Peverley, Very Rev. Courtney, 72

Phalange (Lebanon), 20, 362, 412, 484, 488–9, 507, 673, 773, 828–9, 831, 832n

Picot, François Georges, 144, 791, 825, 1031

Pilger, John, 708, 718

Pim, Richard, 160

Pines-Paz, Ophir, 448n

Pinochet, General Augusto, 460

Piranshahr, 210

Pirouzi, Hossein, 266

Poland: massacres and deportations in, 336–7

Po-le-charkhi prison, Kabul, 54–5, 79, 84

Political Organisation of the Arab People of Arabistan, 167

Pollack, Kenneth: *The Threatening Storm*, 922–3

Pollard, Jonathan, 437n

Pontecorvo, Gillo, 520, 539, 1014

Popper, Ellen, 839

Popular Arab and Islamic Conference, Khartoum, 9–10, 11–12

Popular Front for the Liberation of Palestine—General Command (PFLP-GC), 272

Port Said, 917–18, 919–20

Post, Marine Sergeant John, 620

Pour, Ghaysar Amin, 287

Powell, Colin: addresses UN Security Council, 927–31; chides emir of Qatar for Al-Jazeera "anti-Americanism," 854; claims Iraqi oil held in trusteeship for Iraqi people, 925–6; and Iraqi actions against Kurds, 684–5; on mission of peace to Israel and West Bank, 500; on options for disposing of Saddam, 663; recognises Arafat as Palestinian leader, 502; re-designates occupied territories as "disputed," 480–1; reinforces sanctions against Iraq, 480–1; seeks Pakistani support in Afghanistan, 858; traduces Saddam, 598; and U.S. actions in Afghanistan, 863; warns Arafat of "last chance," 509; warns Syria and Iran for supporting "terror" groups, 957; warns Taliban against sheltering bin Laden, 846

Powell, Eileen, 211
Powers, Francis Gary, 90
Price, Sergeant Frederick William, 956
Primakov, Yevgeni, 819
prisoners-of-war: exchanged after Iran-Iraq
    ceasefire, 276; in Iran-Iraq war, 192–3,
    200, 205–6, 228, 232–3, 256, 285
Protsjuk, Taras "Sasha," 970–1
Provide Comfort, Operation, 667, 670–1
Purcell-O'Byrne, Noel, 244
Pushtunistan, 44
Putin, Vladimir, 760, 819, 905

Qadir, Haji, 16
Qadisiya, Iraq, 964; battle of (633 AD), 205,
    208–9
al-Qahtani, Mohamed Ibn Abdullah, 848
Qana, Lebanon, 20, 439, 456–8, 773n, 778,
    806
al-Qaraghuli, Wahbi, 170
Qardaha, Syria, 820–1
Qasimiyh security station, Baghdad, 994–5
Qasqari, Hassan, 203–4
Qassem, Dhamia, 731, 738
Qassem, Youssef, 739
Qassim, Abdul-Karim, 148–9, 278
Qatar: and al-Jazeera broadcasts, 854; forces
    in First Gulf War, 620, 636; opposes
    bombing of Iraq, 726; supports Afghans,
    857
Qom, Iran, 106, 108, 122–3
Qotb, Saïd, 525
Qotbzadeh, Sadeq, 62, 110, 118, 124, 126,
    177
Quayle, Dan, 245
Quddusi, Ayatollah Ali, 199
Quemener, Olivier, 552
Quraishi tribe, 88

Rabin, Yitzhak: agrees Oslo accords with
    Arafat, 393, 399, 407–9, 413–14, 415,
    436–7; aided by French, 546; and Araba
    agreement with Jordan, 798;
    assassinated, 430, 450, 462, 799;
    background, 506; concludes Oslo II
    (Taba) agreement (1995), 420n; cruelty
    under, 429–30, 466n; funeral, 807; on
    Gaza, 506; holds on to occupied land,
    427, 430; shares Nobel prize with Arafat,
    424; on suicide attacks, 406, 429; on
    supplying arms to China, 772
Radwan, Ahmed Hassan Abu, 463–4
Radwan, Mariam Abu, 463
Rafah, 414–15, 469
Rafiqdoost, Mohsen, 284
Rafsanjani, Hojatolislam Ali Akbar, 201,
    214–15, 229, 231–2, 234, 244–5, 251,
    273
al-Rahimi, Dr. Osama, 973–4
Rahman, Mullah Abdul, 867
Raïs, Algeria, 569–70, 572

Rajai, Mohamed, 199
Rajoub, Jibril, 483
Ramadan, Taha Yassin, 944, 954–5, 957
Ramadan: Islamic violence in, 559n, 569
Ramadi, Iraq, 232, 1002, 1004, 1006
Ramallah: Arafat in, 494, 501–2, 1024;
    Arafat's funeral in, 1026; attacked by
    Israelis, 442, 444–5, 456, 467, 473,
    494–6
Ramsay (of Cartvale), Meta, Baroness, 346
Ramseh, Colonel (Iraqi army), 190
Rantissi, Abdul-Aziz, 431, 504–6, 1025–6
rape: in Algeria, 520, 563–4, 568–9, 572; in
    Bosnia, 718; in Iran, 228; in occupied
    Iraq, 1010; as political weapon by Iraqis,
    681–2; by Taliban, 850
Rashed, Major-General Maher Abdul, 240
Rashid, Prince of Jordan, 799
Rashid, Ahmed, 863
Rashidian brothers, 92, 95–6
Rather, Dan, 615
al-Rawi, General Hazim, 954–5
Reagan, Ronald: accuses Libya of organising
    Berlin bombing, 883; on Afghan
    "freedom fighters," 62; apologises for
    shooting down Iranian civil airplane,
    260; on arms supply to Iraq, 230; blames
    Iran for attack on USS *Stark*, 219–21,
    222; bombing of Libya, 886, 888; and
    collapsing NATO forces in Beirut, 814;
    disparages Iran, 266; elected, 120; gifts
    to Rafsanjani, 244–5; and Iran-Contra
    scandal, 243, 768–9; offers protection to
    Kuwait-flagged ships, 247; pledge to
    Afghan mujahedin, 859; relations with
    Saddam, 1004; sends envoy to meet
    Saddam (1983), 903–4; strategic
    cooperation with Israel, 227; and supply
    of U.S. cluster bombs to Israel, 786n; on
    U.S. presence in Gulf, 222, 223–4, 226
Reda (Algerian soldier), 577–9
Red Cross, *see* International Red Cross
Rediehs, Laura, 923
Rees-Mogg, William, Baron, 50, 170
Reeves, Phil, 453, 497, 928
Refik, Ahmed, 339
*Reid,* USS, 223
Rennison, Heather, 632
Reporters Without Borders, 972
Reuter, Paul Julius, Freiherr von, 117–18
Reuters news agency, 117–18
Rey-Goldzeiguer, Annie, 523
Rezai, Mohsen, 273
Rezaian, Hossein, 267–8
Rezaian, Captain Mohsen, 262, 264–7, 271
Reza Pahlavi, Shah of Iran, 44n
Rezki, Nabila, 548
Rhame, Major General Tom, 734
Riad, Isra, 940–1
Riarat, Ali Nasser, 257
Ribas-Dominicci, Captain Fernando, 884, 886

Ribbentrop, Joachim von, 362
Rice, Condoleezza, 904
Richards, Charles, 395, 397, 408
Rikabi, Fouad, 152
Ritter, Scott, 720–1, 923
Rivera, Geraldo, 877
Riyadh: bombings in, 20, 21, 31
Rizk, Hani, 463–4
Roberts, Field Marshal Frederick Sleigh, 1st Earl, 38–9, 41, 846*n*
Robertson, Pat, 428, 910
Robinson, Mary, 580
Rodgers, Walter, 877
Rogan, Chanagh, 479
Roger, Philippe, 758
Rogers, Sharon, 263*n*, 267
Rogers, Captain Will III, USN, 262–5, 267–8, 272
Roosevelt, Franklin D., 925
Roosevelt, Kermit, 92, 95, 96, 98, 597
Rose, General Sir Michael, 725–7
Roseman, Aharon, 474
Ross, Dennis, 438
Ross, John Sperrin, 71
Rossetti, Christina, 1038
Rothschild, Danny, 388–9
Rothschild, Rabbi Walter, 792
Royal Marines: in confrontation with Turks in Iraq, 676–7
Rubin, James, 726
Rudeina, Shahira Abu, 831
Rufa, Mounir, 152
al-Rumaydh, Badr, 145
Rumeleh, Hani, 498
Rumsfeld, Donald: and administration of Iraq, 1010; approves air strikes resulting in civilian deaths, 983; on bombing in Afghanistan, 864; campaigns for war against Iraq, 931; on conduct of Iraq war, 958; denies killings in Afghanistan, 862, 869–70; denies widespread looting in Baghdad, 997; describes West Bank, 900; dismisses accusation of anarchy in Baghdad, 989; on evidence for Iraq's nuclear potential, 900; and new world order, 1014; offers to Saddam, 925; on "old Europe," 932; optimism over actions against al-Qaeda, 911; "shock and awe" policy in Iraq, 175, 942; threatens Belgium over complaint against Sharon, 507; and UN weapons inspectors, 926; on U.S. attack on Baghdad, 939–40; visits Saddam (1983), 166, 169–70, 207, 209, 904, 913, 1004
Runcie, Robert, Archbishop of Canterbury, 622
Russell, Sir William Howard, 41, 876
Russia (and USSR): acquires Caucasian states, 333; actions in Chechnya, 905; agents in Iran, 122; arms sales, 749, 750, 758–9, 766, 769; atrocities in

Afghanistan, 175; bin Laden fights, 4, 7–8; casualties in Afghanistan, 50, 60, 86; claims success in Afghanistan, 78; cost of war in Afghanistan, 90; forces and equipment in Afghanistan, 40, 45–50, 52, 89–90; helicopter attacks and air raids in Afghanistan, 80–2, 84; invades Afghanistan (1979), 5, 7–8, 17, 40–2, 45, 173; invades Hungary (1956), 921; Iran denounces for invasion of Afghanistan, 62; Iranian hostility to, 201; military equipment upgraded by Israelis, 771–2; naval ships in Gulf, 224; offers protection to Kuwait-flagged ships, 247; officials and military in Kabul, 85; popular hostility to in Afghanistan, 89–90; rivalry with Britain over Afghanistan, 37, 40; road building in Afghanistan, 44, 60; soldiers attacked in Afghanistan, 60, 66–7; Soviet collapse, 69*n*; supplies arms to China, 771–2; supplies arms to Iraq, 689–90; supports Iraq against Iran, 227; supports PLO, 173; supposed detention of Afghans, 84; supposed support from satellite states, 78*n*; technicians attacked in Afghanistan, 82
Rustomi, Warrant Officer, 106–8
Ruzicka, Marla, 1003

Saad, Mohamed, 8
Saadi, Colonel Abdulaziz, 996
Saadi of Shiraz, 937
Saba, Marine Rafee, 618
al-Sabah, Sheikh Ahmed (Kuwaiti Foreign Minister), 227
al-Sabah, Sheikh Jaber al-Ahmed al-Jaber, 13th Emir of Kuwait, 712
Sabah, Sheikh Mubarak, 613*n*
al-Sabah, Saad Abdullah, 712
al-Sabeq, Wadha, 830
Sabra and Chatila massacre, 449, 458–9, 461, 484, 488–9, 507, 791, 806, 827–32, 840–1, 879, 1038
Sabri, Naji, 956, 969
Sabri, Rawa, 968
Sadafi, Mohamed, 112
Sadat, Anwar: Begin's peace overtures to, 426; at Camp David summit (1977), 426; criticised at Baghdad summit, 150; election (1974), 841*n*; improvises speeches, 159; loyalty to Shah, 109; murdered, 410, 546, 805; named after Enver Pasha, 324*n*; removes Egypt from Arab-Israeli conflict, 149; spies for Rommel, 362
Saddam Hussein al-Tikriti: agrees border with Iran, 101; apologises for attack on USS *Stark*, 220–1; appearance and manner, 158–60; Arafat supports, 358, 382; attacks Kuwait's Sabah family, 711–12;

Saddam Hussein al-Tikriti: *(continued)*
attempts to kill, 983; bans medicine
imports, 737; bin Laden's hostility to,
22–3, 722, 908, 1033–4; boasting in
First Gulf War, 600; capture and
imprisonment awaiting trial, 109,
1003–7; compared with Hitler, 924*n*,
925; condemns Khomeini, 159; courts
Arab favour, 711; criticises UNSCOM,
719; cruelty, 246, 623, 692, 1021; cult,
160, 811; demands Israeli withdrawal
from Palestinian territories, 590; denies
plans for nuclear weapons, 158–9;
denigrated, 95, 95*n*, 922, 924, 985;
disregards warnings of U.S. firepower,
935; drains marshlands, 246, 687, 1017;
economic problems, 689; and effect of
sanctions, 705–6, 723; election victories,
841*n*; employs chemical weapons,
209–15, 692, 698, 719, 904; encourages
Iraqis in war, 944; and execution of
Bazoft, 169; George W. Bush condemns,
889–90; gives gates to Najaf shrine, 164;
gives to tribal guerrillas, 948–9; hangs
deserters, 227; Haughey meets, 167;
imitates Stalin, 160*n*; impedes UN
weapons inspectors, 720; and internal
dissent, 198, 199; invades Kuwait
(1990), 5, 7, 21, 272–3, 588–90, 593,
612–13, 689–90, 699, 769; joins Baath
party, 149; Khomeini calls for overthrow,
173, 201, 229; King Fahd's dispute with,
612–13, 625; King Hussein embraces,
802; meets President Assad of Syria with
King Hussein, 247; memorials and
monuments to, 278; and Mossadeq, 95;
and Mouffak's filming of war, 291–2;
names military leaders against Anglo-
U.S. forces, 943; offers ceasefire to Iran
(1982), 286; orders war memorial in
Baghdad, 276–8; palaces and
possessions, 947, 984–6, 1005;
personally executes political opponents,
152–3; public appearances, 605; repeats
claims on Kuwait, 710–11; represented
as threat, 722, 758; repressive measures,
153–5, 169–70, 173; retreat from
Kuwait, 149, 151–3,
801; Rumsfeld's visit to (1983), 166,
169–70, 207, 209, 904, 913; Saudis
support in war against Iran, 21, 613–14;
Saudi view of, 608; on Shia threat,
204–5; statues and posters, 948; statues
toppled and portraits smashed, 975–6,
978, 983; supports Sunnis, 161;
supposed links with bin Laden, 722, 958;
supposed massing of troops in southern
Iraq (October 1994), 716, 718; uncle's
anti-British sentiments, 148; U.S.A. sells
helicopters to, 557*n*; U.S. calls for
overthrow of, 646–7; U.S. fails to pursue
after First Gulf War, 665; and US's anti-
Iran stance, 251; U.S. support for, 597;
U.S. view of after First Gulf War, 684–5,
705–6; visits France, 166; visits
wounded in war with Iran, 194; war with
Iran, 170–1, 172, 176–7, 181, 187, 190,
199–200, 201, 205, 207–8, 227, 246,
252, 254, 769; welcomes arms
inspectors, 900–1; West supports against
Khomeini, 170–1

Sadeq, Abolhassan, 116, 134–6
Sadler, Brent, 255, 713
Sadr, Imam Moussa, 163
Sadr, Mohamed, 995
al-Sadr, Muqtada, 165, 995, 1010
al-Sadr, Sayed Mohamed Sadiq, 165
Sadr City *(formerly* Saddam City), 165
Sadri, General Jaffar Qoli, 103
Saf, Dr. Salah, 390
Safavi, Mujtaba, 284–5, 289–90
al-Safi, Lieutenant Ehsan, 641
Safian, Alex, 879
Safwan, 641, 657
al-Sahaf, Mohamed Saeed ("Comical Ali"),
    153, 945*n*, 963, 966, 969
Sahnoun, Sheikh Ahmed, 524–5
Said, Edward, 358, 395, 420–1, 1036
Saifullah of Turangzai, 860–1
Saladin, 625, 812
Salah, Bilal, Hilal and Zuheir, 446–7
Salam, Mohamed, 207–8, 210–11, 212, 1017
Salamatian, Dr. (Iranian politician), 111
Salang road tunnel (Afghanistan), 44, 63
Salawi, Captain Abdulsalam, 996
al-Saleh, Ali Abdullah, 152
Saleh, Amal Hassan, 734
Saleh, Hala, 738, 739
al-Saleh, Taleb Abdullah, 152
Salem, Hossam, 1017
Salha, Israel, 372–3
Salibi, Kamal, 847–8
Salman, Adnan, 156
Salman, Hassan, 734
Salman, Mohamed, 680
Salman, Tamam, 652*n*
Salman, Yahia, 738–9
Samadali (Kabul taxi driver), 46–7, 52–3, 60,
    61, 69, 80
Samara, Iraq, 1007, 1008–9
Samet, Gideon, 468
Samuel, Sir Herbert, 881
*Samuel Bo Roberts,* USS, 251
Sana, Hassan, 112
Sanchez, Ilich Ramirez ("Carlos the Jackal"),
    12, 25
Sanchez, General Ricardo, 1015–16
Sandburg, Carl, 316
Sanders, J. Y., 735
*Saratoga,* USS, 624
Sarbullzaharb, Kurdistan, 229
Sardai, Habib, 137

Sarenac, Sladjana, 740n-1n
Sarfati, Albert, 515
Sartawi, Isaam, 379
Sarvath, Princess of Jordan, 799
Satar, Abdul, 892, 894
Sattar, Latif Abdul, 728, 737
Saud al-Feisal, Prince, 957
Saudi Arabia: arms for Iraq transported over,
    222; attitude to U.S. presence, 607–8;
    backs Saddam against Iran, 207, 224,
    227, 613–14; bin Laden criticises, 20–2,
    24, 590; British and French forces in,
    908–9; deprives bin Laden of citizenship,
    9; destruction of idolatrous sites in, 847;
    dismisses Egyptian and Syrian forces,
    700; distress at bombing of Iraq, 626–7;
    fears U.S. presence in Gulf, 227; financial
    contribution to First Gulf War, 637n;
    financial support for Palestinian-Gaza-
    Jericho accord, 691; hostility to Iran, 250;
    increasing conservatism, 690; Iraqi
    planes refuel in, 246; and 9/11 attacks,
    840, 847; offers money to Iran to rebuild,
    286; participation in First Gulf War, 617,
    618–19, 620–1, 631, 636–7; potential
    disintegration, 900; questions New World
    Order, 624–5; refuses assault on Iraq,
    607–8; regulates U.S. army practices,
    598; relations with Iran, 224; royal family
    accused of corruption, 13; supports
    Afghanistan against Soviet invasion, 5,
    90; supports Iraq opposition group, 661;
    supports Syrian peace mission to Tehran
    and Riyadh, 227; U.S. arms supplies for,
    690–1, 758; U.S. forces in, 5, 19–22,
    590–2, 594, 599, 636–7, 848; U.S.
    influence in, 596; as U.S. vassal state,
    637; Wahhabism in, 847–9
*Saudi Gazette,* 595
Savak (Iranian security service), 99, 103, 105,
    111–12, 128
Sawari, Asadullah, 59, 86
Sayah, Abdul-Hadi, 523–4, 526
Schindler, Oskar, 351n
Schmidt, Helmut, 769
Schmitt, Eric, 927
Schnabel, Rockwell, 924n
Schwarzkopf, General H. Norman (Sr.), 96,
    597
Schwarzkopf, General Norman (Jr.): and
    attack on Khajfi, 621; background,
    597–8; bombards Iraq, 616; British
    collaboration with, 610; claims Scud
    missile destruction, 720, 751; denies oil
    as motive for defending Saudi Arabia,
    597; denigrates Iraqi army, 598;
    dismissive over Iraqi casualties, 692;
    favours advance on Baghdad, 665; and
    Iraqi helicopters, 663; and killing of
    Palestinians in Kuwait, 638–9; leads U.S.
    forces in 1991 Gulf War, 96, 280, 598;

and loss of British war plans, 611;
    military strength, 599; professes
    admiration for Arabs, 638; relations with
    Prince Khaled, 636–7, 639; on return of
    Kuwaiti civilians, 701; on U.S. advance
    and successes, 649
*Scotsman* (newspaper), 375–6
Scowcroft, Brent, 667
Sebag-Montefiore, Simon, 160n
Sebri, Yousef, 552
Second Afghan War (1879), 37–40
Seeckt, Lieutenant General Hans von, 329
Sehrai, Saeb Jan, 86
Selim, Colonel Abdul Aziz, 917
Selim, Saad and Omar, 940–1
*seqina* (tranquillity), 8
Serbia, 508, 984
Sersawi, Hassan, 828
Sersawi, Sana, 828–9
Sétif, Algeria: massacre (1945), 520
settlement: as term, 425
Sevan, Benon, 726
Sèvres, Treaty of (1920), 331–2, 858–9, 1032
Shabla, Sid-Ahmad, 556
al-Shaer, Mohamed, 488
Shafi, Haidar Abdul, 384–6, 387
al-Shahadat, Major Ismail Bin Khalaf, 817
Shahak, Amnon, 465
Shahak, Israel, 458
Shah-Cherghi, Sayad Hassan, 233
Shaheed, Akil, 994
Shahin, Jamal Eid, 470n
Shah of Iran (Mohamed Reza Shah Pahlavi):
    Anniversary celebration and Abadan
    cinema fire, 103; attempted
    assassination, 131; death and burial,
    109–10, 172; demands for return and
    execution, 109, 120, 124, 131; downfall,
    102, 1036; executes opposition leaders,
    121; exiled, 101; illness and treatment,
    109; on Iraqi military strength, 176; life-
    style, 115–17; lovers, 115; moves to
    Panama, 134; regime, 101–2, 103,
    112–13; reinstated (1953), 41, 92,
    94–100; relations with British
    intelligence, 112; repression of religion,
    129; Saddam's attitude to, 161; and
    seizure of U.S. embassy in Tehran,
    118–19; 30th anniversay celebration,
    100–1; "White Revolution," 100, 137;
    *see also* Iran; Reza Pahlavi, Shah
Shahristani, Ala, 154
Shahristani, Bernice, 158
Shahristani, Hussain, 154–8, 161, 996
Shai, Major, 467–8
Shaker, Major-General Hussain, 177
Shakr, Saadoun, 979
al-Shamaari, Badr, 715
Shami, Sheikh Abdullah, 474–5
Shamir, Yitzhak, 376n, 382, 384–6
Shamra, Captain Abu, 415

Shansal, Siddik, 152
al-Sharaa, Farouq, 384–5, 387, 409, 856
Sharbaji, Zakaria, 391–2
Shariatmadari, Ayatollah Kazem, 79, 108, 127
Sharif, Bassam Abu, 470n
Sharif, Nawaz, 851
Sharjah, 26
Sharm el-Sheikh: anti-terrorism conference, 20, 421n
Sharon, Ariel: accuses Arafat of supporting bin Laden, 846; acts against Palestinians, 499–501, 511; attacks Muslim holy places, 440; besieges Beirut, 379; blocks Palestinian travel to London conference, 932; builds wall, 479n, 1024; Bush describes as "man of peace," 1014; and Bush's acceptance of settlements, 1027; claims Israel under siege, 468; closes Jewish settlements in Gaza, 506–7, 1027; contempt for Oslo agreement, 506; and control of army, 419; criticises NATO's war against Serbia, 508–9; denigrates Arafat, 483–4; hawkishness, 449, 463, 468–9; joins war against "world terror," 846; at King Hussein's funeral, 806; meets Colin Powell, 500; meets George W.Bush, 509–10; mocks Arafat, 858; on murder of Bashir Gemayel, 484, 488–9; and 9/11 attack on U.S.A., 490; opposes Hamas, 505; orders killing of Hamas official, 465; record of views and achievements, 506–7; and Sabra/Chatila killings, 412, 442, 449, 484, 828, 830–1, 838; suggests abandoning Gaza, 506; on targeted killing, 905; urges settlers to seize land, 438, 442, 463
Shatt al-Arab, 178, 179, 181, 185–8, 195, 197, 235, 237, 240, 242, 253, 745
Shaw, George Bernard, 106, 748, 751, 753, 755, 767
Shaw, Tony, 916
Shawcross, William, 105
al-Shebaki, Abdul-Rahman, 390–1
Shebaro, Ahmed, 796
Shefi, Danielle, 499
Shehab, Nour, 738
Shehada, Salah, 511
Shekerdemian, Yervant, 349
Sherati, Ikhlef, 564–5
Sherman, Captain Mike, 599, 600–1
Sheubner-Richter, Max Erwin von, 329–30
Shewmaker, Private Andrew, 602–5
Shia Muslims: dispute leadership of Islam, 161; dominate 2005 Iraq government, 1036; expelled from Iraq, 159; internal conflicts, 995; in Iran, 129, 161; in Iraq, 148, 161–5, 170, 204; in Lebanon and Syria, 204; in "liberated" Iraq, 1028–30; massacred by Saddam, 658–9, 668; minority in Afghanistan, 79; opposition to Saddam, 661; plunder Sunnis after

liberation, 990; rebel in Iraq after First Gulf War, 657–9, 661–2, 664, 1017; in southern Iraq, 702; in Syria, 820–1; Taliban persecution of, 849; understanding of martyrdom, 281–2; and U.S. call for overthrow of Saddam, 646–7; Wahhabi hostility to, 849; women tortured and killed, 1021
Shikaki, Fatih, 433
Shin Bet, 465, 466n, 470n, 829
Shir Ali Khan, Afghan king, 37
Shiraz, 174
Shlaim, Avi, 429–30
al-Shomari, Saadia Hussein, 974
Shoulder, Mike, 933n
Shoval, Zalman, 926
Shubeilath, Leith, 807
Shultz, George Pratt, 210
*Sides*, USS, 262, 263–4
Sidi Bel Abbès, Algeria, 517
Sifi, Mokdad, 527
Simmons, Jack, 195
Simon Wiesenthal Centre, Paris, 508n
Sinn Fein, 307
Sirri, Midhat al-Haj, 152
Sirri Island, 246
al-Sistani, Grand Ayatollah Ali, 145, 165
Six Day War (1967), 377
Smaja, Josette, 515
Smati, Aziz, 559n
Smith, Colin, 650–1
Smith, Howard K.: *Last Train from Berlin*, 922
Smyrna, *see* Izmir
Snow, Jon, 194–7, 607
Soares, Mario, 580
Sobhi, Mohamed, 1023
Solehi, Ibrahim, 137
Soltani, Abdul Latif, 524–5
Somali, Mahmoud, 698, 699
Somalia: U.S. presence in, 32, 713
Sorkh Rud (village), Afghanistan, 80–2
Souaida, Lieutenant Habib: *La Sale Guerre*, 584
al-Soufi, Colonel Yassir, 256n
Soustelle, Jacques, 516, 543
South Africa: arms trade, 758, 773
Soviet Union, *see* Russia
Spanish Civil War: atrocities in, 336
*Spark, The* (PUK's magazine), 165
Spence, Hamilton, 770–1
Sponeck, Hans von, 708–9, 725
Squires, Chris, 195–6
Srourian, Nevart, 321
Stafford, Colonel R.S., 336
Stahl, Leslie, 704
Stalin, Josef, 160, 362
*Stark*, USS, 218–22, 251, 267n
Steinbeck, John, 775
Stern, Eva, 456–9, 488, 507
Sternberg, Sy, 348

Stern Gang, 369, 373, 376n
Stevely, Trooper Kevin, 607
Steven, Stewart, 489
Stevenson, Adlai, 931
Steyn, Mark, 489, 875, 876
stoning to death: in Iran, 132
Straw, Jack, 929
Strong, Dean, 208
Stroop, Brigadeführer Jürgen, 510
*Struma* (Jewish refugee ship), 374
Suad Bey, Ali, 320
Sudan: bin Laden in, 6–7, 9; civil war
    atrocities in, 11; Clinton bombs, 722,
    791; conditions, 10–11
Suez crisis and war (1956), 377, 913–21
Suheil, Doha, 940–1
suicide bombers: and Arab fearlessness, 481;
    attack U.S. base in Beirut, 226, 478, 673,
    791, 835, 886, 954; attack USS *Cole* at
    Aden, 225, 443; efficacy, 842; explained
    and justified, 476–80; in Hama, Syria,
    822; by Hamas, 406–7, 422, 493, 495,
    499; in, 480n; in Iraq, 953–6, 981n-2n,
    1003, 1008, 1028, 1034, 1036; Israeli
    reaction to, 425; Lebanese Hizballah,
    406, 476–7; and 9/11 attacks, 842–5;
    Palestinian, 22, 406–7, 422, 429, 433,
    442, 471–6, 479–80, 502–3, 509, 1014,
    1024; re-named "homicide bombers,"
    462; women, 955
Suleimaniya, 147, 292
Suleimanjar, Colonel Beyrouz, 200–1
Sullivan, Captain Stephen, 717–18
Sullivan, William, 127
Sultan, Adnan Fathi, 470n
Sultan Ibn Abdul Aziz, Prince of Saudi
    Arabia, 607–8, 640
Sultan Yacoub, battle of (1982), 812, 814
Summayl (village), Iraq, 336
*Sunday Express*, 910n
*Sunday Press* (Dublin), 166–7
*Sunday Times*, 624
*Sunday Tribune* (Dublin), 271
Sungar, Murat, 680
Sunni Muslims: decline to vote in Iraq, 1003;
    form Islamic committees, 955;
    insurgency, 1007, 1011; plundered by
    Shias after liberation, 990; power, 161;
    protest demonstrations against
    Americans, 1007; status in Afghanistan,
    79; in Syria, 820–1; *see also* Wahhabism
Supreme Muslim Council, 359
Suwaidi, Sheikh, 752
Sway, Yousef Abu, 470n
Sweden: arms sales, 751
Switzerland: arms sales, 751
Sykes, Ella, 39
Sykes, Sir Mark, 144, 791, 825, 1031
Symonds, Matthew, 610–11
Syria: accused of aiding 2003–5 Iraq
    insurrection, 145; author travels in,

808–11; besieges Arafat, 379n;
    conditions and regime, 810–17; conflicts
    with Israel, 812, 813–14, 816–17;
    cooperation with al-Bakr, 150; fears
    separate Jordan agreement with Israel,
    389–90; French mandate in, 145, 306,
    334, 792, 812–13; and Hindawi's attempt
    to destroy El Al aircraft, 460n, 461; at
    Madrid Middle East Conference, 384,
    385–8; peace mission to Tehran and
    Riyadh, 226; rebellion suppressed, 546;
    refugees in Saudi Arabia, 608–9;
    religious sects in, 820–1; ruled by
    Alawites, 204; seeks autonomy within
    Ottoman empire, 822–3; seeks return of
    Golan, 439, 1037; supports anti-Saddam
    conference (1991), 660; supports U.S.A.
    in First Gulf War, 594; suppresses
    Muslim Brotherhood uprising (Hama),
    814–16; territory and boundaries,
    817–18; torture methods, 173; troops in
    Lebanon, 150, 821; troops leave
    Lebanon (2005), 1035–6
*Syria Times*, 809

Taba agreement (Oslo II, 1995), 420n
Tabrizi, Hojatolislam Sayed Emadeddin
    Tabatai, 162
Tahri, Mohamed, 573–4
Tahsin Bey, 350–1
Tajikistan, 850
Tajik troops: disavow loyalty to USSR, 87–8
Taki, Ahmed, 233
Tal, Rami, 439n
Talaat Pasha, 318, 331
Talal, Walid bin, 799
Taliban: attacked by U.S.A., 847, 855, 857,
    861–2; bin Laden on, 31–3; in civil
    conflict, 90; cruelty, 849–50; destroy
    Bamiyan Buddhas, 85, 847, 988;
    embassy in Islamabad closed, 866;
    hostility to Northern Alliance, 863–4;
    massacred, 864, 869–70, 871, 911;
    reaction to bombing, 860; regime and
    ideology, 25–7, 849–51, 860; return to
    Afghanistan, 1014; U.S.A.'s initial
    welcome of, 864
Tamarchin, 210
Tansel, Ibrahim, 338
Tanzim militia, 443, 466n
Taraki, Nur Mohamed, 44–5, 56, 59, 62,
    76, 79
targeted killing: by Israelis, 1024–5; as term,
    905; U.S. potential victims, 1026
Tartouche, Roger, 513
Tat, Aygen, 338
Tavernier, Bertrand: *La Guerre sans Nom*,
    521
Taylor, Denis, 270
Tebin, Private, 64
Tehlirian, Soghoman, 331

Tehran: cemeteries, 256–8; Iraqi air raids on, 229–30; life under Ayatollah's regime, 115–17; prayer meetings in, 231–2; street names changed, 117; student demonstrations in, 120; U.S. embassy seized and occupied, 118–19, 120–1, 124–5, 177; *see also* Iran
*Tehran Journal*, 111
Teissier, Mgr. Henri, Archbishop of Algiers, 566–7
Tel el-Kbir, 671–2
Tenet, George, 449–50, 929
terrorism: bin Laden and, 7; discussed at Madrid Middle East Conference, 385–6; in Palestine/Israel, 373–8, 436–7; as term, 62–3, 378–9, 411–12, 436
*Texaco Caribbean* (tanker), 250
Texas Instruments Inc., 629*n*
Thabet, Dr. Thabet, 466*n*
al-Thani, Sheikh Hamad bin Jassim, 726, 856–7
Thatcher, Margaret (*later* Baroness), 65, 86, 109, 250, 265, 269, 353, 597, 609, 881, 913, 1026
Thesiger, Wilfrid, 1018
Third Afghan War (1919), 44
Thompson, Nigel, 195–6
Thomson, Alex, 644, 728, 733
Thomson, Kenneth Roy, 2nd Baron, 102, 269
Tibherine monastery, Algeria: monks killed, 566–7, 583
Tigris river: contaminated, 707
al-Tikrit, Hashem, 994
Tikriti, Barzan, 157
al-Tikriti, Lieutenant Hussain, 1019
al-Tikriti, Dr. Saadun Khalifa, 184–5
*Time* magazine: journalists expelled from Iran, 135
*Times, The*: author reports for, 41, 43, 50–1, 70, 73–4; and author's interview with Khomeini, 125*n*; closed by strike, 102; emasculates author's report on 1988 U.S. destruction of Iranian airliner, 269–71; Murdoch buys, 268; on shooting down of Iranian civil airplane, 260–1, 263, 269–71; on Suez crisis, 915–16; Tripoli bombing, 886
Timur (Tamburlaine), 37*n*
Tito, Josip Broz, 362, 527
Tizi-Ouzou, Algeria, 584
Tlass, Lieutenant General Mustafa, 755, 818
Tmaizeh, Mohamed Salameh, 437
Tolstoy, Count Leo, 71, 586
Tora Bora mountains, Afghanistan, 17, 866
Torrijos, General Omar, 109
torture: in Algeria, 468, 506, 520–1, 530, 553, 555–6, 564, 568, 572, 574–9, 583; of Bahais in Iran, 173–4; Dershowitz favours limited use, 490; in Egypt, 411; in Iran, 130, 228; in Iraq, 155–8, 166, 170, 994–5; by Iraqi intelligence service,

994; by Iraqis in Kuwait, 632; by Israelis, 430, 433, 436, 486; at Israel's Khiam prison, 269; in Khuzestan, 168; by Palestinians, 433; practised by U.S.A. in Iraq, 1011–12, 1015, 1021–2; by Russians in Afghanistan, 175; by Savak in Iran, 99, 101, 112; in Syria, 173; of women in Iraq, 1019; *see also* atrocities
Toutungi, Ayub Hamis, 427
Tower Commission (on Iran-Contra affair), 243
Towmeh, Nouri, 162
Townshend, Major-General Charles, 142
Toynbee, Arnold, 325
Transcaucasia, 333
Travnik, Bosnia, 9
Trefgarne, David, 2nd Baron, 168
Trenchard, Air Marshal Sir Hugh, 146
Trevor-Roper, Hugh (Baron Dacre), 261*n*
Tripoli, Libya, 880–1, 882, 884, 885–6
Truman, Harry S., 95
Tudeh party (communist), Iran, 121–2, 227
Tulfa, Khairallah, 148
Turabi, Hassan Abdullah, 9–10, 11–12, 527
Turkey: and Alexandretta referendum, 335; application to join European Union, 344, 348; bombs Kurds, 718–19; confrontation with Royal Marines in Iraq, 676–7; Dardanelles victory, 320–1; in First World War, 823; joins Allies (1945), 335; and Kurdish problem, 674, 683; perpetrates and denies Armenian massacres, 316–31, 333, 337–51, 353–5, 865; in post-1919 peace settlement, 331–2, 858–9; suppresses Arab autonomy under Ottomans, 822–6; troops steal relief supplies from Kurdish refugees, 676–7
Turkmenistan: oil pipeline to Pakistan, 28
Turnbull, Derek, 753–4, 761
Turungzai, 861
Tusi, Anish, 232
Tutweiler, Margaret, 533
Tveit, Karsten, 832, 837, 839

U-2 intelligence plane (U.S.), 90
Uganda: proposed as Jewish homeland, 368
Ukraine: arms sales, 754–5; terror famine (1930–33), 336
Ulemas, Association of (Algeria), 520, 524
Um al-Rassas, 246
Um Qasr, Iraq, 704, 710, 713
Umran, Major General Mustafa Mahmoud, 943
Ungar, Joseph I., 879
Union Oil Company of California Asian Oil Pipeline Project (Unocal), 28
United Arab Emirates: arms bazaar, 752–3; arms purchases, 758
United Nations: Arafat addresses, 381–2; Convention on Genocide, 865; George

W. Bush addresses General Assembly, 888–90, 929; and import of medicines into Iraq, 737; investigates Algerian atrocities, 580; observers in Afghanistan, 14; and Suez crisis, 916; suicide-bombed in Baghdad, 1015; supports eradication of Afghan opium, 16; weapons inspectors in Iraq, 719–21, 723, 901, 909, 910, 925–6; weapons inspectors leave Iraq, 935

United Nations Children's Fund (UNICEF), 704, 707, 721, 978

United Nations Iraq-Kuwait Observer Mission, 710

United Nations Security Council: appeals to Iran and Iraq, 228; Colin Powell addresses on Iraqi weapons, 927–31; declares Israeli annexation of Jerusalem null and void, 606n; demands end to Israeli reoccupation of West Bank, 500; ignores expulsion of Palestinians from Kuwait, 695; and Iranian air attacks in Gulf, 227, and Iran-Iraq war, 178; Resolution 181 on state of Israel, 384, 1032; Resolution 194 on Palestinians' return, 399; Resolution 242 on Israeli withdrawal from Arab lands, 383, 384, 386, 399, 420, 440, 443, 448, 451, 481–2, 501, 821, 889; Resolution 338 on Israeli withdrawal from Arab lands, 386, 399, 440, 889; Resolution 425 on Israeli withdrawal from Lebanon, 386; Resolution 476 on status of Jerusalem, 426; Resolution 598 on Iran-Iraq ceasefire, 273; Resolution 661 on sanctions against Iraq, 703; Resolution 688 allowing humanitarian intervention in foreign countries, 683, 719; Resolution 1224 on Iraq oil for food programme, 709; Resolution 1441 on Iraqi disarmament, 906, 930, 935; votes to disarm Iraq, 905–6

United Nations Special Commission on Monitoring (UNSCOM), 704, 719–21, 724

United States of America: actions in Afghanistan, 891–8; administration in Iraq, 1012–13; air actions in Iraq, 147; air and missile strikes against Iraq, 710, 712, 714, 721, 724–7, 732–4; Algerian suspicions of conspiracy by, 546–7; Arab suspicions of, 590n; arms supplies to Middle East, 690–1, 750–2, 755–6, 758, 779; arms to Iran, 177; arms used against Palestinians, 761–2; assessment of Iranian society, 128–9; assessment of Iran-Iraq military strengths, 176; attacked on 11 September 2001, 490, 794–5, 827, 832–4, 840–1, 852, 854–6, 900, 1003, 1013; attempted rescue of Iranian embassy hostages, 130n; author

takes evidence of used Hellfire missile to, 779–88; bin Laden addresses, 1033n; bin Laden analyses motives, 31–2; bombing of Afghanistan, 841, 846–7, 854–5, 857, 858, 859–63; bombing of Iraqi civilians, 621, 624, 625–9; calls for overthrow of Saddam, 646–7, 661, 666–7; casualties in Afghanistan, 1014; casualties in First Gulf War, 649–50, 693; casualties in Iraq, 1003, 1009, 1011, 1027; casualties in second war against Iraq, 981; condemns Jewish settlements in West Bank and Gaza, 426; and deaths of Iraqi and Palstinian prisoners, 1023; delegation at Madrid Middle East Conference, 382–7; demands UN arms embargo on Iran, 247; and denial of Armenian massacres, 340–4; disbelieves UN's assurances on Iraq's lack of weapons, 720; and drug prevention, 16; efficacy of military, 650; expenditure in Afghanistan, 90; fails to acknowledge attacks on forces in Iraq, 1011; and financial cost of First Gulf War, 637n; forces invited into Saudi Arabia, 590–2, 599, 636; given local cultural advice in Saudi Arabia, 595–6; helps fund IRA, 796; humanitarian organisations in Afghanistan, 896–7; intelligence cooperation with Iran, 112–14; intelligence failures on 9/11 attacks, 855; intervenes in Suez war, 920–1; invades Iraq (2003), 22–3, 434, 517, 722–3; and Iraqi attack on USS *Stark,* 218–22; isolates Sudan, 12; Jewish diplomats, 438–9; Jewish press coverage of Israel, 457–8; Joint Intelligence Bureau in Dhahran, 599–601; journalists expelled from Afghanistan, 69; judicial system, 891; justifies peace process in Middle East, 413–14; and liberation of Baghdad, 977–93; massacres retreating Iraqi army, 640–2; militancy against Iraq, 931–2; military alliance with Britain, 609–11; military constraints in Saudi Arabia, 598; naval presence in Gulf, 222–3, 225–6, 248–51; neglects Iraqi dead, 691–4; and New World Order, 624–5; ordnance diverted to Israel, 785–6n; and Oslo agreement, 408, 421, 432; personnel attacked in Afghanistan, 896; policy on Iraq after First Gulf War, 660–6, 680–1, 683–4; popular Iraqi hostility to, 993; post-9/11 attacks on Afghanistan, 841, 846–7; and post-1918 peace settlement in Middle East, 331–2; praises Arafat's secret courts, 423; prepares for war against Iraq, 900–2, 921–3; presence and actions in Iraq, 999–1012; reaction to *From Beirut to Bosnia* TV series, 878–9;

United States of America *(continued)*
    records Armenian massacres, 325,
    326–7; recruits Iraqi former policemen to
    restore order, 989; and reinstatement of
    Shah of Iran, 94–5, 96, 98–9; relations
    with Algeria, 581–2; relations with
    Saddam, 589; relations with Taliban, 28;
    relief operations in Iraq, 667, 670–1; in
    Second World War, 925; sends additional
    troops on mission to Iraq, 712–14; and
    Shah's exile, 134; shredded diplomatic
    papers reassembled and published by
    Iranians, 126–30; soldiers killed in
    Dhahran, 19; Special Forces' behaviour
    in liberated Kuwait, 650–2; Special
    Forces in Afghanistan, 892, 895, 911–12;
    Special Forces operate in Algeria, 584–5;
    strategic cooperation with Israel, 227;
    supplies arms to Iraq, 690; supplies arms
    to Israel, 443, 469–70, 493, 509;
    supports Iraq in war with Iran, 69,
    207–8, 213–14, 220, 230; supports
    mujahedin in Afghanistan, 62; supports
    Zia ul-Haq, 69; tactics in Iraq, 963–4,
    965–6; "targeted killings," 1025; Tehran
    embassy occupied, 118–19, 120–1,
    124–5, 177; troop reinforcements in Gulf
    (1994), 717; troops attacked by Iraqi
    insurgents, 1000; troops in Saudi Arabia,
    5, 19–22, 590–2, 594, 599, 636–7, 848;
    troops killed in Beirut suicide attack,
    226, 478, 791, 835, 886, 954; on use of
    chemical weapons in Middle East,
    211–12; vetoes UN resolution on Israeli
    construction of settlement, 427; warship
    shoots down Iranian civil airliner,
    259–67, 272; and Wye agreement, 437–8
Uquili, General Abdul Aziz, 151
Uruzgan, Afghanistan, 894, 897, 899*n*
Usborne, David, 839
al-Utayba, Juhayman Ibn Mohamed, 848

*Valley Forge,* USS, 249
Vanunu, Mordechai, 905
Velayati, Ali Akbar, 30
Veliotes, Nicholas, 380
Veloukhiotis, Aris, 97
Verenis, Maria, 754
Vietnam: invoked in Afghanistan, 86;
    journalists in, 876
Viktor, Captain, 64
Villiers, Gérard de, 95
*Vincennes,* USS, 260–7, 269, 270–3, 752
Vincent, General Sir Richard, 611
Viney, Mike, 46, 48, 52, 53, 60
Voice of America (radio service), 647
Voice of Britain (radio service), 919*n*
*Voice of Free Iraq, The* (CIA radio station),
    646–7
Voice of Hope (radio station), 774
Voorst, Bruce van, 135

Waez, Mullah, 84
Wahab, Zaki Abdul, 152
Wahebi, Sergeant Mikael Srour bin, 817
Wahhabi, Mullah Omar, 847
Wahhabism, 27, 125, 847
Waldegrave, William, 168–9
Waldheim, Kurt, 94, 802*n*-3*n*
Waldron, Karl, 656–7
Walid, Ahmed, 731
Walker, Christopher, 426
Walker, Tony, 593
Wallenberg, Raoul, 656
*Wall Street Journal,* 342, 468–9, 875, 928,
    931
Waqqas, Saad bin Ali, 205
Warburton, Sir Robert: *Eighteen Years in the
    Khyber,* 71
Ward, John, 744
Warner, John H., 221, 718
Washburn, John, 129
Washington: attacked on 11 September 2003,
    794, 832, 834, 839, 1013; Middle East
    talks (1992), 389–90
*Washington Post,* 452, 582, 624, 663, 706,
    844, 900, 909
al-Wazzir, Jihad, 464–5
Webster, Lance Corporal, 310–13
Wegner, Armin, 326, 346, 348
Weinberger, Caspar, 219, 221, 251, 886
Weiss, Lilly and Barry, 839
Weizmann, Chaim, 366
Werfel, Franz, 331, 334
West Bank: annexed by Jordan, 364;
    appropriated by Israel, 1027; Israeli
    names for, 388; Israelis fight in, 374,
    419; Jewish settlements in, 425–7, 429,
    432, 438, 1014, 1027; occupied by
    Israel, 377, 388–9, 425–6; Palestine
    police militia in, 481; Palestinians in,
    425; UN demands Israeli withdrawal,
    500, 509; violence in, 388; zoned under
    Oslo agreement, 420–1
White, Marine Lieutenant Colonel Dick, 624
Whittam Smith, Andreas, 270, 397, 610–11
Widad, Abu, 1019, 1021
Wiesel, Elie, 338–9, 343, 509
Wigg, Richard, 42
Wilk, Yehuda, 440–1
Williams, Michael, 511*n*
Wills, Frank, 310–14, 321, 742
Wilson, Sir Arnold Talbot, 145, 1029
Wilson, Thomas Woodrow, 332–3, 383, 674,
    890*n*
Winkleman, Barry, 117*n*
Wippermann, Wolfgang, 330*n*
*Wisconsin,* USS, 598
Witwet, Colonel Ali Hadi, 151
Wolfowitz, Paul, 931, 974, 1014
women: abducted, 573–4; executed in Iran,
    174, 275; killed and violated in Algeria,
    520, 565, 568–9, 572; mujahedin

treatment of, 82–3; raped in Iran, 275; religious repression of, 80; Soviet treatment of in Afghanistan, 59; stoned to death, 132; suicide bombers, 955; under Taliban in Afghanistan, 26–8; tortured and killed in Iraq, 1019–22; tortured and molested in Afghanistan, 175

Woodberry, George, 593n

Woodhouse, Christopher Montague, 5th Baron Terrington: and coup in Iran, 92, 94–8, 138, 598, 1028–9

Woodhouse, Davina, 97

Woolsey, James, 97n

Wordsworth, William, 92

al-Wougayan, Najib, 715

Wren, P. C.: *Beau Geste*, 294

Wye River agreement (Israel-Palestinian, 1998), 436–8

Yabad, West Bank, 446–7

al-Yacoubi, Sheikh Mohamed, 995

Yalon, Moshe, 507

Yalta agreement (1945), 924n

Yamin, Asil, 962

Yammine, Father Antoine, 824

Yaqub Khan, 37, 39

Yaron, Brigadier General Amos, 507, 509

Yasilova, 675, 677, 679–80

Yasin, Shakr, 400–1

Yassin, Sheikh Ahmed, 415, 1024–5

Yates, Liz, 502

Yazdani, Dr. Faizullah, 213

Yazdani, Hojabr, 131

Yazdi, Ibrahim, 114, 121, 176

Yazdi, Sayed Khadum, 145

Yeltsin, Boris: and Chechnya war, 175; at King Hussein's funeral, 807

Yılmaz, Mesut, 335

Yonkers, Captain (USN), 248

*York,* HMS, 598

Yossef, Rabbi Ovadia, 466n

Young Turks (Committee of Union and Progress), 320

Younis, Mahmoud, 914–15

Youssef, Hassan, 505

Ypres, 307–8

Yugoslavia: created as state, 306

*Yung Chun* (Chinese ship), 191

Yuri, Major (Soviet army), 65–7, 68–9

Zaehner, Robin, 92, 96

Zaghlani, Laïd, 543

Zahedi, Ardeshir, 131

Zaher, Abu, 285

Zahera, Abdul, 291

Zahir Khan, 44n

Zakhem, Sam, 220n-1n

Zakho, 680, 685–6

Zaki, Shukri Saleh, 152

Zalum, Marwan, 492–3

Zalzal, Philippe, 825

Zant, Abdul Monim Abu, 955

Zaqout, Bassem, 503

al-Zarakani, Fadil Hamidi, 1020

Zaude, Sheikh Ibrahim, 136–7

Zawahari, Ayman, 859

Zayed al-Nahyan, Sheikh Mohamed bin, 638, 748

Zeevi, Rehavem, 507

Zeidan, Ahmed, 904n

Zeidan, Mohamed, *see* Abul Abbas, Mohamed

Zeki Bey, 320

Zerani, Rashid, 550

Zeroual, General Liamine, 551–2, 572

Zervas, Napoleon, 97

Zeyid, Abbas, 471

Ziarad, Mohamed, 76–8, 83

Zia ul-Haq, General Mohamed, 69–70

Zidan, Margot, 443–4

Zilkha, Izra Naji, 151

Zinn, Howard, 343

Zionists: at Paris Peace Conference (1919), 383

Zitouni, Djamel, 583

Zorba, S., 338

Zouabri, Antar, 583

Zoubar, Salah, 558

Zoubeidi, Jawad, 155

Zrein, Bahija, 830–1

Zucchino, David: *Thunder Run,* 981n-2n

Zucker, Dedi, 404

Zughayer, Kemal, 498–9

Zuheir (Iraqi cameraman), 970

Zuri, Eliyahu Bet, 374–5

PERMISSIONS ACKNOWLEDGEMENTS

Grateful acknowledgement is made to the following for permission to reprint previously published material:

Alfred A. Knopf: Quotation from *The Prophet* by Kahlil Gibran. Copyright 1923 by Kahlil Gibran and renewed 1951 by administrators C.T.A. of Kahlil Gibran Estate and Mary G. Gibran. Reprinted by permission of Alfred A. Knopf a division of Random House, Inc.

A. P. Watt Ltd.: Quotation from "Lapis Lazuli" by W. B. Yeats. Reprinted by permission of A. P. Watt, Ltd. on behalf of Michael B. Yeats.

Faber and Faber Ltd.: Quotation from T. S. Eliot's preface to *The Dark Side of the Moon*. Reprinted by permission of Faber and Faber Ltd.

Harcourt, Inc.: Quotation from "Grass" from *Chicago Poems* by Carl Sandburg. Copyright © 1916 by Holt, Reinhart and Winston and renewed 1944 by Carl Sandburg. Reprinted by permission of Harcourt, Inc.

Oxford University Press: Quotation from *War and Peace* by Leo Tolstoy, edited and translated by Louis and Aylmer Maude, 1954. Reprinted by permission of Oxford University Press.

Random House, Inc.: Quotation from "Epitaph on a Tyrant" copyright 1940 & renewed 1968 by W. H. Auden. Quotation from "Musée des Beaux Arts" copyright 1940 & renewed 1968 by W. H. Auden. Both from *Collected Poems* by W. H. Auden. Reprinted by permission of Random House, Inc.

The Society of Authors: Quotation from *Major Barbara* by G. B. Shaw. Reprinted by permission of The Society of Authors on behalf of the George Bernard Shaw Estate.

A NOTE ABOUT THE AUTHOR

ROBERT FISK received a Ph.D. in political science from Trinity College, Dublin, and was *The Times*'s Belfast correspondent from 1971 to 1975 and its Middle East correspondent from 1976 to 1987. Currently based in Beirut as Middle East correspondent for *The Independent*, he has lived in the region for almost three decades and has received more British and international journalism awards than any other foreign correspondent.

A NOTE ABOUT THE TYPE

THE TEXT OF THIS BOOK was set in a typeface called Times New Roman, designed by Stanley Morison (1889–1967) for The Times (London) and first introduced by that newspaper in 1932.

Among typographers and designers of the twentieth century, Stanley Morison was a strong forming influence—as a typographical adviser to the Monotype Corporation, as a director of two distinguished publishing houses, and as a writer of sensibility, erudition, and keen practical sense.

Composed by North Market Street Graphics,
Lancaster, Pennsylvania
Printed and bound by R. R. Donnelley,
Crawfordsville, Indiana
Designed by Virginia Tan